E-commerce

business. technology. society.

GLOBAL EDITION

THIRTEENTH EDITION

Kenneth C. Laudon
New York University

Carol Guercio Traver
Azimuth Interactive, Inc.

Pearson

Boston   Columbus   Indianapolis   New York   San Francisco   Amsterdam
Cape Town   Dubai   London   Madrid   Milan   Munich   Paris   Montréal   Toronto   Delhi
Mexico City   São Paulo   Sydney   Hong Kong   Seoul   Singapore   Taipei   Tokyo

VP Editorial Director: Andrew Gilfillan
Senior Portfolio Manager: Samantha Lewis
Managing Editor, Global Edition: Steven Jackson
Senior Project Editor, Global Edition: Daniel Luiz
Manager, Media Production, Global Edition: M. Vikram Kumar
Program Monitor: Ann Pulido/SPi Global
Editorial Assistant: Michael Campbell
Product Marketing Manager: Kaylee Carlson

Project Manager: Revathi Viswanathan/Cenveo Publisher Services
Senior Manufacturing Controller, Production, Global Edition: Trudy Kimber
Cover Designer: Lumina Datamatics, Inc.
Cover Image: © Syda Productions/Shutterstock
Chapter Images: Marinini/Fotolia
Full Service Project Management: Azimuth Interactive, Inc.
Composition: Azimuth Interactive, Inc.

Pearson Education Limited
Edinburgh Gate
Harlow
Essex CM20 2JE
England
and Associated Companies throughout the world

Visit us on the World Wide Web at:
www.pearsonglobaleditions.com

Credits and acknowledgements borrowed from other sources and reproduced, with permission, in this textbook appear on page 909.

ISBN 10: 1-292-21168-7
ISBN 13: 978-1-292-21168-8

British Library Cataloguing-in-Publication Data
A catalogue record for this book is available from the British Library

10 9 8 7 6 5 4

Typeset in ITC Veljovic Std. Book 9.5pt by Azimuth Interactive Inc.
Printed and bound by Ashford Colour Press Ltd.

PREFACE

E-commerce 2017. business. technology. society. Global Edition, 13e, provides you with an in-depth introduction to the field of e-commerce. We focus on key concepts, and the latest empirical and financial data, that will help you understand and take advantage of the evolving world of opportunity offered by e-commerce, which is dramatically altering the way business is conducted and driving major shifts in the global economy. E-commerce is a global phenomenon affecting economic and social life throughout the world. The Global Edition is aimed at students and professionals in the European Union, the Middle East, Asia Pacific, Australia, and South Africa. Case studies reflect e-commerce firms in these regions, and figures and tables relate to these regional sources wherever possible.

Just as important as our global orientation, we have tried to create a book that is thought-provoking and current. We use the most recent data available, and focus on companies that you are likely to encounter on a daily basis in your everyday life, such as Uber, Facebook, Google, Twitter, Amazon, YouTube, Pinterest, eBay, WhatsApp, Snapchat, and many more that you will recognize, as well as some exciting startups that may be new to you. Global Edition cases include Puma, *Financial Times,* Ace & Tate, InMobi, Spotify, Deezer, Souq, Alibaba, and Rocket Internet, among others. We also have up-to-date coverage of the key topics in e-commerce today, from privacy and piracy, to government surveillance, cyberwar, social, local, and mobile marketing, Internet sales taxes, intellectual property, and more. You will find here the most up-to-date and comprehensive overview of e-commerce today.

The e-commerce concepts you learn in this book will make you valuable to potential employers. The e-commerce job market is expanding rapidly. Many employers expect new employees to understand the basics of e-commerce, social and mobile marketing, and how to develop an e-commerce presence. Every industry today is touched in at least some way by e-commerce. The information and knowledge you find in this book will be valuable throughout your career, and after reading this book, we expect that you will be able to participate in, and even lead, management discussions of e-commerce for your firm.

WHAT'S NEW IN THE 13TH EDITION

Currency

The 13th Global Edition features all new or updated opening, closing, and "Insight on" cases. The text as well as all of the data, figures, and tables in the book have been updated through October 2016 with the latest marketing and business intelligence available from eMarketer, Pew Research Center, Forrester Research, comScore, Gartner Research, and other industry and government sources.

In addition, we have added new, expanded, and/or updated material throughout the text on a number of e-commerce topics that have appeared in the headlines during 2016, including the following:

- The latest developments with respect to on-demand service companies such as Uber, Airbnb, Instacart, and many others (Chapters 1, 5, and 11)

- Developments in wearable computing, including Apple Watch 2; Border Gateway Protocol; HTTP/2; depletion of IPv4 Internet addresses; Tier 1, Tier 2, and Tier 3 ISPs and peering arrangements; Facebook's satellite Internet access plans; the transition of control over IANA from the U.S. Department of Commerce to ICANN; 5G wireless; Google's Project Loon and Facebook's Internet access drone Aquila; IoT developments; the rise of mobile messaging applications and mobile search; virtual and augmented reality; artificial intelligence, intelligent personal assistants, and chatbots (Chapter 2)

- Open source Web and app development tools; mobile-first and responsive design; large companies, such as Dick's Sporting Goods, reclaim their e-commerce infrastructure (Chapter 3)

- New research on tensions between ease of use and security; new security threats (such as the growth of ransomware; hacktivist attacks such as Wikileaks; the Yahoo data breach; the DDoS attack on Dyn); bug bounty programs; HSTS; Cybersecurity Information Sharing Act; end-to-end encryption and national security issues; mobile wallets; Bitcoin and blockchain technology; P2P (Venmo; Facebook Messenger) and mobile payment systems (Chapter 4)

- Twitter's difficulties in finding a workable business model, new federal equity crowdfunding regulations, developing new business models based on the Internet of Things (Chapter 5)

- Google search engine algorithm updates; FTC regulation of native advertising; ad fraud issues; new proposed rules on mobile ad viewability; the continuing rise in usage of ad blocking software; mobile supercookie issues; industry and FTC guidelines on cross-device tracking; big data and marketing (Chapter 6)

- Mobile marketing spending overtakes spending on desktop advertising; new social marketing and social e-commerce tools from Facebook, Twitter, Pinterest, Instagram, LinkedIn, and Snapchat; proximity marketing; BLE; Google Eddystone; Apple iBeacons (Chapter 7)

- New, revised section on privacy issues, including facial recognition issues; the impact of the Supreme Court's Spokeo decision; new E.U. General Data Protection Regulation (Privacy Shield); new FCC privacy regulations on ISPs; Apple/U.S. government iPhone privacy fight; Google Library Project final court decision; new DMCA litigation; Apple/Samsung patent battles new section on trade secrets and federal Trade Secrets act; Internet sales tax developments; net neutrality developments; online fantasy sports gambling issues (Chapter 8)

- Cord cutters, cord shavers, and cord nevers; industry structure convergence (AT&T/Time Warner; Verizon/Yahoo mergers); native digital news sites; FCC open set top box plan; streaming of pirated content; streaming music services; streaming TV devices; the impact of Pokemon GO (Chapter 9)

- Acquisition of LinkedIn by Microsoft; new section on the the use of algorithms by social networks, such as Facebook's algorithm for generating personalized content; Facebook Workplace; Verizon acquires AOL and Yahoo (Chapter 10)

- The rise of social e-commerce; investments in fintech companies and online lending services; consolidation in the online recruitment industry; on-demand service companies (Chapter 11)
- Amazon Business; the rise of B2B sell-side marketplaces; supply chain visibility; cloud-based B2B; mobile B2B; B2B marketing (Chapter 12)

Themes

E-commerce has significantly evolved over the last decade. The iPhone was introduced in 2007. The iPad tablet was first introduced in 2010 and has already gone through several generations! Cloud services for storing and streaming content, and hosting thousands of apps, were not widely available until 2011. Smartphone and tablet devices have changed e-commerce into a social, local, and mobile experience. The 13th edition spotlights the following themes and content:

Headlines

- Social, Mobile, Local: We include an entire chapter describing social, mobile, and local marketing. Content about social networks, the mobile platform, and local e-commerce appears throughout the book.
  » The mobile platform composed of smartphones and tablet computers takes off and becomes a major factor in search, marketing, payment, retailing and services, and online content, as well as on-demand service companies. Mobile device use poses new security and privacy issues as well.
  » Social networks such as Facebook, Twitter, Pinterest, Instagram, LinkedIn, and Snapchat continue their rapid growth, laying the groundwork for a social network marketing platform.
  » Location-based services lead to explosive growth in local advertising and marketing.
- Online privacy continues to deteriorate, driven by a culture of self-revelation and powerful technologies for collecting personal information online without the knowledge or consent of users. A growing number of consumers adopt ad blockers.
- Internet security risks increase; cyberwarfare becomes a new way of conducting warfare among nation-states and a national security issue. A growing perception of online risk supports a growing lack of trust in e-commerce firms and transactions.

Business

- Global e-commerce revenues surge, despite slow economic growth.
- Internet advertising growth continues to outpace traditional advertising, including television.
- Social marketing grows faster than traditional online marketing like search and display advertising.
- E-books sales plateau but continue as a major channel for books. Consumers increasingly use smartphones and tablets as reader devices.
- Newspapers struggle to define a digital first news service.

- Streaming of popular TV shows and movies (Netflix, Amazon, YouTube, and Hulu. com) becomes a reality, as Internet distributors and Hollywood and TV producers strike deals for Web distribution that also protects intellectual property.
- "Free" and "freemium" business models compete to support digital content. Subscription services show unexpected strength.
- New mobile payment platforms continue to emerge to challenge PayPal, including Apple Pay, Android Pay, Samsung Pay, and Venmo.
- B2B e-commerce exceeds pre-recession levels as firms become more comfortable with digital supply chains.

Technology

- Smartphones, tablets, and e-book readers, along with associated cloud-based software applications, and coupled with 4G cellular network expansion, fuel rapid growth of the mobile platform.
- Investment in cloud computing increases, providing the computing infrastructure for a massive increase in online digital information content, and e-commerce.
- Cloud-based streaming services for music and video challenge sales of downloads and physical product.
- Software apps fuel growth in app sales, marketing, and advertising; transforming software production and distribution.
- The cost of developing sophisticated websites continues to drop due to declining software and hardware prices and open source software tools.
- Internet and cellular network capacity is challenged by the rapid expansion in digital traffic generated by mobile devices; the use of bandwidth caps tier-pricing expands.

Society

- The mobile, "always on" culture in business and family life continues to grow.
- European countries develop much stronger privacy policies, including Right to be Forgotten laws, add a new General Data Protection Regulation (Privacy Shield), and continue to expand the rights of citizens vis-à-vis Internet data giants.
- U.S. state governments heat up the pursuit of taxes on Internet sales by e-commerce firms.
- Intellectual property issues remain a source of conflict with significant movement toward resolution in some areas, such as Google's deals with Hollywood and the publishing industry, and Apple's and Amazon's deals with e-book and magazine publishers.
- Net neutrality regulations forbid Internet providers from discriminating against types of content, or providing differential service to large players.
- P2P piracy traffic declines as paid streaming music and video gains ground, although digital piracy of online content remains a significant threat to Hollywood and the music industry.

- Governments around the world increase surveillance of Internet users and web sites in response to national security threats; Google continues to tussle with China and other countries over censorship and security issues. Europe ends safe harbor protections for U.S. Internet firms.
- Venture capital investing in e-commerce explodes for social, mobile, and local software applications. Crowdfunding becomes a new source of funding for e-commerce start-ups.

WELCOME TO E-COMMERCE 2017

Since it began in 1995, global e-commerce has grown from a standing start to a $600 billion business-to-consumer and a $6.7 trillion business-to-business juggernaut, bringing about enormous change in business firms, markets, and consumer behavior. Economies and business firms around the globe are being similarly affected. During this relatively short time, e-commerce has itself been transformed from its origin as a mechanism for online retail sales into something much broader. Today, e-commerce has become the platform for media and new, unique services and capabilities that aren't found in the physical world. There is no physical world counterpart to Facebook, Twittter, Google search, or a host of other recent online innovations from Pinterest and iTunes to Tumblr. The Internet is about to replace television as the largest entertainment platform. Welcome to the new e-commerce!

E-commerce is projected to continue growing at double-digit rates over the next five years, remaining the fastest growing form of commerce. Just as automobiles, airplanes, and electronics defined the twentieth century, so will e-commerce of all kinds define business and society in the twenty-first century. The rapid movement toward an e-commerce economy and society is being led by both established business firms such as Tesco, Ford, IBM, Carrefours, and General Electric, and online firms such as Google, Amazon, Apple, Facebook, Yahoo, Twitter, and YouTube. Students of business and information technology need a thorough grounding in e-commerce in order to be effective and successful managers in the next decade.

While firms such as Facebook, YouTube, Twitter, Pinterest, and Uber have grown explosively in the last two years and grab our attention, the traditional forms of retail e-commerce and services also remain vital and have proven to be more resilient than traditional retail channels in facing the economic recession. The experience of these firms from 1995 to the present is also a focus of this book. The defining characteristic of these firms is that they are profitable, sustainable, efficient, and innovative, with powerful brand names. Many of these now-experienced retail and service firms, such as eBay, Amazon, E*Trade, Priceline, and Expedia, are survivors of the first era of e-commerce. These surviving firms have evolved their business models, integrated their online and offline operations, and changed their revenue models to become profitable. Understanding how these online businesses succeeded will help students to manage their own firms in the current omni-channel business environment.

It would be foolish to ignore the lessons learned in the early period of e-commerce. Like so many technology revolutions in the past—automobiles, electricity, telephones, television, and biotechnology—there was an explosion of entrepreneurial efforts, followed by consolidation. By 2005, the survivors of the early period were moving to establish profitable businesses while maintaining rapid growth in revenues. In 2016, e-commerce was in the midst of a new period of explosive entrepreneurial activity focusing on on-demand services, social networks, and the mobile platform created by smartphones and tablet computers. These technologies and social behaviors are bringing about extraordinary changes to our personal lives, markets, industries, individual businesses, and society as a whole. E-commerce is generating thousands of new jobs in all fields from marketing to management, entrepreneurial studies, and information systems. Today, e-commerce has moved into the mainstream life of established businesses that have the market brands and financial muscle required for the long-term deployment of e-commerce technologies and methods. If you are working in an established business, chances are the firm's e-commerce capabilities are important factors for its success. If you want to start a new business, chances are very good that the knowledge you learn in this book will be very helpful.

BUSINESS. TECHNOLOGY. SOCIETY.

We believe that in order for business and technology students to really understand e-commerce, they must understand the relationships among e-commerce business concerns, Internet technology, and the social and legal context of e-commerce. These three themes permeate all aspects of e-commerce, and therefore, in each chapter, we present material that explores the business, technological, and social aspects of that chapter's main topic.

Given the continued growth and diffusion of e-commerce, all students—regardless of their major discipline—must also understand the basic economic and business forces driving e-commerce. E-commerce has created new digital markets where prices are more transparent, markets are global, and trading is highly efficient, though not perfect. E-commerce has a direct impact on a firm's relationship with suppliers, customers, competitors, and partners, as well as how firms market products, advertise, and use brands. Whether you are interested in marketing and sales, design, production, finance, information systems, or logistics, you will need to know how e-commerce technologies can be used to reduce supply chain costs, increase production efficiency, and tighten the relationship with customers. This text is written to help you understand the fundamental business issues in e-commerce.

We spend a considerable amount of effort analyzing the business models and strategies of both online companies and established businesses now employing "bricks-and-clicks" business models. We explore why e-commerce firms fail and the strategic, financial, marketing, and organizational challenges they face. We also discuss how e-commerce firms learned from the mistakes of early firms, and how established firms are using e-commerce to succeed. Above all, we attempt to bring a strong sense of business realism and sensitivity to the often exaggerated descriptions of e-commerce.

The Web and mobile platform have caused a major revolution in marketing and advertising in the United States. We spend two chapters discussing online marketing and advertising. Chapter 6 discusses "traditional" online marketing formats like search engine marketing, display advertising, and e-mail, as well as various Internet marketing technologies underlying those efforts, and metrics for measuring marketing success. Chapter 7 provides an in-depth examination of social, mobile, and local marketing, which relies on mobile devices and social networks.

E-commerce is driven by Internet technology. Internet technology, and information technology in general, is perhaps the star of the show. Without the Internet, e-commerce would be virtually nonexistent. Accordingly, we provide three chapters specifically on the Internet and e-commerce technology, and in every chapter we provide continuing coverage by illustrating how the topic of the chapter is being shaped by new information technologies. For instance, Internet technology drives developments in security and payment systems, marketing strategies and advertising, financial applications, media distribution, business-to-business trade, and retail e-commerce. We discuss the rapid growth of the mobile platform, the emergence of cloud computing, new open source software tools and applications, and new types of Internet-based information systems that support digital business-to-business markets.

E-commerce is not only about business and technology, however. The third part of the equation for understanding e-commerce is society. E-commerce and Internet technologies have important social consequences that business leaders can ignore only at their peril. E-commerce has challenged our concepts of privacy, intellectual property, and even our ideas about national sovereignty and governance. Google, Facebook, Amazon, and assorted advertising networks maintain profiles on millions of shoppers and consumers worldwide. The proliferation of illegally copied music, videos, and books on the Internet, and the growth of social network sites often based on displaying copyrighted materials without permission, are challenging the intellectual property rights of record labels, Hollywood studios, artists, and writers. And many countries—including the United States—are demanding to control the content of websites displayed within their borders for political and social reasons. Tax authorities in the United States and Europe are demanding that e-commerce sites pay sales taxes just like ordinary brick and mortar stores on Main Street. As a result of these challenges to existing institutions, e-commerce and the Internet are the subject of increasing investigation, litigation, and legislation. Business leaders need to understand these societal developments, and they cannot afford to assume any longer that the Internet is borderless, beyond social control and regulation, or a place where market efficiency is the only consideration. In addition to an entire chapter devoted to the social and legal implications of e-commerce, each chapter contains material highlighting the social implications of e-commerce.

FEATURES AND COVERAGE

Strong Conceptual Foundation The book emphasizes the three major driving forces behind e-commerce: business development and strategy, technological innovations, and social controversies and impacts. Each of these driving forces is represented in every chapter, and together they provide a strong and coherent conceptual framework for understanding e-commerce. We analyze e-commerce, digital markets, and e-business firms just as we would ordinary businesses and markets using concepts from economics, marketing, finance, sociology, philosophy, and information systems. We strive to maintain a critical perspective on e-commerce and avoid industry hyperbole.

Some of the important concepts from economics and marketing that we use to explore e-commerce are transaction cost, network externalities, information asymmetry, social networks, perfect digital markets, segmentation, price dispersion, targeting, and positioning. Important concepts from the study of information systems and technologies play an important role in the book, including Internet standards and protocols, client/server computing, cloud computing, mobile platform and wireless technologies, and public key encryption, among many others. From the literature on ethics and society, we use important concepts such as intellectual property, privacy, information rights and rights management, governance, public health, and welfare.

From the literature on business, we use concepts such as business process design, return on investment, strategic advantage, industry competitive environment, oligopoly, and monopoly. We also provide a basic understanding of finance and accounting issues, and extend this through an "E-commerce in Action" case that critically examines the financial statements of Amazon. One of the witticisms that emerged from the early years of e-commerce and that still seems apt is the notion that e-commerce changes everything except the rules of business. Businesses still need to make a profit in order to survive in the long term.

Currency Important new developments happen almost every day in e-commerce and the Internet. We try to capture as many of these important new developments as possible in each annual edition. You will not find a more current book for a course offered for the 2017 academic year. Many other texts are already six months to a year out of date before they even reach the printer. This text, in contrast, reflects extensive research through October 2016.

Real-World Global Business Firm Focus and Cases From Akamai Technologies to Google, Microsoft, Apple, and Amazon, to Facebook, Twitter, and Tumblr, to Netflix, Pandora, and Elemica, this book contains hundreds of real-company examples and over 60 more extensive cases that place coverage in the context of actual e-commerce businesses. You'll find these examples in each chapter, as well as in special features such as chapter-opening, chapter-closing, and "Insight on" cases. The book takes a realistic look at the world of e-commerce, describing what's working and what isn't, rather than presenting a rose-colored or purely "academic" viewpoint.

In-depth Coverage of Marketing and Advertising The text includes two chapters on marketing and advertising, both traditional online marketing and social, mobile, and local marketing. Marketing concepts, including market segmentation, personalization, clickstream analysis, bundling of digital goods, long-tail marketing, and dynamic pricing, are used throughout the text.

In-depth Coverage of B2B E-commerce We devote an entire chapter to an examination of B2B e-commerce. In writing this chapter, we developed a unique and easily understood classification schema to help students understand this complex arena of e-commerce. This chapter covers e-distributors, e-procurement companies, exchanges, and industry consortia, as well as the development of private industrial networks and collaborative commerce.

Current and Future Technology Coverage Internet and related information technologies continue to change rapidly. The most important changes for e-commerce include dramatic price reductions in e-commerce infrastructure (making it much less expensive to develop a sophisticated e-commerce presence), the explosive growth in the mobile platform such as iPhones, iPads, and tablet computers, and expansion in the development of social technologies, which are the foundation of online social networks. What was once a shortage of telecommunications capacity has now turned into a surplus, PC prices have continued to fall, smartphone and tablet sales have soared, Internet high-speed broadband connections are now typical and are continuing to show double-digit growth, and wireless technologies such as Wi-Fi and cellular broadband are transforming how, when, and where people access the Internet. While we thoroughly discuss the current Internet environment, we devote considerable attention to describing emerging technologies and applications such as the Internet of Things, advanced network infrastructure, fiber optics, wireless and 4G technologies, Wi-Fi, IP multicasting, and future guaranteed service levels.

Up-to-Date Coverage of the Research Literature This text is well grounded in the e-commerce research literature. We have sought to include, where appropriate, references and analysis of the latest e-commerce research findings, as well as many classic articles, in all of our chapters. We have drawn especially on the disciplines of economics, marketing, and information systems and technologies, as well as law journals and broader social science research journals including sociology and psychology.

We do not use references to Wikipedia in this text, for a variety of reasons. Most colleges do not consider Wikipedia a legitimate or acceptable source for academic research and instruct their students not to cite it. Material found on Wikipedia may be out of date, lack coverage, lack critical perspective, and cannot necessarily be trusted. Our references are to respected academic journals; industry sources such as eMarketer, comScore, Hitwise, Nielsen, and Gartner; newspapers such as the *New York Times* and *Wall Street Journal*; and industry publications such as *Computerworld* and *InformationWeek*, among others. Figures and tables sourced to "authors' estimates" reflect analysis of data from the U.S. Department of Commerce, estimates from various research firms, historical trends, revenues of major online retailers, consumer online buying trends, and economic conditions.

Special Attention to the Social and Legal Aspects of E-commerce We have paid special attention throughout the book to the social and legal context of e-commerce. Chapter 8 is devoted to a thorough exploration of four ethical dimensions of e-commerce: information privacy, intellectual property, governance, and protecting public welfare on the Internet. We have included an analysis of the latest Federal Trade Commission and other regulatory and nonprofit research reports, and their likely impact on the e-commerce environment.

A major theme throughout this chapter, and the remainder of the book, is the impact of social, mobile, and local commerce on how consumers use the Internet.

Writing That's Fun to Read Unlike some textbooks, we've been told by many students that this book is actually fun to read and easy to understand. This is not a book written by committee—you won't find a dozen different people listed as authors, co-authors, and contributors on the title page. We have a consistent voice and perspective that carries through the entire text and we believe the book is the better for it.

OVERVIEW OF THE BOOK

The book begins with a chapter that provides an introduction to the major themes of the book. Chapter 1 defines e-commerce, distinguishes between e-commerce and e-business, and defines the different types of e-commerce. Chapter 2 traces the historical development of the Internet and thoroughly describes how today's Internet works. A major focus of this chapter is mobile technology, new software applications, and the near-term future Internet that is now under development and will shape the future of e-commerce. Chapter 3 builds on the Internet chapter by focusing on the steps managers need to follow in order to build an e-commerce presence. This e-commerce infrastructure chapter covers the process that should be followed in building an e-commerce presence; the major decisions regarding outsourcing site development and/or hosting; how to choose software, hardware, and other tools that can improve website performance; and issues involved in developing a mobile website and mobile applications. Chapter 4 focuses on e-commerce security and payments, building on the e-commerce infrastructure discussion of the previous chapter by describing the ways security can be provided over the Internet. This chapter defines digital information security, describes the major threats to security, and then discusses both the technology and policy solutions available to business managers seeking to secure their firm's sites. This chapter concludes with a section on e-commerce payment systems. We identify the various types of online payment systems (credit cards, stored value payment systems such as PayPal, digital wallets such as Google Wallet, and others), and the development of mobile and social payment systems such as Apple Pay, Venmo, and Facebook Messenger.

The next four chapters focus directly on the business concepts and social-legal issues that surround the development of e-commerce. Chapter 5 introduces and defines the concepts of business model and revenue model, describes the major e-commerce business and revenue models for both B2C and B2B firms, and introduces the basic business concepts required throughout the text for understanding e-commerce firms including industry structure, value chains, and firm strategy. Chapter 6 focuses on e-commerce consumer behavior, the Internet audience, and introduces the student to the basics of online marketing and branding, including traditional online marketing technologies and marketing strategies. Topics include the website as a marketing platform, search engine marketing and advertising, display ad marketing, e-mail campaigns, affiliate and lead generation marketing programs, multichannel marketing, and various customer retention strategies such as personalization (including interest-based advertising, also known as behavioral targeting) and customer service tools. The chapter also covers other marketing strategies such as pricing and long-tail marketing. Internet marketing technologies (web transaction logs, tracking files, data mining, and Big Data) and marketing automation and CRM systems are also explored. The chapter concludes with a section on understanding the costs and benefits of various types of online marketing, including a new section on marketing analytics software. Chapter 7 is devoted to an in-depth analysis of social, mobile, and local marketing. Topics include Facebook, Twitter, and Pinterest marketing platforms, the evolution of mobile marketing, and the growing use of geo-aware technologies to support proximity marketing. Chapter 8 provides a thorough introduction to the social and legal environment of e-commerce. Here, you will find a description of the ethical and legal dimensions of e-commerce, including a thorough discussion of the latest developments in personal information privacy, intellectual property, Internet governance, jurisdiction, and public health and welfare issues such as pornography, gambling, and health information.

The final four chapters focus on real-world e-commerce experiences in retail and services, online media, auctions, portals, and social networks, and business-to-business e-commerce. These chapters take a sector approach rather than the conceptual approach used in the earlier chapters. E-commerce is different in each of these sectors. Chapter 9 explores the world of online content and digital media and examines the enormous changes in online publishing and entertainment industries that have occurred over the last two years, including streaming movies, e-books, and online newspapers and magazines. Chapter 10 explores the online world of social networks, auctions, and portals. Chapter 11 takes a close look at the experience of firms in the retail marketplace for both goods and services, as well as on-demand service companies such as Uber and Airbnb. Chapter 11 also includes an "E-commerce in Action" case that provides a detailed analysis of the business strategies and financial operating results of Amazon, which can be used as a model to analyze other e-commerce firms. Chapter 12 concentrates on the world of B2B e-commerce, describing both Net marketplaces and the less-heralded, but very large arena of private industrial networks and the movement toward collaborative commerce.

PEDAGOGY AND CHAPTER OUTLINE

The book's pedagogy emphasizes student cognitive awareness and the ability to analyze, synthesize, and evaluate e-commerce businesses. While there is a strong data and conceptual foundation to the book, we seek to engage student interest with lively writing about e-commerce businesses and the transformation of business models at traditional firms.

Each chapter contains a number of elements designed to make learning easy as well as interesting.

Learning Objectives A list of learning objectives that highlights the key concepts in the chapter guides student study.

Chapter-Opening Cases Each chapter opens with a story about a leading e-commerce company that relates the key objectives of the chapter to a real-life e-commerce business venture.

The Financial Times:
A Remodel for 21st Century Publishing Profitability

© Azimuth Interactive, Inc.

When London-based The Financial Times Ltd. (FT) updated its apps with a new browser-based HTML5 Web app in 2011, it became the first major news outlet to employ responsive design tools to create a single app for multiple platforms. FT believed that the HTML5 app would yield significant cost savings in comparison to building multiple native apps for different platforms and would also liberate it from app stores and their attendant commission fees. The decision was also triggered by Apple's pronouncement that it would no longer share subscriber data from subscriptions purchased through its App Store.

FT's next major goal was to satisfy the yearning of a significant portion of its readership who still wanted to be able to read the paper as they always did, from cover to cover. Released in 2013, FT's web app has two modes: Live and Morning. The Live version provides frequently updated stories and shifting article arrangement. The Morning version, on the other hand, reproduces the experience of yesteryear, presenting a snapshot of the previous day's news just like the print edition. A navigation bar allows readers to easily toggle between the two versions and also presents thumbnails for easy navigation to newspaper sections, a search bar, and a refresh button. A new section, myFT, provides article recommendations based on reading history and a place to store personal portfolios and articles. Articles can be clipped from one platform and viewed on another. Subscribers can also create personalized charts to monitor investment performance vs. performance benchmarks and organize how they view their portfolio. While some of these tools had been available in the original web app, myFT consolidated them in a handy single-page hub.

But while FT.com subscribers have access to the latest tools and technologies for managing, monitoring, and sharing articles with fellow readers, they now also experience a digital design that simulates the reading of a newspaper. A fixed-height page and two-column layout limits the amount of up and down scrolling needed to read an article, and a left-to-right swipe navigates to the next article. This format keeps readers engaged longer as they dig deeper into the site. Full-page ads, often including multimedia content, are interspersed between articles and display at each section change. Simulating a television commercial break or an advertisement encountered while

175

"Insight on" Cases Each chapter contains three real-world cases illustrating the themes of technology, business, and society. These cases take an in-depth look at relevant topics to help describe and analyze the full breadth of the field of e-commerce. The cases probe such issues as the ability of governments to regulate Internet content, how to design websites for accessibility, the challenges faced by luxury marketers in online marketing, and smartphone security.

Margin Glossary
Throughout the text, key terms and their definitions appear in the text margin where they are first introduced.

Real-Company Examples
Drawn from actual e-commerce ventures, well over 100 pertinent examples are used throughout the text to illustrate concepts.

Chapter-Closing Case Studies Each chapter concludes with a robust case study based on a real-world organization. These cases help students synthesize chapter concepts and apply this knowledge to concrete problems and scenarios such as evaluating Pandora's freemium business model, ExchangeHunterJumper's efforts to build a brand, and the evolution of eBay.

Chapter-Ending Pedagogy Each chapter contains extensive end-of-chapter materials designed to reinforce the learning objectives of the chapter.

Key Concepts Keyed to the learning objectives, Key Concepts present the key points of the chapter to aid student study.

Review Questions Thought-provoking questions prompt students to demonstrate their comprehension and apply chapter concepts to management problem solving.

Projects At the end of each chapter are a number of projects that encourage students to apply chapter concepts and to use higher level evaluation skills. Many make use of the Internet and require students to present their findings in an oral or electronic presentation or written report. For instance, students are asked to evaluate information about a company's financials that can be obtain from the U.S. Securities and Exchange Commission website, assess payment system options for companies across international boundaries, or search for the top 10 cookies on their own computer and the sites they are from.

Web Resources Web resources that can extend students' knowledge of each chapter with projects, exercises, and additional content are available at www.azimuth-interactive.com/ecommerce13e. The website contains the following content provided by the authors:

- Additional projects, exercises, and tutorials
- Information on how to build a business plan and revenue models
- Essays on careers in e-commerce

INSTRUCTOR RESOURCES

At the Instructor Resource Center, www.pearsonglobaleditions.com/laudon, instructors can easily register to gain access to a variety of instructor resources available with this text in downloadable format. If assistance is needed, our dedicated technical support team is ready to help with the media supplements that accompany this text at https://support.pearson.com/getsupport.

The following supplements are available with this text:

- **Instructor's Resource Manual**
- **Test Bank**
- **TestGen® Computerized Test Bank**
- **PowerPoint Presentation**
- **Image Library**
- **Video Cases** The authors have created a collection of video case studies that integrate short videos, supporting case study material, and case study questions. Video cases can be used in class to promote discussion or as written assignments. There are 29 video cases for the 13th edition, of which 14 are entirely new, and the remainder with updated supporting case study material.

  Chapter 1
  1.1 The Importance of the Internet for E-commerce
  1.2 The Growth of the On-Demand Economy

  Chapter 2
  2.1 How Freshdesk Uses Amazon Web Services
  2.2 Compare.com Turns to Microsoft Azure and the Cloud
  2.3 Facebook's Data Centers
  2.4 Amazon Echo

  Chapter 3
  3.1 WL Gore Expands Using Demandware
  3.2 National Kidney Registry Turns to Rackspace for Managed Hosting

  Chapter 4
  4.1 The Rise of Cyberwarfare
  4.2 Tech Titans Clash over Future of Mobile Payments

  Chapter 5
  5.1 Twitter for Business
  5.2 Angel Investing
  5.3 Deals Galore at Groupon

  Chapter 6
  6.1 To Ad Block or Not to Ad Block
  6.2 Pandora's Recommendation System

- **Learning Tracks** These additional essays, created by the authors, provide instructors and students with more in-depth content on selected topics in e-commerce.

ACKNOWLEDGMENTS

Pearson Education has sought the advice of many excellent reviewers, all of whom have strongly influenced the organization and substance of this book. The following individuals provided extremely useful evaluations of this and previous editions of the text:

Deniz Aksen, Koç University (Istanbul)

Carrie Andersen, Madison Area Technical College

Subhajyoti Bandyopadhyay, University of Florida

Christine Barnes, Lakeland Community College

Reneta Barneva, SUNY Fredonia

Rathin Basu, Ferrum College

Dr. Shirley A. Becker, Northern Arizona University

Prasad Bingi, Indiana-Purdue University, Fort Wayne

Joanna Broder, Pima Community College

Lisa Bryan, Southeastern Community College

James Buchan, College of the Ozarks

Ashley Bush, Florida State University

Cliff Butler, North Seattle Community College

Carl Case, St. Bonaventure University

Teuta Cata, Northern Kentucky University

Adnan Chawdhry, California University of Pennsylvania

Mark Choman, Luzerne City Community College

Andrew Ciganek, Jacksonville State University

Daniel Connolly, University of Denver

Tom Critzer, Miami University

Dr. Robin R. Davis, Claflin University

Dursan Delen, Oklahoma State University

Abhijit Deshmukh, University of Massachusetts

Brian L. Dos Santos, University of Louisville

Robert Drevs, University of Notre Dame

Akram El-Tannir, Hariri Canadian University, Lebanon

Kimberly Furumo, University of Hawaii at Hilo

John H. Gerdes, University of California, Riverside

Gurram Gopal, Illinois Institute of Technology

Philip Gordon, University of California at Berkeley

Allan Greenberg, Brooklyn College

Bin Gu, University of Texas at Austin

Norman Hahn, Thomas Nelson Community College

Peter Haried, University of Wisconsin-La Crosse

Sherri Harms, University of Nebraska at Kearney

Sharon Heckel, St. Charles Community College

David Hite, Virginia Intermont College

Gus Jabbour, George Mason University

Thaddeus Janicki, University of Mount Olive

Kevin Jetton, Texas State University, San Marcos

Jim Keogh, Saint Peter's University

Ellen Kraft, Georgian Court University

Gilliean Lee, Lander University

Zoonky Lee, University of Nebraska, Lincoln

Andre Lemaylleux, Boston University, Brussels

Haim Levkowitz, University of Massachusetts, Lowell

Yair Levy, Nova Southeastern University

Richard Lucic, Duke University

Brenda Maynard, University of Pikeville

Vincent McCord, Foothill College

John Mendonca, Purdue University

John Miko, Saint Francis University

Dr. Abdulrahman Mirza, DePaul University

Natalie Nazarenko, SUNY - Fredonia

Barbara Ozog, Benedictine University

Kent Palmer, MacMurray College

Karen Palumbo, University of St. Francis

James Pauer, Lorain County Community College

Wayne Pauli, Dakota State University

Sam Perez, Mesa Community College

Jamie Pinchot, Thiel College

Selwyn Piramuthu, University of Florida

Kai Pommerenke, University of California at Santa Cruz

Barry Quinn, University of Ulster, Northern Ireland

Mahesh (Michael) Raisinghani, TWU School of Management, Executive MBA Program

Michelle Ramim, Nova Southeastern University

Jay Rhee, San Jose State University

Jorge Romero, Towson University

John Sagi, Anne Arundel Community College

Carl Saxby, University of Southern Indiana

Patricia Sendall, Merrimack College

Dr. Carlos Serrao, ISCTE/DCTI, Portugal

Neerja Sethi, Nanyang Business School, Singapore

Amber Settle, DePaul CTI

Vivek Shah, Texas State University-San Marcos

Wei Shi, Santa Clara University

Seung Jae Shin, Mississippi State University

Sumit Sircar, University of Texas at Arlington

Toni Somers, Wayne State University Mike Ilitch School of Business

Hongjun Song, University of Memphis

Pamela Specht, University of Nebraska at Omaha

Esther Swilley, Kansas State University

Tony Townsend, Iowa State University

Bill Troy, University of New Hampshire

Susan VandeVen, Southern Polytechnic State University

Hiep Van Dong, Madison Area Technical College

Michael Van Hilst, Nova Southeastern University

Mary Vitrano, Palm Beach Community College

Andrea Wachter, Point Park University

Nitin Walia, Ashland University

Catherine Wallace, Massey University, New Zealand

Biao Wang, Boston University

Haibo Wang, Texas A&M International University

Harry Washington, Lincoln University

Irene Wheeler, CVCC

Rolf Wigand, University of Arkansas at Little Rock

Erin Wilkinson, Johnson & Wales University

Alice Wilson, Cedar Crest College

Dezhi Wu, Southern Utah University

Gene Yelle, SUNY Institute of Technology

Kaimei Zheng, Isenberg School of Management, UMass, Amherst

David Zolzer, Northwestern State University

We would like to thank eMarketer, Inc. and David Iankelevich for their permission to include data and figures from their research reports in our text. eMarketer is one of the leading independent sources for statistics, trend data, and original analysis covering many topics related to the Internet, e-business, and emerging technologies. eMarketer aggregates e-business data from multiple sources worldwide.

In addition, we would like to thank all those who have worked so hard to make sure this book is the very best it can be, including Steven Jackson, Managing Editor, Global Editions, and Daniel Luiz, Senior Project Editor, Global Editions, for all their help and support in creating this Global Edition. We would also like to thank Samantha McAfee Lewis, Senior Portfolio Manager at Pearson and Revathi Viswanathan, Project Manager at Cenveo Publisher Services for their help and support with respect to the U.S. edition. Very special thanks to Megan Miller and Will Anderson at Azimuth Interactive, Inc., for all their hard work on the production of, and supplements for, both the global and U.S. editions.

Finally, last but not least, we would like to thank our family and friends, without whose support this book would not have been possible.

Kenneth C. Laudon
Carol Guercio Traver

Brief Contents

Contents

2   E-COMMERCE INFRASTRUCTURE   **94**

3 BUILDING AN E-COMMERCE PRESENCE   174

9 ONLINE MEDIA 624

| 10 | ONLINE COMMUNITIES | 692 |

11   E-COMMERCE RETAILING AND SERVICES   736

CHAPTER 1

Introduction to E-commerce

After reading this chapter, you will be able to:

- Understand why it is important to study e-commerce.
- Define e-commerce, understand how e-commerce differs from e-business, identify the primary technological building blocks underlying e-commerce, and recognize major current themes in e-commerce.
- Identify and describe the unique features of e-commerce technology and discuss their business significance.
- Describe the major types of e-commerce.
- Understand the evolution of e-commerce from its early years to today.
- Describe the major themes underlying the study of e-commerce.
- Identify the major academic disciplines contributing to e-commerce.

Uber:

The New Face of E-commerce?

If you were trying to pick iconic examples of e-commerce in the two decades since it began in 1995, it is likely that companies such as Amazon, eBay, Google, Apple, and Facebook would be high on the list. Today, there's a new company that is becoming the face of e-commerce as it enters its third decade: Uber. Uber and other firms with similar business models, such as Lyft (a ride service similar to Uber's), Airbnb (rooms for rent), Trusk (movers), TaskRabbit (part-time household helpers), Deliveroo (food delivery), ZipJet (laundry service), and BloomThat (flower delivery), are the pioneers of a

© Lenscap/Alamy Stock Photo

new on-demand service e-commerce business model that is sweeping up billions of investment dollars and disrupting major industries, from transportation to hotels, real estate, house cleaning, maintenance, and grocery shopping. On-demand service firms in the United States have collected over $26 billion in venture capital funding over the last five years, making this the hottest business model in e-commerce.

Uber offers a variety of different services. The two most common are UberX, which uses compact sedans and is the least expensive, and UberBlack, which provides higher-priced town car service. UberPool is a ride-sharing service that allows users to share a ride with another person who happens to be going to the same place. In several cities, Uber is developing UberEats, a food delivery service; UberRush, a same-day delivery service; and UberCargo, a trucking service.

Uber, headquartered in San Francisco, was founded in 2009 by Travis Kalanick and Garrett Camp, and has grown explosively since then to over 480 cities in 69 countries. Drivers are signing up at an exponential rate: as of the beginning of 2016, there were over 1 million drivers worldwide. According to an Uber-sponsored survey, over 44% of Uber drivers have college degrees (compared to 15% of taxi drivers), 71% say they have boosted their income and financial security by driving for Uber, and 73% say they prefer a job where they choose their hours rather than a 9-to-5 job. It is estimated that Uber's revenue will reach around $2 billion in 2016, but it is still not expected to generate an overall profit, with losses in developing markets such as China and India swallowing up profits being generated in North America, Europe, and elsewhere. Uber's strategy is to expand as fast as possible while foregoing short-term profits in the hope of long-term returns. As of July 2016, Uber has raised over $12.5 billion in venture capital. Uber is currently valued at around $68 billion, more than all of its competitors combined. In August 2016, Uber agreed to sell Uber China, where it had been engaged in a costly turf war for Chinese riders, to Didi Chuxing Technology, its primary Chinese rival. Uber will receive a 18% interest in Didi Chuxing and Didi will invest $1 billion in Uber. In doing so, Uber converted a reported $2 billion loss on its Chinese operations into a new merged entity valued at around $7 billion, and freed up capital to invest more heavily in other emerging markets such as Indonesia and India, where it does not have such significant competition.

Uber offers a compelling value proposition for both customers and drivers. Customers can sign up for free, request and pay for a ride (at a cost Uber claims is 40% less than a traditional taxi) using a smartphone and credit card, and get picked up within a few minutes. No need to stand on a street corner frantically waving, competing with others, or waiting and waiting for an available cab to drive by, without knowing when that might happen. Instead, customers using the Uber app know just how long it will take for the ride to arrive and how much it will cost. With UberPool ride-sharing, the cost of a ride drops by 50%, making it cost-competitive with owning a car in an urban area, according to Uber. Uber's value proposition for drivers is that it allows them to set their own hours, work when they like, and put their own cars to use generating revenue.

Uber is the current poster child for "digital disruption." It is easy to see why Uber has ignited a firestorm of opposition from existing taxi services both in the United States and around the world. Who can compete in a market where a new upstart firm offers a 50% price reduction? If you've paid €240,000 for a license to drive a taxi in Paris, what is it worth now that Uber has arrived? Even governments find Uber to be a disruptive threat. Governments do not want to give up regulatory control over passenger safety, driver training, nor the healthy revenue stream generated by charging taxi firms for a taxi license and sales taxes.

Uber's business model differs from traditional retail e-commerce. Uber doesn't sell goods. Instead, it has created a smartphone-based platform that enables people who want a service—like a taxi—to find a provider with the resources, such as a personal automobile and a driver with available time, to fill the demand. It's important to understand that although Uber and similar firms are often called "sharing economy" companies, this is a misnomer. Uber drivers are selling their services as drivers and the temporary use of their car. Uber itself is not in the sharing business either: it charges a hefty fee for every transaction on its platform. Uber is not an example of true "peer-to-peer" e-commerce because Uber transactions involve an online intermediary: a third party that takes a cut of all transactions and arranges for the marketplace to exist in the first place.

Uber has disrupted the traditional taxi business model because it offers a superior, fast, convenient taxi-hailing service when compared to traditional taxi companies. With a traditional taxi service, there is no guarantee you will find a cab. Uber reduces that uncertainty: the customer enters a request for pickup using his or her smartphone and nearly instantly (under the best of circumstances), Uber finds a provider and notifies the customer of the estimated time of arrival and price. Riders can accept the price or find an alternative.

Uber's business model is much more efficient than a traditional taxi firm. Uber does not own taxis and has no maintenance and financing costs. Uber calls its drivers "independent contractors," not employees. Doing so enables Uber to avoid costs for workers' compensation, minimum wage requirements, driver training, health insurance, and commercial licensing.

Quality control would seem to be a nightmare with over 1 million contract drivers. But Uber relies on user reviews to identify problematic drivers and driver reviews to identify problematic passengers. Drivers are evaluated by riders on a 5-point scale. Drivers that fall below 4.5 are warned and may be dropped if they don't improve. Customers are also rated with a 5-point system. Drivers can refuse to pick up troublesome customers, and the Uber server can delay service to potential customers with low ratings or ban them entirely. Uber does not publicly report how many poorly rated drivers or passengers there are in its system. Academic articles have found that in similar on-demand companies, such as Airbnb, there is a built-in bias for both sellers and buyers to give good reviews regardless of the actual experience. If you routinely give low reviews to sellers (drivers), they will think you are too demanding and not service you in the future. If a driver gives low reviews to passengers, they might not rate you highly in return.

Rather than having a dispatcher in every city, Uber has an Internet-based app service running on cloud servers located throughout the world. It does not provide radios to its drivers, who instead must use their own smartphones and cell service, which the drivers pay for. It does not provide insurance or maintenance for its drivers' cars. Uber has shifted the costs of running a taxi service entirely to the drivers. Uber charges prices that vary dynamically with demand: the higher the demand, the greater the price of a ride. Therefore, it is impossible using public information to know if Uber's prices are lower than traditional taxis. Clearly, in high-demand situations they are higher, sometimes ten times higher, than a regulated taxi. There is no regulatory taxi commission setting uniform per mile fares. Consumers do face some traditional uncertainties regarding availability: during a rain storm, a convention, or a sports event, when demand peaks, not enough drivers may be available at any price.

If Uber is the poster child for the new on-demand service economy, it's also an iconic example of the social costs and conflicts associated with this new kind of e-commerce. Uber has been accused in many countries of misclassifying its drivers as contractors as opposed to employees, thereby denying the drivers the benefits of employee status, such as minimum wages, social security, workers' compensation, and health insurance.

Uber has also been accused of violating public transportation laws and regulations throughout the world; abusing the personal information it has collected on users of the service; seeking to use personal information to intimidate journalists; failing to protect public safety by refusing to do adequate criminal, medical, and financial background checks on its drivers; taking clandestine actions against its chief competitor Lyft in order to disrupt its business; and being tone-deaf to the complaints of its own drivers against the firm's efforts to reduce driver fees. Uber has met with heavy resistance in many

SOURCES: "In Europe, Is Uber a Transportation Service or a Digital Platform," by Mark Scott, *New York Times*, November 27, 2016; "Uber Drivers Entitled to UK Minimum Wage, London Tribunal Rules," Theregister.co.uk, by Gareth Corfield, October 28, 2016; "Uber Takes Legal Action Against Tough New London Regulations," News.sky.com, August 17, 2016; "Even Uber Couldn't Bridge the China Divide," by Farhad Manjoo, *New York Times*, August 1, 2016; "Uber Sells China Operations to Didi Chuxing," by Alyssa Abkowitz and Rick Carew, *Wall Street Journal*, August 1, 2016; "Uber Faces Permit Pressure in France," by Robert Williams, FT.com, July 6,

2016; "Why Uber Keeps Raising Billions," by Andrew Ross Sorkin, *New York Times*, June 20, 2016; "On-Demand Economy Not Slowing Down in Europe," by Rory Grieve, Pivotl.com, June 16, 2016; "Uber Points to Profits in All Developed Markets," by Leslie Hook, FT.com, June 16, 2016; "Legal Challenges for Uber in the European Union and in Germany," by Jenny Gesley, Blogs.loc.gov, March 14, 2016; "Uber Paid €450,000 in Dutch Fines Last Year," Dutchnews.nl, March 14, 2016; "Leaked: Uber's Financials Show Huge Growth, Even Bigger Losses," by Brian Solomon, *Forbes*, January 12, 2016; "Twisting Words to Make 'Sharing' Apps Seem Selfless," by Natasha Singer, *New York Times*, August 9, 2015; "The $50 Billion Question: Can Uber Deliver?," by Douglas Macmillan, *Wall Street Journal*, June 15, 2015; "How Everyone Misjudges the Sharing Economy," by Christopher Mims, *Wall Street Journal*, May 25, 2015; "The On-Demand Economy Is Reshaping Companies and Careers," *The Economist*, January 4, 2015; "The On-Demand Economy: Workers on Tap," *The Economist*, January 3, 2015.

countries in Europe. In London, a Employment Tribunal judge has ruled that Uber drivers are entitled to the British minimum wage and Uber is suing to overturn recent enacted Transport for London regulations that require its car drivers to pass a written test and have commercial insurance. In Paris, Uber faces continuing protests, at times violent, from taxi unions, as well as proposed regulation that would give additional protection to traditional taxis. In June 2016, a French court fined Uber €800,000, as well as two of its executives, for operating an illegal car service. In the Netherlands, Uber has been fined €450,000 for breaking taxi regulations. Uber has filed complaints with the European Commission against France, Germany, and Spain in response to efforts in those countries to ban some or all of its services and is attempting to convince the EU's most powerful court, the European Court of Justice, that Uber is is an information society service (digital platform) and not a transportation service that violates the existing laws in many countries.

Critics also fear that on-demand service firms will create a society of part-time, low-paid, temp work, displacing traditionally full-time, secure jobs—the so-called "uber-ization" of work. As one critic put it, Uber is not the Uber for rides so much as it is the Uber for low-paid jobs. Uber responds to this fear by claiming that it is lowering the cost of transportation, making better use of spare human and financial resources, expanding the demand for ride services, and expanding opportunities for car drivers, whose pay is about the same as other taxi drivers.

Despite the controversy surrounding it, Uber continues to have no trouble attracting additional investors and, according to CEO Kalanick, plans to remain a private company for the foreseeable future. Although Uber currently has a host of rivals, both big and small, most analysts expect that ultimately, only one or two major players will remain. Uber is doing everything it can to assure that it will be the one to prevail.

In 1994, e-commerce as we now know it did not exist. In 2016, just 22 years later, around 1.62 billion consumers worldwide are expected to spend about €2.35 trillion, and businesses around €19.8 trillion, purchasing goods and services via a desktop computer or mobile device. And in this short period of time, e-commerce has been reinvented not just once, but twice.

The early years of e-commerce, during the late 1990s, were a period of business vision, inspiration, and experimentation. It soon became apparent, however, that establishing a successful business model based on those visions would not be easy. There followed a period of retrenchment and reevaluation, which led to the stock market crash of 2000–2001, with the value of e-commerce, telecommunications, and other technology stocks plummeting. After the bubble burst, many people were quick to write off e-commerce. But they were wrong. The surviving firms refined and honed their business models, and the technology became more powerful and less expensive, ultimately leading to business firms that actually produced profits. Between 2002–2008, retail e-commerce grew at more than 25% per year.

Today, we are in the middle of yet another transition. Social networks such as Facebook, Twitter, YouTube, Pinterest, Instagram, and Tumblr, which enable users to distribute their own content (such as videos, music, photos, personal information, commentary, and blogs), have rocketed to prominence. Never before in the history of media have such large audiences been aggregated and made so accessible. At the same time, mobile devices, such as smartphones and tablet computers, and mobile apps have supplanted the traditional desktop/laptop platform and web browser as the most common method for consumers to access the Internet. Facilitated by technologies such as cloud computing, cellular networks, and Wi-Fi, mobile devices have become advertising, shopping, reading, and media viewing machines, and in the process, are transforming consumer behavior yet again. Mobile, social, and local have become driving forces in e-commerce. The mobile platform infrastructure has also given birth to yet another e-commerce innovation: on-demand services that are local and personal. From hailing a taxi, to shopping, to washing your clothes, these new businesses are creating a marketspace where owners of resources such as cars, spare bedrooms, and spare time can find a market of eager consumers looking to buy a service in a few minutes using their smartphones. Uber, profiled in the opening case, is a leading example of these new on-demand service firms that are disrupting traditional business models.

1.1 THE FIRST THIRTY SECONDS: WHY YOU SHOULD STUDY E-COMMERCE

The rapid growth and change that has occurred in the first two decades of e-commerce represents just the beginning—what could be called the first 30 seconds of the e-commerce revolution. Technology continues to evolve at exponential rates. This underlying ferment presents entrepreneurs with new opportunities to create new business models and businesses in traditional industries and in the process, disrupt, and in some instances, destroy existing business models and firms.

Improvements in underlying information technologies and continuing entrepreneurial innovation in business and marketing promise as much change in the next decade as was seen in the previous two decades. The twenty-first century will be the age of a digitally enabled social and commercial life, the outlines of which we can still only barely perceive at this time. Analysts estimate that by 2020, U.S. consumers will be spending around $933 billion and businesses around $9.1 trillion in digital transactions. It appears likely that e-commerce will eventually impact nearly all commerce, and that most commerce will be e-commerce by the year 2050, if not sooner.

Business fortunes are made—and lost—in periods of extraordinary change such as this. The next five years hold exciting opportunities—as well as risks—for new and traditional businesses to exploit digital technology for market advantage. For society as a whole, the next few decades offer the possibility of extraordinary gains in social wealth as the digital revolution works its way through larger and larger segments of the world's economy.

It is important to study e-commerce in order to be able to perceive and understand the opportunities and risks that lie ahead. By the time you finish this book, you will be able to identify the technological, business, and social forces that have shaped, and continue to shape, the growth of e-commerce, and be ready to participate in, and ultimately guide, discussions of e-commerce in the firms where you work. More specifically, you will be able to analyze an existing or new idea for an e-commerce business, identify the most effective business model to use, and understand the technological underpinnings of an e-commerce presence, including the security and ethical issues raised, as well as how to optimally market and advertise the business, using both traditional e-marketing tools and social, mobile, and local marketing.

1.2 INTRODUCTION TO E-COMMERCE

In this section, we'll first define e-commerce and then discuss the difference between e-commerce and e-business. We will also introduce you to the major technological building blocks underlying e-commerce: the Internet, Web, and mobile platform. The section concludes with a look at some major current trends in e-commerce.

WHAT IS E-COMMERCE?

e-commerce
the use of the Internet, the Web, and mobile apps and browsers running on mobile devices to transact business. More formally, digitally enabled commercial transactions between and among organizations and individuals

E-commerce involves the use of the Internet, the World Wide Web (Web), and mobile apps and browsers running on mobile devices to transact business. Although the terms Internet and Web are often used interchangeably, they are actually two very different things. The *Internet* is a worldwide network of computer networks, and the *Web* is one of the Internet's most popular services, providing access to billions of web pages. An *app* (short-hand for application) is a software application. The term is typically used when referring to mobile applications, although it is also sometimes used to refer to desktop computer applications as well. A *mobile browser* is a version of web browser software accessed via a mobile device. (We describe the Internet, Web, and mobile platform more fully later in this chapter and in Chapters 2 and 3.) More formally, e-commerce can be defined as digitally enabled commercial transactions between and among organizations and individuals. Each of these components of our working definition of e-commerce is important. *Digitally enabled transactions* include all transactions mediated by digital technology. For the most part, this means transactions that occur over the Internet, the Web, and/or via mobile devices. *Commercial transactions* involve the exchange of value (e.g., money) across organizational or individual boundaries in return for products and services. Exchange of value is important for understanding the limits of e-commerce. Without an exchange of value, no commerce occurs.

The professional literature sometimes refers to e-commerce as digital commerce. For our purposes, we consider e-commerce and digital commerce to be synonymous.

THE DIFFERENCE BETWEEN E-COMMERCE AND E-BUSINESS

There is a debate about the meaning and limitations of both e-commerce and e-business. Some argue that e-commerce encompasses the entire world of electronically based organizational activities that support a firm's market exchanges—including a firm's entire information system infrastructure (Rayport and Jaworski, 2003). Others argue, on the other hand, that e-business encompasses the entire world of internal and external electronically based activities, including e-commerce (Kalakota and Robinson, 2003).

We think it is important to make a working distinction between e-commerce and e-business because we believe they refer to different phenomena. E-commerce is not "anything digital" that a firm does. For purposes of this text, we will use the term **e-business** to refer primarily to the digital enabling of transactions and processes *within* a firm, involving information systems under the control of the firm. For the most part, in our view, e-business does not include commercial transactions involving an exchange of value across organizational boundaries. For example, a company's online inventory control mechanisms are a component of e-business, but such internal processes do not directly generate revenue for the firm from outside businesses or consumers, as e-commerce, by definition, does. It is true, however, that a firm's e-business infrastructure provides support for online e-commerce exchanges; the same infrastructure and skill sets are involved in both e-business and e-commerce. E-commerce and e-business systems blur together at the business firm boundary, at the point where internal business systems link up with suppliers or customers (see **Figure 1.1**). E-business applications turn into e-commerce precisely when an exchange of value occurs (see Mesenbourg, U.S. Department of Commerce, 2001, for a similar view). We will examine this intersection further in Chapter 12.

e-business
the digital enabling of transactions and processes within a firm, involving information systems under the control of the firm

TECHNOLOGICAL BUILDING BLOCKS UNDERLYING E-COMMERCE: THE INTERNET, WEB, AND MOBILE PLATFORM

The technology juggernauts behind e-commerce are the Internet, the Web, and increasingly, the mobile platform. We describe the Internet, Web, and mobile platform in some detail in Chapter 2. The **Internet** is a worldwide network of computer networks built on common standards. Created in the late 1960s to connect a small number of

Internet
worldwide network of computer networks built on common standards

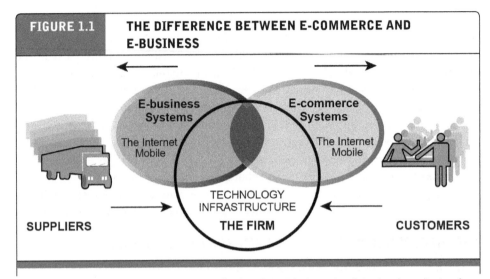

E-commerce primarily involves transactions that cross firm boundaries. E-business primarily involves the application of digital technologies to business processes within the firm.

mainframe computers and their users, the Internet has since grown into the world's largest network. It is impossible to say with certainty exactly how many computers and other mobile devices such as smartphones and tablets are connected to the Internet worldwide at any one time, but some experts estimate the number to be more than 5 billion (Camhi, 2015). The Internet links businesses, educational institutions, government agencies, and individuals together, and provides users with services such as e-mail, document transfer, shopping, research, instant messaging, music, videos, and news.

One way to measure the growth of the Internet is by looking at the number of Internet hosts with domain names. (An *Internet host* is defined by the Internet Systems Consortium as any IP address that returns a domain name in the in-addr.arpa domain, which is a special part of the DNS namespace that resolves IP addresses into domain names.) In January 2016, there were more than 1 billion Internet hosts in over 245 countries, up from just 70 million in 2000 (Internet Systems Consortium, 2016).

The Internet has shown extraordinary growth patterns when compared to other electronic technologies of the past. It took radio 38 years to achieve a 30% share of U.S. households. It took television 17 years to achieve a 30% share. It took only 10 years for the Internet/Web to achieve a 53% share of U.S. households once a graphical user interface was invented for the Web in 1993. Today, in the United States, around 267 million people of all ages (about 82% of the U.S. population) use the Internet at least once a month (eMarketer, Inc. 2016a).

World Wide Web (the Web)

an information system running on Internet infrastructure that provides access to billions of web pages

The **World Wide Web (the Web)** is an information system that runs on the Internet infrastructure. The Web was the original "killer app" that made the Internet commercially interesting and extraordinarily popular. The Web was developed in the early 1990s and hence is of much more recent vintage than the Internet. We describe the Web in some detail in Chapter 2. The Web provides access to billions of web pages indexed by Google and other search engines. These pages are created in a language called *HTML (HyperText Markup Language)*. HTML pages can contain text, graphics, animations, and other objects. The Internet prior to the Web was primarily used for text communications, file transfers, and remote computing. The Web introduced far more powerful and commercially interesting capabilities of direct relevance to commerce. In essence, the Web added color, voice, and video to the Internet, creating a communications infrastructure and information storage system that rivals television, radio, magazines, and libraries.

There is no precise measurement of the number of web pages in existence, in part because today's search engines index only a portion of the known universe of web pages. Google has identified over 30,000 trillion unique uniform resource locators (URLs), commonly known as web addresses, up from 1 trillion in 2008, although many of these pages do not necessarily contain unique content (Schwartz, 2015). In addition to this "surface" or "visible" Web, there is also the so-called deep Web that is reportedly 500 to 1,000 times greater than the surface Web. The deep Web contains databases and other content that is not routinely indexed by search engines such as Google (see **Figure 1.2**). Although the total size of the Web is not known, what is indisputable is that web content has grown exponentially since 1993.

The mobile platform is the newest development in Internet infrastructure. The **mobile platform** provides the ability to access the Internet from a variety of mobile

mobile platform
provides the ability to access the Internet from a variety of mobile devices such as smartphones, tablets, and other ultra-lightweight laptop computers

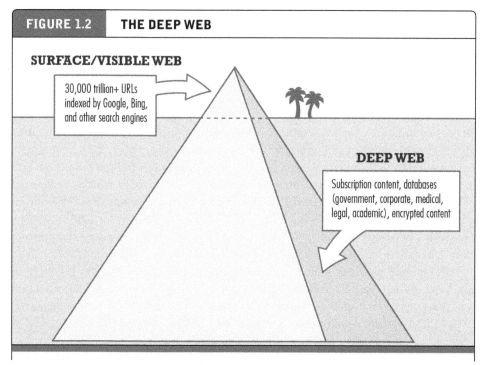

FIGURE 1.2 THE DEEP WEB

SURFACE/VISIBLE WEB

30,000 trillion+ URLs indexed by Google, Bing, and other search engines

DEEP WEB

Subscription content, databases (government, corporate, medical, legal, academic), encrypted content

Search engines index only a small portion of online content.

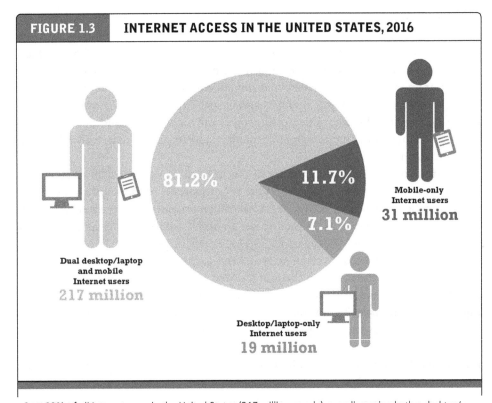

FIGURE 1.3 **INTERNET ACCESS IN THE UNITED STATES, 2016**

81.2%

Dual desktop/laptop
and mobile
Internet users
217 million

11.7%

Mobile-only
Internet users
31 million

7.1%

Desktop/laptop-only
Internet users
19 million

Over 80% of all Internet users in the United States (217 million people) go online using both a desktop/laptop and mobile device. Almost 12% (31 million) only go online by using a mobile device. Just over 7% (19 million) use only a desktop or laptop computer to access the Internet.

SOURCE: Based on data from eMarketer, Inc., 2016c.

devices such as smartphones, tablets, and other ultra-lightweight laptop computers via wireless networks or cell phone service. Mobile devices are playing an increasingly prominent role in Internet access. In 2016, there are over 360 million mobile devices in the United States that can be connected to the Internet (more than 1 device for each person in the United States), and almost 93% of Americans who access the Internet use a mobile device to do so at least some of the time (eMarketer, Inc., 2016b, 2016c). **Figure 1.3** illustrates the variety of devices used by Americans to access the Internet in 2016.

The mobile platform is not just a hardware phenomenon. The introduction of the Apple iPhone in 2007, followed by the Apple iPad in 2010, has also ushered in a sea-change in the way people interact with the Internet from a software perspective. In the early years of e-commerce, the Web and web browsers were the only game in town. Today, in contrast, more Americans access the Internet via a mobile app than by using a desktop computer and web browser. *Insight on Technology: Will Apps Make the Web Irrelevant?* examines the challenge that apps and the mobile platform pose to the Web's dominance of the Internet ecosphere in more depth.

INSIGHT ON TECHNOLOGY

WILL APPS MAKE THE WEB IRRELEVANT?

Nowadays, it's hard to recall a time before the Web. How did we get along without the ability to pull up a web browser and search for any item, learn about any topic, or play just about any type of game? Though the Web has come a remarkably long way from its humble beginnings, many experts claim that the Web's best days are behind it, and that there's a new player on the field: apps. Opinions vary widely over the future role of the Web in a world where apps have become an ever larger portion of the Internet marketspace. In 10 years, will web browsers be forgotten relics, as we rely entirely on apps to do both our work and our play on the Internet? Will the Web and apps coexist peacefully as vital cogs in the Internet eco-system? Or will the app craze eventually die down as tech users gravitate back toward the Web as the primary way to perform Internet-related tasks?

Apps have grown into a disruptive force ever since Apple launched its App Store in 2008. The list of industries apps have disrupted is wide-ranging: communications, media and entertainment, logistics, education, healthcare, and most recently, with Uber, the taxi industry. Despite not even existing prior to 2008, in 2016, sales of apps are expected to account for over $59 billion in revenues worldwide, and the app economy is continuing to show robust growth, with estimates of over $100 billion in revenue by 2020. More of those revenues are likely to come from in-app purchases than from paid app downloads. Not only that, but the growth is not coming from more users trying the same small number of apps. Although usage of apps tends to be highly concentrated, with nearly 75% of smartphone app minutes spent on an individual's top 3 apps, consumers are trying new apps all the time and visit about 27 apps per month, leaving plenty of room

for new app developers to innovate and create best-selling apps. In fact, according to mobile advertising company Flurry, 280 million people worldwide qualify as mobile addicts, which they define as someone who launches a smartphone app more than 60 times a day. According to Flurry, the number of such addicts increased by about 350% from 2013 to 2015.

In January 2014, for the first time ever, Americans used mobile apps more than desktop computers to access the Internet. The time U.S. adults are spending using mobile apps has exploded, growing by over 110% over the past three years, and now accounting for 58% of total digital media time spent; time spent on the desktop now accounts for just 33%, and mobile browsers just 9%. U.S. adults are spending over 96 hours a month (about 3¼ hours a day) within apps on their smartphones and tablet computers. Consumers have gravitated to apps for several reasons. First, smartphones and tablet computers enable users to use apps anywhere, instead of being teth-ered to a desktop or having to lug a heavy laptop around. Of course, smartphones and tablets enable users to use the Web too, but apps are often more convenient and boast more streamlined, elegant interfaces than mobile web browsers.

Not only are apps more appealing in certain ways to consumers, they are much more appealing to content creators and media companies. Apps are much easier to control and monetize than websites, not to mention they can't be crawled by Google or other services. On the Web, the average price of ads per thousand impressions is falling, and many content providers are still mostly strug-gling to turn the Internet into a profitable content delivery platform. Much of software and media companies' focus has shifted to developing mobile apps for this reason.

(continued)

These trends are why some pundits boldly proclaim that the Web is dead, and that the shift from the Web to apps has only just started. These analysts believe that the Internet will be used to transport data, but individual app interfaces will replace the web browser as the most common way to access and display content. Even the creator of the Web, Tim Berners-Lee, feels that the Web as we know it is being threatened. That's not a good sign.

But there is no predictive consensus about the role of the Web in our lives in the next decade and beyond. Many analysts believe the demise of the Web has been greatly exaggerated, and that the Web boasts many advantages over today's apps that users will be unwilling to relinquish. Although apps may be more convenient than the Web in many respects, the depth of the web browsing experience trumps that of apps. The Web is a vibrant, diverse array of sites, and browsers have an openness and flexibility that apps lack. The connections between websites enhance their usefulness and value to users, and apps that instead seek to lock users in cannot offer the same experience.

Other analysts who are more optimistic about the Web's chances to remain relevant in an increasingly app-driven online marketplace feel this way because of the emergence of HTML5. HTML5 is a markup language that enables more dynamic web content and allows for browser-accessible web apps that are as appealing as device-specific apps. In fact, there is another group of analysts who believe that apps and the Web are going to come together, with HTML5 bringing the best of the app experience to the Web, and with apps developing new web-like capabilities. Already, work is underway to create more "smart" apps that handle a wider array of tasks than today's apps can handle, such as apps with Siri integration.

A shift towards apps and away from the Web could have a ripple effect on e-commerce firms. As the pioneer of apps and the market leader in apps, smartphones, and tablet computers, Apple stands to gain from a shift towards apps, and although it also faces increasing competition from other companies, including Google, the established success of the App Store will make it next to impossible to dethrone Apple. For instance, while Google's Google Play store had double the number of downloads compared to Apple's App Store in 2015, the App Store still made 75% more revenue than Google Play. Google's search business is likely to suffer from all of the "walled garden" apps that it cannot access, but it also has a major stake in the world of smartphones, tablets, and apps itself with its Android operating system, which is used by over 80% of smartphones worldwide. Facebook has already seen its members make the transition from using its website to using its mobile app and has made, and continues to make, significant investments in standalone apps, such as Instagram and WhatsApp. Web-based companies that fail to find an answer to the growth of mobile apps may eventually fall by the wayside.

SOURCES: "The 2016 U.S. Mobile App Report," comScore, September 2016; "US Mobile StatPack," by Cathy Boyle, eMarketer, March 2016; "Gartner Says Worldwide Smartphone Sales Grew 9.7 Percent in Fourth Quarter of 2015," Gartner.com, February 18, 2016; "App Forecast: Over $100 Billion in Revenue by 2020," by Danielle Levitas, Blog.Appannie.com, February 10, 2016; "App Annie 2015: Google Play Saw 100% More Downloads Than the iOS App Store, but Apple Generated 75% More Revenue," by Emil Protalinski, Venturebeat.com, January 20, 2016; "Publisher Straddle the Apple-Google, App-Web Divide," by Katie Benner and Conor Dougherty, *New York Times*, October 18, 2015; "Mobile Addicts Multiply Across the Globe," by Simon Khalaf, Flurrymobile.tumblr.com, July 15, 2015; "How Apps Won the Mobile Web," by Thomas Claburn, Informationweek.com, April 3, 2014; "Mobile Apps Overtake PC Internet Usage in U.S.," by James O'Toole, Money.cnn.com, February 28, 2014; "Is The Web Dead In the Face of Native Apps? Not Likely, But Some Think So," by Gabe Knuth, Brianmadden.com, March 28, 2012; "The Web Is Dead. Long Live the Internet," by Chris Anderson and Michael Wolff, Wired.com, August 17, 2010; "The Web Is Dead? A Debate," by Chris Anderson, Wired.com, August 17, 2010.

MAJOR TRENDS IN E-COMMERCE

Table 1.1 describes the major trends in e-commerce in 2016–2017 from a business, technological, and societal perspective, the three major organizing themes that we use in this book to understand e-commerce (see Section 1.6).

From a business perspective, one of the most important trends to note is that all forms of e-commerce continue to show very strong growth. Retail e-commerce has been growing at double-digit rates for the last few years, and by 2017, is expected to reach €2.37 trillion, while mobile e-commerce will make up more than 50% of all e-commerce sales in China, India, and South Korea, and over 33% in the U.K. and Germany. Social networks such as Facebook, Pinterest, and Instagram are enabling social e-commerce by providing advertising, search, and buy buttons that enable consumers to actually purchase products. Local e-commerce is being fueled by the explosion of interest in on-demand services such as Uber and Airbnb. B2B e-commerce, which dwarfs all other forms, also is continuing to strengthen and grow.

From a technology perspective, the mobile platform based on smartphones and tablet computers has finally arrived with a bang, driving astronomical growth in mobile advertising and making true mobile e-commerce a reality. The use of mobile messaging services such as WhatsApp and Snapchat has created an alternative communications platform that are beginning to be leveraged for commerce as well. Cloud computing is inextricably linked to the development of the mobile platform by enabling the storage of consumer content and software on cloud (Internet-based) servers, and making it available to mobile devices as well as desktops. Other major technological trends include the increasing ability of companies to track and analyze the flood of online data (typically referred to as big data) being produced. The Internet of Things, comprised of billions of Internet-connected devices, continues to grow exponentially, and will only add to this flood of data in the years to come.

At the societal level, other trends are apparent. The Internet and mobile platform provide an environment that allows millions of people to create and share content, establish new social bonds, and strengthen existing ones through social network, photo- and video-posting, and blogging sites and apps, while at the same time creating significant privacy issues. Privacy seems to have lost some of its meaning in an age when millions create public online personal profiles, while at the same time concerns over commercial and governmental privacy invasion continue to increase. The major digital copyright owners have increased their pursuit of online piracy with mixed success, while reaching agreements with the big technology players such as Apple, Amazon, and Google to protect intellectual property rights. Taxation of online sales continues to pose challenges for governments. Sovereign nations have expanded their surveillance of, and control over, online communications and content as a part of their anti-terrorist activities and their traditional interest in law enforcement. Online security, or lack thereof, remains a significant issue, as new stories about security breaches, malware, hacking, and other attacks emerge seemingly daily.

TABLE 1.1	MAJOR TRENDS IN E-COMMERCE 2016–2017

BUSINESS

- Retail e-commerce continues to grow worldwide, with a global growth rate of over 20%, and even higher in emerging markets such as China, India, and Brazil.
- Mobile retail e-commerce explodes and in the EU-5 is expected to reach almost €70 billion in 2016.
- The mobile app ecosystem continues to grow, with over 2 billion people using mobile apps worldwide.
- Social e-commerce, based on social networks and supported by advertising, emerges and continues to grow, generating $3.9 billion in revenue for the top 500 social media retailers in the United States in 2015.
- Local e-commerce, the third dimension of the mobile, social, local e-commerce wave, also is growing, fueled by an explosion of interest in on-demand services such as Uber.
- B2B e-commerce worldwide continues to strengthen and grow to €19.8 trillion.
- On-demand service firms like Uber and Airbnb attract billions in capital, garner multi-billion dollar valuations, and show explosive growth.
- Mobile advertising continues growing at astronomical rates, accounting for almost two-thirds of all digital ad spending.
- Small businesses and entrepreneurs continue to flood into the e-commerce marketplace, often riding on the infrastructures created by industry giants such as Apple, Facebook, Amazon, Google, and eBay.

TECHNOLOGY

- A mobile computing and communications platform based on smartphones, tablet computers, wearable devices, and mobile apps becomes a reality, creating an alternative platform for online transactions, marketing, advertising, and media viewing. The use of mobile messaging services such as WhatsApp and Snapchat continues to expand, and these services are now used by over 60% of smartphone users.
- Cloud computing completes the transformation of the mobile platform by storing consumer content and software on "cloud" (Internet-based) servers and making it available to any consumer-connected device from the desktop to a smartphone.
- The Internet of Things, comprised of billions of Internet-connected devices, continues to grow exponentially.
- As firms track the trillions of online interactions that occur each day, a flood of data, typically referred to as big data, is being produced.
- In order to make sense out of big data, firms turn to sophisticated software called business analytics (or web analytics) that can identify purchase patterns as well as consumer interests and intentions in milliseconds.

SOCIETY

- User-generated content, published online as social network posts, tweets, blogs, and pins, as well as video and photo-sharing, continues to grow and provides a method of self-publishing that engages millions.
- Social networks encourage self-revelation, while threatening privacy.
- Participation by adults in social networks increases; Facebook becomes ever more popular in all demographic categories.
- Conflicts over copyright management and control continue, but there is substantial agreement among online distributors and copyright owners that they need one another.
- Taxation of online sales poses challenges for governments.
- Surveillance of online communications by both repressive regimes and Western democracies grows.
- Concerns over commercial and governmental privacy invasion increase.
- Online security continues to decline as major sites are hacked and lose control over customer information.
- Spam remains a significant problem.
- On-demand service e-commerce produces a flood of temporary, poorly paid jobs without benefits.

FIGURE 1.4	EIGHT UNIQUE FEATURES OF E-COMMERCE TECHNOLOGY

E-commerce technologies provide a number of unique features that have impacted the conduct of business.

1.3 UNIQUE FEATURES OF E-COMMERCE TECHNOLOGY

Figure 1.4 illustrates eight unique features of e-commerce technology that both challenge traditional business thinking and help explain why we have so much interest in e-commerce. These unique dimensions of e-commerce technologies suggest many new possibilities for marketing and selling—a powerful set of interactive, personalized, and rich messages are available for delivery to segmented, targeted audiences.

Prior to the development of e-commerce, the marketing and sale of goods was a mass-marketing and salesforce–driven process. Marketers viewed consumers as passive targets of advertising campaigns and branding "blitzes" intended to influence their long-term product perceptions and immediate purchasing behavior. Companies sold their products via well-insulated channels. Consumers were trapped by geographical and social boundaries, unable to search widely for the best price and quality. Information about prices, costs, and fees could be hidden from the consumer, creating profitable information asymmetries for the selling firm. **Information asymmetry** refers to any disparity in relevant market information among parties in a transaction. It was so expensive to change national or regional prices in traditional retailing (what are called *menu costs*) that one national price was the norm, and dynamic pricing to

information asymmetry
any disparity in relevant market information among parties in a transaction

the marketplace (changing prices in real time) was unheard of. In this environment, manufacturers prospered by relying on huge production runs of products that could not be customized or personalized.

E-commerce technologies make it possible for merchants to know much more about consumers and to be able to use this information more effectively than was ever true in the past. Online merchants can use this information to develop new information asymmetries, enhance their ability to brand products, charge premium prices for high-quality service, and segment the market into an endless number of subgroups, each receiving a different price. To complicate matters further, these same technologies also make it possible for merchants to know more about other merchants than was ever true in the past. This presents the possibility that merchants might collude on prices rather than compete and drive overall average prices up. This strategy works especially well when there are just a few suppliers (Varian, 2000a). We examine these different visions of e-commerce further in Section 1.4 and throughout the book.

Each of the dimensions of e-commerce technology illustrated in Figure 1.4 deserves a brief exploration, as well as a comparison to both traditional commerce and other forms of technology-enabled commerce.

UBIQUITY

marketplace

physical space you visit in order to transact

ubiquity

available just about everywhere, at all times

marketspace

marketplace extended beyond traditional boundaries and removed from a temporal and geographic location

In traditional commerce, a **marketplace** is a physical place you visit in order to transact. For example, television and radio typically motivate the consumer to go someplace to make a purchase. E-commerce, in contrast, is characterized by its **ubiquity**: it is available just about everywhere, at all times. It liberates the market from being restricted to a physical space and makes it possible to shop from your desktop, at home, at work, or even from your car, using mobile e-commerce. The result is called a **marketspace**—a marketplace extended beyond traditional boundaries and removed from a temporal and geographic location.

From a consumer point of view, ubiquity reduces *transaction costs*—the costs of participating in a market. To transact, it is no longer necessary that you spend time and money traveling to a market. At a broader level, the ubiquity of e-commerce lowers the cognitive energy required to transact in a marketspace. *Cognitive energy* refers to the mental effort required to complete a task. Humans generally seek to reduce cognitive energy outlays. When given a choice, humans will choose the path requiring the least effort—the most convenient path (Shapiro and Varian, 1999; Tversky and Kahneman, 1981).

GLOBAL REACH

E-commerce technology permits commercial transactions to cross cultural, regional, and national boundaries far more conveniently and cost-effectively than is true in traditional commerce. As a result, the potential market size for e-commerce merchants is roughly equal to the size of the world's online population (an estimated 3.3 billion in 2016) (eMarketer, Inc., 2016d). More realistically, the Internet makes it much easier for startup e-commerce merchants within a single country to achieve a national audience than was ever possible in the past. The total number of users or customers an e-commerce business can obtain is a measure of its **reach** (Evans and Wurster, 1997).

In contrast, most traditional commerce is local or regional—it involves local merchants or national merchants with local outlets. Television, radio stations, and newspapers, for instance, are primarily local and regional institutions with limited but powerful national networks that can attract a national audience. In contrast to e-commerce technology, these older commerce technologies do not easily cross national boundaries to a global audience.

reach
the total number of users or customers an e-commerce business can obtain

UNIVERSAL STANDARDS

One strikingly unusual feature of e-commerce technologies is that the technical standards of the Internet, and therefore the technical standards for conducting e-commerce, are **universal standards**—they are shared by all nations around the world. In contrast, most traditional commerce technologies differ from one nation to the next. For instance, television and radio standards differ around the world, as does cell phone technology.

The universal technical standards of e-commerce greatly lower *market entry costs*—the cost merchants must pay just to bring their goods to market. At the same time, for consumers, universal standards reduce *search costs*—the effort required to find suitable products. And by creating a single, one-world marketspace, where prices and product descriptions can be inexpensively displayed for all to see, *price discovery* becomes simpler, faster, and more accurate (Banerjee et al., 2005; Bakos, 1997; Kambil, 1997). Users, both businesses and individuals, also experience *network externalities*—benefits that arise because everyone uses the same technology. With e-commerce technologies, it is possible for the first time in history to easily find many of the suppliers, prices, and delivery terms of a specific product anywhere in the world, and to view them in a coherent, comparative environment. Although this is not necessarily realistic today for all or even most products, it is a potential that will be exploited in the future.

universal standards
standards that are shared by all nations around the world

RICHNESS

Information **richness** refers to the complexity and content of a message (Evans and Wurster, 1999). Traditional markets, national sales forces, and retail stores have great richness: they are able to provide personal, face-to-face service using aural and visual cues when making a sale. The richness of traditional markets makes them a powerful selling or commercial environment. Prior to the development of the Web, there was a trade-off between richness and reach: the larger the audience reached, the less rich the message.

E-commerce technologies have the potential for offering considerably more information richness than traditional media such as printing presses, radio, and television because they are interactive and can adjust the message to individual users. Chatting with an online sales person, for instance, comes very close to the customer experience in a small retail shop. The richness enabled by e-commerce technologies allows retail and service merchants to market and sell "complex" goods and services that heretofore required a face-to-face presentation by a sales force to a much larger audience.

richness
the complexity and content of a message

INTERACTIVITY

interactivity

technology that allows for two-way communication between merchant and consumer

Unlike any of the commercial technologies of the twentieth century, with the possible exception of the telephone, e-commerce technologies allow for **interactivity**, meaning they enable two-way communication between merchant and consumer and among consumers. Traditional television or radio, for instance, cannot ask viewers questions or enter into conversations with them, or request that customer information be entered into a form.

Interactivity allows an online merchant to engage a consumer in ways similar to a face-to-face experience. Comment features, community forums, and social networks with social sharing functionality such as Like and Share buttons all enable consumers to actively interact with merchants and other users. Somewhat less obvious forms of interactivity include responsive design elements, such as websites that change format depending on what kind of device they are being viewed on, product images that change as a mouse hovers over them, the ability to zoom in or rotate images, forms that notify the user of a problem as they are being filled out, and search boxes that autofill as the user types.

INFORMATION DENSITY

information density

the total amount and quality of information available to all market participants

E-commerce technologies vastly increase **information density**—the total amount and quality of information available to all market participants, consumers and merchants alike. E-commerce technologies reduce information collection, storage, processing, and communication costs. At the same time, these technologies greatly increase the currency, accuracy, and timeliness of information—making information more useful and important than ever. As a result, information becomes more plentiful, less expensive, and of higher quality.

A number of business consequences result from the growth in information density. One of the shifts that e-commerce is bringing about is a reduction in information asymmetry among market participants (consumers and merchants). Prices and costs become more transparent. *Price transparency* refers to the ease with which consumers can find out the variety of prices in a market; *cost transparency* refers to the ability of consumers to discover the actual costs merchants pay for products. Preventing consumers from learning about prices and costs becomes more difficult with e-commerce and, as a result, the entire marketplace potentially becomes more price competitive (Sinha, 2000). But there are advantages for merchants as well. Online merchants can discover much more about consumers; this allows merchants to segment the market into groups willing to pay different prices and permits them to engage in *price discrimination*—selling the same goods, or nearly the same goods, to different targeted groups at different prices. For instance, an online merchant can discover a consumer's avid interest in expensive exotic vacations, and then pitch expensive exotic vacation plans to that consumer at a premium price, knowing this person is willing to pay extra for such a vacation. At the same time, the online merchant can pitch the same vacation plan at a lower price to more price-sensitive consumers. Merchants also have enhanced abilities to differentiate their products in terms of cost, brand, and quality.

PERSONALIZATION AND CUSTOMIZATION

E-commerce technologies permit **personalization**: merchants can target their marketing messages to specific individuals by adjusting the message to a person's name, interests, and past purchases. Today this is achieved in a few milliseconds and followed by an advertisement based on the consumer's profile. The technology also permits **customization**—changing the delivered product or service based on a user's preferences or prior behavior. Given the interactive nature of e-commerce technology, much information about the consumer can be gathered in the marketplace at the moment of purchase.

With the increase in information density, a great deal of information about the consumer's past purchases and behavior can be stored and used by online merchants. The result is a level of personalization and customization unthinkable with traditional commerce technologies. For instance, you may be able to shape what you see on television by selecting a channel, but you cannot change the contents of the channel you have chosen. In contrast, the online version of the *Financial Times* allows you to select the type of news stories you want to see first, and gives you the opportunity to be alerted when certain events happen. Personalization and customization allow firms to precisely identify market segments and adjust their messages accordingly.

personalization
the targeting of marketing messages to specific individuals by adjusting the message to a person's name, interests, and past purchases

customization
changing the delivered product or service based on a user's preferences or prior behavior

SOCIAL TECHNOLOGY: USER-GENERATED CONTENT AND SOCIAL NETWORKS

In a way quite different from all previous technologies, e-commerce technologies have evolved to be much more social by allowing users to create and share content with a worldwide community. Using these forms of communication, users are able to create new social networks and strengthen existing ones.

All previous mass media in modern history, including the printing press, used a broadcast model (one-to-many): content is created in a central location by experts (professional writers, editors, directors, actors, and producers) and audiences are concentrated in huge aggregates to consume a standardized product. The telephone would appear to be an exception but it is not a mass communication technology. Instead the telephone is a one-to-one technology. E-commerce technologies have the potential to invert this standard media model by giving users the power to create and distribute content on a large scale, and permit users to program their own content consumption. E-commerce technologies provide a unique, many-to-many model of mass communication.

Table 1.2 provides a summary of each of the unique features of e-commerce technology and their business significance.

1.4   TYPES OF E-COMMERCE

There are a number of different types of e-commerce and many different ways to characterize them. For the most part, we distinguish different types of e-commerce

TABLE 1.2	BUSINESS SIGNIFICANCE OF THE EIGHT UNIQUE FEATURES OF E-COMMERCE TECHNOLOGY
E-COMMERCE TECHNOLOGY DIMENSION	**BUSINESS SIGNIFICANCE**
Ubiquity—E-commerce technology is available everywhere: at work, at home, and elsewhere via mobile devices, anytime.	The marketplace is extended beyond traditional boundaries and is removed from a temporal and geographic location. "Marketspace" is created; shopping can take place anywhere. Customer convenience is enhanced, and shopping costs are reduced.
Global reach—The technology reaches across national boundaries, around the earth.	Commerce is enabled across cultural and national boundaries seamlessly and without modification. "Marketspace" includes potentially billions of consumers and millions of businesses worldwide.
Universal standards—There is one set of technology standards.	There is a common, inexpensive, global technology foundation for businesses to use.
Richness—Video, audio, and text messages are possible.	Video, audio, and text marketing messages are integrated into a single marketing message and consuming experience.
Interactivity—The technology works through interaction with the user.	Consumers are engaged in a dialog that dynamically adjusts the experience to the individual, and makes the consumer a co-participant in the process of delivering goods to the market.
Information density—The technology reduces information costs and raises quality.	Information processing, storage, and communication costs drop dramatically, while currency, accuracy, and timeliness improve greatly. Information becomes plentiful, cheap, and accurate.
Personalization/Customization—The technology allows personalized messages to be delivered to individuals as well as groups.	Personalization of marketing messages and customization of products and services are based on individual characteristics.
Social technology—User-generated content and social networks.	New online social and business models enable user content creation and distribution, and support social networks.

by the nature of the market relationship—who is selling to whom. Mobile, social, and local e-commerce can be looked at as subsets of these types of e-commerce.

BUSINESS-TO-CONSUMER (B2C) E-COMMERCE

business-to-consumer (B2C) e-commerce

online businesses selling to individual consumers

The most commonly discussed type of e-commerce is **business-to-consumer (B2C) e-commerce**, in which online businesses attempt to reach individual consumers. B2C e-commerce includes purchases of retail goods, travel and other types of services, and online content. B2C has grown exponentially since 1995 and is the type of e-commerce that most consumers are likely to encounter (see **Figure 1.5**).

Within the B2C category, there are many different types of business models. Chapter 5 has a detailed discussion of seven different B2C business models: online

---

FIGURE 1.5   **THE WORLDWIDE GROWTH OF B2C E-COMMERCE**

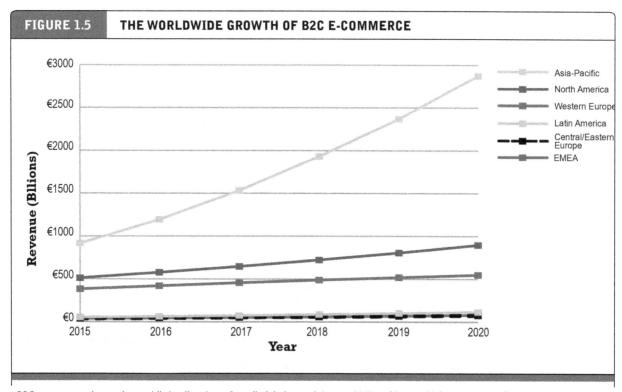

B2C e-commerce is growing rapidly in all regions. Overall global growth is over 22% and is even higher in Asia-Pacific.
SOURCES: Based on data from eMarketer, Inc., 2016e, 2016f.

---

retailers, service providers, transaction brokers, content providers, community providers/social networks, market creators, and portals. Then, in Part 4, we look at each of these business models in action. In Chapter 11, we examine online retailers, service providers, including on-demand services, and transaction brokers. In Chapter 9, we focus on content providers. In Chapter 10, we look at community providers (social networks), market creators (auctions), and portals.

The data suggests that, over the next five years, B2C e-commerce in the United States will grow by over 10% annually. There is tremendous upside potential. Today, for instance, retail e-commerce (which currently comprises the lion's share of B2C e-commerce revenues) is still a very small part (around 8%) of the overall $4.8 trillion retail market in the United States. There is obviously much room to grow (see **Figure 1.6**). However, it's not likely that B2C e-commerce revenues will continue to expand forever at current rates. As online sales become a larger percentage of all sales, online sales growth will likely eventually decline. However, this point still appears to be a long way off. Online content sales, everything from music, to video, medical information, games, and entertainment, have an even longer period to grow before they hit any ceiling effects.

BUSINESS-TO-BUSINESS (B2B) E-COMMERCE

Business-to-business (B2B) e-commerce, in which businesses focus on selling to other businesses, is the largest form of e-commerce, with around $6.7 trillion in

business-to-business (B2B) e-commerce
online businesses selling to other businesses

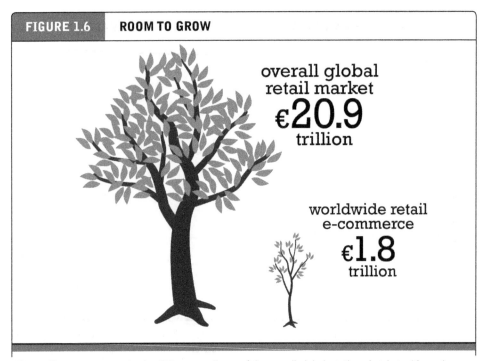

FIGURE 1.6   **ROOM TO GROW**

overall global
retail market
€20.9
trillion

worldwide retail
e-commerce
€1.8
trillion

The retail e-commerce market is still just a small part of the overall global retail market, but with much room to grow in the future.

transactions in the United States in 2016 (see **Figure 1.7**) and about €19.8 trillion worldwide (UNCTAD, 2016). This is a small portion of total B2B commerce (which remains largely non-automated), suggesting that B2B e-commerce has significant growth potential. The ultimate size of B2B e-commerce is potentially huge.

There are two primary business models used within the B2B arena: Net marketplaces, which include e-distributors, e-procurement companies, exchanges and industry consortia, and private industrial networks. We review various B2B business models in Chapter 5 and examine them in further depth in Chapter 12.

CONSUMER-TO-CONSUMER (C2C) E-COMMERCE

consumer-to-consumer (C2C) e-commerce
consumers selling to other consumers

Consumer-to-consumer (C2C) e-commerce provides a way for consumers to sell to each other, with the help of an online market maker (also called a platform provider) such as eBay or Etsy, the classifieds site Craigslist, or on-demand service companies such as Airbnb and Uber. In C2C e-commerce, the consumer prepares the product for market, places the product for auction or sale, and relies on the market maker to provide catalog, search engine, and transaction-clearing capabilities so that products can be easily displayed, discovered, and paid for.

Given that in 2015, eBay by itself generated around $82 billion in gross merchandise volume, it is probably safe to estimate that the size of the C2C market in 2016 is more than €100 billion (eBay, 2016).

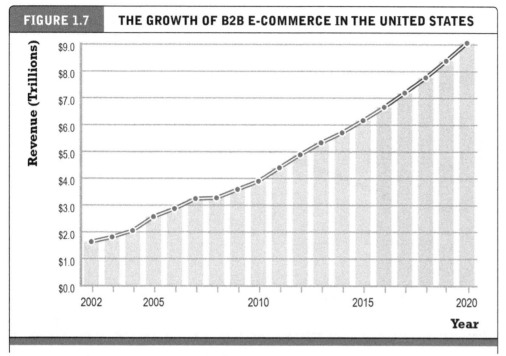

| FIGURE 1.7 | THE GROWTH OF B2B E-COMMERCE IN THE UNITED STATES |

B2B e-commerce in the United States is about 10 times the size of B2C e-commerce. In 2020, B2B e-commerce is projected to be over $9 trillion. (Note: Does not include EDI transactions.)

SOURCES: Based on data from U.S. Census Bureau, 2016; authors' estimates.

MOBILE E-COMMERCE (M-COMMERCE)

Mobile e-commerce (m-commerce), refers to the use of mobile devices to enable online transactions. M-commerce involves the use of cellular and wireless networks to connect smartphones and tablet computers to the Internet. Once connected, mobile consumers can purchase products and services, make travel reservations, use an expanding variety of financial services, access online content, and much more.

    M-commerce purchases are expected to reach almost €70 billion in the EU-5 (France, Germany, Italy, Spain and the United Kingdom) in 2016 and to grow rapidly over the next five years (see **Figure 1.8**). Factors that are driving the growth of m-commerce include the increasing amount of time consumers are spending using mobile devices, larger smartphone screen sizes, greater use of responsive design enabling e-commerce sites to be better optimized for mobile use and mobile checkout and payment, and enhanced mobile search functionality (eMarketer, Inc., 2016e).

mobile e-commerce (m-commerce)
use of mobile devices to enable online transactions

SOCIAL E-COMMERCE

Social e-commerce is e-commerce that is enabled by social networks and online social relationships. The growth of social e-commerce is being driven by a number of factors, including the increasing popularity of social sign-on (signing onto websites using your Facebook or other social network ID), network notification (the sharing of approval or disapproval of products, services, and content), online collaborative

social e-commerce
e-commerce enabled by social networks and online social relationships

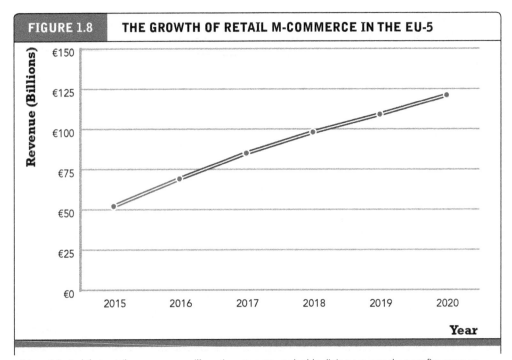

FIGURE 1.8	THE GROWTH OF RETAIL M-COMMERCE IN THE EU-5

It is anticipated that retail m-commerce will continue to grow at double-digit rates over the next five years as consumers become more and more accustomed to using mobile devices to purchase products and services.
SOURCES: Based on data from eMarketer, Inc., 2016e.

shopping tools, social search (recommendations from online trusted friends), and the increasing prevalence of integrated social commerce tools such as Buy buttons, Shopping tabs, and virtual shops on Facebook, Instagram, Pinterest, YouTube, and other social network sites.

Social e-commerce is still in its relative infancy, but in 2015, the top 500 retailers in Internet Retailer's Social Media 500 earned about $3.9 billion from social e-commerce. Website traffic from social networks to the top 500 retailers also increased by almost 20% in 2015 (Internet Retailer, 2016).

Social e-commerce is often intertwined with m-commerce, particularly as more and more social network users access those networks via mobile devices. A variation of social e-commerce known as *conversational commerce* leverages the mobile connection even further. Conversational commerce involves the use of mobile messaging apps such as Facebook Messenger, WhatsApp, Snapchat, Slack, and others as a vehicle for companies to engage with consumers.

LOCAL E-COMMERCE

local e-commerce
e-commerce that is focused on engaging the consumer based on his or her current geographic location

Local e-commerce, as its name suggests, is a form of e-commerce that is focused on engaging the consumer based on his or her current geographic location. Local merchants use a variety of online marketing techniques to drive consumers to their stores.

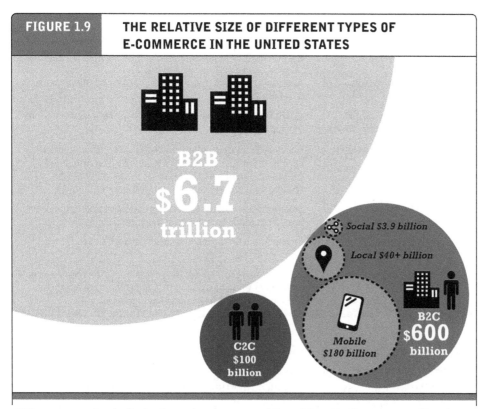

FIGURE 1.9 | **THE RELATIVE SIZE OF DIFFERENT TYPES OF E-COMMERCE IN THE UNITED STATES**

B2B e-commerce dwarfs all other forms of e-commerce; mobile, social, and local e-commerce, although growing rapidly, are still relatively small in comparison to "traditional" e-commerce.

Local e-commerce is the third prong of the mobile, social, local e-commerce wave and, fueled by an explosion of interest in local on-demand services such as Uber, is expected to grow in the United States to over $40 billion in 2016.

Figure 1.9 illustrates the relative size of all of the various types of e-commerce while **Table 1.3** provides examples for each type.

1.5 E-COMMERCE: A BRIEF HISTORY

It is difficult to pinpoint just when e-commerce began. There were several precursors to e-commerce. In the late 1970s, a pharmaceutical firm named Baxter Healthcare initiated a primitive form of B2B e-commerce by using a telephone-based modem that permitted hospitals to reorder supplies from Baxter. This system was later expanded during the 1980s into a PC-based remote order entry system and was widely copied throughout the United States long before the Internet became a commercial environment. The 1980s saw the development of Electronic Data Interchange (EDI) standards that permitted firms to exchange commercial documents and conduct digital commercial transactions across private networks.

TABLE 1.3	MAJOR TYPES OF E-COMMERCE
TYPE OF E-COMMERCE	**EXAMPLE**
B2C—business-to-consumer	Amazon is a general merchandiser that sells consumer products to retail consumers.
B2B—business-to-business	Go2Paper is an independent third-party marketplace that serves the paper industry.
C2C—consumer-to-consumer	Auction sites such as eBay, and listing sites such as Craigslist, enable consumers to auction or sell goods directly to other consumers. Airbnb and Uber provide similar platforms for services such as room rental and transportation.
M-commerce—mobile e-commerce	Mobile devices such as tablet computers and smartphones can be used to conduct commercial transactions.
Social e-commerce	Facebook is both the leading social network and social e-commerce site.
Local e-commerce	Groupon offers subscribers daily deals from local businesses in the form of Groupons, discount coupons that take effect once enough subscribers have agreed to purchase.

In the B2C arena, the first truly large-scale digitally enabled transaction system was the Minitel, a French videotext system that combined a telephone with an 8-inch screen. The Minitel was first introduced in 1981, and by the mid-1980s, more than 3 million had been deployed, with more than 13,000 different services available, including ticket agencies, travel services, retail products, and online banking. The Minitel service continued in existence until December 31, 2006, when it was finally discontinued by its owner, France Telecom.

However, none of these precursor systems had the functionality of the Internet. Generally, when we think of e-commerce today, it is inextricably linked to the Internet. For our purposes, we will say e-commerce begins in 1995, following the appearance of the first banner advertisements placed by AT&T, Volvo, Sprint, and others on Hotwired in late October 1994, and the first sales of banner ad space by Netscape and Infoseek in early 1995.

Although e-commerce is not very old, it already has a tumultuous history, which can be usefully divided into three periods: 1995–2000, the period of invention; 2001–2006, the period of consolidation; and 2007–present, a period of reinvention with social, mobile, and local expansion. The following examines each of these periods briefly, while **Figure 1.10** places them in context along a timeline.

E-COMMERCE 1995–2000: INVENTION

The early years of e-commerce were a period of explosive growth and extraordinary innovation. During this Invention period, e-commerce meant selling retail goods, usually quite simple goods, on the Internet. There simply was not enough bandwidth for more complex products. Marketing was limited to unsophisticated static display ads and not very powerful search engines. The web policy of most large firms, if they had one at all, was to have a basic static website depicting their brands. The rapid growth in e-commerce was fueled by over $125 billion in U.S. venture capital. This period of e-commerce came to a close in 2000 when stock market valuations plunged, with thousands of companies disappearing (the "dot-com crash").

The early years of e-commerce were also one of the most euphoric of times in commercial history. It was also a time when key e-commerce concepts were developed. For computer scientists and information technologists, the early success of e-commerce was a powerful vindication of a set of information technologies that had developed over a period of 40 years—extending from the development of the early Internet, to the PC, to local area networks. The vision was of a universal communications and computing environment that everyone on Earth could access with cheap, inexpensive computers—a worldwide universe of knowledge stored on HTML pages created by hundreds of millions of individuals and thousands of libraries, governments, and scientific institutes. Technologists celebrated the fact that the Internet was not controlled by anyone or any nation, but was free to all. They believed the Internet—and the e-commerce that rose on this infrastructure—should remain a self-governed, self-regulated environment.

For economists, the early years of e-commerce raised the realistic prospect of a nearly perfect competitive market: where price, cost, and quality information are equally distributed, a nearly infinite set of suppliers compete against one another, and customers have access to all relevant market information worldwide. The Internet would spawn digital markets where information would be nearly perfect—something that is rarely true in other real-world markets. Merchants in turn would have equal

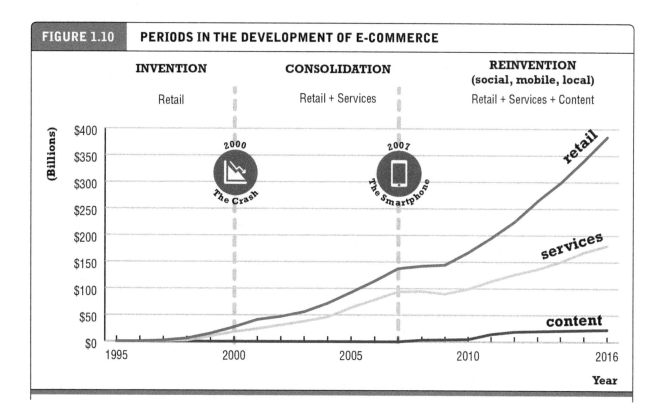

FIGURE 1.10   PERIODS IN THE DEVELOPMENT OF E-COMMERCE

direct access to hundreds of millions of customers. In this near-perfect information marketspace, transaction costs would plummet because search costs—the cost of searching for prices, product descriptions, payment settlement, and order fulfillment—would all fall drastically (Bakos, 1997). For merchants, the cost of searching for customers would also fall, reducing the need for wasteful advertising. At the same time, advertisements could be personalized to the needs of every customer. Prices and even costs would be increasingly transparent to the consumer, who could now know exactly and instantly the worldwide best price, quality, and availability of most products. Information asymmetry would be greatly reduced. Given the instant nature of Internet communications, the availability of powerful sales information systems, and the low cost involved in changing prices on a website (low menu costs), producers could dynamically price their products to reflect actual demand, ending the idea of one national price, or one suggested manufacturer's list price. In turn, market middle-men—the distributors and wholesalers who are intermediaries between producers and consumers, each demanding a payment and raising costs while adding little value—would disappear (**disintermediation**). Manufacturers and content originators would develop direct market relationships with their customers. The resulting intense competition, the decline of intermediaries, and the lower transaction costs would eliminate product brands, and along with these, the possibility of *monopoly profits* based on brands, geography, or special access to factors of production. Prices for products and services would fall to the point where prices covered costs of production plus a fair, "market rate" of return on capital, plus additional small payments for entrepreneurial effort (that would not last long). Unfair competitive advantages (which occur when one competitor has an advantage others cannot purchase) would be reduced, as would extraordinary returns on invested capital. This vision was called **friction-free commerce** (Smith et al., 2000).

For real-world entrepreneurs, their financial backers, and marketing professionals, e-commerce represented an extraordinary opportunity to earn far above normal returns on investment. This is just the opposite of what economists hoped for. The e-commerce marketspace represented access to millions of consumers worldwide who used the Internet and a set of marketing communications technologies (e-mail and web pages) that was universal, inexpensive, and powerful. These new technologies would permit marketers to practice what they always had done—segmenting the market into groups with different needs and price sensitivity, targeting the segments with branding and promotional messages, and positioning the product and pricing for each group—but with even more precision. In this new marketspace, extraordinary profits would go to **first movers**—those firms who were first to market in a particular area and who moved quickly to gather market share. In a "winner take all" market, first movers could establish a large customer base quickly, build brand name recognition early, create an entirely new distribution channel, and then inhibit competitors (new entrants) by building in *switching costs* for their customers through proprietary interface designs and features available only at one site. The idea for entrepreneurs was to create near monopolies online based on size, convenience, selection, and brand. Online businesses using the new technology could create informative, community-like features unavailable to traditional merchants. These "communities of consumption"

---

disintermediation

displacement of market middlemen who tradition-ally are intermediaries between producers and consumers by a new direct relationship between producers and consumers

friction-free commerce

a vision of commerce in which information is equally distributed, trans-action costs are low, prices can be dynamically adjusted to reflect actual demand, intermediaries decline, and unfair compet-itive advantages are eliminated

first mover

a firm that is first to market in a particular area and that moves quickly to gather market share also would add value and be difficult for traditional merchants to imitate. The thinking was that once customers became accustomed to using a company's unique web interface and feature set, they could not easily be switched to competitors. In the best case, the entrepreneurial firm would invent proprietary technologies and techniques that almost everyone adopted, creating a network effect. A **network effect** occurs where all participants receive value from the fact that everyone else uses the same tool or product (for example, a common operating system, telephone system, or software application such as a proprietary instant messaging standard or an operating system such as Windows), all of which increase in value as more people adopt them.[1]

network effect
occurs where users receive value from the fact that everyone else uses the same tool or product

To initiate this process, entrepreneurs argued that prices would have to be very low to attract customers and fend off potential competitors. E-commerce was, after all, a totally new way of shopping that would have to offer some immediate cost benefits to consumers. However, because doing business on the Web was supposedly so much more efficient when compared to traditional "bricks-and-mortar" businesses (even when compared to the direct mail catalog business) and because the costs of customer acquisition and retention would supposedly be so much lower, profits would inevitably materialize out of these efficiencies. Given these dynamics, market share, the number of visitors to a site ("eyeballs"), and gross revenue became far more important in the earlier stages of an online firm than earnings or profits. Entrepreneurs and their financial backers in the early years of e-commerce expected that extraordinary profitability would come, but only after several years of losses.

Thus, the early years of e-commerce were driven largely by visions of profiting from new technology, with the emphasis on quickly achieving very high market visibility. The source of financing was venture capital funds. The ideology of the period emphasized the ungoverned "Wild West" character of the Web and the feeling that governments and courts could not possibly limit or regulate the Internet; there was a general belief that traditional corporations were too slow and bureaucratic, too stuck in the old ways of doing business, to "get it"—to be competitive in e-commerce. Young entrepreneurs were therefore the driving force behind e-commerce, backed by huge amounts of money invested by venture capitalists. The emphasis was on *disrupting* (destroying) traditional distribution channels and disintermediating existing channels, using new pure online companies who aimed to achieve impregnable first-mover advantages. Overall, this period of e-commerce was characterized by experimentation, capitalization, and hypercompetition (Varian, 2000b).

E-COMMERCE 2001–2006: CONSOLIDATION

In the second period of e-commerce, from 2000 to 2006, a sobering period of reassessment of e-commerce occurred, with many critics doubting its long-term prospects. Emphasis shifted to a more "business-driven" approach rather than being technology driven; large traditional firms learned how to use the Web to strengthen their market positions; brand extension and strengthening became more important than creating

---

[1] The network effect is quantified by Metcalfe's Law, which argues that the value of a network grows by the square of the number of participants.

new brands; financing shrunk as capital markets shunned startup firms; and traditional bank financing based on profitability returned.

During this period of consolidation, e-commerce changed to include not just retail products but also more complex services such as travel and financial services. This period was enabled by widespread adoption of broadband networks in American homes and businesses, coupled with the growing power and lower prices of personal computers that were the primary means of accessing the Internet, usually from work or home. Marketing on the Internet increasingly meant using search engine advertising targeted to user queries, rich media and video ads, and behavioral targeting of marketing messages based on ad networks and auction markets. The web policy of both large and small firms expanded to include a broader "web presence" that included not just websites, but also e-mail, display, and search engine campaigns; multiple websites for each product; and the building of some limited community feedback facilities. E-commerce in this period was growing again by more than 10% a year.

E-COMMERCE 2007–PRESENT: REINVENTION

Web 2.0

set of applications and technologies that enable user-generated content

Beginning in 2007 with the introduction of the iPhone, to the present day, e-commerce has been transformed yet again by the rapid growth of **Web 2.0** (a set of applications and technologies that enable user-generated content, such as online social networks, blogs, video and photo sharing sites, and wikis), widespread adoption of mobile devices such as smartphones and tablet computers, the expansion of e-commerce to include local goods and services, and the emergence of an on-demand service economy enabled by millions of apps on mobile devices and cloud computing. This period can be seen as both a sociological, as well as a technological and business, phenomenon.

The defining characteristics of this period are often characterized as the "social, mobile, local" online world. Entertainment content has developed as a major source of e-commerce revenues and mobile devices have become entertainment centers, as well as on-the-go shopping devices for retail goods and services. Marketing has been transformed by the increasing use of social networks, word-of-mouth, viral marketing, and much more powerful data repositories and analytic tools for truly personal marketing. Firms have greatly expanded their online presence by moving beyond static web pages to social networks such as Facebook, Twitter, Pinterest, and Instagram in an attempt to surround the online consumer with coordinated marketing messages. These social networks share many common characteristics. First, they rely on user-generated content. "Regular" people (not just experts or professionals) are creating, sharing, and broadcasting content to huge audiences. They are inherently highly interactive, creating new opportunities for people to socially connect to others. They attract extremely large audiences (about 1.7 billion monthly active users worldwide as of June 2016 in the case of Facebook). These audiences present marketers with extraordinary opportunities for targeted marketing and advertising.

More recently, the reinvention of e-commerce has resulted in a new set of on-demand, personal service businesses such as Uber, Airbnb, Instacart, and Handy. These businesses have been able to tap into a large reservoir of unused assets (cars, spare rooms, and personal spare time) and to create lucrative markets based on the mobile platform infrastructure. The *Insight on Business* case, *Rocket Internet*, takes a look at Rocket Internet, which has mentored a number of these new social, mobile, and local e-commerce ventures.

Table 1.4 summarizes e-commerce in each of these three periods.

ASSESSING E-COMMERCE: SUCCESSES, SURPRISES, AND FAILURES

Looking back at the evolution of e-commerce, it is apparent that e-commerce has been a stunning technological success as the Internet and the Web ramped up from a few thousand to billions of e-commerce transactions per year, and this year will generate an estimated €2.35 trillion in total B2C revenues and around €19.8 trillion in B2B revenues, with around 1.62 billion online buyers worldwide. With enhancements and strengthening, described in later chapters, it is clear that e-commerce's digital infrastructure is solid enough to sustain significant growth in e-commerce during the next decade. The Internet scales well. The "e" in e-commerce has been an overwhelming success.

From a business perspective, though, the early years of e-commerce were a mixed success, and offered many surprises. Only a very small percentage of dot-coms formed

TABLE 1.4	EVOLUTION OF E-COMMERCE	
1995–2000 INVENTION	2001–2006 CONSOLIDATION	2007–PRESENT REINVENTION
Technology driven	Business driven	Mobile technology enables social, local, and mobile e-commerce
Revenue growth emphasis	Earnings and profits emphasis	Audience and social network connections emphasis
Venture capital financing	Traditional financing	Return of venture capital financing; buy-outs of startups by large firms
Ungoverned	Stronger regulation and governance	Extensive government surveillance
Entrepreneurial	Large traditional firms	Entrepreneurial social, mobile, and local firms
Disintermediation	Strengthening intermediaries	Proliferation of small online intermediaries renting business processes of larger firms
Perfect markets	Imperfect markets, brands, and network effects	Continuation of online market imperfections; commodity competition in select markets
Pure online strategies	Mixed "bricks-and-clicks" strategies	Return of pure online strategies in new markets; extension of bricks-and-clicks in traditional retail markets
First-mover advantages	Strategic-follower strength; complementary assets	First-mover advantages return in new markets as traditional web players catch up
Low-complexity retail products	High-complexity retail products and services	Retail, services, and content

INSIGHT ON BUSINESS

ROCKET INTERNET

By now we've all heard the story of code written by Mark Zuckerberg in a Harvard dorm room blossoming into a multi-billion dollar business. These days, it's harder than ever to keep track of all the tech startups being bought for millions and even billions of euros, often even without any revenue to show for themselves. Many of them have something in common—they have been nurtured, and in some cases, whipped into shape, with the help of an "incubator."

Incubators have come to occupy a vital role in tech, helping new businesses move from little more than a great idea to an established, vibrant business. Rocket Internet is one such incubator. Founded in 2007 by German entrepreneurs Oliver Samwer and his brothers Alexander and Marc, Rocket Internet launches e-commerce and other Internet start-ups in emerging markets, with the goal of becoming the world's largest Internet platform outside the United States and China. Headquartered in Berlin and with 25 international offices, Rocket Internet has launched over 100 companies with 30,000 employees in 120 countries. In 2014, Rocket went public on the Frankfurt Stock Exchange in the largest German technology IPO in the past decade. The initial pricing valued the company at around €6.5 billion. Since its IPO, the company's stock price has steadily fallen from a high of nearly €60 before settling in at approximately €20 per share for the majority of 2016, and the company's market capitalization is now down to about €3 billion. The company's tumble is a cautionary tale about the perils of chasing growth at all costs above profitability.

Rocket bills itself as more than a venture capital firm or typical incubator. Rocket has a variety of teams that work closely with each of its ventures, including teams focused on engineering and product development, online marketing, CRM, business intelligence, operations, HR, and finance. Rocket also helps its start-ups by providing access to centralized logistics and other back-office functions to help them cut down on operational costs. In many emerging markets, the most talented workers end up in established industries, but Rocket is ensuring that e-commerce also captures top talent in those regions. Prominent companies launched via Rocket Internet include Germany's Zalando, India's Jabong, Russia's Lamoda, Nigeria's Jumia, Australia's The Iconic and Zanui, Pakistan's Azmalo (now Kaymu) and Daraz, and Southeast Asia's Zalora.

Former Rocket Internet employees describe Oliver Samwer's attention to detail and emphasis on making decisions using data. Rocket Internet start-ups collect and analyze as much data as possible on their markets and customers. They also report that their association with Rocket Internet gives them more credibility with major investors.

Rocket Internet has yet to launch many new businesses in the United States, where the competitive environment is much more difficult than in emerging markets and even Europe. Many of Rocket's ventures focus on emerging markets because the profit margins are higher although the markets are smaller. This is in contrast to Amazon, for example, which has razor-thin margins but enormous scope and market reach. Critics of Rocket Internet claim that the company is less concerned with innovation than it is with launching clones of successful United States–based businesses in other markets. Rocket counters that it improves upon established businesses by refining their business processes and by localizing them to better fit specific areas. Investors are also concerned about the profitability of Rocket's portfolio. Many of Rocket's companies have market-leader status in their respective areas, but hardly any of them are currently profitable. Rocket contends that by focusing on growth in emerging markets first, profits will come in time, but its strategy has attracted increasing scrutiny as it continues to post disappointing growth and revenue figures. Rocket did report a 32% increase in aggregate revenue among its largest companies, inching it closer to profitability, but among its nine largest companies, only Middle East–based fashion retailer Namshi recorded a profit, and its largest investment, grocery delivery firm HelloFresh, posted mounting losses and flagging growth in 2016. The company has been struggling in many of its key areas of operation, such as India, where it sold fashion retailer Jabong and online furniture retailer FabFurnish in 2016 and was forced to consolidate food delivery company FoodPanda with Delivery Hero, another one of its holdings. Analysts have also criticized Rocket for the way it calculates the valuations of its companies, which tend to be much higher than the valuations of its investors.

Nevertheless, Rocket has captured significant market share in many industries by launching companies modeled after established businesses in emerging markets and then selling these ventures to those established businesses when they're looking to expand into those markets. eBay's acquisition of Germany's leading auction site, Alando, where the Samwers got their start, is an example, and the company sold a controlling stake in Southeast Asian Amazon clone Lazada to Alibaba for $1 billion in 2016, a price exceeding investor valuations of the company. Increasingly, however, Rocket is looking to create sustainable companies who are focused less on their eventual sale to bigger companies and more on their own growth. Oliver Samwer believes that in the past, it may have sold some businesses, such as Alando, too early, but that it was necessary in order for Rocket to build a track record. Now that it has one, it can afford to take a longer-term view. Rocket is increasingly focusing on quality and profitability over quantity, selling or liquidating many of its smaller companies, especially in food delivery, where it sold companies at a loss in Spain, Italy, Brazil, and Mexico in 2016. Companies like Uber and Airbnb are proving that many startups are able to quickly expand globally without the aid of firms like Rocket. Rocket's shift in strategy seems to acknowledge this reality. Still, as the global economy continues to rely more on the Internet and Internet-based services, accelerators like Rocket Internet will have a prominent role in markets around the world.

▬ **SOURCES:** "Rocket Internet's Trajectory Shift," by Leila Abboud, Bloomberg.com, November 23, 2016; "German Tech Incubator Rocket Internet to Focus on Biggest Companies," Nasdaq.com, November 16, 2016; "Rocket Internet Leaves Us Groping in the Dark," by Leila Abboud, Bloomberg.com, October 12, 2016; "Inside Rocket Internet's Ailing Startup Factory," by Jeremy Kahn, Stefan Nicola, Aaron Ricadela, and Adam Satariano, Bloomberg.com, October 7, 2016; "Deliver Hero Buys Foodpanda in Sought After Food Delivery Market," Reuters, December 10, 2016; "Rocket Internet's Portfolio Firms Narrow Losses on Higher Revenue," by Friedrich Geiger, *Wall Street Journal*, September 22, 2016; "The Rise and Fall of Rocket Internet in India," by Shrutika Verma and Mihir Dalal, Livemint.com, September 2, 2016; "Rocket Internet's Deal with Alibaba Validates Its Opaque, Unproven Model," by Joon Ian Wong, Qz.com, April 13, 2016; "Is Rocket Internet Finally on the Path to Profitability?" by Friedrich Geiger, *Wall Street Journal*, April 12, 2016; "Rocket Internet Sells Food Startups in Spain, Italy, Brazil, Mexico for $140M To Just Eat," by Ingrid Lunden, Techcrunch.com, February 5, 2016; "Rocket Internet: Waiting for Lift-Off," by Sarah Gordon and Dan McCrum, *Financial Times*, October 19, 2015; "Revenue Jumps at Rocket Internet's Top Start-ups," by Emma Thomason, Reuters, September 30, 2015; "Rocket Internet Plans to Sell Its Top Companies in India," by Biswarup Gooptu and Krithika Krishnamurthy, *Economic Times*, September 22, 2015; "Fear and Laundry in London as Rocket Internet's ZipJet Launches in the U.K. Capital City," by Steve O'Hear, Techcrunch.com, November 3, 2014; "With ShopWings, Instacart Gets a Wink and a Clone from Rocket Internet," by Ingrid Lunden, Techcrunch.com, October 13, 2014; "Rocket Internet – First Mover in Asia?" by Susan Cunningham, *Forbes*, October 5, 2014; "Rocket Internet Drops 13% in Debut," by Chase Gummer, *Wall Street Journal*, October 2, 2014; "Rocket Internet's Marc Samwar on Cloning: We Make Business Models Better Because We Localize," by Leena Rao, Techcrunch.com, October 28, 2013; "5 Reasons Why Rocket Internet Graduates Become Good Entrepreneurs," Ventureburn.com, October 17, 2013; "eBay Acquires Germany's Leading Onine Person-to-Person Trading Site – Alando.de AG," Prnewswire.com, June 22, 2013; "Rocket Internet's New Site Reveals a Huge Global Cloning Operation in Full Flow," by Mike Butcher, TechCrunch.com, July 20, 2012.

since 1995 have survived as independent companies in 2016, and even fewer of these survivors are profitable. Yet online retail sales of goods and services are still growing very rapidly. Contrary to economists' hopes, however, online sales are increasingly concentrated. For instance, according to Internet Retailer, the top 500 retailers account for 84% of all online retail sales (Internet Retailer, 2016). So thousands of firms have failed, and those few that have survived dominate the market. The idea of thousands of suppliers competing on price has been replaced by a market dominated by giant firms. Consumers use the Web as a powerful source of information about products they often actually purchase through other channels, such as at a traditional bricks-and-mortar store. For instance, a 2014 study found that almost 90% of those surveyed "webroomed" (researched a product online before purchasing at a physical store) (Interactions Consumer Experience Marketing, Inc., 2014). This is especially true of expensive consumer durables such as automobiles, appliances, and electronics. This offline "Internet-influenced" commerce is very difficult to estimate, but definitely significant. For instance, Forrester Research estimated the amount to be somewhere around $1.3 trillion in 2015 (Forrester Research, 2016). All together then, retail e-commerce (actual online purchases) and purchases influenced by online shopping but actually bought in a store (Internet-influenced commerce) are expected to amount to almost $1.7 trillion in 2016. The "commerce" in e-commerce is basically very sound, at least in the sense of attracting a growing number of customers and generating revenues and profits for large e-commerce players.

Although e-commerce has grown at an extremely rapid pace in customers and revenues, it is clear that many of the visions, predictions, and assertions about e-commerce developed in the early years have not been fulfilled. For instance, economists' visions of "friction-free" commerce have not been entirely realized. Prices are sometimes lower online, but the low prices are sometimes a function of entrepreneurs selling products below their costs. In some cases, online prices are higher than those of local merchants, as consumers are willing to pay a small premium for the convenience of buying online (Cavallo, 2016). Consumers are less price sensitive than expected; surprisingly, the websites with the highest revenue often have the highest prices. There remains considerable persistent and even increasing price dispersion: online competition has lowered prices, but price dispersion remains pervasive in many markets despite lower search costs (Levin, 2011; Ghose and Yao, 2010). In a study of 50,000 goods in the United Kingdom and the United States, researchers found Internet prices were sticky even in the face of large changes in demand, online merchants did not alter prices significantly more than offline merchants, and price dispersion across online sellers was somewhat greater than traditional brick and mortar stores (Gorodnichenko, et al., 2014). The concept of one world, one market, one price has not occurred in reality as entrepreneurs discover new ways to differentiate their products and services. Merchants have adjusted to the competitive Internet environment by engaging in "hit-and-run pricing" or changing prices every day or hour (using "flash pricing" or "flash sales") so competitors never know what they are charging (neither do customers); by making their prices hard to discover and sowing confusion among consumers by "baiting and switching" customers from low-margin products to high-margin products with supposedly "higher quality." Finally, brands remain very important in e-commerce—consumers trust some firms more than others to deliver a high-quality product on time and they are willing to pay for it (Rosso and Jansen, 2010).

The "perfect competition" model of extreme market efficiency has not come to pass. Merchants and marketers are continually introducing information asymmetries. Search costs have fallen overall, but the overall transaction cost of actually completing a purchase in e-commerce remains high because users have a bewildering number of new questions to consider: Will the merchant actually deliver? What is the time frame of delivery? Does the merchant really stock this item? How do I fill out this form? Many potential e-commerce purchases are terminated in the shopping cart stage because of these consumer uncertainties. Some people still find it easier to call a trusted catalog merchant on the telephone than to order on a website. Finally, intermediaries have not disappeared as predicted. Most manufacturers, for instance, have not adopted the manufacturer-direct sales model of online sales, and some that had, such as Sony, have returned to an intermediary model. Dell, one of the pioneers of online manufacturer-direct sales, has moved toward a mixed model heavily reliant on in-store sales where customers can "kick the tires;" Apple's physical stores are among the most successful stores in the world. People still like to shop in a physical store.

If anything, e-commerce has created many opportunities for middlemen to aggregate content, products, and services and thereby introduce themselves as the "new" intermediaries. Third-party travel sites such as Travelocity, Orbitz, and Expedia are an example of this kind of intermediary. E-commerce has not driven existing retail chains and catalog merchants out of business, although it has created opportunities for entrepreneurial online-only firms to succeed.

The visions of many entrepreneurs and venture capitalists for e-commerce have not materialized exactly as predicted either. First-mover advantage appears to have succeeded only for a very small group of companies, albeit some of them extremely well-known, such as Google, Facebook, Amazon, and others. Getting big fast sometimes works, but often not. Historically, first movers have been long-term losers, with the early-to-market innovators usually being displaced by established "fast-follower" firms with the right complement of financial, marketing, legal, and production assets needed to develop mature markets, and this has proved true for e-commerce as well. Many e-commerce first movers, such as eToys, FogDog (sporting goods), Webvan (groceries), and Eve.com (beauty products), failed. Customer acquisition and retention costs during the early years of e-commerce were extraordinarily high, with some firms, such as E*Trade and other financial service firms, paying up to $400 to acquire a new customer. The overall costs of doing business online—including the costs of technology, site design and maintenance, and warehouses for fulfillment—are often no lower than the costs faced by the most efficient bricks-and-mortar stores. A large warehouse costs tens of millions of dollars regardless of a firm's online presence. The knowledge of how to run the warehouse is priceless, and not easily moved. The startup costs can be staggering. Attempting to achieve or enhance profitability by raising prices has often led to large customer defections. From the e-commerce merchant's perspective, the "e" in e-commerce does not stand for "easy."

On the other hand, there have been some extraordinary and unanticipated surprises in the evolution of e-commerce. Few predicted the impact of the mobile platform. Few anticipated the rapid growth of social networks or their growing success as advertising platforms based on a more detailed understanding of personal behavior than even Google has achieved. And few, if any, anticipated the emergence of on-demand e-commerce, which enables people to use their mobile devices to order up everything from taxis, to groceries, to laundry service.

1.6   UNDERSTANDING E-COMMERCE: ORGANIZING THEMES

Understanding e-commerce in its totality is a difficult task for students and instructors because there are so many facets to the phenomenon. No single academic discipline is prepared to encompass all of e-commerce. After teaching the e-commerce course for a number of years and writing this book, we have come to realize just how difficult it is to "understand" e-commerce. We have found it useful to think about e-commerce as involving three broad interrelated themes: technology, business, and society. We do not mean to imply any ordering of importance here because this book and our thinking freely range over these themes as appropriate to the problem we are trying to understand and describe. Nevertheless, as in previous technologically driven commercial revolutions, there is a historic progression. Technologies develop first, and then those developments are exploited commercially. Once commercial exploitation of the technology becomes widespread, a host of social, cultural, and political issues arise, and society is forced to respond to them.

TECHNOLOGY: INFRASTRUCTURE

The development and mastery of digital computing and communications technology is at the heart of the newly emerging global digital economy we call e-commerce. To understand the likely future of e-commerce, you need a basic understanding of the information technologies upon which it is built. E-commerce is above all else a technologically driven phenomenon that relies on a host of information technologies as well as fundamental concepts from computer science developed over a 50-year period. At the core of e-commerce are the Internet and the Web, which we describe in detail in Chapter 2. Underlying these technologies are a host of complementary technologies: cloud computing, desktop computers, smartphones, tablet computers, local area networks, relational and non-relational databases, client/server computing, data mining, and fiber-optic switches, to name just a few. These technologies lie at the heart of sophisticated business computing applications such as enterprise-wide information systems, supply chain management systems, manufacturing resource planning systems, and customer relationship management systems. E-commerce relies on all these basic technologies—not just the Internet. The Internet, while representing a sharp break from prior corporate computing and communications technologies, is nevertheless just the latest development in the evolution of corporate computing and part of the continuing chain of computer-based innovations in business. **Figure 1.11** illustrates the major stages in the development of corporate computing and indicates how the Internet and the Web fit into this development trajectory.

To truly understand e-commerce, you will need to know something about packet-switched communications, protocols such as TCP/IP, client/server and cloud computing, mobile digital platforms, web servers, HTML5, CSS, and software programming tools such as Flash and JavaScript on the client side, and Java, PHP, Ruby on Rails, and ColdFusion on the server side. All of these topics are described fully in the book (Chapters 2–4).

FIGURE 1.11	THE INTERNET AND THE EVOLUTION OF CORPORATE COMPUTING

Computer Technology   **Business Application**

Mainframe Computers
- 1950 – 1975

Transaction automation
Payroll
Accounts receivable

Minicomputers
1970 – 1980

Business function automation
Marketing
Human resources
Design

Personal Computers
- 1980 – Present

Desktop automation
Word processing
Spreadsheets
Databases

Local Area Networks Client/Server Computing
1980 – Present

Workgroup automation
Document sharing
Project management
Messaging, e-mail

Enterprise-wide Computing
- 1990 – Present

Enterprise-wide automation
Resource planning systems
Integrated finance-manufacturing systems
Human resource planning

Internet and Web Mobile Platform Cloud Computing
1995 – Present

Industrial system automation
Supply chain management
Customer relationship management
Channel management systems
Web and cloud services

The Internet and Web, and the emergence of a mobile platform held together by the Internet cloud, are the latest in a chain of evolving technologies and related business applications, each of which builds on its predecessors.

BUSINESS: BASIC CONCEPTS

While technology provides the infrastructure, it is the business applications—the potential for extraordinary returns on investment—that create the interest and excitement in e-commerce. New technologies present businesses and entrepreneurs with new ways of organizing production and transacting business. New technologies change the strategies and plans of existing firms: old strategies are made obsolete and new ones need to be invented. New technologies are the birthing grounds where thousands of new companies spring up with new products and services. New technologies are the graveyard of many traditional businesses. To truly understand e-commerce, you will need to be familiar with some key business concepts, such as the nature of digital markets, digital goods, business models, firm and industry value chains, value webs, industry structure, digital disruption, and consumer behavior in digital markets, as well as basic concepts of financial analysis. We'll examine these concepts further in Chapters 5, 6, 7, and 9 through 12.

SOCIETY: TAMING THE JUGGERNAUT

With around 3.3 billion now using the Internet worldwide, the impact of the Internet and e-commerce on society is significant and global. Increasingly, e-commerce is subject to the laws of nations and global entities. You will need to understand the pressures that global e-commerce places on contemporary society in order to conduct a successful e-commerce business or understand the e-commerce phenomenon. The primary societal issues we discuss in this book are individual privacy, intellectual property, and public welfare policy.

Because the Internet and the Web are exceptionally adept at tracking the identity and behavior of individuals online, e-commerce raises difficulties for preserving privacy—the ability of individuals to place limits on the type and amount of information collected about them, and to control the uses of their personal information. Read the *Insight on Society* case, *Facebook and the Age of Privacy*, to get a view of some of the ways e-commerce sites use personal information.

Because the cost of distributing digital copies of copyrighted intellectual property—tangible works of the mind such as music, books, and videos—is nearly zero on the Internet, e-commerce poses special challenges to the various methods societies have used in the past to protect intellectual property rights.

The global nature of e-commerce also poses public policy issues of equity, equal access, content regulation, and taxation. For instance, in the United States, public telephone utilities are required under public utility and public accommodation laws to make basic service available at affordable rates so everyone can have telephone service. Should these laws be extended to the Internet and the Web? If goods are purchased by a New York State resident from a website in California, shipped from a center in Illinois, and delivered to New York, what state has the right to collect a sales tax? Should some heavy Internet users who consume extraordinary amounts of bandwidth by streaming endless movies be charged extra for service, or should the Internet be neutral with respect to usage? What rights do nation-states and their citizens have with respect to the Internet, the Web, and e-commerce? We address issues such as these in Chapter 8, and also throughout the text.

INSIGHT ON SOCIETY

FACEBOOK AND THE AGE OF PRIVACY

In a January 2010 interview, Mark Zuckerberg, the founder of Facebook, proclaimed that the age of privacy had to come to an end. According to Zuckerberg, people were no longer worried about sharing their personal information with friends, friends of friends, or even the entire Web. Supporters of Zuckerberg's viewpoint believe the twenty-first century is a new era of openness and transparency. If true, this is good news for Facebook because its business model is based on selling access to a database of personal information.

However, not everyone is a true believer. Privacy—limitations on what personal information government and private institutions can collect and use—is a founding principle of democracies. A decade's worth of privacy surveys in the United States show that well over 80% of the American public fear the Internet is a threat to their privacy.

With about 1.7 billion monthly users worldwide, and around 175 million in North America, Facebook's privacy policies are going to shape privacy standards on the Internet for years to come. The economic stakes in the privacy debate are quite high, involving billions in advertising and transaction dollars. Facebook's business model is based on building a database of billions of users who are encouraged, or even perhaps deceived, into relinquishing control over personal information, which is then sold to advertisers and other third parties. The less privacy Facebook's users want or have, the more Facebook profits. Eliminating personal information privacy is built into Facebook's DNA.

Facebook's current privacy policies are quite a flip-flop from its original policy in 2004, which promised users near complete control over who could see their personal profile. However,

every year since 2004, Facebook has attempted to extend its control over user information and content, often without notice. For instance, in 2007, Facebook introduced the Beacon program, which was designed to broadcast users' activities on participating websites to their friends. After a public outcry, Facebook terminated the Beacon program, and paid $9.5 million to settle a host of class action lawsuits. In 2009, undeterred by the Beacon fiasco, Facebook unilaterally decided that it would publish users' basic personal information on the public Internet, and announced that whatever content users had contributed belonged to Facebook, and that its ownership of that information never terminated. However, as with the Beacon program, Facebook's efforts to take permanent control of user information resulted in users joining online resistance groups and it was ultimately forced to withdraw this policy as well.

In 2011, Facebook began publicizing users' "likes" of various advertisers in Sponsored Stories (i.e., advertisements) that included the users' names and profile pictures without their explicit consent, without paying them, and without giving them a way to opt out. This resulted in yet another class action lawsuit, which Facebook settled for $20 million in June 2012. (Facebook dropped Sponsored Stories in April 2014.) In 2011, Facebook enrolled all Facebook subscribers into its facial recognition program without notice. This too raised the privacy alarm, forcing Facebook to make it easier for users to opt out.

In May 2012, Facebook went public, creating even more pressure to increase revenues and profits to justify its stock market value. Shortly thereafter, Facebook announced that it was launching a mobile advertising product that pushes ads to the mobile news feeds of users based on the apps they use through the Facebook Connect feature, without explicit permission from the user to do so. It also

(continued)

announced Facebook Exchange, a program that allows advertisers to serve ads to Facebook users based on their browsing activity while not on Facebook. Privacy advocates raised the alarm yet again and more lawsuits were filed by users. In 2013, Facebook agreed to partner with several data marketing companies that deliver targeted ads based on offline data. The firms provide customer data to Facebook, which then allows Facebook advertisers to target their ads to those users based on that data.

In December 2013, another class action lawsuit was filed against Facebook by users alleging that it violated their privacy by scanning users' private Facebook messages and mining them for data such as references to URLs that Facebook could then sell to advertisers. In May 2014, an enhancement to Facebook's mobile app that allows the app to recognize the music, television show, or movie playing in the background when a user makes a status update raised a new privacy alarm.

Facebook's newest privacy issue involves its facial recognition software used to tag users in photos. The "tag suggestions" feature is automatically enabled when you sign up, without user consent. A federal court in 2016 is allowing a lawsuit to go forward contesting Facebook's right to tag users in photos without their consent. This feature appears to be in violation of several state laws which seek to secure the privacy of biometric data.

After all these lawsuits and online public protests, one might think that Facebook's privacy policy would improve. But an academic analysis of Facebook's privacy policies from 2008 to 2015 found that on most measures of privacy protection, Facebook's policies have worsened. Since 2008, Facebook has made it more difficult for users to find out what information is being shared with whom, how it builds profiles, or how to change privacy settings. Its privacy policies have become less readable, even inscrutable, according to the researchers.

Facebook is certainly aware of consumer suspicion of its privacy policies, and it changes its policies almost yearly in response to criticism. But the response is often not helpful for users, and typically extends the company's claims to do whatever it wants with personal information. Its latest privacy policy, implemented in 2015, claims to switch its default privacy settings for new users from Public to Friends, provide a Privacy Checkup tool for users, give users the ability to see the data it keeps on their likes and interests, and enable users to change, delete, or add to that data. Facebook argues this new policy gives users more control of the ads they are shown. Analysts point out, however, that using these new features requires users to navigate a maze of check boxes and menus that are difficult to understand even for expert Facebook users. Users have come to realize that everything they post or say on Facebook will be given over to advertisers. There is no privacy on Facebook. People who are concerned about their privacy, analysts have concluded, should delete their Facebook accounts.

▬▬ **SOURCES:** "Facebook's Newest Privacy Problem: 'Faceprint' Data" by Katie Collins, Cnet.com, May 16, 2016; "In Re Facebook Biometric Information Privacy Litigation," U.S. District Court, Northern District of California, Case No. 15-cv-03747-JD, May 6, 2016; "Facebook to Face Privacy Lawsuit Over Photo Tagging," by Jessica Guynn, *USA Today*, May 6, 2016; "Facebook Rescinds Internship to Harvard Student Who Exposed a Privacy Flaw in Messenger," by Robert Gabelhoff, *Washington Post*, August 14, 2015; "Did You Really Agree to That? The Evolution of Facebook's Privacy Policy," by Jennifer Shore and Jill Steinman, *Technology Science*, August 11, 2015; "Facebook's Privacy Incident Response: A Study of Geolocation Sharing on Facebook Messenger," by Aran Khanna, *Technology Science*, August 11, 2015; "Sharing Data, but Not Happily," by Natasha Singer, *New York Times*, June 4, 2015; "How Your Facebook Likes Could Cost You a Job," by Anna North, *New York Times*, January 20, 2015; "Facebook Stops Irresponsibly Defaulting Privacy of New Users' Posts to 'Public,' Changes to 'Friends,'" by Josh Constine, Techcrunch.com, May 22, 2014; "Facebook Users Revolt Over Privacy Feature—Enables Microphone in Apps," by Jan Willem Aldershoff, Myce.com, June 9, 2014; "Didn't Read Those Terms of Service? Here's What You Agreed to Give Up," by Natasha Singer, *New York Times*, April 28, 2014; "Facebook Eliminates Sponsored Stories—Will It Matter to Advertisers?," by Amy Durbin, Mediapost.com, February 25, 2014; "Facebook Sued for Allegedly Intercepting Private Messages," by Jennifer Van Grove, Cnet.com, January 2, 2014; "Facebook to Partner with Data Brokers," by Bob Sullivan, Redtape.nbcnews.com, February 26, 2013; "Facebook Exchange Ads Raise Privacy Concerns," by Mikal E. Belicove, Cnbc.com, June 21, 2012; "Facebook Suit Over Subscriber Tracking Seeks $15 Billion," by Kit Chellel and Jeremy Hodges, Bloomberg.com, May 19, 2012; "How Facebook Pulled a Privacy Bait and Switch," by Dan Tynan, *PC World*, May 2010.

1.7   ACADEMIC DISCIPLINES CONCERNED WITH E-COMMERCE

The phenomenon of e-commerce is so broad that a multidisciplinary perspective is required. There are two primary approaches to e-commerce: technical and behavioral.

TECHNICAL APPROACHES

Computer scientists are interested in e-commerce as an exemplary application of Internet technology. They are concerned with the development of computer hardware, software, and telecommunications systems, as well as standards, encryption, and database design and operation. Operations management scientists are primarily interested in building mathematical models of business processes and optimizing these processes. They are interested in e-commerce as an opportunity to study how business firms can exploit the Internet to achieve more efficient business operations. The information systems discipline spans the technical and behavioral approaches. Technical groups within the information systems specialty focus on data mining, search engine design, and artificial intelligence.

BEHAVIORAL APPROACHES

From a behavioral perspective, information systems researchers are primarily interested in e-commerce because of its implications for firm and industry value chains, industry structure, and corporate strategy. Economists have focused on online consumer behavior, pricing of digital goods, and on the unique features of digital electronic markets. The marketing profession is interested in marketing, brand development and extension, online consumer behavior, and the ability of e-commerce technologies to segment and target consumer groups, and differentiate products. Economists share an interest with marketing scholars who have focused on e-commerce consumer response to marketing and advertising campaigns, and the ability of firms to brand, segment markets, target audiences, and position products to achieve above-normal returns on investment.

Management scholars have focused on entrepreneurial behavior and the challenges faced by young firms who are required to develop organizational structures in short time spans. Finance and accounting scholars have focused on e-commerce firm valuation and accounting practices. Sociologists—and to a lesser extent, psychologists—have focused on general population studies of Internet usage, the role of social inequality in skewing Internet benefits, and the use of the Web as a social network and group communications tool. Legal scholars are interested in issues such as preserving intellectual property, privacy, and content regulation.

No one perspective dominates research about e-commerce. The challenge is to learn enough about a variety of academic disciplines so that you can grasp the significance of e-commerce in its entirety.

Puma
Goes Omni

W hen Puma, one of the world's top sports footwear, apparel, and accessories brands, conceived its Love=Football campaign in 2010, the goal was to create a memorable tagline in a language that would be understood the world over—pictures. In the process, the company stumbled upon the power of social marketing. Puma's ad agency, Droga5, filmed a light-hearted commercial featuring scruffy everyday men in a Tottenham pub singing love songs to their Valentines. The video went viral, garnering more than 130 million impressions and spawning hundreds of homemade response videos. Today, Puma's marketing campaigns are all branded with the slogan Forever Faster, which, according to Ruth How, Puma's Head of Marketing Communications, is a sentiment that applies not only to its marketing message to consumers, but also to Puma's approach to marketing itself. As How notes, since so much of Puma's target market lives and breathes in the digital space, its imperative for Puma to fuse marketing with technology to reach those consumers.

© René van den Berg/Alamy Stock Photo

Puma maintains an extensive presence on Facebook, Twitter, Instagram, Pinterest, Snapchat, and YouTube and closely integrates its social strategy with its other marketing channels with an eye toward driving the conversation and deepening its engagement with consumers. It uses social media in part to better understand the different regional and sub-brand audiences within more than 120 countries in which it operates. Not all content is suitable for every one of its nearly 17 million global Facebook fans. Dedicated sport, country, region, and product category pages were created for each social network. For several years, Puma took a trial-and-error approach, focusing on building its follower base. Today, Puma uses a data-driven approach, geo-targeting posts at the appropriate times of the day to maximize fan engagement and generate the right mix of online content to best drive sales. For instance, it has begun working with a platform named My Appy, which allows it to aggregate all of the social media conversations involving Puma into one space, enabling Puma to better understand how consumers are engaging with its content. A tab for its iPhone app sends followers directly to Apple's App Store, substantially boosting sales. The company also sends personalized messages based on customers' website activity, using items abandoned in shopping carts and other information to generate customized messages and surveys. This integration of channels into a cohesive customer acquisition strategy is in fact a key element of the emerging world of omni-channel retailing.

The advent of the term "omni-channel" signals the evolution of multi-channel or cross-channel retailing to encompass all digital and social technologies. The idea is that customers can examine, access, purchase, and return goods from any channel, and even change channels during the process, and receive timely and relevant product information at each step along the way and in each channel. The rise of social networks and the personalized retail it engenders is a primary driver of omni-channel—the complete integration of the shopping and brand experience. Marketing efforts must be unified undertakings combining offline events and sales and online promotions and brand building that not only employ all available channels but provide multiple opportunities for customer involvement. For a company like Puma, with e-commerce sites in the United States, Russia, Canada, China, India, Switzerland, Germany, France, the United Kingdom, and a European site that serves multiple countries in multiple languages, this presents quite a challenge.

Puma's Global Head of E-Commerce, Tom Davis, has overseen a major restructuring of its e-commerce business. Puma was not fully prepared to compete with Adidas, Nike, and other sports apparel companies in a global market that was rapidly shifting away from mature Western markets and desktop commerce. To coordinate market rollouts and ensure a unified brand image, Puma's regional e-commerce teams needed oversight. A command center took over brand strategy and investment decisions, leaving daily operational and locality-based decision-making to the regional teams. Unified content and product strategies were developed in addition to a centralized product database. One central website replaced multiple e-commerce sites on different platforms. The company developed new content and product strategies and launched a centralized product database. Demandware, Puma's main e-commerce platform, was used to simplify managing global e-commerce operations from a central digital platform, though several other e-commerce platforms are still used. The goal was to achieve a consistent and cohesive brand building strategy so that the teams would all be on the same page.

SOURCES: "Puma on Track to Hit Upper End of Earnings Target," by James Shotter, Ft.com, November 10, 2016; "What Puma Is Doing Right in Asia," by Byravee Iyer, Campaignasia.com, October 12, 2016; "Puma Personalizes Targeted Messages Based on Site Visits, Cart Abandonment," by Laurie Sullivan, Mediapost.com, June 15, 2016; "Which Sneaker Brand Wins the E-commerce Foot Race?" by Zach Blatt, Internetretailer.com, May 17, 2016; "How Puma Is Turning to Startups to Become 'the Fastest Sports Brand in the World'," by Natalie Mortimer, Thedrum.com, March 29, 2016; "Puma and Adidas to Start Their Own E-commerce Portals in India," Businessinsider.in, March 7, 2016; "eCommerce Trend Alert 2016— Personalized Products," by Amy Watson, Brainsins.com, 2016; "Inside Puma's Branded Content Strategy," by Lucia Moses, Digiday. com, December 15, 2014; "The Case of Puma: Can Tmall and In-House E-Store Co-Exist in China?" by Gelati Ting, Fashionbi. com, June 26, 2014; "Puma Understands the Importance of Local Needs in a Global E-commerce Rollout," by Derek Du Preez, Diginomica.com, June 24, 2014; "Puma and Newegg Discuss Their Entry into the China E-commerce Market," Cdnetworks.

Puma assigned the overhaul of its website to Viget, a web design firm. It created templates to unite several Puma sites into one and unify the look across numerous categories and content types. A dozen category sites now complement Puma.com, with a custom-built content management system (CMS) ensuring that consistent Puma branding and navigation are maintained across all sub-sites and pages. Category managers can customize home pages outside of the template layout. The flexibility to roll out local, regional, or global campaigns is thus built into the website design. What's more, the CMS integrates with a language translation tool, a Storefinder tool that helps visitors locate Puma stores, and Puma's product inventory manager. These design changes have improved site visualization and navigation, prompting customers to spend twice as much time on the site and raising the order rate by 7.1%. Other features like the ability to design Puma shoes from the ground up using a built-in web app across all of its sites have made Puma's online presence even more compelling.

The Viget team then turned to the mobile site, first incorporating Storefinder into the interface. Using the GPS capability of the mobile device, Puma stores nearest to the user can be located, along with address and contact information. Users experience the same content and appearance as Puma.com and each of the category sites, managed by the same CMS. Viget also rebuilt Puma's mobile site using responsive design features. Puma also incorporated mobile into its omni-channel marketing strategy. For instance, it developed PUMATRAC, an iPhone app that automatically analyzes environmental conditions to give runners feedback on how these variables impact their performance. The app offers multiple options to share statistics and routes with other runners.

In addition to focusing on unifying its branding efforts and e-commerce websites, Puma has also streamlined its e-commerce teams. In the past, Puma maintained nine independent e-commerce teams on five continents. Currently, it is working towards teams divided into the three major segments that comprise the majority of its sales—North America, Europe, and Asia-Pacific—as well as a global unit that operates at a level above these regional segments. At the same time, the company hopes to pursue a strategy that is flexible and focused more on the precise local needs in individual markets, even though it has moved to fewer individual e-commerce teams. For example, Puma found that in the Asia-Pacific region, traditional paid media advertising was very ineffective compared to social marketing, particularly that featuring compelling influencers like Usain Bolt and Kylie Jenner. The company's shift in strategy in that region has led to a 10% increase in sales in 2016, making it the company's strongest segment. Overall, Puma's approach has worked across all its segments, improving conversion rates from 10% to 20% and boosting average order value by 12%. Centralizing its e-commerce operations under a single site also helps Puma better collect customer data to personalize marketing and develop more appealing products.

Over the past several years Puma has gained invaluable omni-channel experience, racked up social marketing accomplishments, and laid the groundwork for resurgent e-commerce success. But it hasn't been easy. Implementing a successful omni-channel strategy is a monumental task. In 2013 and 2014, Puma's profits sagged, and the company claimed its growing marketing budget was the reason while insisting that its strategy would pay dividends in the future. Puma knows it cannot compete on price with mass merchandisers such as Amazon and Zappos, and it cannot control Puma product presentation in those venues. External loss of brand control necessitates superior product content, product information management, and shopping experience internally, precisely the skills it has been nurturing. Puma's ability to adapt its strategy to individual areas has also helped the company advance into in India, where Puma received permission from the Indian government to open a portal after the country changed its rules regarding foreign direct investment. (Puma had formerly only been able to sell products wholesale, as opposed to traditional retail and e-commerce directly to the consumer), and China, a growing market where Puma has traditionally had minimal presence. In 2015, Puma finally began to see results from its innovative advertising, product development, and centralization efforts as its earnings rebounded to beat analysts' estimates. Puma CEO Bjorn Gulden believes that 2015 represented a turning point for the Puma brand back to profitability. In 2016, Puma ranked behind only Nike and New Balance in e-commerce footwear, ahead of brands like Adidas and Reebok, which spend much larger amounts on advertising, and its quarterly earnings reflect that strength. Puma reported third-quarter earnings of €39.5m, nearly double the €20m it recorded in the same period of 2015, and projected its 2016 yearly earnings to come in at the high end of expectations. Puma's e-commerce strategy has been the main driver of that success.

com, June 3, 2014; "How Puma Is Improving Sales Operations Through E-commerce," by Paul Demery, internetretailer.com, May 20, 2014; "Clients: Puma," Demandware.com, accessed October 20, 2013; "Droga5 Case Studies: The HardChorus," Droga5.com, accessed October 20, 2013; "Puma Launches Innovative New Running App," News.puma.com, October 2, 2013; "Puma's Unified Approach to Global E-commerce," Ecommercefacts.com, August 5, 2013; "Puma's Head of E-Commerce: Changes and Challenges of Customization in the Apparel Industry," Masscustomization.de, July 16, 2013; "PUMA: Challenges in an Omni-channel World," Embodee.com, May 3, 2013; "3 Shoe Brands Kicking Butt with Social Media," by Lauren Indvik, Mashable.com, February 6, 2012; "Why Brands Like Puma and GE Are Flocking to Instagram," by Cotton Delo, Adage.com, January 17, 2012.

Case Study Questions

1. What is the purpose of Puma's content management system?

2. Why did Puma build a single centralized website rather than continue with multiple websites serving different countries and regions?

3. What social media sites does Puma use, and what do they contribute to Puma's marketing effort?

1.9 REVIEW

KEY CONCEPTS

■ Understand why it is important to study e-commerce.

- The next five years hold out exciting opportunities—as well as risks—for new and traditional businesses to exploit digital technology for market advantage. It is important to study e-commerce in order to be able to perceive and understand these opportunities and risks that lie ahead.

■ Define e-commerce, understand how e-commerce differs from e-business, identify the primary technological building blocks underlying e-commerce, and recognize major current themes in e-commerce.

- E-commerce involves digitally enabled commercial transactions between and among organizations and individuals.

- E-business refers primarily to the digital enabling of transactions and processes within a firm, involving information systems under the control of the firm. For the most part, unlike e-commerce, e-business does not involve commercial transactions across organizational boundaries where value is exchanged.
- The technology juggernauts behind e-commerce are the Internet, the Web, and increasingly, the mobile platform.
- From a business perspective, one of the most important trends to note is that all forms of e-commerce continue to show very strong growth. From a technology perspective, the mobile platform has finally arrived with a bang, driving astronomical growth in mobile advertising and making true mobile e-commerce a reality. At a societal level, major issues include privacy and government surveillance, protection of intellectual property, online security, and governance of the Internet.

■ Identify and describe the unique features of e-commerce technology and discuss their business significance.

There are eight features of e-commerce technology that are unique to this medium:
- *Ubiquity*—available just about everywhere, at all times, making it possible to shop from your desktop, at home, at work, or even from your car.
- *Global reach*—permits commercial transactions to cross cultural and national boundaries far more conveniently and cost-effectively than is true in traditional commerce.
- *Universal standards*—shared by all nations around the world, in contrast to most traditional commerce technologies, which differ from one nation to the next.
- *Richness*—enables an online merchant to deliver marketing messages in a way not possible with traditional commerce technologies.
- *Interactivity*—allows for two-way communication between merchant and consumer and enables the merchant to engage a consumer in ways similar to a face-to-face experience, but on a much more massive, global scale.
- *Information density*—is the total amount and quality of information available to all market participants. The Internet reduces information collection, storage, processing, and communication costs while increasing the currency, accuracy, and timeliness of information.
- *Personalization* and *customization*—the increase in information density allows merchants to target their marketing messages to specific individuals and results in a level of personalization and customization unthinkable with previously existing commerce technologies.
- *Social technology*—provides a many-to-many model of mass communications. Millions of users are able to generate content consumed by millions of other users. The result is the formation of social networks on a wide scale and the aggregation of large audiences on social network platforms.

■ Describe the major types of e-commerce.

There are six major types of e-commerce:
- *B2C e-commerce* involves businesses selling to consumers and is the type of e-commerce that most consumers are likely to encounter.
- *B2B e-commerce* involves businesses selling to other businesses and is the largest form of e-commerce.
- *C2C e-commerce* is a means for consumers to sell to each other. In C2C e-commerce, the consumer prepares the product for market, places the product for auction or sale, and relies on the market maker to provide catalog, search engine, and transaction clearing capabilities so that products can be easily displayed, discovered, and paid for.
- *Social e-commerce* is e-commerce that is enabled by social networks and online social relationships.
- *M-commerce* involves the use of wireless digital devices to enable online transactions.
- *Local e-commerce* is a form of e-commerce that is focused on engaging the consumer based on his or her current geographic location.

■ Understand the evolution of e-commerce from its early years to today.

E-commerce has gone through three stages: innovation, consolidation, and reinvention.
- The early years of e-commerce were a technological success, with the digital infrastructure created during the period solid enough to sustain significant growth in e-commerce during the next decade, and a mixed business success, with significant revenue growth and customer usage, but low profit margins.
- E-commerce entered a period of consolidation beginning in 2001 and extending into 2006.
- E-commerce entered a period of reinvention in 2007 with the emergence of the mobile digital platform, social networks, and Web 2.0 applications that attracted huge audiences in a very short time span.

■ Describe the major themes underlying the study of e-commerce.

E-commerce involves three broad interrelated themes:
- *Technology*—To understand e-commerce, you need a basic understanding of the information technologies upon which it is built, including the Internet, the Web, and mobile platform, and a host of complementary technologies—cloud computing, desktop computers, smartphones, tablet computers, local area networks, client/server computing, packet-switched communications, protocols such as TCP/IP, web servers, HTML, and relational and non-relational databases, among others.
- *Business*—While technology provides the infrastructure, it is the business applications—the potential for extraordinary returns on investment—that create the interest and excitement in e-commerce. Therefore, you also need to understand some key business concepts such as electronic markets, information goods, business models, firm and industry value chains, industry structure, and consumer behavior in digital markets.
- *Society*—Understanding the pressures that global e-commerce places on contemporary society is critical to being successful in the e-commerce marketplace. The primary societal issues are intellectual property, individual privacy, and public policy.

■ Identify the major academic disciplines contributing to e-commerce.

There are two primary approaches to e-commerce: technical and behavioral. Each of these approaches is represented by several academic disciplines.
- On the technical side, this includes computer science, operations management, and information systems.
- On the behavioral side, it includes information systems as well as sociology, economics, finance and accounting, management, and marketing.

QUESTIONS

1. What does omni-channel mean in terms of e-commerce presence?
2. What is information asymmetry?
3. What are some of the unique features of e-commerce technology?
4. What are some of the factors driving the growth of social e-commerce?
5. What are three benefits of universal standards?
6. How does the ubiquity of e-commerce impact consumers?
7. Name three of the business consequences that can result from growth in information density.
8. What difficulties are presented in trying to measure the number of web pages in existence?
9. Why is the mobile platform not just a hardware phenomenon?
10. What is conversational commerce and how does it relate to social e-commerce and m-commerce?
11. Describe the three different stages in the evolution of e-commerce.
12. Define disintermediation and explain the benefits to Internet users of such a phenomenon. How does disintermediation impact friction-free commerce?

13. What are some of the major advantages and disadvantages of being a first mover?
14. What is a network effect, and why is it valuable?
15. Discuss the ways in which the early years of e-commerce can be considered both a success and a failure.
16. What are five of the major differences between the early years of e-commerce and today's e-commerce?
17. Why is a multidisciplinary approach necessary if one hopes to understand e-commerce?
18. Why is the term "sharing economy" a misnomer?
19. What are those who take a technical approach to studying e-commerce interested in?
20. Why has Rocket Internet been criticized, and how do the Samwer brothers respond to that criticism?

PROJECTS

1. Choose an e-commerce company and assess it in terms of the eight unique features of e-commerce technology described in Table 1.2. Which of the features does the company implement well, and which features poorly, in your opinion? Prepare a short memo to the president of the company you have chosen detailing your findings and any suggestions for improvement you may have.

2. Search the Web for an example of each of the major types of e-commerce described in Section 1.4 and listed in Table 1.3. Create a presentation or written report describing each company (take a screenshot of each, if possible), and explain why it fits into the category of e-commerce to which you have assigned it.

3. Given the development and history of e-commerce in the years from 1995–2016, what do you predict we will see during the next five years of e-commerce? Describe some of the technological, business, and societal shifts that may occur as the Internet continues to grow and expand. Prepare a brief presentation or written report to explain your vision of what e-commerce will look like in 2020.

4. Prepare a brief report or presentation on how companies are using Pinterest, Instagram, or another company of your choosing as a social e-commerce platform.

5. Follow up on events at Uber since December 2016 (when the opening case was prepared). Prepare a short report on your findings.

REFERENCES

Bakos, Yannis. "Reducing Buyer Search Costs: Implications for Electronic Marketplaces." *Management Science* (December 1997).

Banerjee, Suman, and Chakravarty, Amiya. "Price Setting and Price Discovery Strategies with a Mix of Frequent and Infrequent Internet Users." (April 15, 2005). SSRN: http://ssrn.com/abstract=650706.

Camhi, Jonathan. "BI Intelligence Projects 34 Billion Devices Will Be Connected by 2020." Businessinsider.com (November 6, 2015).

Cavallo, Alberto F. "Are Online and Offline Prices Similar? Evidence from Large Multi-Channel Retailers." NBER Working Paper No. 22142. (March 2016).

eBay, Inc. "Form 10-K for the fiscal year ended December 31, 2015." (February 1, 2016).

eMarketer, Inc. "US Internet Users and Penetration, 2015–2020." (August 3, 2016a).

eMarketer, Inc. "US Mobile Connections, 2014–2020." (February 2016b).

eMarketer, Inc. "US Internet Users, by Device, 2015–2020." (August 2, 2016c).

eMarketer, Inc. "Internet Users and Penetration Worldwide, 2015–2020." (September 1, 2016d).

eMarketer, Inc. (Cindy Liu), "Worldwide Retail Ecommerce Sales: The eMarketer Forecast for 2016." (August 16, 2016e).

eMarketer, Inc. "Worldwide Digital Travel Sales: The Complete eMarketer Forecast for 2016." (July 21, 2016f).

Evans, Philip, and Thomas S. Wurster. "Getting Real About Virtual Commerce." *Harvard Business Review* (November–December 1999).

Evans, Philip, and Thomas S. Wurster. "Strategy and the New Economics of Information." *Harvard Business Review* (September–October 1997).

Forrester Research. "U.S. Cross-Channel Retail Forecast, 2015 to 2020." (January 26, 2016).

Ghose, Anindya, and Yuliang Yao. "Using Transaction Prices to Re-Examine Price Dispersion in Electronic Markets." *Information Systems Research*, Vol. 22 No. 2. (June 2011).

Gorodnichenko, Yuriy, et al. "Price Setting in Online Markets: Does IT Click?" NBER Working Paper No. 20819 (December 2014).

Interactions Consumer Experience Marketing, Inc., "The Rise of Webrooming." (May 2014).

Internet Retailer. "Top 500 Guide 2016 Edition." (2016).

Internet Systems Consortium, Inc. "ISC Internet Domain Survey." (January 2016).

Kalakota, Ravi, and Marcia Robinson. *e-Business 2.0: Roadmap for Success, 2nd edition.* Reading, MA: Addison Wesley (2003).

Kambil, Ajit. "Doing Business in the Wired World." *IEEE Computer* (May 1997).

Levin, Jonathon. "The Economics of Internet Markets." NBER Working Paper No 16852 (February 2011).

Mesenbourg, Thomas L. "Measuring Electronic Business: Definitions, Underlying Concepts, and Measurement Plans." U. S. Department of Commerce Bureau of the Census (August 2001).

Rayport, Jeffrey F., and Bernard J. Jaworski. *Introduction to E-commerce, 2nd edition.* New York: McGraw-Hill (2003).

Rosso, Mark, and Bernard Jansen. "Smart Marketing or Bait & Switch: Competitors' Brands as Keywords in Online Advertising." Proceedings of the 4th Workshop on Information Credibility. ACM (2010).

Schwartz, Barry. "Google: We Know About 30 Thousand Trillion URLS on the Web, But..." Seroundtable.com (June 3, 2015).

Shapiro, Carl, and Hal R. Varian. *Information Rules. A Strategic Guide to the Network Economy.* Cambridge, MA: Harvard Business School Press (1999).

Sinha, Indrajit. "Cost Transparency: The Net's Threat to Prices and Brands." *Harvard Business Review* (March-April 2000).

Smith, Michael, Joseph Bailey, and Erik Brynjolfsson. "Understanding Digital Markets: Review and Assessment." In Erik Brynjolfsson and Brian Kahin (eds.), *Understanding the Digital Economy.* Cambridge, MA: MIT Press (2000).

Tversky, A., and D. Kahneman. "The Framing of Decisions and the Psychology of Choice." *Science* (January 1981).

United Nations Conference on Trade and Development. "New Initiative to Help Developing Countries Grasp the Opportunity of E-commerce-Worth Around $22.1 Trillion in 2015—or Risk Falling Behind." Unctad.org (July 19, 2016).

U.S. Census Bureau. "E-Stats." (June 7, 2016).

Varian, Hal R. "When Commerce Moves On, Competition Can Work in Strange Ways." *New York Times* (August 24, 2000a).

Varian, Hal R. "5 Habits of Highly Effective Revolution." *Forbes ASAP* (February 21, 2000b).

E-commerce Infrastructure

After reading this chapter, you will be able to:

- Discuss the origins of, and the key technology concepts behind, the Internet.
- Explain the current structure of the Internet.
- Understand the limitations of today's Internet and the potential capabilities of the Internet of the future.
- Understand how the Web works.
- Describe how Internet and web features and services support e-commerce.
- Understand the impact of mobile applications.

Wikitude and Blippar:

Augment My Reality

Walk down the street in any city and count the number of people pecking away at their smartphones. Ride the train, and observe how many fellow travelers are using a tablet. Today, one of the primary means of accessing the Internet is via a mobile device. Traditional desktop computers still play a role, but in 2016, around 2.5 billion people worldwide

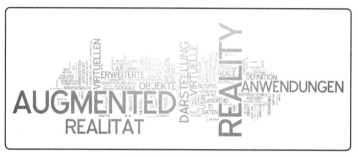

© skdesign/123RF

used a mobile device to access the Internet. The mobile platform provides the foundation for a number of unique new services, including augmented reality, which involves content (text, video, and sound) that is superimposed over live images in order to enrich the user's experience.

Augmented reality combines the geolocation functionality built into smartphones to bring together location and context, helping the user understand his or her environment better. Wikitude is one of the leading providers of augmented reality technology for smartphones, tablets, and digital eyewear. It is a "points of interest" location-based service that uses the same kind of wiki tools that power Wikipedia, the online encyclopedia. The Wikitude 8 app is available for all major mobile operating systems, and the company released the latest edition of its developer kit, SDK 5.3, in September 2016. When users examine objects and locations using the Wikitude app on their smartphones, the app uses smartphone features like GPS and the accelerometer to display information on over 100 million points of interest gathered from Wikipedia, Yelp, and other third-party services. Wikitude most often functions as a very sophisticated travel guide as well as an advertising platform, allowing merchants to advertise their local offerings and discount coupons based on where the user is located.

Organizations throughout Europe and the rest of world are using Wikitude to create custom apps for a variety of purposes. Fashion retailer Zalando and concept car manufacturer Rinspeed collaborated with Wikitude to produce an augmented reality display inside Rinspeed's latest vehicle. Wikitude and eoVision, which offers services and products related to Earth's observation and geoinformation, collaborated on a book entitled *one earth,* which has 119 pages of satellite images that analyze the environment and display maps, descriptions, 3D modeling, and advanced augmented reality technology to deliver an entirely new media experience. Wikitude technology also features prominently in the companion app to *Who We Are: One Direction,* an autobiography of the popular band One Direction, released in 2014. App users can place their mobile device over photographs and other areas of the book, allowing them to view exclusive videos, interviews, and other interactive material. The app was downloaded more than 60,000 times in the two weeks after its launch.

Blippar, a Wikitude competitor that also offers an augmented reality browser, uses image recognition to allow users to hold up a smartphone to a real-life object and receive an overlay of data about it, including advertising offers. Blippar creates "blipps" in which users snap pictures of products to view content-rich, interactive experiences via mobile devices. Although Blippar is not yet profitable, the company's revenue grew 45% in financial 2015, and after a $45 million round of funding, Blippar reached a valuation of $1.5 billion. Advertisers are lining up to work with Blippar, including hundreds of the top newsstand magazines in the world that have agreed to make their magazines compatible with Blippar advertising and interactive features. In late 2016, retailers from the Covent Garden district of London partnered with Blippar to create the world's first augmented reality retail environment. Shoppers were able to go on an interactive augmented reality treasure hunt, access fashion and gift guides for many outlets through the Blippar app, and use an interactive map to view events happening in the area for the holiday season. In the near future, events like this could become a regular occurrence.

Blippar is working to develop new applications for its technology. In 2016, Blippar unveiled what it calls the "Blipparsphere." The feature allows users to point their phones at any object using the Blippar app and get suggestions on what the object might be. User answers are recorded and used to improve future searches using machine learning techniques. Blippar can also learn about the objects that are most relevant to each user, much to the delight of advertisers. Blippar also added facial recognition capability in 2016. Blippar has been indexing "face profiles" for public figures prior to the launch of the service, which will provide images and information about people of interest like historical figures or celebrities. Eventually users will be able to create their own face profiles, complete with social media updates, "likes", and celebrity look-alikes. Privacy groups have raised concerns about this feature, though Blippar states it will be fully opt-in.

More and more commercial applications of augmented reality technology are being introduced every day. Yellow Pages has tested the use of augmented reality to overlay advertisements, paid for by businesses, to street views where its app is used. Another variation is a real estate app tested by RightMove that allows users to point their phone up and down a street and find out what is for sale or for rent, and how much it costs. It also provides contact information for each of the properties. Yelp, TripAdvisor, and Lonely Planet are just a few of the travel companies that have introduced some aspects of augmented reality to their apps.

Another current use of augmented reality is to allow users to simulate "trying on" the product. For instance, eBay's Fashion iPhone app lets users virtually try on sunglasses using the phone's front-facing camera to take a picture of themselves and then virtually "fit" the sunglasses to their face. Watchmaker Neuvo offers a similar app that lets users virtually try on watches, while a Converse app lets you do the same with Converse shoes. Software from Zugara allows you try on clothing from online shops.

Gaming is another area where augmented reality has made a big splash. In 2016, AR gaming landed its first huge hit in the form of Pokemon GO, a reboot of the classic Nintendo franchise. Pokemon GO is a smartphone app that works as a kind of worldwide

SOURCES: "The Snapchat Spectacles Craze, Explained," by Xavier Harding, Vox.com, December 14, 2016; "AR Startup Blippar Added Real-Time Facial Recognition to Its App," by Hannah Roberts, Businessinsider.com, December 6, 2016; "Blippar Smartphone App Raises Privacy Concerns by Planning to Add Facial Recognition," by Jason Murdock, Ibtimes.co.uk, December 6, 2016; "Blippar turns Covent Garden into Augmented Reality Wonderland for Christmas," Netimperative.com, scavenger hunt, as users navigate the physical world using an in-game map and explore real-life landmarks to find and capture virtual monsters. Shortly after its release, Pokemon GO became the most popular mobile phone game of all time, amassing 100 million downloads within weeks. The game still boasts over 15 million active users as of late 2016, and special events have kept players both interested and invested; for example, Niantic earned $23.3 million during its Halloween event in October 2016. Pokemon GO was an introduction to augmented reality for most of its users, and other companies are now exploring the possibilities of similar games and services. For example, in 2016, Porsche and Blippar partnered to create an augmented reality game using a five-page magazine advertisement showing the Swiss Alps. Readers could scan the ad using the Blippar app to view a digital version of the mountains and a game where app users could race a Porsche through them.

Other AR gaming options from smaller outfits are poised to make an impact as well, including Kickstarter-supported CastAR and its augmented reality gaming system. CastAR includes glasses, an RFID grid, and a controller to overlay 3D holographic images within the user's field of vision without requiring a full headset like the current generation of VR headsets. Though CastAR was forced to delay the shipping of its prototype glasses to its Kickstarter backers in 2015, the company refunded its Kickstarter donations in full and plans to launch the device in 2017.

Rumor also has it that Apple may be planning its own augmented reality foray. Apple has applied for and won a number of patents involving augmented reality technologies between 2013 and 2016, and has started the process of adding augmented reality technology to iPhone cameras. Apple appears to be developing a system that can provide virtual overlays of their surroundings akin to Blippar's, but which also will include "x-ray vision" that allows users to look behind walls of select structures. A combination of a live feed from the iPhone's camera and local sensor information would pinpoint a user's position and generate an interactive wireframe model of their immediate surroundings. Users will be able to manipulate the frame so that it matches their view. Applications for the service could be as an advanced version of Apple's Maps service, complete with capability for local businesses to advertise and generate special offers based on Apple's granular user data. Apple is also rumored to be developing a pair of smart glasses that will interact with an iPhone to display information.

Apple's push into augmented reality may put AR squarely in the mainstream, but as Google discovered, one tech giant putting its weight behind a technology doesn't guarantee its success. One of the most promising platforms for augmented reality was Google Glass, a pair of glasses capable of a variety of augmented and virtual reality applications, but the device failed to gain traction and was discontinued in 2015. In 2016, Snapchat announced its Spectacles product, which resembles Google Glass superficially but is far simpler in functionality. Snapchat Spectacles are designed for one purpose only: to take 10 second videos and send them to your phone. Demand for the device has been overwhelming, with customers waiting in line for up to ten hours to get their hands on the glasses. Google may simply have been slightly ahead of the times.

November 21, 2016; "Apple Has a Secret Team Working to Make the iPhone's Camera a Portal to Augmented Reality," by Kif Leswing, Businessinsider.com, November 16, 2016; "Expect 'Pokemon GO' to Make More Halloween-Like Events After Huge 133% Revenue Jump," by Paul Tassi, *Forbes*, November 1, 2016; "The Wikitude SDK 5.3 Is Ready: Support for iOS 10, Android 7 and New Features," Wikitude.com, September 13, 2016; "Is Pokemon Go Finally Making Augmented Reality Mainstream?" by Marty Swant, Adweek.com, August 7, 2016; "AR Startup Blippar Has Launched the Visual Browser It Says Could Be 'Bigger Than the Internet Itself,'" by Lara O'Reilly, Businessinsider.com, June 9, 2016; "Blippar Bringing Augmented Reality to Newsstand Mags," by Peter Graham, Vrfocus.com, October 15, 2015; "Why It's Taken So Long for the Oculus Rift to Ship," by Lily Prasuethsut, Techradar.com, September 24, 2015; "Here's Everything We Know About Apple's Augmented Reality Plans," by Chris Neiger, Fool.com, September 3, 2015; "How Will the Vive Headset Delay Affect the IR Market?" by Chris Morris, *Fortune*, August 28, 2015; "British Tech Startup Blippar Eyes New Funding After £4.96m Loss," by Stuart Dredge, *The Guardian*, August 18, 2015; "Watch What castAR's Projected Augmented Reality Can Do," by Nicole Lee, Engadget.com, February 21, 2015; "castAR Bets Big on Its Augmented Reality Hardware with Move to Silicon Valley," by Nicole Lee, Engadget.com, October 17, 2014; "Apple's iPhone-based Augmented Reality Navigation Concept Has 'X-Ray Vision' Features," by Mikey Campbell, Appleinsider.com, September 4, 2014; "UK Startup Blippar Confirms It Has Acquired AR Pioneer Layar," by Mike Butcher, Techcrunch.com, June 18, 2014; "Augmented Reality Augmentation: Blippar Has Bought Layar," by Ingrid Lunden, Techcrunch.com, June 10, 2014; "Apple Patent Hints at Augmented Reality Camera App," by Josh Lowensohn, News.cnet.com; August 18, 2011.

T his chapter examines the Internet, Web, and mobile platform of today and tomorrow, how they evolved, how they work, and how their present and future infrastructure enable new business opportunities.

The opening case illustrates the importance of understanding how the Internet and related technologies work, and being aware of what's new. The Internet and its underlying technology are not static phenomena, but instead continue to change over time. Computers have merged with cell phone services; broadband access in the home and broadband wireless access to the Internet via smartphones, tablet computers, and laptops are expanding rapidly; self-publishing via social networks and blogging now engages millions of Internet users; and software technologies such as cloud computing and smartphone apps are revolutionizing the way businesses are using the Internet. Looking forward a few years, the business strategies of the future will require a firm understanding of these technologies and new ones, such as different types of wearable technology like the Apple Watch profiled in the opening case, the Internet of Things, the "smart/connected" movement (smart homes, smart TVs, and connected cars), augmented and virtual reality, and artificial intelligence to deliver products and services to consumers. **Table 2.1** summarizes some of the most important developments in e-commerce infrastructure for 2016–2017.

2.1 THE INTERNET: TECHNOLOGY BACKGROUND

What is the Internet? Where did it come from, and how did it support the growth of the Web? What are the Internet's most important operating principles? How much do you really need to know about the technology of the Internet?

Let's take the last question first. The answer is: it depends on your career interests. If you are on a marketing career path, or general managerial business path, then you need to know the basics about Internet technology, which you'll learn in this and the following chapter. If you are on a technical career path and hope to become a web designer, or pursue a technical career in web infrastructure for businesses, you'll need to start with these basics and then build from there. You'll also need to know about the business side of e-commerce, which you will learn about throughout this book.

Internet

an interconnected network of thousands of networks and millions of computers linking businesses, educational institutions, government agencies, and individuals

As noted in Chapter 1, the **Internet** is an interconnected network of thousands of networks and millions of computers (sometimes called *host computers* or just *hosts*), linking businesses, educational institutions, government agencies, and individuals. The Internet provides approximately 3.3 billion people around the world with services such as e-mail, apps, newsgroups, shopping, research, instant messaging, music, videos, and news (eMarketer, Inc., 2016a, 2016b). No single organization controls the Internet or how it functions, nor is it owned by anybody, yet it has provided the infrastructure for a transformation in commerce, scientific research, and culture. The word *Internet* is derived from the word *internetwork*, or the connecting together of two

TABLE 2.1	TRENDS IN E-COMMERCE INFRASTRUCTURE 2016–2017

BUSINESS

- Mobile devices become the primary access point to social network services and a rapidly expanding social marketing and advertising platform, and create a foundation for location-based web services and business models.
- Explosion of Internet content services and mobile access devices strains the business models of Internet backbone providers (the large telecommunication carriers).
- The growth in cloud computing and bandwidth capacity enables new business models for distributing music, movies, and television.
- Search becomes more social and local, enabling social and local commerce business models.
- Big data produced by the Internet creates new business opportunities for firms with the analytic capability to understand it.

TECHNOLOGY

- Mobile devices such as smartphones and tablet computers have become the dominant mode of access to the Internet. The new client is mobile.
- The explosion of mobile apps threatens the dominance of the Web as the main source of online software applications and leads some to claim the Web is dead.
- Cloud computing reshapes computing and storage, and becomes an important force in the delivery of software applications and online content.
- The Internet runs out of IPv4 addresses; the transition to IPv6 continues.
- The decreased cost of storage and advances in database software lead to explosion in online data collection known as big data, and creates new business opportunities for firms with the analytic capability to understand it.
- The Internet of Things, with millions of sensor-equipped devices connecting to the Internet, starts to become a reality, and is powering the development of smart connected "things" such as televisions, houses, cars, and wearable technology.
- Augmented reality applications such as Pokemon GO, and virtual reality hardware such as Facebook's Oculus Rift, Google's Cardboard, and Samsung's Gear VR, begin to gain traction.
- Interest in and funding of artificial intelligence technologies explode, with potential applications ranging from supply chain logistics, to self-driving cars, to consumer-oriented personal assistants.
- HTML5 grows in popularity among publishers and developers and makes possible web applications that are just as visually rich and lively as native mobile apps.

SOCIETY

- Governance of the Internet becomes more involved with conflicts between nations; the United States gives up control over IANA, which administers the Internet's IP addressing system.
- Government control over, and surveillance of, the Internet is expanded in most advanced nations, and in many nations the Internet is nearly completely controlled by government agencies.
- The growing infrastructure for tracking online and mobile consumer behavior conflicts with individual claims to privacy and control over personal information.

or more computer networks. The **Web** is one of the Internet's most popular services, providing access to billions, perhaps trillions, of web pages, which are documents created in a programming language called HTML that can contain text, graphics, audio, video, and other objects, as well as "hyperlinks" that permit users to jump easily from one page to another. Web pages are navigated using web browser software.

Web
one of the Internet's most popular services, providing access to billions, and perhaps trillions, of web pages

THE EVOLUTION OF THE INTERNET: 1961—THE PRESENT

Although journalists talk glibly about "Internet" time—suggesting a fast-paced, nearly instant, worldwide global change mechanism—in fact, today's Internet had its start about 55 years ago and has slowly evolved since then.

The history of the Internet can be segmented into three phases (see **Figure 2.1**). During the *Innovation Phase,* from 1961 to 1974, the fundamental building blocks of the Internet—packet-switching hardware, a communications protocol called TCP/IP, and client/server computing (all described more fully later in this section)—were conceptualized and then implemented in actual hardware and software. The Internet's original purpose was to link large mainframe computers on different college campuses. This kind of one-to-one communication between campuses was previously possible only via the telephone system or private networks owned by the large computer manufacturers.

During the *Institutionalization Phase*, from 1975 to 1995, large institutions such as the U.S. Department of Defense (DoD) and the National Science Foundation (NSF) provided funding and legitimization for the fledging Internet. Once the concepts behind the Internet had been proven in several government-supported demonstration projects, the DoD contributed $1 million to further develop them into a robust military communications system. This effort created what was then called ARPANET (Advanced Research Projects Agency Network). In 1986, the NSF assumed responsibility for the development of a civilian Internet (then called NSFNET) and began a 10-year-long $200 million expansion program.

During the *Commercialization Phase*, from 1995 to the present, the U.S. government encouraged private corporations to take over and expand the Internet backbone as well as local service beyond military installations and college campuses to the rest of the population around the world. See **Table 2.2** for a closer look at the development of the Internet from 1961 on.

| FIGURE 2.1 | STAGES IN THE DEVELOPMENT OF THE INTERNET |

Innovation
1961 – 1974

Institutionalization
1975 – 1995

Commercialization
1995 →

The Internet has developed in three stages over approximately a 55-year period from 1961 to the present. In the Innovation stage, basic ideas and technologies were developed; in the Institutionalization stage, these ideas were brought to life; in the Commercialization stage, once the ideas and technologies had been proven, private companies brought the Internet to millions of people worldwide.

TABLE 2.2	DEVELOPMENT OF THE INTERNET TIMELINE	
YEAR	EVENT	SIGNIFICANCE
INNOVATION PHASE 1961–1974		
1961	Leonard Kleinrock (MIT) publishes a paper on "packet switching" networks.	The concept of packet switching is born.
1962	J.C.R. Licklider (MIT) writes memo calling for an "Intergalactic Computer Network."	The vision of a global computer network is born.
1969	BBN Technologies awarded ARPA contract to build ARPANET.	The concept of a packet-switched network moves closer toward physical reality.
1969	The first packet-switched message is sent on ARPANET from UCLA to Stanford.	The communications hardware underlying the Internet is implemented for the first time. The initial ARPANET consisted of four routers (then called Interface Message Processors (IMPs)) at UCLA, Stanford, UCSB, and the University of Utah.
1972	E-mail is invented by Ray Tomlinson of BBN. Larry Roberts writes the first e-mail utility program permitting listing, forwarding, and responding to e-mails.	The first "killer app" of the Internet is born.
1973	Bob Metcalfe (Xerox PARC Labs) invents Ethernet and local area networks.	**Client/server computing is invented.** Ethernet permitted the development of local area networks and client/server computing in which thousands of fully functional desktop computers could be connected into a short-distance (<1,000 meters) network to share files, run applications, and send messages.
1974	"Open architecture" networking and TCP/IP concepts are presented in a paper by Vint Cerf (Stanford) and Bob Kahn (BBN).	**TCP/IP invented.** The conceptual foundation for a single common communications protocol that could potentially connect any of thousands of disparate local area networks and computers, and a common addressing scheme for all computers connected to the network, are born. Prior to this, computers could communicate only if they shared a common proprietary network architecture. With TCP/IP, computers and networks could work together regardless of their local operating systems or network protocols.
INSTITUTIONALIZATION PHASE 1975–1995		
1977	Lawrence Landweber envisions CSNET (Computer Science Network).	CSNET is a pioneering network for U.S. universities and industrial computer research groups that could not directly connect to ARPANET, and was a major milestone on the path to the development of the global Internet.
1980	TCP/IP is officially adopted as the DoD standard communications protocol.	The single largest computing organization in the world adopts TCP/IP and packet-switched network technology.
1980	Personal computers are invented.	Altair, Apple, and IBM personal desktop computers are invented. These computers become the foundation for today's Internet, affording millions of people access to the Internet and the Web.
1984	Apple Computer releases the HyperCard program as part of its graphical user interface operating system called Macintosh.	The concept of "hyperlinked" documents and records that permit the user to jump from one page or record to another is commercially introduced.

(continued)

TABLE 2.2	DEVELOPMENT OF THE INTERNET TIMELINE (CONTINUED)	
YEAR	**EVENT**	**SIGNIFICANCE**
1984	Domain Name System (DNS) introduced.	DNS provides a user-friendly system for translating IP addresses into words that people can easily understand.
1989	Tim Berners-Lee of CERN in Switzerland proposes a worldwide network of hyperlinked documents based on a common markup language called HTML—HyperText Markup Language.	**The concept of an Internet-supported service called the World Wide Web based on HTML pages is born**. The Web would be constructed from "pages" created in a common markup language, with "hyperlinks" that permitted easy access among the pages.
1990	NSF plans and assumes responsibility for a civilian Internet backbone and creates NSFNET.[1] ARPANET is decommissioned.	The concept of a "civilian" Internet open to all is realized through nonmilitary funding by NSF.
1993	The first graphical web browser called Mosaic is invented by Marc Andreessen and others at the National Center for Supercomputing Applications at the University of Illinois.	Mosaic makes it very easy for ordinary users to connect to HTML documents anywhere on the Web. The browser-enabled Web takes off.
1994	Andreessen and Jim Clark form Netscape Corporation.	The first commercial web browser—Netscape—becomes available.
1994	The first banner advertisements appear on Hotwired.com in October 1994.	**The beginning of e-commerce**.
COMMERCIALIZATION PHASE 1995–PRESENT		
1995	NSF privatizes the backbone, and commercial carriers take over backbone operation.	**The fully commercial civilian Internet is born**. Major long-haul networks such as AT&T, Sprint, GTE, UUNet, and MCI take over operation of the backbone. Network Solutions (a private firm) is given a monopoly to assign Internet addresses.
1995	Jeff Bezos founds Amazon; Pierre Omidyar forms AuctionWeb (eBay).	E-commerce begins in earnest with pure online retail stores and auctions.
1998	The U.S. federal government encourages the founding of the Internet Corporation for Assigned Names and Numbers (ICANN).	Governance over domain names and addresses passes to a private nonprofit international organization.
1999	The first full-service Internet-only bank, First Internet Bank of Indiana, opens for business.	Business on the Web extends into traditional services.
2003	The Internet2 Abilene high-speed network is upgraded to 10 Gbps.	A major milestone toward the development of ultra-high-speed transcontinental networks several times faster than the existing backbone is achieved.
2005	NSF proposes the Global Environment for Network Innovations (GENI) initiative to develop new core functionality for the Internet.	Recognition that future Internet security and functionality needs may require the thorough rethinking of existing Internet technology.
2006	The U.S. Senate Committee on Commerce, Science, and Transportation holds hearings on "Network Neutrality."	The debate grows over differential pricing based on utilization that pits backbone utility owners against online content and service providers and device makers.

[1] "Backbone" refers to the U.S. domestic trunk lines that carry the heavy traffic across the nation, from one metropolitan area to another. Universities are given responsibility for developing their own campus networks that must be connected to the national backbone.

TABLE 2.2	DEVELOPMENT OF THE INTERNET TIMELINE (CONTINUED)	
YEAR	EVENT	SIGNIFICANCE
2007	The Apple iPhone is introduced.	The introduction of the iPhone represents the beginning of the development of a viable mobile platform that will ultimately transform the way people interact with the Internet.
2008	The Internet Society (ISOC) identifies Trust and Identity as a primary design element for every layer of the Internet, and launches an initiative to address these issues.	The leading Internet policy group recognizes the current Internet is threatened by breaches of security and trust that are built into the existing network.
2008	Internet "cloud computing" becomes a billion-dollar industry.	Internet capacity is sufficient to support on-demand computing resources (processing and storage), as well as software applications, for large corporations and individuals.
2009	Internet-enabled smartphones become a major new web access platform.	Smartphones extend the reach and range of the Internet to more closely realize the promise of the Internet anywhere, anytime, anyplace.
2009	Broadband stimulus package and Broadband Data Improvement Act enacted.	President Obama signs stimulus package containing $7.2 billion for the expansion of broadband access in the United States.
2011	ICANN expands domain name system.	ICANN agrees to permit the expansion of generic top-level domain names from about 300 to potentially thousands using any word in any language.
2012	World IPv6 Launch day.	Major Internet service providers (ISPs), home networking equipment manufacturers, and online companies begin to permanently enable IPv6 for their products and services as of June 6, 2012.
2013	The Internet of Things (IoT) starts to become a reality.	Internet technology spreads beyond the computer and mobile device to anything that can be equipped with sensors, leading to predictions that up to 100–200 billion uniquely identifiable objects will be connected to the Internet by 2020.
2014	Apple introduces Apple Pay and Apple Watch.	Apple Pay is likely to become the first widely adopted mobile payment system; Apple Watch may usher in a new era of wearable Internet-connected technology and is a further harbinger of the Internet of Things.
2015	Federal Communications Commission adopts regulations mandating net neutrality.	ISPs are required to treat all data on the Internet equally and are not allowed to discriminate or charge differentially based on user, content, site, platform, application, type of equipment, or mode of communication.
2016	FCC proposes "Open Set Top Box" rules; net neutrality regulations upheld by U.S. Court of Appeals.	FCC continues to promote concept of an open Internet, despite continued resistance from telecommunications industry.

SOURCES: Based on Leiner et al., 2000; Zakon, 2005; Gross, 2005; Geni.net, 2007; ISOC.org, 2010; Arstechnica.com, 2010; ICANN, 2011a; Internet Society, 2012; IEEE Computer Society, 2013; Craig, 2016.

THE INTERNET: KEY TECHNOLOGY CONCEPTS

In 1995, the U.S. Federal Networking Council (FNC) passed a resolution formally defining the term *Internet* as a network that uses the IP addressing scheme, supports the Transmission Control Protocol (TCP), and makes services available to users much like a telephone system makes voice and data services available to the public (see **Figure 2.2**).

Behind this formal definition are three extremely important concepts that are the basis for understanding the Internet: packet switching, the TCP/IP communications protocol, and client/server computing. Although the Internet has evolved and changed dramatically in the last 35 years, these three concepts are at the core of the way the Internet functions today and are the foundation for the Internet of the future.

Packet Switching

Packet switching is a method of slicing digital messages into discrete units called **packets**, sending the packets along different communication paths as they become available, and then reassembling the packets once they arrive at their destination (see **Figure 2.3**). Prior to the development of packet switching, early computer networks used leased, dedicated telephone circuits to communicate with terminals and other computers. In circuit-switched networks such as the telephone system, a complete point-to-point circuit is put together, and then communication can proceed. However, these "dedicated" circuit-switching techniques were expensive and wasted available communications capacity—the circuit would be maintained regardless of whether any data was being sent. For nearly 70% of the time, a dedicated voice circuit is not being fully used because of pauses between words and delays in assembling the circuit

packet switching

a method of slicing digital messages into packets, sending the packets along different communication paths as they become available, and then reassembling the packets once they arrive at their destination

packets

the discrete units into which digital messages are sliced for transmission over the Internet

---

FIGURE 2.2	RESOLUTION OF THE U.S. FEDERAL NETWORKING COUNCIL

"The Federal Networking Council (FNC) agrees that the following language reflects our definition of the term 'Internet.'

'Internet' refers to the global information system that—

(i) is logically linked together by a globally unique address space based on the Internet Protocol (IP) or its subsequent extensions/follow-ons;

(ii) is able to support communications using the Transmission Control Protocol/Internet Protocol (TCP/IP) suite or its subsequent extensions/follow-ons, and/or other IP-compatible protocols; and

(iii) provides, uses or makes accessible, either publicly or privately, high level services layered on the communications and related infrastructure described herein."

Last modified on October 30, 1995.

SOURCE: Federal Networking Council, 1995

FIGURE 2.3	PACKET SWITCHING
I want to communicate with you.	Original text message
00101101100010011011110001101	Text message digitized into bits
01100010 10101100 11000011	Digital bits broken into packets
0011001 10101100 11000011	Header information added to each packet indicating destination, and other control information, such as how many bits are in the total message and how many packets

In packet switching, digital messages are divided into fixed-length packets of bits (generally about 1,500 bytes). Header information indicates both the origin and the ultimate destination address of the packet, the size of the message, and the number of packets the receiving node should expect. Because the receipt of each packet is acknowledged by the receiving computer, for a considerable amount of time, the network is not passing information, only acknowledgments, producing a delay called latency.

segments, both of which increase the length of time required to find and connect circuits. A better technology was needed.

The first book on packet switching was written by Leonard Kleinrock in 1964 (Kleinrock, 1964), and the technique was further developed by others in the defense research labs of both the United States and England. With packet switching, the communications capacity of a network can be increased by a factor of 100 or more. (The communications capacity of a digital network is measured in terms of bits per second.[2]) Imagine if the gas mileage of your car went from 15 miles per gallon to 1,500 miles per gallon—all without changing too much of the car!

In packet-switched networks, messages are first broken down into packets. Appended to each packet are digital codes that indicate a source address (the origination point) and a destination address, as well as sequencing information and error-control information for the packet. Rather than being sent directly to the destination address, in a packet network, the packets travel from computer to computer until they reach their destination. These computers are called routers. A **router** is a special-purpose computer that interconnects the different computer networks that make up the Internet and routes packets along to their ultimate destination as they travel. To ensure that packets take the best available path toward their destination, routers use a computer program called a **routing algorithm**.

Packet switching does not require a dedicated circuit, but can make use of any spare capacity that is available on any of several hundred circuits. Packet switching

router
special-purpose computer that interconnects the computer networks that make up the Internet and routes packets to their ultimate destination as they travel the Internet

routing algorithm
computer program that ensures that packets take the best available path toward their destination

---

[2] A bit is a binary digit, 0 or 1. A string of eight bits constitutes a byte. A home telephone dial-up modem connects to the Internet usually at 56 Kbps (56,000 bits per second). Mbps refers to millions of bits per second, whereas Gbps refers to billions of bits per second.

makes nearly full use of almost all available communication lines and capacity. Moreover, if some lines are disabled or too busy, the packets can be sent on any available line that eventually leads to the destination point.

Transmission Control Protocol/Internet Protocol (TCP/IP)

While packet switching was an enormous advance in communications capacity, there was no universally agreed-upon method for breaking up digital messages into packets, routing them to the proper address, and then reassembling them into a coherent message. This was like having a system for producing stamps but no postal system (a series of post offices and a set of addresses). The answer was to develop a **protocol** (a set of rules and standards for data transfer) to govern the formatting, ordering, compressing, and error-checking of messages, as well as specify the speed of transmission and means by which devices on the network will indicate they have stopped sending and/or receiving messages.

Transmission Control Protocol/Internet Protocol (TCP/IP) has become the core communications protocol for the Internet (Cerf and Kahn, 1974). **TCP** establishes the connections among sending and receiving computers, and makes sure that packets sent by one computer are received in the same sequence by the other, without any packets missing. **IP** provides the Internet's addressing scheme and is responsible for the actual delivery of the packets.

TCP/IP is divided into four separate layers, with each layer handling a different aspect of the communication problem (see **Figure 2.4**). The **Network Interface Layer** is responsible for placing packets on and receiving them from the network medium, which could be a LAN (Ethernet) or Token Ring network, or other network technology. TCP/IP is independent from any local network technology and can adapt to changes at the local level. The **Internet Layer** is responsible for addressing, packaging, and routing messages on the Internet. The **Transport Layer** is responsible for providing communication with other protocols (applications) within the TCP/IP protocol suite by acknowledging and sequencing the packets to and from the applications. The **Application Layer** includes a variety of protocols used to provide user services or exchange data. One of the most important is the **Border Gateway Protocol (BGP)**, which enables the exchange of routing information among different autonomous systems on the Internet. BGP uses TCP as its transport protocol. Other important protocols included in the Application layer include HyperText Transfer Protocol (HTTP), File Transfer Protocol (FTP), and Simple Mail Transfer Protocol (SMTP), all of which we will discuss later in this chapter.

IP Addresses

The IP addressing scheme answers the question "How can billions of computers attached to the Internet communicate with one another?" The answer is that every computer connected to the Internet must be assigned an address—otherwise it cannot send or receive TCP packets. For instance, when you sign onto the Internet using a dial-up, DSL, or cable modem, your computer is assigned a temporary address by your

protocol
set of rules and standards for data transfer

Transmission Control Protocol/Internet Protocol (TCP/IP)
core communications protocol for the Internet

TCP
establishes connections among sending and receiving computers and handles assembly and reassembly of packets

IP
provides the Internet's addressing scheme and is responsible for delivery of packets

Network Interface Layer
responsible for placing packets on and receiving them from the network medium

Internet Layer
responsible for addressing, packaging, and routing messages on the Internet

Transport Layer
responsible for providing communication with other protocols within TCP/IP suite

Application Layer
includes protocols used to provide user services or exchange data

Border Gateway Protocol
enables exchange of routing information among systems on the Internet

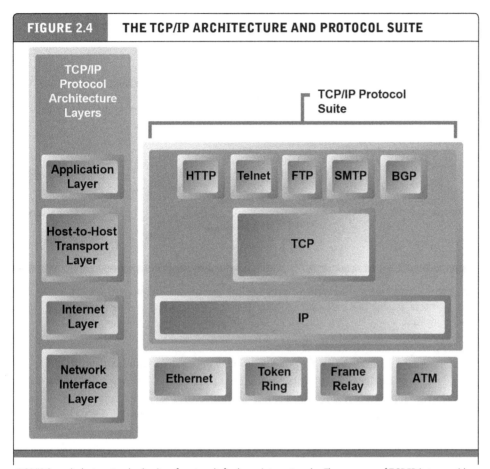

FIGURE 2.4 | THE TCP/IP ARCHITECTURE AND PROTOCOL SUITE

TCP/IP is an industry-standard suite of protocols for large internetworks. The purpose of TCP/IP is to provide high-speed communication network links.

Internet Service Provider. Most corporate and university computers attached to a local area network have a permanent IP address.

There are two versions of IP currently in use: IPv4 and IPv6. An **IPv4 Internet address** is a 32-bit number that appears as a series of four separate numbers marked off by periods, such as 64.49.254.91. Each of the four numbers can range from 0–255. This "dotted quad" addressing scheme supports up to about 4 billion addresses (2 to the 32nd power). In a typical Class C network, the first three sets of numbers identify the network (in the preceding example, 64.49.254 is the local area network identification) and the last number (91) identifies a specific computer.

Because many large corporate and government domains have been given millions of IP addresses each (to accommodate their current and future work forces), and with all the new networks and new Internet-enabled devices requiring unique IP addresses being attached to the Internet, the number of IPv4 addresses available to be assigned has shrunk significantly. Registries for North America, Europe, Asia, and Latin

IPv4 Internet address
Internet address expressed as a 32-bit number that appears as a series of four separate numbers marked off by periods, such as 64.49.254.91

FIGURE 2.5 **ROUTING INTERNET MESSAGES: TCP/IP AND PACKET SWITCHING**

① TCP/IP breaks data into packets

② The packets travel from router to router over the Internet

③ TCP/IP reassembles the packets into the original whole

To:
From:

Router

Router

Router

Router

Router

Router

Sender

To:
From:

Recipient

The Internet uses packet-switched networks and the TCP/IP communications protocol to send, route, and assemble messages. Messages are broken into packets, and packets from the same message can travel along different routes.

IPv6 Internet address
Internet address expressed as a 128-bit number

America have all essentially run out. IPv6 was created to address this problem. An **IPv6 Internet address** is 128 bits, so it can support up to 2^{128} (3.4×10^{38}) addresses, many more than IPv4. According to Akamai, in the United States, about 20% of Internet traffic now occurs over IPv6. Belgium leads the way globally, with over 40% of Internet traffic converted to IPv6 (Akamai, 2016a).

Figure 2.5 illustrates how TCP/IP and packet switching work together to send data over the Internet.

domain name
IP address expressed in natural language

Domain Name System (DNS)
system for expressing numeric IP addresses in natural language

Uniform Resource Locator (URL)
the address used by a web browser to identify the location of content on the Web

Domain Names, DNS, and URLs

Most people cannot remember 32-bit numbers. An IP address can be represented by a natural language convention called a **domain name**. The **Domain Name System (DNS)** allows expressions such as Cnet.com to stand for a numeric IP address (cnet.com's numeric IP is 216.239.113.101).[3] A **Uniform Resource Locator (URL)**, which is the address used by a web browser to identify the location of content on the Web, also uses a domain name as part of the URL. A typical URL contains the protocol to be used when accessing the address, followed by its location. For instance, the URL http://www.azimuth-interactive.com/flash_test refers to the IP address 208.148.84.1 with the domain name "azimuth-interactive.com" and the protocol being used to access the address, HTTP. A resource called "flash_test" is located on the server directory path /flash_test. A URL can have from two to four parts; for example, name1.name2.name3.org. We discuss domain names and URLs further in Section 2.4.

---

[3] You can check the IP address of any domain name on the Internet. If using a Windows operating system, open the command prompt. Type ping < Domain Name >. You will receive the IP address in return.

FIGURE 2.6 — THE HIERARCHICAL DOMAIN NAME SYSTEM

The Domain Name System is a hierarchical namespace with a root server at the top. Top-level domains appear next and identify the organization type (such as .com, .gov, .org, etc.) or geographic location (such as .uk [Great Britain] or .ca [Canada]). Second-level servers for each top-level domain assign and register second-level domain names for organizations and individuals such as IBM.com, Microsoft.com, and Stanford.edu. Finally, third-level domains identify a particular computer or group of computers within an organization, e.g., www.finance.nyu.edu.

Figure 2.6 illustrates the Domain Name System and **Table 2.3** summarizes the important components of the Internet addressing scheme.

Client/Server Computing

While packet switching exploded the available communications capacity and TCP/IP provided the communications rules and regulations, it took a revolution in

TABLE 2.3	PIECES OF THE INTERNET PUZZLE: NAMES AND ADDRESSES
IP addresses	Every device connected to the Internet must have a unique address number called an Internet Protocol (IP) address.
Domain names	The Domain Name System allows expressions such as Pearsoned.com (Pearson Education's website) to stand for numeric IP locations.
DNS servers	DNS servers are databases that keep track of IP addresses and domain names on the Internet.
Root servers	Root servers are central directories that list all domain names currently in use for specific domains; for example, the .com root server. DNS servers consult root servers to look up unfamiliar domain names when routing traffic.

computing to bring about today's Internet and the Web. That revolution is called client/server computing and without it, the Web—in all its richness—would not exist. **Client/server computing** is a model of computing in which **client** computers are connected in a network with one or more **servers**, which are computers that are dedicated to performing common functions that the client computers on the network need, such as file storage, software applications, printing, and Internet access. The client computers are themselves sufficiently powerful to accomplish complex tasks. Servers are networked computers dedicated to common functions that the client computers on the network need, such as file storage, software applications, utility programs that provide web connections, and printers (see **Figure 2.7**). The Internet is a giant example of client/server computing in which millions of web servers located around the world can be easily accessed by millions of client computers, also located throughout the world.

To appreciate what client/server computing makes possible, you must understand what preceded it. In the mainframe computing environment of the 1960s and 1970s, computing power was very expensive and limited. For instance, the largest commercial mainframes of the late 1960s had 128k of RAM and 10-megabyte disk drives, and occupied hundreds of square feet. There was insufficient computing capacity to support graphics or color in text documents, let alone sound files, video, or hyperlinked documents. In this period, computing was entirely centralized: all work was done by a single mainframe computer, and users were connected to the mainframe using terminals.

With the development of personal computers and local area networks during the late 1970s and early 1980s, client/server computing became possible. Client/server computing has many advantages over centralized mainframe computing. For instance, it is easy to expand capacity by adding servers and clients. Also, client/server networks are less vulnerable than centralized computing architectures. If one server goes down,

client/server computing
a model of computing in which client computers are connected in a network together with one or more servers

client
a powerful desktop computer that is part of a network

server
networked computer dedicated to common functions that the client computers on the network need

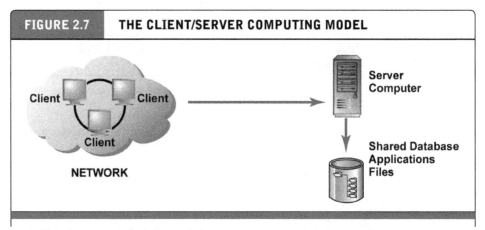

| FIGURE 2.7 | THE CLIENT/SERVER COMPUTING MODEL |

In the client/server model of computing, client computers are connected in a network together with one or more servers.

backup or mirror servers can pick up the slack; if a client computer is inoperable, the rest of the network continues operating. Moreover, processing load is balanced over many powerful smaller computers rather than being concentrated in a single huge computer that performs processing for everyone. Both software and hardware in client/server environments can be built more simply and economically.

In 2016, there are an estimated 1.8 billion "traditional" personal computers in use around the world (Cox, 2016). Personal computing capabilities have also moved to smartphones and tablet computers (all much "thinner" clients with a bit less computing horsepower, and limited memory, but which rely on Internet servers to accomplish their tasks). In the process, more computer processing will be performed by central servers.

THE NEW CLIENT: THE MOBILE PLATFORM

There's a new client in town. The primary means of accessing the Internet worldwide is now through highly portable smartphones and tablet computers, and not traditional desktop or laptop PCs. This means that the primary platform for e-commerce products and services is also changing to a mobile platform.

The change in hardware has reached a tipping point. The form factor of PCs has changed from desktops to laptops and tablet computers such as the iPad (and more than 100 other competitors). Tablets are lighter, do not require a complex operating system, and rely on the Internet cloud to provide processing and storage. In the United States, about 155 million people access the Internet using a tablet computer (eMarketer, Inc., 2016c).

Smartphones are a disruptive technology that radically alters the personal computing and e-commerce landscape. Smartphones have created a major shift in computer processors and software that has disrupted the dual monopolies long established by Intel and Microsoft, whose chips, operating systems, and software applications began dominating the PC market in 1982. Few smartphones use Intel chips, which power 90% of the world's PCs; only a small percentage of smartphones use Microsoft's operating system (Windows Mobile). Instead, smartphone manufacturers either purchase operating systems such as Symbian, the world leader, or build their own, such as Apple's iPhone iOS, typically based on Linux and Java platforms. Smartphones do not use power-hungry hard drives but instead use flash memory chips with storage up to 128 gigabytes that also require much less power. In 2016, over 2.5 billion people use mobile phones to access the Internet (eMarketer, Inc., 2016d).

The mobile platform has profound implications for e-commerce because it influences how, where, and when consumers shop and buy.

THE INTERNET "CLOUD COMPUTING" MODEL: HARDWARE AND SOFTWARE AS A SERVICE

Cloud computing is a model of computing in which computer processing, storage, software, and other services are provided as a shared pool of virtualized resources over the Internet. These "clouds" of computing resources can be accessed on an as-needed

cloud computing
model of computing in which computer processing, storage, software, and other services are provided as a shared pool of virtualized resources over the Internet

FIGURE 2.8 **THE CLOUD COMPUTING MODEL**

THE INTERNET

Software and
   hardware services
Collaboration
Integration of devices

In the cloud computing model, hardware and software services are provided on the Internet by vendors operating very large server farms and data centers.

basis from any connected device and location. **Figure 2.8** illustrates the cloud computing concept.

The U.S. National Institute of Standards and Technology (NIST) defines cloud computing as having the following essential characteristics:

- **On-demand self-service:** Consumers can obtain computing capabilities such as server time or network storage as needed automatically on their own.

- **Ubiquitous network access:** Cloud resources can be accessed using standard network and Internet devices, including mobile platforms.

- **Location-independent resource pooling:** Computing resources are pooled to serve multiple users, with different virtual resources dynamically assigned according to user demand. The user generally does not know where the computing resources are located.

- **Rapid elasticity:** Computing resources can be rapidly provisioned, increased, or decreased to meet changing user demand.

- **Measured service:** Charges for cloud resources are based on the amount of resources actually used.

Cloud computing consists of three basic types of services:

- **Infrastructure as a service (IaaS):** Customers use processing, storage, networking, and other computing resources from third-party providers called cloud service providers (CSPs) to run their information systems. For example, Amazon used the spare capacity of its information technology infrastructure to develop Amazon Web Services (AWS), which offers a cloud environment for a myriad of different IT infrastructure services. See **Table 2.4** for a description of the range of services that AWS offers, such as its Simple Storage Service (S3) for storing customers' data and

TABLE 2.4	AMAZON WEB SERVICES
NAME	**DESCRIPTION**
COMPUTING SERVICES	
Elastic Compute Cloud (EC2)	Scalable cloud computing services
Elastic Load Balancing (ELB)	Distributes incoming application traffic among multiple EC2 instances
STORAGE SERVICES	
Simple Storage Service (S3)	Data storage infrastructure
Glacier	Low-cost archival and backup storage
DATABASE SERVICES	
DynamoDB	NoSQL database service
Redshift	Petabyte-scale data warehouse service
Relational Database Service (RDS)	Relational database service for MySQL, Oracle, SQL Server, and PostgreSQL databases
ElastiCache	In-memory cache in the cloud
SimpleDB	Non-relational data store
NETWORKING AND CONTENT DELIVERY SERVICES	
Route 53	DNS service in the cloud, enabling business to direct Internet traffic to web applications
Virtual Private Cloud (VPC)	Creates a VPN between the Amazon cloud and a company's existing IT infrastructure
CloudFront	Content delivery services
Direct Connect	Provides alternative to using the Internet to access AWS cloud services
ANALYTICS	
Elastic MapReduce (EMR)	Web service that enables users to perform data-intensive tasks
Kinesis	Big Data service for real-time data streaming ingestion and processing
APPLICATION SERVICES	
AppStream	Provides streaming services for applications and games from the cloud
CloudSearch	Search service that can be integrated by developers into applications
MESSAGING SERVICES	
Simple Email Service (SES)	Cloud e-mail sending service
Simple Notification Service (SNS)	Push messaging service
Simple Queue Service (SQS)	Queue for storing messages as they travel between computers

(continued)

TABLE 2.4	AMAZON WEB SERVICES (CONT.)
DEPLOYMENT AND MANAGEMENT SERVICES	
Identity and Access Management (IAM)	Enables securely controlled access to AWS services
CloudWatch	Monitoring service
Elastic Beanstalk	Service for deploying and scaling web applications and services developed with Java, .Net, PHP, Python, Ruby, and Node.js
CloudFormation	Service that allows developers an easy way to create a collection of related AWS resources
MOBILE	
Cognito	Allows developers to securely manage and synchronize app data for users across mobile devices
Mobile Analytics	Can collect and process billions of events from millions of users a day
PAYMENT SERVICES	
Flexible Payment Service (FPS)	Payment services for developers
DevPay	Online billing and account management service for developers who create an Amazon cloud application
MISCELLANEOUS	
Amazon Mechanical Turk	Marketplace for work that requires human intelligence
Alexa Web Information Service	Provides web traffic data and information for developers

its Elastic Compute Cloud (EC2) service for running applications. Users pay only for the amount of computing and storage capacity they actually use.

- **Software as a service (SaaS):** Customers use software hosted by the vendor on the vendor's cloud infrastructure and delivered as a service over a network. Leading SaaS examples are Google Apps, which provides common business applications online, and Salesforce.com, which provides customer relationship management and related software services over the Internet. Both charge users an annual subscription fee, although Google Apps also has a pared-down free version. Users access these applications from a web browser, and the data and software are maintained on the providers' remote servers.

- **Platform as a service (PaaS):** Customers use infrastructure and programming tools supported by the CSP to develop their own applications. For example, IBM offers Bluemix for software development and testing on its cloud infrastructure. Another example is Salesforce.com's Force.com, which allows developers to build applications that are hosted on its servers as a service.

A cloud can be private, public, or hybrid. A **public cloud** is owned and maintained by CSPs, such as Amazon Web Services, IBM, HP, and Dell, and made available

public cloud

third-party service providers that own and manage large, scalable data centers that offer computing, data storage, and high speed Internet to multiple customers who pay for only the resources they use to multiple customers, who pay only for the resources they use. A public cloud offers relatively secure enterprise-class reliability at significant cost savings. Because organizations using public clouds do not own the infrastructure, they do not have to make large investments in their own hardware and software. Instead, they purchase their computing services from remote providers and pay only for the amount of computing power they actually use (utility computing) or are billed on a monthly or annual subscription basis. The term *on-demand computing* is also used to describe such services. As such, public clouds are ideal environments for small and medium-sized businesses who cannot afford to fully develop their own infrastructure; for applications requiring high performance, scalability, and availability; for new application development and testing; and for companies that have occasional large computing projects. Gartner estimates that spending on public cloud services worldwide grew over 15% in 2016 to €193 billion (Gartner, Inc., 2016a). Companies such as Google, Apple, Dropbox, and others also offer public clouds as a consumer service for online storage of data, music, and photos. Google Drive, Dropbox, and Apple iCloud are leading examples of this type of consumer cloud service.

A **private cloud** provides similar options as a public cloud but is operated solely for the benefit of a single tenant. It might be managed by the organization or a third party and hosted either internally or externally. Like public clouds, private clouds can allocate storage, computing power, or other resources seamlessly to provide computing resources on an as-needed basis. Companies that have stringent regulatory compliance or specialized licensing requirements that necessitate high security, such as financial services or healthcare companies, or that want flexible information technology resources and a cloud service model while retaining control over their own IT infrastructure, are gravitating toward these private clouds.

private cloud
provides similar options as public cloud but only to a single tenant

Large firms are most likely to adopt a **hybrid cloud** computing model, in which they use their own infrastructure for their most essential core activities and adopt public cloud computing for less-critical systems or for additional processing capacity during peak business periods. **Table 2.5** compares the three cloud computing models.

hybrid cloud
offers customers both a public cloud and a private cloud

TABLE 2.5	CLOUD COMPUTING MODELS COMPARED		
TYPE OF CLOUD	DESCRIPTION	MANAGED BY	USES
Public cloud	Third-party service offering computing, storage, and software services to multiple customers	Third-party service providers (CSPs)	Companies without major privacy concerns. Companies seeking pay-as-you-go IT services. Companies lacking IT resources and expertise
Private cloud	Cloud infrastructure operated solely for a single organization and hosted either internally or externally	In-house IT or private third-party host	Companies with stringent privacy and security requirements. Companies that must have control over data sovereignty
Hybrid cloud	Combination of private and public cloud services that remain separate entities	In-house IT, private host, third-party providers	Companies requiring some in-house control of IT that are also willing to assign part of their IT infrastructures to a public cloud partition on their IT infrastructures

Cloud computing will gradually shift firms from having a fixed infrastructure capacity toward a more flexible infrastructure, some of it owned by the firm, and some of it rented from giant data centers owned by CSPs.

Cloud computing has some drawbacks. Unless users make provisions for storing their data locally, the responsibility for data storage and control is in the hands of the provider. Some companies worry about the security risks related to entrusting their critical data and systems to an outside vendor that also works with other companies. Companies expect their systems to be available 24/7 and do not want to suffer any loss of business capability if cloud infrastructures malfunction. Nevertheless, the trend is for companies to shift more of their computer processing and storage to some form of cloud infrastructure.

Cloud computing has many significant implications for e-commerce. For e-commerce firms, cloud computing radically reduces the cost of building and operating websites because the necessary hardware infrastructure and software can be licensed as a service from CSPs at a fraction of the cost of purchasing these services as products. This means firms can adopt "pay-as-you-go" and "pay-as-you-grow" strategies when building out their websites. For instance, according to Amazon, hundreds of thousands of customers use Amazon Web Services. For individuals, cloud computing means you no longer need a powerful laptop or desktop computer to engage in e-commerce or other activities. Instead, you can use much less-expensive tablet computers or smartphones that cost a few hundred dollars. For corporations, cloud computing means that a significant part of hardware and software costs (infrastructure costs) can be reduced because firms can obtain these services online for a fraction of the cost of owning, and they do not have to hire an IT staff to support the infrastructure.

OTHER INTERNET PROTOCOLS AND UTILITY PROGRAMS

There are many other Internet protocols and utility programs that provide services to users in the form of Internet applications that run on Internet clients and servers. These Internet services are based on universally accepted protocols—or standards—that are available to everyone who uses the Internet. They are not owned by any organization, but they are services that have been developed over many years and made available to all Internet users.

HyperText Transfer Protocol (HTTP)
the Internet protocol used for transferring web pages

HyperText Transfer Protocol (HTTP) is the Internet protocol used to transfer web pages (described in the following section). HTTP was developed by the World Wide Web Consortium (W3C) and the Internet Engineering Task Force (IETF). HTTP runs in the Application Layer of the TCP/IP model shown in Figure 2.4 on page 107. An HTTP session begins when a client's browser requests a resource, such as a web page, from a remote Internet server. When the server responds by sending the page requested, the HTTP session for that object ends. Because web pages may have many objects on them—graphics, sound or video files, frames, and so forth—each object must be requested by a separate HTTP message. For more information about HTTP, you can consult RFC 2616, which details the standards for HTTP/1.1, the version of HTTP most commonly used today (Internet Society, 1999). (An RFC is a document published by the Internet Society [ISOC] or one of the other organizations involved in Internet governance that sets forth the standards for various Internet-related technologies. You will learn more about the organizations involved in setting standards for the Internet later in the chapter.) An updated version of HTTP, known as HTTP/2, was published as RFC 7540 in May 2015 (IETF, 2015). HTTP/2 addresses a number of HTTP 1.1 shortcomings and is designed to enhance performance by eliminating the need to open multiple TCP connections between a client and server (known as multiplexing), allowing servers to push resources to a client without the client having to request them (known as server push), and reducing the HTTP header size (header compression). HTTP/2 will also have security benefits, with improved performance for encrypted data running over HTTP/2. HTTP/2 is supported by almost all the leading web browsers, but as of August 2016, it has only been adopted by around 10% of the top 10 million websites, in part due to the challenges involved for organizations in transitioning their applications from HTTP to HTTP/2 (Akamai, 2016; W3techs.com, 2016).

E-mail is one of the oldest, most important, and frequently used Internet services. Like HTTP, the various Internet protocols used to handle e-mail all run in the Application Layer of TCP/IP. **Simple Mail Transfer Protocol (SMTP)** is the Internet protocol used to send e-mail to a server. SMTP is a relatively simple, text-based protocol that was developed in the early 1980s. SMTP handles only the sending of e-mail. To retrieve e-mail from a server, the client computer uses either **Post Office Protocol 3 (POP3)** or **Internet Message Access Protocol (IMAP)**. You can set POP3 to retrieve e-mail messages from the server and then delete the messages on the server, or retain them on the server. IMAP is a more current e-mail protocol. IMAP allows users to search, organize, and filter their mail prior to downloading it from the server.

File Transfer Protocol (FTP) is one of the original Internet services. FTP runs in TCP/IP's Application Layer and permits users to transfer files from a server to their client computer, and vice versa. The files can be documents, programs, or large database files. FTP is the fastest and most convenient way to transfer files larger than 1 megabyte, which some e-mail servers will not accept. More information about FTP is available in RFC 959 (Internet Society, 1985).

Telnet is a network protocol that also runs in TCP/IP's Application Layer and is used to allow remote login on another computer. The term Telnet also refers to the Telnet program, which provides the client part of the protocol and enables the client to emulate a mainframe computer terminal. (The industry-standard terminals defined in the days of mainframe computing are VT-52, VT-100, and IBM 3250.) You can then attach yourself to a computer on the Internet that supports Telnet and run programs or download files from that computer. Telnet was the first "remote work" program that permitted users to work on a computer from a remote location.

Secure Sockets Layer (SSL)/Transport Layer Security (TLS) are protocols that operate between the Transport and Application Layers of TCP/IP and secure communications between the client and the server. SSL/TLS helps secure e-commerce communications and payments through a variety of techniques, such as message encryption and digital signatures, that we will discuss further in Chapter 4.

Simple Mail Transfer Protocol (SMTP)
the Internet protocol used to send mail to a server

Post Office Protocol 3 (POP3)
a protocol used by the client to retrieve mail from an Internet server

Internet Message Access Protocol (IMAP)
a more current e-mail protocol that allows users to search, organize, and filter their mail prior to downloading it from the server

File Transfer Protocol (FTP)
one of the original Internet services. Part of the TCP/IP protocol that permits users to transfer files from the server to their client computer, and vice versa

Telnet
a terminal emulation program that runs in TCP/IP

Secure Sockets Layer (SSL)/Transport Layer Security (TLS)
protocols that secure communications between the client and the server

FIGURE 2.9 THE RESULT OF A PING

A ping is used to verify an address and test the speed of the round trip from a client computer to a host and back.

SOURCE: Command Prompt, Microsoft Windows, Microsoft Corporation.

Ping

a program that allows you to check the connection between your client and the server

Packet InterNet Groper (Ping) is a utility program that allows you to check the connection between a client computer and a TCP/IP network (see **Figure 2.9**). Ping will also tell you the time it takes for the server to respond, giving you some idea about the speed of the server and the Internet at that moment. You can run Ping from the command prompt on a personal computer with a Windows operating system by typing: ping < domain name >. Ping can also be used to slow down or even crash a domain server by sending it millions of ping requests.

Tracert

one of several route-tracing utilities that allow you to follow the path of a message you send from your client to a remote computer on the Internet

Tracert is one of several route-tracing utilities that allow you to follow the path of a message you send from your client to a remote computer on the Internet. **Figure 2.10** shows the result of a message sent to a remote host using a visual route-tracing program called VisualRoute (available from Visualware).

2.2 THE INTERNET TODAY

In 2016, there are an estimated 3.3 billion Internet users worldwide, up from 100 million users at year-end 1997. While this is a huge number, it still represents less than half (about 45%) of the world's population (eMarketer, Inc., 2016a). Although Internet user growth has slowed in the United States and Western Europe to about 1%–2% annually, worldwide, the growth rate is about 7%, with the highest growth areas being the Middle East/Africa and Asia-Pacific (both still growing at over 8%). By 2020, it is expected that there will be over 3.9 billion Internet users worldwide. One would think the Internet would be overloaded with such incredible growth; however, this has not been true for several reasons. First, client/server computing is highly extensible. By simply adding servers and clients, the population of Internet users can grow indefinitely. Second, the Internet architecture is built in layers so that each layer can change without disturbing developments in other layers. For instance, the technology used to move messages through the Internet can go through radical changes to make service faster without being disruptive to your desktop applications running on the Internet.

FIGURE 2.10   TRACING THE ROUTE A MESSAGE TAKES ON THE INTERNET

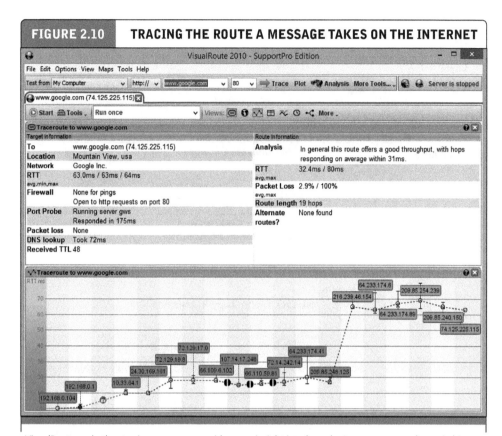

VisualRoute and other tracing programs provide some insight into how the Internet uses packet switching. This particular message traveled to a Google server in Mountain View, California.

SOURCE: © Visualware, Inc., 2014.

Figure 2.11 illustrates the "hourglass" and layered architecture of the Internet. The Internet can be viewed conceptually as having four layers: Network Technology Substrates, Transport Services and Representation Standards, Middleware Services, and Applications.[4] The **Network Technology Substrate layer** is composed of telecommunications networks and protocols. The **Transport Services and Representation Standards layer** houses the TCP/IP protocol. The **Applications layer** contains client applications such as the Web, e-mail, and audio or video playback. The **Middleware Services layer** is the glue that ties the applications to the communications networks and includes such services as security, authentication, addresses, and storage repositories. Users work with applications (such as e-mail) and rarely become aware of middleware that operates in the background. Because all layers use TCP/IP and other common standards linking all four layers, it is possible for there to be significant

Network Technology Substrate layer
layer of Internet technology that is composed of telecommunications networks and protocols

Transport Services and Representation Standards layer
layer of Internet architecture that houses the TCP/IP protocol

Applications layer
layer of Internet architecture that contains client applications

Middleware Services layer
the "glue" that ties the applications to the communications networks and includes such services as security, authentication, addresses, and storage repositories

---

[4] Recall that the TCP/IP communications protocol also has layers, not to be confused with the Internet architecture layers.

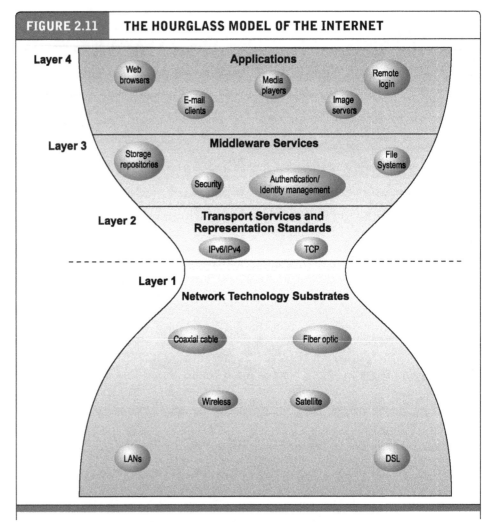

FIGURE 2.11   **THE HOURGLASS MODEL OF THE INTERNET**

The Internet can be characterized as an hourglass modular structure with a lower layer containing the bit-carrying infrastructure (including cables and switches) and an upper layer containing user applications such as e-mail and the Web. In the narrow waist are transportation protocols such as TCP/IP.

changes in the Network Technology Substrate layer without forcing changes in the Applications layer.

THE INTERNET BACKBONE

Tier 1 Internet Service Providers (Tier 1 ISPs)

own and control the major long-haul fiber-optic cable networks comprising the Internet's backbone

Figure 2.12 illustrates some of the main physical elements of today's physical Internet. Originally, the Internet had a single backbone, but today's Internet is woven together from numerous privately owned networks comprised of high-bandwidth fiber-optic cable that are physically connected with each other and that transfer information from one private network to another. These long-haul fiber-optic networks are owned by firms sometimes referred to as **Tier 1 Internet Service Providers (Tier 1 ISPs)** (also sometimes called *transit ISPs*) (see **Table 2.6**). Tier 1 ISPs have "peering"

FIGURE 2.12 | **INTERNET NETWORK ARCHITECTURE**

Today's Internet has a multi-tiered open network architecture featuring multiple backbones, regional hubs, campus/corporate area networks, and local client computers.

---

arrangements with other Tier 1 ISPs to allow Internet traffic to flow through each other's cables and equipment without charge. Tier 1 ISPs deal only with other Tier 1 or Tier 2 ISPs (described in the next section) and not with end consumers.

For the sake of simplicity, we will refer to these networks of backbones as a single "backbone." The **backbone** has been likened to a giant pipeline that transports data around the world in milliseconds. The backbone is typically composed of fiber-optic cable with bandwidths ranging from 155 Mbps to 2.5 Gbps. **Bandwidth** measures how much data can be transferred over a communications medium within a fixed period of time and is usually expressed in bits per second (Bps), kilobits (thousands of bits)

backbone
high-bandwidth fiber-optic cable that transports data across the Internet

bandwidth
measures how much data can be transferred over a communications medium within a fixed period of time; is usually expressed in bits per second (bps), kilobits per second (Kbps), megabits per second (Mbps), or gigabits per second (Gbps)

TABLE 2.6 | **MAJOR TIER 1 (TRANSIT) INTERNET SERVICE PROVIDERS**

AT&T	Sprint
CenturyLink	Tata Communications
Cogent Communications	Verizon
Level 3 Communications	Zayo Group

per second (Kbps), megabits (millions of bits) per second (Mbps), or gigabits (billions of bits) per second (Gbps).

Connections to other continents are made via a combination of undersea fiber-optic cable and satellite links. Increasingly, rather than leasing bandwidth from Tier 1 ISPs, Internet giants such as Google, Microsoft, and Facebook are laying down their own fiber-optic networks. For instance, Google has one cable stretching from the California to Japan and another connecting the United States to Brazil, while Facebook and Microsoft have allied to lay a cable across the Atlantic, connecting Virginia to Spain. The backbone in foreign countries typically is operated by a mixture of private and public owners. The backbone has built-in redundancy so that if one part breaks down, data can be rerouted to another part of the backbone. **Redundancy** refers to multiple duplicate devices and paths in a network. A recent study of the Internet's physical structure in the United States has created one of the first maps of the Internet's long-haul fiber network as it currently exists. The map reveals that, not surprisingly, there are dense networks of fiber in the Northeast and coastal areas of the United States, while there is a pronounced absence of infrastructure in the Upper Plains and Four Corners regions. The U.S. Department of Homeland Security has made the map, as well as the data that underlies it, available to government, private, and public researchers, believing that doing so could make the Internet more resilient by improving knowledge (Simonite, 2015; Durairajan et al., 2015).

redundancy

multiple duplicate devices and paths in a network

INTERNET EXCHANGE POINTS

Regional hubs where Tier 1 ISPs physically connect with one another and/or with regional (Tier 2) ISPs were originally called Network Access Points (NAPs) or Metropolitan Area Exchanges (MAEs), but now are more commonly referred to as Internet Exchange Points (IXPs) (see Figure 2.13). Tier 2 ISPs exchange Internet traffic both through peering arrangements as well as by purchasing Internet transit, and they connect Tier 1 ISPs with Tier 3 ISPs, which provide Internet access to consumers and business. Tier 3 ISPs are described further in the next section.

TIER 3 INTERNET SERVICE PROVIDERS

The firms that provide the lowest level of service in the multi-tiered Internet architecture by leasing Internet access to home owners, small businesses, and some large institutions are sometimes called **Tier 3 Internet Service Providers (ISPs)**. Tier 3 ISPs are retail providers. They deal with "the last mile of service" to the curb—homes and business offices. Tier 3 ISPs typically connect to IXPs with high-speed telephone or cable lines (45 Mbps and higher).

Tier 3 Internet Service Provider (Tier 3 ISP)

firm that provides the lowest level of service in the multi-tiered Internet architecture by leasing Internet access to home owners, small businesses, and some large institutions

There are a number of major ISPs throughout Europe, such as Plusnet, Sky Broadband, Virgin Media, and TalkTalk in the U.K; Orange, SFR, Bouyges Telecom, and Free Mobile in France; and Tiscali, BT Italia, and Fastweb in Italy. If you have home or small business Internet access, a Tier 3 ISP likely provides the service to you. (It's important to note that many Tier 3 ISPs are also Tier I ISPs; the two roles are not mutually exclusive.) Satellite firms also offer Internet access, especially in remote areas where broadband service is not available.

FIGURE 2.13	SOME MAJOR U.S. INTERNET EXCHANGE POINTS (IXPs)

Region	Name	Location	Operator
EAST	Boston Internet Exchange (BOSIX)	Boston	Markley
	New York International Internet Exchange (NYIIX)	New York	Telehouse
	Peering and Internet Exchange (PAIX)	New York, Virginia, Atlanta	Equinix
	NAP of the Americas	Miami	Verizon Terremark
CENTRAL	Any2 Exchange	Chicago	CoreSite
	Peering and Internet Exchange (PAIX)	Dallas	Equinix
	Midwest Internet Cooperative Exchange (MICE)	Minneapolis	Members
WEST	Peering and Internet Exchange (PAIX)	Seattle, Palo Alto	Equinix
	Los Angeles International Internet Exchange (LAIIX)	Los Angeles	Telehouse
	Any2 Exchange	San Jose, Los Angeles	CoreSite
	Seattle Internet Exchange (SIX)	Seattle	Members

TABLE 2.7	INTERNET ACCESS SERVICE LEVELS AND BANDWIDTH CHOICES	
SERVICE	COST/MONTH	DOWNLOAD SPEED
Telephone modem	$10–$25	30–56 Kbps
DSL	$20–$30	1–15 Mbps
FiOS	$50–$300	25 Mbps–500 Mbps
Cable Internet	$35–$199	1 Mbps–500 Mbps
Satellite	$39–$129	5–15 Mbps
T1	$200–$300	1.54 Mbps
T3	$2,500–$10,000	45 Mbps

narrowband

the traditional telephone modem connection, now operating at 56.6 Kbps

broadband

refers to any communication technology that permits clients to play streaming audio and video files at acceptable speeds

Table 2.7 summarizes the variety of services, speeds, and costs of Internet access available to consumers and businesses. There are two types of service: narrowband and broadband. **Narrowband** service is the traditional telephone modem connection now operating at 56.6 Kbps (although the actual throughput hovers around 30 Kbps due to line noise that causes extensive resending of packets). This used to be the most common form of connection worldwide but it has been largely replaced by broadband connections in the United States, Europe, and Asia. Broadband service is based on DSL (including high speed fiber-optic service), cable, telephone (T1 and T3 lines), and satellite technologies. **Broadband**, in the context of Internet service, refers to any communication technology that permits clients to play streaming audio and video files at acceptable speeds. In January 2015, the U.S. Federal Communications Commission updated its broadband benchmark speeds to 25 Mbps for downloads and 3 Mbps for uploads. The FCC found that 17% of all Americans lack access to 25 Mbps/3 Mbps service, and that rural America is particularly underserved, with more than half lacking such access (Federal Communication Commission, 2015). According to Akamai, the global average connection speed in 2016 was 6.3 Mbps, and the global average peak connection speed was 34.7 Mbps. South Korea is a leader in both categories, ranking first in average connection speed at 26.3 Mbps and third in average peak connection speed at 114.2 Mbps (Akamai, 2016c). In the United Kingdom, broadband household penetration is estimated to have reached 87% in 2016, with a similar penetration rate in Germany (86%) (eMarketer, Inc., 2016e).

The actual throughput of data will depend on a variety of factors including noise in the line and the number of subscribers requesting service. Service-level speeds quoted are typically only for downloads of Internet content; upload speeds tend to be slower, although a number of broadband ISPs have plans that offer the same upload as download speed. T1 and T3 lines are publicly regulated utility lines that offer a guaranteed level of service, but the actual throughput of the other forms of Internet service is not guaranteed.

Digital Subscriber Line (DSL) service is a telephone technology that provides high-speed access to the Internet through ordinary telephone lines found in a home or business. Service levels typically range from about .5 to 15 Mbps. DSL service requires that customers live within two miles (about 4,000 meters) of a neighborhood telephone switching center. In order to compete with cable companies, telephone companies now also offer an advanced form of DSL called **FiOS (fiber-optic service)** that provides up to 500 Mbps to homes and businesses.

Cable Internet refers to a cable television technology that piggybacks digital access to the Internet using the same analog or digital video cable providing television signals to a home. Cable Internet is a major broadband alternative to DSL service, generally providing faster speeds and a "triple play" subscription: telephone, television, and Internet for a single monthly payment. However, the available bandwidth of cable Internet is shared with others in the neighborhood using the same cable. When many people are attempting to access the Internet over the cable at the same time, speeds may slow and performance will suffer. Cable Internet services typically range from 1 Mbps up to 500 Mbps. Deutsche Telekom, Vodafone, Telefonica, and Liberty Global are some of the major cable Internet providers in Europe.

T1 and T3 are North American telephone standards for digital communication. **T1** lines offer guaranteed delivery at 1.54 Mbps, while **T3** lines offer 45 Mbps. T1 lines cost about $200–$300 per month, and T3 lines around $2,500–$6,000 per month. These are leased, dedicated, guaranteed lines suitable for corporations, government agencies, and businesses such as ISPs requiring high-speed guaranteed service levels.

Satellite Internet is offered by satellite companies that provide high-speed broadband Internet access primarily to homes and offices located in rural areas where DSL or cable Internet access is not available. Access speeds and monthly costs are comparable to DSL and cable, but typically require a higher initial payment for installation of a small (18-inch) satellite dish. Upload speeds tend to be slower, typically 1–5 Mbps. Satellite providers typically have policies that limit the total megabytes of data that a single account can download within a set period, usually monthly. Major satellite providers in Europe include Hughes, Telefonica, Europasat, and Bentley Walker, among others. In August 2016, Facebook announced plans to launch a satellite aimed at bringing Internet connectivity to parts of sub-Saharan Africa, but those plans were put on hold when the SpaceX rocket that was to launch the satellite exploded while being tested during pre-launch activities.

Nearly all business firms and government agencies have broadband connections to the Internet. Demand for broadband service has grown so rapidly because it greatly speeds up the process of downloading web pages and large video and audio files (see **Table 2.8**). As the quality of Internet service offerings continues to expand, the demand for broadband access will continue to swell.

CAMPUS/CORPORATE AREA NETWORKS

Campus/corporate area networks (CANs) are generally local area networks operating within a single organization—such as New York University or Microsoft Corporation. In fact, most large organizations have hundreds of such local area networks.

Digital Subscriber Line (DSL) delivers high-speed access through ordinary telephone lines found in homes or businesses

FiOS (fiber-optic service) a form of DSL that provides speeds of up to 500 Mbps

cable Internet piggybacks digital access to the Internet on top of the analog video cable providing television signals to a home

T1 North American telephone standard for digital communication that offers guaranteed delivery at 1.54 Mbps

T3 North American telephone standard for digital communication that offers guaranteed delivery at 45 Mbps

satellite Internet high-speed broadband Internet access provided via satellite

campus/corporate area network (CAN) generally, a local area network operating within a single organization that leases access to the Web directly from regional and national carriers

TABLE 2.8	TIME TO DOWNLOAD A 10-MEGABYTE FILE BY TYPE OF INTERNET SERVICE
TYPE OF INTERNET SERVICE	TIME TO DOWNLOAD
NARROWBAND SERVICES	
Telephone modem	25 minutes
BROADBAND SERVICES	
DSL @ 1 Mbps	1.33 minutes
Cable Internet @ 10 Mbps	8 seconds
T1	52 seconds
T3	2 seconds

These organizations are sufficiently large that they lease access to the Web directly from regional and national carriers. These local area networks generally are running Ethernet (a local area network protocol) and have network operating systems such as Windows Server or Linux that permit desktop clients to connect to the Internet through a local Internet server attached to their campus networks. Connection speeds in campus area networks are in the range of 10–100 Mbps to the desktop.

INTRANETS

intranet
a TCP/IP network located within a single organization for purposes of communications and information processing

The very same Internet technologies that make it possible to operate a worldwide public network can also be used by private and government organizations as internal networks. An **intranet** is a TCP/IP network located within a single organization for purposes of communications and information processing. Internet technologies are generally far less expensive than proprietary networks, and there is a global source of new applications that can run on intranets. In fact, all the applications available on the public Internet can be used in private intranets. The largest provider of local area network software is Microsoft, followed by open source Linux, both of which use TCP/IP networking protocols.

WHO GOVERNS THE INTERNET?

Aficionados and journalists often claim that the Internet is governed by no one, and indeed cannot be governed, and that it is inherently above and beyond the law. What these people forget is that the Internet runs over private and public telecommunications facilities that are themselves governed by laws, and subject to the same pressures as all telecommunications carriers. In fact, the Internet is tied into a complex web of governing bodies, national governments, and international professional societies. There is no one single governing organization that controls activity on the Internet.

Instead, there are a number of organizations that influence the system and monitor its operations. Among the governing bodies of the Internet are:

- The *Internet Corporation for Assigned Names and Numbers (ICANN)*, which coordinates the Internet's systems of unique identifiers: IP addresses, protocol parameter registries, and the top-level domain systems. ICANN was created in 1998 as a non-profit organization and manages the *Internet Assigned Numbers Authority (IANA)*, which is in charge of assigning IP addresses.

- The *Internet Engineering Task Force (IETF)*, which is an open international community of network operators, vendors, and researchers concerned with the evolution of the Internet architecture and operation of the Internet. The IETF has a number of working groups, organized into several different areas, that develop and promote Internet standards, which influence the way people use and manage the Internet.

- The *Internet Research Task Force (IRTF)*, which focuses on the evolution of the Internet. The IRTF has a number of long-term research groups working on various topics such as Internet protocols, applications, applications, and technology.

- The *Internet Engineering Steering Group (IESG)*, which is responsible for technical management of IETF activities and the Internet standards process.

- The *Internet Architecture Board (IAB)*, which helps define the overall architecture of the Internet and oversees the IETF and IRTF.

- The *Internet Society (ISOC)*, which is a consortium of corporations, government agencies, and nonprofit organizations that monitors Internet policies and practices.

- The *Internet Governance Forum (IGF)*, which is a multi-stakeholder open forum for debate on issues related to Internet governance.

- The *World Wide Web Consortium (W3C)*, which is a largely academic group that sets HTML and other programming standards for the Web.

- The *Internet Network Operators Groups (NOGs)*, which are informal groups that are made up of ISPs, IXPs, and others that discuss and attempt to influence matters related to Internet operations and regulation.

While none of these organizations has actual control over the Internet and how it functions, they can and do influence government agencies, major network owners, ISPs, corporations, and software developers with the goal of keeping the Internet operating as efficiently as possible. ICANN comes closest to being a manager of the Internet and reflects the powerful role that the U.S. Department of Commerce has played historically in Internet governance. The United States has been responsible for the IANA function since the beginning of the Internet. After the creation of ICANN, however, the expectation was the function would eventually be transferred out of the U.S. government's control. In 2006, however, the U.S. Department of Commerce announced that the U.S. government would retain oversight over the root servers, contrary to initial expectations. There were several reasons for this move, including the use of the Internet for basic communications services by terrorist groups and the uncertainty that might be caused should an international body take over. In 2008, the Department of Commerce reaffirmed this stance, stating that it did not have any plans to transition management of the authoritative root zone file to ICANN (U.S. Department of Commerce, 2008). At the same time, growing Internet powers China and Russia were lobbying for more functions of the Internet to be brought under the control of the United Nations, raising fears that governance of the Internet could become even more politicized (Pfanner, 2012). In 2014, the United States, under continued pressure from other countries, finally announced its willingness to transition control of IANA, provided that certain stipulations are met, including that the organization managing the IANA functions not be specifically controlled by any other government or inter-governmental organization (such as the United Nations). The transition took place on October 1, 2016.

In addition to these professional bodies, the Internet must also conform to the laws of the sovereign nation-states in which it operates, as well as the technical infrastructures that exist within each nation-state. Although in the early years of the Internet there was very little legislative or executive interference, this situation is changing as the Internet plays a growing role in the distribution of information and knowledge, including content that some find objectionable.

Read *Insight on Society: Government Regulation and Surveillance of the Internet* for a further look at the issue of censorship of Internet content and substance.

2.3   THE FUTURE INTERNET INFRASTRUCTURE

The Internet is changing as new technologies appear and new applications are developed. The next era of the Internet is being built today by private corporations, universities, and government agencies. To appreciate the potential benefits of the Internet of the future, you must first understand the limitations of the Internet's current infrastructure.

LIMITATIONS OF THE CURRENT INTERNET

Much of the Internet's current infrastructure is several decades old (equivalent to a century in Internet time). It suffers from a number of limitations, including:

- *Bandwidth limitations.* There is insufficient capacity throughout the backbone, the metropolitan switching centers, and most importantly, the "last mile" to the house and small businesses. The result is slow peak-hour service (congestion) and a limited ability to handle high volumes of video and voice traffic.

latency
delays in messages caused by the uneven flow of information packets through the network

- *Quality of service limitations.* Today's information packets take a circuitous route to get to their final destinations. This creates the phenomenon of **latency**—delays in messages caused by the uneven flow of information packets through the network. In the case of e-mail, latency is not noticeable. However, with streaming video and synchronous communication, such as a telephone call, latency is noticeable to the user and perceived as "jerkiness" in movies or delays in voice communication. Today's Internet uses "best-effort" quality of service (QoS), which makes no guarantees about when or whether data will be delivered, and provides each packet with the same level of service, no matter who the user is or what type of data is

INSIGHT ON SOCIETY

GOVERNMENT REGULATION AND SURVEILLANCE OF THE INTERNET

Hardly a week goes by without reports that a massive protest has occurred in the streets of a big city somewhere in the world. Invariably, the Internet, social media, and mobile phones are either blamed or praised for enabling these popular expressions of discontent with political regimes, corrupt officials, unemployment, or wealth inequality. Such events encourage us to think of the Internet and the Web as an extraordinary technology unleashing torrents of human creativity, innovation, expression, popular rebellion, and sometimes, even democracy.

How ironic then that the same Internet has also spawned an explosion in government control and surveillance of individuals on the Internet. Totalitarian dictators of the mid-twentieth century would have given their eyeteeth for a technology such as this, that can track what millions of people do, say, think, and search for in billions of e-mails, searches, blogs, and Facebook posts every day.

In the early years of the Internet and the Web, many people assumed that because the Internet is so widely dispersed, it must be difficult to control or monitor. But the reality is quite different. We now know that just about all governments assert some kind of control and surveillance over Internet content and messages, and in many nations this control over the Internet and the people who use it is very extensive.

While the Internet is a decentralized network, Internet traffic in all countries runs through large fiber-optic trunk lines that are controlled by national authorities or private firms. In China, there are three such lines, and China requires the companies that own these lines to configure their routers for both internal and external service requests. When a request originates in China for a web page in Chicago, Chinese routers examine the request to see if the site is on a blacklist, and then examine words in the requested web page to see if it contains blacklisted terms. The system is often referred to as "The Great Firewall of China" (but formally by China as the "Golden Shield") and was implemented with the assistance of Cisco Systems (the U.S. firm that is the largest manufacturer of routers in the world), Juniper Networks, and California-based Blue Coat (now owned by Symantec), which provides deep packet inspection software. A number of other U.S. Internet firms have also been involved in China's censorship and surveillance efforts.

Over the past several years, China has strengthened and extended its regulation of the Internet in the name of social stability. Recently passed legislation allows web users to be jailed for up to three years if they post defamatory rumors that are read by more than 5,000 people. China has also issued rules to restrict the dissemination of political news and opinions on instant messaging applications such as WeChat, a text messaging app similar to Twitter and WhatsApp. Users are required to post political opinions and news only to state-authorized media outlets and are required to use their own names when establishing accounts. In 2016, China issued new rules barring foreign companies or their affiliates from publishing online content without government approval. It also began to subject online programs to the same censorship regulations as regular TV shows. In July 2016, it said it would punish websites that publish unverified social media content as news, and ordered several of the most popular Chinese portals, such as Sinu, Sohu, and NetEase, to cease original news reporting.

(continued)

While China is often criticized for its extensive Internet controls, other countries are not far behind. Iran's Internet surveillance of its citizens is considered by security experts to be one of the world's most sophisticated mechanisms for controlling and censoring the Internet, allowing it to examine the content of individual online communications on a massive scale. The Iranian system goes beyond merely preventing access to specific sites such as Google, Twitter, and Facebook and reportedly also utilizes deep packet inspection. Deep packet inspection allows governments to read messages, alter their contents for disinformation purposes, and identify senders and recipients. It is accomplished by installing computers in the line between users and ISPs, opening up every digitized packet, inspecting for keywords and images, reconstructing the message, and sending it on. This is done for all Internet traffic including Skype, Facebook, e-mail, tweets, and messages sent to proxy servers. In 2016, Iran announced that it had completed the first stage of establishing an isolated, domestic version of the Internet, purportedly one that will be faster and less costly, but which subjects its users to even more heightened surveillance.

In Russia, a 2014 law allows the government to close websites without a court decision if the General Prosecutor's office declares the material on a site to be "extremist." Russia also regulates the blogosphere, requiring bloggers with more than 3,000 daily readers to register their real names and contact information with Russia's communications regulator. In 2015, Russia passed laws requiring domestic Internet companies to store their data on Russian soil, allowing the government to control it and limit access, and in July 2016, passed additional laws that provide for mandatory data retention by ISPs and telecommunications providers for between 6 months and three years, require those companies to provide access to all such data without a warrant, and also require a government backdoor that will enable it to access all encrypted communications.

Turkey is another country that has increasingly attempted to control and censor Internet content. These efforts have increased after the terrorist attack on Istanbul's Ataturk Airport and the failed coup against President Recep Tayyip Erdogan.

But it is not just totalitarian nations that have sought to regulate and surveil the Internet. Both Europe and the United States have, at various times, also taken steps to control access to certain websites, censor web content, and engage in extensive surveillance of communications. For instance, Great Britain has a list of blocked sites, as do Germany, France, and Australia. The United States and European countries generally ban the sale, distribution, and/or possession of online child pornography. France, Germany, and Austria all bar the online sale of Nazi memorabilia. Even in South Korea, one of the world's most wired countries, there are restrictions on content that is deemed subversive and harmful to the public order.

In response to terrorism threats and other crimes, European governments and the U.S. government also perform deep packet inspection on e-mail and text communications of terrorist suspects. This surveillance is not limited to cross-border international data flows and includes large-scale domestic surveillance and analysis of routine e-mail, tweets, and other messages. In 2013, National Security Agency (NSA) contractor Edward Snowden made headlines by leaking classified NSA documents shedding light on the NSA's PRISM program, which allowed the agency access to the servers of major Internet companies such as Facebook, Google, Apple, Microsoft, and many others. Additionally, the documents revealed the existence of the NSA's XKeyscore program, which allows analysts to search databases of e-mails, chats, and browsing histories of individual citizens without any authorization. Warrants, court clearance, or other forms of legal documentation are not required for analysts to use the technology. Snowden's documents also showed spy agencies were tapping data from smartphone apps like Candy Crush, and most others, and that the NSA was tapping the flow of personal user information between Google and Yahoo. The NSA claimed that the program was only used to monitor foreign intelligence targets and that the information it collects has assisted in apprehending terrorists. The FBI also has an Internet surveillance unit, the National Domestic Communications Assistance Center. The NDCAC's mission is to assist in the development of new surveillance technologies that will allow authorities to increase the interception of Internet, wireless, and VoIP communications.

In 2016, many European powers moved ahead with plans to fortify their online surveillance with new start-of-the-art networks. In England, potential new laws would force Internet service companies to maintain "Internet connection records" that would be subject to review by law enforcement at any time. In response to multiple terror attacks on French soils in 2015, the French government passed very similar rules that force ISPs to maintain browsing data, as well as additional provisions for surveillance of phone calls, e-mails, and all mobile phone communications. And De-Cix, the world's largest IXP, pushed back against the German government regarding requests to allow surveillance

of all communications passing through its Frankfurt hub. De-Cix sued the German intelligence service for what it views as illegal overreach, but the German government hopes to pass new laws that would legitimize the practice, just as England, France, and other nations have done.

However, in the United States, efforts are underway to curb domestic and international counter-terrorist agencies like the NSA from conducting dragnet surveillance of the entire American population, strengthen court oversight of surveillance, limit surveillance to specific individuals, and ease disclosure rules for Internet firms who receive requests from government agencies. In 2015, Congress passed the USA Freedom Act, which limits the bulk collection of Americans' phone records. However, equally concerted efforts are underway to expand these types of spying powers. For instance, the Obama administration has expanded the NSA's ability to perform warrantless wiretaps on suspected malicious hackers, allowing them to monitor international Internet traffic from these suspects as well as domestic traffic. Concerns about the use of the Internet and other methods of encrypted communications by the Islamic State to recruit new members and engage in terrorism have further heightened the tension.

■■■ **SOURCES:** "World's Biggest Internet Hub Sues German Government Over Surveillance," by David Meyer, *Fortune*, September 16, 2016; "Iran Launches New 'National Internet' That Censors Content, Encourages Regime Surveillance," Thetower.org, August 30, 2016; "China Clamps Down on Online News Reporting," by Michael Forsythe, *New York Times*, July 25, 2016; "Russia Asks for the Impossible with Its New Surveillance Laws," by Eva Galperin and Danny O'Brien, Eff.org, July 19, 2016; "China Cracks Down on News Reports Spread via Social Media," by Edward Wong and Vanessa Pia, July 5, 2016; "Britain to Pay Billions for Monster Internet Surveillance Network," by Duncan Campbell, Computerweekly.com, March 21, 2016; "China Cracks Down on Online Television," by Amy Qin, *New York Times*, March 3, 2016; "New Chinese Rules on Foreign Firms' Online Content," by David Barboza and Paul Mozer, *New York Times*, February 19, 2016; "ISIS Influence on Web Prompts Second Thoughts on First Amendment," by Erik Eckholm, *New York Times*, December 7, 2015; "France Has a Powerful and Controversial New Surveillance Law," by Arik Hesseldahl, Recode.net, November 14, 2015 "Freedom on the Net 2015," Freedomhouse.org, October 28, 2015; "Russian Data Law Fuels Web Surveillance Fears," by Shaun Walker, *The Guardian*, September 1, 2015; "China Passes New National Security Law Extending Control Over Internet," *The Guardian*, July 1, 2015; "Hunting for Hackers, N.S.A. Secretly Expands Internet Spying at U.S. Border," by Charlie Savage et al., *New York Times*, June 4, 2015; "The State of Surveillance in Iran," by Arta Shams, Ifex.org, May 22, 2015; "House Moves to Curb Government Surveillance of Phone, Internet Records," by Cristina Maza, Csmonitor.com, May 1, 2015; "Turkey's Parliament Issues Contested Security, Surveillance Laws," Bloombergnews.com, March 27, 2015; "Russia Forces Its Popular Bloggers to Register—Or Else," by Ilya Khrennikov, Bloomberg.com, August 19, 2014; "NSA Top Lawyer Says Tech Giants Knew About Data Collection," Cnet.com, March 19, 2014; "Documents Say NSA Pretends to Be Facebook in Surveillance," by Reed Albergotti, *Wall Street Journal*, March 12, 2014; "Amid Flow of Leaks, Turkey Moves to Crimp Internet," by Tim Arango and Ceylan Yeginsu, *New York Times*, February 6, 2014; "Spy Agencies Tap Data Streaming From Phone Apps," by James Glanz, Jeff Larson, and Andrew Lehren, *New York Times*, January 27, 2014; "NSA Surveillance Covers 75 Percent of U.S. Internet Traffic: WSJ," by Reuters, News.Yahoo.com, August 20, 2013; "New Snowden Leak: NSA Program Taps All You Do Online," by Amanda Wills, Mashable.com, August 1, 2013; "Snowden: NSA Collects 'Everything,' Including Content of Emails," by Eyder Peralta, NPR.org, June 17, 2013; "FBI Quietly Forms Secret Net-Surveillance Unit," by Declan McCullagh, News.cnet.com, May 22, 2012.

contained in the packet. A higher level of service quality is required if the Internet is to keep expanding into new services, such as video on demand and telephony.

- *Network architecture limitations*. Today, a thousand requests for a single music track from a central server will result in a thousand efforts by the server to download the music to each requesting client. This slows down network performance, as the same music track is sent out a thousand times to clients that might be located in the same metropolitan area. This is very different from television, where the program is broadcast once to millions of homes.
- *Wired Internet*. The Internet is still largely based on cables—fiber-optic and coaxial copper cables. Copper cables use a centuries-old technology, and fiber-optic cable is expensive to place underground. The wired nature of the Internet restricts mobility of users although it is changing rapidly as Wi-Fi hotspots proliferate, and cellular phone technology advances. However, cellular systems are often overloaded due to the growth in the number of smartphones.

Now imagine an Internet at least 1,000 times as powerful as today's Internet, one that is not subjected to the limitations of bandwidth, protocols, architecture, physical connections, and language detailed previously. Welcome to the world of the future Internet, and the next generation of e-commerce services and products!

THE INTERNET2® PROJECT

Internet2®

advanced networking consortium of more than 450 member institutions working in partnership to facilitate the development, deployment, and use of revolutionary Internet technologies

Internet2® is an advanced networking consortium of more than 450 member institutions including universities, corporations, government research agencies, and not-for-profit networking organizations, all working in partnership to facilitate the development, deployment, and use of revolutionary Internet technologies. The broader Internet2 community includes more than 90,000 institutions across the United States and international networking partners in more than 100 countries. Internet2's work is a continuation of the kind of cooperation among government, private, and educational organizations that created the original Internet.

The advanced networks created and in use by Internet2 members provide an environment in which new technologies can be tested and enhanced. For instance, Internet2 provides a next-generation, nationwide 100 gigabit-per-second network that not only makes available a reliable production services platform for current high-performance needs but also creates a powerful experimental platform for the development of new network capabilities. See **Table 2.9** to get some sense of just how fast a 100-Gbps network is in terms of data transmission times. The fourth generation of this network, built through a federal stimulus grant from the National Telecommunications and Information Administration's Broadband Technology Opportunities Program, has now been deployed. The hybrid optical and packet network provides 8.8 terabits of capacity with the ability to seamlessly scale as requirements grow, includes over 15,000 miles of owned fiber optic cable, and reaches into underserved areas of the country, supporting connectivity for approximately 200,000 U.S. community anchor institutions (schools, local libraries, and museums), and enabling them to provide citizens across the country with telemedicine, distance learning, and other advanced applications not possible with consumer-grade Internet services. The infrastructure supports a wide range of IP and optical services already available today and also will stimulate a new

TABLE 2.9	HOW FAST IS A 100-GBPS NETWORK?
DATA	TIME TO TRANSMIT
8.5 million electronic records	1 minute
300,000 X-rays	1 minute
1.8 million e-books simultaneously downloaded	2 minute

generation of innovative services. The goal is to create an intelligent global ecosystem that will enable researchers, scientists, and others to "turn on" high-capacity network connections whenever and wherever they are needed. **Table 2.10** describes some of the projects that Internet2's 100-Gbps network is enabling. Other initiatives involve science and engineering (advanced network applications in support of distributed lab environments, remote access to rare scientific instruments, and distributed large-scale computation and data access), health sciences and health networks (telemedicine, medical and biological research, and health education and awareness), and arts and humanities (collaborative live performances, master classes, remote auditions, and interactive performing arts education and media events).

THE FIRST MILE AND THE LAST MILE

The Internet2 project is just the tip of the iceberg when it comes to future enhancements to the Internet. In 2007, the NSF began work on the Global Environment for Network Innovations (GENI) initiative. GENI is a unique virtual laboratory for exploring future internets at scale. GENI aims to promote innovations in network science, security technologies, services, and applications. GENI is a partnership of leading

TABLE 2.10	PROJECTS BEING ENABLED BY INTERNET2'S 100-GBPS NETWORK
PROJECT	DESCRIPTION
XSEDE (Extreme Science and Engineering Discovery Environment)	XSEDE is a collection of integrated, advanced digital resources and services that enables scientists to interactively share computing resources, data, and expertise. XSEDE supports over 8,000 members of the scientific community, and 16 supercomputers. In 2013, XSEDE upgraded from a 10-Gbps network to Internet2's 100-Gbps network. In 2016, the NSF awarded XSEDE $110 million in funding to enable it to continue to provide advanced cyberinfrastructure resources and services to the nation's scientists and engineers.
CloudLab	Cloud computing test beds based at the University of Utah, Clemson, and the University of Wisconsin-Madison, connected by Internet2's 100-Gbps network. Focusing on the development of novel cloud architectures and new cloud computing applications. Enables researchers to build their own clouds and experiment with applications such as real-time disaster response and medical record security.
University of Florida	Support for Compact Muon Solenoid (CMS) experiments at CERN's Hadron collider (contributed to discovery of the Higgs boson particle, which earned 2013 Nobel Prize).

academic centers and private corporations such as Cisco, IBM, and HP, among many others. To date, awards have been made to 83 academic/industry teams for various projects to build, integrate, and operate early prototypes of the GENI virtual laboratory (Geni.net, 2014). Between 2015 and 2017, GENI will transition from being overseen by NSF's GENI Project Office to a community governance model (Geni.net, 2016).

The most significant privately initiated (but often government-influenced) changes are coming in two areas: fiber-optic trunk line bandwidth and wireless Internet services. Fiber optics is concerned with the first mile or backbone Internet services that carry bulk traffic long distances. Wireless Internet is concerned with the last mile—from the larger Internet to the user's smartphone, tablet computer, or laptop.

Fiber Optics and the Bandwidth Explosion in the First Mile

fiber-optic cable

consists of up to hundreds of strands of glass or plastic that use light to transmit data

Fiber-optic cable consists of up to hundreds of strands of glass that use light to transmit data. It often replaces existing coaxial and twisted pair cabling because it can transmit much more data at faster speeds, with less interference and better data security. Fiber-optic cable is also thinner and lighter, taking up less space during installation. The hope is to use fiber optics to expand network bandwidth capacity in order to prepare for the expected increases in web traffic once next-generation Internet services are widely adopted.

Telecommunication firms have made substantial investments in global, national, and regional fiber optic cable systems in the last decade. For instance, Verizon has spent over $23 billion since 2004, building and expanding its FiOS fiber-optic Internet service that can provide speeds of up to 500 Mbps, and currently has about 6.6 million FiOS customers. In 2012, Google joined the fray with Google Fiber, a 1-Gbps fiber-optic network, that is currently available in 7 cities. This installed base of fiber-optic cable represents a vast digital highway that is currently being exploited by YouTube (Google), Facebook, and other high-bandwidth applications. But despite the interest in fiber, only about 12.3% of U.S. homes had fiber connections as of 2015, a much lower percentage than a number of other countries around the world (Buckley, 2015; Richter, 2016). **Table 2.11** illustrates several optical bandwidth standards and compares them to traditional T lines.

The Last Mile: Mobile Internet Access

Fiber-optic networks carry the long-haul bulk traffic of the Internet and play an important role in bringing high-speed broadband to the household and small business. The goal of the Internet2 and GENI projects is to bring gigabit and ultimately terabit bandwidth to the household over the next 20 years. But along with fiber optics, arguably the most significant development for the Internet and Web has been the emergence of mobile Internet access.

Wireless Internet is concerned with the last mile of Internet access to the user's home, office, car, smartphone, or tablet computer, anywhere they are located. Up until 2000, the last-mile access to the Internet—with the exception of a small satellite Internet connect population—was bound up in land lines of some sort: copper coaxial TV cables or telephone lines or, in some cases, fiber-optic lines to the office. Today,

TABLE 2.11	HIGH-SPEED OPTICAL BANDWIDTH STANDARDS
STANDARD	SPEED
T1	1.544 Mbps
T3	43.232 Mbps
OC-3	155 Mbps
OC-12	622 Mbps
OC-48	2.5 Gbps
OC-192	10 Gbps
OC-768	40 Gbps

Note: "OC" stands for Optical Carrier and is used to specify the speed of fiber-optic networks conforming to the SONET standard. SONET (Synchronous Optical Networks) includes a set of signal rate multiples for transmitting digital signals on optical fiber. The base rate (OC-1) is 51.84 Mbps.

in comparison, high-speed cell phone networks and Wi-Fi network hotspots provide a major alternative.

Today, sales of desktop computers have been eclipsed by sales of smartphones and tablet and ultramobile laptop computers with built-in wireless networking functionality. Clearly, a large part of the Internet is now mobile, access-anywhere broadband service for the delivery of video, music, and web search. According to eMarketer, there are almost 2.5 billion mobile Internet users worldwide in 2016 (eMarketer, Inc., 2016d).

Telephone-based versus Computer Network-based Wireless Internet Access

There are two different basic types of wireless Internet connectivity: telephone-based and computer network-based systems.

Telephone-based wireless Internet access connects the user to a global telephone system (land, satellite, and microwave) that has a long history of dealing with millions of users simultaneously and already has in place a large-scale transaction billing system and related infrastructure. Cellular telephones and the telephone industry are currently the largest providers of wireless access to the Internet today. Around 1.5 billion smartphones are expected to be sold worldwide in 2016 (Gartner, Inc., 2016b). Smartphones combine the functionality of a cell phone with that of a laptop computer with Wi-Fi capability. This makes it possible to combine in one device music, video, web access, and telephone service. Tablet computers can also access cellular networks. **Table 2.12** summarizes the various telephone technologies currently being used and under development for wireless Internet access. 5G wireless is the next frontier. Although official standards are not expected to be fully rolled out for a few years, telecommunications companies will likely start to introduce technology branded as "5G" as soon as 2017.

TABLE 2.12	WIRELESS INTERNET ACCESS TELEPHONE TECHNOLOGIES		
TECHNOLOGY	SPEED	DESCRIPTION	PLAYERS
3G (THIRD GENERATION)			
CDMA2000 EV-DO HSPA (W-CDMA)	144 Kbps–2 Mbps	High-speed, mobile, always on for e-mail, browsing, and instant messaging. Implementing technologies include versions of CDMA2000 EV-DO (used by CDMA providers) and HSPDA (used by GSM providers). Nearly as fast as Wi-Fi.	Verizon, Sprint, AT&T, T-Mobile, Vodafone
3.5G (3G+)			
CDMA2000 EV-DO, Rev.B	Up to 14.4 Mbps	Enhanced version of CDMA 2000 EV-DO.	Verizon, Sprint
HSPA+	Up to 11 Mbps	Enhanced version of HSPA.	AT&T, T-Mobile
4G (FOURTH GENERATION)			
Long-Term Evolution (LTE)	Up to 100 Mbps	True broadband on cell phone; lower latency than previous generations.	AT&T, Verizon, Sprint, T-Mobile (in 2013)
5G (FIFTH GENERATION)			
Standards under development; expected by 2020	Up to 10 Gbps	Goals include 1–10 Gbps connectivity; sub-1 millisecond latency enabling services such as autonomous driving, augmented reality, virtual reality, and immersive/tactile Internet.	Ericsson, SK Telecom, Huawei, Samsung, NTT DoCoMo, Verizon, national governments

Wi-Fi

Wireless standard for Ethernet networks with greater speed and range than Bluetooth

Wireless local area network (WLAN)-based Internet access derives from a completely different background from telephone-based wireless Internet access. Popularly known as **Wi-Fi**, WLANs are based on computer local area networks where the task is to connect client computers (generally stationary) to server computers within local areas of, say, a few hundred meters. Wi-Fi functions by sending radio signals that are broadcast over the airwaves using certain radio frequency ranges (2.4 GHz to 5.875 GHz, depending on the type of standard involved). The major technologies here are the various versions of the Wi-Fi standard, WiMax, and Bluetooth (see **Table 2.13**).

In a Wi-Fi network, a *wireless access point* (also known as a "hot spot") connects to the Internet directly via a broadband connection (cable, DSL telephone, or T1 line) and then transmits a radio signal to a transmitter/receiver installed in a tablet or laptop computer or smartphone. **Figure 2.14** illustrates how a Wi-Fi network works.

Wi-Fi provided under the 802.11 a/b/g/n specifications offers high-bandwidth capacity from 11 Mbps up to a maximum of 7 Gbps—far greater than any 3G or 4G service currently in existence—but has a limited range of 300 meters, with the exception of WiMax discussed below. Wi-Fi is also exceptionally inexpensive. The cost of creating a corporate Wi-Fi network in a single 14-story building with an access point for each floor is less than $100 an access point. It would cost well over $500,000 to

TABLE 2.13	WIRELESS NETWORK INTERNET ACCESS TECHNOLOGIES		
TECHNOLOGY	RANGE/SPEED	DESCRIPTION	PLAYERS
Wi-Fi (IEEE 802.11 a/b/g/n)	300 feet/11–70 Mbps	Evolving high-speed, fixed broadband wireless local area network for commercial and residential use	Linksys, Cisco, and other Wi-Fi router manufacturers; entrepreneurial network developers
802.11ac	500 Mbps–1 Gbps		
802.11ad	less than 10 meters/ up to 7 Gbps		
WiMax (IEEE 802.16)	30 miles/50–70 Mbps	High-speed, medium-range, broadband wireless metropolitan area network	Clearwire, Sprint, Fujitsu, Intel, Alcatel, Proxim
Bluetooth (wireless personal area network)	1–30 meters/1–3 Mbps	Modest-speed, low-power, short-range connection of digital devices	Sony Ericsson, Nokia, Apple, HP, and other device makers

wire the same building with Ethernet cable. IEEE 802.11ac is a version of the 802.11 specification adopted in December 2013 that provides for effective throughputs of 500 Mbps to over 1 Gbps. The newest standard, IEEE 802.11ad, provides for theoretical maximum throughput up to 7 Gbps. The first 802.11ad devices began shipping at the beginning of 2016. Next-generation Wi-Fi standards currently being worked on by

FIGURE 2.14	WI-FI NETWORKS

In a Wi-Fi network, wireless access points connect to the Internet using a land-based broadband connection. Clients, which could be desktops, laptops, tablet computers, or smartphones, connect to the access point using radio signals.

the IEEE 802.11 Working Group include 802.11ay, which deals with 60 GHz wireless operations, and will provide for data rates of up to 20 Gbps, and 802.11ax, aimed at high-efficiency WLANs used for stadiums and other areas where many people want to access a Wi-Fi network at the same time. A next-generation 802.11ah standard aimed at the Internet of Things is also being developed (Weiss, 2015; Hsu, 2015).

While initially a grass roots, "hippies and hackers" public access technology, billions of dollars have subsequently been poured into private ventures seeking to create for-profit Wi-Fi networks. One of the most prominent networks has been created by Boingo Wireless with more than 1 million hotspots around the globe. Optimum WiFi (available to Optimum Online customers for free) also offers over 1.5 million hotspots around the world. AT&T Wi-Fi Services (formerly Wayport) has another large network that provides Wi-Fi service at hotels, airports, McDonald's, and IHOP restaurants, and Hertz airport rental offices, with thousands of hotspots throughout the United States and access to Boingo's wireless network internationally. T-Mobile and Sprint also have Wi-Fi services at Starbucks coffee shops and thousands of other public locations in the United States. Apple, in turn, has made Wi-Fi automatically available to iPhone and iPad devices as an alternative to the more expensive and much slower 3G and 4G cellular systems. In 2015, for the first time, a majority (51%) of mobile Internet traffic originated from Wi-Fi rather than cellular systems, and it is expected that Wi-Fi will be carrying over half of all Internet traffic by 2019 (Cisco, 2016).

Bluetooth

technology standard for short-range wireless communication under 30 feet

A second WLAN technology for connecting to the Internet, and for connecting Internet devices to one another, is called Bluetooth. **Bluetooth** is a personal connectivity technology that enables links between mobile devices and connectivity to the Internet (Bluetooth.com, 2016). Bluetooth is the universal cable cutter, promising to get rid of the tangled mess of wires, cradles, and special attachments that plague the current world of personal computing. With Bluetooth, users can wear a wireless earbud, share files in a hallway or conference room, synchronize their smartphone with their laptop without a cable, send a document to a printer, and even pay a restaurant bill from the table to a Bluetooth-equipped cash register. Bluetooth is also an unregulated media operating in the 2.4 GHz spectrum but with a very limited range of 30 feet or less. It uses a frequency hopping signal with up to 1,600 hops per second over 79 frequencies, giving it good protection from interference and interception. Bluetooth-equipped devices constantly scan their environments looking for connections to compatible devices. Today, almost all mobile devices are Bluetooth-enabled. Bluetooth may also play a role in the future as a platform for the Internet of Things (see page 140).

INTERNET ACCESS DRONES

A new method of providing Internet access to areas that are not well served by wired or cellular networks is being explored by companies such as Google and Facebook. Both companies have recently purchased companies that make drones (unmanned aircraft/ satellites) that may be used to provide Internet access to remote parts of the world.

In 2014, Google purchased Titan Aerospace, which makes solar-powered drones that can fly for several years at 65,000 feet. Google is reportedly experimenting with using drones to deliver 5G wireless Internet service. Google is also experimenting with high-altitude balloons with its Project Loon. Google envisions a network of balloons circling high above the earth in the stratosphere, establishing a ring of uninterrupted connectivity. In 2014, Google sent a prototype of a networked hot-air balloon around the world in 22 days, even taking photos for its Street View program, and in 2015, the government of Sri Lanka announced that Sri Lanka would be the first country to use Project Loon to provide universal Internet access across Sri Lanka. In August 2016, Google is reportedly taking steps to move Project Loon from a research project into a profitable business.

In a similar effort, Facebook has put together the Facebook Connectivity Lab, where engineers are focusing on solar-powered drones, satellites, and infrared lasers capable of providing Internet access. To propel that effort, Facebook purchased the British company Ascenta, whose founders helped create the world's longest flying solar-powered drone. In 2016, Facebook completed a full-scale test flight of its first Internet access solar-powered drone, Aquila. Created from carbon fiber, the drone has the wingspan of a Boeing 737 but weighs less than a small car, and is designed to fly at 60,000 to 90,000 feet for up to three months at a time. It reportedly uses a laser communications system that can beam data from the sky.

THE FUTURE INTERNET

The increased bandwidth and expanded wireless network connectivity of the Internet of the future will result in benefits beyond faster access and richer communications. First-mile enhancements created by fiber-optic networks will enhance reliability and quality of Internet transmissions and create new business models and opportunities. Some of the major benefits of these technological advancements include latency solutions, guaranteed service levels, lower error rates, and declining costs. Widespread wireless access to the Internet will also essentially double or even triple the size of the online shopping marketspace because consumers will be able to shop and make purchases just about anywhere. We describe some of these benefits in more detail in the following sections.

Latency Solutions

One of the challenges of packet switching, where data is divided into chunks and then sent separately to meet again at the destination, is that the Internet does not differentiate between high-priority packets, such as video clips, and those of lower priority, such as self-contained e-mail messages. Because the packets cannot yet be simultaneously reassembled, the result can be distorted audio and video streams.

Differentiated quality of service (diffserv) is a technology that assigns levels of priority to packets based on the type of data being transmitted. Video conference packets, for example, which need to reach their destination almost instantaneously, receive much higher priority than e-mail messages. In the end, the quality of video and audio will skyrocket without undue stress on the network. Differential service is very controversial because it means some users may get more bandwidth than others, and potentially they may have to pay a higher price for more bandwidth.

differentiated quality of service (diffserv)
a new technology that assigns levels of priority to packets based on the type of data being transmitted

Guaranteed Service Levels and Lower Error Rates

In today's Internet, there is no service-level guarantee and no way to purchase the right to move data through the Internet at a fixed pace. Today's Internet promises only "best effort." The Internet is democratic—it speeds or slows everyone's traffic alike. In the future, it might be possible to purchase the right to move data through the network at a guaranteed speed in return for higher fees.

Declining Costs

As the Internet pipeline is upgraded, the availability of broadband service will expand beyond major metropolitan areas, significantly reducing the cost of access. More users mean lower cost, as products and technology catch on in the mass market. Higher volume usage enables providers to lower the cost of both access devices, or clients, and the service required to use such products. Both broadband and wireless service fees are expected to decline as geographic service areas increase, in part due to competition for that business.

The Internet of Things

Internet of Things (IoT)

Use of the Internet to connect a wide variety of devices, machines, and sensors

No discussion of the future Internet would be complete without mentioning the **Internet of Things (IoT)**, also sometimes referred to as the Industrial Internet. Internet technology is spreading beyond the desktop, laptop, and tablet computer, and beyond the smartphone, to consumer electronics, electrical appliances, cars, medical devices, utility systems, machines of all types, even clothing—just about anything that can be equipped with sensors that can collect data and connect to the Internet, enabling the data to be analyzed with data analytics software.

IoT builds on a foundation of existing technologies, such as radio frequency identification (RFID) tags, and is being enabled by the availability of low-cost sensors, the drop in price of data storage, the development of "big data" analytics software that can work with trillions of pieces of data, as well as implementation of IPv6, which will allow Internet addresses to be assigned to all of these new devices. Although IoT devices don't necessarily have to be wireless, most use wireless communications technology previously discussed, such as cellular networks, Wi-Fi, Bluetooth, or other wireless protocols such as ZigBee or Z-Wave, to connect either directly or via a mobile app to the Internet (often a cloud service).

IoT technology is powering the development of "smart" connected "things"—televisions, houses, and cars, as well as wearable technology—clothing and devices like the Apple Watch, profiled in the opening case. Smart televisions that integrate directly with the Internet and can run apps have become very popular, with more than half (52%) of all U.S. Internet homes having at least one TV connected to the Internet (NPD Group Inc, 2016). Smart houses have attracted even more interest, fueled by Google's purchase of Nest Labs for $3.2 billion in 2014. Nest Labs makes smart thermostats, home security cameras, and smoke and carbon monoxide alarms. In 2015, Nest Labs announced that it was making Nest Weave, a protocol it had developed that enables appliances, thermostats, door locks, and other devices to communicate with each other and other Nest products, available to third-party developers and manufacturers. Apple announced a smart home platform that it calls HomeKit in 2014. HomeKit is a framework and network protocol for controlling devices in the home that is programmed directly into Apple's iOS software for iPhones and iPads, and is integrated with Siri, Apple's voice-activated artificial intelligence assistant. By 2016, a number of devices had been designed specifically for use with HomeKit, such as a smart thermostat, a smart deadbolt lock, a home sensor that provides temperature, humidity, and air quality readings, and an iDevices switch that enables you to turn electronic devices on and off using Siri. Many cable companies such as Time Warner Cable, Comcast, and AT&T already offer connected home systems that include appliances and lights. All in all, the global market for smart house products is expected to grow from about €45 billion in 2015 to over €114 billion by 2022 (Research and Markets, 2016).

In September 2014, Apple introduced the Apple Watch. The Apple Watch features a fitness/activity tracker similar to offerings from Fitbit, Nike +, FuelBand, and Jawbone Up, is able to access a wide variety of apps and also works with Apple Pay, Apple's mobile payment service. A number of other manufacturers, such as Samsung, LG, Motorola, and Swatch, have also introduced smartwatches. Wearable computing is expected to grow into a €160 billion business by 2021.

Connected cars that have built-in Internet access have also arrived (see the *Insight on Technology* case, *Are Connected Cars the Next Hot Entertainment Vehicle?* in Chapter 5). Here too, Google and Apple are major players. In 2014, Google announced the Open Automotive Alliance, a group of leading automakers and technology companies focused on bringing the Android platform to cars. Shortly thereafter, Apple announced CarPlay, a software platform that synchronizes iPhones to the car's infotainment system. Android Auto and CarPlay-enabled vehicles began to be introduced in 2015, and have become more widely available in 2016. Connected cars are likely to be integrated with smart home initiatives in the future. Already, iControl, which provides the software underlying automated home systems from Comcast, TimeWarner, ADT, and others, has entered into a partnership with Zubie, a provider of connected car services. The next frontier on the connected car front is the the self-driving car, combining IoT and artificial intelligence technologies. Many Internet technology companies, ranging from giants such as Google, Baidu (China's version of Google), Uber, and Intel to start-ups like Drive.ai and Mobileye, have jumped into the fray alongside automotive companies such as Tesla, BMW, Volvo, GM, Ford, and others, with the goal of offering self-driving, autonomous cars by 2019 or sooner.

Despite all of the IoT activity, however, interoperability remains a major concern. As with many technologies in the early stages of development, many organizations are fighting to create the standards that participants in the market will follow. The AllSeen Alliance, formed by Qualcomm in 2013 with 50 other companies, including Microsoft and Cisco, is one group that hopes to create an open source standard. Membership in the Alliance has soared since its initial founding and in 2016, it has over 200 members. Another group, the Open Connectivity Foundation (formerly the Open Interconnect Consortium), formed in 2014 by Intel, Broadcom, Dell, and others apparently not happy with the AllSeen effort, has also seen its membership soar to over 200 members. A different group, the Industrial Internet Consortium, has been formed by AT&T,

Cisco, GE, IBM, and Intel to focus on engineering standards for industrial assets. The Wolfram Connected Devices Project is aimed at developing a database of IoT devices, and currently includes more than 3,000. And as with many other types of Internet-related technology, Google with its Android operating system and Apple with AirPlay wireless streaming protocol may be trying to create their own standards.

Other concerns include security and privacy. Security experts believe that IoT devices could potentially be a security disaster, with the potential for malware being spread through a connected network, and difficulty in issuing patches to devices, leaving them vulnerable (Internet Society, 2015). Data from stand-alone smart devices can reveal much personal detail about a consumer's life, and if those devices are all ultimately interconnected, there will be little that is truly private.

Although challenges remain before the Internet of Things is fully realized, it is coming closer and closer to fruition. As of 2016, experts estimate that there are anywhere from 6.4 billion to 9 billion IoT devices (not including smartphones, tablets, or desktop computers), with some projecting as many as 100 billion connected IoT devices and global economic impact of more than €10 trillion by 2025 (Nordstrom, 2016; Internet Society, 2015).

2.4   THE WEB

Without the Web, there would be no e-commerce. The invention of the Web brought an extraordinary expansion of digital services to millions of amateur computer users, including color text and pages, formatted text, pictures, animations, video, and sound. In short, the Web makes nearly all the rich elements of human expression needed to establish a commercial marketplace available to nontechnical computer users worldwide.

While the Internet was born in the 1960s, the Web was not invented until 1989–1991 by Dr. Tim Berners-Lee of the European Particle Physics Laboratory, better known as CERN (Berners-Lee et al., 1994). Several earlier authors—such as Vannevar Bush (in 1945) and Ted Nelson (in the 1960s)—had suggested the possibility of organizing knowledge as a set of interconnected pages that users could freely browse (Bush, 1945; Ziff Davis Publishing, 1998). Berners-Lee and his associates at CERN built on these ideas and developed the initial versions of HTML, HTTP, a web server, and a browser, the four essential components of the Web.

First, Berners-Lee wrote a computer program that allowed formatted pages within his own computer to be linked using keywords (hyperlinks). Clicking on a keyword in a document would immediately move him to another document. Berners-Lee created the pages using a modified version of a powerful text markup language called Standard Generalized Markup Language (SGML).

Berners-Lee called this language HyperText Markup Language, or HTML. He then came up with the idea of storing his HTML pages on the Internet. Remote client computers could access these pages by using HTTP (introduced earlier in Section 2.1 and described more fully in the next section). But these early web pages still appeared as black and white text pages with hyperlinks expressed inside brackets. The early Web was based on text only; the original web browser only provided a line interface.

Information shared on the Web remained text-based until 1993, when Marc Andreessen and others at the National Center for Supercomputing Applications (NCSA) at the University of Illinois created a web browser with a graphical user interface (GUI) called **Mosaic** that made it possible to view documents on the Web graphically—using colored backgrounds, images, and even primitive animations. Mosaic was a software program that could run on any graphically based interface such as Macintosh, Windows, or Unix. The Mosaic browser software read the HTML text on a web page and displayed it as a graphical interface document within a GUI operating system such as Windows or Macintosh. Liberated from simple black and white text pages, HTML pages could now be viewed by anyone in the world who could operate a mouse and use a Macintosh or PC.

Aside from making the content of web pages colorful and available to the world's population, the graphical web browser created the possibility of **universal computing**, the sharing of files, information, graphics, sound, video, and other objects across all computer platforms in the world, regardless of operating system. A browser could be made for each of the major operating systems, and the web pages created for one system, say, Windows, would also be displayed exactly the same, or nearly the same, on computers running the Macintosh or Unix operating systems. As long as each operating system had a Mosaic browser, the same web pages could be used on all the different types of computers and operating systems. This meant that no matter what kind of computer you used, anywhere in the world, you would see the same web pages. The browser and the Web have introduced us to a whole new world of computing and information management that was unthinkable prior to 1993.

In 1994, Andreessen and Jim Clark founded Netscape, which created the first commercial browser, **Netscape Navigator**. Although Mosaic had been distributed free of charge, Netscape initially charged for its software. In August 1995, Microsoft Corporation released its own free version of a browser, called **Internet Explorer**. In the ensuing years, Netscape fell from a 100% market share to less than .5% in 2009. The fate of Netscape illustrates an important e-commerce business lesson. Innovators usually are not long-term winners, whereas smart followers often have the assets needed for long-term survival. Much of the Netscape browser code survives today in the Firefox browser produced by Mozilla, a nonprofit heavily funded by Google.

HYPERTEXT

Web pages can be accessed through the Internet because the web browser software on your PC can request web pages stored on an Internet host server using the HTTP protocol. **Hypertext** is a way of formatting pages with embedded links that connect documents to one another and that also link pages to other objects such as sound, video, or animation files. When you click on a graphic and a video clip plays, you have clicked on a hyperlink. For example, when you type a web address in your browser such as http://www.sec.gov, your browser sends an HTTP request to the sec.gov server requesting the home page of sec.gov.

Mosaic
Web browser with a graphical user interface (GUI) that made it possible to view documents on the Web graphically

universal computing
the sharing of files, information, graphics, sound, video, and other objects across all computer platforms in the world, regardless of operating system

Netscape Navigator
the first commercial web browser

Internet Explorer
Microsoft's web browser

hypertext
a way of formatting pages with embedded links that connect documents to one another, and that also link pages to other objects such as sound, video, or animation files

HTTP is the first set of letters at the start of every web address, followed by the domain name. The domain name specifies the organization's server computer that is housing the document. Most companies have a domain name that is the same as or closely related to their official corporate name. The directory path and document name are two more pieces of information within the web address that help the browser track down the requested page. Together, the address is called a Uniform Resource Locator, or URL. When typed into a browser, a URL tells it exactly where to look for the information. For example, in the following URL:

http://www.megacorp.com/content/features/082602.html

http = the protocol used to display web pages

www.megacorp.com = domain name

content/features = the directory path that identifies where on the domain web server the page is stored

082602.html = the document name and its format (an HTML page)

The most common domain extensions (known as general top-level domains, or gTLDs) currently available and officially sanctioned by ICANN are shown in **Table 2.14**. Countries also have domain names, such as .uk, .au, and .fr (United Kingdom, Australia, and France, respectively). These are sometimes referred to as country-code top-level domains, or ccTLDs. In 2008, ICANN approved a significant expansion of gTLDs, with potential new domains representing cities (such as .berlin), regions (.africa), ethnicity (.eus), industry/activities (such as .health), and even brands (such as .deloitte). In 2009, ICANN began the process of implementing these guidelines. In 2011, ICANN removed nearly all restrictions on domain names, thereby greatly expanding the number of different domain names available. As of August 2016, over 1,150 gTLDs have been applied for, acquired, and launched. The new gTLDs are in multiple languages and scripts/characters (including Arabic, Chinese, Japanese, and Russian) and include geographic place names such as .nyc, .london, and .paris; business identifiers such as .restaurant, .realtor, .technology, and .lawyer; brand names such as .bmw and .suzuki; and a whole host of other descriptive names.

MARKUP LANGUAGES

Although the most common web page formatting language is HTML, the concept behind document formatting actually had its roots in the 1960s with the development of Generalized Markup Language (GML).

HyperText Markup Language (HTML)

HyperText Markup Language (HTML) is a GML that is relatively easy to use. HTML provides web page designers with a fixed set of markup "tags" that are used to format a web page (see **Figure 2.15**). When these tags are inserted into a web page, they are read by the browser and interpreted into a page display. You can see the source HTML

HyperText Markup Language (HTML)
GML that is relatively easy to use in web page design. HTML provides web page designers with a fixed set of markup "tags" that are used to format a web page

TABLE 2.14	EXAMPLES OF TOP-LEVEL DOMAINS		
GENERAL TOP-LEVEL DOMAIN (GTLD)	YEAR(S) INTRODUCED	PURPOSE	SPONSOR/ OPERATOR
.com	1980s	Unrestricted (but intended for commercial registrants)	VeriSign
.edu	1980s	U.S. educational institutions	Educause
.gov	1980s	U.S. government	U.S. General Services Administration
.mil	1980s	U.S. military	U.S. Department of Defense Network Information Center
.net	1980s	Unrestricted (but originally intended for network providers, etc.)	VeriSign
.org	1980s	Unrestricted (but intended for organizations that do not fit elsewhere)	Public Interest Registry (was operated by VeriSign until December 31, 2002)
.int	1998	Organizations established by international treaties between governments	Internet Assigned Numbers Authority (IANA)
.aero	2001	Air-transport industry	Societé Internationale de Telecommunications Aeronautiques SC (SITA)
.biz	2001	Businesses	NeuLevel
.coop	2001	Cooperatives	DotCooperation LLC
.info	2001	Unrestricted use	Afilias LLC
.museum	2001	Museums	Museum Domain Name Association (MuseDoma)
.name	2001	For registration by individuals	Global Name Registry Ltd.
.pro	2002	Accountants, lawyers, physicians, and other professionals	RegistryPro Ltd
.jobs	2005	Job search	Employ Media LLC
.travel	2005	Travel search	Tralliance Corporation
.mobi	2005	Websites specifically designed for mobile phones	mTLD Top Level Domain, Ltd.
.cat	2005	Individuals, organizations, and companies that promote the Catalan language and culture	Fundació puntCAT
.asia	2006	Regional domain for companies, organizations, and individuals based in Asia	DotAsia Organization
.tel	2006	Telephone numbers and other contact information	ICM Registry
.xxx	2010	New top-level domain for pornographic content	None yet approved

SOURCE: Based on data from ICANN, 2011b.

FIGURE 2.15   **EXAMPLE HTML CODE (A) AND WEB PAGE (B)**

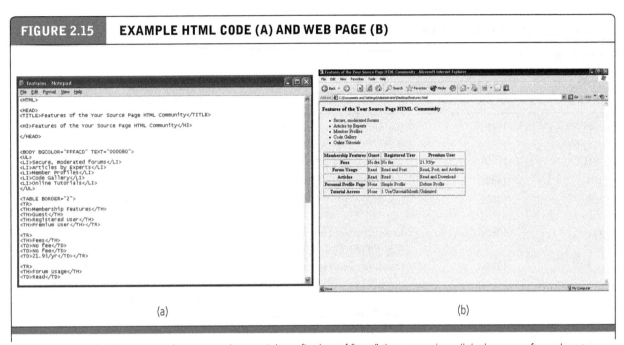

(a)   (b)

HTML is a text markup language used to create web pages. It has a fixed set of "tags" that are used to tell the browser software how to present the content on screen. The HTML shown in Figure 2.15 (a) creates the web page seen in Figure 2.15 (b).

SOURCES: (A) Notepad, Microsoft Windows, Microsoft Corporation; (B) Internet Explorer, Microsoft Windows, Microsoft Corporation.

---

code for any web page by simply clicking on the "Page Source" command found in all browsers. In Figure 2.15, the HTML code in the first screen produces the display in the second screen.

HTML defines the structure and style of a document, including the headings, graphic positioning, tables, and text formatting. Since its introduction, the major browsers have continuously added features to HTML to enable programmers to further refine their page layouts. Unfortunately, some browser enhancements may work only in one company's browser. Whenever you build an e-commerce site, you should take care that the pages can be viewed by the major browsers, even outdated versions of browsers. HTML web pages can be created with any text editor, such as Notepad or WordPad, using Microsoft Word (simply save the Word document as a web page), or any one of several web page development tools such as Microsoft Expression Web or Adobe Dreamweaver CC.[5]

The most recent version of HTML is HTML5. HTML5 introduces features like video playback and drag-and-drop that in the past were provided by plug-ins like Adobe Flash. HTML5 is also used in the development of mobile websites and mobile apps, and is an important tool in both responsive web design and adaptive web delivery, all of which are discussed more fully in Chapter 3. The *Insight on Technology* case, *The Rise of HTML5*, examines the increasing use of HTML5.

---

[5] A detailed discussion of how to use HTML is beyond the scope of this text.

INSIGHT ON TECHNOLOGY

THE RISE OF HTML5

In 2010, Apple founder Steve Jobs lambasted Adobe Flash for its poor security, poor performance on mobile devices, and for being an energy hog. Jobs instead trumpeted HTML5 as the preferred method for displaying video online. Fast forward to 2016. Two years after its official ratification by the W3C, the Web's standards-setting organization, HTML5 has become a de facto standard, proving once again Jobs' uncanny ability to see and perhaps shape the future.

HTML5 has become a catch-all term that encompasses not only the video element but also the use of the newest versions of Cascading Style Sheets (CSS3) and JavaScript, and another new tool, HTML5 Canvas, that is used with a set of JavaScript functions to render simple animations, which reduces page load time. HTML5 provides not only device independence, but can also access the built-in functionality of mobile devices, such as GPS and swiping, enabling the creation of web-based mobile apps that can replicate the native app experience. Web-based mobile apps (HTML5 apps) work just like web pages, with page content, including graphics, images, and video, loaded into the browser from a web server, rather than residing in the mobile device hardware like a native app. This concept has been embraced by mobile developers who naturally dream of being able to reach all platforms with a single product.

For businesses, the cost savings of HTML5 are obvious. A single HTML5 app requires far less effort to build than multiple native apps for the iOS, Android, Windows Phone, and other platforms. HTML5 apps can more easily be linked to and shared on social networks, encouraging viral distribution. Some HTML5 apps can even be designed so that they can be run on mobile devices when they are offline. Differences in how apps run across different platforms and workarounds are eliminated.

In the past, HTML5 apps couldn't approach the smooth and speedy user experience of a native app, but thanks to advancements in the underlying technologies behind HTML5 and improvements in the expertise of HTML5 developers, that is no longer the case. Flash also requires installation, whereas HTML5 does not.

In 2014, the Interactive Advertising Bureau (IAB), together with a number of the largest online publishers and advertising firms, urged advertisers to implement HTML5 as the standard for mobile ads in order to guarantee that ads will run and look good on different platforms, and in 2015 released guidelines that fully embrace HTML5, citing interoperability and the improved effectiveness of HTML5 ads. The rise of HTML5 has mirrored the growth of the mobile platform as it supplants Flash, which was developed for the desktop, as the preferred media delivery platform on the Web. During this time, Flash has continued to struggle with critical security vulnerabilities. In response, the online advertising industry has responded by reducing or eliminating the use of Flash. For instance, in 2016, Facebook mandated HTML5 instead of Flash for all videos posted to its site, reporting improved loading times, fewer bugs, and better engagement, and Google signaled a shift towards HTML5 by blocking Flash advertisements from autoplaying in Chrome, in part due to their notorious security issues. In 2016, Chrome began to automatically block any non-visible Flash content, like tracking cookies, and by year's end, HTML5 will be the "default" for Chrome, except where sites only support Flash. Google also announced that its display ads would be 100 percent HTML5 by the beginning of 2017. Mozilla Firefox made a similar announcement shortly thereafter regarding non-visible Flash content and its own plans to make HTML5 its default by 2017, meaning that over 80% of the web browser market is now blocking Flash. Apple's

(continued)

Safari browser, one of the first to impose restrictions on Flash, has taken steps to prevent sites offering both Flash and HTML5 from displaying Flash content. Twitch, one of the largest sites still using Flash video streaming, announced it would begin a switch to HTML5 in 2016, just as YouTube did a year earlier. The moves from these advertising and tech juggernauts have solidified the downfall of Flash and the rise of HTML5 as the future of advertising. Even Adobe itself has begun to recommend that content creators use HTML5 instead of Flash and has renamed its Flash Professional tool to 'Adobe Animate CC,' adding HTML5 support and the ability to convert Flash advertisements to HTML5.

Retailers have taken notice. One example of a company using HTML5 with success is Rakuten Shopping, an online retailer that offers a wide variety of goods online, and is currently ranked as one of Internet Retailer's top 30 mobile retailers. Using HTML5 has enabled Rakuten to shift away from using cookies to store customer attributes and has lightened the load on its servers.

Another example is the *Financial Times,* whose HTML5 app has proven to be an important driver for FT's business. FT first switched from a native app to HTML5 in 2011, in part to make maintaining the app across multiple platforms and devices easier. In 2013, FT rolled out a redesign of the app, featuring even more videos and personalization features.

In fact, according to Indeed, which searches millions of jobs from thousands of different job sites, "HTML5" continues to be one of the fastest growing keywords found in online job postings. Many online advertisers that have relied heavily on Flash are also struggling to adapt to the emergence of HTML5 ads, which are larger in size and require testing on more platforms. Content creators and advertisers alike are also uneager to manage two different formats. In the past, they only had to deal with Flash, and many have been unwilling to make the transition just yet.

However, even given all its benefits, HTML5 is not without flaws. For instance, HTML5 has not consistently supported digital rights management (DRM). In the past, media companies developed their own copy protection standards based on geographical region and/or whether payment had been proffered. These were enforced through their own media players. Because HTML5 does not require plug-ins to play video (or audio), and further, because HTML5 is an official W3C standard charged with remaining vendor neutral, this presents a challenge to HTML5 developers. HTML5 also allows websites to track how much battery power their site visitors have remaining. This feature was implemented so that sites could warn users to recharge their battery, but the reporting is so detailed that sites can determine what sites you've come from last solely based on your battery information, presenting privacy concerns. However, the security issues with HTML5 pale in comparison to those associated with Flash, and it's still early in the development cycle for HTML5.

SOURCES: "Google Nixes Flash, Embraces HTML5 in Chrome Browser," by Paul Krill, Infoworld.com, August 11, 2016; "Publishers Must Embrace Transition From Flash to HTML5 Before It's Too Late," by Brian DeFrancesco, Publishersdaily.com, August 5, 2016; "Firefox Sets Kill-Flash Schedule," by Gregg Keizer, Infoworld.com, July 22, 2016; "Twitch Begins Shift from Flash to HTML5 with Closed Beta," by Devin Coldewey, Techcrunch.com, July 14, 2016; "Safari 10 To Turn Off Flash by Default," by John Ribeiro, Infoworld.com, June 15, 2016; "As Flash Apocalypse Approaches, Here are HTML5 Rules of Thumb to Keep in Mind," by Barry Levine, Marketingland.com, May 26, 2016; "Facebook's Website Now Uses HTML5 Instead of Flash for All Videos," by Chris Welch, Theverge.com, December 18, 2015; "Why We Chose to Move to HTML5 Video," by Daniel Baulig, Code.facebook.com, December 18, 2015; "Adobe Tells Developers to Use HTML5 Instead of Flash," by Fahmida Y. Rashid, Infoworld.com, December 2, 2015; "Adobe Bows to HTML5 and Renames Its Flash Professional App," by Steve Dent, Engadget.com, December 1, 2015; "Transforming the Web with HTML5," by Christina Mulligan, Sdtimes.com, October 5, 2015; "With Digital Ads Shifting to HTML5, the Industry Now Has a New Set of Guidelines," by Christopher Heine, Adweek.com, September 28, 2015; "HTML5 Looks Good in Light of Google, Facebook and IAB Moves," by Carl Weinschenk, September 22, 2015; "How Your Smartphone's Battery Life Can Be Used to Invade Your Privacy," by Alex Hern, *The Guardian,* August 4, 2015; "RIP Flash: Why HTML5 Will Finally Take Over Video and the Web This Year," by Erika Trautman, Thenextweb.com, April 19, 2014; "Financial Times: 'There Is No Drawback to Working in HTML5'," by Stuart Dredge, Theguardian.com, April 29, 2013; "Adobe's Flash Surrender Proves Steve Jobs and Apple Were Right All Along with HTML5," by Nigam Arora, *Forbes,* November, 9, 2011.

| FIGURE 2.16 | **A SIMPLE XML DOCUMENT** |

```
<?xml version="1.0"?>
<note>
<to>George</to>
<from>Carol</from>
<heading>Just a Reminder</heading>
<body>Don't forget to order the groceries from FreshDirect!</body>
</note>
```

The tags in this simple XML document, such as <note>, <to>, and <from>, are used to describe data and information, rather than the look and feel of the document.

eXtensible Markup Language (XML)

eXtensible Markup Language (XML) takes web document formatting a giant leap forward. XML is a markup language specification developed by the W3C that is similar to HTML, but has a very different purpose. Whereas the purpose of HTML is to control the "look and feel" and display of data on the web page, XML is designed to describe data and information. For example, consider the sample XML document in **Figure 2.16**. The first line in the sample document is the XML declaration, which is always included; it defines the XML version of the document. In this case, the document conforms to the 1.0 specification of XML. The next line defines the first element of the document (the root element): < note >. The next four lines define four child elements of the root (to, from, heading, and body). The last line defines the end of the root element. Notice that XML says nothing about how to display the data, or how the text should look on the screen. HTML is used for information display in combination with XML, which is used for data description.

Figure 2.17 shows how XML can be used to define a database of company names in a company directory. Tags such as < Company >, < Name >, and < Specialty > can be defined for a single firm, or an entire industry. On an elementary level, XML is extraordinarily easy to learn and is very similar to HTML except that you can make up your own tags. At a deeper level, XML has a rich syntax and an enormous set of software tools, which make XML ideal for storing and communicating many types of data on the Web.

XML is "extensible," which means the tags used to describe and display data are defined by the user, whereas in HTML the tags are limited and predefined. XML can also transform information into new formats, such as by importing information from a database and displaying it as a table. With XML, information can be analyzed and displayed selectively, making it a more powerful alternative to HTML. This means that business firms, or entire industries, can describe all of their invoices, accounts payable, payroll records, and financial information using a web-compatible markup language. Once described, these business documents can be stored on intranet web servers and shared throughout the corporation.

Really Simple Syndication (RSS) is an XML format that allows users to have digital content, including text, articles, blogs, and podcast audio files, automatically

eXtensible Markup Language (XML)
a markup language specification developed by the World Wide Web Consortium (W3C) that is designed to describe data and information

Really Simple Syndication (RSS)
program that allows users to have digital content, including text, articles, blogs, and podcast audio files, automatically sent to their computers over the Internet

---

| **FIGURE 2.17** | **SAMPLE XML CODE FOR A COMPANY DIRECTORY** |

```
<?xml version="1.0"?>
<Companies>
    <Company>
          <Name>Azimuth Interactive Inc.</Name>
        <Specialties>
               <Specialty>HTML development</Specialty>
                <Specialty>technical documentation</Specialty>
              <Specialty>ROBO Help</Specialty>
              <Country>United States</Country>
        </Specialties>
        <Location>
               <Country>United States</Country>
            <State />
             <City>Chicago</City>
        </Location>
            <Telephone>301-555-1212</Telephone>
    </Company>
    <Company>
      . . .
    </Company>
  . . .
</Companies>
```

This XML document uses tags to define a database of company names.

sent to their computers over the Internet. An RSS aggregator software application that you install on your computer gathers material from the websites and blogs that you tell it to scan and brings new information from those sites to you. Sometimes this is referred to as "syndicated" content because it is distributed by news organizations and other syndicators (or distributors). Users download an RSS aggregator and then "subscribe" to the RSS "feeds." When you go to your RSS aggregator's page, it will display the most recent updates for each channel to which you have subscribed. RSS has rocketed from a "techie" pastime to a broad-based movement. Although Google has closed down Google Reader, a popular RSS product, a number of other RSS reader options remain, including Feedly, Reeder, and NewsBlur.

WEB SERVERS AND CLIENTS

We have already described client/server computing and the revolution in computing architecture brought about by client/server computing. You already know that a server is a computer attached to a network that stores files, controls peripheral devices, interfaces with the outside world—including the Internet—and does some processing for other computers on the network.

web server software
software that enables a computer to deliver web pages written in HTML to client computers on a network that request this service by sending an HTTP request

But what is a web server? **Web server software** refers to the software that enables a computer to deliver web pages written in HTML to client computers on a network that request this service by sending an HTTP request. Apache, which works with Linux and Unix operating systems, is the most commonly used type of web server software. Microsoft's Internet Information Services (IIS) also has significant market share (Netcraft, 2016).

Aside from responding to requests for web pages, all web servers provide some additional basic capabilities such as the following:

- *Security services*—These consist mainly of authentication services that verify that the person trying to access the site is authorized to do so. For websites that process payment transactions, the web server also supports SSL and TLS, the protocols for transmitting and receiving information securely over the Internet. When private information such as names, phone numbers, addresses, and credit card data needs to be provided to a website, the web server uses SSL to ensure that the data passing back and forth from the browser to the server is not compromised.
- *FTP*—This protocol allows users to transfer files to and from the server. Some sites limit file uploads to the web server, while others restrict downloads, depending on the user's identity.
- *Search engine*—Just as search engine sites enable users to search the entire Web for particular documents, search engine modules within the basic web server software package enable indexing of the site's web pages and content and permit easy keyword searching of the site's content. When conducting a search, a search engine makes use of an index, which is a list of all the documents on the server. The search term is compared to the index to identify likely matches.
- *Data capture*—Web servers are also helpful at monitoring site traffic, capturing information on who has visited a site, how long the user stayed there, the date and time of each visit, and which specific pages on the server were accessed. This information is compiled and saved in a log file, which can then be analyzed. By analyzing a log file, a site manager can find out the total number of visitors, the average length of each visit, and the most popular destinations, or web pages.

The term *web server* is also used to refer to the physical computer that runs web server software. Leading manufacturers of web server computers include Lenovo, Dell, and Hewlett-Packard. Although any desktop computer can run web server software, it is best to use a computer that has been optimized for this purpose. To be a web server, a computer must have the web server software installed and be connected to the Internet. Every public web server computer has an IP address. For example, if you type http://www.pearsonhighered.com/laudon in your browser, the browser software sends a request for HTTP service to the web server whose domain name is pearsonhighered.com. The server then locates the page named "laudon" on its hard drive, sends the page back to your browser, and displays it on your screen. Of course, firms also can use web servers for strictly internal local area networking in intranets.

Aside from the generic web server software packages, there are actually many types of specialized servers on the Web, from **database servers** that access specific information within a database, to **ad servers** that deliver targeted banner ads, to **mail servers** that provide e-mail messages, and **video servers** that provide video clips. At a small e-commerce site, all of these software packages might be running on a single computer, with a single processor. At a large corporate site, there may be hundreds or thousands of discrete server computers, many with multiple processors, running specialized web server functions. We discuss the architecture of e-commerce sites in greater detail in Chapter 3.

database server
server designed to access specific information within a database

ad server
server designed to deliver targeted banner ads

mail server
server that provides e-mail messages

video server
server that serves video clips

web client

any computing device attached to the Internet that is capable of making HTTP requests and displaying HTML pages, most commonly a Windows PC or Macintosh

A **web client**, on the other hand, is any computing device attached to the Internet that is capable of making HTTP requests and displaying HTML pages. The most common client is a Windows or Macintosh desktop computer, with various flavors of Unix/Linux computers a distant third. However, the fastest growing category of web clients is not computers at all, but mobile devices. In general, a web client can be any device—including a printer, refrigerator, stove, home lighting system, or automobile instrument panel—capable of sending and receiving information from a web server.

WEB BROWSERS

web browser

software program whose primary purpose is to display web pages

A **web browser** is a software program whose primary purpose is to display web pages. Browsers also have added features, such as e-mail and newsgroups (an online discussion group or forum). As of July 2016, the leading desktop web browser is Google's Chrome, a small, yet technologically advanced open source browser, with about 51% of the market. Chrome is also the leading mobile/tablet browser, with about a 52% share of that market. The second most popular desktop browser is Microsoft's Internet Explorer, with about a 30% share. However, Internet Explorer's share of the mobile/tablet market is miniscule, with less than a 2% share. Mozilla Firefox is in third place in the desktop browser marketplace, with only about 8% share. It has less than a 1% share of the mobile/tablet browser market. First released in 2004, Firefox is a free, open source web browser for the Windows, Linux, and Macintosh operating systems, based on Mozilla open source code (which originally provided the code for Netscape). It is small and fast and offers many features such as pop-up blocking and tabbed browsing. Apple's Safari browser has only about a 4.5% share of the desktop browser market, but is the second most popular mobile/tablet browser, with a 28% share, due in large part to its use on iPhones and iPads (Marketshare.hitslink.com, 2016a, 2016b). In 2015, Microsoft introduced Edge, an entirely new browser bundled with its new operating system, Windows 10. Edge was designed to replace Internet Explorer. However, despite the popularity of Windows 10, Edge has thus far been largely ignored by Windows 10 adopters and has been installed on only about 5% of desktops.

2.5 THE INTERNET AND THE WEB: FEATURES AND SERVICES

The Internet and the Web have spawned a number of powerful software applications upon which the foundations of e-commerce are built. You can think of all these as web services, and it is interesting as you read along to compare these services to other traditional media such as television or print media. If you do, you will quickly realize the richness of the Internet environment.

COMMUNICATION TOOLS

The Internet and Web provide a number of communication tools that enable people around the globe to communicate with one another, both on a one-to-one basis as well as a one-to-many basis. Communication tools include e-mail, messaging applications, online message boards (forums), Internet telephony applications, and video conferencing, video chatting, and telepresence. We'll look at each of these in a bit more depth in the following sections.

E-mail

Since its earliest days, **electronic mail**, or **e-mail**, has been the most-used application of the Internet. Worldwide, there are over 2.6 billion e-mail users, sending over 2.15 billion e-mails a day. There are an estimated 1.7 billion mobile e-mail users worldwide, with over 65% of all e-mail users worldwide accessing e-mail on a mobile device (Radicati Group, 2016). Estimates vary on the amount of spam, ranging from 40% to 90%. E-mail marketing and spam are examined in more depth in Chapter 6.

E-mail uses a series of protocols to enable messages containing text, images, sound, and video clips to be transferred from one Internet user to another. Because of its flexibility and speed, it is now the most popular form of business communication—more popular than the phone, fax, or snail mail (the U.S. Postal Service). In addition to text typed within the message, e-mail also allows **attachments**, which are files inserted within the e-mail message. The files can be documents, images, sounds, or video clips.

electronic mail (e-mail)
the most-used application of the Internet. Uses a series of protocols to enable messages containing text, images, sound, and video clips to be transferred from one Internet user to another

attachment
a file inserted within an e-mail message

Messaging Applications

Instant messaging (IM) allows you to send messages in real time, unlike e-mail, which has a time lag of several seconds to minutes between when messages are sent and received. IM displays text entered almost instantaneously. Recipients can then respond immediately to the sender the same way, making the communication more like a live conversation than is possible through e-mail. To use IM, users create a buddy list they want to communicate with, and then enter short text messages that their buddies will receive instantly (if they are online at the time). And although text remains the primary communication mechanism in IM, more advanced systems also provide voice and video chat functionality. Instant messaging over the Internet competes with cell phone Short Message Service (SMS) and Multimedia Messaging Service (MMS) texting, which is far more expensive than IM. Major IM systems include Skype, Yahoo Messenger, Google Hangouts, and AIM (AOL Instant Messenger). IM systems were initially developed as proprietary systems, with competing firms offering versions that did not work with one another. Today, there still is no built-in interoperability among the major IM systems.

Mobile messaging apps, such as Facebook Messenger, WhatsApp (purchased by Facebook for $22 billion in 2014), Snapchat (which allows users to send pictures, videos, and texts that will disappear after a short period of time), Kik, Viber, and others have also become wildly popular, providing competition for both traditional desktop IM systems and SMS text messaging. In the United States in 2016, over 130 million people (about 40% of the population) use mobile messaging apps, and companies are increasingly turning their attention to using these apps to market their brands (eMarketer, Inc., 2016g).

instant messaging (IM)
displays text entered almost instantaneously. Recipients can then respond immediately to the sender the same way, making the communication more like a live conversation than is possible through e-mail

Online Message Boards

online message board
a web application that allows Internet users to communicate with each other, although not in real time

An **online message board** (also referred to as a forum, bulletin board, discussion board, discussion group, or simply a board or forum) is a web application that enables Internet users to communicate with each other, although not in real time. A message board provides a container for various discussions (or "threads") started (or "posted") by members of the board, and depending on the permissions granted to board members by the board's administrator, enables a person to start a thread and reply to other people's threads. Most message board software allows more than one message board to be created. The board administrator typically can edit, delete, move, or otherwise modify any thread on the board. Unlike an electronic mailing list (such as a listserv), which automatically sends new messages to a subscriber, an online message board typically requires that the member visit the board to check for new posts. Some boards offer an "e-mail notification" feature that notifies users that a new post of interest to them has been made.

Internet Telephony

If the telephone system were to be built from scratch today, it would be an Internet-based, packet-switched network using TCP/IP because it would be less expensive and more efficient than the alternative existing system, which involves a mix of circuit-switched legs with a digital backbone. In fact, AT&T has begun testing all-digital IP phone networks in several U.S. cities. Likewise, if cable television systems were built from scratch today, they most likely would use Internet technologies for the same reasons.

IP telephony
a general term for the technologies that use VoIP and the Internet's packet-switched network to transmit voice and other forms of audio communication over the Internet

Voice over Internet Protocol (VoIP)
protocol that allows for transmission of voice and other forms of audio communication over the Internet

IP telephony is a general term for the technologies that use **Voice over Internet Protocol (VoIP)** and the Internet's packet-switched network to transmit voice, fax, and other forms of audio communication over the Internet. VoIP can be used over a traditional handset as well as over a mobile device. VoIP avoids the long distance charges imposed by traditional phone companies.

There were about 230 million residential VoIP subscribers worldwide in 2015, and in the United States, more than half of residential customers are now using VoIP, and this number is expanding rapidly as cable systems provide telephone service as part of their "triple play": voice, Internet, and TV as a single package. This number is dwarfed, however, by the number of mobile VoIP subscribers, which has grown explosively over the last several years, fueled by the rampant growth of mobile messaging apps that now also provide free VoIP services, such as Facebook Messenger, WhatsApp (also owned by Facebook), Viber (owned by Japanese e-commerce giant Rakuten), WeChat, Line, KakaoTalk, and others (IHS, 2016; BuddeComm, 2016).

VoIP is a disruptive technology. In the past, voice and fax were the exclusive provenance of the regulated telephone networks. With the convergence of the Internet and telephony, however, this dominance is already starting to change, with local and long distance telephone providers and cable companies becoming ISPs, and ISPs getting into the phone market. Key players in the VoIP market include independent service providers such as VoIP pioneers Vonage and Skype (now owned by Microsoft), as well as traditional players such as telephone and cable companies that have moved aggressively into the market. Skype currently dominates the international market.

Skype carries over 3 billion minutes per day (translating into about 90 billion minutes per month) from 300 million users around the world (Anurag, 2016).

Video Conferencing, Video Chatting, and Telepresence

Internet video conferencing is accessible to anyone with a broadband Internet connection and a web camera (webcam). The most widely used web conferencing suite of tools is WebEx (now owned by Cisco). VoIP companies such as Skype and ooVoo also provide more limited web conferencing capabilities, commonly referred to as video chatting. Apple's FaceTime is another video chatting technology available for iOS mobile devices with a forward-facing camera and Macintosh computers equipped with Apple's version of a webcam, called a FaceTime camera.

Telepresence takes video conferencing up several notches. Rather than single persons "meeting" by using webcams, telepresence creates an environment in a room using multiple cameras and screens, which surround the users. The experience is uncanny and strange at first because as you look at the people in the screens, they are looking directly at you. Broadcast quality and higher screen resolutions help create the effect. Users have the sensation of "being in the presence of their colleagues" in a way that is not true for traditional webcam meetings. Providers of telepresence software and hardware include Cisco, LifeSize, BlueJeans Network, and Polycom ATX.

SEARCH ENGINES

Search engines identify web pages that appear to match keywords, also called queries, entered by a user and then provide a list of the best matches (search results). Almost 85% of U.S. Internet users regularly use search engines from either desktop or mobile devices, and they generate around 16 billion queries a month on desktop computers, about 10.2 billion of which are conducted using Google. Desktop search volume is declining, as more and more search activity moves to mobile devices. In fact, Google has reported that mobile search queries exceeded desktop queries in the United States and numerous other countries for the first time in 2015 (eMarketer, Inc., 2016h, 2016i; Sterling, 2016). There are hundreds of different search engines, but in the United States, the vast majority of the search results are supplied by the top three providers: Google, Microsoft's Bing, and Yahoo. Google, Bing, and Yahoo are also major search providers in Europe. Other European search providers include T-Online (Germany) and Qwant (France). In China, Baidu, Qihoo 360, and Sohu Sogou are major search engine providers.

Web search engines started out in the early 1990s shortly after Netscape released the first commercial web browser. Early search engines were relatively simple software programs that roamed the nascent Web, visiting pages and gathering information about the content of each web page. These early programs were called variously crawlers, spiders, and wanderers; the first full-text crawler that indexed the contents of an entire web page was called WebCrawler, released in 1994. AltaVista (1995), one of the first widely used search engines, was the first to allow "natural language" queries such as "history of web search engines" rather than "history + web + search engine."

The first search engines employed simple keyword indexes of all the web pages visited. They would count the number of times a word appeared on the web page, and store this information in an index. These search engines could be easily fooled by web

search engine
identifies web pages that appear to match keywords, also called queries, entered by the user and then provides a list of the best matches

designers who simply repeated words on their home pages. The real innovations in search engine development occurred through a program funded by the Department of Defense called the Digital Library Initiative, designed to help the Pentagon find research papers in large databases. Stanford, Berkeley, and three other universities became hotbeds of web search innovations in the mid-1990s. At Stanford in 1994, two computer science students, David Filo and Jerry Yang, created a hand-selected list of their favorite web pages and called it "Yet Another Hierarchical Officious Oracle," or Yahoo!. Yahoo initially was not a real search engine, but rather an edited selection of web sites organized by categories the editors found useful. Yahoo later developed "true" search engine capabilities.

In 1998, Larry Page and Sergey Brin, two Stanford computer science students, released their first version of the Google search engine. This search engine was different: not only did it index each web page's words, but Page had discovered that the AltaVista search engine not only collected keywords from sites but also calculated what other sites linked to each page. By looking at the URLs on each web page, they could calculate an index of popularity. AltaVista did nothing with this information. Page took this idea and made it a central factor in ranking a web page's appropriateness to a search query. He patented the idea of a web page ranking system (PageRank System), which essentially measures the popularity of the web page. Brin contributed a unique web crawler program that indexed not just keywords on a web page, but combinations of words (such as authors and their article titles). These two ideas became the foundation for the Google search engine (Brandt, 2004). **Figure 2.18(A)** illustrates how Google indexes the Web. **Figure 2.18(B)** shows you what happens when you enter a search query.

Initially, few understood how to make money from search engines. That changed in 2000 when Goto.com (later Overture) allowed advertisers to bid for placement on their search engine results, and Google followed suit in 2003 with its AdWords program, which allowed advertisers to bid for placement of short text ads on Google search results. The spectacular increase in Internet advertising revenues (which have been growing at around 20%–25% annually over the last few years) has helped search engines transform themselves into major shopping tools and created an entire new industry called "search engine marketing."

When users enter a search term at Google, Bing, Yahoo, or any of the other websites serviced by these search engines, they receive two types of listings: sponsored links, for which advertisers have paid to be listed (usually at the top of the search results page), and unsponsored "organic" search results. Advertisers can also purchase small text ads on the right side of the search results page. In addition, search engines have extended their services to include news, maps, satellite images, computer images, e-mail, group calendars, group meeting tools, and indexes of scholarly papers.

Although the major search engines are used for locating general information of interest to users, search engines have also become a crucial tool within e-commerce sites. Customers can more easily search for the product information they want with the help of an internal search program; the difference is that within websites, the search engine is limited to finding matches from that one site. For instance, more online shoppers use Amazon's internal search engine to look for products than conducting a

FIGURE 2.18   **HOW GOOGLE WORKS**

(A) Indexing the Web

1 A Googlebot (software code) crawls the Web, going from link to link.

2 Crawled pages are analyzed: links, semantic analysis and JavaScript/CSS content.

3 New data is added to an index of keywords and the pages on which they appear.

4 To deal with the scale of the Web (Google has already indexed an estimated 30 trillion pages), Google breaks it up into thousands of "index shards"—groups of millions of pages.

5 The index shards are stored on Google servers (approximately 1 million), located in data centers around the world.

6 The indexing process runs continuously, processing billions of web pages a day. Pages with frequently updated content and links from other highly ranked sites are crawled more regularly and deeply, and given higher rank themselves.

(B) Processing a Search Query

1 A user enters a search query on a desktop computer or mobile device. Google will make suggestions as the user types.

2 The search request is sent to one of Google's many servers.

3 The server uses an algorithm to access the index database, find matching pages, and compute a score, representing how good a match the page is for the query. The algorithm has 200+ variables, including PageRank, the quality and relevance of the content on the page to the query, the context of the search (such as the user's location and device being used), and the user's previous search history. Google also applies various penalties and filters to prevent attempts to "game" the algorithm.

4 Short text summaries (snippets) are generated for each result.

5 Results are delivered to the user, 10 to a page.

product search using Google, a fact noted by Google's executive chairman Eric Schmidt, who believes that Amazon search poses a significant threat to Google (Mangalindan, 2014). Pinterest hopes to challenge Google in the realm of visual search.

DOWNLOADABLE AND STREAMING MEDIA

download

transfers a file from a web server and stores it on a computer for later use

streaming media

enables video, music, and other large-bandwidth files to be sent to a user in a variety of ways that enable the user to play the files as they are being delivered

When you **download** a file from the Web, the file is transferred from a web server and is stored on your computer for later use. With the low-bandwidth connections of the early Internet, audio and video files were difficult to download, but with the huge growth in broadband connections, these files are not only commonplace but today constitute the majority of web traffic. **Streaming media** is an alternative to downloaded media and enables video, music, and other large-bandwidth files to be sent to a user in a variety of ways that enable the user to play the files as they are being delivered. In some situations, the files are broken into chunks and served by specialized video servers to client software that puts the chunks together and plays the video. In other situations, a single large file is delivered from a standard web server to a user who can begin playing the video before the entire file is delivered. Streamed files must be viewed in real time; they cannot be stored on client hard drives without special software. Streamed files are "played" by a software program such as Windows Media Player, Apple QuickTime, Adobe Flash, and Real Player. There are a number of tools used to create streaming files, including HTML5 and Adobe Flash, as well as technologies specifically adapted for the mobile platform such as the Meerkat and Periscope apps. As the capacity of the Internet grows, streaming media will play an even larger role in e-commerce.

Spurred on by the worldwide sales of more than 2.5 billion iOS (iPhones, iPads, and iPod Touches) and Android devices, the Internet has become a virtual digital river of music, audio, and video files. The Apple iTunes store is probably the most well-known repository of digital music online, with a catalog of more than 43 million songs worldwide in its catalog as of September 2016. Google Play offers over 35 million, and there are hundreds of other sites offering music downloads as well. In addition, streaming music services and Internet radio, such as Apple Music, Spotify, Pandora, Amazon Prime Music, Tidal, and hundreds of others, add to the bandwidth devoted to the delivery of online music.

podcast

an audio presentation—such as a radio show, audio from a movie, or simply a personal audio presentation—stored online as a digital media file

Podcasting (the name originates from a mashup of the word "iPod" and the word "broadcasting") is also surging in popularity. A **podcast** is an audio presentation—such as a radio show, audio from a conference, or simply a personal presentation—stored online as digital media file. Listeners can download the file and play it on their mobile devices or computers. Podcasting has transitioned from an amateur independent producer media in the "pirate radio" tradition to a professional news and talk content distribution channel. For instance, This American Life's *Serial* podcast has been downloaded over 175 million times. NPR is the top U.S. producer of podcasts, with an aggregate monthly audience of almost 8 million, followed by WNYC Studios, a NYC-based public broadcasting organization, with a monthly audience of about 6 million (Podtrac, Inc., 2016).

Online video viewing has also exploded in popularity. In 2016, for instance, there are around 215 million Americans that watch streaming or downloaded video content on a desktop or mobile device at least once a month (eMarketer, Inc., 2016j). Cisco estimates that consumer Internet video traffic constituted a whopping 70% of all consumer Internet traffic in 2015, and this percentage is expected to grow to 82% by 2020 (Cisco, 2016b). The Internet has become a major distribution channel for movies, television shows, and sporting events (see Chapter 9). Another common type of Internet video is provided by YouTube, with more than 1 billion users worldwide, who each day watch hundreds of millions of hours of video content, ranging from a wide variety of user-generated content, to branded content from major corporations, music videos, original programming, and more. Sites such as YouTube, Metacafe, and Facebook have popularized user-generated video streaming. Many apps such as Instagram, Twitter, Snapchat, and others also include video capabilities.

Online advertisers increasingly use video to attract viewers. Companies that want to demonstrate use of their products have found video clips to be extremely effective. Streaming video segments used in web ads and news stories are perhaps the most frequently used streaming services. High-quality interactive video and audio makes sales presentations and demonstrations more effective and lifelike and enables companies to develop new forms of customer support.

WEB 2.0 APPLICATIONS AND SERVICES

Today's broadband Internet infrastructure has greatly expanded the services available to users. These capabilities have formed the basis for new business models. Web 2.0 applications and services are "social" in nature because they support communication among individuals within groups or social networks.

Online Social Networks

Online social networks are services that support communication within networks of friends, colleagues, and entire professions. Online social networks have developed very large worldwide audiences (over 2.3 billion people in 2016, almost one-third of the world's population) and form the basis for new advertising platforms and for social e-commerce (see Chapters 6, 7, and 10). The largest social networks are Facebook (1.7 billion monthly active users worldwide), Instagram (500 million members worldwide), LinkedIn (more than 450 million members worldwide), Twitter (more than 310 million active users worldwide), and Pinterest (over 110 million active users). These networks rely on user-generated content (messages, photos, and videos) and emphasize sharing of content. All of these features require significant broadband Internet connectivity and equally large cloud computing facilities to store content.

Blogs

A **blog** (originally called a **weblog**) is a personal web page that typically contains a series of chronological entries (newest to oldest) by its author, and links to related web pages. The blog may include a blogroll (a collection of links to other blogs) and trackbacks (a list of entries in other blogs that refer to a post on the first blog). Most blogs allow readers to post comments on the blog entries as well. The act of creating a blog

blog
personal web page that is created by an individual or corporation to communicate with readers

is often referred to as "blogging." Blogs are either hosted by a third-party site such as WordPress, Tumblr, Blogger, LiveJournal, TypePad, and Xanga, or prospective bloggers can download software such as Movable Type to create a blog that is hosted by the user's ISP. Blog pages are usually variations on templates provided by the blogging service or software and hence require no knowledge of HTML. Therefore, millions of people without HTML skills of any kind can post their own web pages, and share content with friends and relatives. The totality of blog-related websites is often referred to as the "blogosphere."

Blogs have become hugely popular. Tumblr and Wordpress together hosted over 400 million blogs as of September 2016, so it is likely that the total number is significantly higher. According to eMarketer, there are an estimated 29 million active U.S. bloggers, and 81 million U.S. blog readers (eMarketer, Inc., 2916k, 2016l). No one knows how many of these blogs are kept up to date or are just yesterday's news. And no one knows how many of these blogs have a readership greater than one (the blog author). In fact, there are so many blogs you need a search engine just to find them, or you can just go to a list of the most popular 100 blogs and dig in.

Wikis

wiki
web application that allows a user to easily add and edit content on a web page

A **wiki** is a web application that allows a user to easily add and edit content on a web page. (The term wiki derives from the "wiki wiki" (quick or fast) shuttle buses at Honolulu Airport.) Wiki software enables documents to be written collectively and collaboratively. Most wiki systems are open source, server-side systems that store content in a relational database. The software typically provides a template that defines layout and elements common to all pages, displays user-editable source code (usually plain text), and then renders the content into an HTML-based page for display in a web browser. Some wiki software allows only basic text formatting, whereas others allow the use of tables, images, or even interactive elements, such as polls and games. Because wikis by their very nature are very open in allowing anyone to make changes to a page, most wikis provide a means to verify the validity of changes via a "Recent Changes" page, which enables members of the wiki community to monitor and review the work of other users, correct mistakes, and hopefully deter "vandalism."

The most well-known wiki is Wikipedia, an online encyclopedia that contains more than 40 million articles in 294 different languages on a variety of topics. The Wikimedia Foundation, which operates Wikipedia, also operates a variety of related projects, including Wikibooks, a collection of collaboratively written free textbooks and manuals; Wikinews, a free content news source; and Wiktionary, a collaborative project to produce a free multilingual dictionary in every language, with definitions, etymologies, pronunciations, quotations, and synonyms.

VIRTUAL REALITY AND AUGMENTED REALITY

virtual reality (VR)
involves fully immersing users within a virtual world, typically through the use of a head-mounted display (HMD) connected to headphones and other devices

In 2016, virtual reality and augmented reality technologies began to enter the consumer market and attract significant attention. **Virtual reality (VR)** involves fully immersing users within a virtual world, typically through the use of a head-mounted display (HMD) connected to headphones and other devices that enable navigation through the experience and allowing users to feel as if they are actually present within the virtual world. High-end VR devices designed to be used with PCs or gaming systems include Facebook's Oculus Rift, HTC's Vive, and Sony's PlayStation VR. Samsung's Gear VR and Google Cardboard are examples of lower-cost, mobile, entry-level devices. A number of publishers are experimented with VR content that can use these lower-cost devices. For example, the New York Times has a VR mobile app that viewers can use with Google Cardboard to view VR films and advertisements that feature 360-degree video. By 2020, some analysts estimate that there will be almost 155 million virtual reality users worldwide (with around 135 million using a smartphone-powered device and another 20 million a higher-end PC/game console-related device). **Augmented reality (AR)** involves overlaying virtual objects over the real world, via smartphones, tablets, or HMDs. Perhaps the highest profile use of AR thus far has been its use in Nintendo's Pokemon GO game. Other uses include Snapchat's Lenses feature, which uses facial recognition technology and 3-D models that allow users to augment their selfies by overlaying animations or other images on top of them, and "try-before-you-buy" apps created for beauty and fashion brands (eMarketer, Inc., 2016m).

augmented reality (AR)
involves overlaying virtual objects over the real world, via smartphones, tablets or HMDs.

INTELLIGENT PERSONAL ASSISTANTS

The idea of having a conversation with a computer, having it understand you and be able to carry out tasks according to your direction, has long been a part of science fiction, from the 1968 Hollywood movie *2001: A Space Odyssey*, to an old Apple promotional video depicting a professor using his personal digital assistant to organize his life, gather data, and place orders at restaurants. That was all fantasy. But Apple's Siri, billed as an intelligent personal assistant and knowledge navigator and released in 2011, has many of the capabilities of the computer assistants found in fiction. Siri has a natural language, conversational interface, situational awareness, and is capable of carrying out many tasks based on verbal commands by delegating requests to a variety of different web services. For instance, you can ask Siri to find a restaurant nearby that serves Italian food. Siri may show you an ad for a local restaurant in the process. Once you have identified a restaurant you would like to eat at, you can ask Siri to make a reservation using OpenTable. You can also ask Siri to place an appointment on your calendar, search for airline flights, and figure out what's the fastest route between your current location and a destination using public transit. The answers are not always completely accurate, but critics have been impressed with its uncanny abilities. Siri is currently available on the Apple Watch, the iPhone 4S and later versions, iPads with Retina display, the iPad Mini, and iPod Touches (fifth generation and later versions).

In 2012, Google released its version of an intelligent assistant for Android-based smartphones, which it calls Google Now. Google Now is part of the Google Search mobile application. While Google Now has many of the capabilities of Apple's Siri, it attempts to go further by predicting what users may need based on situational awareness, including physical location, time of day, previous location history, calendar, and expressed interests based on previous activity, as described in its patent application (United States Patent Office, 2012). For instance, if you often search for a particular musician or style of music, Google Now might provide recommendations for similar music. If it knows that you go to a health club every other day, Google Now will remind you not to schedule events during these periods. If it knows that you typically read articles about health issues, the system might monitor Google News for similar articles and make recommendations. In 2016, Google unveiled Google Assistant, a similar virtual assistant for its Allo chat app and integrated into its Google Home products and its new Pixel phones. Other intelligent personal assistants include Samsung's S Voice, LG's Voice Mate, and Microsoft's Cortana. The *Insight on Business* case, *AI, Intelligent Assistants, and Chatbots*, focuses on the increasing use of AI technologies in e-commerce.

2.6   MOBILE APPS: THE NEXT BIG THING IS HERE

When Steve Jobs introduced the iPhone in January 2007, no one, including himself, envisioned that the device would launch a software revolution or become a major e-commerce platform, let alone a game platform, advertising platform, and general media platform for television shows, movies, videos, and e-books. The iPhone's original primary functions, beyond being a cell phone, were to be a camera, text messaging device, and web browser. What Apple initially lacked for the iPhone were software applications ("apps") that would take full advantage of its computing capabilities. The solution was apps developed by outside developers. In July 2008, Apple introduced the App Store, which provides a platform for the distribution and sale of apps by Apple as well as by independent developers. Around the same time, Google was developing Android as an open source operating system for mobile devices. In October 2008, the first smartphone using Android was released, and Google launched the Android Market (now called Google Play) as the official app store for Android. In 2010, tablet computers such as Apple's iPad and the Samsung Galaxy Tab, which provided additional platforms for mobile apps, were introduced.

As of June 2016, more than 130 billion apps have been downloaded from the App Store worldwide, and there are over 2 million approved apps available for download. There are over 2 million apps available for Android devices on Google Play as well. And while the number of cumulative downloads of Android apps is not publicly available, Google has announced that Android users downloaded over 65 billion apps between May 2015 and May 2016 alone.

The mobile app phenomenon has spawned a new digital ecosystem: tens of thousands of developers, a wildly popular hardware platform, and millions of consumers now using a mobile device to replace their clunky desktop-laptop Microsoft Windows computer and act as a digital media center as well. In the United Kingdom, adults spend almost 2 hours using mobile apps, over 80% of the entire time they spend using their mobile devices for non-voice related activities (eMarketer, Inc., 2016n). More consumers are opting to consume media on their phones and tablet computers than ever before, which is more good news for app developers.

The implications of the app ecosystem for e-commerce are significant. The smartphone in your pocket or the tablet computer on your lap becomes not only a general-purpose computer, but also an always-present shopping tool for consumers, as well as

INSIGHT ON BUSINESS

AI, INTELLIGENT ASSISTANTS, AND CHATBOTS

Despite the frequent appearances of robots and advanced artificial intelligence (AI) in books and movies over the past several decades, real-world equivalents have lagged hopelessly behind. However, today's tech titans are doubling their efforts to improve AI technologies in an effort to get a jump on the competition. We may still be a long way away from R2-D2, but AI in the form of personalization systems, chatbots, and intelligent assistants is finally entering the mainstream.

AI systems of the past have had frustratingly limited capabilities. Asking them to perform tasks outside of their purpose or to interpret and respond to the variation and nuances of human language simply doesn't work. Even tools like search engines, which have the ability to distinguish between different types of language and queries, can't incorporate context.

Although companies like Amazon have made use of more complex forms of AI to power their personalization and recommendation engines, this mostly occurs behind the scenes—customers aren't interacting directly with these types of AI technologies. However, advances in natural language processing techniques have enabled Amazon to develop exciting new technologies like the Amazon Echo and its underlying AI technology, which Amazon calls Alexa. The Echo is marketed as a home assistant that can perform a variety of tasks using speech recognition, but is still in its infancy as a product. Currently, the Echo can update to-do lists, adjust home appliances, play games, and stream music, all controlled by voice.

Echo and Alexa are powered by these and other "skills," which function much like apps do on the iPhone, and which third-party developers are lining up in droves to develop. For example,

1-800-Flowers was one of the first large retailers to develop a skill that allows users to place orders by voice alone on any device running Alexa, including the Echo and the Amazon Fire TV. Although customers interested in using this capability must have account info, payment info, and addresses already on file, this represents a major breakthrough. Other companies developing skills for Alexa include Domino's, Capital One, Ford Motor, and many more. Amazon is hoping that in the future, people will be able to ask Alexa what they should buy and receive an intelligent, relevant response.

Although Echo and Alexa are perhaps the most visible sign of growth in artificial intelligence and natural language processing, the modern technological landscape is defined by its multitude of platforms. Retailers are trying to encourage their customers to do business with them on each and every one of them. Many of these platforms are text-based, and the number of people using messaging apps is skyrocketing in the United States, from 113 million in 2015 to a projected 177 million by 2019. To that end, companies have been rolling out "chatbots"—AI that can interact with users via text and automate many parts of the purchasing process that are currently manual, such as talking on the phone or navigating online menus.

Facebook Messenger is one of the most popular messaging apps, trailing only WhatsApp in monthly active users. Facebook M is a virtual assistant within Messenger launched in 2015 that can perform a variety of tasks via text, including making restaurant reservations, booking travel plans, and helping find birthday gifts. Facebook has also opened the Messenger platform to third-party chatbots from other companies, including the previously mentioned 1-800-Flowers as well

(continued)

as others like Uber. Increasingly, popular workplace messaging tool Slack has done the same with its platform, and companies like Taco Bell have developed tools like TacoBot that allow Slack users to order food through a brief text conversation.

Seemingly every prominent tech company and messaging platform has an AI that it hopes will dominate the emerging marketplace. Amazon has Alexa and Facebook has M; Apple has Siri, perhaps the best known intelligent assistant; Google has Google Now and Google Assistant; Microsoft has Cortana. Google also unveiled its Google Home appliance, which is modeled after the Echo but which reportedly has better conversational functionality and ability to integrate with home speakers. In the same vein, Samsung announced the Samsung Otto device, which comes equipped with features Echo lacks like an HD camera and facial recognition capability. These companies are all positioning themselves to take part in the impending boom in virtual assistant technologies. Analysts anticipate that virtual assistants of all types will have 1.8 billion active global users by 2021, up from 390 million in 2016.

Other players have emerged as well. The developers of the AI that powers Apple's Siri have developed a new platform called Viv that goes far beyond Siri's functionality. Viv can answer much more complicated questions than Siri, such as "Will it be warmer than 70 degrees near the Golden Gate Bridge after 5 PM the day after tomorrow?" Viv can also book flights by using your preferred airline, frequent flyer number, and seating preference, all without any human guidance, and might someday have the ability to automatically detect low fares.

A primary goal of all of these technologies is to facilitate sales. Intelligent personal assistants and chatbots might be able to understand what it is that we're looking for as consumers even when we're not sure how to phrase it or what we're even looking for. If AI continues to improve and people learn to trust technologies like chatbots, the importance of websites and native apps is likely to greatly diminish, and web search may also take a hit. That's part of the reason why Google has been so active in this area, perhaps sensing a threat to its core business model.

Interestingly, Microsoft has eight full-time writers who formulate Cortana's responses to user queries. The team's goal is for Cortana to exhibit the type of multi-dimensional intelligence that humans display—social intelligence, emotion, humor, and a point of view. Whichever intelligent assistant is most successful at this is likely to have a leg up on the others. Although these technologies still require plenty of human guidance (Facebook M reportedly has a staff of human customer service agents on hand to handle difficult queries), the time may finally have arrived where interacting directly with AI becomes a part of our everyday lives.

SOURCES: "What Alexa & AI Means for the Future of Commerce," by Richard MacManus, Richardmacmanus.com, August 25, 2016; "Why Dominos' Virtual Assistant Struggles to Understand Your Orders," by Clint Boulton, Cio.com, August 24, 2016; "What Retailers Need to Know, and Expect, About Virtual Digital Technology," by Judy Motti, Retailcustomerexperience.com, August 5, 2016; "3 Ways Artificial Intelligence Is Transforming E-commerce," by Ben Rossi, Information-age.com, July 18, 2016; "These Three Virtual Assistants Point the Way to the Future," by Mike Elgan, Computerworld.com, June 8, 2016; "The Search for the Killer Bot," by Sharon Gaudin, Casey Newton, Theverge.com, June 1, 2016; "When a Robot Books Your Airline Ticket," by Jane L. Levere, *New York Times,* May 30, 2016; "Google Makes Push Into Artificial Intelligence with New Offerings," by Jack Nicas, *Wall Street Journal,* May 18, 2016; "Google Home vs. Amazon Echo: Why Home Could Win," by Andrew Gebhart, Cnet.com, May 18, 2016; "New Siri Sibling Viv May Be Next Step in A.I. Evolution," Computerworld.com, May 11, 2016; "Siri-Creator Shows Off First Public Demo of Viv, 'The Intelligent Interface for Everything,'" by Lucas Matney, Techcrunch. com, May 9, 2016; "1-800-Flowers Chats Up Amazon's Alexa," by Allison Enright, Internetretailer.com, April 26, 2016; "The Chatbots are Coming - and They Want to Help You Buy Stuff," by Sarah Halzack, *Washington Post,* April 13, 2016; "What Can Chatbots Do for Ecommerce?" by Mike O'Brien, Clickz.com, April 11, 2016; "2 Ways Artificial Intelligence Is Changing Customer Engagement," by Randy Kohl, The-future-of-commerce.com, February 18, 2016; "How Real People Help Cortana, Siri, and Other Virtual Assistants Feel Alive," by Mike Elgan, Pcworld.com, February 1, 2016; "The North Face Brings AI to Ecommerce," by Rebecca Harris, Marketingmag.ca, January 12, 2016.

an entirely new marketing and advertising platform for vendors. Early e-commerce applications using desktops and laptops were celebrated as allowing people to shop in their pajamas. Smartphones and tablets extend this range from pajamas to office desktops to trains, planes, and cars, all while you're fully clothed. You can shop anywhere, shop everywhere, and shop all the time, in between talking, texting, watching videos, and listening to music. Almost all of the top 100 brands have a presence in at least one of the major app stores, and more than 90% have an app in the Apple App Store. Retail m-commerce in the EU-5 is expected to generate almost €70 billion in 2016, with the highest percentage of buyers via smartphone in the United Kingdom (over 33% of smartphone users), compared to the rest of the EU-5, where rates range from 28% for Italy to just 13.5% for France. Buyers in the United Kingdom were also the most likely to make purchases via apps, with almost 60% of smartphone m-commerce buyers doing so (eMarketer, Inc., 2016o, 2016p).

PLATFORMS FOR MOBILE APPLICATION DEVELOPMENT

Unlike mobile web sites, which can be accessed by any web-enabled mobile device, native apps, which are designed specifically to operate using the mobile device's hardware and operating system, are platform-specific. Applications for the iPhone, iPad, and other iOS devices are written in the Objective-C programming language using the iOS SDK (software developer kit). Applications for Android operating system–based phones typically are written using Java, although portions of the code may be in the C or C++ programming language. Applications for Windows mobile devices are written in C or C++. In addition to creating native apps using a programming language such as Objective C or Java, there are also hundreds of low-cost or open source app development toolkits that make creating cross-platform mobile apps relatively easy and inexpensive without having to use a device-specific programming language. See Section 3.6 in Chapter 3 for more information.

APP MARKETPLACES

Once written, applications are distributed through various marketplaces. Android apps for Android-based phones are distributed through Google Play, which is controlled by Google. iPhone applications are distributed through Apple's App Store. Microsoft operates the Windows Phone Marketplace for Windows mobile devices. Apps can also be purchased from third-party vendors such as Amazon's Appstore. It is important to distinguish "native" mobile apps, which run directly on a mobile device and rely on the device's internal operating system, from web apps, which install into your browser, although these can operate in a mobile environment as well.

CASE STUDY

Akamai Technologies:
Attempting to Keep Supply Ahead of Demand

I n 2016, the amount of Internet traffic generated by YouTube alone is greater than the amount of traffic on the entire Internet in 2000. Because of video streaming and the explosion in mobile devices demanding high-bandwidth applications, Internet traffic has increased over 500% since 2010 and is predicted to nearly triple by 2019 (see **Figure 2.19**). Internet video is now a majority of Internet traffic and will reach 82% by 2020, according to Cisco. Experts call services like YouTube, Netflix, and high definition streaming video "net bombs" because they threaten the effective operation of the Internet. Mobile platform traffic grew by almost 75% in 2015 and may soon push cellular networks and the Internet to their capacities.

FIGURE 2.19	THE GROWTH OF INTERNET TRAFFIC

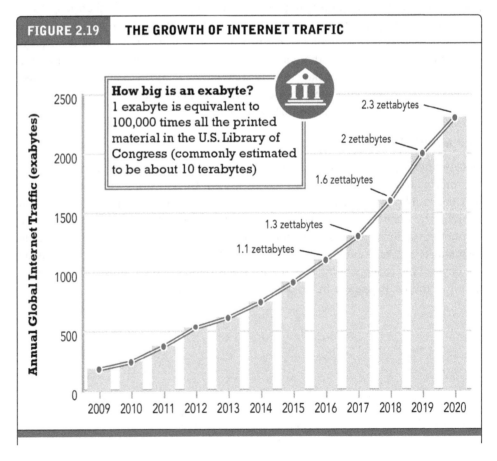

Cisco estimates that annual global Internet traffic will be around 2.3 zettabytes in 2020: that's 2,300 exabytes, or, in other words, 23 with 19 zeroes behind it!

In today's broadband environment, the threshold of patience is very low. Increased video and audio customer expectations are bad news for anyone seeking to use the Web for delivery of high-quality multimedia content and high definition video. Akamai is one of the Web's major helpers, and an overwhelming majority of the Web's top companies use Akamai's services to speed the delivery of content. Akamai serves more than 30 terabits of web traffic per second.

Slow-loading web pages and content sometimes result from poor design, but more often than not, the problem stems from the underlying infrastructure of the Internet. The Internet is a collection of networks that has to pass information from one network to another. Sometimes the handoff is not smooth. Every 1,500-byte packet of information sent over the Internet must be verified by the receiving server and an acknowledgment sent to the sender. This slows down not only the distribution of content such as music, but also slows down interactive requests, such as purchases, that require the client computer to interact with an online shopping cart. Moreover, each packet may go through many different servers on its way to its final destination, multiplying by several orders of magnitude the number of acknowledgments required to move a packet from New York to San Francisco. The Internet today spends much of its time and capacity verifying packets, contributing to a problem called "latency" or delay. For this reason, a single e-mail with a 1-megabyte attached PDF file can create more than 50 megabytes of Internet traffic and data storage on servers, client hard drives, and network backup drives.

Akamai Technologies was founded by Tom Leighton, an MIT professor of applied mathematics, and Daniel Lewin, an MIT grad student, with the idea of expediting Internet traffic to overcome these limitations. Lewin's master's thesis was the theoretical starting point for the company. It described storing copies of web content such as pictures or video clips at many different locations around the Internet so that one could always retrieve a nearby copy, making web pages load faster.

Officially launched in August 1998, Akamai's current products are based on the Akamai Intelligent Platform, a cloud platform made up of over 216,000 servers in 120 countries within over 1,500 networks around the world, and all within a single network hop of 85% of all Internet users. Akamai software on these servers allows the platform to identify and block security threats and provide comprehensive knowledge of network conditions, as well as instant device-level detection and optimization. Akamai's site performance products allow customers to move their online content closer to end users so a user in New York City, for instance, will be served L.L.Bean pages from the New York Metro area Akamai servers, while users of the L.L.Bean site in San Francisco will be served pages from Akamai servers in San Francisco. Akamai has a wide range of large corporate and government clients: 1 out of every 3 global Fortune 500 companies, the top 30 media and entertainment companies, 96 of the top 100 online U.S. retailers, all branches of the U.S. military, all the major U.S. sports leagues, and so on. In 2015, Akamai delivers between 15% and 30% of all web traffic, and over 3 trillion daily Internet interactions. Other competitors in the content delivery network (CDN) industry include Limelight Networks, Level 3 Communications, and Mirror Image Internet.

Accomplishing this daunting task requires that Akamai monitor the entire Internet, locating potential sluggish areas and devising faster routes for information to travel. Frequently used portions of a client's website, or large video or audio files that would be difficult to send to users quickly, are stored on Akamai's servers. When a user requests a song or a video file, his or her request is redirected to an Akamai server nearby and the content is served from this local server. Akamai's servers are placed in Tier 1 backbone supplier networks, large ISPs, universities, and other networks. Akamai's software determines which server is optimal for the user and then transmits the "Akamaized" content locally. Web sites that are "Akamaized" can be delivered anywhere from 4 to 10 times as fast as non-Akamaized content. Akamai has developed a number of other business services based on its Internet savvy, including targeted advertising based on user location and zip code, content security, business intelligence, disaster recovery, on-demand bandwidth and computing capacity during spikes in Internet traffic, storage, global traffic management, and streaming services. You can see several interesting visualizations of the Internet that log basic real-time online activity by visiting the Akamai website.

The shift toward cloud computing and the mobile platform as well as the growing popularity of streaming video have provided Akamai with new growth opportunities. As more businesses and business models are moving to the Web, Akamai has seen its client base continue to grow beyond the most powerful Internet retailers and online content providers. In 2014, Akamai made a push to encourage Hollywood studios to use the cloud for feature films, touting its ability to handle uploads and downloads of large video files, to quickly convert files from one format to another, and to apply DRM protections. Establishing partnerships with movie studios represented big business for Akamai, with an increasing amount of media consumption taking place on mobile devices through the cloud. Akamai has also made agreements to become the primary content delivery platform for cloud service providers like Microsoft Azure and Google Cloud Platform.

However, the growth of streaming video has also created new challenges for Akamai, including increased competition from Comcast and Amazon, which have built competing content delivery services. Amazon's Cloudfront content delivery network is already bringing in $1.8 billion in revenues. Larger clients like Apple and Facebook are also increasingly shifting their content delivery operations away from Akamai's platforms and onto in-house content delivery networks. Reducing carbon emissions and energy expenditure as demand grows has been another challenge for Akamai. In response, the company has undertaking sweeping efforts to reduce its greenhouse gas emissions to below 2015 levels by 2020 despite significantly higher demand.

Akamai is also acutely aware of the increase in cybercrime as more traffic migrates to the Internet. Growth in Internet traffic is good news for Akamai, but the company must also now deal with politically motivated cyberattacks, organized crime online, and state-sponsored cyberwarfare. Akamai has continued to improve its Kona Site Defender tool, which offers a variety of security measures for Akamai clients. The tool protects against Distributed Denial of Service (DDoS) attacks and includes a firewall for web applications. In 2016, Akamai rolled out new improvements to Kona's web application firewall and analytics features. Akamai also upgraded Site Defender's Web Application Firewall feature and developed modifications to the tool that make it easier

SOURCES: "Facts & Figures," Akamai.com, accessed September 8, 2016; "Amazon, Comcast Content Delivery Network Push Could Hurt Akamai," by Reinhardt Krause, Investors.com, May 11, 2016; "Akamai Will Power Internet with Sun and Wind," by Nicola Peill-Moelter, Greenbiz.com, May 11, 2016; "Akamai Advances Kona Site Defender to Meet the Challenges Posed by Constantly Evolving Web Application and DDoS Threat Landscape," Akamai.com, February 29, 2016; "Akamai Shares Surge on Earnings Beat, Reorganization, Buybacks," by Wallace Witkowski, Marketwatch.com, February 9, 2016; "Google and Akamai Partner on Speeding Up Cloud Network," by Steven J. Vaughan-Nichols, Zdnet.com, November 20, 2015; "How Akamai Plans to Make a Comeback," Bloomberg.com, October 28, 2015; "Microsoft and Akamai Bring CDN to Azure Customers," by Sudheer Sirivara, Azure.microsoft.com, for its users to use. With so many businesses now dependent on the uninterrupted flow of content over the Internet, Akamai is in a very strong position to sell security services to its customers. In 2015, Akamai partnered with top information security firm Trustwave to cross-sell each other's services and products, expanding their offerings and reaching even further. Akamai made a similar agreement with China Unicom, a provider of cloud services in the fast-growing Chinese market. Akamai has also set itself up for future growth by moving into areas of the world with less developed broadband infrastructure, such as the Middle East. In 2015, Akamai opened an office in Dubai, hoping to bolster its presence in an area where the adoption rate for broadband is skyrocketing.

In 2016, experiencing rapidly increasing demand from its clients for security tools, Akamai announced it would restructure its business into two distinct units, one focusing on content delivery and media, and the other on website security. The improvements in Akamai's security businesses have offset any slowdown in their content delivery business, as the company registered earnings well above analyst estimates in 2016 despite increased competition in content delivery. Akamai has plans to increase its suite of security tools going forward, with tools designed to protect employees from phishing and malware due to be released in 2017. While the future of its content delivery business is cloudier due to increased competition and the challenges of Internet growth, the company is still very profitable.

September 29, 2015; "Akamai Opens Dubai Office to Support Its Growing Middle East Business," Akamai.com, June 14, 2015; "Akamai, Trustwave to Promote, Sell Each Other's Security Services," by Sean Michael Kerner, Eweek.com, June 1, 2015; "Akamai and China Unicom Establish Strategic Cloud Services Partnership," Akamai.com, May 26, 2015; "Akamai Appeals to Hollywood Studios at NAB 2014," by Troy Dreier, Streamingmedia.com, April 7, 2014; "Akamai Completes Acquisition of Prolexic," Akamai.com, February 18, 2014; "You Think the Internet Is Big Now? Akamai Needs to Grow 100-Fold," by Mathew Ingram, GigaOM.com, June 20, 2012; "Akamai Eyes Acceleration Boost for Mobile Content," by Stephen Lawson, Computerworld, March 20, 2012; "To Cash In on Wave of Web Attacks, Akamai Launches Stand-alone Security Business," by Andy Greenberg, Forbes.com, February 21, 2012.

Case Study Questions

1. Why does Akamai need to geographically disperse its servers to deliver its customers' web content?

2. If you wanted to deliver software content over the Internet, would you sign up for Akamai's service? Why or why not?

3. Do you think Internet users should be charged based on the amount of bandwidth they consume, or on a tiered plan where users would pay in rough proportion to their usage?

2.8 REVIEW

KEY CONCEPTS

■ Discuss the origins of, and the key technology concepts behind, the Internet.

- The Internet has evolved from a collection of mainframe computers located on a few U.S. college campuses to an interconnected network of thousands of networks and millions of computers worldwide.
- The history of the Internet can be divided into three phases: the Innovation Phase (1961–1974), the Institutionalization Phase (1975–1995), and the Commercialization Phase (1995 to the present).

- Packet switching, TCP/IP, and client/server technology are key technology concepts behind the Internet.
- The mobile platform has become the primary means for accessing the Internet.
- Cloud computing refers to a model of computing in which firms and individuals obtain computing power and software applications over the Internet, rather than purchasing the hardware and software and installing it on their own computers.
- Internet protocols and utility programs such as BGP, HTTP, SMTP and POP, SSL and TLS, FTP, Telnet, Ping, and Tracert provide a number of Internet services.

■ **Explain the current structure of the Internet.**

- The main structural elements of the Internet are the backbone (composed primarily high-bandwidth fiber optic cable), IXPs (hubs that use high-speed switching computers to connect to the backbone), CANs (campus/corporate area networks), and ISPs (which deal with the "last mile" of service to homes and offices).
- *Governing bodies*, such as IAB, ICANN, IESG, IETF, ISOC, and W3C, have influence over the Internet and monitor its operations, although they do not control it.

■ **Understand the limitations of today's Internet and the potential capabilities of the Internet of the future.**

- To envision what the Internet of tomorrow will look like, we must first look at the limitations of today's Internet, which include bandwidth limitations, quality of service limitations, network architecture limitations, language limitations, and limitations arising from the wired nature of the Internet.
- Internet2 is a consortium working together to develop and test new technologies for potential use on the Internet. Other groups are working to expand Internet bandwidth via improvements to fiber optics. Wireless and cellular technologies are providing users of mobile devices with increased access to the Internet and its various services. The increased bandwidth and expanded connections will result in a number of benefits, including latency solutions; guaranteed service levels; lower error rates; and declining costs. The Internet of Things will be a big part of the Internet of the future, with more and more sensor-equipped machines and devices connected to the Internet.

■ **Understand how the Web works.**

- The Web was developed during 1989–1991 by Dr. Tim Berners-Lee, who created a computer program that allowed formatted pages stored on the Internet to be linked using keywords (hyperlinks). In 1993, Marc Andreessen created the first graphical web browser, which made it possible to view documents on the Web graphically and created the possibility of universal computing.
- The key concepts you need to be familiar with in order to understand how the Web works are hypertext, HTTP, URLs, HTML, XML, web server software, web clients, and web browsers.

■ **Describe how Internet and web features and services support e-commerce.**

- Together, the Internet and the Web make e-commerce possible by allowing computer users to access product and service information and to complete purchases online.
- Some of the specific features that support e-commerce include communication tools such as e-mail, messaging applications, online message boards, Internet telephony, video conferencing, video chatting, and telepresence; search engines; and downloadable and streaming media.
- Web 2.0 applications and services include social networks, blogs, and wikis.
- Virtual reality, augmented reality and artificial intelligence technologies have begun to enter the consumer market and attract significant attention.

■ **Understand the impact of mobile applications.**

- The mobile app phenomenon has spawned a new digital ecosystem.

- Smartphone and tablet users spent the majority of their time using mobile apps rather than the mobile Web.
- There are a variety of different platforms for mobile application development including Objective-C (for iOS devices), Java (Android smartphones), and C and C++ (Windows mobile devices).
- Mobile apps for the iPhone are distributed through Apple's App Store, for Android devices through Google Play, and for Windows mobile devices through Microsoft's Windows Phone Marketplace. There are also third-party vendors such as Amazon's Appstore.

QUESTIONS

1. What advantages does client/server computing have over mainframe computing?
2. What are three different types of cloud computing models that have been developed?
3. Why is packet switching so essential to the Internet?
4. What are four Internet protocols besides HTTP (the Web) and sending e-mail (SMTP)?
5. What are the three main phases in the evolution of the Internet? Briefly describe each.
6. How does virtual reality differ from augmented reality?
7. Why are smartphones a disruptive technology?
8. How is Google aiming to provide Internet access to remote areas?
9. Identify the various types of narrowband and broadband ISP Internet connections. Of all, which is the fastest and which is the slowest?
10. What is the Internet of Things and how is it being created and enabled?
11. Explain what domain names, URLs, and IP addresses are and provide an example of each. How are they used when a user is browsing the Web?
12. What are the main mobile platforms used by mobile devices?
13. How does HTTP/2 improve on HTTP? Why isn't it being used by more websites?
14. Identify the layers used in Internet technology. What is their importance to Internet communications?
15. Describe at least two differences between a public web server connected to the Internet and an end-user's computer connected to the Internet.
16. Define and contrast the "First Mile" and "Last Mile." What is the importance of making these distinctions in Internet telecommunications?
17. What are three concerns about the Internet of Things?
18. What is the difference between HTML and XML?
19. What are some of the drawbacks of cloud computing?
20. Explain how apps are distributed once they have been created.

PROJECTS

1. Review the opening case. What developments have occurred since this case was written in December 2016?

2. Call or visit the websites of a cable provider, DSL provider, and satellite provider to obtain information on their Internet services. Prepare a brief report summarizing the features, benefits, and costs of each. Which is the fastest? What, if any, are the downsides of selecting any of the three for Internet service (such as additional equipment purchases)?

3. Select two countries (excluding the United States) and prepare a short report describing their basic Internet infrastructure. Are they public or commercial? How and where do they connect to backbones within the United States?

4. Investigate the Internet of Things. Select one example and describe what it is and how it works.

REFERENCES

Akamai Inc. "IPV6 Adoption Visualization." (August 2016a).

Akamai Inc. "HTTP/2: The Future of the Internet." (accessed August 29, 2016b).

Akamai Inc. "Akamai's State of the Internet Q3 2016 Report." (December 14, 2016c).

Anurag. "New Statistics on Skype." Geekycube.com (April 11, 2016).

Arstechnica.com. "Capitol Hill, The Internet, and Broadband: An Ars Technica Quarterly Report." (September 2010).

Berners-Lee, Tim, Robert Cailliau, Ari Luotonen, Henrik Frystyk Nielsen, and Arthur Secret. "The World Wide Web." *Communications of the ACM* (August 1994).

Bluetooth SIG, Inc. "What Is Bluetooth Technology." (Accessed August 25, 2016).

Brandt, Richard. "Net Assets: How Stanford's Computer Science Department Changed the Way We Get Information." *Stanford Magazine* (November/December 2004).

Buckley, Tom. "U.S. FTTH Deployment Rose 13 Percent in 2015, Says Council." Fiercetelecom.com (November 16, 2015).

BuddeCom. "BuddeCom Intelligence Report - VoIP and Mobile VoIP Statistics and Insights." (March 10, 2016).

Bush, Vannevar. "As We May Think." *Atlantic Monthly* (July 1945).

Cerf, V., and R. Kahn, "A Protocol for Packet Network Intercommunication." *IEEE Transactions on Communications*, Vol. COM-22, No. 5, pp 637–648 (May 1974).

Cisco. "Cisco Visual Networking Index: Global Mobile Data Traffic Forecast Update, 2015–2020." (February 3, 2016a)

Cisco. "Cisco Visual Networking Index: Forecast and Methodology, 2015–2020." (June 1, 2016).

Cox, Mark. "Dell Promises to Continue Doubling Down on PCs." Channelbuzz.ca (April 14, 2016).

Craig, Caroline. "Sorry ISPs: The FCC Finally Has the Dopes on the Ropes." Infoworld.com (June 17, 2016).

Durairajan, Ramakrishnan, Paul Barford, Joel Sommers, and Walter Willinger. "InterTubes: A Study of the US Long-haul Fiber-optic Infrastructure." SIGCOMM '15 (August 17–21, 2015).

eMarketer, Inc. "Internet Users and Penetration Worldwide, 2015–2020." (September 1, 2016a).

eMarketer, Inc. "US Internet Users and Population, 2015–2020." (August 3, 2016b).

eMarketer, Inc. "US Tablet Internet Users and Penetration, 2014–2020." (August 2, 2016c).

eMarketer, Inc., (Cindy Liu). "Worldwide Internet and Mobile Users: eMarketer's Estimates for 2016." (June 2016d).

eMarketer, Inc. "Fixed Broadband Penetration in Europe, by Country, 2011–2016 (% of total households)." December 20, 2016.

eMarketer, Inc. "Mobile Phone Internet Users and Penetration Worldwide, 2015–2020." (September 1, 2016f)

eMarketer, Inc., "Mobile Phone Messaging App Users and Penetration, 2013–2020." (June 3, 2016g).

eMarketer, Inc. "US Search Users and Penetration, 2015–2020." (August 3, 2016h).

eMarketer, Inc. "Monthly Online Searches in the US, by Search Engine, Jan–June 2016." (July 22, 2016i).

eMarketer, Inc. "US Digital Video Viewers and Penetration, 2015–2020." (August 3, 2016j).

eMarketer, Inc., "US Bloggers and Penetration, 2015–2020." (August 3, 2016k).

eMarketer, Inc. "US Blog Readers and Penetration, 2015–2020." (August 3, 2016l).

eMarketer, Inc. (Brian Yeager) "Immersive Media Update: Fall 2016." (September 2016m).

eMarketer, Inc. "How Users in the UK Engage with Mobile Apps." (January 26, 2016n).

eMarketer, Inc. "UK Smartphone Shoppers Do It In-App." (August 3, 2016o).

eMarketer, Inc. "Retail Mcommerce Sales in the EU-5, 2015–2020." (August 1, 2016p).

Federal Communications Commission. "FCC Finds U.S. Broadband Deployment Not Keeping Pace." (January 29, 2015).

Federal Networking Council. "FNC Resolution: Definition of 'Internet.'" (October 24, 1995).

Gartner, Inc. "Gartner Says Worldwide Public Cloud Services Market Is Forecast to Reach $204 Billion in 2016." (January 25, 2016a).

Gartner, Inc. "Gartner Says Worldwide Smartphone Sales to Slow in 2016." (June 7, 2016).

Geni.net. "Have Your Say: GENI Sustainment and Governance & Future Network Research Infrastructure." (accessed August 25, 2016).

Gross, Grant. "NSF Seeks Ambitious Next-Generation Internet Project." *Computerworld* (August 29, 2005).

Hsu, Jeremy. "What's Next After 25 Years of Wi-Fi?" Spectrum.ieee.org (September 10, 2015).

IEEE Computer Society. "Top Trends for 2013." (2013).

IHS. "Voice over IP Services Market Up 5 Percent in 2015." Infonetics.com (April 19, 2016).

Internet Corporation for Assigned Names and Numbers (ICANN). "ICANN Approves Historic Change to Internet's Domain System." (June 20, 2011a).

Internet Corporation for Assigned Names and Numbers (ICANN). "Top-Level Domains (gTLDs)." (2011b).

Internet Engineering Task Force (IETF). "RFC 7540: Hypertext Transfer Protocol Version 2 (HTTP/2)." (May 2015).

Internet Retailer. "2015 Lite Edition Mobile 500 Executive Summary." (2015).

Internet Society. "The Internet of Things: An Overview." (October 2015).

Internet Society. "World IPv6 Launch on June 6, 2012, To Bring Permanent IPv6 Deployment." (January 2012).

Internet Society. "ISOC's Standards Activities." (September 2010).

Internet Society. "RFC 2616: Hypertext Transfer Protocol-HTTP/1.1." (June 1999).

Internet Society. "RFC 0959: File Transfer Protocol." (October, 1985).

Kleinrock, Leonard. *1964 Communication Nets: Stochastic Message Flow and Delay.* New York: McGraw-Hill (1964).

Leiner, Barry M., Vinton G. Cerf, David D. Clark, Robert E. Kahn, Leonard Kleinrock, Daniel C. Lynch, Jon Postel, Larry G. Roberts, and Stephen Wolff. "All About the Internet: A Brief History of the Internet." *Internet Society* (ISOC) (August 2000).

Mangalindan, JP. "In Online Search War, It's Google vs. Amazon." *Fortune* (October 15, 2014).

National Research Foundation. "NSP Leadership in Discovery and Initiative Sparks White House US Ignite Initiative." (June 13, 2012).

Netcraft. "August 2016 Web Server Survey." (August 24, 2016).

Netmarketshare. "Desktop Browser Market Share." Marketshare.hitslink.com (accessed August 31, 2016a).

Netmarketshare. "Market/Tablet Browser Market Share." Marketshare.hitslink.com (accessed August 31, 2016b).

Nordstrom, Amy. "Popular Internet of Things Forecast of 50 Billion Devices by 2020 Is Outdated." Spectrum. ieee.org (August 18, 2016).

NPD Group. "49 Million U.S. Internet Homes Now Own a Connected TV or Attached Content Device, According to the NPD Group." Npd.com (March 7, 2016).

Pfanner, Eric. "Ethics Fight Over Domain Names Intensifies." *New York Times* (March 18, 2012).

Podtrac, Inc. "Podcast Industry Audience Rankings." Podtrac.com (accessed September 5, 2016).

Radicati Group. "Email Statistics Report, 2016–2020—Executive Summary." (March 2016).

Research and Markets. "Smart Home Market by Product, Software & Service, and Geography -- Global Forecast to 2022." (May 17, 2016).

Richter, Felix. "The U.S. Lags Behind in Fiber Adoption." Statista.com (August 5, 2015).

SANS Institute (John Pescatore). "Security the 'Internet of Things' Survey." (January 2014).

Simonite, Tom. "First Detailed Public Map of U.S. Internet Backbone Could Make It Stronger." Technologyreview.com (September 15, 2015).

Sterling, Greg. "Google Down 1 Billion PC Searches From 2014, But Mobile Volumes Likely Way Up." Searchengineland.com (January 22, 2016).

U.S. Department of Commerce. "Letter to ICANN Chairman." Ntia.doc.gov (July 30, 2008).

Visualware, Inc., "VisualRoute Traceroute Server." (2014).

W3Techs.com. "Usage of HTTP/2 for Websites." (Accessed August 29, 2016).

Weiss, Todd R. "802.11ac WiFi Products Gaining Market Share as Older Devices Decline." Eweek.com (April 22, 2015).

Zakon, Robert H. "Hobbes' Internet Timeline v8.1." Zakon.org (2005).

Ziff-Davis Publishing. "Ted Nelson: Hypertext Pioneer." Techtv.com (1998).

CHAPTER 3

Building an E-commerce Presence

After reading this chapter, you will be able to:

- Understand the questions you must ask and answer, and the steps you should take, in developing an e-commerce presence.
- Explain the process that should be followed in building an e-commerce presence.
- Identify and understand the major considerations involved in choosing web server and e-commerce merchant server software.
- Understand the issues involved in choosing the most appropriate hardware for an e-commerce site.
- Identify additional tools that can improve website performance.
- Understand the important considerations involved in developing a mobile website and building mobile applications.

The Financial Times:

A Remodel for 21st Century Publishing Profitability

When London-based The Financial Times Ltd. (FT) updated its apps with a new browser-based HTML5 Web app in 2011, it became the first major news outlet to employ responsive design tools to create a single app for multiple platforms. FT believed that the HTML5 app would yield significant cost savings in comparison to building multiple native apps for different platforms and would also liberate it from app stores and their attendant commission fees. The decision was also triggered by Apple's pronouncement that it would no longer share subscriber data from subscriptions purchased through its App Store.

© Azimuth Interactive, Inc.

FT's next major goal was to satisfy the yearning of a significant portion of its readership who still wanted to be able to read the paper as they always did, from cover to cover. Released in 2013, FT's web app has two modes: Live and Morning. The Live version provides frequently updated stories and shifting article arrangement. The Morning version, on the other hand, reproduces the experience of yesteryear, presenting a snapshot of the previous day's news just like the print edition. A navigation bar allows readers to easily toggle between the two versions and also presents thumbnails for easy navigation to newspaper sections, a search bar, and a refresh button. A new section, myFT, provides article recommendations based on reading history and a place to store personal portfolios and articles. Articles can be clipped from one platform and viewed on another. Subscribers can also create personalized charts to monitor investment performance vs. performance benchmarks and organize how they view their portfolio. While some of these tools had been available in the original web app, myFT consolidated them in a handy single-page hub.

But while FT.com subscribers have access to the latest tools and technologies for managing, monitoring, and viewing their investments and sharing articles with fellow readers, they now also experience a digital design that simulates the reading of a newspaper. A fixed-height page and two-column layout limits the amount of up and down scrolling needed to read an article, and a left-to-right swipe navigates to the next article. This format keeps readers engaged longer as they dig deeper into the site. Full-page ads, often including multimedia content, are interspersed between articles and display at each section change. Simulating a television commercial break or an advertisement encountered while turning the pages of a magazine, these ads command a premium. FT's digital subscriptions have long since surpassed print circulation, and the new app design provides additional opportunities for digital advertising growth, including space on article pages in addition to the interstitials. In 2016, more than half of FT's total traffic comes via mobile devices.

Unsatisfied with its progress, FT unveiled the fastest version of its website yet in 2016. The site fully loads articles within 1.5 seconds on the desktop, and within 2.1 seconds on mobile devices, down from 6 seconds before the update. Rollout of Google's Accelerated Mobile Pages (AMP) across the FT platform was the primary reason for the speed boost. The company live-tested the new site along with the older version for months to compare data and engagement metrics between the two. FT's analytics showed that the faster a page loads, the more likely it engages readers, and that the new version was up to 30% more engaging to users overall. The new site also improved the myFT feature, introducing the much-requested ability to send a free article to friends as a gift. FT anticipates the upgrades attracting more advertising, especially via the cost-per-hour option it began offering in 2015, where advertisers pay by the actual time users spend watching ads instead of traditional metrics like clicks or impressions.

The overarching goal of FT's ongoing upgrades is to balance the desires of FT's older but technologically proficient audience with the expectations of its newer, younger audience. FT wants to provide its older subscribers with a soothingly familiar experience while introducing them to the convenience and efficiencies of modern tools. At the same time, it hopes to keep its younger audience on the site longer, giving FT advertisers more marketing opportunities. To that end, FT has explored the use of cutting-edge technologies, such as virtual reality documentaries about prominent world locations, including Dublin, London, Rio de Janeiro, and Brussels. FT has partnered with Google to supply Google Cardboard VR headsets to view the content, which is freely available to view even for non-subscribers. The technology is still in its infancy, but FT hopes that its early adoption of VR and 360-degree video will be useful if it becomes more commonplace.

Thus far, the results of FT's efforts have been a resounding success. In 2016, FT announced that its circulation had reached an all-time high at 805,000 subscribers, a 9.2% increase over the previous year. The digital subscriber segment of FT's subscriber base grew 16% over the previous year to 601,000, comprising almost 75% of total subscribers, and digital accounts for more than 40% of FT's total income, compared to 10% to 15% for most other modern newspapers.

Because its subscribers are increasingly using multiple channels to access FT content, FT has invested significant time and resources into adapting storage tools and methods including cookies, the application cache (AppCache), IndexDB, and the bootstrap process so that subscribers have access even when they have no network connection. The majority of each web page is JavaScript, Cascading Style Sheets (CSS), templates, advertising, and UI images that do not change from page to page. Most go into local storage. The web app automatically caches the content on load, and the page is assembled in the browser using JavaScript. When an online reader goes to an article page, the server only has to send the article content. Everything else is added to the page in the browser. For FT's audience, many of whom switch back and forth between workplace computers and mobile devices, and which also includes a sizable business traveler audience, this means

SOURCES: The FT Web App," Labs.ft.com/articles, accessed January 16, 24, 2017; "FT and Google Shine a Light on Dublin in New VR Video," FT.com, December 2, 2016; "Financial Times Unveils Next Generation Website," FT.com, October 4, 2016; "The Financial Times Flips the Switch on Its Speedy New Website, After Months of Beta-Testing in the Open," by Shan Wang, Niemanlab.org, October 4, 2016; "Financial Times Hopes Speedy New Website Will Boost Subscribers," by Jack Marshall, *Wall Street Journal,* October 4, 2016; "'Financial Times' Revamps Site," by Sara Guaglione, Mediapost.com, October 4, 2016; "Game On: Financial Times Makes Its VR Debut for Rio Olympics," by Jessica Davies, Digiday.com, August 5, 2016; "The FT Doubles Its Branded Content Initiative," by Ken Doctor, Politico.com, June 28, 2016; "Financial Times Stresses Importance of Google AMP for Its Subscriptions," Businessinsider. com, June 25, 2016; "The FT's that cached articles, clipped articles, myFT, and even video content are available offline and can even be streamed to in-flight entertainment screens without a network connection.

What's more, FT has discovered that tablet use is more conducive to the consumption of longer, more in-depth pieces. While the smartphone is clearly a device designed for the consumption of short bursts of pertinent information, tablet reading more closely approximates how people read books and magazines.

FT has discovered that during normal business hours, the desktop site gets the most traffic, but during weekends, a whopping 75% of traffic comes from mobile devices. This informed FT's decision in 2014 to split its Weekend section into a separate app, FT Weekend. FT Weekend is a graphically rich, premium print product focusing on lifestyle, and the app focuses more on these qualities than the flagship site. FT is confident that new subscribers who wouldn't otherwise pay for digital editions will do so for premium content from FT Weekend, and that many readers will want access to both. FT is also able to upsell FT Weekend subscribers, offering them deals on the full version.

Although FT's revenue is now driven primarily by subscriptions, the company continues to bolster its advertising products whenever possible. With ad blockers severely damaging sites supported primarily by advertising revenue, FT has found that the use of a paywall and its subscription-supported model has kept it in a strong position. Still, advertising is a critical component of its business. FT has focused on quality over quantity in advertising, particularly with rich media ads. Rich media ads don't require a click and are embedded within the content stream. FT launched a marketing unit in 2015 called FT Squared (FT²) to develop branded content for the site. FT² uses reader feedback and analytics to inform its choices. Prominent brands like BP are using FT's Paid Posts feature, which launched in 2016. Paid Posts display advertising prominently on FT's home page and allow FT to provide companies with precise feedback about how their advertisements are performing, from individual mouse movements and scrolling depth to click-through rates. Paid Posts revenue has grown 30% in the past year and is FT's fastest growing digital advertising option. FT continued to bolster its advertising capability in 2016, acquiring Alpha Grid, a branded content marketing firm based in London.

In 2015, FT's parent company, Pearson, sold FT Group to the Japanese business newspaper publisher Nikkei for $1.3 billion. FT's market-leading status in mobile and digital was likely a significant reason for its lofty valuation. The opportunity to buy a respected news organization is also exceedingly rare. Nikkei has vowed not to alter the day-to-day operation of FT, and has even committed to returning the paper's headquarters back to its original location in England.

Warning to Its Media Rivals: 'If You're Trying to Play a Game of Scale, You're Going to Lose,'" by Ian Burrell, Thedrum.com, June 23, 2016; "How the Financial Times Uses Reader Insight to Evolve Its Native Ad Offering," by Lucinda Southern, Digiday.com, April 7, 2016; "Financial Times Brings Multimedia Content to Its Paid Post Offering FT²," by Jessica Goodfellow, Thedrum.com, April 7, 2016; "Nikkei's Surprising Purchase of the Financial Times," *The Economist*, July 24, 2015; "The Financial Times' Mobile-Led Weekend Evolution," *World News Publishing Focus*, July 26, 2014; "More Products, Better Treatment: How and Why the Financial Times Built a Digital FT Weekend," by Jasper Jackson, Themediabriefing.com, July 22, 2014; "Financial Times Debuts FT Weekend App for Growing Lifestyle Audience," FT.com, July 3, 2014; "Financial Times Weighs In on Web vs. Native App Debate, How Technology Has Shaped Its Own Digital Strategy," by Graham Hinchly, Inma.org, January 20, 2014; "Building the New Financial Times Web App (A Case Study)," by Wilson Page, Smashingmagazine.com, May 23rd, 2013; "FT App Blends Features of Print, Web," by Charlotte Woolard, BtoB Media Business, May 7, 2013; "Financial Times: 'There Is No Drawback to Working in HTML5'," by Stuart Dredge, Theguardian.com, April 29, 2013; "'Financial Times' Relaunches Web App with 'Live' and 'Morning' Editions," by Lauren Indvik, Mashable.com, April 3, 2013 "FT Relaunches Web App: New App Facilitates Tighter Integration with FT.com," by Bill Mickey, Foliomag.com, April 3, 2013; "The 'Financial Times' Has a Secret Weapon: Data," by Lauren Indvik, Mashable.com, April, 2, 2013.

I n Chapter 2, you learned about e-commerce's technological foundation: the Internet, the Web, and the mobile platform. In this chapter, you will examine the important factors that a manager needs to consider when building an e-commerce presence. The focus will be on the managerial and business decisions you must make before you begin, and that you will continually need to make. Although building a sophisticated e-commerce presence isn't easy, today's tools are much less expensive and far more powerful than they were during the early days of e-commerce. At the same time, the proliferation of mobile devices and social networks adds complexity because firms need to build a presence on three platforms: the Web, mobile, and social networks. In this chapter, we focus on both small and medium-sized businesses as well as much larger corporate entities that serve thousands of customers a day, or even an hour. As you will see, although the scale may be very different, the principles and considerations are basically the same.

3.1 IMAGINE YOUR E-COMMERCE PRESENCE

Before you begin to build a website or app of your own, there are some important questions you will need to think about and answer. The answers to these questions will drive the development and implementation of your e-commerce presence.

WHAT'S THE IDEA? (THE VISIONING PROCESS)

Before you can plan and actually build an e-commerce presence, you need to have a vision of what you hope to accomplish and how you hope to accomplish it. The vision includes not just a statement of mission, but also identification of the target audience, characterization of the market space, a strategic analysis, a marketing matrix, and a development timeline. It starts with a dream of what's possible, and concludes with a timeline and preliminary budget for development.

If you examine any successful website, you can usually tell from the home page what the vision that inspires the site is. If the company is a U.S. public company, you can often find a succinct statement of its vision or mission in the reports it files with the U.S. Securities and Exchange Commission. For Amazon, it's to become the largest marketplace on earth. For Facebook, it's to make the world more open and connected. For Google, it's to organize the world's information and make it universally accessible and useful. The e-commerce presence you want to build may not have such all-encompassing ambitions, but a succinct statement of mission, purpose, and direction is the key factor in driving the development of your project. For instance, the mission of TheKnot is to be the Internet's comprehensive, one-stop wedding planning solution.

WHERE'S THE MONEY: BUSINESS AND REVENUE MODEL

Once you have defined a mission statement, a vision, you need to start thinking about where the money will be coming from. You will need to develop a preliminary idea of your business and revenue models. You don't need detailed revenue and cost projections at this point. Instead, you need a general idea of how your business will generate revenues. The basic choices will be described in Chapter 5. Basic business models include portal, e-tailer, content provider, transaction broker, market creator, service provider, and community provider (social network).

The basic revenue model alternatives are advertising, subscriptions, transaction fees, sales, and affiliate revenue. There's no reason to adopt a single business or revenue model, and in fact, many firms have multiple models. For instance, the *Financial Times'* digital business model is to both sell subscriptions and sell ad space. In addition, they sell unique photographs and gifts. At TheKnot, a vertical portal for the wedding industry, you will find ads, affiliate relationships, and sponsorships from major creators of wedding products and services, including a directory to local wedding planners, all of which produce revenue for TheKnot. PetSmart, the most popular pet website in the United States, has a more focused sales revenue model, and presents itself almost entirely as an e-tailer of pet supplies.

WHO AND WHERE IS THE TARGET AUDIENCE?

Without a clear understanding of your target audience, you will not have a successful e-commerce presence. There are two questions here: who is your target audience and where can you best reach them? Your target audience can be described in a number of ways: demographics, behavior patterns (lifestyle), current consumption patterns (online vs. offline purchasing), digital usage patterns, content creation preferences (blogs, social networks, sites like Pinterest), and buyer personas (profiles of your typical customer). Understanding the demographics of your target audience is usually the first step. Demographic information includes age, income, gender, and location. In some cases, this may be obvious and in others, much less so. For instance, Harley-Davidson sells motorcycles to a very broad demographic range of varying ages, incomes, and locations, from 34-year-olds to 65-year-olds. Although most of the purchasers are middle-aged men, with middle incomes, many of the men ride with women, and the Harley-Davidson website has a collection of women's clothing and several web pages devoted to women riders. While the majority of men who purchase Harley-Davidsons have modest incomes, a significant group of purchasers are professionals with above-average incomes. Hence, the age and income demographic target is quite broad. What ties Harley-Davidson riders together is not their shared demographics, but their love of the motorcycles and the brand, and the lifestyle associated with touring the highways of America on a powerful motorcycle that sounds like a potato popper. In contrast, a company like TheKnot is aimed at women in the 18–34-year-old range who are in varying stages of getting married, with lifestyles that include shopping online, using smartphones and tablets, downloading apps, and using Facebook. This audience is technologically hip. These women read and contribute to blogs, comment on forums, and use Pinterest to find ideas for fashion. A "typical" visitor to TheKnot would be a 28-year-old woman who has an engagement ring, is just starting the wedding planning process, has an income of $45,000, lives in the Northeast United States, and is interested in a beach wedding. There are, of course, other "typical" profiles. For each profile for your website you will need to develop a detailed description.

WHAT IS THE BALLPARK? CHARACTERIZE THE MARKETPLACE

The chances of your success will depend greatly on the characteristics of the market you are about to enter, and not just on your entrepreneurial brilliance. Enter into a declining market filled with strong competitors, and you will multiply your chances of failure. Enter into a market that is emerging, growing, and has few competitors, and you stand a better chance. Enter a market where there are no players, and you will either be rewarded handsomely with a profitable monopoly on a successful product no one else thought of (Apple) or you will be quickly forgotten because there isn't a market for your product at this point in time (the Franklin e-book reader circa 1999).

Features of the marketplace to focus on include the demographics of the market and how an e-commerce presence fits into the market. In addition, you will want to know about the structure of the market: competitors and substitute products.

What are the features of the marketplace you are about to enter? Is the market growing, or receding in size? If it's growing, among which age and income groups? Is the marketplace shifting from offline to online delivery? If so, is the market moving toward traditional websites, mobile, and/or tablets? Is there a special role for a mobile presence in this market? What percentage of your target audience uses a website, smartphone, or tablet? What about social networks? What's the buzz on products like yours? Are your potential customers talking about the products and services you want to offer on Facebook, Twitter, Instagram, or blogs? How many blogs focus on products like yours? How many Twitter posts mention similar offerings? How many Facebook Likes (signs of customer engagement) are attached to products you want to offer?

The structure of the market is described in terms of your direct competitors, suppliers, and substitute products. You will want to make a list of the top five or ten competitors and try to describe their market share, and distinguishing characteristics. Some of your competitors may offer traditional versions of your products, while others will offer new renditions or versions of products that have new features. You need to find out everything you can about your competitors. What's the market buzz on your competitors? How many unique monthly visitors (UMVs) do they have? How many Facebook Likes, Twitter followers, and/or Pinterest followers? How are your competitors using social sites and mobile devices as a part of their online presence. Is there something special you could do with social networks that your competitors do not? Do a search on customer reviews of their products. You can find online services (some of them free) that will measure the number of online conversations about your competitors, and the total share of Internet voice each of your competitors receives. Do your competitors have a special relationship with their suppliers that you may not have access to? Exclusive marketing arrangements would be one example of a special supplier relationship. Finally, are there substitutes for your products and services? For instance, your site may offer advice to the community of pet owners, but local pet stores or local groups may be a more trusted source of advice on pets.

WHERE'S THE CONTENT COMING FROM?

Websites are like books: they're composed of a lot of pages that have content ranging from text, to graphics, photos, and videos. This content is what search engines catalog as they crawl through all the new and changed web pages on the Internet. The content is why your customers visit your site and either purchase things or look at ads that generate revenue for you. Therefore, the content is the single most important foundation for your revenue and ultimate success.

There are generally two kinds of content: static and dynamic. Static content is text and images that do not frequently change, such as product descriptions, photos, or text that you create to share with your visitors. Dynamic content is content that changes regularly, say, daily or hourly. Dynamic content can be created by you, or increasingly, by bloggers and fans of your website and products. User-generated content has a number of advantages: it's free, it engages your customer fan base, and search engines are more likely to catalog your site if the content is changing. Other sources of content, especially photos, are external websites that aggregate content such as Pinterest.

KNOW YOURSELF: CONDUCT A SWOT ANALYSIS

A **SWOT analysis** is a simple but powerful method for strategizing about your business and understanding where you should focus your efforts. In a SWOT analysis you describe your strengths, weaknesses, threats, and opportunities. In the example SWOT analysis in **Figure 3.1**, you will see a profile of a typical startup venture that includes a unique approach to an existing market, a promise of addressing unmet needs in this market, and the use of newer technologies (social and mobile platforms) that older competitors may have overlooked. There are many opportunities to address a large market with unmet needs, as well as the potential to use the initial website as a home base and spin-off related or nearby sites, leveraging the investment in design and

SWOT analysis
describes a firm's strengths, weaknesses, opportunities, and threats

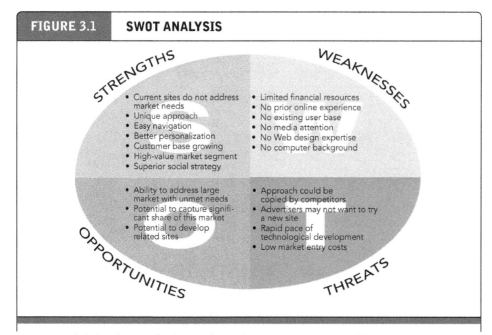

FIGURE 3.1   **SWOT ANALYSIS**

STRENGTHS
- Current sites do not address market needs
- Unique approach
- Easy navigation
- Better personalization
- Customer base growing
- High-value market segment
- Superior social strategy

WEAKNESSES
- Limited financial resources
- No prior online experience
- No existing user base
- No media attention
- No Web design expertise
- No computer background

OPPORTUNITIES
- Ability to address large market with unmet needs
- Potential to capture significant share of this market
- Potential to develop related sites

THREATS
- Approach could be copied by competitors
- Advertisers may not want to try a new site
- Rapid pace of technological development
- Low market entry costs

A SWOT analysis describes your firm's strengths, weaknesses, opportunities, and threats.

technology. But there are also weaknesses and threats. Lack of financial and human resources are typically the biggest weakness of startup companies. Threats include competitors that could develop the same capabilities as you, and low market entry costs, which might encourage many more startups to enter the marketplace.

Once you have conducted a SWOT analysis, you can consider ways to overcome your weaknesses and build on your strengths. For instance, you could consider hiring or partnering to obtain technical and managerial expertise, and looking for financing opportunities (including friends and relatives).

DEVELOP AN E-COMMERCE PRESENCE MAP

E-commerce has moved from being a PC-centric activity on the Web to a mobile and tablet-based activity as well. While around 70% of e-commerce retail and travel revenues are still generated by purchases made from a desktop computer, increasingly smartphones and tablets are being used for purchasing. Smartphones and tablets are also used by a majority of Internet users in the United States to shop for goods and services, explore purchase options, look up prices, and access social sites. Your potential customers use these various devices at different times during the day, and involve themselves in different conversations depending on what they are doing—touching base with friends, viewing photos on Instagram, tweeting, or reading a blog. Each of these are "touch points" where you can meet the customer, and you have to think about how you develop a presence in these different virtual places. **Figure 3.2** provides a

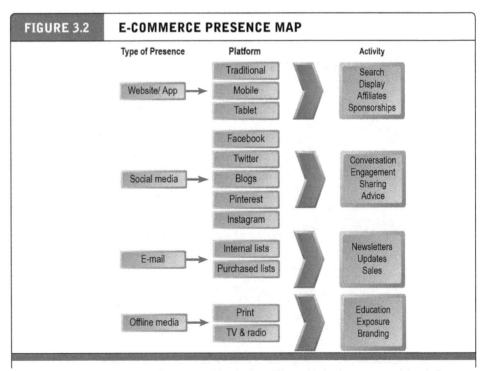

FIGURE 3.2   **E-COMMERCE PRESENCE MAP**

An e-commerce presence requires firms to consider the four different kinds of presence, and the platforms and activities associated with each type of presence.

roadmap to the platforms and related activities you will need to think about when developing your e-commerce presence.

Figure 3.2 illustrates four different kinds of e-commerce presence: website/app, e-mail, social media, and offline media. For each of these types there are different platforms that you will need to address. For instance, in the case of websites and/or apps, there are three different platforms: traditional desktop, tablets, and smartphones, each with different capabilities. And for each type of e-commerce presence there are related activities you will need to consider. For instance, in the case of websites and apps, you will want to engage in search engine marketing, display ads, affiliate programs, and sponsorships. Offline media, the fourth type of e-commerce presence, is included here because many firms use multiplatform or integrated marketing where print, television, or radio ads refer customers to websites and apps. The marketing activities in Figure 3.2 are described in much greater detail in Chapters 6 and 7.

DEVELOP A TIMELINE: MILESTONES

Where would you like to be a year from now? It's a good idea for you to have a rough idea of the time frame for developing your e-commerce presence when you begin. You should break your project down into a small number of phases that could be completed within a specified time. Six phases are usually enough detail at this point. **Table 3.1** illustrates a one-year timeline for the development of a startup e-commerce company.

Note that this example timeline defers the development of a mobile plan until after a website and social media plan have been developed and implemented. There is a growing trend, however, to flip this timeline around, and begin with a mobile plan instead (sometimes referred to as mobile first design). Mobile first design has both advantages and disadvantages that will be examined more fully in Section 3.6.

TABLE 3.1	E-COMMERCE PRESENCE TIMELINE	
PHASE	**ACTIVITY**	**MILESTONE**
Phase 1: Planning	Envision e-commerce presence; determine personnel	Mission statement
Phase 2: Website development	Acquire content; develop a site design; arrange for hosting the site	Website plan
Phase 3: Web implementation	Develop keywords and metatags; focus on search engine optimization; identify potential sponsors	A functional website
Phase 4: Social media plan	Identify appropriate social platforms and content for your products and services	A social media plan
Phase 5: Social media implementation	Develop Facebook, Twitter, and Pinterest presence	Functioning social media presence
Phase 6: Mobile plan	Develop a mobile plan; consider options for porting your website to smartphones	A mobile media plan

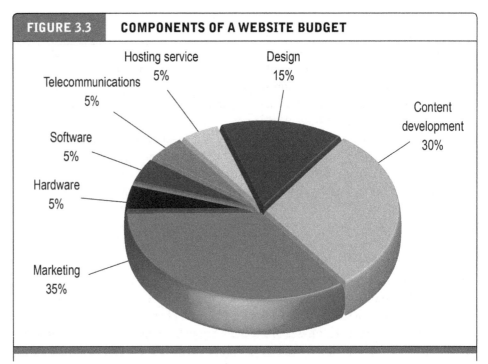

| FIGURE 3.3 | COMPONENTS OF A WEBSITE BUDGET |

While hardware and software costs have fallen dramatically, websites face significant design, content development, and marketing costs.

HOW MUCH WILL THIS COST?

It's too early in the process to develop a detailed budget for your e-commerce presence, but it is a good time to develop a preliminary idea of the costs involved. How much you spend on a website, for instance, depends on what you want it to do. Simple websites can be built and hosted with a first-year cost of €5,000 or less if all the work is done in-house by yourself and others willing to work without pay. A more reasonable budget for a small startup using available tools and design services such as WordPress, might be €10,000 to €25,000. Here the firm owner would develop all the content at no cost, and a web designer and programmer would be hired to implement the initial website. As discussed later, the website would be hosted on a cloud-based server. The websites of large firms that offer high levels of interactivity and linkage to corporate systems can cost several hundred thousand to millions of dollars a year to create and operate. Large firms often outsource their web development and hosting entirely although many large firms have recently changed and brought the entire web effort in-house. (see the closing case study, *Dick's Sporting Goods: Taking Control of Its E-commerce Operations*).

While how much you spend to build a website depends on how much you can afford, and, of course, the size of the opportunity, **Figure 3.3** provides some idea of the relative size of various website costs. In general, the cost of hardware, software, and telecommunications for building and operating a website has fallen dramatically (by over 50%) in the last decade, making it possible for very small entrepreneurs to build fairly sophisticated sites. At the same time, while technology has lowered the costs of system development, the costs of marketing, content development, and design have risen to make up more than half of typical website budgets. The longer-term costs would also have to include site and system maintenance, which are not included here. The costs of developing a mobile site and apps are discussed in Section 3.6.

3.2 BUILDING AN E-COMMERCE PRESENCE: A SYSTEMATIC APPROACH

Once you have developed a vision of the e-commerce presence you want to build, it's time to start thinking about how to build and implement that presence. Building a successful e-commerce presence requires a keen understanding of business, technology, and social issues, as well as a systematic approach. E-commerce is just too important to be left totally to technologists and programmers.

The two most important management challenges are (1) developing a clear understanding of your business objectives and (2) knowing how to choose the right technology to achieve those objectives. The first challenge requires you to build a plan for developing your firm's presence. The second challenge requires you to understand some of the basic elements of e-commerce infrastructure. Let the business drive the technology.

Even if you decide to outsource the development effort and operation to a service provider, you will still need to have a development plan and some understanding of the basic e-commerce infrastructure issues such as cost, capability, and constraints. Without a plan and a knowledge base, you will not be able to make sound management decisions about e-commerce within your firm.

Let's assume you are a manager for a medium-sized industrial parts firm in Munich, Germany. You have been given a budget of €100,000 to develop an e-commerce presence for the firm. The purpose will be to sell and service the firm's customers, who are mostly small machine and metal fabricating shops, and to engage your customers through the website, perhaps via a blog and user forum. Where do you start? In the following sections, we will examine developing an e-commerce website, and then, at the end of the chapter, discuss some of the more specific considerations involved in developing a mobile site and building mobile applications.

First, you must be aware of the main areas where you will need to make decisions (see **Figure 3.4**). On the organizational and human resources fronts, you will have to bring together a team of individuals who possess the skill sets needed to build and manage a successful e-commerce presence. This team will make the key decisions about business objectives and strategy, technology, design, and social and information policies. The entire development effort must be closely managed if you hope to avoid the disasters that have occurred at some firms.

You will also need to make decisions about hardware, software, and telecommunications infrastructure. The demands of your customers should drive your choices of technology. Your customers will want technology that enables them to find what they want easily, view the product, purchase the product, and then receive the product from your warehouses quickly. You will also have to carefully consider design. Once you have identified the key decision areas, you will need to think about a plan for the project.

| FIGURE 3.4 | FACTORS TO CONSIDER IN DEVELOPING AN E-COMMERCE PRESENCE |

Building an e-commerce presence requires that you systematically consider the many factors that go into the process.

PLANNING: THE SYSTEMS DEVELOPMENT LIFE CYCLE

systems development life cycle (SDLC)

a methodology for understanding the business objectives of any system and designing an appropriate solution

Your second step in building an e-commerce website will be creating a plan document. In order to tackle a complex problem such as building an e-commerce site, you will have to proceed systematically through a series of steps. One methodology is the systems development life cycle. The **systems development life cycle (SDLC)** is a methodology for understanding the business objectives of any system and designing an appropriate solution. Adopting a life cycle methodology does not guarantee success, but it is far better than having no plan at all. The SDLC method also helps in creating documents that communicate objectives, important milestones, and the uses of resources to management. **Figure 3.5** illustrates the five major steps involved in the systems development life cycle for an e-commerce site:

- Systems analysis/planning
- Systems design
- Building the system
- Testing
- Implementation

SYSTEMS ANALYSIS/PLANNING: IDENTIFY BUSINESS OBJECTIVES, SYSTEM FUNCTIONALITY, AND INFORMATION REQUIREMENTS

In the systems analysis/planning step of the SDLC, you try to answer the question, "What do we want this e-commerce site to do for our business?" The key point is to let the business decisions drive the technology, not the reverse. This will ensure that your technology platform is aligned with your business. We will assume here that you have identified a business strategy and chosen a business model to achieve your strategic objectives (see Chapter 5). But how do you translate your strategies, business models, and ideas into a working e-commerce website?

FIGURE 3.5 **WEBSITE SYSTEMS DEVELOPMENT LIFE CYCLE**

One way to start is to identify the specific business objectives for your site, and then develop a list of system functionalities and information requirements. **Business objectives** are simply capabilities you want your site to have.

System functionalities are types of information systems capabilities you will need to achieve your business objectives. The **information requirements** for a system are the information elements that the system must produce in order to achieve the business objectives. You will need to provide these lists to system developers and programmers so they know what you as the manager expect them to do.

Table 3.2 describes some basic business objectives, system functionalities, and information requirements for a typical e-commerce site. As shown in the table, there are ten basic business objectives that an e-commerce site must deliver. These objectives must be translated into a description of system functionalities and ultimately into a set of precise information requirements. The specific information requirements for a system typically are defined in much greater detail than Table 3.2 indicates. To a large extent, the business objectives of an e-commerce site are not that different from those of an ordinary retail store. The real difference lies in the system functionalities and information requirements. In an e-commerce site, the business objectives must be provided entirely in digital form without buildings or salespeople, 24 hours a day, 7 days a week.

SYSTEM DESIGN: HARDWARE AND SOFTWARE PLATFORMS

Once you have identified the business objectives and system functionalities, and have developed a list of precise information requirements, you can begin to consider just how all this functionality will be delivered. You must come up with a **system design specification**—a description of the main components in the system and their relationship to one another. The system design itself can be broken down into two

business objectives
capabilities you want your site to have

system functionalities
types of information systems capabilities you will need to achieve your business objectives

information requirements
the information elements that the system must produce in order to achieve the business objectives

system design specification
description of the main components in a system and their relationship to one another

TABLE 3.2	SYSTEM ANALYSIS: BUSINESS OBJECTIVES, SYSTEM FUNCTIONALITIES, AND INFORMATION REQUIREMENTS FOR A TYPICAL E-COMMERCE SITE	
BUSINESS OBJECTIVE	SYSTEM FUNCTIONALITY	INFORMATION REQUIREMENTS
Display goods	Digital catalog	Dynamic text and graphics catalog
Provide product information (content)	Product database	Product description, stocking numbers, inventory levels
Personalize/customize product	Customer on-site tracking	Site log for every customer visit; data mining capability to identify common customer paths and appropriate responses
Engage customers in conversations	On-site blog; user forums	Software with blogging and community forum functionality
Execute a transaction	Shopping cart/payment system	Secure credit card clearing; multiple payment options
Accumulate customer information	Customer database	Name, address, phone, and e-mail for all customers; online customer registration
Provide after-sale customer support	Sales database	Customer ID, product, date, payment, shipment date
Coordinate marketing/advertising	Ad server, e-mail server, e-mail, campaign manager, ad banner manager	Site behavior log of prospects and customers linked to e-mail and banner ad campaigns
Understand marketing effectiveness	Site tracking and reporting system	Number of unique visitors, pages visited, products purchased, identified by marketing campaign
Provide production and supplier links	Inventory management system	Product and inventory levels, supplier ID and contact, order quantity data by product

logical design
describes the flow of information at your e-commerce site, the processing functions that must be performed, the databases that will be used, the security and emergency backup procedures that will be instituted, and the controls that will be used in the system

physical design
translates the logical design into physical components

components: a logical design and a physical design. A **logical design** includes a data flow diagram that describes the flow of information at your e-commerce site, the processing functions that must be performed, and the databases that will be used. The logical design also includes a description of the security and emergency backup procedures that will be instituted, and the controls that will be used in the system.

A **physical design** translates the logical design into physical components. For instance, the physical design details the specific model of server to be purchased, the software to be used, the size of the telecommunications link that will be required, the way the system will be backed up and protected from outsiders, and so on.

Figure 3.6(a) presents a data flow diagram for a simple high-level logical design for a very basic website that delivers catalog pages in HTML in response to HTTP requests from the client's browser, while **Figure 3.6(b)** shows the corresponding physical design. Each of the main processes can be broken down into lower-level designs that are much more precise in identifying exactly how the information flows and what equipment is involved.

BUILDING THE SYSTEM: IN-HOUSE VERSUS OUTSOURCING

Now that you have a clear idea of both the logical and physical designs for your site, you can begin considering how to actually build the site. You have many choices, and

FIGURE 3.6   A LOGICAL AND A PHYSICAL DESIGN FOR A SIMPLE WEBSITE

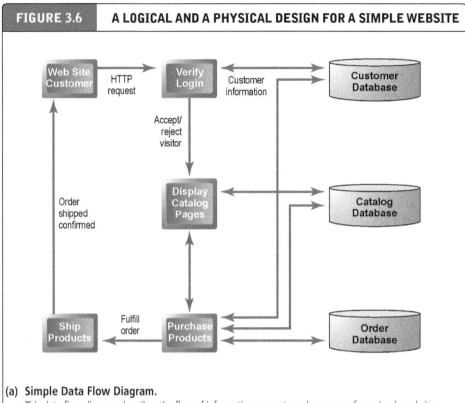

(a) Simple Data Flow Diagram.
This data flow diagram describes the flow of information requests and responses for a simple website.

(b) Simple Physical Design.
A physical design describes the hardware and software needed to realize the logical design.

FIGURE 3.7 **CHOICES IN BUILDING AND HOSTING**

You have a number of alternatives to consider when building and hosting an e-commerce site.

much depends on the amount of money you are willing to spend. Choices range from outsourcing everything (including the actual systems analysis and design) to building everything yourself (in-house). **Outsourcing** means that you will hire an outside vendor to provide the services involved in building the site rather than using in-house personnel. You also have a second decision to make: will you host (operate) the site on your firm's own servers or will you outsource the hosting to a web host provider? These decisions are independent of each other, but they are usually considered at the same time. There are some vendors who will design, build, and host your site, while others will either build or host (but not both). **Figure 3.7** illustrates the alternatives.

Build Your Own versus Outsourcing

Let's take the building decision first. If you elect to build your own site, there are a range of options. Unless you are fairly skilled, you should use a pre-built template to create the website. For example, Yahoo Aabaco Small Business (formerly Yahoo Stores) provides templates that merely require you to input text, graphics, and other data, as well as the infrastructure to run a sales-oriented website once it has been created.

If your website is not a sales-oriented site requiring a shopping cart, one of the least expensive and most widely used site building tools is WordPress. **WordPress** is a website development tool with a sophisticated content management system. A **content management system (CMS)** is a database software program specifically designed to manage structured and unstructured data and objects in a website environment. A CMS provides web managers and designers with a centralized control structure to manage website content. WordPress also has thousands of user-built plug-ins and widgets that you can use to extend the functionality of a website. Websites built in WordPress are treated by search engines like any other website: their content is indexed and made available to the entire web community. Revenue-generating ads, affiliates, and sponsors are the main sources of revenue for WordPress sites. Other

outsourcing
hiring an outside vendor to provide the services you cannot perform with in-house personnel

WordPress
open source content management and website design tool

content management system (CMS)
organizes, stores, and processes website content

FIGURE 3.8 **THE SPECTRUM OF TOOLS FOR BUILDING YOUR OWN E-COMMERCE SITE**

similar website building tools are provided by Google Sites, Wix, Squarespace, and Weebly. While these are the least costly ways to create a website, you will be limited to the "look and feel" and functionality provided by the templates and infrastructure supplied by these vendors.

If you have some programming experience, you might decide to build the site yourself "from scratch." There are a broad variety of tools, ranging from those that help you build everything truly "from scratch," such as Adobe Dreamweaver CC and Microsoft Visual Studio, to top-of-the-line prepackaged site-building tools that can create sophisticated sites customized to your needs. **Figure 3.8** illustrates the spectrum of tools available. We will look more closely at the variety of e-commerce software available in Section 3.3.

The decision to build a website on your own has a number of risks. Given the complexity of features such as shopping carts, credit card authentication and processing, inventory management, and order processing, the costs involved are high, as are the risks of doing a poor job. You will be reinventing what other specialized firms have already built, and your staff may face a long, difficult learning curve, delaying your entry to market. Your efforts could fail. On the positive side, you may be better able to build a site that does exactly what you want, and, more importantly, develop the in-house knowledge to allow you to change the site rapidly if necessary due to a changing business environment.

If you choose more expensive site-building packages, you will be purchasing state-of-the art software that is well tested. You could get to market sooner. However, to make a sound decision, you will have to evaluate many different packages, and this can take a long time. You may have to modify the package to fit your business needs and perhaps hire additional outside vendors to do the modifications. Costs rise rapidly as modifications mount. A €4,000 package can easily become a €40,000 to €60,000 development project (see **Figure 3.9**).

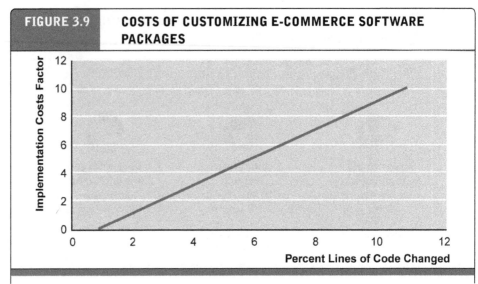

FIGURE 3.9 | **COSTS OF CUSTOMIZING E-COMMERCE SOFTWARE PACKAGES**

While sophisticated site development software packages appear to reduce costs and increase speed to market, as the modifications required to fit the package to your business needs rise, costs rise rapidly.

In the past, bricks-and-mortar retailers in need of an e-commerce site typically designed the site themselves (because they already had the skilled staff in place and had extensive investments in information technology capital such as databases and telecommunications). However, as web applications have become more sophisticated, larger retailers today rely heavily on vendors to provide sophisticated website capabilities, while also maintaining a substantial internal staff. Small startups may build their own sites from scratch using in-house technical personnel in an effort to keep costs low. Medium-size startups will often purchase a website design and programming expertise from vendors. Very small mom-and-pop firms seeking simple storefronts will use templates like WordPress. For e-commerce sites, the cost of building has dropped dramatically in the last five years, resulting in lower capital requirements for all players (see *Insight on Business: Weebly Makes Building Websites Easy*).

Host Your Own versus Outsourcing

Now let's look at the hosting decision. Most businesses choose to outsource hosting and pay a company to host their website, which means that the hosting company is responsible for ensuring the site is "live," or accessible, 24 hours a day. By agreeing to a monthly fee, the business need not concern itself with many of the technical aspects of setting up a web server and maintaining it, telecommunications links, nor with staffing needs.

You can also choose to *co-locate*. With a **co-location** agreement, your firm purchases or leases a web server (and has total control over its operation) but locates the server in a vendor's physical facility. The vendor maintains the facility, communications lines, and the machinery. Co-location has expanded with the spread of virtualization where one server has multiple processors (4 to 16) and can operate multiple websites at once with multiple operating systems. In this case, you do not buy the

co-location

when a firm purchases or leases a web server (and has total control over its operation) but locates the server in a vendor's physical facility. The vendor maintains the facility, communications lines, and the machinery

INSIGHT ON BUSINESS

WEEBLY MAKES CREATING WEBSITES EASY

With so many big companies dominating the e-commerce scene, you may wonder if there's a chance for the little guy anymore. The answer is yes: there are still billions left in potential online retail sales, with additional money to be made from advertising revenues. In fact, there's an e-commerce frenzy going on that nearly rivals the dot-com era with one exception: the startups have access to cheap technology and social media that can provide inexpensive marketing and sales.

Weebly provides valuable website solutions for smaller businesses and entrepreneurs. Founded in 2007 by Penn State University graduates David Rusenko, Chris Fanini, and Dan Veltri, Weebly provides templates that allow small businesses to create their own websites with a full suite of features, including blogs, online stores, and mobile compatibility. Weebly's customers have built 40 million sites, which together have 300 million monthly unique visitors. Users create sites using a drag-and-drop, widget-based tool that works within a web browser. Weebly's typical customers are the "little guys" without website coding experience, and who are hoping to harness the site tools traditionally available only to bigger websites and retailers.

Weebly is just one option in an increasingly crowded marketplace for website creation services. Today's offerings are a far cry from early services like GeoCities and Angelfire, which look crude by today's standards. Weebly and its competitors, including Squarespace, Wix, and WordPress, offer a much more polished product than their predecessors. The company has a free option with basic features as well as premium plans starting at $8 per month and increasing to $49 per month for its high-end Power Sellers plan. Over the course of its

growth, Weebly has added Google AdSense monetization features, CSS/ HTML editing support, and the ability to generate a mobile version of each website automatically. Weebly is a strong player in this marketplace, boasting 40 million registered users, though it does not disclose how many are paid subscribers. By contrast, Wix has 82 million registered users, but less than 2 million of those are paid subscribers.

Weebly has increasingly focused on improving its e-commerce services, such as a mobile store and checkout capability, integrated shopping cart, and filtered product search. It also offers basic support for PayPal, Google Checkout, and Square. By revamping its e-commerce tools, Weebly hopes to better compete with Amazon, as well as similar user-friendly marketplaces such as Etsy and Shopify. Sixty percent of Weebly users identify themselves as entrepreneurs hoping to create an online presence for their business.

The inventors of the Dharma Yoga Wheel, Dov Vargas and Raquel Vamos, fit this description. The two yoga instructors developed the wheel, which helps new yoga practitioners learn to improve the flexibility of their back, chest, shoulders, abdomen, and hip flexors, release tension in those areas, and perform other exercises, in 2014. After launching their site, their sales grew to over $1 million within a year. Wheels are hand-made in the United States, and start from approximately $80, with options of both environmentally-friendly plastic and wooden wheels. The Dharma Yoga Wheel store also offers yoga apparel and other equipment like handstand canes and yoga straps. The two founders credit Weebly with the ability to reach Canada, Europe, Asia, and other markets that would have been unreachable without a website.

Although Weebly doesn't disclose its revenue, the company is profitable and has been since

(continued)

2009. This is an attractive quality for a startup company, many of which have historically sought growth first and profitability later. In 2014, Weebly received $35 million in venture capital funding that valued the company at $455 million. As of 2016, the founders have yet to spend the money, though they expect to use it to drive future growth. The company's hiring of a former Google executive to serve as chief financial officer suggests it plans to begin using its venture capital actively. Weebly is one of the more valuable companies to graduate from the technology incubator Y Combinator, which its founders attended in 2007.

Because so many businesses still don't have an online presence, Weebly's prospects for growth are bright. Less than 40% of restaurants have online menus, for example. Although its competitors are also growing fast, there appears to be enough room in this market for several companies. In 2013, Wix launched an initial public offering, but the response was lukewarm, with investors expressing concern over its lack of profitability. So far, that's an advantage for Weebly, but when Weebly begins an aggressive push for growth, the company's profitability may suffer.

Weebly has continued adapting its platform. In September 2016, it released Weebly 4, the fourth generation of its website creation platform, focusing on integrating website design with e-commerce functionality specifically aimed at small and medium-sized businesses, together with marketing solutions such as an easy-to-use e-mail marketing module. For example, sites can now incorporate abandoned cart functionality, which allows stores to message customers when they leave the site without completing a purchase, as well as functionality that allows stores to more easily calculate taxes and real-time shipping prices. Targeted e-mail campaigns, such as to customers who have not purchased an item within a specified time period, can be easily implemented. Weebly hopes the new platform will enable it to better compete with other e-commerce platform providers, such as Shopify, as well as its traditional website creation competitors. The new features, which are also available for mobile devices, build on the functionality of Carbon, Weebly's third generation platform. Weebly launched Carbon, which necessitated a complete rebuild of its platform, in 2015. Carbon focused on mobile development, providing users with new mobile apps for iPhone, iPad, and Android that allow users to update their sites on the go. Carbon also included an App Center, which allows customers to quickly and easily choose from over 40 partner apps to improve their sites, as well as a Dashboard that gives customers a detailed analytical view of their business.

Weebly is just one example of a larger trend toward leaner business models that rely on outside help for many business functions. Although hardware has become less expensive over time, many startup firms have found that cloud computing and social marketing greatly reduce the costs of starting a company. Market intelligence, public relations, and even design services can be found online for a fraction of the cost of traditional service firms. It's never been cheaper to start an e-commerce company.

SOURCES: "Weebly Updates Its Website Builder with a Focus on E-commerce and Marketing," by Anthony Ha, Techcrunch.com, September 21, 2016; "How Weebly 4 Is Leading an E-commerce Revolution," by Stephan Rabimov, *Forbes*, September 21, 2016; "Weebly's Online Platform Adds Email Marketing," by David Rusenko, Venturebeat.com, September 21, 2016; "Raquel & Dov," Weebly.com/stories, accessed May 2016; "Why Weebly Is the Warp Drive of Website Building," by Murray Newlands, *Forbes*, November 24, 2015; "Tech Startup Weebly Hires Former Google Executive Kim Jabal As Its First CFO," by James Kosur, Businessinsider.com, November 13, 2015; "Weebly Targets Europe with Localized Services for Its Drop-and-Drag Websites," by Paul Sawers, Venturebeat.com, October 27, 2015; "Weebly Introduces Carbon," Weebly.com, October 1, 2015; "Website Builder Weebly Gets a Revamp and Its First App Center," by Anthony Ha, Techcrunch.com, October 1, 2015; "About Weebly," Weebly.com, accessed September 21, 2015; "Weebly for Apple Watch," Weebly.com, April 28, 2015; "Weebly Brings Industry-First App to Android Tablets," *Business Wire*, March 11, 2015; "Weebly and Square Bring Simple, High-Quality Business Solutions to Stores Looking to Get Online," *Business Wire*, February 25, 2015; "Looking Back on a Very Special Year," Weebly.com, November 30, 2014; "Weebly Debuts An iPad App for Building and Managing Websites," by Ryan Lawler, Techcrunch.com, October 9, 2014; "New Weebly App Lets You Build a Website Using the iPad," by Michael Muchmore, Pcmag.com, October 9, 2014; "Weebly Valued at $455 Million Amid Website-Building Boom," by Douglas Macmillan, *Wall Street Journal*, April 22, 2014.

TABLE 3.3	KEY PLAYERS: HOSTING/CO-LOCATION/CLOUD SERVICES	
Amazon Web Services (AWS) EC2		Microsoft
CenturyLink		SoftLayer (IBM)
Digital Realty Trust		Rackspace
Fujitsu		Verizon Cloud
Joyent (Samsung)		Virtualstream

server but rent its capabilities on a monthly basis, usually at one-quarter of the cost of owning the server itself. See **Table 3.3** for a list of some of the major hosting/co-location/cloud providers. There is an extraordinary range of prices for co-location, ranging from a few euros a month, to several hundred thousands of euros per month depending on the size of the website, bandwidth, storage, and support requirements.

While co-location involves renting physical space for your hardware, you can think of using a cloud service provider as renting virtual space in your provider's infrastructure. Cloud services are rapidly replacing co-location because they are less expensive, and arguably more reliable. Unlike with co-location, your firm does not own the hardware. Cloud service providers offer a standardized infrastructure, virtualization technology, and employ a pay-as-you-go billing system.

Hosting, co-location, and cloud services have become a commodity and a utility: costs are driven by very large providers (such as IBM) who can achieve large economies of scale by establishing huge "server farms" located strategically around the country and the globe. This means the cost of pure hosting has fallen as fast as the fall in server prices, dropping about 50% every year! Telecommunications costs have also fallen. As a result, most hosting services seek to differentiate themselves from the commodity hosting business by offering extensive site design, marketing, optimization, and other services. Small, local ISPs also can be used as hosts, but service reliability is an issue. Will the small ISPs be able to provide uninterrupted service, 24 hours a day, 7 days a week, 365 days a year? Will they have service staff available when you need it?

There are several disadvantages to outsourcing hosting. If you choose a vendor, make sure the vendor has the capability to grow with you. You need to know what kinds of security provisions are in place for backup copies of your site, internal monitoring of activity, and security track record. Is there a public record of a security breach at the vendor? Most Fortune 500 firms have their own private cloud data centers so they can control the web environment. On the other hand, there are risks to hosting your own site if you are a small business. Your costs will be higher than if you had used a large outsourcing firm because you don't have the market power to obtain low-cost hardware and telecommunications. You will have to purchase hardware and software, have a physical facility, lease communications lines, hire a staff, and build security and backup capabilities yourself.

TESTING THE SYSTEM

Once the system has been built and programmed, you will have to engage in a testing process. Depending on the size of the system, this could be fairly difficult and lengthy. Testing is required whether the system is outsourced or built in-house. A complex e-commerce site can have thousands of pathways through the site, each of which must be documented and then tested. It is important to note that testing is generally under-budgeted. As much as 50% of the budget can be consumed by testing and rebuilding (usually depending on the quality of the initial design). **Unit testing** involves testing the site's program modules one at a time. **System testing** involves testing the site as a whole, in the same way a typical user would when using the site. Because there is no truly "typical" user, system testing requires that every conceivable path be tested. Final **acceptance testing** requires that the firm's key personnel and managers in marketing, production, sales, and general management actually use the system as installed on a test Internet or intranet server. This acceptance test verifies that the business objectives of the system as originally conceived are in fact working.

Another form of testing is called **A/B testing** (or **split testing**). This form of testing involves showing two versions (A and B) of a web page or website to different users to see which one performs better. There are several different types of A/B testing that can be used for a website design project. A *template test* compares the same general page content using two different layouts and or design treatments. A *new concept test* compares a control page with one that is very different. A *funnel test* compares the flow through a series of pages (such as a product page, to a registration page, to shopping cart page, versus skipping the registration page) to see which one results in a higher percentage of conversions. **Multivariate testing** is a much more sophisticated form of testing than A/B testing. Multivariate testing involves identifying specific elements, or variables, on a web page, such as a headline, image, button and text, creating versions for each element, and then creating a unique combination of each element and version to test. So for example, if there are three elements and two versions of each, there will be eight possible combinations ($2*2*2 = 8$) to test. When used correctly, multivariate testing enables designers to identify the most optimal layout, color, content and format.

IMPLEMENTATION AND MAINTENANCE

Most people unfamiliar with systems erroneously think that once an information system is installed, the process is over. In fact, while the beginning of the process is over, the operational life of a system is just beginning. Systems break down for a variety of reasons—most of them unpredictable. Therefore, they need continual checking, testing, and repair. Systems maintenance is vital, but sometimes not budgeted for. In general, the annual system maintenance cost will roughly parallel the development cost. An e-commerce site that cost €40,000 to develop is likely to require a €40,000 annual expenditure to maintain. Very large e-commerce sites experience some economies of scale, so that, for example, a site that cost €1 million to develop is likely to require an annual maintenance budget of perhaps half to three-quarters of that cost.

Why does it cost so much to maintain an e-commerce site? Unlike payroll systems, for example, e-commerce sites are always in a process of change, improvement, and correction. Studies of traditional systems maintenance have found 20% of the time

---

unit testing

involves testing the site's program modules one at a time

system testing

involves testing the site as a whole, in a way the typical user will use the site

acceptance testing

verifies that the business objectives of the system as originally conceived are in fact working

A/B testing (split testing)

involves showing two versions of a web page or website to different users to see which one performs better

multivariate testing

involves identifying specific elements, creating versions for each element, and then creating a unique combination of each element and version to test is devoted to debugging code and responding to emergency situations (for example, a new server was installed by your ISP, and all your hypertext links were lost and CGI scripts disabled—the site is down!). Another 20% of the time is concerned with changes in reports, data files, and links to backend databases. The remaining 60% of maintenance time is devoted to general administration (making product and price changes in the catalog) and making changes and enhancements to the system. E-commerce sites are never finished: they are always in the process of being built and rebuilt. They are dynamic—much more so than payroll systems.

The long-term success of an e-commerce site will depend on a dedicated team of employees (the web team) whose sole job is to monitor and adapt the site to changing market conditions. The web team must be multi-skilled; it will typically include programmers, designers, and business managers drawn from marketing, production, and sales support. One of the first tasks of the web team is to listen to customers' feedback on the site and respond to that feedback as necessary. A second task is to develop a systematic monitoring and testing plan to be followed weekly to ensure all the links are operating, prices are correct, and pages are updated. A large business may have thousands of web pages, many of them linked, that require systematic monitoring. Other important tasks of the web team include **benchmarking** (a process in which the site is compared with those of competitors in terms of response speed, quality of layout, and design) and keeping the site current on pricing and promotions. The Web is a competitive environment where you can very rapidly frustrate and lose customers with a dysfunctional site.

benchmarking
a process in which the site is compared with those of competitors in terms of response speed, quality of layout, and design

FACTORS IN OPTIMIZING WEBSITE PERFORMANCE

If you are a small firm using one of the available design and hosting sites like WordPress, you do not have to worry about hardware, software, and website optimizing techniques because the vendor will provide this expertise. However, if you are developing your firm's website in-house, you will need to consider these issues. The purpose of a website is to deliver content to customers and to complete transactions. The faster and more reliably these two objectives are met, the more effective the website is from a commerce perspective. If you are a manager or marketing executive, you will want the website operating in a way that fulfills customers' expectations. You'll have to make sure the website is optimized to achieve this business objective. The optimization of website performance is more complicated than it seems and involves at least three factors: page content, page generation, and page delivery (see **Figure 3.10**). In this chapter, we describe the software and hardware choices you will need to make in building an e-commerce site; these are also important factors in website optimization.

Using efficient styles and techniques for *page design* and *content* can reduce response times by two to five seconds. Simple steps include reducing unnecessary HTML comments and white space, using more efficient graphics, and avoiding unnecessary links to other pages in the site. *Page generation* speed can be enhanced by segregating computer servers to perform dedicated functions (such as static page generation, application logic, media servers, and database servers), and using various devices from vendors to speed up these servers. Using a single server or multiple servers to perform multiple tasks reduces throughput by more than 50%. *Page delivery* can be speeded up by using specialized content delivery networks such as Akamai, or by increasing local bandwidth.

FIGURE 3.10 | **FACTORS IN WEBSITE OPTIMIZATION**

Page Delivery
Content delivery networks
Edge caching
Bandwidth

Page Generation
Server response time
Device-based accelerators
Efficient resource allocation
Resource utilization thresholds
Monitoring site performance

Page Content
Optimize HTML
Optimize images
Site architecture
Efficient page style

Website optimization requires that you consider three factors: page content, page generation, and page delivery.

We will discuss some of these factors throughout the chapter, but a full discussion of optimizing website performance is beyond the scope of this text.

3.3 CHOOSING SOFTWARE

Along with telecommunications, software and hardware constitute the infrastructure of an e-commerce presence. As a business manager in charge of creating an e-commerce presence, you will need to know some basic information about both.

SIMPLE VERSUS MULTI-TIERED WEBSITE ARCHITECTURE

Prior to the development of e-commerce, websites simply delivered web pages to users who were making requests through their browsers for HTML pages with content of various sorts. Website software was appropriately quite simple—it consisted of a server computer running basic web server software. We might call this arrangement a single-tier system architecture. **System architecture** refers to the arrangement of software, machinery, and tasks in an information system needed to achieve a specific functionality (much like a home's architecture refers to the arrangement of building materials to achieve a particular functionality). Many websites started this way—there are no monetary transactions. Tens of thousands of sites still perform this way. Orders can always be called in by telephone and not taken online.

However, the development of e-commerce required a great deal more interactive functionality, such as the ability to respond to user input (name and address forms), take customer orders for goods and services, clear credit card transactions on the fly, consult price and product databases, and even adjust advertising on the screen based on user characteristics. This kind of extended functionality required the development of web application servers and a multi-tiered system architecture to handle the processing loads. *Web application servers*, described more fully later in this section, are

system architecture
the arrangement of software, machinery, and tasks in an information system needed to achieve a specific functionality

specialized software programs that perform a wide variety of transaction processing required by e-commerce.

In addition to having specialized application servers, e-commerce sites must be able to pull information from and add information to pre-existing corporate databases. These older databases that predate the e-commerce era are called *backend* or *legacy* databases. Corporations have made massive investments in these systems to store their information on customers, products, employees, and vendors. These backend systems constitute an additional layer in a multi-tiered site.

Figure 3.11 illustrates a simple two-tier and a more complex multi-tier e-commerce site architecture. In **two-tier architecture**, a web server responds to requests

two-tier architecture
e-commerce system architecture in which a web server responds to requests for web pages and a database server provides backend data storage

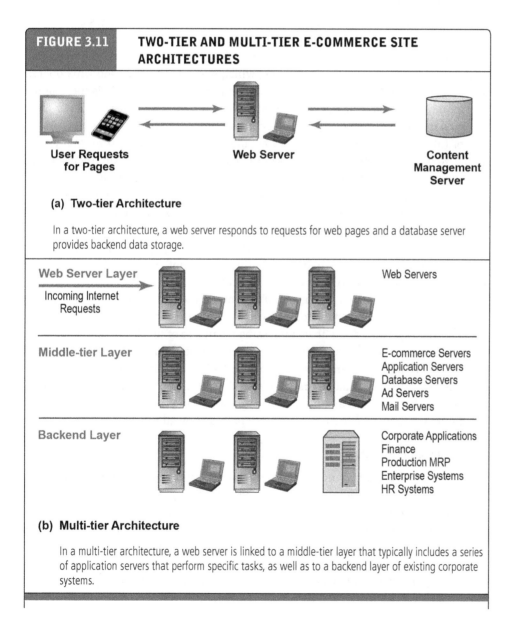

| FIGURE 3.11 | TWO-TIER AND MULTI-TIER E-COMMERCE SITE ARCHITECTURES |

User Requests for Pages   **Web Server**   **Content Management Server**

(a) Two-tier Architecture

In a two-tier architecture, a web server responds to requests for web pages and a database server provides backend data storage.

Web Server Layer
Incoming Internet Requests
Web Servers

Middle-tier Layer
E-commerce Servers
Application Servers
Database Servers
Ad Servers
Mail Servers

Backend Layer
Corporate Applications
Finance
Production MRP
Enterprise Systems
HR Systems

(b) Multi-tier Architecture

In a multi-tier architecture, a web server is linked to a middle-tier layer that typically includes a series of application servers that perform specific tasks, as well as to a backend layer of existing corporate systems.

multi-tier architecture
e-commerce system architecture in which the web server is linked to a middle-tier layer that typically includes a series of application servers that perform specific tasks as well as a backend layer of existing corporate systems

for web pages and a database server provides backend data storage. In a **multi-tier architecture**, in contrast, the web server is linked to a middle-tier layer that typically includes a series of application servers that perform specific tasks, as well as to a backend layer of existing corporate systems containing product, customer, and pricing information. A multi-tiered site typically employs several physical computers, each running some of the software applications and sharing the workload across many physical computers.

The remainder of this section describes basic web server software functionality and the various types of web application servers.

WEB SERVER SOFTWARE

All e-commerce sites require basic web server software to answer requests from customers for HTML and XML pages.

When you choose web server software, you will also be choosing an operating system for your site's computers. Apache, which works with Linux and Unix operating systems, is the leading web server software (Netcraft, 2016). Unix is the original programming language of the Internet and Web, and Linux is a derivative of Unix designed for the personal computer. Apache was developed by a worldwide community of Internet innovators. Apache is free and can be downloaded from many sites on the Web; it also comes installed on most IBM web servers. Literally thousands of programmers have worked on Apache over the years; thus, it is extremely stable. There are thousands of utility software programs written for Apache that can provide all the functionality required for a contemporary e-commerce site. In order to use Apache, you will need staff that is knowledgeable in Unix or Linux.

Microsoft Internet Information Services (IIS) is another popular type of web server software. IIS is based on the Windows operating system and is compatible with a wide selection of Microsoft utility and support programs.

There are also at least 100 other smaller providers or open source versions of web server software. Note that the choice of web server has little effect on users of your system. The pages they see will look the same regardless of the development environment. There are many advantages to the Microsoft suite of development tools—they are integrated, powerful, and easy to use. The Unix operating system, on the other hand, is exceptionally reliable and stable, and there is a worldwide open software community that develops and tests Unix-based web server software.

Table 3.4 shows the basic functionality provided by all web servers.

Site Management Tools

site management tools
verify that links on pages are still valid and also identify orphan files

In Chapter 2, we described most of the basic functionality of the web servers listed in Table 3.4. Another functionality not described previously is site management tools. **Site management tools** are essential if you want to keep your site working, and if you want to understand how well it is working. Site management tools verify that links on pages are still valid and also identify orphan files, or files on the site that are not linked to any pages. By surveying the links on a website, a site management tool can quickly report on potential problems and errors that users may encounter. Your

TABLE 3.4	BASIC FUNCTIONALITY PROVIDED BY WEB SERVERS
FUNCTIONALITY	DESCRIPTION
Processing of HTTP requests	Receive and respond to client requests for HTML pages
Security services (Secure Sockets Layer)/ Transport Layer Security	Verify username and password; process certificates and private/public key information required for credit card processing and other secure information
File Transfer Protocol	Permits transfer of very large files from server to server
Search engine	Indexing of site content; keyword search capability
Data capture	Log file of all visits, time, duration, and referral source
E-mail	Ability to send, receive, and store e-mail messages
Site management tools	Calculate and display key site statistics, such as unique visitors, page requests, and origin of requests; check links on pages

customers will not be impressed if they encounter a "404 Error: Page Does Not Exist" message on your website. Links to URLs that have moved or been deleted are called dead links; these can cause error messages for users trying to access that link. Regularly checking that all links on a site are operational helps prevent irritation and frustration in users who may decide to take their business elsewhere to a better functioning site.

Even more importantly, site management tools can help you understand consumer behavior on your website. Site management software and services, such as those provided by Webtrends, can be purchased in order to more effectively monitor customer purchases and marketing campaign effectiveness, as well as keep track of standard hit counts and page visit information. These services can track your e-commerce presence on the Web, mobile, and social network platforms. **Figure 3.12** shows a screenshot that illustrates Webtrends Analytics 10.

Dynamic Page Generation Tools

One of the most important innovations in website operation has been the development of dynamic page generation tools. Prior to the development of e-commerce, websites primarily delivered unchanging static content in the form of HTML pages. While this capability might be sufficient to display pictures of products, consider all the elements of a typical e-commerce site today by reviewing Table 3.2 (on page 188), or visit what you believe is an excellent e-commerce site. The content of successful e-commerce sites is always changing, often day by day. There are new products and promotions, changing prices, news events, and stories of successful users. E-commerce sites must intensively interact with users who not only request pages but also request product, price, availability, and inventory information. One of the most dynamic sites is eBay—the auction site. There, the content is changing minute by minute. E-commerce sites are just like real markets—they are dynamic. News sites, where stories change constantly, also are dynamic.

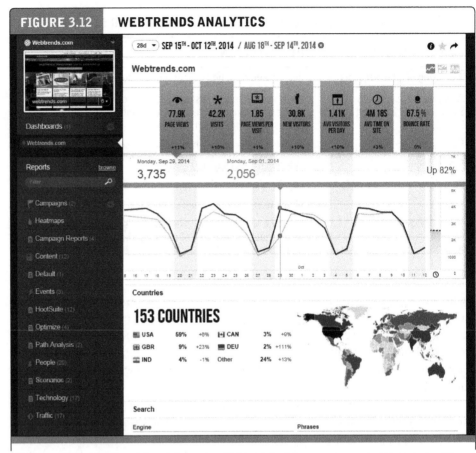

Using a sophisticated web analytics solution such as Webtrends Analytics, managers can quickly understand the return on investment of their online marketing efforts and determine how to improve conversion by drilling down into abandonment paths, product preferences, and successful campaign elements for different types of customers. SOURCE: © Webtrends, Inc., 2014.

dynamic page generation

the contents of a web page are stored as objects in a database, rather than being hard-coded in HTML. When the user requests a web page, the contents for that page are then fetched from the database

The dynamic and complex nature of e-commerce sites requires a number of specialized software applications in addition to static HTML pages. Perhaps one of the most important is dynamic page generation software. With **dynamic page generation**, the contents of a web page are stored as objects in a database, rather than being hard-coded in HTML. When the user requests a web page, the contents for that page are then fetched from the database. The objects are retrieved from the database using Common Gateway Interface (CGI), Active Server Pages (ASP), Java Server Pages (JSP), or other server-side programs. CGI, ASP, and JSP are described in the last section of this chapter. This technique is much more efficient than working directly in HTML code. It is much easier to change the contents of a database than it is to change the coding of an HTML page. A standard data access method called *Open Database Connectivity (ODBC)* makes it possible for applications written in the C programming language to access data from any database regardless of the database and operating system software being used via an ODBC driver that serves as a translator between the application and the database. ODBC drivers are available for most of the major database management systems offered by companies such as Oracle, SAP, Sybase, and IBM. Java Database Connectivity (JDBC) is a version of ODBC that provides connectivity between applications written in the Java programming language and a wide range of databases. However, while ODBC remains the de facto standard for cross-platform data access, today many web development platforms provide functionality that allows a programmer to directly link to a target database, making ODBC/JDBC drivers unnecessary.

Dynamic page generation gives e-commerce several significant capabilities that generate cost and profitability advantages over traditional commerce. Dynamic page generation lowers *menu costs* (the costs incurred by merchants for changing product descriptions and prices). Dynamic page generation also permits easy online *market segmentation*—the ability to sell the same product to different markets. For instance, you might want variations on the same banner ad depending on how many times the customer has seen the ad. In the first exposure to a car ad, you might want to emphasize brand identification and unique features. On the second viewing you might want to emphasize superlatives like "most family friendly" to encourage comparison to other brands. The same capability makes possible nearly cost-free *price discrimination*—the ability to sell the same product to different customers at different prices. For instance, you might want to sell the same product to corporations and government agencies but use different marketing themes. Based on a cookie you place on client computers, or in response to a question on your site that asks visitors if they are from a government agency or a corporation, you would be able to use different marketing and promotional materials for corporate clients and government clients. You might want to reward loyal customers with lower prices, say on DVDs or musical tracks, and charge full price to first-time buyers. Dynamic page generation allows you to approach different customers with different messages and prices.

Dynamic page generation also enables the use of a content management system (CMS). As previously described, a CMS is used to create and manage web content. A CMS separates the design and presentation of content (such as HTML documents, images, video, audio) from the content creation process. The content is maintained in a database and dynamically linked to the website. A CMS usually includes templates that can be automatically applied to new and existing content, WYSIWYG editing tools that make it easy to edit and describe (tag) content, and collaboration, workflow, and document management tools. Typically, an experienced programmer is needed to install the system, but thereafter, content can be created and managed by non-technical staff. There are a wide range of commercial CMSs available, from top-end enterprise systems offered by OpenText, IBM, Adobe, and Oracle, to mid-market systems by Sitecore, PaperThin, and Episerver, as well as hosted software as a service (SaaS) versions by Acquia, Clickability (Upland), and Crownpeak Technology among others. There are also several open source content management systems available, such as WordPress, Joomla, Drupal, OpenCms, and others.

TABLE 3.5	APPLICATION SERVERS AND THEIR FUNCTION
APPLICATION SERVER	FUNCTIONALITY
Catalog display	Provides a database for product descriptions and prices
Transaction processing (shopping cart)	Accepts orders and clears payments
List server	Creates and serves mailing lists and manages e-mail marketing campaigns
Proxy server	Monitors and controls access to main web server; implements firewall protection
Mail server	Manages Internet e-mail
Audio/video server	Stores and delivers streaming media content
Chat server	Creates an environment for online real-time text and audio interactions with customers
News server	Provides connectivity and displays Internet news feeds
Fax server	Provides fax reception and transmission using a web server
Groupware server	Creates workgroup environments for online collaboration
Database server	Stores customer, product, and price information
Ad server	Maintains web-enabled database of advertising banners that permits customized and personalized display of advertisements based on consumer behavior and characteristics
Auction server	Provides a transaction environment for conducting online auctions
B2B server	Implements buy, sell, and link marketplaces for commercial transactions

APPLICATION SERVERS

web application server
software program that provides specific business functionality required of a website

Web application servers are software programs that provide the specific business functionality required of a website. The basic idea of application servers is to isolate the business applications from the details of displaying web pages to users on the front end and the details of connecting to databases on the back end. Application servers are a kind of middleware software that provides the glue connecting traditional corporate systems to the customer as well as all the functionality needed to conduct e-commerce. In the early years, a number of software firms developed specific separate programs for each function, but increasingly, these specific programs are being replaced by integrated software tools that combine all the needed functionality for an e-commerce site into a single development environment, a packaged software approach.

Table 3.5 illustrates the wide variety of application servers available in the marketplace. The table focuses on "sell-side" servers that are designed to enable selling products on the Web. So-called "buy-side" and "link" servers focus on the needs of businesses to connect with partners in their supply chains or find suppliers for specific parts and assemblies. There are several thousand software vendors that provide application server software. For Linux and Unix environments, many of these capabilities are available free on the Internet from various sites. Most businesses—faced with this bewildering array of choices—choose to use integrated software tools called merchant server software.

E-COMMERCE MERCHANT SERVER SOFTWARE FUNCTIONALITY

E-commerce merchant server software provides the basic functionality needed for online sales, including an online catalog, order taking via an online shopping cart, and online credit card processing.

Online Catalog

A company that wants to sell products online must have a list, or **online catalog**, of its products, available on its website. Merchant server software typically includes a database capability that will allow for construction of a customized online catalog. The complexity and sophistication of the catalog will vary depending on the size of the company and its product lines. Small companies, or companies with small product lines, may post a simple list with text descriptions and perhaps color photos. A larger site might decide to add sound, animations, or videos (useful for product demonstrations) to the catalog, or interactivity, such as customer service representatives available via instant messaging to answer questions. Today, larger firms make extensive use of streaming video.

Shopping Cart

Online **shopping carts** are much like their real-world equivalent; both allow shoppers to set aside desired purchases in preparation for checkout. The difference is that the online variety is part of a merchant server software program residing on the web server, and allows consumers to select merchandise, review what they have selected, edit their selections as necessary, and then actually make the purchase by clicking a button. The merchant server software automatically stores shopping cart data.

Credit Card Processing

A site's shopping cart typically works in conjunction with credit card processing software, which verifies the shopper's credit card and then puts through the debit to the card and the credit to the company's account at checkout. Integrated e-commerce software suites typically supply the software for this function. Otherwise, you will have to make arrangements with a variety of credit card processing banks and intermediaries.

MERCHANT SERVER SOFTWARE PACKAGES (E-COMMERCE SOFTWARE PLATFORMS)

Rather than build your site from a collection of disparate software applications, it is easier, faster, and generally more cost-effective to purchase a **merchant server software package** (also called an **e-commerce software platform**). Merchant server software offers an integrated environment that promises to provide most or all of the functionality and capabilities you will need to develop a sophisticated,

e-commerce merchant server software
software that provides the basic functionality needed for online sales, including an online catalog, order taking via an online shopping cart, and online credit card processing

online catalog
list of products available on a website

shopping cart
allows shoppers to set aside desired purchases in preparation for checkout, review what they have selected, edit their selections as necessary, and then actually make the purchase by clicking a button

merchant server software package (e-commerce software platform)
offers an integrated environment that provides most or all of the functionality and capabilities needed to develop a sophisticated, customer-centric site

customer-centric site. An important element of merchant sofware packages is a built-in shopping cart that can display merchandise, manage orders, and clear credit card transactions. E-commerce software platforms come in three general ranges of price and functionality.

While existing firms often have the financial capital to invest in commercial merchant server software, many small firms and startup firms do not. There are really two options here, the key factor being how much programming experience and time you have. One option is to utilize the e-commerce merchant services provided by sites that makes it easy to create an e-commerce website with customizable templates, such as Yahoo Aabaco Small Business, which offers a Basic plan for $29 a month and a 1.5% transaction fee for each transaction processed through the store. An e-commerce template is a predesigned website that allows users to customize the look and feel of the site to fit their business needs and provides a standard set of functionalities. Most templates today contain ready-to-go site designs with built-in e-commerce functionality like shopping carts, payment clearance, and site management tools. The Basic plan also includes a mobile storefront, search engine optimization tools, social media support, and a variety of other marketing tools. Many others, such as Bigcommerce, Homestead, Vendio, and Shopify offer similar services.

open source software
software that is developed by a community of programmers and designers, and is free to use and modify

If you have considerable, or at least some, programming background, you can consider open source merchant server software. **Open source software** is software developed by a community of programmers and designers, and is free to use and modify. **Table 3.6** provides a description of some open source options. The advantage of using open source web building tools is that you get exactly what you want, a truly customized unique website. The disadvantage is that it will take several months for a single programmer to develop the site and get all the tools to work together seamlessly. How many months do you want to wait before you get to market with your ideas?

Midrange e-commerce software platforms include IBM WebSphere Commerce Express Edition and Sitecore Commerce Server (formerly Microsoft Commerce Server). High-end enterprise solutions for large global firms are provided by IBM Websphere Professional and Enterprise Editions, IBM Commerce on Cloud, Oracle ATG Web Commerce, Salesforce Commerce Cloud (formerly Demandware), Magento, NetSuite, and others. Many of these e-commerce software platforms are now available on a Software as a Service (SaaS) basis, a model in which the software is hosted in the cloud and run by the client via a web browser. This model enables a firm to launch an e-commerce site very quickly. For instance, Williams-Sonoma, a housewares retail chain in the United States, used web-hosted e-commerce software from NetSuite to launch an e-commerce site in Australia in only 3 months time (Dusto, 2014). There are several hundred software firms that provide e-commerce software, which raises the costs of making sensible decisions on this matter.

Choosing an E-commerce Software Platform

With all of these vendors, how do you choose the right one? Evaluating these tools and making a choice is one of the most important and uncertain decisions you will make in building an e-commerce site. The real costs are hidden—they involve training

TABLE 3.6	OPEN SOURCE SOFTWARE OPTIONS
FUNCTIONALITY	OPEN SOURCE SOFTWARE
Web server	Apache (the leading web server for small and medium businesses)
Shopping cart, online catalog	Many providers: osCommerce, Zen Cart, AgoraCart, X-cart, AspDotNetStorefront
Credit card processing	Credit card acceptance is typically provided in shopping cart software but you may need a merchant account from a bank as well.
Database	MySQL (the leading open source SQL database for businesses)
Programming/scripting language	PHP is a scripting language embedded in HTML documents but executed by the server, providing server-side execution with the simplicity of HTML editing. Perl is an alternative language. JavaScript programs are client-side programs that provide user interface components. Ruby on Rails (RoR, Rails) and Django are other popular open source web application frameworks.
Analytics	Analytics keep track of your site's customer activities and the success of your web advertising campaign. You can also use Google Analytics if you advertise on Google, which provides good tracking tools; most hosting services will provide these services as well. Other open source analytic tools include Piwik, CrawlTrack, and Open Web Analytics.

your staff to use the tools and integrating the tools into your business processes and organizational culture. The following are some of the key factors to consider:

- Functionality, including availability on an SaaS basis
- Support for different business models, including m-commerce
- Business process modeling tools
- Visual site management tools and reporting
- Performance and scalability
- Connectivity to existing business systems
- Compliance with standards
- Global and multicultural capability
- Local sales tax and shipping rules

For instance, although e-commerce software platforms promise to do everything, your business may require special functionality—such as streaming audio and video. You will need a list of business functionality requirements. Your business may involve several different business models—such as a retail side and a business-to-business side; you may run auctions for stock excess as well as fixed-price selling.

Be sure the package can support all of your business models. You may wish to change your business processes, such as order taking and order fulfillment. Does the platform contain tools for modeling business process and work flows? Understanding how your site works will require visual reporting tools that make its operation transparent to many different people in your business. A poorly designed software package will drop off significantly in performance as visitors and transactions expand into the thousands per hour, or minute. Check for performance and scalability by stress-testing a pilot edition or obtaining data from the vendor about performance under load. You will have to connect the e-commerce platform to your traditional business systems. How will this connection to existing systems be made, and is your staff skilled in making the connection? Because of the changing technical environment—in particular, changes in m-commerce platforms—it is important to document exactly what standards the platform supports now, and what the migration path will be toward the future. Finally, your e-commerce site may have to work both globally and locally. You may need a foreign language edition using foreign currency denominations. And you will have to collect sales taxes across many local, regional, and national tax systems. Does the e-commerce platform support this level of globalization and localization?

3.4   CHOOSING HARDWARE

hardware platform

refers to all the underlying computing equipment that the system uses to achieve its e-commerce functionality

Whether you host your own site or outsource the hosting and operation of your site, you will need to understand certain aspects of the computing hardware platform. The **hardware platform** refers to all the underlying computing equipment that the system uses to achieve its e-commerce functionality. Your objective is to have enough platform capacity to meet peak demand (avoiding an overload condition), but not so much platform that you are wasting money. Failing to meet peak demand can mean your site is slow, or actually crashes. How much computing and telecommunications capacity is enough to meet peak demand? How many hits per day can your site sustain?

To answer these questions, you will need to understand the various factors that affect the speed, capacity, and scalability of an e-commerce site.

RIGHT-SIZING YOUR HARDWARE PLATFORM: THE DEMAND SIDE

The most important factor affecting the speed of your site is the demand that customers put on the site. **Table 3.7** lists the most important factors to consider when estimating the demand on a site.

Demand on a website is fairly complex and depends primarily on the type of site you are operating. The number of simultaneous users in peak periods, the nature of customer requests, the type of content, the required security, the number of items in inventory, the number of page requests, and the speed of legacy applications that may be needed to supply data to the web pages are all important factors in overall demand on a website system.

TABLE 3.7	**FACTORS IN RIGHT-SIZING AN E-COMMERCE PLATFORM**				
SITE TYPE	PUBLISH/ SUBSCRIBE	SHOPPING	CUSTOMER SELF-SERVICE	TRADING	WEB SERVICES/ B2B
Examples	WSJ.com	Amazon	Travelocity	E*Trade	Ariba e-procurement exchanges
Content	Dynamic Multiple authors High volume Not user-specific	Catalog Dynamic items User profiles with data mining	Data in legacy applications Multiple data sources	Time sensitive High volatility Multiple suppliers and consumers Complex transactions	Data in legacy applications Multiple data sources Complex transactions
Security	Low	Privacy Nonrepudiation Integrity Authentication Regulations	Privacy Nonrepudiation Integrity Authentication Regulations	Privacy Nonrepudiation Integrity Authentication Regulations	Privacy Nonrepudiation Integrity Authentication Regulations
Percent secure pages	Low	Medium	Medium	High	Medium
Cross session information	No	High	High	High	High
Searches	Dynamic Low volume	Dynamic High volume	Nondynamic Low volume	Nondynamic Low volume	Nondynamic Moderate volume
Unique items (SKUs)	High	Medium to high	Medium	High	Medium to high
Transaction volume	Moderate	Moderate to high	Moderate	High to extremely high	Moderate
Legacy integration complexity	Low	Medium	High	High	High
Page views (hits)	High to very high	Moderate to high	Moderate to low	Moderate to high	Moderate

Certainly, one important factor to consider is the number of simultaneous users who will likely visit your site. In general, the load created by an individual customer on a server is typically quite limited and short-lived. A web session initiated by the typical user is **stateless**, meaning that the server does not have to maintain an ongoing, dedicated interaction with the client. A web session typically begins with a page request, then a server replies, and the session is ended. The sessions may last from tenths of a second to a minute per user. Nevertheless, system performance does degrade as more and more simultaneous users request service. Fortunately, degradation (measured as "transactions per second" and "latency" or delay in response) is

stateless
refers to the fact that the server does not have to maintain an ongoing, dedicated interaction with the client

fairly graceful over a wide range, up until a peak load is reached and service quality becomes unacceptable (see **Figure 3.13**).

I/O intensive
requires input/output operations rather than heavy-duty processing power

Serving up static web pages is **I/O intensive**, which means it requires input/output (I/O) operations rather than heavy-duty processing power. As a result, website performance is constrained primarily by the server's I/O limitations and the telecommunications connection, rather than the speed of the processor.

Other factors to consider when estimating the demand on a website are the user profile and the nature of the content. If users request searches, registration forms, and order taking via shopping carts, then demands on processors will increase markedly.

RIGHT-SIZING YOUR HARDWARE PLATFORM: THE SUPPLY SIDE

scalability
the ability of a site to increase in size as demand warrants

vertical scaling
increasing the processing power of individual components

horizontal scaling
employing multiple computers to share the workload

Once you estimate the likely demand on your site, you will need to consider how to scale up your site to meet demand. We have already discussed one solution that requires very little thought: outsource the hosting of your website to a cloud-based service. You can also engage the services of a content delivery network (CDN) such as Akamai. See Chapter 2 for a discussion of cloud-based computing services and a case study on Akamai. However, if you decide to host your own website, scalability is an important consideration. **Scalability** refers to the ability of a site to increase in size as demand warrants. There are three steps you can take to meet the demands for service at your site: scale hardware vertically, scale hardware horizontally, and/or improve the processing architecture of the site (see **Table 3.8**). **Vertical scaling** refers to increasing the processing power of individual components. **Horizontal scaling** refers to employing multiple computers to share the workload and increase the "footprint" of the installation (IBM, 2002).

You can scale your site vertically by upgrading the servers from a single processor to multiple processors. You can keep adding processors to a computer depending on the operating system and upgrade to faster chip speeds as well.

TABLE 3.8	VERTICAL AND HORIZONTAL SCALING TECHNIQUES
TECHNIQUE	APPLICATION
Use a faster computer	Deploy edge servers, presentation servers, data servers, etc.
Create a cluster of computers	Use computers in parallel to balance loads.
Use appliance servers	Use special-purpose computers optimized for their task.
Segment workload	Segment incoming work to specialized computers.
Batch requests	Combine related requests for data into groups, process as group.
Manage connections	Reduce connections between processes and computers to a minimum.
Aggregate user data	Aggregate user data from legacy applications in single data pools.
Cache	Store frequently used data in cache rather than on the disk.

FIGURE 3.13 **DEGRADATION IN PERFORMANCE AS NUMBER OF USERS INCREASES**

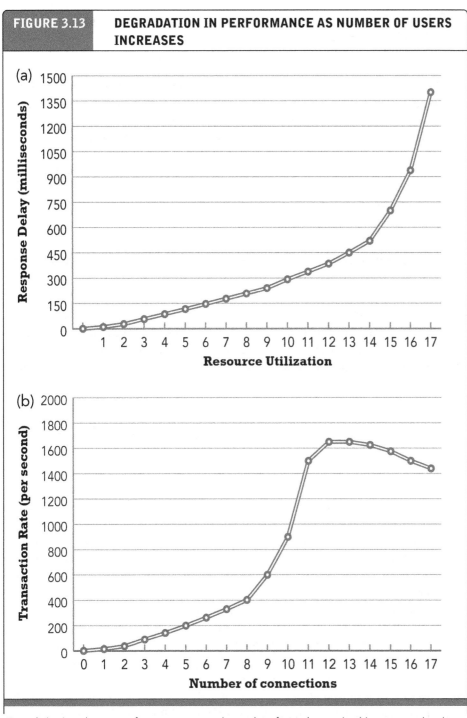

Degradation in web server performance occurs as the number of users (connections) increases, and as the system's resources (processors, disk drives) become more utilized. In (a), user-experienced delay rises gracefully until an inflection point is reached, and then delay rises exponentially to an unacceptable level. In (b), the transaction rate rises gracefully until the number of users rapidly escalates the transaction rate, and at a certain inflection point, the transaction rate starts declining as the system slows down or crashes.

TABLE 3.9	IMPROVING THE PROCESSING ARCHITECTURE OF YOUR SITE
ARCHITECTURE IMPROVEMENT	DESCRIPTION
Separate static content from dynamic content	Use specialized servers for each type of workload.
Cache static content	Increase RAM to the gigabyte range and store static content in RAM.
Cache database lookup tables	Use cache tables used to look up database records.
Consolidate business logic on dedicated servers	Put shopping cart, credit card processing, and other CPU-intensive activity on dedicated servers.
Optimize ASP code	Examine your code to ensure it is operating efficiently.
Optimize the database schema	Examine your database search times and take steps to reduce access times.

There are two drawbacks to vertical scaling. First, it can become expensive to purchase additional processors with every growth cycle, and second, your entire site becomes dependent on a small number of very powerful computers. If you have two such computers and one goes down, half of your site, or perhaps your entire site, may become unavailable.

Horizontal scaling involves adding multiple single-processor servers to your site and balancing the load among the servers. You can then partition the load so some servers handle only requests for HTML or ASP pages, while others are dedicated to handling database applications. You will need special load-balancing software (provided by a variety of vendors such as Cisco, Microsoft, and IBM) to direct incoming requests to various servers.

There are many advantages to horizontal scaling. It is inexpensive and often can be accomplished using older PCs that otherwise would be disposed of. Horizontal scaling also introduces redundancy—if one computer fails, chances are that another computer can pick up the load dynamically. However, when your site grows from a single computer to perhaps 10 to 20 computers, the size of the physical facility required (the "footprint") increases and there is added management complexity.

A third alternative—improving the processing architecture—is a combination of vertical and horizontal scaling, combined with artful design decisions. **Table 3.9** lists some of the more common steps you can take to greatly improve performance of your site. Most of these steps involve splitting the workload into I/O-intensive activities (such as serving web pages) and CPU-intensive activities (such as taking orders). Once you have this work separated, you can fine-tune the servers for each type of load. One of the least expensive fine-tuning steps is to simply add RAM to a few servers and store all your HTML pages in RAM. This reduces load on your hard drives and increases speed dramatically. RAM is thousands of times faster than hard disks, and RAM is inexpensive. The next most important step is to move your CPU-intensive activities, such as order taking, onto a high-end, multiple-processor server that is dedicated to handling orders and accessing the necessary databases. Taking these steps can permit you to reduce the number of servers required to service 10,000 concurrent users from 100 down to 20, according to one estimate.

3.5 OTHER E-COMMERCE SITE TOOLS

Now that you understand the key factors affecting the speed, capacity, and scalability of your website, we can consider some other important requirements. You will need a coherent website design that makes business sense—not necessarily a site to wow visitors or excite them, but to sell them something. You will also need to know how to build active content and interactivity into your site—not just display static HTML pages. You must be able to track customers who come, leave, and return to your site in order to be able to greet return visitors ("Hi Sarah, welcome back!"). You will also want to track customers throughout your site so you can personalize and customize their experience. You will definitely want the ability for customers to generate content and feedback on your site to increase their engagement with your brand. Finally, you will need to establish a set of information policies for your site—privacy, accessibility, and access to information policies.

In order to achieve these business capabilities, you will need to be aware of some design guidelines and additional software tools that can cost-effectively achieve the required business functionality.

WEBSITE DESIGN: BASIC BUSINESS CONSIDERATIONS

This is not a text about how to design websites. (In Chapter 6, we discuss website design issues from a marketing perspective.) Nevertheless, from a business manager's perspective, there are certain design objectives you must communicate to your website designers to let them know how you will evaluate their work. At a minimum, your customers will need to find what they need at your site, make a purchase, and leave. A website that annoys customers runs the risk of losing the customer forever. See **Table 3.10** for a list of the most common consumer complaints about websites.

TABLE 3.10	E-COMMERCE WEBSITE FEATURES THAT ANNOY CUSTOMERS
• Requiring user to view ad or intro page before going to website content • Pop-up and pop-under ads and windows • Too many clicks to get to the content • Links that don't work • Confusing navigation; no search function • Requirement to register and log in before viewing content or ordering • Slow loading pages • Content that is out of date	• Inability to use browser's Back button • No contact information available (web form only) • Unnecessary splash/flash screens, animation, etc. • Music or other audio that plays automatically • Unprofessional design elements • Text not easily legible due to size, color, format • Typographical errors • No or unclear returns policy

TABLE 3.11	THE EIGHT MOST IMPORTANT FACTORS IN SUCCESSFUL E-COMMERCE SITE DESIGN
FACTOR	DESCRIPTION
Functionality	Pages that work, load quickly, and point the customer toward your product offerings
Informational	Links that customers can easily find to discover more about you and your products
Ease of use	Simple foolproof navigation
Redundant navigation	Alternative navigation to the same content
Ease of purchase	One or two clicks to purchase
Multi-browser functionality	Site works with the most popular browsers
Simple graphics	Avoids distracting, obnoxious graphics and sounds that the user cannot control
Legible text	Avoids backgrounds that distort text or make it illegible

Some critics believe poor design is more common than good design. It appears easier to describe what irritates people about websites than to describe how to design a good website. The worst e-commerce sites make it difficult to find information about their products and make it complicated to purchase goods; they have missing pages and broken links, a confusing navigation structure, and annoying graphics or sounds that you cannot turn off. **Table 3.11** restates these negative experiences as positive goals for website design.

TOOLS FOR SEARCH ENGINE OPTIMIZATION

A website is only as valuable from a business perspective as the number of people who visit. The first stop for most customers looking for a product or service is to start with a search engine, and follow the listings on the page, usually starting with the top three to five listings, then glancing to the sponsored ads to the right. The higher you are on the search engine pages, the more traffic you will receive. Page 1 is much better than Page 2. So how do you get to Page 1 in the natural (unpaid) search listings? While every search engine is different, and none of them publish their algorithms for ranking pages, there are some basic ideas that work well:

- **Metatags, titles, page contents:** Search engines "crawl" your site and identify keywords as well as title pages and then index them for use in search arguments. Pepper your pages with keywords that accurately describe what you say you do in your metatag site "description" and "keywords" sections of your source code. Experiment: use different keywords to see which work. "Vintage cars" may attract more visitors than "antique cars" or "restored cars."

- **Identify market niches:** Instead of marketing "jewelry," be more specific, such as "Victorian jewelry," or "1950s jewelry" to attract small, specific groups who are intensely interested in period jewelry and closer to purchasing.

- **Offer expertise:** White papers, industry analyses, FAQ pages, guides, and histories are excellent ways to build confidence on the part of users and to encourage them to see your website as the place to go for help and guidance.

- **Get linked up:** Encourage other sites to link to your site; build a blog that attracts people and who will share your URL with others and post links in the process. Build a Facebook page for your company, and think about using Instagram or Pinterest to develop a following or fan base for your products.

- **Buy ads:** Complement your natural search optimization efforts with paid search engine keywords and ads. Choose your keywords and purchase direct exposure on web pages. You can set your budget and put a ceiling on it to prevent large losses. See what works, and observe the number of visits to your site produced by each keyword string.

- **Local e-commerce:** Developing a national market can take a long time. If your website is particularly attractive to local people, or involves products sold locally, use keywords that connote your location so people can find you nearby. Town, city, and region names in your keywords can be helpful, such as "Vermont cheese" or "San Francisco blues music."

TOOLS FOR INTERACTIVITY AND ACTIVE CONTENT

The more interactive a website is, the more effective it will be in generating sales and encouraging return visitors. Although functionality and ease of use are the supreme objectives in site design, you will also want to interact with users and present them with a lively, "active" experience. You will want to personalize the experience for customers by addressing their individual needs, and customize the content of your offerings based on their behavior or expressed desires. In order to achieve these business objectives, you will need to consider carefully the tools necessary to build these capabilities. Simple interactions such as a customer submitting a name, along with more complex interactions involving credit cards, user preferences, and user responses to prompts, all require special programs. The following sections provide a brief description of some commonly used software tools for achieving high levels of site interactivity.

Common Gateway Interface (CGI)

Common Gateway Interface (CGI) is a set of standards for communication between a browser and a program running on a server that allows for interaction between the user and the server. CGI permits an executable program to access all the information within incoming requests from clients. The program can then generate all the output required to make up the return page (the HTML, script code, text, etc.), and send it back to the client via the web server. For instance, if a user clicks the My Shopping Cart button, the server receives this request and executes a CGI program. The CGI program retrieves the contents of the shopping cart from the database and returns it to the server. The server sends an HTML page that displays the contents of the shopping cart on the user's screen. Notice that all the computing takes place on the server

Common Gateway Interface (CGI)
a set of standards for communication between a browser and a program running on a server that allows for interaction between the user and the server

side (this is why CGI programs and others like it are referred to as "server-side" programs).

CGI programs can be written in nearly any programming language as long as they conform to CGI standards. Currently, Perl is one of the most popular languages for CGI scripting. Generally, CGI programs are used with Unix servers. CGI's primary disadvantage is that it is not highly scalable because a new process must be created for each request, thereby limiting the number of concurrent requests that can be handled. CGI scripts are best used for small to medium-sized applications that do not involve a high volume of user traffic. There are also web server extensions available, such as FastCGI, that improve CGI's scalability and SCGI, which is a simpler version of FastCGI (Doyle and Lopes, 2005).

CGI scripts also face security issues. In 2014, a major security hole in the command-line shell used by many Linux and Unix operating systems was discovered. Nicknamed Shellshock, the hole allowed hackers to target vulnerable CGI scripts on Apache web servers. These types of security issues have resulted in some web hosting services, such as Rackspace, requiring their customers to use alternatives to CGI.

Active Server Pages (ASP) and ASP.NET

Active Server Pages (ASP)
a proprietary software development tool that enables programmers using Microsoft's IIS package to build dynamic pages

Active Server Pages (ASP) is Microsoft's original version of server-side programming for Windows. Invented by Microsoft in late 1996, ASP grew rapidly to become the major technique for server-side web programming in the Windows environment. ASP enables developers to easily create and open records from a database and execute programs within an HTML page, as well as handle all the various forms of interactivity found on e-commerce sites. Like CGI, ASP permits an interaction to take place between the browser and the server. ASP uses the same standards as CGI for communication with the browser. ASP programs are restricted to use on Windows servers running Microsoft's IIS web server software. **ASP.NET**, first released in January 2002, and part of Microsoft's .NET framework, is the successor to ASP. As of September 2015, ASP.NET 4.6 is the most current version of ASP.NET. ASP.NET 5, a major rewrite aimed at providing an improved, modern, cross-platform web framework for cloud and regular application servers, is also under development.

ASP.NET
successor to ASP

Java, Java Server Pages (JSP), and JavaScript

Java
a programming language that allows programmers to create interactivity and active content on the client computer, thereby saving considerable load on the server

Java is a programming language that allows programmers to create interactivity and active content on the client computer, thereby saving considerable load on the server. Java was initially developed by Sun Microsystems as a platform-independent programming language for consumer electronics. The idea was to create a language whose programs (so-called Write Once Run Anywhere [WORA] programs) could operate on any computer regardless of operating system. This would be possible if every operating system at the time (Macintosh, Windows, Unix, DOS, and mainframe MVS systems) had a Java Virtual Machine (VM) installed that would interpret the Java programs for that environment.

By 1995, however, when Sun Microsystems released Java 1.0, the first public version of the language, it had become clear that Java was more applicable to the Web than to consumer electronics. Java programs (known as Java applets) could be downloaded to the client over the Web and executed entirely on the client's computer. Applet tags could be included in an HTML page. To enable this, each browser would have to include a Java VM. Today, the leading browsers include a VM to run Java programs and according to Oracle, which inherited oversight over Java when it acquired Sun Microsystems, Java is used on 97% of enterprise desktop computers. When the browser accesses a page with an applet, a request is sent to the server to download and execute the program and allocate page space to display the results of the program. Java can be used to display interesting graphics, create interactive environments (such as a mortgage calculator), and directly access the web server. JDK (Java Development Kit) 8 and the Java SE 8 Runtime Environment (for running Java applications) were released in 2014, and Java 9, which reportedly will focus on modularization of the platform, is expected to be released in 2016. Today, Java remains one of the most popular programming languages, with many critical technologies, such as the Google Android mobile platform (although not Apple's iOS), leveraging aspects of the language. However, Java does face some challenges. In recent years, it has been plagued by security flaws, which Oracle has been attempting to address with the frequent release of new versions and security patches (Krill, 2015).

Java Server Pages (JSP), like CGI and ASP, is a web page coding standard that allows developers to use a combination of HTML, JSP scripts, and Java to dynamically generate web pages in response to user requests. JSP uses Java "servlets," small Java programs that are specified in the web page and run on the web server to modify the web page before it is sent to the user who requested it. JSP is supported by most of the popular application servers on the market today.

JavaScript is a programming language invented by Netscape that is used to control the objects on an HTML page and handle interactions with the browser. It is most commonly used on the client side to handle verification and validation of user input, as well as to implement business logic. For instance, JavaScript can be used on customer registration forms to confirm that a valid phone number, zip code, or even e-mail address has been given. Before a user finishes completing a form, the e-mail address given can be tested for validity. JavaScript appears to be much more acceptable to corporations and other environments in large part because it is more stable and also it is restricted to the operation of requested HTML pages. JavaScript is also used as part of Node.js, a cross-platform environment for server-side applications (including mobile), which has been used by companies such as PayPal, Walmart, and LinkedIn. In 2015, Node.js v4.0 was released, combining Node.js and io.js, a variant of the JavaScript platform built on V8, the JavaScript virtual machine used in Google Chrome, into a single codebase for the first time. *Ajax (asynchronous JavaScript and XML)* uses a variety of different tools, including JavaScript, to allow web pages to be updated asynchronously (i.e., updating only parts of the page rather than having to reload the entire page to change just part of the content).

ActiveX and VBScript

Microsoft invented the **ActiveX** programming language to compete with Java and **VBScript** to compete with JavaScript. When a browser receives an HTML page with an ActiveX control (comparable to a Java applet), the browser simply executes the

Java Server Pages (JSP)
like CGI and ASP, a web page coding standard that allows developers to dynamically generate web pages in response to user requests

JavaScript
a programming language invented by Netscape that is used to control the objects on an HTML page and handle interactions with the browser

ActiveX
a programming language created by Microsoft to compete with Java

VBScript
a programming language invented by Microsoft to compete with JavaScript

program. Unlike Java, however, ActiveX has full access to all the client's resources—printers, networks, and hard drives. VBScript performs in the same way as JavaScript. ActiveX and VBScript work only if you are using Internet Explorer. Otherwise, that part of the screen is blank. However, the days of ActiveX and VBScript are numbered. Microsoft has dropped support for both in Microsoft Edge, the browser that has replaced Internet Explorer in the Windows 10 operating system. Microsoft believes that the need for ActiveX and VBScript has been significantly reduced given the capabilities of HTML5, and that eliminating them will enhance browser security.

ColdFusion

ColdFusion

an integrated server-side environment for developing interactive web applications

ColdFusion is an integrated server-side environment for developing interactive web and mobile applications. Originally developed by Macromedia and now offered by Adobe, ColdFusion combines an intuitive tag-based scripting language and a tag-based server scripting language (CFML) that lowers the cost of creating interactive features. ColdFusion offers a powerful set of visual design, programming, debugging, and deployment tools. The most recent version of ColdFusion, released in 2016, provides enhanced ability to create mobile apps, as well as a number of new security features and programming language enhancements, as well as increased support for interoperability.

PHP, Ruby on Rails (RoR), and Django

PHP

open source, general purpose scripting language

PHP is an open source, general purpose scripting language that is most frequently used in server-side web applications to generate dynamic web page content, although it can also be used for client-side graphical user interface applications. PHP is also a part of many web application development frameworks, such as CakePHP, CodeIgniter, and others, and is also part of the LAMP (Linux, Apache, MySQL, PHP) open source web development model for building dynamic websites and web applications (Perl and Python are sometimes substituted for PHP in some LAMP projects). According to W3Techs, PHP is, by far and away, the most commonly used server-side scripting language (used by over 80% of the websites whose server-side programming language it was able to identify), with ASP.NET a distant second, used by around 16%, followed by Java, with 3%. ColdFusion, Ruby on Rails, Perl, JavaScript, and Python were all less than 1% (W3techs.com, 2016). PHP is also popular with hackers; according to Netcraft, nearly all phishing kits are written in PHP (Mutton, 2015).

Ruby on Rails (RoR/Rails)

open source web application framework based on Ruby programming language

Ruby on Rails (RoR or Rails) is an open source web application framework based on the Ruby programming language. RoR is based on a philosophy known as convention over configuration, or coding by convention (CoC), which means that the framework provides a structured layout that minimizes the number of decisions that the programmer needs to make, thereby simplifying and speeding development. JavaScript and Ajax are highly integrated into RoR, which makes it easy to handle Ajax requests for page updates. Some well-known websites based on RoR include Shopify, Groupon, Indiegogo, and Airbnb (Hegde, 2015).

Django is also an open source web application framework. It is based on the Python programming language. Django is optimized for the creation of complex, database-driven websites. It allows for fast development, focuses on automating as much as possible, emphasizes the reusability of various components, and follows the DRY (Don't Repeat Yourself) programming principle. Some well-known websites based on Django include Instagram, Pinterest, and the satirical news site, The Onion (Pinkham, 2015).

Django
open source web application framework based on Python programming language

Other Design Elements

One easy way to pump up the energy on your website is to include some appropriate widgets (sometimes called gadgets, plug-ins, or snippets). **Widgets** are small chunks of code that execute automatically in your HTML web page. They are prebuilt and many are free. Social networks and blogs use widgets to present users with content drawn from around the Web (news headlines from specific news sources, announcements, press releases, and other routine content), calendars, clocks, weather, live TV, games, and other functionality. You can copy the code to an HTML web page. You can find widgets at Apple's Dashboard Widgets, Wolfram|Alpha Widgets, and SIMILE Widgets. There are also widgets for specific platforms such as WordPress, Amazon Widgets, and Pinterest's Widget Builder.

widget
a small, prebuilt chunk of code that executes automatically in your HTML web page; capable of performing a wide variety of tasks

Mashups are a little more complicated and involve pulling functionality and data from one program and including it in another. The most common mashup involves using Google Maps data and software and combining it with other data. For instance, if you have a local real estate website, you can download Google Maps and satellite image applications to your site so visitors can get a sense of the neighborhood. There are thousands of Google Map mashups, from maps of Myanmar political protests, to maps of the Fortune 500 companies, all with associated news stories and other content. Other mashups involve sports, photos, video, shopping, and news.

PERSONALIZATION TOOLS

You will definitely want to know how to treat each customer on an individual basis and emulate a traditional face-to-face marketplace. *Personalization* (the ability to treat people based on their personal qualities and prior history with your site) and *customization* (the ability to change the product to better fit the needs of the customer) are two key elements of e-commerce that potentially can make it nearly as powerful as a traditional marketplace, and perhaps even more powerful than direct mail or shopping at an anonymous suburban shopping mall. Speaking directly to the customer on a one-to-one basis, and even adjusting the product to the customer is quite difficult in the usual type of mass marketing, one-size-fits-all commercial transaction that characterizes much of contemporary commerce.

There are a number of methods for achieving personalization and customization. For instance, you could personalize web content if you knew the personal background of the visitor. You could also analyze the pattern of clicks and sites visited for every customer who enters your site. We discuss these methods in later chapters on marketing.

The primary method for achieving personalization and customization is through the placement of cookie files on the user's client computer. A cookie is a small text file placed on the user's client computer that can contain any kind of information about the customer, such as customer ID, campaign ID, or purchases at the site. And then, when the user returns to the site, or indeed goes further into your site, the customer's prior history can be accessed from a database. Information gathered on prior visits can then be used to personalize the visit and customize the product.

For instance, when a user returns to a site, you can read the cookie to find a customer ID, look the ID up in a database of names, and greet the customer ("Hello Mary! Glad to have you return!"). You could also have stored a record of prior purchases, and then recommend a related product ("How about the wrench tool box now that you have purchased the wrenches?"). And you could think about customizing the product ("You've shown an interest in the elementary training programs for Word. We have a special 'How to Study' program for beginners in Office software. Would you like to see a sample copy online?").

We further describe the use of cookies in Chapter 6.

THE INFORMATION POLICY SET

In developing an e-commerce site, you will also need to focus on the set of information policies that will govern the site. You will need to develop a **privacy policy**—a set of public statements declaring to your customers how you treat their personal information that you gather on the site. You also will need to establish **accessibility rules**—a set of design objectives that ensure disabled users can effectively access your site. There are more than 650 million people worldwide who are disabled, many of whom may require special help in order to be able to access computer systems (see *Insight on Society: Designing for Accessibility*). E-commerce information policies are described in greater depth in Chapter 8.

3.6	**DEVELOPING A MOBILE WEBSITE AND BUILDING MOBILE APPLICATIONS**

Today, building a website is just one part of developing an e-commerce presence. Given that almost 2.5 billion people worldwide (over 75% of all Internet users) access the Web at least part of the time from mobile devices, businesses today need to develop mobile websites, and mobile web apps, native apps, or hybrid apps, in order to interact with customers, suppliers, and employees. Deciding which of these extended web presence tools to use is a first step.

There are different kinds of m-commerce platform offerings to consider, each with unique advantages and costs. A **mobile website** is a version of a regular website that is scaled down in content and navigation so that users can find what they want and move quickly to a decision or purchase. You can see the difference between a regular website and a mobile site by visiting the Amazon website from your desktop computer and then a smartphone or tablet computer. Amazon's mobile site is a cleaner, more

privacy policy
a set of public statements declaring to your customers how you treat their personal information that you gather on the site

accessibility rules
a set of design objectives that ensure disabled users can effectively access your site

mobile website
version of a regular desktop website that is scaled down in content and navigation

INSIGHT ON SOCIETY

DESIGNING FOR ACCESSIBILITY

About 10% of the population worldwide has a disability that affects their ability to use the Internet. There are approximately 360 million people worldwide with hearing loss and 285 million with significant vision loss. These and other disabilities, such as motor and mobility impairments, can often be addressed with intelligent software and hardware design. But, for the most part, this has not yet occurred. As a result, the Internet and mobile devices are unfriendly places for many disabled.

So how should designers build in accessibility for the blind? One tool is screen-reader software. A blind person navigates a web page by checking the hypertext links on the page, usually by jumping from link to link with the Tab key; the screen-reader software automatically reads the highlighted text as the focus moves from link to link. The screen-reader software is looking for ASCII text, which it can convert to speech or Braille. Examples of such software include Freedom Scientific's Job Access with Speech (JAWS) and MacForTheBlind's VoiceOver.

There are also several simple strategies web designers can use to improve accessibility. Embedding text descriptions behind images is one example that allows screen readers to announce those descriptions. Allowing users to set the color and font schemes also can make a difference for the visually impaired. Adding screen magnification tools and sound labels where hyperlinks appear are two additional ways to increase accessibility. For those who are hearing impaired, access to close-captioned video with subtitles, as mandated by the United States' 21st Century Communications and Video Accessibility Act, can also be helpful.

These are examples of "equivalent alternatives" that disability advocates suggest should be required for both visual and auditory content to ensure that individuals with disabilities have equal access to information that appears on-screen. Guidelines for creating accessible web pages include ensuring that text and graphics are understandable when viewed without color, using features that enable activation of page elements via a variety of input devices (such as keyboard, head wand, and Braille reader), and providing clear navigation mechanisms (such as navigation bars or a site map) to aid users.

The World Wide Web Consortium (W3C) issued Web Content Accessibility Guidelines (WCAG) 2.0 in June 2010 (final draft form) that provide all organizations with strategies in web design for accommodating people with many different kinds of disabilities.

Ensuring accessibility of mobile devices has its own set of issues, in many instances ones that are even more challenging than those associated with the Web. There is only a limited selection of mobile devices with built-in accessibility features. The small size of the device, screen, and keypad presents its own problems. Third-party applications, such as text-to-speech/screen readers and screen magnifiers, are starting to become available, but much work still needs to be done. For instance, many mobile devices come equipped with voice control capabilities and audio alerts, which could be helpful to those with vision or motor difficulties, but in most cases, these are still limited to simple tasks, and do not provide access to the full functionality of the device. In addition, the deaf community cannot rely on audio content or alerts, so developers need to provide text or other alternatives for auditory information. Those with impaired motor functionality also face great challenges in dealing with input to mobile devices. To deal with these challenges, the WC3 recommends that mobile content developers follow WCAG 2.0 and its guidelines on best practices.

Web accessibility is not just a concern for web developers or a question of technical web standards, but is also a matter of government policy. Article 9 of the United Nations' *Convention on the Rights of Persons with Disabilities* requires that appropriate measures must be taken to ensure access to information and communications technologies for persons with disabilities on an equal basis with others as a matter of basic human rights. All member states of the EU have signed the Convention and over 130 have ratified it. Despite this, actual accessibility of both government and private websites remains quite low. For instance, a recent European Commission report on monitoring accessibility found that only one-third of the content generated by public authorities was accessible. In December 2015, the European Commission proposed a European Accessibility Act, which will set accessibility requirements for certain products and services, including computers and operating systems, banking services, smartphones, digital television services, transportation services, e-books, and e-commerce. The requirements set forth what features must be accessible, such as a user interface, but do not mandate specific technical solutions. In February 2016, the European Parliament appointed a Rapporteur on the proposal and in November 2016, the European Council issued a progress report, noting that Council preparatory bodies would continue working toward developing a Council position with the goal of starting negotiations with the European Parliament, which is expected to formulate its position during early 2017.

Various countries have also implemented accessibility legislation. In many cases, standards apply only to government agency websites and not private websites. For example, French law requires all French public websites to comply with its standard, RGAA 2.2.1, which is based on WCAG2. In Germany, all government websites must comply with BITV 2 (also based on WCAG 2). One exception is Australia, which requires non-government as well as government websites to comply with WCAG 2. In the United Kingdom, service providers must make reasonable adjustments to ensure that their websites are accessible to all users. In determining what is reasonable, the Statutory Code of Practice indicates that factors to be taken into account include the service provider's financial and other resources, the amount of resources already spent on making adjustments, and the extent of any disruption that it would cause the service provider. Large companies will clearly have a more difficult time justifying any failure to make their websites accessible. In the United States, several statutes, including the Rehabilitation Act (Section 508), the Americans with Disabilities Act (the ADA), and the 21st Century Communications and Video Accessibility Act, impose various obligations with respect to accessibility.

Disability advocates are also using lawsuits as a way to get the ball rolling. In 2012, the Royal National Institute of the Blind (RNIB) brought a court case against BMI Baby, a British travel agency. BMI Baby ultimately agreed to make changes to its website to enable the blind to book flights. Other, similar cases have been settled out of court. Despite these successes, however, much remains to be done to make websites, mobile sites, and apps fully accessible to the disabled.

SOURCES: "European Accessibility Act/After 2015-12," Europarl.europa.eu, accessed January 16, 2017; "EU Ready to Set Laws for Accessibility Testing," Qa-financial.com, December 9, 2016; "Proposal for a Directive of the European Parliament and of the Council on the Approximation of the Laws, Regulations, and Administrative Proposals of the Member States as Regards the Accessibility Requirements for Products and Services—Progress Report," Council of the European Union, November 18, 2016; "Commission Proposes to Make Products and Services More Accessible," European Commission, December 2, 2015; "Digital Agenda for Europe: A Europe 2020 Initiative/Web Accessibility," European Commission, accessed December 1, 2014; "Tough New EU Public Sector Web Accessibility Rules Take Shape," by Dan Jellinek, UKAuthority.com, March 4, 2014; "Disabled Consumers' Ownership of Communications Services," Ofcom, September 25, 2013; "Digital Britain 2: Putting Users at the Heart of Government's Digital Services," National Audit Office, March 28, 2013; "Government Accessiblity Standards and WCAG 2.0," by Mark Rodgers, Powermapper.com, November 13, 2012; "Mobile Web Accessibility," by Tim Shelton, Accessibletech.com, July 2011; "People with Disabilities Face Digital Divide," by Michael Collins, Diversitybestpractices.com, January 26, 2011; "W3C Web Accessibility Initiative [Final Draft]," WC3.org, June 2010; "Web Accessibility: Making Your Site Accessible to the Blind," by Curtis Chong, National Federation of the Blind, accessed August 14, 2009.

interactive site suitable for finger navigation and efficient consumer decision making. Like traditional websites, mobile websites run on a firm's servers and are built using standard web tools such as server-side HTML, Linux, PHP, and SQL. Like all websites, the user must be connected to the Web and performance will depend on bandwidth. Generally, mobile websites operate more slowly than traditional websites viewed on a desktop computer connected to a broadband office network. Most large firms today have mobile websites.

A **mobile web app** is an application built to run on the mobile web browser built into a smartphone or tablet computer. In the case of Apple, the native browser is Safari. Generally it is built to mimic the qualities of a native app using HTML5 and Java. Mobile web apps are specifically designed for the mobile platform in terms of screen size, finger navigation, and graphical simplicity. Mobile web apps can support complex interactions used in games and rich media, perform real-time, on-the-fly calculations, and can be geo-sensitive using the smartphone's built-in global positioning system (GPS) function. Mobile web apps typically operate faster than mobile websites but not as fast as native apps.

mobile web app
application built to run on the mobile web browser built into a smartphone or tablet computer

A **native app** is an application designed specifically to operate using the mobile device's hardware and operating system. These stand-alone programs can connect to the Internet to download and upload data, and can operate on this data even when not connected to the Internet. Download a book to an app reader, disconnect from the Internet, and read your book. Because the various types of smartphones have different hardware and operating systems, apps are not "one size fits all" and therefore need to be developed for different mobile platforms. An Apple app that runs on an iPhone cannot operate on Android phones. As you learned in Chapter 2, native apps are built using different programming languages depending on the device for which they are intended, which is then compiled into binary code, and which executes extremely fast on mobile devices, much faster than HTML or Java-based mobile web apps. For this reason, native apps are ideal for games, complex interactions, on-the-fly calculations, graphic manipulations, and rich media advertising.

native app
application designed specifically to operate using the mobile device's hardware and operating system

Increasingly, developers are combining elements of native apps and mobile web apps into hybrid apps. A **hybrid app** has many of the features of both a native app and a mobile web app. Like a native app, it runs inside a native container on the mobile device and has access to the device's APIs, enabling it to take advantage of many of the device's features, such as a gyroscope, that are normally not accessible by a mobile web app. It can also be packaged as an app for distribution from an App store. Like a mobile web app, it is based on HTML5, CSS3, and JavaScript, but uses the device's browser engine to render the HTML5 and process the JavaScript locally.

hybrid app
has many of the features of both a native app and a mobile web app

PLANNING AND BUILDING A MOBILE PRESENCE

What is the "right" mobile presence for your firm? The answer depends on identifying the business objectives, and from these, deriving the information requirements of your mobile presence. The same kind of systems analysis and design (SAD) reasoning described earlier in the chapter is needed for planning and building a mobile presence, although there are important differences.

TABLE 3.12	SYSTEMS ANALYSIS FOR BUILDING A MOBILE PRESENCE	
BUSINESS OBJECTIVE	SYSTEM FUNCTIONALITY	INFORMATION REQUIREMENTS
Driving sales	Digital catalog; product database	Product descriptions, photos, SKUs, inventory
Branding	Showing how customers use your products	Videos and rich media; product and customer demonstrations
Building customer community	Interactive experiences, games with multiple players	Games, contests, forums, social sign-up to Facebook
Advertising and promotion	Coupons and flash sales for slow-selling items	Product descriptions, coupon management, and inventory management
Gathering customer feedback	Ability to retrieve and store user inputs including text, photos, and video	Customer sign-in and identification; customer database

The first step is to identify the business objectives you are trying to achieve. **Table 3.12** illustrates the thought process for the analysis stage of building a mobile presence. Why are you developing a mobile presence? Is it to drive sales by creating an easily browsed catalog where users can shop and purchase? Strengthen your brand by creating an engaging, interactive experience? Enable customers to interact with your customer community? How are your competitors using their mobile presence? Once you have a clear sense of business objectives, you will be able to describe the kind of system functionality that is needed and specify the information requirements for your mobile presence.

After you have identified the business objectives, system functionality, and information requirements, you can think about how to design and build the system. Now is the time to consider which to develop: a mobile website, a mobile web app, or a native app. For instance, if your objective is branding or building community, a native app might be the best choice because it enables you to deliver a rich, interactive, and immersive experience that can strengthen the emotional connection with the brand. Because native apps are stored locally on the device, they can be accessed even when the user is offline, enabling the user to more deeply engage. In addition, native apps can take advantage of the mobile device's unique characteristics, such as using the gyroscope to deliver a 360-degree view. If your objective, on the other hand, is to create broad awareness, provide specific information on particular products, or drive sales, then a mobile website or mobile web app makes more sense, because it is relatively easy and inexpensive to simply publish information to the mobile Web and consumers are still most comfortable completing transactions on the Web (although this is changing as more and more retailers add e-commerce functionality directly into apps). Increasingly, however, the choice will not be an either/or decision. Mobile apps and mobile websites each offer distinct benefits, and in most cases, the best strategy will be to plan to deliver compelling content across all devices.

MOBILE PRESENCE: DESIGN CONSIDERATIONS

Designing a mobile presence is somewhat different from traditional desktop website design because of different hardware, software, and consumer expectations. **Table 3.13** describes some of the major differences.

Designers need to take mobile platform constraints into account when designing for the mobile platform. File sizes should be kept smaller and the number of files sent to the user reduced. Focus on a few, powerful graphics, and minimize the number of images sent to the user. Simplify choice boxes and lists so the user can easily scroll and touch-select the options.

Mobile presence has become so important that it is fueling a growing trend to flip the traditional e-commerce development process and begin instead with development of a mobile presence rather than a desktop website (known as **mobile first design**). Mobile first design has several advantages. Instead of creating a full-featured design for a desktop website that then needs to be scaled back, mobile first design focuses on creating the best possible experience given mobile platform constraints and then adding back elements for the desktop platform, progressively enhancing the functionality of the site. Proponents of mobile first design argue that it forces designers to focus on what is most important, and this helps create a lean and efficient mobile design that functions much better than a design that begins with a traditional platform that must be stripped down to work on mobile. Mobile first design is not without its challenges, however. It can be more difficult for designers who are more comfortable with the more traditional process (Byers, 2013).

Other important trends in the development of mobile websites include responsive web design and adaptive web design.

Responsive web design (RWD) tools and design techniques make it possible to design a website that automatically adjusts its layout and display according to

mobile first design
beginning the e-commerce development process with a mobile presence rather than a desktop website

responsive web design (RWD)
tools and design principles that automatically adjust the layout of a website depending on the screen resolution of the device on which it is being viewed

TABLE 3.13	UNIQUE FEATURES THAT MUST BE TAKEN INTO ACCOUNT WHEN DESIGNING A MOBILE PRESENCE
FEATURE	IMPLICATIONS FOR MOBILE PLATFORM
Hardware	Mobile hardware is smaller, and there are more resource constraints in data storage and processing power.
Connectivity	The mobile platform is constrained by slower connection speeds than desktop websites.
Displays	Mobile displays are much smaller and require simplification. Some screens are not good in sunlight.
Interface	Touch-screen technology introduces new interaction routines different from the traditional mouse and keyboard. The mobile platform is not a good data entry tool but can be a good navigational tool.

the screen resolution of the device on which it is being viewed, whether a desktop, tablet, or smartphone. RWD tools include HTML5 and CSS3 and its three key design principles involve using flexible grid-based layouts, flexible images and media, and media queries. RWD uses the same HTML code and design for each device, but uses CSS (which determines the layout of the web page) to adjust the layout and display to the screen's form factor. RWD sites typically work well for sites with relatively simple functionality (i.e., sites that primarily deliver content) and that users engage with in a similar manner no matter the device being used. However, using RWD can be costly, often requiring a complete redesign of the website's interface. Another problem with RWD, particularly if not coupled with mobile first design, is that the responsive website still has the size and complexity of a traditional desktop site, sometimes making it slow to load and perform on a mobile device. Another technique, known as adaptive web design, has been developed to deal with this issue.

adaptive web design (AWD)

server-side technique that detects the attributes of the device making the request and, using predefined templates based on device screen size along with CSS and Java-Script, loads a version of the site that is optimized for the device

With **adaptive web design (AWD)** (sometimes also referred to as *adaptive delivery* or *responsive web design with server-side components (RESS)*), the server hosting the website detects the attributes of the device making the request and, using predefined templates based on device screen size along with CSS and JavaScript, loads a version of the site that is optimized for the device. AWD has a number of advantages, including faster load times, the ability to enhance or remove functionality on the fly, and typically a better user experience, particularly for businesses where user intent differs depending on the platform being used. For example, creating its mobile website with AWD enabled Lufthansa to focus on actions its mobile users are most likely to take, such as checking in, getting flight status information, and looking up travel itineraries, and to provide a differentiated experience from its traditional desktop site (Pratap, 2013). A variation on AWD uses a cloud-based platform to provide similar functionality.

CROSS-PLATFORM MOBILE APP DEVELOPMENT TOOLS

In addition to creating native apps from scratch using a programming language such as Objective C or Java (as described in Chapter 2), there are hundreds of low-cost or open source app development toolkits that make creating cross-platform mobile apps relatively easy and inexpensive without having to use a device-specific programming language.

Tools include Appery.io, a cloud-based platform that enables you to a drag-and-drop visual builder tool to create HTML5 apps using jQuery Mobile. Appery.io supports Android, iOS, and Windows Phone applications. Codiqa is a similar tool that is even easier to use. It also provides a drag-and-drop interface and builds an app with 100% HTML5 components, without the need to do any coding. For those who are even less technical, Conduit is a free mobile app builder that allows you to include a variety of functionality, including e-commerce, notifications, and a social feed.

On the more technical side, PhoneGap is a mobile development framework that uses software called Apache Cordova to enable building hybrid mobile applications using HTML, CSS, and JavaScript. MoSync is another advanced tool for developing cross-platform apps for iOS, Android, Linux Mobile, Windows Mobile, and Symbian operating systems. Appcelerator is a similar, less technical tool for creating and managing hybrid mobile apps.

MOBILE PRESENCE: PERFORMANCE AND COST CONSIDERATIONS

If you don't have an existing website, the most efficient process may be to use a mobile first design philosophy and design a mobile site first. Alternatively, you may choose to build a traditional website using RWD or AWD techniques. If you already have a website that you don't want to totally redevelop, the least expensive path is to resize it to create a smartphone-friendly mobile site. Doing so typically will not require a complete redesign effort. You will need to reduce the graphics and text, simplify the navigation, and focus on improving the customer experience so you do not confuse people. Because your customers might still need to use a relatively slow cell connection at times, you will need to lighten up the amount of data you send. Also, given the difficulty of customer data entry on a mobile device, you cannot expect customers to happily enter long strings of numbers or text characters. For marketing clarity, make sure the brand images used on the mobile website match those on the traditional website. The cost of developing a mobile website can range widely, from upwards of €1 million for a custom-designed site for a large global enterprise to well under €1,000 for a small business who chooses a company such as Wix or MoFuse that offers a template or mobile website creator.

Building a mobile web app that uses the mobile device's browser requires more effort and cost than developing a mobile website and suffers from the same limitations as any browser-based application. However, it does offer some advantages such as better graphics, more interactivity, and faster local calculations as, for instance, in mobile geo-location applications like Foursquare that require local calculations of position and then communication with the site's web server.

The most expensive path to a mobile presence is to build a native app. Native apps can require more programming expertise, although there are many new development packages that can build mobile native apps with minimal programming expertise. In addition, virtually none of the elements used in your existing website can be reused, and you will need to redesign the entire logic of the interface and carefully think out the customer experience. For instance, there is a fairly stable HTML traditional website interface with buttons, graphics, videos, and ads that has developed over the last decade. This is not true for apps. There is no set of standards or expectations even on the part of users—every app looks different from every other app. This means the user confronts large variations in app design, so your interface must be quite simple and obvious. Many of the bells and whistles found on the large desktop website screen cannot be used in mobile apps. You'll need even greater simplification and focus. These weaknesses are also native apps' greatest strength: you have the opportunity to create a really stunning, unique customer experience where users can interact with your brand. If you want an intense branding experience with your customers, where interaction between your brand and customers is effortless and efficient, then native apps are the best choice.

INSIGHT ON TECHNOLOGY

CARNIVAL CRUISE SHIPS GO MOBILE

If you want to take an ocean cruise, it's hard to avoid taking it on a Carnival-brand ship. Through a series of mergers, acquisitions, and partnerships, the British-American firm now includes 10 different cruise lines, including such well-known brands as Cunard, Princess, Holland America, Seaborn, and Carnival. Carnival operates over 100 cruise ships, carries 1.7 million guests each year, and has over 200,000 berths. It controls 50% of the global cruise market. In 2015, it had revenues of $15 billion. In 2016, revenues have been stable, but profits have soared 50% as the price of fuel has fallen by half. In 2016, Carnival had a market worth of $38 billion.

So suppose the time has come to finally take that cruise of a lifetime. You've signed up for a week-long cruise through the Caribbean Islands on a Carnival Cruise ship. You've thought about this for years. You will relax on a sun-drenched deck by the pool. It will be a time to think about the important questions in life, a time for you to disconnect from all the digital tools that dominate your life on land, such as smartphones, e-mail, and computers in general.

Once onboard, though, reality sets in: you're on the latest Carnival Cruise ship, the Carnival Breeze. At 130,000 tons, she's big: 3,600 guests on board, 1,000 feet long (3 football fields), and 1,300 crew to keep you well-fed, entertained, exercised, and delighted. There are 10 restaurants, from Chinese and BBQ to Italian and a steak house, eight drinking establishments, several live theaters, several feature film theaters, a thrill theater for the kids, a 300-foot water slide, a number of spas for adults, a comedy show, and even an adults-only meditation center. All of this is laid out on 15 decks that run the length of the ship—each of them 1,000 feet long. It soon becomes apparent to you that just discovering what exists on board, let alone finding where on the ship it's located, and how to get there, is a significant challenge. Is this a vacation? Where to start? You need help!

In the past, Carnival attacked this problem of product discovery and navigation through ship maps, brochures, video displays on the decks, in-room television, and stewards walking the decks, directing traffic and answering questions like, "Where's the water slide," and "How do I get to Bonsai Sushi?" But technology has changed and customers increasingly show up with smartphones, along with a new set of expectations and behaviors. They want to find things out for themselves on their smartphones, just like they do at home with Google Maps. They want the ship's map on their screens, with directions. They expect to text with and send photos to their friends both back home and aboard. They don't want to ditch all their digital connections, but instead expect Carnival to serve their digital needs and desires. Customers want an on-board mobile companion. Carnival needed a new model of how to serve its customers.

Carnival's solution was the Carnival Hub App, a snazzy, complete, at-a-glance guide to the ship, available for both Apple and Android devices. The app includes a daily schedule of hundreds of events, a list of restaurants and prices, ship maps, and of considerable importance to travelers, their on-board charges. The app also has a Chat function so friends on board can keep track of and share experiences. Carnival Hub was introduced on a single ship, the Carnival Breeze, in 2015. Over 33% of the passengers downloaded and used the app in its first trial run. Carnival launched Carnival

Hub throughout its fleet in summer 2016, and as of September 2016, it is now available on 14 of its ships, with the rest expected to be added by March 2017. To keep customers closely connected to friends back home, Carnival introduced a $5 social media package providing unlimited access to selected social networks like Facebook and Instagram, but not the entire Internet.

Designing this snazzy app took over a year of research. Designers started by interviewing guests and employees to discover what concerned them most when on board. The key areas for guests, in rank order, were how to keep track of their charges at all the venues, how to discover what events were available, and how to find and communicate with their friends on board. With this basic information, designers constructed journey maps, showing how customers moved through the process of being on board, what were they looking for, where they found information on events and locations, and how they tracked their friends. This information helped them design behavioral maps for the app describing what information would be on each of the app screens, and the user-flows or navigation patterns of users. The idea of journeys was to diagram how users would naturally want to navigate the app. The maps were then used to create working models of the app screens, and the links between the screens.

Carnival is moving quickly to go beyond mobile apps just as ship guides to making apps an integral part of the total cruise experience. A part of its mobile strategy is to integrate betting and gaming services into its mobile apps library and onboard entertainment lineup. Using the iGaming Mobile Platform, Carnival is now offering a mobile casino experience through wager-based and free-to-play games, including blackjack, poker, sports betting, and bingo. Travelers will be able to access a Mobile Casino app for Apple and Android devices that provides games from leading firms like Scientific Games and PokerTrek. Hanging out around the pool, or relaxing in their staterooms, guests can play poker and bet on the horses and sport events. Now this is a vacation!

SOURCES: "They're the Biggest, Costliest Cruise Ships Ever Built. And They're Coming Here," by Chabeli Herrera, *Miami Herald*, October 30, 2016; "Carnival Expands Mobile App To More Ships," by Richard Simms, Cruiseradio.net, August 22, 2016; "Carnival Cruise Lines Art Direction Product Design UI/UX," by Brad Harris, Behance.net, May 18, 2016; "Princess Plays Travel Matchmaker with New 'Places to Sea' Mobile Experience: Swipe Technology First of its Kind for Cruise Industry and Travel Planning," by Carnival Corporation & LLC, March 22, 2016; "Carnival Corporation & PLC Form 10-K 2015," filed with the Securities and Exchange Commission, November 30, 2015; "Carnival to Expand Chatting App Fleetwide," by Fran Golden, *USA Today*, August 10, 2015; "Carnival Corporation, MSC Ramp Up Mobile Offerings with Shipboard Gaming Platforms, Apps," by Alex Samuely, Mobilecommercedaily.com, January 27, 2015; "Carnival Corporation Launches Shipboard Mobile Gaming Solution for Mid-Cruise Wagering Powered by Scientific Games," Prnewswire.com, January 23, 2015; "Carnival Cruise Line Launches New Shipboard Mobile App," Prnewswire.com, January 15, 2015.

Dick's Sporting Goods:
Taking Control of Its E-commerce Operations

Founded in 1948 by Dick Stack in Binghamton, New York, Dick's Sporting Goods has grown from a small local company selling fishing and camping supplies into a Fortune 500 business with stores throughout the United States. After Stack's retirement in 1984, his son Edward bought the business with his siblings and took over as president. Edward spearheaded the company's growth from a handful of local stores into a sporting goods powerhouse. The company sells athletic apparel, outerwear, sportswear, a variety of shoes, fitness equipment, and outdoor equipment. Now headquartered in Pennsylvania, Dick's also runs two smaller franchises: its Field & Stream outdoor goods division, and Golf Galaxy for golfing supplies. Dick's prides itself on combining small-business customer service with big-box retailer selection and values, and routinely outperforms competitors in customer service metrics such as phone and e-mail response time and delivery speed.

© Ian Dangall/Alamy Stock Photo

Unlike some of its competitors, Dick's was quick to embrace the online channel and has maintained very strong e-commerce sales relative to its competitors in the sporting goods industry. Industry surveys in 2015 showed that Dick's increased its e-commerce revenue by 40% since 2010, whereas its competitors' e-commerce revenues have increased by roughly 20% over that span. For most of that period, Dick's relied on external vendors for its IT and e-commerce needs. The company's primary e-commerce vendor was eBay and its eBay Enterprise suite of e-commerce services. EBay handled Dick's back-end fulfillment processes and most aspects of their e-commerce presence for approximately 10 successful years. In 2014, Dick's reached 70th on Internet Retailer's Top 500 list, and the company's 2015 yearly revenue grew 19% to $748 million, up from $638 million in 2014. E-commerce represented 10% of total sales for the year.

However, Dick's overall revenues slumped in 2014, and continued to lag in 2015 thanks to unseasonably warm weather in the winter. Analysts were also skeptical of Dick's significant financial commitment to large physical stores in an era dominated by online shopping. Dick's had grown to a size where its agreement with eBay was costing the company significant revenue. eBay collected a fixed commission on all items Dick's sold online, no matter how big, despite the fact that expensive items cost no more for eBay to process than cheaper ones. As Dick's e-commerce sales continued to grow, its deal with eBay was costing it more and more money.

Many bigger businesses have begun migrating their e-commerce operations away from external vendors and back within the control of the company to avoid these types of expenses. Also, it can be difficult to customize pre-made software and services from external vendors. However, once in-house, companies can more easily differentiate their web presences from competitors and adjust their software and services to best suit their capabilities. Companies that reclaim their e-commerce operations also maintain easier access to their proprietary customer data. Examples of companies following this path include Target, which left Amazon Web Services to build its own e-commerce platform, and Toys 'R' Us, who had also used eBay Enterprise, like Dick's.

Facing pressure to slow down physical growth and reduce the high cost of maintaining physical real estate, and sensing the trend towards e-commerce at the expense of in-store sales, Dick's made the difficult decision to follow suit and formulate a plan to take over its own e-commerce operations by the year 2017. The company's rapidly increasing online sales gave Dick's both the incentive and the budget to undertake the transition. Edward Stack explained that the money the company was going to recoup from no longer paying transaction commissions to eBay would pay for the temporary increase in expenditure required to build and maintain an e-commerce infrastructure. Stack estimated that the company stood to immediately save between $20 and $25 million per year, and with a total expenditure relating to the switch of about $80 million, the move would pay for itself within four years.

Having total control of its e-commerce operations will allow Dick's to provide better support for unique omnichannel features, such as shipping online orders from physical Dick's stores. To that end, Dick's has also made plans to convert its stores into distribution centers as well as traditional retail showrooms. This will increase efficiency and improve delivery times, turning its perceived weakness of excessive bricks-and-mortar infrastructure into a strength. Approximately 80% of Dicks' e-commerce orders are shipped within the geographical area of a physical store. Dick's foresees its stores functioning not only as traditional retail showcases, but also as miniature distribution centers. In addition, customers can order online and pickup orders at local stores. Customizing its infrastructure and website capabilities to capitalize on this unusual arrangement was one of the reasons it wanted to reclaim operation of its e-commerce platform.

The process has three steps. In 2014, Dick's completed development of its e-commerce platform and began integrating its existing systems. In 2015, Dick's began moving two of its lesser brands, Field & Stream and Golf Galaxy, onto the platform, and continued development work on the e-commerce platform. In 2016 and 2017, the company plans to re-launch its flagship Dick's Sporting Goods site on the platform. Dick's has launched its smaller sites one at a time to ensure that there are no major issues with any aspects of the platform. Both went live without incident in 2015.

Dick's selected IBM Websphere Commerce Suite for its e-commerce technology stack because of its emphasis on omnichannel shopping and fulfillment capability. Core components of the stack also include Apache ServiceMix service-oriented architecture, Manhattan Associates Order Management System for supply chain management, JDA Software Group software for merchandising, allocation, and replenishment, Oracle PeopleSoft for human resource management, IBM hardware, and Cisco networking technology. Manhattan Associates runs Dick's four Pittsburgh distribution centers, and JDA Software Group data is directed into a data warehouse that allows Dick's to access real-time information from any area of their business.

Specific features of the new e-commerce platform that Dick's has prioritized include the ability to buy online and pick up items at a store, the ability to ship from or to a store, and its associate ordering system. The platform also features the ability to break down and test different pricing and marketing approaches by region, an improved search function, and better analytics capabilities. Dick's has found that e-commerce sales double in regions where it opens new stores, and that multichannel customers spend three times as much as single-channel customers. That's why Dick's has focused so much on integrating physical and virtual sales and omnichannel features. Bringing all of its e-commerce infrastructure in house also allows the company better control over development cycles and speeds up its testing and implementation time frames.

The process wasn't without risk. Installing a completely new e-commerce platform is no easy task. It involves integrating legacy systems and new systems without losing access to information, hiring a slew of new employees to manage the system, and avoiding implementation delays, cost overruns, outages, and other delays. Shifting much of its focus to the lower-margin online channel with extremely experienced competitors like Amazon lurking is also a challenge. Other competitors of Dick's have struggled to adapt to the omnichannel challenge. For example, Sports Authority finalized plans to close all of its remaining stores after it went bankrupt and could not find a buyer in 2016. Many retailers have found that their e-commerce growth has not been sufficient to offset their struggling bricks-and-mortar segment of their businesses.

SOURCES: "Why Dick's Sporting Goods Decided to Play Its Own Game in E-commerce," by Larry Dignan, Techrepublic.com, April 21, 2016; "Dick's Sporting Goods Touts Omnichannel Success and New Store Growth," by Mike Troy, Chainstoreage.com, March 8, 2016; "E-commerce Wins Q4 for Dick's Sporting Goods," by Don Davis, Internetretailer.com, March 8, 2016; "Dick's Sporting Goods Posts Nearly 18% Growth in Q3 Web Sales," Don Davis, by Internetretailer.com, November 18, 2015; "Dick's Sporting Goods Opens a New Online Store," by Matt Lindner, Internetretailer.com, November 12, 2015; "Dick's Sporting Goods Could Get a Boost From E-Commerce," by Chris Laudani, Thestreet.com, September 30, 2015; "Dick's Sporting Goods Scores a 24.4% Gain in Q2 E-commerce Sales," by Don Davis, Internetretailer.com, August 18,

However, in 2016, Dick's has continued its strong e-commerce growth, which it believes will allow it to avoid a similar fate. Dick's hopes to increase its e-commerce revenue to $1.2 billion by 2017, or approximately double what it was before ending its arrangement with eBay. Dick's also hopes to continue building physical stores. At the end of 2015, Dick's had 644 stores in 47 states, as well as 73 Golf Galaxy stores and 19 Field & Stream stores. However, the company believes that if its physical stores continue to drive online sales, it can reach as many as 1,100 stores in the United States. In 2016, Dick's opened approximately 40 new stores and relocated several more. The company hopes that its revamped e-commerce platform and emphasis on omnichannel retailing will continue to drive both physical and online growth.

2015; "Toys 'R' Us Makes a Big E-commerce Play," by Don Davis, Internetretailer.com, July 9, 2015; "Dick's Sporting Goods Aims to Control Its E-commerce Destiny," by Larry Dignan, Zdnet.com, May 21, 2015; "Dick's Sporting Goods Plans to Double E-commerce Revenue by 2017," by Matt Lindner, Internetretailer.com, April 15, 2015; "A Slam-Dunk Year Online for Dick's Sporting Goods," by Don Davis, Internetretailer.com, March 3, 2015.

Case Study Questions

1. Why did Dick's decide to leave eBay and take over its own e-commerce operations?
2. What is Dick's omnichannel strategy?
3. What are the three steps in Dick's migration to its new website?
4. What are the primary benefits of Dick's new system?

3.8 REVIEW

KEY CONCEPTS

- **Understand the questions you must ask and answer, and the steps you should take, in developing an e-commerce presence.**
- Questions you must ask and answer when developing an e-commerce presence include:
  - What is your vision and how do you hope to accomplish it?
  - What is your business and revenue model?
  - Who and where is the target audience?
  - What are the characteristics of the marketplace?
  - Where is the content coming from?
  - Conduct a SWOT analysis.
  - Develop an e-commerce presence map.
  - Develop a timeline.
  - Develop a detailed budget.

- **Explain the process that should be followed in building an e-commerce presence.**
- Factors you must consider when building an e-commerce site include hardware, software, telecommunications capacity, website and mobile platform design, human resources, and organizational capabilities.
- The systems development life cycle (a methodology for understanding the business objectives of a system and designing an appropriate solution) for building an e-commerce website involves five major steps:
  - Identify the specific business objectives for the site, and then develop a list of system functionalities and information requirements.

234 | CHAPTER 3   Building an E-commerce Presence

- Develop a system design specification (both logical design and physical design).
- Build the site, either by in-house personnel or by outsourcing all or part of the responsibility to outside contractors.
- Test the system (unit testing, system testing, acceptance testing, A/B (split) testing, and multivariate testing).
- Implement and maintain the site.
- The basic business and system functionalities an e-commerce site should contain include a digital catalog, a product database, customer tracking, shopping cart/payment system, an on-site blog, a customer database, an ad server, a site tracking and reporting system, and an inventory management system.
- Advantages of building a site in-house include the ability to change and adapt the site quickly as the market demands and the ability to build a site that does exactly what the company needs.
- Disadvantages of building a site in-house include higher costs, greater risks of failure, a more time-consuming process, and a longer staff learning curve that delays time to market.
- Using design templates cuts development time, but preset templates can also limit functionality.
- A similar decision is also necessary regarding outsourcing the hosting of the site versus keeping it in-house. Relying on an outside vendor places the burden of reliability on someone else in return for a monthly hosting fee. The downside is that if the site requires fast upgrades due to heavy traffic, the chosen hosting company may or may not be capable of keeping up. Reliability versus scalability is the issue in this instance.

■ **Identify and understand the major considerations involved in choosing web server and e-commerce merchant server software.**

- Early websites used single-tier system architecture and consisted of a single-server computer that delivered static web pages to users making requests through their browsers. The extended functionality of today's websites requires the development of a multi-tiered systems architecture, which utilizes a variety of specialized web servers, as well as links to pre-existing backend or legacy corporate databases.
- All e-commerce sites require basic web server software to answer requests from customers for HTML and XML pages. When choosing web server software, companies are also choosing what operating system the site will run on. Apache, which runs on the Unix system, is the market leader.
- Web servers provide a host of services, including processing user HTML requests, security services, file transfer, a search engine, data capture, e-mail, and site management tools.
- Dynamic server software allows sites to deliver dynamic content, rather than static, unchanging information. Web application server programs enable a wide range of e-commerce functionality, including creating a customer database, creating an e-mail promotional program, and accepting and processing orders, as well as many other services.
- E-commerce merchant server software is another important software package that provides catalog displays, information storage and customer tracking, order taking (shopping cart), and credit card purchase processing. E-commerce software platforms can save time and money, but customization can significantly drive up costs. Factors to consider when choosing an e-commerce software platform include its functionality, support for different business models, visual site management tools and reporting systems, performance and scalability, connectivity to existing business systems, compliance with standards, and global and multicultural capability.

■ **Understand the issues involved in choosing the most appropriate hardware for an e-commerce site.**

- Speed, capacity, and scalability are three of the most important considerations when selecting an operating system, and therefore the hardware that it runs on.

- To evaluate how fast the site needs to be, companies need to assess the number of simultaneous users the site expects to see, the nature of their requests, the type of information requested, and the bandwidth available to the site. The answers to these questions will provide guidance regarding the processors necessary to meet customer demand. In some cases, additional processing power can increase capacity, thereby improving system speed.
- Scalability is also an important issue. Increasing processing supply by scaling up to meet demand can be done through vertical or horizontal scaling or by improving processing architecture.

■ Identify additional tools that can improve website performance.

- In addition to providing a speedy website, companies must also strive to have a well-designed site that encourages visitors to buy. Building in interactivity improves site effectiveness, as do personalization techniques.
- Commonly used software tools for achieving high levels of website interactivity and customer personalization include Common Gateway Interface (CGI) scripts, Active Server Pages (ASP) and ASP.NET, Java applets, JavaScript, ActiveX and VBScript, Ajax, PHP, Ruby on Rails (RoR or Rails), and Django.

■ Understand the important considerations involved in developing a mobile website and building mobile applications.

- When developing a mobile presence, it is important to understand the difference between a mobile website, mobile web apps, native apps, and hybrid apps.
- The first step is to identify business objectives, because they help determine which type of mobile presence is best.
- Design should take into account mobile platform constraints. Recent trends include mobile first design, responsive web design, and adaptive web delivery.
- Developing a mobile website is likely to be the least expensive option; mobile web apps require more effort and cost; native apps are likely to be the most expensive to develop.

QUESTIONS

1. What are the main factors to consider when developing an e-commerce presence?
1. What elements do you need to address when developing a vision for an e-commerce presence?
2. Name the four main kinds of e-commerce presence and the different platforms for each type.
3. Identify the different phases used in a one-year timeline for the development of an e-commerce presence and the related milestones for each phase.
4. Define the systems development life cycle and discuss the various steps involved in creating an e-commerce site.
5. What are the various components of a Web site budget?
6. What is multivariate testing and how does it differ from A/B testing (split testing)?
7. What are the disadvantages of outsourcing hosting? What risks does a small business face when hosting its own website?
8. What is a content management system and what function does it serve?
9. What is open source software and how can it be used in creating an e-commerce presence?
10. What are the main factors to consider when choosing an e-commerce suite?
11. What are some methods for achieving personalization and customization?
12. Discuss some of the ways that you can optimize a website so that it will appear higher up in search engine listings.
13. What is CGI and how does it enable interactivity?

14. What are some of the unique features that must be taken into account when designing a mobile Web presence?
15. What is PHP? What role does it play in website design?
16. What are the advantages and disadvantages of mobile first design?
17. What is the difference between a mobile Web app and a native app?
18. In what ways does a hybrid mobile app combine the functionality of a mobile Web app and a native app?
19. What is a widget and what are they used for?
20. How does responsive Web design differ from adaptive Web delivery?

PROJECTS

1. Go to the website of Wix, Weebly, or another provider of your choosing that allows you to create a simple e-tailer website for a free trial period. Create a website. The site should feature at least four pages, including a home page, product page, shopping cart, and contact page. Extra credit will be given for additional complexity and creativity. Come to class prepared to present your e-tailer concept and website.

2. Visit several e-commerce sites, not including those mentioned in this chapter, and evaluate the effectiveness of the sites according to the eight basic criteria/functionalities listed in Table 3.11. Choose one site you feel does an excellent job on all the aspects of an effective site and create an electronic presentation, including screen shots, to support your choice.

3. Imagine that you are in charge of developing a fast-growing startup's e-commerce presence. Consider your options for building the company's e-commerce presence in-house with existing staff, or outsourcing the entire operation. Decide which strategy you believe is in your company's best interest and create a brief presentation outlining your position. Why choose that approach? And what are the estimated associated costs, compared with the alternative? (You'll need to make some educated guesses here—don't worry about being exact.)

4. Choose two e-commerce software packages and prepare an evaluation chart that rates the packages on the key factors discussed in the section "Choosing an E-commerce Software Platform." Which package would you choose if you were developing a website of the type described in this chapter, and why?

5. Choose one of the open source web content management systems such as WordPress, Joomla, or Drupal or another of your own choosing and prepare an evaluation chart similar to that required by Project 4. Which system would you choose and why?

REFERENCES

Byers, Josh. "Three Reasons a 'Mobile First' Philosophy Is Critical to Achieving Your Business Goals." Copyblogger.com (May 11, 2013).

Doyle, Barry, and Cristina Videira Lopes. "Survey of Technologies for Web Application Development." *ACM*, Vol. 2., No. 3. (June 2005).

Dusto, Amy. "The Top E-commerce Platform Vendors for Midmarket Retailers." Internetretailer.com (January 10, 2014).

Hegde, Raviraj. "Top Sites Built with Ruby on Rails." Codebrahma.com (December 25, 2015).

IBM (High Volume Web Sites Team). "Best Practices for High-Volume Web Sites." *IBM Redbooks* (December 2002).

Krill, Paul. "Java at 20: The Programming Juggernaut Rolls On." Infoworld.com (May 18, 2015).

Mutton, Paul. "Hostinger Hosts Over 90% of All Steam Phishers." News.netcraft.com (April 28, 2015).

Netcraft. "September 2016 Web Server Survey." (September 19, 2016).

Pinkham, Andrew. "Starting a New Django Project: Building a Startup Categorizer with Blog." Informit.com (December 29, 2015).

Pratap, Ravi. "Responsive Design vs. Adaptive Delivery: Which One's Right for You?" Venturebeat.com (November 19, 2013).

W3Techs. "Usage of Server-side Programming Languages for Websites." (accessed September 29, 2016).

Webtrends, Inc. "Webtrends Analytics 10." (2014).

E-commerce Security and Payment Systems

After reading this chapter, you will be able to:

- Understand the scope of e-commerce crime and security problems, the key dimensions of e-commerce security, and the tension between security and other values.
- Identify the key security threats in the e-commerce environment.
- Describe how technology helps secure Internet communications channels and protect networks, servers, and clients.
- Appreciate the importance of policies, procedures, and laws in creating security.
- Identify the major e-commerce payment systems in use today.
- Describe the features and functionality of electronic billing presentment and payment systems.

Europol

Takes on Cybercrime with EC3

From the earliest of days, humans have warred against and stolen from each other, with the tools evolving over time from sticks and stones, to arrows and spears, to guns and bombs. Physical weaponry is familiar and readily recognizable. But today, algorithms and computer code have moved to the forefront. Cyberspace has become a new battlefield, one that often involves targets such as financial systems and communications networks.

In 2013, the European Cybercrime Center (EC3) was created at Europol, the European law enforcement agency in The Hague, to combat the rise of cybercrime and cyberattacks throughout Europe and the rest of the world. More than half of the EU's population is now online, meaning that an organization like the EC3 is needed in Europe now more than ever before.

© Rafal Olechowski / Fotolia

A major challenge in fighting cybercrime is concretely defining and measuring it. Estimates vary widely, but a 2015 study by the Center for Strategic and International Studies estimates that the economic impact of cybercrime and cyberespionage worldwide is in a range between €345 billion and €530 billion, and that both the cost and frequency of attacks are on the rise. Sharing information about cybercrime is critical for success in apprehending cybercriminals, making Europol an excellent vehicle to combat multinational criminal operations. The EC3 is helping to set guidelines regarding what incidents constitute cybercrime and standardizing approaches to better counteract it.

The EC3 began operations out of The Hague on January 1, 2013 with a focus on three areas of cybercrime: crime committed by organized groups or rings; crime that causes harm to a victim, like child pornography; and cyberattacks on EU infrastructure, such as government websites, databases, and storage centers. In the wake of the 2015 terrorist attacks in Paris, the EC3 received a boost in financial backing and powers, including the ability to coordinate police units to counter emerging threats and the capacity to directly force companies like Facebook and Twitter to remove posts containing terrorist communications. The EC3 has also joined forces with private security firms, such as cybersecurity company FireEye and digital currency security company Chainalysis, forming agreements to share knowledge and expertise on cybercrime prevention techniques, as well as with Internet registry services, such as RIPE NCC, which manage IP addresses and other

Internet number resources that law enforcement can use to track down cybercriminals. Members of the EC3 staff also contribute to the Joint Cybercrime Action Taskforce (J-CAT), a group that also includes team members from EU member states as well as non-EU law enforcement partners like Australia, Canada, and the United States. J-CAT pursues criminals operating across multiple countries and facilitates cooperation between its members. The EC3 started with 43 anti-cybercrime experts but has increased its size to more than 70 people and is guided by a 12-member advisory board on Internet security featuring some of the foremost experts from a variety of different fields.

The EC3's operations have five main functions. The first is data fusion, which involves gathering and processing information on cybercrime. The EC3 functions as a central repository for statistics on cybercrime and its apprehension. Its second function is cybercrime prevention operations, including conducting cybercrime investigations within individual EU states and facilitating joint investigations across multiple EU states. Its third major function is developing strategies for fighting cybercrime, analyzing crime trends, and forecasting future trends in cybercrime. Its fourth function is research and development as well as training of law enforcement agencies in the skills required to effectively investigate and combat cybercrime. The organization educates judges and prosecutors on cybercrime. Lastly, the EC3 conducts outreach, working with the private sector, academia, and society at large to better handle cybercrime.

The majority of credit card numbers used in cybercrime in the EU have historically originated from United States data breaches, so a major focus of the EC3 has been preventing card-not-present (CNP) fraud. Europol has reported that organized crime makes around €1.5 billion annually from credit card fraud, €900 million of which originates from CNP fraud. As technological infrastructure improves in developing nations, it is expected that incidences of online credit card fraud originating in Africa and other similar countries will increase. In 2016, the EC3 staged an exercise that simulated widespread attacks on the retail sector and companies that process credit card transactions.

The early results of the EC3 have been positive. In its first year of operation, it took down Operation Ransom, the largest ransomware cybercrime network in Russia, spanning 33 countries, including 22 in the EU, arresting the leader of the ring in Dubai along with 10 more members of the group, and then later in the year, two more Ukranian cybercriminals who sold access to a botnet with over 21,000 compromised servers located in 80 different countries, as well as operating a sophisticated money laundering scheme that processed around €10,000 a day through various electronic payment systems and virtual currencies. These two investigations were part of the EC3's "Focal Point Cyborg," which assisted in a total of 19 cybercrime operations in the EC3's first year of existence.

As part of its "Focal Point Terminal" division, the EC3 busted an Asian criminal network responsible for the theft of 15,000 credit card numbers and for conducting illegal Internet transactions and purchases of airline tickets. In 2014, the EC3 held a "day of action" to target criminals using stolen credit cards to buy airline tickets as part of a different ring. Europol and individual law enforcement officers worked in concert in each country to make the arrests, which yielded further links to other criminal organizations. A third area, "Focal Point Twins," focused on nine sophisticated online child sexual exploitation rings. The EC3 has continued to shut down high-profile cybercriminal operations,

SOURCES: "Joint Cybercrime Action Taskforce (J-CAT)," Europol. europa.eu, accessed December 2016; "RIPE NCC and Europol Enhance Cooperation to Tackle Cybercrime and Internet Security," Europol.europa.eu, December 15, 2016; "International Cyber Sweep Nets DDoS Attackers," Fbi.gov, December 12, 2016; "Europol Hosts Simulated Cyber Attack on Retail Sector," by Warwick Ashford, Computerweekly.com, December 5, 2016; "'Avalanche' Network Dismantled in International Cyber Operation," Eurojust.europa.eu, December 1, 2016; "178 Arrests in Successful Hit Against Money Muling," Eurojust.europa.eu, November 22, 2016; "First European-Wide Action on E-Commerce Fraud Sees Arrest of 42," Europol.europa.eu, October 31, 2016; "Europol and Chainalysis Reinforce Their Cooperation in the Fight Against Cybercrime," Europol.europa.eu, February 19, 2016; "Europol Get New Powers to including the Ramnit and Beebone botnets in 2015. J-CAT was also responsible for shutting down several high profile operations in 2015, including the Triangle phishing scheme and the Dridex banking malware, which accounted for £20 million in losses in the United Kingdom and $10 million in the United States. In 2016, the EC3 brought down arguably its biggest criminal operation to date, the "Avalanche" malware network. Avalanche was particularly difficult to bring down because of its use of the "Fast Flux" technique of rapidly changing both the server name and the IP addresses of affected computers in its network. The EC3's investigation into Avalanche took over four years, during which time Avalanche was responsible for €6 million in damages and fraud in Germany alone and an estimated hundreds of millions of euros worldwide. The operation resulted in 5 arrests, 39 servers seized, and 221 servers taken offline due to the presence of Avalanche malware. Also in 2016, the EC3 made its first arrests for e-commerce fraud, apprehending 42 individuals for systematically ordering expensive goods worth a combined €3.5 million with stolen credit card information.

The EC3 has increasingly focused on fighting "cybercrime-as-a-service." Experienced cybercriminals are selling programs and services that buyers can use to commit cybercrime without the same knowledge of criminal techniques. When cybercrime is committed outside the EU's jurisdiction, it is more difficult to police, so many skilled cybercriminals within EU borders have taken to cybercrime-as-a-service to reduce their risk, allowing others to execute the cybercrime instead. In 2016, law enforcement from 13 countries arrested nearly three dozen suspects for their participation in a "DDoS for hire" scheme of this type. Criminals are also increasingly making use of legitimate tools to stay anonymous on the Web, such as encryption techniques; virtual currencies like Bitcoin; and anonymization services such as Tor, which are used to navigate areas on the Web known as the Darknet, private networks where connections are made without sharing IP addresses. Many cybercriminals have migrated their efforts to mobile devices, forcing the EC3 to begin targeting these operations. In its first major success in that area, the EC3 brought down the DroidJack mobile phone malware in 2015. The EC3 has also targeted "money muling," where individuals not directly responsible for cybercrime act as money launderers for criminal operations. Money muling is critical to the ongoing operation of cybercriminal operations. In 2016, the EC3 and J-CAT worked in tandem with over 100 participating banks to make 178 arrests of suspected money mules.

The EC3 believes that worldwide cybercrime is driven by a small number of skilled programmers, and that focusing on these top-level criminals is the best way to combat cybercrime going forward. J-CAT operations in particular frequently target these top-level criminals, since only multiple countries acting in tandem can apprehend them. Many of these criminals conduct their operations using the Darknet to thwart law enforcement. However, in 2014, the EC3 demonstrated its ability to shut down sites on the Darknet when it put an end to the second iteration of the underground black market Silk Road 2.0 and arrested its operator, a 26-year-old former Google programmer. In 2015, it continued to bring down illicit sites on the Darknet, including a service for distributing child pornography. The EC3's challenge will be to continue making these high-profile arrests while adapting to the ever-changing array of techniques cybercriminals use.

Target Terrorists and Cyber-gangs," Scmagazineuk.com, December 1, 2015; "International Law Enforcement Action Against DroidJack Mobile Phone Malware," Europol, October 28, 2015; "FireEye Latest Security Firm to Join Forces with Europol," by Warwick Ashford, Computerweekly.com, August 17, 2015; "Darknet Hidden Service for Child Sexual Abuse Material Shut Down," Europol, July 31, 2015; Maxwell Cooter, "Europol Leads Takedown of Beebone Botnet," Scmagazineuk.com, April 10, 2015; "Europol Shuts Down Ramnit Botnet in Global Operation," by Dave Neal, Theinquirer.net, February 26, 2015; "FBI, Europol Make Large 'Dark Web' Bust," Reuters, November 7, 2014; "'Every Day Is a Challenge'— Inside Europol's Fight Against Cybercrime," by Doug Drinkwater, Scmagazineuk.com, November 1, 2014; "Only 100 Cybercrime Brains Worldwide Says Europol Boss," BBC News, October 10, 2014; "Service Model Driving Cyber Crime, Says Europol Report," by Warwick Ashford, Computerweekly. com, September 29, 2014; "Europol's EC3 Launches Pan-Euro Cybercrime Taskforce J-CAT," by Phil Muncaster, Info Security, September 2, 2014; "Europol Launches Taskforce to Fight World's Top Cybercriminals," by Tom Brewster, Theguardian.com, September 1, 2014; "First Year Report," EC3, February 9, 2014; "Europol-Interpol Cybercrime Conference Steps Up Policing in Cyberspace," Europol, September 25, 2013; "International Network of On-Line Card Fraudsters Dismantled," Europol, March 8, 2013; "European Cybercrime Centre Dismantles Its First Criminal Network," by Nerea Rial, Neurope. eu, February 14, 2013; "Opening of the European Cybercrime Center — A Journey Begins," by Neil Robinson, Rand.org, January 11, 2013; "Europe's Cybercrime Fighters Get New Digs...Complete with Faraday Room," by John Leyden, Theregister.co.uk, January 11, 2013; "Europe's New Cybercrime Center to Open Its Doors This Week: EC3 to Act as Hub for EU-Wide Collaboration to Combat E-Crime," by Natasha Lomas, Techcrunch.com, January 9, 2013.

As the opening case illustrates, the Internet and Web are increasingly vulnerable to large-scale attacks and potentially large-scale failure. Increasingly, these attacks are led by organized gangs of criminals operating globally—an unintended consequence of globalization. Even more worrisome is the growing number of large-scale attacks that are funded, organized, and led by various nations against the Internet resources of other nations. Anticipating and countering these attacks has proved a difficult task for both business and government organizations. However, there are several steps you can take to protect your websites, your mobile devices, and your personal information from routine security attacks. Reading this chapter, you should also start thinking about how your business could survive in the event of a large-scale "outage" of the Internet.

In this chapter, we will examine e-commerce security and payment issues. First, we will identify the major security risks and their costs, and describe the variety of solutions currently available. Then, we will look at the major payment methods and consider how to achieve a secure payment environment. **Table 4.1** highlights some of the major trends in online security in 2016–2017.

TABLE 4.1	WHAT'S NEW IN E-COMMERCE SECURITY 2016–2017

- Large-scale data breaches continue to expose data about individuals to hackers and other cybercriminals.
- Mobile malware presents a tangible threat as smartphones and other mobile devices become more common targets of cybercriminals, especially as their use for mobile payments rises.
- Malware creation continues to skyrocket and ransomware attacks rise.
- Distributed Denial of Service (DDoS) attacks are now capable of slowing Internet service within entire countries.
- Nations continue to engage in cyberwarfare and cyberespionage.
- Hackers and cybercriminals continue to focus their efforts on social network sites to exploit potential victims through social engineering and hacking attacks.
- Politically motivated, targeted attacks by hacktivist groups continue, in some cases merging with financially motivated cybercriminals to target financial systems with advanced persistent threats.
- Software vulnerabilities, such as the Heartbleed bug and other zero day vulnerabilities, continue to create security threats.
- Incidents involving celebrities raise awareness of cloud security issues.

4.1 THE E-COMMERCE SECURITY ENVIRONMENT

For most law-abiding citizens, the Internet holds the promise of a huge and convenient global marketplace, providing access to people, goods, services, and businesses worldwide, all at a bargain price. For criminals, the Internet has created entirely new—and lucrative—ways to steal from the more than 1.6 billion Internet consumers worldwide in 2016. From products and services, to cash, to information, it's all there for the taking on the Internet.

It's also less risky to steal online. Rather than rob a bank in person, the Internet makes it possible to rob people remotely and almost anonymously. Rather than steal a CD at a local record store, you can download the same music for free and almost without risk from the Internet. The potential for anonymity on the Internet cloaks many criminals in legitimate-looking identities, allowing them to place fraudulent orders with online merchants, steal information by intercepting e-mail, or simply shut down e-commerce sites by using software viruses and swarm attacks. The Internet was never designed to be a global marketplace with billions of users and lacks many basic security features found in older networks such as the telephone system or broadcast television networks. By comparison, the Internet is an open, vulnerable-design network. The actions of cybercriminals are costly for both businesses and consumers, who are then subjected to higher prices and additional security measures. The costs of malicious cyberactivity include not just the cost of the actual crime, but also the additional costs that are required to secure networks and recover from cyberattacks, the potential reputational damage to the affected company, as well as reduced trust in online activities, the loss of potentially sensitive business information, including intellectual property and confidential business information, and the cost of opportunities lost due to service disruptions. Ponemon Institute estimates that the average total cost of a data breach to the 383 companies from 12 different countries participating in its 2016 study was approximately €3.8 million (Ponemon Institute, 2016).

THE SCOPE OF THE PROBLEM

Cybercrime is becoming a more significant problem for both organizations and consumers. Bot networks, DDoS attacks, Trojans, phishing, ransomware, data theft, identity fraud, credit card fraud, and spyware are just some of the threats that are making daily headlines. Social networks also have had security breaches. But despite the increasing attention being paid to cybercrime, it is difficult to accurately estimate the actual amount of such crime, in part because many companies are hesitant to report it due to the fear of losing the trust of their customers, and because even if the crime is reported, it may be difficult to quantify the actual dollar amount of the loss. A 2014 study by the Center for Strategic and International Studies examined the difficulties in accurately estimating the economic impact of cybercrime and cyberespionage, with its research indicating a range of €355 billion to €540 billion worldwide. Further research is planned to try to help determine an even more accurate estimate (Center for Strategic and International Studies, 2014).

One source of information is a survey conducted by Ponemon Institute. Ponemon's 2015 survey included 252 companies in seven countries: Germany, the United Kingdom, Russia, Australia, Japan, Brazil, and the United States. There were 1,928 total attacks reported, a 12.3% increase from the previous year. The average annualized cost for organizations in the study was around €7.1 million. In all countries, virtually all organizations experienced attacks involving viruses, worms, Trojans, and malware. More than 50% of the companies also suffered Web-based attacks, phishing and social engineering attacks, malicious code, botnets, and denial of service attacks.

The most costly types of attacks were those by malicious insiders, denial of service and web-based attacks (Ponemon Institute, 2015a).

Reports issued by security product providers, such as Symantec, are another source of data. Symantec issues a semi-annual *Internet Security Threat Report* based on 57.6 million sensors monitoring Internet activity in more than 157 countries. Advances in technology have greatly reduced the entry costs and skills required to enter the cybercrime business. Low-cost and readily available web attack kits enable hackers to create malware without having to write software from scratch. In addition, there has been a surge in polymorphic malware, which enables attackers to generate a unique version of the malware for each victim, making it much more difficult for pattern-matching software used by security firms to detect. According to Symantec, the number of data breaches increased by 23% in 2015, over half a billion personal records were stolen, the number of spear-phishing attacks increased by 55%, malware increased by 36%, and ransomware attacks grew by 35% (Symantec, 2016). However, Symantec does not attempt to quantify actual crimes and/or losses related to these threats.

Online credit card fraud is one of the most high-profile forms of e-commerce crime. Although the average amount of credit card fraud loss experienced by any one individual is typically relatively small, the overall amount is substantial. The overall rate of online credit card fraud is estimated to be about 0.8% of all online card transactions, including both mobile and web transactions (Cybersource, 2016). The nature of credit card fraud has changed greatly from the theft of a single credit card number and efforts to purchase goods at a few sites to the simultaneous theft of millions of credit card numbers and their distributions to thousands of criminals operating as gangs of thieves. The emergence of identity fraud, described in detail later in this chapter, as a major online/offline type of fraud may well markedly increase the incidence and amount of credit card fraud, because identity fraud often includes the use of stolen credit card information and the creation of phony credit card accounts.

The Underground Economy Marketplace: The Value of Stolen Information

Criminals who steal information on the Internet do not always use this information themselves, but instead derive value by selling the information to others on the so-called underground or shadow economy market. Data is currency to cybercriminals and has a "street value" that can be monetized. For example, in 2013, Vladislav Horohorin (alias "BadB") was sentenced to over 7 years in federal prison for using online criminal forums to sell stolen credit and debit card information (referred to as "dumps"). At the time of his arrest, Horohorin possessed over 2.5 million stolen credit and debit card numbers. There are several thousand known underground economy marketplaces around the world that sell stolen information, as well as malware, such as exploit kits, access to botnets, and more. **Table 4.2** lists some recently observed prices for various types of stolen data, which typically vary depending on the quantity being purchased, supply available, and "freshness." For example, when credit card information from the Target data breach first appeared on the market, individual card numbers went for up to $120 each. After a few weeks, however, the price dropped

TABLE 4.2	THE CYBER BLACK MARKET FOR STOLEN DATA
DATA	PRICE*
Individual U.S. card number with expiration date and CVV2 (the three-digit number printed on back of card) (referred to as a CVV)	$5–$8
Individual U.S. card number with full information, including full name, billing address, expiration date, CVV2, date of birth, mother's maiden name, etc. (referred to as a Fullz or Fullzinfo)	$30
Dump data for U.S. card (the term "dump" refers to raw data such as name, account number, expiration data, and CVV encoded on the magnetic strip on the back of the card)	$110–$120
Online payment service accounts	$20–$300
Bank account login credentials	$80–$700
Online account login credentials (Facebook, Twitter, eBay)	$10–$15
Medical information/health credentials	$10–$20
1,000 e-mail addresses	$1–$10
Scan of a passport	$1–$2

SOURCES: Based on data from McAfee, 2016; Intel Security, 2015; Symantec, 2015; Maruca, 2015; Infosec Institute, 2015; RAND Corporation, 2014.

*Prices vary based on supply and quality (freshness of data, account balances, validity, etc.).

dramatically (Leger, 2014). Experts believe the cost of stolen information has generally fallen as the tools of harvesting have increased the supply. On the demand side, the same efficiencies and opportunities provided by new technology have increased the number of people who want to use stolen information. It's a robust marketplace.

Finding these marketplaces and the servers that host them can be difficult for the average user (and for law enforcement agencies), and prospective participants are typically vetted by other criminals before access is granted. This vetting process takes place through Twitter, Tor, and VPN services, and sometimes e-mail exchanges of information, money (often Bitcoins, a form of digital cash that we discuss further in Section 4.5 and in the *Insight on Business* case study on pages 304–305), and reputation. There is a general hierarchy of cybercriminals in the marketplace, with low-level, nontechnical criminals who frequent "carder forums," where stolen credit and debit card data is sold, aiming to make money, a political statement, or both, at the bottom; resellers in the middle acting as intermediaries; and the technical masterminds who create malicious code at the top.

So, what can we can conclude about the overall size of cybercrime? Cybercrime against e-commerce sites is dynamic and changing all the time, with new risks appearing often. The amount of losses to businesses is significant and growing. The managers of e-commerce sites must prepare for an ever-changing variety of criminal assaults, and keep current in the latest security techniques.

WHAT IS GOOD E-COMMERCE SECURITY?

What is a secure commercial transaction? Anytime you go into a marketplace you take risks, including the loss of privacy (information about what you purchased). Your prime risk as a consumer is that you do not get what you paid for. As a merchant in the market, your risk is that you don't get paid for what you sell. Thieves take merchandise and then either walk off without paying anything, or pay you with a fraudulent instrument, stolen credit card, or forged currency.

E-commerce merchants and consumers face many of the same risks as participants in traditional commerce, albeit in a new digital environment. Theft is theft, regardless of whether it is digital theft or traditional theft. Burglary, breaking and entering, embezzlement, trespass, malicious destruction, vandalism—all crimes in a traditional commercial environment—are also present in e-commerce. However, reducing risks in e-commerce is a complex process that involves new technologies, organizational policies and procedures, and new laws and industry standards that empower law enforcement officials to investigate and prosecute offenders. **Figure 4.1** illustrates the multi-layered nature of e-commerce security.

To achieve the highest degree of security possible, new technologies are available and should be used. But these technologies by themselves do not solve the problem. Organizational policies and procedures are required to ensure the technologies are not subverted. Finally, industry standards and government laws are required to enforce payment mechanisms, as well as to investigate and prosecute violators of laws designed to protect the transfer of property in commercial transactions.

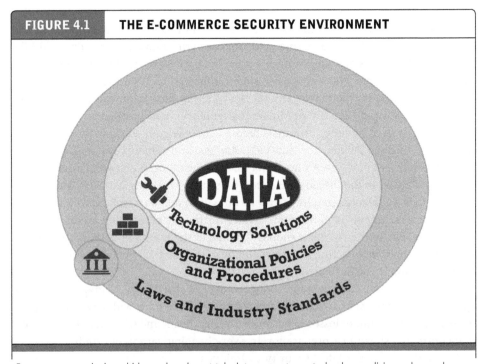

FIGURE 4.1   **THE E-COMMERCE SECURITY ENVIRONMENT**

E-commerce security is multi-layered, and must take into account new technology, policies and procedures, and laws and industry standards.

The history of security in commercial transactions teaches that any security system can be broken if enough resources are put against it. Security is not absolute. In addition, perfect security of every item is not needed forever, especially in the information age. There is a time value to information—just as there is to money. Sometimes it is sufficient to protect a message for a few hours or days. Also, because security is costly, we always have to weigh the cost against the potential loss. Finally, we have also learned that security is a chain that breaks most often at the weakest link. Our locks are often much stronger than our management of the keys.

We can conclude then that good e-commerce security requires a set of laws, procedures, policies, and technologies that, to the extent feasible, protect individuals and organizations from unexpected behavior in the e-commerce marketplace.

DIMENSIONS OF E-COMMERCE SECURITY

There are six key dimensions to e-commerce security: integrity, nonrepudiation, authenticity, confidentiality, privacy, and availability.

Integrity refers to the ability to ensure that information being displayed on a website, or transmitted or received over the Internet, has not been altered in any way by an unauthorized party. For example, if an unauthorized person intercepts and changes the contents of an online communication, such as by redirecting a bank wire transfer into a different account, the integrity of the message has been compromised because the communication no longer represents what the original sender intended.

Nonrepudiation refers to the ability to ensure that e-commerce participants do not deny (i.e., repudiate) their online actions. For instance, the availability of free e-mail accounts with alias names makes it easy for a person to post comments or send a message and perhaps later deny doing so. Even when a customer uses a real name and e-mail address, it is easy for that customer to order merchandise online and then later deny doing so. In most cases, because merchants typically do not obtain a physical copy of a signature, the credit card issuer will side with the customer because the merchant has no legally valid proof that the customer ordered the merchandise.

Authenticity refers to the ability to identify the identity of a person or entity with whom you are dealing on the Internet. How does the customer know that the website operator is who it claims to be? How can the merchant be assured that the customer is really who she says she is? Someone who claims to be someone he is not is "spoofing" or misrepresenting himself.

Confidentiality refers to the ability to ensure that messages and data are available only to those who are authorized to view them. Confidentiality is sometimes confused with **privacy**, which refers to the ability to control the use of information a customer provides about himself or herself to an e-commerce merchant.

E-commerce merchants have two concerns related to privacy. They must establish internal policies that govern their own use of customer information, and they must protect that information from illegitimate or unauthorized use. For example, if hackers break into an e-commerce site and gain access to credit card or other information, this violates not only the confidentiality of the data, but also the privacy of the individuals who supplied the information.

integrity
the ability to ensure that information being displayed on a website or transmitted or received over the Internet has not been altered in any way by an unauthorized party

nonrepudiation
the ability to ensure that e-commerce participants do not deny (i.e., repudiate) their online actions

authenticity
the ability to identify the identity of a person or entity with whom you are dealing on the Internet

confidentiality
the ability to ensure that messages and data are available only to those who are authorized to view them

privacy
the ability to control the use of information about oneself

TABLE 4.3	CUSTOMER AND MERCHANT PERSPECTIVES ON THE DIFFERENT DIMENSIONS OF E-COMMERCE SECURITY	
DIMENSION	**CUSTOMER'S PERSPECTIVE**	**MERCHANT'S PERSPECTIVE**
Integrity	Has information I transmitted or received been altered?	Has data on the site been altered without authorization? Is data being received from customers valid?
Nonrepudiation	Can a party to an action with me later deny taking the action?	Can a customer deny ordering products?
Authenticity	Who am I dealing with? How can I be assured that the person or entity is who they claim to be?	What is the real identity of the customer?
Confidentiality	Can someone other than the intended recipient read my messages?	Are messages or confidential data accessible to anyone other than those authorized to view them?
Privacy	Can I control the use of information about myself transmitted to an e-commerce merchant?	What use, if any, can be made of personal data collected as part of an e-commerce transaction? Is the personal information of customers being used in an unauthorized manner?
Availability	Can I get access to the site?	Is the site operational?

availability

the ability to ensure that an e-commerce site continues to function as intended

Availability refers to the ability to ensure that an e-commerce site continues to function as intended.

Table 4.3 summarizes these dimensions from both the merchants' and customers' perspectives. E-commerce security is designed to protect these six dimensions. When any one of them is compromised, overall security suffers.

THE TENSION BETWEEN SECURITY AND OTHER VALUES

Can there be too much security? The answer is yes. Contrary to what some may believe, security is not an unmitigated good. Computer security adds overhead and expense to business operations, and also gives criminals new opportunities to hide their intentions and their crimes.

Ease of Use

There are inevitable tensions between security and ease of use. When traditional merchants are so fearful of robbers that they do business in shops locked behind security gates, ordinary customers are discouraged from walking in. The same can be true with respect to e-commerce. In general, the more security measures added to an e-commerce site, the more difficult it is to use and the slower the site becomes. As you will discover reading this chapter, digital security is purchased at the price of slowing down processors and adding significantly to data storage demands on storage devices. Security is a technological and business overhead that can detract from doing business. Too much security can harm profitability, while not enough security can potentially put you out of business. One solution is to adjust security settings to the user's preferences. A recent McKinsey report found that when consumers find authentication at websites easy, they purchased 10% to 20% more. About 30% of the Internet population prioritizes ease of use and convenience over security, while 10% prioritize security. The report suggests it is possible to have both ease of use and security by adjusting the authentication process for each customer, providing options from automatic login (low security), to downloadable one-time passwords (high security) (Hasham, et al., 2016).

Public Safety and the Criminal Uses of the Internet

There is also an inevitable tension between the desires of individuals to act anonymously (to hide their identity) and the needs of public officials to maintain public safety that can be threatened by criminals or terrorists. This is not a new problem, or even new to the electronic era. The U.S. government began tapping telegraph wires during the Civil War in the mid-1860s in order to trap conspirators and terrorists, and the first police wiretaps of local telephone systems were in place by the 1890s—20 years after the invention of the phone (Schwartz, 2001). No nation-state has ever permitted a technological haven to exist where criminals can plan crimes or threaten the nation-state without fear of official surveillance or investigation. In this sense, the Internet is no different from any other communication system. Drug cartels make extensive use of voice, fax, the Internet, and encrypted e-mail; a number of large international organized crime groups steal information from commercial websites and resell it to other criminals who use it for financial fraud. Over the years, the U.S. government has successfully pursued various "carding forums" (websites that facilitate the sale of stolen credit card and debit card numbers), such as Shadowcrew, Carderplanet, and Cardersmarket, resulting in the arrest and prosecution of a number of their members and the closing of the sites. However, other criminal organizations have emerged to take their place.

The Internet and mobile platform also provide terrorists with convenient communications channels. Encrypted files sent via e-mail were used by Ramzi Yousef—a member of the terrorist group responsible for bombing the World Trade Center in 1993—to hide plans for bombing 11 U.S. airliners. The Internet was also used to plan and coordinate the subsequent attacks on the World Trade Center on September 11, 2001. The case of Umar Farouk Abdulmutallab further illustrates how terrorists make effective use of the Internet to radicalize, recruit, train, and coordinate youthful terrorists. Abdulmutallab allegedly attempted to blow up an American airliner in Detroit on Christmas Day 2009. He was identified, contacted, recruited, and trained, all within six weeks, according to a Pentagon counterterrorism official. In an effort to combat such terrorism, the U.S. government has significantly ramped up its surveillance of communications delivered via the Internet over the past several years. The extent of that surveillance created a major controversy with National Security Agency contractor Edward Snowden's release of classified NSA documents that revealed that the NSA had obtained access to the servers of major Internet companies such as Facebook, Google, Apple, Microsoft, and others, as well as that NSA analysts have been searching e-mail, online chats, and browsing histories of U.S. citizens without any court approval. Security agencies have shifted from mass surveillance to smaller, targeted surveillance of terrorists and terrorist groups, and the use of predictive algorithms to focus their efforts (N.F. Johnson, et al., 2016). The proper balance between public safety and privacy in the effort against terrorism has proven to be a very thorny problem for the U.S. government.

4.2 SECURITY THREATS IN THE E-COMMERCE ENVIRONMENT

From a technology perspective, there are three key points of vulnerability when dealing with e-commerce: the client, the server, and the communications pipeline. **Figure 4.2** illustrates a typical e-commerce transaction with a consumer using a credit

---

FIGURE 4.2 A TYPICAL E-COMMERCE TRANSACTION

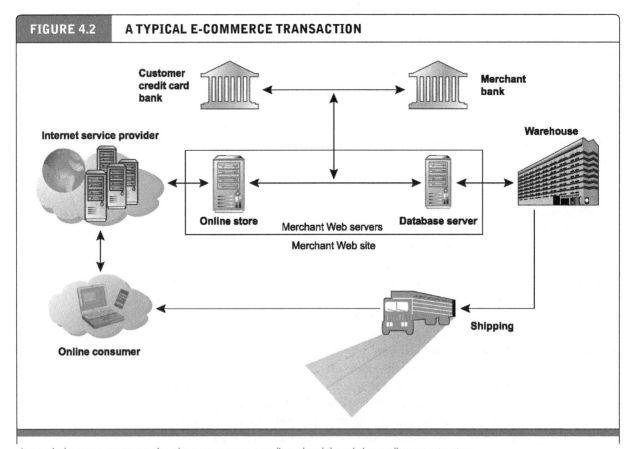

In a typical e-commerce transaction, the customer uses a credit card and the existing credit payment system.

| FIGURE 4.3 | **VULNERABLE POINTS IN AN E-COMMERCE TRANSACTION** |

There are three major vulnerable points in e-commerce transactions: Internet communications, servers, and clients.

card to purchase a product. **Figure 4.3** illustrates some of the things that can go wrong at each major vulnerability point in the transaction—over Internet communications channels, at the server level, and at the client level.

In this section, we describe a number of the most common and most damaging forms of security threats to e-commerce consumers and site operators: malicious code, potentially unwanted programs, phishing, hacking and cybervandalism, credit card fraud/theft, spoofing, pharming, spam (junk) websites (link farms), identity fraud, Denial of Service (DoS) and DDoS attacks, sniffing, insider attacks, poorly designed server and client software, social network security issues, mobile platform security issues, and finally, cloud security issues.

MALICIOUS CODE

Malicious code (sometimes referred to as "malware") includes a variety of threats such as viruses, worms, Trojan horses, ransomware, and bots. Some malicious code, sometimes referred to as an *exploit,* is designed to take advantage of software vulnerabilities in a computer's operating system, web browser, applications, or other software components. **Exploit kits** are collections of exploits bundled together and rented or sold as a commercial product, often with slick user interfaces and in-depth analytics functionality. Use of an exploit kit typically does not require much technical skill, enabling novices

malicious code (malware)
includes a variety of threats such as viruses, worms, Trojan horses, and bots

exploit kit
collection of exploits bundled together and rented or sold as a commercial product

to become cybercriminals. Exploit kits typically target software that is widely deployed, such as Microsoft Windows, Internet Explorer, Adobe Flash and Reader, and Oracle Java. In 2014, according to Cisco, Angler, an exploit kit that uses Flash, Java, Microsoft Internet Explorer, and Microsoft Silverlight vulnerabilities, was one of the exploit kits most observed "in the wild" (Cisco, 2016). According to Symantec, more than 430 million new variants of malware were created in 2015, an average of more than a million strains a day, up 36% in one year (Symantec, 2016). In the past, malicious code was often intended to simply impair computers, and was often authored by a lone hacker, but increasingly it involves a small group of hackers or a nation-state supported group, and the intent is to steal e-mail addresses, logon credentials, personal data, and financial information. It's the difference between petty crime and organized crime.

Malware is often delivered in the form of a malicious attachment to an email or embedded as a link in the email. Malicious links can also be placed in innocent-looking Microsoft Word or Excel documents. The links lead directly to a malicious code download or websites that include malicious code (Symantec, 2016). One of the latest innovations in malicious code distribution is to embed it in the online advertising chain (known as **maladvertising**), including in Google, AOL, and other ad networks (Goodin, 2016). As the ad network chain becomes more complicated, it becomes more and more difficult for websites to vet ads placed on their sites to ensure they are malware-free. A 2014 research study indicated that as many as 1% of all ads served may be maladvertising (Zarras et al., 2014). The largest advertising malware infection occurred at Yahoo where more than 6.9 million daily visitors were exposed to malicious pop-up ads (Blue, 2016). These malicious ads can be stopped by turning on pop-up blockers in users' browsers. Much of the maladvertising in the recent years has been in the form of drive-by downloads that exploited the frequent zero-day vulnerabilities that have plagued Adobe Flash, which is often used for online advertisements. As a result, the Internet Advertising Bureau has urged advertisers to abandon Adobe Flash in favor of HTML5, and Mozilla Firefox, Apple's Safari, and Google's Chrome browser all now block Flash advertisements from autoplaying. Amazon has also stopped accepting Flash ads (see the Chapter 2 *Insight on Technology* case, *The Rise of HTML5*). A **drive-by download** is malware that comes with a downloaded file that a user intentionally or unintentionally requests. Drive-by is now one of the most common methods of infecting computers. For instance, websites as disparate as the New York Times, MSN, Yahoo, and AOL have experienced instances where ads placed on their sites either had malicious code embedded or directed clickers to malicious sites. According to Symantec, drive-by download exploit kits, including updates and 24/7 support, can be rented for between $100 to $700 per week. Malicious code embedded in PDF files also is common. Equally important, there has been a major shift in the writers of malware from amateur hackers and adventurers to organized criminal efforts to defraud companies and individuals. In other words, it's now more about the money than ever before.

A **virus** is a computer program that has the ability to replicate or make copies of itself, and spread to other files. In addition to the ability to replicate, most computer viruses deliver a "payload." The payload may be relatively benign, such as the display of a message or image, or it may be highly destructive—destroying files, reformatting the computer's hard drive, or causing programs to run improperly.

maladvertising
online advertising that contains malicious code

drive-by download
malware that comes with a downloaded file that a user requests

virus
a computer program that has the ability to replicate or make copies of itself, and spread to other files

Viruses are often combined with a worm. Instead of just spreading from file to file, a **worm** is designed to spread from computer to computer. A worm does not necessarily need to be activated by a user or program in order for it to replicate itself. The Slammer worm is one of the most notorious. Slammer targeted a known vulnerability in Microsoft's SQL Server database software and infected more than 90% of vulnerable computers worldwide within 10 minutes of its release on the Internet; crashed Bank of America cash machines, especially in the southwestern part of the United States; affected cash registers at supermarkets such as the Publix chain in Atlanta, where staff could not dispense cash to frustrated buyers; and took down most Internet connections in South Korea, causing a dip in the stock market there. The Conficker worm, which first appeared in November 2008, is the most significant worm since Slammer, and reportedly infected 11 million computers worldwide (Microsoft, 2015). Originally designed to establish a global botnet, a massive industry effort has defeated this effort, but Conficker still resides on over 800,000 Internet devices in 2016. It is the most widely detected malware on the Internet.

worm
malware that is designed to spread from computer to computer

Ransomware (scareware) is a type of malware (often a worm) that locks your computer or files to stop you from accessing them. Ransomware will often display a notice that says an authority such as the FBI, Department of Justice, or IRS has detected illegal activity on your computer and demands that you pay a fine in order to unlock the computer and avoid prosecution. One type of ransomware is named CryptoLocker. CryptoLocker encrypts victims' files with a virtually unbreakable asymmetric encryption and demands a ransom to decrypt them, often in Bitcoins. If the victim does not comply within the time allowed, the files will not ever be able to be decrypted. Other variants include CryptoDefense and Cryptowall. Ransomware attacks increased by over 400% in 2016, and the U.S. Department of Justice reports that there are over 4,000 ransomware attacks daily, up from 1,000 daily in 2015 (U.S. Department of Justice, 2016). Crypto-ransomware infections often take place via a malicious e-mail attachment that purports to be an invoice (Symantec, 2016). The growth of ransomware is also related to the growth of the virtual currency Bitcoin. Hackers often demand victims pay using Bitcoin so their transactions are hidden from authorities (McMillan, 2016).

ransomware (scareware)
malware that prevents you from accessing your computer or files and demands that you pay a fine

A **Trojan horse** appears to be benign, but then does something other than expected. The Trojan horse is not itself a virus because it does not replicate, but is often a way for viruses or other malicious code such as bots or *rootkits* (a program whose aim is to subvert control of the computer's operating system) to be introduced into a computer system. The term *Trojan horse* refers to the huge wooden horse in Homer's *Iliad* that the Greeks gave their opponents, the Trojans—a gift that actually contained hundreds of Greek soldiers. Once the people of Troy let the massive horse within their gates, the soldiers revealed themselves and captured the city. In today's world, a Trojan horse may masquerade as a game, but actually hide a program to steal your passwords and e-mail them to another person. Miscellaneous Trojans and Trojan downloaders and droppers (Trojans that install malicious files to a computer they have infected by either downloading them from a remote computer or from a copy contained in their own code) are a common type of malware. According to Panda Security, Trojans accounted for over 50% of all malware created in 2015, and over 60% of all malware infections (Panda Security, 2016). In 2011, Sony experienced the largest data

Trojan horse
appears to be benign, but then does something other than expected. Often a way for viruses or other malicious code to be introduced into a computer system

breach in history up to that time when a Trojan horse took over the administrative computers of Sony's PlayStation game center and downloaded personal and credit card information involving 77 million registered users (Wakabayashi, 2011). Trojan horses are often used for financial malware distributed via botnets. One example is Zeus, which steals information by keystroke logging and has infected over 10 million computers since it first became known in 2007. Other examples include SpyEye, a Trojan that can steal banking information via both a keylogging application and the ability to take screenshots on a victim's computer; Torpig, a botnet that is spread by a Trojan horse called Meboot; and Vawtrak, a Trojan that spreads via social media, e-mail, and FTP, and is able to hide evidence of fraud by changing bank balances shown to the victim on the fly (Cyphort, 2015).

backdoor

feature of viruses, worms, and Trojans that allows an attacker to remotely access a compromised computer

A **backdoor** is a feature of viruses, worms, and Trojans that allows an attacker to remotely access a compromised computer. Downadup is an example of a worm with a backdoor, while Virut, a virus that infects various file types, also includes a backdoor that can be used to download and install additional threats.

bot

type of malicious code that can be covertly installed on a computer when connected to the Internet. Once installed, the bot responds to external commands sent by the attacker

Bots (short for robots) are a type of malicious code that can be covertly installed on your computer when attached to the Internet. Once installed, the bot responds to external commands sent by the attacker; your computer becomes a "zombie" and is able to be controlled by an external third party (the "bot-herder"). **Botnets** are collections of captured computers used for malicious activities such as sending spam, participating in a DDoS attack, stealing information from computers, and storing network traffic for later analysis. The number of botnets operating worldwide is not known but is estimated to be well into the thousands, controlling millions of computers. Bots and bot networks are an important threat to the Internet and e-commerce because they can be used to launch very large-scale attacks using many different techniques. In 2011, federal marshals accompanied members of Microsoft's digital crimes unit in raids designed to disable the Rustock botnet, at that time the leading source of spam in the world with nearly 500,000 slave PCs under the control of its command and control servers located at six Internet hosting services in the United States. Officials confiscated the Rustock control servers at the hosting sites, which claimed they had no idea what the Rustock servers were doing. The actual spam e-mails were sent by the slave PCs under the command of the Rustock servers (Wingfield, 2011). In 2013, Microsoft and the FBI engaged in another aggressive botnet operation, targeting 1,400 of Zeus-derived Citadel botnets, which had been used in 2012 to raid bank accounts at major banks around the world, netting over $500 million (Chirgwin, 2013). In April 2015, an international cybersquad took down the Beebone botnet, made up of 12,000 computers that had been infecting about 30,000 computers a month around the world via drive-by downloads with Changeup, a polymorphic worm used to distribute Trojans, worms, backdoors, and other types of malware (Constantin, 2015). In 2015, the FBI and British police were also able to stop a botnet that had stolen over $10 million from banks (Pagliery, 2015). As a result of efforts such as these, the number of bots has significantly declined, especially in the United States (Symantec, 2016).

botnet

collection of captured bot computers

Malicious code is a threat at both the client and the server levels, although servers generally engage in much more thorough anti-virus activities than do consumers. At

TABLE 4.4	NOTABLE EXAMPLES OF MALICIOUS CODE	
NAME	TYPE	DESCRIPTION
Cryptolocker	Ransomware/ Trojan	Hijacks users' photos, videos, and text documents, encrypts them with virtually unbreakable asymmetric encryption, and demands ransom payment for them.
Citadel	Trojan/botnet	Variant of Zeus Trojan, focuses on the theft of authentication credentials and financial fraud. Botnets spreading Citadel were targets of Microsoft/FBI action in 2012.
Zeus	Trojan/botnet	Sometimes referred to as king of financial malware. May install via drive-by download and evades detection by taking control of web browser and stealing data that is exchanged with bank servers.
Reveton	Ransomware worm/Trojan	Based on Citadel/Zeus Trojans. Locks computer and displays warning from local police alleging illegal activity on computer; demands payment of fine to unlock.
Ramnit	Virus/worm	One of the most prevalent malicious code families still active in 2013. Infects various file types, including executable files, and copies itself to removable drives, executing via AutoPlay when the drive is accessed on other computers
Sality.AE	Virus/worm	Most common virus in 2012; still active in 2013. Disables security applications and services, connects to a botnet, then downloads and installs additional threats. Uses polymorphism to evade detection.
Conficker	Worm	First appeared November 2008. Targets Microsoft operating systems. Uses advanced malware techniques. Largest worm infection since Slammer in 2003. Still considered a major threat.
Netsky.P	Worm/Trojan	First appeared in early 2003. It spreads by gathering target e-mail addresses from the computers, then infects and sends e-mail to all recipients from the infected computer. It is commonly used by bot networks to launch spam and DoS attacks.
Storm (Peacomm, NuWar)	Worm/Trojan	First appeared in January 2007. It spreads in a manner similar to the Netsky.P worm. May also download and run other Trojan programs and worms.
Nymex	Worm	First discovered in January 2006. Spreads by mass mailing; activates on the 3rd of every month, and attempts to destroy files of certain types.
Zotob	Worm	First appeared in August 2005. Well-known worm that infected a number of U.S. media companies.
Mydoom	Worm	First appeared in January 2004. One of the fastest spreading mass-mailer worms.
Slammer	Worm	Launched in January 2003. Caused widespread problems.
CodeRed	Worm	Appeared in 2001. It achieved an infection rate of over 20,000 systems within 10 minutes of release and ultimately spread to hundreds of thousands of systems.
Melissa	Macro virus/ worm	First spotted in March 1999. At the time, the fastest spreading infectious program ever discovered. It attacked Microsoft Word's Normal.dot global template, ensuring infection of all newly created documents. It also mailed an infected Word file to the first 50 entries in each user's Microsoft Outlook Address Book.
Chernobyl	File-infecting virus	First appeared in 1998. It wipes out the first megabyte of data on a hard disk (making the rest useless) every April 26, the anniversary of the nuclear disaster at Chernobyl.

the server level, malicious code can bring down an entire website, preventing millions of people from using the site. Such incidents are infrequent. Much more frequent malicious code attacks occur at the client level, and the damage can quickly spread to millions of other computers connected to the Internet. **Table 4.4** lists some well-known examples of malicious code.

POTENTIALLY UNWANTED PROGRAMS (PUPS)

In addition to malicious code, the e-commerce security environment is further challenged by **potentially unwanted programs (PUPs)** such as adware, browser parasites, spyware, and other applications that install themselves on a computer, such as rogue security software, toolbars, and PC diagnostic tools, typically without the user's informed consent. Such programs are increasingly found on social network and user-generated content sites where users are fooled into downloading them. Once installed, these applications are usually exceedingly difficult to remove from the computer. One example of a PUP is System Doctor, which infects PCs running Windows operating systems. System Doctor poses as a legitimate anti-spyware program when in fact it is malware that, when installed, disables the user's security software, alters the user's web browser, and diverts users to scam websites where more malware is downloaded.

Adware is typically used to call for pop-up ads to display when the user visits certain sites. While annoying, adware is not typically used for criminal activities. A **browser parasite** is a program that can monitor and change the settings of a user's browser, for instance, changing the browser's home page, or sending information about the sites visited to a remote computer. Browser parasites are often a component of adware. In early 2015, Lenovo faced a barrage of criticism when it became known that, since September 2014, it had been shipping its Windows laptops with Superfish adware preinstalled. Superfish injected its own shopping results into the computer's browser when the user searched on Google, Amazon, or other websites. In the process, Superfish created a security risk by enabling others on a Wi-Fi network to silently hijack the browser and collect anything typed into it. Lenovo ultimately issued a removal tool to enable customers to delete the adware. Microsoft and legitimate security firms have redefined adware programs to be malware and discourage manufacturers from shipping products with adware programs (Loeb, 2016).

Spyware, on the other hand, can be used to obtain information such as a user's keystrokes, copies of e-mail and instant messages, and even take screenshots (and thereby capture passwords or other confidential data).

PHISHING

Social engineering relies on human curiosity, greed, and gullibility in order to trick people into taking an action that will result in the downloading of malware. Kevin Mitnick, until his capture and imprisonment in 1999, was one of America's most wanted computer criminals. Mitnick used simple deceptive techniques to obtain passwords, social security, and police records all without the use of any sophisticated technology (Mitnick, 2011).

Phishing is any deceptive, online attempt by a third party to obtain confidential information for financial gain. Phishing attacks typically do not involve malicious code but instead rely on straightforward misrepresentation and fraud, so-called "social engineering" techniques. One of the most popular phishing attacks is the e-mail scam letter. The scam begins with an e-mail: a rich former oil minister of Nigeria is seeking a bank account to stash millions of dollars for a short period of time, and requests your bank account number where the money can be deposited. In return, you will receive

potentially unwanted program (PUP)
program that installs itself on a computer, typically without the user's informed consent

adware
a PUP that serves pop-up ads to your computer

browser parasite
a program that can monitor and change the settings of a user's browser

spyware
a program used to obtain information such as a user's keystrokes, e-mail, instant messages, and so on

social engineering
exploitation of human fallibility and gullibility to distribute malware

phishing
any deceptive, online attempt by a third party to obtain confidential information for financial gain

FIGURE 4.4	AN EXAMPLE OF A NIGERIAN LETTER E-MAIL SCAM

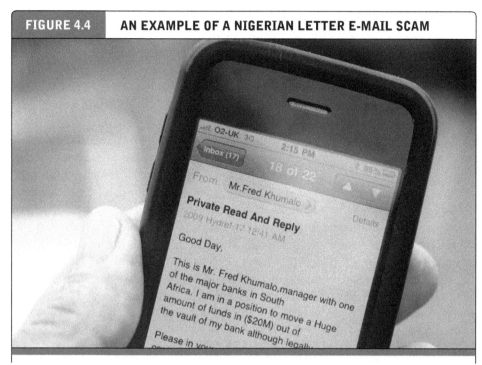

This is an example of a typical Nigerian letter e-mail scam.
© keith morris/Alamy Stock Photo

a million dollars. This type of e-mail scam is popularly known as a "Nigerian letter" scam (see **Figure 4.4**).

Thousands of other phishing attacks use other scams, some pretending to be eBay, PayPal, or Citibank writing to you for account verification (known as *spear phishing,* or targeting a known customer of a specific bank or other type of business). Click on a link in the e-mail and you will be taken to a website controlled by the scammer, and prompted to enter confidential information about your accounts, such as your account number and PIN codes. On any given day, millions of these phishing attack e-mails are sent, and, unfortunately, some people are fooled and disclose their personal account information.

Phishers rely on traditional "con man" tactics, but use e-mail to trick recipients into voluntarily giving up financial access codes, bank account numbers, credit card numbers, and other personal information. Often, phishers create (or "spoof") a website that purports to be a legitimate financial institution and cons users into entering financial information, or the site downloads malware such as a keylogger to the victim's computer. Phishers use the information they gather to commit fraudulent acts such as charging items to your credit cards or withdrawing funds from your bank account, or in other ways "steal your identity" (identity fraud). Symantec reported that in 2015, about 1 in every 1,875 e-mails contained a phishing attack. The number of spear-phishing campaigns in 2015 increased by 55%, but the number of attacks, recipients within each campaign, and the average duration of the campaign all declined, indicating that perpetrators are becoming stealthier about them, since campaigns that target fewer recipients and are smaller and shorter are less likely to arouse suspicion. In 2015, according to Symantec, 43% of spear-phishing e-mails were directed at small businesses with less than 250 employees, and 35% of large organizations reported they were targeted in spear-phishing campaigns (Symantec, 2016). According to Verizon, 30% of phishing emails were opened by their targets, and 12% were clicked on to open attachments (Verizon, 2016).

To combat phishing, in January 2012, leading e-mail service providers, including Google, Microsoft, Yahoo, and AOL, as well as financial services companies such as PayPal, Bank of America, and others, joined together to form DMARC.org, an organization aimed at dramatically reducing e-mail address spoofing, in which attackers use real e-mail addresses to send phishing e-mails to victims who may be deceived because the e-mail appears to originate from a source the receiver trusts. DMARC offers a method of authenticating the origin of the e-mail and allows receivers to quarantine, report, or reject messages that fall to pass its test. Yahoo and AOL have reported significant success against email fraud as a result of using DMARC, and, effective as of June 2016, Google joined them in implementing a stricter version of DMARC, in which e-mail that fails DMARC authentication checks will be rejected (Vijayan, 2015).

HACKING, CYBERVANDALISM, AND HACKTIVISM

hacker
an individual who intends to gain unauthorized access to a computer system

cracker
within the hacking community, a term typically used to denote a hacker with criminal intent

cybervandalism
intentionally disrupting, defacing, or even destroying a site

hacktivism
cybervandalism and data theft for political purposes

A **hacker** is an individual who intends to gain unauthorized access to a computer system. Within the hacking community, the term **cracker** is typically used to denote a hacker with criminal intent, although in the public press, the terms hacker and cracker tend to be used interchangeably. Hackers and crackers gain unauthorized access by finding weaknesses in the security procedures of websites and computer systems, often taking advantage of various features of the Internet that make it an open system that is easy to use. In the past, hackers and crackers typically were computer aficionados excited by the challenge of breaking into corporate and government websites. Sometimes they were satisfied merely by breaking into the files of an e-commerce site. Today, hackers have malicious intentions to disrupt, deface, or destroy sites (**cybervandalism**) or to steal personal or corporate information they can use for financial gain (data breach).

Hacktivism adds a political twist. Hacktivists typically attack governments, organizations, and even individuals for political purposes, employing the tactics of cybervandalism, distributed denial of service attacks, data thefts, and doxing (gathering and exposing personal information of public figures, typically from emails, social network posts, and other documents). The most prominent hacktivist organization is Wikileaks, founded by Julian Assange and others, which released documents and e-mails of the U.S. Department of State, U.S. Department of Defense, and Democratic National Committee in 2016. LulzSec and Anonymous are two other prominent hacktivist groups. In 2015, another hacktivist group called the Impact Team allegedly hacked the Ashley Madison website to call attention to its weak security, and after its owner Avid Life Media refused to shut it down as they demanded, the group released millions of sensitive customer records. See the *Insight on Society* case study, *The Ashley Madison Data Breach*, for a more in-depth look at implications of this high-profile hack.

INSIGHT ON SOCIETY

THE ASHLEY MADISON DATA BREACH

As the Internet continues to permeate even the most intimate aspects of our lives, the stigma attached to online dating has largely disappeared. Online dating has grown into a $2.2 billion industry annually in the United States, led by companies like eHarmony, OKCupid, and Match. There are also a number of smaller niche sites that cater to people with more specific interests or lifestyles. One such site is Ashley Madison.

Based in Canada and launched in 2001 by its parent company, Avid Life Media, Ashley Madison specifically markets itself to people in marriages or committed relationships, which has earned the site a tawdry reputation. Users purchase credits, rather than a monthly subscription, and then redeem the credits to participate in conversations with other members, which can be through messages or real-time chat. Women are not charged money to create a profile on the site, nor are they charged to send or receive messages, while men are charged for both. Even with those incentives, the ratio of men to women on the site skews dramatically toward men, which led Ashley Madison to create fictitious female profiles to create the appearance of balance.

The perception of secrecy is critical for prospective users of Ashley Madison. But in 2015, that veil of secrecy came crashing down. The site was hacked by a group known as The Impact Team, which stated that its motivations were to harm the site and its unethical business model, as well as to protest the site's use of a $19 data deletion fee for users seeking to close their accounts. The Impact Team stated that after creating a plan to make an undetectable breach, they discovered they were easily able to access the entire cache of company data. They released the data in two batches of 10 and 12 gigabytes, and the data is now easily searchable on the Web. Names, street addresses, and dates of birth were all stolen and made public, as well as other personal information. They also stole company documents, including the e-mails of CEO Noel Biderman, many of which caused further damage to the company's shattered reputation. For example, Biderman's e-mails revealed that the CTO of Ashley Madison had hacked a competitor's database, revealing key security flaws (perhaps he should have been paying more attention to his own company's security systems). Partial credit card information of Ashley Madison users was also leaked, but not enough for identity thieves to use.

Demographic information gleaned from the data dump shows that of the site's 36 million users, 31 million were males, but only 10 million actively used the site. The other 5 million profiles were female, but less than 2,500 of those were involved in chats with other users, suggesting that fake female profiles were the overwhelming majority of female profiles on the site. A full third of the accounts on the site were created with dummy e-mail addresses. North Americans had the highest number of accounts as a percentage of population, with the United States coming in at 5.1%. E-mail addresses associated with government accounts were well-represented, as were big banks, large tech companies, and other high-powered industries. This stands in stark demographic contrast to a service like Tinder, which consists of much younger members; Ashley Madison users tended to be more established financially and willing to pay for what they perceived to be a discreet and upscale service. After the hack, researchers found that companies with a disproportionately high number of Ashley Madison members took bigger financial risks and had poor scores in corporate responsibility.

Ashley Madison's own corporate profile suggests risk-taking of its own. How could a site

(continued)

that advertises the ability to discreetly have an affair allow its data to be breached and stolen so easily? Security experts reviewing Ashley Madison's setup claimed that the site lacked even simplistic security measures. For example, all of the data belonging to users who paid the $19 data deletion fee persisted on Ashley Madison servers and was obtained in the hack. Additionally, none of the data was encrypted. Encryption would have incurred hefty additional expense for the company, but it might have saved it considerable embarrassment during a breach like this one.

Most data breaches allow criminals to engage in identity theft and other types of online fraud. But in this case, the Ashley Madison hack has even more significant ramifications on the personal lives of its users. There are already multiple reported incidents of suicides committed by former users, and a handful of notable public figures have been publicly embarrassed by the release of their profile data. The hack has the potential to ruin the marriages and personal lives of thousands of people. Although many of Ashley Madison's users were engaged in infidelity, these people were still the victims of a crime and an invasion of privacy that goes beyond typical data breaches. Spammers and blackmailers have used the now-public data to extort users, demanding Bitcoin in exchange for silence and threatening to share Ashley Madison data with users' families and social media contacts.

As a result of the hack, Biderman quickly stepped down from his post as CEO, and in 2016 a new executive team was installed and immediately began distancing themselves from the previous regime. Going forward, the revelations about fake profiles, impending lawsuits, and overall negative coverage of the breach will likely derail plans for growth. Ashley Madison had already struggled to market its business and raise funds in the past, despite its very solid financial profile. The company had been growing so fast that Biderman had started investigating launching an IPO in England to fuel its expansion. Not only are those plans on hold indefinitely, but the Federal Trade Commission has begun investigating Ashley Madison's usage of bots and other fake profiles. Ashley Madison has also begun to receive what may become a barrage of lawsuits alleging negligence and personal damages, though many potential plaintiffs may be unwilling to reveal their identities, which they must do to be included in any suit after a judge ruled in 2016 that plaintiffs could not use aliases such as John Doe. And the results of a joint investigation by the Canadian and Australian governments completed in 2016 confirmed that the company had fabricated a "trusted security award" displayed on its homepage. The investigation also confirmed the company's failure to delete profile information of users who canceled their accounts.

Despite the turmoil, the company estimates that its membership base has actually grown over the past year. However, a third-party analysis showed that traffic to the site has dropped by 82% since the breach, calling the site's self-reported numbers into question.

■■■ **SOURCES:** "Ashley Madison Blasted Over Fake Security Award as Lawsuit Moves Forward," by Jeff John Roberts, *Fortune*, August 25, 2016; "You Blew It, Ashley Madison: Dating Site Slammed for Security 'Shortcomings,'" by Claire Reilly Cnet.com, August 23, 2015; "Ashley Madison Parent, Under FTC Investigation, Launches Turnaround Plans," by Maria Armental and Austen Hufford, *Wall Street Journal*, July 5, 2016; "Infidelity Website Ashley Madison Facing FTC Probe, Apologizes," Alastair Sharp and Allison Martell, by Reuters.com, July 5, 2016; "Ashley Madison Hacking Victims Face Big Decision," by Robert Hackett, *Fortune*, April 20, 2016; "The Ashley Madison Effect on Companies," by Justin Lahart, *Wall Street Journal*, March 6, 2016; "Life After the Ashley Madison Affair," by Tom Lamont, Theguardian.com, February 27, 2016; "It's Been Six Months Since the Ashley Madison Hack. Has Anything Changed?" by Caitlin Dewey, *Washington Post*, January 15, 2016; "Ashley Madison Hack Victims Receive Blackmail Letters," BBC, December 15, 2015; "Ashley Madison Hack: 6 Charts That Show Who Uses the Infidelity Website," by Zachary Davies Boren, Independent.co.uk, August 21, 2015; "Ashley Madison Hackers Speak Out: 'Nobody Was Watching,'" by Joseph Cox, Motherboard.vice.com, August 21, 2015; "The Ashley Madison Hack, Explained," by Timothy B. Lee, Vox.com, August 19, 2015; "Who Is Ashley Madison," by Paul R. LaMonica, CNN Money, July 20, 2015.

Groups of hackers called *tiger teams* are sometimes used by corporate security departments to test their own security measures. By hiring hackers to break into the system from the outside, the company can identify weaknesses in the computer system's armor. These "good hackers" became known as **white hats** because of their role in helping organizations locate and fix security flaws. White hats do their work under contract, with agreement from the target firms that they will not be prosecuted for their efforts to break in. Hardware and software firms such as Apple and Microsoft pay bounties of $25,000 to $200,000 to white hat hackers for discovering bugs in their software and hardware (Perlroth, 2016).

In contrast, **black hats** are hackers who engage in the same kinds of activities but without pay or any buy-in from the targeted organization, and with the intention of causing harm. They break into websites and reveal the confidential or proprietary information they find. These hackers believe strongly that information should be free, so sharing previously secret information is part of their mission.

Somewhere in the middle are the **grey hats**, hackers who believe they are pursuing some greater good by breaking in and revealing system flaws. Grey hats discover weaknesses in a system's security, and then publish the weakness without disrupting the site or attempting to profit from their finds. Their only reward is the prestige of discovering the weakness. Grey hat actions are suspect, however, especially when the hackers reveal security flaws that make it easier for other criminals to gain access to a system.

white hats
"good" hackers who help organizations locate and fix security flaws

black hats
hackers who act with the intention of causing harm

grey hats
hackers who believe they are pursuing some greater good by breaking in and revealing system flaws

DATA BREACHES

A **data breach** occurs whenever organizations lose control over corporate information to outsiders. According to Symantec, the total number of data breaches in 2015 grew by only 2% compared to 2014, which was a record year for breaches. There were nine mega-breaches in 2015, up from eight in 2014. The total identities exposed reached 429 million, up 23%, with over 190 million identities exposed in a single breach (Symantec, 2016). The Identity Theft Resource Center is another organization that tracks data breaches. It recorded 780 breaches in 2015, the second highest total on record. Breaches involving the medical/healthcare industry had the highest impact, representing 35% of all breaches and almost 70% of all records exposed. Hackers were the leading cause of data breaches, responsible for almost 40% of breaches, followed by employee error/negligence (15%), accidental e-mail/Internet exposure (14%) and insider theft (11%). The number of breaches involving social security numbers involved almost 165 million people (Identity Theft Resource Center, 2016). Among the high profile breaches that occurred in 2015 were those affecting the Office of Personnel Management and the Internal Revenue Service, as well as others against health-care insurers such as Anthem and Premera, retailers such as CVS and Walgreens, and the credit rating agency Experian. In 2016, the trend has continued with the Yahoo data breach, which is believed to be the largest breach at a single company in history, exposing the records of 500 million. Compared to others like Google and Microsoft, Yahoo management was reportedly slow to invest in security measures (Perlroth and Goel, 2016).

data breach
occurs when an organization loses control over its information to outsiders

CREDIT CARD FRAUD/THEFT

Theft of credit card data is one of the most feared occurrences on the Internet. Fear that credit card information will be stolen prevents users from making online purchases in many cases. Interestingly, this fear appears to be largely unfounded. Incidences of stolen credit card information are actually much lower than users think, around 0.8% of all online card transactions (CyberSource, 2016). Online merchants use a variety of techniques to combat credit card fraud, including using automated fraud detection tools, manually reviewing orders, rejection of suspect orders, and requiring additional levels of security such as email address, zip code, and CCV security codes.

In addition, U.S. federal law limits the liability of individuals to $50 for a stolen credit card. For amounts more than $50, the credit card company generally pays the amount, although in some cases, the merchant may be held liable if it failed to verify the account or consult published lists of invalid cards. Banks recoup the cost of credit card fraud by charging higher interest rates on unpaid balances, and by merchants who raise prices to cover the losses. In 2016, the U.S. credit card system is in the midst of a shift to EMV credit cards, also known as smart cards or chip cards. Already widely used in Europe, EMV credit cards have a computer chip instead of a magnetic strip that can be easily copied by hackers and sold as dump data (see Table 4.2). While EMV technology cannot prevent data breaches from occurring, the hope is that it will make it harder for criminals to profit from the mass theft of credit card numbers that could be used in commerce.

In the past, the most common cause of credit card fraud was a lost or stolen card that was used by someone else, followed by employee theft of customer numbers and stolen identities (criminals applying for credit cards using false identities). Today, the most frequent cause of stolen cards and card information is the systematic hacking and looting of a corporate server where the information on millions of credit card purchases is stored. For instance, in 2010, Albert Gonzalez was sentenced to 20 years in prison for organizing one of the largest thefts of credit card numbers in American history. Along with several Russian co-conspirators, Gonzalez broke into the central computer systems of TJX, BJ's, Barnes & Noble, and other companies, stealing over 160 million card numbers and costing these firms over $200 million in losses (Fox and Botelho, 2013).

International orders have a much higher risk of being fraudulent, with fraud losses twice those of domestic orders. If an international customer places an order and then later disputes it, online merchants often have no way to verify that the package was actually delivered and that the credit card holder is the person who placed the order. As a result, most online merchants will not process international orders.

A central security issue of e-commerce is the difficulty of establishing the customer's identity. Currently there is no technology that can identify a person with absolute certainty. For instance, a lost or stolen EMV card can be used until the card is cancelled, just like a magnetic strip card. Until a customer's identity can be guaranteed, online companies are at a higher risk of loss than traditional offline companies. The federal government has attempted to address this issue through the Electronic Signatures in Global and National Commerce Act (the "E-Sign" law), which gives digital signatures the same authority as hand-written signatures in commerce. This law also intended to make digital signatures more commonplace and easier to use. Although the use of e-signatures is still uncommon in the B2C retail e-commerce arena, many businesses are starting to implement e-signature solutions, particularly for B2B contracting, financial services, insurance, health care, and government and professional services. DocuSign, Adobe eSign, RightSignature, and Silanis eSignLive are currently among the most widely adopted e-signature solutions. They use a variety of techniques, such as remote user identification through third-party databases or personal information verification such as a photo of a driver's license; multi-factor user authentication methods (user ID and password, e-mail address verification, secret question and answer); and public/private key encryption to create a digital signature and embedded audit trail that can be used to verify the e-signature's integrity (Silanis Technology, 2014). The use of fingerprint identification is also one solution to positive identification, but the database of print information can be hacked. Mobile e-signature solutions are also beginning to be adopted (DocuSign, 2015).

IDENTITY FRAUD

Identity fraud involves the unauthorized use of another person's personal data, such as social security, driver's license, and/or credit card numbers, as well as user names and passwords, for illegal financial benefit. Criminals can use such data to obtain loans, purchase merchandise, or obtain other services, such as mobile phone or other utility services. Cybercriminals employ many of the techniques described previously, such as spyware, phishing, data breaches, and credit card theft, for the purpose of identity fraud. Data breaches, in particular, often lead to identity fraud.

identity fraud
involves the unauthorized use of another person's personal data for illegal financial benefit

Identity fraud is a significant problem in the United States and around the world. In 2015, according to Javelin Strategy & Research, 13 million U.S. consumers suffered identity fraud. The total dollar losses as a result of identity fraud were approximately $15 billion (Javelin Research & Strategy, 2016).

SPOOFING, PHARMING, AND SPAM (JUNK) WEBSITES

Spoofing involves attempting to hide a true identity by using someone else's e-mail or IP address. For instance, a spoofed e-mail will have a forged sender e-mail address designed to mislead the receiver about who sent the e-mail. IP spoofing involves the creation of TCP/IP packets that use someone else's source IP address, indicating that the packets are coming from a trusted host. Most current routers and firewalls can offer protection against IP spoofing. Spoofing a website sometimes involves **pharming**, automatically redirecting a web link to an address different from the intended one, with the site masquerading as the intended destination. Links that are designed to lead to one site can be reset to send users to a totally unrelated site—one that benefits the hacker.

spoofing
involves attempting to hide a true identity by using someone else's e-mail or IP address

pharming
automatically redirecting a web link to an address different from the intended one, with the site masquerading as the intended destination

Although spoofing and pharming do not directly damage files or network servers, they threaten the integrity of a site. For example, if hackers redirect customers to a fake website that looks almost exactly like the true site, they can then collect and process orders, effectively stealing business from the true site. Or, if the intent is to disrupt rather than steal, hackers can alter orders—inflating them or changing products ordered—and then send them on to the true site for processing and delivery. Customers become dissatisfied with the improper order shipment, and the company may have huge inventory fluctuations that impact its operations.

In addition to threatening integrity, spoofing also threatens authenticity by making it difficult to discern the true sender of a message. Clever hackers can make it almost impossible to distinguish between a true and a fake identity or web address.

spam (junk) websites
also referred to as link farms; promise to offer products or services, but in fact are just collections of advertisements

Spam (junk) websites (also sometimes referred to as *link farms*) are a little different. These are sites that promise to offer some product or service, but in fact are just a collection of advertisements for other sites, some of which contain malicious code. For instance, you may search for "[name of town] weather," and then click on a link that promises your local weather, but then discover that all the site does is display ads for weather-related products or other websites. Junk or spam websites typically appear on search results, and do not involve e-mail. These sites cloak their identities by using domain names similar to legitimate firm names, and redirect traffic to known spammer-redirection domains such as topsearch10.com.

SNIFFING AND MAN-IN-THE-MIDDLE ATTACKS

sniffer
a type of eavesdropping program that monitors information traveling over a network

A **sniffer** is a type of eavesdropping program that monitors information traveling over a network. When used legitimately, sniffers can help identify potential network trouble-spots, but when used for criminal purposes, they can be damaging and very difficult to detect. Sniffers enable hackers to steal proprietary information from anywhere on a network, including passwords, e-mail messages, company files, and confidential reports. For instance, in 2013, five hackers were charged in another worldwide hacking scheme that targeted the corporate networks of retail chains such as 7-Eleven and the French retailer Carrefour SA, using sniffer programs to steal more than 160 million credit card numbers (Voreacos, 2013).

E-mail wiretaps are a variation on the sniffing threat. An e-mail wiretap is a method for recording or journaling e-mail traffic generally at the mail server level from any individual. E-mail wiretaps are used by employers to track employee messages, and by government agencies to surveil individuals or groups. E-mail wiretaps can be installed on servers and client computers. In the United States, the USA PATRIOT Act permits the FBI to compel ISPs to install a black box on their mail servers that can impound the e-mail of a single person or group of persons for later analysis. In the case of American citizens communicating with other citizens, an FBI agent or government lawyer need only certify to a judge on the secret 11-member U.S. Foreign Intelligence Surveillance Court (FISC) that the information sought is relevant to an ongoing criminal investigation to get permission to install the program. Judges have no discretion. They must approve wiretaps based on government agents' unsubstantiated assertions. In the case of suspected terrorist activity, law enforcement does not have to inform a court prior to installing a wire or e-mail tap. A 2007 amendment to the 1978 Foreign Intelligence Surveillance Act, known as FISA, provided new powers to the National Security Agency to monitor international e-mail and telephone communications where one person is in the United States, and where the purpose of such interception is to collect foreign intelligence (Foreign Intelligence Surveillance Act of 1978; Protect America Act of 2007). The FISA Amendments Reauthorization Act of 2012 extends the provisions of FISA for five more years, until 2017. NSA's XKeyscore program, revealed by Edward Snowden, is a form of "wiretap" that allows NSA analysts to search through vast databases containing not only e-mail, but online chats, and browsing histories of millions of individuals (Wills, 2013).

The U.S. Communications Assistance for Law Enforcement Act (CALEA) requires all communications carriers (including ISPs) to provide near-instant access to law enforcement agencies to their message traffic. Many Internet services (such as Facebook and LinkedIn) that have built-in ISP services technically are not covered by CALEA. One can only assume these non-ISP e-mail operators cooperate with law enforcement. Unlike the past where wiretaps required many hours to physically tap into phone lines, in today's digital phone systems, taps are arranged in a few minutes by the large carriers at their expense.

A **man-in-the-middle (MitM) attack** also involves eavesdropping but is more active than a sniffing attack, which typically involves passive monitoring. In a MitM attack, the attacker is able to intercept communications between two parties who believe they are directly communicating with one another, when in fact the attacker is controlling the communications. This allows the attacker to change the contents of the communication.

DENIAL OF SERVICE (DOS) AND DISTRIBUTED DENIAL OF SERVICE (DDOS) ATTACKS

In a **Denial of Service (DoS) attack**, hackers flood a website with useless pings or page requests that inundate and overwhelm the site's web servers. Increasingly, DoS attacks involve the use of bot networks and so-called "distributed attacks" built from thousands of compromised client computers. DoS attacks typically cause a website to shut down, making it impossible for users to access the site. For busy e-commerce sites, these attacks are costly; while the site is shut down, customers cannot make purchases. And the longer a site is shut down, the more damage is done to a site's reputation. Although such attacks do not destroy information or access restricted areas of the server, they can destroy a firm's online business. Often, DoS attacks are accompanied by attempts at blackmailing site owners to pay tens or hundreds of thousands of dollars to the hackers in return for stopping the DoS attack.

A **Distributed Denial of Service (DDoS) attack** uses hundreds or even thousands of computers to attack the target network from numerous launch points. DoS and DDoS attacks are threats to a system's operation because they can shut it down indefinitely. Major websites have experienced such attacks, making the companies aware of their vulnerability and the need to continually introduce new measures to prevent future attacks. According to Akamai, the number of DDoS attacks in the 2nd quarter of 2016 increased by about 130% compared to the same period in 2015. One new technique increasingly being used targets insecure routers and other home devices such as webcams that use UPnP (Universal Plug and Play) to amplify the attacks (Akamai, 2016a). With the growth of the Internet of Things (IoT), billions of Internet-connected things from refrigerators to security cameras can be used to launch service requests against servers. In October 2016, a large scale DDoS attack using Internet devices such as these was launched against an Internet domain resolving firm, Dyn. Twitter, Amazon, Netflix, Airbnb, the New York Times, and many other sites across the

man-in-the-middle (MitM) attack
attack in which the attacker is able to intercept communications between two parties who believe they are directly communicating with one another, when in fact the attacker is controlling the communications

Denial of Service (DoS) attack
flooding a website with useless traffic to inundate and overwhelm the network

Distributed Denial of Service (DDoS) attack
using numerous computers to attack the target network from numerous launch points

country were affected. Hackers were able to guess the administrator passwords of common devices (often set to factory defaults like admin, or 12345), and then insert instructions to launch an attack against Dyn servers (Sanger and Perlroth, 2016). DDoS attacks are typically isolated to a single firm, but in the Dyn attack, the firm attacked happened to be one of the switchboards for a large part of the Internet in the United States. In another measure of the prevalence of DDoS attacks, in an Arbor Networks survey of 354 ISP and network operators around the world, respondents noted that DDoS attacks against customers constituted the number one operational threat, with over 50% of respondents experiencing DDoS attacks during the survey period. Arbor Networks also reported that the size of reported DDoS attacks in terms of bandwidth consumed continued to increase in 2015, with attackers using reflection/amplification techniques to create attacks reaching 500 Gpbs (Arbor Networks, 2016). Another trend is DDoS smokescreening, in which attackers use DDoS as a distraction while they also insert malware or viruses or steal data. A 2016 survey of 760 security and IT professionals in companies in North America and Europe, the Middle East, and Africa conducted by Neustar found that 45% reported that a virus or malware was installed as a result of the DDoS attack, while 57% also experienced a theft of data or funds (Neustar, 2016). And not surprisingly, now that mobile data connections have become faster and more stable, hackers are beginning to harness mobile devices for mobile-based DDoS attacks. A recent attack originating from China used malicious ads loaded inside mobile apps and mobile browesrs as the attack mechanism (Majkowski, 2015).

China also appears to have been behind another major DDoS attack in 2015 against the software development platform GitHub, aimed specifically at two Chinese anti-censorship projects hosted on the platform. Researchers say the attack was an example of a new tool they have nicknamed the Great Cannon. Although originally thought to be part of China's Great Firewall censorship system, further investigation revealed that the Great Cannon is a separate distinct offensive system that is co-located with the Great Firewall. The Great Cannon enables hackers to hijack traffic to individual IP addresses and uses a man-in-the-middle attack to replace unencrypted content between a web server and the user with malicious Javascript that would load the two GitHub project pages every two seconds (Kirk, 2015b; Essers, 2015).

INSIDER ATTACKS

We tend to think of security threats to a business as originating outside the organization. In fact, the largest financial threats to business institutions come not from robberies but from embezzlement by insiders. Bank employees steal far more money than bank robbers. The same is true for e-commerce sites. Some of the largest disruptions to service, destruction to sites, and diversion of customer credit data and personal information have come from insiders—once trusted employees. Employees have access to privileged information, and, in the presence of sloppy internal security procedures, they are often able to roam throughout an organization's systems without leaving a trace. Research from Carnegie Mellon University documents the significant damage insiders have done to both private and public organizations (Software Engineering Institute, 2012). Survey results also indicate that insiders are more likely to be the source of cyberattacks than outsiders, and to cause more damage to an organization than external attacks (PWC, 2015). In some instances, the insider might not have criminal intent, but inadvertently exposes data that can then be exploited by others. For instance, a Ponemon Institute study found that negligent insiders are a top cause of data breaches (Ponemon Institute, 2015b). Another study based on an analysis of the behavior of 10 million users during 2015 estimated that 1% of employees are responsible for 75% of cloud-related enterprise security risk, by reusing or sending out plain-text passwords, indiscriminately sharing fiiles, using risky applications, or accidentally downloading malware or clicking phishing links (Korolov, 2015).

POORLY DESIGNED SOFTWARE

Many security threats prey on poorly designed software, sometimes in the operating system and sometimes in the application software, including browsers. The increase in complexity and size of software programs, coupled with demands for timely delivery to markets, has contributed to an increase in software flaws or vulnerabilities that hackers can exploit. For instance, **SQL injection attacks** take advantage of vulnerabilities in poorly coded web application software that fails to properly validate or filter data entered by a user on a web page to introduce malicious program code into a company's systems and networks. An attacker can use this input validation error to send a rogue SQL query to the underlying database to access the database, plant malicious code, or access other systems on the network. Large web applications have hundreds of places for inputting user data, each of which creates an opportunity for an SQL injection attack. A large number of web-facing applications are believed to have SQL injection vulnerabilities, and tools are available for hackers to check web applications for these vulnerabilities.

SQL injection attack
takes advantage of poorly coded web application software that fails to properly validate or filter data entered by a user on a web page

Each year, security firms identify thousands of software vulnerabilities in Internet browsers, PC, Macintosh, and Linux software, as well as mobile device operating systems and applications. According to Microsoft, vulnerability disclosures across the software industry in the second half of 2015 increased by 9% compared to the same period in 2014. Over 3,300 vulnerabilities were identified (Microsoft, 2016). Browser vulnerabilities in particular are a popular target, as well as browser plug-ins such as for Adobe Reader. A **zero-day vulnerability** is one that has been previously unreported and for which no patch yet exists. In 2015, 54 zero-day vulnerabilities were reported, up from 24 in 2014 (Symantec, 2016). The very design of the personal computer includes many open communication ports that can be used, and indeed are designed to be used, by external computers to send and receive messages. Ports that are frequently attacked include TCP port 445 (Microsoft-DS), port 80 (WWW/HTTP), and 443 (SSL/HTTPS). Given their complexity and design objectives, all operating systems and application software, including Linux and Macintosh, have vulnerabilities.

zero-day vulnerability
software vulnerability that has been previously unreported and for which no patch yet exists

In 2014, a flaw in the OpenSSL encryption system, used by millions of websites, known as the **Heartbleed bug**, was discovered (see Section 4.3 for a further discussion of SSL). The vulnerability allowed hackers to decrypt an SSL session and discover user names, passwords, and other user data, by using OpenSSL in combination with a communications protocol called the RFC6520 heartbeat that helps a remote user remain in touch after connecting with a website server. In the process a small chunk of the server's memory content can leak out (hence the name heartbleed), potentially large

Heartbleed bug
flaw in OpenSSL encryption system that allowed hackers to decrypt an SSL session and discover user names, passwords, and other user data

enough to hold a password or encryption key that would allow a hacker to exploit the server further. The Heartbleed bug also affected over 1,300 Android apps. Later in 2014, another vulnerability known as ShellShock or BashBug that affected most versions of Linux and Unix, as well as Mac OS X, was revealed. ShellShock enabled attackers to use CGI (see Chapter 3) to add malicious commands (Symantec, 2015). In 2015, researchers announced that they had discovered a new SSL/TLS vulnerability that they named FREAK (Factoring Attack on RSA-Export Keys) that allows man-in-the-middle attacks that enable the interception and decryption of encrypted communications between clients and servers, which would then allow the attackers to steal passwords and other personal information. More than 60% of encrypted websites were reportedly open to attack via this security vulnerability, including those for the White House, the FBI, and the National Security Agency (Hackett, 2015; Vaughan-Nichols, 2015). A recent study found over 1,200 of the largest firms' websites have not fixed the problem entirely.

SOCIAL NETWORK SECURITY ISSUES

Social networks like Facebook, Twitter, LinkedIn, Pinterest, and Tumblr provide a rich and rewarding environment for hackers. Viruses, site takeovers, identity fraud, malware-loaded apps, click hijacking, phishing, and spam are all found on social networks. According to Symantec, the most common type of scam on social media sites in 2015 were manual sharing scams, where victims unwittingly shared videos, stories, and pictures that included links to malicious sites. Fake offerings that invite victims to join a fake event or group with incentives such as free gift cards and that require a user to share his or her information with the attacker were another common technique. Other techniques include fake Like buttons that, when clicked, install malware and post updates to the user's Newsfeed, further spreading the attack, and fake apps (Symantec, 2016). By sneaking in among our friends, hackers can masquerade as friends and dupe users into scams.

Social network firms have thus far been relatively poor policemen because they have failed to aggressively weed out accounts that send visitors to malware sites (unlike Google, which maintains a list of known malware sites and patrols its search results looking for links to malware sites). Social networks are open: anyone can set up a personal page, even criminals. Most attacks are social engineering attacks that tempt visitors to click on links that sound reasonable. Social apps downloaded from either the social network or a foreign site are not certified by the social network to be clean of malware. It's "clicker beware."

MOBILE PLATFORM SECURITY ISSUES

The explosion in mobile devices has broadened opportunities for hackers. Mobile users are filling their devices with personal and financial information, and using them to conduct an increasing number of transactions, from retail purchases to mobile banking, making them excellent targets for hackers. In general, mobile devices face all the same risks as any Internet device as well as some new risks associated with wireless network security. For instance, public Wi-Fi networks that are not secured are very susceptible to hacking. While most PC users are aware their computers and websites may be hacked and contain malware, most cell phone users believe their cell phone is as secure as a traditional landline phone. As with social network members, mobile users are prone to think they are in a shared, trustworthy environment.

Mobile cell phone malware (sometimes referred to as malicious mobile apps (MMAs) or rogue mobile apps) was developed as early as 2004 with Cabir, a Bluetooth worm affecting Symbian operating systems (Nokia phones) and causing the phone to continuously seek out other Bluetooth-enabled devices, quickly draining the battery. The iKee.B worm, first discovered in 2009, only two years after the iPhone was introduced, infected jailbroken iPhones, turning the phones into botnet-controlled devices. An iPhone in Europe could be hacked by an iPhone in the United States, and all its private data sent to a server in Poland. IKee.B established the feasibility of cell phone botnets.

In 2015, Symantec analyzed 10 million apps and found 3 million were malware. Symantec expects the growth in mobile malware to continue in 2016 and become more aggressive in targeting mobile payment and mobile banking applications. The majority of mobile malware still targets the Android platform. For instance, Symantec has already discovered Android malware that can intercept text messages with bank authentication codes and forward them to attackers, as well as fake versions of legitimate mobile banking applications. However, the Apple iPhone platform is beginning to be increasingly targeted as well, and in 2015, Chinese hackers infected Xcode, Apple's integrated suite of development tools for creating iOS appps, and as a result, unsuspecting Chinese iOS developers unknowingly created thousands of apps with the malicious code (Keizer, 2015). And it is not just rogue applications that are dangerous, but also popular legitimate applications that simply have little protection from hackers. For instance, in 2014, security researchers revealed that the Starbucks mobile app, the most used mobile payment app in the United States, was storing user names, e-mail addresses, and passwords in clear text, in such a way that anyone with access to the phone could see the passwords and user names by connecting the phone to a computer. According to researchers, Starbucks erred in emphasizing convenience and ease of use in the design of the app over security concerns (Schuman, 2014).

Vishing attacks target gullible cell phone users with verbal messages to call a certain number and, for example, donate money to starving children in Haiti. *Smishing* attacks exploit SMS/text messages. Compromised text messages can contain e-mail and website addresses that can lead the innocent user to a malware site. Criminal SMS spoofing services have emerged, which conceal the cybercriminal's true phone number, replacing it with a false alpha-numeric name. SMS spoofing can also be used by cybercriminals to lure mobile users to a malicious website by sending a text that appears to be from a legitimate organization in the From field, and suggesting the receiver click on a malicious URL hyperlink to update an account or obtain a gift card. A small number of downloaded apps from app stores have also contained malware. *Madware*—innocent-looking apps that contain adware that launches pop-up ads and text messages on your mobile device—is also becoming an increasing problem. An examination of 3 million apps in 2015 that Symantec classified as grayware (programs that do not contain viruses and are not overtly malicious, but which can be annoying or harmful) found that 2.3 million of those ads were madware (Symantec, 2016).

Read the *Insight on Technology* case, *Think Your Smartphone Is Secure?* for a further discussion of some of the issues surrounding smartphone security.

INSIGHT ON TECHNOLOGY

THINK YOUR SMARTPHONE IS SECURE?

So far, there have been few publicly identified, large-scale, smartphone security breaches, but just because it hasn't happened yet doesn't mean it won't. With about 210 million smartphone users in the United States, business firms increasingly switching their employees to the mobile platform, and consumers using their phones for financial transactions and paying bills, the size and richness of the smartphone target for hackers is growing.

Many users believe their smartphones are unlikely to be hacked because Apple and Google are protecting them from malware, and that Verizon and AT&T can keep the cell phone network secure just as they do the land-line phone system. Telephone systems are "closed" and therefore not subject to the kinds of attacks that occur on the open Internet.

But hackers can do to a smartphone just about anything they can do to any Internet device: request malicious files without user intervention, delete files, transmit files, install programs running in the background that can monitor user actions, and potentially convert the smartphone into a robot that can be used in a botnet to send e-mail and text messages to anyone.

Apps are an emerging avenue for potential security breaches. Apple and Google now offer over 5 million apps collectively. Apple claims that it examines each and every app to ensure that it plays by Apple's App Store rules, but risks remain. In 2014, malware known as WireLurker attacked iPhone and iPad users in China via the Mac OS X operating system, representing the first attack on iPhones that were not jailbroken. Apple quickly moved to remove affected apps, but the attack was a warning sign that the iOS system is not likely to be a malware-

free environment going forward. In March 2016, new malware called AceDeceiver that infected non-jailbroken Apple devices circulated widely, scanning the App Store for other corrupted apps and automatically downloading them. That these corrupted apps were initially accepted by the App Store staff of reviewers suggests Apple cannot effectively review new apps prior to their use. This problem was further highlighted by a barrage of fake retail and product apps, primarily from developers in China, that also apparently slipped through Apple's review process and began appearing in the App Store preceding the 2016 holiday shopping season. Updates to the iOS operating system in 2016 exposed a series of vulnerabilities, collectively known as Trident, which allow attackers to take complete control of a phone remotely, without any indication that something has gone awry. Though Apple quickly scrambled to fix the vulnerability, releasing an operating system update in ten days, Trident showed that the iOS operating system is not as impervious to malware as many users believe. Any problems Apple has, it will have to fix by itself: third parties are not able to develop services to protect Apple devices as easily as they may be able to with Android because of Apple's "walled garden" approach. Overall, more malware affected iOS devices in 2015 than in the previous five years combined.

Android's security future appears just as murky. The amount of malware on the Android platform has skyrocketed over the past few years, with the number of spyware apps more than quadrupling from just a few years ago and doubling from 2015 to 2016. According to the Pulse Secure Mobile Threat Center, 97% of all mobile malware in 2015 targeted Android devices, and according to Nokia, more than 9 million Android apps are vulnerable to remote attacks. In part this is due to the fact that security on the Android platform is much less under the control of Google because it employs an "open" app model compared to Apple's, which makes security flaws easier to detect. In 2016, security firm Check Point reported that malware known as Hummingbad, which installs fraudulent apps and generates unwanted advertising, has infected approximately 10 million Android devices.

Android apps can use any personal information found on a phone but they must also inform the user what each app is capable of doing, and what personal data it requires. Google uses a universal scanning system that checks apps for malicious code and removes any apps that break its rules against malicious activity. Google can also perform a remote wipe of offending apps from all Droid phones without user intervention. In one incident, Google pulled down dozens of mobile banking apps made by a developer called 09Droid. The apps claimed to give users access to their accounts at many banks throughout the world. In fact, the apps were unable to connect users to any bank, and were removed before they could do much harm. Google does take preventive steps to reduce malware apps such as requiring developers to register and be approved by Google before they can distribute apps through Google Play.

Beyond the threat of rogue apps, smartphones of all stripes are susceptible to browser-based malware that takes advantage of vulnerabilities in all browsers. In addition, most smartphones, including the iPhone, permit the manufacturers to remotely download configuration files to update operating systems and security protections. Unfortunately, flaws in the public key encryption procedures that permit remote server access to iPhones have been discovered, raising further questions about the security of such operations. Attackers have also developed methods of hijacking phones using weaknesses in SIM cards. There are at least 500 million vulnerable SIM cards in use today, and the defects allow hackers to obtain the encryption key that guards users' personal information, granting them nearly complete access over the phone in the process. Many users don't even take advantage of the security features they have available to them, such as the use of a lock screen, which only one-third of Android users have enabled.

In 2015, documents obtained by Edward Snowden indicated that the United States and Great Britain had hacked into Gemalto, a manufacturer of SIM cards, and obtained encryption keys that allowed them to surveil mobile phone users across the globe. The investigation is still ongoing, but after these revelations and a turbulent year of security breaches on both iOS and Android, our smartphones and tablets don't seem quite as safe anymore.

SOURCES: "Beware, iPhone Users: Fake Retail Apps Are Surging Before Holidays," by Vindu Goel, *New York Times,* November 6, 2016; "Microsoft: 'Apple Can No More Secure Your iPhone Than Google Can Secure Android,'" by Zdnet.com, October 14, 2016; "Top 10 Ways to Secure Your Mobile Phone," by Wendy Zamora, Blog.malwarebytes.com, September 21, 2016; "Smartphone Infections Double, Hotspots Are Also a Trouble Area," by Patrick Nelson, Networkworld.com, September 7, 2016; "iPhone Malware That Steals Your Data Proves No Platform is Truly Secure," by Liam Tung and Raymond Wong, Mashable.com, August 26, 2016; "This App Can Tell If an iPhone Was Hacked With Latest Pegasus Spy Malware," by Janko Roettgers, Variety.com, August 26, 2016; "IPhone Users Urged to Update Software After Security Flaws Are Found," by Nicole Perlroth, *New York Times,* August 25, 2016; "Hummingbad Malware Infects 10 Million Devices: How to Check If Your Phone or Tablet Is Among Them," by Aaron Mamiit, Techtimes.com, July 6, 2016; "This Nasty New Malware Can Infect Your Apple iPhone or iPad," by Jonathan Vanian, *Fortune,* March 16, 2016; "Mobile Malware on Smartphones and Tablets: The Inconvenient Truth," by Shaked Vax, Securityintelligence.com, February 15, 2016; "Android Accounts for 97 Percent of All Mobile Malware," by Carly Page, Theinquirer.net, June 25, 2015; "Digital-Security Firm Gemalto Probes Alleged U.S., U.K. Hack," by Amir Mizroch and Lisa Fleisher, *Wall Street Journal,* February 20, 2015; "US and UK Accused of Hacking SIM Card Firm to Steal Codes," by Bbc.com, February 20, 2015; "XAgent iPhone Malware Attack Steals Data Without Jailbreaking," by Jeff Gamet, Macobserver.com, February 5, 2015; "Apple Blocks Apps Infected with WireLurker Malware Targeting iPhones and iPads," by Carly Page, Theinquirer.net, November 6, 2014; "NSA Secretly Broke Smartphone Security," by Cory Doctorow, Boingboing.com, September 8, 2013; "Obama Administration Had Restrictions on NSA Reversed in 2011," by Ellen Nakashima, September 7, 2013; "How Google Just Quietly Made Your Android Phone More Secure," by JR Raphael, *Computerworld,* July 26, 2013.

CLOUD SECURITY ISSUES

The move of so many Internet services into the cloud also raises security risks. From an infrastructure standpoint, DDoS attacks threaten the availability of cloud services on which more and more companies are relying. For instance, as previously noted, the DDoS attack on Dyn in 2016 caused a major disruption to cloud services across the United States. According to Alert Logic, which analyzed 1 billion security events in the IT environments of more than 3,000 enterprise customers, attacks against cloud-based services and applications increased by 45%. Alert Logic also found a a 36% increase in suspicious activity in cloud environment, such as attempts to scan the infrastructure (Alert Logic, 2015). Safeguarding data being maintained in a public cloud environment is also a major concern (Cloud Security Alliance, 2016). For example, researchers identified several ways data could be accessed without authorization on Dropbox, which offers a popular cloud file-sharing service. In 2014, compromising photos of as many as 100 celebrities such as Jennifer Lawrence were posted online, reportedly stolen from Apple's iCloud. Although initially it was thought that the breach was made possible by a vulnerability in Apple's Find My iPhone API, it instead apparently resulted from lower-tech phishing attacks that yielded passwords that could be used to connect to iCloud. A similar hack into writer Mat Honan's Apple iCloud account using social engineering tactics in 2012 allowed the hackers to wipe everything from his Mac computer, iPhone, and iPad, which were linked to the cloud service, as well as take over his Twitter and Gmail accounts (Honan, 2012). These incidents highlight the risks involved as devices, identities, and data become more and more interconnected in the cloud. A 2016 Ponemon Insititute study of 3,400 IT executives found that the majority of IT and IT security practitioners surveyed felt that the likelihood of a data breach increases due to the cloud, in part due to the fact that many organizations do not thoroughly examine cloud security before deploying cloud services. The study also found that only one-third of sensitive data in cloud-based applications was encrypted, and that half of the firms involved do not have a proactive approach to cloud security, relying instead on the cloud providers to ensure security (Loten, 2016; Gemalto and Ponemon, 2016).

INTERNET OF THINGS SECURITY ISSUES

As you learned in Chapter 2, the Internet of Things (IoT) involves the use of the Internet to connect a wide variety of sensors, devices, and machines, and is powering the development of a multitude of smart connected things, such as home electronics (smart TVs, thermostats, home security systems, and more), connected cars, medical devices, and industrial equipment that supports manufacturing, energy, transportation, and other industrial sectors. IoT raises a host of security issues that are in some ways similar to existing security issues, but even more challenging, given the need to deal with a wider range of devices, operating in a less controlled, global environment, and with an expanded range of attack. In a world of connected things, the devices, the data produced and used by the devices, and the systems and applications supported by those devices, can all potentially be attacked (IBM, 2015). **Table 4.5** takes a closer look at some of the unique security challenges posed by IoT identified

TABLE 4.5	INTERNET OF THINGS SECURITY CHALLENGES
CHALLENGE	POSSIBLE IMPLICATIONS
Many IoT devices, such as sensors, are intended to be deployed on a much greater scale than traditional Internet-connected devices, creating a vast quantity of interconnected links that can be exploited.	Existing tools, methods, and strategies need to be developed to deal with this unprecedented scale.
Many instances of IoT consist of collections of identical devices that all have the same characteristics.	Magnifies the potential impact of a security vulnerability.
Many IoT devices are anticipated to have a much longer service life than typical equipment.	Devices may "outlive" manufacturer, leaving them without long-term support that creates persistent vulnerabilities.
Many IoT devices are intentionally designed without the ability to be upgraded, or the upgrade process is difficult.	Raises the possibility that vulnerable devices cannot or will not be fixed, leaving them perpetually vulnerable.
Many IoT devices do not provide the user with visibility into the workings of the device or the data being produced, nor alert the user when a security problem arises.	Users may believe an IoT device is functioning as intended when in fact, it may be performing in a malicious manner.
Some IoT devices, such as sensors, are unobtrusively embedded in the environment such that a user may not even be aware of the device.	Security breach might persist for a long time before being noticed.

by the Internet Society (ISOC), a consortium of corporations, government agencies, and nonprofit organizations that monitors Internet policies and practices (Internet Society, 2016, 2015).

Already, alarming reports of hacked IoT devices are starting to pop up in the popular press. For example, in July 2015, researchers demonstrated the ability to hack into a Jeep Cherokee through its entertainment system, sending commands to the dashboard, steering, brakes, and transmission system from a remote laptop that turned the steering wheel, disabled the brakes, and shut down the engine (Greenberg, 2015). Fiat Chrysler Automobiles immediately issued a recall notice to fix the software vulnerability involved, but it is almost certain that such incidents will continue to occur, as auto manufacturers add more and more wireless "connected car" features to automobiles. Other reports have surfaced of wireless baby monitors being hacked, as well as medical devices such as hospital lab blood gas analyzers, radiology picture archive and communication systems, drug infusion pumps, and hospital x-ray systems (Storm, 2015a, 2015b). The previously mentioned DDoS 2016 attack on Dyn relied in part on millions of Internet-connected security cameras (Sanger and Perlroth, 2016).

FIGURE 4.5 — TOOLS AVAILABLE TO ACHIEVE SITE SECURITY

There are a number of tools available to achieve site security.

4.3 TECHNOLOGY SOLUTIONS

At first glance, it might seem like there is not much that can be done about the onslaught of security breaches on the Internet. Reviewing the security threats in the previous section, it is clear that the threats to e-commerce are very real, widespread, global, potentially devastating for individuals, businesses, and entire nations, and likely to be increasing in intensity along with the growth in e-commerce and the continued expansion of the Internet. But in fact a great deal of progress has been made by private security firms, corporate and home users, network administrators, technology firms, and government agencies. There are two lines of defense: technology solutions and policy solutions. In this section, we consider some technology solutions, and in the following section, we look at some policy solutions that work.

The first line of defense against the wide variety of security threats to an e-commerce site is a set of tools that can make it difficult for outsiders to invade or destroy a site. **Figure 4.5** illustrates the major tools available to achieve site security.

PROTECTING INTERNET COMMUNICATIONS

Because e-commerce transactions must flow over the public Internet, and therefore involve thousands of routers and servers through which the transaction packets flow, security experts believe the greatest security threats occur at the level of Internet communications. This is very different from a private network where a dedicated communication line is established between two parties. A number of tools are available to protect the security of Internet communications, the most basic of which is message encryption.

ENCRYPTION

Encryption is the process of transforming plain text or data into **cipher text** that cannot be read by anyone other than the sender and the receiver. The purpose of encryption is (a) to secure stored information and (b) to secure information transmission. Encryption can provide four of the six key dimensions of e-commerce security referred to in Table 4.3 on page 248:

- *Message integrity*—provides assurance that the message has not been altered.
- *Nonrepudiation*—prevents the user from denying he or she sent the message.
- *Authentication*—provides verification of the identity of the person (or computer) sending the message.
- *Confidentiality*—gives assurance that the message was not read by others.

This transformation of plain text to cipher text is accomplished by using a key or cipher. A **key** (or **cipher**) is any method for transforming plain text to cipher text.

Encryption has been practiced since the earliest forms of writing and commercial transactions. Ancient Egyptian and Phoenician commercial records were encrypted using substitution and transposition ciphers. In a **substitution cipher**, every occurrence of a given letter is replaced systematically by another letter. For instance, if we used the cipher "letter plus two"—meaning replace every letter in a word with a new letter two places forward—then the word "Hello" in plain text would be transformed into the following cipher text: "JGNNQ." In a **transposition cipher**, the ordering of the letters in each word is changed in some systematic way. Leonardo Da Vinci recorded his shop notes in reverse order, making them readable only with a mirror. The word "Hello" can be written backwards as "OLLEH." A more complicated cipher would (a) break all words into two words and (b) spell the first word with every other letter beginning with the first letter, and then spell the second word with all the remaining letters. In this cipher, "HELLO" would be written as "HLO EL."

Symmetric Key Cryptography

In order to decipher (decrypt) these messages, the receiver would have to know the secret cipher that was used to encrypt the plain text. This is called **symmetric key cryptography** or **secret key cryptography**. In symmetric key cryptography, both the sender and the receiver use the same key to encrypt and decrypt the message. How do the sender and the receiver have the same key? They have to send it over some communication media or exchange the key in person. Symmetric key cryptography was used extensively throughout World War II and is still a part of Internet cryptography.

The possibilities for simple substitution and transposition ciphers are endless, but they all suffer from common flaws. First, in the digital age, computers are so powerful and fast that these ancient means of encryption can be broken quickly. Second, symmetric key cryptography requires that both parties share the same key. In order to share the same key, they must send the key over a presumably *insecure* medium where it could be stolen and used to decipher messages. If the secret key is lost or stolen, the entire encryption system fails. Third, in commercial use, where we are not all part of the same team, you would need a secret key for each of the parties with whom you transacted, that is, one key for the bank, another for the department store,

encryption
the process of transforming plain text or data into cipher text that cannot be read by anyone other than the sender and the receiver. The purpose of encryption is (a) to secure stored information and (b) to secure information transmission

cipher text
text that has been encrypted and thus cannot be read by anyone other than the sender and the receiver

key (cipher)
any method for transforming plain text to cipher text

substitution cipher
every occurrence of a given letter is replaced systematically by another letter

transposition cipher
the ordering of the letters in each word is changed in some systematic way

symmetric key cryptography (secret key cryptography)
both the sender and the receiver use the same key to encrypt and decrypt the message

and another for the government. In a large population of users, this could result in as many as $n^{(n-1)}$ keys. In a population of billions of Internet users, billions of keys would be needed to accommodate all e-commerce customers. Clearly this situation would be too unwieldy to work in practice.

Modern encryption systems are digital. The ciphers or keys used to transform plain text into cipher text are digital strings. Computers store text or other data as binary strings composed of 0s and 1s. For instance, the binary representation of the capital letter "A" in ASCII computer code is accomplished with eight binary digits (bits): 01000001. One way in which digital strings can be transformed into cipher text is by multiplying each letter by another binary number, say, an eight-bit key number 0101 0101. If we multiplied every digital character in our text messages by this eight-bit key and sent the encrypted message to a friend along with the secret eight-bit key, the friend could decode the message easily.

The strength of modern security protection is measured in terms of the length of the binary key used to encrypt the data. In the preceding example, the eight-bit key is easily deciphered because there are only 2^8 or 256 possibilities. If the intruder knows you are using an eight-bit key, then he or she could decode the message in a few seconds using a modern desktop PC just by using the brute force method of checking each of the 256 possible keys. For this reason, modern digital encryption systems use keys with 56, 128, 256, or 512 binary digits. With encryption keys of 512 digits, there are 2^{512} possibilities to check out. It is estimated that all the computers in the world would need to work for 10 years before stumbling upon the answer.

The **Data Encryption Standard (DES)** was developed by the National Security Agency (NSA) and IBM in the 1950s. DES uses a 56-bit encryption key. To cope with much faster computers, it has been improved by the *Triple DES Encryption Algorithm (TDEA)*—essentially encrypting the message three times, each with a separate key. Today, the most widely used symmetric key algorithm is **Advanced Encryption Standard (AES)**, which offers key sizes of 128, 192, and 256 bits. AES had been considered to be relatively secure, but in 2011, researchers from Microsoft and a Belgian university announced that they had discovered a way to break the algorithm, and with this work, the "safety margin" of AES continues to erode. There are also many other symmetric key systems that are currently less widely used, with keys up to 2,048 bits.[1]

Public Key Cryptography

In 1976, a new way of encrypting messages called **public key cryptography** was invented by Whitfield Diffie and Martin Hellman. Public key cryptography (also referred to as *asymmetric cryptography*) solves the problem of exchanging keys. In this method, two mathematically related digital keys are used: a public key and a private key. The private key is kept secret by the owner, and the public key is widely disseminated. Both keys can be used to encrypt and decrypt a message. However, once the keys are used

---

[1] For instance: DESX, GDES, and RDES with 168-bit keys; the RC Series: RC2, RC4, and RC5 with keys up to 2,048 bits; and the IDEA algorithm, the basis of PGP, e-mail public key encryption software described later in this chapter, which uses 128-bit keys.

Data Encryption Standard (DES)

developed by the National Security Agency (NSA) and IBM. Uses a 56-bit encryption key

Advanced Encryption Standard (AES)

the most widely used symmetric key algorithm, offering 128-, 192-, and 256-bit keys

public key cryptography

two mathematically related digital keys are used: a public key and a private key. The private key is kept secret by the owner, and the public key is widely disseminated. Both keys can be used to encrypt and decrypt a message. However, once the keys are used to encrypt a message, that same key cannot be used to unencrypt the message

FIGURE 4.6	PUBLIC KEY CRYPTOGRAPHY—A SIMPLE CASE

STEP	DESCRIPTION
1. The sender creates a digital message.	The message could be a document, spreadsheet, or any digital object.
2. The sender obtains the recipient's public key from a public directory and applies it to the message.	Public keys are distributed widely and can be obtained from recipients directly.
3. Application of the recipient's key produces an encrypted cipher text message.	Once encrypted using the public key, the message cannot be reverse-engineered or unencrypted using the same public key. The process is irreversible.
4. The encrypted message is sent over the Internet.	The encrypted message is broken into packets and sent through several different pathways, making interception of the entire message difficult (but not impossible).
5. The recipient uses his/her private key to decrypt the message.	The only person who can decrypt the message is the person who has possession of the recipient's private key. Hopefully, this is the legitimate recipient.

In the simplest use of public key cryptography, the sender encrypts a message using the recipient's public key, and then sends it over the Internet. The only person who can decrypt this message is the recipient, using his or her private key. However, this simple case does not ensure integrity or an authentic message.

to encrypt a message, the same key cannot be used to unencrypt the message. The mathematical algorithms used to produce the keys are one-way functions. A *one-way irreversible mathematical function* is one in which, once the algorithm is applied, the input cannot be subsequently derived from the output. Most food recipes are like this. For instance, it is easy to make scrambled eggs, but impossible to retrieve whole eggs from the scrambled eggs. Public key cryptography is based on the idea of irreversible mathematical functions. The keys are sufficiently long (128, 256, and 512 bits) that it would take enormous computing power to derive one key from the other using the largest and fastest computers available. **Figure 4.6** illustrates a simple use of public key cryptography and takes you through the important steps in using public and private keys.

Public Key Cryptography Using Digital Signatures and Hash Digests

In public key cryptography, some elements of security are missing. Although we can be quite sure the message was not understood or read by a third party (message confidentiality), there is no guarantee the sender really is the sender; that is, there is no authentication of the sender. This means the sender could deny ever sending the message (repudiation). And there is no assurance the message was not altered somehow in transit. For example, the message "Buy Cisco @ $16" could have been accidentally or intentionally altered to read "Sell Cisco @ $16." This suggests a potential lack of integrity in the system.

A more sophisticated use of public key cryptography can achieve authentication, nonrepudiation, and integrity. **Figure 4.7** illustrates this more powerful approach.

hash function

an algorithm that produces a fixed-length number called a hash or message digest

To check the integrity of a message and ensure it has not been altered in transit, a hash function is used first to create a digest of the message. A **hash function** is an algorithm that produces a fixed-length number called a *hash* or *message digest*. A hash function can be simple, and count the number of digital 1s in a message, or it can be more complex, and produce a 128-bit number that reflects the number of 0s and 1s, the number of 00s and 11s, and so on. Standard hash functions are available (MD4 and MD5 produce 128- and 160-bit hashes) (Stein, 1998). These more complex hash functions produce hashes or hash results that are unique to every message. The results of applying the hash function are sent by the sender to the recipient. Upon receipt, the recipient applies the hash function to the received message and checks to verify the same result is produced. If so, the message has not been altered. The sender then encrypts both the hash result and the original message using the recipient's public key (as in Figure 4.6 on page 277), producing a single block of cipher text.

One more step is required. To ensure the authenticity of the message and to ensure nonrepudiation, the sender encrypts the entire block of cipher text one more time using the sender's private key. This produces a **digital signature** (also called an *e-signature*) or "signed" cipher text that can be sent over the Internet.

digital signature (e-signature)

"signed" cipher text that can be sent over the Internet

A digital signature is a close parallel to a handwritten signature. Like a handwritten signature, a digital signature is unique—only one person presumably possesses the private key. When used with a hash function, the digital signature is even more unique than a handwritten signature. In addition to being exclusive to a particular individual, when used to sign a hashed document, the digital signature is also unique to the document, and changes for every document.

The recipient of this signed cipher text first uses the sender's public key to authenticate the message. Once authenticated, the recipient uses his or her private key to obtain the hash result and original message. As a final step, the recipient applies the same hash function to the original text, and compares the result with the result sent by the sender. If the results are the same, the recipient now knows the message has not been changed during transmission. The message has integrity.

Early digital signature programs required the user to have a digital certificate, and were far too difficult for an individual to use. Newer programs are Internet-based and do not require users to install software, or understand digital certificate technology. DocuSign, Adobe eSign, and Sertifi are among a number of companies offering online

FIGURE 4.7 PUBLIC KEY CRYPTOGRAPHY WITH DIGITAL SIGNATURES

STEP	DESCRIPTION
1. The sender creates an original message.	The message can be any digital file.
2. The sender applies a hash function, producing a 128-bit hash result.	Hash functions create a unique digest of the message based on the message contents.
3. The sender encrypts the message and hash result using the recipient's public key.	This irreversible process creates a cipher text that can be read only by the recipient using his or her private key.
4. The sender encrypts the result, again using his or her private key.	The sender's private key is a digital signature. There is only one person who can create this digital mark.
5. The result of this double encryption is sent over the Internet.	The message traverses the Internet as a series of independent packets.
6. The receiver uses the sender's public key to authenticate the message.	Only one person can send this message, namely, the sender.
7. The receiver uses his or her private key to decrypt the hash function and the original message. The receiver checks to ensure the original message and the hash function results conform to one another.	The hash function is used here to check the original message. This ensures the message was not changed in transit.

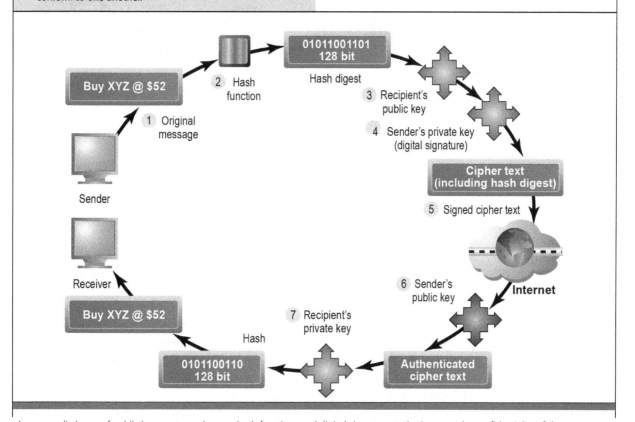

A more realistic use of public key cryptography uses hash functions and digital signatures to both ensure the confidentiality of the message and authenticate the sender. The only person who could have sent the above message is the owner or the sender using his/her private key. This authenticates the message. The hash function ensures the message was not altered in transit. As before, the only person who can decipher the message is the recipient, using his/her private key.

FIGURE 4.8 **PUBLIC KEY CRYPTOGRAPHY: CREATING A DIGITAL ENVELOPE**

A digital envelope can be created to transmit a symmetric key that will permit the recipient to decrypt the message and be assured the message was not intercepted in transit.

digital signature solutions. Many insurance, finance, and surety companies now permit customers to electronically sign documents.

Digital Envelopes

Public key cryptography is computationally slow. If one used 128- or 256-bit keys to encode large documents—such as this chapter or the entire book—significant declines in transmission speeds and increases in processing time would occur. Symmetric key cryptography is computationally faster, but as we pointed out previously, it has a weakness—namely, the symmetric key must be sent to the recipient over insecure transmission lines. One solution is to use the more efficient symmetric encryption and decryption for large documents, but public key cryptography to encrypt and send the symmetric key. This technique is called using a **digital envelope**. See **Figure 4.8** for an illustration of how a digital envelope works.

In Figure 4.8, a diplomatic document is encrypted using a symmetric key. The symmetric key—which the recipient will require to decrypt the document—is itself encrypted, using the recipient's public key. So we have a "key within a key" (a *digital envelope*). The encrypted report and the digital envelope are sent across the Web. The recipient first uses his/her private key to decrypt the symmetric key, and then

digital envelope

a technique that uses symmetric encryption for large documents, but public key cryptography to encrypt and send the symmetric key

FIGURE 4.9   DIGITAL CERTIFICATES AND CERTIFICATION AUTHORITIES

The PKI includes certification authorities that issue, verify, and guarantee digital certificates that are used in e-commerce to assure the identity of transaction partners.

the recipient uses the symmetric key to decrypt the report. This method saves time because both encryption and decryption are faster with symmetric keys.

Digital Certificates and Public Key Infrastructure (PKI)

There are still some deficiencies in the message security regime described previously. How do we know that people and institutions are who they claim to be? Anyone can make up a private and public key combination and claim to be someone they are not. Before you place an order with an online merchant such as Amazon, you want to be sure it really is Amazon you have on the screen and not a spoofer masquerading as Amazon. In the physical world, if someone asks who you are and you show a social security number, they may well ask to see a picture ID or a second form of certifiable or acceptable identification. If they really doubt who you are, they may ask for references to other authorities and actually interview these other authorities. Similarly, in the digital world, we need a way to know who people and institutions really are.

Digital certificates, and the supporting public key infrastructure, are an attempt to solve this problem of digital identity. A **digital certificate** is a digital document issued by a trusted third-party institution known as a **certification authority (CA)** that contains the name of the subject or company, the subject's public key, a digital certificate serial number, an expiration date, an issuance date, the digital signature of the certification authority (the name of the CA encrypted using the CA's private key), and other identifying information (see **Figure 4.9**).

digital certificate
a digital document issued by a certification authority that contains a variety of identifying information

certification authority (CA)
a trusted third party that issues digital certificates

public key infrastructure (PKI)
CAs and digital certificate procedures that are accepted by all parties

Worldwide, thousands of organizations issue CAs. GlobalSign was the first certification authority created in Europe. EU member states and other European nations maintain lists of approved CAs. A hierarchy of CAs has emerged with less-well-known CAs being certified by larger and better-known CAs, creating a community of mutually verifying institutions. **Public key infrastructure (PKI)** refers to the CAs and digital certificate procedures that are accepted by all parties. When you sign into a "secure" site, the URL will begin with "https" and a closed lock icon will appear on your browser. This means the site has a digital certificate issued by a trusted CA. It is not, presumably, a spoof site.

To create a digital certificate, the user generates a public/private key pair and sends a request for certification to a CA along with the user's public key. The CA verifies the information (how this is accomplished differs from CA to CA). The CA issues a certificate containing the user's public key and other related information. Finally, the CA creates a message digest from the certificate itself (just like a hash digest) and signs it with the CA's private key. This signed digest is called the *signed certificate*. We end up with a totally unique cipher text document—there can be only one signed certificate like this in the world.

There are several ways the certificates are used in commerce. Before initiating a transaction, the customer can request the signed digital certificate of the merchant and decrypt it using the merchant's public key to obtain both the message digest and the certificate as issued. If the message digest matches the certificate, then the merchant and the public key are authenticated. The merchant may in return request certification of the user, in which case the user would send the merchant his or her individual certificate. There are many types of certificates: personal, institutional, web server, software publisher, and CAs themselves.

PKI and CAs can also be used to secure software code and content for applications that are directly downloaded to mobile devices from the Internet. Using a technique referred to as code signing, mobile application developers use their private key to encrypt a digital signature. When end users decrypt the signature with the corresponding public key, it confirms the developer's identity and the integrity of the code.

Pretty Good Privacy (PGP)
a widely used e-mail public key encryption software program

You can easily obtain a public and private key for personal, noncommercial use at the International PGP Home Page website, Pgpi.org. **Pretty Good Privacy (PGP)** was invented in 1991 by Phil Zimmerman, and has become one of the most widely used e-mail public key encryption software tools in the world. Using PGP software installed on your computer, you can compress and encrypt your messages as well as authenticate both yourself and the recipient. There are also a number of Firefox, Chrome, Internet Explorer, and Safari add-ons, extensions, or plug-ins that enable you to encrypt your e-mail.

Limitations of PKI

PKI is a powerful technological solution to security issues, but it has many limitations, especially concerning CAs. PKI applies mainly to protecting messages in transit on the Internet and is not effective against insiders—employees—who have legitimate access to corporate systems including customer information. Most e-commerce sites do not store customer information in encrypted form. Other limitations are apparent. For one, how is your private key to be protected? Most private keys will be stored on insecure desktop or laptop computers.

There is no guarantee the person using your computer—and your private key—is really you. For instance, you may lose your laptop or smartphone, and therefore lose the private key. Likewise, there is no assurance that someone else in the world cannot use your personal ID papers, such as a social security card, to obtain a PKI authenticated online ID in your name. If there's no real world identification system, there can be no truly secure Internet identification system. Under many digital signature laws, you are responsible for whatever your private key does even if you were not the person using the key. This is very different from mail-order or telephone order credit card rules, where you have a right to dispute the credit card charge. Second, there is no guarantee the verifying computer of the merchant is secure. Third, CAs are self-selected organizations seeking to gain access to the business of authorization. They may not be authorities on the corporations or individuals they certify. For instance, how can a CA know about all the corporations within an industry to determine who is or is not legitimate? A related question concerns the method used by the CA to identify the certificate holder. Was this an e-mail transaction verified only by claims of the applicants who filled out an online form? For instance, VeriSign acknowledged in one case that it had mistakenly issued two digital certificates to someone fraudulently claiming to represent Microsoft. Digital certificates have been hijacked by hackers, tricking consumers into giving up personal information. For example, in 2014, India's National Informatics Centre, an intermediate CA that was trusted by the Indian Controller of Certifying Authorities, whose certificates were included in the Microsoft Root Store and thus trusted by the vast majority of programs running on Windows, including Internet Explorer and Chrome, was hacked and a number of unauthorized digital certificates were issued for domains operated by Google and Yahoo (Datta, 2014). Last, what are the policies for revoking or renewing certificates? The expected life of a digital certificate or private key is a function of the frequency of use and the vulnerability of systems that use the certificate. Yet most CAs have no policy or just an annual policy for reissuing certificates. If Microsoft, Apple, or Cisco ever rescinded a number of CAs, millions of users would not be able to access sites. The CA system is difficult and costly to police.

SECURING CHANNELS OF COMMUNICATION

The concepts of public key cryptography are used routinely for securing channels of communication.

Secure Sockets Layer (SSL) and Transport Layer Security (TLS)

The most common form of securing channels is through the *Secure Sockets Layer (SSL)* and *Transport Layer Security (TLS)* protocols. When you receive a message from a server on the Web with which you will be communicating through a secure channel, this means you will be using SSL/TLS to establish a secure negotiated session. (Notice that the URL changes from HTTP to HTTPS.) A **secure negotiated session** is a client-

secure negotiated session
a client-server session in which the URL of the requested document, along with the contents, contents of forms, and the cookies exchanged, are encrypted

FIGURE 4.10	SECURE NEGOTIATED SESSIONS USING SSL/TLS

Certificates play a key role in using SSL/TLS to establish a secure communications channel.

server session in which the URL of the requested document, along with the contents, contents of forms, and the cookies exchanged, are encrypted (see **Figure 4.10**). For instance, your credit card number that you entered into a form would be encrypted. Through a series of handshakes and communications, the browser and the server establish one another's identity by exchanging digital certificates, decide on the strongest shared form of encryption, and then proceed to communicate using an agreed-upon session key. A **session key** is a unique symmetric encryption key chosen just for this single secure session. Once used, it is gone forever. Figure 4.10 shows how this works.

session key
a unique symmetric encryption key chosen for a single secure session

In practice, most private individuals do not have a digital certificate. In this case, the merchant server will not request a certificate, but the client browser will request the merchant certificate once a secure session is called for by the server.

SSL/TLS provides data encryption, server authentication, optional client authentication, and message integrity for TCP/IP connections. SSL/TLS addresses the issue of authenticity by allowing users to verify another user's identity or the identity of a server. It also protects the integrity of the messages exchanged. However, once the merchant receives the encrypted credit and order information, that information is typically stored in unencrypted format on the merchant's servers. While SSL/TLS provides secure transactions between merchant and consumer, it only guarantees server-side authentication. Client authentication is optional.

In addition, SSL/TLS cannot provide irrefutability—consumers can order goods or download information products, and then claim the transaction never occurred. Recently, social network sites such as Facebook and Twitter have begun to use SSL/TLS for a variety of reasons, including the ability to thwart account hijacking using Firesheep over wireless networks. Firesheep, an add-on for Firefox, can be used by hackers to grab unencrypted cookies used to "remember" a user and allow the hacker to immediately log on to a website as that user. SSL/TLS can thwart such an attack because it encrypts the cookie. In June 2015, the White House's Office of Management and Budget issued a memorandum requiring that all publicly accessible federal websites and web services use HTTPS by December 31, 2016. HTTPS encrypts user requests to website servers. It is implemented by the server adopting the HTTP Strict Transport Security (HSTS) feature that forces browsers to only access the server using HTTPS (CIO.gov, 2016).

Virtual Private Networks (VPNs)

A **virtual private network (VPN)** allows remote users to securely access a corporation's local area network via the Internet, using a variety of VPN protocols. VPNs use both authentication and encryption to secure information from unauthorized persons (providing confidentiality and integrity). Authentication prevents spoofing and misrepresentation of identities. A remote user can connect to a remote private local network using a local ISP. The VPN protocols will establish the link from the client to the corporate network as if the user had dialed into the corporate network directly. The process of connecting one protocol through another (IP) is called *tunneling,* because the VPN creates a private connection by adding an invisible wrapper around a message to hide its content. As the message travels through the Internet between the ISP and the corporate network, it is shielded from prying eyes by an encrypted wrapper.

A VPN is "virtual" in the sense that it appears to users as a dedicated secure line when in fact it is a temporary secure line. The primary use of VPNs is to establish secure communications among business partners—larger suppliers or customers, and employees working remotely. A dedicated connection to a business partner can be very expensive. Using the Internet and VPN as the connection method significantly reduces the cost of secure communications.

virtual private network (VPN)
allows remote users to securely access internal networks via the Internet, using the Point-to-Point Tunneling Protocol (PPTP)

Wireless (Wi-Fi) Networks

Accessing the Internet via a wireless (Wi-Fi) network has its own particular security issues. Early Wi-Fi networks used a security standard called Wired Equivalent Privacy (WEP) to encrypt information. WEP was very weak, and easy for hackers to crack. A new standard, Wi-Fi Protected Access (WPA), was developed that provided a higher standard of protection, but this too soon became vulnerable to intrusion. Today, the current standard is **WPA2**, which uses the AES algorithm for encryption and CCMP, a more advanced authentication code protocol.

WPA2
wireless security standard that uses the AES algorithm for encryption and CCMP, a more advanced authentication code protocol

PROTECTING NETWORKS

Once you have protected communications as well as possible, the next set of tools to consider are those that can protect your networks, as well as the servers and clients on those networks.

Firewalls

Firewalls and proxy servers are intended to build a wall around your network and the attached servers and clients, just like physical-world firewalls protect you from fires for a limited period of time. Firewalls and proxy servers share some similar functions, but they are quite different.

firewall

refers to either hardware or software that filters communication packets and prevents some packets from entering the network based on a security policy

A **firewall** refers to either hardware or software that filters communication packets and prevents some packets from entering or exiting the network based on a security policy. The firewall controls traffic to and from servers and clients, forbidding communications from untrustworthy sources, and allowing other communications from trusted sources to proceed. Every message that is to be sent or received from the network is processed by the firewall, which determines if the message meets security guidelines established by the business. If it does, it is permitted to be distributed, and if it doesn't, the message is blocked. Firewalls can filter traffic based on packet attributes such as source IP address, destination port or IP address, type of service (such as WWW or HTTP), the domain name of the source, and many other dimensions. Most hardware firewalls that protect local area networks connected to the Internet have default settings that require little if any administrator intervention and employ simple but effective rules that deny incoming packets from a connection that does not originate from an internal request—the firewall only allows connections from servers that you requested service from. A common default setting on hardware firewalls (DSL and cable modem routers) simply ignores efforts to communicate with TCP port 445, the most commonly attacked port. The increasing use of firewalls by home and business Internet users has greatly reduced the effectiveness of attacks, and forced hackers to focus more on e-mail attachments to distribute worms and viruses.

There are two major methods firewalls use to validate traffic: packet filters and application gateways. *Packet filters* examine data packets to determine whether they are destined for a prohibited port or originate from a prohibited IP address (as specified by the security administrator). The filter specifically looks at the source and destination information, as well as the port and packet type, when determining whether the information may be transmitted. One downside of the packet filtering method is that it is susceptible to spoofing, because authentication is not one of its roles.

Application gateways are a type of firewall that filters communications based on the application being requested, rather than the source or destination of the message. Such firewalls also process requests at the application level, farther away from the client computer than packet filters. By providing a central filtering point, application gateways provide greater security than packet filters but can compromise system performance.

Next-generation firewalls use an application-centric approach to firewall control. They are able to identify applications regardless of the port, protocol, or security evasion tools used; identify users regardless of device or IP address; decrypt outbound SSL; and protect in real-time against threats embedded in applications.

FIGURE 4.11	FIREWALLS AND PROXY SERVERS

The primary function of a firewall is to deny access by remote client computers to local computers. The primary purpose of a proxy server is to provide controlled access from local computers to remote computers.

Proxy Servers

Proxy servers (proxies) are software servers (often a dedicated computer) that handle all communications originating from or being sent to the Internet by local clients, acting as a spokesperson or bodyguard for the organization. Proxies act primarily to limit access of internal clients to external Internet servers, although some proxy servers act as firewalls as well. Proxy servers are sometimes called *dual-home systems* because they have two network interfaces. To internal computers, a proxy server is known as the *gateway*, while to external computers it is known as a *mail server* or *numeric address*.

When a user on an internal network requests a web page, the request is routed first to the proxy server. The proxy server validates the user and the nature of the request, and then sends the request onto the Internet. A web page sent by an external Internet server first passes to the proxy server. If acceptable, the web page passes onto the internal network web server and then to the client desktop. By prohibiting users from communicating directly with the Internet, companies can restrict access to certain types of sites, such as pornographic, auction, or stock-trading sites. Proxy servers also improve web performance by storing frequently requested web pages locally, reducing upload times, and hiding the internal network's address, thus making it more difficult for hackers to monitor. **Figure 4.11** illustrates how firewalls and proxy servers protect a local area network from Internet intruders and prevent internal clients from reaching prohibited web servers.

proxy server (proxy)
software server that handles all communications originating from or being sent to the Internet, acting as a spokesperson or bodyguard for the organization

Intrusion Detection and Prevention Systems

In addition to a firewall and proxy server, an intrusion detection and/or prevention system can be installed. An **intrusion detection system (IDS)** examines network traffic, watching to see if it matches certain patterns or preconfigured rules indicative of an attack. If it detects suspicious activity, the IDS will set off an alarm alerting administrators and log the event in a database. An IDS is useful for detecting malicious activity that a firewall might miss. An **intrusion prevention system (IPS)** has all the functionality of an IDS, with the additional ability to take steps to prevent and block suspicious activities. For instance, an IPS can terminate a session and reset a connection, block traffic from a suspicious IP address, or reconfigure firewall or router security controls.

PROTECTING SERVERS AND CLIENTS

Operating system features and anti-virus software can help further protect servers and clients from certain types of attacks.

Operating System Security Enhancements

The most obvious way to protect servers and clients is to take advantage of automatic computer security upgrades. The Microsoft, Apple, and Linux/Unix operating systems are continuously updated to patch vulnerabilities discovered by hackers. These patches are autonomic; that is, when using these operating systems on the Internet, you are prompted and informed that operating system enhancements are available. Users can easily download these security patches for free. The most common known worms and viruses can be prevented by simply keeping your server and client operating systems and applications up to date. In April 2014, Microsoft ended security support and updates for its Windows XP operating system. Despite this, many organizations continue to use XP-based systems, and as a result, many security experts anticipate a wave of strikes against such systems. Application vulnerabilities are fixed in the same manner. For instance, most popular Internet browsers are updated automatically with little user intervention.

Anti-Virus Software

The easiest and least-expensive way to prevent threats to system integrity is to install anti-virus software. Programs by Malwarebytes, McAfee, Symantec (Norton AntiVirus), and many others provide inexpensive tools to identify and eradicate the most common types of malicious code as they enter a computer, as well as destroy those already lurking on a hard drive. Anti-virus programs can be set up so that e-mail attachments are inspected before you click on them, and the attachments are eliminated if they contain a known virus or worm. It is not enough, however, to simply install the software once. Because new viruses are developed and released every day, daily routine updates are needed in order to prevent new threats from being loaded. Some premium-level anti-virus software is updated hourly.

Anti-virus suite packages and stand-alone programs are available to eliminate intruders such as bot programs, adware, and other security risks. Such programs work much like anti-virus software in that they look for recognized hacker tools or signature actions of known intruders.

FIGURE 4.12 DEVELOPING AN E-COMMERCE SECURITY PLAN

There are five steps involved in building an e-commerce security plan.

4.4 MANAGEMENT POLICIES, BUSINESS PROCEDURES, AND PUBLIC LAWS

Worldwide, in 2016, companies are expected to spend over €76 billion on security hardware, software, and services, up 8% from the previous year (Gartner, 2016). However, most CEOs and CIOs believe that technology is not the sole answer to managing the risk of e-commerce. The technology provides a foundation, but in the absence of intelligent management policies, even the best technology can be easily defeated. Public laws and active enforcement of cybercrime statutes also are required to both raise the costs of illegal behavior on the Internet and guard against corporate abuse of information. Let's consider briefly the development of management policy.

A SECURITY PLAN: MANAGEMENT POLICIES

In order to minimize security threats, e-commerce firms must develop a coherent corporate policy that takes into account the nature of the risks, the information assets that need protecting, and the procedures and technologies required to address the risk, as well as implementation and auditing mechanisms. **Figure 4.12** illustrates the key steps in developing a solid security plan.

risk assessment
an assessment of the risks and points of vulnerability

A security plan begins with **risk assessment**—an assessment of the risks and points of vulnerability. The first step is to inventory the information and knowledge assets of the e-commerce site and company. What information is at risk? Is it customer information, proprietary designs, business activities, secret processes, or other internal information, such as price schedules, executive compensation, or payroll? For each type of information asset, try to estimate the dollar value to the firm if this information were compromised, and then multiply that amount by the probability of the loss occurring. Once you have done so, rank order the results. You now have a list of information assets prioritized by their value to the firm.

security policy
a set of statements prioritizing the information risks, identifying acceptable risk targets, and identifying the mechanisms for achieving these targets

Based on your quantified list of risks, you can start to develop a **security policy**— a set of statements prioritizing the information risks, identifying acceptable risk targets, and identifying the mechanisms for achieving these targets. You will obviously want to start with the information assets that you determined to be the highest priority in your risk assessment. Who generates and controls this information in the firm? What existing security policies are in place to protect the information? What enhancements can you recommend to improve security of these most valuable assets? What level of risk are you willing to accept for each of these assets? Are you willing, for instance, to lose customer credit card data once every 10 years? Or will you pursue a 100-year hurricane strategy by building a security edifice for credit card data that can withstand the once-in-100-year disaster? You will need to estimate how much it will cost to achieve this level of acceptable risk. Remember, total and complete security may require extraordinary financial resources. By answering these questions, you will have the beginnings of a security policy.

implementation plan
the action steps you will take to achieve the security plan goals

Next, consider an **implementation plan**—the steps you will take to achieve the security plan goals. Specifically, you must determine how you will translate the levels of acceptable risk into a set of tools, technologies, policies, and procedures. What new technologies will you deploy to achieve the goals, and what new employee procedures will be needed?

security organization
educates and trains users, keeps management aware of security threats and breakdowns, and maintains the tools chosen to implement security

To implement your plan, you will need an organizational unit in charge of security, and a security officer—someone who is in charge of security on a daily basis. For a small e-commerce site, the security officer will likely be the person in charge of Internet services or the site manager, whereas for larger firms, there typically is a dedicated team with a supporting budget. The **security organization** educates and trains users, keeps management aware of security threats and breakdowns, and maintains the tools chosen to implement security.

access controls
determine who can gain legitimate access to a network

The security organization typically administers access controls, authentication procedures, and authorization policies. **Access controls** determine which outsiders and insiders can gain legitimate access to your networks. Outsider access controls include firewalls and proxy servers, while insider access controls typically consist of login procedures (usernames, passwords, and access codes).

authentication procedures
include the use of digital signatures, certificates of authority, and public key infrastructure

Authentication procedures include the use of digital signatures, certificates of authority, and PKI. Now that e-signatures have been given the same legal weight as an original pen-and-ink version, companies are in the process of devising ways to test and confirm a signer's identity. Companies frequently have signers type their full name and click on a button indicating their understanding that they have just signed a contract or document.

Biometric devices can also be used to verify physical attributes associated with an individual, such as a fingerprint or retina (eye) scan or speech recognition system. (**Biometrics** is the study of measurable biological, or physical, characteristics.) A company could require, for example, that an individual undergo a fingerprint scan before being allowed access to a website, or before being allowed to pay for merchandise with a credit card. Biometric devices make it even more difficult for hackers to break into sites or facilities, significantly reducing the opportunity for spoofing. Newer Apple iPhones (5S and later) feature a fingerprint sensor called Touch ID built into the iPhone's home button that can unlock the phone and authorize purchases from the iTunes, iBooks, and App Stores without requiring users to enter a PIN or other security code. According to Apple, the system does not store an actual fingerprint, but rather biometric data, which will be encrypted and stored only on a chip within the iPhone, and will not be made available to third parties.

Security tokens are physical devices or software that generate an identifier that can be used in addition to or in place of a password. Security tokens are used by millions of corporation and government workers to log on to corporate clients and servers. One example is RSA's SecurID token, which continously generates six-digit passwords.

Authorization policies determine differing levels of access to information assets for differing levels of users. **Authorization management systems** establish where and when a user is permitted to access certain parts of a website. Their primary function is to restrict access to private information within a company's Internet infrastructure. Although there are several authorization management products currently available, most operate in the same way: the system encrypts a user session to function like a passkey that follows the user from page to page, allowing access only to those areas that the user is permitted to enter, based on information set at the system database. By establishing entry rules up front for each user, the authorization management system knows who is permitted to go where at all times.

The last step in developing an e-commerce security plan is performing a security audit. A **security audit** involves the routine review of access logs (identifying how outsiders are using the site as well as how insiders are accessing the site's assets). A monthly report should be produced that establishes the routine and nonroutine accesses to the systems and identifies unusual patterns of activities. As previously noted, tiger teams are often used by large corporate sites to evaluate the strength of existing security procedures. Many small firms have sprung up in the last five years to provide these services to large corporate sites.

THE ROLE OF LAWS AND PUBLIC POLICY

The public policy environment today is very different from the early days of e-commerce. The net result is that the Internet is no longer an ungoverned, unsupervised, self-controlled technology juggernaut. Just as with financial markets in the last 70 years, there is a growing awareness that e-commerce markets work only when a powerful institutional set of laws and enforcement mechanisms are in place. These laws

biometrics
the study of measurable biological or physical characteristics

security token
physical device or software that generates an identifier that can be used in addition to or in place of a password

authorization policies
determine differing levels of access to information assets for differing levels of users

authorization management system
establishes where and when a user is permitted to access certain parts of a website

security audit
involves the routine review of access logs (identifying how outsiders are using the site as well as how insiders are accessing the site's assets)

help ensure orderly, rational, and fair markets. This growing public policy environment is becoming just as global as e-commerce itself. Despite some spectacular internationally based attacks on U.S. e-commerce sites, the sources and persons involved in major harmful attacks have almost always been uncovered and, where possible, prosecuted.

Voluntary and private efforts have played a very large role in identifying criminal hackers and assisting law enforcement. Since 1995, as e-commerce has grown in significance, national and local law enforcement activities have expanded greatly. New laws have been passed that grant local and national authorities new tools and mechanisms for identifying, tracing, and prosecuting cybercriminals. For instance, a majority of states now require companies that maintain personal data on their residents to publicly disclose when a security breach affecting those residents has occurred. **Table 4.6** lists the most significant federal e-commerce security legislation and regulation. In addition, the Federal Trade Commission has asserted that it has authority over corporations' data security practices. The FTC sued the Wyndham hotel chain after hacking attacks in 2008 and 2009 resulted in a data breach that led to fraudulent credit charges of more than $10 million. According to the FTC, its investigation showed that Wyndham had failed to follow basic data security practices, while at the same time assuring customers that their data was safe. In August 2015, the U.S. Court of Appeals for the Third Circuit ruled that the FTC was within the scope of its authority, opening the door for it to take a greater role, especially in light of the failure of Congress to adopt legislation governing data security. By increasing the punishment for cybercrimes, the U.S. government is attempting to create a deterrent to further hacker actions. And by making such actions federal crimes, the government is able to extradite international hackers and prosecute them within the United States.

After September 11, 2001, Congress passed the USA PATRIOT Act, which broadly expanded law enforcement's investigative and surveillance powers. The act has provisions for monitoring e-mail and Internet use. The Homeland Security Act of 2002 also attempts to fight cyberterrorism and increases the government's ability to compel information disclosure by computer and ISP sources. Recent proposed legislation that focuses on requiring firms to report data breaches to the FTC, protection of the national electric grid, and cybersecurity has all failed to pass. However, in December 2015, the Cybersecurity Information Sharing Act (CISA) was signed into law by President Obama. The Act, which creates a system that lets companies share evidence about attacks without the risk of being sued, had been opposed by many large technology companies and privacy advocates on the grounds that it did not do enough to protect individual privacy and could lead to increased government surveillance. However, implementation of the CISA is still a work in progress and it remains to be seen how effective it will be (Chew and Newby, 2016; Peterson, 2015).

Private and Private-Public Cooperation Efforts

The good news is that e-commerce sites are not alone in their battle to achieve security on the Internet. Several organizations—some public and some private—are

TABLE 4.6	U.S. E-COMMERCE SECURITY LEGISLATION AND REGULATION
LEGISLATION/REGULATION	SIGNIFICANCE
Computer Fraud and Abuse Act (1986)	Primary federal statute used to combat computer crime.
Electronic Communications Privacy Act (1986)	Imposes fines and imprisonment for individuals who access, intercept, or disclose the private e-mail communications of others.
National Information Infrastructure Protection Act (1996)	Makes DoS attacks illegal; creates NIPC in the FBI.
Health Insurance Portability and Accountability Act (1996)	Requires certain health care facilities to report data breaches.
Financial Modernization Act (Gramm-Leach-Bliley Act) (1999)	Requires certain financial institutions to report data breaches.
Cyberspace Electronic Security Act (2000)	Reduces export restrictions.
Computer Security Enhancement Act (2000)	Protects federal government systems from hacking.
Electronic Signatures in Global and National Commerce Act (the "E-Sign Law") (2000)	Authorizes the use of electronic signatures in legal documents.
USA PATRIOT Act (2001)	Authorizes use of computer-based surveillance of suspected terrorists.
Homeland Security Act (2002)	Authorizes establishment of the Department of Homeland Security, which is responsible for developing a comprehensive national plan for security of the key resources and critical infrastructures of the United States; DHS becomes the central coordinator for all cyberspace security efforts.
CAN-SPAM Act (2003)	Although primarily a mechanism for civil and regulatory lawsuits against spammers, the CAN-SPAM Act also creates several new criminal offenses intended to address situations in which the perpetrator has taken steps to hide his or her identity or the source of the spam from recipients, ISPs, or law enforcement agencies. Also contains criminal sanctions for sending sexually explicit e-mail without designating it as such.
U.S. SAFE WEB Act (2006)	Enhances FTC's ability to obtain monetary redress for consumers in cases involving spyware, spam, Internet fraud, and deception; also improves FTC's ability to gather information and coordinate investigations with foreign counterparts.
Improving Critical Infrastructure Cybersecurity Executive Order (2013)	After Congress failed to pass cybersecurity legislation in 2012, this executive order issued by the Obama administration directs federal agenices to share cybersecurity threat intelligence with private sector companies that may be targets, and the development and implementation of a cybersecurity framework for private industry, incorporating best practices and voluntary standards.
Cybersharing Information Sharing Act (2015)	Encourages businesses and the federal government to share cyber threat information in the interests of national security,

devoted to tracking down criminal organizations and individuals engaged in attacks against Internet and e-commerce sites. On the federal level, the Office of Cybersecurity and Communications (CS&C) within the U.S. Department of Homeland Security (DHS) is responsible for overseeing the security, resilience, and reliability of the United States' cyber and communications infrastructure. The National Cybersecurity and Communications Integration Center (NCCIC) acts as a 24/7 cyber monitoring, incident response, and management center. In addition, the DHS also operates the **United States Computer Emergency Readiness Team (US-CERT)**, which coordinates cyber incident warnings and responses across both the government and private sectors. One of the better-known private organizations is the **CERT Coordination Center** (formerly known as the Computer Emergency Response Team) at Carnegie Mellon University. CERT monitors and tracks online criminal activity reported to it by private corporations and government agencies that seek out its help. CERT is composed of full-time and part-time computer experts who can trace the origins of attacks against sites despite the complexity of the Internet. Its staff members also assist organizations in identifying security problems, developing solutions, and communicating with the public about widespread hacker threats. The CERT Coordination Center also provides product assessments, reports, and training in order to improve the public's knowledge and understanding of security threats and solutions.

US-CERT
division of the U.S. Department of Homeland Security that coordinates cyber incident warnings and responses across government and private sectors

CERT Coordination Center
monitors and tracks online criminal activity reported to it by private corporations and government agencies that seek out its help

Government Policies and Controls on Encryption

In the United States, both Congress and the executive branch have sought to regulate the uses of encryption and to restrict availability and export of encryption systems as a means of preventing crime and terrorism. At the international level, four organizations have influenced the international traffic in encryption software: the Organization for Economic Cooperation and Development (OECD), G-7 (the heads of state of the top seven industrialized countries in the world, not including Russia, which was suspended from participation in 2014), the European Council, and the Wassenaar Arrangement (which includes 41 countries that produce sensitive industrial equipment or weapons). Various governments have proposed schemes for controlling encryption software or at least preventing criminals from obtaining strong encryption tools (see **Table 4.7**). The U.S. and U.K. governments are also devoting a large amount of resources to cryptography-related programs that will enable them to break encrypted communications collected on the Internet. Documents leaked by former NSA contractor Edward Snowden indicate that both the NSA and its U.K. counterpart, the GCHQ, may be able to break encryption schemes used by SSL/TLS, VPNs, and on 4G smartphones (Vaughan-Nichols, 2013). In recent years, the fight between the U.S. government and technology companies over encryption has shifted to the mobile platform, with Apple resisting U.S. government efforts to break Apple's iCloud and Apple iPhone encryption systems (see the Chapter 8 *Insight on Society* case, *Apple: Defender of Privacy?*) and concerns over encryption messaging apps such as WhatsApp, Signal, and Telegram, that offer end-to-end encryption for texts, photos, and videos that make it difficult, if not impossible, for authorities to intercept communications using such services (Isaac, 2016).

TABLE 4.7	GOVERNMENT EFFORTS TO REGULATE AND CONTROL ENCRYPTION
REGULATORY EFFORT	IMPACT
Restricted export of strong security systems	Supported primarily by the United States. Widespread distribution of encryption schemes weakens this policy. The policy is changing to permit exports except to pariah countries.
Key escrow/key recovery schemes	France, the United Kingdom, and the United States supported this effort in the late 1990s but now have largely abandoned it. There are few trusted third parties.
Lawful access and forced disclosure	Growing support in U.S. legislation and in OECD countries.
Official hacking	All countries are rapidly expanding budgets and training for law enforcement "technical centers" aimed at monitoring and cracking computer-based encryption activities of suspected criminals.

4.5 E-COMMERCE PAYMENT SYSTEMS

For the most part, existing payment mechanisms such as cash, credit cards, debit cards, checking accounts, and stored value accounts have been able to be adapted to the online environment, albeit with some significant limitations that have led to efforts to develop alternatives. In addition, new types of purchasing relationships, such as between individuals online, and new technologies, such as the development of the mobile platform, have also created both a need and an opportunity for the development of new payment systems. In this section, we provide an overview of the major e-commerce payment systems in use today. **Table 4.8** lists some of the major trends in e-commerce payments in 2016–2017.

Worldwide, online payments by consumers represented a market of almost €2.35 trillion in 2016. Institutions and business firms that can handle this volume of trans-

TABLE 4.8	MAJOR TRENDS IN E-COMMERCE PAYMENTS 2016–2017

- Payment by credit and/or debit card remains the dominant form of online payment.
- Mobile retail payment volume skyrockets.
- PayPal remains the most popular alternative payment method online.
- Apple, Google, Samsung, and PayPal extend their reach in mobile payment apps.
- Large banks enter the mobile wallet and P2P payments market.
- Square gains further traction with a smartphone app, credit card reader, and credit card processing service that permits anyone to accept credit card payments.
- Google refocuses Google Wallet, which had met with tepid response, solely on sending and receiving money.
- Mobile P2P payment systems such as Venmo take off.

| FIGURE 4.13 | ALTERNATIVE PAYMENT METHODS USED BY U.S. CONSUMERS |

PayPal is still, by far, the most popular alternative payment method.
SOURCE: Based on data from eMarketer, 2016a.

actions (mostly the large banking and credit firms) generally extract 2%–3% of the transactions in the form of fees. Given the size of the market, competition for online payments is spirited. New forms of online payment are expected to attract a substantial part of this growth.

In the United States, the primary form of online payment is still the existing credit and debit card system. Alternative payment methods such as PayPal continue to make inroads into traditional payment methods. Mobile payments are also expected to grow significantly. **Figure 4.13** illustrates the percentage of consumers that use various alternative payment methods in 2016. However, none of these alternative payment methods have become substitutes for the bank and credit cards, but instead provide consumers with alternative methods of accessing their existing bank and credit accounts.

In other parts of the world, e-commerce payments can be very different depending on traditions and infrastructure. Credit cards are not nearly as dominant a form of online payment as they are in the United States. If you plan on operating an e-commerce site in Europe, Asia, or Latin America, you will need to develop different payment systems for each region. For instance, in Denmark, Norway, and Finland payment is primarily with debit or credit cards, while in Sweden, payment after being tendered an invoice and by bank transfer are very popular in addition to credit/debit cards. In the Netherlands, the online payments service iDEAL is the most popular retail e-commerce payment method. In Italy, consumers rely heavily on both credit

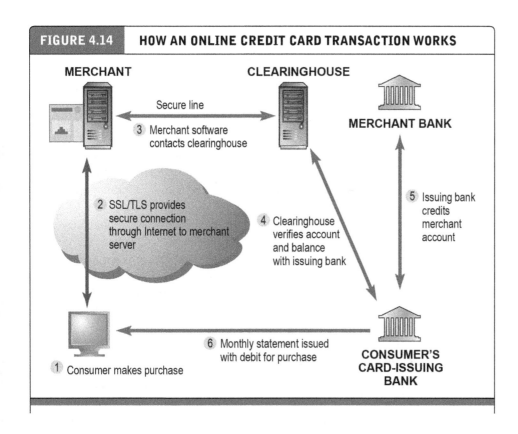

FIGURE 4.14   HOW AN ONLINE CREDIT CARD TRANSACTION WORKS

cards and PayPal. In Japan, although credit card is the primary payment method, many consumers still pick up and pay for goods using cash at local convenience stores (konbini) (eMarketer, Inc., 2015).

ONLINE CREDIT CARD TRANSACTIONS

Because credit and debit cards are the dominant form of online payment, it is important to understand how they work and to recognize the strengths and weaknesses of this payment system. Online credit card transactions are processed in much the same way that in-store purchases are, with the major differences being that online merchants never see the actual card being used, no card impression is taken, and no signature is available. Online credit card transactions most closely resemble Mail Order-Telephone Order (MOTO) transactions. These types of purchases are also called Cardholder Not Present (CNP) transactions and are the major reason that charges can be disputed later by consumers. Because the merchant never sees the credit card, nor receives a hand-signed agreement to pay from the customer, when disputes arise, the merchant faces the risk that the transaction may be disallowed and reversed, even though he has already shipped the goods or the user has downloaded a digital product.

Figure 4.14 illustrates the online credit card purchasing cycle. There are five parties involved in an online credit card purchase: consumer, merchant, clearinghouse, merchant bank (sometimes called the "acquiring bank"), and the consumer's card-issuing bank. In order to accept payments by credit card, online merchants must have

merchant account

a bank account that allows companies to process credit card payments and receive funds from those transactions

a merchant account established with a bank or financial institution. A **merchant account** is simply a bank account that allows companies to process credit card payments and receive funds from those transactions.

As shown in Figure 4.14, an online credit card transaction begins with a purchase (1). When a consumer wants to make a purchase, he or she adds the item to the merchant's shopping cart. When the consumer wants to pay for the items in the shopping cart, a secure tunnel through the Internet is created using SSL/TLS. Using encryption, SSL/TLS secures the session during which credit card information will be sent to the merchant and protects the information from interlopers on the Internet (2). SSL does not authenticate either the merchant or the consumer. The transacting parties have to trust one another.

Once the consumer credit card information is received by the merchant, the merchant software contacts a clearinghouse (3). As previously noted, a clearinghouse is a financial intermediary that authenticates credit cards and verifies account balances. The clearinghouse contacts the issuing bank to verify the account information (4). Once verified, the issuing bank credits the account of the merchant at the merchant's bank (usually this occurs at night in a batch process) (5). The debit to the consumer account is transmitted to the consumer in a monthly statement (6).

Credit Card E-commerce Enablers

Companies that have a merchant account still need to buy or build a means of handling the online transaction; securing the merchant account is only step one in a two-part process. Today, Internet payment service providers (sometimes referred to as payment gateways) can provide both a merchant account and the software tools needed to process credit card purchases online.

For instance, Authorize.net is an Internet payment service provider. The company helps a merchant secure an account with one of its merchant account provider partners and then provides payment processing software for installation on the merchant's server. The software collects the transaction information from the merchant's site and then routes it via the Authorize.net "payment gateway" to the appropriate bank, ensuring that customers are authorized to make their purchases. The funds for the transaction are then transferred to the merchant's merchant account. CyberSource is another well-known Internet payment service provider.

PCI-DSS Compliance

PCI-DSS (Payment Card Industry-Data Security Standards)

data security standards instituted by the five major credit card companies

The **PCI-DSS (Payment Card Industry-Data Security Standard)** is a data security standard instituted by the five major credit card companies (Visa, MasterCard, American Express, Discover, and JCB). PCI-DSS is not a law or governmental regulation, but an industry-mandated standard. Every online merchant must comply with the appropriate level of PCI-DSS in order to accept credit card payments. Those that fail to comply and are involved in a credit card breach may ultimately be subjected to fines and other expenses. PCI-DSS has various levels, related to the number of credit and/or debit cards processed by the merchant each year. Level 1, the strictest level, applies to very large merchants that process more than 6 million transactions a year, while Level 2 applies to those who process between 1 million and 6 million. Level 3 applies to organizations that process between 20,000 and 1 million transactions, while Level 4 applies to smaller merchants that process less than 20,000 transactions. PCI-DSS has six major control objectives. It requires the merchant to (a) build and maintain a secure network, (b) protect cardholder data, (c) maintain a vulnerability management program, (d) implement strong access control measures, (e) regularly test and monitor networks, and (f) maintain an information security policy. Each of these six broad control objectives has further specific requirements that must be met. The most current version of PCI-DSS is Version 3.1, which went into effect as of April 2015 (PCI Security Standards Council, 2015).

Limitations of Online Credit Card Payment Systems

There are a number of limitations to the existing credit card payment system. The most important limitations involve security, merchant risk, administrative and transaction costs, and social equity.

The existing system offers poor security. Neither the merchant nor the consumer can be fully authenticated. The merchant could be a criminal organization designed to collect credit card numbers, and the consumer could be a thief using stolen or fraudulent cards. The risk facing merchants is high: consumers can repudiate charges even though the goods have been shipped or the product downloaded. The banking industry attempted to develop a secure electronic transaction (SET) protocol, but this effort failed because it was too complex for consumers and merchants alike. The rate of online credit card fraud is expected to reach $4 billion in 2016, up from $2 billion in 2011. As banks switch to EMV cards with computer chips, offline credit card fraud becomes more difficult, encouraging criminals to focus on online fraud (Sidel, 2016).

The administrative costs of setting up an online credit card system and becoming authorized to accept credit cards are high. Transaction costs for merchants also are significant—roughly 3% of the purchase plus a transaction fee of 20–35 cents per transaction, plus other setup fees.

Credit cards are not very democratic, even though they seem ubiquitous. Millions of young adults do not have credit cards, along with millions of others who cannot afford cards or who are considered poor risks because of low incomes.

ALTERNATIVE ONLINE PAYMENT SYSTEMS

The limitations of the online credit card system have opened the way for the development of a number of alternative online payment systems. Chief among them is PayPal. PayPal (purchased by eBay in 2002 and then spun-off as an independent company again in 2015) enables individuals and businesses with e-mail accounts to make and receive payments up to a specified limit. Paypal is an example of an **online stored value payment system**, which permits consumers to make online payments to merchants and other individuals using their bank account or credit/debit cards. It is available in 202 countries and 25 currencies around the world. PayPal builds on the existing financial infrastructure of the countries in which it operates. You establish a PayPal account by specifying a credit, debit, or checking account you wish to have charged or paid when conducting online transactions. When you make a payment

online stored value payment system
permits consumers to make instant, online payments to merchants and other individuals based on value stored in an online account

using PayPal, you e-mail the payment to the merchant's PayPal account. PayPal transfers the amount from your credit or checking account to the merchant's bank account. The beauty of PayPal is that no personal credit information has to be shared among the users, and the service can be used by individuals to pay one another even in small amounts. However, one issue with PayPal is its relatively high cost. For example, when using a credit card as the source of funds, to send or request money, the cost ranges from 2.9% to 5.99% of the amount (depending on the type of transaction) plus a small fixed fee (typically $0.30) per transaction. PayPal is discussed in further depth in the case study at the end of the chapter.

Although PayPal is by far the most well-known and commonly used online credit/ debit card alternative, there are a number of other alternatives as well. Pay with Amazon is aimed at consumers who have concerns about entrusting their credit card information to unfamiliar online retailers. Consumers can purchase goods and services at non-Amazon websites using the payment methods stored in their Amazon accounts, without having to reenter their payment information at the merchant's site. Amazon provides the payment processing. Visa Checkout (formerly V.me) and MasterCard's MasterPass substitute a user name and password for an actual payment card number during online checkout. Both MasterPass and Visa Checkout are supported by a number of large payment processors and online retailers. However, they have not yet achieved the usage of Paypal.

Bill Me Later (owned by PayPal as well) also appeals to consumers who do not wish to enter their credit card information online. Bill Me Later describes itself as an open-ended credit account. Users select the Bill Me Later option at checkout and are asked to provide their birth date and the last four digits of their social security number. They are then billed for the purchase by Bill Me Later within 10 to 14 days. Bill Me Later is currently offered by more than 1,000 online merchants.

WU Pay (formerly eBillme, and now operated by Western Union) offers a similar service. WU Pay customers who select the WU Pay option at firms such as Sears, Kmart, and other retailers do not have to provide any credit card information. Instead they are e-mailed a bill, which they can pay via their bank's online bill payment service, or in person at any Western Union location. Dwolla is a similar cash-based payment network for both individuals and merchants. It bypasses the credit card network and instead connects directly into a bank account. In 2015, Dwolla eliminated its transaction and processing fees, changing its focus from consumer-to-consumer payments to larger businesses. Dwolla has its own network that bypasses the Automated Clearing House (ACH), the traditional system for processing financial transactions in the United States, and in 2015, signed up major U.S. bank BBVA Compass. Earlier in the year, the U.S. Treasury had selected Dwolla (along with PayPal) to process payments to federal agencies, and in October 2015, the Chicago Mercantile Exchange chose Dwolla to replace ACH. Dwolla now processes nearly $2 billion a year and has over 1 million accounts (Pendell, 2016; Patane, 2015; Leising, 2015).

Like Dwolla, Stripe is another company that is attempting to provide an alternative to the traditional online credit card system. Stripe focuses on the merchant side of the process. It provides simple software code that enables companies to bypass much of the administrative costs involved in setting up an online credit card system, and instead lets companies begin accepting credit card payments almost immediately without the need to obtain a merchant account or use a gateway provider. Stripe recently introduced merchant apps that can accept NFC payments. Unlike PayPal, the customer doesn't need a Stripe account to pay, and all payments are made directly to the company rather than being routed through a third party.

MOBILE PAYMENT SYSTEMS: YOUR SMARTPHONE WALLET

The use of mobile devices as payment mechanisms is already well established in Europe and Asia and is now exploding in the United States, where the infrastructure to support mobile payment is finally being put in place.

Near field communication (NFC) is the primary enabling technology for mobile payment systems. **Near field communication (NFC)** is a set of short-range wireless technologies used to share information among devices within about 2 inches of each other (50 mm). NFC devices are either powered or passive. A connection requires one powered device (the initiator, such as a smartphone), and one target device, such as a merchant NFC reader, that can respond to requests from the initiator. NFC targets can be very simple forms such as tags, stickers, key fobs, or readers. NFC peer-to-peer communication is possible where both devices are powered. Consumers can swipe their NFC-equipped phone near a merchant's reader to pay for purchases. In September 2014, Apple introduced the iPhone 6, which is equipped with NFC chips designed to work with Apple's mobile payments platform, Apple Pay. Building on Apple Passbook and Touch ID biometric fingerprint scanning and encryption that Apple previously introduced in September 2012, Apple Pay is able to be used for mobile payments at the point-of-sale at a physical store as well as online purchases using an iPhone. Other competitors in NFC-enabled mobile payments include Android Pay, Samsung Pay, PayPal, and Square. Surveys reveal that about 20%–30% of smartphone users have downloaded mobile wallet apps, but that only about 20% of these adopters have made a payment in the last month using these apps. **Figure 4.15** shows that Apple and PayPal are the most widely used mobile payment apps among adopters of mobile wallets. The promise of riches beyond description to a firm that is able to dominate the mobile payments marketplace has set off what one commentator has called a goat rodeo surrounding the development of new technologies and methods of mobile payment. The end-of-chapter case study, *Mobile Payment Marketplace: Goat Rodeo*, provides a further look at the future of online and mobile payment in the United States, including the efforts of Apple, Google, Samsung, Square, PayPal, and major financial institutions.

near field communication (NFC)
a set of short-range wireless technologies used to share information among devices

SOCIAL/MOBILE PEER-TO-PEER PAYMENT SYSTEMS

In addition to using a mobile device as a vehicle for e-commerce and as a payment method at physical point-of-sale, another type of mobile payment transaction is becoming increasingly popular: social/mobile peer-to-peer payments. Services such as Venmo, Square Cash, Snapcash, the newly refocused Google Wallet, and the new Facebook Messenger Payment service all enable users to send another person money through a mobile application or website, funded by a bank debit card. There is no charge for this service. Currently, these services are the most popular among Millennials, which is the key demographic driving their growth. Venmo, owned by PayPal,

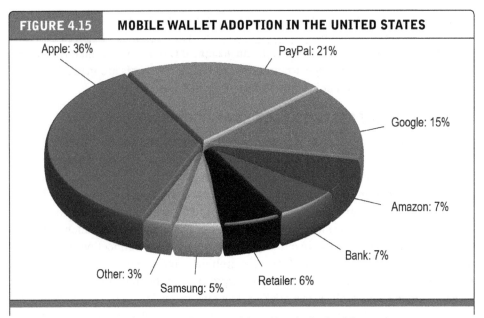

| FIGURE 4.15 | MOBILE WALLET ADOPTION IN THE UNITED STATES |

Apple Pay and PayPal's mobile wallet are the most widely used methods of mobile payment.
SOURCE: Based on data from eMarketer, Inc., 2016b.

is particularly popular, with its success in part due to its integration with Facebook and its social network newsfeed, which lets users see when friends are paying other friends or paying for products and services. In 2015, Venmo processed an estimated $8 billion in transactions and is growing at over 200% annually. In 2016, Facebook and PayPal announced that Facebook subscribers could use PayPal to purchase goods and services, with notifications coming through Facebook Messenger. Analysts forecast that mobile P2P will grow to $174 billion, worth 30% of total P2P payment volume, by 2020. That's up from $5.6 billion, or just 1%, in 2014 (BI Intelligence, 2016).

REGULATION OF MOBILE WALLETS AND RECHARGEABLE CARDS

In October 2016, the Bureau of Consumer Financial Protection (BCFP), a U.S. federal regulatory agency, issued the first regulations on what it called General Purpose Reloadable (GPR) cards. The regulations apply to some mobile digital wallets and to physical cards that can be loaded with prepaid funds, as well as cards that can be purchased at retail locations or recharged with funds at a bank ATM or merchant point-of-sale terminal (but not to gift cards purchased at retail locations). Previously, GPR cards were not subject to existing federal consumer banking regulations that provide protection from unauthorized transfers and require disclosure with respect to their terms and error resolution procedures. The BCFP estimates that GPR transactions in the United States grew from $1 billion in 2003 to $65 billion in 2012, with a projected growth to $117 billion in 2019 (BCFP, 2016). Physical GPR cards are generally sold to people who do not have a bank or credit account, and who use them as a substitute for a checking account and cash for mobile payments. Mobile digital wallets, in comparison, are typically used by people who already have these banking credentials. Venmo and similar peer-to-peer payment services, as well as Android Pay and Samsung Pay, are subject to these regulations because they allow for the storage of prepaid funds. Apple Pay and similar wallets are not subject to these regulations because they do not store prepaid funds and simply act as an intermediary between the banks and consumers using existing bank credentials.

The new regulations require disclosure of financial terms to consumers prior to and after acquisition of a prepaid account, access to periodical statements, a means for consumers to correct errors in payments, consumer opt-in for over-draft and credit features, and a 21-day minimum repayment period. The regulations prohibit requiring customers to set up preauthorized electronic fund transfers to repay credit extended through an overdraft service or credit feature. These requirements are extensions of the existing Electronic Funds Transfer Act (Regulation E) and the Truth in Lending Act (Regulation Z) that apply to products of bank and credit institutions such as credit and debit cards.

DIGITAL CASH AND VIRTUAL CURRENCIES

Although the terms digital cash and virtual currencies are often used synonymously, they actually refer to two separate types of alternative payment systems. **Digital cash** typically is based on an algorithm that generates unique authenticated tokens representing cash value that can be used "in the real world." Bitcoin is the best known example of digital cash. Bitcoins are encrypted numbers (sometimes referred to as cryptocurrency) that are generated by a complex algorithm using a peer-to-peer network in a process referred to as "mining" that requires extensive computing power. Like real currency, Bitcoins have a fluctuating value tied to open-market trading. Like cash, Bitcoins are anonymous—they are exchanged via a 34-character alphanumeric address that the user has, and do not require any other identifying information. Bitcoins have recently attracted a lot of attention as a potential money laundering tool for cybercriminals and illicit drug markets like Silk Road, and have also been plagued by security issues, with some high-profile heists. Nonetheless, there are companies now using Bitcoins as a legitimate alternative payment system. Read the *Insight on Business* case, *Bitcoin*, for a further look at Bitcoin and some of the issues surrounding it.

digital cash
an alternative payment system in which unique, authenticated tokens represent cash value

Virtual currencies, on the other hand, typically circulate primarily within an internal virtual world community, such as Linden Dollars, created by Linden Lab for use in its virtual world, Second Life. Virtual currencies are typically used for purchasing virtual goods.

virtual currency
typically circulates within an internal virtual world community or is issued by a specific corporate entity, and used to purchase virtual goods

4.6 ELECTRONIC BILLING PRESENTMENT AND PAYMENT

In 2007, for the first time, the number of bill payments made online exceeded the number of physical checks written in the United States (Fiserv, 2007). In the $19 trillion U.S. economy with a $13.3 trillion consumer sector for goods and services, there are billions of bills to pay. According to the U.S. Postal Service, U.S. households received about 21 billion bills in 2015 via the mail. No one knows for sure, but some experts believe the life-cycle cost of a paper bill for a business, from point of issuance to point of payment, ranges from $3 to $7. This calculation does not include the value of time to consumers, who must open bills, read them, write checks, address envelopes, stamp, and then mail

INSIGHT ON BUSINESS

BITCOIN

In recent years, a number of countries around the world have experienced banking crises, eroding trust in the system. Enter Bitcoin, a form of electronic currency that can be transferred from one person to another via peer-to-peer networks, without the need for a bank or other financial institution as intermediary. This ability to operate outside the banking system has made Bitcoin a favorite of hackers and buyers and sellers of illicit goods and services; but more recently, it has made Bitcoin a darling among many in the technological elite who believe that Bitcoin and the technology behind it could be the next big thing in the payments industry.

Bitcoin has many unique attributes that differentiate it from traditional currencies. Bitcoins are not physically minted, but are generated by computer software at a predetermined rate beginning in 2009. A finite amount of coins are "built into the software," such that in the year 2140, all of the coins will be mined and present in the market. The program that is used to generate Bitcoins runs on a peer-to-peer network and requires powerful computer systems to operate. "Mining" a Bitcoin is the result of these powerful computers solving cryptographic problems in tandem with other similar computers—the computer that hits upon the solution is awarded the coin, and a record of all of the involved computers' attempts at mining the coin is logged. Bitcoins derive some of their initial value because of the time and computational effort required to mine them.

There are, however, many reasons to be skeptical of Bitcoin. Although law enforcement has improved its ability to apprehend criminals using Bitcoin, including the founder of the online black market Silk Road in 2015, governments are justifiably concerned about the emergence of a new currency without any tangible form whose purpose is to avoid regulation. Bitcoin has also been lauded for its democratic structure, under which anyone running the underlying software has a say in making future changes. However, in 2016, Bitcoin is embroiled in a bitter civil war. As the currency continues to gain in popularity, limits on the Bitcoin transactions that can be processed each second, originally imposed as a safeguard, have begun to create backlogs and cripple transaction speed. Some of Bitcoin's long-time supporters want to raise these limits to bring Bitcoin processing speed in line with services like PayPal; others argue that doing so could abandon the decentralized nature of the currency and place Bitcoin in the control of the few companies with the computing power to handle such a significant load, and out of the hands of the people. In 2016, there are now competing versions of Bitcoin, one which has removed transaction limits, and the other which remains faithful to the currency's original vision, poor processing speed notwithstanding. Because of Bitcoin's uncertainties and legal quandaries, the governments of many countries, including China, Denmark, Russia, and Israel, have taken a firm stand against digital cash.

Each of these developments has put downward pressure on Bitcoin's value and slowed its growth, although Chinese exchanges accounted for 42% of all Bitcoin transactions in 2016, suggesting that China's attempts to limit Bitcoin's usage have been unsuccessful. A 2015 analysis of Bitcoin usage suggested that Bitcoins are still used primarily for gambling, illicit goods, and hoarding by speculators. Security concerns have also ravaged the largest Bitcoin exchanges to date, including Mt. Gox and Flexcoin. Hackers stole $425 million and $600,000 in Bitcoins from the two exchanges, respectively, and in 2016 the identity of the thieves and location of the Bitcoins stolen from Mt. Gox is still shrouded in mystery. These regulatory pressures and security concerns have driven Bitcoin's dizzying volatility.

In 2012, Bitcoin's value was $6; in 2013, it rose to $1,200; and in 2016, it has surged back to $650 after plummeting to nearly $200 in 2015.

Despite all of these drawbacks, Bitcoin continues to move forward, and more banks and regulators are recognizing that the underlying technology may be here to stay. In 2015, Goldman Sachs invested heavily in Circle Internet Financial, a Bitcoin peer-to-peer payment platform, noting that Bitcoin could gain international acceptance over time. In September 2015, New York issued the first license to operate a virtual currency business, called a BitLicense, to Circle Internet, giving it the right to operate in the state, while subjecting it to strict capital, consumer protection, and anti-money laundering requirements. Many large U.S. banks, the New York Stock Exchange, Japanese telecom giant DoCoMo, the Bank of Tokyo, and other companies have invested in Coinbase, an intermediary for Bitcoin transactions. The first Bitcoin bank and the first Bitcoin investment fund launched in 2015 and the IRS began taxing Bitcoin earnings, further legitimizing it in the eyes of regulators. The EU, Japan, and a host of other countries proposed rules for the regulation, use, and trading of virtual currencies in 2016.

Companies like Circle Internet Financial hope to harness Bitcoin's decentralized network of computers to enable frictionless and inexpensive movement of currencies across international borders. Bitcoins and Bitcoin transactions are all logged on a public ledger known as the blockchain, which is updated and maintained by all of the members of the network. Contrast this with a bank, which is a central hub where all currency and financial information resides. With the blockchain, there isn't a single point of failure or vulnerability the way there may be with a bank, and no single entity must update and maintain the ledger. For Bitcoin to truly gain acceptance, regular people will need to begin using it for everyday transactions. In countries where the banking system is less developed than in the United States, this has already begun to happen. In Argentina, the Philippines, Kenya, and other similar countries, banking regulations have made Bitcoin a more appealing alternative for ordinary people making normal commercial transactions.

A number of high-profile online businesses accept Bitcoin, such as Dell, Microsoft Expedia, and Newegg, as well as reportedly over 80,000 other merchants around the world. Bitcoin trading volume is still down significantly from its peak in 2014, but by July 2016, volume had spiked up again. Industry analysts predict that the number of active Bitcoin users will grow to 4.7 million in 2019, up from roughly 1.3 million today. Analysts also believe that the number of transactions per day will grow to 200,000 per day in 2016, with a value of more than $92 billion, up from $27 billion in 2015. For Bitcoin to continue to grow, however, it must become more than just a trading commodity and prove itself to be a useful tool to actually purchase goods and services.

SOURCES: "Coinbase Eyes Japan Expansion After Landing Investment from Bank of Tokyo," by Jon Russell, Techcrunch.com, July 8, 2016; "EU Proposes Stricter Rules on Bitcoin, Prepaid Cards, Terrorism Fight," by Foo Yun Chee, Reuters.com, July 5, 2016; "How China Took Center Stage in Bitcoin's Civil War," by Nathaniel Popper, New York Times, June 29, 2016; "Bitcoin Transactions Values to Triple This Year, Reaching Over $92BN," by Juniper Research, June 4, 2016; "Bitcoin Is on the Verge of Splitting in Two," by Ben Popper, Theverge.com, February 9, 2016; "Mt. Gox Creditors Seek Trillions Where There Are Only Millions," by Nathaniel Popper, New York Times, May 25, 2016; "We Must Regulate Bitcoin. Problem Is, We Don't Understand It," by Primavera De Filippi, Wired.com, March 1, 2016; "A Bitcoin Believer's Crisis of Faith," by Nathaniel Popper, New York Times, January 14, 2016; "BitCoin's Big Challenge in 2016: Reaching 100 Million Users," by Michael Jackson, Coindesk.com, January 1, 2016; "Circle Gets First 'BitLicense,' Releases Circle Pay, New Service," by Paul Vigna, Wall Street Journal, September 22, 2015; "Goldman and IDG Put $50 Million to Work in a Bitcoin Company," by Nathaniel Popper, New York Times, April 30, 2015; "Bitcoin Behemoth Coinbase launches in the UK," by Alex Hern, The Guardian, April 29, 2015; "The World's First Proper Bitcoin Exchange Will Go Live in a Month," by Kieren McCarthy, The Register, April 29, 2015; "Final New York Bitcoin Regulation Released: Bitlicense," by P.H. Madore, Cryptocoinnews.com, April 6, 2015; "Bitcoin's Golden Moment: BIT Gets FINRA Approval," by Brian Kelly, Cnbc.com, March 4, 2015; "Tokyo Court: Bitcoin Exchange Mt. Gox Will Liquidate," by Donna Leinwand, USA Today, April 16, 2014; "China Cracks Down on Bitcoin," by Chao Deng and Lingling Wei, Wall Street Journal, April 1, 2014; "The Mt. Gox Bitcoin Scandal Is the Best Thing to Happen to Bitcoin In Years," by Heidi Moore, Theguardian.com, February 26, 2014; "Israel's Central Bank Warns on Potential Fraud With Bitcoin," by Calev Ben-David, Bloomberg.com, February 19, 2014; "Russian Authorities Say Bitcoin Illegal," by Gabriela Baczynska, Reuters.com, February 9, 2014; "Bitcoin Pitchman Busted for 'Selling $1M in Currency to Silk Road,'" by Kaja Whitehouse and Rich Calder, New York Post, January 27, 2014; "Following the Bitcoin Trail," Economist.com, August 28, 2013.

remittances. The billing market represents an extraordinary opportunity for using the Internet as an electronic billing and payment system that potentially could greatly reduce both the cost of paying bills and the time consumers spend paying them. Estimates vary, but online payments are believed to cost between only 20 to 30 cents to process.

electronic billing presentment and payment (EBPP) system

form of online payment system for monthly bills

Electronic billing presentment and payment (EBPP) systems are systems that enable the online delivery and payment of monthly bills. EBPP services allow consumers to view bills electronically using either their desktop PC or mobile device and pay them through electronic funds transfers from bank or credit card accounts. More and more companies are choosing to issue statements and bills electronically, rather than mailing out paper versions, especially for recurring bills such as utilities, insurance, and subscriptions.

MARKET SIZE AND GROWTH

In 2002, 61% of bill payments in the United States were made by check, and only 12% by online bill payments. In 2015, in contrast, online bill payments accounted for more than 55% of all bill payments, while paper checks now account for less than 20%. Among online households, almost three-quarters pay at least one bill online each month, and almost half receive at least one bill electronically each month. Mobile bill payments are surging, with 33% U.S. households in 2015 paying at least one bill on a mobile device. Most consumers cited the convenience and time saved by using mobile bill payment (Fiserv, 2016).

One major reason for the surge in EBPP usage is that companies are starting to realize how much money they can save through online billing. Not only is there the savings in postage and processing, but payments can be received more quickly (3 to 12 days faster, compared to paper bills sent via regular mail), thereby improving cash flow. Online bill payment options can also reduce the number of phone calls to a company's customer service line. In order to realize these savings, many companies are becoming more aggressive in encouraging their customers to move to EBPP by instituting a charge for the privilege of continuing to receive a paper bill.

Financials don't tell the whole story, however. Companies are discovering that a bill is both a sales opportunity and a customer retention opportunity, and that the electronic medium provides many more options when it comes to marketing and promotion. Rebates, savings offers, cross-selling, and upselling are all possible in the digital realm, and much less expensive than mailed envelopes stuffed with offers.

EBPP BUSINESS MODELS

There are four EBPP business models: online banking, biller-direct, mobile, and consolidator.

The online banking model is the most widely used today. Consumers share their banking or credit card credentials with the merchant and authorize the merchant to charge the consumer's bank account. This model has the advantage of convenience for the consumer because the payments are deducted automatically, usually with a notice from the bank or the merchant that their account has been debited.

In the biller-direct model, consumers are sent bills by e-mail notification, and go to the merchant's website to make payments using their banking credentials. This model has the advantage of allowing the merchant to engage with the consumer by sending coupons or rewards. The biller-direct model is a two-step process, and less convenient for consumers.

The mobile model allows consumers to make payments using mobile apps, once again relying on their bank credentials as the source of funds. Consumers are notified of a bill by text message and authorize the payment. An extension of this is the social-mobile model, where social networks like Facebook integrate payment into their messaging services. The mobile model has several advantages, not least of which is the convenience for consumers of paying bills while using their phones, but also the speed with which bills can be paid in a single step. This is the fastest growing form of EBPP. In 2016, Facebook and PayPal announced a deal in which Facebook users can pay for purchases on Facebook using PayPal (Demos, 2016). Consumers will not have to leave Facebook in order to purchase and pay for products.

In the consolidator model, a third party, such as a financial institution or a focused portal such as Intuit's Paytrust, Fiserv's MyCheckFree, Mint Bills, and others, aggregates all bills for consumers and permits one-stop bill payment. This model has the advantage of allowing consumers to see all their bills at one website or app. However, because bills come due at different times, consumers need to check their portals often. The consolidator model faces several challenges. For billers, using the consolidator model means an increased time lag between billing and payment, and also inserts an intermediary between the company and its customer.

Supporting these primary business models are infrastructure providers such as Fiserv, Yodlee, FIS Global, ACI Worldwide, MasterCard RPPS (Remote Payment and Presentment Service), and others that provide the software to create the EBPP system or handle billing and payment collection for the biller. **Figure 4.16** categorizes the major players in the EBPP marketspace.

FIGURE 4.16   **MAJOR PLAYERS IN THE EBPP MARKETSPACE**

The main business models in the EBPP marketspace are biller-direct, online banking, consolidator, and mobile. Infrastructure providers support all of these competing models.

CASE STUDY

The Mobile Payment Marketplace:

Goat Rodeo

Nearly every day, it seems, a new mobile payment system is announced by giant tech companies, startups, merchants, and banks. The mobile payment marketplace is experiencing an explosion of innovative ideas, plans, and announcements, which one commentator has likened to a goat rodeo, a chaotic situation in which powerful players with different agendas compete with one another for public acceptance, and above all, huge potential revenues. The mobile payment market is expected to generate to somewhere between $27 billion and $75 billion in U.S. transaction volume in 2016, more than doubling the 2015 number. This wide-range estimate indicates how little is really known about the size of mobile payments, except that they are rapidly growing, especially among Millennials who have stopped using checks, and unlike their parents, are comfortable handling their financial

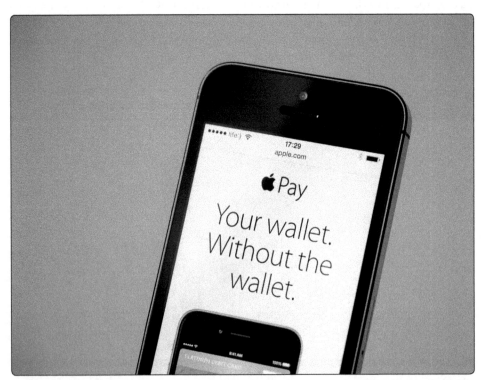

© Anatolii Babii/Alamy Stock Photo

transactions and banking using a smartphone. Times are changing: for the first time, more people are using mobile banking on their phones and laptops than going to a bank branch.

American consumers spent over $5.1 trillion on credit and debit card transactions in 2015, and mobile payments are still just a tiny percentage of the existing credit and debit card system. But even if a small percentage of the $5 trillion credit card transactions move from plastic to mobile, the potential revenue is very large. On the other hand, moving consumers away from over 800 million credit and debit cards, which can be swiped at millions of merchants and used online with ease and safety, is proving to be a difficult task. The rosy future of mobile payments painted by tech companies may be a long time coming.

The mobile payment market is a battle among the titans of online payment and retailing: PayPal, credit card companies like Visa and MasterCard, Google, Apple, Samsung, and startup tech companies like Venmo and Square. The startups are backed by millions in venture capital. Even large retailers like Walmart, Best Buy, and Target are getting into the game by developing their own mobile payment apps. Major banks are in the line of fire: who needs a checking account when you can pay with a mobile phone? Rising to this challenge, the banks are slowly building their own mobile payment systems, and investing in startups to lead the charge.

There are, by one count, already about 8,000 startups in the mobile payment market. The most recent startups focus on peer-to-peer mobile payments. Venmo is a good example. Venmo is a social-mobile payment app that lets users transfer money to one another. It can also be used to pay at a small number of participating merchants. Founded in 2010 by two college students who wanted to send cash to one another for sharing restaurant tabs and paying small debts without the hassle of cash or writing checks, Venmo was purchased by PayPal in 2013. Users sign up for a Venmo account and link their account to a bank account, a debit card, or credit card. Users can also create a Venmo balance by sending money to their Venmo account, and then charge payments against that balance. There is no charge for the service when users have a Venmo balance or use a debit card, and a 3% charge for using a credit card as the source of funds. There is a social aspect of Venmo that allows users to share their purchase events (but with amount paid stripped from the notification). Users have the option to keep all transactions private as well. When they want to make a payment to another person, they enter the person's e-mail and the funds are transferred when the recipient, who must also have a Venmo account, accepts the payment. Venmo relies on NFC technology to make in-person payments to individuals by tapping their phones. Venmo's popularity has skyrocketed, especially among Millennials, and in January 2016 it processed $1 billion in transactions, a 250% increase over the previous year. The company does not release information on its subscriber base, and because it is largely a free service, it does not contribute significantly to PayPal's gross revenues. PayPal has begun to monetize its investment in Venmo by expanding beyond peer-to-peer small payments, and extending its use to merchants who accept PayPal payments, a much larger user base, which includes large retailers like Home Depot, Target, Sears, and OfficeMax.

Startups like Venmo are small fry compared to the three other giants in the mobile payment market. First in terms of subscribers are the technology companies like

Apple, Google, Samsung, PayPal, and Square, all of which have major hardware and software mobile payment initiatives. Apple, Google, and Samsung own and license the hardware and software platform of the ubiquitous smartphone, while PayPal and Square operate large-scale payment processing platforms. Second, the large national merchants are developing their own mobile payment systems in an effort, in part, to sidestep the credit card companies (Visa, MasterCard, Discover, and American Express), which charge them a 3% transaction fee that gets passed along to the consumer as 3% higher prices, and in part to maintain control over the point-of-sale consumer moment at the cash register. These firms have tens of millions of loyal customers. Banks like JPMorgan Chase, Wells Fargo, Citi, and other money center banks, and of course, the credit card companies Visa, Master Card, and others, are the third major player. These firms have the advantage of owning and operating the global banking and credit card systems, with hundreds of millions of loyal banking and credit card customers, and the expertise to provide security and financial stability for their products. They are, however, very slow movers and are just now entering the mobile payment marketplace.

Let's take a look at the technology companies first, all of whom offer variations on contactless payments, often referred to as digital or mobile wallets. Apple Pay is an app that comes with iPhone 6 phones and later. It uses built-in NFC technology. Users set up an account, and enter their banking credentials, using either their credit/debit card account information, or their checking or savings account, as the source of funds.

When a customer wants to make a payment, he or she presses the iPhone Touch ID button, which reads the customer's fingerprint and ensures the phone does indeed belong to the person. On the Apple Watch, there's a special button just for Apple Pay transactions. Next, the consumer swipes the device near a merchant's NFC point-of-sale terminal, which begins the transaction process. The iPhone 6 and later comes with a hardware-defined secure area on a chip that contains a unique device number and the ability to generate a one-time 16-digit code. Together they form a digital token. The token information is encrypted and sent to Apple servers to verify the authenticity of the device and the person. Apple sends the payment request to the credit card issuer. Credit card issuers verify the account owner and available credit. In about one second, the transaction is approved or denied. Credit card information is not shared with the merchant and not transmitted from the iPhone. The 800 million credit cards stored on Apple's servers are also encrypted. If hackers intercept the NFC communication at the point-of-sale, or intercept the stream of data moving over the cellular network, it would be useless, and incapable of supporting additional transactions because the message is encrypted, and involves a one-time-only digital token.

Apple Pay is free to consumers, and the credit card companies charge their usual fee of 3% for each transaction. Apple collects .15% from the credit companies and banks, and in return, guarantees the transaction is valid. Apple Pay does not store any user funds and is solely a technology-based intermediary between consumers and banks, and, unlike Venmo, is not subject to federal banking regulations. Merchants' point-of-sale terminals need to be NFC-enabled, and merchants need to install Apple software to accept payments. Apple Pay can be used by any consumer that has a credit card from a major issuer bank.

Apple has developed relationships with many of the key players in the payment ecosystem, including credit giants Visa, MasterCard, American Express, and Discover, as well as 11 large bank credit card issuers including JPMorgan Chase, Bank of America, Citigroup, and Wells Fargo, which together account for 83% of U.S. credit card payment volume. Apple has also signed up national merchants such as Walgreens, Duane Reade, McDonald's, Disney, Macy's, Bloomingdale's, Staples, and Whole Foods. Groupon and Uber have integrated Apple Pay into their systems.

Android Pay is a Google app that provides an NFC-based payment system much like Apple Pay. Android is the most widely used smartphone operating system in the world. Launched in 2015, Android Pay replaces Google Wallet, which has been repurposed as a peer-to-peer payment service that allows users to pay friends using only their e-mail address, similar to PayPal and Venmo. Users sign up for an Android Pay account by entering their existing bank credit or debit card account information, or by depositing a prepaid balance of funds in their Android Pay account. Google is for some users a prepaid digital card where users transfer funds to their Android Pay account, and therefore is subject to federal regulations. To use Android Pay, customers hold their phone near the merchant's NFC terminal at checkout. Users are asked to enter their PIN and then choose to pay with either the credit or debit card on file with Android Pay or with their cash balance. If the user chooses to pay with a bank card, the app creates a unique digital token and sends this as an encrypted message to Android servers, which then communicate with the issuing bank, for approval. Approval messages are sent to the merchant's point-of-sale terminal. No card information is transmitted from the point of purchase. Android Pay is free for subscribers except when they use their credit card, which entails a 3% credit card transaction fee charged by the credit card companies. However, Google may offer consumers rewards, and in the future, display ads. Because Android Pay can store user funds, it is subject to federal banking regulations.

Samsung Pay was introduced by Samsung in the United States in September 2015, after an earlier roll-out in Samsung's home country, South Korea. Samsung smartphones are the most widely used smartphones in the world. As with Apple Pay and Android Pay, users create an account, and submit their bank credit or debit card information. Samsung Pay prioritizes the use of NFC technology when merchants have the appropriate terminal, but when that is not available, switches to a technology called Magnetic Secure Transmission that sends the card data stored on the user's device to traditional magnetic stripe terminals. This means that Samsung Pay can be used by the millions of existing point-of-sale card swiping terminals without upgrading to NFC terminals or installing any apps. Samsung Pay also stores coupons and reward cards, but does not store user funds and is not a prepaid card. Therefore, it most likely will not be subject to U.S. federal regulations. Like the other mobile wallets, it is essentially a place where users can store all their credit cards.

Currently, the most popular mobile payment systems are offered by PayPal and Square, some of which do not use NFC. While claiming to be financial services firms, both PayPal and Square are financial service software platform firms, technology companies in disguise. PayPal was late to the mobile payment market, beaten to the punch by Square. Square started in 2009 with Square Reader, a square plastic device that plugged into an iPhone or iPad, and allowed users to easily set up a merchant license to accept credit cards, and then swipe the cards locally on the Square Reader device. Using the Square app, it allows merchants to easily accept credit card payments from customers on the go. Square also developed Square Register (now called Point of Sale), which is a software app that turns a tablet into a point-of-sale terminal and cash register. Square has morphed into a small business services company, serving coffee shops, newsstands, small retailers, and farmers' market merchants, as well as piano teachers, baby sitters, and taxi drivers, allowing them to easily accept credit card payments. Square generated $1 billion in revenue in 2015, and showed a loss of $174 million.

PayPal is currently the most successful and profitable non-traditional online payment system, used mostly on desktops and tablets, but rapidly becoming a mobile payment force. PayPal is currently the largest alternative (non-credit card) online payment service, processing $282 billion in transactions in 2015, and has 188 million subscribers. PayPal processed $66 billion in mobile payments in 2015, up from $27 billion in 2013. PayPal is growing payment volume at around 20% annually.

PayPal currently enables mobile payments in three ways. First, PayPal sells a device that allows merchants (mostly small businesses) to swipe credit cards using a smartphone or tablet, just like the Square device. Second, the most common PayPal mobile payment occurs when customers use their mobile device browser on a tablet or smartphone to make a purchase or payment at a website. This is not very helpful for merchants like Starbucks, Macys, or local restaurants, who would like customers to be able to purchase goods in their stores and outlets on the fly without keying in information to a smartphone. A third method is PayPal's updated app for iOS and Android devices. On entering a merchant's store that accepts PayPal app payments, the app establishes a link using Bluetooth with the merchant's app that is also running on an iOS or Android device. This step authenticates the user's PayPal account. On checkout, the customer tells the merchant he or she will pay with PayPal. The merchant app charges the customer's PayPal account. After the payment is authorized, a message is sent to the customer's phone. No credit card information is being transmitted or shared with the merchant. Users do not have to enter a pin code or swipe their phone at a special merchant device, so merchants are not required to purchase an expensive NFC point-of-sale device, but they must have the PayPal merchant app stored on a PC which is really acting like a digital cash register. In 2012, PayPal launched PayPal Here, a device that will both read credit cards equipped with computer chips, as well as accept payments from Android Pay and Apple Pay. The service includes a card reader that plugs into a tablet or smartphone, and a stand-alone contactless device that can accept NFC payments, as well as swipe credit cards. In 2015, PayPal launched the PayPal.me app, a peer-to-peer payment service that allows users to make and receive payments from friends. Users share their PayPal.me link with friends and can transfer money to their PayPal accounts. The service is free and is a direct competitor with Venmo and other P2P payment services. Venmo, which PayPal also owns, only works with U.S. banks, credit and debit cards, while PayPal.me is targeted at PayPal's global user base. In 2016 PayPal launched NFC payments for locations that accept VISA's contactless payments.

SOURCES: "Consumer Bill Payments Shifts & Strategies," by Jim Gilligan and Kellie Thomas, Payments.com, 2016; "PayPal Gets Friendlier With Facebook," by Telis Demos, *New York Times*, October 24, 2016; "Apple Pay at Two Years: Not Much to Celebrate (Yet)," by Mark Hamblen, Computerworld.com, October 20, 2016; "How Millennials Became Spooked by Credit Cards," by Nathaniel Popper,

While mobile payment systems developed by technology companies are experiencing rapid growth, mobile wallets developed by large national merchants have sputtered. Large national merchants have had a contentious relationship with credit card firms because of the 3% fees charged by credit card companies, which raise prices to consumers by the same amount. Merchants would much prefer customers pay with store credit cards that are linked to the customer's bank account, or debit accounts, where banks do not charge a fee, or customer-supplied prepayment funds. Some merchants also offer their own store credit cards and have developed their own transaction processing systems, circumventing the bank credit card system entirely. Merchants also want to control the point-of-sale moment, where they can offer coupons, loyalty rewards, and special discounts, rather than rely on mobile wallets provided by the technology companies, which do not offer these capabilities.

In 2012, a joint venture of the 15 largest merchants announced the Merchant Customer Exchange (MCX). MCX was backed by Walmart, Target, Sears, 7-Eleven, Sunoco, and 10 other national pharmacies, supermarkets, and restaurant chains. The backers of this effort have annual sales of more than $1 trillion dollars. That was enough to make everyone involved in mobile payments stand up and listen, even Google and Apple. Their initial effort was coined CurrentC, and was piloted in 2014. CurrentC was an app that allowed customers to pay using their bank accounts, bank debit cards, or store-issued credit cards, but not traditional bank credit cards. The idea was to circumvent the bank credit system entirely, and avoid paying the credit companies their typical 3% fee. CurrentC was withdrawn in 2016, and the MCX joint venture has ended due to squabbles among the partners, and an excessively long development time for the app. In 2016, Walmart introduced its own Walmart Pay app for both iOS and Android phones. Using QR recognition technology, not NFC, Walmart Pay now accepts all bank credit and debit cards, as well as Walmart store credit cards. It can also read coupons and offer rewards to loyal customers. Walmart Pay can only be used at Walmart stores, but given that Walmart has 140 million customers a week in the United States, that's not a terrible disadvantage. As of October 2016, 22 million customers are using the Walmart Pay app every month. The advantage to Walmart is that it owns the customer transaction, and information, without the intervention of the tech giants. Walmart, and the other large national merchants, will have to live with the credit card companies and their 3% fees for now.

The third entrant to the mobile payment market is composed of the large national banks and credit card companies. Banks and credit card firms have been very slow moving into the mobile payment space, in part because the existing credit system works so well and their cards are widely accepted by consumers and merchants. Mobile payment systems from tech companies and merchants are competitors for the loyalty of bank customers who deposit billions of dollars in bank checking, savings, and debit cards, where banks can charge fees, and use the deposits essentially free of cost, given the low or non-existent interest rates on these accounts. JP Morgan Chase has launched Retail Checkout, a card reader that accepts tap card and mobile wallet NFC payments, and the Chase Mobile app for smartphones and tablets, which allows bank customers to perform a wide variety of banking functions like peer-to-peer payments by e-mail (QuickPay), pay bills, deposit checks, check balances, and even apply for

New York Times, August 14, 2016; "Under Pressure, Big Banks Vie for Instant Payment Market," by Michael Corkery, *New York Times,* August 1, 2016; "PayPal to Roll Out NFC Mobile Payments Across the US Through Visa Deal," by Rian Boden, NFCworld.com, July 25, 2016; "Walmart Pay vs. Apple Pay: Hardware Age Dictates All," by Evan Shuman, Computerworld.com, July 8, 2016; "In Mobile Payments War, Big Banks Strike Back," by Aaron Black, *Wall Street Journal,* July 8, 2016; "The Mobile Payments Report," by Evan Baker, Businessinsider.com, June 3, 2016; "Reasons that US Smartphone Users Don't Use Mobile Payments," eMarketer, Inc., June 2016; "Why Apple Pay and Other Mobile Wallets Beat Chip Cards," by Brian Chen, *New York Times,* May 4, 2016; "Apple Pay's Big Drop," Pymnts.com, March 18, 2016; "Latest Mobile-Banking Research Shows Laptops Still Reign," by Robin Sidel, *Wall Street Journal,* January 27, 2016; "As More Pay by Smartphone, Banks Scramble to Keep Up," by Steve Lohr, *New York Times,* January 18, 2016; "For the First Time, More Are Mobile-Banking Than Going to a Branch," by Telis Demos, *Wall Street Journal,* January 12, 2016; "US Mobile Payments Forecast," by Bryan Yeager, eMarketer, Inc., November 2015; "Bold Bet That Banking Industry Is Poised for Serious Disruption," by Michael Casey, *Wall Street Journal,* June 5, 2015; "'Pretty Useless': Consumer Frustrations Grow Over New Credit Card Chip," by Alexandra Zaslow, Todaymoney.com, October 16, 2015; "Square's IPO Filing: It's Complicated," Recode.net, by Jason Del Rey, October 14, 2015; "PayPal Here Launches a Mobile Card Reader That Accepts Android Pay and Apple Pay," by Ruth Reader, Venturebeat.com, September 28, 2015; "Samsung Pay: What You Need to Know (FAQ)," by Lexy Savvides, Cnet.com, September 28, 2015; "Revamped Google Wallet Arrives on iOS," by Stephanie Mlot, Pcmagazine.com, September 22, 2015; "Apple Pay Competitor CurrentC May Not Launch Until Next Year," by Jason Del Rey, Recode.net, August 12, 2015;

"PayPal Returns to Market with $52 Billion Valuation," by Devika Krishna Kumar and Mari Saito, Reuters.com, July 20, 2015; "There Are No Transaction Fees for Android Pay, Which Is Good for Us, Bad for Google," by Robert Nazarian, Digitaltrends.com, June 8, 2015; "The State of Mobile Payments in 2015," by James A. Martin, CIO.com, April 22, 2015; "Apple Sees Mobile-Payment Service Gaining in Challenge to PayPal," by Olga Kharif, Bloomberg.com, January 27, 2015; "What Apple Pay Means for Retailers," by Abby Callard, Internetretailer.com, September 12, 2014; "Apple Pay: No Charge for Merchants, But Transaction-Security Fees for Issuers," by Jim Daly, Digitaltransaction.net, September 11, 2014.

mortgages. Citi has launched Citi Mobile with similar functionality. Banks so far have not introduced apps for making NFC payments for consumer purchases, but these will surely be introduced shortly. The large banks are investing heavily in payment startups to acquire these capabilities.

The future for smartphone mobile wallets is assured given the size of the players involved, the potential rewards for successful players, and the demands of consumers for a payment system that does not involve swiping plastic cards, dealing with slips of paper receipts, and digging for cash in their pockets and purses.

But the transition is going much slower than pundits initially thought, with millions of consumers trying the new methods once, and then not using them again because not enough merchants accept them, lack of familiarity, and concerns about security and privacy. One recent study found there are now 11 million contactless mobile payment users in the United States, but just 2.3 million who are active users. It is unlikely that all the mobile payment systems described above will survive, and also quite likely that consumers will remain confused by all their payment options for some time yet to come. A full transition to mobile payments will be a long time coming.

Case Study Questions

1. Who are the three major players in the mobile payment market?

2. Why is Venmo considered a social-mobile payment system?

3. How does Apple Pay differ from Android Pay and Samsung Pay?

4. How does PayPal enable mobile payments?

4.8 REVIEW

KEY CONCEPTS

■ **Understand the scope of e-commerce crime and security problems, the key dimensions of e-commerce security, and the tension between security and other values.**

- While the overall size of cybercrime is unclear, cybercrime against e-commerce sites is growing rapidly, the amount of losses is growing, and the management of e-commerce sites must prepare for a variety of criminal assaults.
- There are six key dimensions to e-commerce security: integrity, nonrepudiation, authenticity, confidentiality, privacy, and availability.
- Although computer security is considered necessary to protect e-commerce activities, it is not without a downside. Two major areas where there are tensions between security and website operations are:
  - *Ease of use*—The more security measures that are added to an e-commerce site, the more difficult it is to use and the slower the site becomes, hampering ease of use. Security is purchased at the price

of slowing down processors and adding significantly to data storage demands. Too much security can harm profitability, while not enough can potentially put a company out of business.

- *Public safety*—There is a tension between the claims of individuals to act anonymously and the needs of public officials to maintain public safety that can be threatened by criminals or terrorists.

■ **Identify the key security threats in the e-commerce environment**

- The most common and most damaging forms of security threats to e-commerce sites include:
  - *Malicious code*—viruses, worms, Trojan horses, ransomware, and bot networks are a threat to a system's integrity and continued operation, often changing how a system functions or altering documents created on the system.
  - *Potentially unwanted programs (adware, spyware, etc.)*—a kind of security threat that arises when programs are surreptitiously installed on your computer or computer network without your consent.
  - *Phishing*—any deceptive, online attempt by a third party to obtain confidential information for financial gain.
  - *Hacking and cybervandalism*—intentionally disrupting, defacing, or even destroying a site.
  - *Credit card fraud/theft*—one of the most-feared occurrences and one of the main reasons more consumers do not participate in e-commerce. The most common cause of credit card fraud is a lost or stolen card that is used by someone else, followed by employee theft of customer numbers and stolen identities (criminals applying for credit cards using false identities).
  - *Identity fraud*—involves the unauthorized use of another person's personal data, such as social security, driver's license, and/or credit card numbers, as well as user names and passwords, for illegal financial benefit.
  - *Spoofing*—occurs when hackers attempt to hide their true identities or misrepresent themselves by using fake e-mail addresses or masquerading as someone else.
  - *Pharming*—involves redirecting a web link to an address different from the intended one, with the site masquerading as the intended destination.
  - *Denial of Service (DoS) and Distributed Denial of Service (DDoS) attacks*—hackers flood a website with useless traffic to inundate and overwhelm the network, frequently causing it to shut down and damaging a site's reputation and customer relationships.
  - *Sniffing*—a type of eavesdropping program that monitors information traveling over a network, enabling hackers to steal proprietary information from anywhere on a network, including e-mail messages, company files, and confidential reports. The threat of sniffing is that confidential or personal information will be made public.
  - *Insider jobs*—although the bulk of Internet security efforts are focused on keeping outsiders out, the biggest threat is from employees who have access to sensitive information and procedures.
  - *Poorly designed server and client software*—the increase in complexity and size of software programs has contributed to an increase in software flaws or vulnerabilities that hackers can exploit.
  - *Social network security issues*—malicious code, PUPs, phishing, data breaches, identity fraud, and other e-commerce security threats have all infiltrated social networks.
  - *Mobile platform security issues*—the mobile platform presents an alluring target for hackers and cybercriminals, and faces all the same risks as other Internet devices, as well as new risks associated with wireless network security.
  - *Cloud security issues*—as devices, identities, and data become more and more intertwined in the cloud, safeguarding data in the cloud becomes a major concern.

■ **Describe how technology helps secure Internet communications channels and protect networks, servers, and clients.**

- Encryption is the process of transforming plain text or data into cipher text that cannot be read by anyone other than the sender and the receiver. Encryption can provide four of the six key dimensions of e-commerce security: message integrity, nonrepudiation, authentication, and confidentiality.

- There are a variety of different forms of encryption technology currently in use. They include:
  - *Symmetric key cryptography*—Both the sender and the receiver use the same key to encrypt and decrypt a message.
  - *Public key cryptography*—Two mathematically related digital keys are used: a public key and a private key. The private key is kept secret by the owner, and the public key is widely disseminated. Both keys can be used to encrypt and decrypt a message. Once the keys are used to encrypt a message, the same keys cannot be used to unencrypt the message.
  - *Public key cryptography using digital signatures and hash digests*—This method uses a mathematical algorithm called a hash function to produce a fixed-length number called a hash digest. The results of applying the hash function are sent by the sender to the recipient. Upon receipt, the recipient applies the hash function to the received message and checks to verify that the same result is produced. The sender then encrypts both the hash result and the original message using the recipient's public key, producing a single block of cipher text. To ensure both the authenticity of the message and nonrepudiation, the sender encrypts the entire block of cipher text one more time using the sender's private key. This produces a digital signature or "signed" cipher text that can be sent over the Internet to ensure the confidentiality of the message and authenticate the sender.
  - *Digital envelope*—This method uses symmetric cryptography to encrypt and decrypt the document, but public key cryptography to encrypt and send the symmetric key.
  - *Digital certificates and public key infrastructure*—This method relies on certification authorities who issue, verify, and guarantee digital certificates (a digital document that contains the name of the subject or company, the subject's public key, a digital certificate serial number, an expiration date, an issuance date, the digital signature of the certification authority, and other identifying information).
- In addition to encryption, there are several other tools that are used to secure Internet channels of communication, including: Secure Sockets Layer (SSL)/Transport Layer Security (TLS), virtual private networks (VPNs), and wireless security standards such as WPA2.
- After communications channels are secured, tools to protect networks, the servers, and clients should be implemented. These include: firewalls, proxies, intrusion detection and prevention systems (IDS/IDP), operating system controls, and anti-virus software.

■ **Appreciate the importance of policies, procedures, and laws in creating security.**

- In order to minimize security threats, e-commerce firms must develop a coherent corporate policy that takes into account the nature of the risks, the information assets that need protecting, and the procedures and technologies required to address the risk, as well as implementation and auditing mechanisms.
- Public laws and active enforcement of cybercrime statutes also are required to both raise the costs of illegal behavior on the Internet and guard against corporate abuse of information.
- The key steps in developing a security plan are:
  - *Perform a risk assessment*—an assessment of the risks and points of vulnerability.
  - *Develop a security policy*—a set of statements prioritizing the information risks, identifying acceptable risk targets, and identifying the mechanisms for achieving these targets.
  - *Create an implementation plan*—a plan that determines how you will translate the levels of acceptable risk into a set of tools, technologies, policies, and procedures.
  - *Create a security team*—the individuals who will be responsible for ongoing maintenance, audits, and improvements.
  - *Perform periodic security audits*—routine reviews of access logs and any unusual patterns of activity.

■ **Identify the major e-commerce payment systems in use today.**

- The major types of e-commerce payment systems in use today include:

- *Online credit card transactions,* which are the primary form of online payment system. There are five parties involved in an online credit card purchase: consumer, merchant, clearinghouse, merchant bank (sometimes called the "acquiring bank"), and the consumer's card-issuing bank. However, the online credit card system has a number of limitations involving security, merchant risk, cost, and social equity.
- *PayPal,* which is an example of an alternative payment system that permits consumers to make instant, online payments to merchants and other individuals based on value stored in an online account. Other examples include Pay with Amazon, Visa Checkout, MasterPass, Bill Me Later, and WU Pay.
- *Mobile payment systems,* which use either credit card readers attached to a smartphone (Square, PayPal Here) or near field communication (NFC) chips, which enable mobile payment at point-of-sale (Apple Pay, Android Pay, and Samsung Pay).
- *Digital cash,* such as Bitcoin and virtual currencies. Digital cash is growing in importance and can be used to hide payments from authorities, as well as support the legitimate exchange of value.

■ **Describe the features and functionality of electronic billing presentment and payment systems.**

- Electronic billing presentment and payment (EBPP) systems are a form of online payment systems for monthly bills. EBPP services allow consumers to view bills electronically and pay them through electronic funds transfers from bank or credit card accounts.
- Major players in the EBPP marketspace include: online banking, biller-direct systems, mobile payment systems, and consolidators.

QUESTIONS

1. What is a VPN and what is its value to an organization?
2. What features or abilities does an intrusion prevention system use to protect a network?
3. Identify and describe the five main steps in establishing a company's security plan.
4. Differentiate between the security dimension of confidentiality and the concept of online privacy.
5. Outside of the United States, what types of payments are popular for online purchases?
6. What is the role that a consumer's card-issuing bank play in an online credit card transaction?
7. Why is the mobile payment industry in such a great state of flux today?
8. What are the general technologies and tools needed by merchants and users to implement a mobile payment system?
9. What risks do Bitcoin users face?
10. What role does ease of use play in ensuring e-commerce security?
11. How are the SSL/TLS protocols used in securing Internet communications?
12. What is nonrepudiation and why is it an important dimension of e-commerce security? What technologies are used to establish nonrepudiation?
13. How are improvements to the overall e-commerce security environment achieved?
14. What kind of payment system is Venmo?
15. What is a man-in-the-middle attack?
16. Why are botnets considered an especially important threat to e-commerce, more so than, say, an individual, destructive virus?
17. Why are security issues associated with the Internet of Things even more challenging than existing security issues related to the Internet?
18. What is the Heartbleed bug and how does it threaten security?
19. How does code signing protect a mobile app?
20. What is a next generation firewall?

PROJECTS

1. Imagine you are the owner of an e-commerce website. What are some of the signs that your site has been hacked? Discuss the major types of attacks you could expect to experience and the resulting damage to your site. Prepare a brief summary presentation.

2. Given the shift toward m-commerce, do a search on m-commerce (or mobile commerce) crime. Identify and discuss the security threats this type of technology creates. Prepare a presentation outlining your vision of the new opportunities for cybercrime that m-commerce may provide.

3. Find three certification authorities and compare the features of each company's digital certificates. Provide a brief description of each company as well, including number of clients. Prepare a brief presentation of your findings.

4. Research the challenges associated with payments across international borders and prepare a brief presentation of your findings. Do most e-commerce companies conduct business internationally? How do they protect themselves from repudiation? How do exchange rates impact online purchases? What about shipping charges? Summarize by describing the differences between a U.S. customer and an international customer who each make a purchase from a U.S. e-commerce merchant.

REFERENCES

Akamai Technologies, Inc. "Akamai's State of the Internet Q2 2016 Report." (September 2016).

Akamai Technologies. "Exploitation of IoT devices for Launching Mass-Scale Attack Campaigns." (October 11, 2016b.)

Alert Logic. "2015 Cloud Security Report." (2015).

Arbor Networks. "Worldwide Infrastructure Security Report Volume XI." (2016).

BI Intelligence. "Chase Adds Real-time P2P Payments." Businessinsider.com (June 15, 2016).

Blue, Violet. "You Say Advertising, I Say Block That Malware." Engadget.com (January 8, 2016).

Bureau of Consumer Financial Protection. "Prepaid Accounts under the Electronic Fund Transfer Act (Regulation E) and the Truth In Lending Act (Regulation Z)." [Docket No. CFPB-2014-0031] RIN 3170-AA22 (October 12, 2016).

Center for Strategic and International Studies. "Net Losses: Estimating the Global Cost of Cybercrime." (June 2014).

Chew, Hanley and Tyler G. Newby. "The Cybersecurity Information Sharing Act of 2015: An Overview." Lexology.com (October 24, 2016).

Chirgwin, Richard. "Microsoft and FBI Storm Ramparts of Citadel Botnets." *The Register* (June 6, 2013).

CIO.gov. "HTTP Strict Transport Security." (2016).

Cisco. "2016 Cisco Annual Security Report." (2016).

Cloud Security Alliance. "State of Cloud Security 2016." CSA Global Enterprise Advisory Board (2016).

Constantin, Lucian. "Police Operation Disrupts Beebone Botnet Used for Malware Distribution." Pcworld.com (April 9, 2015).

Cybersource, Inc. "Online Fraud Management Benchmarks: North American Edition." (2016).

Cyphort. "Cyphort Labs Knocks Down the Top 8 Financial Malware." (October 15, 2015).

Daly, Jim. "Report Documents the March of Online Alternatives to the Payments Mainstream." Digital-transactions.net (March 9, 2014).

Datta, Saikat. "Security Breach in NIC Allowed Hackers to Issue Fake Digital Certifcates—Hindustan Times." Medianama.com (August 14, 2014).

Dell Inc. "Determining the True Costs of a Data Breach." (2015).

Demos, Telis. "PayPal Gets Friendlier With Facebook." *Wall Street Journal* (October 24, 2016).

DocuSign. "Going Mobile with Electronic Signatures." (2015).

eMarketer, Inc. "Digital Payment Methods Used by US Internet Users, Aug 2016." (October 19, 2016a).

eMarketer, Inc. "Mobile Wallet Adoption Among US Smartphone Users, by Provider, June 2016." (August 24, 2016b).

eMarketer, Inc. (Rahul Chadha). "Global Ecommerce Platforms 2015: A Country-by-Country Look at the Top Retail Ecommerce Sites." (October 2015).

Essers, Loek. "The 'Great Cannon' of China Enforces Censorship." Computerworld.com (April 10, 2015).

Fiserv. "Eight Annual Billing Household Survey." (March 2016).

Fiserv. "2007 Consumer Bill Payments Trends Survey: Volume of Electronic Payments." (2007).

Fox, Emily Jane and Greg Botelho. "5 Charged in Credit Card Hacking Scheme Feds Call Largest Ever Prosecuted in the U.S." Cnn.com (July 25, 2013).

Gartner. "Gartner Says Worldwide Information Security Spending Will Grow 7.9 Percent to Reach $81.6 Billion in 2016." (August 16, 2016).

Gemalto and Ponemon Institute. "Gemalto 2016 Global Cloud Data Security Study." (July 26, 2016).

Goodin, Dan. "Big-Name Sites Hit by Rash of Malicious Ads Spreading Crypto Ransomware." Arstechnica (March 15, 2016).

Greenberg, Andy. "Hackers Remotely Kill a Jeep on the Highway—With Me In It." Wired.com (July 21, 2015).

Hackett, Robert. "On Heartbleed's Anniversary, 3 of 4 Big Companies Are Still Vulnerable." *Fortune* (April 7, 2015).

Hasham, Salim, Chris Rezek, Maxence Vancauwenberghe, and Josh Weiner. "Is Cybersecurity Incompatible with Digital Convenience?," Mckinsey.com (August 2016).

Honan, Mat. "How Apple and Amazon Security Flaws Led to My Epic Hacking." Wired.com (August 6, 2012).

IBM. "IBM Point of View: Internet of Things Security." (April 2015).

Identity Theft Resource Center. "ITRC Data Breach Report." (January 25, 2016).

Infosec Institute. "A Buyers Guide to Stolen Data on the Deep Web." Darkmatters.norsecorp.com (April 7, 2015).

Internet Society. "Policy Brief: The Internet of Things." (October 7, 2016).

Internet Society. "The Internet of Things: An Overview." (2015).

Isaac, Mike. "WhatsApp Introduces End-to-End Encryption." *New York Times* (April 5, 2016).

Javelin Strategy & Research. "2016 Identity Survey Report." (February 2, 2016).

Johnson, N.F., M. Zheng, Y. Vorobyeva, A. Gabriel, H. Qi, N. Velasquez, P. Manrique, D. Johnson, E. Restrepo, C. Song, and S. Wuchty. "New Online Ecology of Adversarial Aggregates: ISIS and Beyond." *Science* (June 17, 2016).

Keizer, Greg. "XcodeGhost Used Unprecedented Infection Strategy Against Apple." Computerworld.com (September 26, 2015).

Kirk, Jeremy. "Zero Day, Web Browser Vulnerabilities Spike in 2014." Networkworld.com (March 25, 2015a).

Korolov, Maria. "Most Corporate Risk Due to Just 1% of Employees." Csoonline.com (August 26, 2015).

Leger, Donna Leinwand. "Credit Card Info Sold on Hacker Sites." *USA Today* (September 4, 2014).

Leising, Matthew. "CME Teams Up with Dwolla to Bring Real-Time Payments to Exchange." Bloomberg.com (October 28, 2015).

Loeb, Larry. "Malwarebytes Thinks Potentially Unwanted Programs Are Malware." SecurityIntelligence.com (October 13, 2016).

Loten, Angus. "Cloud Security Fears Persist." Wall Street Journal (October 17, 2016).

Majkowski, Marek. "Mobile Ad Networks as DDoS Vectors: A Case Study." Blog.cloudfare.com (September 25, 2015).

Maruca, William. "Hacked Health Records Prized for their Black Market Value." Hipaahealthlaw.foxrothschild.com (March 16, 2015).

McAfee. "The Hidden Data Economy: The Marketplace for Stolen Digital Information." (October 15, 2016).

McMillan, Robert. "In the Bitcoin Era, Ransomware Attacks Surge." *Wall Street Journal* (August 19, 2016).

Microsoft. "Microsoft Security Intelligence Report Volume 20: July–December 2015." (May 5, 2016).

Mitnick, Kevin. *Ghost in the Wires.* Little, Brown & Co. (2011).

Neustar. "April 2016 Neustar DDoS Attacks and Protection Report: North America & EMEA." (April 2016).

Pagliery, Jose. "FBI Teams Up with Hackers to Bust Bank Robbing Botnet." Cnn.com (October 13, 2015).

Panda Security. "PandaLabs' Annual Report 2015." (2016).

Patane, Matthew. "Dwolla Drops Transaction Fees to Gain Ground." *Des Moines Register* (June 4, 2015).

PCI Security Standards Council. "Payment Card Industry (PCI) Data Security Standard: Requirements and Security Assessment Procedure Version 3.1." (April 2015).

Pendell, Ryan. "Why Dwolla Made Its Transactions Free (And What Happened Next)," Siliconprairienews.com (June 21, 2016).

Perlroth, Nicole. "Apple Will Pay a 'Bug Bounty' to Hackers Who Report Flaws." *New York Times* (August 4, 2016).

Perlroth, Nicole, and Vindu Goel. "Defending Against Hackers Took a Back Seat at Yahoo, Insiders Say." *New York Times* (September 28, 2016).

Peterson, Andrea. "Senate Passes Cybersecurity Information Sharing Bill Despite Privacy Fears." *Washington Post* (October 27, 2015).

Ponemon Institute. "2016 Cost of Data Breach Study: Global Analysis." (June 2016).

Ponemon Institute. "2015 Cost of Cyber Crime Study: Global." (October 2015a).

Ponemon Institute. "The Unintentional Insider Risk in the United States and German Organizations." (July 2015b).

PWC. "US Cybersecurity: Progress Stalled. Key Findings from the 2015 US State of Cybercrime Survey." (June 2015).

RAND Corporation. "Markets for Cybercrime Tools and Stolen Data: Hackers' Bazaar." (2014).

Sanger, David and Nicole Perlroth. "A New Era of Internet Attacks Powered by Everyday Devices." *New York Times* (October 22, 2016).

Sidel, Robin. "Credit Card Scammers Flock to Online Shopping." *Wall Street Journal* (October 25, 2016).

Schuman, Evan. "Starbucks Caught Storing Mobile Passwords in Clear Text." *Computerworld* (January 15, 2014).

Schwartz, John. "Fighting Crime Online: Who Is in Harm's Way?" *New York Times* (February 8, 2001).

Silanis Technology. "Security for E-Signatures and E-Transactions: What to Look for in a Vendor." (2014).

Software Engineering Institute. "Common Sense Guide to Mitigating Insider Threats, 4th Edition." Sei.cmu.edu (December 2012).

Stein, Lincoln D. *Web Security: A Step-by-Step Reference Guide*. Reading, MA: Addison-Wesley (1998).

Storm, Darlene. "MEDJACK: Hackers Hijacking Medical Devices Create Backdoors in Hospital Networks." Computerworld.com (June 8, 2015a).

Storm, Darlene. "2 More Wireless Baby Monitors Hacked: Hackers Remotely Spied on Babies and Parents." Computerworld.com (April 22, 2015b).

Symantec, Inc. "Internet Security Threat Report 2016 Volume 21." (April 2016).

Symantec, Inc. "Internet Security Threat Report 2015 Volume 20." (April 2015).

U.S. Department of Justice. "How to Protect Your Networks From Ransomware." (2016).

Vaughan-Nichols, Steven J. "FREAK: Another Day, Another Serious SSL Security Hole." Zdnet.com (March 3, 2015).

Vaughan-Nichols, Steven J. "Has the NSA Broken SSL? TLS? AES?" Zdnet.com (September 6, 2013).

Verizon. "2016 Data Breach Investigations Report." (2016).

Vijayan, Jaikumar. "Google Joins Yahoo, AOL, in Adopting Stricter Email Authentication." Eweek.com (October 20, 2015).

Voreacos, David. "5 Hackers Charged in Largest Data Breach Scheme in U.S." Bloomberg.com (July 26, 2013).

Wakabayashi, Daisuke. "A Contrite Sony Vows Tighter Security." *Wall Street Journal* (May 1, 2011).

Wills, Amanda. "New Snowden Leak: NSA Program Taps All You Do Online." Mashable.com (August 1, 2013).

Wingfield, Nick. "Spam Network Shut Down." *Wall Street Journal* (March 18, 2011).

Zarras, Apostolis, Alexander Kapravelos, Gianluca Stringhini, Thorsten Holz, Christopher Krugel, and Giovanni Vigna. "The Dark Alleys of Madison Avenue: Understanding Malicious Advertisements." ICM '14 Vancouver, BC, Canada (November 5–7, 2014).

CHAPTER 5

E-commerce Business Strategies

After reading this chapter, you will be able to:

- Identify the key components of e-commerce business models.
- Describe the major B2C business models.
- Describe the major B2B business models.
- Understand key business concepts and strategies applicable to e-commerce.

Ace & Tate:

Disrupting the European Eyewear Industry

The rise of e-commerce has disrupted countless traditional retail market segments, but even today there remain areas where e-commerce innovation has yet to fully take place. Until recently, one of those areas was the optical industry. The supply chain for selling glasses typically includes a host of different players, including frame manufacturers, lens manufacturers, opticians, franchises, and very few individual direct retailers. Several companies have emerged looking to change that paradigm, including Amsterdam-based Ace & Tate.

© nomadsoul1/123RF

Ace & Tate sells eyewear in the United Kingdom, Netherlands, Germany, and several other major European markets, and is planning expansion into other areas. Named after acetate, the flexible, durable, lightweight material used in all of its glasses, Ace & Tate has used the cost savings made possible by disrupting the traditional eyewear supply chain to offer quality glasses at a low price point of €98. The company has a full-time staff of 25 employees in Amsterdam, including its eyewear designers. Key processes like manufacturing and shipping are performed by external vendors. Ace & Tate's lean business model allows it to keep costs low and focus on its core goal: creating a strong, stylish product at a fraction of the usual price.

Ace & Tate's CEO Mark de Lange was motivated by the premise that changing eyewear should be as simple as changing a pair of sneakers. To de Lange, the fact that many of us have several pairs of sneakers but only one pair of glasses is indicative of inefficiency in the marketplace. Opticians are a good choice for people with complicated prescriptions, extremely bad eyesight, or a need for a multi-focal prescription. For the majority of people who wear glasses without such specific requirements, the high prices of glasses are difficult to justify, and the middlemen that come between the glasses and the customer are simply unnecessary. By selling directly to consumers, Ace & Tate can avoid the markups introduced by third-party, bricks-and-mortar retailers, as well as opticians and other entities along the supply chain. Ace & Tate represents a cost-effective option for simpler prescriptions as well as for non-prescription eyewear worn purely for style.

Ace & Tate sells primarily online, using a flat fee payment system for each pair of glasses. Many extra services are bundled into the base price, including free shipping and returns, a flexible return policy, and the ability to try on up to four pairs of glasses, also delivered for free, over the span of five days. Any more than four glasses per delivery would compromise Ace & Tate's ability to maintain sufficient inventory and increase the size of the box beyond normal mailboxes. Ace & Tate relies on a family-owned eyewear manufacturer in Northern Italy for most of its glasses, a well-regarded Dutch laboratory for its synthetic lenses, and a third-party logistics company based in the Netherlands for most of its shipping. The company also selects the correct synthetic glasses and lens coatings for users at no extra charge, and includes ultraviolet protection, also at no extra charge.

Technologically, as a company that sells its products almost exclusively online, a robust e-commerce infrastructure is a must. Ace & Tate uses Bootstrap CSS, an open source front-end framework, for its website home page. Bootstrap allows Ace & Tate customers to shop on mobile devices just as effectively as on desktops, quickly and efficiently scaling websites and applications in accordance with the device each customer is using to access the site. The full site uses responsive web design with Magento, an e-commerce software and platform provider. The Magento Web store and custom Magento extensions further enrich the customer experience on the site. For Ace & Tate, using responsive design features on its site is critical to allowing consumers to shop on any device of their choosing.

Ace & Tate's typical demographic is younger, style-conscious consumers who are open to the idea of buying glasses in a new way. The company's heavy involvement in social media reflects this focus; Ace & Tate maintains active presences on the platforms most popular with its target demographic, such as Instagram (nearly 60,000 followers), Facebook (over 100,000 followers), Twitter, YouTube, and Vimeo. The cost savings compared to the traditional optical industry supply chains are also appealing to the typical Ace & Tate consumer. CEO de Lange and other top executives personally oversee every area of the business, including design, where their goal is to blend classic frame designs with modern Dutch style. Ace & Tate also places great importance on conservation and philanthropy; its "Black is the New Green" collection is fully biodegradable and made mostly from natural sources, and the company also donates to Sightsavers, a charity with a focus on eliminating blindness in developing and impoverished countries, with every pair of glasses it sells.

While Ace & Tate is likely to remain an e-commerce retailer first and foremost, the company has experimented with various forms of physical presence. The company opened its first full-time physical store in Amsterdam using a local design studio to create a space that complements Ace & Tate's sleek, fashionable style and modern feel. In 2015, it added a second location in Berlin to bolster its presence in Germany, its most recent area of expansion. Encouraged by the success of these two physical outlets, the company has continued to add more physical locations in 2016, including Munich and Hamburg in Germany, Antwerp in Belgium, and Copenhagen in Denmark. Ace & Tate also has agreements with individual outlets like Hutspot in Amsterdam, where customers can view and try on different styles of glasses—but even in these individual outlets, ordering is still done online.

SOURCES: "Warby Parker's Neil Blumenthal on Building an Eyewear Unicorn," by Ryan Mac, *Forbes*, October 18, 2016; "Warby Parker, Bonobos Have Big Plans for Physical Stores," by Khadeeja Safdar, *Wall Street Journal*, October 6, 2016; "Ace & Tate's CEO Talks

The U.S. equivalent to Ace & Tate is Warby Parker, also an online retailer of eyeglasses and sunglasses. Warby Parker was founded in 2010, and provided many entrepreneurs, including the founders of Ace & Tate, with inspiration that the business direct-to-consumer model could work. Billing itself as "the Netflix of eyewear," Warby Parker has had little trouble raising venture capital and growing quickly. Warby Parker charges $95 for all of its glasses and sells direct to consumers online, just like Ace & Tate. However, Warby Parker has quickly expanded from a handful of physical stores to 37 stores across the United States with immediate plans for at least 50 by 2017 and long-term plans for potentially hundreds of stores. Other retailers that grew primarily via e-commerce, such as men's clothing retailer Bonobos and online jeweler Blue Nile, have taken similar steps to expand via physical outlets that often function more as showrooms for their products than traditional retail outlets. For example, 85% of Warby Parker's walk-in customers at physical stores are already familiar with the company's site.

Warby Parker is renowned for its hip, trendy brand, carefully cultivated by its founders, Neil Blumenthal and David Gilboa, and for its obsessive attention to customer service. With revenue over $100 million and over a million pairs of glasses sold, Warby Parker is a thriving business and has blazed the trail not only for Ace & Tate, but also for a variety of other companies, including GlassesDirect in the United Kingdom and Quattrocento in Italy, both of whom represent competition for Ace & Tate in Europe. Other industries have taken note of the direct-to-consumer e-commerce business model, such as razor blades and other shaving implements (Harry's), mattresses (Casper and Novosbed), and backpacks (Just Porter). By bypassing traditional retailers and selling directly to consumers, these companies can all offer savings and improvements in quality and customer service. These companies are commanding respect from investors and venture capitalists because of their profitability and potential for growth. Ace & Tate should be able to ride this wave to sustained success.

Berlin Store Opening, Japanese Design & More," by Aaron Howes, Highsnobiety.com, July 4, 2016; "Why This Billion Dollar Startup Is Moving Offline," by Robert Sevilla, Channon Hodge, Abigail Brooks, and Molly Shiels, Money.cnn.com, May 26, 2016; "Mark De Lange, Ace & Tate," Themakersamsterdam.com, accessed November 2015; "Our Story," Aceandtate.com, accessed November 2015; "Ace & Tate Eyewear Store by Occult Studio, Amsterdam - Netherlands," Retaildesignblog.net, August 13, 2015; "The Warby Parker of Backpacks Is Reinventing a Popular Startup Model," by Barbara Tasch, Businessinsider.com, August 9, 2015; "Ace & Tate," Inspiration-alshops.com, August 8, 2013; "Ace & Tate," Expo.getbootstrap.com, July 27, 2015; "Italy's Quattrocento Joins the Race to Become the Warby Parker of Europe," by Mike Butcher, Techcrunch.com, July 9, 2015; "Is Dutch Eyewear Startup Ace & Tate the European Answer to Warby Parker?," by Charmaine Li, Tech.eu, March 17, 2015; "Warby Parker Sees the Future of Retail," by Max Chafkin, *Fast Company*, March 2015; "'Ace & Tate:' It Feels a Little Like Being a Band of Pirates," by John Koblin, Fashion-united.co.uk, May 16, 2014; "Investors Bet Big on Harry's, the Warby Parker of Shaving," *New York Times*, December 3, 2014.

T he story of Ace & Tate illustrates the process of turning a good business idea into a successful business model that produces revenues and even profits.

Thousands of firms have discovered that they can spend other people's invested capital much faster than they can get customers to pay for their products or services. In most instances of failure, the business model of the firm is faulty from the beginning. In contrast, successful e-commerce firms have business models that are able to leverage the unique qualities of the Internet, the Web, and the mobile platform, provide customers real value, develop highly effective and efficient operations, avoid legal and social entanglements that can harm the firm, and produce profitable business results. In addition, successful business models must scale. The business must be able to achieve efficiencies as it grows in volume. But what is a business model, and how can you tell if a firm's business model is going to produce a profit?

In this chapter, we focus on business models and basic business concepts that you must be familiar with in order to understand e-commerce.

5.1 E-COMMERCE BUSINESS MODELS

INTRODUCTION

business model
a set of planned activities designed to result in a profit in a marketplace

business plan
a document that describes a firm's business model

e-commerce business model
a business model that aims to use and leverage the unique qualities of the Internet, the Web, and the mobile platform

A **business model** is a set of planned activities (sometimes referred to as *business processes*) designed to result in a profit in a marketplace. A business model is not always the same as a business strategy, although in some cases they are very close insofar as the business model explicitly takes into account the competitive environment (Magretta, 2002). The business model is at the center of the business plan. A **business plan** is a document that describes a firm's business model. A business plan always takes into account the competitive environment. An **e-commerce business model** aims to use and leverage the unique qualities of the Internet, the Web, and the mobile platform.

EIGHT KEY ELEMENTS OF A BUSINESS MODEL

If you hope to develop a successful business model in any arena, not just e-commerce, you must make sure that the model effectively addresses the eight elements listed in **Figure 5.1**. These elements are value proposition, revenue model, market opportunity, competitive environment, competitive advantage, market strategy, organizational development, and management team. Many writers focus on a firm's value proposition and revenue model. While these may be the most important and most easily identifiable aspects of a company's business model, the other elements are equally important when evaluating business models and plans, or when attempting to understand why a particular company has succeeded or failed (Kim and Mauborgne, 2000). In the following sections, we describe each of the key business model elements more fully.

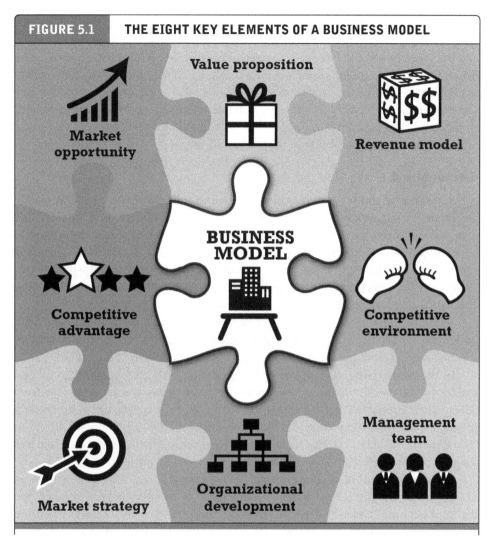

FIGURE 5.1   THE EIGHT KEY ELEMENTS OF A BUSINESS MODEL

A business model has eight key elements. Each element must be addressed if you hope to be successful.

Value Proposition

A company's value proposition is at the very heart of its business model. A **value proposition** defines how a company's product or service fulfills the needs of customers (Kambil, Ginsberg, and Bloch, 1998). To develop and/or analyze a firm's value proposition, you need to understand why customers will choose to do business with the firm instead of another company and what the firm provides that other firms do not and cannot. From the consumer point of view, successful e-commerce value propositions include personalization and customization of product offerings, reduction of product search costs, reduction of price discovery costs, and facilitation of transactions by managing product delivery.

value proposition
defines how a company's
product or service fulfills
the needs of customers

For instance, before Amazon existed, most customers personally traveled to book retailers to place an order. In some cases, the desired book might not be available, and the customer would have to wait several days or weeks, and then return to the bookstore to pick it up. Amazon makes it possible for book lovers to shop for virtually any book in print from the comfort of their home or office, 24 hours a day, and to know immediately whether a book is in stock. Amazon's Kindle takes this one step further by making e-books instantly available with no shipping wait. Amazon's primary value propositions are unparalleled selection and convenience.

Revenue Model

revenue model
describes how the firm will earn revenue, produce profits, and produce a superior return on invested capital

A firm's **revenue model** describes how the firm will earn revenue, generate profits, and produce a superior return on invested capital. We use the terms *revenue model* and *financial model* interchangeably. The function of business organizations is both to generate profits and to produce returns on invested capital that exceed alternative investments. Profits alone are not sufficient to make a company "successful" (Porter, 1985). In order to be considered successful, a firm must produce returns greater than alternative investments. Firms that fail this test go out of existence.

Although there are many different e-commerce revenue models that have been developed, most companies rely on one, or some combination, of the following major revenue models: advertising, subscription, transaction fee, sales, and affiliate.

advertising revenue model
a company provides a forum for advertisements and receives fees from advertisers

In the **advertising revenue model**, a company that offers content, services, and/or products also provides a forum for advertisements and receives fees from advertisers. Companies that are able to attract the greatest viewership or that have a highly specialized, differentiated viewership and are able to retain user attention ("stickiness") are able to charge higher advertising rates. Yahoo, for instance, derives a significant amount of revenue from display and video advertising.

subscription revenue model
a company offers its users content or services and charges a subscription fee for access to some or all of its offerings

In the **subscription revenue model**, a company that offers content or services charges a subscription fee for access to some or all of its offerings. For instance, the digital version of *Consumer Reports* provides online and mobile access to premium content, such as detailed ratings, reviews, and recommendations, only to subscribers, who have a choice of paying a $6.95 monthly subscription fee or a $30.00 annual fee. Experience with the subscription revenue model indicates that to successfully overcome the disinclination of users to pay for content, the content offered must be perceived as a high-value-added, premium offering that is not readily available elsewhere nor easily replicated. Companies successfully offering content or services online on a subscription basis include eHarmony (dating services), Ancestry (genealogy research), Microsoft's Xbox Live (video games), Pandora, Spotify, and Apple Music (music), Scribd and Amazon's Kindle Unlimited program (e-books), and Netflix and Hulu (television and movies). See **Table 5.1** for examples of various subscription services.

freemium strategy
companies give away a certain level of product or services for free, but then charge a subscription fee for premium levels of the product or service

Recently, a number of companies have been combining a subscription revenue model with a freemium strategy. In a **freemium strategy**, the companies give away a certain level of product or services for free, but then charge a subscription fee for premium levels of the product or service. See the case study, *Freemium Takes Pandora Public*, at the end of the chapter, for a further look at the freemium strategy.

TABLE 5.1	EXAMPLES OF SUBSCRIPTION SERVICES
NAME	DESCRIPTION
eHarmony.co.uk (dating)	• Free: Create profile and view profiles of matches • Basic (see photos, send and receive messages): £44.95 for 1 month; £65.85 for 3 months; £113.7 for 6 months; £119.4 for 12 months • Total Connect (Basic plus additional services): £44.95 for 1 month; £68.85 for 3 months; £119.7 for 6 months; £155.4 for 12 months
Ancestry.co.uk (genealogical research)	• Essentials (UK census, birth, marriage, and death records): £10.99 for 1 month; £95.99 for 12 months • Premium (unlimited access to entire library): £13.99 for 1 month; £119.99 for 12 months
Kindle Unlimited UK	• Unlimited books for £7.99/month (over 1 million books from which to choose)
Spotify (music)	• Many different permutations, depending on device (mobile, tablet, or desktop) and plan chosen (Free, Unlimited, or Premium)

In the **transaction fee revenue model**, a company receives a fee for enabling or executing a transaction. For example, eBay provides an auction marketplace and receives a small transaction fee from a seller if the seller is successful in selling the item. E*Trade, a financial services provider, receives transaction fees each time it executes a stock transaction on behalf of a customer.

transaction fee revenue model
a company receives a fee for enabling or executing a transaction

In the **sales revenue model**, companies derive revenue by selling goods, content, or services to customers. Companies such as Amazon, L.L.Bean, and Gap all have sales revenue models. A number of companies are also using a subscription-based sales revenue model. Birchbox, which offers home delivery of beauty products for a $10 monthly or $100 annual subscription price, is one example. Dollar Shave Club, which sells razor blades by subscription and was recently acquired by Unilever for $1 billion, is another.

sales revenue model
a company derives revenue by selling goods, information, or services

In the **affiliate revenue model**, companies that steer business to an "affiliate" receive a referral fee or percentage of the revenue from any resulting sales. For example, MyPoints makes money by connecting companies with potential customers by offering special deals to its members. When they take advantage of an offer and make a purchase, members earn "points" they can redeem for freebies, and MyPoints receives a fee. Community feedback companies typically receive some of their revenue from steering potential customers to websites where they make a purchase.

affiliate revenue model
a company steers business to an affiliate and receives a referral fee or percentage of the revenue from any resulting sales

Table 5.2 summarizes these major revenue models. The *Insight on Society* case, *Foursquare: Check Your Privacy at the Door,* examines some of the issues associated with Foursquare's business and revenue model.

INSIGHT ON SOCIETY

FOURSQUARE: CHECK YOUR PRIVACY AT THE DOOR

Foursquare is one of a host of companies that combine a social network business model with location-based technology. Foursquare offers mobile social applications that know where you are located and can provide you with information about popular spots nearby, as well as reviews from other Foursquare users. Its apps also allow you to check in to a restaurant or other location, and automatically let friends on Facebook and other social networks learn where you are. Founded in 2008 by Dennis Crowley and Naveen Selvadurai, Foursquare has more than 55 million monthly active users worldwide, split fairly evenly between the United States and the rest of the world, who have checked in over 8 billion times. There's potentially a great deal of money to be made by combining a social network with smartphone-based technology that can identify your location precisely. Location-based data has extraordinary commercial value because advertisers can then send you advertisements, coupons, and flash bargains, based on where you are located.

In 2014, Foursquare shook up its business model when it split its app into two separate apps with different focuses. Its redesigned Foursquare app became a recommender system akin to a travel guide, using passive location tracking to offer suggestions to users for where to eat or visit. A separate app, Swarm, absorbed Foursquare's check-in feature. The redesigned app asks the user to identify things he or she likes, known as "tastes," from over 10,000 possibilities (ranging from barbecue to museums to board games), and then provides recommendations. Rather than earn badges, users are encouraged to add tips to work toward becoming an expert. Many loyal Foursquare users were driven away by the change. In 2015, the company added many of the old features, such as status levels, mayorships (awards

offered to users with the most check-ins at a particular location), and leaderboards, back to Swarm. Foursquare's decision was influenced primarily by its continued struggles to find profitability, though it's not for lack of trying. Foursquare has continued to develop in-app advertising products that serve advertising based on users' locations and has formed partnerships with companies like American Express to offer discounts to cardholders after using Foursquare to check-in. Unfortunately for Foursquare, Facebook and seemingly every other social network now offer the ability to check-in and share that information with friends. However, in 2015, Foursquare shifted in a different direction with the launch of its Pinpoint product, an advertising tool that allows marketers unprecedented ability to target users based on its accumulated historical location data and to filter out inaccurate data. Most importantly, Pinpoint can even reach mobile users without the Foursquare app, a major advantage considering the company's relatively low number of in-network users compared to other top social networks.

In 2016, Foursquare is likely to focus more on Pinpoint and other technologies that it can offer other companies than on its flagship check-in app. From 2014 to 2016, Foursquare's revenue doubled on a year-to-year basis, including a 170% increase in its advertising solutions business in 2015. This growth has been driven primarily by data licensing agreements with other tech and social networking giants. For example, in 2014, Foursquare struck just such an agreement with Microsoft, which may use the data to customize Bing on a user-by-user basis with specific search results and advertisements based on their location data. Foursquare has also struck similar deals with Twitter, Google, Yahoo, and Pinterest to provide location-based functions and to share location data, increasing the richness and accuracy of its own data in the process. All of these partnerships greatly enrich the value of Pinpoint and allow Foursquare to track users that are not even a part of its platform. All of a sudden, Foursquare's "lowly" 55 million users and unimpressive user growth don't matter quite as much. In 2016, Foursquare received $45 million in new financing, albeit at a much lower valuation than its last round of financing in 2013. Crowley also stepped down as CEO as the company restructured its executive team to focus on continued development of both advertising products as well as techniques to monetize its location data. The company believes that its renewed focus on its advertising products will help it overcome the stigma of its stalled user growth.

As the popularity of location-based services like Foursquare has grown, so too have concerns about privacy. Privacy advocates point out that many apps have no privacy policy, that most of the popular apps transmit location data to their developers, after which the information is not well controlled, and that these services are creating a situation where government, marketers, creditors, and telecommunications firms will end up knowing nearly everything about citizens, including their whereabouts. Many users may not truly understand how much of their location history is available to their friends. A 2016 study indicated that algorithms that analyze Twitter posts in tandem with Foursquare or Instagram posts can identify users' identities with relative ease. One advantage Foursquare does have, though, is that many of its users are actually interested in having their location tracked and their data collected—users are less likely to revolt when they find that Foursquare is collecting and sharing their data.

The Foursquare app automatically provides Foursquare with the phone's GPS coordinates any time the phone is turned on, even when the app is closed, unless the user specifically opts out of such tracking. In contrast, Facebook's Nearby Friends feature requires users to opt in. Persistent location tracking of this sort further enhances the value of Foursquare's location data. Foursquare claims that the services it provides are a fair trade for the data it collects; privacy experts are concerned that users cannot delete archived location data from Foursquare's servers. Striking a balance between respecting user privacy and continuing to drive profitability will continue to be a challenge for Foursquare moving forward. Signaling a desire to meet its users' demands for privacy, in 2016, Swarm began allowing users to check in without sharing their locations publicly; but at approximately the same time, Foursquare released its Attribution product, which mines daily location information of over 1.3 million Foursquare users who have consented to location tracking in order to determine whether or not the advertising they've seen has actually influenced their purchasing decisions. In July 2016, Foursquare released a digital dashboard for advertising using Attribution that lets marketers drill down into the data even further, with even more detailed audience metrics.

SOURCES: "Foursquare Is Debuting a Dashboard for Its Intriguing Foot Traffic Measurement System," by Christoper Heine, Adweek.com, July 25, 2016; "Swarm Now Lets Users Check-In Without Sharing Their Location," by Jordan Crook, Techcrunch.com, April 21, 2016; "Location Data From Just Two of Your Apps Is Enough to Reveal Your Identity," by Brian Mastroianni, Cbsnews.com, April 14, 2016; "Foursquare 'Attribution' Takes On Nielsen By Selling Foot Traffic From 1.2 Million Daily Mobile Audience," by Kerry Flynn, Ibtimes.com, February 22, 2016; "Foursquare's Potentially Game-Changing New Tool Can Measure Foot Traffic Generated by Digital Ads," by Christopher Heine, Adweek.com, February 22, 2016; "Inside Foursquare's Plan to Become Profitable," by Andrew Nusca, *Fortune*, January 25, 2016; "Foursquare's Plan to Use Your Data to Make Money—Even If You Aren't a User," by Klint Finley, Wired.com, January 19, 2016; "Foursquare Raises $45 Million, Cutting Its Valuation Nearly in Half," by Mike Isaac, *New York Times*, January 14, 2016; "Swarm Gets Back into the Game with Leaderboards," by Jordan Crook, Techcrunch.com, August 20, 2015; "Foursquare by the Numbers: 60M Registered Users, 50M MAUs, and 75M Tips to Date," by Harrison Weber and Jordan Novet, Venturebeat.com, August 18, 2015; "Foursquare Returns to Its Roots in Bid to Win Back Users," by Jason Cipriani, *Fortune*, May 13, 2015; "Foursquare Unveils Pinpoint for Location-Based Ad Targeting," by Melanie White, Clickz.com, April 14, 2015; "Foursquare Unveils Pinpoint to Show You Ads Based on Where You've Been," by Harrison Weber, Venturebeat.com, April 14, 2015; "Why Twitter and Foursquare Just Struck a Deal," by Erin Griffith, *Fortune*, March 23, 2015; "Radical New Foursquare App Thinks You Want Even Less Privacy," by Jason Cipriani, Wired.com, August 6, 2014; "Foursquare Now Tracks Users Even When the App is Closed," by Douglas Macmillan, *Wall Street Journal*, August 6, 2014; "Foursquare Updates Swarm to Soothe Check-in Blues," by Caitlin McGarry, Techhive.com, July 8, 2014; "How Foursquare Uses Location Data to Target Ads on PCs, Phones," by Cotton Delo, Adage.com, February 27, 2014; "With Foursquare Deal, Microsoft Aims for Supremacy in Hyper-Local Search," by Ryan Tate, Wired.com, February 5, 2014.

TABLE 5.2	FIVE PRIMARY REVENUE MODELS	
REVENUE MODEL	EXAMPLES	REVENUE SOURCE
Advertising	Yahoo	Fees from advertisers in exchange for advertisements
Subscription	eHarmony Consumer Reports Online Netflix	Fees from subscribers in exchange for access to content or services
Transaction Fee	eBay E*Trade	Fees (commissions) for enabling or executing a transaction
Sales	Amazon L.L.Bean Birchbox iTunes	Sales of goods, information, or services
Affiliate	MyPoints	Fees for business referrals

Market Opportunity

market opportunity
refers to the company's intended marketspace and the overall potential financial opportunities available to the firm in that marketspace

The term **market opportunity** refers to the company's intended **marketspace** (i.e., an area of actual or potential commercial value) and the overall potential financial opportunities available to the firm in that marketspace. The market opportunity is usually divided into smaller market niches. The realistic market opportunity is defined by the revenue potential in each of the market niches where you hope to compete.

marketspace
the area of actual or potential commercial value in which a company intends to operate

For instance, let's assume you are analyzing a software training company that creates online software-learning systems for sale to businesses. The overall size of the software training market for all market segments is approximately €65 billion. The overall market can be broken down, however, into two major market segments: instructor-led training products, which comprise about 70% of the market (€45.5 billion in revenue), and computer-based training, which accounts for 30% (€19.5 billion). There are further market niches within each of those major market segments, such as the FT 500 online training market and the small business computer-based training market. Because the firm is a start-up firm, it cannot compete effectively in the large business, online training market (about €13.65 billion). Large brand-name training firms dominate this niche. The start-up firm's real market opportunity is to sell to the thousands of small business firms that spend about €5.85 billion on online software training. This is the size of the firm's realistic market opportunity (see **Figure 5.2**).

competitive environment
refers to the other companies operating in the same marketspace selling similar products

Competitive Environment

A firm's **competitive environment** refers to the other companies selling similar products and operating in the same marketspace. It also refers to the presence of substitute products and potential new entrants to the market, as well as the power of customers and suppliers over your business. We discuss the firm's environment

---

FIGURE 5.2   **MARKETSPACE AND MARKET OPPORTUNITY IN THE SOFTWARE TRAINING MARKET**

Small Business €18.2 Billion

Small Business €5.85 Billion

Instructor-Led Training €45.5 Billion

Online Training €19.5 Billion

FT 500 €13.65 Billion

FT 500 €27.3 Billion

Marketspaces are composed of many market segments. Your realistic market opportunity will typically focus on one or a few market segments.

---

later in the chapter. The competitive environment for a company is influenced by several factors: how many competitors are active, how large their operations are, what the market share of each competitor is, how profitable these firms are, and how they price their products.

Firms typically have both direct and indirect competitors. Direct competitors are companies that sell very similar products and services into the same market segment. For example, Priceline and Travelocity, both of whom sell discount airline tickets online, are direct competitors because both companies sell identical products—cheap tickets. Indirect competitors are companies that may be in different industries but still compete indirectly because their products can substitute for one another. For instance, automobile manufacturers and airline companies operate in different industries, but they still compete indirectly because they offer consumers alternative means of transportation. CNN, a news outlet, is an indirect competitor of ESPN, not because they sell identical products, but because they both compete for consumers' time online.

The existence of a large number of competitors in any one segment may be a sign that the market is saturated and that it may be difficult to become profitable. On the other hand, a lack of competitors could signal either an untapped market niche ripe for the picking, or a market that has already been tried without success because there is no money to be made. Analysis of the competitive environment can help you decide which it is.

Competitive Advantage

Firms achieve a **competitive advantage** when they can produce a superior product and/or bring the product to market at a lower price than most, or all, of their

competitive advantage
achieved by a firm when it can produce a superior product and/or bring the product to market at a lower price than most, or all, of its competitors

competitors (Porter, 1985). Firms also compete on scope. Some firms can develop global markets, while other firms can develop only a national or regional market. Firms that can provide superior products at the lowest cost on a global basis are truly advantaged.

Firms achieve competitive advantages because they have somehow been able to obtain differential access to the factors of production that are denied to their competitors—at least in the short term (Barney, 1991). Perhaps the firm has been able to obtain very favorable terms from suppliers, shippers, or sources of labor. Or perhaps the firm has more experienced, knowledgeable, and loyal employees than any competitors. Maybe the firm has a patent on a product that others cannot imitate, or access to investment capital through a network of former business colleagues or a brand name and popular image that other firms cannot duplicate. An **asymmetry** exists whenever one participant in a market has more resources—financial backing, knowledge, information, and/or power—than other participants. Asymmetries lead to some firms having an edge over others, permitting them to come to market with better products, faster than competitors, and sometimes at lower cost.

For instance, when Apple announced iTunes, a service offering legal, downloadable individual song tracks for 99 cents a track that would be playable on any digital device with iTunes software, the company had better-than-average odds of success simply because of Apple's prior success with innovative hardware designs, and the large stable of music firms that Apple had meticulously lined up to support its online music catalog. Few competitors could match the combination of cheap, legal songs and powerful hardware to play them on.

One rather unique competitive advantage derives from being a first mover. A **first-mover advantage** is a competitive market advantage for a firm that results from being the first into a marketplace with a serviceable product or service. If first movers develop a loyal following or a unique interface that is difficult to imitate, they can sustain their first-mover advantage for long periods (Arthur, 1996). Amazon provides a good example. However, in the history of technology-driven business innovation, most first movers often lack the **complementary resources** needed to sustain their advantages, and often follower firms reap the largest rewards (Rigdon, 2000; Teece, 1986). Indeed, many of the success stories we discuss in this book are those of companies that were slow followers—businesses that gained knowledge from the failure of pioneering firms and entered into the market late.

Some competitive advantages are called "unfair." An **unfair competitive advantage** occurs when one firm develops an advantage based on a factor that other firms cannot purchase (Barney, 1991). For instance, a brand name cannot be purchased and is in that sense an "unfair" advantage. Brands are built upon loyalty, trust, reliability, and quality. Once obtained, they are difficult to copy or imitate, and they permit firms to charge premium prices for their products.

In **perfect markets**, there are no competitive advantages or asymmetries because all firms have access to all the factors of production (including information and knowledge) equally. However, real markets are imperfect, and asymmetries leading to competitive advantages do exist, at least in the short term. Most competitive

---

asymmetry

exists whenever one participant in a market has more resources than other participants

first-mover advantage

a competitive market advantage for a firm that results from being the first into a marketplace with a serviceable product or service

complementary resources

resources and assets not directly involved in the production of the product but required for success, such as marketing, management, financial assets, and reputation

unfair competitive advantage

occurs when one firm develops an advantage based on a factor that other firms cannot purchase

perfect market

a market in which there are no competitive advantages or asymmetries because all firms have equal access to all the factors of production advantages are short term, although some can be sustained for very long periods. But not forever. In fact, many respected brands fail every year.

Companies are said to **leverage** their competitive assets when they use their competitive advantages to achieve more advantage in surrounding markets. For instance, Amazon's move into the online grocery business leverages the company's huge customer database and years of e-commerce experience.

leverage
when a company uses its competitive advantages to achieve more advantage in surrounding markets

Market Strategy

No matter how tremendous a firm's qualities, its marketing strategy and execution are often just as important. The best business concept, or idea, will fail if it is not properly marketed to potential customers.

Everything you do to promote your company's products and services to potential customers is known as marketing. **Market strategy** is the plan you put together that details exactly how you intend to enter a new market and attract new customers.

For instance, Twitter, YouTube, and Pinterest have a social network marketing strategy that encourages users to post their content for free, build personal profile pages, contact their friends, and build a community. In these cases, the customer becomes part of the marketing staff!

market strategy
the plan you put together that details exactly how you intend to enter a new market and attract new customers

Organizational Development

Although many entrepreneurial ventures are started by one visionary individual, it is rare that one person alone can grow an idea into a multi-million dollar company. In most cases, fast-growth companies—especially e-commerce businesses—need employees and a set of business procedures. In short, all firms—new ones in particular—need an organization to efficiently implement their business plans and strategies. Many e-commerce firms and many traditional firms that attempt an e-commerce strategy have failed because they lacked the organizational structures and supportive cultural values required to support new forms of commerce (Kanter, 2001).

Companies that hope to grow and thrive need to have a plan for **organizational development** that describes how the company will organize the work that needs to be accomplished. Typically, work is divided into functional departments, such as production, shipping, marketing, customer support, and finance. Jobs within these functional areas are defined, and then recruitment begins for specific job titles and responsibilities. Typically, in the beginning, generalists who can perform multiple tasks are hired. As the company grows, recruiting becomes more specialized. For instance, at the outset, a business may have one marketing manager. But after two or three years of steady growth, that one marketing position may be broken down into seven separate jobs done by seven individuals.

organizational development
plan that describes how the company will organize the work that needs to be accomplished

For instance, eBay founder Pierre Omidyar started an online auction site, according to some sources, to help his girlfriend trade Pez dispensers with other collectors, but within a few months the volume of business had far exceeded what he alone could handle. So he began hiring people with more business experience to help out. Soon the company had many employees, departments, and managers who were responsible for overseeing the various aspects of the organization.

Management Team

management team

employees of the company responsible for making the business model work

Arguably, the single most important element of a business model is the **management team** responsible for making the model work. A strong management team gives a model instant credibility to outside investors, immediate market-specific knowledge, and experience in implementing business plans. A strong management team may not be able to salvage a weak business model, but the team should be able to change the model and redefine the business as it becomes necessary.

Eventually, most companies get to the point of having several senior executives or managers. How skilled managers are, however, can be a source of competitive advantage or disadvantage. The challenge is to find people who have both the experience and the ability to apply that experience to new situations.

To be able to identify good managers for a business start-up, first consider the kinds of experiences that would be helpful to a manager joining your company. What kind of technical background is desirable? What kind of supervisory experience is necessary? How many years in a particular function should be required? What job functions should be fulfilled first: marketing, production, finance, or operations? Especially in situations where financing will be needed to get a company off the ground, do prospective senior managers have experience and contacts for raising financing from outside investors?

Table 5.3 summarizes the eight key elements of a business model and the key questions that must be answered in order to successfully develop each element.

RAISING CAPITAL

Raising capital is one of the most important functions for a founder of a start-up business and its management team. Not having enough capital to operate effectively is a primary reason why so many start-up businesses fail. Many entrepreneurs initially "bootstrap" to get a business off the ground, using personal funds derived from savings,

TABLE 5.3	KEY ELEMENTS OF A BUSINESS MODEL
COMPONENTS	KEY QUESTIONS
Value proposition	Why should the customer buy from you?
Revenue model	How will you earn money?
Market opportunity	What marketspace do you intend to serve, and what is its size?
Competitive environment	Who else occupies your intended marketspace?
Competitive advantage	What special advantages does your firm bring to the marketspace?
Market strategy	How do you plan to promote your products or services to attract your target audience?
Organizational development	What types of organizational structures within the firm are necessary to carry out the business plan?
Management team	What kinds of experiences and background are important for the company's leaders to have?

TABLE 5.4	KEY ELEMENTS OF AN ELEVATOR PITCH
ELEMENT	DESCRIPTION
Introduction	Your name and position; your company's name, and a tagline in which you compare what your company does to a well-known company. Example: "My name is X, I am the founder of Y, and we are the Uber/Amazon of Z."
Background	The origin of your idea and the problem you are trying to solve.
Industry size/market opportunity	Brief facts about the (hopefully very large) size of the market.
Revenue model/numbers/ growth metrics	Insight into your company's revenue model and results thus far, how fast it is growing, and early adopters, if there are any.
Funding	The amount of funds you are seeking and what it will help you achieve.
Exit strategy	How your investors will achieve a return on their investment.

credit card advances, home equity loans, or from family and friends. Funds of this type are often referred to as **seed capital**. Once such funds are exhausted, if the company is not generating enough revenue to cover operating costs, additional capital will be needed. Traditional sources of capital include incubators, commercial banks, angel investors, venture capital firms, and strategic partners. One of the most important aspects of raising capital is the ability to boil down the elements of the company's business plan into an **elevator pitch**, a short two-to-three minute (about the length of an elevator ride, giving rise to its name) presentation aimed at convincing investors to invest. **Table 5.4** lists the key elements of an elevator pitch.

Incubators (sometimes also referred to as accelerators) such as Rocket Internet (profiled in Chapter 1's *Insight on Business* case) typically provide a small amount of funding, but more importantly, also provide an array of services to start-up companies that they select to participate in their programs, such as business, technical, and marketing assistance, as well as introductions to other sources of capital. Well-known European incubator programs include INiTS (Austria), Accelerace (Denmark), Numa (Le Camping) (France), and SeedRocket (Spain).

Obtaining a loan from a commercial bank is often difficult for a start-up company without much revenue, but it may be worthwhile to investigate programs offered by the U.S. Small Business Administration, and its state or local equivalents. The advantage of obtaining capital in the form of a loan (debt) is that, although it must be repaid, it does not require an entrepreneur to give up any ownership of the company.

Angel investors are typically wealthy individuals (or a group of individuals) who invest their own money in an exchange for an equity share in the stock in the business. In general, angel investors make smaller investments (typically €1 million or less) than venture capital firms, are interested in helping a company grow and succeed, and invest on relatively favorable terms compared to later stage investors. The first round of external investment in a company is sometimes referred to as Series A financing.

seed capital
typically, an entrepreneur's personal funds derived from savings, credit card advances, home equity loans, or from family and friends

elevator pitch
short two-to-three minute presentation aimed at convincing investors to invest

incubators
typically provide a small amount of funding and also an array of services to start-up companies

angel investors
typically wealthy individuals or a group of individuals who invest their own money in exchange for an equity share in the stock of a business; often are the first outside investors in a start-up

venture capital investors

typically invest funds they manage for other investors; usually later-stage investors

Venture capital investors typically become more interested in a start-up company once it has begun attracting a large audience and generating some revenue, even if it is not profitable. **Venture capital investors** invest funds they manage for other investors such as investment banks, pension funds, insurance companies, or other businesses, and usually want to obtain a larger stake in the business and exercise more control over the operation of the business. Venture capital investors also typically want a well-defined "exit strategy," such as a plan for an initial public offering or acquisition of the company by a more established business within a relatively short period of time (typically 3 to 7 years), that will enable them to obtain an adequate return on their investment. Venture capital investment often ultimately means that the founder(s) and initial investors will no longer control the company at some point in the future.

crowdfunding

involves using the Internet to enable individuals to collectively contribute money to support a project

Crowdfunding involves using the Internet to enable individuals to collectively contribute money to support a project. The concepts behind crowdfunding have been popularized by Kickstarter and Indiegogo, but they could not be used for equity investments in for-profit companies due to various laws and regulations. However, this is changing in the United States with the passage of the JOBS Act in 2012 and the issuance of regulations by the U.S. Securities and Exchange Commission, which now enables companies to use the Internet to solicit investors to invest in small and early-stage start-ups in exchange for stock. In Europe, the European Commission has indicated an intention to support crowdfunding and has issued several reports aimed at promoting understanding this form of financing at the EU level and laying the groundwork for possible future action, as well as a guide to crowdfunding for small and medium enterprises as part of its effort to inform citizens about both its benefits and risks (European Commission, 2016; 2015; 2014). See the *Insight on Business* case, *Crowdfunding Takes Off*, for a further look at the issues surrounding crowdfunding.

CATEGORIZING E-COMMERCE BUSINESS MODELS: SOME DIFFICULTIES

There are many e-commerce business models, and more are being invented every day. The number of such models is limited only by the human imagination, and our list of different business models is certainly not exhaustive. However, despite the abundance of potential models, it is possible to identify the major generic types (and subtle variations) of business models that have been developed for the e-commerce arena and describe their key features. It is important to realize, however, that there is no one correct way to categorize these business models.

Our approach is to categorize business models according to the different major e-commerce sectors—B2C and B2B—in which they are utilized. You will note, however, that fundamentally similar business models may appear in more than one sector. For example, the business models of online retailers (often called e-tailers) and e-distributors are quite similar. However, they are distinguished by the market focus of the sector in which they are used. In the case of e-tailers in the B2C sector, the business model focuses on sales to the individual consumer, while in the case of the e-distributor, the business model focuses on sales to another business. Many companies use a variety of

INSIGHT ON BUSINESS

CROWDFUNDING TAKES OFF

Think you have the next big idea but lack the resources to make it happen? Crowdfunding sites might be your best shot. Sites such as Kickstarter, Indiegogo, RocketHub, and Tilt have led the growth of crowdfunding. A World Bank study predicts that capital raised via crowdfunding will exceed around €75 billion by 2025. The Internet is the ideal medium for crowdfunding because it allows individuals and organizations in need of funds and potential backers to find one another around the globe. For instance, Kickstarter is available for projects in 14 European countries, as well as the United States, Canada, Mexico, Australia, New Zealand, Singapore, and Hong Kong. Indiegogo is also focusing on international growth, with campaigns having been started in almost 225 different countries and territories to date.

How do sites like Kickstarter and Indiegogo work? The idea is simple—an inventor, artist, or activist looking to raise money for a project uses the site to create a page for that project. The sites take a small commission, usually about 5%, on completed projects. Backers often receive some type of reward, often corresponding to the size of their contribution to the project.

Crowdfunding is becoming a mainstay in the development of movies, video games, art installations, and many other types of projects. For instance, in the United Kingdom, one of the top projects funded is a new 3-D game called Yooka-Laylee created by Playtonic Games that raised almost £2.1 million from over 80,000 backers. The game is expected to be released in April 2017.

Successful crowdfunding projects typically share some common elements. One of the most important is a clear and concise presentation of the idea, especially through the use of video. The crowdfunding campaign is in many ways similar to presenting a business plan and should touch on the same eight elements of a business model, such as the project's value proposition and its target market.

Not every crowdfunding project gets off the ground—Kickstarter reports that only about 35% of its approximately 335,000 projects thus far have reached their funding goals. Sometimes projects that do get off the ground simply flame out, disappointing their backers. For instance, Europe's biggest Kickstarter project, for the development of the Zano, an autonomous, intelligent, swarming nano drone, went bankrupt before ever completing its product despite raising over £2.34 million from over 12,000 backers. Another high-profile Kickstarter project, the Coolest Cooler, has been marred by price increases, delays in production, and failure to deliver the product to its original backers despite shipping it to those who pay full retail price on Amazon. Kickstarter now requires fundraisers to disclose the risks associated with their project and now also requires photos of prototype products (instead of simply drawings, simulations, or renderings) for inventions.

A new use of crowdfunding is to provide seed capital for startup companies in return for equity (shares) in the company, known as equity crowdfunding. Under the JOBS Act passed by the U.S. Congress in 2012, a company will be able to crowdfund up to $1 million over a 12-month period, and in 2016, the rules requiring potential investors to be accredited (having a net worth of at least $1 million dollars) were relaxed to allow smaller investors to purchase equity stakes

(continued)

of $2,000 or more. Twenty-five states in the United States have their own crowdfunding rules that allow local businesses to raise money in this way, and the 2016 regulations will also fix a loophole preventing these businesses from advertising to investors from outside their respective states. However, equity crowdfunding will require extensive compliance from businesses, with steep penalties for any irregularities, and potential investors will be subject to all the same risks that professional investors experience but may put themselves in more precarious financial positions as a result. They'll also be forced to hold their investments for at least one year.

Many expect the use of crowdfunding for this purpose to skyrocket once regulations allowing it are fully implemented. However, studies from MIT and the College of William and Mary suggest that equity crowdfunding isn't as likely to lead to positive outcomes for smaller investors. Many of the highest-quality startups won't need to use equity crowdfunding and will instead pursue more traditional venture capitalists, and smaller investors may be more likely to fall prey to misleading claims from businesses seeking funding. It's likely that more regulations will need to be developed to protect smaller equity crowdfunding investors in coming months and years.

In Europe, the situation is more complicated. Although the European Commission is considering how best to promote equity crowdfunding, currently national laws in countries throughout Europe vary widely, with the United Kingdom, Italy, and France each taking their own unique approaches. In the United Kingdom, crowdfunding is regulated by the Financial Conduct Authority, which issued new rules in 2014. Italy was one of the first European countries to regulate equity crowdfunding in 2013, and since then it has updated those regulations twice, first in 2015 to enlarge the category of companies that can be crowdfunded, and most recently in 2016, to simplify the regulatory framework and reduce the costs associated with crowdfunding, and expand the number of people able to invest. In France, companies are able to raise up to €1 million via equity crowdfunding without having to notify the French financial markets authority.

In Europe, much of the crowdfunding still takes the form of peer-to-peer lending rather than equity investment. Some of the leading companies in this area include Zopa and Ratesetter. Funding Circle is one of the biggest crowdfunding platforms in the United Kingdom, and has facilitated loans to small businesses totalling more than £1 billion since its launch in 2010. Auxmoney is Germany's largest credit marketplace and continental Europe's second-largest P2P lender, after French firm Younited Credit, and has facilitated €268 million worth of loans since its launch in 2013.

▬ **SOURCES:** "Yook-Laylee," Playtonicgames.com, accessed January 23, 2017; "The Current State of Crowdfunding in the UK," Crowdfundinghub.eu, accessed January 22, 2017; "The Current State of Crowdfunding in France," Crowdfundinghub.eu, accessed January 22, 2017; "Leading German Crowdfunding Platform, P2P Lender Auxmoney Powers On," by Therese Torris, Crowdfunderinsider.com, July 13, 2016; Kickstarter.com, accessed January 22, 2017; Indiegogo.com, accessed January 22, 2017; "New Crowdfunding Rules Could Do More Harm Than Good for Some Startups," by Samantha Drake, *Forbes*, June 27, 2016; "New Crowdfunding Rules Let the Small Fry Swim with Sharks," by Stacy Cowley, *New York Times*, May 14, 2016; "Can Equity Crowdfunding Democratize Access to Capital and Investment Opportunities?," by Christian Catalini, Catherine Fazio, and Fiona Murray, MIT Innovation Initiative, May 2016; "As Equity Crowdfunding Debuts in U.S., Will More Regulations Follow?," by Jeff Engel, Xconomy.com, March 25, 2016; "New Rules for Equity Crowdfunding in Italy," by Grow VC Group, Growvc.com, March 2016; "Zano: The Rise and Fall of Kickstarter's Mini-Drone," by Rory Cellan-Jones, BBC.com, January 20, 2016; "Funding Circle's Lending to Small Businesses Passes £1bn," by Peter Campbell, FT.com, December 29, 2015; "Trouble on Kickstarter as Two Massive Projects Hit the Rocks," by Alex Hern, *The Guardian*, November 19, 2015; "S.E.C. Gives Small Investors Access to Equity Crowdfunding," by Stacy Cowley, *New York Times*, October 30, 2015; "Equity Crowdfunding: A Market for Lemons?," by Darian M. Ibrahim, College of William & Mary Law School, 2015; "Here Are Australia's Most Successful Kickstarter Projects," by Junglist, Gizmodo.com.au, November 13, 2014; "The Ultimate Guide to Crowdfunding in New Zealand," by Vaughn Davis, Idealog.co.nz, February 7, 2014; "Invest in Next Facebook...for a Few Bucks," by Patrick M. Sheridan, CNNMoney.com, April 14, 2014; "World Bank: Crowdfunding Investment Market to Hit $93 Billion by 2025," by Richard Swart, PBS.org, December 10, 2013.

different business models as they attempt to extend into as many areas of e-commerce as possible. We look at B2C business models in Section 5.2 and B2B business models in Section 5.3.

A business's technology platform is sometimes confused with its business model. For instance, "mobile e-commerce" refers to the use of mobile devices and cellular and wide area networks to support a variety of business models. Commentators sometimes confuse matters by referring to mobile e-commerce as a distinct business model, which it is not. All of the basic business models we discuss below can be implemented on both the traditional Internet/Web and mobile platforms. Likewise, although they are sometimes referred to as such, social e-commerce and local e-commerce are not business models in and of themselves, but rather subsectors of B2C and B2B e-commerce in which different business models can operate.

You will also note that some companies use multiple business models. For instance, Amazon has multiple business models: it is an e-retailer, content provider, market creator, e-commerce infrastructure provider, and more. eBay is a market creator in the B2C and C2C e-commerce sectors, using both the traditional Internet/Web and mobile platforms, as well as an e-commerce infrastructure provider. Firms often seek out multiple business models as a way to leverage their brands, infrastructure investments, and assets developed with one business model into new business models.

Finally, no discussion of e-commerce business models would be complete without mention of a group of companies whose business model is focused on providing the infrastructure necessary for e-commerce companies to exist, grow, and prosper. These are the e-commerce enablers. They provide the hardware, operating system software, networks and communications technology, applications software, web design, consulting services, and other tools required for e-commerce (see **Table 5.5** on page 342). While these firms may not be conducting e-commerce per se (although in many instances, e-commerce in its traditional sense is in fact one of their sales channels), as a group they have perhaps profited the most from the development of e-commerce. We discuss many of these players in the following chapters.

5.2 MAJOR BUSINESS-TO-CONSUMER (B2C) BUSINESS MODELS

Business-to-consumer (B2C) e-commerce, in which online businesses seek to reach individual consumers, is the most well-known and familiar type of e-commerce. **Table 5.6** illustrates the major business models utilized in the B2C arena.

E-TAILER

Online retail stores, often called **e-tailers**, come in all sizes, from giant Amazon to tiny local stores. E-tailers are similar to the typical bricks-and-mortar storefront, except that customers only have to connect to the Internet or use their smartphone to place an order. Some e-tailers, which are referred to as "bricks-and-clicks," are subsidiaries or

e-tailer
online retail store

TABLE 5.5	E-COMMERCE ENABLERS
INFRASTRUCTURE	**PLAYERS**
Hardware: Web Servers	HP • Dell • Lenovo
Software: Web Server Software	Microsoft • IBM • Red Hat Linux (Apache) • Oracle
Cloud Providers	Amazon Web Services • Google • IBM • Rackspace
Hosting Services	Rackspace • WebIntellects • 1&1 • HostGator • Hostway
Domain Name Registration	GoDaddy • Network Solutions • Dotster
Content Delivery Networks	Akamai • Limelight
Site Design	Weebly • Wix • Squarespace
E-commerce Platform Providers	Magento • IBM • Oracle • Salesforce
Mobile Commerce Hardware Platform	Apple • Samsung • LG
Mobile Commerce Software Platform	Apple • Google • Adobe • Usablenet • Unbound Commerce
Streaming, Rich Media, Online Video	Adobe • Apple • Webcollage
Security and Encryption	VeriSign • Check Point • GeoTrust • Entrust • Thawte • Intel Security
Payment Systems	PayPal • Authorize.net • Chase Paymentech • Cybersource
Web Performance Management	Compuware • SmartBear • Keynote
Comparison Engine Feeds/Marketplace Management	ChannelAdvisor • CommerceHub • CPC Strategy
Customer Relationship Management	Oracle • SAP • Salesforce • Microsoft Dynamics
Order Management	JDA Software • Jagged Peak • Monsoon Commerce
Fulfillment	JDA Software • Jagged Peak • CommerceHub
Social Marketing	Buffer • HootSuite • SocialFlow
Search Engine Marketing	iProspect • ChannelAdvisor • Merkle
E-mail Marketing	Constant Contact • Experian CheetahMail • Bronto Software • MailChimp
Affiliate Marketing	CJ Affiliate • Rakuten LinkShare
Customer Reviews and Forums	Bazaarvoice • PowerReviews • BizRate
Live Chat/Click-to-Call	LivePerson • BoldChat • Oracle
Web Analytics	Google Analytics • Adobe Analytics • IBM Digital Analytics • Webtrends

divisions of existing physical stores and carry the same products. REI, JCPenney, Barnes & Noble, Walmart, and Staples are examples of companies with complementary online stores. Others, however, operate only in the virtual world, without any ties to physical locations. Amazon, Blue Nile, and Bluefly are examples of this type of e-tailer. Several other variations of e-tailers—such as online versions of direct mail catalogs, online malls, and manufacturer-direct online sales—also exist.

Given that the overall global retail market in 2016 is estimated to be around €20.9 trillion, the market opportunity for e-tailers is very large. Every Internet and smartphone user is a potential customer. Customers who feel time-starved are even better prospects, because they want shopping solutions that will eliminate the need

TABLE 5.6	B2C BUSINESS MODELS			
BUSINESS MODEL	VARIATIONS	EXAMPLES	DESCRIPTION	REVENUE MODELS
E-tailer	Virtual Merchant	Amazon Blue Nile Bluefly	Online version of retail store, where customers can shop at any hour of the day or night without leaving their home or office	Sales of goods
	Bricks-and-Clicks	Walmart Sears	Online distribution channel for a company that also has physical stores	Sales of goods
	Catalog Merchant	L.L.Bean LillianVernon	Online version of direct mail catalog	Sales of goods
	Manufacturer-Direct	Dell Mattel	Manufacturer uses online channel to sell direct to customer	Sales of goods
Community Provider		Facebook LinkedIn Twitter Pinterest	Sites where individuals with particular interests, hobbies, common experiences, or social networks can come together and "meet" online	Advertising, subscription, affiliate referral fees
Content Provider		Wall Street Journal CNN ESPN Netflix Apple Music	Offers customers newspapers, magazines, books, film, television, music, games, and other forms of online content	Advertising, subscription fees, sales of digital goods
Portal	Horizontal/ General	Yahoo AOL MSN Facebook	Offers an integrated package of content, search, and social network services: news, e-mail, chat, music downloads, video streaming, calendars, etc. Seeks to be a user's home base	Advertising, subscription fees, transaction fees
	Vertical/ Specialized (Vortal)	Sailnet	Offers services and products to specialized marketplace	Advertising, subscription fees, transaction fees
	Search	Google Bing Ask	Focuses primarily on offering search services	Advertising, affiliate referral
Transaction Broker		E*Trade Expedia Monster Travelocity Orbitz	Processors of online sales transactions, such as stockbrokers and travel agents, that increase customers' productivity by helping them get things done faster and more cheaply	Transaction fees
Market Creator		eBay Etsy Amazon Priceline	Businesses that use Internet technology to create markets that bring buyers and sellers together	Transaction fees
Service Provider		VisaNow Wave RocketLawyer	Companies that make money by selling users a service, rather than a product	Sales of services

to drive to the mall or store (Bellman, Lohse, and Johnson, 1999). The e-tail revenue model is product-based, with customers paying for the purchase of a particular item.

This sector, however, is extremely competitive. Because **barriers to entry** (the total cost of entering a new marketplace) into the e-tail market are low, tens of thousands of small e-tail shops have sprung up. Becoming profitable and surviving is very difficult, however, for e-tailers with no prior brand name or experience. The e-tailer's challenge is differentiating its business from existing competitors.

Companies that try to reach every online consumer are likely to deplete their resources quickly. Those that develop a niche strategy, clearly identifying their target market and its needs, are best prepared to make a profit. Keeping expenses low, selection broad, and inventory controlled is key to success in e-tailing, with inventory being the most difficult to gauge. Online retail is covered in more depth in Chapter 11.

COMMUNITY PROVIDER

Although community providers are not a new phenomenon, the Internet has made such sites for like-minded individuals to meet and converse much easier, without the limitations of geography and time to hinder participation. **Community providers** create an online environment where people with similar interests can transact (buy and sell goods); share interests, photos, videos; communicate with like-minded people; receive interest-related information; and even play out fantasies by adopting online personalities called avatars. Facebook, LinkedIn, Twitter, and Pinterest, and hundreds of other smaller, niche social networks all offer users community-building tools and services.

The basic value proposition of community providers is to create a fast, convenient, one-stop site where users can focus on their most important concerns and interests, share the experience with friends, and learn more about their own interests. Community providers typically rely on a hybrid revenue model that includes subscription fees, sales revenues, transaction fees, affiliate fees, and advertising fees from other firms that are attracted by a tightly focused audience.

Community providers make money from advertising and through affiliate relationships with retailers. Some of the oldest online communities are The Well, which provides a forum for technology and Internet-related discussions, and The Motley Fool, which provides financial advice, news, and opinions. The Well offers various membership plans ranging from $10 to $15 a month. Motley Fool supports itself through ads and selling products that start out "free" but turn into annual subscriptions.

Consumers' interest in communities is mushrooming. Community is, arguably, the fastest growing online activity. While many community providers have had a difficult time becoming profitable, many have succeeded over time, with advertising as their main source of revenue. Both the very large social networks such as Facebook, Twitter, and LinkedIn, as well as niche social networks with smaller dedicated audiences, are ideal marketing and advertising territories. Traditional online communities such as The Motley Fool and WebMD (which provides medical information to members) find that the breadth and depth of knowledge offered is an important factor. Community

barriers to entry
the total cost of entering a new marketplace

community provider
creates an online environment where people with similar interests can transact (buy and sell goods); share interests, photos, and videos; communicate with like-minded people; and receive interest-related information

members frequently request knowledge, guidance, and advice. Lack of experienced personnel can severely hamper the growth of a community, which needs facilitators and managers to keep discussions on course and relevant. For the newer community social networks, the most important ingredients of success appear to be ease and flexibility of use, and a strong customer value proposition. For instance, Facebook leapfrogged over its rival MySpace by encouraging the development of third-party revenue-producing applications.

Online communities benefit significantly from offline word-of-mouth, viral marketing. Online communities tend to reflect offline relationships. When your friends say they have a profile on Facebook and ask you to "friend" them, you are encouraged to build your own online profile.

CONTENT PROVIDER

Content providers distribute information content, such as digital video, music, photos, text, and artwork. Content providers can make money via a variety of different revenue models, including advertising, subscription fees, and sales of digital goods. For instance, in the case of Spotify, a monthly subscription fee provides users with access to millions of music tracks. Other content providers, such as the *Financial Times* online newspaper, *Harvard Business Review*, and many others, charge customers for content downloads in addition to, or in place of, a subscription fee.

content provider
distributes information content, such as digital news, music, photos, video, and artwork

Of course, not all online content providers charge for their information: just look at the websites or mobile apps for the BBC, Football365, and Silicon.co.uk, and the online versions of many newspapers and magazines. Users can access news and information without paying a cent, although sometimes they may be required to register as a member. These popular online content providers make money in other ways, such as through advertising and partner promotions. Increasingly, however, "free content" may be limited to headlines and text, whereas premium content—in-depth articles or videos—is sold for a fee.

Generally, the key to becoming a successful content provider is owning the content. Traditional owners of copyrighted content—publishers of books and newspapers, broadcasters of radio and television content, music publishers, and movie studios—have powerful advantages over newcomers who simply offer distribution channels and must pay for content, often at very high prices.

Some content providers, however, do not own content, but syndicate (aggregate) and then distribute content produced by others. *Syndication* is a major variation of the standard content provider model. Aggregators, who collect information from a wide variety of sources and then add value to that information through post-aggregation services, are another variation. For instance, Shopzilla collects information on the prices of thousands of goods online, analyzes the information, and presents users with tables showing the range of prices and links to the sites where the products can be purchased. Shopzilla adds value to content it aggregates, and resells this value to advertisers.

Any e-commerce start-up that intends to make money by providing content is likely to face difficulties unless it has a unique information source that others cannot access. For the most part, this business category is dominated by traditional content providers. The *Insight on Technology* case, *Will the Connected Car Become the Next Hot Entertainment Vehicle?*, discusses how changes in Internet technology are driving the development of new business models in the online content market.

Online content is discussed in further depth in Chapter 9.

PORTAL

portal

offers users powerful search tools as well as an integrated package of content and services all in one place

Portals such as Yahoo, MSN, and AOL offer users powerful search tools as well as an integrated package of content and services, such as news, e-mail, instant messaging, calendars, shopping, music downloads, video streaming, and more, all in one place. Initially, portals sought to be viewed as "gateways" to the Internet. Today, however, the portal business model is to be a destination. They are marketed as places where consumers will hopefully stay a long time to read news, find entertainment, and meet other people (think of destination resorts). Portals do not sell anything directly—or so it seems—and in that sense they can present themselves as unbiased. Portals generate revenue primarily by charging advertisers for ad placement, collecting referral fees for steering customers to other sites, and charging for premium services.

Although there are numerous portals/search engines, the top five (Google, Microsoft's Bing, Yahoo, Ask, and AOL) in the United States gather more than 95% of U.S. search engine traffic because of their superior brand recognition. Many of the top portal/search engines were among the first to appear on the Web and therefore had first-mover advantages. Being first confers an advantage because customers come to trust a reliable provider and experience switching costs if they change to late arrivals in the market. By garnering a large chunk of the marketplace, first movers—just like a single telephone network—can offer customers access to commonly shared ideas, standards, and experiences (something called *network externalities,* which we describe in later chapters).

The traditional portals have company: Facebook and other social networks are now the initial start or home page (portal) for millions of Internet users.

Yahoo, AOL, and others like them are considered to be horizontal portals because they define their marketspace to include all users of the Internet. Vertical portals (sometimes called vortals) attempt to provide similar services as horizontal portals, but are focused around a particular subject matter or market segment. For instance, Sailnet focuses on the world's sailing community, and provides sailing news, articles, discussion groups, free e-mail, and a retail store. Although the total number of vortal users may be much lower than the number of portal users, if the market segment is attractive enough, advertisers are willing to pay a premium in order to reach a targeted audience. Also, visitors to specialized niche vortals spend more money than the average Yahoo visitor. Google and Ask can also be considered portals of a sort, but focus primarily on offering search and advertising services. They generate revenues primarily from search engine advertising sales and also from affiliate referral fees.

INSIGHT ON TECHNOLOGY

WILL THE CONNECTED CAR BECOME THE NEXT HOT ENTERTAINMENT VEHICLE?

You're in the driver's seat of your car, commuting to work. But instead of keeping your eyes on the road, you're watching a Netflix movie, logging on to Facebook, and checking your e-mail. And no, you are not an accident waiting to happen.

This scenario is one that is likely to become commonplace in the not too distant future. In 2016, we are on the cusp of yet another revolution in the way we live our lives, this time driven by technology known as the Internet of Things (IoT). IoT refers to the use of sensors connected to the Internet and cloud computers, coupled with powerful data analytics programs, to track things and make sense out of their behavior (you'll learn more about IoT in Chapter 3). The technology behind IoT already exists, and now businesses are working on using it to develop products and services that consumers and businesses are willing to pay for.

From a business perspective, IoT is not just a collection of technologies, but an enabler for services that can be sold to other businesses and consumers. For businesses, IoT may mean more effective and efficient maintenance, remote monitoring of equipment, tracking assets in the supply chain, and identifying patterns of behavior of machines and operators. These services translate into cost reduction, and greater profits for firms that truly understand IoT. For consumers, IoT means self-driving smart cars, intelligent media systems, smart homes, personal health monitoring, and retail and e-commerce automation.

Gartner estimates that 6.4 billion connected things are in use worldwide in 2016, 5.5 million new things are added every day, and over 20 billion will be connected by 2020. McKinsey estimates

that IoT will produce from $4 to $11 trillion in value by 2025, with 70% of this value occurring in B2B commerce, and the rest in B2C commerce. For suppliers of IoT hardware, software, and telecommunications, it's a bonanza of potential sales revenue. Along the way, IoT is going to transform business processes and enable a host of new business models in a variety of different industries.

One arena that IoT is expected to have a significant impact on is the content industry, especially when coupled with its increasing use in the automobile industry to create connected, and ultimately, self-driving cars that will free drivers from having to focus on the road. Today, your car is still probably one of the least connected devices in your digital life, but that is rapidly changing, in part due to consumer demand. A recent survey found that almost two-thirds of U.S. car owners with broadband Internet access in their homes wanted similar access in their cars. A connected car is equipped with hundreds of sensors and has direct access to the Internet, as well as links to hundreds of other connected objects. Tiny sensors will be able to report on your route and destination, the state of your tires, air conditioning, what music you are listening to, and in the future, perhaps even your state of mind, using sentiment sensors that can pick up anger, tears, crying, and laughing.

The number of connected cars on the road is rapidly increasing. According to one industry analysis, more than 40 million cars in the United States were already connected to the Internet by the beginning of 2016. Telecommunications companies are, not surprisingly, very interested in connected cars as platforms for their services and are facilitating their development. AT&T, for example, introduced an expanded connected car platform in

(continued)

2016, which allows unlimited plan smartphone customers to add their car to the service for $40 a month, or $10 a month for 1 gigabyte of data. In 2016, AT&T also signed an agreement with Ford to connect 10 million Ford cars using Ford's new SYNC Connect system. AT&T is also working with a number of other auto companies to install wireless access devices in cars. Aside from selling its wireless network to consumers, AT&T is planning to sell data collected from cars and drivers that will allow ads to be targeted, based on car model, locations, and even the kind of music listened to.

For content distributors, IoT offers a whole new venue. Connected cars provide a potentially huge market for media companies. People (drivers and passengers) spend about 500 hours in a vehicle per year, including 42 hours in traffic. This captive audience is an ideal target for both marketers and media companies. Today, although we primarily think of cars as transportation, they are also entertainment and media centers. For instance, cars are already the main source of radio revenues in the United States, with more than half of all radio consumption taking place in a car. But using online radio services in today's cars is most often a painful process that often fails to work properly. Both carmakers and content providers have been hard at work fixing this problem.. Pandora Media, seeking to build on its existing dominance in the online radio market, has entered into agreements with 24 auto brands to embed its music service into over 160 car models. Spotify,

Apple's CarPlay, and Google's Android Auto also have new services for connected cars. Cars will eventually become like a mobile living room, with video services that deliver ads along with movies and TV shows (currently, for the rear seats only, but moving to the front seats in a self-driving car). As cars become more and more automated and drivers are able to shift from driving to watching video content, consulting firm EY estimates that video industry revenue may increase by more than $20 billion. Connected cars are also likely to feature enhanced dashboard interfaces that will enable easy access to email, music streaming, and social networks.

In addition to changing the type of content available in automobiles, IoT is also expected to have the ability to deliver much more personalized content. IoT sensors will make it possible for sensors to recognize individual consumers and offer suggested content on the basis of their past behavior and preferences. Advertisers are already imagining ways to use the shape of a car to create immersive, 360-degree ad experiences. To that end, Ford patented a driverless car windshield entertainment system that could be the basis for this type of advertising as well as consuming traditional video content. Other forms of personalization could include the ability to find the nearest available parking place, locating nearby favorite restaurants or other attractions, and the ability to take your "driving profile" with you from car to car, including preferences and tendencies.

SOURCES: "5 Reasons the Music Industry Should Care About Driverless Cars," by Cherie Hu, Hypebot.com, October 26, 2016; "Detroit's Music Chops and Auto Shops Could Drive Connected-Car Entertainment," by Scott Keeney, Techcrunch.com, August 30, 2016; "The Internet of Things Is Here, and It Isn't a Thing," by Christopher Mims, *Wall Street Journal*, August 21, 2016; "DASH Podcast Episode 7: Audio Entertainment in Self-Driving Cars (Andreas Mai)," by Seth Resler, Jacobsmedia.com, August 17, 2016; "Will IoT Totally Reshape How, When, and Where We Get Content," By Chris Gianutsos, Readwrite.com, July 8, 2016; "Verizon Acquisition of Telogis Expands Company's Connected Car Footprint," by Doug Newcomb, Forbes.com, June 30, 2016; "Media and Entertainment Meet the Internet of Things," by Chase Martin, Mediapost.com, June 22, 2016; "The Connected Car Report: Forecasts, Competing Technologies, and Leading Manufacturers," by John Greenough, BusinessInsider.com, June 10, 2016; "The Internet of Things," by Victoria Petrock, eMarketer, Inc., May 2016; "AT&T Just Took a Big Step to Maintain Its Lead in Wireless Service for Connected Cars," by Andrew Meola, Businessinsider.com, May 23, 2016; "How Ford Is Building the Connected Car," by Steven Norton, *Wall Street Journal*, February 21, 2016; "The Internet of Media and Entertainment Things," by Victoria Petrock, eMarketer, Inc., February 2016; "The Internet of Automotive Things," by Victoria Petrock, eMarketer, Inc., February 2016; "The Top Five Trends for the Connected Car in 2016," by Mahbubul Alam, Techcrunch.com, January 2, 2016 "AT&T and the Connected Car Making Cars Smarter and Safer," Business.att.com, 2016; "State of the Market: Internet of Things 2016," by Verizon, 2016; "Gartner Says 6.4 Billion Connected "Things" Will Be in Use in 2016, Up 30 Percent from 2015," Gartner.com, November 10, 2015; "The Internet of Things: Mapping the Value Beyond the Hype," McKinsey & Company, June 2015.

TRANSACTION BROKER

Companies that process transactions for consumers normally handled in person, by phone, or by mail are **transaction brokers**. The largest industries using this model are financial services, travel services, and job placement services. The online transaction broker's primary value propositions are savings of money and time. In addition, most transaction brokers provide timely information and opinions. Companies such as Monster offer job searchers a national marketplace for their talents and employers a national resource for that talent. Both employers and job seekers are attracted by the convenience and currency of information. Online stock brokers charge commissions that are considerably less than traditional brokers, with many offering substantial deals, such as cash and a certain number of free trades, to lure new customers.

Given rising consumer interest in financial planning and the stock market, the market opportunity for online transaction brokers appears to be large. However, while millions of customers have shifted to online brokers, some are still wary about switching from their traditional broker who provides personal advice and a brand name. Fears of privacy invasion and the loss of control over personal financial information also contribute to market resistance. Consequently, the challenge for online brokers is to overcome consumer fears by emphasizing the security and privacy measures in place, and, like physical banks and brokerage firms, providing a broad range of financial services and not just stock trading. This industry is covered in greater depth in Chapter 11.

Transaction brokers make money each time a transaction occurs. Each stock trade, for example, nets the company a fee, based on either a flat rate or a sliding scale related to the size of the transaction. Attracting new customers and encouraging them to trade frequently are the keys to generating more revenue for these companies. Travel sites generate commissions from travel bookings and job sites generate listing fees from employers up front, rather than charging a fee when a position is filled.

transaction broker
processes transactions for consumers that are normally handled in person, by phone, or by mail

MARKET CREATOR

Market creators build a digital environment in which buyers and sellers can meet, display and search for products and services, and establish prices. Prior to the Internet and the Web, market creators relied on physical places to establish a market. Beginning with the medieval marketplace and extending to today's New York Stock Exchange, a market has meant a physical space for transacting business. There were few private digital network marketplaces prior to the Web. The Web changed this by making it possible to separate markets from physical space. Prime examples are Priceline, which allows consumers to set the price they are willing to pay for various travel accommodations and other products (sometimes referred to as a reverse auction), and eBay, the online auction site utilized by both businesses and consumers. Market creators make money by either charging a percentage of every transaction made, or charging merchants for access to the market.

For example, eBay's auction business model is to create a digital environment for buyers and sellers to meet, agree on a price, and transact. This is different from transaction brokers who actually carry out the transaction for their customers, acting as agents in larger markets. At eBay, the buyers and sellers are their own agents. Each

market creator
builds a digital environment where buyers and sellers can meet, display products, search for products, and establish a price for products

sale on eBay nets the company a commission based on the percentage of the item's sales price, in addition to a listing fee. eBay is one of the few e-commerce companies that has been profitable virtually from the beginning. Why? One answer is that eBay has no inventory or production costs. It is simply a middleman.

The market opportunity for market creators is potentially vast, but only if the firm has the financial resources and marketing plan to attract sufficient sellers and buyers to the marketplace. As of June 30, 2016, eBay had more than 164 million active buyers, and this makes for an efficient market (eBay Inc., 2016). There are many sellers and buyers for each type of product, sometimes for the same product, for example, laptop computer models. Many other digital auctions have sprung up in smaller, more specialized vertical market segments such as jewelry and automobiles.

Uber, Airbnb, and Lyft are another example of the market creator business model (although they could also be categorized as service providers). On-demand service companies (also sometimes called sharing economy companies) are market creators that have developed online platforms that allow people to sell services, such as transportation or spare rooms, in a marketplace that operates in the cloud and relies on the Web or smartphone apps to conduct transactions. It is important to note that, although referred to as sharing economy or mesh economy companies, these companies do not in fact share resources. Users of these services are either selling something or buying something, and the companies produce revenue by extracting fees for each transaction. However, they do unlock the economic value in spare resources (personal cars and rooms) that might otherwise have been lost. In the process they have created huge online markets. For instance, Uber (founded in 2009) currently operates in over 480 cities in 69 countries around the world. Airbnb, founded in 2008, operates in more than 190 countries and 34,000 cities, lists over 2 million rooms available for rent, and has had over 60 million people use its services to book a room. Airbnb has raised around $2.4 billion in funding thus far and is valued at $30 billion; Uber has raised over $12.5 billion and is valued at around $68 billion.

SERVICE PROVIDER

service provider
offers services online

While e-tailers sell products online, **service providers** offer services online. There's been an explosion in online services that is often unrecognized. Photo sharing, video sharing, and user-generated content (in blogs and social networks) are all services provided to customers. Google has led the way in developing online applications such as Google Maps, Google Docs, and Gmail. Other personal services such as online medical bill management, financial and pension planning, and travel recommendation are showing strong growth.

Service providers use a variety of revenue models. Some charge a fee, or monthly subscriptions, while others generate revenue from other sources, such as through advertising and by collecting personal information that is useful in direct marketing. Many service providers employ a freemium revenue model, in which some basic services are free, but others require the payment of additional charges. Much like retailers who trade products for cash, service providers trade knowledge, expertise, and capabilities for revenue.

Obviously, some services cannot be provided online. For example, dentistry, plumbing, and car repair cannot be completed via the Internet. However, online arrangements can be made for these services. Online service providers may offer computer services, such as data storage (Dropbox and Carbonite), provide legal services (RocketLawyer), or accounting or bookkeeping services (Wave, Bench). Grocery shopping sites such as FreshDirect and Peapod are also providing services.[1] To complicate matters a bit, most financial transaction brokers (described previously) provide services such as college tuition and pension planning. Travel brokers also provide vacation-planning services, not just transactions with airlines and hotels. Indeed, mixing services with your products is a powerful business strategy pursued by many hard-goods companies (for example, warranties are services).

The basic value proposition of service providers is that they offer consumers valuable, convenient, time-saving, and low-cost alternatives to traditional service providers or provide services that are truly unique. Where else can you search billions of web pages, or share photos with as many people instantly? Research has found, for instance, that a major factor in predicting online buying behavior is *time starvation*. Time-starved people tend to be busy professionals who work long hours and simply do not have the time to pick up packages, buy groceries, send photos, or visit with financial planners (Bellman, Lohse, and Johnson, 1999). The market opportunity for service providers is as large as the variety of services that can be provided and potentially is much larger than the market opportunity for physical goods. We live in a service-based economy and society; witness the growth of fast-food restaurants, package delivery services, and wireless cellular phone services. Consumers' increasing demand for convenience products and services bodes well for current and future online service providers.

Marketing of service providers must allay consumer fears about hiring a vendor online, as well as build confidence and familiarity among current and potential customers. Building confidence and trust is critical for service providers just as it is for retail product merchants.

5.3 MAJOR BUSINESS-TO-BUSINESS (B2B) BUSINESS MODELS

In Chapter 1, we noted that business-to-business (B2B) e-commerce, in which businesses sell to other businesses, is more than 10 times the size of B2C e-commerce, even though most of the public attention has focused on B2C. For instance, it is estimated that revenues for all types of B2B e-commerce worldwide will total around €19.8 trillion in 2016, compared to about €2.35 trillion for retail and travel-related B2C e-commerce. Clearly, most of the revenues in e-commerce involve B2B e-commerce.

---

[1] FreshDirect and other e-commerce businesses can also be classified as online retailers insofar as they warehouse commonly purchased items and make a profit based on the spread between their buy and sell prices.

TABLE 5.7	B2B BUSINESS MODELS		
BUSINESS MODEL	EXAMPLES	DESCRIPTION	REVENUE MODEL
(1) NET MARKETPLACE			
E-distributor	Grainger Amazon Business	Single-firm online version of retail and wholesale store; supply maintenance, repair, operation goods; indirect inputs	Sales of goods
E-procurement	Ariba Supplier Network PerfectCommerce	Single firm creating digital markets where sellers and buyers transact for indirect inputs	Fees for market-making services, supply chain management, and fulfillment services
Exchange	Go2Paper	Independently owned vertical digital marketplace for direct inputs	Fees and commissions on transactions
Industry Consortium	TheSeam SupplyOn	Industry-owned vertical digital market open to select suppliers	Fees and commissions on transactions
(2) PRIVATE INDUSTRIAL NETWORK			
	Walmart Procter & Gamble	Company-owned network that coordinates supply chains with a limited set of partners	Cost absorbed by network owner and recovered through production and distribution efficiencies

Much of this activity is unseen and unknown to the average consumer. **Table 5.7** lists the major business models utilized in the B2B arena.

E-DISTRIBUTOR

Companies that supply products and services directly to individual businesses are **e-distributors**. W.W. Grainger, for example, is the largest distributor of maintenance, repair, and operations (MRO) supplies. In the past, Grainger relied on catalog sales and physical distribution centers in metropolitan areas. Its catalog of equipment went online in 1995. In 2015, Grainger's e-commerce platform, which includes websites and mobile apps, produced $3.3 billion in sales (41% of its total revenue) for the company.

E-distributors are owned by one company seeking to serve many customers. However, as with exchanges (described on the next page), critical mass is a factor. With e-distributors, the more products and services a company makes available, the more attractive it is to potential customers. One-stop shopping is always preferable to having to visit numerous sites to locate a particular part or product.

e-distributor
a company that supplies products and services directly to individual businesses

E-PROCUREMENT

Just as e-distributors provide products to other companies, **e-procurement firms** create and sell access to digital markets. Firms such as Ariba, for instance, have created software that helps large firms organize their procurement process by creating mini-digital markets for a single firm. Ariba creates custom-integrated online catalogs

e-procurement firm
creates and sells access to digital markets

(where supplier firms can list their offerings) for purchasing firms. On the sell side, Ariba helps vendors sell to large purchasers by providing software to handle catalog creation, shipping, insurance, and finance. Both the buy and sell side software is referred to generically as "value chain management" software.

B2B service providers make money through transaction fees, fees based on the number of workstations using the service, or annual licensing fees. They offer purchasing firms a sophisticated set of sourcing and supply chain management tools that permit firms to reduce supply chain costs. In the software world, firms such as Ariba are sometimes also called Software as a Service (SaaS) or Platform as a Service (PaaS) providers; they are able to offer firms much lower costs of software by achieving scale economies. **Scale economies** are efficiencies that result from increasing the size of a business, for instance, when large, fixed-cost production systems (such as factories or software systems) can be operated at full capacity with no idle time. In the case of software, the marginal cost of a digital copy of a software program is nearly zero, and finding additional buyers for an expensive software program is exceptionally profitable. This is much more efficient than having every firm build its own supply chain management system, and it permits firms such as Ariba to specialize and offer their software to firms at a cost far less than the cost of developing it.

B2B service provider
sells business services to other firms

scale economies
efficiencies that arise from increasing the size of a business

EXCHANGES

Exchanges have garnered most of the B2B attention and early funding because of their potential market size even though today they are a small part of the overall B2B picture. An **exchange** is an independent digital marketplace where hundreds of suppliers meet a smaller number of very large commercial purchasers (Kaplan and Sawhney, 2000). Exchanges are owned by independent, usually entrepreneurial start-up firms whose business is making a market, and they generate revenue by charging a commission or fee based on the size of the transactions conducted among trading parties. They usually serve a single vertical industry such as steel, polymers, or aluminum, and focus on the exchange of direct inputs to production and short-term contracts or spot purchasing. For buyers, B2B exchanges make it possible to gather information, check out suppliers, collect prices, and keep up to date on the latest happenings all in one place. Sellers, on the other hand, benefit from expanded access to buyers. The greater the number of sellers and buyers, the lower the sales cost and the higher the chances of making a sale. The ease, speed, and volume of transactions are summarily referred to as *market liquidity*.

exchange
an independent digital marketplace where suppliers and commercial purchasers can conduct transactions

In theory, exchanges make it significantly less expensive and time-consuming to identify potential suppliers, customers, and partners, and to do business with each other. As a result, they can lower transaction costs—the cost of making a sale or purchase. Exchanges can also lower product costs and inventory-carrying costs—the cost of keeping a product on hand in a warehouse. In reality, as will be discussed in Chapter 12, B2B exchanges have had a difficult time convincing thousands of suppliers to move into singular digital markets where they face powerful price competition, and an equally difficult time convincing businesses to change their purchasing behavior away from trusted long-term trading partners. As a result, the number of exchanges has fallen significantly.

INDUSTRY CONSORTIA

industry consortia
industry-owned vertical marketplaces that serve specific industries

Industry consortia are industry-owned *vertical marketplaces* that serve specific industries, such as the automobile, aerospace, chemical, floral, or logging industries. In contrast, *horizontal marketplaces* sell specific products and services to a wide range of companies. Vertical marketplaces supply a smaller number of companies with products and services of specific interest to their industry, while horizontal marketplaces supply companies in different industries with a particular type of product and service, such as marketing-related, financial, or computing services. For example, SupplyOn, founded in 2000 and owned by industrial giants Bosch (one of the world's largest suppliers of automotive components), Continental (a leading automotive manufacturing company), and Schaeffler (a global manufacturer of various types of bearings), among others, provides a shared supply chain collaboration platform for companies in various manufacturing industries. In 2016, in addition to its shareholders, its customers include Airbus, BMW, BorgWarner, Siemens, Thales, and many other major global manufacturing companies.

Industry consortia have tended to be more successful than independent exchanges in part because they are sponsored by powerful, deep-pocketed industry players, and also because they strengthen traditional purchasing behavior rather than seek to transform it.

PRIVATE INDUSTRIAL NETWORKS

private industrial network
digital network designed to coordinate the flow of communications among firms engaged in business together

A **private industrial network** (sometimes referred to as a private trading exchange or PTX) is a digital network designed to coordinate the flow of communications among firms engaged in business together. The network is owned by a single large purchasing firm. Participation is by invitation only to trusted long-term suppliers of direct inputs. These networks typically evolve out of a firm's own enterprise resource planning (ERP) system, and are an effort to include key suppliers in the firm's own business decision making. For instance, Walmart operates one of the largest private industrial networks in the world for its suppliers, who on a daily basis use Walmart's network to monitor the sales of their goods, the status of shipments, and the actual inventory level of their goods.

We discuss the nuances of B2B e-commerce in more detail in Chapter 12.

5.4 HOW E-COMMERCE CHANGES BUSINESS: STRATEGY, STRUCTURE, AND PROCESS

Now that you have a clear grasp of the variety of business models used by e-commerce firms, you also need to understand how e-commerce has changed the business environment in the last decade, including industry structures, business strategies, and industry and firm operations (business processes and value chains). We return to these concepts throughout the book as we explore the e-commerce phenomenon. In general, the Internet is an open standards system available to all players, and this fact inherently makes it easy for new competitors to enter the marketplace and offer substitute

TABLE 5.8	EIGHT UNIQUE FEATURES OF E-COMMERCE TECHNOLOGY
FEATURE	SELECTED IMPACTS ON BUSINESS ENVIRONMENT
Ubiquity	Alters industry structure by creating new marketing channels and expanding size of overall market. Creates new efficiencies in industry operations and lowers costs of firms' sales operations. Enables new differentiation strategies.
Global reach	Changes industry structure by lowering barriers to entry, but greatly expands market at the same time. Lowers cost of industry and firm operations through production and sales efficiencies. Enables competition on a global scale.
Universal standards	Changes industry structure by lowering barriers to entry and intensifying competition within an industry. Lowers costs of industry and firm operations by lowering computing and communications costs. Enables broad scope strategies.
Richness	Alters industry structure by reducing strength of powerful distribution channels. Changes industry and firm operations costs by reducing reliance on sales forces. Enhances post-sales support strategies.
Interactivity	Alters industry structure by reducing threat of substitutes through enhanced customization. Reduces industry and firm costs by reducing reliance on sales forces. Enables differentiation strategies.
Personalization/ Customization	Alters industry structure by reducing threats of substitutes, raising barriers to entry. Reduces value chain costs in industry and firms by lessening reliance on sales forces. Enables personalized marketing strategies.
Information density	Changes industry structure by weakening powerful sales channels, shifting bargaining power to consumers. Reduces industry and firm operations costs by lowering costs of obtaining, processing, and distributing information about suppliers and consumers.
Social technologies	Changes industry structure by shifting programming and editorial decisions to consumers. Creates substitute entertainment products. Energizes a large group of new suppliers.

products or channels of delivery. The Internet tends to intensify competition. Because information becomes available to everyone, the Internet inherently shifts power to buyers who can quickly discover the lowest-cost provider. On the other hand, the Internet presents many new opportunities for creating value, for branding products and charging premium prices, and for enlarging an already powerful offline physical business such as Walmart or Sears.

Recall Table 1.2 in Chapter 1 that describes the truly unique features of e-commerce technology. **Table 5.8** suggests some of the implications of each unique feature for the overall business environment—industry structure, business strategies, and operations.

INDUSTRY STRUCTURE

industry structure

refers to the nature of the players in an industry and their relative bargaining power

E-commerce changes industry structure, in some industries more than others. **Industry structure** refers to the nature of the players in an industry and their relative bargaining power. An industry's structure is characterized by five forces: *rivalry among existing competitors*, the *threat of substitute products, barriers to entry into the industry*, the *bargaining power of suppliers*, and the *bargaining power of buyers* (Porter, 1985). When you describe an industry's structure, you are describing the general business environment in an industry and the overall profitability of doing business in that environment. E-commerce has the potential to change the relative strength of these competitive forces (see **Figure 5.3**).

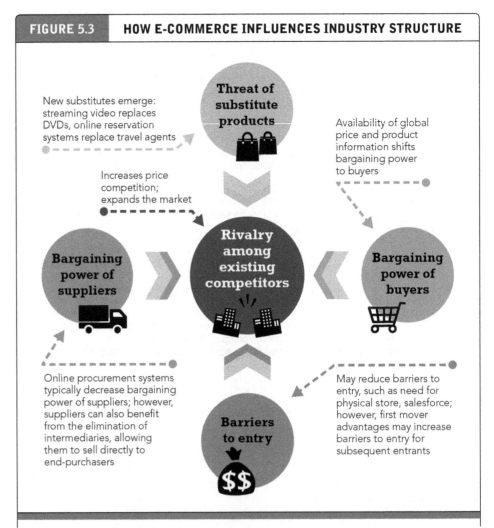

FIGURE 5.3 **HOW E-COMMERCE INFLUENCES INDUSTRY STRUCTURE**

New substitutes emerge: streaming video replaces DVDs, online reservation systems replace travel agents

Threat of substitute products

Availability of global price and product information shifts bargaining power to buyers

Increases price competition; expands the market

Bargaining power of suppliers

Rivalry among existing competitors

Bargaining power of buyers

Online procurement systems typically decrease bargaining power of suppliers; however, suppliers can also benefit from the elimination of intermediaries, allowing them to sell directly to end-purchasers

Barriers to entry

May reduce barriers to entry, such as need for physical store, salesforce; however, first mover advantages may increase barriers to entry for subsequent entrants

E-commerce has many impacts on industry structure and competitive conditions. From the perspective of a single firm, these changes can have negative or positive implications depending on the situation. In some cases, an entire industry can be disrupted, while at the same time, a new industry is born. Individual firms can either prosper or be devastated.

When you consider a business model and its potential long-term profitability, you should always perform an industry structural analysis. An **industry structural analysis** is an effort to understand and describe the nature of competition in an industry, the nature of substitute products, the barriers to entry, and the relative strength of consumers and suppliers.

E-commerce can affect the structure and dynamics of industries in very different ways. Consider the recorded music industry, an industry that has experienced significant change because of e-commerce. Historically, the major record companies owned the exclusive rights to the recorded music of various artists. With the entrance into the marketplace of substitute providers such as Napster and Kazaa, millions of consumers began to use the Internet to bypass traditional music labels and their distributors entirely. In the travel industry, entirely new middlemen such as Travelocity entered the market to compete with traditional travel agents. After Travelocity, Expedia, CheapTickets, and other travel services demonstrated the power of e-commerce marketing for airline tickets, the actual owners of the airline seats—the major airlines—banded together to form their own Internet outlet for tickets, Orbitz, for direct sales to consumers (although ultimately selling the company to a private investor group). Clearly, e-commerce creates *new industry dynamics* that can best be described as the give and take of the marketplace, the changing fortunes of competitors.

Yet, in other industries, e-commerce has strengthened existing players. In the chemical and automobile industries, e-commerce is being used effectively by manufacturers to strengthen their traditional distributors. In these industries, e-commerce technology has not fundamentally altered the competitive forces—bargaining power of suppliers, barriers to entry, bargaining power of buyers, threat of substitutes, or rivalry among competitors—within the industry. Hence, each industry is different and you need to examine each one carefully to understand the impacts of e-commerce on competition and strategy.

New forms of distribution created by new market entrants can completely change the competitive forces in an industry. For instance, consumers gladly substituted free access to Wikipedia for a $699 set of World Book encyclopedias, or a $40 DVD, radically changing the competitive forces in the encyclopedia industry. As we describe in Chapter 10, the content industries of newspapers, books, movies, games, and television have been transformed by the emergence of new distribution platforms.

Inter-firm rivalry (competition) is one area of the business environment where e-commerce technologies have had an impact on most industries. In general, e-commerce has increased price competition in nearly all markets. It has been relatively easy for existing firms to adopt e-commerce technology and attempt to use it to achieve competitive advantage vis-à-vis rivals. For instance, e-commerce inherently changes the scope of competition from local and regional to national and global. Because consumers have access to global price information, e-commerce produces pressures on firms to compete by lowering prices (and lowering profits). On the other hand, e-commerce has made it possible for some firms to differentiate their products or services from others. Amazon patented one-click purchasing, for instance, while eBay created a unique, easy-to-use interface and a differentiating brand name. Therefore, although e-commerce has increased emphasis on price competition, it has also enabled businesses to create new strategies for differentiation and branding so that they can retain higher prices.

industry structural analysis
an effort to understand and describe the nature of competition in an industry, the nature of substitute products, the barriers to entry, and the relative strength of consumers and suppliers

It is impossible to determine if e-commerce technologies have had an overall positive or negative impact on firm profitability in general. Each industry is unique, so it is necessary to perform a separate analysis for each one. Clearly, e-commerce has shaken the foundations of some industries, in particular, content industries (such as the music, newspaper, book, and software industries) as well as other information-intense industries such as financial services. In these industries, the power of consumers has grown relative to providers, prices have fallen, and overall profitability has been challenged. In other industries, especially manufacturing, e-commerce has not greatly changed relationships with buyers, but has changed relationships with suppliers. Increasingly, manufacturing firms in entire industries have banded together to aggregate purchases, create industry exchanges or marketplaces, and outsource industrial processes in order to obtain better prices from suppliers. Throughout this book, we document these changes in industry structure and market dynamics introduced by e-commerce.

INDUSTRY VALUE CHAINS

value chain

the set of activities performed in an industry or in a firm that transforms raw inputs into final products and services

While an industry structural analysis helps you understand the impact of e-commerce technology on the overall business environment in an industry, a more detailed industry value chain analysis can help identify more precisely just how e-commerce may change business operations at the industry level. One of the basic tools for understanding the impact of information technology on industry and firm operations is the value chain. The concept is quite simple. A **value chain** is the set of activities performed in an industry or in a firm that transforms raw inputs into final products and services. Each of these activities adds economic value to the final product; hence, the term *value chain* as an interconnected set of value-adding activities. **Figure 5.4** illustrates the six generic players in an industry value chain: suppliers, manufacturers, transporters, distributors, retailers, and customers.

| FIGURE 5.4 | **E-COMMERCE AND INDUSTRY VALUE CHAINS** |

Every industry can be characterized by a set of value-adding activities performed by a variety of actors. E-commerce potentially affects the capabilities of each player as well as the overall operational efficiency of the industry.

By reducing the cost of information, e-commerce offers each of the key players in an industry value chain new opportunities to maximize their positions by lowering costs and/or raising prices. For instance, manufacturers can reduce the costs they pay for goods by developing Internet-based B2B exchanges with their suppliers. Manufacturers can develop direct relationships with their customers, bypassing the costs of distributors and retailers. Distributors can develop highly efficient inventory management systems to reduce their costs, and retailers can develop highly efficient customer relationship management systems to strengthen their service to customers. Customers in turn can search for the best quality, fastest delivery, and lowest prices, thereby lowering their transaction costs and reducing prices they pay for final goods. Finally, the operational efficiency of the entire industry can increase, lowering prices and adding value for consumers, and helping the industry to compete with alternative industries.

FIRM VALUE CHAINS

The concept of value chain can be used to analyze a single firm's operational efficiency as well. The question here is: How does e-commerce technology potentially affect the value chains of firms within an industry? A **firm value chain** is the set of activities a firm engages in to create final products from raw inputs. Each step in the process of production adds value to the final product. In addition, firms develop support activities that coordinate the production process and contribute to overall operational efficiency. **Figure 5.5** illustrates the key steps and support activities in a firm's value chain.

firm value chain
the set of activities a firm engages in to create final products from raw inputs

E-commerce offers firms many opportunities to increase their operational efficiency and differentiate their products. For instance, firms can use the Internet's communications efficiency to outsource some primary and secondary activities to specialized, more efficient providers without such outsourcing being visible to the

FIGURE 5.5	E-COMMERCE AND FIRM VALUE CHAINS

Administration
Human Resources
Information Systems
Procurement
Finance/Accounting

SECONDARY ACTIVITIES

PRIMARY ACTIVITIES

Inbound Logistics · Operations · Outbound Logistics · Sales and Marketing · After Sales Service

Every firm can be characterized by a set of value-adding primary and secondary activities performed by a variety of actors in the firm. A simple firm value chain performs five primary value-adding steps: inbound logistics, operations, outbound logistics, sales and marketing, and after sales service.

consumer. In addition, firms can use e-commerce to more precisely coordinate the steps in the value chains and reduce their costs. Finally, firms can use e-commerce to provide users with more differentiated and high-value products. For instance, Amazon provides consumers with a much larger inventory of books to choose from, at a lower cost, than traditional book stores. It also provides many services—such as instantly available professional and consumer reviews, and information on buying patterns of other consumers—that traditional bookstores cannot.

FIRM VALUE WEBS

value web

networked business ecosystem that coordinates the value chains of several firms

While firms produce value through their value chains, they also rely on the value chains of their partners—their suppliers, distributors, and delivery firms. E-commerce creates new opportunities for firms to cooperate and create a value web. A **value web** is a networked business ecosystem that uses e-commerce technology to coordinate the value chains of business partners within an industry, or at the first level, to coordinate the value chains of a group of firms. **Figure 5.6** illustrates a value web.

A value web coordinates a firm's suppliers with its own production needs using an Internet-based supply chain management system. We discuss these B2B systems

| FIGURE 5.6 | INTERNET-ENABLED VALUE WEB |

STRATEGIC ALLIANCE AND PARTNER FIRMS

DIRECT SUPPLIERS

CUSTOMERS

FIRM/INDUSTRY

ERP Systems
Legacy Systems

Supply Chain
Management Systems:
Private Industrial Networks
Net Marketplaces

Customer Relationship
Management (CRM) Systems

INDIRECT SUPPLIERS (MRO)

Internet technology enables firms to create an enhanced value web in cooperation with their strategic alliance and partner firms, customers, and direct and indirect suppliers.

in Chapter 12. Firms also use the Internet to develop close relationships with their logistics partners. For instance, Amazon relies on UPS tracking systems to provide its customers with online package tracking, and it relies on the U.S. Postal Service systems to insert packages directly into the mail stream. Amazon has partnership relations with hundreds of firms to generate customers and to manage relationships with customers. In fact, when you examine Amazon closely, you realize that the value it delivers to customers is in large part the result of coordination with other firms and not simply the result of activities internal to Amazon. The value of Amazon is, in large part, the value delivered by its value web partners. This is difficult for other firms to imitate in the short run.

BUSINESS STRATEGY

A **business strategy** is a set of plans for achieving superior long-term returns on the capital invested in a business firm. A business strategy is therefore a plan for making profits in a competitive environment over the long term. **Profit** is simply the difference between the price a firm is able to charge for its products and the cost of producing and distributing goods. Profit represents economic value. Economic value is created anytime customers are willing to pay more for a product than it costs to produce. Why would anyone pay more for a product than it costs to produce? There are multiple answers. The product may be unique (there are no other suppliers), it may be the least costly product of its type available, consumers may be able to purchase the product anywhere in the world, or it may satisfy some unique needs that other products do not. Each of these sources of economic value defines a firm's strategy for positioning its products in the marketplace. There are four generic strategies for achieving a profitable business: differentiation, cost, scope, and focus. We describe each of these below. The specific strategies that a firm follows will depend on the product, the industry, and the marketplace where competition is encountered.

Although the Internet is a unique marketplace, the same principles of strategy and business apply. As you will see throughout the book, successful e-commerce strategies involve using the Internet and mobile platform to leverage and strengthen existing business (rather than destroy your business), and to provide products and services your competitors cannot copy (in the short term anyway). That means developing unique products, proprietary content, distinguishing processes (such as Amazon's one-click shopping), and personalized or customized services and products (Porter, 2001). There are five generic business strategies: product/service differentiation, cost competition, scope, focus, and customer/supplier intimacy. Let's examine these ideas more closely.

Differentiation refers to all the ways producers can make their products or services unique and distinguish them from those of competitors. The opposite of differentiation is **commoditization**—a situation where there are no differences among products or services, and the only basis of choosing is price. As economists tell us, when price alone becomes the basis of competition and there are many suppliers and

business strategy
a set of plans for achieving superior long-term returns on the capital invested in a business firm

profit
the difference between the price a firm is able to charge for its products and the cost of producing and distributing goods

differentiation
refers to all the ways producers can make their products or services unique and different to distinguish them from those of competitors

commoditization
a situation where there are no differences among products or services, and the only basis of choosing is price

many customers, eventually the price of the good/service falls to the cost to produce it (marginal revenues from the nth unit equal marginal costs). And then profits are zero! This is an unacceptable situation for any business person. The solution is to differentiate your product or service and to create a monopoly-like situation where you are the only supplier.

There are many ways businesses differentiate their products or services. A business may start with a core generic product or service, but then create expectations among users about the "experience" of consuming the product or using the service— "Nothing equals the experience of driving a BMW." Businesses may also augment products and services by adding features to make them different from those of competitors. And businesses can differentiate their products and services further by enhancing their abilities to solve related consumer problems. For instance, tax programs such as TurboTax can import data from spreadsheet programs, as well as be used to file tax returns online. These capabilities are enhancements to the product that solve a customer's problems. The purpose of marketing is to create these differentiation features and to make the consumer aware of the unique qualities of products and services, creating in the process a "brand" that stands for these features. We discuss marketing and branding in Chapters 6 and 7.

In their totality, the differentiation features of a product or service constitute the customer value proposition we described in earlier sections of this chapter. E-commerce offers some unique ways to differentiate products and services, such as the ability to personalize the shopping experience and to customize the product or service to the particular demands of each consumer. E-commerce businesses can also differentiate products and services by making it possible to purchase the product from home, work, or on the road (ubiquity); by making it possible to purchase anywhere in the world (global reach); by creating unique interactive content, videos, stories about users, and reviews by users (richness and interactivity); and by storing and processing information for consumers of the product or service, such as warranty information on all products purchased through a site or income tax information online (information density).

strategy of cost competition
offering products and services at a lower cost than competitors

Adopting a **strategy of cost competition** means a business has discovered some unique set of business processes or resources that other firms cannot obtain in the marketplace. Business processes are the atomic units of the value chain. For instance, the set of value-creating activities called Inbound Logistics in Figure 5.5 is in reality composed of many different collections of activities performed by people on the loading docks and in the warehouses. These different collections of activities are called *business processes*—the set of steps or procedures required to perform the various elements of the value chain.

When a firm discovers a new, more efficient set of business processes, it can obtain a cost advantage over competitors. Then it can attract customers by charging a lower price, while still making a handsome profit. Eventually, its competitors go out of business as the market decisively tilts toward the lowest-cost provider. Or, when a business discovers a unique resource, or lower-cost supplier, it can also compete effectively on cost. For instance, switching production to low-wage-cost areas of the world is one way to lower costs.

Competing on cost can be a short-lived affair and very tricky. Competitors can also discover the same or different efficiencies in production. And competitors can also move production to low-cost areas of the world. Also, competitors may decide to lose money for a period as they compete on cost.

E-commerce offers some ways to compete on cost, at least in the short term. Firms can leverage ubiquity by lowering the costs of order entry (the customer fills out all the forms, so there is no order entry department); leverage global reach and universal standards by having a single order entry system worldwide; and leverage richness, interactivity, and personalization by creating customer profiles online and treating each individual consumer differently—without the use of an expensive sales force that performed these functions in the past. Finally, firms can leverage information intensity by providing consumers with detailed information on products, without maintaining either expensive catalogs or a sales force.

While e-commerce offers powerful capabilities for intensifying cost competition, which makes cost competition appear to be a viable strategy, the danger is that competitors have access to the same technology. The *factor markets*—where producers buy supplies—are open to all. Assuming they have the skills and organizational will to use the technology, competitors can buy many of the same cost-reducing techniques in the marketplace. Even a skilled labor force can be purchased, ultimately. However, self-knowledge, proprietary tacit knowledge (knowledge that is not published or codified), and a loyal, skilled workforce are in the short term difficult to purchase in factor markets. Therefore, cost competition remains a viable strategy.

Two other generic business strategies are scope and focus. A **scope strategy** is a strategy to compete in all markets around the globe, rather than merely in local, regional, or national markets. The Internet's global reach, universal standards, and ubiquity can certainly be leveraged to assist businesses in becoming global competitors. Yahoo, for instance, along with all of the other top 20 e-commerce companies, has readily attained a global presence. A **focus/market niche strategy** is a strategy to compete within a narrow market segment or product segment. This is a specialization strategy with the goal of becoming the premier provider in a narrow market. For instance, L.L.Bean uses e-commerce to continue its historic focus on outdoor sports apparel; and W.W. Grainger focuses on the narrow MRO market segment. E-commerce offers some obvious capabilities that enable a focus strategy. Firms can leverage richness and interactivity to create highly focused messages to different market segments; information intensity makes it possible to focus e-mail and other marketing campaigns on small market segments; personalization—and related customization—means the same product can be customized and personalized to fulfill the very focused needs of specific market segments and consumers.

Another generic strategy is **customer intimacy**, which focuses on developing strong ties with customers. Strong linkages with customers increase *switching costs* (the costs of switching from one product or service to a competing product or service) and thereby enhance a firm's competitive advantage. For example, Amazon's one-click shopping that retains customer details and recommendation services based on previous purchases makes it more likely that customers will return to make subsequent purchases.

scope strategy
competing in all markets around the globe, rather than just local, regional, or national markets

focus/market niche strategy
competing within a narrow market or product segment

customer intimacy
focuses on developing strong ties with customers in order to increase switching costs

TABLE 5.9	BUSINESS STRATEGIES	
STRATEGY	DESCRIPTION	EXAMPLE
Differentiation	Making products and services unique and different in order to distinguish them from those of competitors	Warby Parker (vintage-inspired prescription eyeglasses)
Cost competition	Offering products and services at a lower cost than competitors	Walmart
Scope	Competing in all markets around the globe, rather than merely in local, regional, or national markets	Apple iDevices
Focus/market niche	Competing within a narrow market or product segment	Bonobos (men's clothing)
Customer intimacy	Developing strong ties with customers	Amazon; Netflix

Table 5.9 summarizes the five basic business strategies.

Industry structure, industry and firm value chains, value webs, and business strategy are central business concepts used throughout this book to analyze the viability of and prospects for e-commerce companies. In particular, the signature case studies found at the end of each chapter are followed by questions that may ask you to identify the competitive forces in the case, or analyze how the case illustrates changes in industry structure, industry and firm value chains, and business strategy.

E-COMMERCE TECHNOLOGY AND BUSINESS MODEL DISRUPTION

While e-commerce has changed most industries in terms of their structure, processes, and strategies, in some cases e-commerce has radically changed entire industries, driving incumbent firms out of business, greatly altering the economics of an industry, and spawning entirely new firms and value chains (Schumpeter, 1942). When new technologies are at the core of a change in the way business is done, they are referred to as **disruptive technologies**. When the technology involved is digital, the term **digital disruption** is used. Usually it is not the technology per se that is disruptive—in fact, it can be rather ordinary and commonplace. Instead, the disruption occurs when an innovative firm applies the technology to pursue a different business model and strategy than existing firms, perhaps discovering a whole new market that existing firms did not even know existed (Bower and Christensen, 1995; Christensen and Leslie, 2000). For instance, personal computers using off-the-shelf inexpensive processors and technologies disrupted the market for mainframe and mini-computers. All the eight elements of a business model identified previously can be affected by disruptive technologies, from the business value proposition to the revenue model, market opportunity, competitive environment, competitive advantage, market strategy, organizational development, and management. In short, it's a whole new world that often confuses and surprises successful companies who tend to ignore, dismiss, and/or mock

disruptive technologies

technologies that underpin a business model disruption

digital disruption

a business model disruption that is driven by changes in information technology the early disruptive products. For instance, the entrepreneurs who introduced personal computers identified an entire new market of customers that had been ignored by the large computer firms, along with new price points, competitive factors, and market strategy, using new organizational, management teams, and employees with different skills. Many existing firms could not compete, and dissolved. Similar dynamics can be found in communications (disrupted by e-mail), data storage, music, photography, publishing, and transportation (Lepore, 2014). In 2016, firms like Uber and Airbnb are beginning to have a significant impact on the taxi and lodging industries.

Not all technologies are disruptive (Christensen, et al., 2015; King and Baatartog-tokh, 2015). In fact, most successful companies use technology to sustain their current business models, industry structure, processes, and strategies. This use of technology is referred to as **sustaining technology** because it helps companies to cope with competitive pressures and improve their products, and serve their customers with less expensive, more powerful, or unique products. But the same technology can be used by innovative entrepreneurs (**disruptors**) to destroy existing business models. Here's how it works.

Successful companies use whatever technology is available to incrementally improve their products, focusing on the customer by improving quality, price, and service. The incumbent and dominant firms seek to maintain the status quo in an industry, and their firms. In the first disruptive stage, disruptors, often funded by new sources of finance, introduce new products that are less expensive, less capable, and of poorer quality. The first personal computers used relatively unsophisticated technology compared to mainframe computers of the 1970s. These early products nevertheless find a niche in a market that incumbents do not serve or are unaware of. In the second stage, disruptors improve their products at a rapid pace, taking advantage of newer technologies at a faster pace than incumbents, expanding their niche market, and eventually attracting a larger customer base from the incumbents' market. When word processors, and eventually Microsoft Office, were married to the more powerful PC of the 1980s, they attracted a new market of business managers and professionals that was not served by incumbents. The concept was entirely new at the time. The successful incumbents never thought business professionals, let alone people working at home, would like to have a computer at their desk to create documents, build spreadsheets, and make presentation slides. The people and companies that developed personal computers were outsiders to the mainframe computer industry. They were disruptors. They had the vision.

In the third stage, the new products and business model become good enough, and even superior to products offered by incumbents. In the fourth stage, incumbent companies lose market share, and either go out of business or are consolidated into other more successful firms that serve a much more limited customer base. Some incumbents survive by finding new customers for their existing product, adopting some of the newer products and business models in separate divisions of their firms, or moving into other often nearby markets. For instance, mainframe computers are still made by IBM, but they are one of the few survivors. They survived by sustaining innovation in their traditional market of large-scale computing for Fortune 500 firms, moving into computing services, data centers, enterprise software, and most recently cloud computing, business analytics, data mining, and machine learning. As for the PC

sustaining technologies
technologies that enable the incremental improvement of products and services

disruptors
the entrepreneurs and their business firms that lead a business model disruption

industry, it is currently being disrupted by smartphones and tablet computers, created by outsiders who played a small role in the personal computer world, and who have identified huge consumer markets that incumbent PC manufacturers did not realize even existed. They have the vision, for now, but they face new digital disruptors sure to follow.

Why don't the existing companies realize the changes that are coming, and take steps to compete directly with the disruptors? Successful incumbents usually have enormous capital reserves, in-depth technology and intellectual skills, and access to prestigious management consulting firms. Why didn't Kodak see the transition to digital photography? Why didn't Canon see the smartphone camera as a powerful competitor to digital cameras? Why don't firms disrupt their own business models? The answers are complex. Incumbent technologists and professionals may be trained in an *unfit fitness*, having the wrong skills for the current environment. Shareholders expect returns on investment, not destruction of a firm's historic and cherished profitable products. The existing customer base comes to expect continuous improvement in existing products—not a business disruption, but business as usual. These powerful practices, all of which make good business sense, prevent incumbent firms from meeting the challenges of business model disruption. It is unclear at this time if the two most innovative firms in the current e-commerce environment, Apple and Google, will prove any different from previous incumbents.

CASE STUDY

Freemium

Takes Pandora Public

Pandora is the Internet's most successful radio service. As of June 2016, it had over 250 million registered users (225 million of whom access the service via a mobile device) and about 80 million active listeners. According to a recent survey, Pandora is the clear leader among Internet radio services, with more than 25% of reporting they had listened to it in the previous week, with Spotify a distant second at 10%. Pandora currently accounts for a 10% share of total U.S. radio listening (both traditional and Internet). In 2015, it streamed over 21 billion hours of music!

At Pandora, users select a genre of music based on a favorite musician, and a computer algorithm puts together a personal radio station that plays not only the music of the selected artist but also closely related music by different artists. Listeners have created over 10 billion different stations. A team of approximately 25 professional musicians listens to new songs each day and classifies the music according to more than 450 musical criteria. These criteria are used in a computer algorithm to classify new songs into various genres. Within each of these genres are hundreds of subgenres. Altogether, Pandora has a database of over 1 million analyzed songs from over 200,000 artists.

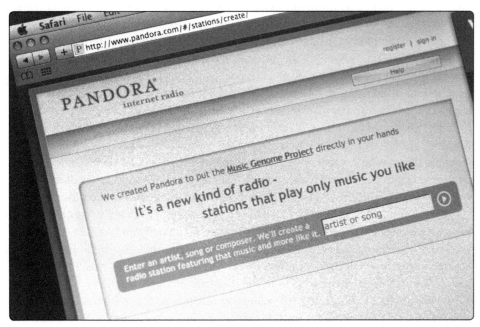

© NetPhotos/Alamy Stock Photo

Pandora's founders, Will Glaser and Tim Westergren, launched Pandora in 2005. Their biggest challenge was making a business out of a totally new kind of online radio station when competing online stations were making music available for free, many without advertising, and online subscription services were streaming music for a monthly fee and finding some advertising support as well. Online music illegally downloaded from P2P networks for free was also a significant factor, as was iTunes, which by 2005 was a roaring success, charging 99 cents a song. The idea of a "personal" radio station playing your kind of music was very new.

Pandora's business strategy is referred to as "freemium." A freemium strategy is based on giving away some products or services for free while relying on a certain percentage of customers to pay for premium versions of the same product or service. Because the marginal cost of digital products is typically close to zero, providing free product does not cost much, and potentially enables you to reach many more people. If the market is very large, even getting just 1% of that market to purchase could be very lucrative. Other notable freemium success stories include LinkedIn, a social network for career-oriented and job networking that offers some basic services for free, such as creating a profile and making connections, but which charges for premium services, and Dropbox, a cloud storage and file sharing service that provides 2 gigabytes of cloud storage for free, but charges for additional storage. Freemium has been the standard business model for most apps, with over 65% of the top 100 apps in Apple's App Store and the most successful mobile gaming apps today using a freemium strategy.

Pandora's first strategy was to give away 10 hours of free access, and then ask subscribers to pay $36 a month for a year after they used up their free 10 hours. The result: 100,000 people listened to their 10 hours for free and then refused to pay for the annual service. People loved Pandora but appeared unwilling to pay for it.

Facing financial collapse, in November 2005 Pandora introduced an ad-supported option. Subscribers could listen to a maximum of 40 hours of music in a calendar month for free. After the 40 hours were used up, subscribers had three choices: (a) pay 99 cents for the rest of the month, (b) sign up for a premium service offering unlimited usage, or (c) do nothing. If they chose (c), the music would stop, but users could sign up again the next month. The ad-supported business model was a risky move because Pandora had no ad server or accounting system, but it attracted so many users that in a few weeks it had a sufficient number of advertisers (including Apple) to pay for its infrastructure. In 2006, Pandora added a "Buy" button to each song being played and struck deals with Amazon, iTunes, and other online retail sites. Pandora now gets an affiliate fee for directing listeners to Amazon where users can buy the music. In 2008, Pandora added an iPhone app to allow users to sign up from their smartphones and listen all day if they wanted. By 2009, this "free" ad-supported model had attracted 20 million users.

After attracting a sufficiently large user base, Pandora turned its attention back to its premium service. In late 2009, the company launched Pandora One, a high-end version of its service that offered no advertising, higher-quality streaming music, a desktop app, and fewer usage limits. The service cost $36 a year. This time around it met with much more success, so much so that Pandora went public in June 2011. By 2016, Pandora had a projected $1.42 billion in revenue with about 80% coming from advertising and the remainder from subscriptions and other sources.

However, Pandora has not yet shown a profit, and its stock price has steadily dropped since its high in 2014. The company is experiencing slowing growth rates and even declines in its number of active users, and competitors like Spotify have made gains at Pandora's expense. Fully paid services like Apple-backed Apple Music, as well as much-hyped new entrants like Tidal, founded by Jay Z and a slew of other high profile artists, represent threats to Pandora as well. But the picture isn't totally bleak: Pandora has continued to show growth in advertising revenue and in listener hours, as its active users are listening more and more. Pandora also made a flurry of acquisitions in 2015, including on-demand music service Rdio. Absorbing Rdio signified Pandora's ambitions to directly compete with Spotify in on-demand music streaming, as opposed to focusing primarily on its radio model. Additionally, music licensing costs were expected to increase sharply in 2016, jeopardizing Pandora's ability to license its music, but a 2015 ruling by the U.S. Copyright Royalty Board raised rates to stream a song one time by a smaller amount than expected. After the ruling, Pandora made deals with the two largest music licensing companies in the United States and continues to make deals with music labels in 2016 as it prepares for the launch of its on-demand service.

While freemium clearly has worked to grow companies like Pandora, LinkedIn, and Dropbox, there is ongoing debate about the effectiveness of the freemium strategy. The crux of the issue is that while freemium can be an efficient way to gather a large group of potential customers, companies have found that it's a challenge to convert eyeballs into those willing to pay. Absent subscriber revenue, firms are forced to rely on advertising revenues.

Apple has led a recent push against freemium competitors. Pandora and Spotify have thrived at the expense of iTunes Music Store, whose revenues have declined steeply for several years, and Apple's first attempt at a streaming service, iTunes Radio, was a bust. Undeterred and sensing a shift in the industry, in 2014 Apple acquired Beats, a streaming music service and maker of popular headphones, for $3 billion. In 2015, Apple launched its own paid subscription streaming service app modeled after Beats called Apple Music, and by offering free three-month trials, quickly made significant inroads against Pandora and Spotify. In 2016, Apple Music has more than 15 million paying users and continues to grow quickly.

Music industry leadership is also unsure about the future of freemium music streaming. The heads of Universal Music Group and Sony Music both expressed skepticism of the long-term prospects of the freemium model in 2015, and in 2014, Taylor Swift removed her entire catalog of music from Spotify in protest of the freemium model, claiming that it devalued her music. Lesser known artists are equally upset with the revenue sharing models used by Pandora and other online music streaming services, with Pandora keeping about 54% of its revenue and only 4% going to music creators. Music labels are optimistic about Apple's ability to make paid streaming work, given Apple's deep pockets and brand cachet. But industry analysts believe that Pandora and Spotify are headed toward profitability as their subscriber numbers continue to expand.

Whether freemium services continue to breathe life back into the music business remains to be seen, but other companies like MailChimp show how freemium can turn

SOURCES: "Pandora's Share of U.S. Radio Listening Time from 1st Quarter 2013 to 4th Quarter 2015," Statista.com, accessed August 22, 2016; "Form 10-Q for the Quarterly Period Ended June 30, 2016," Pandora Media, Inc., July 26, 2016; "US Usage, Sales and Ad Spending Trends for Digital Music, Digital Radio, and Podcasting," by eMarketer, Inc., May 20, 2016; "Pandora Reports Q4 and Full Year 2015 Financial Results," Businesswire.com, February 11, 2016; "The Battle of Subscription Business Models: A Look at Their Strengths and Weaknesses," by Glenn Peoples, Billboard.com, January 29, 2016;

"203 Billion Emails in a Year: The Untold Growth Story of Mailchimp," Appvirality.com, December 24, 2015; "2016 Is Shaping Up to Be a Critical Year for Pandora, If Not All Music Streaming," by Amy X. Wang, Quartz.com, December 23, 2015; "A Big Music Copyright Ruling Has Managed to Make Both Pandora and Record Labels Happy – Mostly," by Amy X. Wang, Quartz.com, December 16, 2015; "Pandora to Acquire Pieces of Rdio," by Ienn Peoples, Billboard.com, November 16, 2015; "How Freemium Nearly Caused Our Business to Implode," by Josh Pigford, Baremetrics.com, November 10, 2015; "Freemium Model Works for Pandora But is Devastating to Songwriters," by David Israelite, Hypebot.com, September 2015; "Should You Consider a Freemium Model For Your Business?" by Chuck Cohn, *Forbes*, July 2, 2015; Amy X. Wang, "No, Apples Music Streaming App Looks Nothing Like Beats," by Liz Stinson, Wired.com, June 11, 2015; "Pandora's Three Biggest Issues Are Both a Blessing and a Curse," by Leon Lazaroff, Thestreet.com, May 20, 2015; "Spotify: Freemium Clampdown Rumours Are 'Completely False,'" by Tim Ingham, Musicbusinessworldwide.com, May 17, 2015; "Apple, Spotify, and the Battle Over Freemium," by Jingping Zhang, Harvard Business Review, May 13, 2015; "Why Apple Wants to End the Era of Free Music Streaming," by James Cook, Businessinsider.com, May 5, 2015; "Apple Pushing Music Labels to Kill Free Spotify Streaming Ahead of Beats Relaunch," by Micah Singleton, Theverge.com, May 4, 2015; "Apple and Beats Developing Streaming Music Service to Rival Spotify," by Ben Sisario and Brian X. Chen, *New York Times*, March 25, 2015; "Sony Music Boss Doug Morris: 'In General, Free is Death,'" by Stuart Dredge, Musically.com, March 12, 2015; "Making 'Freemium' Work," by Vineet Kumar, *Harvard Business Review*, May 2014; "How MailChimp Learned to Treat Data Like Orange Juice and Rethink the Email in the Process," by Derrick Harris, Gigaom.com, May 5, 2013; "When Freemium Fails," by Sarah E.

a company's fortunes around. The company lets anyone send e-mail to customers, manage subscriber lists, and track the performance of an e-mail marketing campaign. Despite the powerful tools it gives marketers, and its open applications programming interface, after 10 years in business, the company had only 85,000 paid subscribers.

In 2009, MailChimp began giving away its basic tools and charging subscription fees for special features, expecting that users would be more willing to pay for analytics and other services as their e-mail lists grew. In just over a year, MailChimp went from 85,000 to 450,000 users. E-mail volume went from 200 million a month to around 700 million. Most importantly, the number of paying customers increased more than 150%, while profit increased more than 650%!

For MailChimp, freemium has been worth the price. It currently supports more than 8 million subscribers worldwide, sending over 200 billion e-mails per year. However, Baremetrics, a developer of analytics compatible with the Stripe payment processing platform, came to a different conclusion. Though it had historically charged even for the lowest tier of its product offerings, Baremetrics introduced a free option in 2015. For the full versions of each of the features in the free plan, customers would have to upgrade. If judged solely by conversion rate, the free plan could have been deemed a success, as over 11% of free plan subscribers eventually became paying customers compared to the 3% to 5% that is typical in the industry. However, Baremetrics wasn't able to keep up with the sudden increase in data processing requirements, and the staff it had available for customer support requests were struggling to meet the higher demand.

Eventually, the total number of Baremetrics customers began to drop below what it had been before the introduction of the free plan as frustrated customers canceled their subscriptions. Baremetrics discovered that its resources were too tight to use the freemium model. Unlike MailChimp or Pandora, whose marginal costs were small enough that they could launch their service for millions of users, Baremetrics is a smaller company with different goals and scope. Baremetrics has since switched to a 14-day free trial strategy, after which customers are forced to pick a paid subscription plan.

So when does it make sense to include freemium in a business plan? It makes sense when the product is easy to use and has a very large potential audience, preferably in the millions. Using a freemium strategy can be a very successful marketing tool, because free features can help attract a user base, and are more attractive to most consumers than 30-day free trials that require a cancellation process. A solid customer value proposition is critical. It's helpful if a large user network increases the perceived value of the product (i.e., a dating service such as Match). Freemium may work when a company has good long-term customer retention rates and the product produces more value over time. An extremely important part of the equation is that the variable costs of providing the product or service to additional customers for free must be low.

Companies also face challenges in terms of determining what products and/or services to offer for free versus what to charge for (this may change over time), the cost of supporting free customers, and how to price premium services. Further, it is difficult to predict attrition rates, which are highly variable at companies using freemium. So, while freemium can be a great way to get early users and to provide a company with a built-in pool for upgrades, it's tough to determine how many users will be willing to pay and willing to stay.

A freemium strategy makes sense for companies such as Pandora, where there is a very low marginal cost, approaching zero, to support free users. It also makes sense for a company where the value to its potential customers depends on a large network, like LinkedIn. Freemium also works when a business can be supported by the percentage of customers who are willing to pay, like Pandora, especially when there are other revenues like advertising fees that can make up for shortfalls in subscriber revenues. The freemium music streaming services don't have to worry about their business model being sound strategy, but they do have to worry about industry goliaths like Apple and the record labels taking a stand against them.

Needleman and Angus Loten, *Wall Street Journal*, August 22, 2012; "Pandora IPO Prices at $16; Valuation $2.6 Billion," by Eric Savitz, Blogs.forbes.com, June 14, 2011; "Going Freemium: One Year Later," by Ben Chestnut, Blog.mailchimp.com, September 27, 2010; "Case Studies in Freemium: Pandora, Dropbox, Evernote, Automattic and MailChimp," by Liz Gannes, Gigaom.com, March 26, 2010; *Free: The Future of a Radical Price*, by Chris Anderson, Hyperion, 2009.

Case Study Questions

1. Compare Pandora's original business model with its current business model. What's the difference between "free" and "freemium" revenue models?

2. What is the customer value proposition that Pandora offers?

3. Why did MailChimp ultimately succeed with a freemium model but Baremetrics did not?

4. What's the most important consideration when considering a freemium revenue model?

5.6 REVIEW

KEY CONCEPTS

■ Identify the key components of e-commerce business models.

A successful business model effectively addresses eight key elements:
- *Value proposition*—how a company's product or service fulfills the needs of customers. Typical e-commerce value propositions include personalization, customization, convenience, and reduction of product search and price delivery costs.
- *Revenue model*—how the company plans to make money from its operations. Major e-commerce revenue models include the advertising model, subscription model, transaction fee model, sales model, and affiliate model.
- *Market opportunity*—the revenue potential within a company's intended marketspace.
- *Competitive environment*—the direct and indirect competitors doing business in the same marketspace, including how many there are and how profitable they are.
- *Competitive advantage*—the factors that differentiate the business from its competition, enabling it to provide a superior product at a lower cost.

- *Market strategy*—the plan a company develops that outlines how it will enter a market and attract customers.
- *Organizational development*—the process of defining all the functions within a business and the skills necessary to perform each job, as well as the process of recruiting and hiring strong employees.
- *Management team*—the group of individuals retained to guide the company's growth and expansion.

■ Describe the major B2C business models.

There are a number of different business models being used in the B2C e-commerce arena. The major models include the following:
- *Portal*—offers powerful search tools plus an integrated package of content and services; typically utilizes a combined subscription/advertising revenue/transaction fee model; may be general or specialized (vortal).
- *E-tailer*—online version of traditional retailer; includes virtual merchants (online retail store only), bricks-and-clicks e-tailers (online distribution channel for a company that also has physical stores), catalog merchants (online version of direct mail catalog), and manufacturers selling directly to the consumer.
- *Content provider*—information and entertainment companies that provide digital content; typically utilizes an advertising, subscription, or affiliate referral fee revenue model.
- *Transaction broker*—processes online sales transactions; typically utilizes a transaction fee revenue model.
- *Market creator*—uses Internet technology to create markets that bring buyers and sellers together; typically utilizes a transaction fee revenue model.
- *Service provider*—offers services online.
- *Community provider*—provides an online community of like-minded individuals for networking and information sharing; revenue is generated by advertising, referral fees, and subscriptions.

■ Describe the major B2B business models.

The major business models used to date in the B2B arena include:
- *E-distributor*—supplies products directly to individual businesses.
- *E-procurement*—single firms create digital markets for thousands of sellers and buyers.
- *Exchange*—independently owned digital marketplace for direct inputs, usually for a vertical industry group.
- *Industry consortium*—industry-owned vertical digital market.
- *Private industrial network*—industry-owned private industrial network that coordinates supply chains with a limited set of partners.

■ Understand key business concepts and strategies applicable to e-commerce.

E-commerce has had a major impact on the business environment in the last decade, and have affected:
- *Industry structure*—the nature of players in an industry and their relative bargaining power by changing the basis of competition among rivals, the barriers to entry, the threat of new substitute products, the strength of suppliers, and the bargaining power of buyers.
- *Industry value chains*—the set of activities performed in an industry by suppliers, manufacturers, transporters, distributors, and retailers that transforms raw inputs into final products and services by reducing the cost of information and other transaction costs.
- *Firm value chains*—the set of activities performed within an individual firm to create final products from raw inputs by increasing operational efficiency.
- *Business strategy*—a set of plans for achieving superior long-term returns on the capital invested in a firm by offering unique ways to differentiate products, obtain cost advantages, compete globally, or compete in a narrow market or product segment.

QUESTIONS

1. What distinguishes an e-commerce business plan from a traditional business plan?
2. Identify and describe the business model element that specifies how the company's product will fulfill the needs of its customers.
3. How can e-commerce technologies be used to improve a firm's value web?
4. What is a freemium strategy?
5. What is a disruptive technology, and how does it differ from a sustaining technology?
6. What types of business models does eBay use?
7. What is an on-demand services company?
8. Why would a firm decide to engage in a strategy of cost competition?
9. What are the benefits offered by incubator investor firms over other traditional sources of capital?
10. What is an unfair competitive advantage?
11. What is an industry structural analysis and what is its place in the e-commerce business plan?
12. What has been the effect of e-commerce technologies on general interfirm rivalry?
13. What revenue models do content providers use, and what is the key to becoming a successful content provider?
14. What disadvantages are faced by "first-mover" companies entering a marketspace?
15. Why is the e-tail sector so competitive?
16. Describe the feature of ubiquity as it applies to e-commerce technology and describe how it has affected the business environment over the past decade.
17. What kinds of firms are considered to be e-commerce enablers?
18. What are five generic business strategies for achieving a profitable business?
19. Define market opportunity and describe how you would determine a new company's realistic market opportunity.
20. What are the main elements of an elevator pitch?

PROJECTS

1. Select an e-commerce company. Visit its website or mobile app and describe its business model based on the information you find there. Identify its customer value proposition, its revenue model, the marketspace it operates in, who its main competitors are, any comparative advantages you believe the company possesses, and what its market strategy appears to be. Also try to locate information about the company's management team and organizational structure. (Check for a page labeled "the Company," "About Us," or something similar.)

2. Examine the experience of shopping online versus shopping in a traditional environment. Imagine that you have decided to purchase a digital camera (or any other item of your choosing). First, shop for the camera in a traditional manner. Describe how you would do so (for example, how you would gather the necessary information you would need to choose a particular item, what stores you would visit, how long it would take, prices, etc.). Next, shop for the item on the Web or via a mobile app. Compare and contrast your experiences. What were the advantages and disadvantages of each? Which did you prefer and why?

3. During the early days of e-commerce, first-mover advantage was touted as one way to success. On the other hand, some suggest that being a market follower can yield rewards as well. Which approach has proven to be more successful—first mover or follower? Choose two e-commerce companies that prove your point, and prepare a brief presentation to explain your analysis and position.

4. Select an e-commerce company that has participated in an incubator program such as Startup Bootcamp, Seedcamp, INiTS, or another of your choosing, and write a short report on its business model and the amount and sources of capital it has raised thus far. Include your views on the company's future prospects for success. Then create an elevator pitch for the company.

5. Select a B2C e-commerce retail industry segment such as pet products, sporting goods, or toys, and analyze its value chain and industry value chain. Prepare a short presentation that identifies the major industry participants in that business and illustrates the move from raw materials to finished product.

REFERENCES

Arthur, W. Brian. "Increasing Returns and the New World of Business." *Harvard Business Review* (July–August 1996).

Barney, J. B. "Firm Resources and Sustained Competitive Advantage." *Journal of Management* Vol. 17, No. 1 (1991).

Bellman, Steven, Gerald L. Lohse, and Eric J. Johnson. "Predictors of Online Buying Behavior." *Communications of the ACM* (December 1999).

Bower, Joseph L., and Clayton Christensen. "Disruptive Technologies: Catching the Wave." *Harvard Business Review* (January–February, 1995).

Christensen, Clayton M., Michael E. Raynor, and Rory McDonald. "What Is Disruptive Innovation?" *Harvard Business Review* (December 2015).

eBay, Inc. "eBay Inc. Reports Second Quarter 2016 Results." (July 20, 2016).

European Commission. "Crowdfunding in the EU Capital Markets Union."(May 3, 2016).

European Commission. "Crowdfunding Explained: A Guide for Small and Medium Enterprises on Crowdfunding and How to Use It." (2015).

European Commission. "Unleashing the Potential of Crowdfunding in the European Union." (March 2014).

Johnson, Mark, and Clayton Christensen. "Reinventing Your Business Model." *Harvard Business Review* (December 2008).

Kambil, Ajit, Ari Ginsberg, and Michael Bloch. "Reinventing Value Propositions." Working Paper, NYU Center for Research on Information Systems (1998).

Kanter, Elizabeth Ross. "The Ten Deadly Mistakes of Wanna-Dots." *Harvard Business Review* (January 2001).

Kaplan, Steven, and Mohanbir Sawhney. "E-Hubs: The New B2B Marketplaces." *Harvard Business Review* (May–June 2000).

Kim, W. Chan, and Renee Mauborgne. "Knowing a Winning Business Idea When You See One." *Harvard Business Review* (September-October 2000).

King, Andrew A. and Baljir Baatartogtokh. "How Useful Is the Theory of Disruptive Innovation?" *Sloan MIT Management Review* (September 15, 2015).

Lepore, Jill. "The Disruption Machine: What the Gospel of Innovation Gets Wrong." *New Yorker* (June 23, 2014).

Magretta, Joan. "Why Business Models Matter." *Harvard Business Review* (May 2002).

Porter, Michael E. "Strategy and the Internet." *Harvard Business Review* (March 2001).

Porter, Michael E. *Competitive Advantage: Creating and Sustaining Superior Performance.* New York: Free Press (1985).

Rigdon, Joan I. "The Second-Mover Advantage." *Red Herring* (September 1, 2000).

Schumpeter, Joseph A. *Capitalism, Socialism and Democracy.* London: Routledge, 1942.

Teece, David J. "Profiting from Technological Innovation: Implications for Integration, Collaboration, Licensing and Public Policy." *Research Policy* 15 (1986).

CHAPTER 6

E-commerce Marketing and Advertising

After reading this chapter, you will be able to:

- Understand the key features of the Internet audience, the basic concepts of consumer behavior and purchasing, and how consumers behave online.
- Identify and describe the basic digital commerce marketing and advertising strategies and tools.
- Identify and describe the main technologies that support online marketing.
- Understand the costs and benefits of online marketing communications.

InMobi's

Global Mobile Ad Network

Watch out, tech titans! InMobi, an innovative startup based in Bangalore, India, is making some serious waves in the global mobile advertising network marketplace currently dominated by Google, Facebook, and Twitter. InMobi was founded in early 2007 by four graduates of the Indian Institute of Technology, including Naveen Tewari. After unsuccessful attempts at SMS-based mobile search and a mobile-based deals company specifically for Mumbai, Tewari and his co-founders scrambled to come up with a new idea. With the last of their personal funds, they honed in on mobile advertising. Apple had just introduced the iPhone in early 2007, and few companies were focusing yet on the cellphone as a mobile advertising platform. This new idea proved to be the company's golden ticket, and in 2008, Tewari convinced venture firms Kleiner Perkins Caufield & Byers and Sherpalo Investments to make an $8 million investment in the company. They then moved to Bangalore, deeming it a better location from which to attract talent, and later changed the name of the company to InMobi.

© fotografiedk/Fotolia.com

InMobi bills itself as a mobile advertising platform and solutions provider. It acts as an intermediary between companies that want to advertise and content owners/publishers that offer mobile content, often in the form of apps. For instance, if you've seen the advertisements that appear when you play the Angry Birds games on an Android smartphone, you've seen InMobi's mobile ad platform at work. InMobi serves almost 138 billion mobile ads a month to over 1 billion consumers in over 200 countries. There are over 30,000 apps and mobile sites on the InMobi network, and the company tracks over 2.5 billion app downloads on its platform. Although it is a private company, InMobi's revenues in 2015 are believed to have been approximately $250 million. It makes money by keeping a percentage of the revenue per ad, typically 30%–40%. Increasingly, InMobi has focused on native advertising as the marketplace abandons banner ads and moves toward more creative and interactive formats. Native advertising appears seamlessly within an app and often as if it were a post from a friend. InMobi's customers include Unilever, Samsung, Microsoft, Adidas, and a rapidly growing number of other prominent companies and brands.

InMobi grew quickly using a "reverse market strategy," establishing leadership positions in Asia and Africa first and then tackling the European Union and U.S. markets.

SOURCES: "India's Early Unicorn Copmany Talks About Maintaining Startup Culture During Tough Times," by Sneha Banerjee, Entrepreneur.com, November 22, 2016; "InMobi Bulks Up on Viewability Via Partnerships with Moat and DoubleVerify," by Tobi Elkin, Mediapost.com, November 1, 2016; "Mobile Adtech Co InMobi to Double Its Investment in China," by Shadma Shaikh,

Economictimes.indiatimes.com, October 13, 2016; "InMobi Launches Suite of Advanced Video Ad Formats," by Shadma Shaikh, Economictimes.indiatimes.com, September 8, 2016; "InMobi to Pay $950,000 Fine to Settle FTC Charges for Tracking Location of Consumers Without Consent," by Vikas SN, Economictimes.india-times.com, June 23, 2016; "The US Has Fined a Mobile Advertising Firm for Tracking the Location of Hundreds of Millions of People," by Itika Sharma Punit, Qz.com, June 23, 2016; "InMobi Technologies to Discontinue Use of Mascot Function on Miip Platform," by Sadhana Chathurvedula, Livemint.com, June 17, 2016; "InMobi Grapples with Senior, Mid-Level Attrition Amid Concerns About Future," by Anirban Sen and Aditi Shrivastava, Economictimes.indiatimes.com, May 26, 2016; "InMobi Vouches 100% Viewability on Mobile Ads," by Dhanya Ann Thoppil, Livemint.com, November 20, 2015; "InMobi Guarantees 100% In-App Mobile Ad View-ability," Prnewswire.com, November 18, 2015; "InMobi and Taboola Partner to Engage over One Billion Mobile Consumers Through Content Discovery on Native Platform," Prnewswire.com, October 29, 2015; "India's Global Ad Giant Taking on Google and Facebook," by Kinjal Pandya-Wagh, Bbc.com, October 20, 2015; "With $100 Million, InMobi Raises the Banner for the Future," by Pankaj Mishra, *Economic Times*, September 29, 2015; "India's InMobi Ties Up with China's APUS to Take On Google," Cnbc.com, September 16, 2015; "Dell, InMobi Forge Alliance for E-Commerce Platform," by Anirban Sen, *Economic Times*, September 14, 2015; "Why InMobi May Be India's Most Innovative Company," by Malini Goyal, *Economic Times*, August 2, 2015; "InMobi, Google & Facebook Mobile Ad Rival, Puts Personalized Discovery Feature into Mobile Ads," by Saritha Rai, Forbes.com, July 15, 2015; "How a Monkey Will Help You Go Beyond Ads on InMobi Ad Network," by Barry Levine, Venturebeat.com, July 15, 2015; "Meet Miip, the Ad Monkey in Your App," by Vindu Goel, *New York Times*, July 14,

Today, the company employs over 1,000 people and has offices around the world, including in Asia (India, China, Singapore, Malaysia, South Korea, Taiwan, and Japan), Australia, the European Union (Germany, the United Kingdom, Spain, France, and Sweden), the Middle East (the UAE), and the United States (San Francisco). Fueled in part by a $200 million investment from Japanese media and telecommunications giant Softbank, which valued InMobi at over $1 billion, InMobi is currently focusing on growth in the United States and plans to focus next on Russia, Latin America, and especially China, where growth in mobile users is expected to rise the fastest. In 2016, InMobi announced plans to double its investments in China, its fastest-growing market, with the expectation that it would exceed revenues from the U.S. market by 2017. InMobi has also used funds to make some strategic purchases, including MMTG Labs, a developer of an application market for Facebook pages, Appstores.com, and Overlay Media, which helps to deliver more highly targeted and context-sensitive ads.

Can InMobi truly hope to challenge Google, which is currently the dominant leader in market share? Its $250 million in revenues trails significantly behind Google's $1.5 billion in revenue from mobile display advertising. InMobi has modeled itself after Google and other tech titans in its hiring and employee policies, which allow employees the latitude and support to come up with the next big, disruptive idea. InMobi boasts a growing number of partnerships with other tech firms, including marketing company Amobee, payment processing firm Stripe, Chinese tech firm APUS, and Dell. Tewari also points to InMobi's primary focus on mobile, compared to Google, which is involved in many different areas. InMobi also claims that its technology is superior and that its data on customers is richer and more granular. InMobi backed up its claims when it became one of the first mobile advertising companies to offer a 100% viewability guarantee, a rarity in the modern landscape of ad blockers and ad fraud. As more advertisers gravitate to the mobile platform, its emphasis on ensuring that ads are viewable should help InMobi differentiate itself from the pack. In 2016, InMobi acquired video measurement analytics firm Moat to further bolster the viewability of its ads and announced a partnership with video advertising and tracking firm DoubleVerify to ensure that its ads are viewable and trackable by third parties.

Tewari's confidence in InMobi's proprietary technology stems from InMobi's ap-pographic targeting system, which uses algorithms and data on how users interact with apps to determine very precise trends and preferences of those users. To develop the system, InMobi studied over 100,000 apps and how different types of consumers used them. The result is a system so accurate that InMobi has guaranteed 2%–3% increases in engagement by app developers using InMobi's services. InMobi has continued to innovate, honing the Geo Context Targeting system used in its Smart Ads, which it says generate ten times the interaction compared to traditional ads, and more than three times the conversion rate of traditional ads. SmartAds support rich media and are tailored based on users' personal details and geographic conditions in the area, such as location and nearby weather. For example, if you're strolling city streets on a hot summer afternoon, you'll be given advertisements for cold beverages from nearby food chains. The company also released an updated suite of its advanced video ad formats in 2016 on the heels of strong growth in video ads served in the first half of the year.

InMobi also maintains several advertising platforms, including an interactive video ad platform as well as a native ad exchange, to help advertisers boost their sales on mobile beyond Facebook and Google. InMobi's video ad platform focuses on contextualized mobile video ads using its advanced targeting system. Developed in tandem with programmatic advertising service provider Rubicon Project, InMobi's native ad exchange is the first that allows buying and selling of mobile native advertising on a global scale.

In 2015, InMobi launched its Miip personalized discovery tool, which is a monkey character that persists throughout multiple apps and offers users options for different types of content, including product feeds and other apps. Over time, Miip improved its accuracy, offering only relevant and thematically consistent products to users, like workout clothes in a fitness app or fashion tips in a dating app. While Miip was announced to great fanfare and lofty earnings projections as high as $1 billion within two years, the company has discontinued much of the functionality of the service due to its lukewarm reception, including the animated monkey character, and instead hopes to use much of its underlying technology with other products.

The failure of Miip is just one of several ways that InMobi is struggling to meet its considerable hype. Users spend much more time on Facebook, Google, and Twitter than they do anywhere else, which complicates things for InMobi. For every dollar that is spent on mobile advertising, 85 cents go to Facebook and Google, leaving little room for smaller players. InMobi touts its cost-effectiveness compared to these widely accepted platforms, and also claims that its margins are a whopping 40% compared to just 5%–10% in the TV and print advertising industry. Still, despite its high margins, the company recorded a loss of $40 million in 2015. In 2016, talk of InMobi becoming the next Facebook or Google has been put on hold, as the company has battled slowing growth; significant attrition within its senior management and staff, including the company's CFO, VP of finance, and VP of engineering; and fallout from a $4 million fine levied by the U.S. Federal Trade Commission for tracking underage users without consent. As if that wasn't bad enough publicity for the company, the FTC reduced the fine to $950,000, citing the perilous financial condition of the company and questioning its ability to pay in full. Analysts had anticipated that InMobi would launch an IPO in the near future, but until the company jumpstarts its growth and stabilizes its workforce and management, that's not likely to happen.

2015; "InMobi Plans to Stay Independent, Dismissing Rumors of Talks with Google," by Vindu Goel, *New York Times*, March 11, 2015; "Think They're Tracking You Now? Wait till InMobi's Unveiling Next Month," by Richard Byrne Reilly, Venturebeat.com, October 16, 2014; "InMobi Takes a Bold Stand: But How Much Can They Really Guarantee?" by Michael Essany, Mobilemarketingwatch.com, October 14, 2014; "InMobi Has Positioned Itself as the Go-To Company In Mobile Advertising," by Deepak Ajwani, *Forbes India*, October 10, 2014; "InMobi Decoded: How Bangalore-based Firm Is Taking On Google and Facebook," by Peerzada Abrar and Krithika Krishnamurthy, *The Economic Times*, March 7, 2014; "How inMobil Grew from a Startup to a Giant Mobile Ad Network," by Willis Wee, Techinasia.com, May 16, 2013; "InMobi Acquires Overlay Media," InMobi, January 8, 2013; "Mobile Ad Network InMobi Continues Buying Spree, Picks Up Metaflow Solutions for App Distribution," by Ingrid Lunden, Techcrunch.con, July 31, 2012; "Softbank Invests $200M in InMobi," by Jamie Yap, ZDnet.com, September 15, 2011; "InMobi Raises Massive $200M to Overtake Google in Mobile Ads," by Matt Marshall, Venturebeat.com, September 15, 2011; "HTML Ad Builder Sprout Acquired by InMobi," by Jason Kincaid, Techcrunch.com, August 2, 2011; "InMobi Signs "Multi-million Dollar" Mobile Ad Partnership with Amobee," by Steve O'Hear, Techcrunch.com, May 11, 2011.

Perhaps no area of business has been more affected by Internet and mobile platform technologies than marketing and marketing communications. As a communications tool, the Internet affords marketers new ways of contacting millions of potential customers at costs far lower than traditional media. The Internet also provides new ways—often instantaneous and spontaneous—to gather information from customers, adjust product offerings, and increase customer value. The Internet has spawned entirely new ways to identify and communicate with customers, including search engine marketing, social marketing, behavioral targeting, and targeted e-mail, among others. And the Internet was just the first transformation. Today, the mobile platform based on smartphones and tablet computers is transforming online marketing and communications yet again. **Table 6.1** summarizes some of the significant new developments in online marketing and advertising for 2016–2017.

The subject of online marketing, branding, and market communications is very broad and deep. We have created two chapters to cover the material. In this chapter, we begin by examining consumer behavior on the Web, the major types of online marketing and branding, and the technologies that support advances in online marketing. We then focus on understanding the costs and benefits of online marketing communications. In Chapter 7, we focus on the social, mobile, and local marketing phenomenon in greater depth.

6.1 CONSUMERS ONLINE: THE INTERNET AUDIENCE AND CONSUMER BEHAVIOR

Before firms can begin to sell their products online, they must first understand what kinds of people they will find online and how those people behave in the online marketplace. In this section, we focus primarily on individual consumers in the business-to-consumer (B2C) arena. However, many of the factors discussed apply to the B2B arena as well, insofar as purchasing decisions by firms are made by individuals. We cover B2B marketing in more depth in Chapter 12. For readers who have no background in marketing, we have created an online Learning Track, Learning Track 6.1, that discusses basic marketing and branding concepts.

INTERNET TRAFFIC PATTERNS: THE ONLINE CONSUMER PROFILE

We will start with an analysis of some basic background demographics of online consumers. The first principle of marketing and sales is "know thy customer." Who is online, who shops online and why, and what do they buy? In 2016, around 3.3 billion people of all ages had access to the Internet. In the United Kingdom, broadband household penetration is estimated to have reached 87% in 2016, with a similar penetration rate in Germany (86%) (eMarketer, Inc., 2016x).

Although the number of new online users increased at a rate of 30% a year or higher in the early 2000s, over the last several years, this growth rate has slowed. E-commerce businesses can no longer count on a double-digit growth rate in the

TABLE 6.1	WHAT'S NEW IN ONLINE MARKETING AND ADVERTISING 2016–2017

BUSINESS

- Online marketing and advertising spending worldwide continues to increase (by over 20% in 2016), compared to only about 1% for traditional media marketing and advertising.
- Mobile advertising in all formats continues to be one of the fastest growing types of digital advertising and is now the platform for over 55% of all digital advertising spending worldwide.
- Search engine marketing and advertising maintains its importance, but its rate of growth is slowing somewhat compared to other formats.
- Social and local marketing spending all continue to rapidly expand.
- Viewability issues and ad fraud raise increasing concerns for marketers.
- Native advertising and other forms of content marketing are on the rise.

TECHNOLOGY

- Ad blocking software usage increases, creating concerns for both online publishers and advertisers.
- Big data: online tracking produces oceans of data, challenging business analytics programs.
- Cloud computing makes rich marketing content and multi-channel, cross-platform marketing a reality.
- Programmatic advertising (an automated, technology-driven method of buying and selling display and video ads) takes off.

SOCIETY

- Targeted advertising based on behavioral tracking leads to growing privacy awareness and fears.

online population to fuel their revenues. The days of extremely rapid growth in the U.S. Internet population are over.

Intensity and Scope of Usage

The slowing rate of growth in the Internet population is compensated for, in part, by an increasing intensity and scope of use. In 2016, more than 80% of the U.S. population regularly used the Internet, spending a total of almost 5 hours and 45 minutes a day (eMarketer, Inc., 2016a, 2016b). Internet use by U.S. teens is even more pervasive, with over 90% saying they go online daily, and about 25% reporting that they use the Internet almost constantly (Pew Research Center, 2015a). In 2016, mobile smartphones and tablets are major access points to the Internet and online commerce. About 2.5 billion people, about 75% of all Internet users, access the Internet using a mobile phone. Owners of mobile devices in the United Kingdom spend about 2 hours and 40 minutes a day using them for nontelephone activities such as playing games, viewing videos, and visiting social networks. Engaging in such activities is widespread—in the United States in 2016, around 180 million mobile users played games, about 140 million watched videos, over 160 million visited a social network, and millions of others listened to music or shopped (eMarketer, Inc., 2016a, 2016b). According to the Pew Research Center, the more time users spend online, becoming more comfortable and familiar with Internet features and services, the more services they are likely to explore.

Demographics and Access

In the United States, the demographic profile of the Internet—and e-commerce—has changed greatly since 1995. Up until 2000, single, white, young, college-educated males with high incomes dominated the Internet. This inequality in access and usage led to concerns about a possible "digital divide." However, in recent years, there has been a marked increase in Internet usage by females, minorities, seniors, and families with modest incomes, resulting in a notable decrease—but not elimination—in the earlier inequality of access and usage.

A roughly equal percentage of men (82%) and women (83%) use the Internet in the U.S. today. Teens (12–17) and young adults (18–24) form the age groups with the highest percentage of Internet use, at 97%. Adults in the 25–54 group are also strongly represented, with percentages of over 90%. Another fast-growing group online is the 65 and over segment, 61% of whom now use the Internet. The percentage of very young children (0–11 years) online has also spurted, to 62% of that age group. Future Internet user growth in the United States will come predominantly from those aged 55 and older and from children in the 0–11 age bracket (eMarketer, Inc., 2016a). Variation across racial and ethnic groups is not as wide as across age groups.

Ten years ago, there were significant differences among such groups in the United States, but this has receded. In 2016, 87% of whites use the Internet, compared to 84% of blacks and Hispanics. About 97% of U.S. households with income levels above $75,000 use the Internet, compared to only 77% of households earning less than $30,000. Over time, income differences have declined but they remain significant with a 20% gap between the highest category of household income and the lowest. Amount of education also makes a significant difference when it comes to Internet usage. Of those individuals with less than a high school education, only 66% went online in 2016, compared to 97% of individuals with a college degree or more. Even some college education boosted Internet usage, with that segment reaching 94% (Pew Research Center, 2016).

Overall, the so-called "digital divide" has indeed moderated, but it still persists along income, education, age, and ethnic dimensions. Gender, income, education, age, and ethnicity also impact online behavior. According to the Pew Research Center, U.S. adults over the age of 65, those who have not completed high school, those who make less than $30,000 a year, and Hispanics are all less likely to purchase products online. Women are slightly more likely to purchase online than men, but not significantly so. With respect to online banking, the demographics are similar—those 65 and older are less likely than any age group to bank online, while those with at least some college are more likely than those with a high school diploma or less. Online banking is also more popular with men than women. No significant differences were found in terms of ethnicity (Pew Research Center, 2012). Other commentators have observed that children of poorer and less educated families spend considerably more time using their access devices for entertainment (movies, games, Facebook, and texting) than do children from wealthier households. For all children and teenagers, the majority of time spent on the Internet is often labeled as "wasted time" because the majority of online use is for entertainment, and not education or learning (Richtel, 2012).

Type of Internet Connection: Broadband and Mobile Impacts

While a great deal of progress has been made in reducing glaring gaps in access to the Internet, there are still inequalities in access to broadband service. In 2016, around 92 million U.S. households had broadband service in their homes—over 75% of all households (eMarketer, Inc., 2016c). Research by the Pew Research Center indicates that broadband adoption levels are lower for older adults, those with low levels of education, and those with low household incomes. Rural residents, African Americans, and Latinos are also less likely to have a home broadband connection (Pew Research Center, 2013). For marketers, the broadband audience offers unique opportunities for the use of multimedia marketing campaigns, and for the positioning of products especially suited for this more educated and affluent audience. It is also important to note that just because a household does not have broadband access, it does not mean that household members do not use the Internet. About 50% of the non-broadband adopters do use the Internet, either from another location or via a smartphone. Certain groups are particularly reliant on smartphones for online access: younger adults in the 18–29 age group, those with low household incomes and levels of education, and non-whites (Pew Research Center, 2015b, 2013). The explosive growth of smartphones and tablet computers connected to broadband cellular and Wi-Fi networks is the foundation for a truly mobile e-commerce and marketing platform, which did not exist a few years ago.

Community Effects: Social Contagion in Social Networks

For a physical retail store, the most important factor in shaping sales is location, location, location. If you are located where thousands of people pass by every day, you will tend to do well. But for Internet retailers, physical location has almost no consequence as long as customers can be served by shipping services such as UPS or the post office or their services can be downloaded to anywhere. What does make a difference for consumer purchases on the Internet is whether or not the consumer is located in "neighborhoods" where others purchase on the Internet. These neighborhoods can be either face-to-face and truly personal, or digital. These so-called neighborhood effects, and the role of social emulation in consumption decisions, are well known for goods such as personal computers. In general, there is a relationship between being a member of a social network and purchasing decisions. Yet the relationship between "connectedness" (either offline or online) and purchase decisions is not straightforward or simple. People who score in the top 10%–15% of connectedness "do their own thing" to differentiate themselves and often do not share purchase decisions with friends. In fact, highly connected users often stop purchasing what their friends purchase. One can think of them as iconoclasts. The middle 50% of connected people very often share purchase patterns of their friends. One can think of these people as "keeping up with the Joneses" (Iyengar et al., 2009). A study of 6,000 social network users found that social networks have a powerful influence on shopping and purchasing behavior. An estimated 40% of social media users have purchased an item after sharing or favoriting it on Facebook, Pinterest, or Twitter. Facebook is the network most likely to drive customers to purchase, followed by Pinterest and Twitter. Unexpectedly, social networks increase research online, followed by purchase offline (sometimes referred to as ROPO), driving purchase traffic into physical stores where the product can be seen, tried, and then purchased. This is the opposite of the showrooming effect where consumers shop in stores, and then purchase online. The ROPO effect was found to be as large as the research offline and purchase online effect (Vision Critical, 2013; Schleifer, 2013; Sevitt and Samuel, 2013).

Membership in social networks has a large influence on discovering new independent music, but less influence on already well-known products (Garg, 2009). Membership in an online brand community like Ford's Facebook page and community has a direct effect on sales (Adjei et al., 2009). Amazon's recommender systems ("Consumers who bought this item also bought ...") create co-purchase networks where people do not know one another personally, but nevertheless triple the influence of complementary products (Oestreicher-Singer and Sundararajan, 2008). The value of social networks to marketers rests on the proposition that brand strength and purchase decisions are closely related to network membership, rank, prominence, and centrality (Guo et al., 2011).

CONSUMER BEHAVIOR MODELS

consumer behavior
a social science discipline that attempts to model and understand the behavior of humans in a marketplace

Once firms have an understanding of who is online, they need to focus on how consumers behave online. The study of **consumer behavior** is a social science discipline that attempts to model and understand the behavior of humans in a marketplace. Several social science disciplines play roles in this study, including sociology, psychology, and economics. Models of consumer behavior attempt to predict or "explain" what consumers purchase and where, when, how much, and why they buy. The expectation is that if the consumer decision-making process can be understood, firms will have a much better idea how to market and sell their products. **Figure 6.1** illustrates a general consumer behavior model that takes into account a wide range of factors that influence a consumer's marketplace decisions. Learning Track 6.2 contains further information about the cultural, social, and psychological background factors that influence consumer behavior.

PROFILES OF ONLINE CONSUMERS

Online consumer behavior parallels that of offline consumer behavior with some obvious differences. It is important to first understand why people choose the Internet channel to conduct transactions. **Table 6.2** lists the main reasons consumers choose the online channel.

While price is an important consideration, consumers also shop online because of convenience, which in turn is produced largely by saving them time. Overall transaction cost reduction appears to be a major motivator for choosing the online channel.

FIGURE 6.1 — A GENERAL MODEL OF CONSUMER BEHAVIOR

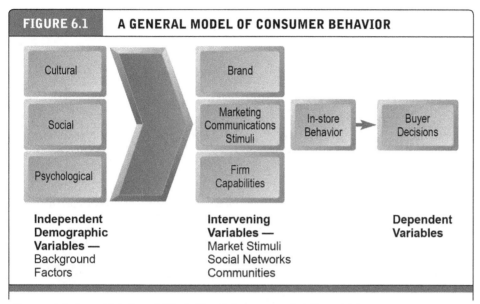

Consumer behavior models try to predict the decisions that consumers make in the marketplace.

SOURCE: Adapted from Kotler and Armstrong, 2009.

THE ONLINE PURCHASING DECISION

Once online, why do consumers actually purchase a product or service at a specific site? Among the most important reasons are price and the availability of free shipping. That the seller is someone whom the purchaser trusts is also a very important factor.

TABLE 6.2 — WHY CONSUMERS CHOOSE THE ONLINE CHANNEL

REASON	PERCENTAGE OF RESPONDENTS
Lower prices	59%
Shop from home	53%
Shop 24/7	44%
Wider variety of products available	29%
Easier to compare and research products and offers	27%
Products only available online	22%
Online customer reviews	18%
Better product information available	7%
Promotion via e-mail or text	7%
Social media influence	1%

SOURCE: Based on data from eMarketer, Inc., 2014.

FIGURE 6.2   THE CONSUMER DECISION PROCESS AND SUPPORTING COMMUNICATIONS

Consumer Decision Process

Awareness—Need Recognition	Search	Evaluation of Alternatives	Purchase	Post-purchase Behavior—Loyalty

Online Marketing Communications

| Targeted display ads • Targeted e-mail ads • Social media | Search engines • Online catalogs • Site visits • Targeted e-mail • Social networks | Search engines • Online catalogs • Site visits • Product reviews • User evaluations • Social networks | Online promotions • Discounts • Targeted e-mail • Flash sales | Communities of consumption • Newsletters • Customer e-mail • Online updates • Social networks |

Offline Marketing Communications

| Mass media • TV • Radio • Print media • Social networks | Catalogs • Print ads • Mass media • Sales people • Product raters • Store visits • Social networks | Reference groups • Opinion leaders • Mass media • Product raters • Store visits • Store visits • Social networks | Promotions • Direct mail • Mass media • Print media | Warranties • Service calls • Parts and repair • Consumer groups • Social networks |

The ability to make a purchase without paying tax and the availability of an online coupon are also significant factors.

You also need to consider the process that buyers follow when making a purchase decision, and how the Internet environment affects consumers' decisions. There are five stages in the consumer decision process: awareness of need, search for more information, evaluation of alternatives, the actual purchase decision, and post-purchase contact with the firm. **Figure 6.2** shows the consumer decision process and the types of offline and online marketing communications that support this process and seek to influence the consumer before, during, and after the purchase decision.

The stages of the consumer decision process are basically the same whether the consumer is offline or online. On the other hand, the general model of consumer behavior requires modification to take into account new factors, and the unique features of e-commerce that allow new opportunities to interact with the customer online also need to be accounted for. In **Figure 6.3**, we have modified the general model of consumer behavior to focus on user characteristics, product characteristics, and website and mobile platform features, along with traditional factors such as brand strength and specific market communications (advertising) and the influence of both online and offline social networks.

In the online model, website and mobile platform features, along with consumer skills, product characteristics, attitudes towards online purchasing, and perceptions

FIGURE 6.3   A MODEL OF ONLINE CONSUMER BEHAVIOR

In this general model of online consumer behavior, the decision to purchase is shaped by background demographic factors, several intervening factors, and, finally, influenced greatly by clickstream behavior very near to the precise moment of purchase.

about control over the online environment come to the fore. Website and mobile platform features include latency (delay in downloads), navigability, and confidence in online security. There are parallels in the analog world. For instance, it is well known that consumer behavior can be influenced by store design, and that understanding the precise movements of consumers through a physical store can enhance sales if goods and promotions are arranged along the most likely consumer tracks. Consumer skills refers to the knowledge that consumers have about how to conduct online transactions (which increases with experience). Product characteristics refers to the fact that some products can be easily described, packaged, and shipped online, whereas others cannot. Combined with traditional factors, such as brand, advertising, and firm capabilities, these factors lead to specific attitudes about purchasing from an e-commerce firm (trust in the firm and favorable customer experience) and a sense that the consumer can control his or her environment online.

Clickstream behavior refers to the transaction log that consumers establish as they move about the Web, from search engine to a variety of sites, then to a single site, then to a single page, and then, finally, to a decision to purchase. These precious moments are similar to "point-of-purchase" moments in traditional retail. A study of over 10,000 visits to an online wine store found that detailed and general clickstream

clickstream behavior
the transaction log that consumers establish as they move about the Web

behavior were as important as customer demographics and prior purchase behavior in predicting a current purchase (Van den Poel and Buckinx, 2005). Clickstream marketing takes maximum advantage of the Internet environment. It presupposes no prior "deep" knowledge of the customer (and in that sense is "privacy-regarding"), and can be developed dynamically as customers use the Internet. For instance, the success of search engine marketing (the display of paid advertisements by search engines) is based in large part on what the consumer is looking for at the moment and how they go about looking (detailed clickstream data). After examining the detailed data, general clickstream data is used (days since last visit, past purchases). If available, demographic data is used (region, city, and gender).

SHOPPERS: BROWSERS AND BUYERS

The picture of Internet use sketched in the previous section emphasizes the complexity of behavior online. Although the Internet audience still tends to be concentrated among the well educated, affluent, and youthful, the audience is increasingly becoming more diverse. Clickstream analysis shows us that people go online for many different reasons. Online shopping is similarly complex. Beneath the surface of the €2.35 trillion B2C e-commerce market in 2016 are substantial differences in how users shop online.

For instance, as shown in **Figure 6.4**, 89% of U.K. Internet users age 14 and older are "buyers" who actually purchase something online. Another 4.8% research products online ("browsers"), but purchase them offline. With the U.K. Internet audience estimated at 53 million in 2016, in 2016, online shoppers (the combination of buyers and browsers, totalling almost 94%) add up to a market size of almost 50 million consumers. Most U.K. marketers find this number exciting.

The significance of online browsing for offline purchasing should not be underestimated. Although it is difficult to precisely measure the amount of offline sales that occur because of online product research, Forrester Research estimates that

| FIGURE 6.4 | ONLINE SHOPPERS AND BUYERS IN THE UNITED KINGDOM |

Online buyers 89%

Did not shop or buy online 6.2%

Shopped online but did not buy 4.8%

Almost 94% of U.K. Internet users age 14 and older shop online on desktop computers and mobile devices, either by researching products or by purchasing products online. Only about 6% do not buy or shop online.
SOURCE: Based on data from eMarketer, Inc., 2016d.

web-influenced retail sales will generate about $1.3 trillion in 2016, growing to around $1.6 trillion by 2020 (Forrester Research, 2016).

E-commerce is a major conduit and generator of offline commerce. The reverse is also true: online traffic is driven by offline brands and shopping. While online research influences offline purchases, it is also the case that offline marketing media heavily influence online behavior including sales. Traditional print media (magazines and newspapers) and television are by far the most powerful media for reaching and engaging consumers with information about new products and directing them to the Web. Online communities and blogging are also very influential but not yet as powerful as traditional media. This may be surprising to many given the attention to social networks as marketing vehicles, but it reflects the diversity of influences on consumer behavior and the real-world marketing budgets of firms that are still heavily dominated by traditional media. Even more surprising in the era of Facebook, face-to-face interactions are a more powerful influence than participation in online social communities.

These considerations strongly suggest that e-commerce and traditional commerce are coupled and should be viewed by merchants (and researchers) as part of a continuum of consuming behavior and not as radical alternatives to one another. Commerce is commerce; the customers are often the same people. Customers use a wide variety of media, sometimes multiple media at once. The significance of these findings for marketers is very clear. Online merchants should build the information content of their sites to attract browsers looking for information, build content to rank high in search engines, put less attention on selling per se, and promote services and products (especially new products) in offline media settings in order to support their online stores.

WHAT CONSUMERS SHOP FOR AND BUY ONLINE

You can look at online sales as divided roughly into two groups: small-ticket and big-ticket items. Big-ticket items include computer equipment and consumer electronics, where orders can easily be more than €1,000. Small-ticket items include apparel, books, health and beauty supplies, office supplies, music, software, videos, and toys, where the average purchase is typically less than $100. In the early days of e-commerce, sales of small-ticket items vastly outnumbered those of large-ticket items. But the recent growth of big-ticket items such as computer hardware, consumer electronics, furniture, and jewelry has changed the overall sales mix. Consumers are now much more confident spending online for big-ticket items. Although furniture and large appliances were initially perceived as too bulky to sell online, these categories have rapidly expanded in the last few years. Free shipping offered by Amazon and other large retailers has also contributed to consumers buying many more expensive and large items online such as air conditioners. Refer to Figure 9.2 to see how much consumers spent online for various categories of goods in 2015.

INTENTIONAL ACTS: HOW SHOPPERS FIND VENDORS ONLINE

Given the prevalence of "click here" display ads, one might think customers are "driven" to online vendors by spur-of-the-moment decisions. In fact, only a tiny percentage of shoppers click on display ads to find vendors. E-commerce shoppers are highly intentional. Typically, they are focused browsers looking for specific products, companies, and services. Once they are online, a majority of consumers use a search engine as their preferred method of research for purchasing a product. Many will go directly to a online marketplace, such as Amazon or eBay, and some will go directly to a specific retail website. Merchants can convert these "goal-oriented," intentional shoppers into buyers if the merchants can target their communications to the shoppers and design their sites in such a way as to provide easy-to-access and useful product information, full selection, and customer service, and do this at the very moment the customer is searching for the product. This is no small task.

WHY SOME PEOPLE DON'T SHOP ONLINE

About 9% of Internet users do not shop or buy online. Why not? One of the most important factors cited by those who don't shop or buy online is the "trust factor," the fear that online merchants will cheat you, lose your credit card information, or use personal information you give them to invade your personal privacy, bombarding you with unwanted e-mail and pop-up ads. Secondary factors can be summarized as "hassle factors," like shipping costs, returns, and inability to touch and feel the product.

TRUST, UTILITY, AND OPPORTUNISM IN ONLINE MARKETS

A long tradition of research shows that the two most important factors shaping the decision to purchase online are utility and trust (Brookings Institute, 2011; Kim et al., 2009; Ba and Pavlou, 2002). Consumers want good deals, bargains, convenience, and speed of delivery. In short, consumers are looking for utility. On the other hand, in any seller-buyer relationship, there is an asymmetry of information. The seller usually knows a lot more than the consumer about the quality of goods and terms of sale. This can lead to opportunistic behavior by sellers (Akerlof, 1970; Williamson, 1985; Mishra, 1998). Consumers need to trust a merchant before they make a purchase. Sellers can develop trust among online consumers by building strong reputations of honesty, fairness, and delivery of quality products—the basic elements of a brand. Feedback forums such as Epinions.com (now part of Shopping.com), Amazon's book reviews from reviewers, and eBay's feedback forum are examples of trust-building online mechanisms (NielsenWire, 2012; Opinion Research Corporation, 2009). Online sellers who develop trust among consumers are able to charge a premium price for their online products and services (Kim and Benbasat, 2006, 2007; Pavlou, 2002). A review of the literature suggests that the most important factors leading to a trusting online relationship are perception of website credibility, ease of use, and perceived risk (Corritore et al., 2006). An important brake on the growth of e-commerce is lack of trust. Newspaper and television ads are far more trusted than online ads (Nielsen, 2011). Personal friends and family are far more powerful determinants of online purchases than membership in social networks (eMarketer, Inc., 2010). These attitudes have grown more positive over time, but concerns about the use of personal information by online marketers continue to raise trust issues among consumers.

DIGITAL COMMERCE MARKETING AND ADVERTISING STRATEGIES AND TOOLS

Online marketing has many similarities to, and differences from, ordinary marketing. (For more information on basic marketing concepts, see Learning Tracks 6.1 and 6.2.) The objective of online marketing—as in all marketing—is to build customer relationships so that the firm can achieve above-average returns (both by offering superior products or services and by communicating the brand's features to the consumer). These relationships are a foundation for the firm's brand. But online marketing is also very different from ordinary marketing because the nature of the medium and its capabilities are so different from anything that has come before.

There are four features of online marketing that distinguish it from traditional marketing channels. Compared to traditional print and television marketing, online marketing can be more personalized, participatory, peer-to-peer, and communal. Not all types of online marketing have these four features. For instance, there's not much difference between a marketing video splashed on your computer screen without your consent and watching a television commercial. However, the same marketing video can be targeted to your personal interests, community memberships, and allow you to share it with others using a Like or + tag. Marketers are learning that the most effective forms of online marketing have all four of these features.

STRATEGIC ISSUES AND QUESTIONS

In the past, the first step in building an online brand was to build a website, and then try to attract an audience. The most common "traditional" marketing techniques for establishing a brand and attracting customers were search engine marketing, display ads, e-mail campaigns, and affiliate programs. This is still the case: building a website is still a first step, and the "traditional" online marketing techniques are still the main powerhouses of brand creation and online sales revenue. But today, marketers need to take a much broader view of the online marketing challenge, and to consider other media channels for attracting an audience such as social media and mobile devices, in concert with traditional websites.

The five main elements of a comprehensive multi-channel marketing plan are: website, traditional online marketing, social marketing, mobile marketing, and offline marketing. **Table 6.3** illustrates these five main platforms, central elements within each type, some examples, and the primary function of marketing in each situation. Each of the main types of online marketing is discussed in this section and throughout the chapter in greater detail.

Immediately, by examining Table 6.3, you can understand the management complexity of building brands online. There are five major types of marketing, and a variety of different platforms that perform different functions. If you're a manager of a startup, or the website manager of an existing commercial website, you face a number of strategic questions. Where should you focus first? Build a website, develop a blog, or jump into developing a Facebook presence? If you have a successful website that already uses search engine marketing and display ads, where should you go next:

TABLE 6.3	THE DIGITAL MARKETING ROADMAP		
TYPE OF MARKETING	PLATFORMS	EXAMPLES	FUNCTION
Website	Traditional website	Ford.com	Anchor site
Traditional Online Marketing	Search engine marketing	Google; Bing; Yahoo	Query-based intention marketing
	Display advertising	Yahoo; Google; MSN	Interest- and context-based marketing; targeted marketing
	E-mail	Major retailers	Permission marketing
	Affiliates	Amazon	Brand extension
Social Marketing	Social networks	Facebook	Conversations; sharing
	Micro blogging sites	Twitter	News, quick updates
	Blogs/forums	Tumblr	Communities of interest; sharing
	Visual marketing	Pinterest/Instagram	Branding; sharing
	Video marketing	YouTube	Engage; inform
	Game marketing	Chipotle Scarecrow Game	Identification
Mobile Marketing	Mobile site	m.ford.com	Quick access; news; updates
	Apps	Ford Mustang Customizer app	Visual engagement
		My Ford	Visual engagement
Offline Marketing	Television	Apple/The Human Family: Shot on iPhone	Brand anchoring; inform
	Newspapers	American Airlines/The World's Greatest Flyers Fly American	Brand anchoring; inform
	Magazines	Apple Watch/Vogue Magazine	Brand anchoring; inform

develop a social network presence or use offline media? Does your firm have the resources to maintain a social media marketing campaign?

A second strategic management issue involves the integration of all these different marketing platforms into a single coherent branding message. Often, there are different groups with different skill sets involved in website design, search engine and display marketing, social media marketing, and offline marketing. Getting all these different specialties to work together and coordinate their campaigns can be very difficult. The danger is that a firm ends up with different teams managing each of the four platforms rather than a single team managing the digital online presence, or for that matter, marketing for the entire firm including retail outlets.

A third strategic management question involves resource allocation. There are actually two problems here. Each of the different major types of marketing, and each of the different platforms, has different metrics to measure its effectiveness. In some cases, for new social marketing platforms, there is no commonly accepted metric, and few that have withstood critical scrutiny or have a deep experience base providing empirical data. For instance, in Facebook marketing, an important metric is how many Likes your Facebook page produces. The connection between Likes and sales is still being explored. In search engine marketing, effectiveness is measured by how many clicks your ads are receiving; in display advertising, by how many impressions of your ads are served. Second, each of these platforms has different costs for Likes, impressions, and clicks. In order to choose where your marketing resources should be deployed, you will have to link each of these activities to sales revenue. You will need to determine how much clicks, Likes, and impressions are worth. We address these questions in greater detail in Chapter 7.

THE WEBSITE AS A MARKETING PLATFORM: ESTABLISHING THE CUSTOMER RELATIONSHIP

A firm's website is a major tool for establishing the initial relationship with the customer. The website performs four important functions: establishing the brand identity and consumer expectations, informing and educating the consumer, shaping the customer experience, and anchoring the brand in an ocean of marketing messages coming from different sources. The website is the one place the consumer can turn to find the complete story. This is not true of apps, e-mail, or search engine ads.

The first function of a website is to establish the brand's identity and to act as an anchor for the firm's other web marketing activities, thereby driving sales revenue. This involves identifying for the consumer the differentiating features of the product or service in terms of quality, price, product support, and reliability. Identifying the differentiating features of the product on the website's home page is intended to create expectations in the user of what it will be like to consume the product. For instance, Snapple's website creates the expectation that the product is a delicious, refreshing drink made from high quality, natural ingredients. Ford's website focuses on automobile technology and high miles per gallon. The expectation created by Ford's website is that if you buy a Ford, you'll be experiencing the latest automotive technology and the highest mileage. At the location-based social network website for Foursquare, the focus is on meeting friends, discovering local places, and saving money with coupons and rewards.

Websites also function to anchor the brand online, acting as a central point where all the branding messages that emanate from the firm's multiple digital presences, such as Facebook, Twitter, mobile apps, or e-mail, come together at a single online location. Aside from branding, websites also perform the typical functions of any commercial establishment by informing customers of the company's products and services. Websites, with their online catalogs and associated shopping carts, are important elements of the online customer experience. **Customer experience** refers to the totality of experiences that a customer has with a firm, including the search, informing, purchase, consumption, and after-sales support for the product. The concept "customer

customer experience
the totality of experiences that a customer has with a firm, including the search, informing, purchase, consumption, and after-sales support for its products, services, and various retail channels

experience" is broader than the traditional concept of "customer satisfaction" in that a much broader range of impacts is considered, including the customer's cognitive, affective, emotional, social, and physical relationship to the firm and its products. The totality of customer experiences will generally involve multiple retail channels. This means that, in the customer's mind, the website, mobile site and apps, Facebook page, Twitter feed, physical store, and television advertisements are all connected as part of his or her experience with the company.

TRADITIONAL ONLINE MARKETING AND ADVERTISING TOOLS

Below we describe the basic marketing and advertising tools for attracting e-commerce consumers: search engine marketing, display ad marketing (including banner ads, rich media ads, video ads, and sponsorships), e-mail and permission marketing, affiliate marketing, viral marketing, and lead generation marketing.

online advertising
a paid message on a website, online service, or other interactive medium

Companies spent an estimated €513 billion on advertising worldwide in 2016 and an estimated €182 billion of that amount on **online advertising**, which includes display (banners, video, and rich media), search, mobile messaging, sponsorships, classifieds, lead generation, and e-mail, on desktop and laptop computers as well as mobile devices (see **Figure 6.5**) (eMarketer, Inc., 2016e).

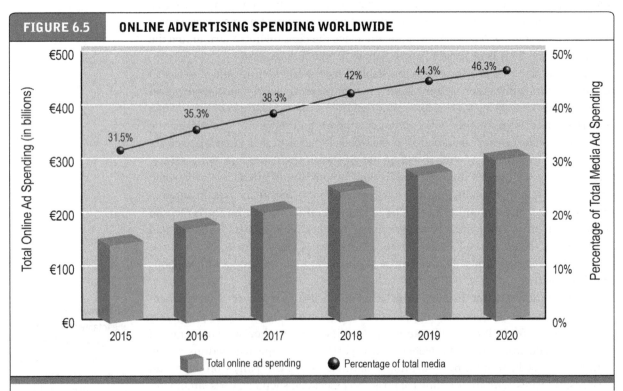

| FIGURE 6.5 | ONLINE ADVERTISING SPENDING WORLDWIDE |

Spending on online advertising worldwide is expected to grow from €182 billion in 2016 to over €312 billion by 2020 and comprise an increasing percentage of total media ad spending.

SOURCE: Based on data from eMarketer, Inc., 2016e.

TABLE 6.4	ONLINE ADVERTISING SPENDING IN THE UNITED STATES FOR SELECTED FORMATS (IN BILLIONS)		
FORMAT	2016	2020	AVERAGE GROWTH RATE
Search	$33.3	$51.4	12.2%
Banner ads	$14.4	$21.5	12.6%
Video	$10.3	$16.3	18.8%
Rich media	$8.0	$14.9	22.1%
Sponsorships	$1.9	$2.4	6.5%
Lead generation	$1.9	$2.1	4.2%
Classifieds	$1.8	$2.4	5.9%
E-mail	$0.31	$0.41	8.4%

SOURCE: Based on data from eMarketer, Inc., 2016f, 2016g.

In the last five years, advertisers have aggressively increased online spending and cut outlays on traditional channels. By 2018, the amount spent on online advertising is expected to exceed the amount spent on television advertising.

Table 6.4 provides some comparative data on the amount of spending for certain advertising formats in the United States. In 2016, the highest amount of spending is for paid search, followed by banner ads, but the fastest growing online ad formats are rich media and video ads.

Spending on U.S. online advertising among different industries is somewhat skewed. Retail accounts for the highest percentage (22%), followed by financial services (13%), automotive (13%), telecommunications (9%), leisure travel (9%), consumer electronics and computers (7%), consumer packaged goods (6%), pharmaceuticals and healthcare (5%), media (5%), and entertainment (4%) (Interactive Advertising Bureau/PricewaterhouseCoopers, 2016). Online advertising has both advantages and disadvantages when compared to advertising in traditional media, such as television, radio, and print (magazines and newspapers). One big advantage for online advertising is that the Internet is where the audience has moved, especially the very desirable 18–34 age group. A second big advantage for online advertising is the ability to target ads to individuals and small groups and to track performance of advertisements in almost real time. **Ad targeting**, the sending of market messages to specific subgroups in the population in an effort to increase the likelihood of a purchase, is as old as advertising itself, but prior to the Internet, it could only be done with much less precision, certainly not down to the level of individuals. Ad targeting is also the foundation of price discrimination: the ability to charge different types of consumers different prices for the same product or service. With online advertising, it's theoretically possible to charge every customer a different price.

ad targeting
the sending of market messages to specific subgroups in the population

Theoretically, online advertising can personalize every ad message to precisely fit the needs, interests, and values of each consumer. In practice, as we all know from spam and constant exposure to ads that are of little interest, the reality is very different. Online advertisements also provide greater opportunities for interactivity—two-way communication between advertisers and potential customers. The primary disadvantages of online advertising are concerns about its cost versus its benefits, how to adequately measure its results, and the supply of good venues to display ads. For instance, the owners of websites who sell advertising space ("publishers") do not have agreed-upon standards or routine audits to verify their claimed numbers as do traditional media outlets. We examine the costs and benefits of online advertising as well as research on its effectiveness in Section 6.4.

Search Engine Marketing and Advertising

In 2016, companies spent an estimated €83 billion worldwide on search engine marketing and advertising, about 46% of all spending for digital marketing (eMarketer, Inc., 2016e). Briefly, this is where the eyeballs are (at least for a few moments) and this is where advertising can be very effective by responding with ads that match the interests and intentions of the user. The click-through rate for search engine advertising is generally 1%–4% (with an average of around 2%) and has been fairly steady over the years. The top search engine throughout Western Europe is Google, with a market share of over 90%. **Search engine marketing (SEM)** refers to the use of search engines to build and sustain brands. **Search engine advertising** refers to the use of search engines to support direct sales to online consumers.

Search engines are often thought of as mostly direct sales channels focused on making sales in response to advertisements. While this is a major use of search engines, they are also used more subtly to strengthen brand awareness, drive traffic to other websites or blogs to support customer engagement, to gain deeper insight into customers' perceptions of the brand, to support other related advertising (for instance, sending consumers to local dealer sites), and to support the brand indirectly. Search engines can also provide marketers insight into customer search patterns, opinions customers hold about their products, top trending search keywords, and what their competitors are using as keywords and the customer response. For example, PepsiCo, home of mega brands like Pepsi and Doritos, makes no sales on the Web, but has several branding websites aimed at consumers, investors, and shareholders. The focus is on building, sustaining, and updating the Pepsi collection of branded consumer goods. A search on Pepsi will generate numerous search results that link to Pepsi marketing materials.

Types of Search Engine Advertising   Search engine sites originally performed unbiased searches of the Web's huge collection of web pages and derived most of their revenue from banner advertisements. This form of search engine results is often called **organic search** because the inclusion and ranking of websites depends on a more or less "unbiased" application of a set of rules (an algorithm) imposed by the search engine. Since 1998, search engine sites slowly transformed themselves into digital yellow

search engine marketing (SEM)
involves the use of search engines to build and sustain brands

search engine advertising
involves the use of search engines to support direct sales to online

organic search
inclusion and ranking of sites depends on a more or less unbiased application of a set of rules imposed by the search engine

pages, where firms pay for inclusion in the search engine index, pay for keywords to show up in search results, or pay for keywords to show up in other vendors' ads.

Most search engines offer **paid inclusion** programs, which, for a fee, guarantee a website's inclusion in its list of search results, more frequent visits by its web crawler, and suggestions for improving the results of organic searching. Search engines claim that these payments—costing some merchants hundreds of thousands a year—do not influence the organic ranking of a website in search results, just inclusion in the results. However, it is the case that page inclusion ads get more hits, and the rank of the page appreciates, causing the organic search algorithm to rank it higher in the organic results.

Google claims that it does not permit firms to pay for their rank in the organic results, although it does allocate two to three sponsored links at the very top of their pages, albeit labeling them as "Sponsored Links." Merchants who refuse to pay for inclusion or for keywords typically fall far down on the list of results, and off the first page of results, which is akin to commercial death.

Pay-per-click (PPC) search ads are the primary type of search engine advertising. In **keyword advertising**, merchants purchase keywords through a bidding process at search sites, and whenever a consumer searches for that word, their advertisement shows up somewhere on the page, usually as a small text-based advertisement on the right, but also as a listing on the very top of the page. The more merchants pay, the higher the rank and greater the visibility of their ads on the page. Generally, the search engines do not exercise editorial judgment about quality or content of the ads although they do monitor the use of language. In addition, some search engines rank the ads in terms of their popularity rather than merely the money paid by the advertiser so that the rank of the ad depends on both the amount paid and the number of clicks per unit time. Google's keyword advertising program is called AdWords.

Network keyword advertising (**context advertising**), introduced by Google as its AdSense product in 2002, differs from the ordinary keyword advertising described previously. Publishers (websites that want to show ads) join these networks and allow the search engine to place "relevant" ads on their sites. The ads are paid for by advertisers who want their messages to appear across the Web. Google-like text messages are the most common. The revenue from the resulting clicks is split between the search engine and the site publisher, although the publisher gets much more than half in some cases.

Search engine advertising is nearly an ideal targeted marketing technique: at precisely the moment that a consumer is looking for a product, an advertisement for that product is presented. Consumers benefit from search engine advertising because ads for merchants appear only when consumers are looking for a specific product. Thus, search engine advertising saves consumers cognitive energy and reduces search costs (including the cost of transportation needed to do physical searches for products).

Because search engine marketing can be very effective, companies optimize their websites for search engine recognition. The better optimized the page is, the higher a ranking it will achieve in search engine result listings, and the more likely it will appear on the top of the page in search engine results. **Search engine optimization**

---

paid inclusion
for a fee, guarantees a website's inclusion in its list of sites, more frequent visits by its web crawler, and suggestions for improving the results of organic searching

pay-per-click (PPC) search ad
primary type of search engine advertising

keyword advertising
merchants purchase keywords through a bidding process at search sites, and whenever a consumer searches for that word, their advertisement shows up somewhere on the page

network keyword advertising (context advertising)
publishers accept ads placed by Google on their websites, and receive a fee for any click-throughs from those ads

search engine optimization (SEO)
techniques to improve the ranking of web pages generated by search engine algorithms

(SEO) is the process of improving the ranking of web pages with search engines by altering the content and design of the web pages and site. By carefully selecting key words used on the web pages, updating content frequently, and designing the site so it can be easily read by search engine programs, marketers can improve the impact and return on investment in their web marketing programs.

Google and other search engine firms make frequent changes to their search algorithms in order to improve the search results and user experience. Google, for instance, reportedly makes over 600 search engine changes in a year. Most are small unannounced tweaks. Recent major changes have included Panda, Penguin, Hummingbird, Knowledge Graph, and an unnamed algorithm that has been nicknamed Mobilegeddon. **Panda** was introduced in 2011 in an effort to weed out low quality sites from search results. Those sites with thin content, duplicate content, content copied from elsewhere on the Web, and content that did not attract high-quality hits from other sources were systematically pushed down in the search results. Google introduced **Penguin** in 2012 in an effort to punish websites and their SEO marketing firms who were manipulating links to their site in order to improve their rankings. The Google search engine rewards sites that have links from many other sites. What some marketers discovered is that Google could not tell the quality of these back links, and they began to manufacture links by putting their clients onto list sites, creating multiple blogs to link to their clients' sites, and paying others to link to their clients' sites. Penguin evaluates the quality of links to a site, and pushes down in the rankings those sites that have poor-quality back links. Between 2012 and 2016, Google released four major Penguin updates and in September 2016 that it had become part of the core Google algorithm.

Many search engines are attempting to capture more of what the user intended, or might like to know about a search subject. This is often referred to as semantic search. Google introduced **Hummingbird** in 2013. Rather than evaluate each word separately in a search, Google's semantically informed Hummingbird will try to evaluate an entire sentence. Semantic search more closely follows conversational search, or search as you would ordinarily speak it to another human being.

Google introduced **Knowledge Graph** in 2012 as an effort to anticipate what you might want to know more about as you search on a topic or answer questions you might not thought of asking. Since 2013, results of Knowledge Graph appear on the right of the screen and contain more information about the topic or person you are searching on. Not all search terms have a Knowledge Graph result. Google displays information based on what other users have searched for in the past, as well as its database on over 1 billion objects (people, places, and things), and more than 18 billion facts.

In 2015, Google released a new algorithm update (nicknamed Mobilegeddon) that made the "mobile-friendliness" of websites a much stronger ranking factor for mobile searches. Websites that are not optimized for mobile now have a much lower ranking in mobile search results. And starting in November 2015, Google began lowering the search rank of mobile websites that display an ad that obscures the screen and asks users whether they would like to install the site's mobile app, on the grounds that such ads are less mobile-friendly. Companies that use such ads, such as Yelp, LinkedIn, Pinterest, and others, have charged that Google's new policy is in part an effort to protect its web search revenue from mobile apps that lure users away from the Web.

Panda
change in the Google algorithm to eliminate low-quality sites from search results

Penguin
change in the Google algorithm to eliminate sites with low-quality back links

Hummingbird
semantic search component of Google's search algorithm

Knowledge Graph
function in Google's search engine that displays a selection of facts related to your search term that you may be interested in knowing more about

Social Search **Social search** is an attempt to use your social contacts (and your entire social graph) to provide search results. In contrast to search engines that use a mathematical algorithm to find pages that satisfy your query, social search reviews your friends' (and their friends') recommendations, past web visits, and use of Like buttons. One problem with traditional search engines is that they are so thorough: enter a search for "smartphone" on Google and in .28 seconds you will receive 569 million results, some of which provide helpful information and others that are suspect. Social search is an effort to provide fewer, more relevant, and trustworthy results based on the social graph. Facebook's first effort to create a social search engine was Facebook Graph Search, which it launched in 2013. Graph Search produced information from within a user's network of friends supplemented with additional results provided by Bing. In 2014, Facebook introduced a series of changes to Graph Search, dropping its relationship with Bing, rebranding the product as Facebook Search, and providing keyword search functionality that enables users to find people, photos, posts, videos, and links on Facebook by searching for words within a post. Results are ranked using a personalization algorithm based in part on the user's relationship to the poster.

social search

effort to provide fewer, more relevant, and trust-worthy results based on the social graph

Search Engine Issues While search engines have provided significant benefits to merchants and customers, they also present risks and costs. For instance, search engines have the power to crush a small business by placing its ads on the back pages of search results. Merchants are at the mercy of search engines for access to the online marketplace, and this access is dominated by a single firm, Google. How Google decides to rank one company over another in search results is not known. No one really knows how to improve in its rankings (although there are hundreds of firms who claim otherwise). Google editors intervene in unknown ways to punish certain websites and reward others. Using paid sponsored listings, as opposed to relying on organic search results, eliminates some, but not all, of this uncertainty.

Other practices that degrade the results and usefulness of search engines include:

- **Link farms** are groups of websites that link to one another, thereby boosting their ranking in search engines that use a PageRank algorithm to judge the "usefulness" of a site. For instance, in the 2010 holiday season, JCPenney was found to be the highest ranked merchant for a large number of clothing products. On examination, it was discovered that this resulted from Penney's hiring a search engine optimization company to create thousands of websites that linked to JCPenney's website. As a result, JCPenney's website became the most popular (most linked-to) website for products like dresses, shirts, and pants. No matter what popular clothing item people searched for, JCPenney came out on top. Experts believe this was the largest search engine fraud in history. Google's Panda series of updates to its search algorithms were aimed in part at eliminating link farms (Castell, 2014).

link farms

groups of websites that link to one another, thereby boosting their ranking in search engines

content farms

companies that generate large volumes of textual content for multiple websites designed to attract viewers and search engines

- **Content farms** are companies that generate large volumes of textual content for multiple websites designed to attract viewers and search engines. Content farms profit by attracting large numbers of readers to their sites and exposing them to ads. The content typically is not original but is artfully copied or summarized from legitimate content sites.

- **Click fraud** occurs when a competitor clicks on search engine results and ads, forcing the advertiser to pay for the click even though the click is not legitimate. Competitors can hire offshore firms to perform fraudulent clicks or hire botnets to automate the process. Click fraud can quickly run up a large bill for merchants, and not result in any growth in sales. A study by the National Association of Advertisers estimated that advertisers would lose $7.2 billion in 2016 due to click fraud (Ragan, 2016).

Display Ad Marketing

In 2016, companies spent around €83 billion worldwide on all forms of display ad marketing, about 46% of all spending for digital marketing. More than 6 trillion display ads will be served on desktop and mobile devices in 2016. The top five display ad companies in the United States are Facebook, Google, Twitter, Yahoo, and Verizon (AOL and Millennial Media), which together account for almost 60% of U.S. display ad revenue. The Interactive Advertising Bureau (IAB), an industry organization, has established voluntary industry guidelines for display ads. Publishers are not required to use these guidelines, but many do. One objective of IAB is to give the consumer a consistent experience across all websites. The various types of ads are designed to help advertisers break through the "noise" and clutter created by the high number of display ad impressions that a typical user is exposed to within a given day. **Figure 6.6** shows examples of the seven core standard ad units as specified by the IAB. According to Google, the top performing ad formats are the large rectangle, the medium rectangle, the leaderboard, and the half-page (Google Inc., 2016). Display ads consist of four different kinds of ads: banner ads, rich media ads (animated ads), sponsorships, and video ads.

banner ad

displays a promotional message in a rectangular box at the top or bottom of a computer screen

Banner Ads   Banner ads are the oldest and most familiar form of display marketing. They are also the least effective and the lowest cost form of online marketing. A banner ad displays a promotional message in a rectangular box on the screen of a desktop computer or mobile device. A **banner ad** is similar to a traditional ad in a printed publication but has some added advantages. When clicked, it brings potential customers directly to the advertiser's website, and the site where the ad appears can observe the user's behavior on the site. The ability to identify and track the user is a key feature of online advertising. Banner ads often feature video and other animations. It's important to note that, although the terms banner ad and display ad are often used interchangeably, banner ads are just one form of display ad. Despite their limited effectiveness, advertisers will still spend about $14 billion on banner ads in 2016, about 42% of all spending on display ads, and 20% of total online ad spending.

rich media ad

ad employing animation, sound, and interactivity, using Flash, HTML5, Java, and JavaScript

Rich Media Ads   Ads that employ animation, sound, and interactivity, using Flash, HTML5, Java, and JavaScript are referred to as **rich media ads**. They are far more effective than simple banner ads. For instance, one research report that analyzed 24,000 different rich media ads with more than 12 billion impressions served in North America over a six-month period found that exposure to rich media ads boosted advertiser site visits by nearly 300% compared to standard banner ads. Viewers of

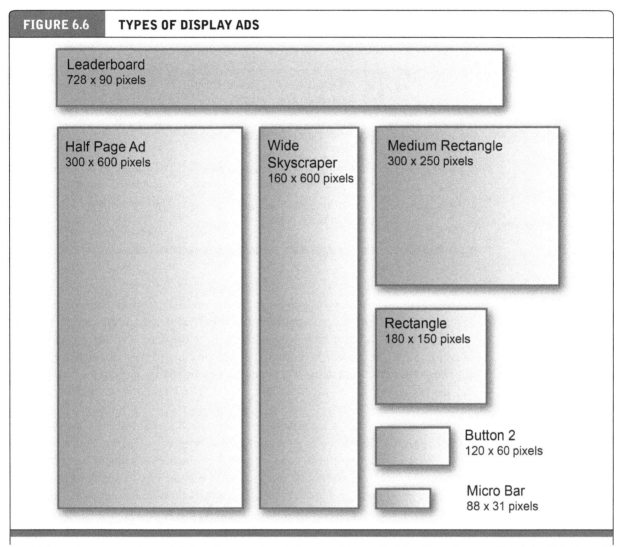

FIGURE 6.6   TYPES OF DISPLAY ADS

Leaderboard
728 x 90 pixels

Half Page Ad
300 x 600 pixels

Wide
Skyscraper
160 x 600 pixels

Medium Rectangle
300 x 250 pixels

Rectangle
180 x 150 pixels

Button 2
120 x 60 pixels

Micro Bar
88 x 31 pixels

In addition to the seven core forms of display ads shown above, IAB also provides standards for six new formats called Display Rising Star ad units.

SOURCE: Based on data from Interactive Advertising Bureau, 2011.

rich media ads that included video were six times more likely to visit the advertiser's website, by either directly clicking on the ad, typing the advertiser's URL, or searching (MediaMind, 2012a). Recent research by the IAB indicates that its Rising Star ad units that can incorporate rich media elements deliver a 30% stronger brand lift than the traditional IAB core display ads with just one full exposure, increasing to over 40% when a consumer interacts with the ad. Rising Star ads also topped traditional display ads in terms of ad recall and were considered less annoying (IAB, 2015).

The IAB provides guidance for a number of different types of rich media ads, such as those that contain in-banner video, those that are expandable/retractable, pop-ups, floating versions, and interstitials. An **interstitial ad** (interstitial means

interstitial ad
a way of placing a full-page message between the current and destination pages of a user

TABLE 6.5	TYPES OF VIDEO ADS	
FORMAT	DESCRIPTION	WHEN USED
Linear video ad	Pre-roll; takeover; ad takes over video for a certain period of time	Before, between, or after video
Nonlinear video ad	Overlay; ad runs at same time as video content and does not take over full screen	During, over, or within video
In-banner video ad	Rich media; ad is triggered within banner, may expand outside banner	Within web page, generally surrounded by content
In-text video ad	Rich media; ad is delivered when user mouses over relevant text	Within web page, identified as a highlighted word within relevant content

"in between") is a way of placing a full-page message between the current and destination pages of a user. Interstitials are usually inserted within a single website, and displayed as the user moves from one page to the next. The interstitial is typically contained in its own browser window and moves automatically to the page the user requested after allowing enough time for the ad to be read. Interstitials can also be deployed over an advertising network and appear as users move among websites.

Because the Web is such a busy place, people have to find ways to cope with overstimulation. One means of coping is known as *sensory input filtering*. This means that people learn to filter out the vast majority of the messages coming at them. Internet users quickly learn at some level to recognize banner ads or anything that looks like a banner ad and to filter out most of the ads that are not exceptionally relevant. Interstitial messages, like TV commercials, attempt to make viewers a captive of the message. Typical interstitials last 10 seconds or less and force the user to look at the ad for that time period. IAB standards for pre-roll ads also limit their length. To avoid boring users, ads typically use animated graphics and music to entertain and inform them. A good interstitial will also have a "skip through" or "stop" option for users who have no interest in the message.

The IAB also provides mobile rich media ad interface definitions (MRAID) in an effort to provide a set of standards designed to work with HTML5 and JavaScript that developers can use to create rich media ads to work with apps running on different mobile devices. The hope is make it easier to display ads across a wide variety of devices without having to rewrite code (Interactive Advertising Bureau, 2012).

video ad

TV-like advertisement that appears as an in-page video commercial or before, during, or after content

Video Ads Online **video ads** are TV-like advertisements that appear as in-page video commercials or before, during, or after a variety of content. **Table 6.5** describes some of the IAB standards for video ads. The most widely used format is the "pre-roll" (followed by the mid-roll and the post-roll) where users are forced to watch a video ad either before, in the middle of, or at the end of the video they originally clicked on. In 2014, the IAB released additional standards for five new in-stream and linear interactive video ad formats that enable advertisers to provide additional opportunities for consumer engagement.

Although from a total spending standpoint, online video ads are still very small when compared to the amount spent on search engine advertising, video ads are another fast growing form of online advertisement. The rapid growth in video ads is due in part to the fact that video ads are far more effective than other display ad formats. For instance, according to research analyzing a variety of ad formats, in-stream video ads had click-through rates 12 times that of rich media and 27 times that of standard banner ads (MediaMind, 2012). Research by the IAB indicates that interactive digital video has even greater impact than typical, non-interactive video formats, with interaction rates three to four times higher, and brand awareness heightened by more than 50% (Interactive Advertising Bureau, 2014).

There are many specialized video advertising networks that run video advertising campaigns for national advertisers and place these videos on their respective networks of websites. Firms can also establish their own video and television sites to promote their products. Retail sites are among the largest users of advertising videos. For instance, Zappos, the largest online shoe retailer, has a video for every one of its over 100,000 products.

Sponsorships A **sponsorship** is a paid effort to tie an advertiser's name to particular information, an event, or a venue in a way that reinforces its brand in a positive yet not overtly commercial manner. Sponsorships typically are more about branding than immediate sales. A common form of sponsorship is targeted content (or advertorials), in which editorial content is combined with an ad message to make the message more valuable and attractive to its intended audience. For instance, WebMD, the leading medical information website in the United States, displays sponsored pages on the WebMD website from companies such as Phillips to describe its home defibrillators, and Lilly to describe its pharmaceutical solutions for attention deficit disorders among children. Social media sponsorships, in which marketers pay for mentions in social media, such as blogs, tweets, or in online video, have also become a popular tactic. Sponsorships have also moved onto the mobile platform. For instance, Subaru sponsors an app called MapMyDogwalk, a GPS-enabled dog walking tool.

sponsorship
a paid effort to tie an advertiser's name to information, an event, or a venue in a way that reinforces its brand in a positive yet not overtly commercial manner

Native Advertising Advertising that looks similar to editorial content is known as **native advertising.** Native advertising is not new. Traditional native advertising includes television infomercials, newspaper advertorials, and entire sections of newspapers and magazines that are given over to advertisers, where the advertising looks similar to the rest of the publication. In the online world, native ads are most often found on social media, especially mobile social media, as part of a Facebook News Feed, Twitter Timeline, or Pinterest Promoted Pin. Mobile social networks do not have room for ads on the right side of the screen (the sidebar or right rail), and therefore native ads in the form of posts that look like other posts are the favored option. Native

native advertising
advertising that looks similar to editorial content

advertising's share of mobile display ad revenues has skyrocketed and together with content marketing now garners 45% of the spending on U.K. mobile display advertising (eMarketer, Inc., 2016h).

Typically, native ads mimic the editorial content around them, and increasingly include video. They appear outside the normal or expected area for ads and are labeled to indicate they are not editorial content, although in most cases the word "ad" is not used. On the Web or mobile screens, native ads are usually distinguished by a "sponsored" tag underneath the headline, often in a different color. Online native advertising is growing rapidly, especially on social networks. The U.S. Federal Trade Commission researchers found that 73% of online publishers offer native advertising, including traditional publishers such as the *New York Times*, the *Wall Street Journal*, *Forbes*, and many others.

Researchers have found that 35% of online consumers cannot distinguish between editorial content and sponsored ads that look like editorial content, even if the ads are labelled as sponsored or promoted. Most consumers do not know what sponsored or promoted means. In a survey of 10,000 consumers, researchers found that consumers skip over labels like sponsored, and many do not understand the difference between paid and unpaid content (Franklyn, 2013). Yet market researchers have found that native ads are far more influential with consumers. Consumers look at native ads for about twice as long as they do banner ads, 53% more frequently than display ads; native ads raise purchase intent by 18%; and consumers are twice as likely to share a native ad with a family member as a regular ad. Marketers and advertisers are opposed to labeling native advertising with the word "ad" and instead prefer other tags.

Native advertising is controversial. Critics contend that the purpose of native ads is to deceive or fool the consumer into thinking the ad has the same validity as the editorial content in media. In December 2015, the Federal Trade Commission issued an enforcement policy statement on deceptively formatted advertisements and guidelines setting forth explicit rules for native ads. The FTC said it would examine the entire ad, including factors such as its overall appearance, its similarity of its style to editorial content on the site on which it appears, and the degree to which it is distinguishable from such content. It further advised that labels indicting the commercial nature of the content need to be prominently displayed upon the viewer's first contact with the contact (Federal Trade Commission, 2015a, 2015b). In 2016, in the first action under the new guidelines, the FTC charged that a native advertising campaign run by national retailer Lord & Taylor's on Instagram deceived consumers. Lord & Taylor agreed to settle the complaint in March 2016 (Feil, 2016).

content marketing
creates a content campaign for a brand and then attempts to secure placement on a variety of websites

Content Marketing Native advertising is usually focused on partnering with a specific publisher. **Content marketing** creates a content campaign for a brand and then tries to secure placement on a variety of websites. Examples of content include articles, infographics, case studies, interactive graphics, white papers and even traditional press releases. The aim of content marketing is to increase visitors to a company's website, organic search rankings, and brand engagement via social media (Libert, 2015).

Advertising Networks In the early years of e-commerce, firms placed ads on the few popular websites in existence, but by early 2000, there were hundreds of thousands

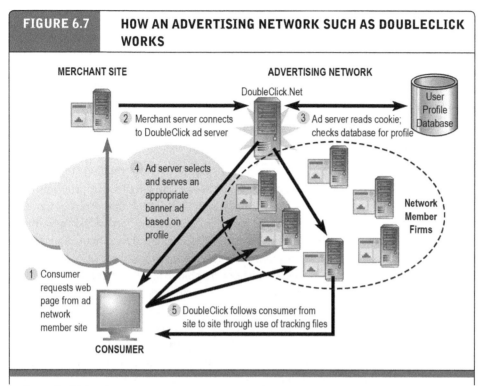

FIGURE 6.7 | **HOW AN ADVERTISING NETWORK SUCH AS DOUBLECLICK WORKS**

Millions of publishers have audiences to sell, and pages to fill with ads. Thousands of advertisers are looking for audiences. Ad networks are intermediaries that connect publishers with marketers.

of sites where ads could be displayed, and it became very inefficient for a single firm to purchase ads on each individual website. Most firms, even very large firms, did not have the capability by themselves to place banner ads and marketing messages on thousands of websites and monitor the results. Specialized marketing firms called **advertising networks** appeared to help firms take advantage of the powerful marketing potential of the Internet, and to make the entire process of buying and selling online ads more efficient and transparent. These ad networks have proliferated and have greatly increased the scale and liquidity of online marketing.

Advertising networks represent the most sophisticated application of Internet database capabilities to date, and illustrate just how different Internet marketing is from traditional marketing. Advertising networks sell advertising and marketing opportunities (slots) to companies who wish to buy exposure to an online audience (advertisers). Advertising networks obtain their inventory of ad opportunities from a network of participating sites that want to display ads on their sites in return for receiving a payment from advertisers everytime a visitor clicks on an ad. These sites are usually referred to as web publishers. Marketers buy audiences and publishers sell audiences by attracting an audience and capturing audience information. Ad networks are the intermediaries who make this market work efficiently.

Figure 6.7 illustrates how these systems work. Advertising networks begin with a consumer requesting a page from a member of the advertising network (1). A

advertising networks
connect online marketers with publishers by displaying ads to consumers based on detailed customer information

connection is established with the third-party ad server (2). The ad server identifies the user by reading the cookie file on the user's hard drive and checks its user profile database for the user's profile (3). The ad server selects an appropriate banner ad based on the user's previous purchases, interests, demographics, or other data in the profile (4). Whenever the user later goes online and visits any of the network member sites, the ad server recognizes the user and serves up the same or different ads regardless of the site content. The advertising network follows users from site to site through the use of web tracking files (5).

Advertising Exchanges, Programmatic Advertising, Real-Time Bidding Today, most online display advertising is being delivered by ad exchanges that use programmatic advertising and real-time bidding. An **ad exchange** is a digital marketplace that uses an automated auction-based method known as **programmatic advertising** to match supply and demand of online display advertising. Programmatic advertising uses a **real-time bidding (RTB) process** to match advertiser demand for display ads with publisher supply of web page space. Publishers are able to sell their inventory of empty web pages, often excess inventory that could not be sold directly. Want to contact males age 18 to 34, recent visitors to a car site, unmarried, high risk-taking profile, located in New York or California, urban home, and financial service industry employment? An ad exchange will allow you to bid in real time on this audience against other advertisers, and then manage the placement of ads, accounting, and measurement for your firm. Ad exchanges offer tremendous global scale and efficiency. One of the best known is Google's DoubleClick Ad Exchange, which is based on more than 100 ad networks (the supply side), and provides a computer-based market for buyers to purchase audiences (the demand side). This exchange sells audiences sliced into 1,600 interest categories. It displays more than 300 billion ad impressions a month across 2 million websites worldwide, and maintains or distributes more than 500 million user profiles of Internet users (Kantrowitz, 2015, 2013). These profiles are based on web tracking files, offline purchase information, and social network data. Marketing firms, the buyers from publishers of websites, can target their audience and control the frequency and timing of ads during the day. The case study at the end of the chapter, *Programmatic Advertising: Real Time Marketing*, provides you with a further look at ad exchanges and real-time bidding.

Display Advertising Issues As with search engine advertising, online display advertising is not without its issues, which include both ad fraud (similar to click fraud) and concerns about viewability (whether display ads are actually being seen).

    Ad Fraud.   In 2016, the advertising industry has become increasingly concerned about the issue of ad fraud. **Ad fraud** involves the practice of falsifying web or mobile traffic in order to charge advertisers for impressions, clicks, or other actions that never actually occurred (eMarketer, Inc., 2016i). A study by the Interactive Advertising Bureau estimated that U.S. online advertisers are losing over $8 billion annually as a result of ad fraud (Scott, 2016). There are four primary sources of ad fraud. Botnets can be hired by publishers to click on their web pages to create phony traffic. Second,

---

ad exchanges

auction-based digital marketplace where ad networks sell ad space to marketers

programmatic advertising

automated, auction-based method for matching demand and supply for online display ads

real-time bidding (RTB) process

used to match advertiser demand for display ads with publisher supply of web page space

ad fraud

falsifying web or mobile traffic in order to charge advertisers for impressions, clicks, or other actions that never actually occurred a browser extension can insert ads into a premium publisher's website, and then list the ads as available on a programmatic ad exchange. Third, ad targeting firms can create bots that imitate the behavior of real shoppers, and then charge advertisers for successfully targeting consumers. Fourth, if you are a publisher looking to attract ads to your site, the simplest technique is simply to hire people in low-wage countries to click on your ads using a proxy server (Kantrowitz, 2014).

Large advertisers have begun to hire online fraud detection firms (a growth industry) to determine the extent of fraud in their campaigns. Verizon Wireless, L'Oreal, and Kellogg are among the firms that found millions of dollars of ad fraud in recent campaigns, and have demanded advertising networks to either reimburse them or generate real web traffic in the amount of the fraud.

Viewability.   Recent research by Google revealed that 56% of the impressions served across its display advertising platforms, including DoubleClick, are not viewable. There are a number of reasons for this situation. First, there is no mechanism for measuring how many people actually see an online ad that has been served. The same is true of most offline print and TV advertising, although several methods and certifications have been developed over decades to accurately measure audience exposure. There are no such mechanisms for online advertising. Second, a large percentage of ads served appear lower down on the screen where users are less likely to go, or video ads on auto-play are playing in areas the user cannot see. Advertisers are still charged for ads that are served but not viewed. Unscrupulous publishers can place multiple ads on top of each other and charge multiple times for the same page space. Third, botnets can be programmed to click on ads on fraudulent websites, generating impressions and ad serves, but no one actually sees the ads. The Media Rating Council, an advertising industry group, released a very low standard for "viewability" in 2014: an ad is considered viewable if half of the ad can be viewed for at least one second. For video ads, half of the video needs to be viewable for two seconds (Hof, 2014). A revised version of the guidelines issued in August 2015 addressed some additional specific issues, but did not alter the baseline standard. In April 2016, the MRC issued proposed rules for mobile ads that set forth the same thresholds: 50% of the pixels in view for at least one second for display ads, and two seconds for video ads (Neff, 2016). The advertisers who pay for online ads are beginning to demand guarantees of viewability. Several companies, including comScore, are offering tagging technology that can partially measure viewability (Vranica, 2014). Unviewed ads are just as profitable as viewed ads for web publishers and advertising agencies. For advertisers, they represent the half of marketing expenditures that is wasted.

Ad Blocking.   Over the past several years, use of ad-blocking software, which can eliminate display ads, pre-roll video ads, retargeted ads, and some types of native ads on desktops and laptops, has been growing. Ad blockers operate in a manner very similar to a firewall, recognizing and eliminating content based on IP address. Ad blockers have become very easy to install, with programs such as Adblock Plus offered as extensions for Firefox, Chrome, and other web browsers. Currently, almost 25% of Internet users in the United States are estimated to be employing ad blockers, with their most prevalent use among the younger, more technically advanced audience.

Gaming, newsgroup/forums, and social network sites are the most frequently affected by ad-blocking. Although advertisers are not yet panicked about ad blocking, it is a trend that they are watching with increasing concern. Some websites, such as Wired, The Guardian, and OKCupid, have made a direct appeal to their users to turn off their ad-blockers or to make a donation instead.

E-mail Marketing

direct e-mail marketing

e-mail marketing messages sent directly to interested users

When e-mail marketing began, unsolicited e-mail was not common. **Direct e-mail marketing** (e-mail marketing messages sent directly to interested users) was one of the first and most effective forms of online marketing communications. Direct e-mail marketing messages are sent to an opt-in audience of Internet users who, at one time or another, have expressed an interest in receiving messages from the advertiser. By sending e-mail to an opt-in audience, advertisers are targeting interested consumers. By far, in-house e-mail lists are more effective than purchased e-mail lists. Because of the comparatively high response rates and low cost, direct e-mail marketing remains a common form of online marketing communications. Other benefits of e-mail marketing include its mass reach, the ability to track and measure response, the ability to personalize content and tailor offers, the ability to drive traffic to websites for more interaction, the ability to test and optimize content and offers, and the ability to target by region, demographic, time of day, or other criteria. In 2016, although companies will spend a relatively small amount on e-mail marketing when compared to search and display ad marketing, e-mail marketing still packs a punch with solid customer response. Click-through rates for legitimate e-mail depend on the promotion (the offer), the product, and the amount of targeting, but average around 3%–4%. Despite the deluge of spam mail, e-mail remains a highly cost-effective way of communicating with existing customers, and to a lesser extent, finding new customers. Mobile devices have become the predominant method for accessing e-mail. A survey by Movable Ink showed that 69% of all e-mails sent on its platform in the fourth quarter of 2015 were opened on a smartphone or tablet computer, while only 31% were opened on a desktop or laptop (eMarketer, Inc., 2016j).

E-mail marketing and advertising is inexpensive and somewhat invariant to the number of mails sent. The cost of sending 1,000 e-mails is about the same as the cost to send 1 million. The primary cost of e-mail marketing is for the purchase of the list of names to which the e-mail will be sent. This generally costs anywhere from 5 to 20 cents a name, depending on how targeted the list is. Sending the e-mail is virtually cost-free. In contrast, the cost to acquire the name, print, and mail a 5 x 7-inch direct mail post card is around 75 to 80 cents a name.

While e-mail marketing often is sales-oriented, it can also be used as an integral feature of a multi-channel marketing campaign designed to strengthen brand recognition. Relevancy in the form of personalization and targeting are major themes in e-mail marketing in 2016. For instance, Jeep created an e-mail campaign to a targeted audience who had searched on SUVs, and visited Chrysler and Jeep Facebook pages. The e-mail campaign announced a contest based on a game users could play online that involved tracking an arctic beast with a Jeep. Recipients could sign up on Facebook, Twitter, or the Jeep blog.

Although e-mail can still be an effective marketing and advertising tool, it faces three main challenges: spam, software tools used to control spam that eliminate much e-mail from user inboxes, and poorly targeted purchased e-mail lists. **Spam** is unsolicited commercial e-mail (sometimes referred to as "junk" e-mail) and *spammers* are people who send unsolicited e-mail to a mass audience that has not expressed any interest in the product. Spammers tend to market pornography, fraudulent deals and services, scams, and other products not widely approved in most civilized societies. Legitimate direct opt-in e-mail marketing is not growing as fast as behaviorally targeted display ads and search engine advertising because of the explosion in spam. Consumer response to even legitimate e-mail campaigns has become more sophisticated. In general, e-mail works well for maintaining customer relationships but poorly for acquiring new customers.

While click fraud may be the Achilles' heel of search engine advertising, spam is the nemesis of effective e-mail marketing and advertising. The percentage of all e-mail that is spam averaged around 53% in 2016 (Symantec, 2016). Most spam originates from bot networks, which consist of thousands of captured PCs that can initiate and relay spam messages (see Chapter 4). Spam volume has declined somewhat since authorities took down the Rustock botnet in 2011. Spam is seasonally cyclical, and varies monthly due to the impact of new technologies (both supportive and discouraging of spammers), new prosecutions, and seasonal demand for products and services.

Legislative attempts in the United States to control spam have been mostly unsuccessful. Thirty-seven states have laws regulating or prohibiting spam (National Conference of State Legislatures, 2015). State legislation typically requires that unsolicited mail (spam) contain a label in the subject line ("ADV") indicating the message is an advertisement, requires a clear opt-out choice for consumers, and prohibits e-mail that contains false routing and domain name information (nearly all spammers hide their own domain, ISP, and IP address).

The U.S. Congress passed the first national anti-spam law ("Controlling the Assault of Non-Solicited Pornography and Marketing" or CAN-SPAM Act) in 2003, and it went into effect in January 2004. The act does not prohibit unsolicited e-mail (spam) but instead requires unsolicited commercial e-mail messages to be labeled (though not by a standard method) and to include opt-out instructions and the sender's physical address. It prohibits the use of deceptive subject lines and false headers in such messages. The FTC is authorized (but not required) to establish a "Do Not E-mail" registry. State laws that require labels on unsolicited commercial e-mail or prohibit such messages entirely are pre-empted, although provisions merely addressing falsity and deception may remain in place. The act imposes fines of $10 for each unsolicited pornographic e-mail and authorizes state attorneys general to bring lawsuits against spammers. The act obviously makes lawful legitimate bulk mailing of unsolicited e-mail messages (what most people call spam), yet seeks to prohibit certain deceptive practices and provide a small measure of consumer control by requiring opt-out notices. In this sense, critics point out, CAN-SPAM ironically legalizes spam as long as spammers follow the rules.

spam
unsolicited commercial e-mail

For this reason, large spammers have been among the bill's biggest supporters, and consumer groups have been the act's most vociferous critics.

In contrast, Canada's anti-spam law is one of the toughest in the world. Unlike the CAN-SPAM Act, Canada's law is based on an opt-in model and prohibits the sending of commercial e-mail, texts, and social media messaging unless the recipient has given his or her consent. Violations of the law can lead to penalties of up to $1 million for individuals and $10 million for organizations. The first phase of the law went into effect in 2014. The law applies anytime a computer within Canada is used to send or access an electronic message, so companies located within the United States that send e-mail to Canada must comply with the law (French, 2014).

There have been a number of state and federal prosecutions of spammers, and private civil suits by large ISPs such as Microsoft. Volunteer efforts by industry are another potential control point. Notably, the Direct Marketing Association (DMA), an industry trade group that represents companies that use the postal mail system as well as e-mail for solicitations, is now strongly supporting legislative controls over spam, in addition to its voluntary guidelines. The DMA would like to preserve the legitimate use of e-mail as a marketing technique. The DMA has formed a 15-person anti-spam group and spends $500,000 a year trying to identify spammers. The DMA is also a supporter of the National Cyber-Forensics & Training Alliance (NCFTA), a nonprofit organization with close ties to the FBI. NCFTA operates a variety of initiatives aimed at combating cybercrime, including digital phishing via spam.

Affiliate Marketing

affiliate marketing
commissions paid by advertisers to affiliate websites for referring potential customers to their website

Affiliate marketing is a form of marketing where a firm pays a commission, typically anywhere between 4% to 20%, to other websites (including blogs) for sending customers to their website. Affiliate marketing generally involves pay-for-performance: the affiliate or affiliate network gets paid only if users click on a link or purchase a product. Industry experts estimate that around 10% of all retail online sales are generated through affiliate programs (as compared to search engine ads, which account for more than 30% of online sales), and affiliate programs run by the Internet Retailer Top 500 have a median of 2,000 participating affiliates.

Visitors to an affiliate website typically click on ads and are taken to the advertiser's website. In return, the advertiser pays the affiliate a fee, either on a per-click basis or as a percentage of whatever the customer spends on the advertiser's site. Paying commissions for referrals or recommendations long predated the Web.

For instance, Amazon has a strong affiliate program consisting of more than 1 million participant sites, called Associates, which receive up to 10% in advertising fees on sales their referrals generate. Affiliates attract people to their blogs or websites where they can click on ads for products at Amazon. Members of eBay's Affiliates Program can earn 40% to 80% of eBay's revenue on winning bids and Buy It Now transactions as well as $20 to $35 for each active registered user sent to eBay. Amazon, eBay, and other large e-commerce companies with affiliate programs typically administer such programs themselves. Smaller e-commerce firms who wish to use affiliate marketing often decide to join an affiliate network (sometimes called an affiliate broker), such as CJ Affiliate and Rakuten Linkshare, which acts as an intermediary. Bloggers often sign up for Google's AdSense program to attract advertisers to their sites. They are paid for each click on an ad and sometimes for subsequent purchases made by visitors.

Viral Marketing

Just as affiliate marketing involves using a trusted website to encourage users to visit other sites, **viral marketing** is a form of social marketing that involves getting customers to pass along a company's marketing message to friends, family, and colleagues. It's the online version of word-of-mouth advertising, which spreads even faster and further than in the real world. In the offline world, next to television, word of mouth is the second most important means by which consumers find out about new products. And the most important factor in the decision to purchase is the face-to-face recommendations of parents, friends, and colleagues. Millions of online adults in the United States are "influencers" who share their opinions about products in a variety of online settings. In addition to increasing the size of a company's customer base, customer referrals also have other advantages: they are less expensive to acquire because existing customers do all the acquisition work, and they tend to use online support services less, preferring to turn back to the person who referred them for advice. Also, because they cost so little to acquire and keep, referred customers begin to generate profits for a company much earlier than customers acquired through other marketing methods. There are a number of online venues where viral marketing appears. E-mail used to be the primary online venue for viral marketing ("please forward this e-mail to your friends"), but venues such as Facebook, Pinterest, Instagram, Twitter, YouTube, and blogs now play a major role. For example, the most viral video ad of 2015 was an ad for Google's Android that featured surprising pairings of different species of animals, such as elephants and dogs and bears and tigers, set to a song from the soundtrack of Disney's animated film *Robin Hood*. The video was shared more than 6.4 million times.

viral marketing
the process of getting customers to pass along a company's marketing message to friends, family, and colleagues

Lead Generation Marketing

Lead generation marketing uses multiple e-commerce presences to generate leads for businesses who later can be contacted and converted into customers through sales calls, e-mail, or other means. In one sense, all Internet marketing campaigns attempt to develop leads. But lead generation marketing is a specialized subset of the Internet marketing industry that provides consulting services and software tools to collect and manage leads for firms, and to convert these leads to customers. Companies will spend an estimated $1.9 billion on lead generation marketing in 2016. Sometimes called "inbound marketing," lead generation marketing firms help other firms build websites, launch e-mail campaigns, use social network sites and blogs to optimize the generation of leads, and then manage those leads by initiating further contacts, tracking interactions, and interfacing with customer relationship management systems to keep track of customer-firm interactions. One of the foremost lead generation marketing firms is Hubspot, which has developed a software suite for generating and managing leads.

lead generation marketing
uses multiple e-commerce presences to generate leads for businesses who later can be contacted and converted into customers

SOCIAL, MOBILE, AND LOCAL MARKETING AND ADVERTISING

In this section we provide a very brief overview of the social, mobile, and local marketing and advertising landscape. Then, in Chapter 7, we provide a much more in-depth examination of social, mobile, and local marketing and advertising tools.

Social Marketing and Advertising

Social marketing and advertising involves the use of online social networks and communities to build brands and drive sales revenues. There are several kinds of social networks, from Facebook, Twitter, Pinterest, and Instagram, to social apps, social games, blogs, and forums (websites that attract people who share a community of interests or skills). In 2016, companies spent about €33 billion worldwide on social network marketing and advertising. Next to mobile marketing, it is the fastest growing type of online marketing. Nevertheless, in 2016, it represented only about 18% of all online marketing and is still dwarfed by the amount spent on search engine advertising and display advertising (eMarketer, Inc., 2016l).

Marketers cannot ignore the huge audiences that social networks such as Facebook, Twitter, Pinterest, and Instagram are gathering, which rival television and radio in size. In 2016, there were about 1.7 billion Facebook members, around 500 million Instagram users, over 300 million active Twitter users, around 500 million Instagram users, and over 100 million Pinterest members worldwide. Almost one-third of the world's population regularly visits social networks. It's little wonder that marketers and advertisers are joyous at the prospect of connecting with this large audience. Research has found that social network users are more likely to talk about and recommend a company or product they follow on a social network.

Social networks offer advertisers all the main advertising formats, including banner ads (the most common), short pre-roll and post-roll ads associated with videos, and sponsorship of content. Having a corporate Facebook page is in itself a marketing tool for brands just like a web page. Many firms, such as Coca-Cola, have shut down product-specific web pages and instead use Facebook pages.

Blogs and online games can also be used for social marketing. Blogs have been around for a decade and are a part of the mainstream online culture (see Chapter 2 for a description of blogs). Around 29 million people write blogs, and around 80 million read blogs in the United States. Blogs play a vital role in online marketing. Although more firms use Twitter and Facebook, these sites have not replaced blogs, and in fact often point to blogs for long-form content. Because blog readers and creators tend to be more educated, have higher incomes, and be opinion leaders, blogs are ideal platforms for ads for many products and services that cater to this kind of audience. Because blogs are based on the personal opinions of the writers, they are also an ideal platform to start a viral marketing campaign. Advertising networks that specialize in blogs provide some efficiency in placing ads, as do blog networks, which are collections of a small number of popular blogs, coordinated by a central management team, and which can deliver a larger audience to advertisers. For more information on social marketing using blogs, see Learning Track 6.3.

The online gaming marketplace continues to expand rapidly as users increasingly play games on smartphones and tablets, as well as PCs and consoles. The story of game advertising in 2016 is social, mobile, and local: social games are ascendant, mobile devices are the high-growth platform, and location-based advertising is starting to show real traction. The objective of game advertising is both branding and driving customers to purchase moments at restaurants and retail stores. In 2016, around 180 million Americans play games on their mobile phones, about 52 million play on consoles, while about 122 million play on tablets. Of the online gamers, about 95 million play social games, such as Jackbox Games' You Don't Know Jack. U.S. advertisers are expected to spend about $336 million on in-game social game advertising in 2016 (eMarketer, Inc., 2016m).

Mobile Marketing and Advertising

Marketing on the mobile platform has exploded and now constitutes over half (56%) of the overall €182 billion spent on online marketing in 2016. Spending on all forms of mobile marketing was also estimated to be about €102 billion, and it will more than double to around €230 billion by 2020 (eMarketer, Inc., 2016e). A number of factors are driving advertisers to the mobile platform, including much more powerful devices, faster networks, wireless local networks, rich media and video ads, and growing demand for local advertising by small business and consumers. Most important, mobile is where the eyeballs are now and increasingly will be in the future: about 210 million people access the Internet at least some of the time from mobile devices.

Mobile marketing includes the use of display banner ads, rich media, video, games, e-mail, text messaging, in-store messaging, Quick Response (QR) codes, and couponing. Mobile is now a required part of the standard marketing budget. In 2016, display ads are expected to be the most popular mobile advertising format in the United States, accounting for about 52% of all U.S. mobile ad spending. Display ads can be served as a part of a mobile website or inside apps and games. Facebook is the leader in mobile display ad revenues, followed by Google and Twitter. Search advertising is also a popular format, and is expected to account for about 44% of mobile ad spending in 2016. Search ads can be further optimized for the mobile platform by showing ads based on the physical location of the user. Mobile messaging generally involves SMS text messaging to consumers offering coupons or flash marketing messages. Messaging is especially effective for local advertising because consumers can be sent messages and coupons as they pass by or visit locations. Video advertising currently accounts for a small percentage of mobile ad spending, but is one of the fastest growing formats. Ad networks such as Google's AdMob, Apple's iAd, Twitter's MoPub, InMobi (see the opening case), and Millennial Media are also important players in the mobile advertising market.

Apps on mobile devices constitute a marketing platform that did not exist a few years ago. Apps are a nonbrowser pathway for users to experience the Web and perform a number of tasks from reading the newspaper to shopping, searching, and buying. Apps provide users much faster access to content than do multi-purpose browsers. Apps have begun to influence the design and function of traditional websites as consumers are attracted to the look and feel of apps, and their speed of operation. There are over 5 million apps available on Apple's App Store and Google Play and another million apps provided by Internet carriers and third-party storefronts. Over 2 billion people worldwide will use apps in 2016.

Local Marketing: The Social-Mobile-Local Nexus

Along with social marketing and mobile marketing, local marketing is the third major trend in e-commerce marketing in 2016–2017. The growth of mobile devices has accelerated the growth of local search and purchasing. New marketing tools like local advertisements on social networks and daily deal sites are also contributing to local marketing growth.

Spending on online local ads in the United States was estimated at around $45 billion in 2016, while the mobile portion of local advertising spending reached $12.8 billion (BIA/Kelsey, 2016a). In contrast, spending on traditional local advertising remained flat during the same time period. The most common local marketing tools are geotargeting using Google Maps (local stores appearing on a Google map), display ads in hyperlocal publications like those created by Patch Properties, daily deals, and coupons.

The most commonly used venues include Facebook, Google, LinkedIn, Yahoo, Bing, and Twitter, as well as more specific location-based offerings such as Google My Business, Yahoo Local, Citysearch, YP, SuperPages, and Yelp. The "daily deal" coupon sites, Groupon and LivingSocial, and location-based mobile firms such as Foursquare are also a significant part of this trend.

We examine social, mobile, and local marketing in much greater depth in Chapter 7.

MULTI-CHANNEL MARKETING: INTEGRATING ONLINE AND OFFLINE MARKETING

Without an audience, marketing is not possible. With the rapid growth of the Internet, media consumption patterns have changed greatly as consumers are more and more likely to engage with online media, from videos and news sites, to blogs, Twitter feeds, Facebook friends, and Pinterest posts. Increasingly, marketers are using multiple online channels to "touch" customers, from e-mail to Facebook, search ads, display ads on mobile devices, and affiliate programs. Forrester Research reports, for instance, that most customers purchased online following some web marketing influence, and nearly half of online purchases followed multiple exposures to web marketing efforts (Forrester Research, 2016).

In 2013, for the first time ever, the average U.K. adult spent more time with digital media per day than the amount viewing TV. In 2016, the average U.K. adult will spend about 5 hours a day online and using a mobile device for something other than telephone calls, compared to about 3 hours watching television (see **Figure 6.8**) (eMarketer, Inc., 2016b). An increasing percentage of American media consumers multitask by using several media at once in order to increase the total media exposure. In this environment, marketers increasingly are developing multi-channel marketing programs that can take advantage of the strengths of various media, and reinforce branding messages across media. Online marketing is not the only way, or by itself the best way, to engage consumers. Internet campaigns can be significantly strengthened

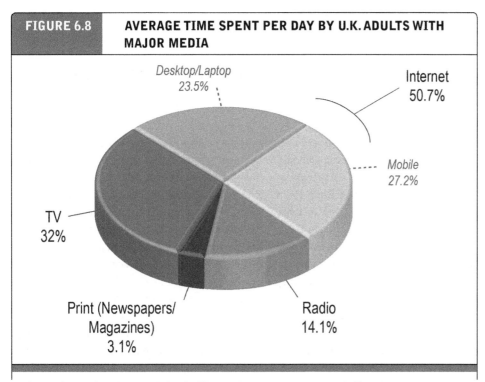

| FIGURE 6.8 | AVERAGE TIME SPENT PER DAY BY U.K. ADULTS WITH MAJOR MEDIA |

Online marketing should be coupled with offline marketing to achieve optimal effectiveness.
SOURCE: Based on data from eMarketer, Inc., 2016b.

by also using e-mail, TV, print, and radio. The marketing communications campaigns most successful at driving traffic to a website have incorporated both online and offline tactics, rather than relying solely on one or the other. Several research studies have shown that the most effective online advertisements are those that use consistent imagery with campaigns running in other media at the same time.

Insight on Business: Are the Very Rich Different from You and Me? examines how luxury goods providers use online marketing in conjunction with their offline marketing efforts.

OTHER ONLINE MARKETING STRATEGIES

In addition to the "traditional" online marketing and advertising tools we have previously discussed, such as search engine, display, and e-mail marketing, and the newer social, mobile, and local marketing and advertising tools, there are also a number of other, more focused online marketing strategies. Here we examine tools aimed at customer retention, pricing, and a strategy known as the "long tail."

Customer Retention Strategies

The Internet offers several extraordinary marketing techniques for building a strong relationship with customers and for differentiating products and services.

INSIGHT ON BUSINESS

ARE THE VERY RICH DIFFERENT FROM YOU AND ME?

"Let me tell you about the very rich. They are different from you and me." So observed F. Scott Fitzgerald in the short story, "The Rich Boy." Palm Beach has its Worth Avenue, New York has its Fifth Avenue, Los Angeles has its Rodeo Drive, and Chicago has the Magnificent Mile. So where do the rich go to get that $5,000 cocktail dress or that $3,000 Italian suit online? It turns out they may not be so different from the rest of us: they look for online deals and situations where quality can be had at a bargain.

Even experts find it hard to define what it means to be affluent. About 25% of all U.S. households (about 31 million) have annual household income of $100,000 or above. These are often referred to as HENRYs (High Earnings, Not Yet Rich). But the really affluent (sometimes called the hyperaffluent) are those 2.5 million (the top 2% of U.S. households) that earn more than $350,000 a year. And then there are the 9 million households (0.7% of households) that earn more than $1 million a year. These are the ultra-rich.

Retail consumption in general is highly skewed: the wealthiest top 10% of households account for about 50% of all retail spending and over 35% of all e-commerce retail spending. Wealthy Americans are opening their wallets to spend on expensive clothing, accessories, jewelry, and beauty products, and increasingly, purchasing luxury products online. A 2016 Boston Consulting Group report notes what consumers hear or see online influences almost 60% of luxury product buying decisions.

The Yoox Net-a-Porter Group is one of the world's leading online luxury fashion retailers, reaching over 170 countries. Luxury goods designers would not even consider selling to Net-a-Porter when it initially launched in 2000. Affluent women in that period only bought clothes they had seen, touched and tried on. That all has changed in the last decade, and in 2015, the Yoox Net-a-Porter group had revenue of over $1.9 billion. Net-a-Porter currently sells over 400 of the world's most fashionable high-end brands from Gucci to Tory Burch and was selected by Chanel as the exclusive online vendor for Chanel's first fine jewelry collection. In 2016, Tiffany began selling select collections on Net-a-Porter as well, the first time it is selling merchandise through another online retailer. In 2015, Net-a-Porter launched an app called the Net Set in an effort to create a mobile social commerce network for luxury consumers. The app provides each designer with its own mobile brand portal, as well as a live feed of trending luxury items. Net-a-Porter also created a new Android native app for its Christmas campaign. These investments played a key role in the increase in the Yoox Net-a-Porter's 2015 revenue, with mobile constituting almost 40% of the Group's sales, boosted by new native app sales, which surged by 180%.

Even the rich are not immune to the lure of a good deal. The problem is that luxury retailers are typically loath to offer sales because they believe sales detract from their reputations. To get around this problem, luxury retailers often offer "secret" discounts via flash e-mail campaigns and private online sales in which selected online customers are e-mailed alerts. Neiman Marcus calls them Midday Dash sales: two-hour online-only sales with 50% off on luxury goods that can be purchased only by clicking a link in the e-mail.

Luxury retailers have another dilemma: they need to attract not just the ultra-affluent, but also the aspirational HENRYs who are far more numerous and anxious to display their wealth. They need to be both exclusive and accessible. One solution is the so-called Mercedes Benz strategy: build luxurious but affordable cars for the HENRYs while maintaining a focus on high-end truly luxury models for the ultra-affluent. Mercedes Benz combines a dual level product strategy with effective use of social and mobile media. Mercedes' Facebook page is a main hub of interaction between the brand and its customers, with over 20 million fans entertained with sweepstakes, videos, images, news, and links to its blog for additional insight into why Mercedes is unique and worth all that money. Mercedes also uses Twitter, YouTube, Instagram, Pinterest, and a dozen mobile apps to engage a broader range of customers by providing personalized video tours of its cars.

The explosion of social media and the increasing investments in the online channel by luxury companies has reinforced and enlarged the community of those who explore, comment upon, and eventually purchase luxury goods. For instance, the Burberry Group, the United Kingdom's largest luxury goods maker, has more than 42 million followers across 20 global platforms. Burberry reports that it obtains the most reach and most response from digital initiatives compared with other media. To promote the Burberry Body fragrance, the London-based company offered exclusive samples to its Facebook fans. It received more than 225,000 requests in little more than a week.

Developing an online marketing approach that increases a company's access to consumers while retaining an image of exclusivity was the challenge faced by Tiffany & Co. The company is in the enviable position of being perhaps the most famous jewelry company in the United States. Tiffany's offline marketing communications seek to engender feelings of beauty, quality, and timeless style—all hallmarks of the Tiffany brand. How does Tiffany maintain its approach on the Web, a medium that often emphasizes speed and flashy graphics over grace and elegance, and low-cost bargains over high-priced exclusive fashion? The Web, for the most part, is all about low prices and great deals—concepts that are anathema to the high-fashion merchants like Tiffany. The answer is apparent in a visit to the Tiffany website. The site features limited inventory, with a focus on high-resolution images of its exclusive and original designs in jewelry and apparel. There are no sales, coupons, discounts, or other offers although visitors can choose jewelry in lower price ranges (less than $250 for instance). The website and Facebook brand page reflect custom service and design, calm, and simplicity. The prices are equally exclusive: an exquisite Atlas Hinged Bangle in 18k rose gold and round brilliant diamonds for $9,000, and sunglasses for $500.

Today, Tiffany has shifted more of its direct marketing effort from the offline catalog to the online catalog and an increasing social media presence, including Facebook (almost 9 million Likes), Instagram, Pinterest, Twitter, Tumblr, and YouTube. In a December 2015 study by Engagement Labs of 100,000 brands, Tiffany ranked second overall on Facebook and first on Twitter among luxury brands in terms of the effectiveness of its engagement with consumers on social media. It has websites in 13 different countries, including Canada, the United Kingdom, Japan, and Australia, and as noted previously, has begun to sell selected products on Net-a-Porter in an effort to increase its global reach. Tiffany sites carry over 2,100 products in six categories of goods: engagement, jewelry, watches, designers and collections, gifts, and accessories.

SOURCES: "Digital or Die: The Choice for Luxury Brands," by Boston Consulting Group, September 22, 2016; "Affluent US Consumers Are Thrifty, Not Spendthrifts," eMarketer, Inc., June 14, 2016; "How Luxury Shoppers Are Changing the Face of Retail," by Cooper Smith and Nancee Halpin, Businessinsider.com, May 2, 2016; "Yoox Net-a-Porter App Investment Pays Off as Sales Surge 180%," by Natalie Mortimer, Thedrum.com, February 8, 2016; "Tiffany Outshines Luxury Competition on Social Media," by Matt Lindner, Internetretailer.com, December 28, 2015; "Affluents Give Digital the Luxury Treatment," eMarketer, Inc., July 9, 2015; "Net-A-Porter Unveils New Weapon in Luxury E-commerce Battle," by Phil Wahba, Fortune.com, May 12, 2015.

Personalization, One-to-One Marketing, and Interest-based Advertising (Behavioral Targeting) No Internet-based marketing technique has received more popular and academic comment than "one-to-one" or "personalized marketing." **One-to-one marketing (personalization)** segments the market on the basis of individuals (not groups), based on a precise and timely understanding of their needs, targeting specific marketing messages to these individuals, and then positioning the product vis-à-vis competitors to be truly unique. One-to-one marketing is the ultimate form of market segmentation, targeting, and positioning—where the segments are individuals.

The movement toward market segmentation has been ongoing since the development of systematic market research and mass media in the 1930s. However, e-commerce and the Internet are different in that they enable personalized one-to-one marketing to occur on a mass scale. A recent survey found that 85% of companies were implementing some form of personalization for online customer interactions in 2016, and of those organizations not yet doing so, over half planned to use website or in-app personalization within the next year. Of those using personalization, almost 90% reported a lift or improvement as a result (Evergage, 2016).

The Amazon and Barnes & Noble websites are good examples of personalization at work. Both sites greet registered visitors (based on cookie files), recommend recent books based on user preferences (stored in a user profile in their database) as well as what other consumers purchased, and expedite checkout procedures based on prior purchases.

Behavioral targeting involves using the online and offline behavior of consumers to adjust the advertising messages delivered to them online, often in real time (milliseconds from the consumer's first URL entry). The intent is to increase the efficiency of marketing and advertising, and to increase the revenue streams of firms who are in a position to behaviorally target visitors. Because behavioral targeting as a label has somewhat unfavorable connotations, the online advertising industry, led by Google, has introduced a new name for behavioral targeting. They call it **interest-based advertising (IBA)**.

One of the original promises of the Web has been that it can deliver a marketing message tailored to each consumer based on this data, and then measure the results in terms of click-throughs and purchases. If you are visiting a jewelry site, you would be shown jewelry ads. If you entered a search query like "diamonds," you would be shown text ads for diamonds and other jewelry. This was taken one step further by advertising networks composed of several thousand sites. An advertising network could follow you across thousands of websites and come up with an idea of what you are interested in as you browse, and then display ads related to those interests. For instance, if you visit a few men's clothing sites in the course of a few hours, you will be shown ads for men's clothing on most other sites you visit subsequently, regardless of their subject content. If you search for a certain pair of shoes at Zappos, and Like them to your friends on Facebook, you will be shown ads for the exact same shoes at other sites (including Facebook). Behavioral targeting combines nearly all of your online behavioral data into a collection of interest areas, and then shows you ads based on those interests, as well as the interests of your friends. What's new about today's behavioral targeting is the breadth of data collected: your e-mail content, social

one-to-one marketing (personalization)
segmenting the market based on a precise and timely understanding of an individual's needs, targeting specific marketing messages to these individuals, and then positioning the product vis-à-vis competitors to be truly unique

behavioral targeting
involves using online and offline behavior of consumers to adjust the advertising messages delivered to them online

interest-based advertising (IBA) (behavioral targeting)
another name for behavioral targeting

network page content, friends, purchases online, books read or purchased, newspaper sites visited, and many other behaviors. And finally, ad exchanges take the marketing of all this information one step further. Most popular websites have more than 100 tracking programs on their home pages that are owned by third-party data collector firms who then sell this information in real time to the highest bidding advertiser in real-time online auctions. Ad exchanges make it possible for advertisers to retarget ads at individuals as they roam across the Internet. **Retargeting** involves showing the same or similar ads to individuals across multiple websites. Retargeting has become a popular tactic, in large part due to its perceived effectiveness. For instance, marketers often use retargeting in an attempt to reach users who have abandoned a shopping cart. A recent survey found that over 90% of marketers believe retargeting ads performs equal or better than search advertising or e-mail. However, as more and more consumers use multiple devices, including mobile devices, for online access, the ability to retarget ads across devices is becoming a topic of great interest to marketers (Marin Software, 2014; AdRoll, 2015; eMarketer, Inc., 2015).

retargeting
showing the same ad to individuals across multiple websites

There are four methods that online advertisers use to behaviorally target ads: search engine queries, the collection of data on individual browsing history online (monitoring the clickstream), the collection of data from social network sites, and increasingly, the integration of this online data with offline data like income, education, address, purchase patterns, credit records, driving records, and hundreds of other personal descriptors tied to specific, identifiable persons. This level of integration of both "anonymous" as well as identifiable information is routinely engaged in by Google, Microsoft, Yahoo, Facebook, and legions of small and medium-sized marketing firms that use their data, or collect data from thousands of websites using web beacons and cookies. On average, online information bureaus maintain 2,000 data elements on each adult person in their database. The currency and accuracy of this data are never examined, and the retention periods are not known. Currently, there are no federal laws or regulations governing this data.

Earlier in the chapter we described search engine advertising in some detail. Search engine advertising has turned out to be the most effective online advertising format by several orders of magnitude, and provides more than 95% of the revenue of Google, the world's largest online advertising agency. Why is search engine advertising so effective? Most agree that when users enter a query into a search engine, it reveals a very specific intention to shop, compare, and possibly purchase. When ads are shown at these very moments of customer behavior, they are 4 to 10 times as effective as other formats. The author John Battelle coined the phrase and the notion that the Web is a database of intentions composed of the results from every search ever made and every path that searchers have followed, since the beginning of the Web. In total, this database contains the intentions of all mankind. This treasure trove of intentions, desires, likes, wants, and needs is owned by Google, Microsoft, and to a lesser extent, Yahoo (Battelle, 2003). Battelle later extended the concept of a database of intentions beyond search to include the social graph (Facebook), status updates (Twitter and Facebook), and the "check-in" (Foursquare and Yelp) (Battelle, 2010). The database of intentions can be exploited to track and target individuals and groups. Not only is this capability unprecedented, but it's growing exponentially into the foreseeable future. The potential for abuse is also growing exponentially.

The decline in the growth rate of search engine advertising caused the major search engine firms to seek out alternative forms of future growth, which include display, rich media, and video advertising on millions of web publisher sites. Web publishers have responded by producing billions of pages of content. In this environment, the effectiveness of display ads has been falling in terms of response rates and prices for ads. Behavioral targeting is an effective way to solve this problem and increase response rates. Behavioral targeting of both search and display advertising is currently driving the expansion in online advertising.

Behavioral targeting seeks to optimize consumer response by using information that web visitors reveal about themselves online, and if possible, to combine this with offline identity and consumption information gathered by companies such as Acxiom. Behavioral targeting is based on real-time information about visitors' use of websites, including pages visited, content viewed, search queries, ads clicked, videos watched, content shared, and products they purchased. Once this information is collected and analyzed on the fly, behavioral targeting programs attempt to develop profiles of individual users, and then show advertisements most likely to be of interest to the user. More than 80% of North American advertisers use some form of targeting in their online display ads (Forrester Research, 2014).

For a variety of technical and other reasons, this vision has, thus far, not been widely achieved. The percentage of ads that are actually targeted is unknown. Many advertisers use less expensive context ads displayed to a general audience without any targeting, or very minimal demographic targeting. The quality of the data, largely owned by the online advertising networks, is quite good but hardly perfect. The ability to understand and respond—the business intelligence and real-time analytics—is still weak, preventing companies from being able to respond quickly in meaningful ways when the consumer is online. The firms who sell targeted ads to their clients claim the targeted ads are two or three times more effective than general ads. There is not very good data to support these claims from independent sources. Generally these claims confound the impact of brands on targeted audiences, and the impact of the ads placed to this targeted audience. Advertisers target groups that are most likely to buy their product even in the absence of targeting ads at them. The additional impact of a targeted ad is much smaller than ad platforms claim. A research report based on real data from 18 ad campaigns on Yahoo, involving 18.4 million users, found that brand interest is the largest single factor in determining targeted ad effectiveness, and not the targeted ad itself (Farahat and Bailey, 2012). And marketing companies are not yet prepared to accept the idea that there needs to be several hundred or a thousand variations on the same display ad depending on the customer's profile. Such a move would raise costs. Last, consumer resistance to targeting continues. A recent survey found that over 90% of Americans are opposed to having companies track their online behavior even if they receive a free service or product (Joe, 2016). Some consumers find marketing messages that are too personalized to be "creepy." For example, suppose you visited the Hanes website to look at underclothing. How would you feel about receiving an unsolicited e-mail from Hanes thanking you for your visit and asking you to come back? How would you feel about getting a similar text message or telephone call, or being served a constant array of underclothing ads as you traverse the Web? What if a company mined your Pinterest pins, Facebook posts, or Twitter feed? Although some consumers might not be disturbed by this, many others find it to be "off-putting" at the very least. The public and congressional reaction to behavioral targeting is described more fully in Chapter 8.

Customization and Customer Co-Production

Customization is an extension of personalization. **Customization** means changing the product—not just the marketing message—according to user preferences. **Customer co-production** means the users actually think up the innovation and help create the new product.

Many leading companies now offer "build-to-order" customized products on the Internet on a large scale, creating product differentiation and, hopefully, customer loyalty. Customers appear to be willing to pay a little more for a unique product. The key to making the process affordable is to build a standardized architecture that lets consumers combine a variety of options. For example, Nike offers customized sneakers through its NIKEiD program on its website. Consumers can choose the type of shoe, colors, material, and even a logo of up to eight characters. Nike transmits the orders via computers to specially equipped plants in China and Korea. At the My M&M's website, customers can get their own message printed on custom-made M&Ms.

Information goods—goods whose value is based on information content—are also ideal for this level of differentiation. For instance, the *New York Times*—and many other content distributors—allows customers to select the news they want to see on a daily basis. Many websites, particularly portal sites such as Yahoo, MSN, and AOL, allow customers to create their own customized version of the website. Such pages frequently require security measures such as usernames and passwords to ensure privacy and confidentiality.

customization
changing the product, not just the marketing message, according to user preferences

customer co-production
in the web environment, takes customization one step further by allowing the customer to interactively create the product

Customer Service

A website's approach to customer service can significantly help or hurt its marketing efforts. Online customer service is more than simply following through on order fulfillment; it has to do with users' ability to communicate with a company and obtain desired information in a timely manner. Customer service can help reduce consumer frustration, cut the number of abandoned shopping carts, and increase sales.

Most consumers want to, and will, serve themselves as long as the information they need to do so is relatively easy to find. Online buyers largely do not expect or desire "high-touch" service unless they have questions or problems, in which case they want relatively speedy answers that are responsive to their individual issue. Researchers have found that online consumers strongly attach to brands when they have a problem with an order. Customer loyalty increases substantially when online buyers learn that customer service representatives are available online or at an 800-number and were willing and able to resolve the situation quickly. Conversely, online buyers who do not receive satisfaction at these critical moments often terminate their relationship with the business and switch to merchants that may charge more but deliver superior customer service (Ba et al., 2010; Wolfinbarger and Gilly, 2001).

There are a number of tools that companies can use to encourage interaction with prospects and customers and provide customer service—FAQs, customer service chat systems, intelligent agents, and automated response systems—in addition to the customer relationship management systems described in the preceding section.

frequently asked questions (FAQs)
a text-based listing of common questions and answers

Frequently asked questions (FAQs), a text-based listing of common questions and answers, provide an inexpensive way to anticipate and address customer concerns. Adding an FAQ page on a website linked to a search engine helps users track down needed information more quickly, enabling them to help themselves resolve questions and concerns. By directing customers to the FAQs page first, websites can give customers answers to common questions. If a question and answer do not appear, it is important for sites to make contact with a live person simple and easy. Offering an e-mail link to customer service at the bottom of the FAQs page is one solution.

real-time customer service chat systems
a company's customer service representatives interactively exchange text-based messages with one or more customers on a real-time basis

Real-time customer service chat systems (in which a company's customer service representatives interactively exchange text-based messages with one or more customers on a real-time basis) are an increasingly popular way for companies to assist online shoppers during a purchase. Chats with online customer service representatives can provide direction, answer questions, and troubleshoot technical glitches that can kill a sale. Leading vendors of customer service chat systems include LivePerson and ClickDesk. Vendors claim that chat is significantly less expensive than telephone-based customer service. However, critics point out this conclusion may be based on optimistic assumptions that chat representatives can assist three or four customers at once, and that chat sessions are shorter than phone sessions. Also, chat sessions are text sessions, and not as rich as talking with a human being over the phone. On the plus side, chat has been reported to raise per-order sales figures, providing sales assistance by allowing companies to "touch" customers during the decision-making process. Evidence suggests that chat can lower shopping cart abandonment rates, increase the number of items purchased per transaction, and increase the dollar value of transactions. "Click to call" or "live call" is another version of a real-time online customer service system, in which the customer clicks a link or accepts an invitation to have a customer service representative call them on the telephone.

automated response system
sends e-mail order confirmations and acknowledgments of e-mailed inquiries

Intelligent agent technology is another way customers are providing assistance to online shoppers. Intelligent agents are part of an effort to reduce costly contact with customer service representatives. **Automated response systems** send e-mail order confirmations and acknowledgments of e-mailed inquiries, in some cases letting the customer know that it may take a day or two to actually research an answer to their question. Automated shipping confirmations and order status reports are also common.

Pricing Strategies

As we noted in Chapter 1, during the early years of e-commerce, many academics and business consultants predicted that the Web would lead to a new world of information symmetry and "frictionless" commerce. In this world, newly empowered customers, using intelligent shopping agents and the nearly infinite product and price information available on the Internet, would shop around the world (and around the clock) with minimal effort, driving prices down to their marginal cost and driving intermediaries out of the market as customers began to deal directly with producers (Wigand and Benjamin, 1995; Rayport and Sviokla, 1995; Evans and Wurster, 1999; Sinha, 2000). The result was supposed to be an instance of the **Law of One Price**: with complete price transparency in a perfect information marketplace, one world price for every product would emerge. Frictionless commerce would, of course, mean the end of marketing based on brands.

But it didn't work out this way. Firms still compete for customers through price as well as product features, scope of operations, and focus. **Pricing** (putting a value on goods and services) is an integral part of marketing strategy. Together, price and quality determine customer value. Pricing of e-commerce goods has proved very difficult for both entrepreneurs and investors to understand.

In traditional firms, the prices of traditional goods—such as books, drugs, and automobiles—are usually based on their fixed and variable costs as well as the market's **demand curve** (the quantity of goods that can be sold at various prices). *Fixed costs* are the costs of building the production facility. *Variable costs* are costs involved in running the production facility—mostly labor. In a competitive market, with undifferentiated goods, prices tend toward their *marginal costs* (the incremental cost of producing the next unit) once manufacturers have paid the fixed costs to enter the business.

Firms usually "discover" their demand curves by testing various price and volume bundles, while closely watching their cost structure. Normally, prices are set to maximize profits. A profit-maximizing company sets its prices so that the *marginal revenue* (the revenue a company receives from the next unit sold) from a product just equals its marginal costs. If a firm's marginal revenue is higher than its marginal costs, it would want to lower prices a bit and sell more product (why leave money on the table when you can sell a few more units?). If its marginal revenue for selling a product is lower than its marginal costs, then the company would want to reduce volume a bit and charge a higher price (why lose money on each additional sale?).

In the early years of e-commerce, something unusual happened. Sellers were pricing their products far below their marginal costs. Some sites were losing money on every sale. How could this be? New economics? New technology? The Internet age? No. Internet merchants could sell below their marginal costs (even giving away products for free) simply because a large number of entrepreneurs and their venture capitalist backers thought this was a worthwhile activity, at least in the short term. The idea was to attract eyeballs with free goods and services, and then later, once the consumer was part of a large, committed audience, charge advertisers enough money to make a profit, and (maybe) charge customers subscription fees for value-added

Law of One Price
with complete price transparency in a perfect information marketplace, there will be one world price for every product

pricing
putting a value on goods and services

demand curve
the quantity of goods that can be sold at various prices

| FIGURE 6.9 | A DEMAND CURVE |

A demand curve shows the quantity of product (Q) that could be sold at various prices (P).

services (the so-called *"piggyback"* *strategy* in which a small number of users can be convinced to pay for premium services that are piggybacked upon a larger audience that receives standard or reduced value services). To a large extent, social network sites and user-generated content sites have resurrected this revenue model with a focus on the growth in audience size and not short-term profits. To understand the behavior of entrepreneurial firms, it is helpful to examine a traditional demand curve (see **Figure 6.9**).

A small number of customers are willing to pay a great deal for the product—far above P_1. A larger number of customers would happily pay P_1, and an even larger number of customers would pay less than P_1. If the price were zero, the demand might approach infinity! Ideally, in order to maximize sales and profits, a firm would like to pick up all the money in the market by selling the product at the price each customer is willing to pay. This is called **price discrimination**—selling products to different people and groups based on their willingness to pay. If some people really want the product, sell it to them at a high price. But sell it to indifferent people at a much lower price; otherwise, they will not buy. This only works if the firm can (a) identify the price each individual would be willing to pay, and (b) segregate the customers from one another so they cannot find out what the others are paying. Therefore, most firms adopt a fixed price for their goods (P_1), or a small number of prices for different versions of their products.

What if the marginal cost of producing a good is zero? What should the price be for these goods? It would be impossible then to set prices based on equalizing marginal revenue and marginal cost—because marginal cost is zero. The Internet is primarily filled with information goods—from music to research reports, to stock quotes, stories, weather reports, articles, pictures, and opinions—whose marginal cost of production is zero when distributed over the Internet. Thus, another reason certain goods, such

price discrimination
selling products to different people and groups based on their willingness to pay

as some information goods, may be free on the Internet is that they are "selling" for what it costs to produce them—next to nothing. Content that is stolen has zero production costs. Content that is contributed by users also has zero production costs for the websites themselves.

Free and Freemium Everyone likes a bargain, and the best bargain is something for free. Businesses give away free PCs, free data storage, free music, free websites, free photo storage, and free Internet connections. Free is not new: banks used to give away "free" toasters to depositors in the 1950s. Google offers free office apps, free e-mail, and free collaboration sites. There can be a sensible economic logic to giving things away. Free content can help build market awareness and can lead to sales of other follow-on products. Finally, free products and services knock out potential and actual competitors (the free browser Internet Explorer from Microsoft spoiled the market for Netscape's browser) (Shapiro and Varian, 1999).

Today, "free" is increasingly being implemented online as "freemium" to borrow a phrase from Chris Anderson's book *Free: The Future of a Radical Price.* The freemium pricing model is a cross-subsidy online marketing strategy where users are offered a basic service for free, but must pay for premium or add-on services. The people who pay for the premium services hopefully will pay for all the free riders on the service. Skype uses a freemium model: millions of users can call other Skype users on the Internet for free, but there's a charge for calling a land line or cell phone. Flickr, Google Sites, Yahoo, and a host of others offer premium services at a price in order to support free services. Pandora offers free Internet radio, but it includes advertisements. Premium service without ads costs about $55 a year. (See the Chapter 5 case study, *Freemium Takes Pandora Public,* for more information on Pandora and the freemium pricing strategy.)

"Free" and "freemium" as pricing strategies do have limits. In the past, many e-commerce businesses found it difficult to convert the eyeballs into paying customers. Free sites attract hundreds of millions of price-sensitive "freeloaders" who have no intention of ever paying for anything, and who switch from one free service to another at the very mention of charges. The piggyback strategy has not been a universal success. "Free" eliminates a rich price discrimination strategy. Clearly some of the free loaders would indeed pay a small amount each month, and this revenue is lost to the firms who offer significant services for free. Some argue that everything digital will one day be free in part because Internet users expect it to be so. But the history of "free" includes broadcast television, which used to be "free" (it was advertising-supported), but the public eventually had no problem moving to cable television and DVDs as paid services. The exceptions to "free" are really valuable streams of information that are exclusive, expensive to produce, not widely distributed, unique, and have immediate consumption or investment value. Even in the age of the Internet, these digital streams will sell for a price greater than zero. There probably is no free lunch after all, at least not one that's worth eating.

Versioning One solution to the problem of free information goods is **versioning**—creating multiple versions of the goods and selling essentially the same product to different market segments at different prices. In this situation, the price depends on the value to the consumer. Consumers will segment themselves into groups that are willing to pay different amounts for various versions (Shapiro and Varian, 1998).

versioning
creating multiple versions of information goods and selling essentially the same product to different market segments at different prices

Versioning fits well with a modified "free" strategy. A reduced-value version can be offered for free, while premium versions can be offered at higher prices. What are characteristics of a "reduced-value version"? Low-priced—or in the case of information goods, even "free"—versions might be less convenient to use, less comprehensive, slower, less powerful, and offer less support than the high-priced versions. Just as there are different General Motors car brands appealing to different market segments (Cadillac, Buick, Chevrolet, and GMC), and within these divisions, hundreds of models from the most basic to the more powerful and functional, so can information goods be "versioned" in order to segment and target the market and position the products. In the realm of information goods, online magazines, music companies, and book publishers offer sample content for free, but charge for more powerful content. The *New York Times*, for instance, allows you to read 10 articles a month online for free, but if you want to read more, you must have a digital subscription. Some websites offer "free services" with annoying advertising, but turn off the ads for a monthly fee.

Bundling "Ziggy" Ziegfeld, a vaudeville entrepreneur at the turn of the twentieth century in New York, noticed that nearly one-third of his theater seats were empty on some Friday nights, and during the week, matinee shows were often half empty. He came up with an idea for bundling tickets into "twofers": pay for one full-price ticket and get the next ticket free. Twofers are still a Broadway theater tradition in New York. They are based on the idea that (a) the marginal cost of seating another patron is zero, and (b) a great many people who would not otherwise buy a single ticket would buy a "bundle" of tickets for the same or even a slightly higher price.

bundling

offers consumers two or more goods for a reduced price

Bundling of information goods online extends the concept of a twofer. **Bundling** offers consumers two or more goods for a price that is less than the goods would cost when purchased individually. The key idea behind the concept of bundling is that although consumers typically have very diverse ideas about the value of a single product, they tend to agree much more on the value of a bundle of products offered at a fixed price. In fact, the per-product price people are willing to pay for the bundle is often higher than when the products are sold separately. Bundling reduces the variance (dispersion) in market demand for goods.

Dynamic Pricing and Flash Marketing The pricing strategies we have discussed so far are all fixed-price strategies. Versions and bundles are sold for fixed prices based on the firm's best effort at maximizing its profits. But what if there is product still left on the shelf along with the knowledge that someone, somewhere, would be willing to pay something for it? It might be better to obtain at least some revenue from the product, rather than let it sit on the shelf, or even perish. Imagine also that there are some people in every market who would pay a hefty premium for a product if they could have it right away. In other situations, such as for an antique, the value of the product has to be discovered in the marketplace (usually because there is a belief that the marketplace would value the product at a much higher price than its owner paid as a cost). In other cases, the value of a good is equal to what the market is willing to pay (and has nothing to do with its cost). Or let's say you want to build frequent visits to your site and offer some really great bargains for a few minutes each day, or the whole day with a set time limit. Here is where dynamic pricing mechanisms come to the fore, and where the strengths of the Internet can be seen. With **dynamic pricing**, the price of the product varies, depending on the demand characteristics of the customer and the supply situation of the seller.

There are a number of different kinds of dynamic pricing mechanisms. For instance, *auctions* have been used for centuries to establish the instant market price for goods. Auctions are flexible and efficient market mechanisms for pricing unique or unusual goods, as well as commonplace goods such as computers, flower bundles, and cameras.

Yield management is quite different from auctions. In auctions, thousands of consumers establish a price by bidding against one another. In *yield management*, managers set prices in different markets, appealing to different segments, in order to sell excess capacity. Airlines exemplify yield management techniques. Every few minutes during the day, they adjust prices of empty airline seats to ensure at least some of the 50,000 empty airline seats are sold at some reasonable price—even below marginal cost of production. Amazon and other large online retailers frequently use yield management techniques that involve changing prices hourly to stimulate demand and maximize revenues. Amazon can also track shopping behavior of individuals seeking a specific product, such as a laser printer. As the consumer searches for the best price, Amazon can observe the offering prices on other websites, and then adjust its prices dynamically so that when the user visits Amazon again, a lower price will be displayed than all other sites visited.

Yield management works under a limited set of conditions. Generally, the product is perishable (an empty airline seat perishes when the plane takes off without a full load); there are seasonal variations in demand; market segments are clearly defined; markets are competitive; and market conditions change rapidly (Cross, 1997). In general, only very large firms with extensive monitoring and database systems in place have been able to afford yield management techniques.

Surge pricing is a kind of dynamic pricing used by companies such as Uber. Uber uses a dynamic pricing algorithm to optimize its revenue, or as the company claims, to balance supply and demand. Prices have surged from two to ten times or higher during storms and popular holiday periods. Uber was sharply criticized for using this scheme in New York City during Hurricane Sandy in 2012. Critics claim the practice amounts to price gouging, which during an emergency is illegal in some states like New York. Uber counters that the higher prices bring more livery cars onto the streets, increasing supply just when needed. But surge pricing, like most dynamic pricing schemes, is not the same as an open auction, where price movements are transparent to all. Uber does not make its data on supply and demand available to the public. Therefore it is impossible to know if Uber prices go up during holidays and storms because demand exceeds supply or because Uber wants to increase profits. In July 2014, Uber reached an agreement with the New York State Attorney General to limit pricing surges during emergencies (Isaac, 2014).

A third dynamic pricing technique is *flash marketing*, which has proved extraordinarily effective for travel services, luxury clothing goods, and other goods. Using e-mail or dedicated website features to notify loyal customers (repeat purchasers), merchants

dynamic pricing
the price of the product varies, depending on the demand characteristics of the customer and the supply situation of the seller

offer goods and services for a limited time (usually hours) at very low prices. JetBlue has offered $14 flights between New York and Los Angeles. Deluxe hotel rooms are flash marketed at $1 a night. Companies like Rue La La, HauteLook, and Gilt Groupe are based on flash marketing techniques. Blink and you can easily miss these great prices. Gilt purchases overstocked items from major fashion brands and then offers them to their subscribers at discounted prices via daily e-mail and SMS flash messages. Typically, the sale of an item lasts for two hours or until the inventory is depleted. On many occasions, Gilt rises to the top of most frequently visited websites when it conducts a sale. Critics point out that these sites take advantage of compulsive shoppers and lead to overshopping for unneeded goods. In another example of mass retail dynamic pricing, in 2011, Amazon used its new cloud music service to offer a flash one-day sale of Lady Gaga's latest album for 99 cents. Response was so great that Amazon's cloud servers could not meet the demand, and the offer has not been repeated.

The Internet has truly revolutionized the possibilities to engage in dynamic, and even misleading, pricing strategies. With millions of consumers using a site every hour, and access to powerful databases, merchants can raise prices one minute and drop them another minute when a competitor threatens. Bait-and-switch tactics become more common: a really low price on one product is used to attract people to a site when in fact the product is not available.

Long Tail Marketing

Consider that Amazon sells a larger number of obscure books than it does of "hit" books (defined as the top 20% of books sold). Nevertheless, the hit books generate 80% of Amazon's revenues. Consumers distribute themselves in many markets according to a power curve where 80% of the demand is for the hit products, and demand for nonhits quickly recedes to a small number of units sold. In a traditional market, niche products are so obscure no one ever hears about them. One impact of the Internet and e-commerce on sales of obscure products with little demand is that obscure products become more visible to consumers through search engines, recommendation engines, and social networks. Hence, online retailers can earn substantial revenue selling products for which demand and price are low. In fact, with near zero inventory costs, and a good search engine, the sales of obscure products can become a much larger percentage of total revenue. Amazon, for instance, has millions of book titles for sale at $2.99 or less, many written by obscure authors. Because of its search and recommendation engines, Amazon is able to generate profits from the sale of this large number of obscure titles. This is called the **long tail effect**. See *Insight on Technology: The Long Tail: Big Hits and Big Misses.*

long tail effect

a colloquial name given to various statistical distributions characterized by a small number of events of high amplitude and a very large number of events with low amplitude

| 6.3 | **INTERNET MARKETING TECHNOLOGIES** |

Internet marketing has many similarities to and differences from ordinary marketing. The objective of Internet marketing—as in all marketing—is to build customer relationships so that the firm can achieve above-average returns (both by offering superior products or services and by communicating the product's features to the

INSIGHT ON TECHNOLOGY

THE LONG TAIL: BIG HITS AND BIG MISSES

The Long Tail is a name given to various statistical distributions characterized by a small group of events of high amplitude and a large group of events with low amplitude. Coined by *Wired Magazine* writer Chris Anderson in 2004, the Web's Long Tail has since gone on to fascinate academics and challenge online marketers. The concept is straightforward. Think Hollywood movies: there are a few big hits and also thousands of films that no one ever hears about. It's the legion of misses that make up the Long Tail. Anderson claimed to have discovered a new rule: no matter how much content you put online, someone, somewhere will show up to buy it, thanks to online search, social networks, and recommendation engines. For example, eBay contains millions of items drawn from every Aunt Tilly's closet in the world and still seems to find a buyer somewhere for just about anything, generating revenue that would not be realized without an online marketplace.

On the Internet, where search costs are tiny and where companies aren't forced to maintain a physical store, reducing storage and distribution costs, online retailers like Amazon and Alibaba offer millions of products for sale compared to a typical bricks-and-mortar retailer like Walmart or Sears. Wherever you look on the Web, you can find a great many items that only a few people are interested in buying. But with over 3.3 billion people online, even a one-in-a-million product could find over 3,000 buyers. Researchers note that most shoppers have a taste for both popular as well as niche products.

One problem with the Long Tail is that people sometimes have difficulty finding niche products because they are—by definition—largely unknown. Here's where recommender systems come into play: although these systems can skew toward the most popular selections, they can sometimes guide consumers to obscure but wonderful works based on the recommendations of others. Netflix has spent millions on improving its recommender system, and Pandora's recommender system focuses on generating quality music without regard to popularity.

Search engine optimization is another area where marketers are trying to unlock the power of the Long Tail. Long Tail keywords are phrases that a small but significant number of people might use to find products. For instance, instead of investing in keywords such as "shoes" or "men's shoes," which are dominated by bigger retailers, a marketer focused on the Long Tail might choose a keyword like "purple all-weather running shoes," where his firm is much likelier to outrank its competition and achieve conversion rates over twice as high as more popular keywords and searches. Google has updated its search algorithms to improve the accuracy of Long Tail searches. According to Hitwise, Long Tail searches comprise as much as 70% of all Web queries, and Google claims that 15% of searches it receives each day have never been searched before. Google offers a feature called broad match, which allows a keyword to trigger an advertisement even when the search phrase is misspelled, contains synonyms, and so on, which further improves the results of Long Tail keywords in search. An increasing number of Internet users are using natural language searches (searches that are phrased in the way we would speak naturally, like "where is the nearest pizza place?") to find products and services. Many of these searches are also part of the Long Tail.

Social networks also make the Long Tail phenomenon even stronger. A recent study found that popularity information of the sort produced in a social network spurs sales of niche products more than mainstream products because of the higher perceived quality of the niche product.

Anderson claimed that the Internet would revolutionize digital content by making even niche products highly profitable, and that the revenues

(continued)

produced by small niche products would ultimately outweigh the revenues of hit movies, songs, and books. But newer research is mixed on the revenue potential in the Long Tail. Solid best sellers have expanded and produce the overwhelming majority of online media revenues. Despite fewer new subscribers than expected, Netflix's most recent earnings report boasted record highs, which it credited to its growing group of original series and recently added blockbuster hits like the television series *Friends*, not the thousands of titles in its Long Tail. In fact, its DVD business, where most of its Long Tail titles are available, has only 4.5 million subscribers, compared to over 80 million subscribers of its streaming service, which consists primarily of new original series and more popular movies and TV shows. The situation is similar in the music industry. As music services compete to offer increasingly large catalogs of songs, the well-known artists do better, while each individual member of the growing Long Tail finds it harder to stand out amidst lesser-known peers. On mobile devices especially, "front end display" for music services and e-books is smaller than on desktop screens, and only the superstars get this valuable marketing real estate.

On the other hand, up-and-coming artists have fewer barriers to entry and more avenues than ever to promote themselves without the aid of major labels. Artists like violinist Lindsey Stirling started out in the Long Tail, putting up videos on YouTube,

and has since become a major commercial success. Other music companies are trying to replicate that success for Long Tail artists. Spotify has focused on improving the visibility of its Discovery Weekly and Fresh Finds features, which connect lesser known artists with wider audiences. In 2016, Kobalt, a music streaming site focused on independent artists, has partnered with multi-platform media company AwesomenessTV to highlight niche and undiscovered artists. AwesomenessTV artists will be able to produce content for distribution on streaming services using Kobalt technology. And although Netflix may be driven primarily by blockbusters, it uses highly specific Long Tail categories such as "Imaginative Time Travel Movies from the 1980s" to narrow down exactly what its subscribers are interested in. One industry analysis found that even Amazon generates 57% of its sales from Long Tail keywords that didn't fall into any "popular" search; on Long Tail Google searches, Amazon results usually rank within the top two or three results.

Both the Long Tail and the winner-take-all approaches have implications for marketers and product designers. In the Long Tail approach, online merchants, especially those selling digital goods such as content, should build up huge libraries of content because they can make significant revenues from niche products that have small audiences. In the winner-take-all approach, the niche products produce little revenue, and firms should concentrate on hugely popular titles and services.

SOURCES: "Long Tail Theory Revisited: AwesomenessTV and Kobalt Partner to Help Up-and-Coming Musicians," by Nelson Granados, *Forbes*, September 23, 2016; "What Netflix Can Teach Us About Long-Tail Keyword Research," by Ryan Shelley, Searchengineland.com, September 20, 2016; "SEO: How to Maximize the Long Tail," by Jill Kocher, Practicalecommerce.com, August 12, 2016; "The Long Tail Theory Can Be Reality for Traditional Megabrands," by Robin Lewis, *Forbes*, May 31, 2016; "Where's the Long Tail? Spotify Touts Its Artist Discovery," by Andrew Flanagan, Billboard.com, May 26, 2016; "The Hidden Value of Long Tail SEO," Hittail.com, April 21, 2016; "7 Brilliant Examples of Brands Driving Long-Tail Organic Traffic," by Neil Patel, Neilpatel.com, December 22, 2015; "Netflix Wags Its Short Tail," by Justin Fox, Bloombergview.com, April 17, 2015; "Hidden in the Long Tail," *The Economist*, January 10, 2015; "The Long Tail And Why Your SEO Keyword Strategy Is Wrong," by Joshua Steimle, *Forbes*, December 23, 2014; "Tales of Long Tail's Death Greatly Exaggerated," by Tracy Maddux, Billboard.com, June 17, 2014; "Why Alibaba's Long Tail Makes Amazon's Look Like a Bobcat's," by Matt Schifrin, *Forbes*, May 8, 2014; "The Death of the Long Tail," Musicindustryblog.com, March 4, 2014; "Winners Take All, But Can't We Still Dream," by Robert H. Frank, *New York Times*, February 22, 2014; "Blockbusters: Why the Long Tail Is Dead and Go-Big Strategies Pay Off," by Ginny Marvin, Marketingland.com, October 23, 2013; "How Google Is Changing Long-Tail Search with Efforts Like Hummingbird," by Rand Fishkin, Moz.com, October 18, 2013; "Microsoft, Apps and the Long Tail," by Ben Bajarin, Time.com, July 8, 2013; "Goodbye Pareto Principle, Hello Long Tail: The Effect of Search Costs on the Concentration of Product Sales," by Eric Brynjolfsson et al., *Management Science*, July 2012; "Recommendation Networks and the Long Tail of Electronic Commerce," by Gail Oestreicher-Singer, New York University, 2012; "Research Commentary—Long Tails vs. Superstars: The Effect of Information Technology on Product Variety and Sales Concentration Patterns," by Erik Brynjolfsson et al., *Information Systems Research*, December 2010; "How Does Popularity Affect Choices? A Field Experiment," by Catherine Tucker and Juanjuan Zhang, *Management Science*, May 2011; "From Niches to Riches: Anatomy of the Long Tail," by Eric Brynjolfsson et al., *MIT Sloan Management Review*, Summer 2006; "The Long Tail," by Chris Anderson, *Wired Magazine*, October 2004.

consumer). But Internet marketing is also very different from ordinary marketing because the nature of the medium and its capabilities are so different from anything that has come before. In order to understand just how different Internet marketing can be and in what ways, you first need to become familiar with some basic Internet marketing technologies.

THE REVOLUTION IN INTERNET MARKETING TECHNOLOGIES

In Chapter 1, we listed eight unique features of e-commerce technology. **Table 6.6** describes how marketing has changed as a result of these new technical capabilities.

TABLE 6.6	IMPACT OF UNIQUE FEATURES OF E-COMMERCE TECHNOLOGY ON MARKETING
E-COMMERCE TECHNOLOGY DIMENSION	SIGNIFICANCE FOR MARKETING
Ubiquity	Marketing communications have been extended to the home, work, and mobile platforms; geographic limits on marketing have been reduced. The marketplace has been replaced by "marketspace" and is removed from a temporal and geographic location. Customer convenience has been enhanced, and shopping costs have been reduced.
Global reach	Worldwide customer service and marketing communications have been enabled. Potentially hundreds of millions of consumers can be reached with marketing messages.
Universal standards	The cost of delivering marketing messages and receiving feedback from users is reduced because of shared, global standards of the Internet.
Richness	Video, audio, and text marketing messages can be integrated into a single marketing message and consuming experience.
Interactivity	Consumers can be engaged in a dialog, dynamically adjusting the experience to the consumer, and making the consumer a co-producer of the goods and services being sold.
Information density	Fine-grained, highly detailed information on consumers' real-time behavior can be gathered and analyzed for the first time. "Data mining" Internet technology permits the analysis of terabytes of consumer data every day for marketing purposes.
Personalization/ Customization	This feature potentially enables product and service differentiation down to the level of the individual, thus strengthening the ability of marketers to create brands.
Social technology	User-generated content and social network sites, along with blogs, have created large new audiences online, where the content is provided by users. These audiences have greatly expanded the opportunity for marketers to reach new potential customers in a nontraditional media format. Entirely new kinds of marketing techniques are evolving. These same technologies expose marketers to the risk of falling afoul of popular opinion by providing more market power to users who now can "talk back."

On balance, the Internet has had four very powerful impacts on marketing. First, the Internet, as a communications medium, has broadened the scope of marketing communications—in the sense of the number of people who can be easily reached as well as the locations where they can be reached, from desktops to mobile smartphones (in short, everywhere). Second, the Internet has increased the richness of marketing communications by combining text, video, and audio content into rich messages. Arguably, the Web is richer as a medium than even television or video because of the complexity of messages available, the enormous content accessible on a wide range of subjects, and the ability of users to interactively control the experience. Third, the Internet has greatly expanded the information intensity of the marketplace by providing marketers (and customers) with unparalleled fine-grained, detailed, real-time information about consumers as they transact in the marketplace. Fourth, the always-on, always-attached, environment created by mobile devices results in consumers being much more available to receive marketing messages. One result is an extraordinary expansion in marketing opportunities for firms.

WEB TRANSACTION LOGS

transaction log

records user activity at a website

How can e-commerce sites know more than a department store or the local grocery store does about consumer behavior? A primary source of consumer information on the Web is the transaction log maintained by all web servers. A **transaction log** records user activity at a website. The transaction log is built into web server software. Transaction log data becomes even more useful when combined with two other visitor-generated data trails: registration forms and the shopping cart database. Users are enticed through various means (such as free gifts or special services) to fill out registration forms. **Registration forms** gather personal data on name, address, phone, zip code, e-mail address (usually required), and other optional self-confessed information on interests and tastes. When users make a purchase, they also enter additional information into the shopping cart database. The **shopping cart database** captures all the item selection, purchase, and payment data. Other potential additional sources of data are information users submit on product forms, contribute to chat groups, or send via e-mail messages using the "Contact Us" option on most sites.

registration forms

gather personal data on name, address, phone, zip code, e-mail address, and other optional self-confessed information on interests and tastes

shopping cart database

captures all the item selection, purchase, and payment data

For a website that has a million visitors per month, and where, on average, a visitor makes 15 page requests per visit, there will be 15 million entries in the log each month. These transaction logs, coupled with data from the registration forms and shopping cart database, represent a treasure trove of marketing information for both individual sites and the online industry as a whole. Nearly all Internet marketing capabilities are based on these data-gathering tools. For instance, here are just a few of the interesting marketing questions that can be answered by examining a site's web transaction logs, registration forms, and shopping cart database:

- What are the major patterns of interest and purchase for groups and individuals?
- After the home page, where do most users go first, and then second and third?
- What are the interests of specific individuals (those we can identify)?
- How can we make it easier for people to use our site so they can find what they want?

- How can we change the design of the site to encourage visitors to purchase our high-margin products?
- Where are visitors coming from (and how can we optimize our presence on these referral sites)?
- How can we personalize our messages, offerings, and products to individual users?

Businesses can choke on the massive quantity of information found in a typical site's log file. We describe some technologies that help firms more effectively utilize this information below.

SUPPLEMENTING THE LOGS: COOKIES AND OTHER TRACKING FILES

While transaction logs create the foundation of online data collection at a single website, marketers use tracking files to follow users across the Web as they visit other sites. There are three primary kinds of tracking files: cookies, Flash cookies, and web beacons. A **cookie** is a small text file that websites place on the hard disk of visitors' client computers every time they visit, and during the visit, as specific pages are visited. Cookies allow a website to store data on a user's computer and then later retrieve it. The cookie typically includes a name, a unique ID number for each visitor that is stored on the user's computer, the domain (which specifies the web server/domain that can access the cookie), a path (if a cookie comes from a particular part of a website instead of the main page, a path will be given), a security setting that provides whether the cookie can only be transmitted by a secure server, and an expiration date (not required). First-party cookies come from the same domain name as the page the user is visiting, while third-party cookies come from another domain, such as ad serving or adware companies, affiliate marketers, or spyware servers. On some websites, there are literally hundreds of tracking files on the main pages.

A cookie provides web marketers with a very quick means of identifying the customer and understanding his or her prior behavior at the site. Websites use cookies to determine how many people are visiting the site, whether they are new or repeat visitors, and how often they have visited, although this data may be somewhat inaccurate because people share computers, they often use more than one computer, and cookies may have been inadvertently or intentionally erased. Cookies make shopping carts and "quick checkout" options possible by allowing a site to keep track of a user as he or she adds to the shopping cart. Each item added to the shopping cart is stored in the site's database along with the visitor's unique ID value.

Ordinary cookies are easy to spot using your browser, but Flash cookies, beacons, and tracking codes are not easily visible. All common browsers allow users to see the cookies placed in their cookies file. Users can delete cookies, or adjust their settings so that third-party cookies are blocked, while first-party cookies are allowed.

With growing privacy concerns, over time the percentage of people deleting cookies has risen. The more cookies are deleted, the less accurate are web page and ad server metrics, and the less likely marketers will be able to understand who is visiting their sites or where they came from. As a result, advertisers have sought other methods. One way is using Adobe Flash software, which creates its own cookie

cookie
small text file that websites place on the hard disk of visitors' client computers that allows the website to store data about the visitor on the computer and later retrieve it

files, known as Flash cookies. Flash cookies can be set to never expire, and can store about 5 MB of information compared to the 1,024 bytes stored by regular cookies.

Although cookies are site-specific (a website can only receive the data it has stored on a client computer and cannot look at any other cookie), when combined with web beacons (also called "bugs"), they can be used to create cross-site profiles. Web beacons are tiny (1-pixel) graphic files embedded in e-mail messages and on websites. Web beacons are used to automatically transmit information about the user and the page being viewed to a monitoring server in order to collect personal browsing behavior and other personal information. For instance, when a recipient opens an e-mail in HTML format or opens a web page, a message is sent to a server calling for graphic information. This tells the marketer that the e-mail was opened, indicating that the recipient was at least interested in the subject header. Web beacons are not visible to users. They are often clear or colored white so they are not visible to the recipient. You may be able to determine if a web page is using web beacons by using the View Source option of your browser and examining the IMG (image) tags on the page. As noted above, web beacons are typically one pixel in size and contain the URL of a server that differs from the one that served the page itself.

Using cookies on mobile devices has been less effective. Regular cookies on the mobile Web are reset every time a user closes his or her mobile browser and in-app cookies can't be shared between apps, making both of limited utility. However, with the increasing numbers of people using mobile devices to access the Internet, it is not surprising that telecommunications companies have begun to use tracking files. In late 2014, it was revealed that Verizon Wireless and AT&T were inserting a tracking header called a Unique Identifier Header (UIDH) into HTTP requests issued to websites from mobile devices, enabling them to track the online activities of their subscribers. Commentators call these tracking headers zombie cookies, perma-cookies, or supercookies because they cannot be deleted the way that regular browser cookies can. Following an outcry by privacy advocates and an FCC investigation, AT&T reportedly stopped using supercookies, and in March 2016, Verizon settled with the FCC, agreeing to pay a $1.35 million fine, and to obtain customer permission before sharing tracking data with other companies and even with other parts of Verizon, including sites owned by AOL. In addition, Verizon agreed to inform customers about its ad targeting practices in the first instance. The FCC also considering whether to outlaw the use of supercookies entirely.

deterministic cross-device tracking
relies on personally identifiable information such as e-mail address used to log into an app and website on different devices

probabilistic cross-device tracking
uses algorithms to analyze thousands of anonymous data points to create a possible match

In an effort to more effectively track consumers across devices, other cross-device tracking methods have begun to be developed. **Deterministic cross-device tracking** relies on personally identifiable information such as e-mail address used to log into an app and website on different devices. Facebook, Google, Apple, Twitter, and other companies that have very large user bases and have both desktop and mobile properties that require logins are the most likely to be able to effectively exploit deterministic matching. **Probabilistic cross-device tracking** uses algorithms developed by vendors such as Drawbridge, BlueCava, and Tapad to analyze thousands of anonymous data points, such as device type, operating system, and IP address, to create a possible match. This type of matching is, not surprisingly, less accurate than deterministic matching (Schiff, 2015; Whitener, 2015).

In November 2015, the Federal Trade Commission hosted a workshop to examine the privacy issues involved with cross-device tracking, and in January 2016, urged the ad industry to allow consumers to opt out of such tracking, noting that consumers' increased use of ad blocking indicates their displeasure with the current state of online advertising. In response, the Digital Advertising Alliance (DAA) has issued guidance that makes clear that the transparency and choice obligations of its existing Self-Regulatory Principles also apply to cross-device tracking. *Insight on Society: Every Move You Take, Every Click You Make, We'll Be Tracking You* further examines the use of tracking files.

DATABASES, DATA WAREHOUSES, DATA MINING, AND BIG DATA

Databases, data warehouses, data mining, and the variety of marketing decision-making techniques loosely called *profiling* are at the heart of the revolution in Internet marketing. **Profiling** uses a variety of tools to create a digital image for each consumer. This image can be quite inexact, even primitive, but it can also be as detailed as a character in a novel. The quality of a consumer profile depends on the amount of data used to create it, and the analytical power of the firm's software and hardware. Together, these techniques attempt to identify precisely who the online customer is and what they want, and then, to fulfill the customer's criteria exactly. These techniques are more powerful, far more precise, and more fine-grained than the gross levels of demographic and market segmentation techniques used in mass marketing media or by telemarketing.

In order to understand the data in transaction logs, registration forms, shopping carts, cookies, web bugs, and other unstructured data sources like e-mails, tweets, and Facebook Likes, Internet marketers need massively powerful and capacious databases, database management systems, and analytic tools.

Databases

The first step in interpreting huge transaction streams is to store the information systematically. A **database** is a software application that stores records and attributes. A telephone book is a physical database that stores records of individuals and their attributes such as names, addresses, and phone numbers. A **database management system** (DBMS) is a software application used by organizations to create, maintain, and access databases. The most common DBMS are DB2 from IBM and a variety of SQL databases from Oracle, Sybase, and other providers. **Structured query language (SQL)** is an industry-standard database query and manipulation language used in relational databases. **Relational databases** such as DB2 and SQL represent data as two-dimensional tables with records organized in rows, and attributes in columns, much like a spreadsheet. The tables—and all the data in them—can be flexibly related to one another as long as the tables share a common data element.

Relational databases are extraordinarily flexible and allow marketers and other managers to view and analyze data from different perspectives very quickly.

Data Warehouses and Data Mining

A **data warehouse** is a database that collects a firm's transactional and customer data in a single location for offline analysis by marketers and site managers. The data

profiling
profiling uses a variety of tools to create a digital image for each consumer

database
a software application that stores records and attributes

database management system (DBMS)
a software application used by organizations to create, maintain, and access databases

structured query language (SQL)
industry-standard database query language used in relational databases

relational databases
represent data as two-dimensional tables with records organized in rows and attributes in columns; data within different tables can be flexibly related as long as the tables share a common data element

data warehouse
a database that collects a firm's transactional and customer data in a single location for offline analysis

INSIGHT ON SOCIETY

EVERY MOVE YOU TAKE, EVERY CLICK YOU MAKE, WE'LL BE TRACKING YOU

Advertising-supported websites depend on knowing as much personal information as possible about you. One of the main ways ad firms discover your personal information is by placing so-called "tracking files" on your computer's browser. There are several kinds of third-party tracking files on web pages. Cookies are the best known. These simple text files are placed in your browser and assign a unique number to your computer, which is then used by advertisers to track you across the Web as you move from one site to another (without telling you). Web beacons (sometimes also referred to as web bugs) are a little more pernicious. Beacons are small software files that track your clicks, choices, purchases, and even location data from mobile devices, and then send that information, often in real time, to advertisers tracking you. Beacons can also assign your computer a unique number and track you across the Web. Tracking may also occur as you watch Adobe Flash-enabled videos, visit websites equipped with HTML5 local storage, and use apps on smartphones. Most Facebook apps, for instance, send personal information, including names, to dozens of advertising and Internet tracking companies. A number of telecommunications companies use supercookies, which are updated whenever a user accesses a website with a mobile device. Mobile service carriers then provide those sites with additional information about the user for a cost.

So how common is web and mobile tracking? In a recent study, researchers found a very widespread surveillance system. Only one site, Wikipedia, had no tracking files. Two-thirds of the tracking files came from companies whose primary business is identifying and tracking Internet users to create consumer profiles that can be sold to advertising firms looking for specific types of customers. The other third came from database firms that gather and bundle the information and then sell it to marketers. Many of the tracking tools gather personal information such as age, gender, race, income, marital status, health concerns, TV shows and movies viewed, magazines and newspapers read, and books purchased. While tracking firms claim the information they gather is anonymous, this is true in name only. Scholars have shown that with just a few pieces of information, such as age, gender, zip code, and marital status, specific individuals can be easily identified. A 2015 Web Privacy Census conducted by the University of California Berkeley Center for Law and Technology found that the total number of cookies on the home pages of top 100 websites had increased by 80%, from 3,600 when first measured in 2009 to almost 6,300. The vast majority of these cookies (about 85%) were third-party tracking cookies from 275 different third-party hosts. Cookies orginating from Google's tracking infrastructure (including Google Analytics, DoubleClick, and YouTube) appeared on over 90% of both the top 100 and top 1000 websites, which the authors noted provides Google with a significant online surveillance structure. Similar results were observed when looking at the top 25,000 websites.

The Privacy Foundation has issued guidelines for web beacon usage. The guidelines suggest that web beacons should be visible as an icon on the screen, the icon should be labeled to indicate its function, and it should identify the name of the company that placed the web beacon on the page. In addition, if a user clicks on the web beacon, it should display a disclosure statement indicating what data is being collected, how the data is used after it is collected, what companies receive the data, what other data the web beacon is combined with, and whether or not a cookie is associated with the web beacon. Users should be able to opt out of any data collection done by the web beacon, and the web beacon should not be used to collect information from web pages of a sensitive nature, such as medical, financial, job-related, or sexual matters. None of these ideas are found in current law. Many sites have adopted the Network Advertising Initiative (NAI)'s self-regulatory guidelines, but these too are only voluntary, and these guidelines have done little to assuage fears from web users that their privacy is at risk.

One roadblock involves the meaning of Do Not Track (DNT). The W3C has been working on a specification with respect to DNT since 2011, but as of 2016, it still remains in draft format. Government and privacy groups have pushed for a DNT feature that would require users to affirmatively allow tracking. The advertising industry, not surprisingly, favors a form of DNT that requires users to affirmatively implement DNT. Nearly all browsers now offer users the option of using a DNT feature, although users have to remember to turn it on. The FCC has refused to make DNT mandatory, and as a result, websites often ignore DNT requests because it is more profitable for them to do so, with advertisers willing to pay up to seven times more for a highly targeted ad. In 2014, major companies such as Yahoo and AOL abandoned the DNT standard, citing the lack of traction that DNT has encountered across the rest of the Web. Although some bigger websites like Twitter and Pinterest do follow DNT guidelines,

these prominent defections are setbacks for the standard. Some users have turned instead to ad-blocking browser plug-ins such as AdBlock and Disconnect to avoid ads entirely. This has put additional pressure on websites as the pool of web users that advertisers can reach slowly shrinks.

The situation in Europe is somewhat different. Directive 2009/136/EC, also known as the EU Cookie Law, provides that websites must ask visitors for their consent before they can install most cookies (although not cookies considered necessary for the basic function of a website, such as session cookies that are used to track a shopping cart). Compliance with the law remains spotty. In January 2017, the European Commission released a proposal to repeal the EU Cookie Law and replace with a new regulation that would simplify the cookie rules, particularly the requirement that websites obtain prior informed consent. Most websites have implemented this requirement by displaying cookie banners at the top or bottom of the screen, which some users find annoying. The proposed rule exempts cookies that are merely used to count the number of visitors to the site, and clarifies that consent is not required for non-privacy intrusive cookies aimed at improving the customer experience, such as for remembering shopping cart history. More significantly, the new rule also proposes to allow users to set privacy settings via web browser software, with websites then detecting a visitor's settings and automatically removing the cookie notice if the use has already been deliberately approved or blocked via the browser's settings.

SOURCES: "Goodbye Cookie Banners? European Commission Proposes to Simply the Cookie Law," by M. James Daley and Natalya Northrip, Carpedatumlaw.com, January 12, 2017; "Understanding 'Do Not Track': Truth or Consequences," by Jason Kint, Recode.net, January 12, 2016; "How 'Do Not Track' Ended Up Going Nowhere," by Dawn Chmielewski, Recode.net, January 4, 2016; "Web Privacy Census," by Ibrahim Altaweel, Nathaniel Good, and Chris Jay Hoofnagle, *Technology Science*, December 12, 2015; "FCC Says Sites Can Ignore 'Do-Not-Track' Requests," by Bill Synder, Cio.com, November 10, 2015; "Supercookies Are Back, and They're as Unappealing as Ever," by Michael Kassner, Techrepublic.com, August 28, 2015; "New Do Not Track Policy Introduced," by Michael Guta, Smallbiztrends.com, August 10, 2015; "Clear Rules of the Road With the Do Not Track Policy," by Peter Eckersley, Rainey Reitman, and Alan Toner, Eff.org, August 8, 2015; "'Do Not Track Compromise' Is Pitched," by Elizabeth Dwoskin, *Wall Street Journal*, August 5, 2015; "Do Not Track—The Privacy Standard That's Melting Away," by Mark Stockley, Nakedsecurity.sophos.com, August 26, 2014; "Yahoo Is the Latest Company Ignoring Web Users' Requests for Privacy," by Jon Brodkin, Arstechnica.com, May 1, 2014; "What Firefox's New Privacy Settings Mean for You," by Sarah A. Downey, Abine.com, March 29, 2013; "Online Tracking Ramps Up," by Julia Angwin, *Wall Street Journal*, June 17, 2012.

originate in many core operational areas of the firm, such as website transaction logs, shopping carts, point-of-sale terminals (product scanners) in stores, warehouse inventory levels, field sales reports, external scanner data supplied by third parties, and financial payment data. The purpose of a data warehouse is to gather all the firm's transaction and customer data into one logical repository where it can be analyzed and modeled by managers without disrupting or taxing the firm's primary transactional systems and databases. Data warehouses grow quickly into storage repositories containing terabytes (trillions of bytes) of data on consumer behavior at a firm's stores and websites. With a data warehouse, firms can answer such questions as: What products are the most profitable by region and city? What regional marketing campaigns are working? How effective is store promotion of the firm's website? Data warehouses can provide business managers with a more complete awareness of customers through data that can be accessed quickly.

data mining
a set of analytical techniques that look for patterns in the data of a database or data warehouse, or seek to model the behavior of customers

Data mining is a set of analytical techniques that look for patterns in the data of a database or data warehouse, or seek to model the behavior of customers. Website data can be "mined" to develop profiles of visitors and customers. A **customer profile** is simply a set of rules that describe the typical behavior of a customer or a group of customers at a website. Customer profiles help to identify the patterns in group and individual behavior that occur online as millions of visitors use a firm's website. For example, almost every financial transaction you engage in is processed by a data mining application to detect fraud. Phone companies closely monitor your cell phone use as well to detect stolen phones and unusual calling patterns. Financial institutions and cell phone firms use data mining to develop fraud profiles. When a user's behavior conforms to a fraud profile, the transaction is not allowed or is terminated (Mobasher, 2007).

customer profile
a description of the typical behavior of a customer or a group of customers at a website

There are many different types of data mining. The simplest type is **query-driven data mining**, which is based on specific queries. For instance, based on hunches of marketers who suspect a relationship in the database or who need to answer a specific question, such as "What is the relationship between time of day and purchases of various products at the website?", marketers can easily query the data warehouse and produce a database table that rank-orders the top 10 products sold at a website by each hour of the day. Marketers can then change the content of the website to stimulate more sales by highlighting different products over time or placing particular products on the home page at certain times of day or night.

query-driven data mining
data mining based on specific queries

model-driven data mining
involves the use of a model that analyzes the key variables of interest to decision makers

Another form of data mining is model-driven. **Model-driven data mining** involves the use of a model that analyzes the key variables of interest to decision makers. For example, marketers may want to reduce the inventory carried on the website by removing unprofitable items that do not sell well. A financial model can be built showing the profitability of each product on the site so that an informed decision can be made.

A more fine-grained behavioral approach that seeks to deal with individuals as opposed to market segments derives rules from individual consumer behavior (along with some demographic information) (Adomavicius and Tuzhilin, 2001a; Chan, 1999; Fawcett and Provost, 1996, 1997). Here, the pages actually visited by specific users are stored as a set of conjunctive rules. For example, if an individual visits a site and typically ("as a rule") moves from the home page to the financial news section to the Asian report section, and then often purchases articles from the "Recent Developments in Banking" section, this person—based on purely past behavioral patterns—might be shown an advertisement for a book on Asian money markets. These rules can be constructed to follow an individual across many different websites.

There are many drawbacks to all these techniques, not least of which is that there may be millions of rules, many of them nonsensical, and many others of short-term duration. Hence, the rules need extensive validation and culling (Adomavicius and Tuzhilin, 2001b). Also, there can be millions of affinity groups and other patterns in the data that are temporal or meaningless. The difficulty is isolating the valid, powerful (profitable) patterns in the data and then acting on the observed pattern fast enough to make a sale that otherwise would not have been made. As we see later, there are practical difficulties and trade-offs involved in achieving these levels of granularity, precision, and speed.

Hadoop and the Challenge of Big Data

Until recently, most data collected by organizations consisted of structured transaction data that could easily fit into rows and columns of relational database management systems. Since then, there has been an explosion of data from web traffic, e-mail messages, social media content (tweets, status messages), even music playlists, as well as machine-generated data from sensors that, due to the plummeting cost of data storage and powerful new processing capabilities, can now be stored and analyzed to draw connections and make inferences and predictions. This data may be unstructured or semi-structured and thus not suitable for relational database products that organize data in the form of columns and rows. The term **big data** refers to this avalanche of digital data that creates huge data sets, often from different sources, in the petabyte and exabyte range. The volumes of data are so large that traditional DBMS cannot capture, store, and analyze the data in a reasonable time. Some examples of big data challenges are analyzing 8 terabytes of tweets generated by Twitter each day to improve your understanding of consumer sentiment towards your products; 100 million e-mails in order to place appropriate ads alongside the e-mail messages; or 500 million call detail records to find patterns of fraud and churn. According to the IDC technology research firm, data is more than doubling every two years, so the amount of data available to organizations is skyrocketing. The next frontier will be data derived from the Internet of Things (IoT).

big data
huge data sets, often from different sources, in the petabyte and exabyte range

Marketers are interested in big data because it allows them to link huge amounts of data from a variety of different sources, which in the past they were unable to do, and mine it for patterns of consumer behavior, with the potential to provide new insights into customer behavior, financial market activity, or other phenomena. For instance, Evrythng, an IoT platform company, has partnered with Trueffect, a digital ad firm, to develop ways that marketers can use data generated by connected appliances and other devices in order to directly communicate with and target advertising with consumers. However, to derive business value from this data, organizations need new technologies and analytic tools capable of managing and analyzing nontraditional data along with their traditional enterprise data. A recent survey found that while marketers say big data is their biggest opportunity, only 14% are confident in their use of big data (Tadena, 2015).

To handle unstructured and semi-structured data in vast quantities, as well as structured data, organizations are using Hadoop. **Hadoop** is an open source software frame-

Hadoop
a software framework for working with various big data sets

work managed by the Apache Software Foundation that enables distributed parallel processing of huge amounts of data across inexpensive computers. It breaks a big data problem down into subproblems, distributes them among up to thousands of inexpensive computer processing nodes, and then combines the result into a smaller data set that is easier to analyze. You've probably used Hadoop to find the best airfare on the Internet, get directions to a restaurant, search on Google, or connect with a friend on Facebook.

Hadoop can process large quantities of any kind of data, including structured transactional data, loosely structured data such as Facebook and Twitter feeds, complex data such as web server log files, and unstructured audio and video data. Hadoop runs on a cluster of inexpensive servers, and processors can be added or removed as needed. Companies use Hadoop to analyze very large volumes of data as well as for a staging area for unstructured and semi-structured data before it is loaded into a data warehouse. Facebook stores much of its data on its massive Hadoop cluster, which holds an estimated 300 petabytes, about 30,000 times more information than the Library of Congress. Yahoo uses Hadoop to track user behavior so it can modify its home page to fit user interests. Life sciences research firm NextBio uses Hadoop and HBase to process data for pharmaceutical companies conducting genomic research. Top database vendors such as IBM, Hewlett-Packard, Oracle, and Microsoft have their own Hadoop software distributions. Other vendors offer tools for moving data into and out of Hadoop or for analyzing data within Hadoop. In addition, there are many new tools being developed for big data analysis in addition to Hadoop. One example is Spark, an open source product being supported by IBM that can deliver results faster than Hadoop.

MARKETING AUTOMATION AND CUSTOMER RELATIONSHIP MANAGEMENT (CRM) SYSTEMS

marketing automation systems
software tools that marketers use to track all the steps in the lead generation part of the marketing process

Marketing automation systems are software tools that marketers use to track all the steps in the lead generation part of the marketing process. The marketing process begins with making the potential customer aware of the firm and product, and recognizing the need for the product. This is the beginning of a lead—someone who might buy. From there, consumers need to find you as they search for products; they will compare your products with your competitors' offerings and at some point, choose to purchase. Software can help in each of these stages of the marketing process. A number of firms sell software packages that can visualize most of the online marketing activities of a firm and then track the progression from exposure to display ads, finding your firm on a search engine, directing follow-up e-mail and communications, and finally a purchase. Once leads become customers, customer relationship management systems take over the maintenance of the relationship.

customer relationship management (CRM) system
a repository of customer information that records all of the contacts that a customer has with a firm and generates a customer profile available to everyone in the firm with a need to "know the customer"

Customer relationship management systems are another important Internet marketing technology. A **customer relationship management (CRM) system** is a repository of customer information that records all of the contacts that a customer has with a firm (including websites) and generates a customer profile available to everyone in the firm with a need to "know the customer." CRM systems also supply the analytical software required to analyze and use customer information. Customers come to firms not just over the Web but also through telephone call centers, customer service representatives, sales representatives, automated voice response systems, ATMs and kiosks, in-store point-of-sale terminals, and mobile devices (m-commerce).

Collectively, these are referred to as "**customer touchpoints**." In the past, firms generally did not maintain a single repository of customer information, but instead were organized along product lines, with each product line maintaining a customer list (and often not sharing it with others in the same firm).

customer touchpoints
the ways in which customers interact with the firm

In general, firms did not know who their customers were, how profitable they were, or how they responded to marketing campaigns. For instance, a bank customer might see a television advertisement for a low-cost auto loan that included an 800-number to call. However, if the customer came to the bank's website instead, rather than calling the 800-number, marketers would have no idea how effective the television campaign was because this web customer contact data was not related to the 800-number call center data. **Figure 6.10** illustrates how a CRM system integrates customer contact data into a single system.

CRMs are part of the evolution of firms toward a customer-centric and marketing-segment–based business, and away from a product-line–centered business. CRMs

| FIGURE 6.10 | A CUSTOMER RELATIONSHIP MANAGEMENT SYSTEM |

This is an example of a CRM system. The system captures customer information from all customer touchpoints as well as other data sources, merges the data, and aggregates it into a single customer data repository or data warehouse where it can be used to provide better service, as well as to construct customer profiles for marketing purposes. Online analytical processing (OLAP) allows managers to dynamically analyze customer activities to spot trends or problems involving customers. Other analytical software programs analyze aggregate customer behavior to identify profitable and unprofitable customers as well as customer activities.

are essentially a database technology with extraordinary capabilities for addressing the needs of each customer and differentiating the product or service on the basis of treating each customer as a unique person. Customer profiles can contain the following information:

- A map of the customer's relationship with the institution
- Product and usage summary data
- Demographic and psychographic data
- Profitability measures
- Contact history summarizing the customer's contacts with the institution across most delivery channels
- Marketing and sales information containing programs received by the customer and the customer's responses
- E-mail campaign responses
- Website visits
- Mobile app downloads

With these profiles, CRMs can be used to sell additional products and services, develop new products, increase product utilization, reduce marketing costs, identify and retain profitable customers, optimize service delivery costs, retain high lifetime value customers, enable personal communications, improve customer loyalty, and increase product profitability. The goal is what is known as a "360-degree" view that enables a company to know what its customers buy, how they browse, what kinds of communications and offers will engage them, and more. Leading CRM vendors include Oracle, SAP, Microsoft, Salesforce, and SugarCRM, many of which offer cloud-based versions of their CRM products. One issue facing cloud CRM providers and global companies that use those products is European Union data regulations that will require them to reassess how they use CRM data in order to avoid violating those regulations. All the major vendors offer cloud-based SaaS CRM applications.

6.4 UNDERSTANDING THE COSTS AND BENEFITS OF ONLINE MARKETING COMMUNICATIONS

As we noted earlier, online marketing communications still comprise only a small part of the total marketing communications universe. While there are several reasons why this is the case, two of the main ones are concerns about how well online advertising really works and about how to adequately measure the costs and benefits of online advertising. We will address both of these topics in this section. But first, we will define some important terms used when examining the effectiveness of online marketing.

ONLINE MARKETING METRICS: LEXICON

In order to understand the process of attracting prospects via marketing communications and converting them into customers, you will need to be familiar with online marketing terminology. **Table 6.7** lists some terms commonly used to describe the impacts and results of "traditional" online marketing such as display ads and e-mail campaigns. Metrics for social, mobile, and local marketing are covered in Chapter 7.

The first nine metrics focus primarily on the success of a website in achieving audience or market share by "driving" shoppers to the site. These measures often substitute for solid information on sales revenue as e-commerce entrepreneurs seek to have investors and the public focus on the success of the website in "attracting eyeballs" (viewers).

Impressions are the number of times an ad is served. **Click-through rate (CTR)** measures the percentage of people exposed to an online advertisement who actually click on the advertisement. Because not all ads lead to an immediate click, the industry has invented a term for a long-term hit called **view-through rate (VTR)**, which measures the 30-day response rate to an ad. **Hits** are the number of HTTP requests received by a firm's server. Hits can be misleading as a measure of website activity because a "hit" does not equal a page. A single page may account for several hits if the page contains multiple images or graphics. A single website visitor can generate hundreds of hits. For this reason, hits are not an accurate representation of web traffic or visits, even though they are generally easy to measure; the sheer volume of hits can be huge—and sound impressive—but not be a true measure of activity. **Page views** are the number of pages requested by visitors. However, with increased usage of web frames that divide pages into separate sections, a single page that has three frames will generate three page views. Hence, page views per se are also not a very useful metric.

Viewability rate is the percentage of ads (either display or video) that are actually seen by people online. See page 407 for a further discussion of the issue of viewability.

The number of unique visitors is perhaps the most widely used measure of a website's popularity. The measurement of **unique visitors** counts the number of distinct, unique visitors to a website, regardless of how many pages they view. **Loyalty** measures the percentage of visitors who return in a year. This can be a good indicator of a site's web following, and perhaps the trust shoppers place in a site. **Reach** is typically a percentage of the total number of consumers in a market who visit a website; for example, 10% of all book purchasers in a year will visit Amazon at least once to shop for a book. This provides an idea of the power of a website to attract market share. **Recency**—like loyalty—measures the power of a website to produce repeat visits and is generally measured as the average number of days elapsed between shopper or customer visits. For example, a recency value of 25 days means the average customer will return once every 25 days.

Stickiness (sometimes called *duration*) is the average length of time visitors remain at a website. Stickiness is important to marketers because the longer the amount of time a visitor spends at a website, the greater the probability of a purchase. However, equally important is what people do when they visit a website and not just how much time they spend there.

The metrics described so far do not say much about commercial activity nor help you understand the conversion from visitor to customer. Several other measures are more helpful in this regard. **Acquisition rate** measures the percentage of visitors who register or visit product pages (indicating interest in the product). **Conversion rate** measures the percentage of visitors who actually purchase something. Conversion

impressions
number of times an ad is served

click-through rate (CTR)
the percentage of people exposed to an online advertisement who actually click on the banner

view-through rate (VTR)
measures the 30-day response rate to an ad

hits
number of http requests received by a firm's server

page views
number of pages requested by visitors

viewability rate
percentage of ads that are actually seen by people online

unique visitors
the number of distinct, unique visitors to a site

loyalty
percentage of purchasers who return in a year

reach
percentage of the total number of consumers in a market who will visit a site

recency
average number of days elapsed between visits

stickiness (duration)
average length of time visitors remain at a site

acquisition rate
percentage of visitors who register or visit product pages

conversion rate
percentage of visitors who purchase something

TABLE 6.7	MARKETING METRICS LEXICON
DISPLAY AD METRICS	**DESCRIPTION**
Impressions	Number of times an ad is served
Click-through rate (CTR)	Percentage of times an ad is clicked
View-through rate (VTR)	Percentage of times an ad is not clicked immediately but the website is visited within 30 days
Hits	Number of HTTP requests
Page views	Number of pages viewed
Viewability rate	Percentage of ads that are actually seen online
Unique visitors	Number of unique visitors in a period
Loyalty	Measured variously as the number of page views, frequency of single-user visits to the website, or percentage of customers who return to the site in a year to make additional purchases
Reach	Percentage of website visitors who are potential buyers; or the percentage of total market buyers who buy at a site
Recency	Time elapsed since the last action taken by a buyer, such as a website visit or purchase
Stickiness (duration)	Average length of stay at a website
Acquisition rate	Percentage of visitors who indicate an interest in the website's products by registering or visiting product pages
Conversion rate	Percentage of visitors who become customers
Browse-to-buy ratio	Ratio of items purchased to product views
View-to-cart ratio	Ratio of "Add to cart" clicks to product views
Cart conversion rate	Ratio of actual orders to "Add to cart" clicks
Checkout conversion rate	Ratio of actual orders to checkouts started
Abandonment rate	Percentage of shoppers who begin a shopping cart purchase but then leave the website without completing a purchase (similar to above)
Retention rate	Percentage of existing customers who continue to buy on a regular basis (similar to loyalty)
Attrition rate	Percentage of customers who do not return during the next year after an initial purchase
VIDEO ADVERTISING METRICS	
View time	How long does the ad actually stay in view while it plays
Completion rate	How many viewers watched the complete video
Skip rate	How many viewers skipped the video
E-MAIL METRICS	
Open rate	Percentage of e-mail recipients who open the e-mail and are exposed to the message
Delivery rate	Percentage of e-mail recipients who received the e-mail
Click-through rate (e-mail)	Percentage of recipients who clicked through to offers
Bounce-back rate	Percentage of e-mails that could not be delivered
Unsubscribe rate	Percentage of recipients who click unsubscribe
Conversion rate (e-mail)	Percentage of recipients who actually buy

rates can vary widely, depending on the success of the site. The average conversion rate in the United States for e-commerce sites on traditional desktop computers was about 4.25% in the first half of 2016, compared to about 3.45% for tablet computers and 1.35% for smartphones. Clearly, websites viewed on desktops still remain the most effective vehicle for converting visitors into purchasers (Monetate, 2016). The **browse-to-buy ratio** measures the ratio of items purchased to product views. The **view-to-cart ratio** calculates the ratio of "Add to cart" clicks to product views. **Cart conversion rate** measures the ratio of actual orders to "Add to cart" clicks. **Checkout conversion rate** calculates the ratio of actual orders to checkouts started. **Abandonment rate** measures the percentage of shoppers who begin a shopping cart form but then fail to complete the form and leave the website. Abandonment rates can signal a number of potential problems—poor form design, lack of consumer trust, or consumer purchase uncertainty caused by other factors. Recent studies on shopping cart abandonment found abandonment rates ranging from 68% to 75% (Baymard Institute, 2016). Among the reasons for abandonment were security concerns, customer just checking prices, couldn't find customer support, couldn't find preferred payment option, and the item being unavailable at checkout. Given that more than 80% of online shoppers generally have a purchase in mind when they visit a website, a high abandonment rate signals many lost sales. **Retention rate** indicates the percentage of existing customers who continue to buy on a regular basis. **Attrition rate** measures the percentage of customers who purchase once but never return within a year (the opposite of loyalty and retention rates).

Specific types of advertising have their own special metrics. For instance, for video ads, **view time** (how long the ad actually stays in view while it plays) and **completion rate** (how many viewers watch the entire video ad) are important factors. Research has shown that brand recall is significantly higher when the entire ad is watched, making the completion rate metric more meaningful to advertisers than the click-through rate (Adler, 2015).

E-mail campaigns also have their own set of metrics. **Open rate** measures the percentage of customers who open the e-mail and are exposed to the message. Generally, open rates are quite high, in the area of 50% or greater. However, some browsers open mail as soon as the mouse cursor moves over the subject line, and therefore this measure can be difficult to interpret. **Delivery rate** measures the percentage of e-mail recipients who received the e-mail. **Click-through rate (e-mail)** measures the percentage of e-mail recipients who clicked through to the offer. Finally, **bounce-back rate** measures the percentage of e-mails that could not be delivered.

There is a lengthy path from simple online ad impressions, website visits, and page views to the purchase of a product and the company making a profit (see **Figure 6.11**). You first need to make customers aware of their needs for your product and somehow drive them to your website. Once there, you need to convince them you have the best value—quality and price—when compared to alternative providers. You then must persuade them to trust your firm to handle the transaction (by providing a secure environment and fast fulfillment). Based on your success, a percentage of customers will remain loyal and purchase again or recommend your website to others.

browse-to-buy ratio
ratio of items purchased to product views

view-to-cart ratio
ratio of "Add to cart" clicks to product views

cart conversion rate
ratio of actual orders to "Add to cart" clicks

checkout conversion rate
ratio of actual orders to checkouts started

abandonment rate
% of shoppers who begin a shopping cart, but then fail to complete it

retention rate
% of existing customers who continue to buy

attrition rate
% of customers who purchase once, but do not return within a year

view time
how long the video ad actually stays in view while it plays

completion rate
how many viewers watch the complete video ad

open rate
% of customers who open e-mail

delivery rate
% of e-mail recipients who received e-mail

click-through rate (e-mail)
% of e-mail recipients who clicked through to the offer

bounce-back rate
percentage of e-mails that could not be delivered

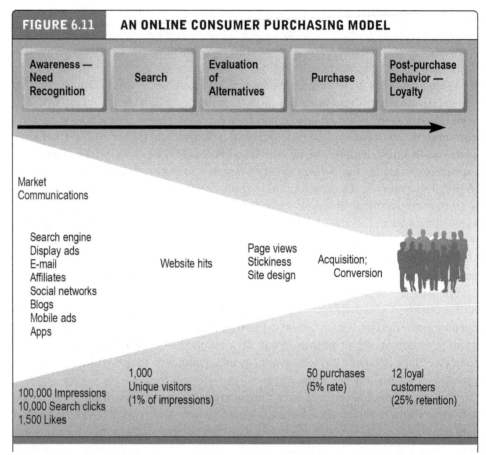

FIGURE 6.11   **AN ONLINE CONSUMER PURCHASING MODEL**

Awareness — Need Recognition · Search · Evaluation of Alternatives · Purchase · Post-purchase Behavior — Loyalty

Market Communications

Search engine
Display ads
E-mail
Affiliates
Social networks
Blogs
Mobile ads
Apps

Website hits

Page views
Stickiness
Site design

Acquisition;
Conversion

100,000 Impressions
10,000 Search clicks
1,500 Likes

1,000
Unique visitors
(1% of impressions)

50 purchases
(5% rate)

12 loyal
customers
(25% retention)

The conversion of visitors into customers, and then loyal customers, is a complex and long-term process that may take several months.

HOW WELL DOES ONLINE ADVERTISING WORK?

What is the most effective kind of online advertising? How does online advertising compare to offline advertising? The answers depend on the goals of the campaign, the nature of the product, and the quality of the website you direct customers toward. The answers also depend on what you measure. Click-through rates are interesting, but ultimately it's the return on the investment (ROI) in the ad campaign that counts. More than 70% of marketing executives said they would spend even more on digital ads if ability to measure ROI improved (Tadena, 2015). Complicating matters is the difficulty of **cross-platform attribution**, which involves understanding how to assign appropriate credit to different marketing initiatives on a variety of platforms that may have influenced a consumer along the way to an ultimate purchase. There is increasing recognition that first-click and last-click models that focus, as their names indicate, on either the first or last marketing channel or advertising format that a consumer engages with prior to a purchase, are no longer sufficient.

cross-platform attribution

understanding how to assign appropriate credit to different marketing initiatives that may have influenced a consumer on the way to a purchase

TABLE 6.8	ONLINE MARKETING COMMUNICATIONS: TYPICAL CLICK-THROUGH RATES	
MARKETING METHODS	**TYPICAL CLICK-THROUGH RATES**	
Banner ads	.03%–.25%	
Google enhanced search ads (Product Listing Ads)	2.8%–3.6%	
Google AdWords search listing	1.35%–3.4%	
Video	.34%–.85%	
Rich media	.13%–.35%	
Sponsorships	1.5%–3.0%	
Native ads	.80-1.8%	
Content marketing	.25%-.40%	
Affiliate relationships	.20%–.40%	
E-mail marketing in-house list	3.0–5.0%	
E-mail marketing purchased list	.01%–1.5%	
Social network display ads	.15%–.25%	
Mobile display ads	.09%–1.25%	

SOURCES: Based on data from Chaffey, 2016; eMarketer, Inc.,2016j, 2016o; PointRoll, 2015; Wordstream, 2016; Viant, 2016; Polar, 2016; industry sources; authors' estimates.

Table 6.8 lists the click-through rates for various types of online marketing communications tools. There is a great deal of variability within any of these types, so the figures should be viewed as general estimates. Click-through rates on all these formats are a function of personalization and other targeting techniques. For instance, several studies have found that e-mail response rates can be increased 20% or more by adding social sharing links. And while the average Google click-through rate is less than 1%, some merchants can hit 10% or more by making their ads more specific and attracting only the most interested people. Permission e-mail click-through rates have been fairly consistent over the last five years, in the 3%–5% range. Putting the recipient's name in the subject line can double the click-through rate. (For unsolicited e-mail and outright spam, response rates are much lower, even though about 20% of U.S. e-mail users report clicking occasionally on an unsolicited e-mail.) The click-through rate for video ads may seem low, but it is twice as high as the rate for banner ads. For instance, research by PointRoll found that adding video to a rich media campaign increased interaction rates by over 17% on average (PointRoll, 2015). "Interaction" means the user clicks on the video, plays it, stops it, or takes some other action.

How effective is online advertising compared to offline advertising? In general, the online channels (e-mail, search engine, display ads, video, and social, mobile, and local marketing) compare very favorably with traditional channels. This explains in large part why online advertising has grown so rapidly in the last five years. Search engine advertising has grown to be one of the most cost-effective forms of marketing communications and accounts for, in large part, the growth of Google. Direct opt-in e-mail is also very cost-effective. This is, in part, because e-mail lists are so inexpensive and because opt-in e-mail is a form of targeting people who are already interested in receiving more information.

A study of the comparative impacts of offline and online marketing concluded that the most powerful marketing campaigns used multiple forms of marketing, including online, catalog, television, radio, newspapers, and retail store. Traditional media like television and print media remain the primary means for consumers to find out about new products even though advertisers have reduced their budgets for print media ads. Consumers who shop multiple channels are spending more than consumers who shop only with a single channel, in part because they have more discretionary income but also because of the combined number of "touchpoints" that marketers are making with the consumers. The fastest growing channel in consumer marketing is the multi-channel shopper.

THE COSTS OF ONLINE ADVERTISING

cost per thousand (CPM)
advertiser pays for impressions in 1,000-unit lots

cost per click (CPC)
advertiser pays prenegotiated fee for each click an ad receives

cost per action (CPA)
advertiser pays only for those users who perform a specific action

Effectiveness cannot be considered without an analysis of costs. Initially, most online ads were sold on a barter or **cost per thousand (CPM)** impressions basis, with advertisers purchasing impressions in 1,000-unit lots. Today, other pricing models have developed, including **cost per click (CPC)**, where the advertiser pays a prenegotiated fee for each click an ad receives; **cost per action (CPA)**, where the advertiser pays a prenegotiated amount only when a user performs a specific action, such as a registration or a purchase; and hybrid arrangements, combining two or more of these models (see **Table 6.9**).

While in the early days of e-commerce, a few online sites spent as much as $400 on marketing and advertising to acquire one customer, the average cost was never that high. While the costs for offline customer acquisition are higher than online, the offline items are typically far more expensive. If you advertise in the *Wall Street Journal*, you are tapping into a wealthy demographic that may be interested in buying islands, jets, and expensive homes in France. A full-page black and white ad in the *Wall Street Journal* National Edition costs about $250,000, whereas other papers are in the $10,000 to $100,000 range.

One of the advantages of online marketing is that online sales can generally be directly correlated with online marketing efforts. If online merchants can obtain offline purchase data from a data broker, the merchants can measure precisely just how much revenue is generated by specific banners or e-mail messages sent to prospective customers. One way to measure the effectiveness of online marketing is by looking at the ratio of additional revenue received divided by the cost of the campaign (Revenue/ Cost). Any positive whole number means the campaign was worthwhile.

TABLE 6.9	DIFFERENT PRICING MODELS FOR ONLINE ADVERTISEMENTS
PRICING MODEL	**DESCRIPTION**
Barter	Exchange of ad space for something of equal value
Cost per thousand (CPM)	Advertiser pays for impressions in 1,000-unit lots
Cost per click (CPC)	Advertiser pays prenegotiated fee for each click ad received
Cost per lead (CPL)	Advertiser pays only for qualified leads or contacts
Cost per action (CPA)	Advertiser pays only for those users who perform a specific action, such as registering, purchasing, etc.
Hybrid	Two or more of the above models used together
Sponsorship	Term-based; advertiser pays fixed fee for a slot on a website

A more complex situation arises when both online and offline sales revenues are affected by an online marketing effort. A large percentage of the online audience uses the Web to "shop" but not buy. These shoppers buy at physical stores. Merchants such as Sears and Walmart use e-mail to inform their registered customers of special offers available for purchase either online or at stores. Unfortunately, purchases at physical stores cannot be tied precisely with the online e-mail campaign. In these cases, merchants have to rely on less precise measures such as customer surveys at store locations to determine the effectiveness of online campaigns.

In either case, measuring the effectiveness of online marketing communications—and specifying precisely the objective (branding versus sales)—is critical to profitability. To measure marketing effectiveness, you need to understand the costs of various marketing media and the process of converting online prospects into online customers.

In general, online marketing communications are more costly on a CPM basis than traditional mass media marketing, but are more efficient in producing sales. **Table 6.10** shows costs for typical online and offline marketing communications. For instance, in 2016, the average cost for 30 seconds of commercial time during a prime-time network television broadcast is about $112,000, not including the cost to produce the advertisement. According to Nielsen, such an ad has an average CPM of $24.76. In contrast, a banner ad costs virtually nothing to produce and can be purchased for a cost of $5–$10 per thousand impressions. Direct postal mail can cost 80 cents to $1 per household drop for a post card, while e-mail can be sent for virtually nothing and costs only $5–$15 per thousand targeted names. Hence, e-mail is far less expensive than postal mail on a CPM basis. **Effective cost-per-thousand (eCPM)** is a metric that measures return on investment from an ad by dividing the total earnings from the ad by the total number of impressions in thousands.

effective cost-per-thousand (eCPM)

measures return on investment from an ad by dividing the total earnings from the ad by the total number of impressions in thousands

TABLE 6.10	TRADITIONAL AND ONLINE ADVERTISING COSTS COMPARED
TRADITIONAL ADVERTISING	
Local television	$1,500–$15,000 for a 30-second commercial; $45,000 for a highly rated show
Network television	$80,000–$600,000 for a 30-second spot during prime time; the average is $112,000
Cable television	$5,000–$8,000 for a 30-second ad during prime time
Radio	$100–$1,000 for a 60-second spot, depending on the time of day and program ratings
Newspaper	$120 per 1,000 circulation for a full-page ad
Magazine	$50 per 1,000 circulation for an ad in a regional edition of a national magazine, versus $120 per 1,000 for a local magazine
Direct mail	$15–$20 per 1,000 delivered for coupon mailings; $25–$40 per 1,000 for simple newspaper inserts
Billboard	$1,500–$30,000 for a large billboard for a 4-week period, with a minimum of 5–20 billboards
ONLINE ADVERTISING	
Banner ads	$5–$10 per 1,000 impressions, depending on how targeted the ad is (the more targeted, the higher the price)
Video and rich media	$20–$25 per 1,000 ads, depending on the website's demographics
E-mail	$5–$15 per 1,000 targeted e-mail addresses
Sponsorships	$30–$75 per 1,000 viewers, depending on the exclusivity of the sponsorship (the more exclusive, the higher the price)
Social network ads	$0.50–$3.00 per 1,000 impressions, with news feed ads at the high end of the range
Mobile display ads	$1.50–$3.25 per 1,000 impressions, including media costs, charges for first- or third-party data and service fees

MARKETING ANALYTICS: SOFTWARE FOR MEASURING ONLINE MARKETING RESULTS

A number of software programs are available to automatically calculate activities at a website or on a mobile device. Tracking the viewing and behavior of consumers across myriad devices and media channels is a much more difficult task. Other software programs and services assist marketing managers in identifying exactly which marketing initiatives are paying off and which are not.

The purpose of marketing is to convert shoppers into customers who purchase what you sell. The process of converting shoppers into customers is often called a

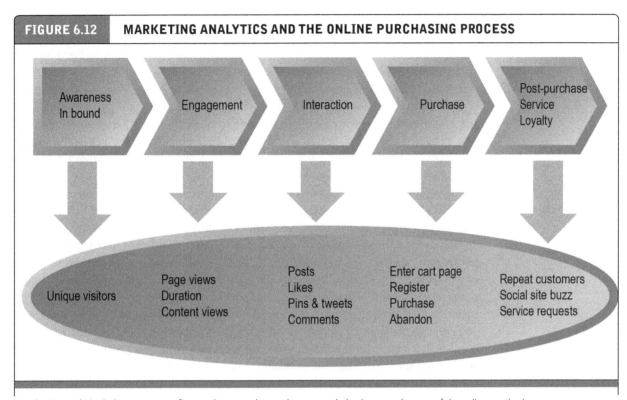

FIGURE 6.12   MARKETING ANALYTICS AND THE ONLINE PURCHASING PROCESS

Marketing analytics help e-commerce firms to better understand consumer behavior at each stage of the online purchasing process.

"purchasing funnel." We have characterized this as a process rather than a funnel that is composed of several stages: awareness, engagement, interaction, purchase, and post-purchase service and loyalty. **Marketing analytics software** collects, stores, analyzes, and graphically presents data on each of the stages in the conversion of shoppers to customers (see **Figure 6.12**).

Marketing analytics packages can tell business managers how people become *aware* of their site, and where they come from (e.g., search, self-entered URL, e-mail, social campaigns, or off-line traditional print and TV ads), along with demographic, behavioral, and geographic information. Are shoppers coming from mobile devices, Facebook, or Pinterest? This information can help managers decide the best ways to drive traffic, the so-called "in-bound" links to a site. Once on the website, analytics packages can record how *engaged* visitors are with the site's content, measured in terms of pages viewed and duration on site. This information can allow managers to change the design or their sites, or change the content viewers are seeing. For instance, video testimonials from product users may be much more engaging than expert reviews or user text comments. In a social marketing world, where consumers' opinions and behavior can be harvested and broadcast to their friends, an important intermediate step in the consumer conversion process is to encourage visitors to *interact* with your

marketing analytics software

collects, stores, analyzes, and graphically presents data on each of the stages in the conversion of shoppers to customers process on e-commerce sites content and share their experiences, opinions, preferences, and behaviors with their friends, as well as other visitors to the site. Marketing analytics packages can track visitor interaction and help managers decide what content leads to higher levels of visitor interaction with friends and other visitors. The *purchase activity* on the shopping cart page is a major focus of analytics tools not just because this is where the revenue is generated, but also because this is where the customer frequently exits the entire site and the firm loses a potential sale. The current shopping cart abandonment is 68% to 75% in the United States, with little change over the last few years, and higher in other countries (Baymard Institute, 2016). This seems like an extraordinary rate but, like most of the indicators discussed in this chapter, abandonment is a complex phenomenon and often not what it seems. Consumers use carts like a shopping list, and don't complete the transaction immediately; they use it for price comparison and to know shipping costs, or taxes; they complete transactions later on a different device, such as a mobile phone. Another measure of near-purchase activity is the add-to-cart rate. Marketing analytics software can help managers tease out the meaning of behavior on a website's shopping cart page. Finally, marketing analytics can help managers discover customer *loyalty and post-purchase* behavior. In an increasingly social marketing environment, marketing managers need to know how their products and services are being talked about on other sites, Facebook pages, or Twitter tweets, often called "buzz" or sentiment analysis. Are the comments positive or negative? What is the source of negative comments? Possible candidates are poor quality, high costs, poor warranty service, and shipping issues.

The end objective of marketing analytics packages is to help business managers optimize the return on investment on their marketing efforts, and to do this by building a detailed understanding of how their consumers behave. Marketing analytics also allows managers to measure the impact of specific marketing campaigns involving, say, discounts, loyalty points, and special offers, as well as regional, or demographic-based campaigns. Aside from its role in enhancing management decision making, and optimizing the effectiveness of building an e-commerce presence, marketing analytics packages also enable a near real-time marketing capability where managers are able to change the content of a website, respond to customer complaints and comments, and align campaigns with trending topics or news developments, all in a near real-time manner (real-time may be a matter of minutes or at most 24 hours) (MarketingLand, 2015).

While there are a great many marketing analytics firms and software packages on the market, the leaders are Google Analytics, Adobe Analytics, IBM Digital Analytics, and Webtrends. Marketing analytics software is often part of a comprehensive package sold to corporations from hardware, to web design tools, cloud services, and management expertise.

CASE STUDY

Programmatic Advertising:
Real-Time Marketing

The holy grail of advertising and marketing is to deliver the right message to the right person at the right time. If this were possible, no one would receive ads they did not want to see, and then no advertising dollars would be wasted, reducing the costs to end users and increasing the efficiency of each ad dollar. In the physical world, only a very rough approximation of this ideal is possible. Advertisers buy television and radio spots, newspaper ads, and billboards based on broad demographics and interests of likely potential customers. The Internet promised to change this by gathering personal information on consumers and targeting ads to just the desired group of people based on their personal characteristics, interests, and recent clickstream behavior. Consumer personal information was gathered through the use of cookies placed on the user's browser, which tracked their behavior and purchases online and could be matched with offline information as well. From the beginning, e-commerce was a trade-off between privacy and efficiency: let us know more about you, and we will show you only the advertising and products you are interested in seeing and would be likely to respond to. E-commerce was supposed to end the mass advertising that began in 19th century newspapers, 20th century radio, and exploded with the growth of television.

But contrary to this rosy scenario, most of the display ads shown to site visitors are irrelevant, sometimes hilariously so, to visitors' interests. For this reason, the click-through rate for banner advertising is stunningly low, well under 1%, and the price of generic display ads is only $1.26 per thousand because of their low response rate. Check this out: visit Yahoo (the largest display advertiser on earth) on a desktop or laptop computer, look at the prominent ads shown on the right, and ask yourself if you are really interested in the ad content at this moment in time. Chances are slim you are interested at this moment, even if the ad is somewhat appropriate to your demographics. Often, it is an ad for something you have recently searched for on Google, or even already purchased at Amazon. These ads will follow you for days. Researchers have found that only 20% of Internet users find that display ads on websites are relevant to their interests. Programmatic advertising promises to improve the targeting of ads, decreasing costs for advertisers, and making the Web less annoying to consumers by showing them ads that really are of interest to them.

Digital display advertising has progressed through three eras. In the early 2000s, a firm with a website interested in ad revenue (a "publisher") would sell space on its site to other firms (advertisers), usually through an ad agency. These were primarily manual transactions. By 2005, ad networks emerged. These networks aggregated thousands of publishers' supply of ad space into a single network where advertisers could buy ad space on thousands of sites in a single purchase, and publishers could sell to hundreds of advertisers more efficiently. By 2011, even larger ad exchanges emerged, which provided advertisers access to an even larger pool of publisher ad spaces. The result today is an extraordinarily complex ecosystem of players, and sophisticated technologies (called a technology stack).

With so much supply available, and so many buyers, automated methods were developed to allocate ad space to ad buyers. These methods are collectively called programmatic advertising. Programmatic advertising is an automated method that publishers use to sell their inventory (empty slots on their web pages) to advertisers who want to buy ad space for their customers (brand and product owners looking to market their products and services). There are two kinds of programmatic advertising: auction-based real time bidding (RTB), and programmatic direct, where advertisers deal directly with publishers who have developed their own supply side platforms.

Programmatic advertising platforms use big data repositories that contain personal information on hundreds of millions of online shoppers and consumers; analytic software to classify and search the database for shoppers with the desired characteristics; and machine learning techniques to test out combinations of consumer characteristics that optimize the chance of a purchase resulting from exposure to an ad. All of this technology is designed to lower the cost, increase the speed, and increase the efficiency of advertising in an environment where there are hundreds of millions of web pages to fill with ads, and millions of online consumers looking to buy at any given moment. Programmatic advertising allows advertisers to potentially show the right ad, at the right time, to just the right person, in a matter of milliseconds. To the extent this is true, display advertising becomes more effective, and perhaps could become as effective as search-based advertising, where it is much more obvious what the searcher is looking for, or interested in, at the moment of search. In 2016, advertisers are expected to spend over $25 billion in the United States (almost three-quarters of all total display ad spending, including on banners, videos, and rich media) on programmatic advertising. This amount is expected to grow to over 80% by 2018. Programmatic advertising is roughly split between RTB and programmatic direct sales. Direct sales offer advertisers more control over ad display, location on the screen, and frequency than RTB.

Currently, just one-third of online display advertising is still done in a non-automated, traditional environment that involves marketers using e-mail, fax, phone, and text messaging. Traditional methods are often used for high value ads, say, the top screen, expanding ads seen at major newspapers, magazines, and portal sites, and native ads appearing alongside organic content. This is the world of the traditional insertion order: if you want to advertise in a newspaper or magazine, call the ad department and fill out an insertion order. In this environment, firms who want to sell products and services online hire advertising agencies to develop a marketing plan. The ad agencies learn from the firms what kinds of people they would like to contact online. The ad agencies pay data brokers or advertising networks like DoubleClick to help them identify where the online ads should be placed given the nature of the product and the specific characteristics the producer firms are looking for. For instance, let's say a firm wants to market a new mountain bike to men and women, ages 24–35, who live in zip codes where mountain biking is a popular activity. Ad networks traditionally would direct the agency to direct purchases of ad space from websites that attract the mountain biking audience.

This traditional environment is expensive, imprecise, and slow, in part because of the number of people involved in the decision about where to place ads. Also, the technology used is slow, and the process of learning which of several ads is optimal could take weeks or months. The ads could be targeted to a more precise group of potential customers. While context advertising on sites dedicated to a niche product is very effective, there are many other websites visited by bikers that might be equally effective, and cost much less.

The process is very different in a programmatic environment. Ad agencies have access to any of several programmatic ad platforms offered by Google, Yahoo, AOL, Facebook, and many smaller firms. Working with their clients, the ad agency more precisely defines the target audience to include men and women, ages 24–35, who live in zip codes where mountain biking is a popular activity, have mentioned biking topics on social network sites, have e-mail where mountain biking is discussed, make more than $70,000 a year, and currently do not own a mountain bike. The ad agency enters a bid expressed in dollars per thousand impressions for 200,000 impressions to people who meet most of the characteristics being sought. The platform returns a quote for access to this population of 200,000 people who meet the characteristics required. The quote is based on what other advertisers are willing to pay for that demographic and characteristics. The quote is accepted or denied. If accepted, the ads are shown to people as they move about the Web, in real time. As people come on to various websites they visit, the automated program assesses whether they meet the desired characteristics, and displays the mountain bike ad within milliseconds to that person. The programmatic platforms also track the responses to the ads in real time, and can change to different ads and test for effectiveness based on the platform's experience. Once the system learns from experience, it will focus on showing the most effective

SOURCES: "US Programmatic Ad Spending Forecast: Most Mobile Display and Video Ad Dollars to be Automated by 2018," by Lauren Fisher, eMarketer, Inc., September 26, 2016; "US Digital Ad Benchmarks: CTR and Conversion Rates, by Format and Device, Q2 2016," eMarketer, Inc., August 31, 2016; "The New Display Ad Tech Stack," by Lauren Fisher, eMarketer, Inc., May 2016; "Programmatic Pays Off Big for P & G, But Obstacles Loom," by Jack Neff, Adage.com, April 1, 2016; "Clorox Is Betting Big on Programmatic Advertising," by Jack Marshall, *Wall Street Journal*, September 4, 2015; "New Breed of Digital Publishers Just Say No to Ad Tech," by Mike Shields, *Wall Street Journal*, July 28, 2015; "US Auto Industry Sets Brisk Pace with Mobile Programmatic," by eMarketer, Inc., July 2, 2014; "Creating Ads on the Fly: Fostering Creativity in the Programmatic Era," by Debra Aho Williamson, eMarketer, Inc., April 2015; "Procter & Gamble CMO Pritchard: Programmatic Delivers Business Lift," by Sarah Sluis, Adexchanger. com, March 6, 2015; "Get With the Programmatic: A Primer on Programmatic Advertising," by Or Shani, Marketingland.com, August 22, 2014; "Programmatic Advertising Spreads Quickly Despite Nagging Problems, Says AOL Survey," by Robert Hof, Adage.com, August 13, 2014; "How Big Media Is Adapting to Automated Ad Buying," *Wall Street Journal*, June 27, 2014; "Procter & Gamble Aims to Buy 70% of Digital Ads Programmatically," Adage.com, June 4, 2014; "Programmatic Buying Roundup," by Lauren Fisher, eMarketer, Inc., June 2014; "Programmatic Guaranteed," by Lauren Fisher, eMarketer Inc., May 2014; "Driving Programmatic Buying: Automotive Industry Will Invest Big in 2014," by Mike Hudson et al., eMarketer, Inc., January 2014; "Programmatic Everywhere? Data, Technology and the Future of Audience Engagement," IAB, November 4, 2013; "RTB Is the Most Overhyped Technology Ever: It's Useful for Extending the Reach of Mediocre Content, but Not for Subtle, Thoughtful Buys," by Joe Mohen, Adage.com, May 30, 2013.

ads on the most productive websites. Programmatic direct (or premium) advertising uses the same platform, but publishers sell blocks of inventory to ad agencies rather than single impressions. This stabilizes their income, and puts them in closer contact with advertisers who can also exercise greater oversight over the publishers.

The auto industry is a large user of programmatic advertising. Car brands are highly focused on specific demographic groups, income levels, and aspirations. A programmatic campaign begins with the advertiser picking a demographic target, establishing a total budget for the campaign, and then choosing an RTB platform and competing for the delivery of an ad to that audience against other advertisers who may be other auto companies, retailers, or telecommunications providers. The ads are awarded and served automatically in millisecond-quick transactions.

Despite its clear advantages, there are also several risks involved for all parties. Programmatic advertisers lose some control over where their ads will appear on the Web. This is a threat to a brand if its products are shown on inappropriate sites. Advertisers lose some accountability for their expenditures because they cannot verify that their ads are actually being shown, and they must take the ad platform's word that indeed the ads are being shown to real people. This is a transparency issue. Ghost sites and ad fraud complicate the picture as well. There are thousands of ghost sites on the Web that do nothing but attract clicks using various ruses. Ad networks record this traffic and have little capability to determine if it is legitimate, and may show ads on these sites, which will generate fraudulent clicks that are paid for by the ad network and the advertising firm.

Given the risks, many of the largest advertisers initially did not use programmatic advertising, but that is rapidly changing. It was first used by publishers to sell inventory that was left over after the major ad campaigns had purchased the premium slots on web pages. Programmatic platforms were inexpensive places to sell excess inventory. However, that is beginning to change as advertisers gain confidence and the platforms themselves improve their abilities to avoid inappropriate websites, purge ghost sites, and learn how to detect click fraud. In addition, a number of firms have stepped into the market with tools that address these concerns.

For instance, in 2014, Procter & Gamble announced that, going forward, it planned to buy 70%–75% of its U.S. digital media using programmatic methods. P&G is the largest advertiser in the country, spending about $4.3 billion on advertising in the United States in 2015. In the past, P&G purchased premium online inventory at the top 100 comScore sites through several different ad agencies and tracked performance using its internal staff. According to P&G's Chief Marketing Officer Marc Pritchard, programmatic advertising has allowed P&G to more precisely target its advertising at a good price, reportedly producing three to five times greater return on investment than through traditional methods. Other companies are following suit. Cleaning supply company Clorox devoted about 50% of its entire digital budget to programmatic advertising in 2015.

However, some upstart web publishers aimed at the millennial demographic are trying to buck the trend. Vox Media, Refinery29, and Mic have all rejected programmatic advertising and will only sell advertising space directly to advertisers. These publishers object on the ground that programmatic advertising can degrade website functionality by slowing down how fast web pages load in browsers while also cluttering the site with ads that will annoy their visitors. Whether other web publishers will follow this lead remains to be seen.

Case Study Questions

1. Pay a visit to your favorite portal and count the total ads on the opening page. Count how many of these ads are (a) immediately of interest and relevant to you, (b) sort of interesting or relevant but not now, and (c) not interesting or relevant. Do this 10 times and calculate the percentage of the three kinds of situations. Describe what you find and explain the results using this case.

2. Advertisers use different kinds of "profiles" in the decision to display ads to customers. Identify the different kinds of profiles described in this case, and explain why they are relevant to online display advertising.

3. How can display ads achieve search-engine–like results?

4. Do you think instant display ads based on your immediately prior clickstream will be as effective as search engine marketing techniques? Why or why not?

6.6   REVIEW

KEY CONCEPTS

■ **Understand the key features of the Internet audience, the basic concepts of consumer behavior and purchasing, and how consumers behave online.**

- Key features of the Internet audience include the number of users online, the intensity and scope of use, demographics and aspects, the type of Internet connection, and community effects.
- Models of consumer behavior attempt to predict or explain what consumers purchase, and where, when, how much, and why they buy. Factors that impact buying behavior include cultural, social, and psychological factors.
- There are five stages in the consumer decision process: awareness of need, search for more information, evaluation of alternatives, the actual purchase decision, and post-purchase contact with the firm.
- The online consumer decision process is basically the same, with the addition of two new factors: website and mobile platform capabilities and consumer clickstream behavior.

■ **Identify and describe the basic digital commerce marketing and advertising strategies and tools.**

- A *website* is the major tool for establishing the initial relationship with the customer.
- *Search engine marketing and advertising* allows firms to pay search engines for inclusion in the search engine index (formerly free and based on "objective" criteria), receiving a guarantee that their firm will appear in the results of relevant searches.
- *Display ads* are promotional messages that users can respond to by clicking on the banner and following the link to a product description or offering. Display ads include banner ads, rich media, video ads, and sponsorships.

- *E-mail marketing* sends e-mail directly to interested users, and has proven to be one of the most effective forms of marketing communications.
- *Lead generation marketing* uses multiple e-commerce presences to generate leads for businesses who later can be contacted and converted into customers.
- *Affiliate marketing* involves a firm putting its logo or banner ad on another firm's website from which users of that site can click through to the affiliate's site.
- *Viral marketing* is a form of social marketing that involves getting customers to pass along a company's marketing message to friends, family, and colleagues.
- *Social marketing and advertising* involves using the social graph to communicate brand images and directly promote sales of products and services.
- *Mobile and local marketing and advertising* involves using display ads, search engine advertising, video ads, and mobile messaging on mobile devices such as smartphones and tablet computers, often using the geographic location of the user.
- *Multi-channel marketing* (combining offline and online marketing efforts) is typically the most effective. Although many e-commerce ventures want to rely heavily on online communications, marketing communications campaigns most successful at driving traffic have incorporated both online and offline tactics.
- *Customer retention techniques* for strengthening customer relationships include personalization, one-to-one marketing, and interest-based advertising, customization and customer co-production, and customer service (such as CRMs, FAQs, live chat, intelligent agents, and automated response systems).
- *Online pricing strategies* include offering products and services for free, versioning, bundling, and dynamic pricing.

■ **Identify and describe the main technologies that support online marketing.**

- *Web transaction logs*—records that document user activity at a website. Coupled with data from the registration forms and shopping cart database, these represent a treasure trove of marketing information for both individual sites and the online industry as a whole.
- *Tracking files*—Various files, like cookies, web beacons, Flash cookies, and apps, that follow users and track their behavior as they visit sites across the Web.
- *Databases, data warehouses, data mining, and profiling*—technologies that allow marketers to identify exactly who the online customer is and what they want, and then to present the customer with exactly what they want, when they want it, for the right price.
- *CRM systems*—a repository of customer information that records all of the contacts a customer has with a firm and generates a customer profile available to everyone in the firm who has a need to "know the customer."

■ **Understand the costs and benefits of online marketing communications.**

- Key terms that one must know in order to understand evaluations of online marketing communications' effectiveness and its costs and benefits include:
  - *Impressions*—the number of times an ad is served.
  - *Click-through rate*—the number of times an ad is clicked.
  - *View-through rate*—the 30-day response rate to an ad.
  - *Hits*—the number of http requests received by a firm's server.
  - *Page views*—the number of pages viewed by visitors.
  - *Stickiness (duration)*—the average length of time visitors remain at a site.
  - *Unique visitors*—the number of distinct, unique visitors to a site.
  - *Loyalty*—the percentage of purchasers who return in a year.
  - *Reach*—the percentage of total consumers in a market who will visit a site.
  - *Recency*—the average number of days elapsed between visits.

- *Acquisition rate*—the percentage of visitors who indicate an interest in the site's product by registering or visiting product pages.
- *Conversion rate*—the percentage of visitors who purchase something.
- *Browse-to-buy ratio*—the ratio of items purchased to product views.
- *View-to-cart ratio*—the ratio of "Add to cart" clicks to product views.
- *Cart conversion rate*—the ratio of actual orders to "Add to cart" clicks.
- *Checkout conversion rate*—the ratio of actual orders to checkouts started.
- *Abandonment rate*—the percentage of shoppers who begin a shopping cart form, but then fail to complete the form.
- *Retention rate*—the percentage of existing customers who continue to buy on a regular basis.
- *Attrition rate*—the percentage of customers who purchase once, but do not return within a year.
- *Open rate*—the percentage of customers who open the mail and are exposed to the message.
- *Delivery rate*—the percentage of e-mail recipients who received the e-mail.
- *Click-through rate (e-mail)*—the percentage of e-mail recipients who clicked through to the offer.
- *Bounce-back rate*—the percentage of e-mails that could not be delivered.

- Studies have shown that low click-through rates are not indicative of a lack of commercial impact of online advertising, and that advertising communication does occur even when users do not directly respond by clicking. Online advertising in its various forms has been shown to boost brand awareness and brand recall, create positive brand perceptions, and increase intent to purchase.
- Effectiveness cannot be considered without analysis of cost. Typical pricing models for online marketing communications include barter, cost per thousand (CPM), cost per click (CPC), cost per action (CPA), hybrid models, and sponsorships.
- Online marketing communications are typically less costly than traditional mass media marketing. Also, online sales can generally be directly correlated with online marketing efforts, unlike traditional marketing communications tactics.

QUESTIONS

1. What are some of the ways that gender, income, education, age, and ethnicity impact online purchasing behavior?
2. What are the primary differences between online and offline consumer behavior?
3. What is clickstream behavior and how is it used by marketers?
4. What is native advertising, and why is it controversial?
5. What are marketing analytics and how do they help e-commerce firms better understand consumer behavior at the various stages of the online purchasing process?
6. What does the issue of ad viewability involve, and how is the ad industry responding to this problem?
7. What are the five main elements of a comprehensive marketing plan? What are some different platforms used for each?
8. Why are marketers interested in big data?
9. What are three strategic questions that online marketing managers need to address?
10. What are the primary marketing functions of a website?
11. Name and describe three different types of search engine advertising.
12. What are some issues associated with the use of search engine advertising?
13. What is lead generation marketing?
14. How are blogs being used for advertising and marketing?
15. Explain why author John Battelle calls the Web a database of intentions.
16. What are two types of cross-device tracking?
17. What is retargeting, and why has it become a popular marketing technique?

18. Shopping cart abandonment rates are typically 70% or higher. Why is this rate so high and what techniques can help improve this rate?

19. Define CTR, CPM, CPC, CPA, and VTR.

20. What advantages do rich media ads have over static display ads?

PROJECTS

1. Go to www.strategicbusinessinsights.com/vals/presurvey.shtml. Take the survey to determine which lifestyle category you fit into. Then write a two-page paper describing how your lifestyle and values impact your use of e-commerce. How is your online consumer behavior affected by your lifestyle?

2. Visit Net-a-porter.com and create an Internet marketing plan for it that includes each of the following:
   - One-to-one marketing
   - Affiliate marketing
   - Viral marketing
   - Blog marketing
   - Social network marketing

   Describe how each plays a role in growing the business, and create a slide presentation of your marketing plan.

3. Use the Online Consumer Purchasing Model (Figure 6.11) to assess the effectiveness of an e-mail campaign at a small website devoted to the sales of apparel to the ages 18–26 young adult market in the United States. Assume a marketing campaign of 100,000 e-mails (at 25 cents per e-mail address). The expected click-through rate is 5%, the customer conversion rate is 10%, and the loyal customer retention rate is 25%. The average sale is $60, and the profit margin is 50% (the cost of the goods is $30). Does the campaign produce a profit? What would you advise doing to increase the number of purchases and loyal customers? What web design factors? What communications messages?

4. Surf the Web for at least 15 minutes. Visit at least two different e-commerce sites. Make a list describing in detail all the different marketing communication tools you see being used. Which do you believe is the most effective and why?

5. Do a search for a product of your choice on at least three search engines. Examine the results page carefully. Can you discern which results, if any, are a result of a paid placement? If so, how did you determine this? What other marketing communications related to your search appear on the page?

6. Examine the use of rich media and video in advertising. Find and describe at least two examples of advertising using streaming video, sound, or other rich media technologies. (Hint: Check the sites of Internet advertising agencies for case studies or examples of their work.) What are the advantages and/or disadvantages of this kind of advertising? Prepare a 3- to 5-page report on your findings.

7. Visit Facebook and examine the ads shown in the right margin. What is being advertised and how do you believe it is relevant to your interests or online behavior? You could also search on a retail product on Google several times, and related products, then visit Yahoo or another popular site to see if your past behavior is helping advertisers track you.

REFERENCES

Adjei, Mavis, and Stephanie Noble. "The Influence of C2C Communications in Online Brand Communities On Purchase Behavior." *Journal of the Academy of Marketing Science*, Vol. 38, No. 5 (2009).

Adomavicius, Gediminas, and Alexander Tuzhilin. "Using Data Mining Methods to Build Customer Profiles." *IEEE Computer* (February 2001a).

Adomavicius, Gediminas, and Alexander Tuzhilin. "Expert-Driven Validation of Rule-Based User Models in Personalization Applications." *Data Mining and Knowledge Discovery* (January 2001b).

AdRoll. "The Performance Marketer's Guide to Retargeting: Part 1." (2015).

Akerlof, G. "The Market for 'Lemons' Quality Under Uncertainty and the Market Mechanism." *Quarterly Journal of Economics* (August 1970).

Ba, Sulin, Jan Stallaert, and Zhongju Zhang. "Balancing IT with the Human Touch: Optimal Investment in IT-Based Customer Service." *Information Systems Research* (September 2010).

Ba, Sulin, and Paul Pavlou. "Evidence on the Effect of Trust Building Technology in Electronic Markets: Price Premiums and Buyer Behavior." *MIS Quarterly* (September 2002).

Bakos, J. Y., and Erik Brynjolfsson. "Bundling and Competition on the Internet: Aggregation Strategies for Information Goods." *Marketing Science* (January 2000).

Battelle, John. "The Database of Intentions Is Far Larger Than I Thought." Battellemedia.com (March 5, 2010).

Battelle, John. "Search Blog." Battellemedia.com (November 13, 2003).

Baymard Institute. "34 Cart Abandonment Rate Statistics." Baymard.com (accessed October 8, 2016).

BIA/Kelsey. "U.S. Local Media Forecast 2016." (June 2, 2016).

Brookings Institute. "Online Identity and Consumer Trust: Assessing Online Risk." (January 2011).

Castell, John. "Google Panda Explained for Website Owners." Linkedin.com (June 12, 2014).

Chaffey, Dave. "Display Advertising Clickthrough Rates." (April 2016).

Chan, P. K. "A Non-Invasive Learning Approach to Building Web User Profiles." In *Proceedings of ACM SIGKDD International Conference* (1999).

Corritore, C. L., B. Kracher, and S. Wiedenbeck, "On-line Trust: Concepts, Evolving Themes, a Model." *International Journal of Human-Computer Studies* (2006).

Cross, Robert. "Launching the Revenue Rocket: How Revenue Management Can Work For Your Business." *Cornell Hotel and Restaurant Administration Quarterly* (April 1997).

eMarketer, Inc. (Cindy Liu) "US Digital Users: eMarketer's Updated Estimates for 2016." (September 22, 2016a).

eMarketer, Inc. Share of "Average Time Spent per Day with Major Media by US Adults, 2012–2018." (April 1, 2016b).

eMarketer, Inc. "Fixed Broadband Households, United States, 2008–2020." (August 8, 2016c).

eMarketer, Inc. "(Cindy Liu) "Worldwide Retail Ecommerce Sales: The eMarketer Forecast for 2016." (August 2016d).

eMarketer, Inc. (Cindy Liu). "Worldwide Ad Spending: eMarketer's Updated Estimates and Forecast for 2015–2020." (October, 2016e).

eMarketer, Inc. "US Digital Ad Spending Growth by Format, 2015–2020 (billions)." (August 24, 2016f).

eMarketer, Inc. "US Digital Ad Spending Growth by Format, 2015–2020 (% change)." (September 1, 2016g).

eMarketer, Inc. "UK Mobile Display Ad Spending Share, by Format, H1 2016." (October 2016h).

eMarketer, Inc. (Lauren T. Fisher). "Ad Fraud in the US: How More Sophisticated Methods Are Hurting, Mobile, Video, and Performance Measurement." (August 2016i).

eMarketer, Inc. (Jillian Ryan). "Email Benchmarks 2016: Relevancy, Frequency, Deliverability and Mobility." (September 6, 2016j).

eMarketer, Inc. "Social Network Ad Spending Worldwide, 2014–2018." (March 9, 2016l).

eMarketer, Inc. "US Social Network Ad Revenues, by Venue, 2015–2018." (September 1, 2016m).

eMarketer, Inc. "Fixed Broadband Penetration in Europe, by Country, 2011–2016 (% of total households)." (December 20, 2016x).

eMarketer, Inc. (Mark Dolliver). "UK Time Spent With Media: The Complete eMarketer Forecast." (May 2016y).

eMarketer, Inc. (Jeremy Kressman). "Cross-Device Search Marketing: As Search Goes Multidevice, Ad Targeting and Measurement Struggle to Keep Pace." (April 9, 2015).

eMarketer, Inc. "Reasons US Internet Users Buy Products Digitally Rather Than In-Store." (February 23, 2014).

eMarketer, Inc. (Paul Verna). "Word of Mouth Marketing." (October 2010).

Evans, P., and T. S. Wurster. "Getting Real About Virtual Commerce." *Harvard Business Review* (November–December 1999).

Evergage. "2016 Trends in Personalization." (June 2016).

Farahat, Ayman, and Michael Bailey. "How Effective is Targeted Advertising." International World Wide Web Conference Committee (April 26–20, 2012).

Fawcett, Tom, and Foster Provost. "Adaptive Fraud Detection." *Data Mining and Knowledge Discovery* (1997).

Fawcett, Tom, and Foster Provost. "Combining Data Mining and Machine Learning for Effective User Profiling." In *Proceedings of the Second International Conference on Knowledge Discovery and Data Mining* (1996).

Federal Trade Commission. "Native Advertising: A Guide for Businesses." (December 2015a).

Federal Trade Commission. "Enforcement Policy Statement on Deceptively Formatted Advertisements." (December 2015b).

Feil, Jessica. "Good Lord, & Taylor! Of Course You Need to Disclose Native Ads." Ftcbeat.com (March 16, 2016).

Forrester Research. "US Cross-Channel Retail Forecast, 2015 to 2020." (January 26, 2016).

Forrester Research. "Refresh Your Approach to 1:1 Marketing: How Real-Time Automation Elevates Personalization." (August 18, 2014).

Franklyn, David J. "Consumer Recognition and Understanding of Native Advertisements." Federal Trade Commission (December 4, 2013).

French, Violet. "Canada's Tough New Anti-Spam Legislation: Beware Its Extra-Territorial Reach." Americanbar.org (January 2014).

Garg, Rajiv. "Peer Influence and Information Difusion in Online Networks: An Empirical Analysis." Carnegie Mellon University, School of Information Systems and Management, Working Paper, 2009.

Google Inc. "Guide to Ad Sizes." (accessed October 8, 2016).

Guo, Stephen, M. Wang, and J. Leskovec. "The Role of Social Networks in Online Shopping Choice: Information Passing, Price of Trust, and Consumer Choice." Stanford University (June 2011).

Hof, Robert. "The One Second Rule: New Viewability Metrics Exposes How Low Online Advertising Standards Still Are." *Forbes* (March 3, 2014).

Interactive Advertising Bureau. "Rising Stars Ads and Brand Equity." (February 9, 2015).

Interactive Advertising Bureau. "Digital Video Rising Starts Added to IAB Standard Ad Portfolio, Augmenting Sight, Sound & Motion with Interactivity at Scale." (February 10, 2014).

Interactive Advertising Bureau. "Mobile Rich Media Ad Definitions (MRAID)." (September 2012).

Interactive Advertising Bureau. "IAB Standards and Guidelines." Iab.net (September 2011).

Interactive Advertising Bureau (IAB)/PriceWaterhouse-Coopers. "IAB Internet Advertising Revenue Report: 2015 Full Year Results." (April 2016).

Isaac, Mike. "Uber Reaches Deal With New York on Surge Pricing in Emergencies." *New York Times* (July 8, 2014).

Iyengar, Raghuram, S. Han, and S. Gupta. "Do Friends Influence Purchases in a Social Network." Harvard Business School. Working Paper, 2009.

Joe, Ryan. "FTC Commissioner Julie Brill: Ad Industry Must Shape Up, or Face the Wrath of Ad Blockers." Adexchanger.com (January 22, 2016).

Kantrowitz, Alex. "Inside Google's Secret War Against Ad Fraud." Adage.com (May 18, 2015).

Kantrowitz, Alex. "Digital Ad Fraud is Rampant. Here's Why So Little Has Been Done about It." Adage.com (March 24, 2014).

Kantrowitz, Alex. "Just Look At How Google Dominates Ad Tech." Adage.com (October 18, 2013).

Kim, D., and I. Benbasat. "The Effects of Trust-Assuring Arguments on Consumer Trust in Internet Stores." *Information Systems Research* (2006).

Kim, D., and I. Benbasat. "Designs for Effective Implementation of Trust Assurances in Internet Stores." *Communications of the ACM* (July 2007).

Kim, Dan, Donald Ferrin, and Raghav Rao. "Trust and Satisfaction, Two Stepping Stones for Successful E-Commerce Relationships: A Longitudinal Exploration." *Journal of Information Systems Research* (June 2009).

Kotler, Philip, and Gary Armstrong. *Principles of Marketing, 13th Edition.* Upper Saddle River, NJ: Prentice Hall (2009).

Libert, Kelsey. "Comparing the ROI of Content Marketing and Native Advertising." *Harvard Business Review* (July 6, 2015).

Marin Software. "The Performance Marketer's Retargeting Guide: Key Benchmarks, Challenges and Best Practices for Cross-Channel Success." (September 2014).

MediaMind Inc. "Consumers 27 Times More Likely to Click-Through Online Video Ads than Standard Banners." (September 12, 2012).

Mishra, D. P., J. B. Heide, and S. G. Cort. "Information Asymmetry and Levels of Agency Relationships." *Journal of Marketing Research* (1998).

Mobasher, Bamshad. "Data Mining for Web Personalization." Center for Web Intelligence, School of Computer Science, Telecommunication, and Information Systems, DePaul University, Chicago, Illinois. (2007).

Monetate. "Ecommerce Quarterly EQ2 2016: Ecommerce Growth Sets New Records in Q2." (September 22, 2016).

National Conference of State Legislatures. "State Laws Relating to Unsolicited Commercial of Bulk E-mail (SPAM)." (December 3, 2015).

Neff, Jack. "Media Rating Council Proposes Mobile Viewability Definition That Matches Desktop." Adage.com (April 1, 2016).

Nielsen Company. "Global Online Consumer Survey." (May 2011).

Oestreicher-Singer, Gail and Arun Sundararajan. "The Visible Hand of Social Networks." *Electronic Commerce Research* (2008).

Opinion Research Corporation. "Online Consumer Product Reviews Have Big Influence." Opinion Research Corporation (April 16, 2009).

Ostermiller, Jeremy. "After Addressing Initial Viewability, These Are the Metrics That Matter." Mediapost.com (June 26, 2015).

Pavlou, Paul. "Institution-Based Trust in Interorganizational Exchange Relationships: The Role of Online B2B Marketplaces on Trust Formation." *Journal of Strategic Information Systems* (2002).

Pew Research Center. (Monica Anderson and Andrew Perrin). "13% of Americans Don't Use the Internet. Who Are They?" (September 7, 2016).

Pew Research Center. (Amanda Lenhart). "Mobile Access Shifts Social Media Use and Other Online Activities." (April 9, 2015a).

Pew Research Center. (Aaron Smith). "U.S. Smartphone Use in 2015." (April 1, 2015b).

Pew Research Center. (Lee Rainie). "The State of the Digital Divides." (November 5, 2013).

Pew Research Center. (Kathryn Zickuhr and Aaron Smith). "Digital Differences." (April 13, 2012).

PointRoll. "2014 Benchmark Report." (March 5, 2015).

Polar. "Q2 2016 Benchmarks: Branded Content Performance." (August 8, 2016).

Ragan, Steve. "Advertisers Expected to Lose $7.2B in 2016 Due to Fraud." Csoonline.com (January 20, 2016).

Rayport, J. F., and J. J. Sviokla. "Exploiting the Virtual Value Chain." *Harvard Business Review* (November–December 1995).

Richtel, Matt. "Wasting Time Is Divide in Digital Era." *New York Times* (May 29, 2012).

Robinson, Jim. "What You Need to Know About the Changing Affiliate Landscape." Marketingprofs.com (August 8, 2014).

Schiff, Allison. "A Marketer's Guide to Cross-Device Identity." Adexhanger.com (April 9, 2015).

Schleifer, Dan. "Which Social Network Makes Your Customers Buy?" *Harvard Business Review* (April 2, 2013).

Scott, Samuel. "The $8.2 Billion Adtech Fraud Everyone Is Ignoring." Techcrunch.com (January 6, 2016).

Sevitt, David, and Alexandra Samuel. "Vision Statement: How Pinterest Puts People in Stores." *Harvard Business Review* (July–August, 2013).

Shapiro, Carl, and Hal Varian. *Information Rules: A Strategic Guide to the Network Economy.* Cambridge, MA: Harvard Business School Press (1999).

Shapiro, Carl, and Hal Varian. "Versioning: The Smart Way to Sell Information." *Harvard Business Review* (November–December 1998).

Sinha, Indrajit. "Cost Transparency: The Net's Real Threat to Prices and Brands." *Harvard Business Review* (March–April 2000).

Symantec. "Symantec Intelligence Report." (September 2016).

Tadena, Nathalie. "Marketers Say They Would Spend Even More on Digital Ads If Measurement Improved." *Wall Street Journal* (July 6, 2015).

Tobii/Mediative. "The Effectiveness of Display Advertising on a Desktop PC vs. a Tablet Device." (August 2012).

Van den Poel, Dirk, and Wouter Buckinx. "Predicting Online Purchasing Behavior." *European Journal of Operations Research*, Vol. 166, Issue 2 (2005).

Viant. "Video Insights Report: 2015 Year in Review." (March 16, 2016).

VisionCritical Corporation. "From Social to Sale: 8 Questions to Ask Your Customers." (June 2013).

Vranica, Suzanne. "A 'Crisis' in Online Ads: One-Third of Traffic is Bogus." *Wall Street Journal* (March 23, 2014).

Whitener, Michael. "Cookies Are So Yesterday; Cross-Device Tracking Is In—Some Tips." Iapp.org (January 27, 2015).

Wigand, R. T., and R. I. Benjamin. "Electronic Commerce: Effects on Electronic Markets." *Journal of Computer Mediated Communication* (December 1995).

Williamson, O. E. *The Economic Institutions of Capitalism.* New York: Free Press (1985).

Wolfinbarger, Mary, and Mary Gilly. "Shopping Online for Freedom, Control and Fun." *California Management Review* (Winter 2001).

Wordstream. "Google AdWords Industry Benchmarks: Average Click Through Rate." (October 12, 2016).

CHAPTER 7

Social, Mobile, and Local Marketing

After reading this chapter, you will be able to:

- Understand the difference between traditional online marketing and the new social-mobile-local marketing platforms and the relationships between social, mobile, and local marketing.
- Understand the social marketing process from fan acquisition to sales and the marketing capabilities of social marketing platforms such as Facebook, Twitter, and Pinterest.
- Identify the key elements of a mobile marketing campaign.
- Understand the capabilities of location-based local marketing.

Pinterest Expands

Around the Globe

Like all successful e-commerce companies, Pinterest taps into a simple truth. In Pinterest's case, the simple truth is that people love to collect things, and show off their collections to others. Founded in 2009 by Ben Silbermann, Evan Sharp, and Paul Sciarra and launched in March 2010, Pinterest allows you to create virtual scrapbooks of images, video, and other content that you "pin" to a virtual bulletin board or pin board on the Web site. Categories range from Animals to Videos, with Food & Drink, DIY & Crafts, Home Décor, and Women's Fashion among the most popular. Find something that you particularly like? In addition to "liking" and perhaps commenting on it, you can re-pin it to your own board, or follow a link back to the original source. Find someone whose taste you admire or who shares your passions? You

© Blaize Pascall/Alamy Stock Photo

can follow one or more of that pinner's boards to keep track of everything she or he pins.

Pinterest originally positioned itself as a social network. Recently, however, it has changed its tune. It now describes itself as "the world's catalog of ideas"—a visual bookmarking tool for discovering and saving creative ideas (and potential purchases), with less emphasis on sharing with friends. Search has become the core part of its mission, with Google, rather than Facebook, Twitter, or Instagram, viewed as its primary competition.

Already extremely popular in the United States, Pinterest has focused its efforts on international expansion as it seeks to continue its explosive growth. In 2016, Pinterest announced that it had reached the 150 million monthly active member mark, with an estimated 80 million coming from outside the United States, representing more than half of its total users. Although estimates of Pinterest's user base suggest that women comprise anywhere from 70% to 80% of the site's total users, a full 40% of its new users in 2016 were men. Pinterest is one of the "stickiest" sites on the Web, with women spending over 1.5 hours (96 minutes) per session, and men about 1.25 hours (75 minutes).

Over the past five years, worldwide investors have poured $1.3 billion in venture capital into Pinterest, with its latest round of funding in March 2015 valuing the company at $11 billion, more than double its previous valuation. Like Facebook, Twitter, and many other start-up companies, Pinterest focused initially on refining its product and building its user base, but not surprisingly, its investors have begun to push it to begin generating revenue.

Pinterest's lofty valuation was based in part on its projections of $2.8 billion in ad revenue by 2018. That's a far cry from its estimated $100 million in revenues in 2015. To bridge the gap, Pinterest has developed a variety of advertising formats. Its first attempts in 2013 included Rich Pins, which allowed advertisers to embed information and links within specific images. Soon after that, it launched Promoted Pins, which appear first in searches using specific keywords, much like Google AdWords. In 2015, Pinterest added video ads called Promoted Video, which display short animations as images but reveal a full length video when clicked, as well as Buyable Pins, which allow advertisers to include a Buy It button on product images on the site. Pinterest has also focused on improving its Guided Search tool, which personalizes search results using user metadata, and on allowing advertisers to target users by specific categories, including gender, interests, age, and demographic. Because ads on Pinterest are virtually indistinguishable from other pins, customers are less apt to hide ads the way they do on platforms like Facebook or Twitter and much more likely to engage with them. In 2016, the company posted significant increases in user engagement, including 10 billion recommendations per day, double its total from 2015, and 2 billion text-based searches per month. Pinterest has over 1 million businesses with a presence on its platform, 10 million buyable products, and thousands of advertisers. Pinterest is also open to experimenting with innovative new ideas, such as the "real-life Pins" it unveiled in Brazil in 2016. Brazilian customers to the country's largest furniture retailer, Tok&Stok, were able to use Bluetooth-enabled physical Pins in store in tandem with a smartphone to mark items for addition to their Pinterest boards.

Pinterest also needs to keep growing if it wants to increase its revenues from millions to billions. In 2016 and beyond, the company is focusing on expanding internationally. Pinterest introduced its first localized site for the United Kingdom in May 2013, and it is now available in 31 different languages. Pinterest has worked to make its platform feel more regional, focusing specifically on the United Kingdom, France, Germany, Japan, and Brazil. Tastes vary from country to country, and Pinterest has embraced the challenge of providing the content that best resonates with users of each country, adjusting details as simple as the fonts used on each country's site and the translation of buttons, and as complicated as the differences in fashion in different parts of the world. For example, in many countries, the word "pin" doesn't make as much sense as it does in the United States, so the company renamed its Pin It button to "Save" in 2016. Pinterest began selling Promoted Pins and Promoted Videos in the United Kingdom in 2016, partnering with prominent national brands like John Lewis, B&Q, and Tesco, and launched the Pinterest UK Shop to allow users to purchase items from specially curated collections. The company's performance there and in other worldwide regions will go a long way in determining its success.

To improve the experience for international users, Pinterest fully overhauled the technology behind its site to ensure that Pinterest runs smoothly for users of any device, even outdated smartphones, and in any country. First, Pinterest standardized its appearance across its Web, iOS, and Android versions as well as across all of its localized sites in different countries. Then, it scaled down its menus to emphasize the images instead of the interface. Pinterest engineers also redesigned the site's swipe function on

SOURCES: "40% of New Pinterest Users Are Men," by Zak Stambor, Internetretailer.com, October 17, 2016; "Pinterest Has Reached a User Milestone," Businessinsider.com, October 17, 2016; "Promoted Video: Now Available in the UK," by Adele Cooper, Business.pinterest.com, October 3, 2016; "Launch of Pinterest UK Shop," by Kate Allchin, Blog.pinterest.com, September 16, 2016; "Pinterest Starts Expanding Its Visual Search Tools to Video," by Matthew Lynley, Techcrunch.com, August 4, 2016; "Interactive Pinterest Pins Let Shoppers in Brazil Bring Offline Items Online," by Saqib Shah, Digitaltrends.com, June 4, 2016; "Pinterest Revamps Pin as Save Button, Promotes Global Expansion," by Gavin O'Malley, Mediapost.com, June 3, 2016; Pinterest Renames 'Pin It' Button as 'Save' in Push for Global Growth," by Kathleen Chaykowski, Forbes.com, June 2, 2016; "Pinterest's Plans for World Domination," by Lara O'Reilly, Businessinsider.com, April 28, 2016; "Pinterest Is a Sleeping Giant—Don't Underestimate It," by Madjumita Murgia, Telegraph.co.uk, April 28, 2016; "Pinterest Announces Complete Overhaul of iOS App with Performance & Visual mobile phones so that the site can prepare to load photos you are likely to scroll to next, ensuring that they appear without delay and reducing the device requirements to use the site. These changes have doubled the site's overall speed and ensured that more users can seamlessly use Pinterest.

Despite all the good news for Pinterest, there are some issues lurking just behind the scenes that may cloud its future, such as the issue of copyright infringement. The basis of Pinterest's business model involves users potentially violating others' copyrights by posting images without permission and/or attribution. Although Pinterest's Terms of Service put the onus on its users to avoid doing so, the site knowingly facilitates such actions by, for example, providing a Pin It tool embedded in the user's browser toolbar. Much content on the site reportedly violates its Terms of Service. Pinterest has provided an opt-out code to enable other sites to bar its content from being shared on Pinterest, but some content owners question why they should be the ones to police Pinterest's site. Another thing Pinterest has done to try to ameliorate the problem is to automatically add citations (attribution) to content coming from certain specified sources, such as Flickr, YouTube, Vimeo, Etsy, Kickstarter, and SlideShare, among others. In 2013, it entered into an agreement with Getty Images in which it agreed to provide attribution for Getty content and pay Getty a fee. Pinterest says it complies with the Digital Millennium Copyright Act, which requires sites to remove images that violate copyright, but this too requires the copyright holder to be proactive and take action to demand the images be removed.

Pinterest is also not immune to the spam and scams that plague many e-commerce initiatives. Security analysts believe Pinterest will have to adapt its systems to deal with scammers and warn users to be wary of requests to pin content before viewing it and to be suspicious of "free" offers, surveys, and links with questionable titles. Pinterest has acknowledged the problem and has promised to improve its technology. In 2015, for instance, Pinterest migrated its website to the HTTPS protocol, which provides more security than the more common HTTP protocol typically used to access Web pages. Pinterest also employs a system known as Stingray that enables it to quickly react to spam and other types of malicious behavior, and has created a program that pays a bounty to white hat hackers who discover security issues.

At the moment, however, the future looks very bright for Pinterest. Although it may encounter some obstacles in the path of its global growth, the company believes it is on track to justify its multi-billion dollar valuation in the near future.

Improvements," by Chance Miller, 9to5mac.com, April 19, 2016; "Pinterest Reinvents Itself to Prove It's Really Worth Billions," by Jessi Hempel, Wired.com, April 19, 2016; "Pinterest Launches Promoted Pins Internationally, Starting with the U.K.," by Paul Sawers, Venturebeat.com, April 7, 2016; "Pinterest Begins Overseas Ad Push," by Yoree Koh, *Wall Street Journal*, April 6, 2016; "Pinterest Opens Up Promoted Pins for UK Advertisers, with John Lewis and Made.com Among Launch Partners," by Rebecca Stewart, Thedrum.com, April 6, 2016; "With Buyable Pins, Pinterest Lets You Buy Stuff Right in the App," by JP Mangalindan, Mashable.com, June 2, 2015; "Why $11 Billion Pinterest Thinks It Has the 'Best Kind of Business Model'," by Jillian D'Onfrio, Businessinsider.com, May 19, 2015; "Pinterest Beefs Up Security with Full HTTPS Support and Bug Bounty Program," by Jordan Novet, Venturebeat.com, March 13, 2015; "Fighting Spam at Pinterest," Engineering.pinterest.com, February 20, 2015; "Pinterest Goes After the Male Demographic with Debut of New Search Filters," by Sarah Perez, Techcrunch.com, January 23, 2015; "Can Pinterest Be Found in Translation," by Sarah Frier, Businessweek.com, May 22, 2014; "Pinning Down Pinterest: Addressing Copyright and Other IP Issues," by Jennifer L. Barry, Lexology.com, October 22, 2013; "Pinterest (Officially) Jumps the Pond," by Zak Stambor, Internetretailer.com, May 10, 2013; "Pinterest Gives Copyright Credit to Etsy, Kickstarter, SoundCloud," by Sarah Kessler, Mashable.com, July 19, 2012.

7.1   INTRODUCTION TO SOCIAL, MOBILE, AND LOCAL MARKETING

Social, mobile, and local marketing have transformed the online marketing landscape. Before 2007, Facebook was a fledgling company limited to college students. Apple had not yet announced the iPhone. Online marketing consisted largely of creating a corporate website, buying display ads on Yahoo, purchasing AdWords on Google, and sending e-mail. The workhorse of online marketing was the display ad that flashed brand messages to millions of users who were not expected to respond immediately, ask questions, or make observations. The primary measure of success was how many "eyeballs" (unique visitors) a website produced, and how many "impressions" a marketing campaign generated. An impression was one ad shown to one person. Both of these measures were carryovers from the world of television, which measures marketing in terms of audience size and ad views.

FROM EYEBALLS TO CONVERSATIONS

After 2007, everything began to change, with the rapid growth of Facebook and other social network sites, the explosive growth of smartphones beginning with Apple iPhone in 2007, and the growing interest in local marketing. What's different about the new world of social-mobile-local marketing and advertising are the related concepts of "conversations" and "engagement." Marketing today is based on businesses marketing themselves as partners in multiple online conversations with their customers, potential customers, and even critics. Your brand is being talked about on the Web and social media (that's the conversation part). Today, marketing your firm and brands requires you to locate, identify, and participate in these conversations. Social marketing means all things social: listening, discussing, interacting, empathizing, and engaging. Rather than bombarding your audience with fancier, louder ads, instead have a conversation with them and engage them in your brand. The emphasis in online marketing has shifted from a focus on eyeballs to a focus on participating in customer-oriented conversations. In this sense, social marketing and advertising is not simply a "new ad channel," but a collection of technology-based tools for communicating with shoppers.

In the past, businesses could tightly control their brand messaging and lead consumers down a funnel of cues that ended in a purchase. That is not true of social marketing. Consumer purchase decisions are increasingly driven by the conversations, choices, tastes, and opinions of the consumer's social network. Social marketing is all about businesses participating in and shaping this social process.

FROM THE DESKTOP TO THE SMARTPHONE AND TABLET

In 2015, for the first time, spending on mobile marketing exceeded that spent on desktop/laptops. **Figure 7.1** illustrates the rapidly changing trajectory of ad spending between 2014 and 2020. In 2014, marketers spent 71% of their online ad spending on desktops and only 29% on mobile. By 2019, that percentage is expected to totally flip,

FIGURE 7.1	THE RAPIDLY CHANGING TRAJECTORY OF WORLDWIDE ONLINE AD SPENDING

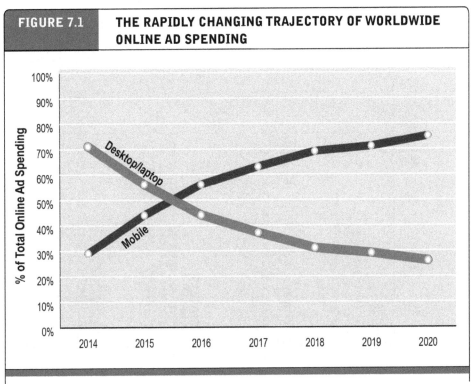

The percentage of online advertising spending worldwide on desktop/laptops versus mobile devices is expected to totally flip from what it was in 2014 by 2019, when over 70% is expected to be spent on the mobile platform compared to only 29% on desktops/laptops.

SOURCES: Based on data from eMarketer, Inc., 2016x, 2015a, 2014.

with 71% of ad spending devoted to mobile and only 29% to desktop/laptops. The marketing dollars are following customers and shoppers from the desktop computer to mobile devices. Today, social, mobile, and local marketing are the fastest growing forms of online marketing (**Figure 7.2**). In 2016, spending on mobile marketing in the United States was almost triple the amount spent on social marketing. By 2018, it is estimated that U.S. mobile marketing spending will account for almost $70 billion annually, while social marketing will be about $24 billion. However, this figure under-estimates the total social marketing spending because of the high percentage of visits to social networks that originate from a mobile device. For instance, Twitter reports that over 80% of their monthly active users access Twitter from a mobile device; over 55% of Facebook's active user base are mobile-only members (Protalinski, 2016; Twitter, 2016). A substantial part of the mobile marketing spending should also be counted as "social" marketing. Nevertheless, the figure indicates the extraordinary impact that mobile devices are having on marketing expenditures. Local online marketing in the United States was almost 25% larger than mobile in 2015, but by 2016, mobile had surpassed local online marketing. As with social and mobile, there is significant overlap between local and mobile and social marketing, with much of local marketing being also either social or mobile, or both.

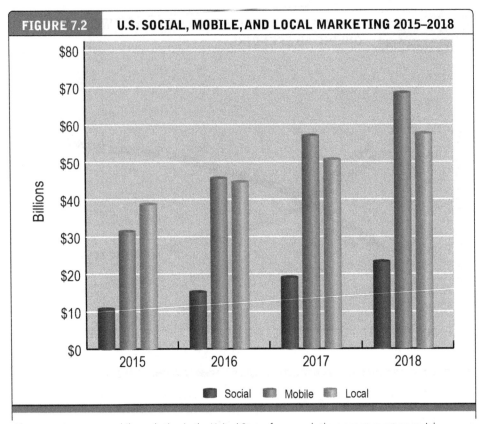

FIGURE 7.2 | **U.S. SOCIAL, MOBILE, AND LOCAL MARKETING 2015–2018**

The amount spent on mobile marketing in the United States far exceeds the amount spent on social marketing and has also overtaken the amount spent on local online marketing as well.

SOURCES: Based on data from eMarketer, Inc., 2016a, 2016b, 2016c.

THE SOCIAL, MOBILE, LOCAL NEXUS

Social, mobile, and local digital marketing are self-reinforcing and connected. For instance, as mobile devices become more powerful, they are more useful for accessing Facebook and other social sites. As mobile devices become more widely adopted, they can be used by customers to find local merchants, and for merchants to alert customers in their neighborhood to special offers. Over time, these will become more overlapped as the three platforms become more tightly coupled.

Over 80% of Facebook's ad revenue is generated by its mobile audience. Mobile constitutes an even larger share of Twitter's ad revenues—90%! Local marketing and mobile are highly related: local advertisers most often target mobile devices. And a considerable amount of mobile ad spending comes from local advertisers. The strong ties among social, mobile, and local marketing have significant implications for managing your own marketing campaign in this new environment. The message is that when you design a social marketing campaign, you must also consider that your customers will be accessing the campaign using mobile devices, and often they will also be

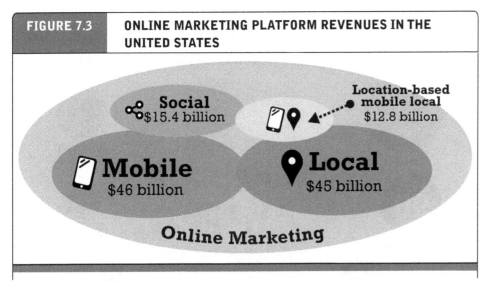

FIGURE 7.3 ONLINE MARKETING PLATFORM REVENUES IN THE UNITED STATES

Mobile marketing is aimed often at local audiences and is the fastest growing form of online marketing, followed closely by social marketing on social networks. Mobile local is in its infancy but it is also growing far faster than traditional desktop marketing.

SOURCES: Based on data from eMarketer, Inc., 2016b, 2016c, 2016d, 2016e.

looking for local content. Social-mobile-local must be seen in an integrated marketing framework. **Figure 7.3** puts social-mobile-local forms of advertising in context.

In the sections that follow we will examine social, mobile, and local marketing more closely. The focus will be on describing the primary marketing tools of each platform and how to envision and manage a marketing campaign on each platform.

7.2 SOCIAL MARKETING

Social marketing differs markedly from traditional online marketing. The objectives of traditional online marketing are to put your business's message in front of as many visitors as possible and hopefully encourage them to come to your website to buy products and services, or to find out more information. The more "impressions" (ad views) you get, and the more unique visitors to your site, the better. Traditional online marketing never expected to listen to customers, much less have a conversation with them, any more than TV advertisers expected to hear from viewers.

In social marketing, the objective is to encourage your potential customers to become fans of your company's products and services, and engage with your business by entering into a conversation with it. Your further objective is to encourage your business's fans to share their enthusiasm with their friends, and in so doing create a community of fans online. Ultimately, the point is to strengthen the brand and drive sales, and to do this by increasing your "share of online conversation." There is some reason to believe that social marketing is more cost effective than traditional marketing although this is still being explored.

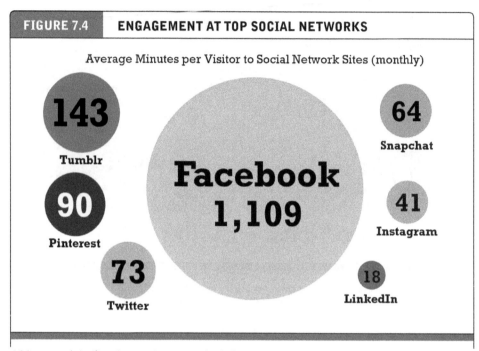

FIGURE 7.4   **ENGAGEMENT AT TOP SOCIAL NETWORKS**

Average Minutes per Visitor to Social Network Sites (monthly)

143 Tumblr

90 Pinterest

73 Twitter

Facebook 1,109

64 Snapchat

41 Instagram

18 LinkedIn

Visitors spend significantly more time on Facebook than any other social network.

SOURCES: Based on data from comScore, 2015a; comScore, 2015b; Statista.com, 2015; MacMillan and Rusli, 2014; Frommer, 2015.

SOCIAL MARKETING PLAYERS

There are hundreds of social network sites worldwide, but the most popular sites (Facebook, Instagram, Twitter, LinkedIn, Pinterest, Snapchat, and Tumblr) account for over 90% of all visits. (See Chapter 10 for a full discussion of social networks.)

While the number of monthly unique visitors is a good measure of market reach, it is not helpful in understanding engagement—the amount and intensity of user involvement in a site. One measure of engagement is the amount of time users spend on a site. **Figure 7.4** illustrates engagement at the top social network sites.

On measures of engagement, Facebook once again dominates, accounting for 85% of the total monthly visitor minutes, a whopping 230 billion minutes per month in the United States. The average U.S. Facebook user spent more than 18 hours a month on Facebook. Tumblr takes second place, followed by Pinterest and Twitter.

For a manager of a social marketing campaign, these findings suggest that in terms of reach and engagement, the place to start a social campaign is Facebook. Yet visitors to the other leading social sites collectively account for an additional 15% of the social market space, and therefore, a social marketing campaign also has to include them at some point. It helps that social network users use multiple social sites. Facebook users are likely to be users at Twitter, Pinterest, LinkedIn, Instagram, and Snapchat. In addition, marketers need to be aware of what has come to be known as dark social. **Dark social** refers to those forms of social sharing that occur off the major social networks, through alternative communication tools such as interpersonal

dark social
those forms of social sharing that occur off the major social networks, through alternative communication tools such as e-mail, instant messages, texts, and mobile messaging apps

FIGURE 7.5   THE SOCIAL MARKETING PROCESS

Fan Acquisition   Engagement   Amplification   Community   Brand Strength (Sales)

The social marketing process has five steps.

conversations, group meetings, and friendships, not to mention e-mail, instant messages, texts, and mobile messaging apps. While online social network users spend over 30 hours a month on average on all networks combined, there are 720 total hours in a month. Therefore, about 4% of all social life in a month involves online social networks, while 96% does not.

THE SOCIAL MARKETING PROCESS

At first glance the large number of different social sites is confusing, each with a unique user experience to offer, from Twitter's micro blogging text messaging service, to Tumblr's blogging capability, and to graphical social sites like Pinterest and Instagram. Yet they can all be approached with a common framework. **Figure 7.5** illustrates a social marketing framework that can be applied to all social, mobile, and local marketing efforts.

There are five steps in the social marketing process: Fan acquisition, engagement, amplification, community, and brand strength (sales). Each of these steps in the process can be measured. The metrics of social marketing are quite different from those of traditional web marketing or television marketing. This is what makes social marketing so different—the objectives and the measures. This will become more apparent as we describe marketing on specific social sites.

Social marketing campaigns begin with **fan acquisition**, which involves using any of a variety of means, from display ads to News Feed and page pop-ups, to attract people to your Facebook page, Twitter feed, or other platform like a web page. It's getting your brand "out there" in the stream of social messages. Display ads on social sites have a social dimension (sometimes called "display ads with social features" or simply "social ads"). Social ads encourage visitors to interact and do something social, such as participate in a contest, obtain a coupon, or obtain free services for attracting friends.

The next step is to generate **engagement,** which involves using a variety of tools to encourage users to interact with your content and brand located on your Facebook or web pages. You can think of this as "starting the conversation" around your brand. You want your fans to talk about your content and products. You can generate engagement through attractive photos, interesting text content, and blogger reports, with

fan acquisition
attracting people to your marketing messages

engagement
encouraging visitors to interact with your content and brand

plenty of opportunities for users to express opinions. You can also provide links to Pinterest photos of your products or fan comments on blog sites like Tumblr.

Once you have engaged visitors, you can begin to use social site features to amplify your messages by encouraging users to tell their friends by clicking a Like or +1 button, or by sending a message to their followers on Twitter. **Amplification** involves using the inherent strength of social networks. On Facebook, the average user has 120 "friends." This includes all people they have ever friended, including people whom they don't really know (and who don't really know them). Facebook users typically have only three to four close friends with whom they can discuss confidential matters, and a larger set of around 20 friends with whom they have two-way communications (mutual friends). Let's use 20 as a reasonable number of mutual friends for marketing purposes. For marketers, this means that if they can attract one fan and encourage that fan to share his or her approval with his or her friends, the message can be amplified twenty times: 20 friends of the one fan can be influenced. Best of all: the friends of fans are free. Marketers pay to attract only the initial fan and they are not charged by social sites (currently) for the amplification that can result.

Once you have gathered enough engaged fans, you will have created the foundation for a **community**—a more or less stable group of fans who are engaged and communicating with one another over a substantial period of time (say several months or more). Marketers have a number of tactics to nurture these communities, including inside information on new products, price breaks for loyalty, and free gifts for bringing in new members. The ultimate goal is to enlarge your firm's "share of the online conversation." The process ends with strengthening the brand and, hopefully, additional sales of products and services. Brand strength can be measured in a variety of ways both online and offline, a subject that is beyond the boundaries of this text (Ailawadi et al., 2003; Aaker, 1996; Simon and Sullivan, 1993; Keller, 1993).

Ultimately, the point of marketing is to drive sales revenue. Measuring the impact of a social marketing campaign on brand strength and sales is still being explored by marketers, social site managers, and researchers, but generally the results are positive: social marketing campaigns drive sales. In 2015, most of the top social network sites, including Facebook, Twitter, Pinterest, and Instagram, added, or were in the processing of adding, social commerce features, such as Buy buttons and other shopping functionality that makes it even easier for the targets of those social marketing campaigns to act on them and make a purchase.

FACEBOOK MARKETING

Nearly everyone reading this book has a Facebook page. There are power users who spend hours a day on the site, some with thousands of "friends," and there are casual users who have a small set of perhaps 20 friends and relatives. While most have a basic understanding of Facebook, it's worthwhile to review the major features of Facebook before discussing its marketing potential.

Basic Facebook Features

Table 7.1 describes various Facebook features that are important in terms of using Facebook as a marketing platform. Reviewing Table 7.1, it is clear that Facebook is

---

amplification

encouraging visitors to share their Likes and comments with their friends

---

community

a stable group of fans engaged and communicating with one another over a substantial period of time about your brand

TABLE 7.1	BASIC FACEBOOK FEATURES
FEATURE	DESCRIPTION
Profile	As part of account creation, you create a profile that includes certain personal information. The profile may also include photos and other media. Establishes baseline information that will be shared with friends.
Friend search	Helps you find friends who are already using Facebook, as well as friends who are not, typically by searching your e-mail contact list. Creates your baseline social network based on prior contacts.
Timeline	A history of your actions on Facebook, including photos, history of posts, and comments to your News Feed, as well as life events that you post and want others to see as a part of your profile. Additions you make to your Timeline may appear on your friends' News Feed. Creates additional links with friends.
Tagging	Ability to tag photos, status updates, check-ins, or comments with the names of friends. Tagging links to that person's Timeline and News Feed. Your friends are notified they have been tagged, and you are linked to their Timeline. Friends of your friends may also be notified. Whenever Facebook detects the person in a new image, it notifies all those who have tagged the photo that this friend appears in a new photo that you can link to. The tagging tool is designed to create additional connections among users.
News Feed	News Feed is a continuously updated list of stories from friends and Pages that you have liked on Facebook. Ads running in the News Feed are the major ad revenue producer for Facebook. News Feed stories include status updates, photos, videos, links, app activity, and Likes. Provides a continual stream of messages from friends and advertisers.
Trending	Facebook's version of trending topics; appears at top of right-hand column next to News Feed.
Status update	A way to post your comments, observations, and location to all your friends.
Reactions buttons	In February 2016, Facebook redesigned its Like button functionality to add five additional buttons and rebranded it as Reactions. In addition to the familiar Like button, users can now register additional reactions, such as Love, laughter (Haha), surprise (Wow), sadness, and anger.
Messenger	Facebook's instant messaging app, used by over 1 billion people every month. In April 2016, Facebook began allowing companies to deploy chatbots on Messenger to provide automated customer support and other e-commerce services, and also began a trial of Sponsored Messages that would allow companies to send messages to customers who had previously engaged with them.
Third-party Apps	Third-party apps add functionality to Facebook. Apps run the gamut from games (Candy Crush Saga; FarmVille) to photos (Instagram, now part of Facebook), music (Spotify), and publications (Washington Post Social Reader). Your personal information and that of your friends is shared with apps that you install. Most apps are free, and most rely on revenues from advertising.
Open Graph	A feature used by app developers to integrate their apps into the Facebook pages of users who sign up for the app, and in that sense, it opens the Facebook social graph to the developer, who can then use all the features of Facebook in the app. For instance, this feature allows your performance on game apps to be sent to your Friend's News Feeds. Supports the development of social apps and increases links among users.
Search	In 2013, Facebook introduced Graph Search, a "social" search engine that searched your social network for answers to queries. It was a "semantic" search engine insofar as it provided a single answer rather than a list of links based on an algorithm's estimate of user intentions. It was also a "hybrid" search engine that relied on Bing to supplement results. In 2015, Facebook significantly expanded its Search functionality. It now focuses on keywords and includes everyone's public posts, Likes, photos, and interests, and makes them available to all users of Facebook, friends or not. In June 2016, Facebook reported that users were doing 2 billion searches a day of its 2.5 trillion posts.

built to encourage people to reveal as much personal information about themselves as feasible, including activities, behavior, photos, music, movies, purchases, and preferences. One result is that Facebook is the world's largest repository of deeply personal behavioral information on the Internet. Facebook knows a great deal more about its users than Google does about its users. Second, Facebook's features are built to maximize the connections among people in the form of notifications, tagging, messaging, posting, and sharing. In many instances, the movement of personal information is so widespread that it is beyond the understanding of users and outside observers. The effect of these two factors is to greatly magnify the social density of the Facebook audience. **Social density** refers to the number of interactions among members of a group and reflects the "connectedness" of a group, even if these connections are forced on users. For instance, some natural groups of people are not very "social" and few messages flow among members. Other natural groups are loquacious and chatty with many messages flowing among members. The scope, intensity, and depth of Facebook's repository of personal information and rich social network present extraordinary marketing opportunities.

social density
refers to the number of interactions among members of a group and reflects the "connectedness" of a group, even if these connections are forced on users

Facebook Marketing Tools

Facebook offers a number of marketing and advertising opportunities and tools for branding and developing community on its site.

Reactions buttons
gives users a chance to share their feelings about content and other objects they are viewing

Reactions Buttons The Reactions and Share buttons on Facebook, and similar buttons on other social sites, are perhaps the single most important element in the rise of social marketing. "Like" is the engine of social marketing. The Like button was introduced by Facebook on its own website in 2009 and rolled out as a plug-in to other websites in 2010. In February 2016, Facebook added five additional buttons (Love, laughter (Haha), surprise (Wow), sadness, and anger) and rebranded the Like button as Reactions. Unlike traditional online advertising, the **Reactions buttons** give users a chance to share their feelings about content and other objects they are viewing and websites they are visiting. For instance, the Like button communicates your support of comments, photos, activities, brands, articles, and products to your friends, and also to the Facebook social graph and third-party marketers. The Reactions buttons are available on virtually all Facebook content, including status updates, photos, comments, brands, timelines, apps, and even ads. The ubiquitous Like button also appears on external sites, mobile and social apps, and ads. These sites are utilizing Facebook's Like social plug-in, and when you Like something outside of Facebook, it appears on your Timeline, where friends can comment on the activity. The Like button is one way Facebook knows what other sites you visit. According to Facebook, the Like button has over 10 billion views a day across millions of websites, with 30% of those impressions coming on mobile devices (Facebook, 2016).

Brand Pages Facebook's early efforts at brand marketing focused on the development of brand pages as a means for firms to establish a direct relationship with their current and potential customers. Nearly all Fortune 1000 companies, and hundreds of thousands of smaller firms, have Facebook brand pages, similar to brand websites, on Facebook as an adjunct to their main website. The purpose of a brand page is to develop fans of the brand by providing users opportunities to interact with the brand through comments, contests, and offerings. Using social calls to action, such as "Like us on Facebook" and "Share," brand pages can escape their isolation and make it more easily into users' social networks, where friends can hear the message. In 2015, Facebook began offering a new Shops tab for Facebook brand pages that features products and services, taking it further into the realm of social e-commerce.

Social brand pages have many more social opportunities for fans to like and comment than are typical of traditional web pages. However, corporate websites have, over time, adopted many social features and the two are now often indistinguishable. Brand pages on Facebook typically attract more visitors than a brand's website.

Brands can get exposure on Facebook either organically or via paid advertisements. Organic reach is free, and happens when fans see the brand's updates and posts in their News Feed, or when others who are not fans see that content because a fan liked, commented, or shared the post (viral reach). In order to ensure that they get the exposure that they want for their marketing messages, most companies choose one of the paid advertising formats discussed below.

Facebook enables you to choose from a variety of different marketing objectives, including promoting your Page posts/ads (Page Post Engagement); obtaining Likes for your Facebook page to grow your company's audience and brand (Page Likes); getting people to click through to your website (Clicks to Websites); getting people to take certain actions on your website (Website Conversions); getting people to install an app (App Installs); getting people to use an app (App Engagement); creating offers for people to redeem (Offer Claims); and getting people to watch a video (Video Views).

Once you have chosen a marketing objective, the next decision is to whom you want to target the advertisement. Facebook ads can be targeted based on location, age, interest, gender, education level, relationship status, and political views, as well as to custom audiences defined by the marketer. Facebook can also create what it calls a "lookalike audience" based on demographics shared with the custom audience identified by the marketer.

Once the marketing objectives and audience have been determined, the next decision is where to place the advertisement. Facebook has four basic locations from which to choose: the News Feed, the right-hand column or sidebar section of Facebook pages, and the mobile News Feed. Ads can also be placed within apps.

News Feed Page Post Ads The News Feed is the most prominent place for advertisements. The News Feed is the center of the action for Facebook users and where Facebook users spend most of their time because that is where posts from their friends appear. Page Post Ads appear in a user's News Feed along with all of the other posts and status updates that normally appear from friends. Page Post Ads have a tiny tag that indicates that they are sponsored (i.e., are advertisements) but otherwise look very similar to posts from friends. Sometimes the ads have a social context ("John Smith and Jane Doe like Pottery Barn") and can be liked, shared, and commented on, just like any other post. Page Post Ads can contain text, photos, video, and links. They can be used for many of the marketing objectives mentioned above, such as increasing brand engagement, obtaining Likes for the brand's Facebook page, and encouraging app installs and engagement. In 2016, Facebook continues to pilot test a Buy button that appears in News Feed Page Post Ads that allows people to purchase items without leaving Facebook. Companies pay to promote or boost Page Post Ads in order to extend their reach. This has become increasingly important as Facebook has reduced the organic reach that brands previously enjoyed for free in an effort to increase advertising revenues (Vahl, 2014; Ernoult, 2014).

Right-Hand Column Sidebar Ads These display ads are located in the right-hand column or sidebar of Facebook pages. They are often used to direct users to off-Facebook content such as website landing pages and content offers. Facebook has recently reduced the number of ads that appear in the right-hand column sidebar from seven to two, increased their size, and made them consistent with the format of News Feed Page Post Ads in an effort to enhance their performance.

Facebook Live Facebook introduced Facebook Live, its free video streaming service, in April 2016. Facebook Live can be used to stream live content that followers can interact with by commenting, liking and sharing. The video can be saved on a brand's page and followers can continue to interact with it.

Video Ads In March 2014, Facebook began showing 15-second video autoplay ads. In July 2014, it acquired Live Rail, an advertising network that now acts as the ad server for Facebook's video ads. Since that time, Facebook video ads have become an increasingly important part of Facebook advertising strategy. In order to continue to grow its advertising revenue without overloading and turning off users by having too many ads, Facebook intends to focus on video ads, which command a premium and therefore generate more revenue. One challenge has been that video ads autoplay in silent mode, requiring advertisers to adapt their video for that medium. Another challenge has been the issue of metrics. In September 2016, Facebook admitted that for two years, it had been overestimating the average viewing time for video ads, possibly by 60%–80%, because it had only been including video views of more than three seconds in its metric.

Mobile Ads Facebook introduced Facebook for Mobile in 2006. It now has over 1 billion daily monthly active users as of June 2016. Users can also access Facebook using a mobile browser although it is slower. In 2016, over 80% of Facebook ad revenue comes from its mobile ad platform, and it is its fastest growing revenue stream.

Because the smartphone screen is much smaller than regular computer screens, there is no room for sidebar ads on the right-hand column, so all mobile ads need to be displayed in the users' News Feed. Mobile ads can include many of the ad formats described above, including video ad. Critics complain that the number of ads in the mobile News Feed becomes distracting and annoying. Mobile ads often take up the entire screen. There also is less targeting of mobile ads, which increases the likelihood users will see irrelevant ads. So far, despite the annoyance, Facebook mobile users continue to sign up and view.

Facebook Messenger In April 2016, Facebook began allowing companies to deploy chatbots on Messenger, Facebook's instant messaging app, to provide automated customer support and other e-commerce services, and also began a trial of Sponsored Messages that would allow companies to send messages to customers who had previously engaged with them. In September 2016, Facebook announced a trial of a Buy button for its Messenger app that enables customers to make payments via Stripe or Paypal to companies advertising on Messenger without having to leave Messenger.

Facebook Exchange (FBX). Facebook Exchange (FBX) is a real-time bidding system that allows advertisers to target their ads based on personal information provided by Facebook. FBX competes with Google's display ad system DoubleClick and other real-time exchanges. Visitors to third-party websites are marked with a cookie, and can then be shown ads related to their web browsing when they return to Facebook.

Table 7.2 summarizes the major tools used by marketers to build their brands on Facebook.

Facebook Exchange (FBX)

a real-time bidding system that allows advertisers to target their ads based on personal information provided by Facebook

TABLE 7.2	BASIC FACEBOOK MARKETING TOOLS
MARKETING TOOL	**DESCRIPTION**
Reactions Buttons	Amplification. A feature that allows users to express support (and as of February 2016, other reactions as well) for content on social sites to their friends and friends of friends. The one tool that marketers cannot control. Currently free.
Brand Pages	Engagement and community building. Similar to a business web page, but much more social by encouraging user interaction and response; ongoing discussions among the community of fans. Brand pages are currently free. Shops tab for brand pages allows companies to feature products and services for sale.
News Feed Page Post Ads	Fan acquisition. Paid brand messages can be inserted into the News Feed. Requires payment. Buy button that can be embedded in News Feed Page Post Ads currently being tested.
Right-Hand Column Sidebar Ads	Fan acquisition. Display ads in the right-hand column (sidebar) similar to display ads elsewhere on the Web. Requires payment.
Facebook Live	Fan acquisition and engagement. Video streaming service within Facebook. Can be used to stream live content that followers can interact with by commenting, liking, and sharing. Video can be saved on a brand's page and followers can continue to interact with it. Free.
Video Ads	Fan acquisition and engagement. Video ads autoplay in silent mode on both desktop and mobile News Feeds. Requires payment.
Mobile Ads	Fan acquisition. Mobile News Feed Page Post Ads are delivered to smartphones and tablets. Requires payment.
Sponsored Messages	Fan acquisition and engagement. Messages to customers who had previously engaged with them via Messenger chatbot. Requires payment.
Facebook Exchange (FBX)	Facebook's real-time ad exchange, which sells ads and retargets ads through online bidding. Advertisers place cookies on user browsers when they visit a site, and when they return to Facebook, they are shown ads on the right side from the site they visited. Requires payment.

Starting a Facebook Marketing Campaign

Prior to starting a Facebook marketing campaign, there are some basic strategy questions you need to address. While every product presumably could benefit from a social marketing campaign, how is this true of your products? Who is your audience? How can you reach them? How have real-world social networks been used in the past to support sales in your industry? Can you be a "thought leader"? Once you have identified your audience, what content will get them excited and interested? Where are you going to get the content? What will it cost and what impact do you expect it to have on your brand and sales? At this point you do not need a detailed budget, but you should be able to develop estimates of the cost of such a campaign, as well as anticipated revenues.

If you're new to Facebook marketing, start simple and build on your fan base based on experience. A typical marketing campaign for Facebook might include the following elements:

● Establish a Facebook page for your brand. Content is king: have interesting, original content that visitors can be enthusiastic about. Acquire fans.

● Use comment and feedback tools to develop fan comments. You want visitors to engage with your content. You can also encourage bloggers to develop content for your page.

● Develop a community of users. Try to encourage fans to talk with one another, and develop new (free) content for your page.

● Encourage brand involvement through videos and rich media showing products being used by real customers.

● Use contests and competitions to deepen fan involvement.

● Develop display ads for use on Facebook.

● Develop display ads for use in response to social search queries.

● Liberally display the Like button so fans share the experience with their friends.

Table 7.3 provides some examples of Facebook marketing campaigns. For more information on social marketing using Facebook, see Learning Track 7.1.

TABLE 7.3	SELECTED FACEBOOK MARKETING CAMPAIGNS
COMPANY	MARKETING CAMPAIGN
Lays	Asked its Facebook followers to submit suggestions for new potato chip flavors, offering a $1 million prize to the winner. Now an annual event.
Kia	Created a racing video game, GT RIDE, to promote the release of the Kia GT. The game allowed players to build their own racetracks and send challenges to Facebook friends, all within a Facebook app. Users were automatically entered into a sweepstakes to win a Kia GT.
Budweiser	Buds for Buds campaign encouraged users in certain cities to buy a beer for a Facebook friend's birthday using a redeemable receipt.
Procter & Gamble	Launched a video along with the Facebook hashtag #LikeAGirl displaying positive representations of "acting like a girl" to promote its Always brand. The video was the most watched in company history.

Measuring Facebook Marketing Results

There are many ways to measure the success of a Facebook marketing campaign, some very sophisticated. This is a very new field that changes daily. Making matters more complicated is that industry sources sometimes use different names to refer to the same thing! Where this occurs we try to give both the most reasonable name and alternative names you might find in trade literature.

Table 7.4 describes some of the basic metrics to use when evaluating a social marketing campaign. It uses the five steps of the social marketing process found in Figure 7.5—fan acquisition, engagement, amplification, community, and ultimately brand strengthening and sales—as an organizing schema.

While the ultimate goal of Facebook marketing is to drive sales (which typically will take place on your website), it is very important to understand what the elements of social marketing that produce these sales are, and how they can be improved.

TABLE 7.4	MEASURING FACEBOOK MARKETING RESULTS
SOCIAL MARKETING PROCESS	MEASUREMENT
Fan acquisition (impressions)	The number of people exposed to your Facebook brand page posts and paid ads (impressions).
	The percentage of those exposed who become fans based on Likes or comments.
	The ratio of impressions to fans.
Engagement (conversation rate)	The number of posts, comments, and responses.
	The number of views of brand page content.
	The number of Likes generated per visitor.
	The number of users who responded to games, contests, and coupons (participation).
	The number of minutes on average that visitors stay on your page (duration).
	The rate of Likes per post or other content (applause rate).
Amplification (reach)	The percentage of Likes, shares, or posts to other sites (the rate at which fans share your content).
Community	The monthly interaction rate with your content (i.e., the monthly total of posts, comments, and actions on your Facebook brand page).
	The average monthly on-site minutes for all fans.
	The ratio of positive to negative comments.
Brand Strength/Sales	The percentage (or revenue) of your online sales that is generated by Facebook links compared to other platforms, such as e-mail, search engines, and display ads.
	The percentage of Facebook-sourced customer purchases compared to other sources of customers (conversion ratio).
	The conversion ratio for friends of fans.

At the most elementary level, the number of fans (or followers) generated is the beginning of all social marketing. Visitors become fans when they like your content. In the early days of social marketing, firms put a great deal of emphasis on the size of the fan base, and collecting Likes. This is less important today, as social marketing managers have become more sophisticated. Fan engagement in your content and brand is the first step toward developing a truly social experience, and arguably is more important than simply the number of impressions or the number of fans. Fans that you never hear from are not valuable. Engagement relates to how your fans are interacting with your content, how intensely, and how often. Understanding the kinds of content (videos, text, photos, or posts from fans) that create the highest levels of engagement is also very important (Unmetric, 2015).

The ability to amplify your marketing message by tapping into the social network of your fans is also at the core of social marketing. This can be measured very simply as the rate at which fans recommend your content to their friends, and how many of their friends further recommend your content to their friends.

Measuring the strength of a Facebook community is not that much different from measuring the strength of an offline community. In both cases you attempt to measure the collective activities of all in the community. Among your fans, how many actively participate? What is the total number of actions taken by fans in a month? How many minutes of involvement are generated each month? What is the percentage of favorable comments?

Finally, measuring sales that result from social campaigns is also straightforward. First, measure the percentage of sales you receive from the Facebook channel. You can easily measure the number of visits to your website that originate on Facebook, and the sales these visits generate. In addition, you can compare purchase rates (conversion rate) for fans and compare these to conversion rates for non-fans from Facebook. More important, you can compare the Facebook conversion rate to other visitors who come from different marketing channels, such as e-mail, display ads, and blogs.

Facebook marketing has entered its second generation even though it's only a few years old. The emphasis today in social marketing has gone beyond collecting Likes and more toward building engagement with high-quality content that fans want to share with their friends; nurturing stable communities of intensely involved fans and friends of fans; and ultimately turning these communities of fans into communities of purchasers.

There are a variety of Facebook analytics tools that provide valuable information about your Facebook marketing efforts. Facebook Page Insights, provided by Facebook, tracks total Page Likes, People Talking About This (PTAT) (which tracks the number of unique people who have clicked on, Liked, commented on, or shared a post), Page Tags and Mentions, Page Check-ins, and other interactions on a page. It also tracks something it calls Engagement Rate. People are considered to have engaged with a post if they Like it, comment on it, share it, or click it (Simply Measured, 2016; AdRoll, 2015).

Social media management system HootSuite enables teams to execute marketing campaigns across multiple networks from one dashboard, and also provides custom reports. Major analytics providers, such as Google Analytics, Webtrends, and IBM Digital Analytics, also provide Facebook reporting modules. Read the *Insight on Technology* case study, *Optimizing Social Marketing with Simply Measured*, for a further look

INSIGHT ON TECHNOLOGY

OPTIMIZING SOCIAL MARKETING WITH SIMPLY MEASURED

Companies of all shapes and sizes are now tapping into the power of social media for marketing and advertising to improve their bottom line and enrich their relationships with their customers. As social media continues to become entrenched in the business and cultural landscape, an ecosystem of companies has sprung up around it to meet growing demand. One major area of growth is in social media analytics—tools that allow companies to track and report social media account performance and generate recommendations on how to optimize social media marketing efforts. Simply Measured is a market leader in this burgeoning field, rating highest in overall customer satisfaction as well as market share.

Founded in 2010, Simply Measured is based in Seattle, Washington, and has quickly grown from humble beginnings (the founders built the original product over a single weekend) to a market-leading company that has raised almost $30 million in venture capital. It currently has 150 employees and more than 1,000 customers. Its rapid growth is due in part to the similarly rapid growth in social media platforms during that time. Marketers eager to tap into this emerging channel may not have the tools to understand what techniques are working and which need refinement. That's where Simply Measured comes in.

Simply Measured offers analytics tools for all major platforms, including Twitter, Facebook, Instagram, Tumblr, LinkedIn, and YouTube. It also offers variations of those products for individual market segments, such as retail, finance and insurance, consumer packaged goods, sports, restaurants, publishing, travel, tech, and telecommunications. Simply Measured's solutions allow companies to plan their social strategy, execute it, and then find out what's working best. Optimizing social marketing techniques in this way leads to better audience engagement and better bottom-line results. Simply Measured generates reports both in Microsoft Excel and on the Web in clear, easily understood formats that can be shared across organizations.

Examples of typical basic reports include Facebook Competitive Analysis, which measures a Facebook page against other competitors in usage and engagement; Traffic Source Analysis, which determines what sources direct the most traffic to your site; and Twitter Follower Analysis, which analyzes an account's followers for demographic information and activity trends. Whatever a company's social marketing needs, odds are good that Simply Measured has solutions to help.

For example, the Seattle Seahawks football team are renowned for their passionate fan base, known as "The 12th Man," and for their fans' deafening crowd noise at home games. The organization hoped to create a similar atmosphere on social media as well, and turned to Simply Measured to help it achieve this goal. During the team's playoff run in 2014, Simply Measured helped the Seahawks increase social engagement across all major platforms by a whopping 173%.

For a team with a large, motivated fan base, managing and understanding that level of social activity is impossible without the assistance of analytics. Using Simply Measured's Cross-Channel Social Performance report, the Seahawks learned which social networks best suited their social media goals and created greater fan engagement. To their surprise, Instagram was extremely effective in this regard, so they focused more energy there. The Twitter Account Report indicated which content was most popular on Twitter and even

(continued)

pointed to particular times of day that were most likely to generate a strong response. And the Twitter Competitive Analysis Report allowed the Seahawks to measure themselves against the rest of their peers in the NFL in key metrics like share of overall "voice" and fan engagement.

Simply Measured also offers a variety of resources detailing the state of social marketing in different market segments. For instance, the company analyzed BMW's industry-leading Instagram account. The luxury carmaker towers over its competitors on Instagram, with over 260,000 more tagged postings than its next closest rival, Jeep, from 2011 to 2015, and the most used branded hashtag on Instagram in 2015, #BMW. Simply Measured tracked BMW's Instagram activity in 2016, and found that over 90% of the company's posts are high-quality still images, which tend to generate the most engagement. They also found that BMW posts at a consistent rate, helping its brand stay in the consciousness of its followers and making it easier to determine which posts work and which posts don't. And Simply Measured found that during its time tracking BMW, over half of the posts the company made were re-grams of photos taken by its followers, further improving brand engagement. BMW's Instagram strategies helped it achieve a 5.6% increase in its audience over the period analyzed by Simply Measured.

Like many startups, Simply Measured is using the money it has raised from venture capital to buy up other firms that can strengthen its main product line and enable it to branch out into related activities. In 2015, Simply Measured acquired Inside Social, a startup that helps marketing firms track the return on investment from social marketing campaigns, and DataRank, a social intelligence platform that helps firms organize and sift through mountains of online comments, helping firms analyze what is being said about them. With these acquisitions Simply Measured can tell its clients not only where to concentrate their efforts in terms of response, but also where they can make the best return on their investment of ad dollars. Simply Measured has also been adding to its executive team, naming two former executives from Salesforce.com as CEO and chief revenue officer in 2015 and a third Salesforce executive as its Vice President of Customer Success in 2016.

In 2016, Simply Measured released a social analytics attribution product that allows marketers to more accurately trace consumer interaction with content and enables marketers to track "dark social" interactions, such as those taking place on messaging services, mobile apps, e-mail, and SMS. The company also released an application programming interface (API) designed for marketers that aggregates data from all major social media platforms. The API will allow marketers to make more specific queries without requiring the expertise of a data scientist.

Using social media correctly can be difficult (see the Chapter 11 *Insight on Society* case, *The Dark Side of Social Networks*, for examples). With Simply Measured and other social media analytics providers, avoiding these pitfalls and getting the most out of social media becomes much easier.

SOURCES: "Simply Measured Continues to Lead Innovation for Social Marketers with Release of Social Attribution," by Simplymeasured.com, September 21, 2016; "What Makes BMW the Most Engaging Car Brand on Instagram?," by Tripti Shrivastava, Simplymeasured.com, September 20, 2016; "Simply Measured Offers 'First Social Measurement API' for Marketers," by Barry Levine, Marketingland.com, July 12, 2016; "Simply Measured Names Exact-Target Vet as CEO and CRO in Bid to Supercharge Growth," by John Cook, Geekwire.com, October 30, 2015; "Simply Measured Found Right Niche at the Right Time," *Seattle Times*, October 24, 2015; "Simply Measured Acquires DataRank, a Social Intelligence Provider," by Maddy Suresh, Thetechbulletin.com, October 14, 2015; "Simply Measured Acquires Inside Social, as Two Seattle Social Media Data Startups Join Forces," by Jacob Demmitt, Geekwire.com, September 1, 2015; "The Top-Rated Social Analytics Tools by Marketers," by Ayaz Nanji, Marketingprofs.com, July 7, 2015; "Simply Measured Takes On $20M More to Grow Its Social Media Analytics Service," by Alex Wilhelm, Techcrunch.com, March 18, 2014; "Winning Your Social Community: A Seattle Seahawks Case Study," by Lindzee McCain, Simplymeasured.com, September 4, 2014.

at how one organization is using analytics tools to help them better understand social marketing.

TWITTER MARKETING

Twitter is a micro-blogging social network site that allows users to send and receive 140-character messages, as well as news articles, photos, and videos. Twitter has around 310 million active users worldwide as of 2016, and its 2015 revenue was $2.2 billion, 50% more than its 2014 revenue. But Twitter lost $521 million in 2015, and has never been profitable since its founding in 2006. Investors have pummeled its stock down to $17 per share as of October 2016. Over 90% of Twitter's users access the service on mobile devices. Almost all of Twitter's revenue comes from pop-ads that appear in users' timelines (tweet stream), but Twitter also has many other marketing tools in its quiver. One major advantage is that Twitter does not pay for the 500 million tweets sent each day. They are supplied for free by active users. Twitter sells ads based on the content of these user messages. See the opening case in Chapter 2 for more information on Twitter.

Twitter was designed from the start as a real-time text messaging service. Twitter offers advertisers and marketers a chance to interact and engage with their customers in real time and in a fairly intimate, one-on-one manner. Advertisers can buy ads that look like organic tweets (the kind you receive from friends), and these ads can tie into and enhance marketing events like new product announcements or pricing changes. Twitter is announcing new marketing tools every quarter in an effort to boost its revenues. On the other hand, there may be a limit to how many ads Twitter users will tolerate.

Basic Twitter Features

While most people probably know what a tweet is, Twitter offers marketers many other ways of communicating using Twitter. In fact, Twitter has introduced a whole new vocabulary that is specific to Twitter's platform. **Table 7.5** on page 444 describes the most common Twitter features.

Twitter Marketing Tools

There are many kinds of Twitter marketing products, and the firm is creating new ones every few months. The current major Twitter marketing tools include the following.

Promoted Tweets. Advertisers pay to have their tweets appear in users' search results. Promoted Tweets are Twitter's version of Google's AdWords. The tweets appear as "promoted" in the search results. Pricing is on a "cost-per-click" basis, based on an auction run by Twitter on the Twitter ad platform and might range from $.50 to $10 per engagement. An "ad carousel" allows up to 12 ads to be shown in a single space, enabling users to swipe through the Promoted Tweets. Promoted Tweets can be geo-targeted and also offer keyword targeting that enables advertisers to send the tweets to specific users based on keywords in their recent tweets or tweets with which they have interacted. Promoted Tweets can be plain text or include a single or multiple images, or can include a website card (link to website), basic app card (link to app), or image

TABLE 7.5	TWITTER FEATURES
FEATURE	**DESCRIPTION**
Tweet	140-character text message. Messages can be private (to a single person or one to one), public (to everyone, one to many), or to a group of followers.
Followers	You can follow someone's tweets and receive them as soon as they are made. Others can follow your tweets.
Message (DM)	A direct private message (DM) is like an e-mail that only you and the recipient can read.
Hashtag #<word>	Like a Twitter search engine, #<word> organizes the conversations on Twitter around a specific topic. Click on a hashtag and you are taken to the search results for that term.
Mention	A public Tweet that includes another user's name "@ username." You can click on mentions and link back to that person's profile. As a public tweet, your followers will be alerted as well.
Moments tab	Curated highlights of what is happening on Twitter at that moment.
Reply	A public response to a tweet using the Reply button. Replies show up on your timeline and that of the person you are responding to.
Timeline	Your timeline is your home page on Twitter listing the tweets you have received in chronological order, the most recent first. Click on a tweet in the timeline and it expands to reveal videos, and photos. Place your mouse over a tweet to reply, retweet, or make it a favorite (which is passed to your followers).
Retweet	Allows you to send along a tweet to all of your followers.
Links	Twitter has a link-shortening feature that allows you to paste in a URL of any link and it will be automatically shortened.

app card (photo plus link to app). Buy buttons embedded within Promoted Tweets enable users to purchase without leaving Twitter. In January 2016, Twitter introduced conversational ads, which enables marketers to include a call to action button with customizable hashtags to encourage consumer engagement within Promoted Tweets.

Promoted Trends. Advertisers pay to move their hashtags (# symbol used to mark keywords in a tweet) to the top of Twitter's Trends List. Otherwise, hashtags are found by the Twitter search engine, and only those that are organically popular make it to the Trends List. Promoted Trends cost about $200,000 a day in the United States and are also available for purchase in 50 different countries.

Promoted Accounts. Advertisers pay to have their branded account suggested to users who are likely to be interested in the account in the "Who to Follow" list, Twitter's account recommendation engine, on the Twitter home page. Promoted Accounts can be targeted by interest, geography, and gender, and are priced on a cost-per-follower basis, with advertisers paying only for new followers gained. Prices range from $.50 to $2.50.

Enhanced Profile Pages. Companies get their own banner and the ability to pin a tweet to the top of the company's timeline. The price reportedly ranges from $15,000 to $25,000.

Amplify. The Twitter Amplify program provides marketers with a real-time digital dashboard so they can see the resulting tweet activity about the show or the brand. Based on this information, marketers can send Promoted Tweets to users who tweeted about a show. They can alter the copy as well based on other information about the tweeters. For example, Jim Beam used Amplify to promote its new Jim Beam Red Stag brand of premium bourbon. The intent was to increase brand awareness, purchase intent, and user engagement. The strength of Twitter, according to Jim Beam marketers, is that it allows the brand to be a part of a real-time conversation, as opposed to Facebook, which is better at reaching a mass audience but not at engaging consumers in real time. The power of social media, including Facebook, is finding consumer advocates who will speak on behalf of the brand.

Promoted Video. In 2014, building on the Amplify program, Twitter announced a beta test of Promoted Video, which allows advertisers to distribute video on the Twitter platform. In 2015, Twitter began allowing advertisers to use Promoted Video to link directly to app installations and also added an ad purchasing feature for videos called "optimized action bidding" that enables marketers to customize ad purchases to improve return on investment.

Television Ad Retargeting. Millions of users tweet with their friends while watching television, and Twitter can follow the conversation to identify who is watching a particular show. Marketers displaying TV ads can retarget those ads or other messages to tweeters in real time to reinforce their marketing message. Advertisers with video content, like the National Basketball Association, insert in-tweet video clips, which are video replays. Advertisers can precede the video with an ad, or place an ad just below the video on screen. Companies can follow up with a Promoted Tweet.

Lead Generation Cards. Marketers can embed a "card" into a tweet. When users click on the tweet, a promotional offer appears and users are asked to sign up. Cards are different from display ads because they are used only by businesses who want to develop new leads, and they always include an offer, such as 50% off your next cup of coffee. This is a one-click process. The users' e-mail and Twitter account names are automatically obtained by Twitter and sent to marketers, who can then follow up with a tweet or an e-mail.

Mobile Ads. Because over 90% of Twitter users access Twitter on a mobile device, most of the above referenced marketing tools can be considered mobile ads tools. Mobile is also proving to be the primary driver of Twitter's business and the source of most of its revenue. In addition to all of the above formats, in April 2014, Twitter

TABLE 7.6	TWITTER MARKETING TOOLS
TWITTER MARKETING TOOLS	**DESCRIPTION**
Promoted Tweets	Advertisers pay to have their tweets appear in users' search results and timelines. The tweets appear as "promoted," and the pricing is on a per-click basis, based on an auction run on the Twitter ad platform. Promoted Tweets can be both keyword- and geo-targeted and can include images and well as links (cards) to websites and apps. An "ad carousel" allows up to 12 ads to be shown in a single space, enabling users to swipe through the Promoted Tweets. Buy buttons embedded within Promoted Tweets enable users to purchase without leaving Twitter.
Promoted Trends	Advertisers pay to move their hashtags (# symbol used to mark keywords in a tweet) to the top of Twitter's Trends List. Otherwise, hashtags are found by the Twitter search engine, and only those that are organically popular make it to the Trends List.
Promoted Accounts	Advertisers pay to have their branded account suggested to users likely to be interested in the account in the "Who to Follow" list, Twitter's account recommendation engine, available on the Twitter home page. Promoted Accounts can be specifically targeted and are priced on a cost-per-follower basis.
Enhanced Profile Pages	Companies can get their own banner to display images and the ability to pin a tweet to the top of the company's timeline.
Amplify	A real-time digital dashboard connecting television commercials and tweet activity.
Promoted Video	Advertisers can use distribute videos on the Twitter platform and use Promoted Videos to link directly to app installlations.
TV Ad Retargeting	Tweeting viewers of TV shows with the same ads targeted at them on a show they are watching.
Lead Generation Card	Promotional offers that appear in users' Twitter timeline of messages with a coupon or other offer. Used for lead generation.
Mobile Ads	All of the above formats delivered on mobile devices, as well as mobile app install and app engagement ads.

added mobile app install and app engagement ads, which have been lucrative formats for Facebook as well.

Table 7.6 summarizes these Twitter marketing tools.

Starting a Twitter Marketing Campaign

If you're new to Twitter marketing, start simple and build on your follower base using experience as a guide for what works. A typical marketing campaign for Twitter may include the following elements:

- Establish a Twitter account. Start following others you are interested in or conversations that you might want to participate with #<topic>. Don't expect any followers at first. Your visibility rises as you follow others, who will begin to tweet back or retweet interesting content. Then start retweeting content you think the group would be interested in, and start encouraging ongoing conversations.

- Try a simple Promoted Tweet. Twitter has a very good online ad facility that will allow you to define an ad, establish the groups you would like to target, and understand the costs. You might start with a regional or metropolitan Promoted Tweet. Test various formats. You don't have to pay for Promoted Tweets unless someone clicks on the tweet, so it is up to you to make those clicks count. Direct users to your website and offer a coupon or discount.

- Promoted Trends can be very expensive—around $200,000. If your budget will allow, and your topic is of general interest to a large audience, you can try this tool. Geo-targeting is possible.

- TV ad retargeting is obviously a big business tool for media companies that have television content and television ads. Retargeting these to the Twitter community strengthens the overall brand image, and can direct people to the firm's website.

- Lead Generation Cards are something that small and medium-sized businesses can use. If you sell anything locally, from pizza to stationery, make up an offer and build a Lead Generation Card specifying the geo-location where your business is located.

As with Facebook, the objective is to establish your brand identity online and seek out engagement with users, not immediate sales. Encourage others to retweet your content and offers to their friends.

Table 7.7 describes some selected Twitter marketing campaigns.

TABLE 7.7	SELECTED TWITTER MARKETING CAMPAIGNS
COMPANY	MARKETING CAMPAIGN
Lowe's	Fix in Six campaign used animated six-second videos displaying quick home improvement tips.
Samsung	Samsung Galaxy users could recharge their phones by tweeting #PowerOn at SXSW festival, which would prompt a Samsung bike messenger to deliver a new battery to that location.
NFL	Promoted live streaming of NFL games on Verizon devices using the #FOMOF campaign (Fear of Missing Out on Football).
Netflix	Used the hashtag #BeLikeDerek to promote its new show, *Derek*.
Bravo	Used a Twitter social voting campaign on its *Top Chef* cooking show to determine the final competitor in the show's finale in its tenth season.

TABLE 7.8	MEASURING TWITTER MARKETING RESULTS
SOCIAL MARKETING PROCESS	**MEASUREMENT**
Fan acquisition (impressions)	The number of people exposed to your Promoted Tweets, Promoted Trends, etc. (impressions).
	The number of followers and monthly growth.
Engagement (conversation rate)	The number of comments, responses to, and retweets of, your tweets.
	The number of views of brand page content.
	The number of users that responded to games, contests, and coupons (participation).
	The number of minutes on average that followers stay on your page (duration).
Amplification (reach)	The rate at which fans retweet or otherwise share your tweets.
Community	The monthly interaction rate (i.e., the monthly total of comments and responses to, and retweets of, your content).
	The average monthly onsite minutes for all followers.
	The ratio of positive to negative tweets.
Brand Strength/Sales	The number of leads generated (people who sign up for news or content).
	Visitor/lead rate: the number of visitors that become leads to compare campaigns.
	The percentage (or revenue) of your online sales generated by Twitter links compared to other platforms, such as e-mail, search engines, and display ads.
	The percentage of Twitter-sourced customer purchases compared to other sources of customers (conversion ratio).

Measuring Twitter Marketing Results

Measuring the results of Twitter marketing is similar to measuring the results of Facebook and other social marketing platforms, with some minor changes to account for the unique qualities of Twitter. **Table 7.8** describes some basic ways to measure the results of a Twitter marketing campaign.

Tools provided by Twitter include a dashboard that provides real-time information on impressions, retweets, clicks, replies, and follows for Promoted Tweets and Promoted Accounts. Twitter's Timeline activity dashboard provides data on how every tweet performs in terms of mentions, follows, and reach. Twitter's Followers dashboard enables marketers to track the growth of the follower base, as well as information about their interests, geography, and engagement.

Third-party tools include TweetDeck, which enables you to track mentions, people, and keywords; Twitalyzer, which provides one-click access to Twitter metrics that analyze followers, mentions, retweets, influencers, and their locations; and Back-Tweets, which allows you to search through a tweet archive for URLs sent via Twitter.

PINTEREST MARKETING

Pinterest provides users with an online board to which they can "pin" interesting pictures. The success of Pinterest is based in part on a shift in consumer behavior enabled by new technologies: people talk about brands using pictures rather than words. Large numbers of users are pinning and instagramming about their lives using pictures.

Pinterest has been one of the fastest growing sites in online history. In 2010, Pinterest had 10,000 users, then 12 million by the end of 2011, and 150 million by 2016. Today, about 17% of online adults in the United States use Pinterest on a regular basis. Pinterest's visitors are overwhelmingly female: about 75% are women, but men were its fastest growing demographic in 2015, and its users cover a broad age demographic range from grandparents to teenagers, with the largest segment (about 25%) between 25 and 44. The hope for marketers, and Pinterest, is that its "referral capacity" (the ability to direct users to retail websites where they can purchase something) will rapidly increase as its audience grows and intensity of use grows.

You can think of Pinterest as a highly interactive and social online magazine. One difference, of course, is that users (including business firms) contribute all the photos. The site currently has 36 categories of boards from gifts, animals, art, cars, and motorcycles to crafts, food, and men's and women's fashion. Users can pin to these boards, create their own boards, and follow other pinners and boards as well. Firms can create their own brand boards and product pins. As of October 2016, there were over 50 billion pins on Pinterest on more than 1 billion different boards.

One way to look at the billions of pictures on Pinterest is as disguised display ads—click, and off you go to a brand website for a purchase. Pinterest pins are much better than display ads because they are unobtrusive, and because they don't look like display ads. Instead, they look like sumptuous catalog or magazine photos. In the future, analysts believe, Pinterest could charge an affiliate fee for any subsequent purchases. Pinterest could also charge businesses for creating brand sites or boards, which currently are free.

Basic Pinterest Features

Marketing on Pinterest requires that you understand the basic features and capabilities of Pinterest. While all users of Pinterest understand how to pin photos to an online scrapbook, many other capabilities are less well understood or used. **Table 7.9** provides a list of Pinterest features.

Pinterest Marketing Tools

Pinterest's first step into the marketing arena was to offer business accounts that provided additional resources for brands. In 2013, it introduced Rich Pins, which allowed companies to embed information, such as current pricing and availability, as well as a direct link to a product page. In 2014, Pinterest took the official leap into paid advertising. It launched Promoted Pins with a select group of national brands and also announced a trial of a Do It Yourself version of Promoted Pins for small and medium-sized businesses, to be paid for on a cost per click basis, similar to the Google AdWords platform. Promoted Pins appear in search results and category feeds. In 2015, Pinterest rolled out Promoted Pins to all its U.S.-based partners and added Cinematic Pins. It also added Buyable Pins for eligible merchants on select e-commerce platforms such as Shopify, BigCommerce, Magento, and Demandware, and a Shop Our Picks feature, allowing users to buy products directly on the Pinterest site, and pay with Apple

TABLE 7.9	PINTEREST FEATURES
FEATURE	DESCRIPTION
Pins	Used to post a photo to a Pinterest board.
Board	An online scrapbook where photos are organized by the user.
Repins	The ability to pin the photos of other users to your own boards, and to share with your friends.
Hashtags and keywords	Use <#hashtags> in the description of your pins, e.g., #style, #cars, #sports cars. Use keywords people are likely to use when searching for specific content.
Share	Sharing your pinned photos with friends. Options: Twitter, Facebook, e-mail, embed.
Image Hover	A widget you can add to your browser. When your mouse hovers over an online image, the Pin It button pops up and you can pin the photo automatically to your Pinterest boards.
Embed	Code that allows you to embed your pinned photos into your blog automatically.
Me+ Contributors	Allows others to contribute to your boards (only if they are already a follower of yours).
Follow	Users can choose to follow other pinners and boards and receive e-mail updates.
Number of Pins and Followers	A count of the number of pins and the number of followers visible at the top of the brand page.
Link to URL; Link to pinner	Click on the URL of the company who pinned a photo; click on a link to the person who pinned a photo.
Price display	Hover over a product and a display pops up with the price and model information.
Integration with Facebook and Twitter	Login from Facebook, Twitter, and other social sites. Your personal profile (but not your photo) information from Facebook comes over to Pinterest; your pins go onto your Facebook Timeline. Twitter and Pinterest profile pages are also integrated.
Pin It browser button (bookmarklet)	Browsers' red Pin It button. Users drag the button onto their browser screen, allowing them to instantly pin photos they see on the Web.
Apps	Smartphone and tablet apps that allow users to pin photos, browse pins and boards, get ideas while shopping, and display pins.
Pinterest widget	Pin It button on your brand page that makes it easy for people to pin images from your site.

Pay. The Shop our Picks feature highlights hand-picked items for users to consider purchasing. It also introduced new ad-targeting and pricing options. In 2016, it added additional ad-targeting options, began offering its search inventory to advertisers for the first time and launched Promoted Video ads. **Table 7.10** identifies and describes some of the primary Pinterest marketing tools.

For instance, Lands' End has several brand pages on Pinterest, one of which is Lands' End Canvas. Search for Lands' End Canvas and it takes you to the page that Lands' End Canvas created and where Lands' End has pinned some of its catalog photos. On this brand page, only Lands' End Canvas products are pinned, and the company is

TABLE 7.10	PINTEREST MARKETING TOOLS
MARKETING TOOL	DESCRIPTION
Rich Pins	Rich Pins enable advertisers to include extra information directly on the pin itself. There are six types of Rich Pin: Product, App, Place, Article, Movie, and Recipe. Product Pins include real time pricing, availability and link to where the item can be purchased. App Pins include an install button that allows a user to download an app without leaving Pinterest. Place Pins include a map, address, and phone number. Article Pins include a headline, author, and story description.
Promoted Pins	A way to promote pins to a targeted audience, and pay for click-through to your website.
Cinematic Pins	A made-for-mobile ad format that displays a short animation when the user scrolls down through the ad; only plays a full-length version when the user clicks on the ad, providing more user control over the experience.
Buyable Pins/Shop Our Picks	Eligible merchants can create Buyable Pins that allow users to purchase product featured in pin without leaving Pinterest. Shop our Picks feature highlights hand-picked items for users to consider purchasing.
Promoted Video	Uses Pinterest's new native video ad player to allow marketers to run video ads.
Add Pin It or Follow button to your website (Pinterest widget)	Makes it easy for visitors to pin photos from your website, and be notified when you post new photos to your site.
Pin as display ad	Pinned photo acts as a display ad by directing users back to a firm's website.
Brand page	Allows companies to create a corporate brand page. In the past, Pinterest did not distinguish between a personal page and a corporate brand page.
Create theme-based boards to reflect your brand messaging	Pinterest recommends that business boards not be strictly sales-oriented, but lifestyle-oriented instead.
URL Link to stores	Makes it easier for consumers to click through links on brand pages and product pins so they can reliably purchase what they see. The goal is to integrate photos of inventory with Pinterest to make items more easily tracked. What this means is retailers can see a definite link between a sale and a photo they pinned. Currently, after thousands of repins, clicking on the URL sometimes leads to a broken link.
Integration with other social sites	Ask your Facebook fans and Twitter followers to pin photos of your products and tag you. Repin these photos to your brand page on Pinterest. Give a shout-out to your loyal users and fans to show potential customers how much current users like using your product.
Network with users, followers, and others	As with Facebook and Twitter, comment, mention, and communicate with others using Pinterest. Participate in the community and you will become better known, and learn more about potential customers and what they believe and to what they aspire.

TABLE 7.11	SELECTED PINTEREST MARKETING CAMPAIGNS
COMPANY	**CAMPAIGN**
Honda	Provided five influential pinners $500 apiece to take a "#Pintermission" from Pinterest and do activities that they had pinned about. The campaign promoted the Honda CR-V and its "seize the day" image.
Mastercard	Launched #AcceptanceMatters hashtag to promote tolerance and acceptance of people, while also drawing attention to its widely accepted credit card.
Nordstrom	Used in-store signage depicting products with the most engagement on Pinterest. Has more followers on Pinterest than on Facebook or Twitter.
Blue Apron	Subscription-based food delivery service pins its most popular recipes to different boards. High quality, compelling photography helps drive engagement.
UNIQLO	Clothing retailer used dozens of accounts to pin graphics in a five-column arrangement on its Pinterest page, allowing users to scroll down and animate the images.

identified. You can see the number of people who have pinned these photos elsewhere, and the total number of others who follow this line of clothing and have posted their own photos. When you click on a photo, you get a larger version of the photo (sometimes called a photo landing page), and the chance to link to the website (canvas.landsend. com) where you can purchase the product and find similar ones. You will also see on this photo landing page a picture of the person who pinned the photo, other boards where it was pinned, and recommendations for related photos and products in a section titled "People who pinned this also pinned...." **Table 7.11** provides a brief description of Pinterest marketing campaigns of selected other retailers.

Starting a Pinterest Marketing Campaign

Before leaping into a Pinterest campaign, ask yourself some questions about your products and services, and then identify some strategic objectives for your Pinterest presence. First, sketch out a vision of what you hope to accomplish with a Pinterest presence. Are you an established company trying to strengthen your brand? Are you the new kid on the block that no one knows and you want to start a marketing campaign? Are your products visual and can your brand be expressed in a set of pictures? Most products have a visual component, some more compelling than others. Is the consumer accustomed to seeing the products in your industry expressed through photos? For instance, food is increasingly a visual experience with the growth of food magazines and websites.

Next, consider the target demographic for your products and services, and compare it to the Pinterest demographic. Currently, about 75% of Pinterest's users are women, and while this might change over time, your offerings will have to be attractive to women. Do your products or services appeal to this demographic?

Think about strategy in your marketspace. What are your competitors doing? Are they on Pinterest? Do they have an effective presence? What types of people follow your competitors and what are the users pinning? How many followers, re-pinners, brand pages, and product pins are there? Because photos are central to a Pinterest presence, where will the photos for your brand pages come from? Are you, or a member of your team, a skilled photographer? You can pin photos from all over the Web, and from other Pinterest boards, but then you're just sharing content, not creating unique and unusual content.

Pinterest is an adjunct to a fully developed marketing plan, both online and offline. You will want to integrate your social and online marketing efforts with a Facebook and Twitter presence. You can share photos from your website, and send web photos to your brand pages. The same photos can be used on your Facebook page and on Twitter. Your customers will be using all these platforms and you will have to follow them to keep up.

Once you have envisioned your Pinterest campaign and developed a marketing plan, you can start implementing your plan. In order to implement your Pinterest plan, you should have a traditional website where your products are displayed (a catalog) and can be purchased. Second, you should also have a Facebook brand page to develop followers and a method for informing your followers of new Pins. Once these are in place, you can begin your Pinterest campaign:

- Create a Pinterest brand page and start pinning photos of your products. Continue to add more pins, and change them regularly. Be sure your photos are the same quality level or higher than those of your competitors. If necessary, hire a skilled photographer. Brand pages generally do not allow followers to pin photos but only to follow and comment. The idea here is to control the content of your brand page, and develop other boards where followers can pin pictures.

- Create multiple theme-based life style boards. Develop several theme-based boards that emphasize life styles or fashions. Pinterest is not just, or even primarily, a selling site. It is also an entertainment and branding site. You want followers to adore your photos. On theme-based boards you will want others besides yourself to be able to pin.

- Use URL links and keywords. Make sure your pins have a URL link to your store, or to vendor stores, so followers can easily buy as well as "see." Be sure to use keywords and hashtags to classify each of your photos so they show up in Pinterest searches. Remember, Pinterest cannot "see" a photo or understand its content. It only "knows" the content based on your tags.

- Use Pinterest Rich Pins. If you are in the food, retail, or movie distribution business, Product Pins are worth a try if you have a popular product at an attractive price, or if you want to use a specific product as a loss-leader to motivate people to come to your website (where you can expose them to your entire catalog of products). Once you have some experience with Rich Pins, you can also experiment with the various types of paid advertising that Pinterest offers, such as Promoted Pins, Cinematic Pins, and Video Ads.

- Use Pin It buttons. Add a Pin It button to your website and Facebook page to encourage fans and followers to pin your photos to their own boards, and to recommend them to friends.

- Use your Facebook and Twitter networks. Start using your Facebook and Twitter networks by adding a Pin It button to Facebook (also called a Pinterest tab), and start sharing your pinned photos with your followers.

- Integrate with Facebook and Twitter. Create Facebook and Twitter logins so that users can go to your pins and boards without leaving the Facebook and Twitter sites.

- Be social. Join the conversation. Follow other pinners and boards and ask to receive e-mail and Facebook updates.

Measuring Pinterest Marketing Results

As with any social marketing platform, the key dimensions to measure for a Pinterest marketing effort are fan (follower) acquisition, engagement, amplification, community, and sales. **Table 7.12** describes some basic ways to measure the results of a Pinterest marketing campaign.

Pinterest provides a built-in web analytics service that offers insights into how people are interacting with pins that originate from their websites. There are several firms that will help produce the metrics referred to in Table 7.12. For instance, Curalate is an online service to measure the impact of Pinterest and other visual social media. It listens and measures visual conversations by seeing what pictures users pin and repin, and also analyzes the colors in the picture. Curalate currently has over 450 brands using its platform.

MARKETING ON OTHER SOCIAL NETWORKS

There are a great many social networks where products and services can be marketed, the largest of which include Instagram, LinkedIn, and Snapchat. Instagram is a visual social network: users and advertisers post photos and videos to their friends, potential customers, and the public at large. In 2016, Instagram (owned by Facebook) has over 500 million users worldwide and over 200,000 active advertisers. Instagram is a mobile-first platform that particularly appeals to Millennials. In 2016, 90% of Instagram's audience is under 35, and by the end of 2016, it is expected to have around 50 million U.S. Millennials as active users. In 2017, analysts estimate Instagram will generate around €3.4 billion in ad revenues (eMarketer, Inc., 2016y).

As with other social networks, users create a profile. There is a Feed that provides a listing of photos and videos (up to 15 seconds long) posted by friends or advertisers. Using a feature called Direct, users can send photos and videos to specific people. Using Explore, users can search for public profiles and photos. Instagram also has a powerful photo editing suite called Layout.

Similar to Facebook, advertisers have brand profiles and run marketing campaigns by sending posts to users' Feeds. Instagram ad campaigns consist of display ads and video ads of exceptional quality, similar to a printed magazine. Carousel ads can include multiple still photos or videos in a single ad. Ads can link to advertiser's websites and now can include a Buy button. For brands that want to drive mass awareness

TABLE 7.12	MEASURING PINTEREST MARKETING RESULTS
SOCIAL MARKETING PROCESS	MEASUREMENT
Fan acquisition (impressions)	The number of people exposed to your pins.
	The number of followers and the rate of growth.
	The number of people that have pinned your product photos.
	The percentage of those exposed to your pins who also pin them to their own or other boards.
Engagement (conversation rate)	The number of posts, comments, and responses to your brand or pins on Pinterest.
	The number of users who are responding to games, contests, and coupons (participation).
	The number of minutes on average fans stay on your brand or product pages (duration).
	The rate of pins per post or other content (applause rate).
Amplification	The rate at which fans share your pinned photos by sharing or repinning to their own or others' boards.
Community	The monthly interaction rate with your content (i.e., the monthly total of pins, comments, and actions on your Pinterest brand page).
	The average monthly onsite minutes for all fans.
	The ratio of positive to negative comments.
Brand Strength/Sales	The percentage of your online sales that are generated by Pinterest links (referrals) compared to other platforms, such as e-mail, search engines, and display ads.
	The percentage of Pinterest-sourced customer purchases, compared to other sources of customers (conversion ratio).
	The conversion ratio for users receiving repinned photos (friends of followers).

around premieres, product launches, and key moments, Instagram developed what it calls its Marquee ad product, which reaches millions of people. Marquee ads generally last a single day, promise to deliver a guaranteed number of impressions, and can be posted several times during the day to catch different audiences. In August 2016, Instagram also added a "Stories" feature to compete with a similar feature offered by Snapchat. Stories typically include a montage of images and/or videos, sometimes annotated with graphics and emoticons, and disappear after 24 hours. Although not yet offered as a paid advertising product, a number of major brands have already eagerly embraced the format and have begun to regularly include Stories in their Instagram marketing efforts (Shields, 2016).

LinkedIn, while generating far less average engagement, nevertheless attracts a highly educated, professional, and managerial audience that is intensively engaged in careers and employment. LinkedIn is a social network focused on professional networking, where users post their resumes, and potential employers hunt for new hires. See the opening case in Chapter 10 for more information on LinkedIn.

As with other social networks, users build a profile, but in this case, sharing their professional background, degrees, employment, and skill set. Companies can create a free company profile page that includes a logo, header image, an About section, and various posts. Companies can also create a showcase page to highlight a specific product or service, as well as a Career page (which requires payment) targeted at recruiting. There is a Feed that provides a listing of posts from colleagues and friends, and sponsored posts (ads) from firms. Display ads also appear on the right and bottom of the page. Advertisers can used LinkedIn's self-serve advertising platform or place ads using LinkedIn Advertising Partner Solutions, which provide more variety and ad options than self-service ads, including premium display advertising, sponsored inMail, and ads that urge users to follow a specific company or join a specific group. LinkedIn also recently began providing a publishing platform called LinkedIn Pulse, which allows users to publish articles to expand their brand and thought leadership.

The primary contribution of LinkedIn is to develop personal brands for professional managers and to create a marketplace where employers can contact suitable candidates. Advertisers tend to use LinkedIn for branding purposes and typically are not soliciting sales.

Snapchat is a mobile messaging app/social network that allows its users to chat and send images and videos (snaps) that disappear after a relatively short period of time once they have been viewed. Snapchat bills itself as method for visually capturing important moments and communicating them creatively via a variety of tools such as geofilters (which tailor an image to the user's location) and lenses (a type of augmented reality that allows users to alter their face in a variety of ways). Snapchat was initially aimed at the under-25 demographic and in 2016, Millennials represent 70% of Snapchat's almost 60 million monthly active U.S. users. However, Snapchat has begun to record significant growth in the 25-to-34-year-old age group, as well as those over 35. In addition to targeting a desirable demographic, Snapchat is also attractive to advertisers because research indicates that it is also very sticky within that demographic, with three out of four college-aged U.S. users indicating that they use the app every day, and over 50% saying that they used it many times a day and even constantly. Snapchat itself reports users worldwide spending 25 to 30 minutes a day using the app.

Since it was initially released, Snapchat has introduced a number of features that present advertising opportunities, including Snapchat Stories (a way for users to simultaneously share snaps, which remain live for 24 hours, with all or just some of their friends), Live Stories (a compilation of snaps from various users at events and locations around the world that are compiled by Snapchat editors into a Live Story that typically has a lifespan of 24 hours), and Discover (unique content from brands chosen by Snapchat). Snapchat offers advertisers three types of "native" ads: Snap Ads (short 10-seconds or less full-screen vertical video ads that have audio turned on by default), Sponsored Geofilters (geofilters that use brand imagery and messaging), and Sponsored Lenses (lenses that use brand imagery). Interactive versions of Snap Ads (known as Snap Ads with Attachments) are also available, and allow a user to swipe to extend the ad to view additional video, an article, a web page, or an app install offer. Ads can be purchased on a flat fee or cost-per-thousand (CPM) impressions basis. Snapchat's targeting capabilities are currently less developed than most of its social network competitors, but plans are in the works for enhanced targeting options. Snapchat is expected to generate around €364 million in ad revenues in 2016, with that number increasing to almost €875 million in 2017. Currently, Snapchat's Discover feature is the primary driver of its U.S. ad revenues (eMarketer, Inc., 2016y; comScore, 2016).

THE DOWNSIDE OF SOCIAL MARKETING

Social marketing is not without its disadvantages. Sometimes social media campaigns backfire. One problem is that brands lose a substantial amount of control over what people say about their brands (see the *Insight on Society* case, *The Dark Side of Social Networks* in Chapter 11 for a variety of examples) and also lose control over where their ads appear in terms of other content on social sites. Ads placed on Facebook according to an algorithm can be placed near content that does not represent the values of the brand. This is not peculiar to social marketing, as advertising using Google's advertising platform faces the same problem. This is very different, however, from TV ads where brands maintain near complete control. Social sites are unique in that disgruntled consumers, or just malicious people, can post material that is inaccurate and/or embarrassing (Vega and Kaufman, 2013).

The *Insight on Society* case, *Marketing to Children of the Web in the Age of Social Networks*, illustrates some additional issues with respect to social marketing.

7.3 MOBILE MARKETING

Mobile marketing involves the use of mobile devices such as smartphones and tablet computers to display banner ads, rich media, video, games, e-mail, text messaging, in-store messaging, QuickResponse (QR) codes, and couponing. Mobile is now a required part of the standard marketing budget. Mobile devices represent a radical departure from previous marketing technologies simply because the devices integrate so many human and consumer activities from telephoning or texting friends to listening to music, watching videos, tracking location, and shopping. The more mobile devices can do, the more people rely on them in daily life. More than 4.3 billion people worldwide are now using mobile phones, while 2.1 billion of these use smartphones. Over 1.1 billion people also use tablet computers (eMarketer, Inc., 2016f, 2016g, 2016h). One report found that people look at their mobile devices at least 40 times a day. Most mobile phone users keep their phone within arm's length 24 hours a day. For many, it's the first thing they check in the morning, the last thing they check at night, and the first tool to use when there's a question of where to go, what to do, and where to meet up.

OVERVIEW: M-COMMERCE TODAY

It's a short number of steps from owning a smartphone or tablet to searching for products and services, browsing, and then purchasing. Retail m-commerce sales in the EU-5 have skyrocketed over the last several years, growing at over 30% in 2016, but are expected to moderate slightly to about 10% annual growth by 2020. Analysts estimate that by 2020, retail m-commerce in the EU-5 will account for over 40% of all retail e-commerce. **Figure 7.6** illustrates the expected growth of mobile and "traditional" e-commerce in the retail industries in the EU-5 to 2020.

Initially, m-commerce was focused primarily on digital goods, such as music, videos, games, and e-books. Today, however, traditional retail products and travel services are the source of much of the growth in m-commerce. Not surprisingly, the

INSIGHT ON SOCIETY

MARKETING TO CHILDREN OF THE WEB IN THE AGE OF SOCIAL NETWORKS

In the United States, over 99% of all 5- to 15-year-olds use the Internet. Social and mobile marketing provides advertisers with an entirely new arsenal to influence children. Using custom banner ads, product characters, videos, games, virtual worlds, and surveys, marketers are both influencing behaviors and gathering valuable data. A children's digital culture has been created with built-in avenues to the psyche of young minds—in some cases, minds that are so young they are unlikely to know when they are being marketed to and when they are being given misleading or even harmful information.

Marketers have moved aggressively to use social networks and viral marketing to get kids hooked on brands early in life. While such moves may be savvy marketing, are they ethical? Some people say no. Research has shown that young children cannot understand the potential effects of revealing their personal information; neither can they distinguish between substantive material on websites and the advertisements surrounding it. Experts argue that since children don't understand persuasive intent until they are eight or nine years old, it is unethical to advertise to them before they can distinguish between advertising and the real world. Others believe that fair advertising is an important and necessary part of the maturation process for future adults in today's society.

In 1998, Congress passed the Children's Online Privacy Protection Act (COPPA) after the FTC discovered that 80% of websites were collecting personal information from children, but only 1% required their parents' permission. Under COPPA, companies must post a privacy policy on their websites, detailing exactly how they collect information from consumers, how they'll use it, and the degrees to which they'll protect consumer privacy. Companies are not permitted to use personal information collected from children under 13 years of age without the prior, verifiable consent of parents.

Since the law took effect, the FTC has obtained a number of settlements and fined a number of companies for violations of COPPA. For instance, Disney's Playdom was fined $3 million, the largest penalty to date, for collecting and disclosing children's information without parental approval.

In 2011, the FTC announced its first-ever COPPA enforcement action involving mobile apps. Shortly thereafter, in response to the increase in the use of mobile devices by children, the FTC announced revisions to its COPPA regulations in an attempt to keep pace with emerging technology. The revisions, which took effect in 2013, expanded the definition of personal information to include a child's location, along with any personal data collected through the use of cookies for the purpose of targeted advertising. They also require that websites that collect a child's information ensure that they can protect it, hold on to it for only as long as reasonably necessary, and thereafter delete the information.

In 2016, the FTC more than doubled the maximum penalties that it levies for violations of COPPA and other consumer protection laws. If firms want to use the personal information of children for internal uses only, the FTC requires an e-mail from the parent plus one other form of verification (such as a credit card or phone number). The FTC now allows parents to take selfies to confirm parental consent in conjunction with facial recognition software. Firms seeking to sell personal information about children are also required to use an additional means of verification, such as a print-and-send consent form, credit card transaction, a toll-free number or video conference staffed by trained personnel, or verification of a parent's identity by checking a form of government-issued identification. Privacy groups applauded the effort, and enforcement of COPPA has improved. For example, in 2016, the FTC levied a fine of $950,000 against mobile advertising firm InMobi, alleging that the company tracked information and locations of hundreds of millions of children without consent and misrepresented the location tracking in its software as being opt-in when it was not. In addition to the fine, the FTC compelled InMobi to delete data collected without consent, implement a comprehensive privacy program, and be audited every two years for the next 20 years. In the past, the FTC had only used COPPA to regulate websites and app developers, as opposed to advertising networks like InMobi. Given that InMobi's data collection policies are widespread in the advertising industry, the FTC could be much more active in 2017 and beyond. Individual states have also started enforcing COPPA regulations. In 2016, New York's attorney general settled with Viacom, Mattel, Hasbro, and JumpStart Games over practices involving the collection of information and online activities of children without parents' consent, and Texas fined mobile app developer Juxta for similar practices.

Major technology companies have also recently been fined and required to adjust their policies with regard to children signing up for their services. Google settled with the FTC in 2014 and agreed to refund $19 million worth of in-app purchases that were made unwittingly by children. Apple had also agreed to refund $32.5 million in similar purchases earlier in the year, and Amazon is likely to follow suit shortly. Yelp was hit with a $450,000 fine despite not having much vested interest in collecting children's information, and even game developers like TinyCo have fallen into the FTC crosshairs, incurring a $300,000 fine for violating children's privacy. The question is whether these FTC fines will be enough to discourage companies from gathering valuable data on future consumers from such a young age. In 2015, Google released YouTube Kids, a child-friendly version of YouTube, but consumer advocates found that it still included inappropriate advertising and explicit content.

In 2015, the Senate launched a bipartisan effort to enact amendments to COPPA, which would include children ages 13 to 15 as well as the requirement of an "eraser button" that allows parents or children to permanently erase personal information online for any site collecting information. However, thus far, the bill has not been passed. The FTC has also toughened its policies toward information gathering, forcing software and app makers to reconsider the inclusion of features that allow for data transfer between devices. App developers will also be required to verify parental consent using a credit or debit card number whether or not the app offers items for purchase.

SOURCES: "The States Also Rise: Recent Settlements Illustrate Potential Pitfalls Regarding Children's Privacy Laws," by Saad Gul and Michael Slipsky, Jdsupra.com, October 17, 2016; "Texas State AG Weighs In on Children's Online Privacy," by Sheila A. Millar et al., Natlawreview.com, October 6, 2016; "New York Attorney General Announces COPPA Settlements," by Tracy P. Marshall et al., Natlawreview.com, September 19, 2016; "Million Dollar Settlement and Online Analytics in an Age of COPPA," by Saad Gul and Michael Slipsky, Linkedin.com, August 10, 2016; "FTC Increases Maximum Civil Penalties for HSR Act, COPPA, and Other Violations From $16,000 to $40,000," by Chris Olsen and Lydia Parnes, Jdsupra.com, July 7, 2016; "InMobi's Illegal Location Tracking Debacle Is Just the Tip of the Iceberg and Regulators Are Chomping at the Bit," by Allison Schiff, Adexchanger.com, June 27, 2016; "Mobile Advertising Network InMobi Settles FTC Charges It Tracked Hundreds of Millions of Consumers' Locations Without Permission," Ftc.gov, June 22, 2016; "FTC Allows Selfies to Verify Parental Consent for Kids Using Online Services," by John Ribeiro, *PCworld*, November 20, 2015; "Significant Amendments to COPPA Proposed in Do Not Track Kids Act," by Ronald London and John Seiver, Jdsupra.com, June 22, 2015; "Mapping the Regulations Protecting Children's Privacy Online," by Josh Yaker, Techcrunch.com, June 4, 2015; "FTC Fines Tech Giants for Violating Kids' Privacy," by Bill Snyder, Cio.com, September 18, 2014; "Amazon Blames Parents for Kids' App Store Purchases," by Jonathan Randles, Law360.com, September 9, 2014; "Google to Refund $19 Million of Children's In-App Purchases," Mashable.com, September 4, 2014; "FTC Changes Privacy Guidelines for Developers of Kids' Apps," by Hayley Tsukayama, *Washington Post*, July 16, 2014; "Child Privacy Online: FTC Updates COPPA Rules," by Mathew Schwartz, Informationweek.com, July 5, 2013; "Revised Children's Online Privacy Protection Rule Goes Into Effect Today," FTC.gov, July 1, 2013; "FTC Announces First-Ever COPPA Enforcement Action Against Mobile Apps," by David Silverman, Privsecblog.com, August 17, 2011; "FTC: Disney's Playdom Violated Child Protection Act," by Don Reisinger, News.cnet.com, May 13, 2011.

FIGURE 7.6 **THE GROWTH OF RETAIL M-COMMERCE IN THE EU-5**

M-commerce in the retail industry in the EU-5 is expected to grow to almost €120 billion by 2020, about 40% of the amount generated by desktop-based "traditional" e-commerce.

SOURCES: Based on data from eMarketer, Inc., 2016i.

giant in the United States is Amazon, with over $17 billion in sales through its mobile website and Amazon app. According to a recent survey, around 45% of shopping trips also include some mobile shopping (eMarketer, Inc., 2016m).

Increasingly, consumers are using their mobile devices to search for people, places, and things—like restaurants and deals on products they saw in a retail store. The rapid switch of consumers from desktop platforms to mobile devices is driving a surge in mobile marketing expenditures. Because search is so important for directing consumers to purchase situations, the mobile search advertising market is very important for search engines like Google and Bing. Desktop search revenues are slowing for both. Google's mobile ad business is growing rapidly, but the prices it can charge for mobile ads are far less than for desktop computer ads. The challenge facing Google and other mobile marketing firms is how to get more consumers to click on mobile ads, and how to charge marketers more for each click. And the answer lies with the consumer who decides what and when to click.

How People Actually Use Mobile Devices

If you plan a mobile marketing campaign, it's important to understand how people actually use their mobile devices (which may be different from what you do or think others do). For instance, most of us think people use their mobile devices on the go, but in fact, according to one of the very few studies of actual mobile behavior, almost 70% of all mobile minutes actually occur in the home. We know Americans spend about 5 hours and 45 minutes with digital media on average daily, and over three of these hours is spent using mobile devices—smartphones and tablets. What are they doing in these three hours, and on what device?

Recent data show that entertainment, not shopping or buying, is the primary focus (at least in terms of time) for mobile device users. Of the three hours (180 minutes) a day that people are spending using their mobile devices, 29 minutes (16%) is spent on social networks. Watching video accounts for 29 minutes as well (16%). A whopping 47 minutes (26%) is spent listening to music, primarily streaming music services. Hence, 42% of mobile device use is for entertainment (music and video), with social networks consuming another 16% (eMarketer, Inc., 2016n). Where else does the time go? A survey by Pew Research Center described the broad range of activities that mobile users accomplish on their mobile devices when they are not entertaining themselves or socializing. People use the mobile devices for pretty much the same activities as they do their desktop computers, from getting information, to banking, and looking for places to live. Unfortunately, this survey did not include data on shopping and purchasing behavior, and did not include information on time spent with the activity (Pew Research Center, 2015).

However, a National Federation of Retailers survey provides insight into how consumers planned to use their mobile devices and which ones—tablet or smartphone—in the 2015 holiday shopping season (**Figure 7.7**). Researching products and comparing prices topped the list, with tablets (47%) leading smartphones (37%) as a vehicle for purchase. However, a very large percentage (35%–40%) did not plan to use either a tablet or a smartphone for shopping or buying at all. Only around one-third of tablet users and less than 25% of smartphone users planned to purchase anything with their tablets or smartphones (National Retail Federation, 2015).

FIGURE 7.7 HOW PEOPLE USE THEIR MOBILE DEVICES TO SHOP

Tablets lead smartphones as an m-commerce shopping and buying platform, but this difference may disappear over time as better tools are developed for smartphones.

SOURCE: Based on data from eMarketer, Inc., 2015b.

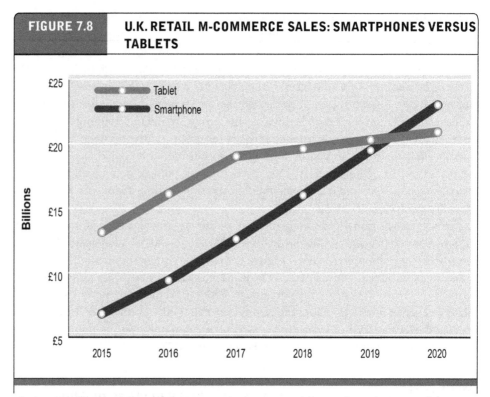

FIGURE 7.8   U.K. RETAIL M-COMMERCE SALES: SMARTPHONES VERSUS TABLETS

Contrary to earlier expectations, retail m-commerce sales on smartphones are increasing at a much faster rate than those on tablet computers.

SOURCES: Based on data from eMarketer, Inc., 2016j.

From this research, we can conclude that mobile devices are still primarily used for entertainment, socializing, and communicating, with less time spent using them for shopping or buying. None of these patterns are permanent, however. M-commerce is surging. Initial expectations were that tablets would provide the primary m-commerce platform, but that has not proven to be the case. As the size of smartphone screens has grown and their resolution improved, coupled with better mobile search, better location- and context-based discovery, and better mobile payment systems, the smartphone buying experience has improved, resulting in rapidly growing smartphone m-commerce sales (**Figure 7.8**).

In-App Experiences and In-App Ads

You may think that using a browser to access the Web on your smartphone or tablet is a typical mobile activity. In reality, however, mobile users in the United States spend almost 60% of their total digital time using apps. Smartphone apps in particular have been the biggest driver in the growth in digital media usage, and they account for almost half of total digital time, as well as almost 75% of the time spent on mobile devices, and 85% of the time spent on mobile apps. Time spent on tablet apps is declining, in contrast, as smartphone screens increase in both size and resolution. On average, users use only about 27 apps a month on their smartphones. Almost 75% of all app time is spent on a user's top three apps. There may be millions of apps on the iOS and Android cloud servers, but just a handful are actually generating sufficient user traffic to be of interest to general advertisers. Facebook is the top app both in audience size and share of time spent, followed by Facebook Messenger in second place. Google has four of the top seven apps (Google Maps, Google Search, Google Play, and Gmail). Most of the other apps in the top 25 are either social networks (Instagram, Snapchat, Pinterest, and Twitter), entertainment-oriented (Pandora Radio, Apple Music, Netflix, and Spotify), or utilities (Apple Maps, Google Drive, Yahoo Stocks, The Weather Channel, Yahoo Mail). There are only four retail-oriented apps in the top 25: Amazon Mobile (10th), Groupon (22nd), Walmart (23rd), and eBay (24th). However, many of the fastest growing apps in terms of unique visitors are those from on-demand service providers, such as Uber and Lyft (comScore, 2016).

The implications for marketers are quite clear: if consumers are primarily using apps rather than browsing the Web on their mobile devices, marketers need to place ads in apps where most of the action is for attracting consumers, and that means social network and entertainment apps. Second, if mobile consumers only use, on average, 27 apps, then marketers need to concentrate their marketing in these popular apps, let's say, the top 100. Niche marketers, on the other hand, can concentrate their ads in apps that support that niche. A distributor of diving equipment, for instance, could place ads in apps devoted to the diving community. There may not be many users of the app, but those who do use it are highly motivated on the topic.

Another implication for marketers is that rather than focus on mobile display ads that are difficult to read, the best ad may be an entertaining video ad that captures the viewer's attention or an ad in an app that is precisely targeted to the consumer's current activities and interests.

How the Multi-Screen Environment Changes the Marketing Funnel

Along with the growth of smartphones and tablets comes a multi-screen world: smartphones, tablets, desktops, and television. The reality, and the future, of computing devices is that consumers will be multi-platform: using desktops and laptops at work and home, and smartphones and tablets at home as well as when moving about. Television will be available all the time, both at home and on the go via tablets and smartphones. Consumer purchasing behavior changes in a multi-screen world. Consumers will often be using two or more screens at once, tweeting when watching a TV show, or moving seamlessly from a TV ad, to a mobile search for more information, to a later tablet purchase screen. Several research studies have found that 90% of multi-device users switch among screens to complete tasks, for instance, viewing an ad on TV, searching on a smartphone for the product, and then purchasing it with a tablet. Consumers move seamlessly among devices, either sequentially or simultaneously. Also, the more screens people use, the more shopping and purchasing they do. One conclusion is that the more screens consumers have, the more consumer touchpoints or marketing opportunities exist (Google, Inc., 2012).

The implications of the multi-device platform, or screen diversity environment, are that marketing needs to be designed for whatever device the consumer is using, and consistent branding across platforms will be important. Screen diversity means that one ad size, for instance, will not fit all situations, and that branding images will need to be adjusted automatically based on the device the consumer is using. From a design perspective, graphics and creative elements will appear differently depending on the screen. This is called responsive design or responsive creative design. Responsive design is a design process that allows your marketing content to resize, reformat, and reorganize itself so that it looks good on any screen. You can see responsive design in action if you look at any portal on a desktop, and then compare the screen to that same portal viewed on a smartphone or tablet. You are likely to find there are three versions of the screen, one for each platform (IAB, 2012). The requirement to find customers on multiple screens can add considerably to the cost of marketing online. Companies need to develop a presence and market not only on websites, but on mobile websites, and/or smartphone and tablet apps as well. Perhaps they may not be able to afford all three of these, and may want to choose only one. In that case, which is the best? Much depends on what the point of the marketing is. To drive sales, a website might be more effective, but to drive brand awareness, and engagement, social and entertainment apps might be better (eMarketer, Inc., 2015c).

But even beyond screen adaptability, a multi-screen world means merchants need to be on all platforms, and to be integrated across platforms, in order to send a coherent message and to create a convenient consumer platform. The marketing environment today is much more complex than placing banner ads on pages or on search engine results pages on the Web.

BASIC MOBILE MARKETING FEATURES

As billions of consumers adopt mobile devices, mobile marketing expenditures worldwide have rapidly grown and in 2016 exceeded the amount spent on advertising on the desktop platform for the first time. This trend is expected to continue through 2020 (see **Figure 7.9**). In 2016, mobile marketing was about 55% of all online marketing worldwide, which is extraordinary given that smartphones appeared only nine years ago in 2007, and tablets not until 2010. Analysts believe that if current mobile marketing growth rates continue, by 2020, mobile marketing will be almost 75% of all online advertising and almost three times as much as desktop advertising.

Mobile advertising in the United States is dominated by Google, with an expected $14.7 billion in mobile ad revenues in 2016, constituting about 32% of the entire market, but down from 40% in 2014 as Facebook and others continue to expand into the mobile market. On the mobile platform, Google is still the king of search, generating an expected $12.7 billion from mobile search ads in 2016, almost two-thirds of all mobile search ad spending. Facebook is second in mobile ads with an expected $10.1 billion in revenue from mobile ads in 2016, about 22% of total mobile ad revenues. Just as Google dominates in mobile search ads, Facebook dominates in mobile display ads, accounting for over 42% of all spending on such ads. Other players in the mobile marketing marketplace are Twitter (with a 2.6% share), Yahoo (2.3%), and Pandora, with 1.8% (see **Figure 7.10**).

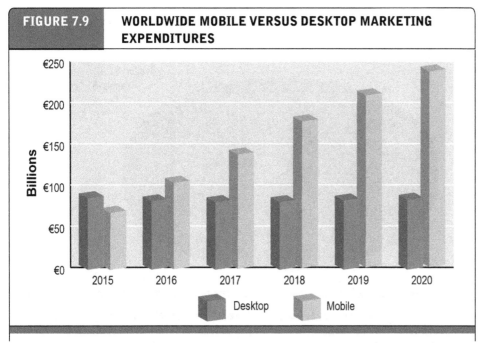

| FIGURE 7.9 | WORLDWIDE MOBILE VERSUS DESKTOP MARKETING EXPENDITURES |

Spending on mobile marketing is growing much more rapidly than spending on advertising aimed at desktop computers, which is expected to remain relatively flat. By 2020, it is expected that advertisers will be spending almost three times as much on mobile marketing as on desktop marketing.
SOURCE: Based on data from eMarketer, Inc., 2016x.

The Technology: Basic Mobile Device Features

Everybody knows the capabilities of smartphones and tablets. But what is it about mobile platforms that make them any different from desktops? What features make them especially suitable for marketing?

For starters, smartphones today play a much more central role in the personal life of consumers than desktops and laptops in large part because smartphones are always physically with us, or close by. In this sense, they are more personal, and almost "wearable." The "always on, always with us" nature of smartphones has several implications for marketers. Because they are perceived as "personal appendages," consumers are less tolerant of commercial intrusion. Have you ever had a telephone conversation interrupted by an advertisement? You probably have not, and if so, you most likely would be annoyed at the interference with a personal conversation. These attitudes extend to any use of the phone or tablet, from reading e-mail, visiting Facebook, or watching a video. Consumers are simply less tolerant of advertising on the small screens of smartphones. Second, the around-the-clock physical proximity of smartphones to our persons greatly expands the time available for marketing materials and increases the supply of screens for marketing materials. This excess supply decreases the price of mobile marketing messages. In turn, there is a tension between marketers and consumers: marketers want to increase the number of mobile ads, while consumers want to see fewer ads, not more, on their mobile devices. Ads inside

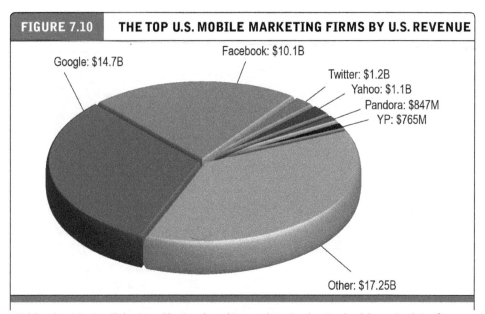

| FIGURE 7.10 | THE TOP U.S. MOBILE MARKETING FIRMS BY U.S. REVENUE |

Google: $14.7B
Facebook: $10.1B
Twitter: $1.2B
Yahoo: $1.1B
Pandora: $847M
YP: $765M
Other: $17.25B

Mobile advertising is still dominated by Google and its search engine, but Facebook has gained significant market share in the last four years.

SOURCE: Based on data from eMarketer, Inc., 2016r.

apps are treated differently by consumers: in return for a free game, consumers are more accepting of ads.

But perhaps the most unique feature of smartphones is that they know users' precise location by virtue of their built-in GPS. This allows marketing messages to be targeted to consumers on the basis of their location, and supports the introduction of location-based marketing and local marketing (described in Section 7.4). While websites may know a desktop's general location, it is a very imprecise fix, and the position of the desktop does not change as the user moves about. **Table 7.13** summarizes the features of mobile devices that marketers can leverage.

MOBILE MARKETING TOOLS: AD FORMATS

Unlike social marketing, mobile marketing does not require much of a new marketing vocabulary. All the marketing formats available on the desktop are also available on mobile devices. With few exceptions, mobile marketing is very much like desktop marketing—except it is smaller. The major marketing opportunities in mobile marketing are search ads, display ads, videos and rich media, messaging (SMS/MMS/PPS), and some familiar other formats like e-mail, classified, and lead generation. **Figure 7.11** illustrates the relative size of U.S. mobile marketing expenditures in 2016 by format. The marketing formats on mobile devices are search ads, display (banners, rich media, and sponsorships), video, text/video messaging, and other (including e-mail, classifieds, and lead generation).

In 2016, search engine advertising continues to be the most popular mobile marketing format, accounting for almost 45% of all mobile ad spending, not surprising given that search is the second most common smartphone application (after voice and

TABLE 7.13	FEATURES OF MOBILE DEVICES
FEATURE	DESCRIPTION
Personal communicator and organizer	Telephone plus calendars and clocks to coordinate life on a personal scale.
Screen size and resolution	Resolution of both tablets and phones is high enough to support vibrant graphics and video.
GPS location	Self-locating GPS capability.
Web browser	Standard browsers will operate all websites and applications.
Apps	Over a million specialized applications running in native code and extending the functionality of mobile devices.
Ultraportable and personal	Fits into a pocket, or a briefcase for tablets, able to be used anywhere and on the go.
Multimedia capable: video, audio, text	Fully capable of displaying all common media from video to text and sound.
Touch/haptic technology	Enhances touch screens by providing feedback in the form of vibration, force, or motion.

text communication). Search engine ads can be further optimized for the mobile platform by showing ads based on the physical location of the user. Display ads (banner ads, rich media, and sponsorships) are the second leading ad format, accounting for about 42% of mobile ad spending. Display ads can be served as a part of a mobile website or inside apps and games. Ad networks such as Google's AdMob, Facebook,

FIGURE 7.11	U.S. MOBILE AD SPENDING BY FORMAT

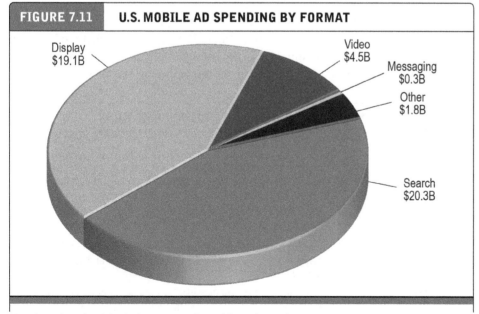

Search engine advertising is the most popular mobile marketing format.
SOURCE: Based on data from eMarketer, Inc., 2016s.

Apple's iAd, Twitter's MoPub, and MillennialMedia are some of the largest providers of mobile display advertising. Video ads are only about 10% of mobile marketing, but are a fast growing segment because of their very high click rates. Most desktop video ads can be resized for use on mobile phones and tablets. Mobile messaging generally involves SMS text messaging to consumers, with coupons or flash marketing messages. Messaging is especially effective for local advertising because consumers can be sent messages and coupons as they pass by or visit locations (see Section 7.4).

Social networks such as Facebook, Twitter, Instagram, and Pinterest have generally brought their desktop advertising techniques over to the mobile platform, with some alterations of the interface for use on small-screen smartphones. In the process, social networks have brought real innovation to the mobile marketing experience, including News Feed posts on Facebook and Promoted Tweets in Twitter. **Table 7.14** provides selected examples of mobile marketing campaigns and techniques used by several well-known firms.

Mobile marketing is uniquely suited for branding purposes, raising awareness through the use of video and rich interactive media such as games. Read the *Insight on Business* case, *Mobile Marketing: Ford Goes 3-D*, for a further look.

STARTING A MOBILE MARKETING CAMPAIGN

As with all marketing campaigns, start by identifying your objectives and understanding just how a mobile marketing campaign might help your firm. Are you a new unknown startup seeking to develop a brand image, or an already existing brand looking to strengthen your presence and sell products? Is there something about your products that makes them especially attractive to a mobile audience? For instance, if you sell to local customers walking by your shop, then you might want to use the GPS capabilities of smartphones to target consumers who are nearby.

Next, consider the target demographic for your campaign and products. The most active purchasers on mobile devices are men, and they are more likely to buy consumer electronics equipment and digital content. Women are more likely to cash in coupons and respond to flash sales and deals. Younger consumers are more likely

TABLE 7.14	SELECTED MOBILE MARKETING CAMPAIGNS
COMPANY	CAMPAIGN
Ikea	Launched an interactive mobile app of its catalog, allowing users to view hidden content by scanning certain pages and to test how furniture looks in your home with augmented reality.
Just for Men	Men's facial care retailer launched a series of mobile ads with interactive sports trivia quizzes, producing brand lift of 24%.
Target	Launched banner ad on Huffington Post mobile site that enabled viewers to browse Procter & Gamble hair products and purchase using a buy button.
McDonald's	Created just-for-fun "Fry Defender" feature of its mobile apps, turning your phone into a motion sensor that goes off if someone approaches your fries.

INSIGHT ON BUSINESS

MOBILE MARKETING: FORD GOES 3-D

Why is mobile marketing any different from ordinary online marketing? In one sense, it isn't. You'll find the same kinds of ad formats on mobile devices that are used on websites— search, display, video, and text messages. On the other hand, the built-in features of the smartphone, such as GPS, gyroscope, and accelerometer, can enable mobile marketers to be much more creative. Not only can marketers use the location of users to market local businesses, but they can also take advantage of the touch interface to serve rich media and video ads that are much more engaging and interactive than traditional desktop computer ads. Other unique smartphone features are that people almost always carry them and keep them turned on. This means that smartphone users can be exposed to marketing messages at nearly any time.

Mobile devices are used by consumers throughout the purchase cycle: About half of the population uses a mobile device to research products online before purchasing. The use of mobile devices to actually purchase products or services online (as opposed to just shopping and browsing online) is growing significantly. Mobile shopping is particularly easy on sites that have one-click shopping capability and for content like books and movies. Also, for local marketing, mobile is an ideal platform for merchants to attract consumers in the neighborhood. Restaurants, museums, and entertainment venues are ideal candidates to use mobile marketing aimed at local consumers. What attracts users to mobile purchasing is the ability to immediately access product information, find deals, and buy products, all with the swipe of a finger. But mobile is also good for introducing new products and building brand recognition, with sales taking place elsewhere and offline. Programmatic advertising, where the purchasing

of ads is automated and ads are served to highly targeted demographics, is also much easier on mobile, where advertisers know much more about their audiences than on a platform like television. Programmatic advertising comprised nearly 80% of mobile display ad spending in 2016.

One increasingly popular method of mobile advertising among companies with big advertising budgets is 3-D advertising, which consists of advertisements with video and other interactive features that take advantage of the capabilities of modern mobile devices. A good example of this type of advertising in action is Ford's "We Own Work" campaign for its F-150 pickup truck, America's top selling truck for 36 years. Ford used a 3-D mobile advertisement for the 2014 edition of the truck as the centerpiece and "lead creative unit" in the campaign, with the stated goals that the ad be innovative, creative, and compatible with all major platforms and devices. They hoped to simulate a showroom experience within the ad, building brand awareness and user engagement in the process.

Ford's advertising team partnered with Amobee, a three-dimensional mobile advertising platform, to create the virtual showroom experience. The ad displays as a motion-sensitive banner ad that expands across the screen into a full 3-D virtual showroom, complete with fully customizable options for the displayed F-150, embedded videos, and a 360-degree view of the vehicle. Users can change the truck to one of fourteen colors with a quick tap of the screen, and can view the F-150 in different environments at any angle by moving their device. The environments are intended to show the F-150 in action performing a wide array of functions, including construction, hauling, farming, and transporting hazardous materials. Users can also tap the screen to load the bed of the virtual F-150, showcasing its payload capacity.

(continued)

By tilting the mobile device in any direction, users can generate reflections of each environment in the mirrors and windows of the truck via the accelerometer of the device.

Unlike traditional rich media ads, 3-D mobile ads respond to users' actions in real time, changing colors, lighting, shading, and other features. But the 3-D ad format offered by Amobee is actually a more light-weight and user-friendly package than traditional HTML5 rich media ads, since the ads take advantage of many features that are used from the phone itself, whereas users must download all of the features used by a rich media ad. Amobee advertisements use WebGL to render interactive 3-D graphics, which allow each ad to run on traditional web browsers as well as an extensive array of mobile devices, and some ads now use 3-D Touch technology to allow users to perform different tasks by applying different levels of pressure to their touch screen. In 2016, Amobee launched an updated set of ad formats and ad creation tools called Amobee Impact, and prominent brands such as PayPal, Red Bull, and Lexus have partnered with Amobee on mobile campaigns.

Amobee also touts that its advertising platform can identify and target individual demographics at scale. Amobee can keep track of engagement with its advertisements in real time, keeping consumers anonymous but measuring how much time different demographics of users spend with individual elements of each ad and how effectively ads engage each type of user. Amobee has an in-house data management platform with over a million profiles with customer information such as gender, age, location, and interests. Needless to say, this capability is extremely useful when measuring the effectiveness of an advertising campaign, and when a brand like Ford Is seeking to target specific types of consumers.

Ford rolled out the ad in conjunction with the launch of the F-150. Using Amobee analytics, Ford determined that the F-150 3-D ad registered 20 million impressions and 595,000 expansions. The 2.9% rate of expansions was 4.6 times the industry average, and the 13% overall engagement rate was twice as high as the industry average. Metrics also indicated that the 3-D mobile campaign generated an increase in brand favorability by 19.9%, an increase in purchase consideration by 40.4%, and an increase in brand awareness of the F-150 and Ford by 11.4%. The ad generated a 71.1% association by consumers of the "We Own Work" slogan with Ford.

Amobee requires a minimum investment of $250,000 for a month-long 3-D advertising campaign, so currently this style of ad is available mostly to bigger brands. Retail brands with physical products are great fits for 3-D ads, but companies offering services such as financial institutions may never be interested in 3-D ads. And while these ads currently offer impressive engagement rates, when their novelty wears off and they become more commonplace, those numbers may come back to earth a bit. Still, the trend toward 3-D advertising is undeniable. Facebook users could see similar posts from brands as a result of its $2 billion purchase of VR app developer Oculus Rift, and Ford was so encouraged by its F-150 campaign that they ran a similar one for the 2015 Mustang. With 3-D advertising, consumers can explore products in greater detail than ever before, at their own pace and with an emphasis on interactivity and fun. It could be closer than ever to a marketer's holy grail: advertising that doesn't feel like advertising.

SOURCES: "360 Degree Mobile Ads: It's All Around You," Fourthsource.com, September 15, 2016; "Amobee Impact Mobile Ad Formats Drive Consumer Engagement Rates," Marketwired.com, May 25, 2016; "Lessons From App Experts: What's New in Mobile Adtech? AppLift Demystifies Programmatic Spending, 3D Ads & More," by Annum Munir, Info.localytics.com, February 11, 2016; "Adello Rolls Out 3D Touch For Its Mobile Creative Ad Units," by Anne Freier, Mobyaffiliates.com, December 23, 2015; "The Future of Mobile Ads Is in 3D," by Noam Neumann, Matomy.com, November 2015; "Bringing the Ford F-150 to Life in Innovative 3D Mobile Ad Experience," Mmaglobal.com, 2015; "Team Detroit and [a•mo•bee] Bring the Ford F-150 to Life with Innovative 3D Mobile Ad Campaign," Amobee.com, 2015; "These 3-D Mobile Ads Are Grabbing Brands' Attention," by Lauren Johnson, Adweek.com, April 13, 2015; "Think Outside the Box: 3-D Mobile Ads Can Boost Engagement," by Yuyu Chen, Clickz.com, October 15, 2014.

to research products and price on mobile devices, and more likely to share experiences using social media. Mobile shoppers and buyers are more affluent than the online population in general. These demographics are averages, and mobile marketing campaigns do not need to restrict themselves to these averages. Find out where your mobile customers are congregating. Are your mobile customers likely to be using apps, and if so, what are they? Are your customers likely to be on Facebook or use Twitter? Or are your customers most likely to find you on a Google mobile search page?

Finally, consider the marketspace where you hope to succeed. What are your competitors doing on the mobile platform? Is their presence effective? Where do they place their marketing efforts: display ads on web portals, or display ads in Google search results? Or can they be found as in-app ads? What apps are they advertising in? How are they represented on Facebook Mobile? Do they also have a Twitter and/or Pinterest brand page? Do your competitors have an app that users can easily download? You'll want to be able to meet your competitors on each of the platforms they have adopted. Once you've developed an initial vision for your marketing campaign, you can develop a timeline and an action plan of how to meet the milestones identified in your timeline.

Once you have envisioned your marketing campaign and identified your market, it is time to start implementing your mobile campaign. Here are some steps to follow:

- Develop a mobile website so mobile consumers can see and buy your products. Make your mobile website social by including Facebook, Twitter, Pinterest, and other social site links.

- Develop a Facebook brand page so your social and mobile marketing efforts are integrated.

- Develop a Twitter brand page so customers can follow your posts.

- If you already use a display advertising program like Google's AdWords or a Facebook display ad account, you can create a new campaign using the same ads designed specifically for mobile platforms.

- Consider opening an iAd account and using Apple's iAd network or Google's AdMob in part because these ad networks can publish and track your ads on multiple platforms simultaneously.

- Develop marketing content that is aimed specifically at the mobile user, with videos and high levels of interactivity designed for the mobile screen.

- Measure and manage your campaign. Apple's iAd and Google's AdWords, along with many other ad networks, will host and manage your mobile campaigns. In addition, they can provide you with a host of campaign measures that will allow you to see which mobile ads and techniques are attracting the most followers, comments, and social activity concerning your brand. With this basic data you can start to manage the mobile marketing campaign by reducing expenditures on ads that do not work and increasing the budget of ads that do work.

MEASURING MOBILE MARKETING RESULTS

There are many different mobile marketing objectives, and therefore different types of mobile marketing campaigns. Some campaigns are sales-oriented, based on display and search ads, offering coupons or discounts, and taking users directly to a website where they can buy something. Measuring the results of these mobile campaigns follows similar campaigns launched on desktops. Other campaigns focus on branding, where the objective is to engage consumers in a conversation, acquire them as fans, and spread the word among their friends. You can use the framework from Figure 7.5 on page 431 to measure the results of these campaigns. The key dimensions to measure for mobile social campaigns are fan acquisition, engagement, amplification, community, brand strength (center of conversation), and sales.

Figure 7.12 illustrates how a brand-oriented marketing campaign utilizing the mobile platform and social marketing might present its effectiveness measures over a six-month period. In a branding campaign, the object is not so much sales as it is strengthening consumers' engagement with the brand. In the example provided in Figure 7.12, acquiring fans is measured by the number of unique visitors. Here you can see that over six months, visitors have risen over 60%. Engagement is reflected in the time on-site (in thousands of minutes); amplification is measured by the number of Likes, and this has expanded threefold. Community is measured by the number of

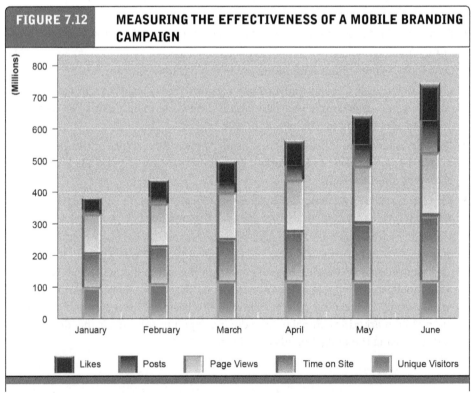

| FIGURE 7.12 | MEASURING THE EFFECTIVENESS OF A MOBILE BRANDING CAMPAIGN |

The effectiveness of a branding campaign utilizing the mobile platform and social marketing can be measured by examining the number of Likes, posts, page views, time on site, and unique visitors.

posts, suggesting fans are actively engaging with one another and the brand. Posts have risen eightfold in the period. Brand strength is best summarized in this figure as the composite picture of fan acquisition, engagement, amplification, and community measures. Measuring the impacts of this mobile campaign on ultimate sales requires going a step further and measuring which sales can be attributed to this mobile campaign.

7.4 LOCAL AND LOCATION-BASED MOBILE MARKETING

Location-based marketing is one of the fastest growing segments of the digital marketing universe. **Location-based marketing** targets marketing messages to users based on their location. Generally, location-based marketing involves marketing of location-based services. **Location-based services** involve providing services to users based on their location. Examples of location-based services are: personal navigation (How do I get there?), point-of-interest (What's that?), reviews (What's the best restaurant in the neighborhood?), friend-finder (Where are you? Where's the crowd?), and family-tracker services (Where is my child?). There is a connection, of course: the more people use their mobile devices to search for and obtain local services, the more opportunities there are for marketers to target consumers with messages at just the right moment, at just the right location, and in just the right way—not too pushy and annoying, but in a way to improve the consumer experience at the moment of local shopping and buying. This is the ideal in any event. Location-based marketing can take place on a desktop as well because browsers and marketers know your approximate location. But in this section we focus primarily on location-based mobile marketing, which is where the greatest growth and opportunities lie.

> **location-based marketing**
> targets marketing messages to users based on their location

> **location-based services**
> involve providing services to users based on their location

Experience and market research suggest that consumers want local ads, offers, information, and content. Consumers have a high likelihood of acting on local ads and purchasing the products and services offered. Because it has evolved so rapidly in the last five years, experience and research with respect to location-based marketing is a work in progress with many different platforms, providers, and techniques. Measures of effectiveness and returns on investment are being developed.

THE GROWTH OF LOCAL MARKETING

Prior to the release of Google Maps in 2005, nearly all local advertising was nondigital and provided by local newspapers, radio and television stations, local yellow pages, and billboards. Of course, some was digital, involving the websites of local merchants. In 2016, total media ad spending in the United States is $196 billion, and approximately $146 billion of this is local media spending by both national and local brands. An estimated 40% of this local advertising (about $58 billion) involves truly local firms like restaurants, grocery stores, theaters, and shoe stores marketing to their local audience. The remaining 60% of local media marketing involves large national firms marketing to local audiences, such as an ad for Coca-Cola in a local newspaper or websites created for local auto dealers by national firms. Of the $146 billion of local media spending, about 31% ($45 billion) will be spent on online marketing, and this amount is expected to grow to about $72 billion by 2020 (BIA/Kelsey, 2016).

After the introduction of Google Maps in 2005 and smartphones in 2007, online local marketing began to rapidly expand. Google Maps on desktop computers enabled the targeting of ads to users based on a general sense of their IP address and enabled merchants to display ads to users based on the general location of potential customers, usually within a several square-mile radius. IP addresses can be used to identify a city, and a neighborhood within the city, but not a zip code, street, or building. Google Maps helped users answer the question "Where can I find an Italian restaurant" in a city or section of a city from their desktop. The arrival of smartphones in 2007, and Google's mobile maps app, took this one step further. The GPS receivers in second-generation smartphones introduced in 2008 (Apple's 3G iPhone), along with other techniques, meant that a user's location (latitude and longitude) could be fairly well known by cell phone manufacturers, marketers, service providers, and carriers like AT&T and Verizon. These developments opened an entirely new growth path for local online advertising that heretofore had been confined to the desktop. In this new world, a local food market could shout out to mobile phone users as they walked by the store, offering discounts to responders, and users in turn could search for specific retail stores nearby, even checking their inventory before walking into the store.

THE GROWTH OF LOCATION-BASED (LOCAL) MOBILE MARKETING

Location-based (local) mobile marketing is currently a small part of the online marketing environment, but it is expected to triple over the next 5 years. **Figure 7.13** helps put the location-based mobile market in perspective. In 2016, total U.S. online marketing will be about $72 billion and local online marketing is expected to be a healthy and surprisingly large $45 billion. The part of local online that is location-based mobile is expected to generate an estimated $12.8 billion.

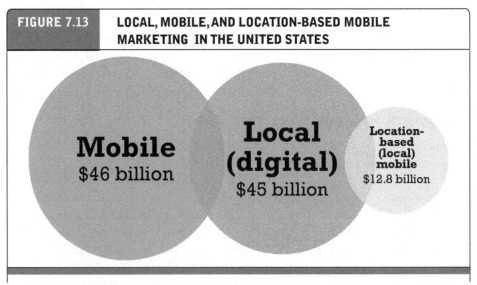

| FIGURE 7.13 | LOCAL, MOBILE, AND LOCATION-BASED MOBILE MARKETING IN THE UNITED STATES |

Mobile
$46 billion

Local (digital)
$45 billion

Location-based (local) mobile
$12.8 billion

Local online marketing in the United States will account for $45 billion in marketing expenditures in 2016, with location-based mobile expected to account for $12.8 billion of that amount.

SOURCES: Based on data from eMarketer, Inc., 2016b, 2016c, 2016e.

| FIGURE 7.14 | **U.S. LOCATION-BASED MOBILE AD FORMAT SPENDING** |

Search is the leading location-based mobile ad format.
SOURCE: Based on data from eMarketer, Inc., 2016e.

The ad formats used in local mobile marketing are familiar—search ads, display, native/social, videos, and SMS text messages. Search ads displayed as a part of user search results comprise the largest location-based mobile ad format, with marketers expected to spend an estimated $7.3 billion in 2016. The local mobile search market is dominated by Google. Social/native ads are the second largest format, generating an estimated $2.5 billion in 2016. Display ads are the third largest format, and are expected to account for about $2.2 billion in spending in 2016. Here the main players are Facebook and Google. Together, Google and Facebook account for vast majority of location-based mobile marketing. **Figure 7.14** illustrates the relative shares of location-based mobile ad format spending in the United States in 2015 (BIA/Kelsey, 2015a).

LOCATION-BASED MARKETING PLATFORMS

The key players in location-based mobile marketing are the same giants who dominate the mobile marketing environment described in a previous section, namely, Google, Facebook, Apple, Twitter, YP (formerly Yellow Pages), Pandora, and Millennial Media. Google is clearly the leading location-based marketer largely because of its widely used Google Maps app on smartphones. When a consumer searches for a location on Google Maps, it is an ideal marketing moment to pop an ad before the consumer's eyes. Google Places is a simple but effective service that provides short business profiles when users search for a specific business. Google's Android operating system has location functionality built into the system, and Google apps, like Google Maps, continuously update the user's location. Google purchased a mobile advertising firm called AdMob in 2009 and claims to be the world's largest mobile advertising firm for both Android and Apple's iOS operating systems. App developers use AdMob to provide their apps with consumer and user location information. Google also sells location information to independent marketing firms. Marketing firms use AdMob to develop full-screen rich media ads. Google's main revenue stream comes from its AdWords service, where marketers bid for keywords on Google's search engine. AdWords used to be the same whether displayed on a desktop computer or a mobile device. Google has upgraded its AdWords service to optimize ads for user contexts and devices, and to provide management of campaigns across all mobile and desktop devices. The new service is called Enhanced AdWords. For instance, if a customer searches for "pizza" on a desktop computer from work at 1 PM, he or she would be shown restaurants nearby and a quick order form. If the customer searched for "pizza" at 8 PM on a smartphone within a half-mile of a pizza restaurant, he or she might be shown a click-to-call phone number and directions to the restaurant. Pizza restaurants pay Google for the chance to show up in these searches.

Google and Apple have advantages in the location-based market: they both have developed extensive maps of Wi-Fi networks throughout the world, allowing them to develop much more precise location information than competitors.

Apple's mobile platform iAd provides location data to iOS app developers and mobile marketing firms. Like AdMob, when users click on an iAd ad, a full-screen ad appears within the app they are using. The ad can be targeted to the user's location.

LOCATION-BASED MOBILE MARKETING: THE TECHNOLOGIES

geo-aware
techniques that identify the location of a user's device and then target marketing to the device

proximity marketing
techniques that identify a perimeter around a physical location, and then target ads to users within that perimeter, recommending actions possible within the fenced-in area

Location-based services and marketing require marketers and local service providers to have a fairly precise idea of where consumer mobile devices are located. There are two general types of location-based marketing techniques: geo-aware and proximity marketing. **Geo-aware** techniques identify the location of a user's device and then target marketing to the device, recommending actions within reach (which, in itself, requires the marketer to know where relevant things like stores are located). For instance, a marketer may target smartphones within several square city blocks to alert them to available offers from participating merchants. **Proximity marketing** techniques identify a perimeter around a physical location, and then target ads to users within that perimeter, recommending actions possible within the fenced-in area. The perimeter can be from hundreds of feet (in urban areas) to several miles (in suburban locations). For instance, if users walk into the geo-fenced perimeter of a store, restaurant, or retail shop, they will receive ads from these businesses. Both of these techniques utilize the same locating technologies.

Ad networks, local-mobile marketing firms, providers of devices and services like Google and Apple, as well as phone companies use several methods for locating mobile devices, none of which are perfect, and all of which have varying degrees of accuracy. **Table 7.15** describes the major locating technologies used to enable location-based services and marketing.

GPS (Global Positioning System) location is the most accurate positioning method in theory. In practice, the signal can be weak in urban areas, nonexistent inside buildings, signals can be deflected, and it can take a long time (30–60 seconds) for the device to acquire the signal and calculate a position. When a clear signal is obtained, GPS can be accurate to within 3–10 meters under ideal conditions, but more frequently, a cell phone's GPS is accurate only to within 50 meters—half a football

TABLE 7.15	MAJOR LOCATING TECHNOLOGIES
TECHNOLOGY	DESCRIPTION
GPS	The user's device downloads GPS data from a GPS satellite. First introduced with the Apple 3G iPhone in 2008. Today, cellphones are required to broadcast their GPS location for emergency assistance purposes.
Wi-Fi	Estimates user's location within a radius of a known Wi-Fi access point.
Bluetooth low energy (BLE)	Used by Apple in iBeacon. Uses less battery power than traditional Bluetooth or GPS and more accurate than targeting through Wi-Fi triangulation.
Geo-search	Uses location information based on the user's search queries.
Cell tower	AT&T, Verizon, and other carriers are in constant contact with their devices, which allows approximation of location by triangulation and refinement of the unit's GPS location. Wireless carriers use a cell phone's MAC address to identify the phone and the location.
Sign in/registration	Estimates users' location when they self-identify their location using sign-in services or social network posts.

field. Also, users have to activate the feature, and many do not for privacy reasons. Assisted GPS (A-GPS) supplements GPS information with other information from the phone network to speed up acquisition. Nearly all smartphones use A-GPS. In Apple's iOS, users can decide whether to turn Location Services on or off. When turned on, the iOS uses GPS, cellular, and Wi-Fi networks to determine the user's approximate location to within 10 meters (30 feet) although in many situations accuracy can be much higher, around 15 feet. The user's iPhone continuously reports its position and reports to Apple servers.

Cell tower location is used by wireless telephone carriers to track the location of their devices, which is required to complete phone calls as devices pass from the range of one tower into the range of another. Cell tower location is also the basis of the wireless emergency response system in the United States. The FCC's wireless Enhanced 9-1-1 (E9-1-1) rules require wireless carriers to track cellphone locations whether or not the user has turned on location services in order to assist emergency responders in locating users who make 911 calls.

Wi-Fi location is used in conjunction with GPS signals to more accurately locate a user based on the known location of Wi-Fi transmitters, which are fairly ubiquitous in urban and suburban locations. Apple, Google, and other mobile service providers have developed global databases of wireless access points simply by driving cars around urban areas in much of the world. Google uses Street View cars to build a global database of wireless access points and their geographic location. Android applications can use this database to determine the approximate location of individuals based on the Wi-Fi networks detected by their mobile devices. All Wi-Fi devices continuously monitor the presence of local Wi-Fi networks, and mobile devices report back this data to Apple and Microsoft, along with other device manufacturers, who use similar methods. The goal of these technologies is to provide consumers and marketers with "micro-location data" accurate to within a few feet to support truly real-time, accurate, local marketing at the personal level. For instance, if you are looking at a rack of dress shirts in a retail store, an accurate positioning system could detect this, and direct you to appropriate accessories like socks and ties on surrounding shelves.

WHY IS LOCAL MOBILE ATTRACTIVE TO MARKETERS?

Consumers who seek information about local businesses using mobile devices are much more active and ready to purchase than desktop users. In part this is because desktop searchers for local information are not in as close proximity to merchants as are mobile searchers. A recent Google survey found that over 80% of U.S. consumers use smartphones and tablet computers to conduct local searches on search engines for a variety of local information such as business hours, local store addresses and directions, and availability of products at local stores. The survey found that consumers search for local information through the purchase process, and 50% of smartphone users visited a store within a day of their local search, and 18% made a purchase within a day. The survey also found that over 60% of smartphone users wanted ads customized both to their city/zip code and to their immediate surroundings (Google, 2014a).

LOCATION-BASED MARKETING TOOLS

Location-based digital marketing, like social marketing, presents students of digital marketing with a confusing array of new services, platforms, and firms that provide these services. While some local-based marketing techniques, like placing ads on Google's AdSense platform aimed at mobile customers, are relatively easy to establish for the small business owner, others require the help of mobile marketing provider firms.

A New Lexicon: Location-Based Digital Marketing Features

Location-based services involve providing services to users based on their location. Examples include personal navigation, point-of-interest, reviews, friend-finder, and family-tracker services. **Table 7.16** describes how some of these features can be used for marketing.

Proximity Marketing with Beacons

While all location-based marketing is in some sense proximity marketing, when Apple introduced iBeacon in 2013 with its iOS 7, it made it possible for retail store retailers to communicate directly and quite precisely with customers as they passed

TABLE 7.16	LOCATION-BASED MARKETING TOOLS AND CAMPAIGNS
LOCATION-BASED MARKETING TOOLS	DESCRIPTION
Geo-social-based services marketing	Users share their location with friends. Can be used for check-in services like Foursquare; friend finders; transportation services.
Location-based services marketing	Provides services to consumers looking for local services and products.
Mobile-local social network marketing based on users' location	Facebook expands local offerings of deals by local firms, display ads using News Feed. Launches Facebook Marketplace, which enables people to easily buy and sell within their local communities, in October 2016.
	Upgraded Foursquare app Swarm focuses on social updates from specific locations and sending recommendations and deals.
	Social network monitoring: sends messages within an app based on mentions of interest in products in Facebook and Twitter posts. MomentFeed allows marketers to listen to social chatter on social networks by location, then target consumers with geo-specific ads. Used by Pizza Hut, Starbucks, and local restaurants.
	Intent marketing: scanning social networks for indications of real-time consumer interest in specific products. H&M partnered with LocalResponse to promote clothing inspired by the movie *Girl With the Dragon Tattoo*.
Proximity marketing	Send messages to consumers in the area of a store or outlet to generate sales using a virtual fence around a retail location (could also be an airport, train station, or arena). Generally opt in. Whole Foods places geofences around its stores to target ads and offers to mobile users passing by.
In-store messaging	Messaging consumers while entering or browsing in a store.
	Retailers collect, analyze, and respond to customers' real-time shopping behavior. Macy's, Lord & Taylor, and Target use beacon marketing to greet customizers and offer deals.
Location-based app messaging	PayPal's mobile app detects customers near a store that offers PayPal payment options and entices them with offers to visit.

within a few feet of in-store beacons. There are many close proximity technologies such as QR codes, Wi-Fi, and NFC (Near Field Communication), but each has drawbacks in terms of precision, cost, and widespread availability. Now that Apple has adopted NFC in its hardware for Apple Pay, NFC will become a good candidate technology for close proximity marketing. Apple's iBeacon uses a different technology called Bluetooth Low Energy (BLE). Android phones also have this capability.

BLE is inexpensive to implement, and uses much less power than traditional Bluetooth. Unlike QR codes, BLE has a two-way, push-pull communication capability. Using QR codes, consumers need to show the code to a QR scanner, and then they see information on a product. With iBeacon, consumers can be contacted as soon as they walk into a store and exposed to special offers, and then when browsing the store, contacted as they pass specific areas, like the jewelry department. This all takes place automatically on the user's iPhone. Consumers can respond to these messages as well. For retailers, in-store beacon marketing is aimed at four objectives. The customer can be engaged immediately on entry to the store, and then accompanied electronically from one area to another, somewhat similar to how luxury retail stores assign a salesperson to high-end consumers. Second, beacons can be used to stimulate loyalty programs. Consumers who buy often can be noticed upon entering the store. Third, retailers can engage in flash sales, instant discounts, and other impulse marketing programs inside their physical stores. Finally, beacons can be used silently, not pushing offers or goods, but instead just gathering data directly about in-store consumer behavior.

Currently, beacon technology, essentially in-store Bluetooth devices that can communicate with user smartphones entering the store, consists of stand-alone apps, each following different standards. But several technology firms are trying to build beacon capabilities into their popular platforms. In 2015, Google announced its Eddystone open-source standard that can work with iOS or Android. In 2016, advertisers are beginning to take advantage of this technology. For example, Google has certified a proximity marketing company Proxama to provide beacon services based on Eddystone to its customers. One application involves alerting consumers to prizes, offers, and apps when they are near a beacon located near tourist attractions and transportation hubs. Facebook has rolled out Place Tips, offering free Bluetooth devices to merchants. When users are recognized as being close to a merchant, Facebook posts to their News Feed suggesting they visit the merchant or buy a product.

Reportedly, 20% of mobile marketing firms that use geo-location marketing are using beacons. One analyst claims that over 400 million beacons will be in place in five years although most will be in the non-retail world from museums to parks and tourist sites.

In 2014, Macy's started to deploy iBeacon in many of its retail stores after a successful test of the system in San Francisco and New York. Using an app from Shopkick (a marketing firm) called shopBeacon, Macy's customers who have downloaded the app receive notifications to open the app when they enter a Macy's store. Customers receive promotions, deals, and discounts. The hope is that by using proximity marketing, retail stores will be able to attract more consumers to their stores, and increase purchases from those who come to their stores. While Macy's initially planned to install 4,000 beacons throughout its retail chain, they have not revealed how many are installed, or what the results have been. Other early adopters of beacon technology include American Eagle Outfitters, Lord & Taylor, Sephora, and Apple.

However, despite the claims of proponents of beacon marketing, beacon technology has not revolutionized mobile marketing. Consumers do not appear to have much interest in the technology. Beacons require users to have Bluetooth turned on. But only 20% of smartphone users in the United States have Bluetooth turned on, and another 20% claimed their smartphones did not have Bluetooth (even though they likely did have it). Consumers are also concerned about the privacy implications of being tracked through a store or on the streets. Many do not want to be bothered with in-store notifications, and may resent the intrusion. One beacon platform firm found that pushing notices to in-store consumers actually led to a decline in the use of the app, and more than one push notice caused a 300% drop in app usage (eMarketer, Inc., 2016t).

STARTING A LOCATION-BASED MARKETING CAMPAIGN

As with all marketing campaigns, start by identifying your objectives and understand just how a location-based mobile marketing campaign might help your business. Location-based marketing is generally much more action-oriented than other forms of online marketing. A person is in a given location only for a short time, measured in minutes and hours, rarely days or weeks. If you want the consumer to do something, it's now. Does your product or service have this quality? Is there something related to a person's location that fits with your product? Is there something about your products that makes them especially attractive to a mobile audience at a specific location and time? There are very few products and services that don't have a location connection.

Next, consider the target demographic for your campaign and products. Location-aware consumers (those with mobile devices and familiar with location-based services) tend to be a younger, more educated, and wealthier demographic. They have many of the same characteristics as all mobile shoppers.

A strategic analysis of your marketspace is very important. The same questions that you would seek to answer if you were doing a nonlocation-aware mobile marketing campaign apply to a location-based marketing effort, such as examining what your competitors are doing.

Once you have envisioned your marketing campaign and identified your market, it is time to start implementing your mobile campaign. The same steps that you would follow in implementing a mobile campaign apply to location-based marketing as well. Note that you can't do everything at once—mobile-centric and location-based. Start by doing something simple like local search. Then consider more sophisticated local-based marketing tactics.

MEASURING LOCATION-BASED MARKETING RESULTS

There are a great many ways to measure the success of a mobile location-based campaign, some very sophisticated. The measures of success will vary depending on the objective of the campaign, which might be to raise the awareness of your brand among consumers, to bring customers to your retail store, or a click-to-call campaign where you want people to make reservations for a concert.

Because mobile local campaigns use the same marketing ad formats as both traditional and mobile web marketing, the basic measures of effectiveness are similar. For instance, the number of impressions (people who see an ad), click-through rate, and unique visitors are basic measures for a mobile local campaign. But mobile location-based marketing is much more personal and social than traditional web marketing

TABLE 7.17	MOBILE LOCATION-BASED MARKETING EFFECTIVENESS
SOCIAL MARKETING PROCESS	**MEASUREMENT**
Acquisition	Impressions; click-through; unique visitors to a mobile or desktop website; pages viewed; time on site.
Engagement	Inquire; reserve; visit a physical store; click-to-call; check maps for directions; register; request more information; posts and comments; responders to offers; Likes generated per visitor; click-to-call rate.
Amplification	SMS to friends; notify friends of location; share location or offers with friends.
Community	Content generated by visitors or responders; reviews; posts; positive comments generated.
Sales	Purchases; percentage increase in sales due to local mobile campaign; percentage of customers from local mobile.

or even simple mobile marketing: it's a marketing message directed to a consumer's personal mobile device based on that person's location. Local mobile marketers hope consumers will take follow-on action almost immediately—inquire, reserve, click-to-call, friend, and ultimately purchase. **Table 7.17** describes some of the basic dimensions and metrics to use when evaluating a mobile marketing campaign. The nature of the location-based campaign makes a difference for how you measure success. For instance, in a click-to-call campaign, you want to measure the volume of calls, duration of call, new versus existing customers, and the number of accidental or hostile calls.

7.5 CASE STUDY

ExchangeHunterJumper.com:
Building an International Brand with Social Marketing

T he Internet and Web have enabled thousands of business ideas to become online realities. The Internet has reduced the costs of starting a small business, and allowed small players to effectively use the same marketing and selling tools as major corporations. Small businesses usually occupy a market niche not occupied by big players or corporations. One such market niche in America, comprising about 10,000 to 30,000 players, is the high-end horse show circuit. These are people who are willing to drop $200,000 on a horse that can jump a five-foot fence with ease. This may be a very small market, but its members are highly motivated to both buy and sell horses, and they are willing to spend in the process. ExchangeHunterJumper.com is one example of how a small business focusing on a tiny niche market was able to successfully build an online brand.

According to Dagny Amber Aslin, founder and owner of ExchangeHunterJumper. com (The Exchange), a website created to help owners and professional trainers sell high-end competition horses, it's hard to "get rich" or even make money on the Internet. She adds, "There are a lot of preconceived notions ... I beat down a path previously

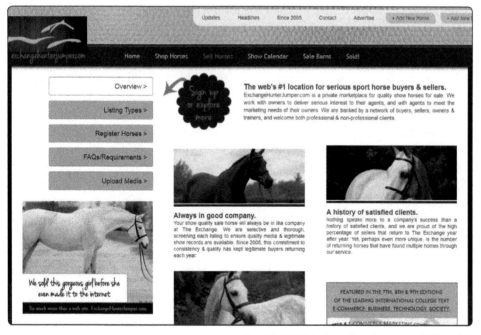

unplowed. It cost us a lot of money and we suffered many setbacks from our mistakes." Yet the site is still growing and has succeeded where others failed. How did Aslin break through and develop a site that works for professionals buying and selling alike? How did she build trust? How did she market her services?

Experience helped. Aslin started with applicable experience—in the horse world and in the world of Internet marketing. In addition to riding and competing as a child, Aslin spent several years working as a professional trainer. Working six-day weeks, including weekends, and spending most of her time outdoors riding, teaching, and competing, she saw first-hand the challenges facing professional horsemen, and she gained valuable credibility with those who would become her audience.

While working in the horse business, and learning how difficult it was to make a living, she took a part-time job as an assistant to a top California real estate agent, helping him market and sell high-end real estate in the Santa Barbara area. Among other activities, she helped him develop and expand his website. Through that experience, she realized that "selling six-figure horses and seven-figure houses are ridiculously similar—both tend to be overpriced, have emotional strings attached, require vettings and exhaustive negotiations, involve agents, and the list goes on." In 2005, when she moved from California back to the Midwest, where she had spent her childhood, The Exchange was born. Eleven years later, the equine marketing model she has built is "a customized copy" of the real estate program she assisted with in Santa Barbara.

Aslin knew that busy horse professionals needed a high-quality, reliable source of suitable mounts for their clients, but their day-to-day business lives left them little time to thoroughly search the market, and they often lacked a good grasp of modern media technology. The same dilemma applied when it came to selling high-end horses. In response, she created an organized, professional process for preparing online horse sale advertisements. It included detailed forms for sellers to fill out, and she insisted that quality photos and video be provided for each horse advertised, enabling her to turn the descriptions into accurate portrayals of each animal and its capabilities. She created a fee structure that was reasonable and affordable, and she developed a multi-channel marketing program.

Aslin understood that her business plan needed to be a living document, evolving over time based on what the market was telling her. This helped her make inroads in a traditional industry that is very resistant to change. Most horse professionals spend their days outside, and tend to do business only with those they know personally—the level of trust is very low. Most existing horse sale websites were little more than online classifieds cluttered with unreliable information. Although professional horsemen were slow to use computers and the Internet, the rise of smartphones and tablet computers has helped increase their comfort level with technology and been a huge factor in the increased online involvement of horse professionals.

The Exchange took all of these things into account, and Aslin went further. In order to remain true to her business goal of providing a *reliable* service to professionals in the horse industry that would become a source of good horses described accurately, Aslin personally reviewed all potential advertisers. In some cases she went back to sellers and insisted on higher quality photographs and video, and in other cases where she determined the horse was not as represented, she turned down their business. The initial business plan process involved strict screening, and it meant turning away money and valuing quality over quantity in every area—horses, buyers, traffic, and ads. It was a hard and expensive premise to adhere to when building a reputation from scratch, but through persistence and dedication it has worked, and today, The Exchange's reputation and "brand" has become one of its most valuable assets.

In discussing some of the obstacles she faced in getting The Exchange up and running, Aslin starts with education—her own or lack thereof, specifically in the areas of graphic design and web technology. While she knew what professional horsemen needed, she did not know how to translate that into graphic design or onto the Web. She says that looking back on the original logo and print designs is "a painful exercise," but she is happy with the current direction.

The budget was also an initial obstacle, as there wasn't a lot of money to spend up front. However, in hindsight, she believes that gave her an advantage because she had to learn what her market wanted and was able to do so without breaking the bank. Conversely, her main competitor took an opposite track, spent big up front, missed the mark with customers, and is now defunct.

In addition, she faced the negative perception among industry professionals and prospective buyers that equine Internet advertising was "worthless." Further, much of her target audience barely knew how to use a computer, didn't have e-mail addresses, and had been doing business in the same old-school manner for decades. For a few key players this worked very well, but it left a void for those outside that inner circle to move horses. Through a combination of knowledge of the marketplace, on-the-job training, perseverance, and listening to what the market was telling her, The Exchange has successfully begun to fill that void. Today, The Exchange typically manages the marketing for 160–180 horses at any given time, and anticipates that this number will likely increase to over 200 in the near future.

Here's how it works. The Exchange handles advertising for sellers and trainers across the country. In 2016, show horses advertised on The Exchange are typically priced from $60,000 to $80,000. The Exchange specializes strictly in hunter-jumper show horses, and specifically those suited for high-level competition.

Trainers/sellers who sign up for a premium listing pay a flat $250 fee for the initial advertisement and a subscription fee of $35/month, which includes a listing on The Exchange's website featuring the horse's details, photos, show record, lineage, and videos. The Exchange provides copy-writing services and professionally edits all videos supplied by sellers, hosting them on its private server and making them available to download, embed, and share. Each listing typically takes 8–10 hours to prepare. In 2012, The Exchange added a second listing alternative—a Sale Barn listing for $300 a month or $3,000 a year, that allows for listing of up to 10 horses. A three-month commitment is required, but there are no initial or other fees. Once the commitment is fulfilled, sellers can deactivate and then reactivate their Sale Barn page as needed at any time without any further charge. Aimed at high-volume operations with frequent turnover, the Sale Barn page can link to the seller's website, YouTube,

Facebook, and Twitter feeds, if available, with the goal of increasing overall brand awareness for the seller's business. Aslin designed the Sale Barn as an affordable option for professionals who might otherwise be reluctant to spend on marketing. The Sale Barn page provides sellers with a mini website and social media advertising, including three sidebar Facebook ads each week. These have the advantage of promoting not only the sellers but also have proved to be a useful promotional tool for the Sale Barn package itself, since those who click on the ad end up on the ExchangeHunterJumper website and are able to see its services first-hand and in depth. International sellers are given a slight additional discount. In 2016, the Sale Barn program has proven to be a major success, with 20 different sale barns listed, including one in Germany and one in France.

Statistics show that a horse's first month online is most successful in terms of the number of web page visits. With the addition of monthly campaign management, The Exchange helps keep each horse's marketing fresh and up to date. Updates can immediately escalate a horse's popularity as much as 30% and attract new potential buyers. Sellers are encouraged to provide updates as frequently as possible. Online videos add to the brand of the horse for sale and are especially important for young horses or those "growing into" their price tags. Updates are added to the website and promoted through various media outlets including Facebook and e-mail campaigns.

Sellers currently fill out two separate forms: a credit card registration form and an equine fact sheet. The fact sheet includes a long series of checkboxes from which sellers select preworded traits, coupled with space for additional written descriptions. This saves some production time, although writing the actual copy is still a major part of the value that The Exchange provides. To implement this option, Aslin spent time investigating form-building tools. Custom-built form solutions were likely to be too expensive, so she played with numerous online form generators and ultimately was able to find some that offered great functionality at a relatively low cost. So, for example, a seller can indicate that the horse is a "jumper" and questions specific to jumpers will be displayed.

The Exchange develops a specific marketing strategy for each horse listed. This includes reviewing information submitted, combing through a horse's official show record, considering impartial impressions, and identifying the most likely buyers. If The Exchange thinks that the photos or videos don't help to sell the horse, they advise the seller on how to improve them. This advice stems from experience in marketing all types of horses from coast to coast, and an understanding of varied buyer profiles and geographic trends that exist in the market.

Social marketing forms the core of the Exchange's marketing efforts. Starting in 2009, The Exchange began experimenting with social media including RSS feeds, YouTube, Facebook, Twitter, and Instagram. Aslin notes that when she began The Exchange, social media was not yet the phenomenon that it is today, but when its significance started to became apparent, she had no choice but to jump in and begin using it, learning as she went. The Exchange has experienced varying success with social media. For instance, The Exchange runs multiple RSS feeds through the free service,

FeedBurner, although thus far, the equestrian set does not appear to be particularly interested in RSS feed subscriptions. The company uses a professional video management system from Vzaar that hosts all of its videos, serves to most smartphones, and provides more control, branding, and flexibility than YouTube without any annoying advertisements. However, it continues to maintain a YouTube channel in order to increase exposure and to be in on YouTube "Horse for Sale" searches. Facebook has been the most resounding social media success. The Exchange now has almost 16,000 fans on Facebook. In addition, Aslin's personal Facebook friends, which number over 1,800, extend her cumulative Facebook reach to almost 18,000 friends and fans, and make her online marketing efforts even more personal. The Exchange's Twitter account has over 2,000 followers, and links with both The Exchange's Facebook page and its YouTube channel. The YouTube channel has over 60,000 views. The Exchange's Instagram feed has over 5,000 followers. Because every business is different, The Exchange's experience suggests it's important for e-commerce sites to experiment with social media to determine which outlets are most effective in reaching their specific target audiences. Currently, The Exchange spends what it characterizes as a "fair amount of money" boosting posts and promotion content on Facebook each month, which she has found has become increasingly necessary in order for her social media marketing on the platform to have any effect. Aslin has also found that posting in various Facebook Groups focused on sales of the types of horses marketed on the Exchange (currently free) often results in good "click-bait" and some increased website traffic.

To track the effectiveness of her social marketing efforts, Aslin uses various tracking systems. For instance, Google Analytics allows her to track exactly how many people are on the ExchangeHunterJumper site in real time and how they got there. Aslin has found that focusing solely on Likes is not sufficient. For example, she notes that a photo she posted advertising a horse on Facebook generated only 10 Likes, but that actually almost 150 people followed the link associated with the photo to the ExchangeHunterJumper website. She also uses a short URL service, bit.ly, to create unique URLs associated with Facebook and other social media posts that have built-in click trackers. This enables her to quickly see the collective success of her social marketing efforts; in a good month, bit.ly stats show around 8,000 click-throughs to the ExchangeHunterJumper site.

Another challenge is developing the actual social media content, which needs to be presented in such as way as to attract attention, and determining the optimal amount and timing of new content to post each day. Aslin notes that if she posts too many times a day, or posts too much content too close together, the reach of her posts seems to drop off.

Although Facebook is currently the primary social marketing platform for ExchangeHunterJumper, the firm also has loyal followers on Instagram and Twitter. Although Aslin doubts that many of these followers are actual buyers or sellers at this time, she notes that in the future they probably will be. Her site has grown up along with her clientele, and children who once drooled over ponies on her site are now, 11 years later, soon-to-be adults and, possibly, young professionals.

SOURCES: Exchangehunterjumper.com, accessed November 1, 2016; Interview with Amber Aslin, founder of ExchangeHunterJumper, November 2016, September 2014, September 2013, and September 2012.

The firm's website is also a key element of its e-commerce presence. Aslin continually reviews the design of the website with an eye to making it the most effective marketing tool possible. She built the original site herself in 2005 and updated it almost yearly in response to her target market's needs. In 2012, Aslin relaunched the site for a fifth time, and for the first time ever hired a professional web development team to convert the static HTML site into a dynamically driven content management system on the Expression Engine platform. While she was able to keep costs low by designing and developing the site's CSS layout, the advanced functionality that was desired, such as the sale horse filter that enables shoppers to sort horses based on price, location, gender, type, and size, still required a hefty five-figure investment. Aslin believes the ability to get to know the market and update the site accordingly has kept The Exchange fresh and innovative. Every iteration of the website has been focused on meeting the target market's needs. For instance, she has also spent considerable time and expense to make sure The Exchange's website, including video, works just as well on mobile devices as it does on a traditional laptop or desktop computer. Aslin has scrapped plans to create a stand-alone mobile site in favor of using responsive design techniques for The Exchange's site.

In addition to the website, The Exchange uses a variety of other marketing strategies, including e-mail campaigns, magazine advertising, and word of mouth. It ceased distributing its four-color, printed National Sales List booklet due to its high cost, and now relies almost totally on various types of online marketing. Aslin has found it has been extremely helpful to have the web development experience she has honed over the years. Here are some of her words of wisdom: She feels that entrepreneurs don't necessarily have to know how to build sites, but do need to be familiar with what is and what is not possible in site construction. It is important to understand which functions are complicated and which are not, so that overly complicated add-ons that don't really add to the user experience can be eliminated from tight budgets. It's also important to know what technology is popular now and what technology is just around the corner. Even if you think you are proficient in all the tasks you will need to launch your business, with the rapid pace of technology, you inevitably spend much of your time learning something totally new, whether you want to or not.

By paying attention to these words of wisdom, as well as to detail at every step of the marketing process, The Exchange has managed to build a successful brand, one the horse community has come to rely upon.

Case Study Questions

1. Find a site on the Web that offers classified ads for horses. Compare this site to exchangehunterjumper.com in terms of the services offered (the customer value proposition). What does The Exchange offer that other sites do not?

2. In what ways were social media effective in promoting The Exchange brand? Which media led to the highest increase in sales and inquiries? Why?

3. Make a list of all the ways The Exchange attempts to personalize its services to both buyers and sellers.

7.6 REVIEW

KEY CONCEPTS

- ■ **Understand the difference between traditional online marketing and the new social-mobile-local marketing platforms and the relationships between social, mobile, and local marketing.**

- Social, mobile, and local marketing have transformed the online marketing landscape. The major trends and concepts include:
  - The emphasis in online marketing has shifted from exposing consumers to messages toward engaging them in conversations about your brand.
  - Social marketing means all things social: listening, discussing, interacting, empathizing, and engaging the consumer.
  - Social marketing and advertising is not simply a "new ad channel," but a collection of technology-based tools for communicating with shoppers.
  - In the past, businesses could tightly control their brand messaging and lead consumers down a funnel of cues that ended in a purchase. This is no longer the case. Instead, consumer purchase decisions are increasingly driven by the conversations, choices, tastes, and opinions of the consumer's social network.
  - Social, mobile, and local marketing are the fastest growing forms of online marketing.
- Social, mobile, and local digital marketing are self-reinforcing and connected.
- Local and mobile marketing are highly related: local advertisers most often target mobile devices.
- The strong ties among social, mobile, and local marketing have significant implications for managing a marketing campaign in this new environment. When you design a social marketing campaign, you must also consider that your customers will be accessing the campaign using mobile devices, and often they will also be looking for local content.

- ■ **Understand the social marketing process from fan acquisition to sales and the marketing capabilities of social marketing platforms such as Facebook, Twitter, and Pinterest.**

- In social marketing, the objective is to encourage your potential customers to become fans of your company's products and services and engage with your business by entering into a conversation with it.
- There are five steps in the social marketing process model: fan acquisition, engagement, amplification, community, and brand strength and sales.
- Facebook is a social network that is designed to encourage people to reveal as much personal information about themselves as feasible, including activities, behavior, photos, music, movies, and purchases.
- Facebook's features are built to maximize the connections among people in the form of notifications, tagging, messaging, posting, and sharing. In many instances, the movement of personal information is so widespread that it is beyond the understanding of users.
- Social density refers to the number of interactions among members of a group and reflects the "connectedness" of a group, even if these connections are forced on users.
- Facebook has many marketing tools, including Reactions buttons, Brand Pages, News Feed ads, Right-hand sidebar ads, mobile ads, video ads, and Facebook Exchange.
- The effectiveness of Facebook ads can be measured using five stages of the social marketing model: fan acquisition, engagement, amplification, community, and ultimately brand strengthening and sales.
- Twitter is a micro-blogging social network site that allows users to send and receive 140-character messages as well as videos, photos, and article previews.

- Twitter marketing tools include Promoted Tweets, Promoted Trends, Promoted Accounts, Enhanced Profile Pages, the Twitter Amplify program, television ad retargeting, Lead Generation Cards, and app install and app engagement ads.
- Measuring the results of Twitter marketing is similar to measuring the results of Facebook and other social marketing platforms, with some minor changes to account for the unique qualities of Twitter.
- Pinterest is the social network site that provides users with an online board to which they can "pin" interesting pictures. The success of Pinterest is based in part on a shift in consumer behavior enabled by new technologies: people talk about brands using pictures rather than words.
- Pinterest marketing tools include Promoted Pins; adding a Pin It logo to your website; pinning photos to Pinterest and direct users to your website; creating theme-based Pin It boards; placing URLs to stores that you support and receive lead generation fees from; integrating your pins and boards with other social sites; networking with users and followers.
- Pinterest campaigns can be measured using the same procedures as for Facebook and Twitter. The key dimensions to measure are fan (follower) acquisition, engagement, amplification, community, and sales.
- Other social networks, such as Instagram, LinkedIn and Snapchat, provide similar advertising opportunites to marketers.
- One downside of social marketing is that brands lose a substantial amount of control over where their ads appear in terms of other content and what people say about their brands on social sites.

■ Identify the key elements of a mobile marketing campaign.

- Although still in its infancy, mobile marketing involves the use of mobile devices such as smartphones and tablet computers to display banner ads, rich media, video, games, e-mail, text messaging, in-store messaging, QuickResponse (QR) codes, and couponing.
- Mobile devices represent a radical departure from previous marketing technologies simply because the devices integrate so many human and consumer activities from telephoning or texting friends, to listening to music, watching videos, and using the Web to shop and purchase goods.
- The mobile platform has changed over the past few years, and there are now almost as many tablet users as smartphone users in the United States.
- Mobile users spend the vast majority of their time using mobile apps as opposed to mobile web browsers. Marketers need to place ads in apps where consumers spend most of their time.
- Mobile devices create a multi-screen world: smartphones, tablets, desktops, and television. The reality, and the future, of computing devices is that consumers will be multi-platform: using desktops and laptops at work and home, and smartphones and tablets at home as well as when moving about.
- The implications of the multi-device platform, or screen diversity, environment are that marketing needs to be designed for whatever device the consumer is using, and consistent branding across platforms will be important.
- Unlike social marketing, mobile marketing does not require a great deal of new marketing vocabulary. All the marketing formats available on the desktop are also available on mobile devices. With few exceptions, mobile marketing is very much like desktop marketing—except it is smaller, mobile, and with the user all the time.
- The major marketing opportunities in mobile marketing are search ads, display ads, videos and rich media, messaging (SMS/MMS/PPS), and other familiar formats like e-mail, classified, and lead generation.
- The effectiveness of mobile marketing can be measured using the dimensions of the social marketing process model: fan acquisition, engagement, amplification, community, brand strength, and sales. Traditional web-browser based metrics also can be used when measuring mobile campaigns.

■ Understand the capabilities of location-based local marketing.

- Location-based marketing is the targeting of marketing messages to users based on their location. Generally, location-based marketing involves marketing of location-based services.

- Examples of location-based services are personal navigation, point-of-interest, reviews, friend-finder, and family-tracker services.
- Location-based marketing is dependent on two technologies: accurate mapping software and mobile device geo-positioning technologies like GPS, Wi-Fi network location data, and Bluetooth low energy (BLE) technology.
- Location-based mobile marketing is currently a small part of the online marketing environment, but is expected to double over the next two years, and is growing far faster than any other form of digital advertising.
- The ad formats used in local mobile marketing are familiar—search ads, display, social/native advertising, video, and SMS text messages. A very large percentage of these local mobile ads will be delivered by search engines such as Google, and social sites such as Facebook.
- The key players in location-based mobile marketing are the same giants of advertising who dominate the mobile marketing environment: Google, Facebook, Apple, Twitter, YP (formerly Yellow Pages), Pandora, and Millennial Media.
- Geo-aware techniques identify the location of a user's device and then target marketing to the device, recommending actions within reach.
- Geo-targeting of ads involves sending ads based on the user's location.
- Proximity marketing techniques identify a perimeter around a physical location, and then target ads to users within that perimeter, recommending actions possible within the fenced-in area.
- In-store messaging involves messaging consumers while entering and browsing in a retail store. This requires a very precise calculation of location.
- Consumers who seek information about local businesses using mobile devices are much more active and ready to purchase than desktop users.
- Measuring the effectiveness of location-based mobile campaigns involves using the same techniques used for browser-based search and display ads (impressions), but also should include the dimensions of the social marketing process model such as acquisition, engagement, amplification, community, and brand strength and sales.

QUESTIONS

1. How and why has online marketing changed since 2007?
2. What are the difficulties in differentiating the social, local, and mobile marketing channels?
3. What is meant by the social marketing term *amplification,* and how is it created and measured?
4. What is meant by the term *conversation* as it applies to online marketing and how do businesses engage in a conversation?
5. What does the term *dark social* refer to?
6. Identify and describe the first step in a social marketing campaign.
7. How would you measure the brand strength of a Facebook marketing campaign?
8. How does LinkedIn differ from other social networks, and how does this impact marketing on LinkedIn?
9. Which of Facebook's various marketing tools is the most important to social marketing, and why?
10. How would you measure engagement for your Twitter marketing campaign?
11. From a business perspective, what are the disadvantages or challenges in social marketing?
12. How can marketers use Instagram for advertising?
13. How is Pinterest blurring the lines between social marketing and social e-commerce?
14. How effective are Facebook ads in comparison to other traditional online marketing channels?
15. Why is Snapchat so attractive to marketers?
16. How does marketing on LinkedIn differ from marketing on other social networks?
17. What are social ads?
18. What is social density and why is it important to social marketing?

19. What is the effect of the growing "multi-screen environment" on e-commerce and marketing?
20. What is Apple's iBeacon technology and how does it differ from using QR codes?

PROJECTS

1. Visit the websites of at least two different online companies. Make a list of the social, mobile, and local marketing efforts you see on the website. Do their pages display Like plug-ins, and/or other social network logos? Do they have a Facebook page? If so, visit the pages to see how they use their Facebook pages. Is it different from their website pages? Can you identify how the firms use mobile marketing? Use your smartphone or tablet to access their websites. Are their websites designed specifically for each platform? In conclusion, compare and critically contrast these firms, and make recommendations for how you, as a marketing manager, would improve their effectiveness.

2. Visit your Facebook page and examine the ads shown in the right margin. What is being advertised and how do you believe it is relevant to your interests or online behavior? Make a list of ads appearing in your News Feed. Are these ads appropriately targeted to you in terms of your demographics, interests, and past purchases? Go to at least two websites, and Like it or Like a product. In the next 24 hours, do you see marketing messages on Facebook related to your Likes?

3. Visit two websites of your choice and apply the social marketing process model to both. Critically compare and contrast the effectiveness of these sites in terms of the dimensions of the social marketing process. How well do these sites acquire fans, generate engagement, amplify responses, create a community, and strengthen their brands? What recommendations can you make for these sites to improve their effectiveness?

4. Identify two Pinterest brand pages. Identify how they use Pinterest marketing tools described in this chapter. Are there some tools they are not using? What recommendations can you make for these sites to improve their Pinterest marketing campaigns?

REFERENCES

Aaker, D. A. "Measuring Brand Equity Across Products and Markets." *California Management Review*, Vol 38, No. 3, pp. 102–20. (1996).

AdRoll. "The Performance Advertiser's Guide to Instagram." (2016).

AdRoll. "Facebook by the Numbers 2015." (September 2015).

Ailawadi, Kusum L., Donald R. Lehmann, and Scott A. Neslin. "Revenue Premium as an Outcome Measure of Brand Equity." *Journal of Marketing*, 67 (October), 1–17 (October 2003).

comScore. "The 2016 US Mobile App Report." (2016).

comScore. "Which Social Networks Have the Most Engaged Audience?" (April 2, 2015a).

comScore. "comScore Ranks the Top 50 U.S. Digital Media Properties for December 2014." (January 27, 2015b).

eMarketer, Inc. "US Digital Ad Spending Share, by Device, and Format, 2015–2020." (August 24, 2016a).

eMarketer, Inc. "US Mobile Ad Spending, 2015–2020." (September 1, 2016b).

eMarketer, Inc. "US Local and Digital Traditional Ad Spending, 2015–2020." (June 2, 2016c).

eMarketer, Inc. "US Social Network Ad Spending, 2015–2018." (September 1, 2016d).

eMarketer, Inc. "US Mobile Local Ad Spending 2015–2020." (June 16, 2016e).

eMarketer, Inc. "Mobile Phone Users and Penetration Worldwide, 2015–2020." (September 1, 2016f).

eMarketer, Inc. "Smartphone Users and Penetration Worldwide, 2014–2020." (September 1, 2016g).

eMarketer, Inc. "Tablet Users and Penetration Worldwide, 2015–2020." (September 1, 2016h).

eMarketer, Inc. (Cindy Liu). "Worldwide Retail Ecommerce Sales: The eMarketer Forecast for 2016." (August 2016i).

eMarketer, Inc. "UK Retail Mcommerce Sales, by Device." (October 1, 2016j).

eMarketer, Inc. (Yory Wurmser) "US Holiday Ecommerce Preview 2016: Mobile to Fuel Explosive Ecommerce Growth." (September 14, 2016m).

eMarketer, Inc. (Mark Dolliver) "US Time Spent with Media: eMarketer's Updated Estimates for Spring 2016." (June 1, 2016n).

eMarketer, Inc. "Net US Mobile Ad Revenues, by Company, 2015–2018." (September 1, 2016r).

eMarketer, Inc. "US Mobile Ad Spending by Format, 2015–2020." (September 1, 2016s).

eMarketer, Inc. "What's Going On with Beacons?" (July 15, 2016t).

eMarketer, Inc. (Cindy Liu). "Worldwide Ad Spending: eMarketer's Updated Estimates and Forecast for 2015–2020." (October 2016x).

eMarketer, Inc. "Instagram vs Snapchat Ad Revenues Worldwide, 2015–2018." (October 1, 2016y).

eMarketer, Inc. (Cindy Liu). "Worldwide Ad Spending: eMarketer's Updated Estimates for 2015." (September 2015a).

eMarketer, Inc. "Ways in Which US Smartphone vs. Tablet Owners Plan to Use Their Device When Holiday Shopping." (October 2015b).

eMarketer, Inc. "Mobile Website, App or Both." (June 2015c).

Ernoult, Emeric. "Guide to Facebook Reach: What Marketers Need to Know." Socialmediaexaminer.com (March 3, 2014).

Facebook. "Developer News: New Ways to Share, Save, and Engage." Developers.facebook.com (June 28, 2016).

Frommer, Dan. "Vine Is a Sleeping Giant (While Everyone Is Focused on Snapchat)." Qz.com (August 7, 2015).

Google, Inc. "Understanding Consumers' Local Search Behavior." (May 2014).

Google, Inc. "The New Multiscreen World." (August 2012).

IAB (Interactive Advertising Bureau). "Response Design and Ad Creative: An IAB Perspective." (September 2012).

Keller, K. L. "Conceptualizing, Measuring and Managing Customer-Based Brand Equity." *Journal of Marketing*, Vol. 57, (January 1993).

Macmillan, Douglas, and Evelyn M. Rusli. "Snapchat Is Said to Have More Than 100 Million Monthly Active Users." *Wall Street Journal* (August 26, 2014).

National Retail Federation (NRF). "2015 Holiday Consumer Spending Survey." (October 20, 2015).

Pew Research Center. "U.S. Smartphone Use in 2015." (April 1, 2015).

Protalinski, Emil. "Facebook Passes 1 Billion Mobile Daily Active Users." Venturebeat.com (July 27, 2016).

Shields, Mike. "Publishers Flock to New Instagram Stories." *Wall Street Journal* (August 12, 2016).

Simon, C. J., and M. J. Sullivan. "The Measurement and Determinants of Brand Equity: A Financial Approach." *Marketing Science*, Vol. 12, No 1, pp. 28–52. (1993).

Simply Measured. "Complete Guide to Analytics on Facebook Third Edition." (2016).

Statista.com. "Number of Unique U.S. Visitors to Tumblr between July 2012 and July 2015 (in millions)." (accessed October 30, 2015).

UnMetric. "29 Must-Know Terms for Every Social Media Analyst." (2015).

Vahl, Andrea. "Boost Posts or Promoted Posts on Facebook: Which is Better?" Socialexaminer.com (May 5, 2014).

Vega, Tanzina, and Leslie Kaufman. "The Distasteful Side of Social Media Puts Advertisers on Their Guard." *New York Times* (June 3, 2013).

CHAPTER 8

Ethics, Law, and E-commerce

After reading this chapter, you will be able to:

- Understand why e-commerce raises ethical, social, and political issues.
- Understand basic concepts related to privacy and information rights, the practices of e-commerce companies that threaten privacy, and the different methods that can be used to protect online privacy.
- Understand the various forms of intellectual property and the challenges involved in protecting it.
- Understand how the Internet is governed and why taxation of e-commerce raises governance and jurisdiction issues.
- Identify major public safety and welfare issues raised by e-commerce.

The Right to Be Forgotten:
Europe Leads on Internet Privacy

In June 2014, Google was forced to begin removing certain search engine query results in Europe after a ruling by the Court of Justice of the European Union, Europe's highest court. The ruling gives individuals the right to request that certain links to personal information found through a search of their names be removed. The court's ruling has come to be known as the "right to be forgotten" (sometimes given the acronym RTBF, or sometimes referred to as the "right to delist"). In an age where it seems there are no limits on the ability or willingness of private Internet firms to collect and dissemi-

© Lee Avison/Alamy Stock Photo

nate personal information, regardless of the user consenting to or knowing of its collection and use, the E.U.'s ruling is possibly the beginning of a new era of digital privacy based on the simple idea that individuals have a right to manage their online personal information and public image. Google, Facebook, Twitter, and many other U.S. Internet-based firms whose business models depend on virtually no limitations on the collection and use of personal information have lobbied strongly against the idea that individuals have a right to manage their personal online information. However, the European Court of Justice's decision is final, and Google, along with Yahoo, Microsoft, and others, have begun to implement the ruling. While simple in concept, the right to be forgotten can be devilishly difficult and expensive to implement in practice.

The court's decision was based on a 2010 lawsuit brought by a Spanish citizen, Mario Costeja Gonzalez, against a Spanish newspaper, and against Google Spain and Google Inc. (the American parent firm), which had linked his name with an auction notice in a newspaper that his house had been repossessed and was being sold in order to pay off debts. A Google search on Gonzalez' name returned a link to the newspaper notice as the most prominent link. Gonzalez' suit said that issues of his debt and foreclosure had been resolved years ago, and that the reference to this event was irrelevant and an invasion of his privacy as defined in the European Union Data Protection Directive—Europe's digital era privacy legislation that governs personal information in the 28 countries that make up the European Union. Gonzalez requested that the newspaper remove or alter the pages it posted on the Web and that Google Spain and Google Inc. be required to remove the link between his name and the auction notice in the newspaper. Gonzalez said he was not worried about his online image as much as the impact on his work and reputation as a lawyer, and the potential of the notice to injure his law business. There had also been thousands of other requests by Europeans asking Google to remove links to their names that they claim are inappropriate, inaccurate, no longer relevant, and interfere with their privacy.

Google and the newspaper argued that because the server providing the results for Google searches in Spain was located outside Europe, the E.U. rules and privacy legislation did not apply. Google also argued that it was a search engine that simply provided links to information stored by others, not a data repository, and that it was not responsible for the accuracy or relevance of information stored by other organizations. Consequently, Google claimed that it should not be subject to the E.U. Data Protection Directive because it pertained only to data repositories. Finally, Google argued that under European law, individuals do not have the right to request that their personal data be removed from accessibility via a search engine. In public statements, Google also said it would be difficult or impossible to respond to thousands or millions of requests to eliminate links; granting these rights would allow criminals, fraudsters, sexual predators, and corrupt public officials to rewrite history; and that it would be very expensive to respond to requests and would potentially limit innovation in the future.

In 2014, the Court of Justice ruled that E.U. data protection policies were not limited by territory and that they apply to search engines no matter where the servers are located. Second, the court found that search engines are "controllers" of individual personal data within the European Union and therefore must comply with E.U. rules. Prior to this ruling, search engines like Google had been considered merely processors of online data, and therefore exempt from data protection rules in Europe. Finally the court found that Europeans do indeed have a right to ask search engines to remove links to personal information about them (the "right to be forgotten") when that information is inaccurate, inadequate, irrelevant, or excessive. The economic interests of the search engine to provide unfettered access to personal information did not justify interfering with the individual's right to be forgotten and personal privacy.

The court also clarified that the right to be forgotten is not absolute, but would have to be balanced against other rights and obligations such as freedom of expression, freedom of the press, and the broader public interest. For instance, the court's ruling did not require the newspaper to change any of the pages in its archives. The original auction notice remains. In other cases, the public has an interest in ensuring that convicted criminals not be allowed to escape their criminal records, which are public records in most jurisdictions. Rather than a blanket right granted to whomever applies to have information removed from search engines, instead the court required a case-by-case assessment that examines the type of information, its potential for harm to the individual's private life, and the interest of the public in having access to that information. Also, for "public figures," those who have thrust themselves into public roles, such as politicians, celebrities, or business leaders, the public interest in knowing may trump the private interest in being forgotten.

As of October 15, 2016, Google said it had received over 570,000 requests from people who wanted, in aggregate, 1.73 million links to online information about them removed, and that it had removed about 43% of those links based on internal guidelines

SOURCES: "Google Transparency Report," Google.com, as of October 15, 2016; "How Italian Courts Used the Right to Be Forgotten to Put an Expiry Date on News," by Athalie Matthews, *The*

that they have developed. However, the process has proved to be problematic. Google has been criticized by various European privacy regulators for its practice of informing websites that their links are being removed from its search results, noting that this may result in even more attention to the links. In the United Kingdom, the U.K.'s Information Commissioner's Office has ordered Google to remove links to news stories about the removal of links, on the grounds that the new links defeat the purpose of the original removal. Other critics complain that the decisions should not be left in the hands of a private company.

In 2016, in response to a ruling from France's data protection authority, Google began filtering delisted links across all of its domains, even its flagship Google.com domain, when searches originate within Europe. Previously, Google had enforced the right to be forgotten only on search results from European domains, allowing residents from European countries to simply use Google's .com domain to obtain information and links that had been purged from searches on its European domains, like Google.co.uk and Google.fr. Microsoft followed suit with its Bing search engine several months later, hoping to avoid potential hefty fines and penalties. Nevertheless, determined sleuths can still use techniques such as searching through archives of online newspapers to find stories with content likely to prompt information removal requests. Also, some new data storage techniques like blockchains are very difficult to manipulate, especially to remove entries; the immutability of blockchains is often cited as one of its great strengths, but could become a weakness when complying with the right to be forgotten. Although Google may remove many links to sensitive stories, forcing the newspapers to censor their own work has dire implications for freedom of the press. Google is also appealing the ruling, arguing that one country's rulings should not apply to a country globally.

The reactions to the Court of Justice's rulings and France's efforts to extend the right to forget beyond the boundaries of Europe reflect a deep digital divide between Europe and the United States when it comes to privacy and the balance between managing personal information (privacy) and freedom of expression and the press. In Europe, many nations celebrated the ruling as a victory over arrogant U.S. Internet companies and their cavalier attitudes towards user privacy. U.S. newspapers and technologists emphasize the importance of a free press and warn against making it possible for individuals to hide their past misdoings. Perhaps the advocates for freedom of the press have a point: in 2016, an Italian court ordered an online newspaper to institute an "expiration date" on their articles, after which the content must be removed if it is requested. This marks the first time that a newspaper has been targeted in an attempt to enforce the right to be forgotten, and has ugly implications for journalism if it is not appealed. Although this ruling is extreme and not likely to become any sort of standard, there is little doubt that European views on privacy, and the idea that data belongs first and foremost to the individual, will have an impact on U.S. privacy claims and laws, especially if France's requirement that Google remove links from all its sites around the world, not just in Europe, prevails.

Guardian, September 20, 2016; "Downside of Bitcoin: A Ledger That Can't Be Corrected," by Richard Lumb, *New York Times*, September 9, 2016; "Blockchain Technologies and the EU 'Right to Be Forgotten' – An Insurmountable Tension?" by Steven Farmer, *International Business Times*, September 7, 2016; "Following Google, Microsoft Expands Right-to-Be-Forgotten Filtering for Bing in Europe," by Paul Sawers, Venturebeat.com, August 12, 2016; "A Loophole in the Right to Be Forgotten," by Samuel Gibbs and Nausicaa Renner, Cjr.org, July 26, 2016; "The Right to Be Forgotten," by Martin von Haller, Digitalbusiness.law, June 16, 2016; "Google Takes Right to Be Forgotten Battle to France's Highest Court," by Alex Hern, *The Guardian*, May 19, 2016; "Google to Extend 'Right to be Forgotten' To All Its Domains Accessed in EU," *The Guardian*, February 11, 2016; "Google Will Further Block Some European Search Results," by Mark Scott, *New York Times*, February 11, 2016; "U.K. Wants to Remove Links to Stories About Removing Links to Stories," by Sam Schechner, *Wall Street Journal*, August 20, 2015; "Google Starts Removing Search Results Under Europe's 'Right to be Forgotten'," by Sam Schechner, *Wall Street Journal*, June 26, 2014; "Google Takes Steps to Comply With 'Right to Be Forgotten' Ruling," by Mark Scott, *New York Times*, May 29, 2014; "Right to Be Forgotten? Not That Easy," by Danny Hakim, *New York Times*, May 29, 2014; "EU Court Ruling a Victory for Privacy," *Der Spiegel*, May 20, 2014; "After European Court Order, Google Works on a Tool to Remove Links," by Mark Scott, *New York Times*, May 15, 2014; "Factsheet on the 'Right to be Forgotten' Ruling," Court of Justice of the European Union, May 14, 2014; "European Court Lets Users Erase Records on Web," by David Streitfield, *New York Times*, May 13, 2014; "Daily Report: Europe Moves to Reform Rules Protecting Privacy," *New York Times*, March 13, 2014.

D etermining how or whether personal information should be retained or deleted on the Internet is just one of many ethical, social, and political issues raised by the rapid evolution of the Internet and e-commerce. For instance, as discussed in the opening case, whether individuals lose control over all personal information once it is placed on the Internet is still up for debate in the United States. In Europe, in contrast, individuals do retain rights to their personal information. These questions are not just ethical questions that we as individuals have to answer; they also involve social institutions such as family, schools, business firms, and in some cases, entire nation-states. And these questions have obvious political dimensions because they involve collective choices about how we should live and what laws we would like to live under.

In this chapter, we discuss the ethical, social, and political issues raised in e-commerce, provide a framework for organizing the issues, and make recommendations for managers who are given the responsibility of operating e-commerce companies within commonly accepted standards of appropriateness.

8.1 UNDERSTANDING ETHICAL, SOCIAL, AND POLITICAL ISSUES IN E-COMMERCE

The Internet and its use in e-commerce have raised pervasive ethical, social, and political issues on a scale unprecedented for computer technology. Entire sections of daily newspapers and weekly magazines are devoted to the social impact of the Internet. But why is this so? Why is the Internet at the root of so many contemporary controversies? Part of the answer lies in the underlying features of Internet technology itself, and the ways in which it has been exploited by business firms. Internet technology and its use in e-commerce disrupt existing social and business relationships and understandings.

Consider for instance Table 1.2 (in Chapter 1), which lists the unique features of Internet technology. Instead of considering the business consequences of each unique feature, **Table 8.1** examines the actual or potential ethical, social, and/or political consequences of the technology.

We live in an "information society," where power and wealth increasingly depend on information and knowledge as central assets. Controversies over information are often disagreements over power, wealth, influence, and other things thought to be valuable. Like other technologies, such as steam, electricity, telephones, and television, the Internet and e-commerce can be used to achieve social progress, and for the most part, this has occurred. However, the same technologies can be used to commit crimes, despoil the environment, and threaten cherished social values. Before automobiles, there was very little interstate crime and very little federal jurisdiction over crime. Likewise with the Internet: before the Internet, there was very little "cybercrime."

Many business firms and individuals are benefiting from the commercial development of the Internet, but this development also exacts a price from individuals, organizations, and societies. These costs and benefits must be carefully considered by those seeking to make ethical and socially responsible decisions in this new envi-

TABLE 8.1	UNIQUE FEATURES OF E-COMMERCE TECHNOLOGY AND THEIR POTENTIAL ETHICAL, SOCIAL, AND/OR POLITICAL IMPLICATIONS
E-COMMERCE TECHNOLOGY DIMENSION	**POTENTIAL ETHICAL, SOCIAL, AND POLITICAL SIGNIFICANCE**
Ubiquity—Internet/web technology is available everywhere: at work, at home, and elsewhere via mobile devices, anytime.	Work and shopping can invade family life; shopping can distract workers at work, lowering productivity; use of mobile devices can lead to automobile and industrial accidents. Presents confusing issues of "nexus" to taxation authorities.
Global reach—The technology reaches across national boundaries, around the Earth.	Reduces cultural diversity in products; weakens local small firms while strengthening large global firms; moves manufacturing production to low-wage areas of the world; weakens the ability of all nations—large and small—to control their information destiny.
Universal standards—There is one set of technology standards, namely Internet standards.	Increases vulnerability to viruses and hacking attacks worldwide, affecting millions of people at once. Increases the likelihood of "information" crime, crimes against systems, and deception.
Richness—Video, audio, and text messages are possible.	A "screen technology" that reduces use of text and potentially the ability to read by focusing instead on video and audio messages. Potentially very persuasive messages that may reduce reliance on multiple independent sources of information.
Interactivity—The technology works through interaction with the user.	The nature of interactivity at commercial sites can be shallow and meaningless. Customer e-mails are frequently not read by human beings. Customers do not really "co-produce" the product as much as they "co-produce" the sale. The amount of "customization" of products that occurs is minimal, occurring within predefined platforms and plug-in options.
Information density—The technology reduces information costs, and raises quality.	While the total amount of information available to all parties increases, so does the possibility of false and misleading information, unwanted information, and invasion of solitude. Trust, authenticity, accuracy, completeness, and other quality features of information can be degraded. The ability of individuals and organizations to make sense out of this plethora of information is limited.
Personalization/Customization—The technology allows personalized messages to be delivered to individuals as well as groups.	Opens up the possibility of intensive invasion of privacy for commercial and governmental purposes that is unprecedented.
Social technology—The technology enables user content generation and social networking.	Creates opportunities for cyberbullying, abusive language, and predation; challenges concepts of privacy, fair use, and consent to use posted information; creates new opportunities for surveillance by authorities and corporations into private lives.

ronment. The question is: How can you as a manager make reasoned judgments about what your firm should do in a number of e-commerce areas—from securing the privacy of your customer's clickstream to ensuring the integrity of your company's domain name?

A MODEL FOR ORGANIZING THE ISSUES

E-commerce—and the Internet—have raised so many ethical, social, and political issues that it is difficult to classify them all, and hence, complicated to see their relationship to one another. Clearly, ethical, social, and political issues are interrelated. One way to organize the ethical, social, and political dimensions surrounding e-commerce is shown in **Figure 8.1**. At the individual level, what appears as an ethical issue—"What should I do?"—is reflected at the social and political levels—"What should we as a society and government do?" The ethical dilemmas you face as a manager of a business using the Web reverberate and are reflected in social and political debates. The major ethical, social, and political issues that have developed around e-commerce over the past 10 years can be loosely categorized into four major dimensions: information rights, property rights, governance, and public safety and welfare.

Some of the ethical, social, and political issues raised in each of these areas include the following:

- **Information rights:** What rights to their own personal information do individuals have in a public marketplace, or in their private homes, when Internet technologies make information collection so pervasive and efficient? What rights do individuals have to access information about business firms and other organizations?

- **Property rights:** How can traditional intellectual property rights be enforced in an Internet world where perfect copies of protected works can be made and easily distributed worldwide in seconds?

- **Governance:** Should the Internet and e-commerce be subject to public laws? And if so, what law-making bodies have jurisdiction—state, federal, and/or international?

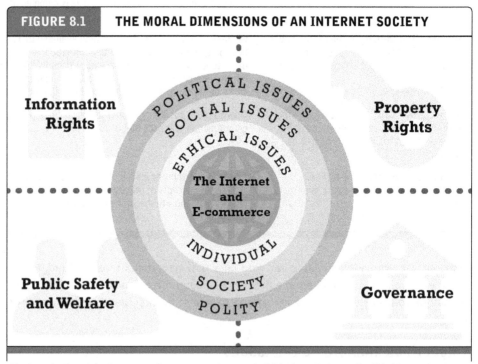

FIGURE 8.1 **THE MORAL DIMENSIONS OF AN INTERNET SOCIETY**

Information Rights

Property Rights

Public Safety and Welfare

Governance

POLITICAL ISSUES
SOCIAL ISSUES
ETHICAL ISSUES
The Internet and E-commerce
INDIVIDUAL
SOCIETY
POLITY

The introduction of the Internet and e-commerce impacts individuals, societies, and political institutions. These impacts can be classified into four moral dimensions: property rights, information rights, governance, and public safety and welfare.

- **Public safety and welfare:** What efforts should be undertaken to ensure equitable access to the Internet and e-commerce channels? Should governments be responsible for ensuring that schools and colleges have access to the Internet? Are certain online content and activities—such as pornography, gambling, or anonymous tweeting of hateful language—a threat to public safety and welfare? What about connected cars? Should mobile commerce be allowed from moving vehicles?

To illustrate, imagine that at any given moment, society and individuals are more or less in an ethical equilibrium brought about by a delicate balancing of individuals, social organizations, and political institutions. Individuals know what is expected of them, social organizations such as business firms know their limits, capabilities, and roles, and political institutions provide a supportive framework of market regulation, banking, and commercial law that provides sanctions against violators.

Now, imagine we drop into the middle of this calm setting a powerful new technology such as the Internet and e-commerce. Suddenly, individuals, business firms, and political institutions are confronted by new possibilities of behavior. For instance, individuals discover that they can download perfect digital copies of music tracks from websites without paying anyone, something that, under the old technology of CDs, would have been impossible. This can be done, despite the fact that these music tracks still legally belong to the owners of the copyright—musicians and record label companies. Then, business firms discover that they can make a business out of aggregating these digital musical tracks—or creating a mechanism for sharing musical tracks—even though they do not "own" them in the traditional sense. The record companies, courts, and Congress were not prepared at first to cope with the onslaught of online digital copying. Courts and legislative bodies will have to make new laws and reach new judgments about who owns digital copies of copyrighted works and under what conditions such works can be "shared." It may take years to develop new understandings, laws, and acceptable behavior in just this one area of social impact. In the meantime, as an individual and a manager, you will have to decide what you and your firm should do in legal "gray" areas, where there is conflict between ethical principles but no clear-cut legal or cultural guidelines. How can you make good decisions in this type of situation?

Before examining the four moral dimensions of e-commerce in greater depth, we will briefly review some basic concepts of ethical reasoning that you can use as a guide to ethical decision making, and provide general reasoning principles about the social and political issues of the Internet that you will face in the future.

BASIC ETHICAL CONCEPTS: RESPONSIBILITY, ACCOUNTABILITY, AND LIABILITY

Ethics is at the heart of social and political debates about the Internet. **Ethics** is the study of principles that individuals and organizations can use to determine right and wrong courses of action. It is assumed in ethics that individuals are free moral agents who are in a position to make choices. When faced with alternative courses of action, what is the correct moral choice? Extending ethics from individuals to business firms and even entire societies can be difficult, but it is not impossible. As long as there is

ethics
the study of principles that individuals and organizations can use to determine right and wrong courses of action

a decision-making body or individual (such as a board of directors or CEO in a business firm, or a governmental body in a society), their decisions can be judged against a variety of ethical principles.

If you understand some basic ethical principles, your ability to reason about larger social and political debates will be improved. In western culture, there are four basic principles that all ethical schools of thought share: responsibility, accountability, liability, and due process. **Responsibility** means that as free moral agents, individuals, organizations, and societies are responsible for the actions they take. **Accountability** means that individuals, organizations, and societies should be held accountable to others for the consequences of their actions. The third principle—liability—extends the concepts of responsibility and accountability to the area of law. **Liability** is a feature of political systems in which a body of law is in place that permits individuals to recover the damages done to them by other actors, systems, or organizations. **Due process** is a feature of law-governed societies and refers to a process in which laws are known and understood, and there is an ability to appeal to higher authorities to ensure that the laws have been correctly applied.

You can use these concepts immediately to understand some contemporary Internet debates. For instance, consider the 2005 U.S. Supreme Court decision in the case of *Metro-Goldwyn-Mayer Studios v. Grokster, et al.* MGM had sued Grokster and other P2P networks for copyright infringement. The court decided that because the primary and intended use of Internet P2P file-sharing services such as Grokster, StreamCast, and Kazaa was the swapping of copyright-protected music and video files, the file-sharing services should be held accountable and shut down. Although Grokster and the other networks acknowledged that the most common use of the software was for illegal digital music file-swapping, they argued that there were substantial, nontrivial uses of the same networks for legally sharing files. They also argued they should not be held accountable for what individuals do with their software, any more than Sony could be held accountable for how people use VCRs, or Xerox for how people use copying machines. Ultimately, the Supreme Court ruled that Grokster and other P2P networks could be held accountable for the illegal actions of their users if it could be shown that they intended their software to be used for illegal downloading and sharing, and had marketed the software for that purpose. The court relied on copyright laws to arrive at its decisions, but these laws reflect some basic underlying ethical principles of responsibility, accountability, and liability.

Underlying the *Grokster* Supreme Court decision is a fundamental rejection of the notion that the Internet is an ungoverned "Wild West" environment that cannot be controlled. Under certain defined circumstances, the courts will intervene into the uses of the Internet. No organized civilized society has ever accepted the proposition that technology can flaunt basic underlying social and cultural values. Through all of the industrial and technological developments that have taken place, societies have intervened by means of legal and political decisions to ensure that the technology serves socially acceptable ends without stifling the positive consequences of innovation and wealth creation. The Internet in this sense is no different, and we can expect societies around the world to exercise more regulatory control over the

---

responsibility

as free moral agents, individuals, organizations, and societies are responsible for the actions they take

accountability

individuals, organizations, and societies should be held accountable to others for the consequences of their actions

liability

a feature of political systems in which a body of law is in place that permits individuals to recover the damages done to them by other actors, systems, or organizations

due process

a process in which laws are known and understood and there is an ability to appeal to higher authorities to ensure that the laws have been correctly applied

Internet and e-commerce in an effort to arrive at a new balance between innovation and wealth creation, on the one hand, and other socially desirable objectives on the other. This is a difficult balancing act, and reasonable people will arrive at different conclusions.

ANALYZING ETHICAL DILEMMAS

Ethical, social, and political controversies usually present themselves as dilemmas. A **dilemma** is a situation in which there are at least two diametrically opposed actions, each of which supports a desirable outcome. When confronted with a situation that seems to present an ethical dilemma, how can you analyze and reason about the situation? The following is a five-step process that should help:

dilemma
a situation in which there are at least two diametrically opposed actions, each of which supports a desirable outcome

1. **Identify and clearly describe the facts.** Find out who did what to whom, and where, when, and how. In many instances, you will be surprised at the errors in the initially reported facts, and often you will find that simply getting the facts straight helps define the solution. It also helps to get the opposing parties involved in an ethical dilemma to agree on the facts.

2. **Define the conflict or dilemma and identify the higher-order values involved.** Ethical, social, and political issues always reference higher values. Otherwise, there would be no debate. The parties to a dispute all claim to be pursuing higher values (e.g., freedom, privacy, protection of property, and the free enterprise system). For example, supporters of the use of advertising networks such as DoubleClick argue that the tracking of consumer movements on the Web increases market efficiency and the wealth of the entire society. Opponents argue this claimed efficiency comes at the expense of individual privacy, and advertising networks should cease their activities or offer web users the option of not participating in such tracking.

3. **Identify the stakeholders.** Every ethical, social, and political issue has stakeholders: players in the game who have an interest in the outcome, who have invested in the situation, and usually who have vocal opinions. Find out the identity of these groups and what they want. This will be useful later when designing a solution.

4. **Identify the options that you can reasonably take.** You may find that none of the options satisfies all the interests involved, but that some options do a better job than others. Sometimes, arriving at a "good" or ethical solution may not always be a balancing of consequences to stakeholders.

5. **Identify the potential consequences of your options.** Some options may be ethically correct but disastrous from other points of view. Other options may work in this one instance but not in other similar instances. Always ask yourself, "What if I choose this option consistently over time?"

Once your analysis is complete, you can refer to the following well-established ethical principles to help decide the matter.

CANDIDATE ETHICAL PRINCIPLES

Although you are the only one who can decide which ethical principles you will follow and how you will prioritize them, it is helpful to consider some ethical principles with deep roots in many cultures that have survived throughout recorded history:

- **The Golden Rule:** Do unto others as you would have them do unto you. Putting yourself into the place of others and thinking of yourself as the object of the decision can help you think about fairness in decision making.

- **Universalism:** If an action is not right for all situations, then it is not right for any specific situation (Immanuel Kant's categorical imperative). Ask yourself, "If we adopted this rule in every case, could the organization, or society, survive?"

- **Slippery Slope:** If an action cannot be taken repeatedly, then it is not right to take at all. An action may appear to work in one instance to solve a problem, but if repeated, would result in a negative outcome. In plain English, this rule might be stated as "once started down a slippery path, you may not be able to stop."

- **Collective Utilitarian Principle:** Take the action that achieves the greater value for all of society. This rule assumes you can prioritize values in a rank order and understand the consequences of various courses of action.

- **Risk Aversion:** Take the action that produces the least harm, or the least potential cost. Some actions have extremely high failure costs of very low probability (e.g., building a nuclear generating facility in an urban area) or extremely high failure costs of moderate probability (speeding and automobile accidents). Avoid the high-failure cost actions and choose those actions whose consequences would not be catastrophic, even if there were a failure.

- **No Free Lunch:** Assume that virtually all tangible and intangible objects are owned by someone else unless there is a specific declaration otherwise. (This is the ethical "no free lunch" rule.) If something someone else has created is useful to you, it has value and you should assume the creator wants compensation for this work.

- **The New York Times Test (Perfect Information Rule):** Assume that the results of your decision on a matter will be the subject of the lead article in the *New York Times* the next day. Will the reaction of readers be positive or negative? Would your parents, friends, and children be proud of your decision? Most criminals and unethical actors assume imperfect information, and therefore they assume their decisions and actions will never be revealed. When making decisions involving ethical dilemmas, it is wise to assume perfect information markets.

- **The Social Contract Rule:** Would you like to live in a society where the principle you are supporting would become an organizing principle of the entire society? For instance, you might think it is wonderful to download illegal copies of Hollywood movies, but you might not want to live in a society that does not respect property rights, such as your property rights to the car in your driveway, or your rights to a term paper or original art.

None of these rules is an absolute guide, and there are exceptions and logical difficulties with all of them. Nevertheless, actions that do not easily pass these guidelines deserve some very close attention and a great deal of caution because the appearance of unethical behavior may do as much harm to you and your company as the actual behavior.

Now that you have an understanding of some basic ethical reasoning concepts, let's take a closer look at each of the major types of ethical, social, and political debates that have arisen in e-commerce.

8.2 PRIVACY AND INFORMATION RIGHTS

Privacy is arguably the most complex ethical issue raised by e-commerce, as well as the changing technology of human communications brought on by the Internet and mobile devices. It may be the most delicate and vexing issue of our digital age, one that will continue to evolve through this century. How can we square the ever-growing power of digital technologies to gather personal information by businesses and government with the notion that individuals have the right to be left alone, free to think what they want without fear?

In ways not anticipated by technologists or politicians, these digital technologies and devices have become the primary means of personal interaction with other people and firms. The smartphone and Internet are now at the center of social, political, and business life. In the fast-growing online marketplace for goods and services, these technologies efficiently and faithfully record human market behavior in ways never imagined. The resulting trove of personal private information gathered by online merchants has no precedent in history. Laws and regulations to govern the use of this information are weak and poorly defined. As a result, consumers often feel they have lost control over their personal information online. And, indeed, they have.

WHAT IS PRIVACY?

The claim to **privacy** rests on the moral right of individuals to be left alone, free from surveillance or interference from other individuals or organizations, including the state. Privacy is one girder supporting freedom: without the privacy required to think, write, plan, and associate independently and without fear, social and political freedom is weakened, and perhaps destroyed.

Information privacy is a subset of privacy that rests on four central premises. First, individuals have a moral right to be able to control the use of whatever information is collected about them, whether or not they consented to the gathering of information in the first place. Individuals should be able to edit, delete, and shape the use of their online personal information by governments and business firms. In this view, individuals even have the "**right to be forgotten**," as discussed in the opening case (Rosen, 2012).

Second, individuals have a moral right to know when information is being collected about them, and must give their consent prior to collecting their personal information. This is the principle of "informed consent," that people are rational actors who

privacy
the moral right of individuals to be left alone, free from surveillance or interference from other individuals or organizations, including the state

information privacy
subset of privacy that rests on four central premises, including the moral rights to control use of information collected and to know whether information is being collected, the right to personal information due process, and the right to have personal information stored in a secure manner

right to be forgotten
the claim of individuals to be able to edit and delete personal information

are informed, and who will make their own choices in the marketplace, including the decision whether to give their information in return for some benefit.

Third, individuals have a right to personal information due process. The process of collecting, sharing, disseminating personal information must be "fair" and transparent to everyone. Systems of personal information—whether public or private—must be publicly known (no secret systems), operate according to a published set of rules (terms of use policies) describing how governments and firms will use personal information, and define ways in which people can edit, correct, and shape their personal information in a system of records.

Fourth, individuals have a right to have their personal information stored in a secure manner. Personal record systems must have procedures in place to protect personal information from intrusion, hacking, and unauthorized uses.

These principles of personal information privacy are reflected in a doctrine called Fair Information Practices (FIP), established by the U.S. Federal Trade Commission (FTC) in 2000 (see **Table 8.2**). We discuss the role of the FTC in protecting personal private information further later in the chapter.

PRIVACY IN THE PUBLIC SECTOR: PRIVACY RIGHTS OF CITIZENS

The concept and practice of privacy, and its legal foundation, are very different in the public versus the private sector. In the public sector, concepts of privacy have a long history that has evolved over two centuries of court rulings, laws, and regulations in the United States and Europe. In the private sector, concepts of privacy are much more recent, and in the age of the Internet, in a state of flux, debate, and argument.

TABLE 8.2	THE FTC'S FAIR INFORMATION PRACTICE PRINCIPLES
Notice/Awareness (core principle)	Sites must disclose their information practices before collecting data. Includes identification of collector, uses of data, other recipients of data, nature of collection (active/inactive), voluntary or required, consequences of refusal, and steps taken to protect confidentiality, integrity, and quality of the data.
Choice/Consent (core principle)	There must be a choice regime in place allowing consumers to choose how their information will be used for secondary purposes other than supporting the transaction, including internal use and transfer to third parties. Opt-in/opt-out must be available.
Access/Participation	Consumers should be able to review and contest the accuracy and completeness of data collected about them in a timely, inexpensive process.
Security	Data collectors must take reasonable steps to assure that consumer information is accurate and secure from unauthorized use.
Enforcement	There must be a mechanism to enforce FIP principles in place. This can involve self-regulation, legislation giving consumers legal remedies for violations, or federal statutes and regulation.

SOURCES: Based on data from Federal Trade Commission, 1998, 2000.

The claim to individual privacy in the public sector, the arena of politics, power, and authority, is largely a European and American phenomenon that started as an attempt to limit the power of political executive leaders—kings, despots, and presidents, and to establish an acceptable relationship between citizens and their leaders.

In the United States, these claims were written into the Constitution and the Bill of Rights. The First Amendment guarantees citizens freedom of speech, association, and religion, and prohibits Congress from passing any laws that challenge these rights. The Fourth Amendment prohibits government agents from unreasonable searches and seizures of a citizen's premises, and requires a court-sanctioned warrant based on probable cause prior to any search of a person's premises. Much later, the Fourth Amendment was extended beyond the home to a very limited set of physical places. Warrants are not required when consent is given, for most motor vehicle searches, or when evidence is in plain view. The Fourteenth Amendment prohibits states from passing laws that deprive persons of life, liberty, or property, which the courts have interpreted as protecting the privacy of personal behavior in the home.

The word privacy is not mentioned in these founding documents, but it is considered to be necessary (implicit) for these amendments to mean anything. If privacy is denied, then freedom of speech, association, and religion is not possible. If one's premises cannot be protected against unreasonable searches by government, then there is no privacy.

However, relying on court decisions involving the U.S. Constitution to protect individuals has turned out to be inadequate in modern times. The founding documents of the 18th century did not define the rights of individuals to their personal information collected by government agencies in the routine course of administration, or the rights of citizens to obtain documents created by government agencies. There were no systems of records containing personal information in the 18th and 19th centuries, and government documents were routinely denied to inquisitive reporters and ordinary citizens by executive fiat and convenience. In 1974, the U.S. Congress passed an omnibus Privacy Act, which for the first time defined the privacy rights of a citizen vis-à-vis U.S. federal government record systems. The Privacy Act regulates the collection and use of data collected by federal agencies and defines fair information practices applicable to federal government systems such as those created by the Internal Revenue Service and the Social Security Administration. It's important to remember that Privacy Act protections apply only to government intrusions on privacy, not private firms' collection and use of personal information.

In addition to the Privacy Act, there are also a host of other U.S. federal laws (and state laws) that protect individuals against unreasonable government intrusions (see **Table 8.3** for a list of federal privacy laws that apply to the U.S. government). These statutes attempt to implement Fair Information Practices in a wide variety of public systems of personal information.

PRIVACY IN THE PRIVATE SECTOR: PRIVACY RIGHTS OF CONSUMERS

When the first large-scale, nationwide computerized systems began to appear in the United States in the 1960s, privacy issues and claims rose. For instance, credit card systems for the first time gave retail merchants and financial institutions the ability

TABLE 8.3	FEDERAL PRIVACY LAWS APPLICABLE TO THE U.S. GOVERNMENT
NAME	**DESCRIPTION**
Freedom of Information Act of 1966	Gives people the right to inspect information about themselves held in government files; also allows other individuals and organizations the right to request disclosure of government records based on the public's right to know.
Privacy Act of 1974, as amended	Regulates the federal government's collection, use, and disclosure of data collected by federal agencies. Gives individuals a right to inspect and correct records.
Privacy Protection Act of 1980	Prohibits government agents from conducting unannounced searches of press offices and files if no one in the office is suspected of committing a crime.
Electronic Communications Privacy Act of 1986	Makes conduct that would infringe on the security of electronic communications illegal.
Computer Security Act of 1987	Makes conduct that would infringe on the security of computer-based files illegal.
Computer Matching and Privacy Protection Act of 1988	Regulates computerized matching of files held by different government agencies.
Driver's Privacy Protection Act of 1994	Limits access to personal information maintained by state motor vehicle departments to those with legitimate business purposes. Also gives drivers the option to prevent disclosure of driver's license information to marketers and the general public.
E-Government Act of 2002	Regulates the collection and use of personal information by federal agencies.
USA Freedom Act of 2015	Imposes limits on the bulk collection by federal agencies of U.S. citizens' telecommunication metadata.

to systematically collect digital information on consumer behavior. For the first time there were very large private national databases that contained a history of whatever people purchased, from whom, and where. Large national private credit rating agencies appeared and began developing consumer credit histories, with details on personal finances from credit card to loan payments. These developments led to the first efforts to claim a right to consumer privacy. Other institutions within the education, health, and financial services sectors also began creating very large scale databases involving millions of citizens. There followed a host of U.S. federal and state legislation that applied to specific industries from credit reporting, finance, and health, to video stores (see **Table 8.4**). The pattern of protecting privacy in the United States is not with a

TABLE 8.4	U.S. PRIVACY LAWS AFFECTING PRIVATE INSTITUTIONS
NAME	DESCRIPTION
SELECTED FEDERAL PRIVACY LAWS	
Fair Credit Reporting Act of 1970	Regulates the credit investigating and reporting industry. Gives people the right to inspect credit records if they have been denied credit and provides procedures for correcting information.
Family Educational Rights and Privacy Act of 1974	Requires schools and colleges to give students and their parents access to student records and to allow them to challenge and correct information; limits disclosure of such records to third parties.
Right to Financial Privacy Act of 1978	Regulates the financial industry's use of personal financial records; establishes procedures that federal agencies must follow to gain access to such records.
Cable Communications Policy Act of 1984	Regulates the cable industry's collection and disclosure of information concerning subscribers.
Video Privacy Protection Act of 1988	Prevents disclosure of a person's video rental records without court order or consent.
Children's Online Privacy Protection Act (1998)	Prohibits deceptive practices in connection with the collection, use, and/or disclosure of personal information from and about children on the Internet.
Telephone Consumer Protection Act of 1991	Regulates telemarketing messages. FCC amended regulations to also apply to such messages delivered via text, mobile app or other forms of wireless communication to a mobile device. Requires consumers' prior express consent. for such messages.
Health Insurance Portability and Accountability Act of 1996 (HIPAA)	Requires healthcare providers and insurers and other third parties to promulgate privacy policies to consumers and establishes due process procedures.
Financial Modernization Act (Gramm-Leach-Bliley Act) (1999)	Requires financial institutions to inform consumers of their privacy policies and permits consumers some control over their records.
SELECTED STATE PRIVACY LAWS	
Online privacy policies	The California Online Privacy Protection Act of 2003 was the first state law in the United States requiring owners of commercial websites or online services to post a privacy policy. The policy must, among other things, identify the categories of PII collected about site visitors and categories of third parties with whom the information may be shared. Failure to comply can result in a civil suit for unfair business practices. Nebraska and Pennsylvania prohibit false and misleading statements in online privacy policies. At least 16 states require government websites to establish privacy policies or procedures or incorporate machine-readable privacy policies into their websites.
Spyware legislation	A number of states, including California, Utah, Arizona, Arkansas, and Virginia, among others, have passed laws that outlaw the installation of spyware on a user's computer without consent.
Disclosure of security breaches	In 2002, California enacted legislation that requires state agencies or businesses that own or license computer data with personal information to notify state residents if they experience a security breach involving that information; today, nearly every state has enacted similar legislation.
Privacy of personal information	Two states, Nevada and Minnesota, require ISPs to keep their customers' PII private unless the customer consents to disclose the information. Minnesota also requires ISPs to get permission from subscribers before disclosing information about subscribers' online surfing habits.
Data encryption	In 2007, Nevada passed the first law that requires encryption for the transmission of customer personal information. The law took effect October 1, 2008.

general privacy statute covering all record systems, but instead to develop privacy statutes piecemeal, one industry at a time, as abuses become known.

While there is a very long history to the discussion of privacy in the public sector in Europe and the United States, and a more recent history of applying these ideas to very large scale private institutions (such as banks, medical providers, and insurance companies), the same is not true of consumer privacy in public markets. E-commerce is based on online markets and transactions. Since village markets appeared in ancient villages, to the present day, there rarely has been a claim to privacy in public, open markets. Think about the local farmers markets today: few, if any, people claim that what they purchase is private, or that others should not see what they are buying or the prices they pay. Merchants in public markets collected personal information in the course of commerce. "Knowing your customer" meant knowing the name, personal preferences, interests, purchases, and background of consumers. Consumer behavior in public markets was not protected by common law or our founding documents.

Yet no one anticipated the rise of Google, Facebook, Amazon, Netflix, and other e-commerce companies that collect personal information on nearly the entire population of the United States (and the world). No one anticipated that e-commerce would involve over 200 million people in the United States; that a single company would dominate book sales (Amazon) or movie rentals (Netflix); that a single company would dominate the online search market and gather very detailed data on consumer intentions and interests (Google); or that a single firm would become a repository of the social life of billions of people (Facebook). The emergence of the Internet, the Web, and now smartphones, and their use in truly huge online markets involving most of the American population, has greatly enlarged the ability of merchants, financial institutions, and marketing firms to gather digital consumer data, use it for their own commercial purposes, and potentially abuse that information. These same forces have also spurred the growth of demands for the protection of consumer personal privacy in the digital era.

As it turns out, the Internet and the Web provide an ideal environment for both business and government to invade the personal privacy of millions of consumers on a scale unprecedented in history. Perhaps no other recent issue has raised as much widespread social and political concern as protecting the privacy of Internet users.

Information Collected by Websites

personally identifiable information (PII)
Any data that can be used to identify, locate, or contact an individual

anonymous information
Demographic and behavioral information that doesn't include any personal identifiers

As you have learned in previous chapters, e-commerce sites routinely collect a variety of information from or about consumers who visit their site and/or make purchases. Some of this data constitutes **personally identifiable information (PII)**, which is defined as any data that can be used to identify, locate, or contact an individual (Federal Trade Commission, 2000). Other data is **anonymous information**, where the identity of the person is not a name but an assigned code. This anonymous information includes demographic and behavioral information, such as age, occupation, income, zip code, ethnicity, and web browsing behavior without identifying who you are. **Table 8.5** lists just a few of the personal identifiers routinely collected by online

TABLE 8.5	PERSONAL INFORMATION COLLECTED BY E-COMMERCE SITES		
Name	Gender	Education
Address	Age	Preference data
Phone number	Occupation	Transaction data
E-mail address	Location	Clickstream data
Social security number	Location history	Device used for access
Bank accounts	Likes	Browser type
Credit card accounts	Photograph	

e-commerce sites including mobile sites and apps. This is not an exhaustive list, and in fact, many websites collect hundreds of different data points on visitors. For instance, a study of nine data brokers identified twelve broad categories of information collected by brokers, and 240 data elements from address history, to liens and political leanings, to vehicle and travel data (Federal Trade Commission, 2014). Although anonymous, this detailed information is still "personal," and a name identifier can be attached to the information quite easily. In general, however, online advertisers and merchants are less interested in your name than in your buying behavior.

Advertising networks and search engines also track the behavior of consumers across thousands of popular sites, not just at one site, via cookies, web beacons, tracking software, spyware, and other techniques. For instance, simply clicking a Like button on a website enables Facebook to track your movements across the Web.

Table 8.6 illustrates some of the major ways online firms gather information about consumers.

Key Issues in Online Privacy of Consumers

In recent polls, 90% of Americans are concerned about their online privacy, and 91% believe they have lost control over their online information (Pew Research Center, 2016a). High on the list of public concerns are four aspects of privacy: profiling (and the use of profiles to target ads), social network privacy, sharing of information by marketers, and mobile phone privacy. On the other hand, Americans have nuanced views about when it is appropriate for firms and government to gather their personal information in return for benefits. More than half (54%) of Americans thinks it acceptable to monitor employees in order to have a safer workplace, to share health information with providers and insurance companies, to share certain personal information with online social networks, and for the government to conduct surveillance of citizens in order to identify terrorists. But only 24% support a home thermostat that would track movements around the house. By large majorities, most Americans do not trust private

TABLE 8.6	THE INTERNET'S MAJOR INFORMATION-GATHERING TOOLS AND THEIR IMPACT ON PRIVACY
INTERNET CAPABILITY	**IMPACT ON PRIVACY**
Smartphones and apps	Used to track location and share photos, addresses, phone numbers, search, and other behavior to marketers.
Advertising networks	Used to track individuals as they move among thousands of websites.
Social networks	Used to gather information on user-provided content such as books, music, friends, and other interests, preferences, and lifestyles.
Cookies and supercookies	Used to track individuals at a single site. Supercookies are nearly impossible to identify or remove.
Third-party cookies (beacons)	Cookies placed by third-party advertising networks. Used to monitor and track online behavior, searches, and sites visited across thousands of sites that belong to the advertising network for the purpose of displaying "relevant" advertising.
Spyware	Can be used to record all the keyboard activity of a user, including websites visited and security codes used; also used to display advertisements to users based on their searches or other behavior.
Search engine behavioral targeting (Google and other search engines)	Uses prior search history, demographics, expressed interests, geographic, or other user-entered data to target advertising.
Deep packet inspection	Uses software installed at the ISP level to track all user clickstream behavior.
Shopping carts	Can be used to collect detailed payment and purchase information.
Forms	Online forms that users voluntarily fill out in return for a promised benefit or reward that are linked with clickstream or other behavioral data to create a personal profile.
Site transaction logs	Can be used to collect and analyze detailed information on page content viewed by users.
Search engines	Can be used to trace user statements and views on newsgroups, chat groups, and other public forums on the Web, and profile users' social and political views. Google returns name, address, and links to a map with directions to the address when a phone number is entered.
Digital wallets (single sign-on services)	Client-side wallets and software that reveal personal information to websites verifying the identity of the consumer.
Digital Rights Management (DRM)	Software (Windows Media Player) that requires users of online media to identify themselves before viewing copyrighted content.
Trusted Computing Environments	Hardware and software that controls the viewing of copyrighted content and requires users' identification, e.g., Amazon Kindle.

TABLE 8.7	INTERNET USERS' EFFORTS TO PRESERVE PRIVACY
ACTION	PERCENTAGE WHO HAVE DONE THIS
Cleared web browser history or cookies.	59%
Refused to provide information if felt wasn't relevant.	57%
Used web browser settings to disable or turn off cookies.	34%
Deleted or edited something previously posted online.	29%
Used a temporary e-mail address or user name.	25%
Provided inaccurate or false information about self.	24%
Refused to use website that required real name.	23%
Used public computer in order to browse anonymously.	12%
Attempted to get something posted online about them removed.	11%
Encrypted phone calls, text messages, or e-mail.	10%
Used proxy server, Tor, or VPN to browse Web anonymously.	9%

SOURCE: Based on data from Pew Research Center, 2015.

firms or governments to protect their information (Pew Research Center, 2016b). **Table 8.7** lists some of the ways Internet users attempt to protect their privacy.

Marketing: Profiling, Behavioral Targeting, and Retargeting

Billions of people around the world go online on an average day. Marketers would like to know who these people are, what they are interested in, and what they buy. The more precise and complete the information, the more valuable it is as a predictive and marketing tool. Armed with this information, marketers can make their ad campaigns more efficient by targeting specific ads at specific groups or individuals, and they can even adjust the ads for specific groups.

Most popular websites allow third parties—including online advertising networks such as DoubleClick, Microsoft Advertising, and others—to place "third-party" cookies and web tracking software on a visitor's computer in order to engage in profiling the user's behavior across thousands of other websites that are also members of the advertising network. **Profiling** is the creation of **data images** (a collection of data records used to create behavioral profiles of consumers) that characterize online individual and group behavior. **Anonymous profiles** identify people as belonging to highly specific and targeted groups, for example, 20- to 30-year-old males, with college degrees and incomes greater than €50,000 a year, and interested in high-fashion clothing (based on recent search engine use). **Personal profiles** add a personal e-mail address, postal address, and/or phone number to behavioral data. Increasingly, online firms are linking their online profiles to personal offline consumer data collected by database firms tracking credit card purchases, as well as established retail and catalog firms. As

profiling
the creation of digital images that characterize online individual and group behavior

data image
collection of data records used to create a behavioral profile of consumers

anonymous profiles
identify people as belonging to highly specific and targeted groups

personal profiles
add a personal e-mail address, postal address, and/or phone number to behavioral data

you learned in Chapter 6, behavioral targeting is the use of personal profile information to determine which ads a consumer will see online. Retargeting is the practice of showing consumers the same ad on many different websites they visit. For instance, if you use Google to search for a new kitchen clock, ads for kitchen clocks will follow you to Yahoo, Facebook, and thousands of other sites you browse.

The online advertising networks have added several new dimensions to established offline marketing techniques. First, they have the ability to precisely track not just consumer purchases, but all online browsing behavior at thousands of websites, including browsing book lists, filling out preference forms, and viewing content pages. Second, they can dynamically adjust what the shopper sees on screen—including prices. Third, they can build and continually refresh high-resolution data images. Most computers have hundreds of these programs installed without consumer consent or understanding.

A different kind of profiling and a more recent form of behavioral targeting is Google's results-based personalization of advertising. Google has a patent on a program that allows advertisers using Google's AdWords program to target ads to users based on their prior search histories and profiles, which Google constructs based on user searches, along with any other information the user submits to Google or that Google can obtain, such as age, demographics, region, and other online activities (such as blogging). Google also has a second patent on a program that allows Google to help advertisers select keywords and design ads for various market segments based on search histories, such as helping a clothing website create and test ads targeted at teenage females. Google uses behavioral targeting to help it display more relevant ads based on keywords. According to Google, the feature is aimed at capturing a more robust understanding of user intent, and thereby delivering a better ad. For instance, Google's Gmail, a free e-mail service, offers a powerful interface, and gigabytes of free storage. In return, Google computers read all incoming and outgoing e-mail and place "relevant" advertising in the margins of the mail. Profiles are developed on individual users based on the content in their e-mail.

Both American and European regulators have objected to Google's policy of integrating personal information from all of its services into a single personal profile, and second, failing to let users know what it is doing with their personal information (Charlton, 2013). Google claims that people who send mail to a friend's Gmail account do not have an expectation of privacy, and that anyone who sends information to a third party does not have an expectation of privacy. Privacy groups expressed concerns when Google announced in 2014 that it was purchasing Nest, the maker of digital home thermostats and smoke detection devices that are connected to the Internet. Although Nest says it is run separately from Google and that Nest accounts are not cross-linked with Google accounts, Nest admits that it does share personal information with Google when connected to Google's "Works with Nest integration" system (Gibbs, 2015a).

Facial recognition software adds a new dimension to profiling and behavioral targeting. In 2016, several uses of facial recognition are already commonplace. Facebook and Google+ use the software to automatically suggest name tags for members or their friends in photographs. Department stores, hotels, and law enforcement use this technology without consent. Originally developed as a tool to recognize terrorists in the field, local police departments have widely adopted the technology to identify wanted persons, finding it much faster than fingerprint databases (Williams, 2015). The technology is evolving rapidly: Google has applied for a patent to identify faces in online videos, and Facebook has developed a highly accurate facial recognition system called DeepFace (Singer, 2014a). It is difficult for people to detect if they are being stalked or followed by persons using facial recognition technology, and currently there are no controls over its use (Consumer Reports, 2016).

Network advertising firms argue that online profiling and targeting ads benefits both consumers and businesses. Profiling permits targeting of ads, ensuring that consumers see advertisements mostly for products and services in which they are actually interested. Businesses benefit by not paying for wasted advertising sent to consumers who have no interest in their product or service. The industry argues that by increasing the effectiveness of advertising, more advertising revenues go to the Internet, which in turn subsidizes free content on the Internet. Last, product designers and entrepreneurs benefit by sensing demand for new products and services by examining user searches and profiles.

Critics argue that profiling undermines the expectation of anonymity and privacy that most people have when using the Internet, and changes what should be a private experience into one where an individual's every move is recorded. As people become aware that their every move is being watched, they will be far less likely to explore sensitive topics, browse pages, or read about controversial issues. How can people experience freedom if they believe their every move on the Internet is being watched? In most cases, the profiling is invisible to users, and even hidden. Consumers are not notified that profiling is occurring. Profiling permits data aggregation on hundreds or even thousands of unrelated sites on the Web.

Critics debate the economic benefits of profiling because it allows firms to engage in price discrimination, charging more for goods based on, for instance, zip code, gender, and ethnicity (Singer, 2015). The cookies placed by ad networks are persistent, and they can be set to last days, months, years, or even forever. Their tracking occurs over an extended period of time and resumes each time the individual logs on to the Internet. This clickstream data is used to create profiles that can include hundreds of distinct data fields for each consumer. Associating so-called anonymous profiles with personal information is fairly easy, and companies can change policies quickly without informing the consumer. Although the information gathered by network advertisers is often anonymous (non-PII data), in many cases, the profiles derived from tracking consumers' activities on the Web are linked or merged with personally identifiable information. Anonymous behavioral data is far more valuable if it can be linked with names, offline consumer behavior, e-mail addresses, and postal addresses.

The Harm of False Data: That's Not Me!

In 2014, Thomas Robins, a California man, sued Spokeo, a company that sells personal data online to employers, and individuals looking for information on prospective partners. Robins sued based on a section of the U.S. Fair Credit Reporting Act that provides damages of up to $1,000 against data gathering firms if these reports are false and cause concrete harm, even if the harm cannot be quantified. Robins claimed the profile distributed by Spokeo was substantially erroneous, claiming that he was employed, married, had children, and held a graduate degree. None of this was true. Robins claims this false data potentially caused him to lose employment and other opportunities although he had no evidence he had experienced any real world harm. Robins also claimed the right to organize a class action group composed of people similarly harmed. A lower court agreed with Robins and his right to organize a class action suit for others similarly harmed. In May 2016, the U.S. Supreme Court decided not to decide the case, but remanded it back to the lower court with instructions to more precisely define "concrete" harm, suggesting it must actually exist and be a real harm (*Spokeo v. Robins, 578 U.S. ___ (2016)*). Real harm, the court agreed, could include intangible harms, and the risk of real harm in the future. The majority argued that mere procedural errors, like misreporting a person's zip code, or minor errors, would not constitute a real harm. Business groups support the Supreme Court's position vis-à-vis Spokeo, arguing that it would cost billions of dollars to defend against these suits, and that people should not be able to bring class action law suits without showing real harm. Privacy advocates argue that individuals should have the right to sue businesses for spreading false information about them. Currently, the law in this area of false data is still evolving (Liptak, 2016).

Social Networks: Privacy and Self Revelation

Social networks pose a unique challenge for the maintenance of personal privacy because they encourage people to reveal details about their personal lives (passions, loves, favorites, photos, videos, and personal interests), and to share them with their friends. Social networks have greatly enlarged the depth, scope, and richness of information collected by private corporations. While Google's search engine is a massive database of personal intentions, Facebook has created a massive database of friends, preferences, Likes, posts, and activities. An Austrian researcher was able to obtain his Facebook file (possible under European laws) and received a 1,222-page document of messages, photos, posts, and friends (Sengupta, 2012). Some social networkers share these personal details with everyone on the social network. On the face of it, this would seem to indicate that people who participate in social networks voluntarily give up their rights to personal privacy. How could they claim an expectation of privacy? When everything is shared, what's private?

But the reality is that many adult participants in social networks have a very keen sense of their personal privacy. Facebook is a prime example of senior management pushing the envelope of privacy, and experiencing a number of public relations reversals and growing government concern. For instance, Facebook deployed facial recognition technology without any previous notice, which compromised its users' privacy by allowing them to be tagged in photos without their consent. Researchers at Carnegie Mellon found that it is possible to identify people, even their social security numbers, based on a single Facebook photograph and using facial recognition programs (Angwin, 2011; Acquisti et al., 2011). After numerous consumer complaints, and challenges from various state attorneys general, Facebook reversed course and made it easier for users to opt out of the technology. In 2012, Facebook began pushing ads on its users based on their use of apps and offering advertisers the ability to serve ads to Facebook users even while not using Facebook. In 2013, Facebook announced a new privacy policy that it claimed clarified its use of personal information. In the new policy, Facebook claimed it could use any personal information for any purpose it wanted to. After howls of protest from users, privacy groups, and legislators, the policy was temporarily withdrawn. In 2014, Facebook changed its default privacy settings to reveal information only to friends, and allowed users to see some of the data Facebook collects about them and to edit that data. Researchers have found that actually performing these tasks is quite difficult. In early 2015, Facebook implemented new privacy policies that stipulate that it may share users' personal data with partnered sites for the delivery of targeted ads. Also in 2015 Facebook changed the privacy policy for its WhatsApp app to permit the site to own and share whatever content users post, including photos as well as messages that were supposed to disappear in a few minutes. For a review of Facebook's various positions on online privacy over the years, and public and governmental reaction to these issues, refer to the *Insight on Society* case, *Facebook and the Age of Privacy*, in Chapter 1.

The result of these public conflicts suggests that social network participants do indeed have a strong expectation of privacy in the sense that they want to control how "their" information is used. People who contribute user-generated content have a strong sense of ownership over the content that is not diminished by posting the information on a social network for one's friends. As for members who post information to everyone, not just friends, these should be seen as "public performances" where the contributors voluntarily publish their performances, just as writers or other artists. In these situations, the claim to privacy is not credible.

Mobile Devices: Location-Based Privacy Issues

As the mobile platform becomes more and more important, issues about mobile and location-based privacy are also becoming a major concern. In 2012, investigators discovered that iOS and Android apps were funneling location information to mobile advertisers, along with users' address books and photos (Bilton, 2012). As a result, the U.S. Congress opened an investigation into the privacy policies of smartphone manufacturers, along with Facebook, Pinterest, Yahoo, Google, and 30 others in the app marketplace. Twitter announced that anyone using its "Find Friends" feature on smartphones was also sending every phone number and e-mail address in their address books to the company (Sarno, 2012).

In 2011 reporters discovered that Apple iPhones and iPads and Google Android smartphones were able to track and store user location information. In 2012, Facebook launched a new mobile advertising service that tracks what apps people use on their smartphones, and what they do while using the apps. Apple and Google track users' apps also. Apple disclosed that it can target ads based on the apps that a person has downloaded, while Google does not currently do this. For instance, Facebook can target a frequent player of a game such as Words with Friends with ads using the player's Facebook News Feed, which is a major channel for Facebook ads. In 2012, investigators discovered that some cell phone companies had installed tracking devices inside phones to improve customer service. In short, smartphones, by their very nature, quickly became storehouses of personal information that users were initially unaware of.

In 2014, the U.S. Supreme Court, in a path-breaking unanimous decision, ruled that police needed a warrant prior to searching a person's cell phone for information. All mobile devices will likely receive this protection against general, warrantless police searches (Savage, 2014). An earlier decision in 2012 requires police to obtain a warrant prior to attaching GPS tracking devices to a suspect's car. In both cases, the Supreme Court found that cell phones held extensive detailed personal information, retained information for many years, and stored many different types of information. Much of a person's intimate and personal life can be stored on cell phones, or cloud servers, making them the modern equivalent of personal papers, which are protected under the Fourth Amendment to the Constitution ("right of the people to be secure in their persons, houses, papers, and effects, against unreasonable searches and seizures"). The U.S. Senate held hearings on proposed legislation (the Consumer Location Privacy Protection Act), which requires firms to notify cell phone users and obtain their consent if they want to gather location data. This legislation was never passed. The FTC signed a 20-year consent order with Snapchat after discovering the app was collecting location data contrary to Snapchat's own privacy policy.

Refer to the *Insight on Society* case, *Foursquare: Check Your Privacy at the Door*, in Chapter 5, for more discussion of some of the issues associated with mobile and location-based privacy.

Consumer Privacy Regulation: The FTC

In the United States, the FTC has taken the lead in conducting research on online privacy and recommending legislation to Congress. The FTC is a cabinet-level agency charged with promoting the efficient functioning of the marketplace by protecting consumers from unfair or deceptive practices and increasing consumer choice by promoting competition. In addition to reports and recommendations, the FTC enforces existing legislation by suing corporations it believes are in violation of federal trade laws, and in some cases, by imposing a federal monitor or reporting system to ensure the firm complies with agency rulings. The FTC also makes recommendations to Congress for new consumer privacy legislation.

informed consent
consent given with knowledge of all material facts needed to make a rational decision

opt-in model
requires an affirmative action by the consumer to allow collection and use of consumer information

opt-out model
the default is to collect information unless the consumer takes an affirmative action to prevent the collection of data

Earlier in this section we described the FTC's Fair Information Practice (FIP) principles (see Table 8.2), on which it bases its assessments of how well firms are protecting consumer privacy. The FTC's FIP principles set the ground rules for what constitutes due process privacy protection procedures at e-commerce and all other websites—including government and nonprofit websites—in the United States. Embedded within FIP principles is the concept of **informed consent** (defined as consent given with knowledge of all material facts needed to make a rational decision). There are traditionally two models for informed consent: opt-in and opt-out. The **opt-in model** requires an affirmative action by the consumer to allow collection and use of information. For instance, using opt-in, consumers would first be asked if they approved of the collection and use of information, and then directed to check a selection box if they agreed. Otherwise, the default is not to approve the collection of data. In the **opt-out model**, the default is to collect information unless the consumer takes an affirmative action to prevent the collection of data by checking a box or by filling out a form. In the United States, most e-commerce companies that offer informed consent use the opt-out model. Unless the consumer checks a box to specifically decline, information is collected. Often, the selection box is at the very bottom of the web page, where the consumer is unlikely to see it, or located within complex menus.

The FTC's FIP principles are guidelines, not laws. In the United States, for example, business firms can gather transaction information generated in the marketplace and then use that information for other purposes, without obtaining the explicit affirmative informed consent of the individual. In Europe, this would be illegal. A business in Europe cannot use marketplace transaction information for any purpose other than supporting the current transaction, unless it obtains the individual's consent in writing or by filling out an on-screen form.

However, the FTC's FIP guidelines are often used as the basis of legislation. The most important online privacy legislation to date that has been directly influenced by the FTC's FIP principles is the Children's Online Privacy Protection Act (COPPA) (1998), which requires websites to obtain parental permission before collecting information on children under 13 years of age.

In the last decade, the FTC has broadened its approach to privacy beyond notice, informed consent, and opt-in/opt-out choice requirements to include a harm-based approach, focusing on practices that are likely to cause harm or unwarranted intrusion in consumers' daily lives. In several reports the FTC has recognized the limitations of its earlier FIP approach. It has found that "informed consent" is not effective when consumers do not know about, or understand, online firms' data collection practices. Consumers do not understand, and often fear, bring tracked from one website to another. Online firms often change their privacy policies without notice, and these policies are written in obscure language that confuses consumers. The FTC has also found the distinction between personal information and anonymous information to be invalid because it is easy for firms to identify consumers personally by name, email, and address based on so-called anonymous data. As a result the FTC developed a new framework to address consumer privacy. **Table 8.8** summarizes the important aspects of this framework.

The FTC also supports a "Do Not Track" mechanism for online behavioral advertising. The mechanism would involve placing a persistent cookie on a consumer's browser and conveying its setting to sites that the browser visits to signal whether or not the consumer wants to be tracked or receive targeted advertisements. A number of bills have been introduced in Congress to implement Do Not Track, but as yet none have been passed. Refer to the *Insight on Technology* case, *Every Move You Take, Every Click You Make, We'll Be Tracking You* in Chapter 6 for a discussion of the difficulties that have developed in implementing Do Not Track.

The FTC's new aggressive policy on consumer privacy has resulted in several judgments and fines. In 2011, the FTC reached an agreement with Google concerning charges it used deceptive tactics and violated its own privacy policies when it launched its Google Buzz social network, forcing people to join the network even if they selected not to join. Under the settlement, Google agreed to start a privacy program, permit independent privacy audits for 20 years, and face $16,000 fines for every future privacy misrepresentation. This was the first time the FTC had charged a company with such violations and ordered it to start a privacy program (Federal Trade Commission, 2011).

TABLE 8.8	THE FTC'S NEW PRIVACY FRAMEWORK
PRINCIPLE	APPLICATION
Scope	Applies to all commercial entities that collect or use consumer data; not limited to those that just collect PII.
Privacy by Design	Companies should promote consumer privacy throughout the organization and at every stage of development of products and services: • Data security • Reasonable collection limits • Reasonable and appropriate data retention policies • Data accuracy • Comprehensive data management procedures
Simplified Choice	Companies should simplify consumer choice. Need not provide choice before collecting and using data for commonly accepted practices: • Product and fulfillment • Internal operations, fraud prevention • Legal compliance • First-party marketing For all other commercial data collection and use, choice is required, and should be clearly and conspicuously offered at a time and in context in which consumer is providing data. Some types of information or practices (children, financial and medical information, deep packet inspection) may require additional protection through enhanced consent. Special choice mechanism for online behavioral advertising: "Do Not Track."
Greater Transparency	Increase transparency of data practices by: • Making privacy notices clearer, shorter, and more standardized to enable better comprehension and comparison • Providing consumers with reasonable access to data about themselves • Providing prominent disclosures and obtaining express affirmative consent before using consumer data in a materially different manner than claimed when data was collected • Educating consumers about commercial data privacy practices

SOURCE: Based on data from Federal Trade Commission, 2010.

In 2012, the FTC fined Google $22.5 million for violating the agreement and for bypassing privacy settings in Apple's Safari browser in order to track users and show them advertisements. This fine—its largest civil penalty to date—followed on the heels of a concerted crackdown on tech companies for privacy violations and a separate investigation of Google for antitrust violations (Federal Trade Commission, 2012a). The FTC also reached a settlement with Facebook resolving charges that Facebook deceived its users by telling them they could keep their information on Facebook private, but then repeatedly allowing it to be shared and made public. The settlement requires Facebook to live up to its promises by giving consumers clear and prominent notice and obtaining their express consent before sharing their information beyond the user's privacy settings. It also requires Facebook to develop a comprehensive privacy program, and obtain independent biennial privacy audits for a period of 20 years (Federal Trade Commission, 2012b).

In 2012, the FTC released another report on consumer privacy. The report describes industry best practices for protecting the privacy of Americans and focuses on five areas: Do Not Track, mobile privacy, data brokers, large platform providers (advertising networks, operating systems, browsers, and social media companies), and the development of self-regulatory codes. The report called for implementation of an easy-to-use, persistent, and effective Do Not Track system; improved disclosures for use of mobile data; making it easier for people to see the files about themselves compiled by data brokers; development of a central website where data brokers identify themselves; development of a privacy policy by large platform providers to regulate comprehensive tracking across the Internet; and enforcement of self-regulatory rules to ensure firms adhere to industry codes of conduct (Federal Trade Commission, 2012c).

In 2014, the FTC issued a report on the data broker industry, which is at the heart of the online and offline privacy debate in the United States. The report found that data brokers operate without transparency, and most users have no idea how their information is being used. The report found that data brokers collect and store billions of data elements covering nearly every U.S. consumer. One of the nine data brokers studied had information on more than 1.4 billion consumer transactions and 700 billion data elements. Another broker adds more than 3 billion new data points to its database each month. The report called for legislation giving consumers more control over their personal information by creating a centralized portal where data brokers would identify themselves, describe their information collection and use practices, and provide links to access tools and opt-outs; require brokers to give consumers access to their data; provide opportunities to opt-out of data collection; describe where they get information and what inferences they make from the data; and require retailers to notify customers when they share information with data brokers (Federal Trade Commission, 2014).

The FTC's most recent emphasis is not on restricting the collection of information (as in previous eras of privacy regulation), but instead on giving consumers rights with respect to the information collected about them in large databases and its use by various businesses and agencies. This is called a "consumer rights-based" privacy policy.

Facing fines, governmental investigations, and public embarrassment over their privacy invading behaviors, with the potential loss of some business and credibility, the major players in the e-commerce industry in the United States are beginning to change some of their policies regarding the treatment of consumer data. Large Internet firms that rely on personal information (Google, Facebook, Microsoft, and many others), along with privacy advocates, are calling on Washington to develop comprehensive consumer privacy protection legislation that would clarify for consumers and business firms the meaning of privacy in the current online commercial environment (Singer, 2013). This represents a change in the meaning of privacy from "leave me alone" to "I want to know and control how my personal information is being used."

Consumer Privacy Regulation: The Federal Communications Commission (FCC)

In 2015, in the context of the controversy over net neutrality (discussed further later in this chapter), broadband Internet service providers (ISPs) such as Verizon, Comcast, and AT&T, which own the fiber optic cables and networks that are the foundation of the Internet, were classified as being like public utility services similar to telephone companies and hence subject to regulation by the FCC. In 2016, the FCC approved new privacy rules applicable to these companies. Up until this time, the focus on Internet privacy issues has centered on how websites and apps use personal information. However, these giant broadband ISPs have also had access to much of the same information, such as data on transactions, location, browsing and app usage, and even social security numbers, which they collected without user consent. The broadband ISPs have been selling this information or using it for targeted advertising, just as Google, Facebook, and hundreds of other websites and apps, do. The FCC's new regulations require broadband ISPs to notify users of their new privacy options by e-mail or on their websites and to obtain user consent to collect this information. ISPs are not allowed to offer service contingent on consumers surrendering their privacy and cannot deny service to consumers who do not permit them to collect personal information (as is typical under Terms of Service policies for websites). For the first time in the decades-long debate over Internet privacy, a U.S. federal regulatory agency declared that personal information gathered by Internet firms belongs to consumers, not the owners of the networks. The new rules do not apply to websites, which are not under FCC regulation (FCC, 2016; King, 2016).

Privacy Policies

As noted previously, one conceptual basis of American privacy law is notification and consent. It is assumed that consumers can read Terms of Use notices (or privacy policies) concerning how a website will use their personal information, and then make a rational choice to either consent to the terms of use, opt out of the data collection (if that is an option), or stop using the site. Until recently, many U.S. e-commerce companies rejected the concept of informed consent and instead simply published their information use policy on their site. Nearly all websites have Terms of Use policies that users can find if they look carefully. These Terms of Use policies are sometimes called privacy policies, and they describe how the firms will use information collected on their sites. These policies are notices, and as noted above, it is assumed that anyone who uses the site has implicitly agreed to the Terms of Use policy. A recent study reviewed 30 popular social network and community sites and found that it would take the average reader about eight hours to simply read the policy. The longest policy was SoundCloud's, with 7,961 words. Obviously a critical flaw with informed consent as the basis of privacy protections is that it assumes the average user can understand what privacy they may be giving up by using a site (Singer, 2014b; Fiesler et al., 2014). For instance, Yahoo's privacy policy begins by stating that Yahoo takes the user's privacy seriously and Yahoo does not rent, sell, or share personal information about users with others or non-affiliated companies. However, there are a number of exceptions that significantly weaken this statement. For instance, Yahoo may share the information with "trusted partners," which could be anyone that Yahoo does business with, although perhaps not a company that the user might choose to do business with. In its privacy policy, Yahoo also says it uses cookies, device identifiers, and web beacons in order to track user clickstream behavior across the Web. To opt-out of interest-based advertising, a user must sign into his or her Yahoo account and allow cookies from

TABLE 8.9	**CRITERIA TO USE WHEN EXAMINING PRIVACY POLICIES**

- Can the privacy policy be easily found, reviewed, and understood by users?
- Does the privacy policy fully disclose how personal information will and will not be used by the organization? Is information about users ever shared or sold without users' explicit permission?
- Can users decide if they want to participate?
- Can users decide and actively indicate that they agree to be profiled, tracked, or targeted?
- Can users decide how and if their sensitive information is shared?
- Are users able to change any information that they input about themselves?
- Can users decide who can access their information?
- Are users notified promptly if their information is lost, stolen, or improperly accessed?
- Can users easily report concerns and get answers?
- Do users receive a copy of all disclosures of their information?

Yahoo. U.S. businesses argue that informing consumers by publishing a terms of use policy is sufficient to establish the users' informed consent. Privacy advocates argue that many terms of use/privacy policy statements on U.S. websites are obscure and difficult to read, and legitimate just about any use of personal information.

While politicians, privacy advocates, and the Internet industry wrangle over what the rules for privacy should be, very little attention has been paid to actually measuring the strength of privacy policies for individual companies, comparing them to other companies, and understanding how privacy policies have changed over time at a specific company. Is Facebook's privacy policy worse, better, or about the same as Apple's, or Google's? Have privacy policies improved after ten years of debate, or have they deteriorated?

A recent research project provides some preliminary answers to these questions. The researchers developed a measure of privacy policies by applying 10 privacy policy principles when reviewing policies (see **Table 8.9**) (Shore and Steinman, 2015). You will recognize these principles because they derive in primary part from the FTC and Fair Information Practices doctrines previously described. The dimensions themselves were measured on a four-point scale from 0 to 4 (0 meaning the privacy policy fails to meet the criterion and 4 indicating the criterion was fully achieved).

You can use the principles in Table 8.9 as a way to measure the privacy policy of your own online business, or another firm like Facebook, or Google. You can measure a single firm at two points in time to see how its policies changed, or compare two or more firms at a single point in time. Shore and Steinman chose to look at Facebook's privacy policies over a ten-year period from 2005 to 2015. They found that Facebook's privacy policies improved from 2005 to 2009, at one point reaching 90% implementation of the criterion, and then steadily declined to 25% in 2015. The areas of notable decline were the amount of information gathered and monitored, informing users about what is shared, clearly identifying data used for profiling, giving users choices in privacy settings, providing information on how Facebook uses cookies, beacons, and weblogs to gather data, and providing an easily understood privacy policy document. The researchers noted that Facebook's privacy policy started out in 2005 with 1,000 words, and by 2015 had ballooned to over 12,000 words!

The European Data Protection Directive

In Europe, privacy protection is much stronger than it is in the United States. In the United States, private organizations and businesses are permitted to use PII gathered in commercial transactions for other business purposes without the prior consent of the consumer (so-called secondary uses of PII). In the United States, there is no federal agency charged with enforcing privacy laws. Instead, privacy laws are enforced largely through self-regulation by businesses, and by individuals who must sue agencies or companies in court to recover damages. This is expensive and rarely done. The European approach to privacy protection is more comprehensive and regulatory in nature. European countries do not allow business firms to use PII without the prior consent of consumers. They enforce their privacy laws by creating data protection agencies to pursue complaints brought by citizens and actively enforce privacy laws.

In 1998, the European Commission's Data Protection Directive went into effect, standardizing and broadening privacy protection in the E.U. nations. The Directive is based on the Fair Information Practices doctrine but extends the control individuals can exercise over their personal information. The Directive required companies to inform people when they collect information about them and to disclose how it will be stored and used. Customers had to provide their consent before a company could legally use data about them, and they had the right to access that information, correct it, and request that no further data be collected. Further, the Directive prohibited the transfer of PII to organizations or countries that do not have similarly strong privacy protection policies. This meant that data collected in Europe by American business firms could not be transferred or processed in the United States (which has weaker privacy protection laws). This would have potentially interfered with a $6.9 trillion annual trade flow in goods, services, and investment between the United States and Europe.

The U.S. Department of Commerce, working with the European Commission, developed a safe harbor framework that permits U.S. firms to move personal data from Europe to the United States. A **safe harbor** is a private self-regulating policy and enforcement mechanism that meets the objectives of government regulators and legislation but does not involve government regulation or enforcement. The United States government played a role in certifying safe harbors, however. However, in October 2015, Europe's highest court struck down the safe harbor agreement entirely, in large part due to the revelations by Edward Snowden that Facebook had shared personal information on European citizens with the National Security Agency, and therefore violated the terms of the agreement (Scott, 2015).

In 2015, the European Council approved a new E.U. General Data Protection Regulation (GDPR) to replace the existing Data Protection Directive. The new GDPR (sometimes referred to as the **Privacy Shield**) took effect in June 2016. The GDPR applies across all E.U. countries, rather than the previous situation in which each member-state regulates privacy matters within its own borders. The GDPR applies to any firm operating in any E.U. country, requires unambiguous consent to use personal data for purposes like tracking individuals across the Web, limits the ability to use data for purposes other than those for which it was collected (tertiary uses, such as constructing user profiles), and strengthens the right to be forgotten, specifically, by allowing individuals to remove personal data from social platforms like Facebook, and

safe harbor

a private self-regulating policy and enforcement mechanism that meets the objectives of government regulators and legislation but does not involve government regulation or enforcement

Privacy Shield

Another name for new European General Data Protection Regulation (GDPR)

prevent them from collecting any new information. Companies operating in the E.U. must delete personal information once it no longer serves the purpose for which it was collected. In addition, an independent ombudsman has been created to investigate complaints and enforce the policy (Drozdiak, 2016; Evans, 2015; Gibbs, 2015b; European Commission, 2014; Pearce and Clarke, 2014; European Commission, 2012). In the end, the Privacy Shield is intended to make it relatively easy for businesses collecting data on Europeans to transfer that data to servers based in the United States.

In 2016, the privacy environment has turned decidedly against American firms like Facebook, Google, and others whose business model requires near unfettered use of personal information to support advertising revenues. Five E.U. nations (Netherlands, Germany, France, Spain, and Belgium) have initiated a series of coordinated investigations into these firms' privacy and data policies.

For instance, in 2015 Belgium sued Facebook for collecting and processing data without user consent, or explaining how it would use the information (Schechner and Drozdiak, 2015). France's privacy data-protection regulator ordered Google to expand the right to be forgotten to the entire world, not just to Europeans (Schechner, 2015). Dutch, German, and Belgian authorities are investigating Facebook's combining of data from its services like Instagram and WhatsApp to target advertising, and its use of its Like buttons for tracking browsing habits across the entire Web.

Industry Self-Regulation

Federal government regulation alone is insufficient to protect consumer privacy. The technology evolves quickly, and provides marketers more tools to collect and use consumer private information before legislatures and government agencies can respond. The online industry in the United States has historically opposed online privacy legislation, arguing that industry can do a better job of protecting privacy than government. The online industry formed the Online Privacy Alliance (OPA) in 1998 to encourage self-regulation in part as a reaction to growing public concerns and the threat of legislation being proposed by the FTC and privacy advocacy groups.

OPA has developed a set of privacy guidelines that members are required to implement. The primary focus of industry efforts has been the development of online "seals" that attest to the privacy policies on a site. The Better Business Bureau (BBB), TRUSTe, WebTrust, and major accounting firms—among them PricewaterhouseCoopers' Better-Web— have established seals for websites. The TRUSTe seal is the most common on the Web. To display a seal, website operators must conform to certain privacy principles, a complaint resolution process, and monitoring by the seal originator. Nevertheless, online privacy seal programs have had a limited impact on online privacy practices. Critics argue that seal programs are not particularly effective in safeguarding privacy. In 2015, for instance, the FTC finalized a settlement in which it fined TRUSTe for failing to annually recertify privacy programs in more than 1,000 instances although claiming that it did so on its website (Davis, 2015). For these reasons, the FTC has not deemed the seal programs as "safe harbors" and the agency continues to push for legislation to enforce privacy protection principles.

The advertising network industry has also formed an industry association, the Network Advertising Initiative (NAI), to develop privacy policies. The NAI policies have two objectives: to offer consumers a chance to opt out of advertising network programs (including e-mail campaigns), and to provide consumers redress from abuses. In order to opt out, the NAI has created a website—Networkadvertising.org—where consumers can use a global opt-out feature to prevent network advertising agencies from placing their cookies on a user's computer. If a consumer has a complaint, the NAI has a link to the Truste.org website where the complaints can be filed (Network Advertising Initiative, 2010; 2011).

The AdChoices program is another industry-sponsored initiative to encourage websites to be more transparent about how they use personal information and to make it more likely that appropriate ads are shown to users by asking users themselves. An AdChoices icon appears next to ads, and clicking on this icon provides more information and the opportunity to provide feedback to the advertiser. There is no data available yet to indicate how well this program is working.

In general, industry efforts at self-regulation in online privacy have not succeeded in reducing fears of privacy invasion during online transactions, or in reducing the level of privacy invasion. At best, self-regulation has offered consumers notice about whether a privacy policy exists, but usually says little about the actual use of the information, does not offer consumers a chance to see and correct the information or control its use in any significant way, offers no promises for the security of that information, and offers no enforcement mechanism (Hoofnagle, 2005).

Technological Solutions

A number of privacy-enhancing technologies have been developed for protecting user privacy during interactions with websites such as spyware blockers, pop-up blockers, cookie managers, and secure e-mail (see **Table 8.10**). However, the most powerful tools for protecting privacy need to be built into browsers. Responding to pressure from privacy advocates, browsers now have a number of tools that can help users protect their privacy, such as eliminating third-party cookies. Potentially one of the most powerful browser-based protections is a built-in Do Not Track capability (refer to the *Insight on Technology* case, *Every Move You Take, Every Click You Make, We'll be Tracking You* in Chapter 6). Most of these tools emphasize security—the ability of individuals to protect their communications and files from illegitimate snoopers. Encryption is also potentially an important technology to preserving privacy of messages and documents. As noted above, Apple implemented encryption of its devices, and iMessage text messaging, and there are many popular apps to encrypt communications among digital devices. Private browsing is another privacy tool available in most browsers that disables browsing history and cookies. This can be useful for protecting a consumer's computer in a shared environment where several users have access to the same computer. Browsing history is still retained on the web server. Some technologies address the security aspects of privacy, especially the threat of man-in-the-middle attacks. Specialized browsers like Epic and Ice Dragon encrypt users' browsing and other data entirely, even at the server level. A very common security protocol is HTTPS, which encrypts the messages between a computer and the computer server and verifies that users are communicating with an authentic website and not an imposter site.

TABLE 8.10	TECHNOLOGICAL PROTECTIONS FOR ONLINE PRIVACY	
TECHNOLOGY	PRODUCTS	PROTECTION
Message encryption	Signal, Gdata, Whisper, Telegram, Ceerus	Apps that encrypt text and other data transferred using smartphones
Spyware blockers	Spyware Doctor, ZoneAlarm, Ad-Aware, and Spybot	Detects and removes spyware, adware, keyloggers, and other malware
Pop-up blockers	Browsers: Firefox, IE, Safari, Opera Toolbars: Google, Yahoo, MSN Add-on programs: Adblock, PopupMaster	Prevents calls to ad servers that push pop-up, pop-under, and leave-behind ads; restricts downloading of images at user request
Ad blockers	Adblock Plus; extensions to most browsers; Crystal	Prevents calls to ad servers; interferes with downloading of ad beacons
Secure e-mail	ZL Technologies, SafeMess, Hushmail.com, Pretty Good Privacy (PGP)	E-mail and document encryption
Anonymous remailers	Jack B. Nymble, Java Anonymous Proxy, Mixmaster	Send e-mail without trace
Anonymous surfing	Freedom Websecure, Anonymizer.com, Tor, GhostSurf	Surf without a trace
Cookie managers	Cookie Monster and most browsers	Prevents client computer from accepting cookies
Disk/file erasing programs	Mutilate File Wiper, Eraser, WipeFile	Completely erases hard drive and floppy files
Policy generators	OECD Privacy Policy Generator	Automates the development of an OECD privacy compliance policy
Public key encryption	PGP Desktop	Program that encrypts your mail and documents

None of these technological solutions address the core issues of consumer privacy, which have to do with what information is being collected, how it is being used, and what rights consumers have vis-à-vis their personal information.

PRIVACY PROTECTION AS A BUSINESS

As websites become more invasive and aggressive in their use of personal information, and as public concern grows, a small number of firms have sprung up to sell products that they claim will help people protect their privacy. Venture capital firms have picked up the scent and are investing in small start-up companies based on the premise that people will pay to protect their reputations. For instance, Reputation.com has received over $67 million in funding as of 2015. For as little as $14.95 a month, you can monitor what people are saying about you, or about your children, on social websites. However, these types of firms can succeed only if people are willing to pay out of pocket for privacy protection. Economists studying this issue have found that people are not willing to pay much to protect their privacy (at most about $30), and

TABLE 8.11	PRIVACY ADVOCACY GROUPS
ADVOCACY GROUP	FOCUS
Electronic Privacy Information Center (EPIC)	Washington, DC-based public interest research center focused on privacy and civil liberties issues
Privacy International	International watchdog organization focused on privacy intrusions by government and businesses
Center for Democracy and Technology (CDT)	Foundation- and business-supported group with a legislative focus
Electronic Frontier Foundation (EFF)	Nonprofit organization focused on defending user privacy, free expression, and other civil liberties
Privacy Rights Clearinghouse	Educational clearinghouse

many are willing to give up their privacy for small discounts of a few dollars (Brustein, 2012; Acquisti et al., 2009). For these reasons the privacy protection business at the retail level has not been successful.

PRIVACY ADVOCACY GROUPS

There are a number of privacy advocacy groups that monitor developments in privacy. Some of these sites are industry-supported, while others rely on private foundations and contributions. Some of the better-known sites are listed in **Table 8.11**.

LIMITATIONS ON THE RIGHT TO PRIVACY: LAW ENFORCEMENT AND SURVEILLANCE

We've emphasized that privacy in the public sector, freedom from government restrictions and searches, is very different from privacy in the private, consumer market sector. But increasingly these different realms of personal information are coming together.

Today, the online and mobile behavior, profiles, and transactions of consumers are routinely available to a wide range of government agencies and law enforcement authorities, contributing to rising fears among online consumers, and in some cases, their withdrawal from the online marketplace. The last few years have not been good for advocates of privacy, with revelations that U.S. federal government agencies have been routinely gathering cell phone call data on Americans and foreigners in the United States for a period of several years with scant judicial oversight. In 2013, Edward Snowden, a security contractor for the National Security Agency (NSA), began releasing NSA documents to *The Guardian*, a U.K. newspaper, providing a detailed description of NSA surveillance programs of both U.S. and foreign citizens. These programs were unprecedented in scope and involved wholesale collection of cell phone metadata around the world, tapping communications lines of Google, Yahoo, and other Internet services, and tapping cell phones of foreign leaders. The NSA enlisted the support of the major telecommunications carriers to give it information about Americans' phone calls and e-mail in a program called Prism. These programs were conceived in the aftermath of the terrorist attack on the United States on September 11, 2001, and were envisaged as necessary to protect the country. The programs were authorized by the USA PATRIOT Act of 2001, and subsequent amendments, and were reviewed by relevant legislative committees. Many in the computer science academic community were aware of these programs, in part because they participated in the development of techniques for discovering patterns in large data sets, as well as so-called machine learning programs. Nevertheless, the revelations alarmed average citizens who previously believed that if they did nothing wrong, surely the government would not be collecting information about them. The revelations also heightened public awareness and criticism of Internet firms like Google and Facebook, and others engaging in extensive tracking and consumer surveillance. Google, Facebook, Microsoft, and others have since tried to resist or prevent warrantless government access to their consumer data (Apuzzo et al., 2015).

Advances in technology for storing, processing, and analyzing unimaginable quantities of personal data, referred to as big data and business analytics (data mining and representation software), have further heightened perceptions that privacy is increasingly difficult to define and protect in the age of e-commerce and social networks (Kakutani, 2013; Mayer-Schonberger and Cukier, 2013).

Striking a balance between security and liberty is at the center of the privacy debate (Ford, 2013). While the Internet used to be thought of as impossible for governments to control or monitor, nothing could be actually further from the truth. Law enforcement authorities have long claimed the right under numerous statutes to monitor any form of electronic communication pursuant to a court order and judicial review and based on the reasonable belief that a crime is being committed. This includes the surveillance of consumers engaged in e-commerce. The Communications Assistance for Law Enforcement Act (CALEA), the USA PATRIOT Act, the Cyber Security Enhancement Act, and the Homeland Security Act all strengthen the ability of U.S. law enforcement agencies to monitor Internet users without their knowledge and, under certain circumstances when life is purportedly at stake, without judicial oversight. The USA PATRIOT Act, designed to combat terrorism inside the borders of the United States, permitted nearly unlimited government surveillance without court oversight, according to several senators (Savage, 2012). However, in general, requests to conduct surveillance by government agencies require the approval of a Federal Intelligence Surveillance Court (FISA court). In 2015, several provisions of the USA PATRIOT Act expired. In response, Congress passed the USA Freedom Act, which imposes some limits on the bulk collection by the National Security Agency and other U.S. intelligence agencies of U.S. citizens' telecommunications metadata, but continues to allow surveillance of individuals pursuant to a FISA court order.

There are many privacy initiatives pending before the U.S. Congress, including the Email Privacy Act, which regulates email providers; the Preserving American Privacy Act, which regulates the collection of information by drones; and the Online Communications and Geolocation Protection Act, which regulates the uses of personal geo-location data. However, at this time, it is not likely that any of these proposed bills will be enacted by Congress.

Taking matters into its own hands, in 2014, Apple introduced the iPhone 6, which offers the ability to encrypt e-mail, photos, and contacts stored on the phone using a strong end-to-end encryption algorithm (E2EE) designed to prevent third parties from reading the messages while in transit. Apple also encrypted data stored on the physical iPhone device. The device data can only be decrypted by using a passcode that only the user possesses, and Apple does not retain the key to the code. As a result, the NSA potentially could not force Apple or Google to reveal such user data. In September 2015, Apple said it could not comply with a court order to turn over text messages in real time involving an investigation of drug and gun runners (Apuzzo et al., 2015). Not surprisingly, the NSA, FBI, and other law enforcement officials are not happy with this prospect and fear that it will enable criminals and terrorists to evade surveillance. Apple and Google contend that in order for them to compete globally, they must be able to convince consumers that their data is secure, a task made more difficult as a result of the Snowden revelations (Sanger and Chen, 2014). In March 2016, the FBI announced it had cracked the iPhone device encryption without Apple's support, and in April 2016, said it would be helping local law enforcement agencies decrypt smartphone and other devices using encryption. With sufficient computing power, common encryption methods can be cracked. Read the *Insight on Technology* case: *Apple: Defender of Privacy?* for a further discussion of this issue.

Government agencies are among the largest users of private sector commercial data brokers, such as Acxiom, Experian, and TransUnion Corporation, that collect a vast amount of information about consumers from various offline and online public sources, such as public records and the telephone directory, and non-public sources, such as "credit header" information from credit bureaus (which typically contains name, aliases, birth date, social security number, current and prior addresses, and phone numbers). Acxiom is the largest private personal database in the world with records on more than 500,000 people and about 1,500 data points per person (Singer, 2012). Information contained in individual reference services' databases ranges from purely identifying information (e.g., name and phone number) to much more extensive data (e.g., driving records, criminal and civil court records, property records, and licensing records). This information can be linked to online behavior information collected from other commercial sources to compile an extensive profile of an individual's online and offline behavior.

8.3 INTELLECTUAL PROPERTY RIGHTS

Congress shall have the power to "promote the progress of science and useful arts, by securing for limited times to authors and inventors the exclusive right to their respective writings and discoveries."

—Article I, Section 8, Constitution of the United States, 1788.

Next to privacy, the most controversial ethical, social, and political issue related to e-commerce is the fate of intellectual property rights. Intellectual property encompasses all the tangible and intangible products of the human mind. As a general rule, in

INSIGHT ON TECHNOLOGY

APPLE: DEFENDER OF PRIVACY?

It's rare, in fact unprecedented, that an Internet giant would take a public stand to support the privacy of individuals from government surveillance, and then back it up by making it impossible for law enforcement agencies hunting criminals and terrorists to gain access to the personal information of these persons. But that's the position that Apple and its CEO, Tim Cook, have taken with respect to iPhones, and potentially all the cloud data Apple stores on its users. Equally unprecedented is the support being given to Apple by giant players Google, Facebook, Microsoft, and others whose very business models are based on the largely unregulated collection of personal information that is sold to advertisers.

On December 3, 2015, two terrorists attacked fellow county employees in San Bernardino, killing fourteen people. The two were ultimately killed in a gun battle with police. The terrorists used an Apple iPhone 5c in their planning and an operating system that encrypts the contents of a locked iPhone 5c and later model iPhones. If the iPhone is unlocked by the user entering the 4-digit pass code, then authorities would have access to the data. The FBI requested Apple to unlock the encryption so it could examine the phone for possible evidence. Apple refused, claiming it discards the unlock keys to its new encrypted phones. Only the owner or user of the phone can access the phone's data using their 4-digit pass code to unlock the phone. In this case, the owner was deceased and his pass code unknown. The operating system was built so that after ten tries at unlocking the phone, the data is permanently encrypted. The only other possibility would be for Apple to update the iPhone with a new operating system that would enable it to bypass the auto erase function and access the data. Apple refused to do this, even though it would work, because it

had not built such an operating system and did not have the computer code. Apple claimed computer code is like speech, and forcing a person or firm to write code was a violation of the First Amendment guarantees of freedom of speech.

In the past, Apple has provided information from its cloud storage service, which has so far remained unencrypted, to federal and state law enforcement officials pursuant to a court order. But in this instance it claimed breaking the encryption on the terrorist's cellphone would set a precedent that would threaten everyone's civil liberties.

The FBI filed a law suit against Apple demanding Apple provide the assistance needed to access the phone. Using the All Writs Act of 1789, the FBI argued it had a court order requiring Apple to provide assistance. In February 2016, a federal court agreed with the FBI, and ordered Apple to provide the FBI reasonable assistance to bypass the auto-erase function of phone. Apple appealed, but just prior to the hearing, the FBI said it had found a third party who could open the iPhone. The appeal hearing was delayed, and the question has not been decided. But going forward, it is clear that Apple and the government will clash again over the right of government investigators to access encrypted iPhone and Apple cloud information in pursuit of a lawful investigation.

In an unrelated case, a New York federal magistrate ruled that the All Writs Act could not be used to force Apple to unlock an iPhone in a drug investigation, or more generally, to force technology companies to provide access to law enforcement agencies to their products. In New York City, police officials say they have hundreds of iPhones used by criminals that cannot be unlocked. In an earlier 1977 Supreme Court case, the court determined that the All Writs Act could be used to compel the New York Telephone Company to

(continued)

install a device on a rotary phone to track the dial numbers of criminals. The CALEA Act (Communications Assistance for Law Enforcement Act, 1994), and other legislation passed in the post–9-11 era contain provisions requiring telecommunications carriers (such as Verizon and AT&T) to design and build their systems in such a way that law enforcement can gain access to communications of suspected criminals and terrorists. CALEA has been extended to include VOiP and Internet broadband traffic, but is limited, for now, to telecommunications carriers, and does not apply to manufacturers of digital devices like iPhones, or their operating systems, like Android and iOS. This is not new on the American scene: government tapping into communications among criminals and terrorists was initiated by Abraham Lincoln during the Civil War in 1862. Tapping telegraph wires was one way to combat the secessionist Confederacy. Whether electrical, electronic, or digital, the federal government has always claimed the right to monitor and record private conversations pursuant to court orders and a legitimate law enforcement action.

Throughout the controversy Tim Cook, Apple's CEO, has maintained that unlocking its iPhones would unleash a torrent of requests from governments around the world, including China and other totalitarian regimes, seeking access to the phones of their citizens. Millions of iPhone users, some in totalitarian countries, would be susceptible to government hacking of all their personal information, messages, and transactions. In addition, Cook claimed that without encryption of iPhone handset data, hackers would be able to capture all the personal information of its customers, exposing them to additional risk of financial, or even personal harm. Hackers would know, for instance, when and where consumers travelled, their schedules, health data, appointments, and contacts. These dangers, Cook claimed, weighed more heavily than dangers brought about by terrorists using iPhones to communicate with impunity.

Cook maintains that Apple has an obligation to protect its customers' data and privacy, and calls for a national debate over the privacy of personal data and how much power the government should have over personal information.

This is not the first time that Tim Cook has taken Apple in the direction of strong privacy protection. In June 2015, Cook gave a most unusual speech for a Silicon Valley executive. Cook attacked other Internet giants like Google, Facebook, Yahoo, and Microsoft for invading their customers' privacy. Apple, he said, rejected the idea that customers have to make a trade-off between privacy and security. Cook believes people have a fundamental right to privacy. Some of the most prominent firms in Silicon Valley, Cook argued, lull their customers into giving up a treasure of personal information in order to receive some service, like cloud storage, social networking, or photo services for "free." In fact, Cook argued, the trade-off comes at a high cost to the consumer in the form of the loss of privacy and fear about what might become of their personal information. In the end, he said, consumers will regret the trade. These companies, he noted, are gobbling up everything they can learn about consumers and trying to monetize it by selling it to advertisers. Cook's strong statements on the importance of privacy are contrary to the views of Mark Zuckerberg, founder and CEO of Facebook, most famously summarized in his January 2011 interview arguing that the age of privacy is over (see the Chapter 1 *Insight on Society* case, *Facebook and the Age of Privacy*). Google, in turn, has built its many apps from search to Google Docs to Gmail on the premise that monitoring the behavior and writing of its users on all platforms, then integrating the data and selling it to advertisers is a successful business model that improves the customer experience.

Critics point to the many ironies in Apple's position. Apple's iPhone platform provides the technical platform for the massive invasion of privacy resulting from Google's mobile search engine and Facebook's mobile social network.

Both of these firms derive from a very significant portion of their ad revenue from mobile advertising targeted to individuals based on their personal information. If Google and Facebook could not show ads on the iPhone platform, they would not provide their services, and instead remain available solely on the Web. This would reduce the value of the iPhone platform and lead to reduced sales of the devices. This kind of commercial privacy invasion may annoy Cook, but Apple allows it go on because it helps sell iPhones. In addition, millions of apps on iOS devices gather data on users, and sell the information to marketers. If commercial invasion of privacy was not allowed, then who would build apps for the iPhone platform? Other critics point to Cook's claim that allowing the government to access the iPhones of criminals, even with a court order, would endanger millions of iPhone users around the world by encouraging governments to monitor their citizens' communications. Worse, if Apple was forced to build a back door, it would inevitably be discovered by hackers, posing further risks for customers.

Are these real risks? Possibly. But there is also the risk that should the iPhone become the preferred and protected communication tool for criminals and terrorists, beyond government surveillance and monitoring, millions of Apple customers, not to mention millions of others, would become more vulnerable to criminals and terrorist attacks.

But Cook, along with the other Internet titans, may be looking towards the future. Tomorrow's smartphone will be quite different from today's. New technologies such as proactive assistants will be gathering your personal information, and predictive analytics will be coming up with suggestions for your car trips, your exercise routine, and your appointments without your prompting. The amount of personal information that smartphone users commit to their handsets, and cloud backup servers, is likely to grow exponentially in the next five years. This incredibly convenient device will contain nearly all the personal private information that customers generate in the course of their life and travels.

Most observers believe the dispute will ultimately go before the Supreme Court, which will have to balance the interests of government gaining access to private information for law enforcement purposes, the interests of consumers to privacy, and the interests of firms like Apple and Google, whose business model is based on consumers committing more and more of their personal information to digital devices. Congress will weigh in as well, trying to establish law in a world of new digital devices where the old laws governing telecommunication carriers may not be applicable, or may need extension to cover not just phone systems, but all digital devices that connect to the Internet. Shareholders may also have a say in the outcome of the coming debate. Making a product that is a protected communications device for terrorists and criminals may not be a promising marketing plan.

SOURCES: "Why the FBI Breach of the iPhone Is a Win for Users," by Christopher Mims, *Wall Street Journal*, April 4, 2016; "Google Also Has Been Ordered to Help Unlock Phones, Records Show," by Devlin Barrett, *Wall Street Journal*, March 30, 2016; "U.S. Says Outside Party Could Unlock Terrorists iPhone," by Daisuke Wakabayashi, *New York Times*, March 22, 2016; "Apple vs. the FBI: How the Case Could Play Out," by Katie Benner and Matt Apuzzo, *New York Times*, March 20, 2016; "Narrow Focus May Aid F.B.I. in Apple Case," by Katie Benner and Matt Apuzzo, *New York Times*, February 22, 2016; "Explaining Apple's Fight With the F.B.I.," by Mike Isaac, *New York Times*, February 17, 2016; "Judge Tells Apple to Help Unlock iPhone Used by San Bernardino Gunman," by Eric Lichtblau, *New York Times*, February 16, 2016; United States v. New York Telephone Co. 434 U.S. 159 (1977); "iPhone 6s's Hands-Free Siri Is an Omen of the Future," by Farhad Manjoo, *New York Times*, September 22, 2015; "Tech That Hangs on Your Every Word Raises Privacy Questions," by Andrea Peterson, *Washington Post*, September 16, 2015; "What Your iPhone Doesn't Tell Apple," by Geoffrey Fowler, *Wall Street Journal*, September 15, 2015; "Apple Dots Its Privacy 'I's In iOS 9, While Google Appears to Back Pedal," by Allison Schiff, Adexchanger. com, September 1, 2015; "The Tradeoff Fallacy: How Marketers Are Misrepresenting American Consumers and Opening Them Up to Exploitation," by Joseph Turow, Michael Hennessy, and Nora Draper, Annenberg School of Communications, University of Pennsylvania, September 2015; "Apple Privacy May Not Be As Private As You Think," by Theo Priestley, *Forbes*, August 24, 2015; "Apple and Google Know What You Want Before You Do," by Daisuke Wakabayashi, *Wall Street Journal*, August 3, 2015; "Apple Moves to Block iPhone App-Scanning," by Amir Efrati, Information.com, June 24, 2015; "Why Edward Snowden Supports Apple's Stance on Privacy," by Jess Bolluyt, Cheatsheet.com, June 27, 2015; "What Apple's Tim Cook Overlooked in His Defense of Privacy," by Farhad Manjoo, *New York Times*, June 10, 2015; "Tim Cook Says Apple 'Doesn't Want Your Data.' Let's Not Say Things We Can't Take Back," by Lily Hay Newman, Slate.com, June 3, 2015; "Apple's Tim Cook Delivers Blistering Speech on Encryption, Privacy," by Matthew Panzarino, Techcrunch.com, June 2, 2015.

the United States, the creator of intellectual property owns it. For instance, if you personally create an e-commerce site, it belongs entirely to you, and you have exclusive rights to use this "property" in any lawful way you see fit. But the Internet potentially changes things. Once intellectual works become digital, it becomes difficult to control access, use, distribution, and copying. These are precisely the areas that intellectual property seeks to control.

Digital media differ from books, periodicals, and other media in terms of ease of replication, transmission, and alteration; difficulty in classifying a software work as a program, book, or even music; compactness—making theft easy; and difficulty in establishing uniqueness. Before widespread use of the Internet, copies of software, books, magazine articles, or films had to be stored on physical media, such as paper, computer disks, or videotape, creating hurdles to distribution, and raising the costs of illegal copies.

The Internet technically permits millions of people to make perfect digital copies of various works—from music to plays, poems, and journal articles—and then to distribute them nearly cost-free to hundreds of millions of online users. The proliferation of innovation has occurred so rapidly that few entrepreneurs have stopped to consider who owns the patent on a business technique or method that they are using on their site. The spirit of the Web has been so free-wheeling that many entrepreneurs ignored trademark law and registered domain names that could easily be confused with another company's registered trademarks. In short, the Internet has demonstrated the potential to disrupt traditional conceptions and implementations of intellectual property law developed over the last two centuries.

The major ethical issue related to e-commerce and intellectual property concerns how we (both as individuals and as business professionals) should treat property that belongs to others. From a social point of view, the main questions are: Is there continued value in protecting intellectual property in the Internet age? In what ways is society better off, or worse off, for having the concept of property apply to intangible ideas, including music, books, and movies? Should society make certain technology illegal or restrict the use of the Internet just because it has an adverse impact on some intellectual property owners? From a political perspective, we need to ask how the Internet and e-commerce can be regulated or governed to protect the institution of intellectual property while at the same time encouraging the growth of e-commerce and the Internet.

TYPES OF INTELLECTUAL PROPERTY PROTECTION

There are four main types of intellectual property protection: copyright, patent, trademark law, and trade secrets law. In the United States, the development of intellectual property law begins with the U.S. Constitution, which mandated Congress to devise a system of laws to promote "the progress of science and the useful arts." Congress passed the first copyright law in 1790 to protect original written works for a period of 14 years, with a 14-year renewal if the author was still alive. Since then, the idea of copyright has been extended to include music, films, translations, photographs, and most recently the designs of vessels under 200 feet (Fisher, 1999). The copyright law has been amended (mostly extended) 11 times in the last 40 years.

The goal of intellectual property law is to balance two competing interests—the public and the private. The public interest is served by the creation and distribution of inventions, works of art, music, literature, and other forms of intellectual expression. The private interest is served by rewarding people for creating these works through the creation of a time-limited monopoly granting exclusive use to the creator.

Maintaining this balance of interests is always challenged by the invention of new technologies. In general, the information technologies of the last century—from radio and television to CD-ROMs, DVDs, and the Internet—have at first tended to weaken the protections afforded by intellectual property law. Owners of intellectual property have often, but not always, been successful in pressuring Congress and the courts to strengthen the intellectual property laws to compensate for any technological threat, and even to extend protection for longer periods of time and to entirely new areas of expression. In the case of the Internet and e-commerce technologies, once again, intellectual property rights are severely challenged. In the next few sections, we discuss the significant developments in each area: copyright, patent, and trademark.

COPYRIGHT: THE PROBLEM OF PERFECT COPIES AND ENCRYPTION

In the United States, **copyright law** protects original forms of expression such as writings (books, periodicals, lecture notes), art, drawings, photographs, music, motion pictures, performances, and computer programs from being copied by others for a period of time. Up until 1998, the copyright law protected works of individuals for their lifetime plus 50 years beyond their life, and works created for hire and owned by corporations, such as Mickey Mouse of the Disney Corporation, for 75 years after initial creation. Copyright does not protect ideas—just their expression in a tangible medium such as paper, cassette tape, or handwritten notes.

copyright law
protects original forms of expression such as writings, art, drawings, photographs, music, motion pictures, performances, and computer programs from being copied by others for a minimum of 70 years

In 1998, the U.S. Congress extended the period of copyright protection for an additional 20 years, for a total of 95 years for corporate-owned works, and life plus 70 years of protection for works created by individuals (the Copyright Term Extension Act, also known as the CTEA). In *Eldred v. Ashcroft*, the U.S. Supreme Court ruled that the CTEA was constitutional, over the objections of groups arguing that Congress had given copyright holders a permanent monopoly over the expression of ideas, which ultimately would work to inhibit the flow of ideas and creation of new works by making existing works too expensive (*Eldred v. Ashcroft*, 2003; Greenhouse, 2003a). Librarians, academics, and others who depend on inexpensive access to copyrighted material opposed the legislation.

In the mid-1960s, the Copyright Office began registering software programs, and in 1980, Congress passed the Computer Software Copyright Act, which clearly provides protection for source and object code and for copies of the original sold in commerce, and sets forth the rights of the purchaser to use the software while the creator retains legal title. For instance, the HTML code for a web page—even though easily available to every browser—cannot be lawfully copied and used for a commercial purpose, say, to create a new website that looks identical.

Copyright protection is clear-cut: it protects against copying of entire programs or their parts. Damages and relief are readily obtained for infringement. The drawback to copyright protection is that the underlying ideas behind a work are not protected, only their expression in a work. A competitor can view the source code on your website to see how various effects were created and then reuse those techniques to create a different website without infringing on your copyright.

Look and Feel

"Look and feel" copyright infringement lawsuits are precisely about the distinction between an idea and its expression. For instance, in 1988, Apple Computer sued Microsoft Corporation and Hewlett-Packard Inc. for infringing Apple's copyright on the Macintosh interface. Among other claims, Apple claimed that the defendants copied the expression of overlapping windows. Apple failed to patent the idea of overlapping windows when it invented this method of presenting information on a computer screen in the late 1960s. The defendants counterclaimed that the idea of overlapping windows could only be expressed in a single way and, therefore, was not protectable under the "merger" doctrine of copyright law. When ideas and their expression merge (i.e., if there is only one way to express an idea), the expression cannot be copyrighted, although the method of producing the expression might be patentable (*Apple Computer, Inc. v. Microsoft*, 1989). In general, courts appear to be following the reasoning of a 1992 case—*Brown Bag Software vs. Symantec Corp.*—in which the court dissected the elements of software alleged to be infringing. There, the U.S. Federal Circuit Court of Appeals found that neither similar concept, function, general functional features (e.g., drop-down menus), nor colors were protectable by copyright law (*Brown Bag vs. Symantec Corp.*, 1992).

Fair Use Doctrine

Copyrights, like all rights, are not absolute. There are situations where strict copyright observance could be harmful to society, potentially inhibiting other rights such as the right to freedom of expression and thought. As a result, the doctrine of fair use has been created. The **doctrine of fair use** permits teachers, writers, and others to use copyrighted materials without permission under certain circumstances. **Table 8.12** describes the five factors that courts consider when assessing what constitutes fair use.

The fair use doctrine draws upon the First Amendment's protection of freedom of speech (and writing). Journalists, writers, and academics must be able to refer to, and cite from, copyrighted works in order to criticize, or even discuss them. Professors are allowed to clip a contemporary article just before class, copy it, and hand it out to students as an example of a topic under discussion. However, they are not permitted to add this article to the class syllabus for the next semester without compensating the copyright holder.

What constitutes fair use has been at issue in a number of recent cases. In *Kelly v. Arriba Soft* (2003) and *Perfect 10, Inc. v. Amazon.com, Inc. et al.*, (2007), the Federal Circuit Court of Appeals for the 9th Circuit held that the display of thumbnail images in response to search requests constituted fair use. A similar result was reached by the district court for the District of Nevada with respect to Google's storage and display of websites from cache memory, in *Field v. Google, Inc.* (2006). In all of these cases, the courts accepted the argument that caching the material and displaying it in response

doctrine of fair use
under certain circumstances, permits use of copyrighted material without permission

TABLE 8.12	FAIR USE CONSIDERATIONS TO COPYRIGHT PROTECTIONS
FAIR USE FACTOR	**INTERPRETATION**
Character of use	Nonprofit or educational use versus for-profit use.
Nature of the work	Creative works such as plays or novels receive greater protection than factual accounts, e.g., newspaper accounts.
Amount of work used	A stanza from a poem or a single page from a book would be allowed, but not the entire poem or a book chapter.
Market effect of use	Will the use harm the marketability of the original product? Has it already harmed the product in the marketplace?
Context of use	A last-minute, unplanned use in a classroom versus a planned infringement.

to a search request was not only a public benefit, but also a form of marketing of the material on behalf of its copyright owner, thereby enhancing the material's commercial value. In what's known as the "dancing baby case," a mother uploaded a 30-second video to YouTube of her baby dancing to a song by Prince called Let's Go Crazy. Universal Music Group, the owner of the copyright to the song, objected and issued a DMCA takedown notice to YouTube. The mother sued, claiming that Universal failed to consider whether use of the song in the video was fair use before issuing the takedown notice. The 9th Circuit Court of Appeals agreed that a copyright owner must consider fair use before sending a takedown notice. The ruling has been appealed to the Supreme Court (Morran, 2016; Bergen, 2015).

Fair use was also at issue in a lawsuit filed by the Authors Guild and five major publishing companies against Google. In 2004, Google announced a book project with two parts. A Partner Program would scan books with the permission of publishers, index the books, post snippets of the books on line, and make bibliographic information available on Google's search engine. In the second project, called the Library Project, Google aimed to scan all the books in several university and public libraries, and then make snippets and parts of the book available online without receiving permission from the publishers or paying royalties. Google said it would never show a full page, just relevant portions of a page in response to searches. In 2005, the Authors Guild and the large book publishers filed a lawsuit seeking to prevent Google from implementing the Library Project.

Google argued that the Library Project constituted fair use of publishers' copyrighted works because it only published snippets. Moreover, Google claimed that it was simply helping libraries do what they are intended to do, namely, lend books. Library lending is considered a fair use following an agreement in the late 1930s with publishers, and such lending was codified into the Copyright Act of 1976. Google claimed that helping libraries make books more available to the public was in the broader public interest, and extended existing rights of libraries to encourage book availability.

In 2013, eight years later, a federal court finally found in favor of Google without reservation by ruling that Google's scanning and making snippets of text available to the public was "fair use" under U.S. copyright law. The judge believed the project had a broad public purpose of making it easier for students, researchers, teachers, and the general public to find books, while also preserving consideration for author and publisher rights. The Google project was "transformative" in the court's view, giving books a new character and purpose, making it easier to discover old books, and leading to increased sales. After a decade of litigation, the U.S. Supreme Court ruled in 2016 that Google's Library Project was fair use, and the matter is settled from a legal perspective (Liptak and Alter, 2016). In the meantime, the project itself has stalled, and efforts to scan so-called orphan books in libraries where the copyright holder could not be identified have ended. Google now appears less than enthusiastic about pursuing the project, in part, analysts believe, because the project offered no hope of ever making a return on the investment, and created a rift with the author and publishing community.

The Digital Millennium Copyright Act of 1998

Digital Millennium Copyright Act (DMCA)

the first major effort to adjust the copyright laws to the Internet age

The **Digital Millennium Copyright Act (DMCA)** of 1998 was the first major effort to adjust the copyright laws of the United States to the Internet age, and remains to this day, the primary statute that defines the relationship between copyright owners, Internet service providers (which in this context also includes website publishers as well as firms that provide Internet service), and end-users of copyrighted material. The law implements two international treaties of the World Intellectual Property Organization (WIPO), a worldwide body formed by the major nations in North America and Europe, as well as Japan. This is one case where law preceded or at least was contemporaneous with digital technology. **Table 8.13** summarizes the major provisions of the DMCA.

There are a number of different actors and conflicting interests involved in the process of delivering content on the Internet. Obviously, copyright owners do not want their work copied and distributed without their consent (and probably compensation), and they do not want their digital rights management software programs broken, compromised, or made ineffectual. ISPs want the freedom to use content within the provisions of "fair use" and do not want to be held liable for content that users may post to their websites. ISPs argue that they are similar to telephone transmission lines, merely providing a method of communication, and they should not be required to monitor their users' activities to see if they are posting copyrighted material. Such surveillance, ISPs and civil libertarians argue, would constitute a restriction on freedom of expression. In addition, the economics of the Internet could be compromised if ISPs were unnecessarily restricted and pay the costs of vetting all content posted by users. The business model of many Internet firms depends on creating large, even huge, audiences, and the more content that can be displayed, the larger the audience, and the more ads can be sold. ISPs also generate revenue from selling bandwidth, so the greater the bandwidth required to support large audiences, the better it is for them. Restricting content is bad for business. Finally, consumers of Internet content want as much content as possible, at the lowest cost possible, or even free. The more content for users to consume, the more they benefit from the Internet.

TABLE 8.13	THE DIGITAL MILLENNIUM COPYRIGHT ACT
SECTION	IMPORTANCE
Title I, WIPO Copyright and Performances and Phonograms Treaties Implementation	Makes it illegal to circumvent technological measures to protect works for either access or copying or to circumvent any electronic rights management information.
Title II, Online Copyright Infringement Liability Limitation	Limits liability of ISPs and search engines for copyright infringement if they comply with safe harbors. Requires ISPs to "take down" sites they host if they are infringing copyrights, and requires search engines to block access to infringing sites if they receive proper notice of infringement from the copyright owner.
Title III, Computer Maintenance Competition Assurance	Permits users to make a copy of a computer program for maintenance or repair of the computer.
Title IV, Miscellaneous Provisions	Requires the Copyright Office to report to Congress on the use of copyright materials for distance education; allows libraries to make digital copies of works for internal use only; extends musical copyrights to include "webcasting."

SOURCE: Based on data from United States Copyright Office, 1998.

The DMCA tries to balance these different interests. Title I of the DMCA implements the WIPO Copyright Treaty of 1996, which makes it illegal to make, distribute, or use devices that circumvent technology-based protections of copyrighted materials, and attaches stiff fines and prison sentences for violations. This makes it illegal, for instance, to break the security software typically found on DVDs, Amazon's Kindle books, and similar devices. There are a number of exceptions to the strong prohibitions against defeating a copyright protection scheme, however, including exceptions for libraries to examine works for adoption, for reverse engineering to achieve interoperability with other software, for encryption research, and for privacy protection purposes.

Title II of the DMCA creates two safe harbors for ISPs. The first safe harbor (the Online Copyright Infringement Liability Limitation Act) provides that ISPs will not be held liable for infringing material that users post to blogs, web pages, or forums, as long as the ISP did not have knowledge that the content was infringing, did not receive any financial benefit attributable to the infringing activity (assuming they can control this activity), and acts expeditiously to remove infringing content when notified by a notice of infringement. This means that users of, say, YouTube, can post material that infringes a copyright and YouTube cannot be held liable (safe harbor) as long as it does not know the material is infringing, and if it demonstrates that it has in place procedures to take down infringing content once it becomes aware of the matter or receives a proper notice from the copyright owner. Such a notice is called a takedown notice, a claim by the copyright owner that the ISP is hosting infringing content. Copyright owners can also subpoena the personal identities of any infringers using an ISP.

The second safe harbor relates to links to infringing material: ISPs will not be held liable for referring or linking users to a site that contains infringing material or infringing activity. So for example, a search engine that directs users to a website that contains pirated songs or movies cannot be held liable. This safe harbor is applicable as long as ISPs did not have knowledge they were linking users to sites containing infringing content, did not receive any financial benefit attributable to the infringing activity (assuming they can control this activity), and acts expeditiously to remove or disable any such link after receiving a proper notice from the copyright owner.

There are a number of administrative requirements for ISPs to be protected by the safe harbor provisions. ISPs must designate an agent to receive takedown notices; adopt and publish a copyright infringement policy (this can be part of a terms of use policy); and comply with takedown notices by removing the content, and/or links to the content. The penalties for willfully violating the DMCA include restitution to the injured parties of any losses due to infringement. Criminal remedies may include fines up to $500,000 or five years imprisonment for a first offense, and up to $1 million in fines and 10 years in prison for repeat offenders. These are serious penalties, but they have rarely been imposed.

The DMCA relieves ISPs of any liability for posting or linking to copyrighted material, if they can meet the safe harbors' conditions. This means users of YouTube can post what they want, and YouTube will not be held liable for infringing content even if it violates YouTube's terms of use policy, which states that users shall not post infringing content. However, it does require YouTube to remove content or links that are infringing once it receives a valid takedown notice. With respect to receiving financial benefits, ISPs may indeed receive financial benefits from posting infringing content if they can show that they can't control the behavior of their users, or that there is no way of knowing prior to the posting that the material is infringing. For instance, how can YouTube be held responsible for users who post copyrighted songs or movies? How could YouTube know, at the time of posting, that the content is infringing?

ISPs and individuals who post content are also protected from frivolous takedown notices. For instance, the ruling in the "dancing baby" case discussed on page 535 put copyright owners on notice that they needed to be careful issuing takedown notices if use of the copyrighted material might constitute fair use and that the DMCA does not supersede the doctrine of fair use.

Safe harbor provisions of the DMCA were also at the heart of a $1 billion lawsuit originally brought by Viacom in 2007 against Google and YouTube for willful copyright infringement. In the Viacom case, Viacom alleged that YouTube and Google engaged in massive copyright infringement by deliberately and knowingly building up a library of infringing works to draw traffic to the YouTube site and enhance its commercial value. Entire episodes of shows like SpongeBob SquarePants and The Daily Show were appearing on YouTube without permission or payment. In response, Google and YouTube claimed that they are protected by the DMCA's safe harbor provisions and that it is impossible to know whether a video is infringing or not. YouTube also does not display ads on pages where consumers can view videos unless it has an agreement with the content owner. In 2007, Google announced a filtering system (Content ID) aimed at addressing the problem. It requires content owners to give Google a copy of their content so Google can load it into an auto-identification system. Then after a video is uploaded to YouTube, the system attempts to match it with its database of copyrighted material and removes any unauthorized material. The copyright owner has several options: it can mute the audio; block a whole video; monetize the video by running ads against it; and track the video's viewer statistics. In 2014, seven years after the billion dollar suit was filed, and multiple court room appearances, Google and Viacom settled out of court. Google's ability to take down copyrighted material using Content ID had become very effective, and Google agreed to rent hundreds of Viacom shows (Kaufman, 2014). Both parties recognized in a joint statement that they could achieve their objectives by collaborating rather than continuing the lawsuit.

The entertainment industry continues to be aggressive in pursuing online copyright infringement. In 2012, the U.S. Department of Justice seized the domain Megaupload.com, one of the largest cyberlockers on the Internet dedicated to storing and sharing copyrighted movies and music. A **cyberlocker** is an online file storage service dedicated to sharing copyrighted material (often movies) illegally. Megaupload's founder, Kim Dotcom, was arrested in New Zealand at his home, and $17 million in assets, and later, $37 million in cash in Hong Kong, was confiscated. Mr. Dotcom is currently back in court, and fighting efforts by the United States to extradite him from New Zealand to face copyright, racketeering, and money laundering charges (Reuters, 2015). In 2016, the U.S. federal government seized Mr. Dotcom's assets that were located in the United States, along with the assets of others associated with him, pending his extradition to the United States to face criminal piracy charges.

cyberlocker
an online file storage service dedicated to sharing copyrighted material illegally

Since the Megaupload case, other cyberlockers have restricted their activities to avoid a similar fate as Megaupload. In 2013, the Center for Copyright Information (CCI), along with 5 of the largest ISPs, major entertainment industry companies, and the Consumer Advisory Board launched the Copyright Alert System (CAS)—a tiered notice and response system aimed at reducing copyright infringement over P2P networks. During its first 10 months of operation, the CAS sent out over 1.3 million alerts to 720,000 ISP account holders of alleged copyright infringement. If the account holder ignores repeated alerts, their ISP may impose consequences, such as a downgrade of the customer's Internet service. The CCI believes that the CAS has great promise for its ability to move user behavior away from copyright infringement and toward legal sources of content (Center for Copyright Information, 2014). Refer to the chapter-ending case study on The Pirate Bay.

In 2016, DMCA litigation continues. In *BMG Rights Management v. Cox Communications*, a federal judge let stand a $25 million jury award against Cox Cable in favor of BMG, a rights management firm, for willful contributory infringement. BMG argued that Cox, an ISP, was allowing subscribers to use BitTorrent to upload copyrighted songs to various websites without an effective policy for preventing this activity, and failing to remove repeat offenders from its service. Cox argued that it was just a pipeline to the Internet and could not be held liable for what its users posted or what software they used. However, although the court left the jury award against Cox in place, it refused to enjoin Cox from continuing to operate, as BMG had requested, noting that while there is a public benefit to reducing copyright infringement, because Cox provides access to the Internet and enables freedom of speech, these interests trumped BMG's interest in copyright protection (Gardner, 2016).

Also in 2016, a U.S. federal court ruled that the video sharing site Vimeo was protected by DMCA against liability for allowing users to post copyrighted video and music created prior to 1972 when DMCA became law. Vimeo did have a procedure of accepting infringement notices and taking down infringing content, but some pre-1972 music tracks were still on the site despite repeated takedown notices (*Capital Records v. Vimeo LLC*, 2016).

Copyright owners from the film and music industry are lobbying Congress for changes in the DMCA that would require websites and ISPs to take more effective actions in removing infringing content (Raymond, 2016). Musicians and film makers have begun to protest the compensation they receive from streaming services (see Chapter 9).

While there has been some progress in limiting infringing content on the Internet, new mobile apps such as Periscope and Meerkat make it easy for people to capture live video and stream it to these apps on mobile devices, making it extremely difficult for content owners to protect the value of their live products. Periscope is owned by Twitter and users can post live videos to Twitter. Meerkat can post live video streams to most social network sites, including Facebook. In 2015, Periscope and Meerkat were used by thousands of users to watch the pay-per-view broadcast of the welterweight fight between Floyd Mayweather and Manny Pacquiao for free. The pay-per-view price on cable networks was $100. Other users have streamed live TV series such as HBO's Game of Thrones. Periscope received 1,400 DMCA takedown requests in the first three months of its existence. Twitter says it has complied with 71% of these (Weber, 2015). But the DMCA takedown notices do not help a unique live event such as a championship boxing match retain its value. The value of the event is largely in attracting viewers willing to pay to see it as it happens, and once a free alternative is available, that value is diminished.

PATENTS: BUSINESS METHODS AND PROCESSES

> "Whoever invents or discovers any new and useful process, machine, manufacture, or composition of matter, or any new and useful improvement thereof, may obtain a patent therefore, subject to the conditions and requirements of this title."
>
> —Section 101, U.S. Patent Act

patent
grants the owner an exclusive monopoly on the ideas behind an invention for 20 years

A **patent** grants the owner a 20-year exclusive monopoly on the ideas behind an invention. The congressional intent behind patent law was to ensure that inventors of new machines, devices, or industrial methods would receive the full financial and other rewards of their labor and still make widespread use of the invention possible by providing detailed diagrams for those wishing to use the idea under license from the patent's owner. Patents are obtained from the United States Patent and Trademark Office (USPTO), which was created in 1812. Obtaining a patent is much more difficult and time-consuming than obtaining copyright protection (which is automatic with the creation of the work). Patents must be formally applied for, and the granting of a patent is determined by Patent Office examiners who follow a set of rigorous rules. Ultimately, federal courts decide when patents are valid and when infringement occurs.

Patents are very different from copyrights because patents protect the ideas themselves and not merely the expression of ideas. There are four types of inventions for which patents are granted under patent law: machines, man-made products, compositions of matter, and processing methods. The U.S. Supreme Court has determined that patents extend to "anything under the sun that is made by man" (*Diamond v. Chakrabarty*, 1980) as long as the other requirements of the Patent Act are met. There are three things that cannot be patented: laws of nature, natural phenomena, and abstract ideas. For instance, a mathematical algorithm cannot be patented unless it is realized in a tangible machine or process that has a "useful" result (the mathematical algorithm exception).

In order to be granted a patent, the applicant must show that the invention is new, original, novel, nonobvious, and not evident in prior arts and practice. As with copyrights, the granting of patents has moved far beyond the original intent of Congress's first patent statute, which sought to protect industrial designs and machines. Patent protection has been extended to articles of manufacture (1842), plants (1930), surgical and medical procedures (1950), and software (1981). The Patent Office did not accept applications for software patents until a 1981 U.S. Supreme Court decision that held that computer programs could be a part of a patentable process. Since that time, thousands of software patents have been granted. Virtually any software program can be patented as long as it is novel and not obvious.

Essentially, as technology and industrial arts progress, patents have been extended to both encourage entrepreneurs to invent useful devices and promote widespread dissemination of the new techniques through licensing and artful imitation of the published patents (the creation of devices that provide the same functionality as the invention but use different methods) (Winston, 1998). Patents encourage inventors to come up with unique ways of achieving the same functionality as existing patents. For instance, Amazon's patent on one-click purchasing caused Barnesandnoble.com to invent a simplified two-click method of purchasing.

The danger of patents is that they stifle competition by raising barriers to entry into an industry. Patents force new entrants to pay licensing fees to incumbents, and thus slow down the development of technical applications of new ideas by creating lengthy licensing applications and delays. Nowhere is the tradeoff between encouraging innovation and yet avoiding raising barriers to market entry (and thereby discouraging innovation) more evident than in the patent battle that has raged between Apple and Samsung in the smartphone market.

In 2011, Apple filed suit in the United States against Samsung alleging that Samsung's Galaxy smartphones violated Apple patents on its iPhone and iPad computer. By 2012, Apple and Samsung were involved in over 50 different patent lawsuits through-

TABLE 8.14	APPLE/SAMSUNG SMARTPHONE PATENT WARS
YEAR	DESCRIPTION
2011–2012	In 2011 Apple filed suit in the United States charging Samsung devices violated Apple patents, and Samsung claimed similar infringement by Apple. The smartphone patent wars begin.
	Apple's patents had been filed in January 2007 shortly after the introduction of the iPhone. The design patents covered the basic shape of the phone, software features (slide-to-unlock, autocorrect, bounce-back effect, and quicklinks), trade dress features, and user interface (home button and icons with rounded and tapered edges). In short, everything that made the iPhone a unique product.
	By 2012, Apple and Samsung are involved in 50 different lawsuits around the world involving the design of tablets and smartphones.
August 2012	First jury verdict mostly favorable to Apple. Found Samsung had infringed on design and utility patents, and Apple's trade dress features. Awarded Apple $1.049 billion. An injunction preventing Samsung from selling infringing products was at first denied, but later granted.
November 2013	A retrial of the first jury trial. Samsung admitted to infringing on Apple patents, but argued the penalty was too high. The jury reduced the damages to $290 million.
May 2014	Another jury trial. Apple wins jury verdict of $119.6 million against Samsung, finding that Samsung infringed on patents for slide-to-unlock, autocorrect, and quicklinks features. Judge declines to force removal of devices from market, instead argues for damages as penalty.
September 2015	Apple and Samsung announced an agreement to participate in court-supervised mediation of their five-year dispute. This is the third effort at mediation (the first two failed).
2016	Apple asks the Supreme Court to rule that Samsung must pay $548 million to Apple for patent infringment based on the value of the entire phone, not just its specific design elements which Samsung argues are a small part of the phone's value.

out the world. See **Table 8.14** for a brief history of the Apple/Samsung smartphone patent wars.

The history of the patent battle is quite complex, and lengthy, lasting over five years. There are three questions raised in this litigation. First, does Apple have valid patents on iPhone and iPad hardware and software? Second, did Samsung's phones and tablets infringe on these Apple patents? And third, if Samsung did infringe, what should the penalty be? There are two possibilities: Samsung pays a fine for damages and/or Samsung removes its infringing products from the market. A fourth question is separate from the lawsuits per se and concerns society, the rest of us: what is the best outcome for society?

After five years and two jury trials, the courts have decided that Apple does have valid patents on the physical iPhone, as well as the operating system, including the physical design (rounded corners and bezel), user interface, and screen functionality. Second, the courts did find that Samsung infringed on some of Apple's patents, and even Samsung admits as much. Third, the courts have generally avoided forcing Samsung to remove its infringing devices from the market, and instead have focused on damages with some exceptions for older phones (Decker, 2015). However, in September 2015, Apple finally won a U.S. appeals court judgment that enjoins Samsung from selling smartphones with Apple's patented slide-to-unlock, autocorrect, and quicklinks features. This was a major victory in principle that Apple can use in the future against other copycat firms (Chen, 2015; Kendall and Wakabayashi, 2015). But Samsung had already designed around these features and came up with its own user interface that accomplishes the same tasks. Hence, the ruling is not likely to have a notable impact on Samsung's sales revenues. The original jury award of $1 billion has been whittled down over the years. Analysts believe the cost to Apple of this litigation is at least equal to the damage award it may ultimately be paid. Over the last five years of litigation, Samsung has changed its interface and functionality to greatly reduce its infringement. Software features can always be designed around. In 2016, Apple asked the U.S. Supreme Court to rule that Samsung must pay for its patent infringement based on all of the profits it made on the entire phone. Samsung argued it should only be liable for that portion of the profits attributable to the design of the phones, a much smaller liability (Kendall, 2016). The final chapter may not be closed until 2017.

An answer to the fourth question, what is the best outcome for society, is more difficult to determine. Apple's forceful defense has put copycat firms on notice that if they infringe on patents owned by large firms such as Apple, it could be harmful to their brands and possibly result in significant damages. Samsung has been pushed into the lower end of the market where it competes with less expensive, copycat smartphones from China. Samsung has a very large chunk of the smartphone market worldwide, but it has been denied pricing power and resulting profits. The litigation may have strengthened Apple's claim that its computers and smartphones are truly unique, and original. Apple today is the largest corporation in the United States by market capitalization and also the most profitable in the world. Samsung's copying of Apple designs and features may only have strengthened Apple's claims to be a superior product.

E-commerce Patents

Much of the Internet's infrastructure and software was developed under the auspices of publicly funded scientific and military programs in the United States and Europe. Unlike Samuel F. B. Morse, who patented the idea of Morse code and made the telegraph useful, most of the inventions that make the Internet and e-commerce possible were not patented by their inventors. The early Internet was characterized by a spirit of worldwide community development and sharing of ideas without consideration of personal wealth (Winston, 1998). This early Internet spirit changed in the mid-1990s with the commercial development of the Web.

In 1998, a landmark legal decision, *State Street Bank & Trust v. Signature Financial Group, Inc.*, paved the way for business firms to begin applying for "business methods" patents. In this case, a Federal Circuit Court of Appeals upheld the claims of Signature Financial to a valid patent for a business method that allows managers to monitor and record financial information flows generated by a partner fund. Previously, it was thought business methods could not be patented. However, the court ruled there was no reason to disallow business methods from patent protection, or any "step by step process, be it electronic or chemical or mechanical, [that] involves an algorithm in the broad sense of the term" (*State Street Bank & Trust Co. v. Signature Financial Group*, 1998). The State Street decision led to an explosion in applications for e-commerce "business methods" patents. In 2010, the U.S. Supreme Court issued a divided opinion on business methods patents in the *Bilski et al. v. Kappos* case (*Bilski et al. v. Kappos*, 2010). The majority argued that business methods patents were allowable even though they did not meet the traditional "machine or transformation test," in which patents are granted to devices that are tied to a particular machine, are a machine, or transform articles from one state to another. The minority wanted to flatly declare that business methods are not patentable in part because any series of steps could be considered a business method (Schwartz, 2010). The Supreme Court struck another blow against business method patents in 2014, with its decision in *Alice Corporation vs. CLS Bank International*. The Court ruled that basic business methods cannot be patented and that while software can be patented, implementing an abstract idea that otherwise could not be patented by using software does not transform the idea into a patentable innovation (*Alice Corporation Pty. Ltd. v. CLS Bank International*, 2014).

Table 8.15 lists some of the better-known e-commerce patents. Some are controversial. Reviewing these, you can understand the concerns of commentators and corporations. Some of the patent claims are very broad (for example, "name your price" sales methods), have historical precedents in the pre-Internet era (shopping carts), and seem "obvious" (one-click purchasing). Critics of online business methods patents argue that the Patent Office has been too lenient in granting such patents, and that in most instances, the supposed inventions merely copy pre-Internet business methods and thus do not constitute "inventions" (Harmon, 2003; Thurm, 2000; Chiappetta, 2001). The Patent Office argues, on the contrary, that its Internet inventions staff is composed of engineers, lawyers, and specialists with many years of experience with Internet and network technologies, and that it consults with outside technology experts before granting patents. To complicate matters, the European Patent Convention and the patent laws of most European countries do not recognize business methods per se unless the method is implemented through some technology (Takenaka, 2001).

TRADEMARKS: ONLINE INFRINGEMENT AND DILUTION

> A trademark is "any word, name, symbol, or device, or any combination thereof ... used in commerce ... to identify and distinguish ... goods ... from those manufactured or sold by others and to indicate the source of the goods."
>
> —The Trademark Act, 1946

trademark
a mark used to identify and distinguish goods and indicate their source

Trademark law is a form of intellectual property protection for **trademarks**—a mark used to identify and distinguish goods and indicate their source. Trademark protections exist at both the federal and state levels in the United States. The purpose of trademark

TABLE 8.15	SELECTED E-COMMERCE PATENTS	
COMPANY	SUBJECT	UPDATE
Amazon	One-click purchasing	Amazon attempted to use patent originally granted to it in 1999 to force changes to Barnes & Noble's website, but a federal court overturned a previously issued injunction. Eventually settled out of court. In 2007, a USPTO panel rejected some of the patent because of evidence another patent predated it. Amazon amended the patent, and the revised version was confirmed in 2010.
Priceline	Buyer-driven "name your price" sales	Originally filed by Walker Digital, an intellectual property laboratory, and then assigned to Priceline. Granted by the USPTO in 1999. Shortly thereafter, Priceline sued Microsoft and Expedia for copying its patented business method.
Akamai	Internet content delivery global hosting system	A broad patent granted in 2000 covering techniques for expediting the flow of information over the Internet. Akamai sued Digital Island for violating the patent and, in 2001, a jury found in its favor.
DoubleClick	Dynamic delivery of online advertising	The patent underlying DoubleClick's business of online banner ad delivery, originally granted in 2000. DoubleClick sued competitors 24/7 Media and L90 for violating the patent and ultimately reached a settlement with them.
Overture	Pay for performance search	System and method for influencing position on search result list generated by computer search engine, granted in 2001. Competitor FindWhat sued Overture, charging that patent was obtained illegally; Overture countered by suing both FindWhat and Google for violating patent. Google agreed to pay a license fee to Overture in 2004 to settle.
Acacia Technologies	Streaming video media transmission	Patents for the receipt and transmission of streaming digital audio and/or video content originally granted to founders of Greenwich Information Technologies in 1990s. Patents were purchased by Acacia, a firm founded solely to enforce the patents, in 2001.
Soverain Software	Purchase technology	The so-called "shopping cart" patent for network-based systems, which involves any transaction over a network involving a seller, buyer, and payment system. In other words, e-commerce! Soverain filed suit against Amazon for patent infringement, which Amazon paid $40 million to settle. In 2013 a federal district court ruled Soverain's claims against Newegg in part invalid.
MercExchange (Thomas Woolston)	Auction technology	Patents on person-to-person auctions and database search, originally granted in 1995. eBay ordered to pay $25 million in 2003 for infringing on patent. In 2007, a motion for permanent patent injunction against eBay was denied. MercExchange and eBay settled the dispute in 2008 on confidential terms.
Google	Search technology	Google PageRank patent filed in 1998 and granted in 2001. Became non-exclusive in 2011 and expires in 2017.
Google	Location technology	Patent for a method of using location information in an advertising system issued to Google in 2010.
Apple	Social technology	Apple applied for a patent in 2010 that allows groups of friends attending events to stay in communication with each other and share reactions to live events as they are occurring.
Facebook	Social technology	A 2010 patent on an algorithm for developing personalized stories and newsfeeds on a social network.

law is twofold. First, trademark law protects the public in the marketplace by ensuring that it gets what it pays for and wants to receive. Second, trademark law protects the owner—who has spent time, money, and energy bringing the product to the market-place—against piracy and misappropriation. Trademarks have been extended from single words to pictures, shapes, packaging, and colors. Some things may not be trade-marked such as common words that are merely descriptive ("clock"). Federal trade-marks are obtained, first, by use in interstate commerce, and second, by registration with the U.S. Patent and Trademark Office (USPTO). Federal trademarks are granted for a period of 10 years and can be renewed indefinitely.

Disputes over federal trademarks involve establishing infringement. The test for infringement is twofold: market confusion and bad faith. Use of a trademark that creates confusion with existing trademarks, causes consumers to make market mis-takes, or misrepresents the origins of goods is an infringement. For instance, in 2015, Multi Time Machine (MTM) sued Amazon for violation of its trademarks and confus-ing consumers looking to buy MTM watches. MTM makes military style watches that are not sold on Amazon. If a user searches on Amazon for an MTM watch, the search results shows watches being offered by MTM competitors that are similar in style to MTM's. MTM argued that this could confuse customers and the court agreed, allow-ing the case to proceed to trial (Levine, 2015). In addition, the intentional misuse of words and symbols in the marketplace to extort revenue from legitimate trademark owners ("bad faith") is proscribed.

dilution

any behavior that would weaken the connection between the trademark and the product

In 1995, the U.S. Congress passed the Federal Trademark Dilution Act (FTDA), which created a federal cause of action for dilution of famous marks. This legislation dispenses with the test of market confusion (although that is still required to claim infringement), and extends protection to owners of famous trademarks against **dilu-tion**, which is defined as any behavior that would weaken the connection between the trademark and the product. In 2006, the FTDA was amended by the Trademark Dilution Revision Act (TDRA), which allows a trademark owner to file a claim based on a "likelihood of dilution" standard, rather than having to provide evidence of actual dilution. The TDRA also expressly provides that dilution may occur through blurring (weakening the connection between the trademark and the goods) and tarnishment (using the trademark in a way that makes the underlying products appear unsavory or unwholesome). Internationally, WIPO handles many cybersquatting cases under its Uniform Dispute Resolution Procedures. In 2014, WIPO warned that the expansion of generic top-level domains authorized by ICANN is likely to be very disruptive in terms of trademark protection (New, 2014). Although the cost of obtaining a new gTLD is not unsubstantial (it is estimated to be more than $180,000), by May 2015, 583 new gTLDs had been approved. Successful applicants become owners of these gTLDs, and can create and sell new domains with the gTLD suffix, such as Avenger.movie. Many of these new domains may potentially conflict with the established trademarks of others.

To deal with these trademark conflicts, ICANN developed a set of procedures to rapidly resolve disputes called the Uniform Rapid Suspension System (URS), a domain name dispute procedure that allows a trademark owner to seek suspension of a domain name in a new generic top-level domain (gTLD). ICANN also established a Trademark Clearing house as a repository of data on registered, court-validated, or statute-protected trademarks. Trademark owners register their marks for a fee.

One successful applicant for a new gTLD is Vox Populi Registry Ltd. Based in the U.K., Vox purchased the gTLD .sucks, and began selling domains such as Apple.sucks and CitiGroup.sucks exclusively to corporations who did not want their brand name associated with .sucks. At some point, .sucks domains will be available to the general public, at which point anyone would be able to create a new domain that potentially embarrasses a major brand name or casts it in a negative light (Bloomberg News, 2015). ICANN has said it may seek remedies and has alerted the FTC and asked for an opinion on the legality of Vox Populi's behavior. ICANN is not a regulatory agency with enforcement powers, and its agreement with new domain owners does not discuss their business models (Fung, 2015).

Trademarks and the Internet

The rapid growth and commercialization of the Internet have provided unusual opportunities for existing firms with distinctive and famous trademarks to extend their brands to the Internet. These same developments have provided malicious individuals and firms the opportunity to squat on Internet domain names built upon famous marks, as well as attempt to confuse consumers and dilute famous or distinctive marks (including your personal name or a movie star's name). The conflict between legitimate trademark owners and malicious firms was allowed to fester and grow because Network Solutions Inc. (NSI), originally the Internet's sole agency for domain name registration for many years, had a policy of "first come, first served." This meant anyone could register any domain name that had not already been registered, regardless of the trademark status of the domain name. NSI was not authorized to decide trademark issues (Nash, 1997).

In response to a growing number of complaints from owners of famous trademarks who found their trademark names being appropriated by web entrepreneurs, the U.S. Congress passed the **Anticybersquatting Consumer Protection Act (ACPA)** in 1999. The ACPA creates civil liabilities for anyone who attempts in bad faith to profit from an existing famous or distinctive trademark by registering an Internet domain name that is identical or confusingly similar to, or "dilutive" of, that trademark. The act does not establish criminal sanctions. It proscribes using "bad-faith" domain names to extort money from the owners of the existing trademark **(cybersquatting)**, or using the bad-faith domain to divert web traffic to the bad-faith domain that could harm the good will represented by the trademark, create market confusion, or tarnish or disparage the mark **(cyberpiracy)**. It is conceivable that domains such as the previously described Apple.sucks might be seen as a kind of cybersquatting and a violation of the ACPA. The act also proscribes the use of a domain name that consists of the name of a living person, or a name confusingly similar to an existing personal name, without that person's consent, if the registrant is registering the name with the intent to profit by selling the domain name to that person.

Anticybersquatting Consumer Protection Act (ACPA)

creates civil liabilities for anyone who attempts in bad faith to profit from an existing famous or distinctive trademark by registering an Internet domain name that is identical or confusingly similar to, or "dilutive" of, that trademark

cybersquatting

involves the registration of an infringing domain name, or other Internet use of an existing trademark, for the purpose of extorting payments from the legitimate owners

cyberpiracy

involves the same behavior as cybersquatting, but with the intent of diverting traffic from the legitimate site to an infringing site

TABLE 8.16	INTERNET AND TRADEMARK LAW EXAMPLES	
ACTIVITY	DESCRIPTION	EXAMPLE CASE
Cybersquatting	Registering domain names similar or identical to trademarks of others to extort profits from legitimate holders	*E. & J. Gallo Winery v. Spider Webs Ltd.*, 129 F. Supp. 2d 1033 (S.D. Tex., 2001) aff'd 286 F. 3d 270 (5th Cir., 2002)
Cyberpiracy	Registering domain names similar or identical to trademarks of others to divert web traffic to their own sites	*Ford Motor Co. v. Lapertosa*, 2001 U.S. Dist. LEXIS 253 (E.D. Mich., 2001); *PaineWebber Inc. v. Fortuny*, Civ. A. No. 99-0456-A (E.D. Va., 1999); *Playboy Enterprises, Inc. v. Global Site Designs, Inc.*, 1999 WL 311707 (S.D. Fla., 1999); *Audi AG and Volkswagen of America Inc. v. Bob D'Amato* (No. 05-2359; 6th Cir., November 27, 2006)
Metatagging	Using trademarked words in a site's metatags	*Bernina of America, Inc. v. Fashion Fabrics Int'l, Inc.*, 2001 U.S. Dist. LEXIS 1211 (N.D. Ill., 2001); *Nissan Motor Co., Ltd. v. Nissan Computer Corp.*, 289 F. Supp. 2d 1154 (C.D. Cal., 2000), aff'd, 246 F. 3rd 675 (9th Cir., 2000)
Keywording	Placing trademarked keywords on web pages, either visible or invisible	*Playboy Enterprises, Inc. v. Netscape Communications, Inc.*, 354 F. 3rd 1020 (9th Cir., 2004); *Nettis Environment Ltd. v. IWI, Inc.*, 46 F. Supp. 2d 722 (N.D. Ohio, 1999); *Government Employees Insurance Company v. Google, Inc.*, Civ. Action No. 1:04cv507 (E.D. VA, 2004); *Google, Inc. v. American Blind & Wallpaper Factory, Inc.*, Case No. 03-5340 JF (RS) (N.D. Cal., April 18, 2007)
Linking	Linking to content pages on other sites, bypassing the home page	*Ticketmaster Corp. v. Tickets.com*, 2000 U.S. Dist. Lexis 4553 (C.D. Cal., 2000)
Framing	Placing the content of other sites in a frame on the infringer's site	*The Washington Post, et al. v. TotalNews, Inc., et al.*, (S.D.N.Y., Civil Action Number 97-1190)

Trademark abuse can take many forms on the Web. **Table 8.16** lists the major behaviors on the Internet that have run afoul of trademark law and some of the court cases that resulted.

Cybersquatting and Brandjacking

In one of the first cases involving the ACPA, E. & J. Gallo Winery, owner of the registered mark "Ernest and Julio Gallo" for alcoholic beverages, sued Spider Webs Ltd. for using the domain name Ernestandjuliogallo.com. Spider Webs Ltd. was a domain name speculator that owned numerous domain names consisting of famous company names. The Ernestandjuliogallo.com website contained information on the risks of alcohol use, anti-corporate articles about E. & J. Gallo Winery, and was poorly constructed. The court concluded that Spider Webs Ltd. was in violation of the ACPA and that its actions constituted dilution by blurring because the Ernestandjuliogallo.com domain name appeared on every page printed off the website accessed by that name, and that Spider Webs Ltd. was not free to use this particular mark as a domain name (*E. & J. Gallo Winery v. Spider Webs Ltd.*, 2001). In 2009, a court upheld the largest cybersquatting judgment to date: a $33 million verdict in favor of Verizon against OnlineNIC, an Internet domain registration company that had used over 660 names that could easily be confused with legitimate Verizon domain names. Although there have not been many cases decided under the ACPA, that does not mean the problem has gone away. Impersonation of individuals and brands on social network sites adds another dimension to the problem. Both Twitter and Facebook make cybersquatting and impersonation a violation of their terms of service.

However, it is not always easy for a firm to prevent trademark infringement by cybersquatters, or to prevent squatters from profiting from their infringing activities. In 2015, for instance, the Academy of Motion Picture Arts and Sciences (AMPAS) accused domain registrar GoDaddy of cybersquatting (*Academy of Motion Picture Arts and Sciences v. GoDaddy.com Inc et al.*, 2015). AMPAS claimed GoDaddy acted in bad faith by allowing customers to purchase 293 domain names such as Academyawards.net, Oscarsredacademyawards.net, Oscarsredcarpet.com, Billycrystal2012oscars.com, and Theoscargoestothehangover.com, and then sharing in the advertising revenues those pages generated. The court ruled that GoDaddy relied on representations of their users that their domain registrations did not infringe any trademarks, and that it took down domains after receiving takedown requests. AMPAS failed to prove intent to profit from AMPAS marks, according to the court. This suit demonstrates that trademark owners need to be vigilant in detecting infringement, sending takedown notices immediately, and following up to make sure the infringing sites are taken down. The burden is clearly on the trademark owner. The suit also demonstrates that cybersquatters have little incentive to stop trying to defraud and confuse consumers. If they are caught, their sites are taken down, but there is no penalty for trying (Stempel, 2015).

Cyberpiracy

Cyberpiracy involves the same behavior as cybersquatting, but with the intent of diverting traffic from the legitimate site to an infringing site. In *Ford Motor Co. v. Lapertosa*, Lapertosa had registered and used a website called Fordrecalls.com as an adult entertainment website. The court ruled that Fordrecalls.com was in violation of the ACPA in that it was a bad-faith attempt to divert traffic to the Lapertosa site and diluted Ford's wholesome trademark (*Ford Motor Co. v. Lapertosa*, 2001).

The Ford decision reflects two other famous cases of cyberpiracy. In the *Paine Webber Inc. v. Fortuny* case, the court enjoined Fortuny from using the domain name www.painewebber.com—a site that specialized in pornographic materials—because it diluted and tarnished Paine Webber's trademark and diverted web traffic from Paine Webber's legitimate site—Painewebber.com (*Paine Webber Inc. v. Fortuny*, 1999). In the *Playboy Enterprises, Inc. v. Global Site Designs, Inc.* case, the court enjoined the defendants from using the Playboy and Playmate marks in their domain names Playboyonline.net and Playmatesearch.net and from including the Playboy trademark in their metatags. In these cases, the defendants' intention was diversion for financial gain (*Playboy Enterprises, Inc. v. Global Site Designs, Inc.*, 1999).

Typosquatting is a form of cyberpiracy in which a domain name contains a common misspelling of another site's name. These domains are sometimes referred to as "doppelganger" domains. Often the user ends up at a site very different from one they intended to visit. For instance, John Zuccarini is an infamous typosquatter who was jailed in 2002 for setting up pornographic websites with URLs based on misspellings of popular children's brands, such as Bob the Builder and Teletubbies. The FTC fined him again in 2007 for engaging in similar practices (McMillan, 2007). Harvard Business School professor Ben Edelman conducted a study that found that there were at least 938,000 domains typosquatting on the top 3,264 ".com" websites, and that 57% of these domains included Google pay-per click ads. In 2011, Facebook filed a lawsuit against 25 typosquatters who established websites with such domain names as Faceboook, Facemook, Faceboik, and Facebooki. In 2013, Facebook was awarded $2.8 million in damages.

Metatagging

The legal status of using famous or distinctive marks as metatags is more complex and subtle. The use of trademarks in metatags is permitted if the use does not mislead or confuse consumers. Usually this depends on the content of the site. A car dealer would be permitted to use a famous automobile trademark in its metatags if the dealer sold this brand of automobiles, but a pornography site could not use the same trademark, nor a dealer for a rival manufacturer. A Ford dealer would most likely be infringing if it used "Honda" in its metatags, but would not be infringing if it used "Ford" in its metatags. (Ford Motor Company would be unlikely to seek an injunction against one of its dealers.)

In the *Bernina of America, Inc. v. Fashion Fabrics Int'l, Inc.* case, the court enjoined Fashion Fabrics, an independent dealer of sewing machines, from using the trademarks "Bernina" and "Bernette," which belonged to the manufacturer Bernina, as metatags. The court found the defendant's site contained misleading claims about Fashion Fabrics' knowledge of Bernina products that were likely to confuse customers. The use of the Bernina trademarks as metatags per se was not a violation of ACPA, according to the court, but in combination with the misleading claims on the site would cause confusion and hence infringement (*Bernina of America, Inc. v. Fashion Fabrics Int'l, Inc.*, 2001).

In the *Nissan Motor Co., Ltd. v. Nissan Computer Corp.* case, Uzi Nissan had used his surname "Nissan" as a trade name for various businesses since 1980, including Nissan Computer Corp. Nissan.com had no relationship with Nissan Motor, but over the years began selling auto parts that competed with Nissan Motor. The court ruled that Nissan Computer's behavior did indeed infringe on Nissan Motor's trademarks, but it refused to shut the site down. Instead, the court ruled Nissan Computer could continue to use the Nissan name and metatags, but must post notices on its site that it was not affiliated with Nissan Motor (*Nissan Motor Co., Ltd. v. Nissan Computer Corp.*, 2000).

Keywording

The permissibility of using trademarks as keywords on search engines is also subtle and depends (1) on the extent to which such use is considered to be a "use in commerce" and causes "initial customer confusion" and (2) on the content of the search results.

In *Playboy Enterprises, Inc. v. Netscape Communications, Inc.*, Playboy objected to the practice of Netscape's and Excite's search engines displaying banner ads unrelated to *Playboy Magazine* when users entered search arguments such as "playboy," "playmate," and "playgirl." The Ninth Circuit Court of Appeals denied the defendant's motion for a summary judgment and held that when an advertiser's banner ad is not labeled so as to identify its source, the practice could result in trademark infringement due to consumer confusion (*Playboy Enterprises, Inc. v. Netscape Communications, Inc.*, 2004).

Google has also faced lawsuits alleging that its advertising network illegally exploits others' trademarks. For instance, insurance company GEICO challenged Google's practice of allowing competitors' ads to appear when a searcher types "Geico" as the search query. A U.S. district court ruled that this practice did not violate federal trademark laws as long as the word "Geico" was not used in the ads' text (*Government Employees Insurance Company v. Google, Inc.*, 2004). Google quickly discontinued allowing the latter, and settled the case (Associated Press, 2005). In 2009, Rosetta Stone, the language-learning software firm, filed a lawsuit against Google for trademark infringement, alleging its AdWords program allowed other companies to use Rosetta Stone's trademarks for online advertisements without permission. In 2012, the 4th Circuit Court of Appeals held that a jury might hold Google liable for trademark infringement, pointing to evidence that an internal Google study found that even sophisticated users were sometimes unaware that sponsored links were advertisements. In 2012, Rosetta Stone and Google settled, which was seen as a strategic win for Google because it eliminated one of the last major cases challenging the legitimacy of its AdWords program. Currently Google allows anyone to buy anyone else's trademark as a keyword. In 2011, Microsoft decided to follow this practice as well with Bing and Yahoo Search.

Linking

Linking refers to building hypertext links from one site to another site. This is obviously a major design feature and benefit of the Web. **Deep linking** involves bypassing the target site's home page and going directly to a content page. In *Ticketmaster Corp. v. Tickets.com*, Tickets.com—owned by Microsoft—competed directly against Ticketmaster in the events ticket market. When Tickets.com did not have tickets for an event, it would direct users to Ticketmaster's internal pages, bypassing the Ticketmaster home page. Even though its logo was displayed on the internal pages, Ticketmaster objected on the grounds that such "deep linking" violated the terms and conditions of use for its site (stated on a separate page altogether and construed by Ticketmaster as equivalent to a shrink-wrap license), and constituted false advertising, as well as the violation of copyright. The court found, however, that deep linking per se is not illegal, no violation of copyright occurred because no copies were made, the terms

linking
building hypertext links from one site to another site

deep linking
involves bypassing the target site's home page, and going directly to a content page

and conditions of use were not obvious to users, and users were not required to read the page on which the terms and conditions of use appeared in any event. The court refused to rule in favor of Ticketmaster, but left open further argument on the licensing issue. In an out-of-court settlement, Tickets.com nevertheless agreed to stop the practice of deep linking (*Ticketmaster v. Tickets.com*, 2000).

Framing

framing

involves displaying the content of another website inside your own website within a frame or window

Framing involves displaying the content of another website inside your own website within a frame or window. The user never leaves the framer's site and can be exposed to advertising while the target site's advertising is distorted or eliminated. Framers may or may not acknowledge the source of the content. In *The Washington Post, et al. v. TotalNews, Inc.,* The Washington Post Company, CNN, Reuters, and several other news organizations filed suit against TotalNews, Inc., claiming that TotalNews's use of frames on its website, TotalNews.com, infringed upon the respective plaintiffs' copyrights and trademarks, and diluted the content of their individual websites. The plaintiffs claimed additionally that TotalNews's framing practice effectively deprived the plaintiffs' websites of advertising revenue.

TotalNews's website employed four frames. The TotalNews logo appeared in the lower left frame, various links were located in a vertical frame on the left side of the screen, TotalNews's advertising was framed across the screen bottom, and the "news frame," the largest frame, appeared in the center and right. Clicking on a specific news organization's link allowed the reader to view the content of that particular organization's website, including any related advertising, within the context of the "news frame." In some instances, the framing distorted or modified the appearance of the linked website, including the advertisements, while the appearance of TotalNews's advertisements, in a separate frame, remained unchanged. In addition, the URL remained fixed on the TotalNews address, even though the content in the largest frame on the website was from the linked website. The "news frame" did not, however, eliminate the linked website's identifying features.

The case was settled out of court. The news organizations allowed TotalNews to link to their websites, but prohibited framing and any attempt to imply affiliation with the news organizations (*The Washington Post, et al. v. TotalNews, Inc.*, 1997).

TRADE SECRETS

trade secret

information that is secret, has commercial value, and has been protected by its owner

Much of the value created by a firm lies not in copyrights, patents, or even trademarks. There is a kind of intellectual property that has to do with business procedures, formulas, and methods of manufacture and service delivery, from which the firm derives value and which it does not want to share with others in the form of a patent application or copyright application. This type of intellectual property is referred to as **trade secrets.** Most famously, the formula for Coca Cola is considered a trade secret, as are the manufacturing techniques for producing General Electric's jet engine turbine blades. Trade secrets differ from other copyright and patent protections because they may not be unique or novel. Information in a firm can be considered a trade secret if (a) it is a secret (something that others do not know), (b) has commercial value to its owner, and (c) the owner has taken steps to protect the secret. U.S. corporations are believed to own trillions of dollars of trade secrets (Gershman, 2016).

Until recently, trade secrets were defined and enforced mostly in state laws because historically businesses were local, as was theft of business trade secrets. In the digital age, when business is national and global, a new level of protection is needed that would make it easier to enforce trade secret laws. In 2016, President Obama signed the Defend Trade Secrets Act (DTSA), which creates a federal private right of action for trade secret protection. DTSA is a response to the large-scale theft of trade secrets (also known as economic sabotage) by hackers and foreign nations from American corporate and government information systems. The European Union is developing a similar Trade Secrets Directive to protect European firms and nations (Crouch, 2016). According to the U.S. Patent and Trade Office, the theft of trade secrets is one of the largest transfers of wealth in history, costing U.S. firms $300 billion a year (Lee, 2016). However, it is unclear if the new Act actually will be capable of protecting firms from theft of trade secrets.

CHALLENGE: BALANCING THE PROTECTION OF PROPERTY WITH OTHER VALUES

The challenge in intellectual property ethics and law is to ensure that creators of intellectual property can receive the benefits of their inventions and works, while also making it possible for their works and designs to be disseminated and used by the widest possible audience. Protections from rampant theft of intellectual property inevitably lead to restrictions on distribution, which then restricts payments to creators for the use of their works—which in itself can slow down the distribution process. Without these protections, however, and without the benefits that flow to creators of intellectual property, the pace of innovation could decline. In the early years of e-commerce, up to 2005, the balance has been struck more toward Internet distributors and their claim to be free from restrictions on intellectual content, particularly music. Since the development of the iTunes store, smartphones, and tablets, after 2005, the balance has swung back toward content owners, largely because Internet distributors depend on high-quality content to attract audiences, but also partly due to the effectiveness of lawsuits in raising the costs to Internet firms that fail to protect intellectual property.

8.4   GOVERNANCE

Governance has to do with social control: Who will control the Internet? Who will control the processes of e-commerce, the content, and the activities? What elements will be controlled, and how will the controls be implemented? A natural question arises and needs to be answered: Why do we as a society need to "control" e-commerce? Because e-commerce and the Internet are so closely intertwined (though not identical), controlling e-commerce also involves regulating the Internet.

governance
has to do with social control: who will control e-commerce, what elements will be controlled, and how will the controls be implemented

CAN THE INTERNET BE CONTROLLED?

Early Internet advocates argued that the Internet was different from all previous technologies. They contended that the Internet could not be controlled, given its inherent decentralized design, its ability to cross borders, and its underlying packet-switching technology that made monitoring and controlling message content impossible. Many still believe this to be true today. The implication is that the content and behavior of e-commerce sites—indeed Internet sites of any kind—cannot be "controlled" in the same way. Content issues such as pornography, gambling, and offensive written expressions and graphics, along with commercial issue of intellectual property protection, ushered in the current era of growing governmental regulation of the Internet and e-commerce throughout the world. Currently, we are in a mixed-mode policy environment where self-regulation through a variety of Internet policy and technical bodies co-exists with limited government regulation (Stone, 2010). See Chapter 2 for a review of the different governing bodies involved in overseeing the Internet, including ICANN and IANA, and changes in the United States' authority over IANA.

In fact, as you learned in the Chapter 2 *Insight on Society* case, *Government Regulation and Surveillance of the Internet*, the Internet is technically very easily controlled, monitored, and regulated from central locations (such as network access points, telecommunication firm or agency fiber trunk lines, as well as servers and routers throughout the network). For instance, in China, Saudi Arabia, Iran, North Korea, Thailand, Singapore, and many other countries, access to the Web is controlled from government-owned centralized routers that direct traffic across their borders and within the country (such as China's "Great Firewall of China," which permits the government to block access to certain U.S. or European websites), or via tightly regulated ISPs operating within the countries. In China, for instance, all ISPs need a license from the Ministry of Information Industry (MII), and are prohibited from disseminating any information that may harm the state or permit pornography, gambling, or the advocacy of cults. In addition, ISPs and search engines such as Google, Yahoo, and Bing typically self-censor their Asian content by using only government-approved news sources or, in the case of Google, exit the country altogether. Twitter is not planning any Chinese presence. China has also instituted regulations that require cafes, restaurants, hotels, and bookstores to install web monitoring software that identifies those using wireless services and monitors web activity. Because of the design of the Internet, a substantial part of global Internet traffic flows through U.S. telecommunication facilities.

Following the outbreak of street demonstrations in 2009 protesting a rigged election, the Iranian government unleashed one of the world's most sophisticated mechanisms for controlling and censoring the Web. Built with the assistance of Western companies like Siemens and Nokia, the system uses deep packet inspection to open every packet, look for keywords, reseal it, and send it on the network.

In the United States, as we have seen in our discussion of intellectual property, e-commerce sites can be put out of business for violating existing laws, and ISPs can be forced to "take down" offending or stolen content. Government security agencies such as the NSA and the FBI can obtain court orders to monitor ISP traffic and engage in widespread monitoring of millions of e-mail messages. Under the USA PATRIOT Act, American intelligence authorities are permitted to tap into whatever Internet traffic they believe is relevant to the campaign against terrorism, in some limited circumstances without judicial review. Working with the large ISP firms such as AT&T, Verizon, and others, U.S. security agencies have access to nearly all Internet communications throughout the country. And many American corporations are developing restrictions on their employees' at-work use of the Web to prevent gambling, shopping, and other activities not related to a business purpose.

In the United States, efforts to control media content on the Web have run up against equally powerful social and political values that protect freedom of expression, including several rulings by the Supreme Court that have struck down laws attempting to limit online content in the United States. The U.S. Constitution's First Amendment says, "Congress shall make no law … abridging the freedom of speech, or of the press." As it turns out, the 200-year-old Bill of Rights has been a powerful brake on efforts to control twenty-first-century online content.

TAXATION

Few questions illustrate the complexity of governance and jurisdiction more potently than taxation of e-commerce sales. In both Europe and the United States, governments rely on sales taxes based on the type and value of goods sold. In Europe, these taxes are collected along the entire value chain, including the final sale to the consumer, and are called "value-added taxes" (VAT). See the *Insight on Business* case, *New Rules Extend EU Taxation of E-commerce*, for a further look at this topic. In the United States, in contrast, taxes are collected by states and localities on final sales to consumers and are called consumption and use taxes. In the United States, there are 50 states, 3,000 counties, and 12,000 municipalities, each with unique tax rates and policies. Cheese may be taxable in one state as a "snack food" but not taxable in another state (such as Wisconsin), where it is considered a basic food. Consumption taxes are generally recognized to be regressive because they disproportionately tax poorer people, for whom consumption is a larger part of their total income. Nevertheless, state and local sales taxes are a major source of revenue, especially in states where there are no income taxes.

Sales taxes were first implemented in the United States in the late 1930s as a Depression-era method of raising money for localities. Ostensibly, the money was to be used to build infrastructure such as roads, schools, and utilities to support business development, but over the years the funds have been used for general government purposes of the states and localities. In most states, there is a state-based sales tax, and a smaller local sales tax. The total sales tax ranges from zero in some states (North Dakota) to as much as 13% in New York City for the combined state and city sales taxes.

The development of "remote sales" such as mail order/telephone order (MOTO) retail in the United States in the 1970s broke the relationship between physical presence and commerce, complicating the plans of state and local tax authorities to tax all retail commerce. States sought to force MOTO retailers to collect sales taxes for them based on the address of the recipient, but U.S. Supreme Court decisions in 1967 and 1992 established that states had no authority to force MOTO retailers to collect state taxes unless the businesses had a "nexus" of operations (physical presence) in the state.

The explosive growth of e-commerce, the latest type of "remote sales," has once again raised the issue of how—and if—to tax remote sales. Since its inception, e-commerce has benefited from a tax subsidy of up to 13% for goods shipped to high sales-tax areas. Local retail merchants have complained bitterly about the e-commerce tax subsidy. E-commerce merchants have argued that this form of commerce needs to be nurtured and encouraged, and that in any event, the crazy quilt of sales and use tax regimes would be difficult to administer for Internet merchants. Online giants like Amazon claim they should not have to pay taxes in states where they have no operations because they do not benefit from local schools, police, fire, and other governmental services. State and local governments meanwhile see billions of tax dollars slipping from their reach. As Amazon's business model has changed with its building of large distribution centers close to urban areas to enable next-day delivery, so has its opposition to paying sales taxes softened. In 2015, the U.S. Supreme Court upheld a challenge to a Colorado law that would have required firms to report online sales to state residents as one step to ensure the residents paid taxes on such sales in Colorado, which is required by state law. So far, 13 states have defied the Supreme Court ruling by imposing their own sales taxes on online purchases made by state residents in the hope of forcing lawsuits and potentially a new Supreme Court ruling, especially because the court also stated that the premise of allowing online sales by out-of-state firms like Amazon to go untaxed in order to support e-commerce sales was no longer appropriate, when e-commerce has exploded to a $600 billion marketplace. A recent study found that states lost $23 billion in revenue since 2012 because of e-commerce sales that went untaxed.

In 1998, the U.S. Congress passed the Internet Tax Freedom Act, which placed a moratorium on "multiple or discriminatory taxes on electronic commerce," as well as on taxes on Internet access, for three years until 2001. Since that time, the moratorium has been extended several times, and in 2016, Congress made the ban permanent.

The taxation situation in Europe, and trade between Europe and the United States, is similarly complex. The Organization for Economic Cooperation and Development (OECD), the economic policy coordinating body of European, American, and Japanese governments, is currently investigating different schemes for applying consumption and business profit taxes for digitally downloaded goods. The European Union began collecting a VAT on digital goods such as music and software delivered to consumers by foreign companies in 2003. Previously, E.U. companies were required to collect the VAT on sales to E.U. customers, but U.S. companies were not. This gave American companies a huge tax edge. European countries have other tax issues with Internet companies like Google, Apple, Yahoo, and others, that sell goods to consumers in one country, but book the sales in a low-tax country like Ireland.

net neutrality
the concept that Internet service providers should treat all Internet traffic equally (or "neutrally")

NET NEUTRALITY

Net neutrality refers to the idea that ISPs, including cable Internet and wireless carriers, should treat all data on the Internet in the same manner, and not discriminate or price differentially by content, protocol, platform, hardware, or application. Prior

INSIGHT ON BUSINESS

NEW RULES EXTEND EU TAXATION OF E-COMMERCE

Most people are happy when they discover they don't have to pay any sales tax on a purchase they make online. However, few stop to consider the implications that this may have. Governments in the last few years have been suffering a persistent budget crunch. Many countries that levy sales taxes have been eyeing the lost revenue from e-commerce sales, estimated to be in the billions in 2016. As e-commerce establishes itself as an ever-increasing percentage of the retail economy, governments worldwide are putting their collective feet down and demanding tax revenue from all online transactions.

The EU and the United States have a combined population of more than 800 million people. In both areas, the tax code is changing to reflect the new online landscape, where goods and services are sold without a physical presence or local representative in the countries where they are purchased. In 2013, the EU standardized its tax collection practices for e-businesses, bringing them more in line with businesses that are not situated in the EU.

In 2014, new EU regulations were implemented that compelled companies providing online services to EU customers to collect a value-added tax, or VAT, regardless of whether the company has a physical presence in that area or not. The customer's location is the determinant of whether the new EU rules apply. VAT was formerly due at the location of the sellers, but is now due at the location of the buyer. In the past, companies would save money by incorporating in countries with low VAT rates, such as Ireland or Luxembourg. The 2014 regulations were intended to combat this trend. Companies outside the EU already had to submit VAT based on its customers' locations when selling to EU B2C customers, but starting in 2015, it became policy for EU companies selling to EU B2C customers as well.

Having VAT due at the location of customers as opposed to the sellers' location requires that EU-based businesses register in every EU country where their customers reside and charge VAT at local rates. Registration can cost upwards of €8,000 per country, representing a major roadblock for smaller firms. In 2015, the hashtag #VATMESS was popular on Twitter with small business owners who were unhappy with the system and demanded change. In 2016, the European Commission responded to these concerns and proposed rules that would dramatically simplify the VAT requirements for online retailers. The new rules require EU companies to register with a "One Stop Shop" online portal controlled by their own national tax authorities, instead of with each individual country in the EU. Smaller businesses making sales of €10,000 or less would be able to treat sales as domestic sales using the VAT rates in their own countries. The requirements for larger businesses to verify the location of their customers were also reduced from two pieces of evidence to one. Many of these rules were already in place for online companies selling services, but not goods; the rules were extended to companies selling goods online as well. Although EU businesses have welcomed the 2016 changes and expected savings in the billions of euros, they still have significant regulatory burdens. They must distinguish between B2C and B2B customers, classify them by residence and store that information, and maintain systems that charge variable tax rates depending on whether customers are within the EU or outside of it.

The United States is one of the rare countries around the world that does not levy a VAT. State

(continued)

and local taxing jurisdictions are responsible for their own taxes and there is no national sales tax. Also, sales taxes apply mostly to end consumers, not intermediaries such as the wholesalers and retailers themselves. Only seven states do not currently levy sales taxes, and within those states, there are thousands of taxing jurisdictions, each with its own set of rules. With the adjustments to the EU's tax collection procedures, it's possible that the United States will follow suit at some point, perhaps as the result of pressure from retailers forced to navigate the confusing patchwork of local regulations. In 2016, through "Brexit," Britain voted in favor of exiting the EU, putting its e-commerce future in limbo. It, too, may need to update its rules and regulations to keep pace with the pro-business changes to the VAT made in 2016 or risk its online retailers falling behind the rest of the EU.

VAT standard percentages in EU countries vary from the high teens, such as in Germany, Luxembourg, and Malta, to the mid-twenties, such as in Sweden, Denmark, and Romania, though the reduced percentages are closer to 10% and below for certain goods and services. The majority of countries have at least a 20% VAT, and the highest rate is Hungary's 27%. The EU has also stipulated that wherever the Internet is used solely as a means of communication, this does not necessarily create a taxable good. However, whereas it was once the case in the United States that e-commerce businesses received special protections against taxation, the EU is considering adjusting its rate reductions to reflect the fact that digital information services may in some cases actually be more valuable than the direct equivalent of traditional products. For example, e-books have search facilities, hyperlinks, and archives, and should perhaps not be sold with a steeply reduced VAT rate. In 2016, along with the changes mentioned previously, the European Commission announced that it would begin applying the same VAT tax rates to e-books and online newspapers, arguing that they no longer need legal protection given the shift from physical to digital media platforms. More countries even outside the EU are toying with adding VAT, including Mexico, the Bahamas, and many more.

Other countries outside the EU and the United States are also grappling with the issue of e-commerce taxes. In China, the Chinese government is working to create new VAT laws that balance the needs of local and central governments. In 2016, China instituted sweeping reductions in the VAT taxes its companies are required to levy in an effort to boost its flagging growth, and also added a sales tax for foreign retailers to encourage more Chinese consumers to purchase products from Chinese retailers. And some academics are even suggesting the possibility of a global tax on cross-border e-commerce, with the funds used to finance global public goods.

■■■ **SOURCES:** "Commission Proposes New Tax Rules to Support E-commerce and Online Businesses in the EU," Europa.eu, December 1, 2016; "Modernising VAT for E-commerce: Questions and Answers," Europa.eu, December 1, 2016; "EU Proposes Simplifying VAT Rules to Boost Online Trade," by Philip Blenkinsop, Reuters.com, December 1, 2016; "EU Online Sellers Hail VAT Reform as 'Game Changer,'" by Joe Kirwin, Bna.com, December 2, 2016; "An Online Retailer's View of the 'Brexit' Debate," by Philip Rooke, Internetretailer.com, May 27, 2016; "China's Tax Overhaul Aims to Cut Business Costs," by Sue-Lin Wong and Jenny Su, Reuters.com, May 1, 2016; "China Changes the Tax Rules on Purchases from Overseas E-retailers," by Frank Tong, Internetretailer.com, February 25, 2016; "Single Vat Return: Is It Back to the Drawing Board?" by Jacek Szufan, Tmf-group.com, December 3, 2015; "#VATMESS Is About to Get Much Messier," by Hugo Grimston, Techcrunch.com, October 10, 2015; "China's VAT Reform Hits Delay," by Mark Melnicoe, Bna.com, August 26, 2015; "EU Targets Single VAT Registration on B2C E-Commerce 2017," Vatlive.com, May 7, 2015; "How the New Value-Added Tax Guidelines for Selling Digital Goods Affect Your Online Store," by Kathy Bricaud, Ecwid.com, January 23, 2015; "How New VAT Regulations Will Affect SMEs—and How to Prepare," by Carol Tricks, *The Guardian*, December 8, 2014; "#VATMess: UK's Army of Start-Up Firms Protest over New European VAT Rules Aimed at Curbing Tax Dodging by Web Giants," by Vicki Owen, Thisismoney.co.uk, November 29, 2014; "New EU VAT Regulations Could Threaten Micro-businesses, by Kitty Dann and Eleanor Ross, *The Guardian*, November 25, 2014; "European VAT: 10 Things Online Sellers Need to Know About Taxes on Digital Goods and Services," by Rick Minor, Forbes.com, May 15, 2014; "Chinese Govt Is Mulling E-commerce Tax," by Wang Ying, Chinadaily.com.cn, June 5, 2013; "A World of Difference: How the EU and US Tax E-commerce," Tmagazine.ey.com, March 15, 2013.

to February 2015, ISPs could discriminate against certain users on the basis of protocol or amount of usage. For instance, users of illegal downloading sites that utilize the BitTorrent protocol were blocked or throttled back (Internet speeds were slowed). Users who watched large volumes of movies on Netflix or other services were occasionally throttled back; wireless cellphone carriers choked off data speeds for heavy users when their networks became clogged; and large Internet services like Netflix and YouTube, that together consume an estimated 50% of the Internet's bandwidth in the United States, were encouraged to strike deals with ISPs and pay a higher fee than ordinary business or home users (Gryta, 2015a).

ISPs had long opposed the idea of net neutrality. ISPs claimed they needed to be able to manage the loads on their networks to ensure stable service, without blackouts or slowdowns. Throttling back heavy users was necessary to manage network load. They also argued that heavy individual or business users should pay more than the average user at home who uses the Web for e-mail, web surfing, and e-commerce, all of which do not require a lot of bandwidth. More to the point, the ISPs claimed the FCC did not have the authority to regulate ISPs because ISPs were not defined by the FCC as common carriers like traditional telephone companies. ISPs instead were classified in FCC regulations of the 1990s as information services in large part because the Internet, at that time, was considered to be a innovative provider of information that should be nurtured and not interfered with or regulated by the FCC. The Internet then was just not that important to the operation of society.

This view ended on February 15, 2015, when the FCC ruled that Internet broadband service providers really should be viewed as public utilities similar to telephone companies, and therefore should be regulated by the FCC in order to ensure fair access to all, deployment of acceptable broadband service levels, and competition among providers. This change reflected the fact that the Internet had evolved by 2015 into one of the primary telecommunications services in the country, and world, necessary to the everyday life of millions of people, businesses, and governments, and therefore a common carrier vital to the operation of society (just like a railroad service). The FCC was created by the Communications Act of 1934 to regulate telegraph and radio, and then later added regulation of television, satellite, and cable in all states. The FCC also overruled state laws that made it difficult for cities to operate their own broadband networks. In this way, a decades-long debate over net neutrality moved a step towards resolution. The ruling does not provide for regulation of ISP pricing, which remains in the hands of the ISPs (Gryta, 2015b). In 2016, a federal appeals court upheld the FCC view that ISPs were utilities that act as neutral indiscriminate platforms for transmission of speech.

However, the debate over net neutrality is not yet over. The large telecommunications carriers are preparing legal challenges to the FCC ruling. Yet there is strong public support for regulation of ISPs to ensure faster broadband deployment, more competition to reduce prices, and service level improvements. Popular services like Netflix, Google, and many other Internet content giants publicly supported the FCC decision as a win for consumers (Ruiz, 2015). Next on the FCC agenda is a proposed rule to end the cable companies' monopoly on TV set-top boxes by allowing the development of devices and apps that would permit consumers to control their cable TV in a manner similar to how they control their Internet access using smartphones or computers (McKinnon, 2016). The cable industry strongly opposes this proposed ruling.

8.5 PUBLIC SAFETY AND WELFARE

Governments everywhere claim to pursue public safety, health, and welfare. This effort produces laws governing everything from weights and measures to national highways, to the content of radio and television programs. Electronic media of all kinds (telegraph, telephone, radio, and television) have historically been regulated by governments seeking to develop a rational commercial telecommunications environment and to control the content of the media—which may be critical of government or offensive to powerful groups in a society. Historically, in the United States, newspapers and print media have been beyond government controls because of constitutional guarantees of freedom of speech. Electronic media such as radio and television have, on the other hand, always been subject to content regulation because they use the publicly owned frequency spectrum and hence come under a variety of federal laws and regulatory agencies, primarily the FCC. Telephones have also been regulated as public utilities and "common carriers," with special social burdens to provide service and access, but with no limitations on content.

In the United States, critical issues in e-commerce center around the protection of children, strong sentiments against pornography in any public media, efforts to control gambling, and the protection of public health through restricting sales of drugs and cigarettes.

PROTECTING CHILDREN

Pornography is an immensely successful Internet business. Statistics with respect to revenues generated by online pornography range widely. Reports of web traffic to pornography sites constituting 30% of all web traffic are likely not true and have no solid foundation. A sample of the million most-visited sites in the world found that 4% of the websites contained pornographic material, and 14% of web searches involved sexual content (Ward, 2013). Online pornography is estimated to generate $10 to $12 billion annually in the United States, and the global revenue is estimated to be $97 billion. Traditional DVD porn revenues have fallen off by 80% as so-called tube sites (YouTube for porn) have rapidly expanded with free and freemium content online. Piracy is rampant as with traditional video content. Revenues are now primarily derived from premium subscriptions and advertising.

To control the Web as a distribution medium for pornography, in 1996, the U.S. Congress passed the Communications Decency Act (CDA). This act made it a felony criminal offense to use any telecommunications device to transmit "any comment, request, suggestion, proposal, image, or other communications which is obscene, lewd, lascivious, filthy, or indecent" to anyone, and in particular, to persons under 18 years of age (Section 502, Communications Decency Act of 1996). In 1997, the U.S. Supreme Court struck down most of the CDA as an unconstitutional abridgement of freedom of speech protected by the First Amendment. While the government argued the CDA was like a zoning ordinance designed to allow "adult" websites for people 18 years of age or over, the Court found the CDA was a blanket proscription on content and rejected the "cyberzoning" argument as impossible to administer. One section of the CDA that did survive scrutiny, Section 230, provides immunity for providers and users of interactive computer services (such as ISPs and websites) from being considered a publisher that might be liable for harmful content posted by others. This is the law that allows social networks, blogs, and online bulletin boards to operate without fear of being held liable for online defamation or libel. In 2002, the Supreme Court struck down another law, the Child Pornography Prevention Act of 1996, which made it a crime to create, distribute, or possess "virtual" child pornography that uses computer-generated images or young adults rather than real children, as overly broad (*Ashcroft v. Free Speech Coalition*). The Children's Online Protection Act (COPA) of 1998 met with a similar fate.

In 2001, the U.S. Congress passed the Children's Internet Protection Act (CIPA), which requires schools and libraries in the United States to install "technology protection measures" (filtering software) in an effort to shield children from pornography. In 2003, the U.S. Supreme Court upheld CIPA, overturning a federal district court that found the law interfered with the First Amendment guarantee of freedom of expression. The Supreme Court, in a 6–3 opinion, held that the law's limitations on access to the Internet posed no more a threat to freedom of expression than limitations on access to books that librarians choose for whatever reason not to acquire. The dissenting justices found this analogy inappropriate and instead argued the proper analogy was if librarians were to purchase encyclopedias and then rip out pages they thought were or might be offensive to patrons. All the justices agreed that existing blocking software was overly blunt, unable to distinguish child pornography from sexually explicit material (which is protected by the First Amendment), and generally unreliable (Greenhouse, 2003b). Other legislation such as the 2002 Domain Names Act seeks to prevent unscrupulous website operators from luring children to pornography using misleading domain names or characters known to children. A plan to create an .xxx domain for adult website content was approved by ICANN in 2010, and in 2011, limited registration for .xxx domains began. Trademark holders who do not wish their brand to be associated with an .xxx domain can block requests by other companies for domain names that include their brand name. The 2003 Protect Act is an omnibus law intended to prevent child abuse that includes prohibitions against computer-generated child pornography. Part of that statute was previously held to be unconstitutional by the Eleventh Circuit Court of Appeals, but in 2008, the Supreme Court reversed the circuit court and upheld the provision (Greenhouse, 2008).

The Children's Online Privacy Protection Act (COPPA) (1998) prohibits websites from collecting information on children under the age of 13. It does permit such data collection if parental consent is obtained. Because COPPA does not interfere with speech or expression, it has not been challenged in the courts. However, since 1998, entirely new technologies like social networks, online tracking, advertising networks, online gaming, and mobile apps have appeared that are now being used to gather data on children and which were not specifically addressed in COPPA or FTC regulations. Responding to these changes in technology and public pressure, the FTC announced a new set of rules that are now in effect. The new rules prohibit online tracking of children across the Web with cookies or any other technology such as persistent identifiers; prohibit ad networks from following children across the Web and advertising to them without parental consent; make clear that mobile devices are subject to COPPA, including games and software apps; and make clear that third-party data collection firms that collect data on websites are responsible for any unlawful data collection. See the Chapter 7 *Insight on Society* case, *Marketing to Children of the Web in the Age of Social Networks*, for more information.

Search engines and ISPs also have a role to play in eliminating child pornography from the Web. The Internet Watch Foundation is a private non-profit organization based in the United Kingdom whose mission is to eliminate child pornography from the Web, and has over 200 corporate members from the Internet technology community (Internet Watch Foundation, 2015). In 2015, Google, Facebook, Microsoft, and Twitter joined together and are using the Internet Watch Foundation's hash list to remove abusive child images from their services. Other companies working with the Internet Watch Foundation include Cisco, Blackberry, Dropbox, and PayPal (Lien, 2015). But when tech companies become censors of content it places them in the tricky position of being media companies that determine the news, opinions, and art shown to their subscribers. Facebook, Google, Yahoo, and others involved in content delivery strongly deny this characterization, and instead claim to be purely pipelines for content. For instance, in 2016 Facebook removed a Pulitzer Prize winning photo of a naked 9-year old girl fleeing napalm bombs during the Vietnam War with tears streaming down her face because it violated their standards on child pornography. After thousands of people around the world protested by posting the picture on their Facebook pages, the company restored the photo, saying it recognized the global importance of this image in documenting a moment in history (Scott and Isaac, 2016). Analysts speculate that Facebook may be the most important editor on earth because it selects the content that billions of people see online.

CIGARETTES, GAMBLING, AND DRUGS: IS THE WEB REALLY BORDERLESS?

In the United States and around the world, governments have adopted legislation to control certain activities and products in order to protect public health and welfare. Cigarettes, gambling, medical drugs, and of course addictive recreational drugs are either banned or tightly regulated (see *Insight on Society: The Internet Drug Bazaar Operates Around the Globe*). Yet these products and services are ideal for distribution over the Internet through e-commerce sites. Because the sites can be located offshore, they can operate beyond the jurisdiction of state and federal prosecutors. Or so it seemed until recently. In the case of cigarettes, state and federal authorities have been quite successful in shutting down tax-free cigarette websites within the United States by pressuring PayPal and credit card firms to drop cigarette merchants from their systems. The major shipping companies—UPS, FedEx, and DHL—have been pressured into refusing shipment of untaxed cigarettes. Philip Morris has also agreed not to ship cigarettes to any resellers that have been found to be engaging in illegal Internet and mail order sales. However, a few offshore websites continue to operate using checks and money orders as payments and the postal system as a logistics partner, but their level of business has plummeted as consumers fear state tax authorities will present

INSIGHT ON SOCIETY

THE INTERNET DRUG BAZAAR OPERATES AROUND THE GLOBE

In June 2016, Interpol announced the results of its ninth-annual Operation Pangea effort to combat sales of illegal drugs online. The operation shut down almost 5,000 websites and resulted in the arrest of 393 people and the seizure of 712 million doses of illegal drugs worth $53 million. Despite successes such as this, however, the Internet drug bazaar operated by rogue Internet drug outlets remains a continuing public health and safety issue. According to a study done by the Treatment Research Institute at the University of Pennsylvania, addictive and potentially lethal medications are available without prescription from more than 2 million websites around the world, with many sites based in countries that impose little if any regulation on pharmaceuticals. A Google search for drugs "no prescription" in 2016, for instance, returned more than 27 million results.

The International Narcotics Control Board, a U.N. narcotics watchdog agency, has provided guidelines and a framework for governments struggling to contain growing abuse of prescription drugs on the Internet. According to the report, only two of 365 so-called Internet pharmacies it surveyed were legitimate. In many countries, the report said, trafficking in illegal prescription drugs now equals or exceeds the sale of heroin, cocaine, and amphetamines. While properly regulated Internet pharmacies offer a valuable service by increasing competition and access to treatments in underserved regions, online pharmacies are a long way from proper regulation.

The sale of drugs without a prescription is not the only danger posed by the Internet drug bazaar. Rogue online pharmacy sites may be selling counterfeit drugs or unapproved drugs.

For instance, in the past, the U.S. Food and Drug Administration (FDA) has issued warnings that a number of consumers who had purchased Ambien, Xanax, and Lexapro online had instead received a product containing haloperial, a powerful antipsychotic drug. Drug pushers on the Internet also include legitimate pharmaceutical firms who have discovered search engine advertising. Google and other search engines have come under fire for their relationships with purveyors of illegal drugs and other unlawful products like stolen credit cards and fake IDs, and both FedEx and UPS have had lawsuits filed against them and millions in fines levied for knowingly shipping packages from illegal online pharmacies, although the U.S. Department of Justice ultimately dismissed its charges against FedEx in 2016.

Despite these dangers, online pharmacies remain alluring and are one of the fastest growing business models with, oddly, senior citizens—usually some of the most law-abiding citizens—leading the charge for cheaper drugs. In 2015, the most popular fake drug was the erectile dysfunction medication Viagra. The main attraction of online drug sites is price. Typically, online pharmacies are located in countries where prescription drugs are price-controlled, or where the price structure is much lower, such as Canada, the United Kingdom, and European countries, as well as India and Mexico. Citizens can save quite a bit of money by purchasing from online pharmacies located in other countries.

Another haven for online purveyors of illegal drugs is the "dark" or "deep" Web, which consists of sites that are not accessible by search engines and often feature security measures designed to allow complete anonymity or to mask illegal activity. In the past, the most prominent online drug

(continued)

marketplace on the deep Web was the Silk Road, which was estimated to attract as much as $45 million a year in illegal drug purchases and $1.2 billion worth of total transactions. The Silk Road required users to run the Tor anonymity software and accepted the virtual currency Bitcoin (see the *Insight on Business* case, *Bitcoin*, in Chapter 4), allowing online drug buyers an unprecedented level of protection. The Silk Road was closer to eBay than to a pharmacy. But in 2013, the Silk Road's founder and chief operator, Ross Ulbricht, was arrested, charged with drug trafficking and money laundering, and eventually sentenced to life in prison in 2015. Although the arrest was seen as a major blow, it it still very easy to purchase illegal drugs on the deep Web. According to researchers at Carnegie Mellon University, more than 50% of the deep Web drug marketplaces (which they call darknet markets) have websites directly derived from the template used by Silk Road. As one market is closed, or closes, another pops up to take its place; for example, in 2016, Silk Road launched its fourth iteration, and although other prominent darknet markets like Agora and Evolution have closed, approximately 50 others have emerged to meet user demand. Together, these darknet markets account for between $150 and $180 million in drug sales each year, more than triple the amount Silk Road had in 2013. Marijuana accounts for about 33% of sales, followed by MDMA, stimulants, psychedelic drugs, prescription drugs, and opioids. And though many Bitcoin exchanges are forcing users to provide their identities, law enforcement agencies have not developed reliable methods for tracking virtual currencies, as criminals have developed methods such as "Bitcoin tumbling," where many users' Bitcoins are mixed together and redistributed to disguise their true owners' identities.

In 2016, Europol and the European Monitoring Centre for Drugs and Drug Addiction issued an in-depth analysis of the illegal drug market within the EU, which found that EU citizens spend between €21 to €31 billion each year on illegal drugs, as well as a related report on the Internet and the drug market. Citing globalization, technology advances, and the Internet as primary causes, the reports noted that the illicit drug market has become increasingly dynamic and innovative, and that Europe has become a major drug production hub. The reports note that the Internet has expanded the possibilities for drug supply and trafficking, allowing drug markets to become hybrid markets that combine traditional social and economic opportunity structures with new opportunities provided by the Internet. In addition, the Internet has not only opened the way for new criminal actors, but has also reconfigured relations among suppliers, intermediaries, and buyers.

These reports suggest that drug regulation enforcement needs to adapt with the times. As e-commerce brings down global borders, the need for a global strategy as opposed to individual countries and a patchwork of enforcement strategies has grown.

▬▬▬ **SOURCES:** "Online Sale of Fake Medicines and Products Targeted in Operation Pangea IX," Europol, June 10, 2016; "Online Sales of Illicit Drugs Triple Since Silk Road Closure," by Steven Musil, Cnet.com, August 10, 2016; "Shedding Light on the Dark Web," *The Economist*, July 16, 2016; "An In-Depth New Study Shows That the Online Market for Illegal Drugs Is Skyrocketing," by James Cook, Businessinsider.com, August 11, 2016; "U.S. Ends $1.6 Billion Criminal Case Against FedEx," by Dan Levine, Reuters, June 17, 2016; "The Internet and Drug Markets," EMCDDA, February 2016; "EU Drug Market Report," EMCDDA and Europol, 2016; "Internet-Facilitated Drugs Trade: An Analysis of the Size, Scope and the Role of the Netherlands," by Kristy Kruithof et al., RAND Corporation, 2016; "Buying Drugs Online Remains Easy, 2 Years After FBI Killed Silk Road," Steven Nelson, Usnews.com, October 2, 2015; "Measuring the Longitudinal Evolution of the Online Anonymous Marketplace," by Kyle Sosa and Nicolas Christin, Proceedings of the 24th USENIX Security Symposium, August 12–15, 2015; "Ross Ulbricht, Creator of Silk Road Website, Is Sentenced to Life in Prison," by Benjamin Weiser, *New York Times*, May 29, 2015; "FedEx Seeks to Show It's Good Guy in Internet Drug Crackdown," by Joel Rosenblatt, Bloomberg.com, May 14, 2015; "Silk Road's Alleged Mastermind Faces More U.S. Charges," by Erik Larson and Bob Van Voris, Bloomberg.com, August 22, 2014; "FedEx Indicted for Shipping Drugs Sold Online," by Katie Lobosco, Money.cnn.com, July 17, 2014; "Eagle Scout. Idealist. Drug Trafficker?," by David Segal, *New York Times*, January 18, 2014; "Meet the Dread Pirate Roberts, The Man Behind Booming Black Market Drug Website Silk Road," by Andy Greenberg, *Forbes*, September 2, 2013.

them with huge tax bills if they are discovered using these sites. In 2010, President Obama signed the Prevent All Cigarette Trafficking Act. The law restricts the sale of untaxed cigarettes and other tobacco products over the Internet and bans the delivery of tobacco products through the U.S. mail.

Gambling also provides an interesting example of the clash between traditional jurisdictional boundaries and claims to a borderless, uncontrollable Web. In the United States, gambling of all kinds is largely a matter of state and local laws, but in 2006 Congress passed the Unlawful Internet Gambling Enforcement Act of 2006 (UIGEA), which prohibited financial institutions from transferring funds to or from Internet gambling sites, but did not remove from the states the ability to regulate gambling of all kinds. While online gambling per se is not prohibited by this act, and no person has ever been arrested for online gambling, this legislation essentially crippled the online gambling industry within the United States. The online gambling market, based almost entirely offshore—primarily in the United Kingdom and various Caribbean Islands—grew by leaps and bounds, between 2009 and 2016, with much of the action (some estimate up to 50%) coming from customers based in the United States. Online gambling is still banned in most of the United States even though the global market is now a $45 billion dollar business, almost entirely offshore, and roughly one-third the size of the entire U.S. gambling business (about $69 billion, including lotteries and public gambling). In the United States, where online gambling is illegal except in three states, online gambling generates less than $2 billion in 2016, but is expected to grow to $9 billion by 2020. The U.S. Department of Justice enforced the law vigorously, denying offshore operators access to American payment systems, seizing assets, crippling their U.S. business, and arresting several executives. However, the mood has changed in the last five years. State revenue needs have grown, and many in the casino gambling industry have switched sides and now support online gambling, seeing it as a revenue growth opportunity. The ethical issues surrounding online gambling may have less influence on the public debate than the need for new tax revenues, and for firms, the hope for additional revenues.

In 2012, Delaware became the first state to legalize online gambling in all its forms, and two others have followed: Nevada and New Jersey. Online gambling is also legal in the U.S. Virgin Islands. In 2016, several states are considering bills that would legalize online gambling: California, Massachusetts, Michigan, New York, and Pennsylvania.

In 2013, Station Casinos, a local Las Vegas company, opened the nation's first legal, pay-to-play poker website. The site claims it can use geo-location technology to ensure that the players are in the State of Nevada and over the age of 21, a condition of its operation insofar as the federal government does not yet permit online poker whereas it is legal in Nevada and supported by the large casinos as an extension of their brands.

However, so far, legal online gambling has disappointed expectations. While online gambling sputters along in a slow-growth economy, fantasy sports and betting is exploding. Two firms dominate the online fantasy sports market: DraftKings and FanDuel. Both firms advertise heavily during college and professional sports games. In fantasy sports, players assemble their ideal fantasy teams, drafting real-life athletes to their team, and then, based on the performance of those players in real games, they can win significant prizes. The most popular sports are college football and basketball, and professional football and baseball. Players are given a budget that they can use to draft players, and some of the combined fees for each game make up the pool for which players compete. Entry fees range widely from less than a dollar, to over $1,000 (Belson, 2015). DraftKings claims that several winner prizes have exceeded $1 million although none of the sites publish a list of winners.

Fantasy sports games are permitted in 45 states. Fantasy sports were exempted from the Unlawful Internet Gambling Enforcement Act of 2006 (UIGEA) under industry pressure from the then much smaller fantasy sports business. The industry argued that fantasy sports are not gambling, but instead games of skill like chess or Scrabble. As the industry has grown to billion-dollar venture capital valuations, however, and with allegations of cheating customers, deceptive practices, lack of transparency, and insider irregularities, state and federal legislators are holding hearings and considering regulations (Russo, 2015; Drape and Williams, 2015). In November 2015, New York State attorney general Eric Schneiderman told both DraftKings and FanDuel to stop taking entries from New York State residents because, in the state's opinion, their operations constitute illegal gambling. After lengthy legislative hearings, and strong support from sports fans, New York reversed its position, arguing that when played fairly, fantasy sports gambling was a game of skill, not gambling, and legalized the practice while imposing a regulatory regime on the industry to ensure its fair operation (Drape, 2016).

CASE STUDY

The Pirate Bay:
Searching for a Safe Haven

he Pirate Bay (TPB) has been one of the world's best-known and most popular pirated music and content sites for over a decade, offering free access to millions of copyrighted songs and thousands of copyrighted Hollywood movies, television shows, and video games. This despite the fact that TPB has been subjected to repeated legal efforts to shut it down. In fact, the authorities pursuing TPB must feel as if they are engaged in a never-ending game of Whack-a-mole, as each time they "whack" TPB, it somehow manages to reappear. But the battle is far from over, and for the first time, it appears possible that the "good guys" are actually winning. The Internet is becoming a tough place for music and video pirates to make a living in part because of enforcement actions, but more importantly because of new mobile and wireless technologies that enable high-quality content to be streamed for just a small fee.

TPB is part of a European social and political movement that opposes copyrighted content and demands that music, videos, TV shows, and other digital content be free

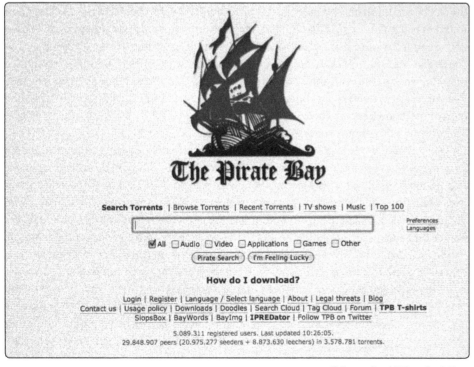

© Tommy (Louth)/Alamy Stock Photo

and unrestricted. TPB does not operate a database of copyrighted content. Neither does it operate a network of computers owned by "members" who store the content, nor does it create, own, or distribute software (like BitTorrent and most other so-called P2P networks) that permits such networks to exist in the first place. Instead, TPB simply provides a search engine that generates a list of search results from P2P networks around the world where the titles can be found. By clicking on a selected link, users gain access to the copyrighted content, but only after downloading software and other files from that P2P network.

TPB claims it is merely a search engine providing pointers to existing P2P networks that it does not itself control. It says that it cannot control what content users ultimately find on those P2P networks, and that it is no different from any other search engine, such as Google or Bing, which are not held responsible for the content found on sites listed in search results. From a broader standpoint, TPB's founders also claim that copyright laws in general unjustly interfere with the free flow of information on the Internet, and that in any event, they were not violating Swedish copyright law, which they felt should be the only law that applied. And they further claimed they did not encourage, incite, or enable illegal downloading. Nevertheless, the defendants have never denied that theirs was a commercial enterprise. Despite all the talk calling for the free, unfettered spread of culture, TPB was a money-making operation from the beginning, designed to produce profits for its founders, with advertising as the primary source of revenue.

However, the First Swedish Court in Stockholm declared TPB's four founders guilty of violating Swedish copyright law, and sentenced each to one year in prison and payment of $3.5 million in restitution to the plaintiffs, all Swedish divisions of the major record firms (Warner Music, Sony, and EMI Group among them). The court found that the defendants had incited copyright infringement by providing a website with search functions, easy uploading and storage possibilities, and a tracker. The court also said that the four defendants had been aware of the fact that copyrighted material was shared with the help of their site and that the defendants were engaged in a commercial enterprise, the basis of which was encouraging visitors to violate the copyrights of owners. In fact, the primary purpose of TPB was to violate copyrights in order to make money for the owners (commercial intent).

Meanwhile, the U.S. government pressured the Swedish government to strengthen its copyright laws to discourage rampant downloading. In Sweden, downloading music and videos from illegal sites was very popular, engaged in by 43% of the Swedish Internet population. To strengthen its laws, Sweden adopted the European Union convention on copyrights, which allows content owners to receive from Internet providers the names and addresses of people suspected of sharing pirated files. In France, participating in these pirate sites will result in banishment from the Internet for up to three years. As a result, Internet traffic in Sweden declined by 40%, and has stayed there.

TPB appealed the court judgment and has not paid any fines. That doesn't mean that TPB has not been affected by the lawsuits, however. In 2011, the firm moved its servers into caves in Sweden, and dispersed multiple copies of its program to other countries. In response to the lawsuits, police raids, and confiscation of servers, TPB has had stints in France, Finland, Italy, Germany, Denmark, Ireland, the U.K., and Greece within the last few years. These countries have in some cases refused to allow Internet service providers in their countries to host or link to TPB, no matter where in the world its servers are located. Authorities have shut down TPB's top-level domains in Sweden, Greenland, and Iceland, but TPB has continued to operate by hopping from country to country, moving to Sint Maarten, to tiny Ascension Island, to Peru, and back again to Sweden. In 2014, co-founder Gottfrid Svartholm Warg began serving a 42-month term in prison in Denmark for both copyright infringement and computer crimes unrelated to TPB, co-founder Peter Sunde was arrested after years on the run, and served a five-month prison term for copyright violation, and Fredrik Neij, another co-founder, was arrested in Thailand, then transferred to Swedish custody to serve a 10-month prison sentence. The company's financial resources also began to run dry. As interest continued to accrue on financial penalties previously levied on TPB, Carl Lundstrom, the site's primary financial backer, declared bankruptcy.

In December 2014, police again raided the site and shut it down. The site remained offline for seven weeks, until January 2015, the longest period of time it had ever been shut down. Members of the hacker group Anonymous claimed it was now in fact an FBI honeypot designed to trap the unwary. Even if rumors about the FBI are not true, many believe that it is not a good idea to use TPB anymore for other reasons: the site is now riddled with ads containing malware, contains downloadable malware and ransomware masquerading as popular movies and TV programs, and frequently goes offline. Even one of its original co-founders, Peter Sunde, has recommended that the site shut down once and for all. Nevertheless, the site continues to prove as elusive as ever for law enforcement, using a distributed approach to minimize the impact of closures in any individual country in which it operates. In 2016, a Swedish court ruled that the state could confiscate its top-level Swedish domains. In response, the company moved back to its original .org domain from 2003, which puts it back within the crosshairs of the United States.

In 2016, several lesser file sharing sites have voluntarily ceased operations, citing falling traffic and revenues and legal concerns. Although TPB recorded increases in site traffic after each of the closures, it's not a good sign for piracy sites in general. Nonetheless, TPB seems to have resilience that other sites lack, celebrating its 13th anniversary in 2016. TPB returned to the top spot among sites of its kind in 2016 after a multi-year hiatus due to its leadership upheaval and frequent closures. TPB has also become the largest video streaming site in the world thanks to a plugin that allows users to stream pirated content directly from their browsers. In typical Pirate Bay fashion, the plug-in behaves suspiciously like malware and is replete with bugs, but for users who are dead set against paying for content, the arrival of streaming to TPB has been a welcome addition. Those users also had to overcome many popular browsers, including Chrome and Firefox, blocking The Pirate Bay as malware.

The record industry's struggle against TPB is just part of the battle that it has been waging for some time. In 2005, the U.S. Supreme Court ruled in the ground-breaking *Metro-Goldwyn Mayer v. Grokster, et al.* case that the original peer-to-peer file sharing services, such as Grokster, Kazaa, and StreamCast, could be held liable for copyright

SOURCES: "The Pirate Bay and ExtraTorrent Traffic Skyrockets as TorrentHound Follows Torrentz in Voluntary Shutdown," by James Geddes, Techtimes.com, September 18, 2016; "Google Doesn't Want You Visiting The Pirate Bay Right Now," by Abhimanyu Ghoshal, Thenextweb.com, September 16, 2016; "Pirate Bay Is the King of Torrents Once Again," by Ernesto, Torrentfreak.com, August 14, 2016; "10 Years After Raid, The Pirate Bay Remains Alive and Well," by Janko Roettgers, *Variety*, May 31, 2016; "The Pirate Bay Sails Back to Its .Org Domain," by Aloysius Low, Cnet.com, May 25, 2016; "Will a Visit to The Pirate Bay End in Malware?" by Paul Ducklin, Nakedsecurity.sophos.com, May 6, 2016; "The Pirate Bay Pulls in a Whopping $9 a Day in Bitcoin Donations," by Jon Martindale, Digitaltrends.com, May 2, 2016; "Malvertising on The Pirate Bay Drops Ransomware," by Jerome Segura, Blog.malwarebytes.com, April 26, 2016; "The Pirate Bay is Now The Largest Video Streaming Site in the World," by Ryan Whitwam, Geek.com, February 8, 2016; "The Pirate Bay Now Supports Video Streaming, But Do So With Caution," by Stan Schroeder, Mashable.com, February 8, 2016; "Don't Trust The Pirate Bay: Movie Torrent Site Down Again, Amid Growing Skepticism and More Malware," by Jeff Stone, ibtimes.com, October 2, 2015; "Last Pirate Bay Co-Founder Released from Prison," by Alex Hern, Theguardian.com, September 29, 2015; "Peter Sunde: The Pirate Bay Should Stay Down," by Ernesto, Torrentfreak.com, December 14, 2014; "Pirate Bay Co-Founder Peter Sunde Arrested Years After Conviction," by Natasha Lomas, Techcrunch.com, June 1, 2014; "The Pirate Bay and the Business of Piracy," by Leo Sun, Fool.com, May 21, 2014; "MPAA Still Hunting for Cash as Pirate Bay Financier Set to Go Bankrupt," by Andy, Torrentfreak.com, June 10, 2013; "Pirate Bay Founder Submits Emotional Plea for Pardon," by Ernesto, Torrentfreak.com, July 7, 2012; "The Pirate Bay Evades ISP Blockade with IPv6, Can Do It 18 Quintillion More Times," by Sebastian Anthony, Extremetech.com, June 8, 2012; "The Pirate Bay: Five Years After the Raid," by Ernesto, Torrentfreak.com, May 31, 2011; "Pirate Bay Keeps Sinking: Another Lawsuit Coming," by Stan Schroeder, Mashable.com, June 22, 2010.

infringement, because they had intentionally sought to encourage users to share copyrighted material. All of these services have since gone out of business. But these legal victories, and stronger government enforcement of copyright laws, have not proven to be the magic bullet that miraculously solves all the problems facing the music industry. The music industry has had to drastically change its business model and decisively move toward streaming digital distribution platforms. They have made striking progress, and sales of music in a purely digital format now account for more revenue than sales of music in a physical format. To accomplish this, the music industry has employed a number of different business models and online delivery platforms, including Apple's iTunes pay-per-download model, subscription models, and cloud-based streaming models.

In each of these new media delivery platforms, the copyright owners—record companies, artists, and Hollywood studios—have struck licensing deals with the technology platform owners and distributors (Apple, Amazon, and Google). These new platforms offer a win-win solution. Consumers benefit by having near instant access to high-quality music tracks and videos without the hassle of P2P software downloads. Content owners get a growing revenue stream and protection for their copyrighted content. And the pirates? TPB and other pirate sites may not be able to compete with new and better ways to listen to music and view videos. In 2015, traffic from the Pirate Bay and its cohorts accounted for 2.76% of Internet traffic during peak hours, compared to 36.48% from Netflix alone. And content pirates don't appear to be particularly loyal to any of the sites they use; for all its traffic, TPB gets an average of only $9 per day in bitcoin donations in 2016, and even that paltry sum still dwarfs the amounts its competitors receive. Like the real pirates of the Caribbean, who are now just a footnote in history books, technology and consumer preference for ease of use may leave them behind.

Case Study Questions

1. Why did TPB believe it was not violating copyright laws? What did the Swedish court rule?

2. How has TPB managed to continue operating despite being found in violation of copyright laws?

3. How has the music industry reacted to the problems created by pirates like TPB?

8.7 REVIEW

KEY CONCEPTS

■ **Understand why e-commerce raises ethical, social, and political issues.**

- Internet technology and its use in e-commerce disrupts existing social and business relationships and understandings. Suddenly, individuals, business firms, and political institutions are confronted by new possibilities of behavior for which understandings, laws, and rules of acceptable behavior have not yet been developed. Many business firms and individuals are benefiting from the commercial development of the Internet, but this development also has costs for individuals, organizations, and societies. These costs and benefits must be carefully considered by those seeking to make ethical and socially responsible decisions in this new environment, particularly where there are as yet no clear-cut legal or cultural guidelines.
- The major issues raised by e-commerce can be loosely categorized into four major dimensions:
  - *Information rights*—What rights do individuals have to control their own personal information when Internet technologies make information collection so pervasive and efficient?
  - *Property rights*—How can traditional intellectual property rights be enforced when perfect copies of protected works can be made and easily distributed worldwide via the Internet?
  - *Governance*—Should the Internet and e-commerce be subject to public laws? If so, what law-making bodies have jurisdiction—state, federal, and/or international?
  - *Public safety and welfare*—What efforts should be undertaken to ensure equitable access to the Internet and e-commerce channels? Do certain online content and activities pose a threat to public safety and welfare?
- Ethical, social, and political controversies usually present themselves as dilemmas. Ethical dilemmas can be analyzed via the following process:
  - Identify and clearly describe the facts.
  - Define the conflict or dilemma and identify the higher-order values involved.
  - Identify the stakeholders.
  - Identify the options that you can reasonably take.
  - Identify the potential consequences of your options.
  - Refer to well-established ethical principles, such as the Golden Rule, Universalism, the Slippery Slope, the Collective Utilitarian Principle, Risk Aversion, the No Free Lunch Rule, the *New York Times* Test, and the Social Contract Rule to help you decide the matter.

■ **Understand basic concepts related to privacy and information rights, the practices of e-commerce companies that threaten privacy, and the different methods that can be used to protect online privacy.**

- To understand the issues concerning online privacy, you must first understand some basic concepts:
  - *Privacy* is the moral right of individuals to be left alone, free from surveillance or interference from others.
  - *Information privacy* includes the right to control personal information, to know what is being collected, the right to due process, and to right to have personal information stored securely.
  - *Due process* as embodied by the Fair Information Practices doctrine, informed consent, and opt-in/opt-out policies also plays an important role in privacy.
- Concepts of privacy are different in the public versus the private sector. In the public sector, privacy is protected by founding documents. In the private sector, privacy is less well defined, and only emerging.
- Almost all e-commerce companies collect some personally identifiable information in addition to anonymous information and use cookies to track clickstream behavior of visitors. Advertising networks and

search engines also track the behavior of consumers across thousands of popular sites, not just at one site, via cookies, spyware, search engine behavioral targeting, and other techniques.

- There are a number of different methods used to protect online privacy. They include:
  - Legal protections deriving from constitutions, common law, federal law, state laws, and government regulations. In the United States, rights to online privacy may be derived from the U.S. Constitution, tort law, federal laws such as the Children's Online Privacy Protection Act (COPPA), the FTC's Fair Information Practice principles, the FCC's broadband ISP privacy regulations, and a variety of state laws. In Europe, the European Commission's Data Protection Directive and GDPR (Privacy Shield) has standardized and broadened privacy protection in the European Union nations.
  - Industry self-regulation via industry alliances, such as the Online Privacy Alliance and the Network Advertising Initiative, that seek to gain voluntary adherence to industry privacy guidelines and safe harbors. Some firms also hire chief privacy officers.
  - Privacy-enhancing technological solutions include spyware and pop-up blockers, secure e-mail, anonymous remailers, anonymous surfing, cookie managers, disk file-erasing programs, policy generators, and public key encryption programs.

■ **Understand the various forms of intellectual property and the challenges involved in protecting it.**

- *Copyright law* protects original forms of expression such as writings, drawings, and computer programs from being copied by others for a minimum of 70 years. It does not protect ideas—just their expression in a tangible medium. Copyrights, like all rights, are not absolute. The doctrine of fair use permits certain parties under certain circumstances to use copyrighted material without permission. The Digital Millennium Copyright Act (DMCA) was the first major effort to adjust copyright law to the Internet age. The DMCA implements a World Intellectual Property Organization treaty, which declares it illegal to make, distribute, or use devices that circumvent technology-based protections of copyrighted materials, and attaches stiff fines and prison sentences for violations.

- *Patent law* grants the owner of a patent an exclusive monopoly to the ideas behind an invention for 20 years. Patents are very different from copyrights in that they protect the ideas themselves and not merely the expression of ideas. There are four types of inventions for which patents are granted under patent law: machines, man-made products, compositions of matter, and processing methods. In order to be granted a patent, the applicant must show that the invention is new, original, novel, nonobvious, and not evident in prior arts and practice. Most of the inventions that make the Internet and e-commerce possible were not patented by their inventors. This changed in the mid-1990s with the commercial development of the Web. Business firms began applying for "business methods" and software patents.

- *Trademark protections* exist at both the federal and state levels in the United States. Trademark law protects the public in the marketplace by ensuring that it gets what it pays for and wants to receive and also protects the owner who has spent time, money, and energy bringing the product to market against piracy and misappropriation. Federal trademarks are obtained, first, by use in interstate commerce, and second, by registration with the U.S. Patent and Trademark Office (USPTO). Trademarks are granted for a period of 10 years and can be renewed indefinitely. Use of a trademark that creates confusion with existing trademarks, causes consumers to make market mistakes, or misrepresents the origins of goods is an infringement. In addition, the intentional misuse of words and symbols in the marketplace to extort revenue from legitimate trademark owners ("bad faith") is proscribed. The Anticybersquatting Consumer Protection Act (ACPA) creates civil liabilities for anyone who attempts in bad faith to profit from an existing famous or distinctive trademark by registering an Internet domain name that is identical or confusingly similar to, or "dilutive" of, that trademark. The major behaviors on the Internet that have run afoul of trademark law include cybersquatting, cyberpiracy, metatagging, keywording, linking, and framing.

- *Trade secret laws* protect intellectual property having to do with business procedures, processes, formulas, and methods of manufacture.

- ■ Understand how the Internet is governed and why taxation of e-commerce raises governance and jurisdiction issues.
- Governance has to do with social control: who will control e-commerce, what elements will be controlled, and how will those controls be implemented. We are currently in a mixed-mode policy environment where self-regulation, through a variety of Internet policy and technical bodies, co-exists with limited government regulation.
- E-commerce raises the issue of how—and if—to tax remote sales. The national and international character of Internet sales has wreaked havoc on taxation schemes in the United States that were built in the 1930s and based on local commerce and local jurisdictions. E-commerce has benefited from a tax subsidy since its inception. E-commerce merchants have argued that this new form of commerce needs to be nurtured and encouraged, and that in any event, the crazy quilt of sales and use tax regimes would be difficult to administer for Internet merchants. In 1998, Congress passed the Internet Tax Freedom Act, which placed a moratorium on multiple or discriminatory taxes on electronic commerce, and any taxation of Internet access, and since that time has extended the moratorium several times, and in 2016 made it permanent. Federal legislation to implement a uniform set of rules for collecting taxes on e-commerce sales is currently pending in Congress. Net neutrality refers to the idea that Internet service providers (ISPs), including cable Internet and wireless carriers, should treat all data on the Internet in the same manner, and not discriminate or price differentially by content, protocol, platform, hardware, or application.

- ■ Identify major public safety and welfare issues raised by e-commerce.
- Critical public safety and welfare issues in e-commerce include:
  - The protection of children and strong sentiments against pornography. Several attempts by Congress to legislate in this area have been struck down as unconstitutional. The Children's Internet Protection Act (CIPA), which requires schools and libraries in the United States to install "technology protection measures" (filtering software) in an effort to shield children from pornography, has, however, been upheld by the U.S. Supreme Court.
  - Efforts to control gambling and restrict sales of cigarettes and drugs. In the United States, cigarettes, gambling, medical drugs, and addictive recreational drugs are either banned or tightly regulated by federal and state laws. Many offshore sites for these products and services have been shut down following government pressure. Online gambling is growing, but slower than anticipated. Online fantasy sports betting is growing rapidly.

QUESTIONS

1. Identify the four main dimensions that e-commerce ethical, political, and social issues fall into and provide an example of how each dimension might apply to an individual.
2. Define the ethical principle of accountability and describe two ways in which Internet technologies have raised accountability issues.
3. What concerns does the use of mobile devices bring to the issue of information privacy?
4. What is an ethical dilemma? Describe the two tactics you can use to resolve or reach a greater understanding of the dilemma.
5. How can the effectiveness of privacy policies be measured?
6. Why has the development of the Internet brought about so many ethical, political, and social issues?
7. Why does a mobile app such as Periscope raise copyright concerns?
8. What are some of the ethical, social, or political issues raised by the information density created by e-commerce technology?
9. What is the FCC and what is its role in consumer privacy protection?

10. What are the primary differences between consumer data privacy protection in Europe and the United States, and how do these differences affect U.S. e-commerce firms?
11. Why do social networks pose a unique problem to the issue of information privacy, and how might sharing personal information on a social site adversely affect a user?
12. What are the overall social benefits that network ad agencies claim derive from the practice of online profiling?
13. Identify and describe the main issues that the Internet and digital content have brought to the wider concerns of protecting intellectual property.
14. Identify the five steps outlined in the text you can use to analyze ethical conflicts.
15. What are some of the potential ethical, social, or political implications raised by the global reach of e-commerce technologies?
16. Why has WIPO warned against ICANN's extension of gTLDs? How has ICANN responded to those concerns?
17. What is a trade secret, and how does it differ from a patent or copyright protections?
18. Define cybersquatting. How is it different from cyberpiracy? What type of intellectual property violation does cybersquatting entail?
19. What is the "right to be forgotten"? What are some of the risks and benefits of establishing this right?
20. What is the doctrine of "fair use"?

PROJECTS

1. Go to Google and find the Advanced Search link. Examine its SafeSearch filtering options. Surf the Web in search of content that could be considered objectionable for children using each of the options. What are the pros and cons of such restrictions? Are there terms that could be considered inappropriate to the filtering software but be approved by parents? Name five questionable terms. Prepare a brief presentation to report on your experiences and to explain the positive and negative aspects of such filtering software.

2. Develop a list of privacy protection features that should be present if a website is serious about protecting privacy. Then, visit at least four well-known websites and examine their privacy policies. Write a report that rates each of the websites on the criteria you have developed.

3. Review the provisions of the Digital Millennium Copyright Act of 1998. Examine each of the major sections of the legislation and make a list of the protections afforded property owners and users of copyrighted materials. Do you believe this legislation balances the interests of owners and users appropriately? Do you have suggestions for strengthening "fair use" provisions in this legislation?

4. Visit at least four websites that take a position on e-commerce taxation, beginning with the National Conference of State Legislatures (Ncsl.org) and the National Governors Association (Nga.org). You might also include national associations of local businesses or citizen groups opposed to e-commerce taxation. Develop a reasoned argument for, or against, taxation of e-commerce.

REFERENCES

Academy of Motion Picture Arts and Sciences v. GoDaddy. com Inc et al. U.S. District Court, Central District of California, No. 10-03738 (2015).

Acquisti, Alessandro, Ralph Gross, and Fred Stutzman. "Faces of Facebook: Privacy in the Age of Augmented Reality," Heinz College & CyLab Carnegie Mellon University (August 4, 2011).

Acquisti, Alessandro, Leslie John, and George Loewenstein. "What Is Privacy Worth?" Twenty First Workshop on Information Systems and Economics (WISE) (December 14–15, 2009).

Alice Corporation Pty. Ltd. v. CLS Bank International, et al., Supreme Court of the United States, No. 13-298. June 19, 2014.

Angwin, Julia. "Face-ID Tools Pose New Risk." *Wall Street Journal* (August 1, 2011).

Apple Computer, Inc. v. Microsoft Corp. 709 F. Supp. 925, 926 (N. D. Cal. 1989); 799 F. Supp. 1006, 1017 (N. D. Cal., 1992); 35 F. 3d 1435 (9th Cir.); cert. denied, 63 U. S. L. W. 3518 (U.S., Feb. 21, 1995) (No. 94-1121).

Apuzzo, Matt, David Sanger, and Michael Schmidt. "Apple and Other Tech Companies Tangle With U.S. Over Data Access." *New York Times* (September 7, 2015).

Ashcroft v. Free Speech Coalition, 535 U.S. 234 (2002).

Associated Press. "Google Settles Final Piece of Geico Case." BizReport.com (September 8, 2005).

Belson, Ken. "A Primer on Daily Fantasy Football Sites." *New York Times* (October 6, 2015).

Bergen, Mark. "'Dancing Baby' Copyright Ruling Hands Temporary Win to YouTube, Facebook." Recode.net (September 14, 2015).

Bernina of America, Inc. v. Fashion Fabrics Int'l., Inc. 2001 U. S. Dist. LEXIS 1211 (N. D. Ill., Feb. 8, 2001).

Bilski et al. v. Kappos, 177 L. Ed. 2d 792, 130 S. Ct. 3218, 561 U.S. 593 (2010).

Bilton, Nick. "Apple Loophole Gives Developers Access to Photos." *New York Times* (February 28, 2012).

Bloomberg News. "Master of Your Domain? Maybe in .Com But Not in .Sucks." (May 13, 2015).

Brown Bag vs. Symantec Corp., 960 F. 2d 1465 (9th Cir. 1992).

Brustein, Joshua. "Start-Ups Seek to Help Users Put a Price on Their Personal Data." *New York Times* (February 12, 2012).

Capitol Records LLC et al. v. Vimeo LLC et al. 2nd U.S. Circuit Court of Appeals, No. 14-1048 (2016).

Center for Copyright Information. "The Copyright Alert System: Phase One and Beyond." (May 28, 2014).

Charlton, Angela. "France Threatens Google with Privacy Fines." *New York Times* (June 20, 2013).

Chen, Brian. "Verizon Publishes First Transparency Report on Data Requests." *Wall Street Journal,* January 22, 2014.

Chen, Brian. "Appeals Court Upholds Apple's Patent Victory Over Samsung." *New York Times* (May 18, 2015).

Chiappetta, Vincent. "Defining the Proper Scope of Internet Patents: If We Don't Know Where We Want to Go, We're Unlikely to Get There." *Michigan Telecommunications Technology Law Review* (May 2001).

Consumer Reports. "Who's Tracking You in Public." (February 2016).

Crouch, Dennis. "A Comparison of the EU Trade Secrets Directive and the US Defend Trade Secrets Act." Patentlyo.com (May 16, 2016).

Davis, Wendy. "TRUSTe Finalizes Settlement with FTC." Mediapost.com (March 18, 2015).

Decker, Susan. "Apple Wins Ruling to Force Samsung to Change Phones, Tablets." Bloomberg.com (September 17, 2015).

Diamond v. Chakrabarty, 447 US 303 (1980).

Drape, Joe. "Win for DraftKings and FanDuel Opens Door for Sports Betting in New York." *New York Times* (August 3, 2016).

Drape, Joe, and Jacqueline Williams. "FanDuel Makes Changes." *New York Times* (October 8, 2015).

Drozdiak, Natalia. "EU Approves 'Privacy Shield' Data-Transfer Pact With U.S." *Wall Street Journal* (July 12, 2016).

E. & J. Gallo Winery v. Spider Webs Ltd. 129 F. Supp. 2d 1033 (S.D. Tex., 2001) aff'd 286 F. 3d 270 (5th Cir., 2002).

Eldred v. Ashcroft, 537 U.S. 186 (2003).

European Commission. "Progress on EU Data Protection Reform Now Irreversible Following European Parliament Vote." (March 12, 2014).

European Commission. "Commission Proposes a Comprehensive Reform of the Data Protection Rules." (January 26, 2012).

Evans, Marcus. "European Council Approves EU General Data Protection Regulation Draft; Final Approval May Come by End of 2015." Dataprotectionreport.com (June 15, 2015).

Federal Communications Commission (FCC). "Protecting the Privacy of Customers of Broadband and Other Telecommunications Services." (October 27, 2016).

Federal Trade Commission. "Data Brokers: A Call for Transparency and Accountability." (May 27, 2014).

Federal Trade Commission. "Google Will Pay $22.5 Million to Settle FTC Charges It Misrepresented Privacy Assurance to Users of Apple's Safari Internet Browser." (August 9, 2012a).

Federal Trade Commission. "Facebook Must Obtain Consumers' Consent Before Sharing Their Information Beyond Established Privacy Settings." (August 10, 2012b).

Federal Trade Commission. "Protecting Consumer Privacy in an Era of Rapid Change." (March 26, 2012c).

Federal Trade Commission. "FTC Charges Deceptive Privacy Practices in Google's Rollout of Its Buzz Network." (March 3, 2011).

Federal Trade Commission. "Protecting Consumer Privacy in an Era of Rapid Change." (December 2010).

Federal Trade Commission. "Privacy Online: Fair Information Practices in the Electronic Marketplace." (May 2000).

Federal Trade Commission. "Privacy Online: A Report to Congress." (June 1998).

Field v. Google, Inc. 412 F.Supp. 2nd 1106 (D. Nev., 2006).

Fiesler, Casey, Jessica L. Feuston, and Amy Bruckman. "Copyright Terms in Online Creative Communities." Georgia Institute of Technology, Working Paper (April 26, 2014).

Fisher, William W. III. "The Growth of Intellectual Property: A History of the Ownership of Ideas in the United States." Law.harvard.edu/Academic_Affairs/coursepages/tfisher/iphistory.html (1999).

Ford, Paul. "Balancing Security and Liberty in the Age of Big Data." Businessweek.com (June 13, 2013).

Ford Motor Co. v. Lapertosa. 2001 U.S. Dist. LEXIS 253 (E. D. Mich. Jan. 3, 2001).

Fung, Brian. "The Group That Created '.sucks' Now Wants Government to Keep It From Spinning Out of Control." *Washington Post* (April 9, 2015).

Gardner, Eriq. "Judge Upholds $25 Million Judgment Against ISP Over User Piracy." *Hollywood Reporter* (August 9, 2016).

Gershman, Jacob. "Congress May Be About to Shake Up Trade Secret Law: Is That a Good Thing?" *Wall Street Journal* (April 27, 2016).

Gibbs, Samuel. "Google's New Nest Cam Is Always Watching, If You Let It into Your Home." *The Guardian* (June 18, 2015a).

Gibbs, Samuel. "EU States Agree on Framework for Pan-European Data Privacy Rules." *The Guardian* (June 15, 2015b).

Government Employees Insurance Company v. Google, Inc. Civ. Action No. 1:04cv507 (E.D. VA, December 15, 2004).

Greenhouse, Linda. "Supreme Court Upholds Child Pornography Law." *New York Times* (May 20, 2008).

Greenhouse, Linda. "20 Year Extension of Existing Copyrights Is Upheld." *New York Times* (January 16, 2003a).

Greenhouse, Linda. "Justices Back Law to Make Libraries Use Internet Filters." *New York Times* (June 24, 2003b).

Gryta, Thomas. "An Early Net-Neutrality Win: Rules Prompt Sprint to Stop Throttling." *Wall Street Journal* (June 17, 2015a).

Gryta, Thomas. "FCC Approves Net Neutrality Rules, Setting Stage for Legal Battle." *Wall Street Journal* (February 26, 2015b).

Harmon, Amy. "Pondering Value of Copyright vs. Innovation." *New York Times* (March 3, 2003).

Hoofnagle, Chris Jay. "Privacy Self-Regulation: A Decade of Disappointment." Electronic Privacy Information Center (Epic.org) (March 4, 2005).

Internet Watch Foundation. "Our Mission." IWF.org (accessed October 10, 2015).

Kakutani, Michiko. "Watched by the Web: Surveillance Is Reborn." *New York Times* (June 10, 2013).

Kaufman, Leslie. "Viacom and YouTube Settle Suit Over Copyright Violations." *New York Times* (March 18, 2014).

Kelly v. ArribaSoft. 336 F3rd 811 (CA 9th, 2003).

Kendall, Brent. "Supreme Court Hears Apple-Samsung Patent Case." *Wall Street Journal* (October 12, 2016).

Kendall, Brent, and Daisuke Wakabayashi, "Apple Wins Ruling in Patent Case Against Samsung." *Wall Street Journal* (September 17, 2015).

King, Cecillia. "Broadband Providers Will Need Permission to Collect Private Data." *New York Times* (October 27, 2016).

Lee, Michelle. "Protecting America's Secret Sauce: The Defend Trade Secrets Act Signed Into Law." Huffingtonpost.com (May 11, 2016).

Levine, Dan. "Amazon Must Face Trademark Lawsuit Over Search Results." Reuters.com (July 6, 2015).

Lien, Tracy. "Google, Facebook, Twitter Join Crackdown On Child Porn." *Los Angeles Times* (August 10, 2015).

Liptak, Adam. "Supreme Court Returns False-Data Case to Appeals Panel." *New York Times* (May 16, 2016).

Liptak, Adam and Alexandra Alter. "Challenge to Google Books Is Declined by Supreme Court." *New York Times* (April 18, 2016).

Mayer-Schonberger, Viktor, and Kenneth Cukier. *Big Data: A Revolution That Will Transform How We Live, Work, and Think.* Eamon Dolan/Houghton Mifflin Harcourt (2013).

McKinnon, John. "FCC Postpones Vote on TV Set-Top Box Plan." *Wall Street Journal* (September 29, 2016).

McMillan, Robert. "Porn Typosquatter Fined Again by FTC." *InfoWorld* (October 16, 2007).

Morran, Chris. "'Dancing Baby' YouTube Lawsuit May Go Before Supreme Court." Consumerist.com (August 12, 2016).

Nash, David B. "Orderly Expansion of the International Top-Level Domains: Concurrent Trademark Users Need a Way Out of the Internet Trademark Quagmire." *The John Marshall Journal of Computer and Information Law,* Vol. 15, No. 3 (1997).

Network Advertising Initiative. "Network Advertising Initiative Releases 2010 Compliance Report." Network-advertising.org (February 18, 2011).

Network Advertising Initiative. "Major Marketing/Media Trade Groups Launch Program to Give Consumers Enhanced Control over Collection and Use of Web Viewing Data for Online Behavioral Advertising." (October 4, 2010).

New, William. "WIPO: Internet Domain Expansion Disruptive to Trademark Strategies." Ip-watch.com (March 17, 2014).

Nissan Motor Co., Ltd. v. Nissan Computer Corp. 289 F. Supp. 2d 1154 (C. D. Cal.), aff'd, 2000 U. S. App. LEXIS 33937 (9th Cir. Dec. 26, 2000).

PaineWebber Inc. v. Fortuny, Civ. A. No. 99-0456-A (E. D. Va. Apr. 9, 1999).

Pearce, Sarah, and Annie Clarke. "EU: European Commission Commits to Finalising Negotiations on the EU Data Protection Regulation in 2015." Lexology.com (September 15, 2014).

Perfect 10, Inc. v. Amazon.com, Inc. 487 F3rd 701 (CA 9th, 2007).

Pew Research Center (Lee Rainie) "The State of Privacy in Post-Snowden America." (September 21, 2016a).

Pew Research Center. (Lee Rainie and Maeve Duggan). "The State of Privacy: Privacy and Information Sharing." (January 14, 2016b).

Pew Research Center. (Mary Madden and Lee Rainie). "Americans' Attitudes About Privacy, Security, and Surveillance." (May 20, 2015).

Pew Research Center (Susannah Fox and Lee Rainie). "The Web at 25 in the U.S." (February 27, 2014).

Playboy Enterprises, Inc. v. Global Site Designs, Inc. 1999 WL 311707 (S. D. Fla. May 15, 1999).

Playboy Enterprises, Inc. v. Netscape Communications, Inc. 354 F. 3rd 1020 (9th Cir., 2004).

Raymond, Nate. "Vimeo Wins U.S. Appeal in Music Copyright Case." *Reuters* (June 16, 2016).

Reuters. "Megaupload Founder Kim Dotcom Appears in Court to Fight U.S. Extradition." Reuters.com (September 21, 2015).

Rosen, Jeffrey. "The Right to be Forgotten." *Stanford Law Review,* 64. Stan. L. Rev. Online 88 (February 13, 2012).

Ruiz, Rebecca. "Publication of New Internet Rules to Prompt Cheers and Challenges." *New York Times* (April 5, 2015).

Russo, Ralph. "Daily Fantasy Football Draws Attention, Ire of NCAA." *Associated Press* (October 8, 2015).

Sanger, David and Brian Chen. "Signaling Post-Snowden Era, New iPhone Locks Out N.S.A." *New York Times* (September 26, 2014).

Sarno, David. "SmartPhone Apps Dial Up Privacy Worries." *Los Angeles Times* (February 16, 2012).

Savage, Charlie. "Between the Lines of the Cellphone Privacy Ruling." *New York Times* (June 25, 2014).

Savage, Charlie. "Democratic Senators Issue Strong Warning About Use of the Patriot Act." *New York Times* (March 16, 2012).

Schechner, Sam. "French Privacy Watchdog Orders Google to Expand Right to Be Forgotten." *Wall Street Journal* (June 12, 2015).

Schechner, Sam, and Natalia Drozdiak. "Belgium Takes Facebook to Court Over Privacy, User Tracking." *Wall Street Journal* (June 16, 2015).

Schwartz, John. "Justices Take Broad View of Business Methods Patents." *New York Times* (June 28, 2010).

Scott, Mark and Mike Isaac. "Facebook Restores Iconic Vietnam War Photo It Censored for Nudity." *New York Times* (September 9, 2016).

Scott, Mark. "European Court Adviser Calls Trans-Atlantic Data-Sharing Pact Insufficient." *New York Times.* (September 23, 2015).

Sengupta, Somini. "Europe Weighs Tough Law on Online Privacy." *New York Times* (January 23, 2012).

Shore, Jennifer and Jill Steinman. "Did You Really Agree to That? The Evolution of Facebook's Privacy Policy." Harvard Dataverse. http://dx.doi.org/10.7910/DVN/JROUKG. (August 6, 2011).

Singer, Natasha. "The Government's Consumer Data Watchdog." *New York Times* (May 23, 2015).

Singer, Natasha. "Never Forgetting a Face." *New York Times* (May 17, 2014a).

Singer, Natasha. "Didn't Read Those Terms of Service? Here's What You Agreed to Give Up." *New York Times* (April 28, 2014b).

Singer, Natasha. "An American Quilt of Privacy Laws, Incomplete." *New York Times* (March 30, 2013).

Singer, Natasha. "Consumer Data, But Not For Consumers." *New York Times* (July 21, 2012).

Spokeo, Inc. v. Robins. 578 U.S. ___ (2016)

State Street Bank & Trust Co. v. Signature Financial Group, 149 F. 3d 1368 (1998).

Stempel, Jonathan. "GoDaddy Prevails in Lawsuit over Oscar Trademarks." Reuters, September 11, 2015.

Stone, Brad. "Scaling the Digital Wall in China." *New York Times* (January 15, 2010).

Takenaka, Toshiko. "International and Comparative Law Perspective on Internet Patents." *Michigan*

Telecommunications Technology Law Review (May 15, 2001).

Thurm, Scott. "The Ultimate Weapon: It's the Patent." *Wall Street Journal* (April 17, 2000).

Ticketmaster v. Tickets.com. 2000 U.S. Dist. Lexis 4553 (C.D. Cal., August 2000).

United States Copyright Office. "Digital Millennium Copyright Act of 1998: U.S. Copyright Office Summary." (December 1998).

Washington Post Co., et al v. TotalNews, Inc., et al., S.D.N.Y., Civil Action Number 97-1190 (February 1997).

Weber, Harrison. "Periscope Has Received 1,391 Copyright Takedown Requests So Far — Twitter Complied with 71% of Them." Venturebeat.com (August 11, 2015).

Williams, Timothy. "Facial Recognition Software Moves From Overseas Wars to Local Police." *New York Times* (August 12, 2015).

Winston, Brian. *Media Technology and Society: A History From the Telegraph to the Internet.* Routledge (1998).

CHAPTER 9

Online Media

LEARNING OBJECTIVES

After reading this chapter, you will be able to:

- Understand the major trends in the consumption of media and online content, the major revenue models for digital content delivery, digital rights management, and the concept of media convergence.
- Understand the key factors affecting the online publishing industry.
- Understand the key factors affecting the online entertainment industry.

Spotify and Deezer:

European Streaming Music Services Spread Around the Globe

Today, streaming music is one of the fastest growing types of online media services. Spotify and Deezer are two prime examples of this type of service.

Spotify, founded in Sweden by Daniel Ek and Martin Lorentzon, is a vibrant music community. Users can choose the artists and music they want to hear, create and share playlists, and control the music while it plays via a mobile device or desktop computer. Spotify launched in Europe in 2008 and in the United States in 2011 and has risen to become the leading streaming music service in Europe. Spotify uses a freemium business model: consumers can listen to up to a certain number of hours of advertising-supported free music each month. Unlimited service without ads is available on computers and mobile phones for an additional cost. As a private company, Spotify does not report financial data, but analysts estimate that the company made $2.18 billion in 2015, up from $1.3 billion

© Felix Choo/Alamy Stock Photo

in 2014 and just $97 million in 2010. Content costs have also risen over that time frame, however, and Spotify has struggled to show a profit, recording a $194 million loss in 2015, only slightly lower than the previous year's $197 million loss. Analysts are skeptical that Spotify's business model can work over the long term, but Spotify believes that as it grows, its margins will improve. To that end, Spotify has continued to slash prices for new users, offering three months of streaming for only $0.99 to new users. In 2015, the company raised $350 million in funding at an incredible $8.5 billion valuation, and in 2016 has made more acquisitions than it made in its previous nine years combined, including music tracking startup Soundwave, voice messaging app Cord Project, social network company CrowdAlbum, and customer retention analytics firm Preact.

Spotify faces strong competition: Apple, Google, and Amazon have all started streaming music services, not to mention entrenched subscription services like Deezer (discussed below), Rhapsody, Pandora, and Rdio. Spotify has also had to deal with prominent artists like Taylor Swift, Adele, and Coldplay withholding their music from the service to protest what they believe to be inadequate compensation. Spotify has countered that as its platform continues to grow, payouts to artists will improve, and that the company had already paid nearly $2 billion to the music industry, including 70% of its revenues to musicians. Many record labels report satisfaction with the royalties their artists receive, but some disputes have continued over the percentage of streaming revenues Spotify pays.

SOURCES: "Music Streaming Hailed as Industry's Savior as Labels Enjoy Profit Surge," by Hannah Ellis-Petersen, *The*

Guardian, December 29, 2016; "Will Spotify Kill the Music Download?," by Charles Arthur, *The Guardian*, December 26, 2016; "Here's Deezer's Grand Plan to Take Over the Music-Streaming World," by Nick Pino, Techradar.com, December 21, 2016; "Tidal Can Keep Lemonade, Deezer Wants Its Original Content to Be More Like Serial," by Nick Pino, Techradar.com, December 9, 2016; "Spotify Is Ramping Up Its Acquisitions," by Hugh McIntyre, *Forbes*, November 15, 2016; "Deezer Launches Direct to Consumers in U.S with the Most Personalized Music Discovery Platform," Deezer-blog.com, October 18, 2016; "At 17 Million Subscribers, Apple Music Is Still Playing a Rocky Game of Catch-Up," by Amy X. Wang, Qz.com, September 7, 2016; "Spotify Revenues Topped $2BN Last Year as Losses Hit $194M," by Tim Ingham, Musicbusinessworldwide.com, May 23, 2016; "Deezer's Music Streaming Service Arrives on the Apple Watch," Mariella Moon, Engadget.com, March 16, 2016; "Deezer Expands Its Offering, Now Supports Hands-Free Driving Experience with Android Auto," Deezer-blog.com, March 7, 2016; "Deezer and Huawei Announce First Global Music Streaming Partnership," Deezer-blog.com, February 4, 2016; "Spotify Rival, Deezer Secures $109M In Latest Funding Round," by Alexandra Gibbs, Cnbc.com, January 20, 2016; "Race to the Bottom? Spotify Launches a 99-cent Premium Subscription Trial," by Charlotte Hassan Digitalmusic-news.com, November 30, 2015; "Music Streaming Service Deezer Abandons IPO Plans," by Stuart Dredge, *The Guardian*, October 28, 2015; "Deezer's IPO Filing Shows Both Potential and Problems," by Glenn Peoples, Billboard.com, September 24, 2015; "Taylor Swift Abruptly Pulls Entire Catalog from Spotify," by Steve Knopper, *Rolling Stone*, November 3, 2014; "Deezer Buys Stitcher, Adds 35K Talk Radio Shows and Podcasts to Its Music Platform," by Ingrid Lunden, TechCrunch.com, October 24, 2014; "Deezer, Entering U.S., Will Sound like Spotify, Act like Netflix," by Joan E. Solsman, Cnet.com, October 11, 2014.

Deezer is a French-based firm and the second-largest streaming music service in Europe behind Spotify. Like Spotify, Deezer offers unlimited access to a catalog of artists and songs, an advanced recommendation engine, and a lively social community. Deezer was founded by Jonathan Benassaya and Daniel Marhely in 2007. In 2008, it received an $8.5 million angel investment and rapidly expanded to dominate the French streaming music market, where it still maintains an edge over Spotify in 2016. Deezer has partnered with mobile operators, ISPs, and telecommunications carriers like French telecom titan Orange to include its service as part of customer contracts, and in 2016, it also partnered with Chinese smartphone manufacturer Huawei to preload the Deezer app on many Huawei smartphones. Deezer has 43 million licensed tracks and approximately 10 million subscribers, the most active of which listen about 60 hours per week. It has nearly tripled its number of paying subscribers within the last two years, trailing only Apple Music and Spotify. Using a freemium business model similar to other streaming services, Deezer offers free unlimited access for two weeks for registered users, who thereafter can continue to listen for free for 10 hours a month. Deezer hasn't focused on growing its advertiser-supported free music option because advertising revenues alone do not cover the cost of musical content. For premium service without ads, Deezer charges $4.99 per PC-only use, and $9.99 for full mobile and PC access. Deezer released apps for both the Apple Watch and Android Auto in 2016. Deezer sees its future growth taking place in China, Asia, and the Middle East.

Deezer stands out in a crowded music streaming marketplace in several ways. In 2016, Deezer operates in 180 countries, more than any of its competitors. This global footprint will help the company stay relevant as music streaming grows in popularity worldwide. The company is also pinning its hopes on its Flow algorithmic playlist feature, which not only analyzes each user's listening history to provide recommendations, as all music streaming sites do, but also takes into account users' activity levels using mobile phone features like GPS and the accelerometer to provide music that is contextually appropriate. Lastly, Deezer has branched out into podcasts and radio shows, acquiring Stitcher, an podcast and radio aggregator, in 2014, and continuing those efforts in 2016, launching compelling original content that can only be heard on Deezer.

In 2015, Deezer announced plans for an IPO, but they were quickly scrapped after the company came under scrutiny from analysts. Although Deezer was valued at a hefty €1 billion and has shown impressive revenue growth, like other music streaming services, it has struggled to show a profit. Deezer was also scrutinized for the relatively low percentage of its subscribers that generated revenue for the company. Several months after its initial announcement, Deezer backtracked and canceled the IPO, claiming that the market conditions were not ideal. However, in 2016, the company secured €100 million in funding from its backers, suggesting that investors are still optimistic about the company's potential.

As Spotify and Deezer struggle with profitability, Apple Music has moved into a comfortable second place position behind Spotify but well ahead of Deezer. However, Apple failed to make significant inroads against Spotify in 2016 and is still facing an uphill battle as it fights for market share. However, record labels have enjoyed rising profits for the first time in years largely thanks to music streaming. Spotify and Deezer still have faith in their long-term prospects, and with less than 3% of the world's population paying for music streaming in 2016, there's ample room for many winners in the near future.

The opening case illustrates how online content distributors like Spotify and Deezer are challenging both traditional and newer digital music distribution channels. If consumers can stream any song whenever they want to on whatever device they want, the demand for physical CDs as well as iTunes downloads is reduced. On the other hand, it is not clear that Spotify or Deezer have viable business models. The case also illustrates how a traditional content business like recorded music has survived the initial digital disruption of its business and begun to develop new innovative digital distribution channels that replace revenues from earlier products like CDs. As Internet users increasingly change their habits, spurred on by the growth of mobile devices, they are challenging existing business models that worked for decades to support newspapers, books, magazines, television, and Hollywood movies. Clearly, the future of content—news, music, and video—is online. Today, the print industry, including newspapers, books, and magazines, is having a difficult time coping with the movement of their readership to digital alternatives. Broadcast and cable television, along with Hollywood and the music industry, are also wrestling with outdated business models based on physical media. Established media giants are continuing to make extraordinary investments in unique online content, new technology, new digital distribution channels, and entirely new business models. Internet giants like Apple, Google, Amazon, and Facebook are competing to dominate online content distribution.

9.1 ONLINE CONTENT

No other sector has been so challenged by the Internet and the Web than the content industries. The online content industries are organized into two major categories: the print industries (newspapers, magazines, and books), and the entertainment industries, which includes television, movies, music (including radio), and games. Together, the online content industries in the United States are expected to generate revenues of at least $23 billion in 2016.

In this chapter, we will look closely at publishing (newspapers, magazines, and books) and entertainment (television and movies, music and radio, and games) as they attempt to transform their traditional media into digitally deliverable forms and experiences for consumers, while at the same time earning profits. These industries make up the largest share of the commercial content marketplace, both offline and online. In each of these industries, there are powerful offline brands, significant new pure-play online providers and distributors, consumer constraints and opportunities, a variety of legal issues, and new mobile technology platforms that offer an entirely new content distribution system in the form of smartphones and tablet computers.

Table 9.1 describes the most recent trends in online content and media for 2016–2017.

CONTENT AUDIENCE AND MARKET: WHERE ARE THE EYEBALLS AND THE MONEY?

In 2016, the average American adult spends around 4,300 hours each year consuming various media, twice the amount of time spent at work (2,000 hours/year) (see

TABLE 9.1	WHAT'S NEW IN ONLINE CONTENT AND MEDIA, 2016–2017

BUSINESS

- Explosive growth of the mobile platform of smartphones and tablets accelerates the transition to digital content.
- Amazon, Google (YouTube), Hulu, and Netflix (owners of the distribution channel) become significant players in the content production business.
- The cable industry continues to be disrupted by growth of Internet content producers and distributors.
- The percentage of Internet users who watch digital video continues to increase, to around 216 million Americans, over 80% of U.S. Internet users.
- The number of Americans watching TV online continues to grow, to over 165 million (over 59% of the U.S. population).
- E-book sales growth slows but represents one-third of all U.S. book revenues.
- Americans continue to spend more on online movies than for DVDs.
- Americans continue to spend more on digital music than on physical units, and more on streaming music than downloaded music.
- Online readership of newspapers exceeds print readership. Online ad revenues grow but not enough to offset declining print ad revenues.
- Console game sales flatten as mobile gaming soars.
- The four Internet Titans compete: Apple, Google, Amazon, and Facebook vie for ownership of the online entertainment and content ecosystem, selling experiences as well as content.
- Cable and satellite companies seek to consolidate: Charter Communications purchases Time Warner Cable for $55 billion, creating the largest cable company in the U.S.

TECHNOLOGY

- Smartphones, tablet computers, and e-readers together create a rich mobile multimedia entertainment environment.
- Netflix remains the largest consumer of bandwidth, consuming about 35% of Internet traffic, while Amazon and Google are ramping up their bandwidth consumption.
- Apps become the foundation for an app economy as they morph into content-distribution platforms that are proprietary, where users can be charged for content.
- Cloud storage services grow to serve the huge market for mobile device content. Apple launches iCloud video service that allows users to watch purchased videos on multiple Apple devices (iPhones, iPads, and Macs). Amazon and Google develop similar cloud services.

SOCIETY

- Media consumption: Americans spend around 4,300 hours a year consuming various types of media, more than twice as many hours as they work.
- Time spent using digital media exceeds time spent with television; time spent on mobile devices exceeds time spent on desktops.
- The Federal Communications Commission issues new net neutrality rules that prohibit broadband providers from blocking, slowing down, or speeding up access to specific websites.

Figure 9.1). U.S. entertainment and media revenues (both online and offline) in 2015 were estimated to be $262 billion, and they are expected to grow at a compound rate of 6% annually to 2020. Sales of tablets and smartphones have created new revenue streams for entertainment and media firms as consumer behavior changes in response to the new technologies. Content is no longer tied to physical products and can be delivered over the Internet from cloud servers to multiple mobile devices, reducing costs for consumers. Currently, online digital entertainment and media revenue is 9% of total entertainment and media revenue, or an estimated $23 billion. Millennials, the generation of people born between 1980 and 2000 (sometimes referred to as Digital Natives), are often thought to consume media very differently from their parents and Baby Boomers. For a discussion of how Millennials differ in media consumption, see *Insight on Society: Are Millennials Really All That Different?*

Media Utilization: A Converging Digital Stream

The proliferation of mobile devices—tablets and smartphones—has led to an increase in the total amount of time spent listening to radio, watching TV and movies, and reading books, newspapers, and even magazines. Internet mobile and desktop account for over 60% of total media time spent. While the number of hours of TV viewing used to be far larger than Internet usage, since the development of mobile devices, time spent on desktops plus the mobile Internet is now expected to consume 5.7 hours compared to 4.15 hours spent watching television on a TV in 2016. On the other hand, a great deal of Internet usage is watching time-shifted television shows! In 2016, over

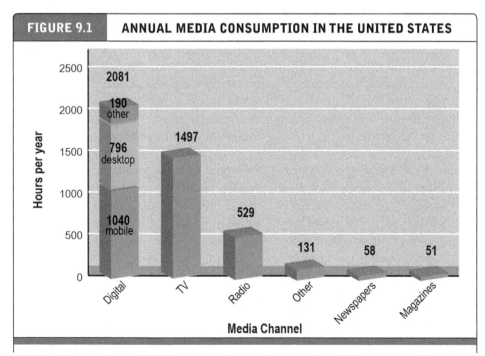

| FIGURE 9.1 | ANNUAL MEDIA CONSUMPTION IN THE UNITED STATES |

Each American spends around 4,300 hours annually on various types of media. Time spent on the Internet (both mobile and desktop) is expected to exceed time spent on traditional television.

SOURCES: Based on data from eMarketer, Inc., 2016a; authors' estimates.

INSIGHT ON SOCIETY

ARE MILLENNIALS REALLY ALL THAT DIFFERENT?

If you were born between 1981 and 2000, congratulations! You are a Millennial and the subject of Millennial mania, which is now gripping the advertising, retailing, educational, and journalistic worlds. Not since the Baby Boomers has so much coverage been given to a single generation.

Some people believe that Millennials are so different from previous generations that they require new kinds of products, new types of marketing and advertising techniques to persuade them to buy, and entirely new educational techniques. Millennials drink more specialty coffee, so coffee makers are responding with multiple new specialty coffee drinks. How about an orange-pineapple latte? And there's a hint of lower prices geared to the fact that Millennials are earning less, have higher rates of unemployment, and extraordinary student debt. There's a lot of money at stake getting the pulse of Millennials and figuring out how to market to them. Millennials now make up the largest generation in the United States, constituting about 80 million consumers, and over 30% of the labor force.

Millennials are just the latest in a long line of generalizations about people who grew up in specific time periods. The Greatest Generation (1901–1924) came of age during the Great Depression and served in World War II. The Baby Boomers (1946–1964) grew up with the civil rights movement, political unrest, and rock and roll. Generation X (1965–1980) continued the trends of the Baby Boomers except more so. Generation Xers were the first to experience a slowdown in living standards, and a growing sense that they might not earn as much as their parents. The

Millennials are continuing many of the trends of previous generations, including an alienation from cultural and political institutions, a decline in religious belief and marriage rates, higher levels of student loan debt, poverty, and unemployment, and the reality—not just the fear—that they will earn less than their parents at a similar age. The Millennials are much more ethnically diverse as well: nearly half of the Millennial generation were not born in the United States.

But perhaps most important according to some is that Millennials are digital natives: they are the first generation to be born into the digital revolution of the 20th century. They grew up with the commercial Internet. According to Marc Prensky, an author and promoter of educational games, Millennials' brains are physically different because of long-term exposure to interactive video games, console controllers (the "twitch" effect), graphical interfaces, and non-linear hypertext experiences on the Internet. Today's digital natives, in his view, cannot learn from books, newspapers, or linear stories even if they are video-based. They are bored by these old-school learning tools. The implications for education are, according to Prensky, to throw out traditional, old-style, linear thinking found in books and school curricula, and replace these with video games and link-clicking for nearly all subjects. This is referred to as the "gamification" of education.

But real-world Millennials don't seem to fit the Prensky mold. In fact, there is no evidence that Millennials think differently from other generations, have physically different brains, or can learn only by using games. More Millennials have a college degree and more graduate school attendance than other generations. They apparently do learn in traditional environments, and they didn't get through all this education by playing games! Academic researchers have dismissed much of the digital native thesis, finding little support for claims that Millennials have adopted learning styles that are radically different from those of their parents.

But clearly Millennials have had a very different experience growing up with technology than their parents, given the incredible advancement of digital technologies in the last three decades that have created entirely new platforms like smartphones, tablets, digital photography, highly interactive console and PC games, all of which have changed how content—books, newspapers, magazines, TV, and Hollywood movies—is created, distributed, and consumed. Millennials probably think like everyone else, but they do have different patterns of content consumption. Let's look at the data.

Given their intense use of the Internet, and absorption in digital experiences, including games, one would think Millennials would read few books (too boring and not twitchy or interactive enough), and that they would believe the Internet contained just about all the content and knowledge worth knowing about. Not so, according to a large study by Pew Research: Millennials are more likely to have read a book in the past 12 months than older adults, 88% vs. 79%. Almost 40% report having read an e-book in the past year, about the same as older adults. They are more likely to use a smartphone to read e-books than a Kindle. And they are more likely to think that there's a lot of useful information that is not on the Internet, more so than older adults. They are just as likely to have used a library in the past twelve months, and more likely to have used a library website. Even more unexpected: a study of 2,000 American and U.K. Millennials found this group overwhelmingly preferred printed books to e-books, and preferred buying them at bookstores rather than online stores like Amazon. Apparently, 600 years of reading printed books has created a print habit that might survive the Internet!

Millennials are only half as likely to subscribe to a print newspaper, but they are more likely to read news on digital news sites or get news (or links to news stories) from social sites, and to use their cell phones to follow news stories. Millennials are not news-less: 69% read news stories every day, some in print and even more online.

Given Millennials' intense exposure to high speed, interactive, "twitch"-oriented video and video games, surely they are not about to watch passive, linear TV series online or offline, like regular cable television, or stream feature-length movies that require concentration. Surely they would not sit for 30 hours to binge watch a TV series already ten years old. Here too, the evidence does not fit the stereotype, although there are some differences. Contrary to the stereotype, Millennials watch 100–130 hours of regular cable TV per month, about the same as older adults. Marketers believe Millennial interest in TV is greater than any generation. Over 70% watch television live, without digital delays or streaming, slightly less than older adults. They like comedy and sitcoms more than older adults, and are more likely to watch TV on a smartphone or tablet. They also adore older TV series that they may have watched as children. In fact, they seem to have transformed the Internet from a media that involves reading to one that involves viewing. About 55% of binge viewers are Millennials.

Millennials are more involved with online video: they watch 200 more videos per month than older adults, mostly on YouTube, in large part because they are more likely to have and use smartphones. Millennials are nearly twice as likely

(continued)

to use streaming services like Netflix, Hulu, and Amazon, and are less likely to have cable or satellite TV service than older adults. About 13% of Millennials have no pay TV service, not that different from 9% of older adults. Millennials are not cutting the cord in large numbers, although they are more likely to have never had cable TV ("cord nevers"). They are using their smartphones and tablets as TV substitutes, viewing TV shows wherever and whenever they want. Almost 20% of Millennials use only a mobile device for Internet access, compared to 5% for older adults. Millennials are driving a surge in YouTube action sports videos (surfing, skateboarding, and snowboarding). When it comes to finding interesting TV shows and videos, Millennials rely much more than other adults on their Facebook friends and newsfeeds. Finally, Millennials play a more active role in creating video content than older adults by posting photos and videos to social sites.

Millennials really do consume content differently than older adults of previous generations, although the differences appear to be far less and more commonsensical than journalists portray. For instance, Millennials take more advantage of the latest technologies from smartphones to

access streaming music and TV services than, say, Baby Boomers, although Baby Boomers, the generation that created the digital revolution, have adopted the new technologies nearly as much. Millennials have not lost interest in society or news about society, they just access it online somewhat more than older adults. Millennials do indeed create and share more content than elders, and control their TV schedules more often, including binge watching, even though they are watching hundreds of hours of cable TV every month.

Reaching Millennials can be a problem for marketers. They are more likely to visit content sites such as Vice and Vox than traditional print sources, but their most frequent news sites include CNN and the New York Times websites. They are more likely to use ad blockers and tune out any kind of online ad. They are more visual and are more likely to use Tumblr, Pinterest, and Instagram. And they are much more likely to use mobile payment methods than Boomers.

Millennials are different, but not so different that we don't recognize them as our children, inheritors of very powerful digital technologies, to be sure, but inheritors also of several thousand years of literature, history, and culture, which they continue to find of enduring value.

SOURCES: "The Majority of Millennials Actively Ignore Ads," eMarketer, Inc., August 25, 2016; "Which Media Companies are Winning the battle for Millennials?," by Ken Doctor, Politico.com, August 9, 2016; "Marketing to Millennials: Visual Buyers," by Curalate, Inc., July 2016; "Younger vs. Older US Adult Millennials as Digital Users," by eMarketer, Inc., January 2016; "For Online Sports Videos, the Action Is Off the Field," by Conor Dougherty, *New York Times*, September 11, 2015; "The Rise of Phone Reading," by Jennifer Maloney, *Wall Street Journal*, August 14, 2015; "Millennials: Seven Insights into Their Evolving Screen Choices and Viewing Habits," by Jeremy Kressman, eMarketer, Inc., August 2015; "State of the News Media 2015," by Amy Mitchell, Pew Research Center, Journalism and Media, April 29, 2015; "Millennials' Media Usage," by Mark Doliver, eMarketer, Inc., April 2015; "New Research Reveals Print Habits Die Hard With Millennial Readers," Publishingtechnology.com, March 26, 2015; "How Millennials Get News: Inside the Habits of America's First Digital Generation," by The Media Insight Project, American Press Institute, March 16, 2015; "15 Economic Facts About Millennials," by The Council of Economic Advisers, The White House, October 2014; "Are Digital Natives a Myth or Reality? University Students' Use of Digital Technologies," by Anoush Margaryan, Allison Littlejohn, and Gabrielle Vojt, *Computers & Education*, Volume 56, Issue 2, February 2011; "Digital Natives, Digital Immigrants," by Marc Prensky, in *On the Horizon* (MCB University Press, Vol. 9 No. 5, October 2001); "Digital Natives, Digital Immigrants, Part II," by Marc Prensky, in *On the Horizon* (MCB University Press, Vol. 9, No. 6, October 2001); "Millennials Rising: The Next Great Generation," by Neil Howe, William Strauss, and R.J. Matson, *Vintage*, September 2000.

165 million Americans will use their computers and/or mobile devices to watch television shows, over 50% of the general population. Therefore, the distinction between Internet usage and television usage is not easy to make. The method of transmission is just different: cable TV versus the Internet. The Internet, television, and movies are converging into a single digital stream. This convergence is described later in the chapter. Well over 80% of television viewers multitask while watching television, usually using a smartphone or tablet computer, texting with friends, reading e-mail, searching the Web, or visiting social networks, activities which have nothing to do with what's happening on the TV screen (eMarketer, 2016b).

Internet and Traditional Media: Cannibalization versus Complementarity

Several studies reveal that time spent on the Internet reduces consumer time available for other media (Pew Research Center, 2013). This is referred to as cannibalization. The alternative argument is that the Internet and traditional media are complementary and mutually supportive rather than substitutive. True, there has been a massive shift of the general audience to the Web, tablets, and smartphones, and once there, a large percentage of time is spent on viewing content. Yet, more recent data finds a more complex picture. Despite the availability of the Internet on high-resolution tablet computers, television viewing remains strong, video viewing on all devices has increased, and the reading of all kinds of books, including physical books, has increased. New television sets are Internet-enabled, allowing consumers to use the Internet to view TV shows on their traditional TVs. Total music consumption measured in hours a day listening to music has increased even as sales of CDs have drastically declined; likewise, movie consumption has increased even as DVD sales also decline markedly. The impact of the Internet on media appears to be increasing the total demand for media, including stimulating demand for products like books. The overall pattern is that physical products like CDs and DVDs are being replaced by digital versions delivered on computers, tablets, and smartphones either as downloaded content or as streaming services.

Media Revenues

An examination of U.S. entertainment and media industry revenues reveals a somewhat different pattern when compared to media consumption (see **Figure 9.2**). In 2015, media of all kinds generated $262 billion in revenue (not including transmission fees for content such as cable TV subscription fees). Television and home video accounted for about 34% and print media (books, newspapers, and magazines) for 32% of total media revenues. Box office (motion pictures and theaters) accounted for 9%, as did Internet media (online music and video), and video games. Radio and recorded music together accounted for 8%. Internet media, while relatively small now, is growing at 12% annually, far faster than traditional media revenues.

Three Revenue Models for Digital Content Delivery: Subscription, A La Carte, and Advertising-Supported (Free and Freemium)

There are three revenue models for delivering content on the Internet. The two pay models are subscriptions (usually "all you can eat") and a la carte (pay for what you use). The third model uses advertising revenue to provide content for free, usually

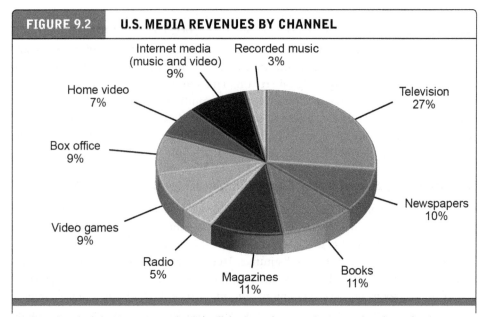

FIGURE 9.2 | **U.S. MEDIA REVENUES BY CHANNEL**

Internet media (music and video) 9%
Recorded music 3%
Television 27%
Home video 7%
Box office 9%
Newspapers 10%
Video games 9%
Radio 5%
Magazines 11%
Books 11%

Traditional media (television, print, and radio) still dominate the entertainment and media market, but Internet media (video, music, and content) is the fastest growing segment.

SOURCES: Based on data from industry sources; authors' estimates.

with a freemium (higher price) option. There is also completely free, user-generated content, which we will discuss later. Contrary to early analysts' projections that "free" would drive "paid" out of business, it turns out that both models are viable now and in the near future. Consumers increasingly choose to pay for high-quality, convenient, and unique content, and they have gladly accepted free advertiser-supported content when that content is deemed not worth paying for but entertaining nevertheless. There's nothing contradictory about all three models working in tandem and cooperatively: free content can drive customers to paid content, as streaming services like Pandora and Spotify have discovered.

Online Content Consumption

Now let's look at what kinds of online content U.S. Internet users purchase or view online in 2016 (**Figure 9.3**). It's not a surprise that 81% of Internet users watch online video of many kinds, but it may be a surprise that 67% of Internet users read online newspapers. Playing games on a mobile device and watching online TV shows and movies are the next most popular. The percentage of Internet users that read e-books (32%) initially grew at triple-digit rates when the Kindle was introduced in 2007 and the iPad in 2010, but has since slowed. What this reveals is that Internet users retain their affinity to traditional formats—newspapers, radio, TV shows and movies, books, and music tracks and albums—and bring these tastes to the Internet and their mobile devices.

Figure 9.4 on page 636 shows estimated U.S. online entertainment content revenues, projected to 2019. Online TV and movies generate the most revenue and are expected to continue to do so through 2019. Revenues from online video games now generate the second largest amount of paid content revenue and are expected to con-

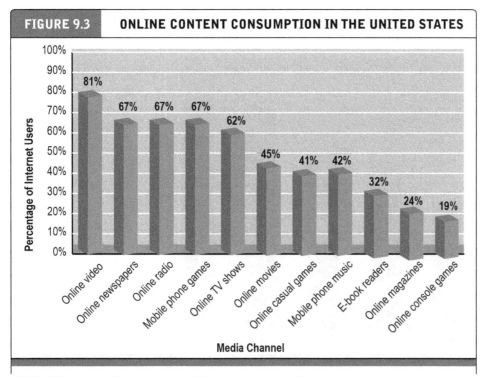

| FIGURE 9.3 | ONLINE CONTENT CONSUMPTION IN THE UNITED STATES |

SOURCES: Based on data from eMarketer, Inc., 2016c; industry sources; authors' estimates.

tinue rising through 2019. Revenue from music sales in the form of downloads has declined slightly, but this is, and will continue to be, offset by the growth of revenues from streaming music, which is growing at 40%.

Free or Fee: Attitudes About Paying for Content and the Tolerance for Advertising

In the early years of online content, multiple surveys found that large majorities of the Internet audience expected to pay nothing for online content although equally large majorities were willing to accept advertising as a way to pay for free content. In reality, on the early Web, there wasn't much high-quality content. However, since then, consumer behavior and attitudes toward paying for content have greatly changed. Until services such as iTunes arrived in 2003, few thought the "fee" model could compete with the "free" model, and many Internet analysts believed that information on the Internet needed to be free. Cable TV systems and cable content providers like ESPN had a totally different history: they always charged for service and content, and cable executives, investors, and TV experts never thought information should be free. Neither did the Hollywood and New York media companies that paid for and provided the content to television and movie theaters. The culture of the Internet began to change when Apple introduced iTunes as a source of relatively inexpensive, high quality music and firms such as YouTube (and its parent Google), which started out with a business model based on amateur videos and illegally uploaded music videos, began cooperating closely with Hollywood and New York production studios

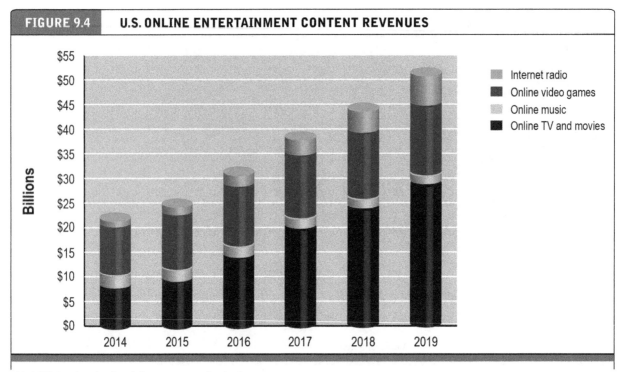

FIGURE 9.4 **U.S. ONLINE ENTERTAINMENT CONTENT REVENUES**

Legend:
- Internet radio
- Online video games
- Online music
- Online TV and movies

SOURCES: Based on data from industry sources; authors' estimates.

for premium content. In 2016, millions of American Internet users are now more than willing to pay for high-quality content delivered on a convenient device such as a smartphone, tablet computer, or e-reader or using services like those offered by Netflix, Apple TV, or Amazon Video.

DIGITAL RIGHTS MANAGEMENT (DRM) AND WALLED GARDENS

digital rights management (DRM) refers to the combination of technical and legal means for protecting digital content from unlimited reproduction without permission

Digital rights management (DRM) refers to a combination of technical (both hardware and software) and legal means for protecting digital content from unlimited reproduction and distribution without permission. DRM hardware and software encrypts content so that it cannot be used without some form of authorization typically based on a payment. The objective is to control the uses of content after it has been sold or rented to consumers. Essentially, DRM can prevent users from purchasing and making copies for widespread distribution over the Internet without compensating the content owners. While music tracks in the iTunes Store were originally protected by DRM, in 2009, Apple abandoned the practice because of user objections, and because Amazon had opened an online music store in 2007 without any DRM protections, with the support of music label firms, who came to realize that DRM prevented them from exploiting the opportunities of the Internet and perhaps even encouraged an illegal market. Streaming content services are inherently difficult to copy and re-distribute. Movies streamed from Netflix are technically difficult for the average user to capture and share although new apps like Meerkat and Periscope

(Twitter) make live re-streaming very easy even if the quality is low. Likewise, music streamed from Pandora is cumbersome to record and share. Streaming services, including both Apple and Amazon, use a kind of DRM called a **walled garden** to restrict the widespread sharing of content. They do this by tying the content to the hardware, operating system, or streaming environment. E-books purchased from Amazon can only be read on Kindles or Kindle apps and Kindle books cannot be converted to other formats. By locking the content to a physical device, or a digital stream with no local storage, the appliance makers derive additional revenues and profits by locking customers into their service or device and satisfy the demands of content producers to be fairly compensated for their work. Google's YouTube identifies and tracks copyrighted music and removes it if music labels have not granted permission, and offers owners the revenue from advertising if they choose to let the music remain on the site.

walled garden
refers to a kind of DRM that uses proprietary file formats, operating systems, and hardware to control the use of content after initial sale

MEDIA INDUSTRY STRUCTURE

The U.S. media content industry prior to 1990 was composed of many smaller independent corporations specializing in content creation and distribution in the separate industries of film, television, book and magazine publishing, and newspaper publishing. During the 1990s and into this century, after an extensive period of consolidation, huge entertainment and publishing media conglomerates emerged.

The U.S. media content industry is still organized largely into three separate vertical stovepipes: print, movies, and music. Each segment is dominated by a few key players, and generally there is very little crossover from one segment to another. For example, newspapers typically do not also produce Hollywood films, and publishing firms do not own newspapers or film production studios. The purchase of the *Washington Post* in 2013 by Jeff Bezos, the founder of Amazon, and an Internet mogul in his own right, was an anomaly. Even within media conglomerates that span several different media segments, separate divisions generally control each media segment.

In the past, we have not included the delivery platform firms, such as Comcast, Time Warner Cable, AT&T, Verizon, Sprint, and Dish Network, in this analysis because in general they did not focus on the creation of content but instead just moved content produced by others across cable, satellite, and telephone networks. However, within the last several years, this has begun to change. Comcast led the way with the acquisition of a majority interest in NBC Universal. AT&T's proposed merger with Time Warner and Verizon's proposed purchase of Yahoo, along with its previous acquisition of AOL, are signs that the telecommunications companies are moving into the content and distribution market, as well as the Internet advertising industry, in a major way.

MEDIA CONVERGENCE: TECHNOLOGY, CONTENT, AND INDUSTRY STRUCTURE

Media convergence is a much used but poorly defined term. There are at least three dimensions of media where the term convergence has been applied: technology, content (artistic design, production, and distribution), and the industry's structure as a whole. Ultimately for the consumer, convergence means being able to get any content you want, when you want it, on whatever platform you want it—from an iPod to an iPad, Android phone, or home PC, or set-top device like Apple TV.

Technological Convergence

Convergence from a technology perspective **(technological convergence)** has to do with the development of hybrid devices that can combine the functionality of two or more existing media platforms, such as books, newspapers, television, movies, radio, and games, into a single device. Examples of technological convergence include the iPad, iPhone, and Android ("smartphones") that combine telephone, print, music, photos, and video in a single device.

Content Convergence

A second dimension of convergence is **content convergence**. There are three aspects to content convergence: design, production, and distribution.

There is a historical pattern in which content created in an older media technology migrates to the new technology largely intact, with little artistic change. Slowly, the different media are integrated so that consumers can move seamlessly back and forth among them, and artists (and producers) learn more about how to deliver content in the new media. Later, the content itself is transformed by the new media as artists learn how to fully exploit the capabilities in the creation process. At this point, content convergence and transformation has occurred—the art is different because of the new capabilities inherent to new tools. For instance, European master painters of the fifteenth century in Italy, France, and the Netherlands (such as van Eyck, Caravaggio, Lotto, and Vermeer) quickly adopted new optical devices such as lenses, mirrors, and early projectors called *camera obscura* that could cast near-photographic quality images on canvases, and in the process they developed new theories of perspective and new techniques of painting landscapes and portraits. Suddenly, paintings took on the qualities of precision, detail, and realism found later in photographs (Boxer, 2001). A similar process is occurring today as artists and writers assimilate new digital and Internet tools into their toolkits. For instance, GarageBand from Apple enables low-budget independent bands (literally working in garages) to mix and control eight different digital music tracks to produce professional sounding recordings on a shoestring budget. Writers of books are beginning to think about video and interactive versions of their books. Online newspapers are changing the news cycle to a 24-hour stream, producing their own video channels, and expanding user comment opportunities on their websites.

On the production side, tools for digital editing and processing (for film and television) are driving content convergence. Given that the most significant cost of content is its creation, if there is a wide diversity of target delivery platforms, then it is wise to develop and produce only once using technology that can deliver to multiple platforms. Generally, this means creating content on digital devices (hardware and software) so that it can be delivered on multiple digital platforms.

technological convergence
development of hybrid devices that can combine the functionality of two or more existing media platforms into a single device

content convergence
convergence in the design, production, and distribution of content

Figure 9.5 depicts the process of media convergence and transformation using the example of books. For example, consider this book. In 2016, this book was written with a view to appearing on iPads and Kindle e-book readers, and is moving closer to the media maturity stage, in which the book will be available mostly as a purely digital product with substantial visual and aural content that can be displayed on many different digital devices. By that time, the learning experience will be transformed by greater use of interactive graphics, videos, as well as an integrated testing system that monitors student performance during the semester. Even the number of pages read by students, and the time on page, will be accounted for by this near-future digital learning system. Traditional bound books will probably still be available (books have many advantages), but most likely, print editions will be printed on demand by customers using their own print facilities.

Industry Structure Convergence

A third dimension of convergence is the structure of the various media industries. **Industry convergence** refers to the merger of media enterprises into powerful, synergistic combinations that can cross-market content on many different platforms and create new works that use multiple platforms. This can take place either through purchases or through strategic alliances. Traditionally, each type of media—film, text,

industry convergence
merger of media enterprises into synergistic combinations that create and cross-market content on different platforms

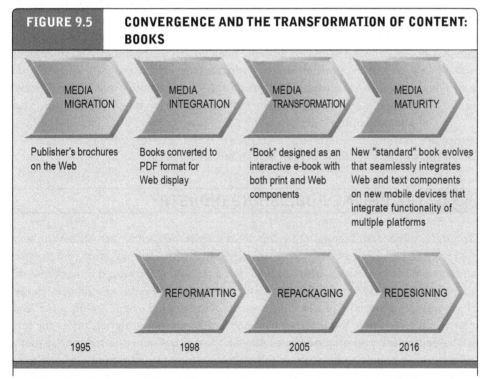

| FIGURE 9.5 | CONVERGENCE AND THE TRANSFORMATION OF CONTENT: BOOKS |

The Internet is making it possible for publishers and writers to transform the standard "book" into a new form that integrates features of both text and the Internet, and also transforms the content of the book itself.

music, television—had its own separate industry, typically composed of very large players. For instance, the entertainment film industry has been dominated by a few large Hollywood-based production studios, book publication is dominated by a few large book publishers, and music production is dominated by four global record label firms.

However, the Internet has created forces that make mergers and partnerships among media and Internet firms a necessary business proposition. Media industry convergence may be necessary to finance the substantial changes in both the technology platform and the content. Traditional media firms who create the content generally do not possess the core competencies or financial heft to distribute it on the Internet. Technology companies that dominate the Internet (Google, Apple, Amazon, and Facebook) have the competency and wealth to pursue Internet channel strategies, but do not currently have the competencies needed to create content. Business combinations and partnerships are made to solve these issues.

While traditional media companies have not done well in purchases of Internet platform companies, the technology owners such as Apple, Amazon, Facebook, Microsoft, and Google have generally avoided merging with media companies, and instead rely on contractual arrangements with media companies to protect intellectual property rights and to create a business pricing model that both parties can accept. However, this pattern is changing. For instance, CBS Inc., a movie and television content producer, produces television shows for Netflix; Netflix, Hulu, and Amazon produce and distribute their own original series; Google is producing original content designed for Internet distribution on YouTube. Amazon created its own book imprint, Amazon Books Publishing, and entered the book publishing business. And in 2016, as noted previously, telecommunications companies are joining the fray, with Verizon proposing to acquire Yahoo and AT&T proposing to merge with Time Warner. In this sense, the Internet is changing the media industry from what it was in the recent past.

In the end, consumers' demands for content anywhere, anytime, and on any device are pushing the technology and content companies toward both strategic alliances and strategic conflicts in their search for advantage.

9.2 THE ONLINE PUBLISHING INDUSTRY

Nothing is quite so fundamental to a civilized society as reading text. Text is the way we record our history, current events, thoughts, and aspirations, and transmit them to all others in the civilization who can read. Even television shows and movies require scripts. Today, the U.S. publishing industry (composed of books, newspapers, magazines, and periodicals) is a $93 billion media sector based originally on print, and now moving rapidly to the Internet and mobile delivery. The Internet offers the text publishing industry an opportunity to move toward a new generation of newspapers, magazines, and books that are produced, processed, stored, distributed, and sold over the Web, available anytime, anywhere, and on any device. The same Internet offers the possibility of destroying many existing print-based businesses that may not be able to make this transition and remain profitable.

ONLINE NEWSPAPERS

Newspapers in 2016 are the most troubled segment of the print publishing industry. U.S. newspaper industry revenues have shrunk from their high of $60 billion in 2000 to about $30 billion in 2015 (see **Figure 9.6**). The newspaper labor force has roughly been cut in half over this period. The newspaper industry has been in an extended period of digital disruption since the rise of the Web in 2000 and the emergence of powerful search engines like Google, which allow consumers to search for news on any subject without having to browse a physical newspaper or an online edition. Social media sites have become a major source of unique visitors, who, unfortunately, do not browse for news and usually stay on the newspaper's site for only a few moments to read a single article. These fleeting visitors typically do not engage with the newspaper as a whole or with its online ads. Even before the Internet and Web, newspaper revenue was falling due to the influence of earlier technologies like broadcast and cable television. In 2014, three of the largest newspaper organizations (Gannett, Tribune Company, and E.W. Scripps) spun off their newspaper operations as independent firms so they could focus on television and other media assets, including in some cases, successful digital properties. Newspapers will now be pure-play print and online enterprises and will have to make it on their own without the protection of television or other media assets (Carr, 2014).

FIGURE 9.6 | **U.S. NEWSPAPER REVENUES 1980–2015**

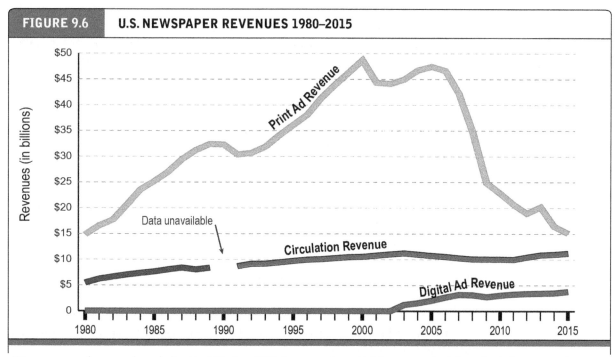

U.S. newspaper ad revenues have declined by 50% since 1980. As a percentage of total revenues, circulation subscription revenues have become more important. Digital is a small source of revenue but growing up until recently.

SOURCES: Based on data from Newspaper Association of America, 2016; Pew Research Center, 2016.

The striking growth of alternative pure digital news sources in the last five years, from Twitter and Facebook, to Vox, Vice, BuzzFeed, Reddit, and Huffington Post, poses additional challenges. Online news sources are attracting millions of consumers everyday and steer potential newspaper readers—both online and offline—away from the most valuable front page of print and digital edition newspapers. The shift of consumers toward the mobile platform and social media deepens the potential for disruption in the newspaper industry. Social media sites are playing a significant factor in directing traffic directly to specific newspaper articles, bypassing the newspaper's valuable front page, and increasingly, are providing their own original reporting and commentary by hiring professional journalists away from troubled newspapers. In 2015, the *New York Times,* along with nine other news media outlets, agreed as an experiment to embed a few of its articles directly into Facebook's News Feed as a way to attract millions of new readers, and hopefully convert them from free readers to paid digital subscribers. Facebook calls these news stories **Instant Articles**. What started as an experiment has become a major source of readers for newspaper articles, but not the entire newspaper. Newspapers are now hiring social media editors to follow trending topics and post articles to newsfeeds. Other news publishers are considering a similar move. The downside is that readers might not ever return to the newspaper websites, which are the most lucrative for digital newspapers. Newspaper survival will depend on how fast newspaper organizations can transform themselves from print to digital, and how fast they can monetize the expanding audience for news all the time, anywhere, on all devices.

Instant Articles
a new Facebook feature that inserts selected articles from mainstream news outlets in a user's News Feed

As can be seen from Figure 9.6, while newspaper circulation revenues (subscriptions plus newsstand sales) have declined 10% since 2000 to around $11 billion, print advertising, which includes display ads, classified ads, and legal notices, has fallen precipitously from a high of $48 billion in 2000 to $15 billion in 2015. Online advertising in newspapers in the last year has shown weak growth, accounting for about $3.7 billion in revenue, and newspapers' revenues from online ads are still only 25% of print ad revenue, and only 12.5% of total revenue. The gains in online digital ad revenue are not large enough to compensate for the loss of print revenue. Only the music industry has suffered a similarly devastating decline in revenue. The 15-year decline in newspaper revenues has resulted from four factors:

- The growth of the Web and mobile devices as an alternative medium for news and advertising. The movement of consumers to an online life style has drained billions of ad dollars (including classified ads) from the printed newspaper. The same has not been true of television advertising as we will discuss later in the chapter. Even radio advertising has stood up well to the digital revolution.

- The rise of alternative digital sources for news, commentary, feature stories, and articles.

- The difficulty of traditional newspaper firms and their managers to develop suitable business and revenue models that could survive and even prosper on the Internet, and the mobile/social platform.

- The rise of social media, and its role in directing traffic to newspaper content, has challenged newspapers to change their business model to accommodate changes in consumer behavior and technology.

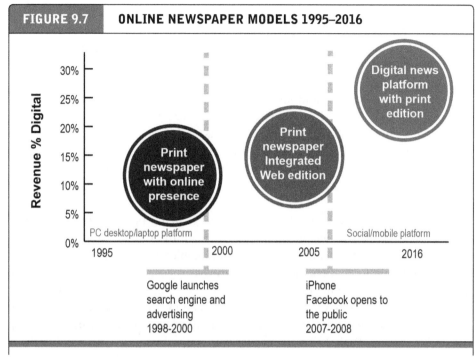

| FIGURE 9.7 | ONLINE NEWSPAPER MODELS 1995–2016 |

Newspapers have gone through three different business models as they adapt to the Internet.

From Print-centric to Digital First: The Evolution of Newspaper Online Business Models, 1995–2016

Since 1995, when e-commerce and digital advertising began, through to the present, newspapers have developed three distinct business models in an effort to adapt to the Internet, and more recently, the mobile and social platform (see **Figure 9.7**). The three models are: Print-centric (1995–2000), Integrated Print/Web (2000–2010), and the most current model, Digital First (2010–present). You can compare these models on four dimensions:

- **Search and discovery:** How do readers find the news?
- **Awareness:** How are potential readers made aware of news?
- **Engagement:** How are readers engaged with the news and journalists?
- **Technology platform:** How, when, and where is the news delivered to readers? (New York Times, 2014).

The milestones reflect important dates in the evolution of the Web and the mobile-social platform. In 1998 to 2000, Google launched its search engine with 60 million pages indexed, and introduced search engine paid advertising based on its Page Rank algorithm. In 2007, Apple introduced its iPhone, creating a truly mobile and universal web device, and Facebook opened its site to the public, and in 2008 signed up over 100 million users, creating the first large-scale, online social network.

Prior to the development of the Web, search engines, mobile devices, and social media platforms, readers discovered the news by browsing (a form of searching) the printed paper. They became aware of stories by reading the front page, section pages, and article titles. Readers did not engage with journalists, editors, or other contributors, except for the few who wrote letters to the editor (less than 1% of all readers). Journalism was considered a profession, and readers were not expected to do much more than read and be fascinated, enlightened, and entertained by people who obviously were more informed than they. Journalists worked all day on their articles and filed them at 5 PM; professional editors revised the copy, and compositors put it on the page for the presses, which ran after midnight. The news stream ended at 5 PM. The technology platform was print, sometimes with color (a major innovation and expense in this period).

With the introduction of the Web and its growing popularity, newspapers retained their existing print-centric strategy and culture. In the Print-centric period from 1995 to 2000, newspapers created digital copies of their print editions and posted them online. Readers discovered stories as they did before, by reading the front page online, following links to stories, and clicking on topic areas or sections (e.g., Sports or Technology). Stories were promoted by a business department that sought to enlarge the print audience and to attract advertisers based on readership and online visitors. Digital advertising was very limited, in part because advertisers did not believe it was effective. Readers were not engaged with journalists except insofar as they read the stories and could identify with the subjects of stories. The business process of creating journalism did not change: articles were filed at 5 PM and went to print editors, and then were sent to the web team and the print group. There was little difference, if any, between the print and online versions. The technology platform for the digital edition was the desktop or laptop, and news was consumed at home and work.

In the Integrated Print/Web period, from 2000 to 2010, newspapers adopted multimedia elements such as video, added more interactive elements like crossword puzzles and contests, and provided more reader feedback opportunities, especially on opinion and editorial pages. There were opportunities to personalize the news using RSS feeds and push news to the reader. Nevertheless, news was discovered by the reader visiting the website; promoting content online was limited, primarily to RSS feeds. Readers were somewhat more engaged. The technology platform remained the desktop or laptop platform.

In the Digital First period, from 2010 to the present, three developments in the technology and popular audience platform occurred: the rapid adoption of smartphones and tablets, and the equally astounding growth of social media sites like Facebook and Twitter, which have come to dominate consumer time on the Web and mobile devices. In addition, the rise of startup news sites specifically focused on using the new technology and platforms has spurred newspapers to radically transform their business—or go out of business. The new platform is not based on personal computers using a browser, but on mobile devices and apps, with desktops and laptops now just one pillar of the delivery platform. In this new environment, the news does not stop at 5 PM, but goes on 24 × 7. Stories might start with a tweet, or from a Facebook post, followed by thousands of tweets, then millions of shares on multiple social sites and finally an article in the online newspaper, and perhaps in the print edition as well. Often amateurs on scene know more about the news in the first hours of a story than any collection of journalists in their offices. Amateurs provide video feeds, commentary, and opinion.

The Digital First business model inverts previous models: the top priority is producing the most engaging, continually updated digital edition, and then producing a print product based on the news developed in the digital edition. In the case of pure digital startups, there is no print edition, and the news is just a continuous stream of updates, blogs, tweets, and posts, rather than a fixed article. News articles are time-stamped, indicating an update is on the way and the reader should return to follow the story. Instead of waiting for readers to discover the news, or search for the news on a search engine, the news is pushed to readers on any of a variety of venues where they happen to be—social media sites, mobile news feeds, Twitter, or Yahoo or Google News. Journalists remain paid professionals, but they follow Twitter feeds and social media sites, and promote their stories and personas on social media sites. Their job is no longer simply reporting and writing, and getting the facts right, but promoting and engaging readers on a personal level through their own efforts. Superior reporting and writing is no longer the sole criterion for hiring and advancement. More emphasis is put on reporters' abilities to attract audiences on their own social media pages and Twitter feeds.

The Digital First business model is not yet a reality for traditional newspapers. The largest print newspaper organizations, such as the *Wall Street Journal*, *New York Times*, *Washington Post*, and others, have begun the journey towards becoming Digital First news organizations. In 2014 the *Wall Street Journal* launched its Real-Time news desk, a headquarters group of 60 editors aiming to produce a continuous and lively flow of digital news and commentary to social media sites, mobile followers, and its online sites (Romenesko, 2014). The *New York Times* also initiated a Digital First model in January 2014. In 2015, the *Wall Street Journal* launched a new digital first website, with redesigned web and video pages, iPad and Android apps, and a greater emphasis on breaking news stories that are refined in the course of a 24-hour news cycle. In the past two years, the *Financial Times*, *New York Times*, the *Washington Post*, *USA Today*, and Bloomberg News have all made similar changes to succeed in a mobile-tablet-desktop digital market place. Most of the major newspaper groups have also joined with social media sites like Facebook to have their articles appear in newsfeeds.

Online Newspaper Industry: Strengths and Challenges

The newspaper industry still has some major strengths, which it will need to draw upon as it faces the challenges of the future. In the following section, we review those strengths and challenges.

Strength: Newspaper Audience Size and Growth. Online readership of newspapers is growing at more than 10% a year. About 67% of U.S. Internet users (about 179 million people) read newspaper content online, making it the second most popular online

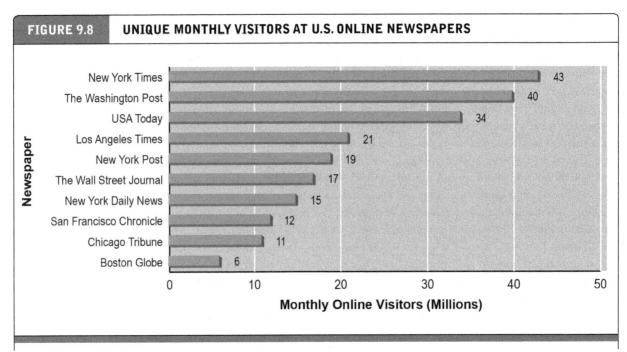

| FIGURE 9.8 | UNIQUE MONTHLY VISITORS AT U.S. ONLINE NEWSPAPERS |

Online newspaper readership is expanding rapidly as consumers shift to mobile devices and participate in social networks.

SOURCE: Based on data from Compete.com, 2016.

activity (Newspaper Association of America, 2016). See **Figure 9.8** for a list of the top ten online newspapers in the United States. The online newspaper is one of the most successful of all online media in terms of audience size. Mobile newspaper readership is especially strong among young persons due to their greater usage of smartphones and tablet computers.

Newspapers have responded to the changing audience by providing access to their content on all digital platforms (see **Figure 9.9**). With 64% of Americans having a smartphone and 52% tablet computer, in a few short years newspapers have become truly multi-platform by developing apps and websites optimized for mobile devices. Only 51% of newspaper readers are exclusively print readers, while 49% use a combination of the Web, print, and/or mobile. Mobile traffic is continuing to grow for most newspapers, while the number of desktop visitors is declining. However, the opposite is true with respect to the amount of time spent by visitors, with minutes per visit on desktops increasing and minutes per visit on mobile devices decreasing (Pew Research Center, 2016).

Online newspapers also attract a wealthy, educated, and consumer-intense demographic, reaching 64% of 25- to 34-year-olds, and 75% of individuals in households earning more than $100,000 a year on average throughout the quarter. Given the large online newspaper audience, it is clear that the future of newspapers lies in the online and mobile market even as readership and subscriptions to the traditional print newspapers continue to decline at a steady pace.

Challenge: Digital Ad Revenue. Newspapers hope that the digital ad revolution and revenue will hit their shores, and lift total ad revenues. But here's the problem: while

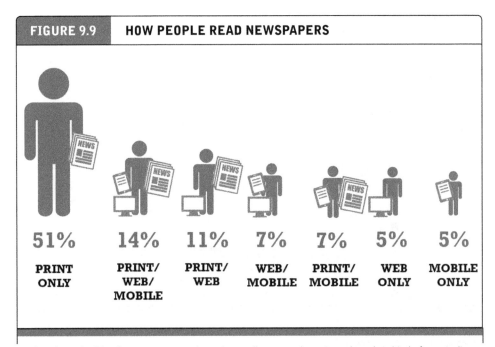

| FIGURE 9.9 | HOW PEOPLE READ NEWSPAPERS |

| 51% | 14% | 11% | 7% | 7% | 5% | 5% |
| PRINT ONLY | PRINT/ WEB/ MOBILE | PRINT/ WEB | WEB/ MOBILE | PRINT/ MOBILE | WEB ONLY | MOBILE ONLY |

Web-only readership of newspapers remains quite small compared to print only and multi-platform reading.
SOURCE: Based on data from Pew Research Center, 2016.

unique visitors to newspaper websites are expanding, increasingly this traffic is less valuable for two reasons. First, the audience is increasingly coming from social media sites and search engines in order to find specific articles, rather than coming directly to the newspaper's home page (so-called side-door entry). Second, these visitors from social sites are less engaged, and less valuable (see **Figure 9.10**).

The less engaged visitors are in terms of pages viewed, minutes on site, and return visits, the less time there is to show them ads and earn revenue. Direct visitors are therefore much more valuable and newspapers are hoping re-designed websites and apps will increase the number of home page visitors. As a result, growth in digital ad revenues at U.S. online newspapers has been tepid despite increasing unique visitors, growing only about 8% in 2015. In comparison, total U.S. digital ad revenue (search, social, and display ads) grew at a robust 20% (eMarketer, Inc., 2016e). If current trends continue, it is unlikely newspapers can rely on growing unique visitors from social sites, or growing digital ad revenues, to reverse the revenue declines of the past decade. Instead they will need to build on their expanding digital subscription market composed of loyal readers who visit the paper everyday for curation and opinion.

Strength: Content Is King. Why do people continue to buy newspapers and pay for news-paper content online? The oft-repeated bon mot that "content is king" appears to be true in the case of print as well as online content of all kinds, including news and pure digital news sites. As in competitive sports, in general, quality counts. The reason why online newspapers attract exceptionally large and loyal audiences who are deeply engaged is simple: quality of content. Compared to other media, newspapers are the most trusted source of news and commentary on local, national, and international stories (Nielsen,

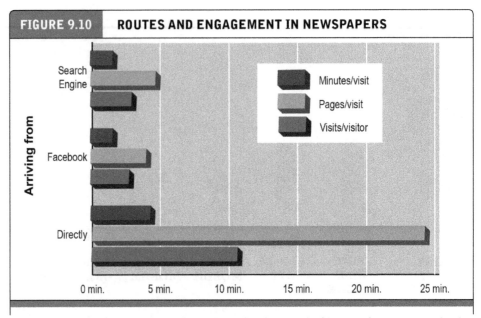

FIGURE 9.10 **ROUTES AND ENGAGEMENT IN NEWSPAPERS**

Newspaper visitors who come to newspaper websites directly in search of news are far more engaged and generate more digital ad revenue.
SOURCE: Based on data from Pew Research Center, 2014a.

2013). Local newspapers produce the highest levels of ad engagement: 35% of consumers report making purchases on the basis of local newspaper ads. Online display ads, e-mail campaigns, and fleeting mobile ads do not even come close to these engagement levels. Newspapers employ about 33,000 full-time professional editorial staff, down from about 56,000 in 2000, but still much larger than television, radio, or newer pure digital news sources, which obtain much of their content from unpaid bloggers, cellphone photographers, and bloggers (Pew Research Center, 2016, 2014b).

Amateur blogs and tweets may be wonderful for expressing opinions, or making instant reports on newsworthy events as they occur, but they are no substitute for professional reporters and editors, who make sense out of the constant stream of reports, and they are not a place for brand-conscious advertisers who do not want their products associated with low-quality content. Google offers Google News Lab Fellowships to journalism students in the stated belief that quality journalism is a key ingredient of a vibrant and functioning society. While Internet news giants are dependent on newspapers to provide them with content to search and index, newspapers are equally dependent on Internet giants for visitors.

Challenge: Finding a Revenue Model. In 1995, when the first newspaper websites appeared, newspapers offered their content for free, with registration. The hope was that advertising would support the website's operation and provide a new revenue stream for the print edition content. In some cases, free content was limited to the most popular articles and did not include the classified ads, a lucrative newspaper franchise. At that time, print advertising provided over 75% of revenues and subscription revenue generated about 25%.

Charging for general newspaper content was an obvious answer, but publications that tried this during the 1995–2005 period were punished by an Internet culture that expected online content such as music and news to be free. For instance, in 1998, Slate, an online magazine owned by Microsoft, began charging its readers a $19.95 annual subscription fee (a so-called **paywall**). There was a free Front Porch section with a few articles. In 1999, Slate dropped its subscription fee after only 20,000 readers signed up. Some specialized content newspapers, like the *Wall Street Journal*, were able to charge an annual subscription fee ($50 annually) and survive. In a year the *Journal* had 200,000 paid subscribers. Similarly, the *Financial Times* introduced a subscription service in 2001, and in 2007 adopted a **metered subscription** model, which allowed readers to access 10 articles for free, but required payment of a $395 subscription fee for further access once that limit was exceeded. Both the *Journal* and *Financial Times* were exceptions to consumer resistance to paying for news, and based on a wealthy, focused readership interested in high-value information.

paywall
paid subscription service

metered subscription
provides access to a limited number of articles for free, but requires payment of a subscription fee once that limit is exceeded

The introduction of the iTunes store in 2003, and the iPhone in 2007, changed the public perception of paid content. While plenty of pirated music was available, Apple devices (iPods and later iPhones and iPads) and iTunes provided a high-quality, convenient, and legal alternative that users were willing to pay for. In 2016, paying a subscription fee for content is the foundation of streaming video and music services from Netflix to Pandora.

In 2011, the *New York Times* introduced a metered subscription model similar to that of the Financial Times, which allowed casual readers to read 20 articles for free, and provided unlimited access to current archived content for $35 annually. Print subscribers received the digital subscription for free. The free-to-print subscribers policy put the emphasis on subscription to the *Times* content, and not to any particular platform. This is important because today's newspaper readers are multi-platform: they read the content with a variety of devices depending on the context. A metered subscription model is similar to a freemium model: some content is free but ad-supported, while unlimited content is only through a subscription. In 2013, the number of free articles was reduced to 10, given the success of the metered model, and in that same year, the *New York Times'* subscription revenue exceeded ad revenue for the first time. In 2016, the *Times* has over 1 million paid digital subscribers. With 43 million online visitors and 30 million mobile readers, there's plenty of room for the *Times* to grow its subscriber base.

Newspapers (and online magazines as well) have benefited from the changes in public perception. Today, 78% of U.S. newspapers with circulations of over 50,000 have some sort of charge for online access. Of these, 64% use a metered subscription model, 12% provide most content for free, but charge a subscription fee to access premium content, and 3% use a paywall model (Williams, 2016).

Challenge: Growth of Pure Digital Competitors. The Web has provided an opportunity for newspapers to extend their print brands, but at the same time it has given digital entrepreneurs the opportunity to disaggregate newspaper content by creating specialized websites for popular content such as weather, classified ads (Craigslist), restaurant and product reviews (Yelp), as well as topical national and international news sites and apps that compete with online newspapers. Despite the declining revenues of the traditional print newspaper industry, entrepreneurs have poured money into news sites, and even newspapers. Since 2011, Warren Buffett has purchased 28 newspapers for an estimated $344 million in a belief that newspapers delivering comprehensive and reliable information to small tightly bound communities, and that have a reasonable Internet strategy, will be viable for a long time (Berkshire Hathaway, 2013). In August 2013, Jeffrey Bezos purchased the iconic *Washington Post* for $250 million in the belief that newspapers are not just papers but news gathering and distribution businesses independent of any technology or platform (Hagey and Bensinger, 2013).

While actual print newspapers are attracting wealthy individual investors, venture capital investors have poured over $1 billion dollars into purely digital online news sites. **Table 9.2** describes some leading native digital news sites and their investment profile. According to the Pew Research Center, 75% of the native digital news sites it

TABLE 9.2	NATIVE DIGITAL NEWS SITES
START UP	**DESCRIPTION**
Huffington Post	Founded in 2005, sold to AOL for $350 million in 2011. Aggregates content from traditional news outlets, invited paid bloggers, legions of unpaid bloggers, and original reporting.
BuzzFeed	Founded in 2006. Focus on using social media to generate viral stories. BuzzFeed focuses on shareable content like quizzes and listicles ("The five most important people"), and photos and gifs. This Digital First media organization also includes more traditional news topics like politics, business, and technology. Originally a news aggregator but now hiring journalists for traditional news reporting. In the top 50 websites in terms of traffic, exceeding *Wall Street Journal* and *Forbes*. Has raised $250 million in venture funding since 2012, and has a market valuation of $1.5 billion.
Flipboard	Founded in 2010. News aggregator app organizes stories in a magazine format that user flips through. Content drawn from traditional media and social sites, such as Twitter and Facebook datastreams, and then reassembled in an easy-to-navigate, personalized format in a mobile—and now a desktop—touchscreen environment. Apple's app of the year in 2014. *Time, New York Times*, and book publishers joining up to push content. In 2016 unable to meet revenue forecasts, and senior executives have left.
Vox	Founded in 2014. Covers politics and general news. Hired Ezra Klein (ex-*Washington Post* writer) to be editor-in-chief. Eschews banner ads for sponsored videos and stories. See the *Insight on Business* case, *Vox: Native Digital News* for more information on Vox and its parent company, Vox Media.
Reddit	Founded in 2005. Purchased by Condé Nast in 2006 and operated as an independent company. A bulletin board of user generated posts made up of 185,000 forums from science trivia, politics, videogames, humor, and photos. Registered community members can submit content, such as text posts or direct links. Mostly male, college-educated members contribute content. Limited advertising on the main pages. Unprofitable, but with 240 million unique visitors. Estimated market value $500 million.
Vice	Founded as a magazine in 1994 and moved on to websites in 2000 as Vice Media. Vice is a bulletin board of user generated articles, aggregated content, and photos. Focuses on irreverent content appealing to young readers, and reporting from dangerous locations. Vice's YouTube channel is a video-based news site. Reportedly valued by investors at $2.5 billion in 2015. Vice has 35 million unique visitors, and reportedly generated over $900 million in revenue in 2015. Earnings are unknown.

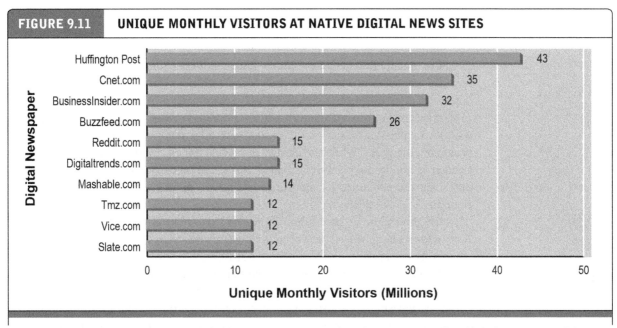

FIGURE 9.11 **UNIQUE MONTHLY VISITORS AT NATIVE DIGITAL NEWS SITES**

Native digital news sites have greatly expanded their unique visitor count and are direct competitors of established newspapers and their online editions.

SOURCE: Based on data from Compete.com, 2016.

studied grew their average monthly unique visitors from 2014 to 2015, with the vast majority of these sites attracting more traffic from mobile devices than from desktops (Pew Research Center, 2016). **Figure 9.11** lists the top native digital news sites in terms of their unique monthly visitors.

Not all digital news services succeed, and few, if any, are profitable so far. For instance, Digg, a news aggregator site, failed in 2011 despite having 230 million unique visitors at one point.

Challenge: Can Newspapers Survive Digital Disruption. The newspaper industry would appear at first glance to be a classic case of a disruptive technology—the Internet, mobile devices, and apps—destroying a traditional business model based on physical products and physical distribution. Incumbents (the existing print newspapers) slowly and incrementally improve their products over time. New firms—disruptors— introduce new products (Huffington Post, BuzzFeed, Vox), which are not as good as the incumbents' products, but are based on newer and more powerful technologies. The new products are less expensive, or free, and target underserved or entirely new markets. They often are founded and promoted by people new to the industry. Eventually the disruptor's products are improved and become more acceptable, or good enough. At this point, the new products and the disruptors start draining significant market share from the incumbents who eventually fail. Incumbents fail for a variety of reasons, from an expensive legacy production process, large human capital investments, a contrary culture, and an inability to perceive rapid changes in the business and technology environment. For a description of a news industry startup that may have a disruptive impact on traditional newspapers, see the *Insight on Business* case, *Vox: Native Digital News*.

Pure digital news sites have many advantages over print newspapers. They don't have the cost of printing papers; they can create new work flows and business processes that are more efficient and timely; they have a lower cost structure, often relying on user generated content and minimal payments to reporters and bloggers, with lower pension costs; and they can take advantage of newer technologies for producing the news. While the quality of journalism on these pure digital sites is not as good as traditional print newspapers, this situation is changing rapidly as the pure digital sites hire talented journalists and editors from print newspapers that are experiencing financial difficulties.

What online news sites often do not have is credibility and trust. For instance, BuzzFeed has been the subject of many lawsuits accusing it of copying content from competing newspapers and sites without attribution, claiming the content as its own. Without trust and quality, online news sites are simply distractions filled with celebrity photos, and there is significant competition for this kind of content.

If the newspaper industry has a future, it will be online and multiplatform. The challenge for newspapers is to create value by focusing on differentiated, timely, and exclusive content available nowhere else; to transform its culture of journalism to provide a continuous news stream just as its pure digital competitors; and to make this content available anywhere, anytime, anyplace, on any device. In short, newspapers will have to become Digital First publications, while maintaining their historic quality edge, and meeting the challenge from their pure digital competitors.

MAGAZINES REBOUND ON THE TABLET PLATFORM

The Internet and the Web did not have much impact on magazine sales at first, in part because the PC was no match for the high-resolution, large-format pictures found in, say, *Life* or *Time*. However, as screens improved, as video on the Web became common, and the economics of color publishing changed, print magazine circulation began to plummet and advertisers turned their attention to the digital platform on the Web, where readers were increasingly getting their news, general-interest journalism, and photographic accounts of events. Magazine newsstand sales have also declined significantly since 2001. Yet special-interest, celebrity, homemaking, and automobile magazines remained stable. News magazines like *Time*, *Newsweek*, and *U.S. News and World Report* have been the hardest hit. In contrast, special-interest, celebrity, fashion, lifestyle, and automobile magazines have remained relatively stable (Trachtenberg, 2015).

Magazines have responded to declining sales of physical magazines by developing digital replica magazines—fairly close copies of the physical magazine. Total U.S. revenues from subscriptions and newsstand sales of magazine were around $28 billion in 2015, down about 4% from 2014 (Sass, 2016). Ad revenues constituted about $18 billion of the total. The good news for magazines is that digital ad revenues are increasing, and accounted for over $4 billion in revenue in 2015. Unfortunately, print advertising (about $14 billion) is expected to remain relatively flat through 2020 (eMarketer,

INSIGHT ON BUSINESS

VOX: NATIVE DIGITAL NEWS

Despite an unprecedented array of entertainment options, people are reading more news online than ever before. In fact, reading news online is the second most popular activity online. Digital news readers are highly engaged with both the content and the journalists who put the words on the screen. All of this is not lost on investors, who have poured over $1 billion dollars into native digital news sites (sites without a print edition or television franchise) in the last few years.

Vox Media is a prime example of a startup media firm grounded in the digital news stream. Founded in 2003, Vox Media is a privately held company based in Washington D.C. with over 700 employees. The company has raised $300 million in venture capital, including $200 million in 2015 from Comcast's NBCUniversal division, valuing the company at a whopping $1 billion. Gaining access to NBCUniversal's content distribution and production capabilities has helped Vox Media to branch out into other forms of media.

Vox Media has pursued a unique strategy from the beginning. Rather than creating a single digital news site, as, say, traditional newspapers have done, and showing tabs for various areas of interest (sports, business, or entertainment), it instead has unbundled the general news site into a number of focused sites, populating them with content from hundreds of different blogs that it has created or purchased. It started with SBNa-tion (SportsBlogNation), a collection of 315 individual sites, most of which focus on individual professional sports teams. Each SBNation site has its own name, URL, brand, and writers.

Vox Media currently owns eight specialty sites, which themselves are often collections of blogs or websites, including Eater (food), Curbed (real estate), Verge (culture), Polygon (game), Racked (fashion), Re/code (tech), and most recently, a general news and commentary site, Vox. com. These niche sites foster much greater intensity of reader engagement. The approach seems to be working: Vox Media reached 91 million unique monthly visitors in August 2016, with the typical visitor being under 35 and with income over $100,000 a year. Almost one-third of its readership belongs to the coveted age 18-to-34 demographic.

Vox.com was created in January 2014 when Vox hired respected political reporter Ezra Klein from the *Washington Post*. Vox.com pioneered the "explanatory journalism" movement by presenting news in card stacks rather than long text articles. Readers can pursue news in small increments, one card at a time, with use of color photos, videos, and graphics on the cards. Readers can go as deep in the card stack as they want or have time for. Vox.com, and other Vox sites that use this technique such as Curbed and Eater, hoped this new format would be more easily consumed by mobile readers, differentiate its product from digital versions of print newspapers, and also be easily placed on social network newsfeeds. This editorial transformation has been viewed as a critical success, and has become a major source of new readers.

Vox Media is often regarded as the future of digital news publishing because of its technology, culture, and business organization. Traditional newspaper firms typically have a melange of technologies, built at different times, to coordinate the flow of news with both print and web versions. One of the first priorities Vox pursued was to invest millions of dollars in a content management system (CMS) called Chorus. Chorus goes beyond content creation and management because it provides the publishing environment as well. When reporters and editors are done,

(continued)

they can use Chorus to publish formatted content to various websites and social media. Chorus offers journalists unprecedented levels of control and customization, including the ability to engage with reader comments and to integrate content from others' stories.

Vox also has a unique organizational structure when compared to traditional newspapers. At Vox, the organization is flat, with fewer middle and senior managers. This empowers reporters and circumvents the lengthy editorial review process at traditional newspapers.

Unbundling news into more focused, vertical websites and harnessing technology to reduce the cost and improve the speed of content creation has been a good start for Vox. But Vox must continue to focus on quality reporting while maintaining an active presence on the myriad other platforms where its audience now gets its news. Whether or not Vox will ultimately succeed depends not only on whether it is able to attract a large audience and enough advertisers, but also on its ability to succeed on other platforms, including Facebook, YouTube, and even Snapchat.

To that end, Vox has been active in its efforts on these platforms, such as its early involvement with Snapchat's Discover service for content creators. For Discover, Vox creates 10-second infographics combining voiceovers and text to plug its latest features. Vox also places heavy emphasis on its YouTube channel, which has well over a million subscribers and whose most popular video has 24 million views. Vox produces high-quality video content to accompany some of its print stories as well as other video content that

stands alone, with 11 full-time Vox employees responsible for video content development. In both its YouTube and Snapchat efforts, Vox is careful to make content that doesn't feel like traditional television or news sources, searching for stories that are specifically well suited for video and weaving graphics, voiceover, interviews, and other techniques together. Much of Vox's video traffic originates from Facebook, where videos shared by Klein garner millions more views. In 2016, Vox launched what it calls its Storytelling Studio, which prepares long-form journalism using these techniques for particularly notable stories. Its first project, an in-depth conversation with and discussion of Hillary Clinton, was well received by Vox users. Vox also announced plans to create a similar team for Snapchat content in 2016. Not content to stop there, Vox also announced a partnership between Curbed and A+E to develop a television show focusing on high-style housing, as well as plans to create other television-style content for BravoTV.com.

Business analysts also point out that few of the digital news sites have generated profits. Most of the digital news sites are private and do not report revenues or profits. The pure digital news sites face the same problems online as traditional newspapers do, namely, the declining revenues from digital advertising. However, internal documents at BuzzFeed, the second most heavily trafficked "new media" company behind Huffington Post suggested that it was profitable and that its revenues were growing signficantly. While the cost of generating traffic to these sites is substantial, Vox and its peers are continuing their push toward profitability.

━━ **SOURCES:** "Two Years In, Vox.com Reconsiders Its 'Card Stacks'," by Lucia Moses, Digiday.com, September 9, 2016; "How Vox Media's New Storytelling Studio Thinks of Stories as Products," by Taylyn Washington-Harmon, Niemanlab.com, July 28, 2016; "Vox Media Launches Its First TV Show on A+E Network's FYI," by Tim Baysinger, Adweek.com, May 4, 2016; "Vox Media Creates a Snapchat Studio, and SB National is Going Bilingual with the Help of Telemundo," by Shan Wang, Niemanlab.com, May 4, 2016; "Vox Media Names First CFO, Adds Former Yahoo President to Board," by Gerry Smith, Bloomberg.com, April 27, 2016; "Inspired By 'Independent YouTubers,' Wary of Cable, Vox.com Takes Its Explainer Mission to Video," by Laura Hazard Owen, Niemanlab.org, April 22, 2016; "Reader's Digest? The Surprising Places Young People Are Getting the News," by Lucia Moses, Digiday.com, April 7, 2016; "Distributed News: The Vox Way of Getting Stories Out to 6 Social Platforms," by Madalina Ciobanu, Journalism.co.uk, January 22, 2016; "Vox Brings Explainer Journalism to Snapchat," by Ashley Norris, Fipp.com, December 2, 2015; "Internal Documents Show BuzzFeed's Skyrocketing Investment in Editorial," by J.K. Trotter, Gawker.com, August 12, 2015; "NBCU Ups Its Share of Vox Media," by Lukas I. Alpert, *Wall Street Journal*, August 12, 2015; "Vox Media Ventures into General News and News Analysis With Vox.com," by Paul Farhi, *Washington Post*, April 7, 2014; "Vox Takes Melding of Journalism and Technology to a New Level," by Leslie Kaufman, *New York Times*, April 6, 2014; "Ezra Klein Is Joining Vox Media as Web Journalism Asserts Itself," by David Carr, *New York Times*, January 26, 2014.

Inc., 2016f). The increasing digital revenue is not quite enough to compensate for the decline in print ad revenue. One possible solution is to begin charging a subscription fee for access to the digital editions, which currently are often free. *The New Yorker*, perhaps the most prestigious magazine in the United States, is also one of the most widely read, with 1 million print subscribers and 13 million unique visitors to its website. In 2014, the magazine introduced a metered paywall. Some articles are free, but frequent readers will be charged an annual subscription fee (Somaiya, 2014). In 2016, *The New Yorker* launched a new iPhone app called The New Yorker Today that is free to download and use for one month, but thereafter switching to the same metered model used for its website. Like newspapers, magazines are experimenting with different revenue models in an effort to monetize the rapidly growing tablet audience. Most magazines participate in Apple's iPad Subscription Service, which allows magazines to offer subscriptions from within their app and have the transaction processed by the App Store billing system. Publishers set the price, and customers can subscribe with one click. Apple keeps 30% of the transaction. Publishers can also direct app readers to their website for a subscription, in which case Apple does not make any fee. Virtual storefronts such as Google Play have helped publishers grow their digital subscriber base. In 2015, Apple introduced its News app. Magazines such as *Time* and 75 others provide articles in an effort to capture a younger, mobile audience (Trachtenberg, 2015).

Despite the shrinkage of print subscription and newsstand sales in the past few years, the total magazine audience size increased by over 6% in 2015, due entirely to growth of digital magazines, especially mobile web editions, and the percentage of adults who read digital edition magazines has more than quadrupled since 2011 (Magazine Publishers Association, 2016). Another study found that over 40% of those surveyed had read an average of 2.5 digital magazine issues in the past month (Mequoda Group LLC, 2016). More than 35% of tablet computer owners read magazine content once a week, and there are an estimated 1,200 magazine apps for mobile readers.

Popular websites like Pinterest, an image-collecting site that attracts millions of viewers, and Facebook, Yahoo, and Twitter are among the largest drivers of traffic to digital magazines. The widespread adoption of tablet computers has helped create the visual Internet, where glossy magazine publishers, who are inherently oriented to richly detailed color photography, can display their works and advertisements to great advantage.

With hundreds of popular online magazines to choose from, magazine aggregators like Zinio, Texture (formerly Next Issue Media), Magzter, and Flipboard make it possible for customers to find their favorite magazines using a single app. A **magazine aggregator** is a website or app that offers users online subscriptions and sales of many digital magazines.

magazine aggregator
a website or app that provides subscriptions and sales of many digital magazines

E-BOOKS AND ONLINE BOOK PUBLISHING

In April 2000, Stephen King, one of America's most popular writers, published a novella called *Riding the Bullet*. This novella was only available as an e-book. King was the first major fiction writer to create an e-book-only volume of a new work. King's publisher, Simon & Schuster, arranged for sales online through online retailers such as Amazon. In the first day, there were 400,000 downloads, so many that Amazon's servers crashed several times. More than 600,000 downloads occurred in the first week. While Amazon gave the book away for free in the first two weeks, when it began charging $2.50 for a 66-page novella—about the same price per page as a standard King hardcover novel—sales continued to be brisk. This experiment showed Simon & Schuster, and Amazon, that there was a mass market for e-book popular fiction. Previous efforts to create a popular e-book had all failed. For publishers, it meant their entire back list of older books suddenly had monetary value if they could be sold as e-book editions.

Ten years later, on April 15, 2010, Amanda Hocking, an unknown and unpublished writer from Austin, Minnesota, uploaded one of her vampire novels, *My Blood Approves*, to Amazon's self-publishing site, and later to the Barnes & Noble e-book store. Her novels had been rejected by many of the publishing houses in New York. By March 2011, she had sold more than 1 million copies of her e-books, which generally sell for 99 cents to $2.99, and earned more than $2 million. In 2012, Hocking was listed as one of the Amazon 99 cent millionaires. In 2013, Hugh Howey's self-published science fiction e-book *Wool* sold more than 500,000 copies and earned him more than $1 million in royalties and film rights. Over 40% of Amazon's top 100 selling e-books are now self-published, generating around 14% of e-book revenue. The Big Five publishers, in contrast, sell less than 25% of Amazon's e-books although they generate over 40% of the revenue with prices around $14.00/per e-book. Twenty-three so-called "indie" (independently published) books have sold more than 250,000 copies, and four Indie authors have sold more than 1 million copies of their books, according to Amazon (Authorearnings.com, 2016). Admittedly these success stories are rare, and the vast majority of Indie authors in 2016 are unable to make a living, let alone $1 million.

The book publishing industry's experience with the Internet is very different from the newspaper and magazine industries. E-book editions of fiction and non-fiction books (so-called trade books) have been very successful, yet printed book sales have not collapsed and have remained about the same over time. Professional books, which includes college textbooks, remain almost entirely printed for a variety of reasons. Book publishing revenues have been stable over the last five years. In 2015, the U.S. book publishing industry generated just under $28 billion in revenue and sold 2.7 billion books (both e-books and printed books). Trade books (general fiction and non-fiction) generated $15.8 billion in revenue on sales of about 2.5 billion books (AAP, 2016).

In the space of a decade, e-books have gone from an unusual experiment by a major author, to an everyday experience for millions of Americans, and an exciting new market for authors, changing the process of writing, selling, and distributing books. U.S. e-books sales in 2016 are expected to be $7.6 billion, 26% of all consumer book sales. Although e-book sales are expected to continue increasing through 2015, e-book sales are not expected to continue to grow nearly as fast as they did in previous years (see **Figure 9.12**). Accounting for e-book sales in the mix of total book sales is difficult because around 30% of the books sold on Amazon do not have ISBNs (International Standard Book Numbers), and therefore, are not counted by the publishing industry, whose books always have ISBN identifying numbers. Industry-based reports on e-book sales only include those published with ISBNs, and indie books generally do not have ISBNs (Authorearnings.com, 2016). Analysts estimate that 25% of Amazon's e-book sales result from indie e-books. The industry estimates presented here likely underestimate e-book sales. An entire new channel for self-published authors now exists, a channel not controlled by the major publishing companies and their professional editors. The book distribution market has been disrupted and yet in 2016 it is apparent that the major publishing firms still maintain their positions as the dominant source of book content. In addition, while bookstore chains like Borders and Waldenbooks have disappeared and while Barnes & Noble faces earnings challenges, small independent bookstores have grown 27% since 2009 to over 2,000 stores. And while the Kindle platform unleashed a torrent of indie manuscripts from thousands of would-be writers, only a few well-publicized authors have achieved popular success and a living income. Unlike the newspaper business, it's too soon to declare that the book industry has been digitally destroyed or wounded, and some reason to believe that printed books will continue to be with us long into the future.

Amazon and Apple: The New Digital Media Ecosystems

Although precursors of e-books and e-book readers began to be introduced in the 1990s and early 2000s, it was not until 2007 that the future of e-books was firmly established. In that year, Amazon introduced the Kindle, which allowed users to download books

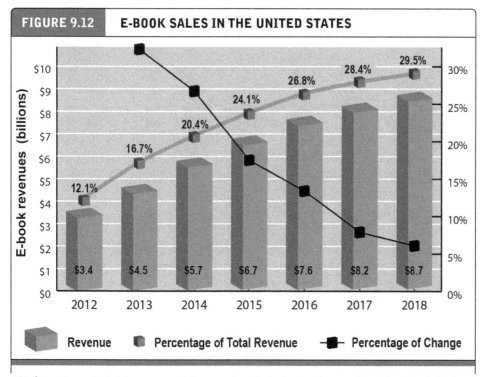

FIGURE 9.12   E-BOOK SALES IN THE UNITED STATES

This figure shows the total revenues and the percentage that e-books sales constitute of total trade book sales revenues in the United States, as well as the change in the growth of revenues. As the graph shows, growth in e-book revenues has slowed significantly since 2013.

SOURCES: Based on data from AAP, 2016; authors' estimates.

from the Kindle store using AT&T's cell network. E-books received another boost in 2009 when Barnes & Noble introduced its Nook e-reader, and in 2010 when Apple introduced its first iPad tablet computer. With its large, high-resolution screen, the iPad was an even better e-book reader than the Kindle, albeit not as easily slipped into a purse. While Amazon got the jump on Apple in dedicated e-book readers, Apple's approach from the beginning was a multipurpose device that could handle movies, music, magazines, and books, as well as having a Wi-Fi connection to the Internet.

Today, Amazon and Apple together account for 85% of the e-book market, with Amazon the leader with a 74% market share and Apple in second at 11% (Barnes & Noble's Nook has experienced declining market share, but still accounts for about 8%) (Authorearnings.com, 2015). Amazon's Kindle Store contains millions of e-book titles while Apple's iBooks Store has over 2.5 million. The result of the Amazon and Apple ecosystems, combining hardware, software, and online mega stores, was an explosion in online book content, readership, authorship, marketing, and at least a partial upending of the traditional book publishing and marketing channels. Traditional book publishing has similarly been altered. In the traditional process, authors worked with agents, who sold book manuscripts to editors and publishers, who sold books through bookstores, at prices determined largely by the publishers. Because bookstores had a vested interest in selling books at a profit, there was only limited discounting during clearance sales. In the new publishing model, authors still write books, but then bypass traditional agent and publisher channels and instead publish digital books that are sold on Amazon or by Apple. Prices are determined by the author, usually much lower than traditional books depending on the popularity of the author, and the digital distributor takes a percentage of the sale (usually 30%). New self-published authors typically give away their early works to develop an audience, and then, when an audience appears, charge a small amount for their books, typically 99 cents to $2.99. Marketing occurs by word of mouth on social networks, author blogs, and public readings. While a small percentage of all books are produced this way, it is a growing and popular form of publishing. Although only a very few self-published authors has thus far struck it rich, the possibility has been enough to arouse the passions of thousands of potential writers of the great American novel, as well as lesser genres from police procedurals to paranormal romance writers.

E-Book Business Models

The e-book industry is composed of intermediary retailers (both brick-and-mortar stores and online merchants), traditional publishers, technology developers, device makers (e-readers), and vanity presses (self-publishing service companies). Together, these players have pursued a wide variety of business models and developed many alliances in an effort to move text onto the computer screen.

There are five large publishers that dominate trade book, education, and religious book publishing. These traditional publishers have the largest content libraries for conversion to e-books and they produce over 80% of new book titles in a year. In the e-book marketplace, the large publishers started out using a **wholesale model** of distribution and pricing, in part because this is the same model they used with hard cover books. In this model, the retail store pays a wholesale price for the book and

wholesale model
prices are determined by the retailer

then decides at what price to sell it to the consumer. The retailer sets the price with, of course, some kind of understanding with the publisher that the book will not be given away for free. In the past, the wholesale price was 50% of the retail price. A retailer would pay the publisher a $10 wholesale price and mark it up to a $20 retail price. However, retailers could also determine to sell the book at a much lower sale price, say $5, as a way to attract readers to the store or as a close-out sale. Brick-and-mortar stores had a vested interest in selling most books above their wholesale cost. With e-books, publishers discovered that some online retailers like Amazon and Apple might sell books below cost in order to encourage customers to purchase their e-book reader devices or to sell them other goods.

In the case of e-books, publishers sought to keep their prices high enough so as not to discourage sales of hard cover books, which typically sell for $26. Generally, this meant publishers wanted e-books to sell at a retail price of $12.99 to $14.99, depending on the popularity of the book and the stage in the product life cycle (months since first publication). E-book distributors like Amazon were charged a wholesale price of about $9 and were expected to mark up the product to around $12.99 to $14.99 or more. Instead, Amazon chose to sell e-books for $9.99, at or below cost, in order to attract buyers to its content store to buy Kindles, and to attract new customers to its online retail store. Amazon lost $1 to $3 on every e-book sold, but recouped the money by selling Kindles for hundreds of dollars, and from additional sales of other products. With Amazon selling e-books at $9.99, the lowest prices on the Web, publishers were forced to sell their e-books on all other websites at the $9.99 Amazon price. Using this strategy, Amazon not only sold millions of Kindles but also sold 90% of all e-book titles on the Web in 2010 and 2011. Amazon had a near monopoly on e-books.

Publishers opposed Amazon's policy as debasing the perceived value of both physical and digital books, and as a mortal threat to the publishers who could not survive if their e-books were priced at $9.99 across the Web. They claimed Amazon was engaging in predatory pricing, designed to destroy traditional book publishers. In 2010, five of the largest publishers secretly met with Steve Jobs and Apple. They agreed to a new pricing model called the agency model. In the **agency model**, the distributor is an agent of the publisher, and can be directed to sell e-books at a price determined by the publisher, around $14.99 and higher for certain titles. In return for a 30% commission, Apple agreed to support this model, as did Google, neither of whom were comfortable watching as Amazon dominated one of the hottest areas of web content sales. In these meetings, publishing executives discussed a common pricing strategy.

agency model
the retailer is an agent and prices are set by the manufacturer

The agency model temporarily turned the tables on Amazon: it now had to charge whatever price the publishers wanted or the publishers would not sell Amazon any books (they would not choose Amazon as an agent for their products). A result of the agency model was that Amazon's prices on e-books rose to the publisher desired levels, and its market share fell to 60% in 2012. Apple, Google, Barnes & Noble, and the five major publishers were delighted. The Justice Department was not delighted: it sued the five publishers and Apple for price fixing in violation of antitrust laws. All five of the publishers settled, but Apple refused to settle and asked for a trial before a judge. In 2013, the United States District Court found that Apple had engaged in price fixing, not because of its agency pricing model, which is quite common throughout retail trade, but because of its "most favored seller" clause in its agreements with publishers, which had the effect of discouraging other sites (like Amazon) from selling e-books for less than Apple's iBooks Store price. In addition, the publishers and Apple conspired to act in concert, rather than as individual publishers. Under the agreements, the publishers, not Amazon, would determine prices on Amazon. If publishers sold their books on Amazon for $9.95, then publishers would have to sell their e-books at the iBooks Store for $9.95. The court found that Apple and the book publishers' plan would result in less price competition, and higher prices, by enforcing a single higher price on all online distributors and e-books. In the field of antitrust, less competition and higher prices for all is considered a cardinal violation of the law. After the ruling, e-book prices on Amazon have fallen to an average of $9.99, with some older titles far less, with limited discounting, and its market share rose to 65%. In August 2014, Apple agreed to pay a $450 million fine to compensate consumers for its price fixing behavior. While the ruling prevents Apple from fixing prices of e-books, it does nothing to solve the issues surrounding Amazon's dominance of the e-book marketplace. Publishers will need to each reach independent marketing agreements with Amazon, one by one. Critics of the court case believe Amazon's market power will force publishers to submit to Amazon's price terms.

In May 2014, following court rulings against the publishers, Amazon and the Hachette group tried to negotiate an agreement on pricing. To demonstrate its market power and strengthen its negotiating position, Amazon withdrew all Hachette books from its website, leading to author-organized protests. In November 2014, Hachette and Simon & Schuster (one of the largest publishers in the United States) agreed on terms with Amazon that allow the publishers to set the prices of their books (the agency model) but allow Amazon to offer incentives to publishers to reduce prices on selected books, and provide for publisher payments to Amazon for listing their books (Streitfield, 2014a; 2014b). Today, prices on e-books as a result are highly variable, ranging from $9.95 to $16.95.

The Challenges of the Digital E-Book Platform

Because of the rapid growth in e-books, the book publishing industry is in stable condition. Yet the industry faces a number of challenges. The early fear of cannibalization, namely inexpensive and less profitable e-books replacing more expensive and profitable print books, has mostly been put to rest. Unlike the newspaper and magazine industries, printed books are surviving in large part because purchasers of e-book readers continue to purchase printed books, and switch back and forth from digital to print as circumstances merit. For instance, according to Pew Research Center, about two-thirds of Americans said they read a printed book last year, about the same as in 2012. Despite the surge of e-books and digital reading platforms, people still prefer printed books (Pew Research Center, 2016b). In the professional and educational book markets, e-books have made some inroads, in part due to their lower costs, but for a variety of reasons, many students still prefer a physical book to an e-book. Students often find the user interface of e-books more difficult to use compared to printed books and that it is easier to concentrate when using a physical book, increasing comprehension and retention. E-books may be like audio books, a useful alternative but not a substitute. The falling growth rate of e-books from double-digit to single-digit growth may reflect this reality.

The biggest challenge facing the book publishing industry is control over pricing on the digital e-book platforms. As previously noted, Amazon accounts for almost 75% of the market, which, while not a monopoly, nevertheless gives it tremendous market power. For critics, Amazon threatens to decimate the traditional book publishing industry, replacing the old print world of a small number of publishers, limited numbers of titles, independent bookstores, elitist editors in New York, and newspaper book critics, with a new digital world of publishing where content is shaped by algorithms identifying what the consumer wants to read about, writers are their own editors, critics are replaced by reader comments, and distribution is controlled by one or a few online stores (Packer, 2014). Efforts by Amazon to create its own book publishing brand, circumventing the traditional book publishers, have only worsened relations between the world's largest book store and the world's largest publishers (Streitfield, 2014c).

Amazon, as the largest player in the e-book market, offers the biggest challenge. This is ironic because Amazon, through its online store and Kindle e-book marketplace and reader, has helped the publishing industry to survive the transition to a digital marketplace, both by providing the largest book store on earth, and by creating the Kindle e-book platform. While the expansion of e-book revenues has offset a small decline in print sales, the industry has lost pricing power vis-à-vis its largest distribution partner, Amazon.

A second serious challenge is the further evolution of the digital distribution platform. In 2014, Amazon announced Kindle Unlimited, a subscription service where for $9.99 a month, customers can read all the books they want. Over 1.4 million titles are available, but this Netflix for books does not include any books from the big five publishers—Hachette, HarperCollins, Simon & Schuster, Macmillan, and Penguin Random House. Major publishers believe subscription e-book services negatively impact book publisher and author revenues. Control over pricing is again the key issue.

While the book publishing industry has survived in the first era of e-books and the digital distribution platform provided by Amazon, Apple, and others, the long-term prospects for book publishing revenues and profits remain an open question.

Interactive Books: Converging Technologies

The future of e-books may depend in part on changes in the concept and design of a book. The modern e-book is not really very different from the first two-facing page, bound books that began to appear in seventeenth-century Europe and had already appeared in the fourth century BCE in ancient China. The traditional Western book has a very simple, nondigital operating system: text appears left to right, pages are numbered, there is a front and a back cover, and text pages are bound together by stitching or glue. In educational and reference books, there is an alphabetical index in the back of the book that permits direct access to the book's content. While these traditional books will be with us for many years given their portability, ease of use, and flexibility, a parallel new world of interactive e-books is expected to emerge in the next five years. Interactive books combine audio, video, and photography with text, providing the reader with a multimedia experience thought to be more powerful than simply reading a book. Apple offers iBooks Author, an app to help authors create interactive books, and iBooks Textbooks, a line of interactive textbooks created by several of the largest textbook publishing firms. Some experts believe that traditional print books will be curiosities by 2025. However, as of 2016, these newer multimedia textbooks have not yet been successful in the marketplace.

9.3 THE ONLINE ENTERTAINMENT INDUSTRY

The entertainment industry is generally considered to be composed of four traditional, commercial players and one new arrival: television, radio broadcasting, Hollywood films, music, and games (the new arrival). Together, these largely separate entertainment players generated $144 billion in annual U.S. revenue in 2015. This includes both digital and traditional format revenues. **Figure 9.13** illustrates the relative sizes of these commercial entertainment markets. By far, the largest entertainment producer is television (broadcast, satellite, and cable), and then motion pictures, followed by video games (both stand-alone and online games), radio, and music. While online, computer, and console revenues have grown to be larger than movie box office revenues (about $11 billion), total Hollywood film revenues dwarf the game industry when other sources of movie revenue are added such as streaming, DVD rental and sales, and licensing (total revenue related to motion pictures is $29.2 billion). Radio remains a strong revenue producer aided in part by the growth of Internet radio services like Spotify and Pandora, but is still largely reliant on FM and AM broadcast technologies,

FIGURE 9.13	THE FIVE MAJOR PLAYERS IN THE U.S. ENTERTAINMENT INDUSTRY

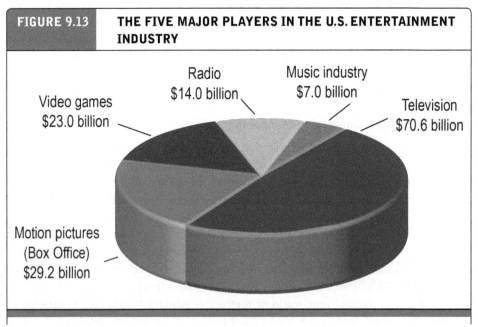

Radio $14.0 billion

Music industry $7.0 billion

Television $70.6 billion

Video games $23.0 billion

Motion pictures (Box Office) $29.2 billion

SOURCES: Based on data from industry sources; authors' estimates.

especially in automobiles. Recorded music is the smallest of the major players at $7 billion, half of its size ten years ago.

Along with the other content industries, the entertainment segment is undergoing a transformation brought about by the Internet and the extraordinary growth of mobile devices. Several forces are at work. Mobile devices, coupled with the easy availability of entertainment content now offered by Amazon, Netflix, and many others, have changed consumer preferences and increased demand for such content, whether in subscription or a la carte pay-per-view forms. Social networks are also spurring the delivery of entertainment content to desktop and mobile devices. Social networks are rapidly adding video and live video-streaming to their services, as well as providing a platform for sharing TV and movie experiences. The iTunes store and Amazon provide successful download music services where users pay for tracks and albums. Music subscription services like Pandora, Spotify, and Apple Music have millions of subscribers. Both kinds of services—download and streaming—have demonstrated that millions of consumers are willing to pay reasonable prices for high-quality content, portability, and convenience. The growth in broadband has obviously made possible both wired and wireless delivery of all forms of entertainment over the Internet, potentially displacing cable and broadcast television networks. Closed platforms, like the Kindle and streaming services like Netflix, also work to reduce the need for DRM. Streaming music and video are inherently protected because the content has been in the past difficult to download to a computer (similar to cable TV). This situation is changing with the advent of streamed video apps like Periscope that can capture live video from a PC or TV screen. All of these forces have combined to bring about a transformation in the entertainment industries.

In an ideal world, consumers would be able to watch any movie, listen to any music, watch any TV show, and play any game, when they want, and where they want, using whatever Internet-connected device is convenient. Consumers would be billed monthly for these services by a single provider of Internet service. This idealized version of a convergent media world is many years away, but clearly this is the direction of the Internet-enabled entertainment industry, in part because technology will enable this outcome, but also because of the emergence of very large-scale, integrated technology media companies like Amazon, Google, Apple, and Netflix. Many analysts believe the large entertainment media giants of the future will be technology companies that have moved into the production of content.

When we think of the producers of entertainment in the offline world, we tend to think about television networks such as ABC, Fox, NBC, HBO, or CBS; Hollywood film studios such as MGM, Disney, Paramount, and Twenty-First Century Fox; and music labels such as Sony BMG, Atlantic Records, Columbia Records, and Warner Records. Interestingly, many of these international brand names are just now moving to have significant entertainment presence on the Internet. Although traditional forms of entertainment such as television shows and Hollywood movies are now commonplace on the Web, neither the television nor film industries have built an industry-wide delivery system. Instead, they are building relationships with tech-based Internet distributors like Netflix, Yahoo, Google, Amazon, Facebook, and Apple, all of which have become significant players in media distribution.

ONLINE ENTERTAINMENT MARKET SIZE AND GROWTH

Figure 9.14 shows the current and projected growth for U.S. commercial online entertainment revenues for the major players: online TV and movies, online games, Internet radio, and online music downloads. Most noticeable is the extraordinary growth of online TV and movies, driven in large part by adoption of mobile devices, as well as the success of TV and movie streaming sites. Other forms of online entertainment will also continue to grow, but at single-digit rates. As the Internet takes on the distribution of TV shows and movies, the role (and revenue) of cable television delivery systems declines.

There will be some interesting changes by 2019. Online TV and movies will grow very rapidly (by more than 15% annually), while online games and Internet radio remain relatively stable generators of revenue, declining in significance when compared to TV and movies.

TELEVISION

In the television industry in 2016, viewers have gone mobile, Internet streaming and downloading distributors like Netflix and Apple have gained market power vis-à-vis TV and movie production firms, and cable television systems are losing ground to

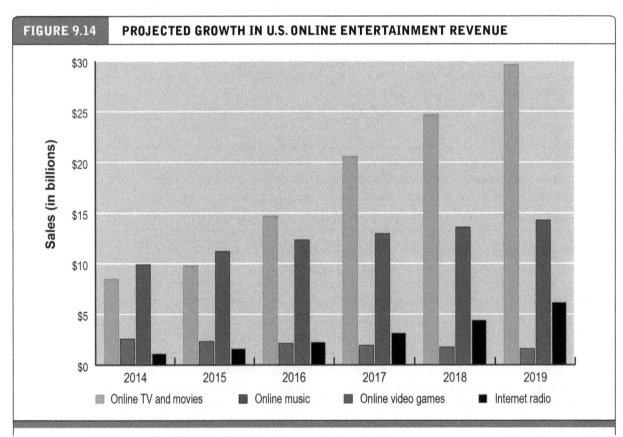

FIGURE 9.14 | **PROJECTED GROWTH IN U.S. ONLINE ENTERTAINMENT REVENUE**

Among commercial forms of mass entertainment, online TV and movies engage the largest number of people and generate the largest online revenues in 2016. By 2019, online TV and movies are expected to account for around 57% of all online entertainment revenues.

SOURCES: Based on data from industry sources; authors' estimates.

Internet and mobile app delivery of content. Streaming services provided by firms like Netflix, Hulu, and Amazon, and convenient downloading of movies and entire TV series, have created powerful alternatives to traditional cable television delivery systems. Cable distribution systems are challenged as the Internet offers alternative, unbundled, a la carte access to TV programs. **Linear TV**—watching a TV series over an entire season as installments—is being supplanted by **binge watching** of entire seasons online over a few days. This is not possible with linear TV on cable or broadcast platforms. Contrary to expectations, the big TV screen in the home is as popular as ever, supported by social networks that buzz with chat about what's on TV right now, and Internet-connected smart TVs. In 2016, over 165 million Americans watch TV online, over 50% of the American population (eMarketer, Inc., 2016g). Increasingly, the TV household is a cross-platform phenomenon. Every day, Americans watch about 4 hours of TV on traditional TV sets, but spend 5¾ hours online using a computer or mobile device. Millennials (ages 16–34) are also avid users of streaming TV services, with over 80% of respondents in that age group in a recent survey reporting that they watched TV programming using such services (eMarketer, Inc., 2016b). Streaming has replaced downloading as the preferred consumer viewing platform. Netflix is the market leader in streaming TV and movies, with revenue of $6.7 billion in 2015.

The television industry is in the midst of a transition to a new delivery platform—the Internet via dedicated streaming devices such as Apple TV, Google Chromecast, Roku, and Amazon Fire TV (see **Table 9.3**), as well as smartphones and tablet computers. As a result, the cable and satellite TV distribution model has been challenged. This transition closely follows an earlier but related transition to DVRs and time-

linear TV
watching a television series in installments over an entire season

binge watching
watching a television series in its entirety in single or multiple sittings in a brief period of time

TABLE 9.3	STREAMING TV DEVICES
DEVICE	**DESCRIPTION**
Apple TV	Provides content from Apple's iTunes store, plus thousands of other channels/apps, including Netflix, Hulu, HBO, Showtime, etc. Does not provide access to Google Play or Amazon Video, although can access Amazon Video using Airplay feature. Available in two models. New Apple TV features touchpad remote control and Siri voice recognition.
Google Chromecast	Stream content from Google Play store as well as from other providers such as Netflix, Hulu, HBO, ESPN, YouTube, and thousands of others. Must have account that provides access to these services. Does not provide access to iTunes or Amazon Video. Unlike other devices with on-screen interfaces that display channels/apps that can be selected and played via use of a remote controller, with Chromecast you find the content you want on the Chrome browser or mobile device and then "cast" it to TV through the Chromecast player. Lowest cost device.
Roku	Stream content from 2500+ channels/apps, including Netflix, Amazon Video, Google Play, HBO, etc. Must have account that provides access to these services. Does not provide access to iTunes. Five different models available, differentiated by performance, features, and price, ranging from set top box to streaming stick.
Amazon Fire TV	Tightly integrated with Amazon Instant Video services, but also provides access to thousands of other content providers, except iTunes and Google Play. Comes in two basic models: set top box (Fire TV) and Fire TV stick.

shifting by consumers who no longer were constrained by television executives' programming and scheduling decisions. The current transition to Internet and especially mobile delivery of television is not leading to a decline in traditional television viewing, which has in fact increased slightly. The new platform is changing how, when, and where consumers can watch TV. Cloud computing, the storage and streaming of content from large Internet datacenters rather than on individual personal devices, has created a large shift away from ownership of content, and a focus instead on access to content anywhere, anytime, from any device as a streaming service. Streaming of movies from subscription services has expanded more rapidly than buying and downloading of movies. Social networks have enabled a new kind of **social TV**, where consumers share comments while viewing television shows. The most important activity in today's television household may not be what's on screen, but instead what's being said about what's on screen. Television rating agencies today do not have a methodology for measuring this kind of engagement.

social TV
involves consumers sharing comments via social networks while viewing television

Expansion of broadband networks, especially those serving mobile devices such as Wi-Fi and high-speed cellular networks, and the growth of cloud servers, has enabled the growth of a whole new class of television distributors. Cloud distributors, like Apple's iCloud service and Walmart's Vudu service, allow users to purchase video and movies, store them in iCloud, and view the entertainment from any device, anywhere. Whereas the dominant way consumers obtained a TV signal in the past was from over-the-air broadcasters, cable TV, or satellite distributors (so-called linear TV), a new "over-the-top" (OTT) channel has developed led by powerful technology companies such as Apple, Google, Hulu, Netflix, and many others, all of whom offer consumers access to television shows and some full-length feature movies using the household Internet service rather than the cable TV service (see **Table 9.4**). **Over-the-top (OTT)** entertainment services refers to the use of the Internet to deliver online entertainment services to the home. "Over-the-top" refers to the fact that the entertainment service rides "on top" of other network services like cable TV and telephone service. It's as if we have a new Internet Broadcasting System with many new players. With OTT entertainment, TV does not have to be linear, and consumers do not have to purchase a bundle of channels, most of which they never watch.Challenging the industry even further, in 2016, the FCC proposed a plan, sometimes referred to as the "open set top box plan" that would enable consumers to get rid of cable set-top boxes and allow them to access cable channels via streaming TV devices such as those referred to in Table 9.3 or through an app on their smart TVs. However, not surprisingly, this plan has met with fierce resistance from the TV industry and cable providers.

Over-the-top (OTT)
use of the Internet to deliver entertainment services to the home on cable TV or FiOS networks

The Internet and the mobile platform have also changed the viewing experience. The best screen when commuting or traveling is the smartphone and tablet. More importantly, Internet-enabled social networks like Facebook and Twitter have made TV viewing a social experience shared among neighbors, friends, and colleagues. In the past, television was often a social event involving family and friends in the same room watching a single TV show. The social circle has expanded to include Facebook and Twitter friends in different locations, changing television from a "lean back and enjoy" experience into a "lean forward and engage" experience. Many viewers are

TABLE 9.4	NEW DIGITAL TV SUBSCRIPTION SERVICES
DIGITAL SERVICE	**PROVIDER**
LIVE AND ON-DEMAND SERVICE	
Sling TV	Dish Network (satellite provider) digital package of 24+ channels. $20/month with additional channel packages available for $5 and up.
Sony PlayStation Vue	Different packages available at a variety of price points ranging from $29.99/month for 55+ channels including live cable TV, movies, and sports channels to $54.99 for 100+ channels, including live national and regional sports networks and major movie and entertainment channels. Requires an Internet connection and a PlayStation Vue. TV-connected devices such as a PS3/PS4, Amazon Fire TV/Fire TV stick, Roku devices, as well as Apple iPhone/iPad and Android devices through the Playstation Vue mobile app. Also can be accessed with Google Chromecast.
Xfinity Stream TV	Comcast's online live and on-demand service of broadcast networks and HBO premium cable shows. $15/month. Available only to Comcast subscribers.
AT&T DirecTV Now	Bundle of 100 on-demand TV channels and movies based on its purchase in 2015 of DirecTV for $49 billion. DirecTV Mobile app will combine premium video with made-for-digital content. Launch expected by end of 2016.
ON-DEMAND ONLY	
Netflix	Thousands of movies and TV episodes along with original series like *House of Cards* and *Unbreakable Kimmy Schmidt*. $8/month.
Amazon Prime	Thousands of movies and TV episodes, free to Amazon Prime subscribers, with some original programming. $99/year.
Hulu Plus	TV shows from broadcasting and cable networks, as well as original HBO shows. $8/month.
Noggin	Video app by Viacom. Aimed at preschool children. Offers access to archive of past shows. $5.99/month.
A LA CARTE NETWORKS*	
Showtime	Premiere cable network original programming available on Apple, Roku, Hulu, and Vue. $11/month.
HBO Now	HBO programming, films, and documentaries available on PlayStation and Apple mobile devices. $15/month.
CBS All Access	Live TV in selected cities and on-demand streaming of past shows in CBS archives. $6/month.

*Current and past shows (original content) from premier content networks multitasking: co-viewing shows while texting, commenting, and chatting online while the show unfolds.

While the Internet so far has had an expansive and positive impact on the television industry, challenges lie ahead. The largest providers of television in virtually all countries are cable television systems that charge consumers a monthly service fee for providing service, often accompanied by Internet and/or telephone service. This service in the United States costs, on average, about $100 per month per household. Cable systems also generate advertising revenues from local and national advertisers. The revenues generated are used to maintain the physical cable network and pay program producers (often called cable networks) for their content. For instance, HBO (Home Box Office network) creates a variety of television shows for the nearly 11,000 local cable systems in the United States, and collects fees from local and national cable systems like Time Warner and their subscribers. ESPN, the largest sports network on TV and the Internet, charges local and national cable systems per-viewer fees. But, as discussed in the opening case, with so much video available online from many different distributors, many users are thinking about "cutting the cable cord" and just relying on the Internet for their video entertainment. Other viewers are "cord shavers," who have reduced their subscriptions to digital channels. Likewise, the improvement in over-the-air digital broadcasting of television signals has resulted in a slight increase in over-the-air viewers (about 15% of all U.S. television viewers). So far, cord cutting and cord shaving has been very limited. There are around 100 million U.S. pay TV consumers, and an estimated 1 million have cut the cord. Millennials are somewhat less likely to have pay TV cable service, and spend more time watching TV online than older consumers. But these differences also reflect differences in income. The vast majority of Millennials watch TV like their parents by watching ordinary cable television (eMarketer, 2016b). Nevertheless, the high service fees for cable television service, and expanding Internet capabilities, suggest that cable television growth is over and that cable subscriptions will fall.

FEATURE-LENGTH MOVIES

In Hollywood, the transition to a digital delivery platform is well underway, and the industry is poised to maintain its revenue stream based on new digital platforms. As consumers have become fully connected to broadband networks on mobile, desktop, and home TVs, Hollywood has responded with a host of new viewing options. As a result, consumer spending on movie entertainment, whether physical or digital, has been stable, with significant growth in several digital platforms.

The key to the success of Hollywood studios in the digital era is their control over original, full-length feature production, and control over who will distribute their movies, when, and how. Distributors—whether Internet providers or cable systems—need to meet the terms of Hollywood studios. The dominance of Hollywood studios in content creation is being challenged, but for now still seems secure. An estimated 120 million Americans will watch movies online in 2016, growing to 145 million in 2020 (see **Figure 9.15**).

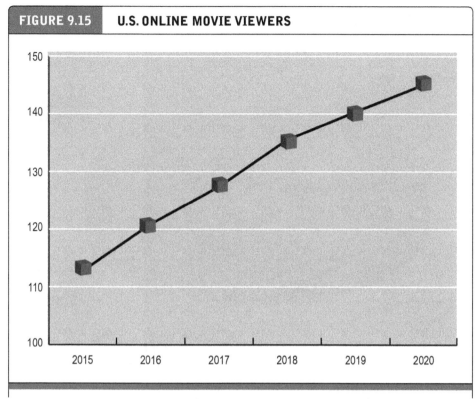

FIGURE 9.15 **U.S. ONLINE MOVIE VIEWERS**

SOURCE: Based on data from eMarketer, Inc., 2016g.

Aside from box office theater revenues, the movie industry derives revenue from both physical formats (DVDs) and digital formats like selling movies for download (called Electronic Sell-Through or EST), selling access on cable or the Internet to specific movies a la carte (called Internet Video On Demand (iVOD)), and subscription streaming over the Internet (see **Figure 9.16**).

Each of these digital formats has a leading player. The EST download leader is Apple's iTunes store. Consumers purchase and own the downloaded movie. Apple is also the leader in iVOD a la carte rentals, but other major players include Amazon, Hulu, and cable systems, which also rent movies on demand (usually referred to as VOD without the 'i' of online video). Netflix is, of course, the leading subscription streaming service, both in terms of the number of subscribers and the time spent using the service, generating $6.7 billion in revenue in 2015. Streaming has grown faster and larger than iVOD, and this is reflected in the market share of Netflix and Apple (see **Figure 9.17** on page 671). New entrants of significant size include Hulu, premium cable television networks such as HBO, Showtime, and Amazon.

Hybrid services such as Walmart's Vudu service allow consumers to purchase a DVD and then also stream it later from any device. Vudu is enabled by a distribution

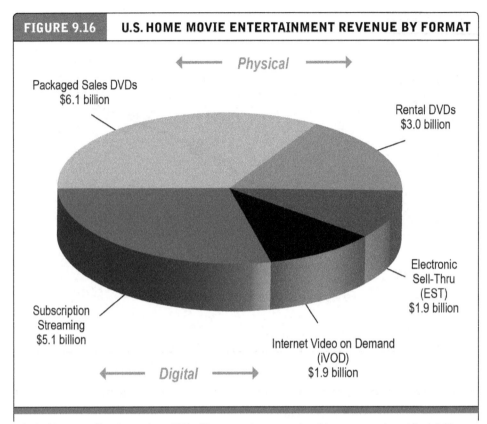

FIGURE 9.16 — U.S. HOME MOVIE ENTERTAINMENT REVENUE BY FORMAT

← Physical →

Packaged Sales DVDs
$6.1 billion

Rental DVDs
$3.0 billion

Electronic
Sell-Thru
(EST)
$1.9 billion

Subscription
Streaming
$5.1 billion

Internet Video on Demand
(iVOD)
$1.9 billion

← Digital →

Physical formats still make up about 59% of home movie revenue, but this percentage is rapidly shrinking. Revenue from digital formats is growing at a much higher rate.

SOURCE: Based on data from Digital Entertainment Group, 2016.

channel called UltraViolet. UltraViolet is an industry-sponsored cloud-based storage and proof-of-purchase system. Users enter a code into their UltraViolet online account, which gives them access to a movie they have purchased from any device, including Android and Apple smartphones. There are an estimated 19 million subscribers using UltraViolet.

Revenue from sale and rental of DVDs in the United States has been declining since 2006, sometimes at double-digit rates. In 2015, DVD revenue was $9 billion, down a whopping 33% compared to 2014. But DVD revenues are still a substantial 51% of total movie revenues. DVDs remain very profitable. The decline in DVD revenues is partially offset by the stunning growth of digital formats, especially subscription streaming, which grew over 25% in 2015 to $5 billion. Of all the content industries, the movie industry has been able to maintain its revenue stream and not be digitally destroyed by new technologies, at least for now.

Hollywood faces a number of challenges as it tries to keep up with a rapidly changing distribution platform, increasingly digital, streaming, and even mobile. The fastest growing digital streaming format does not produce much revenue on a per unit basis.

Studios make about $4.50 on each DVD, but only $2.00 for each VOD downloaded movie sale, and only 50 cents for each streamed movie. This means the studios are under pressure to keep their new movies in the physical format of DVDs, digital theater display, or video downloads, and use the streaming channel (Netflix) for older movies that might not sell at any price without the Internet, or have already been seen by millions of customers. Hollywood achieves this market segmentation by controlling the "release window" of movies, staggering market release. This is a form of price discrimination: those who really want to see the movie as soon as possible are willing to pay a higher price. The first tier is the theater box office, followed by DVDs, cable video-on-demand, then Internet video-on-demand, and finally subscription streaming services. Of course, the longer the studios hold a first-rate movie off the Internet, the greater the likelihood it will be pirated. The **release window** is changing under pressure from consumers to release films earlier to streaming and VOD services. Release windows are shrinking from nine months to four months, especially for poorly performing movies where DVD and box office sales are weak.

release window
Staging the release of new movies across different distribution channels with different prices

A second challenge involves the growing strength of online movie distributors, which may become competitors. Prior to the Internet, distributors such as movie theater chains and DVD rental and sales stores were never in a position to create their own movies and enter the movie production business. But in the digital era, it is conceivable that distributors like Netflix, Amazon, Hulu, and Google have the financial strength to attempt to make feature-length movies, and reduce their licensing costs.

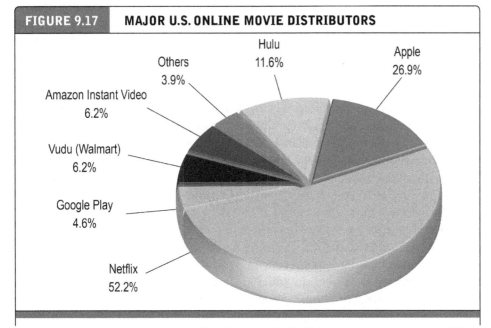

FIGURE 9.17   **MAJOR U.S. ONLINE MOVIE DISTRIBUTORS**

- Hulu 11.6%
- Apple 26.9%
- Others 3.9%
- Amazon Instant Video 6.2%
- Vudu (Walmart) 6.2%
- Google Play 4.6%
- Netflix 52.2%

Apple dominates downloading and purchasing of movies, while Netflix leads in streaming movies and TV shows.
SOURCES: Based on data from industry sources, authors' estimates.

Netflix, Hulu, and Amazon have already demonstrated their ability to create popular TV series. Firms based on streaming are incentivized to produce their own content to avoid steep licensing fees demanded by Hollywood studios. For instance, in 2015, Netflix had an estimated $9 billion obligation to pay movie studios for content, and this accounted for 70% of its operating costs. Therefore, Netflix is investing heavily in original content production. *Insight on Technology: Hollywood and the Internet: Let's Cut a Deal* describes how Hollywood studios and Internet distributors are cutting deals to provide more movie content online.

Although the emergence of multiple legitimate sources for streaming and downloading movies in a convenient and safe manner appears to have reduced the overall amount of piracy, it still remains a threat to the movie and television industry, despite years of effort by the industry and government to reduce piracy. In the past, bit torrents and cyberlockers/file hosting sites (like Megaupload) were the most common methods of piracy, but today, sites that offer streaming of pirated content have become much more popular. For instance, one recent study found that out of a total of almost 80 billion visits worldwide to 14,000 different film and TV piracy sites, almost 75% were to streaming sites, while only 17% were to bit torrent-based sites (Spangler, 2016).

The monetary amount the movie industry loses as a result of piracy is unknown. In the past, the industry estimated that it lost over $6 billion a year in pirated movies distributed over the Internet, copied from DVDs, early production copies, and in-theater videoing (Bialik, 2013). Other academic research estimates the loss is closer to $2 to $3 billion in the United States (Danaher et al., 2013). A Google research paper found that searches for pirated movies have been dropping steadily, while searches for online rentals and streaming are up (Google, 2011). As Google has moved into a closer relationship with TV and movie studios, and has its own ambitions to create original content, it has strengthened its efforts to reduce access to pirate sites. In 2015, Google changed its search algorithm to push pirated movie sites far down in search results, or removed sites altogether, making it difficult to find movies through its search engine. Insofar as searches are an indicator of consumer interest and intent, the public interest in pirated movies is declining. Services like Netflix and iTunes that permit access to streams of movies for a small monthly fee, or download rentals for a few dollars, have arguably reduced the motivation to pirate movies for many potential pirates.

In countries like France, which has passed strong laws to protect artists and discourage illegal downloading (the HADOPI laws), once the laws were implemented, sales of movies on DVDs and legitimate downloading sites increased by 25% in the following twelve months (Danaher et al., 2013).

Government actions to close down cyberlockers also can have a powerful impact on movie sales. In 2012, the U.S. government, along with other governments, closed down the world's largest cyberlocker, Megaupload. In a few days, 25 petabytes of music and movies disappeared from the Internet. In 12 countries where Megaupload was the most widely used, digital revenues for two movie studios in the study were 6–12% higher in the 18 weeks following the shutdown (Danaher and Smith, 2014; Fritz, 2013). With few exceptions, the academic literature produced since 2000 shows that piracy causes a significant reduction in sales of legitimate movies (Danaher et al., 2013).

INSIGHT ON TECHNOLOGY

HOLLYWOOD AND THE INTERNET: LET'S CUT A DEAL

All things considered, 2015 was a good year for the movie industry. Box office receipts were $11 billion in North America, up 6% from the previous year. Global box office sales were also up, to $38 billion in 2015, a record, and 5% higher than the previous year. Sales in China grew over 40%. Admissions were up slightly, with 1.32 billion tickets sold in the United States, and the average ticket price and number of films released were both stable. Online revenues from downloading and streaming continued to increase, to $8.8 billion (about 31% of the home movie market). By any measure, the Hollywood money machine has been transformed by the Internet. But, so far the movie business has avoided the kind of disruption that has occurred in the music business. People still crowd into theaters to see the latest movies, many still rent or purchase DVDs (over half of total home movie revenue), and many are willing to pay for streamed movies even if they are older than what they can see in the theater.

The reasons why Hollywood has survived the disruptive potential of the Internet are complex. The Internet has made older movies more valuable simply because they can be inexpensively stored on cloud servers, are easily discovered by consumers, and can be streamed for nearly zero cost, producing a new revenue stream. Continuing sales of DVDs, and revenues from online streaming services and download sales, drive revenues higher for even older movies. *Avatar*, originally released in 2009, now has grossed over $3 billion, as has *Titanic*, released in 1997. More recent blockbusters include *Star Wars: The Force Awakens* (2015), which hit over $2 billion in its first year, and *Jurassic World* (2015), which generated over $1.6 billion. If only all movies could

produce results like these, Hollywood would be golden again. The Internet has made Hollywood's backlist much more valuable.

But all is not totally well in Tinseltown. Once movies are shown in theaters, where Hollywood generates 30% of its revenue, they move on to less-profitable venues, from DVDs (which are very profitable) to cable television video-on-demand services, and then to Internet distributors like Netflix and Apple for either purchase, rental download, or streaming. Internet streaming services are low on the Hollywood food chain in part because they don't have the revenues to pay for the latest movies. Hollywood prefers to deal with Amazon, which sells and rents millions of DVDs, or Apple, which charges its customers $12–$14 to download recently released movies, compared to Netflix, which charges only $8 a month for access to thousands of movies. Next in line are cable network video-on-demand services, which charge anywhere from $5 to $12 a view. Eventually, movies end up with cable networks and broadcast television stations years after they were released. Even cable networks have greatly reduced their distribution of feature-length movies and replaced them with much less expensive unscripted reality shows. This "release window" differs for various films based on the studio's estimate of the revenue potential for each film. A very popular film will be delayed all along the release window.

Hollywood is facing several problems moving forward to a world where most people will be watching movies on the Internet, either at home, or on the go, using tablet computers and smartphones. One problem is that the fastest growing segment of its business, the Internet, is also the least profitable. A second problem is that Hollywood does not control its own Internet distri-

(continued)

bution network, but instead is forced to rely on the likes of Netflix, Apple, Amazon, and Google, each of which attract large online audiences. Likewise, the big Internet distributors face a content problem: they cannot attract large audiences unless they can access recently made movies. Old movies and movie libraries on Netflix have limited appeal; consumers are looking for the latest releases. But Hollywood charges a very high premium for recent movies.

Initially, Hollywood was highly dependent on Amazon's sales of DVDs as rental revenue from physical stores declined. iTunes is still the largest downloading service of movies a la carte (so-called electronic sell-through, or EST). But recently, the market dynamics have changed, in large part because of Netflix's success with its streaming video model. Why download to own when you can subscribe to a steady stream of movies? Hollywood is in the enviable position of being pursued by Internet distributors who are short of high-quality content. This is very different from what happened in the music business over the last decade. Multiple buyers of movies have appeared, not just Amazon or iTunes. Google has developed its own streaming media device (like Apple TV) that is a platform for movie streaming. Hulu is also ramping up again as a distribution platform.

Netflix continues to dominate online movie revenues, with a 52% market share compared to Apple's 15%. At one time, Apple had a 70% share of Internet movie revenue, and Hollywood studios feared Apple would be able to dominate Internet distribution and dictate prices. Now with Netflix dominating the streaming market, Hollywood fears it will be forced to sell its product for a pittance compared to DVD prices. For this reason, Hollywood restricts the release of movies to Netflix and other streaming services, doling out access to recent movies very carefully. Hollywood would much prefer that fans download movies from Apple rather than wait to rent or stream

them. To encourage this, Hollywood has created a new product called Digital HD that allows fans to download high definition copies of movies three weeks prior to their release on DVD or video-on-demand services. There are different versions of Digital HD. For example, Disney Movies Anywhere allows consumers to pay for recent HD movies stored on a cloud server, and play them anywhere, anytime. Vudu (owned by Walmart) enables downloading of HD movies and digital locker storage for play later. Another service, UltraViolet, allows consumers to buy a digital copy once, store it in the cloud, and view anytime and on any device. Amazon's Digital Copy service enables the purchase of a digital-only movie, as well as a DVD with digital copy access. In these ways Hollywood can afford to release new movies into digital distribution channels because consumers are willing to pay a premium, or buy the DVD for full price and receive a digital cloud copy for "free."

Digital HD movies are priced so that they produce as much revenue as traditional DVDs. This is the first time Hollywood has changed its release window strategy in order to drive digital download sales. The studios can charge a premium price for new movie digital downloads, making this outlet more valuable than either the DVD channel or the video-on-demand channel offered by cable networks. In some cases, movie producers such as Disney and Sony have opened up their own online stores for selling recent releases directly to consumers. This opens the possibility that Hollywood studios can circumvent Internet distributors entirely.

More and more, large firms are entering the premium video downloading and streaming market, competing with one another for Hollywood movies and driving up prices. For instance, beginning in September 2016, Netflix will have the exclusive right to stream Disney, Marvel, Pixar, and Lucasfilm titles during the first pay TV window, blocking their release on HBO or Starz, and keeping them off of Amazon Prime, Hulu, and other streaming services as well. But Amazon and Hulu remain major competitors with Netflix for movies.

All three competitors have also moved into the development of original content as a method of reducing their reliance on Hollywood for movies. In 2016, Amazon had a total of 36 original TV series, a number of which have received critical acclaim. It has even hired Woody Allen to write and direct his own series. Amazon, Hulu, and Netflix could be moving into feature movie production via the TV series route, which is less expensive to produce and more profitable to sell. But it's a long way from producing relatively inexpensive TV series to full-length motion pictures.

In the end, Hollywood and the Internet need each other, and the only question is how to find the price, define the terms of trade, and cut a deal where both parties come out winners. The flurry of deals bodes well for consumers and probably for Internet distributors and Hollywood studios, as well. Given the shift of eyeballs to online entertainment, Hollywood is expanding its audience, maintaining and even enhancing its prices. With lots of Internet distributors competing, Hollywood gains in power from the competition among alternative distributors. Netflix will not have a stranglehold over the Hollywood studios. How all these calculations will work out remains to be seen. Tune in next year on the same channel.

▄▄▄ **SOURCES:** "Netflix's Big Exclusivity Deal for Disney's Latest Movies Starts in September," by Chris Welch, Theverge.com, May 23, 2016; "Hollywood Divided Over Movie Streaming Service," by Brooks Barnes, *New York Times,* March 20, 2016; "Amazon, Retail Behemoth, Taking Small Steps Into Hollywood," by Brent Lang, *Variety,* March 8, 2016; "Global 2015 Box Office: Revenue Hits Record $38 Billion Plus," by Pamela McClintock, *Hollywood Reporter,* January 3, 2016; "Theatrical Market Statistics, 2015," Motion Picture Industry Association, 2016; "Amazon Pushes to Deliver More Prime Time," by Emily Steel, *New York Times,* July 31, 2015; "Hulu Will Offer Showtime for Extra $8.99 a Month, Differentiating Itself From Netflix," by Keach Hagey, *New York Times,* June 23, 2015; "How the New iPhone Helps Hollywood," by Andy Lewis, *Hollywood Reporter,* September 6, 2013; "Amazon Invests Millions in Original TV Shows to Get You to Buy More Diapers," by Timothy Senovac, *Huffington Post,* May 31, 2013.

MUSIC

Perhaps no other content industry has been so severely disrupted by the Internet and new business models as the recorded music industry. Revenues for the industry have fallen by more than half since 1999. By 2010, revenues stabilized and since then, have remained relatively flat. Global sales of music grew by 3% in 2015 to around €14.1 billion, compared to €25 billion in 1999 (IFPI, 2016).

Digital revenues now make up about 70% of all U.S. music revenues (about $4.8 billion) (see **Figure 9.18**). Revenues from CDs continue to decline but still account for 30% of the industry's revenue (about $2 billion). Streaming music sales from ad supported streaming and subscription streaming sites now total $2.4 billion, or about 34% of industry revenue. Digital revenues have not made up for the loss of revenue caused by the drastic decline in CD sales. Revenue from vinyl LP albums grew 32% in 2015, to $416 million. Vinyl is escaping the niche market of hobbyists, in part due to its superior sound reproduction when compared to digital tracks, and a growing number of groups are issuing vinyl editions alongside CD editions although these are only 7% of industry revenues.

For most of its history, the music industry depended on a variety of physical media to distribute music—acetate records, vinyl recordings, cassette tapes, and finally CD-ROMs. At the core of its revenue was a physical product. Since the 1950s, that physical product was an album—a collection of bundled songs that sold for a much higher

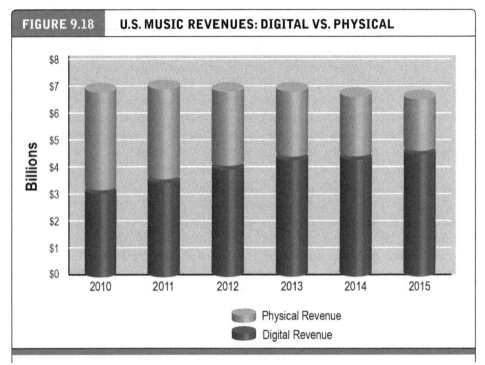

| FIGURE 9.18 | **U.S. MUSIC REVENUES: DIGITAL VS. PHYSICAL** |

Music industry revenues have fallen by 50% since 2000, and have only recently stabilized at around $7 billion. Digital music now makes up about 70% of all music revenues.

SOURCES: Based on data from RIAA, 2016, 2015.

price than singles. The Internet changed all that when, in 2000, a music service called Napster begin distributing pirated music tracks over the Internet to consumers using their PCs as record players. Despite the collapse of Napster due to legal challenges, hundreds of other illegal sites showed up, resulting in music industry revenues falling from $14 billion in 1999 to around $7 billion in 2015. The appearance of powerful mobile media players beginning in 2001 that could be connected to the Internet, like Apple's iPod, and later, the iPhone and iPad, and then the stunning growth of music streaming sites, further eroded sales of CD albums. Streaming has fundamentally altered the sale of physical music formats because it is no longer necessary to "own" a physical unit in order to hear the music consumers want.

The music industry initially resisted the development of legal digital channels of distribution, but ultimately and reluctantly struck deals with Apple's new iTunes Store in 2003, as well as with several small subscription music services, for online distribution. By the time streaming music services appeared on the scene in 2006, the music industry had dropped its opposition to digital formats, and quickly reached agreements with Pandora, Spotify, and others to stream music on their subscription and "free" ad-supported services in return for fees. At that time, digital downloads of tracks and albums and fees from streaming music services were widely perceived as the savior of the music industry, which was losing sales to piracy and file sharing. Nevertheless, revenues from these sources pale in comparison to revenues that used to be produced by CD albums. **Figure 9.19** shows consumer spending on digital music in four different formats: singles, albums, streaming, and ringtones.

While some have argued that Apple's iTunes music service offering single tracks for 99 cents destroyed the sales of albums, this clearly is not the case. Album downloads have held up well against single downloads, and actually have grown faster than single downloads. For instance, in 2014, Adele's *25*, first released in November 2015, sold over 18 million physical and digital copies within six months. Sales of digital or CD albums appear to be a function more of the music quality and popularity than the format.

There are two kinds of digital music services, each with a different business model: streaming music services and digital download. Streaming music services (also known as Internet radio) like Pandora, Spotify, Apple Music, Rdio, Rhapsody, and iHeartRadio, deliver music to listeners from cloud servers; the music is not stored on user devices. Pandora offers a curated service that allows users to select an artist they want to listen to, and then the site uses an algorithm to build a list of artists similar to the artist selected by the user. Users do not control what they hear and cannot repeat a selection. Spotify allows users to specify artists and songs. Streaming music services have two revenue streams: ad-supported and subscription service. Ad-supported streaming is a freemium model that allows users access to free streamed music for a limited number of hours per month and relies on advertising to generate

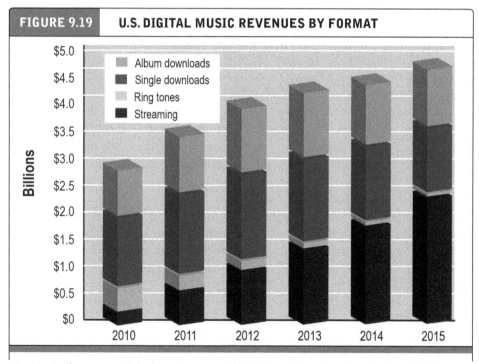

FIGURE 9.19 — **U.S. DIGITAL MUSIC REVENUES BY FORMAT**

Legend: Album downloads, Single downloads, Ring tones, Streaming. Y-axis: Billions. X-axis years: 2010, 2011, 2012, 2013, 2014, 2015.

Downloads of songs are still the largest component of digital music, but streaming digital music is the fastest growing format.

SOURCES: Based on data from eMarketer, Inc., 2016h, 2015.

revenue. Streaming music services also typically offer a subscription option, which enables users to listen to ad-free music for a monthly fee. However, typically only a small percentage of listeners pay a subscription fee, and ad revenues typically exceed subscription revenues by a substantial margin. Apple Music does not have free music and requires a monthly fee of $10 for ad-free streaming.

Digital download services (also known as download to own) are exemplified by iTunes, Amazon, and Google Play, where users download tracks and albums a la carte and pay a fee for each song. Increasingly, the songs are stored on a cloud server so users can listen to the music from any of several personal devices. All revenue derives from the sale of music albums or single tracks. Digital download is the second part of the digital music industry, generating $2.3 billion or 33% of the industry's revenue. While illegal pirated file sharing and downloads of music were the leading edge of a digital tide that deeply disrupted the music industry beginning in the 1990s, legal digital download and streaming services have put a damper on illegal music piracy. Legal digital music sources have saved the music label firms by generating solid revenues and profits, albeit not as generous as in the heyday of CDs. While music labels might make $7 on a CD sold at $16, they only make about 32 cents for a single track downloaded from iTunes for 99 cents. Digital albums produce about $3.00 for the music labels, roughly half of a CD album sale. Artists are similarly impacted, facing a halving of their incomes in the digital environment.

Digital downloads from services like iTunes have declined, and the fastest growing segment is the streaming music services. It appears that the success of music streaming services is cannibalizing the sales of downloads, and in 2015 the sales of downloads declined by 10%, a trend that started in 2012. With the growth of cloud computing and cloud-based music services, the very concept of owning music began to shift instead to accessing music from any device, anywhere. However, while music streaming services are growing listeners at a torrid pace, few, if any, have managed to earn a profit because of infrastructure costs, the costs of acquiring music content from the music labels, and freemium revenue models supported by advertising revenues. As a result, it is unclear if streaming music services have a viable business model. For artists and music label firms, streaming services have little to offer. While music labels might receive 32 cents for every iTunes track they sell, they receive only .63 of a penny on a streamed version of the same song. This revenue is split with the artists, who receive .32 of a penny. *Rolling Stone* calculated that a very popular song selling 1 million streams would produce revenue of $3,166 for the artist and a similar amount for the music label. For artists, ad-supported streaming pays considerably less than subscription streaming. For this reason, many artists and groups refuse to allow streaming of their music.

In 2014, Taylor Swift, one of the world's most popular singers, pulled her music from Spotify's free service because it pays such a low royalty rate. In 2015, she similarly pulled her album *1989* from Apple's newly announced Apple Music service because Apple was planning to not charge for the first three months of the service. Many other singers have withdrawn their performances from free streaming services, and there is a growing movement among musicians toward seeking higher compensation from streaming sites.

FIGURE 9.20   **POKEMON GO**

The augmented reality game *Pokemon GO* took the world by storm in the summer of 2016.
© Anna Stowe/Alamy Stock Photo.

The reason for investor optimism is growth. As music streaming sites proliferate, and major artists withhold their recent albums, many analysts believe that the music industry's business model is broken, and that streaming will not save the industry. It is conceivable that in the future major artists will own their own streaming services and charge what the market will bear.

GAMES

In July 2016, the Pokemon Company (partly owned by Nintendo) released its free augmented reality game, *Pokemon GO* for Apple iOS and Android phones (see **Figure 9.20**). *Pokemon GO* overlays exotic monsters on the phone's screen. The aim is to locate, capture, and train these characters. Users are rewarded with stardust (virtual currency). The game identifies PokeStops, points of interest or historic locations, where users can pick up Poke Balls used to capture Pokemon, and Pokemon gyms, where users can train their monsters, capture others, and receive rewards. There are plenty of opportunities to buy virtual tools to speed up the capture of Pokemons (Poke Balls cost $1 in the store but are free at PokeStops), and advertisers can pay to have their streets or businesses become a PokeStop, attracting huge crowds of players and potential customers. In one month *Pokemon GO* became the most popular download from iTunes and Google Play. In two months, *Pokemon GO* had 200 million players worldwide and generated over $300 million in revenue. No one knows how long the

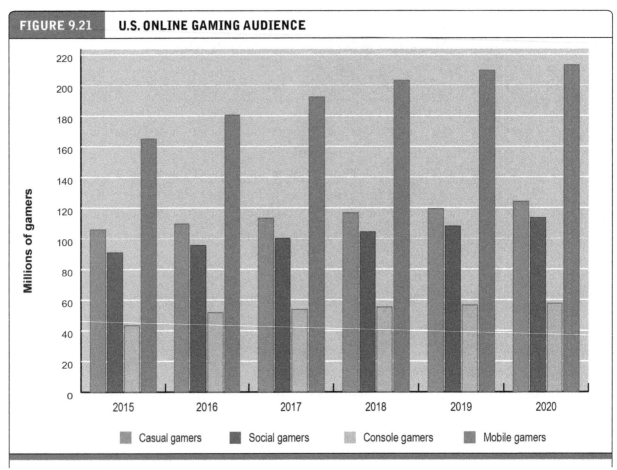

FIGURE 9.21 **U.S. ONLINE GAMING AUDIENCE**

SOURCE: Based on data from eMarketer, 2016c.

Pokemon GO craze will last, but it provides an example of how the online gaming world is changing from its initial focus on console and PC desktop gaming to mobile phone gaming and professional e-sport gaming as a stadium and spectator sport.

Console gaming used to be the heart of the digital gaming industry, and still is from a revenue perspective. But this changed rapidly with the introduction of smartphones and tablets, as well as social and casual gaming, which do not require users to purchase an expensive console or packaged software. Smartphones and tablets have ushered in an era of free-to-play and $1.99 game apps and much simpler game scenarios that do not require millions of investment dollars to develop. Well over 200 million Internet users play some kind of game online in the United States, and that number swells to over 400 million worldwide. In 2016, over 180 million Americans will play games on mobile devices (smartphones and tablets), over three times as many who play games on game consoles. Casual PC gamers are twice as common as console gamers (see **Figure 9.21**) (eMarketer, Inc., 2016c; PriceWaterhouseCoopers, 2016).

In the United States, revenue from digital games in all formats (mobile, PC based, massive multiplayer, social, and console) in 2015 was estimated at nearly $18 billion

(PriceWaterhouseCoopers, 2016). To put this in perspective, the $18 billion game sector is about one-half of the total Hollywood movie sector, and about twice the size of all digital music revenue in 2015.

There are five types of digital gamers. Casual gamers play games on a desktop or laptop computer. They are called casual gamers because they play games for a few minutes at a time, stop and start games, and are not intensively involved. Social gamers are those who play games using a web browser or app on a social network like Facebook, often with friends. Mobile gamers play games using their smartphones or tablet computers. Mobile gamers are casual gamers as well, with fleeting involvement. Massively multiplayer online gamers (MMO) use their computers to play with a large number of players around the globe. Console gamers play games online (or offline) using a dedicated console like Xbox, PlayStation, or Wii. Often, console gamers are connected over the Internet to enable group play.

While many more people play mobile and desktop games online, more than half of the $18 billion online gaming revenue is generated by console gamers, largely through the purchase of expensive physical games on DVDs or online digital downloads of the games, which in 2015 accounted for about $9.6 billion in U.S. revenue. PC games generated around $3.7 billion, about one-quarter of total revenues. Mobile games generated an estimated $3 billion (PriceWaterhouseCoopers, 2016). In terms of the future, overall game revenues are expected to grow by 30% to 2020.

The rapid growth in the number of people playing mobile games based on tablets and smartphones is a sea change for the gaming industry that was previously dominated by closed-platform console games and hardware firms like Microsoft, Nintendo, and Sony, and software firms like Activision and Electronic Arts. The growth of smartphones, tablets, and mobile games has catapulted Apple's App Store and the Google Play store into the leading merchants of digital games, which, of course, use Apple and Google Android hardware and software. Apple and Google take 30% of game sales and also benefit from the sales of the hardware and software needed to play the games. Mobile games appeal to a younger demographic, offer lower prices, and initially are often free. You can play mobile games anywhere you can use a phone, which is nearly everywhere. Console games take much longer to develop, have very large budgets, and are expensive to purchase.

The mobile platform is a more open platform that allows thousands of developers to create entertaining games on much smaller budgets, as well as new and innovative games on a faster schedule. In contrast, the console platform has evolved much more slowly than mobile computing. In 2014, a new Sony PlayStation replaced a seven-year-old model, and a new Microsoft Xbox replaced an eight-year-old model. In a fast-moving online world, such long replacement cycles inevitably lead to declines in hardware sales, and limit software innovation. While console, PC, and online social games will continue to grow their audience size slowly, the fastest audience growth in the future will be in mobile games that can be played anywhere and anytime.

One solution to PC and mobile game revenue growth is likely to be professional gaming, otherwise known as e-sports. E-sports, like other professional sports, is based on competition among teams of players. The competition at the championship level takes place in auditoriums attended by thousands of fans, and is watched by millions more on the Internet. In August 2015, for instance, 11,000 fans packed into Madison Square Garden in New York to watch 10 professional players play the online game *League of Legends* (Needleman, 2015). The International 2016 Tournament in Seattle has a prize pool of $20 million, and the events can draw participants equal to professional football games, including millions of online and TV viewers.

The games are broadcast over cable television channels, but more commonly over Internet channels like Twitch.tv. Twitch accounts for over 80% of online e-sports viewing in the United States, and was purchased by Amazon in 2015 for $1.1 billion. Twitch.tv draws peak-time audiences of over 1 million viewers in 2016, as many as MTV, TruTV, and MSNBC, to name a few cable networks. Other broadcasters include YouTube and Dailymotion.

The organization of the tournaments, and the prize money for the players, is provided by the games' publishers. The leading publisher of PC games played at professional levels is Riot Games, publisher of *League of Legends,* a multiplayer online battle game. There are twenty *League of Legends* professional teams that compete with one another. The league requires teams to hire professional video game coaches. Other multiplayer games suited to arena play include *StarCraft II* and *Call of Duty*.

Advertisers are attracted to e-sports because the audience is predominantly composed of young males between the ages of 21 and 34, who are hard to reach using traditional media. Coca Cola, Nissan, Ford, and Google are among the largest sponsors of e-sports. College teams have sprung up across the country, including Harvard and Princeton, and Robert Morris University in Chicago now offers several scholarships for students who will play on its video game team (Wingfield, 2014). At current rates of growth, e-sports will approach Hollywood in terms of global revenues, and eclipse console game revenue by 2020, transforming online gaming into a popular sport.

Netflix:
How Does This Movie End?

I n the Netflix online television comedy-drama series, *Orange is the New Black*, the lead character is Piper Chapman (Taylor Schilling), a recently engaged blond New Yorker sent to a federal prison for a crime committed years before. Critically acclaimed, and widely followed, *Orange* follows in the footsteps of Netflix's earlier successful online TV series *House of Cards*, a political insider's tale of Washington politics starring Kevin Spacey. *House of Cards* was the first-ever online television series to win an Emmy award (for best director). *Orange* won three Emmy creative awards in 2014. In 2014, Netflix racked up 31 nominations, and in 2015, 34 nominations. In 2016, the number soared to 56 nominations, making Netflix the third leading platform/network behind HBO (96) and FX Networks (38). Besides returning series like *Orange is the New Black*, its new series *Making a Murderer* and the documentary *What Happened, Miss Simone?* each scored six nominations. Netflix is quickly becoming the non-cable alternative to cable TV. By producing its own content, Netflix is able to differentiate itself from cable TV shows and attract new subscribers looking for new shows, not retreads from the cable networks. However, original productions are much more expensive to produce than licensing existing content.

While Netflix does not release the number of viewers for any of its original TV shows, executives credit these shows with driving the streaming service to a record

© Digitallife/Alamy Stock Photo

83 million worldwide subscribers by the second quarter of 2016 (45 million in the United States where 60% of its subscribers come from). In 2016, Netflix announced its presence in all foreign markets except China, and that it had gained 3.5 million new subscribers outside the United States. Its goal is to hit 100 million subscribers by 2017. Its subscriber growth rate in the United States has slowed considerably in the last few years because its market penetration is so high. Netflix shares have increased by over 8,000% since it first went public in 2002, but it has hit a rough spot in 2016, with the stock market punishing the company for failing to achieve expected subscriber growth targets in the United States, amid concerns about growing competition in the streaming marketplace. Many subscribers dropped the service in 2016 because Netflix raised its prices and Amazon grew its own video streaming service. It is currently selling at over 300 times its projected earnings, much more expensive than Google, Facebook, or other tech companies because it is still perceived as a growth company. Revenues in 2015 were $6.7 billion, up 22% from 2014, but profits were a paltry $122 million, less than half the previous year. Netflix's profit margin is less than 2%, far less than a retailer like Walmart (4% margin).

Netflix got its start as a mail order company renting DVDs of older Hollywood movies using the postal system. Founded by two Silicon Valley entrepreneurs, Marc Randolph and Reed Hastings, in 1997, the company started by renting individual copies of 900 DVD movie titles and delivering them to customers by postal mail. In 2000, it switched to a subscription model where customers could receive DVDs on a regular basis for a monthly fee. By 2006, it had delivered its billionth DVD and became the largest subscription provider of DVDs. In 2007, Netflix began a video-on-demand streaming service of movies although it still retains a DVD subscription business. In 2016, Netflix is the largest player in the movie and TV series streaming market, and consumes over 35% of the U.S. Internet bandwidth to serve its customers.

Netflix is one of those Silicon Valley stories that might make a good movie, or even a television series, because of its potential for disrupting the American television and movie landscape (or what's called premium video). It's a dream-come-true story of accomplishment, pluck, innovation, and Internet technology. In a few short years Netflix created the largest DVD rental business in the country, then created the largest streaming video service. Today Netflix accounts for over 90% of digital movie streaming, while its chief streaming competitors, Amazon and Hulu, make up the remaining market. Netflix has created the largest database on consumer video preferences and built a recommendation system that encourages consumers to see more movies. Netflix is as much a technology company as a content company: it has developed its own proprietary video encoding system and distributes its video using over 1,000 servers in the United States located close to its customers to ensure high speed and quality delivery. Netflix discovered that older TV series had strong niche followings and built a new model of "binge watching" where consumers could watch all the episodes of a series in several sittings. Netflix has entered the content creation business by developing original TV series. For this reason, Netflix is an example of convergence in the media industry where an Internet company becomes a media content producer. Other pure media companies have taken notice and begun to develop their own streaming services, but what they lack is a database of viewer preferences that Netflix has developed over a ten-year period and which helps Netflix make recommendations to subscribers.

In the movie and TV business there are only two ways to make money: either own the content or own the pipes that deliver the content. All the better if you can do both. Netflix has become recognized as an important pipeline to a very large audience. For instance, Netflix has a deal with the Weinstein Company, a major American film studio and producer of ten Academy Award films, to become the exclusive subscription TV home for the film studio's content, beginning in 2016. This move puts Netflix into the same league of premium channel distributors and in direct competition with other cable networks like HBO, Starz, Showtime, and A&E for the rights to show movies about eight months after their theater run is complete. Netflix also has a deal with Warner Brothers to be the exclusive Internet distributor of the Batman prequel *Gotham*, and with Twenty-First Century Fox in 2016 for the FX series *American Crime Story*.

In one possible ending scenario for the Netflix movie, the company challenges the much larger cable television industry, which is based on an entirely different technology and business model, namely, selling expensive bundles of hundreds of TV channels that few people watch, then raising monthly fees faster than the rate of inflation. Given Netflix's large national audience of streamers, the company makes new friends in Hollywood and New York that are looking for ways to distribute their shows to a new online, mobile, and social world; Hollywood stretches the distribution window so that Internet distributors like Netflix get the same treatment as cable systems by allowing them to show the latest movies and shows at about the same time as cable systems. And the cable television industry is forced to retreat from its bundling practices and offer customers the ability to select just those channels they actually watch. Cable industry revenues plunge as a result. In this dream scenario, Netflix goes on to challenge the cable networks by producing its own original TV dramas, and adds comedy and documentaries to the mix. A story with a happy ending for Netflix! But happy endings happen mostly in Hollywood.

The outcome of this movie depends on how well Netflix can deal with some considerable challenges. For instance, one source of Netflix's poor profitability is that the costs of content are very high, both purchased older series as well as new content, which is far more risky. The owners of older cable TV series and Hollywood movies charge Netflix for the privilege of distributing their content as much as they do established cable TV networks. In 2016 Netflix reported streaming content obligations to content producers of $12 billion! With $6.7 billion in gross revenue, it paid out $5.7 billion in payments to content owners (mostly cable networks) and production studios for original content. Netflix barely makes any profit. Netflix is, after all, mostly a database and delivery platform, and the company is in a constant bidding war with both cable and Internet giants all looking for the same thing—popular TV series with a built-in or potential audience. But content owners have wised up to the value of their backlist TV series and have raised their prices accordingly. Series just a year old are very expensive or non-existent. Netflix is paying hundreds of millions to Disney, Paramount, Lionsgate, and MGM to license hit shows and movies. As a result of content owners charging more for older cable shows, Netflix has taken the more risky option of developing its own original series. But this is very expensive as well. The critically acclaimed *House of Cards* cost Netflix $100 million for 26 episodes, $4 million an episode. Newer shows like *Between*, *Narcos*, and *Bloodline* are running around $20 million a season. It's possible that Netflix does not scale, and that the more subscribers it has and the more it attracts them with original expensive content, the less profit it makes because the cost of doing business rises faster than revenue.

A second challenge Netflix faces is the risk of creating new content. It's not as if wealthy Silicon Valley entrepreneurs can fly to Hollywood or New York with lots of cash and simply purchase new content. As one pundit noted, this might lead to a mugging, but not a successful TV series or movie. Silicon Valley is generally not the place to go if you're looking for story tellers, writers, producers, directors, talent agents, and cinematographers. Algorithms don't come up with new ideas for novels, plays, movies, or TV series, and they have not proven to be good at guessing what series will succeed in the future. Older series are proven series, and Netflix can identify which of its customers watched the series in previous years, and estimate the audience size, and whether new subscribers will be attracted by the re-plays. But when it comes to new TV series, Netflix has tried to use its algorithms to predict what new series its customers might be interested in with mixed results. Netflix has produced some real winners according to critics, but it has also produced some losers that did not get critical acclaim like *Lillyhammer*, *Hemlock Grove*, *Bad Samaritans*, *Richie Rich*, and *Mitt*. There has been only one tech company in history that was successful with content production for movies or television, and that is Pixar, which pioneered computer-generated animated feature-length movies. It is impossible to know how well Netflix's original content is performing because the company refuses to release this data. Nielsen has begun a rating service for Netflix shows. This service is paid for by the content producers who will base their charges in part on how many Netflix subscribers stream their shows.

While Netflix stands out as a powerful Internet brand today, Netflix has many powerful competitors. Netflix does not have unique technology. In fact, streaming technology is widespread and well understood. The success of Netflix's streaming model has attracted Amazon, Apple, Yahoo, Google, and content producers like Hulu and HBO to the fray. In 2015, Verizon announced a free, ad-supported mobile streaming service call go90, aimed at Millennials who routinely watch video on their smartphones. Some of these firms are tech firms with very large Internet audiences, strong brand names, and a good understanding of what their millions of online customers want.

Apple is the leader in downloaded movies where customers own or rent movies, and of course, it owns iTunes, the world's largest online media store for the purchase of music, videos, and TV series. HBO, founded in 1972, is the oldest and most successful pay television service in the United States with over 140 million cable TV subscribers worldwide, and the originator of a long list of highly successful original TV series and movies such as *Sex and the City*, *The Sopranos*, *The Wire*, *Game of Thrones*, and *True Blood*. If Netflix has a direct competitor on the creative front, it is HBO, a more traditional programmer that does not use computer algorithms to design its content, but

SOURCES: "Netflix Fuels a Surge in Scripted TV Shows. Some See a Glut," by John Koblinaug, *New York Times*, August 9, 2016; Netflix and 20th Century Fox Television Distribution Announce First Global Agreement," Netflix Media Center, July 25, 2016; "Netflix Stock History: What You Need to Know," by Dan Caplinger, Fool.com, July 11, 2016; "Netflix to Be Exclusive Global Streaming Home of FX's American Crime Story instead relies on the hunches and gifts of editors, producers, and directors to produce its content.

Netflix's competitors have very deep pockets. This means Netflix also has competitors for talent and the production of new content, and perhaps price pressure as well. Along with Hulu, Amazon has emerged as the biggest competitor to Netflix streaming. For instance, Amazon offers free streaming to its 60 million Amazon Prime customers, and has taken on HBO TV series to stream to Prime customers without additional fees. Amazon has also moved into original series production with *The Man in the High Castle, Transparent, Mozart in the Jungle,* and others, winning 16 Emmy awards in 2016. Apple iTunes and Amazon have far larger databases of subscribers and their preferences. Google is actively pursuing long-form content creators for its video channel program. There is no cost to Google users because the service is ad supported.

So another possible ending for the Netflix movie is that ultimately it can't compete with Apple, Google, Yahoo, Hulu, and Amazon, or the content producers like CBS and HBO Now, which have started their own streaming services. Generating a negative cash flow of $1 billion a year, Netflix may run out of investors who make up the difference. Netflix can be imitated by its competitors, and its profitability reduced to less than shareholders can tolerate. Apple's 2015 revenue was a staggering $234 billion, 30 times larger than Netflix, and it has a cash reserve of $234 billion. It is entirely within Apple's capabilities, or Amazon's or Google's, and others to develop a competing streaming video service. Equally worrisome, major cable networks like CBS and NBC have started their own streaming networks for their original content. In July 2016, Wall Street finally got the message that Netflix was facing a slew of streaming competitors, and its stock fell over 30%. Netflix may have created a new world of streaming, bingeing, and content production, but it may not be able to survive the world it created. This show is not over until the last episode is finished. Stay tuned.

Franchise in 2017," Netflix Media Press Release, July 25, 2016; "Netflix Chews Up Less Bandwidth, as Amazon Video Streaming Surges," by Todd Splanger, *Variety*, July 22, 2016; "No Surprises Here: Netflix Scores Big with Emmy Nominations," by Saba Hamedy, Mashable.com, July 14, 2016; "Amazon Prime Members Now Outnumber Non-Prime Customers," by Audrey Shi, *Fortune*, July 11, 2016; "Can Netflix Survive the New World It Created?," by Joe Nocera, *New York Times*, June 16, 2016; "Amazon Challenges Netflix by Opening Prime to Monthly Subscribers," by Nick Wingfield, *New York Times*, April 17, 2016; "Verizon to Offer Free Mobile TV Service, Hoping to Draw Millennials," by Emily Steel, *New York Times*, September 8, 2015; "Netflix Viewership Finally Gets a Yardstick," by Joe Flint and Ben Fritz, *Wall Street Journal*, August 26, 2015; "Here Are the Original Shows Netflix Viewers Say They're Watching," by Peter Kafka, Recode.net, August 26, 2015; "Netflix, Amazon Rack Up Emmy Nominations," by Daniel Bukszpan, *Fortune*, July 16, 2015; "Netflix Soars to All-Time High as Customers Top 62 Million," by Lucas Shaw, Bloomberg News, April 16, 2015; "Netflix Inc. Form 10k for the Fiscal Year Ended December 31, 2015," filed with Securities and Exchange Commission, January 26, 2016.

Case Study Questions

1. What are three challenges that Netflix faces?

2. What are the key elements of Netflix's strategy today?

3. What are the implications of Netflix's new strategy for the cable television systems like Comcast and TimeWarner?

4. Why is Netflix in competition with Apple, Amazon, and Google, and what strengths does Netflix bring to the market?

9.5 REVIEW

KEY CONCEPTS

■ Understand the major trends in the consumption of media and online content, the major revenue models for digital content delivery, digital rights management, and the concept of media convergence.

- Major trends in the consumption of media and online content include the following:
  - The average American adult spends around 4,300 hours per year consuming various media. The most hours are spent online, using a desktop or mobile device, followed by watching television and listening to the radio.
  - Although several studies indicate that time spent on the Internet reduces consumer time available for other media, recent data reveals a more complex picture, as Internet users multitask and consume more media of all types than do non-Internet users.
  - In terms of all media revenue, television and home video accounted for about 34% of media revenues, print media (books, newspapers, and magazines) for 32%, video games, 9%, box office, 9%, Internet media (online music and video), 8%, and music (radio and recorded music), 8%. Internet media, while relatively small now, is growing at 12% annually, far faster than traditional media revenues.
  - The three major revenue models for digital content delivery are the subscription, a la carte, and advertising-supported (free and freemium) models.
  - In terms of paid online content, online TV and movies is the largest and fastest growing form of online entertainment.
  - Digital rights management (DRM) refers to the combination of technical and legal means for protecting digital content from reproduction without permission. Walled gardens are a kind of DRM that restrict the widespread sharing of content.
- The concept of media convergence has three dimensions:
  - Technological convergence, which refers to the development of hybrid devices that can combine the functionality of two or more media platforms, such as books, newspapers, television, radio, and stereo equipment, into a single device.
  - Content convergence, with respect to content design, production, and distribution.
  - Industry convergence, which refers to the merger of media enterprises into powerful, synergistic combinations that can cross-market content on many different platforms and create works that use multiple platforms.
  - In the early years of e-commerce, many believed that media convergence would occur quickly. However, many early efforts failed, and new efforts are just now appearing.

■ Understand the key factors affecting the online publishing industry.

- Key factors affecting online newspapers include:
  - *Audience size and growth.* Although the newspaper industry as a whole is the most troubled part of the publishing industry, online readership of newspapers is growing, fueled by smartphones, e-readers, and tablet computers.
  - *Revenue models and results.* Online newspapers predominantly rely on both advertising and subscription revenues. Digital ad revenues are not sufficient to cover losses in print advertising.
- Key factors affecting online magazines include:
  - *Online audience and growth:* Digital magazine sales have soared, with almost a third of the Internet population now reading magazines online.

- *Magazine aggregation:* Magazine aggregators (websites or apps) offer users online subscriptions and sales of many digital magazines.
- Key factors affecting e-books and online book publishing include:
  - *Audience size and growth.* E-book sales growth has leveled off following an explosive growth period. Growth today is fueled by the Amazon Kindle, Apple iPad, and smartphones. The mobile platform of smartphones and tablets has made millions of books available online at a lower price than print books. The future of the book will be digital although printed books are unlikely to disappear in the foreseeable future.
  - *Challenges.* The two primary challenges facing e-book publishing are control over pricing and the continued evolution of the e-book model, including rentals and subscription services.
  - *Competing business models.* E-book business models include the wholesale model and the agency model.
  - *Convergence.* The publishing industry is making steady progress toward media convergence. Newly authored e-books are appearing with interactive rich media, which allow the user to click on icons for videos or other material, and take notes.

- **Understand the key factors affecting the online entertainment industry.**
- There are five main players in the entertainment sector: television, motion pictures, music, games, and radio broadcasting. The entertainment segment is currently undergoing great change, brought about by the Internet and the mobile platform. Consumers have begun to accept paying for content and also to expect to be able to access online entertainment from any device at any time.
- Key factors include the following:
  - *Audience size and growth.* The audience for online movies and television is growing dramatically.
  - *The emergence of streaming services and the mobile platform.* In the movie and television industries, two major trends are the move to streaming services, from Amazon and Apple to Hulu and other channels, and the continued increase in online purchases and rentals. Although physical sales of products (DVDs) are dropping significantly, more and more consumers are purchasing or renting movies and television episodes on mobile devices.
  - The music industry is experiencing similar trends as the movie industry: the growth of streaming services, or Internet radio, the continued decline of online purchases, and increased downloads on mobile devices. However, the unbundling of a traditional music product, the album, into individual songs, and the growth of streaming, have decimated music industry revenues.
  - The greatest growth is anticipated in mobile gaming, as the mobile market is rapidly expanding along all e-commerce fronts.

QUESTIONS

1. Does time spent on the Internet cannibalize or complement traditional media?
2. What are the basic revenue models for online content?
3. How have attitudes about paying for content changed since the early years of the Web?
4. What is DRM?
5. Describe the structure of the media content industry.
6. What factors are needed to support successfully charging the consumer for online content?
7. What are the different revenue models that newspapers have used?
8. Today, Amazon and Apple dominate the e-book marketplace. What impact has this had on the book publishing industry?
9. What features make it difficult for gaming firms to monetize their user base?
10. How has the Internet transformed television viewing?

11. Discuss the impact of *Pokemon GO* on the online gaming industry.
12. What impact did shutting down Megaupload have?
13. What are OTT entertainment services?
14. What are the two kinds of online movie sales and business models? Give an example of each type.
15. Why are advertisers attracted to e-sports?
16. What type of convergence does the Kindle Fire represent?
17. What are some of the different revenue models with which the magazine industry is experimenting?
18. How has the book publishing industry's experience with the Internet differed from the newspaper and magazine industries' experience?
19. What are some of the challenges currently facing the book publishing industry?
20. What are the four factors that have caused the decline of newspaper revenues over the past 15 years?

PROJECTS

1. Research the issue of media convergence in the newspaper industry. Do you believe that convergence will be good for the practice of journalism? Develop a reasoned argument on either side of the issue and write a 3- to 5-page report on the topic. Include in your discussion the barriers to convergence and whether these restrictions should be eased.

2. Go to Amazon and explore the different digital media products that are available. For each kind of digital media product, describe how Amazon's presence has altered the industry that creates, produces, and distributes this content. Prepare a presentation to convey your findings to the class.

3. Identify three online sources of content that exemplify one of the three digital content revenue models (subscription, a la carte, and advertising-supported) discussed in the chapter. Describe how each site works, and how it generates revenue. Describe how each site provides value to the consumer. Which type of revenue model do you prefer, and why?

4. Identify a popular online magazine that also has an offline subscription or newsstand edition. What advantages (and disadvantages) does the online edition have when compared to the offline physical edition? Has technology platform, content design, or industry structure convergence occurred in the online magazine industry? Prepare a short report discussing this issue.

5. In 2014, Amazon purchased Twitch, which lets users stream their video game sessions, for almost $1 billion. Why would Amazon spend so much money on Twitch? Create a short presentation either defending the purchase or explaining why you think it was a bad idea.

REFERENCES

Association of American Publishers. "US Publishing Industry's Annual Survey Reveals Nearly $28 Billion in Revenue in 2015." (July 11 2016).

Authorearnings.com. "February 2016 Author Earnings Report: Amazon's Ebook, Print, and Audio Sales." (February 6, 2016).

Authorearnings.com. "October 2015—Apple, B&N, Kobo, and Google: A Look at the Rest of the Ebook Market." (October 9, 2015).

Berkshire Hathaway Corporation. "Annual Report 2013." (March 1, 2013).

Bialik, Carl. "Studios Struggle for Focus on Film Pirates Booty." *Wall Street Journal* (April 5, 2013).

Boxer, Sarah. "Paintings Too Perfect? The Great Optics Debate." *New York Times* (December 4, 2001).

Carr, David. "Print Is Down, and Now Out." *New York Times* (August 10, 2014).

Compete.com. "August 2016 Unique Visitors." (accessed September 18, 2016).

Danaher, Brett, and Michael D. Smith. "Gone in 60 Seconds: The Impact of the Megaupload Shutdown on

Movie Sales." *International Journal of Industrial Organization* (March 2014).

Danaher, Brett, Michael D. Smith, and Rahul Tang. "Piracy and Copyright Enforcement Mechanisms," *Innovation Policy and the Economy*, Vol. 14 (May 3, 2013).

Digital Entertainment Group. "DEG 2015 Year End Home Entertainment Grid." (January 6, 2016).

eMarketer, Inc. "Average Time Spent per Day with Major Media by US Adults, 2012--2018." (April 1, 2016a)

eMarketer, Inc. (Paul Verna) "US TV and Digital Video StatPack." (May 25, 2016b).

eMarketer, Inc. (Cindy Liu) "US Digital Users: eMarketer's Updated Estimates for 2016." (September 2016c).

eMarketer, Inc. "US Digital Viewers and Penetration, 2015–2020." (August 3, 2016d).

eMarketer, Inc. "US Digital Ad Spending, 2015–2020." (September 1, 2016e).

eMarketer, Inc. "US Magazine Ad Spending, by Segment, 2015–2020." (September 1, 2016f).

eMarketer, Inc. "US Digital TV* and Movie** Viewers and Penetration, 2015–2020." (August 3, 2016g).

eMarketer, Inc. "US Digital Music Shipments and Revenue, by Segment, 2014 & 2015." (March 22, 2016h).

eMarketer, Inc. "US Digital Music Shipments and Revenues, by Format, 2013 & 2014." (March 18, 2015)

Fritz, Ben. "Movie Sales Increase With Shutdown of Piracy Site." *Wall Street Journal* (March 7, 2013).

Google. (Deborah Schwartz) "A Window Into Film." (April 2011).

Hagey, Keach and Greg Bensinger. "Jeff Bezos's Tool Kit for the Post." *Wall Street Journal* (August 6, 2013).

IFPI. "Global Music Report 2016." (April 12, 2016).

MPA—The Association of Magazine Media. "Magazine Media Factbook 2016/2017." (August 29, 2016).

Mequoda Group LLC (Don Nicholas and Kim Mateus). "2016 Mequoda American Magazine Reader Study & Handbook." (2016).

Needleman, Sarah. "Inside the 'League of Legends.'" *Wall Street Journal* (August 23, 2015).

Needleman, Sarah. "The Newest Job in Sports: Video-game Coach," *Wall Street Journal*, July 29, 2015.

New York Times. "Innovation." (May 2014).

Newspaper Association of America. "Newspaper Digital Audience." NAA.com (July 2016).

Nielsen. "2013 Nielsen National Cross Media Engagement Study." (April 16, 2013).

Packer, George. "Cheap Words: Amazon Is Good for Customers. But Is It Good for Books?" *New Yorker* (February 17, 2014).

Pew Research Center (Amy Mitchell and Jesse Holcomb) "State of the News Media 2016." Journalism.org (June 15, 2016).

Pew Research Center (Amy Mitchell, Mark Jurkowitz, and Kenneth Olmstead). "Audience Routes: Direct, Search, and Facebook." (March 12, 2014a.)

Pew Research Center. "State of the News Media 2014." Journalism.org (2014b).

PriceWaterhouseCoopers (PWC). "Global Entertainment and Media Outlook 2015–2019." (2016).

PriceWaterhouseCoopers (PWC). "Global Video Games Report: Key Insights at a Glance." Pwc.com (2015b).

Recording Industry Association of America (RIAA). "News and Notes on 2015 RIAA Shipment and Revenue Statistics." (2016)

Recording Industry Association of America (RIAA). "News and Notes on 2014 RIAA Music Industry Shipments and Revenue Statistics." (2015).

Romenesko, Jim. "Wall Street Journal Memo: Newsroom Changes Mean a Faster-moving, Digital First News Operation." Jimromenesko.com. (January 21, 2014.)

Sass, Erik. "Newspaper, Magazine Revenues Fell in 2015." Mediapost.com (March 11, 2016).

Somaiya, Ravi. "The New Yorker Alters Its Online Strategy." *New York Times* (July 8, 2014).

Spangler, Todd. "Piracy: Streaming Video Accounts for 74% of Illegal Film and TV Activity, Study Finds." Variety.com (July 28, 2016).

Streitfield, David. "Writers Feel an Amazon-Hachette Spat." *New York Times* (May 14, 2014a).

Streitfield, David. "Amazon and Hachette Resolve Dispute." *New York Times* (November 13, 2014b).

Streitfield, David. "Amazon, a Friendly Giant As Long As It's Fed." *New York Times* (July 12, 2014c).

Trachtenberg, Jeffrey. "Clock is Ticking for Time Inc.'s CEO." *Wall Street Journal* (July 27, 2015).

Williams, Alex. "Paying for Digital News: The Rapid Adoption and Current Landscape of Digital Subscriptions at U.S. Newspapers." Americanpressinstitute.org. (February 29, 2016).

Wingfield, Nick. "E-Sports at College, With Stars and Scholarships." *New York Times* (December 8, 2014).

Online Communities

After reading this chapter, you will be able to:

- Describe the different types of social networks and online communities and their business models.
- Describe the major types of auctions, their benefits and costs, how they operate, when to use them, and the potential for auction abuse and fraud.
- Describe the major types of Internet portals and their business models.

LinkedIn:

A Tale of Two Countries

By most measures, LinkedIn is a highly successful social network, ranking behind only Facebook and Twitter in site traffic and boasting steadily growing membership and revenues. It bills itself as the world's largest professional network, allowing prospective employees to connect with people and businesses who can help their careers and giving employers the tools to find talented prospective hires. As more businesses have sought to expand globally, so too has LinkedIn. However, LinkedIn is learning a lesson that many businesses have encoun-

© gigra/Fotolia.com

tered before: the cultural and regulatory landscape can vary greatly from country to country. The company's experiences in China and Russia exemplify this phenomenon.

In 2014, LinkedIn launched a fully localized version of its site in China. Companies often look to expand into China to dramatically grow their user bases, but many western technology giants have struggled to succeed there. For instance, companies often fail to adjust their products to meet the preferences of Chinese users. LinkedIn, on the other hand, cultivated a look and feel that appealed to Chinese users by forming partnerships with popular Chinese services such as cross-platform messaging service WeChat, Twitter-like microblogging service Weibo, and instant messaging service QQ. LinkedIn uses these services to encourage people to sign up for its network. The company used offline advertising located in subways and other high-traffic urban areas featuring Chinese celebrities to promote its brand and quickly established partnerships with large Chinese corporations Lenovo and Huawei to recruit employees.

However, for many companies, China's regulatory policies have been the more significant stumbling block. LinkedIn's success in China thus far has been at least partially contingent on the company's willingness to adhere to the Chinese government's policies regarding content censorship. China targets and blocks any content viewed as unfavorable to the country's political leadership, and the country has detained its own citizens for what it views as inflammatory speech. Any company that is interested in entering the Chinese market, no matter how powerful, must remove this type of content or risk being blocked by the government. Facebook, Twitter, and YouTube are fully blocked in China, and Apple's iTunes was blocked in 2016. Microsoft, which purchased LinkedIn for $26 billion in 2016, has also battled with China over piracy of its products and regulatory penalties that favor domestic Chinese brands. It's not clear what impact, if any, the acquisition will have on LinkedIn's operations in China.

SOURCES: "Russian Regulator Says Had Constructive Meeting with LinkedIn," Reuters.com, December 8, 2016; "LinkedIn Blocked in Russia: A Welcome Warning for Global Players?" by Adrien Henni, Venturebeat.com, November 29, 2016; "The U.S. Is 'Deeply Concerned' with Russia's Decision to Block LinkedIn," *Fortune*, November 18, 2016; "LinkedIn Is Now Officially Blocked in Russia," by Ingrid Lunden, Techcrunch.com, November 17, 2016; "Russia Moves to Block Professional Networking Site LinkedIn," by Adam Taylor, *Washington Post*, November 17, 2016; "Facebook, Microsoft, LinkedIn and Others Must Resist China's Orwellian Vision of the Internet," by Roseann Rife, Amnesty.org, November 16, 2016; "Russia Prepares to Block LinkedIn After Court Ruling," by Mark Scott, *New York Times*, November 10, 2016; "Russian Hacker Suspected of LinkedIn Attack Indicted in U.S.," by Alejandro Lazo, *Wall Street Journal*, October 21, 2016; "Can Foreign Tech Companies Win in China?" by Edward Tse, Techcrunch.com, August 28, 2016; "LinkedIn China New Social Platform Chitu, Interview with Dong Bin," by Roberto V Zicari, Odbms.org, August 4, 2016; "LinkedIn's China Strategy—When Localization Isn't Enough," by Xunshu Li, Blog.btrax.com, August 3, 2016; "For LinkedIn China, Microsoft Deal Is a Complicated Connection," by Alyssa Abkowitz, *Wall Street Journal*, June 23, 2016; "Censorship Is LinkedIn's China Friend as It Boasts User Milestone," Chinatechnews.com, April 25, 2016; "Why Some Social Networks Still Aren't Blocked in China," by Erik Crouch, Techinasia.com, April 15, 2016; "LinkedIn's Biggest Rival in China Just Suddenly and Unexpectedly Shut Down," by Steven Millward, Techinasia.com, December 28, 2015; "Take Two for LinkedIn China with New Youth-Focused App Red Rabbit as Job Networking Site Aims to Tap Resistant Market," by Zen Soo, Scmp.com, November 5, 2015; "How LinkedIn China Learnt How to Win Friends and Influence People," by Li Hui, CKGSB Knowledge, July 14, 2015; "Microsoft Faces New Scrutiny in China," by Paul Mozur and Nick Wingfield, *New York Times*, January 5, 2016; "LinkedIn Goes After China with a new Joint Venture and a Localized Chinese-Language Site," by Josh Ong, Thenextweb.com, February 24, 2014.

Critics of Chinese Internet policies suggest that the government's restrictions force companies to become accomplices in the Chinese government's censorship. Many companies have balked at this prospect. For example, Google has withdrawn many of its services from China because it is unwilling to comply with the Chinese government's regulatory demands. However, LinkedIn has had a more conciliatory attitude, partnering with Chinese Internet companies Sequoia China and China Broadband Capital to ensure a smooth transition into the Chinese market. While LinkedIn CEO Jeff Weiner has publicly stated that he opposes Chinese censorship policies, the company has complied with them to deepen the company's global penetration. LinkedIn is also a professional network, as opposed to a social network like Facebook or Twitter, making it much less likely to contain sensitive political content.

Just two years after launching its localized Chinese site, LinkedIn's Chinese membership has grown from 4 million users to 20 million to become the company's fastest growing market. The company has also unveiled a second professional network aimed at younger users who may not speak English and who are less likely to have lengthy employment histories. The new network, called Chitu, or Red Rabbit in English, is designed to be a bit more exciting than the straight-laced flagship LinkedIn site. As of 2016, Chitu has only about 1 million users, but LinkedIn is bullish on its prospects for growth.

China may be the most high-profile country with heavy-handed requirements for foreign companies, but it is far from alone. LinkedIn discovered this first-hand in 2016 when it became the first site to be blocked in Russia under a new law that revamped the country's data storage policies, and which provides, among other requirements, that the personal data of Russian users be stored on databases located within Russia's physical borders.

The law meant that global companies operating in Russia without a physical presence had to quickly establish one or run the risk of being blocked. Many companies, such as Apple, Google, Uber, and Alibaba, had already complied with the demands of the new law and moved data on Russian users to their existing servers located within the country, but other companies without servers there simply took a wait-and-see approach. LinkedIn was the Russian government's first target despite the fact that only 5 million of the site's 467 million users are registered in Russia. Other sites have much larger numbers of Russian users, particularly Facebook, which has had a strained relationship with Russia since it rejected several requests from the Russian government for data on specific accounts related to domestic protests. LinkedIn itself was the target of a Russian hacker in 2012 who stole the passwords of over 100 million LinkedIn users. In 2016 the hacker was indicted in the Czech Republic, but Russia has no plans to extradite him to the U.S. for trial.

LinkedIn company representatives are in the process of meeting with Russian regulators to find a solution and reportedly have had constructive discussions. Given LinkedIn's willingness to work with regulatory requirements in China, it's possible that the company will move quickly to develop a solution that Russian regulators find acceptable. Many other countries have adopted laws that restrict the storage of their citizens' personal data, and as more countries seek to establish borders on the Internet, companies with global ambitions like LinkedIn may have to remain flexible.

I n this chapter, we discuss social networks, auctions, and portals. What do social networks, auctions, and portals have in common? They are all based on feelings of shared interest and self-identification—in short, a sense of community. Social networks and online communities explicitly attract people with shared affinities, such as ethnicity, gender, religion, and political views, or shared interests, such as hobbies, sports, and vacations. The auction site eBay started as a community of people interested in trading unwanted but functional items for which there was no ready commercial market. That community turned out to be huge—much larger than anyone expected. Portals also contain strong elements of community by providing access to community-fostering technologies such as e-mail, chat groups, bulletin boards, and discussion forums.

10.1 SOCIAL NETWORKS AND ONLINE COMMUNITIES

The Internet was designed originally as a communications medium to connect scientists in computer science departments around the continental United States. From the beginning, the Internet was intended, in part, as a community-building technology that would allow scientists to share data, knowledge, and opinions in a real-time online environment (see Chapter 2) (Hiltzik, 1999). The result of this early Internet was the first "virtual communities" (Rheingold, 1993). As the Internet grew in the late 1980s to include scientists from many disciplines and university campuses, thousands of virtual communities sprang up among small groups of scientists in very different disciplines that communicated regularly using Internet e-mail, listservs, and bulletin boards. The first articles and books on the new electronic communities began appearing in the mid- to late 1980s (Kiesler et al., 1984; Kiesler, 1986). One of the earliest online communities, The Well (originally Whole Earth 'Lectronic Link), was formed in San Francisco in 1985 by a small group of people who once shared an 1,800-acre commune in Tennessee. The Well continues to have thousands of members devoted to discussion, debate, advice, and help (Hafner, 1997; Rheingold, 1998). With the development of the Web in the early 1990s, millions of people began obtaining Internet accounts and e-mail, and the community-building impact of the Internet strengthened. By the late 1990s, the commercial value of online communities was recognized as a potential new business model (Hagel and Armstrong, 1997).

The early online communities involved a relatively small number of web aficionados, and users with intense interests in technology, politics, literature, and ideas. The technology was largely limited to posting text messages on bulletin boards sponsored by the community, and one-to-one or one-to-many e-mails. In addition to The Well, early networks included GeoCities, a website hosting service based on neighborhoods. By 2002, however, the nature of online communities had begun to change. User-created websites called blogs became inexpensive and easy to set up without any technical expertise. Photo sites enabled convenient sharing of photos. Beginning in 2007, the growth of mobile devices like smartphones, tablet computers, digital cameras, and portable media devices cnabled sharing of rich media such as photos, music, and videos. Suddenly there was a much wider audience for sharing interests and activities, and much more to share.

A new culture emerged as well. The broad democratization of the technology and its spread to the larger population meant that online social networks were no longer limited to a small group but instead broadened to include a much wider set of people and tastes, especially pre-teens, teens, and college students who were the fastest to adopt many of these new technologies. Entire families and friendship networks soon joined. The new social network culture is very personal and "me" centered, displaying photos and broadcasting personal activities, interests, hobbies, and relationships on social network profiles. In an online social network, the "news" is not something that happened somewhere else to other people; instead, the news is what happened to you today, and what's going on with your friends and colleagues. Today's social networks are as much a sociological phenomenon as they are a technology phenomenon.

Currently, social network participation is one of the most common usages of the Internet. Over two-thirds of all Internet users worldwide (about 2.3 billion people) use social networks (eMarketer, Inc., 2016a). Facebook has over 1.7 billion active users and a little over 1.5 billion mobile monthly users (Facebook, 2016). There is obviously an overlap between these two sets of users. Other large social networks include LinkedIn (profiled in the opening case), Twitter, Pinterest, Instagram, Snapchat, and Tumblr. While Facebook is the most popular social network, it is also the slowest growing, up just a few percentage points since 2012. Facebook appears to have hit a plateau in the United States, and its real hope for growth is offshore, where it is pushing to create basic Internet access so more people will join the network. Newer social networks, such as Pinterest, Instagram, and Snapchat, are growing much more quickly.

Worldwide, the social network phenomena is even stronger with over 2.3 billion users worldwide, 32% of the world's population, and still growing at 9% annually. Social networks are a top online destination in every country, accounting for the majority of time spent online, and reaching almost 79% of active Internet users. Asia-Pacific has the largest social network audience, followed by the Middle East and Africa, and Latin America, while North America has the highest penetration of social network usage among the general population (eMarketer, Inc., 2016c). Although Facebook dominates the global social network marketspace, in some countries, localized social networks are signficant, such as Orkut (owned by Google) in Brazil, Mixi and social messaging app Line in Japan, Qzone, QQ, Sina Weibo, and RenRen in China, XING in Germany, Tuenti in Spain, and VK in Russia. There is an online social network for you to join almost anywhere you go!

WHAT IS AN ONLINE SOCIAL NETWORK?

social network
involves a group of people, shared social interaction, common ties among members, and people who share an area for some period of time

So exactly how do we define an online social network, and how is it any different from, say, an offline social network? Sociologists, who frequently criticize modern society for having destroyed traditional communities, unfortunately have not given us very good definitions of social networks and community. One study examined 94 different sociological definitions of community and found four areas of agreement. **Social networks** involve (a) a group of people, (b) shared social interaction, (c) common ties among members, and (d) people who share an area for some period of time (Hillery, 1955). This will be our working definition of a social network. Social networks do not necessarily have shared goals, purposes, or intentions. Indeed, social networks can be places where people just "hang out," share space, and communicate.

It's a short step to defining an **online social network** as an online location where people who share common ties can interact with one another. This definition is very close to that of Howard Rheingold's—one of The Well's early participants—who coined the term *virtual communities* as "cultural aggregations that emerge when enough people bump into each other often enough in cyberspace." It is a group of people who may or may not meet one another face to face, and who exchange words and ideas through the mediation of an online social meeting space. The Internet removes the geographic and time limitations of offline social networks. To be in an online network, you don't need to meet face to face, in a common room, at a common time.

online social network
an area online, where people who share common ties can interact with one another

THE GROWTH OF SOCIAL NETWORKS AND ONLINE COMMUNITIES

Figure 10.1 shows the top social networks in the United States, which together account for well over 90% of the Internet's social network activity.

The largest group of Facebook users in the United States are 25 to 34 years old (36 million), followed by 35- to 45-year-olds (30 million). Over one-third (35%) of U.S. Facebook users are older than 44. Adults over 65 constitute the fastest growing group on Facebook (eMarketer, Inc., 2016d). In contrast, Twitter is far more popular among young adults under 34. Similar patterns are observed worldwide as older populations use social networks to stay in touch with children and relatives. Facebook is the most popular social network among teens, with Instagram and Snapchat not far behind.

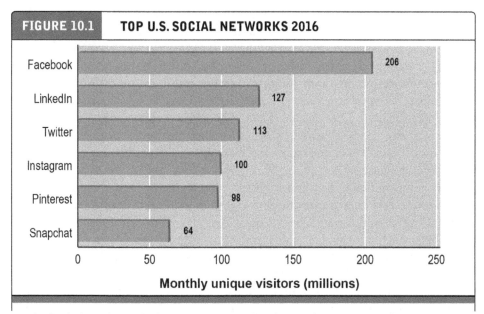

FIGURE 10.1   TOP U.S. SOCIAL NETWORKS 2016

Facebook is by far and away the dominant social network in the United States in terms of monthly unique visitors.

SOURCES: Based on data from comScore, 2016a; Instagram, 2016.

Newer social networks tend to follow this same pattern, with young people being the first adopters.

While Facebook and Twitter still tend to dominate the news, a new kind of social network is appearing and growing much faster than Facebook with respect to unique visitors and subscribers. These new social networks are attracting marketers and advertisers as well. For instance, Pinterest, described in the opening case in Chapter 7, is a visually oriented site that allows users to curate their tastes and preferences, expressed in visual arts. You can think of Pinterest as a visual blog. Users post images to an online "pinboard." The images can come from any source. Users can also "re-pin" images they see on Pinterest. Pinterest's membership has skyrocketed since its launch, accumulating 150 million active members worldwide as of October 2016. Instagram is another social network that focuses on video and photo sharing. A mobile app that enables a user to easily share images to social networks, Instagram was acquired by Facebook for $1 billion in 2012 and has over 500 million members in September 2016.

Other social networks are not necessarily competing with Facebook, but adding to the social network mix and enlarging the total social network audience. **Table 10.1** describes some other popular social networks.

Contributing to the continued growth and commercial success of networks is the rapid adoption and intense use of mobile devices. Over 90% of Facebook's users worldwide are mobile users, although not exclusively. According to comScore, Facebook's flagship Facebook app has the highest number of unique visitors (150 million) of all mobile apps and appears on the home screen of 46% of all smartphone users, with the average person spending 13 hours on the app a month (comScore, 2016b). Several of the largest newer social networks like Instagram and Snapchat are almost entirely mobile.

A new crop of social networks launched since 2008 focuses on messaging. Snapchat (2009) lets users send photos and videos to friends that self-extinguish in ten seconds. Snapchat Stories have a longer lifespan: 24 hours. Snapchat has very high reach among its core audience of 18- to 24-year-olds, but in 2016, it also began to break into the mainstream, with significant growth in the over-25 age group demographic (comScore, 2016b). WhatsApp (2009; acquired by Facebook in 2014) is a messaging service that lets users send text, photos, and videos to their friends' cellphones using the Internet and without having to pay telecommunications companies for cellphone SMS messaging services. Six of the world's most-used apps are messaging services.

The number of unique visitors is just one way to measure the influence of a site. Time on site is another important metric. The more time people spend on a site, called engagement, the more time to display ads and generate revenue. In this sense, Facebook is much more addictive and immersive than the other top social networks. Over time, Facebook has tweaked its content and algorithms in order to keep users on the site longer. In 2014, Facebook added videos (both ads and user-contributed), and in 2016 is now displaying around 8 billion videos a day. It tries to show videos that reflect the user's interests and friends and also plays them automatically in the News Feed, forcing users to turn them off but also ensuring that they are seen for at

TABLE 10.1	OTHER SOCIAL NETWORKS
SOCIAL NETWORK	DESCRIPTION
Myspace	Early leader in social networking was overtaken by Facebook; being reinvented as a music-oriented social network by pop star Justin Timberlake.
Meetup	Helps groups of people with shared interests plan events and meet offline.
Tagged	A network aimed at introducing members to one another through games, shared interests, friend suggestions, and browsing profiles.
MeetMe	Another social network aimed at meeting new people.
Polyvore	Topic-focused social network (fashion).
deviantART	Website focused on art, sharing of images.
Vevo	Video and music sharing site.

least a few moments. Facebook has also made changes to its News Feed algorithm to capture more user attention: increasing content from users' favorite friends; decreasing content from friends of users' friends; and showing multiple posts in a row from the same source for users with few friends (Gaudin, 2015). **Table 10.2** illustrates the different levels of engagement with the top social networks.

The amount of revenue generated is the ultimate metric for measuring a company's business potential. The top three search engine companies (Google, Yahoo, and Microsoft) generated about €65 billion in digital advertising revenue in 2016 (eMarketer, Inc., 2016c). In contrast, social networks generated about €31 billion

TABLE 10.2	TIME SPENT ON TOP SOCIAL NETWORKS
WEB SITE	MINUTES/MONTH (IN BILLIONS)
Facebook	230
Instagram	12.2
Twitter	6.6
Pinterest	6.5
Snapchat	6.4
Tumblr	5.0
LinkedIn	1.7

SOURCES: Based on data from comScore, 2015.

worldwide in advertising revenue in 2016. Social networks are the fastest growing form of Internet usage and advertising revenue, but they are not yet as lucrative as traditional search engines/portals in terms of ad dollars generated. A part of the problem is that subscribers do not go to social networks to seek ads for relevant products, nor do they pay attention to the ads that are flashed before their eyes (see Chapters 6 and 7). In addition, the small screen of the smartphone, the dominant social network platform, is not ideal for display advertising of retail goods. Here, tablets and desktop PCs are more suitable for browsing and purchasing.

TURNING SOCIAL NETWORKS INTO BUSINESSES

While the early social networks had a difficult time raising capital and revenues, today's top social networks are now monetizing their huge audiences. Early social networks relied on subscriptions, but today, most social networks rely on advertising or the investments of venture capitalists. Users of portals and search engines have come to accept advertising as the preferred means of supporting web experiences rather than paying for it. One important exception is LinkedIn, which offers basic free memberships for individuals but charges for premium services. **Figure 10.2** shows the comparative amount of ad spending on various social networks. Facebook, with almost $12 billion in ad revenue, towers over the other sites.

Social networks do not always succeed as businesses. For instance, Twitter began as a social messaging service on which users could communicate with followers. It quickly turned into an Internet broadcasting network for millions of on-scene observers acting as citizen reporters, as well as political organizers, celebrities, and politicians. In 2016, it has just over 300 million users. Twitter's growth has stagnated, and in 2015, it lost $521 million, disappointing investors who expect more advertising dollars and real revenue. Twitter has never shown a profit. In 2015, co-founder Jack Dorsey returned in October 2015 in an effort to reinvigorate Twitter's user and revenue growth. But despite a number of incremental changes designed to streamline the service and make it easier to use, as well as several new strategic efforts, such as live-streaming video partnerships with the sports leagues like the NFL, Twitter's share of U.S. social networks has continued to drop. In September 2016, Twitter is reportedly up for sale. See the Chapter 5 opening case on Twitter for a more detailed discussion of Twitter's business model.

The rapid adoption of mobile devices initially posed a challenge to social networks like Facebook, as well as Google's search engine, because they were largely based on the desktop platform. Google dominated mobile ad revenues up until 2013 because its search engine and Google Maps were among the most popular apps. Facebook quickly developed its own mobile app, and purchased others, and within the space of four years has been able to capture a significant part of the mobile ad market, using its mobile News Feed to provide users a continual stream of ads. The top seven apps, and eight of the top nine, are owned by either Google or Facebook. For Facebook, that includes the main Facebook app (1st), Facebook Messenger (2nd), and Instagram (9th). Today, around 85% of Facebook's revenue (around $10.1 billion) comes from mobile

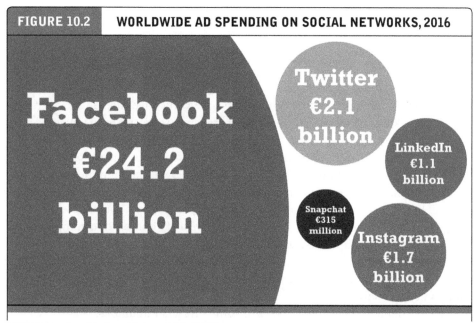

FIGURE 10.2 **WORLDWIDE AD SPENDING ON SOCIAL NETWORKS, 2016**

Facebook
€24.2
billion

Twitter
€2.1
billion

LinkedIn
€1.1
billion

Snapchat
€315
million

Instagram
€1.7
billion

SOURCE: Based on data from eMarketer, 2016c; 2016d.

advertising. Other social network apps within the top 25 are Snapchat (13th), Pinterest (14th), and Twitter (17th) (comScore, 2016b).

Social networks have had an important impact on how businesses operate, communicate, and serve their customers. A 2015 survey of Fortune 500 firms found that 93% used LinkedIn, 78% used Twitter, and 74% used Facebook (Barnes et al., 2015). The most visible business firm use of social networks is as a marketing and branding tool. A less visible marketing use of networks is as a powerful listening tool that has strengthened the role of customers and customer feedback systems inside a business. Public social networks like Facebook have not been used extensively in firms as collaboration tools thus far. However, in 2015, Facebook launched its Facebook at Work app, designed to spur collaboration and networking inside large firms, as a pilot project. In October 2016, it finally released the commercial version of the app, now called Workplace. The new app faces stiff competition from a wide array of collaboration tools provided by Cisco, Microsoft, IBM, and along with other technologies like instant messaging and teleconferencing.

Social networks are where corporate brands and reputations are formed, and firms today take very seriously the topic of "online reputation," as evidenced by social network posts, commentary, chat sessions, and Likes. In this sense, social networks become an extension of corporate customer relationship management systems and extend existing market research programs. Beyond branding, social networks are being used increasingly as advertising platforms to contact a younger audience than websites and e-mail, and as customers increasingly shift their eyeballs to social networks. Rosetta Stone, for instance, uses its Facebook page to display videos of its learning technology, encourage discussions and reviews, and post changes in its learning tools. Yet the business use of social networks does not always go well. The *Insight on Society* case, *The Dark Side of Social Networks*, discusses some of the risks associated with social networks.

TYPES OF SOCIAL NETWORKS AND THEIR BUSINESS MODELS

There are many types and many ways of classifying social networks and online communities. While the most popular general social networks have adopted an advertising model, other kinds of networks have different revenue sources. Social networks have different types of sponsors and different kinds of members. For instance, some are created by firms such as IBM for the exclusive use of their sales force or other employees (intra-firm communities or B2E [business-to-employee] communities); others are built for suppliers and resellers (inter-organizational or B2B communities); and others are built by dedicated individuals for other similar persons with shared interests (P2P [people-to-people] communities). In this chapter, we will discuss B2C communities for the most part, although we also discuss briefly P2P communities of practice.

Table 10.3 describes in greater detail the five generic types of social networks and online communities: general, practice, interest, affinity, and sponsored. Each type of community can have a commercial intent or commercial consequence. We use this schema to explore the business models of commercial communities.

general communities
offer members opportunities to interact with a general audience organized into general topics

General communities offer members opportunities to interact with a general audience organized into general topics. Within the topics, members can find hundreds of specific discussion groups attended by thousands of like-minded members who share an interest in that topic. The purpose of the general community is to attract enough members to populate a wide range of topics and discussion groups. The busi-

TABLE 10.3	TYPES OF SOCIAL NETWORKS AND ONLINE COMMUNITIES
TYPE OF SOCIAL NETWORK / COMMUNITY	DESCRIPTION
General	Online social gathering place to meet and socialize with friends, share content, schedules, and interests. Examples: Facebook, Pinterest, Instagram, Tumblr, and Twitter.
Practice	Social network of professionals and practitioners, creators of artifacts such as computer code or music. Examples: Just Plain Folks (musicians' community), LinkedIn (business), and Doximity (physicians and health care professionals).
Interest	Community built around a common interest, such as games, sports, music, stock markets, politics, health, finance, foreign affairs, or lifestyle. Examples: Debatepolitics.com (political discussion group) and PredictWallStreet (stock market site).
Affinity	Community of members who self-identify with a demographic or geographic category, such as women, African Americans, or Arab Americans. Examples: BlackPlanet (African American community and social network site) and Healthboards.com (focusing on women's health issues).
Sponsored	Network created by commercial, government, and nonprofit organizations for a variety of purposes. Examples: Nike, IBM, Cisco, and political candidates.

INSIGHT ON SOCIETY

THE DARK SIDE OF SOCIAL NETWORKS

In 2015, theme park chain SeaWorld thought it had a great marketing idea when it launched a Twitter hashtag campaign to improve its public image. Using the hashtag #AskSeaWorld, the company solicited questions from Twitter users in an attempt to be more transparent about its operations. SeaWorld is a frequent target for animal rights activists, who object to the company's treatment of sea animals, and was the subject of the 2013 documentary Blackfish, which told the story of a whale whose mistreatment and resulting erratic behavior led to the deaths of three people. After the documentary, SeaWorld's ticket sales plunged and its already spotty public image was devastated. The company hoped that the hashtag campaign would be a much needed step in its rehabilitation.

That's not exactly how the campaign turned out. First, People for the Ethical Treatment of Animals (PETA) used the hashtag to attack SeaWorld for its poor animal care. SeaWorld failed to respond. Soon, many more activists and regular people jumped on the bandwagon, relentlessly attacking SeaWorld and its animal handling techniques. Some users asked why the parking lots at SeaWorld are bigger than the whale tanks, for example.

Instead of demonstrating its awareness of the improvement it needs to make in these areas, Sea-World finally answered these and other concerns by stating, "No time for bots and bullies. We want to answer your questions," completely dismissing its skeptics. The company posted several more tweets with crying babies and memes of Internet trolls to represent the animal rights activists. Needless to say, this only made things worse for SeaWorld. In 2016, well over a year later, angry animal lovers continue to use the hashtag to attack SeaWorld's treatment of whales, dolphins, and other marine animals. SeaWorld's stock price hit an all-time low in August 2016. By any measure, SeaWorld pre-sented us with a textbook case in how social network advertising and branding can go horribly wrong.

Attempts at humor can also often go horribly awry, as Budweiser discovered in advertising for its Bud Light brand. The company introduced the hashtag #upforwhatever in 2015, supported by TV ads and advertising on other platforms. One of the 47 slogans that accompanied the hashtag on its beer bottles was "The perfect beer for removing 'no' from your vocabulary for the night." Many of Bud Light's followers were shocked that the company would make such a controversial statement. The company claimed that its slogans were intended to inspire spontaneous fun, but admitted that this particular slogan was a misfire and immediately apologized and discontinued its use.

Soft drink giant Coca-Cola also encountered the dark side of social networks after its 2016 campaign to wish its customers in different countries Happy New Year. First, the company sent a message on VK, the most popular Russian social network, consisting of a map of Russia decorated with holiday ornaments. There was nothing offensive about the decorations, but Coca-Cola omitted the disputed territory of Crimea. Russian followers of Coca-Cola were enraged. In response, Coca-Cola adjusted the map, adding the Crimea as well as other territories it had neglected the first time around. This time, it was Ukraine's turn to take offense. Ukraine and Russia have been battling over the area since 2014, and Ukrainians believe the territory has been unlawfully annexed by Russia. Many Ukrainians vowed to boycott Coca-Cola, with some tweeting pictures of themselves pouring Coke down the toilet in disgust. Coca-Cola eventually deleted the second image without replacing the first image.

The SeaWorld, Bud Light, and Coca-Cola fiascos are instructive. SeaWorld was totally unprepared for a hashtag campaign gone wrong. Bud Light didn't consider how its messaging might be

(continued)

interpreted as offensive by many customers. Coca-Cola failed to fully recognize the unique aspects of each geopolitical region in which it operates. Companies need to be prepared to handle negative comments appropriately and take responsibility for mistakes.

Companies don't appear to be learning from the earlier mistakes of their peers. For example, in 2014, homemade pizza maker DiGiorno's blundered when it used a hashtag meant to bring awareness to domestic violence, #WhyIStayed, in a tweet promoting its pizza. Outrage came swiftly and DiGiorno's took the tweet down amid a storm of criticism. The New England Patriots football team ran a campaign that automatically retweeted users' Twitter account names superimposed on team jerseys when users tweeted the #1MillionPatriots hashtag. Users seized the opportunity to wreak havoc, creating offensive Twitter handles that embarrassed the Patriots. And US Airways inadvertently tweeted a graphic pornographic image in response to a customer service complaint. Perhaps most surprisingly of all, Twitter's own chief financial officer accidentally publicly tweeted a message about an acquisition the company was still considering.

But in 2014, KFC set a good example when the news broke that a 3-year-old girl from Mississippi who had been mauled by her grandfather's dogs had subsequently been asked to leave a local KFC because she reportedly was scaring the other patrons. The visit to the restaurant had been a special treat for the girl from her family after a doctor's visit. When the news hit social media, KFC was caught in a firestorm of enraged customers. The company took the next several days to respond to as many individual comments as it could, posted a personal apology to the girl's Facebook page, and pledged $30,000 toward her medical bills.

Marketing is not the only social media hazard. For employees, privacy protection for Facebook posts is still being determined in the courts. For example, Danielle Mailhoit was the manager of a Home Depot store in Burbank, California. After she was fired, she filed suit claiming gender and disability discrimination due to her vertigo. The defense attorney filed a broad request for all of Mailhoit's social media activity. In September 2012, a federal judge ruled this request overly broad and limited discovery to only communications between the plaintiff and current or former Home Depot employees. Stating that they were unlikely to be relevant unless they were directly related to the lawsuit or her former employment, she also denied Home Depot's request for photos.

Employers must be careful with personal information gleaned from social networks. If it can be proven that membership in a protected group was discovered during the hiring process and used to reject a candidate or later used to terminate an employee, a claim can be filed under one of the Federal Equal Employment Opportunity (EEO) laws. These include Title VII of the Civil Rights Act of 1964, the Age Discrimination in Employment Act of 1967 (ADEA), Title I and Title V of the Americans with Disabilities Act of 1990 (ADA), and Title II of the Genetic Information Nondiscrimination Act of 2008 (GINA), which prohibits employment discrimination based on genetic information about an applicant, employee, or former employee. GINA's regulations provide a distinction between whether genetic information is acquired purposefully or inadvertently. Inadvertent acquisition includes acquisition through social networks, equating it to accidentally overhearing a conversation at work.

However, data on a social media site protected by privacy controls should not be able to be "inadvertently" acquired. The Stored Communications Act (SCA) covers privacy protection for e-mail and digital communications. The latest court rulings on its application to social network communications have held that Facebook wall postings and other social media comments are protected as long as they have not been made public.

Facebook, to protect its business model, is speaking out against recent hiring practices that have come to its attention—and threatening legal action. According to both Facebook and the American Civil Liberties Union (ACLU), some companies have been asking new hires either to friend the hiring manager or to submit their password. Facebook's Privacy Page condemns this practice, stating that it violates both individual users' and their friends' expectations of privacy, jeopardizes security, and could reveal a user's membership in a protected group. The legal implications of interactions on social media are still being determined; for example, in 2016, a judge ruled that "tagging" someone in a photo represents the violation of a protective order limiting communication.

Legislators in a growing number of states have decided to be proactive. In 2012, California banned employers from asking prospective employees for their social media user names and passwords. In 2016, Illinois became the 25th state to enact a law that prevents employers from accessing potential employees' social media accounts, with Massachusetts and Ohio poised to add to that number in 2017. Additionally, 15 states have enacted laws that forbid educational institutions from doing so for their prospective students. At the federal level, the House passed a bill in 2016 that requires the President to submit a strategy to address the use of social media by terrorist groups.

Carefully crafted policies can help companies to avoid the dark side of social networking. Advertising and hiring are but two of the areas that must be monitored. Companies must also develop policies regarding employee use of social networks. Employee education programs must be implemented to apprise employees of infractions that can be grounds for disciplinary action. IT departments must develop stringent policies to protect proprietary data and defend company networks from cyberscams. Social networking is an exciting new tool, but one that requires safeguards.

SOURCES: "States Lock Up Social Media Access From Employers," by KSE Focus, Cqrollcall.com, September 7, 2016; "State Social Media Privacy Laws," Nscl.org, July 6, 2016; "Ernst-Backed Bill to Combat Terrorist Use of Social Media Passes Committee," Ernst.senate.gov, February 10, 2016; "Why Googling Candidates Before You Decide to Interview Them is Against the Law," by Diane Faulkner, Adp.com, February 4, 2016; Mariella Moon, "Judge Says Facebook Tagging Violates Protective Orders," Engadget.com, January 17, 2016; "The Top 10 Most Embarrassing Social Media Fails from 2015," by Carlos Matias, Socialmediaweek.org, January 5, 2016; "Top 5 Worst Social Media Brand Blunders of 2015," by Erin Carson, Techrepublic.com, December 18, 2015; "'Ask SeaWorld' Marketing Campaign Backfires," by Katie Lobosco, Cnnmoney.com, March 27, 2015; "Virginia's New Social Media Law Protects Employees," Troutmansanders.com, July 1, 2015; "The 5 Worst Twitter Marketing Fails of 2014," by Kim Lachance Shandrow, Entrepreneur.com, December 18, 2014; "10 Worst Social Media Fails of 2014," by Emily Alford, Clickz.com, December 18, 2014; "The Top 10 Social Media Fails of 2014," by Rebecca Borison, Inc.com, December 10, 2014; "RI Passes Social Media Privacy Law," by Bill Tomison, Wpri.com, July 3, 2014; "Facebook's Facing a Losing Battle to Protect Users' Privacy," by Lisa Vaas, Nakedsecurity.sophos.com, June 30, 2014; "KFC Shows How to Handle a Social Media Disaster," by Mary Elizabeth Williams, Salon.com, June 17, 2014; "The Dangers of Using Social Media Data in Hiring," by Gregg Skall, *Radio Business Report,* June 6, 2011; "Stored Communications Act Protects Facebook and MySpace Users' Private Communication," by Kathryn Freund, Jolt.law.harvard.edu, June 11, 2010.

ness model of general communities is typically advertising supported by selling ad space on pages and videos.

Practice networks offer members focused discussion groups, help, information, and knowledge relating to an area of shared practice. For instance, Linux.org is a nonprofit community for the open source movement, a worldwide global effort involving thousands of programmers who develop computer code for the Linux operating system and share the results freely with all. Other online communities involve artists, educators, art dealers, photographers, and nurses. Practice networks can be either profit-based or nonprofit, and support themselves by advertising or user donations.

Interest-based social networks offer members focused discussion groups based on a shared interest in some specific subject, such as business careers, boats, horses, health, skiing, and thousands of other topics. Because the audience for interest communities is necessarily much smaller and more targeted, these communities have usually relied on advertising and

practice networks
offer members focused discussion groups, help, information, and knowledge relating to an area of shared practice

interest-based social networks
offer members focused discussion groups based on a shared interest in some specific topic

tenancy/sponsorship deals. Social networks such as Fool.com, Military.com, Sailing Anarchy, and Chronicle Forums all are examples of social networks that attract people who share a common pursuit. Job markets and forums such as LinkedIn can be considered interest-based social networks as well.

affinity communities
offer members focused discussions and interaction with other people who share the same affinity

Affinity communities offer members focused discussions and interaction with other people who share the same affinity. "Affinity" refers to self- and group identification. For instance, people can self-identify themselves on the basis of religion, ethnicity, gender, sexual orientation, political beliefs, geographical location, and hundreds of other categories. For instance, Bloom is a network for pregnant women and moms that enables them to give and seek advice, discuss concerns and share stories, as well as find local services, and buy and sell related products (Bloomapp.co, 2016). These social networks are supported by advertising along with revenues from sales of products.

sponsored communities
online communities created for the purpose of pursuing organizational (and often commercial) goals

Sponsored communities are online communities created by government, non-profit, or for-profit organizations for the purpose of pursuing organizational goals. These goals can be diverse, from increasing the information available to citizens; for instance, a local county government site such as Westchestergov.com, the website for Westchester County (New York) government; to an online auction site such as eBay; to a product site such as Tide.com, which is sponsored by an offline branded product company (Procter & Gamble). Cisco, IBM, HP, and hundreds of other companies have developed their internal corporate social networks as a way of sharing knowledge.

algorithms
set of step-by-step instructions, similar to a recipe, for producing a desired output from required inputs

SOCIAL NETWORK TECHNOLOGIES AND FEATURES

Algorithms are one of the most important technologies used by social networks. **Algorithms** are a set of step-by-step instructions, similar to a recipe, for producing a desired output from required inputs. **Computer algorithms** are computer programs that carry out step-by-step instructions to produce desired outputs (Coremen, et. al., 2009). Algorithms are an ancient concept, but are fundamental to how computers are used today to do everything from calculating pay checks, the amount you owe when purchasing online, selecting movies on Netflix that you are likely to watch, or recommending products you may be interested in based on your prior purchases. How, for instance, does Facebook decide what trending news to list in your Trending section, which of your posts to post on your friends' News Feeds, and which Instant Articles to make available on your mobile News Feed?

computer algorithms
computer programs that carry out step-by-step instructions to produce desired outputs

The problem Facebook and other social sites need to solve is how to select content (actions of their friends and news stories) for display on users' pages that they will find interesting, and likely click on. Also, Facebook needs to prevent information that is irrelevant from appearing on user pages. **Figure 10.3** illustrates the generic algorithm Facebook uses to produce what it calls relationship-based content personalized for members of a social network based on a patent it filed in 2010. It shows the generic eight steps in the algorithm (left column), and a translation of each step (right column). Facebook users organize themselves into affinity groups by selecting and accepting one another as friends. **Affinity groups** are a key concept here and in all social networks: they are generally composed of like-minded people who share views, attitudes, purchase patterns, and tastes in music and videos. Facebook attempts to discover exactly what those views, attitudes, purchase patterns, and tastes in music and videos

affinity groups
generally composed of like-minded people who share views, attitudes, purchase patterns, and tastes in music and videos

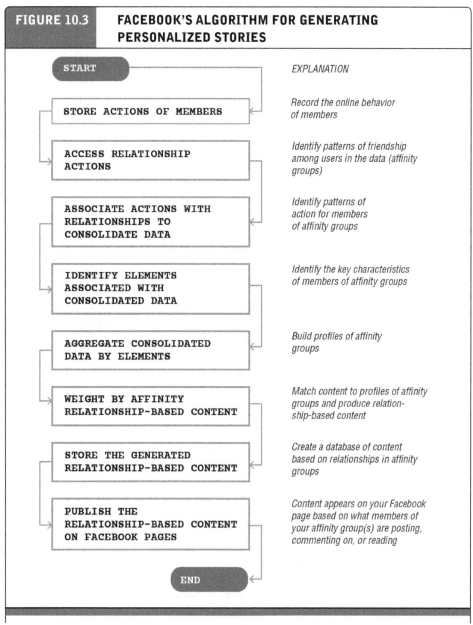

FIGURE 10.3 | FACEBOOK'S ALGORITHM FOR GENERATING PERSONALIZED STORIES

START

EXPLANATION

STORE ACTIONS OF MEMBERS — Record the online behavior of members

ACCESS RELATIONSHIP ACTIONS — Identify patterns of friendship among users in the data (affinity groups)

ASSOCIATE ACTIONS WITH RELATIONSHIPS TO CONSOLIDATE DATA — Identify patterns of action for members of affinity groups

IDENTIFY ELEMENTS ASSOCIATED WITH CONSOLIDATED DATA — Identify the key characteristics of members of affinity groups

AGGREGATE CONSOLIDATED DATA BY ELEMENTS — Build profiles of affinity groups

WEIGHT BY AFFINITY RELATIONSHIP-BASED CONTENT — Match content to profiles of affinity groups and produce relationship-based content

STORE THE GENERATED RELATIONSHIP-BASED CONTENT — Create a database of content based on relationships in affinity groups

PUBLISH THE RELATIONSHIP-BASED CONTENT ON FACEBOOK PAGES — Content appears on your Facebook page based on what members of your affinity group(s) are posting, commenting on, or reading

END

Facebook uses a very complex algorithm to identify content that users are likely to click on. Each step in the algorithm is implanted by computer programs involving tens of thousands of lines of computer code and thousands of hours of software engineering and system development.

SOURCE: Based on data from U.S. Patent and Trademark Office, 2010.

are, as well as demographic and other personal information. Once these are identified, Facebook attempts to find out what content is being consumed by each affinity group and matches the content to each group (relation-base content). Facebook creates a database of this relationship-based content, and serves it to other members of the group, as well as other affinity groups that share similar features.

In the end, you will be informed of what your friends are doing, liking, viewing and listening to. You will find this interesting and engaging. You will be spared hearing about other affinity groups who are very dissimilar to your affinity groups. New content (news, music, videos) that is similar to what your affinity group has liked in the past will also be served to you. For instance, if you are a staunch conservative or liberal, and you choose to click on articles that confirm your views, other members of your affinity group who share your views will have the content and your behavior displayed on their pages. They in turn may share this content with other Facebook friends, and other affinity groups of which they are a part.

While the generic algorithm appears simple, each step in the algorithm is implemented by computer programs involving tens of thousands of lines of computer code, and thousands of hours of software engineering and system development. The data produced by over 167 million users in the United States, and 1.7 billion other users worldwide requires three data centers in the United States and one in Sweden, a total of a million square feet containing tens of thousands of servers, all connected by several fiber optic networks (Data Center Knowledge, 2016). According to Facebook, loading a user's home page involves hundreds of servers, processing tens of thousands of individual pieces of data, and delivering the information selected in less than one second. The *Insight on Technology* case, *Trapped Inside the Facebook Bubble?*, examines the impact of algorithms in further depth.

Social networks also have developed a number of other software applications that allow users to engage in a number of activities. **Table 10.4** describes several additional social network functionalities.

TABLE 10.4	SOCIAL NETWORK FEATURES
FEATURE	DESCRIPTION
Profiles	User-created web pages that describe the owner on a variety of dimensions
Newsfeed	A listing of updates from friends, advertisements, and notifications in chronological order
Timeline	A history of updates, posts from friends, photos, and other objects in chronological order
Friends networks	Ability to create a linked group of friends, a social community
Network discovery	Ability to find other social networks, find new groups and friends, and discover friends of friends
Favorites (Like)	Ability to communicate favorite sites, bookmarks, content, and destinations
Games and apps	Games developed for the social network, and apps that extend its functionality
Instant messaging	Instant messaging, chat
Storage	Storage for photos, videos, text
Message boards	Ability to post updates to friends, e.g., Wall
Groups	Discussion groups, forums, and consumer groups organized by interest, e.g., For Sale Groups

INSIGHT ON TECHNOLOGY

TRAPPED INSIDE THE FACEBOOK BUBBLE?

In May 2016, the blog Gizmodo published a report claiming that Facebook suppressed conservative political stories in its Trending section by allowing its news curators to intervene in the operation of Facebook's Trending algorithm, which allegedly chose trending topics based organically on Facebook's users' likes, mentions, posts, and clicks. There was, so the article claimed, a liberal bias at Facebook. The article, based on claims of former employees, led to a flurry of critical news articles, a potential Congressional investigation, a public debate over Facebook's role in promoting its own political agenda, and a great deal of commentary about the role of Facebook in shaping the news that Americans read everyday.

A related debate arose concerning the role of Facebook's entire News Feed algorithm, which displays posts by your Facebook friends, as well as ads based in part on Facebook's knowledge of you and your friends. Critics fear that both the News Feed and Trending section are helping to create a highly polarized society: users see only the social and political views of their friends on controversial topics, creating a self-reinforcing, bubble world. Sometimes referred to as the Facebook filter trap, echo chamber, or bubble, critics believe this results in groups who never share news or interact with one another, and who therefore cannot find a middle ground to share. Worse, extremist groups proliferate based on their own unchallenged facts and theories, which are never subjected to accuracy checking. It's called homophily: given a choice, people tend to associate with people like themselves. In the social network world, this translates to only being exposed to views of people who share your views, creating an echo chamber. Contrary views will rarely make it to your News Feed or your Trending feed. Every click, every Like, and

keystroke creates a reality for users that may or may not be a fiction.

From Facebook's point of view, both the News Feed and Trending algorithms solve an important problem for today's users of social networks: there is so much information online that users may become inundated with information that does not interest them, and makes it difficult for them to find information that does interest them. The resulting frustration could turn users away from social networks that increasingly are the source of news and opinion for web users. Therefore there is a need for what Facebook refers to, in its patent applications for both algorithms, as "a system to generate dynamic, relationship-based content personalized for members of a Social Network." Translated, this means the algorithms are set up to engage you and keep you on the site, exposing you to more ads.

The Trending algorithm is a complex chunk of code that operates in real time. The algorithm monitors the behavior of over 200 million users in the United States and over 1 billion worldwide, and posts the results on the top right of users' News Feed pages, changing periodically through the day. The algorithm is also sensitive to rates of change: if mentions spike in a short period of time, the topic gets boosted in ranking. Facebook certainly gave users the impression that Trending was a computer-driven process that accurately and objectively reflects what other users were reacting to on the social network and what you are likely to click on.

But the reality was really quite different, according to Gizmodo and former employees. The process of selecting trends evolved over several years, but from the beginning news curators (journalists) intervened and had the last say about what was, or was not, included in Trending. As it turns out, the algorithm could not distinguish between a

(continued)

real event (a SpaceX rocket exploded on the pad) versus a phony event (spacemen land in New Mexico), or if a topic was covered elsewhere as a live topic on Facebook. The algorithm was not allowed to include stories about Facebook itself. If the algorithm missed important news events for some reason, curators injected these events and views as Trending topics. Often, with complex algorithms, how they produce results is not precisely understood even by their authors, and the results of the algorithm may not quite hit the mark. Hot topics identified by the algorithm that involved sex, pornography, nudity, graphic violence, or "R" rated content were removed by editors. Humans played an important editorial role in creating the Trending topics, and like journalists and editors everywhere, could exercise their discretion and perhaps insert their political views, in the process. In many ways, this sounds just like an ordinary newspaper or television news program: selecting news that editors think will be of interest to its readership, using headlines, lists, and sidebars to other stories.

An examination of Facebook's patent describing the Trending algorithm reveals that a variety of other factors are used to create the Trending list. The algorithm uses keywords to process mentions and other activities of users (such as Super Bowl, skiing, baseball, etc.) and groups them into topics. Each topic is given a trending score based on the geographic location of users posting about the topic, the number of mentions, and the rate of increase in activity. Then the trending topics are matched to the personal interests of your friends on the social network, and of each user, as well as other factors like gender, race, national origin, religion, age, marital status, disability, sexual orientation, educational level, and socioeconomic statuses. In short, just about everything you have ever shared with Facebook!

The net result is that the Trending topics you see are likely different from those displayed to your next-door neighbor, friends who live in a different state, colleagues at work, or millions of others who see their own personalized topics. The Trending topics do not reflect the Facebook user audience, but instead are Facebook's best estimate of what you would find engaging, what your friends have found engaging, and what you are more likely to click on, thereby keeping you on Facebook for the display of ads. Facebook is in the business of manufacturing advertising revenues through increasing engagement, i.e., time on site. Facebook is not a news organization in the traditional sense, but a redistributor of content created by others, whether professional journalists or amateur bloggers.

One of the vulnerabilities of the Trending algorithm is its sensitivity to the number of mentions (which could be Likes, posts, clicks, or other behavior), and the rate of increase over short periods of time. Social scientists established a long time ago that on most controversial issues, 90% of the population appears near the middle of opinion, or close by. The other 10% of the population has views that are significantly further away from the average opinion. Sometimes called "fringe groups" or "extremists," people in these groups often are highly engaged, very active contributors to Facebook and other opinion sites, often espouse conspiracy theories, engage in hate speech, and do so in a concerted short-term burst of online posting in the hope of influencing a very large online audience by encouraging a viral sharing of their posts. Fringe groups try to take advantage of the viral nature of social networks. Facebook's algorithm tries to counter this tendency by demoting content posted by very frequent contributors.

In response to the public concern about liberal bias in the Trending section, and the difficulty Facebook encountered in trying to clearly explain how its Trending section works, Facebook fired its staff of 26 Trending editors in 2016, and promised to rely only on the Trending algorithm in order to eliminate human bias and be more objective. The early results suggest that more false news stories, conspiracy theories, and offensive material are appearing in

Trending than before. As one pundit noted, with its human editors dismissed, Facebook has let the inmates—Facebook users—run the asylum.

The News Feed also faces similar criticism. To illustrate the strength of the News Feed echo chamber, and how reality differs for different Facebook users, the *Wall Street Journal* publishes a graphical representation of how very liberal and very conservative users of Facebook linked to (reacted to) news articles drawn from over 500 sources, from bloggers to reputable news organizations. The data was originally produced in a large study of user behavior funded by Facebook, conducted by Facebook researchers, and reported in the magazine *Science*. The News Feeds of 10 million users were examined. The results of the *Journal*'s online data is that very liberal and very conservative Facebook users create for themselves, through their selection of news articles enabled by the News Feed algorithm, two highly divergent world views on most topics, from guns, to abortion, ISIS, political candidates, and so forth. For instance, on guns, very liberal users linked to news posts critical of the National Rifle Association, school shootings, and the ready availability of guns, among others. Very conservative users linked to news posts critical of gun control legislation, invasions of homes by armed criminals, and the use of guns for self-defense, among others. Facebook's researchers concluded in the *Science* article that Facebook's users do get some contrary views in their News Feeds and Trend-

ing sections, and that any bias is not caused by its algorithms, but rather by users selecting as friends people who share their views. The algorithms simply reflect what users have chosen in terms of friends and the articles they click on.

If you want to know why liberals and conservatives have a difficult time communicating with one another, let alone acting on key issues together, it's because they reside in two very different, polarized news streams. Since well over half of the online population gets its news from social networks like Facebook, what Facebook determines is news has a significant impact on public debate and policy.

On the other hand, is Facebook any different from a traditional newspaper or cable news channel, both of which select the news and views that they believe their readers and viewers find engaging? One difference is that for traditional news producers, human beings are doing the selection of news, and viewers understand this, and select among the offerings. At Facebook, algorithms, written by humans, automate this process of determining what is news.

The algorithms of Trending cannot discern the validity of articles, the difference between a crackpot conspiracy theory, and a quality piece of well-researched journalism. Those who join any community on Facebook are algorithmically driven to receive more and more content supported by that group, and less content from opposing groups or views.

SOURCES: "Blue Feed, Red Feed: See Liberal Facebook and Conservative Facebook, Side by Side," *Wall Street Journal,* May 18, 2016; "The Algorithm Is an Editor," by Jeffrey Herbst, *Wall Street Journal,* April 13, 2016; "Facebook's 'Trending' Feature Exhibits Flaws Under New Algorithm," by Georgia Wells, *Wall Street Journal,* September 6, 2016; "Almost No One Really Knows How Facebook's Trending Algorithm Works, But Here's An Idea," by Joseph Lichterman, NiemanLab.org, September 1, 2016; "Inside Facebook's (Totally Insane, Unintentionally Gigantic, Hyperpartisan) Political-Media Machine," by John Herrman, *New York Times,* August 24, 2016; "The Reason Your Feed Became An Echo Chamber—And What To Do About It," NPR.com, July 24, 2016; "Your Facebook Echo Chamber Just Got a Whole Lot Louder," by Brian Barrett, Wired.com, June 29, 2016; "Exposure to Ideologically Diverse News and Opinion on Facebook," by E. Bakshy, S. Messing, and L. Adamic, *Science,* June 5, 2016; "How Facebook Warps Our Worlds," by Frank Bruni, *New York Times,* May 21, 2016; "The Wall Street Journal's New Tool Gives a Side-by-Side Look at the Facebook Political News Filter Bubble," by Ricardo Bilton, *Wall Street Journal,* May 18, 2016; "Facebook Study Finds People Only Click on Links That They Agree With, Site Is an 'Echo Chamber'," by Andrew Griffin, Independent.co.uk, May 8, 2015; *The Filter Bubble,* by Eli Pariser. Penguin Books; Reprint edition (April 24, 2012); Facebook, "Generating a Feed of Stories Personalized For Members of a Social Network," US Patent 7827208 B2, United States Patent Office, published November 2, 2010.

10.2 ONLINE AUCTIONS

consumer-to-consumer (C2C) auctions

auction house acts as an intermediary market maker, providing a forum where consumers can discover prices and trade

Auctions are used throughout the e-commerce landscape. The most widely known auctions are **consumer-to-consumer (C2C) auctions**, in which the auction house is simply an intermediary market maker, providing a forum where consumers—buyers and sellers—can discover prices and trade. The market leader in C2C auctions is eBay, which, as of June 2016, had around 164 million active users and over 800 million items listed on any given day within thousands of different categories. In 2015, eBay had about $6.1 billion in net revenues from its Marketplaces segment, a 4% decline from 2014, and the total worth of goods sold or auctioned was around $78 billion, a 2% decline from 2014 (eBay, 2016). eBay is expanding rapidly in emerging markets, which its CEO has stated are now its fastest growing markets. eBay is further discussed in the case study at the end of this chapter. There are hundreds of auction sites, some specializing in unique collectible products such as stamps and coins, others adopting a more generalist approach in which almost any good can be found for sale.

business-to-consumer (B2C) auctions

business sells goods it owns, or controls, using various dynamic pricing models

Less well known are **business-to-consumer (B2C) auctions**, where a business owns or controls assets and uses dynamic pricing to establish the price. Increasingly, online retail sites, such as Sam's Club, are adding auctions to their sites. Auctions also constitute a significant part of B2B e-commerce in 2016, and more than a third of procurement officers use auctions to procure goods.

Some leading online auction sites are listed in **Table 10.5**. Auctions are not limited to goods and services. They can also be used to allocate resources, and bundles of resources, among any group of bidders. For instance, if you wanted to establish an optimal schedule for assigned tasks in an office among a group of clerical workers, an auction in which workers bid for assignments would come close to producing a nearly optimal solution in a short amount of time (Parkes and Ungar, 2000). In short, auctions—like all markets—are ways of allocating resources among independent agents (bidders).

BENEFITS AND COSTS OF AUCTIONS

The Internet is primarily responsible for the resurgence in auctions. The Internet provides a global environment and very low fixed and operational costs for the aggregation of huge buyer audiences, composed of millions of consumers worldwide, who can use a universally available technology (Internet browsers) to shop for goods.

Benefits of Auctions

Aside from the sheer game-like fun of participating in auctions, consumers, merchants, and society as a whole derive a number of economic benefits from participating in Internet auctions. These benefits include:

- **Liquidity:** Sellers can find willing buyers, and buyers can find sellers. Sellers and buyers can be located anywhere around the globe. Just as important, buyers and

TABLE 10.5	LEADING ONLINE AUCTION SITES
GENERAL	
eBay	The world market leader in auctions: 110 million visitors a month and hundreds of millions of products.
eBid	In business since 1998. Operates in 23 countries, including the United States. Currently, one of the top competitors to eBay. Offers much lower fees.
uBid	Marketplace for excess inventory from pre-approved merchants.
OnlineAuction	Allows sellers to list for a low monthly fee, without a per-item listing or additional fees when the item sells.
SPECIALIZED	
Racersauction	Specialized site for automobile racing parts.
Philatelicphantasies	Stamp site for professionals, monthly online stamp auction.
Stacksbowers	America's largest fully automated auction company of certified coins including ancient gold, silver, and copper coins. Also offers sports cards.
Bid4Assets	Liquidation of distressed real estate assets from government and the public sector, corporations, restructurings, and bankruptcies.
Oldandsold	Online auction service specializing in quality antiques. Dealers pay a 3% commission on merchandise sold.
B2C AUCTIONS	
Auctions.samsclub	Merchandise from Sam's Club in a variety of categories.
Shopgoodwill	Goodwill's online auction site. Offers a wide variety of collectibles, books, and antiques chosen from the goods donated to Goodwill.

sellers can find a global market for rare items that would not have existed before the Internet.

- **Price discovery:** Buyers and sellers can quickly and efficiently develop prices for items that are difficult to assess, where the price depends on demand and supply, and where the product is rare.

- **Price transparency:** Public Internet auctions allow everyone in the world to see the asking and bidding prices for items.

- **Market efficiency:** Auctions can, and often do, lead to reduced prices, and hence reduced profits for merchants, leading to an increase in consumer welfare—one measure of market efficiency.

- **Lower transaction costs:** Online auctions can lower the cost of selling and purchasing products, benefiting both merchants and consumers. Like other Internet markets, such as retail markets, Internet auctions have very low (but not zero) transaction costs.

- **Consumer aggregation:** Sellers benefit from large auction sites' ability to aggregate a large number of consumers who are motivated to purchase something in one marketspace.

- **Network effects:** The larger an auction site becomes in terms of visitors and products for sale, the more valuable it becomes as a marketplace for everyone by providing liquidity and several other benefits listed previously, such as lower transaction costs, higher efficiency, and better price transparency.

Risks and Costs of Auctions

There are a number of risks and costs involved in participating in auctions. In some cases, auction markets can fail—like all markets at times. (We describe auction market failure in more detail later.) Some of the more important risks and costs to keep in mind are:

- **Delayed consumption costs:** Internet auctions can go on for days, and shipping will take additional time.
- **Monitoring costs:** Participation in auctions requires your time to monitor bidding.
- **Equipment costs:** Internet auctions require you to purchase a computer system and pay for Internet access.
- **Trust risks:** Online auctions are a significant source of Internet fraud. Using auctions increases the risk of experiencing a loss.
- **Fulfillment costs:** Typically, the buyer pays fulfillment costs of packing, shipping, and insurance, whereas at a physical store these costs are included in the retail price.

Auction sites such as eBay have taken a number of steps to reduce consumer participation costs and trust risk. For instance, auction sites attempt to solve the trust problem by providing a rating system in which previous customers rate sellers based on their overall experience with the merchant. Although helpful, this solution does not always work. Auction fraud is a leading source of e-commerce complaints to federal law enforcement officials. Another partial solution to high monitoring costs is, ironically, fixed pricing. At eBay, consumers can reduce the cost of monitoring and waiting for auctions to end by simply clicking on the Buy It Now button and paying a premium price. The difference between the Buy It Now price and the auction price is the cost of monitoring.

Nevertheless, given the costs of participating in online auctions, the generally lower cost of goods on Internet auctions is in part a compensation for the other additional costs consumers experience. On the other hand, consumers experience lower search costs and transaction costs because there usually are no intermediaries (unless, of course, the seller is an online business operating on an auction site, in which case there is a middleman cost), and usually there are no local or state taxes.

Merchants face considerable risks and costs as well. At auctions, merchants may end up selling goods for prices far below what they might have achieved in conventional markets. Merchants also face risks of nonpayment, false bidding, bid rigging, monitoring, transaction fees charged by the auction site, credit card transaction processing fees, and the administration costs of entering price and product information.

AUCTIONS AS AN E-COMMERCE BUSINESS MODEL

Online auctions have been among the most successful business models in retail and B2B commerce. eBay, the Internet's most lucrative auction site, has been profitable nearly since its inception. The strategy for eBay has been to make money off every stage in the auction cycle. eBay earns revenue from auctions in several ways: transaction fees based on the amount of the sale, listing fees for display of goods, financial service fees from payment systems such as PayPal, and advertising or placement fees where sellers pay extra for special services such as particular display or listing services. PayPal has been faster growing and more profitable than eBay's markets, growing to more than half of eBay's revenue. In 2015, eBay spun off PayPal into a separate company, and going forward will have to make its profits from its markets operation.

However, it is on the cost side that online auctions have extraordinary advantages over ordinary retail or catalog sites. Auction sites carry no inventory and do not perform any fulfillment activities—they need no warehouses, shipping, or logistical facilities. Sellers and consumers provide these services and bear these costs. In this sense, online auctions are an ideal digital business because they involve simply the transfer of information.

Even though eBay has been extraordinarily successful, the success of online auctions is qualified by the fact that the marketplace for online auctions is highly concentrated. eBay dominates the online auction market, followed by eBid and uBid. In the last several years eBay's growth has slowed considerably as consumers shift toward Buy It Now purchases rather than auctions. Many of the smaller auction sites are not profitable because they lack sufficient sellers and buyers to achieve liquidity. In auctions, network effects are highly influential, and the tendency is for one or two very large auction sites to dominate, with hundreds of smaller specialty auction sites (sites that sell specialized goods such as stamps) being barely profitable.

TYPES AND EXAMPLES OF AUCTIONS

The primary types of auctions found on the Internet are English auctions, Dutch Internet auctions, Name Your Own Price auctions, and so-called penny auctions.

The **English auction** is the easiest to understand and the most common form of auction on eBay. Typically, there is a single item up for sale from a single seller. There is a time limit when the auction ends, a reserve price below which the seller will not sell (usually secret), and a minimum incremental bid set. Multiple buyers bid against one another until the auction time limit is reached. The highest bidder wins the item (if the reserve price of the seller has been met or exceeded). English auctions are considered to be seller-biased because multiple buyers compete against one another—usually anonymously.

English auction
most common form of auction; the highest bidder wins

The **Dutch Internet auction** format is perfect for sellers that have many identical items to sell. Sellers start by listing a minimum price, or a starting bid for one item, and the number of items for sale. Bidders specify both a bid price and the quantity they want to buy. The uniform price reigns. Winning bidders pay the same price per item, which is the lowest successful bid. This market clearing price can be less than some bids. If there are more buyers than items, the earliest successful bids get the goods. In general, high bidders get the quantity they want at the lowest successful price, whereas low successful bidders might not get the quantity they want (but they will get something).

Dutch Internet auction
public ascending price, multiple unit auction. Final price is lowest successful bid, which sets price for all higher bidders

The **Name Your Own Price auction** was pioneered by Priceline, and is the second most-popular auction format on the Web. Although Priceline also acts as an intermediary, buying blocks of airline tickets, hotel rooms, and vacation packages at

Name Your Own Price auction
auction where users specify what they are willing to pay for goods or services

a discount and selling them at a reduced retail price or matching its inventory to bidders, it is best known for its Name Your Own Price auctions, in which users specify what they are willing to pay for goods or services, and multiple providers bid for their business. Prices do not descend and are fixed: the initial consumer offer is a commitment to purchase at that price. In 2015, Priceline had more than $9.2 billion in revenues, and in 2016, it attracts around 20 million unique visitors a month. It is one of the top-ranked travel sites in the United States.

But how can Priceline offer such steep discounts off prices for services provided by major brand-name providers? There are several answers. First, Priceline "shields the brand" by not publicizing the prices at which major brands sell. This reduces conflict with traditional channels, including direct sales. Second, the services being sold are perishable: if a Priceline customer did not pay something for the empty airline seat, rental car, or hotel room, sellers would not receive any revenue. Hence, sellers are highly motivated to at least cover the costs of their services by selling in a spot market at very low prices. The strategy for sellers is to sell as much as possible through more profitable channels and then unload excess capacity on spot markets such as Priceline. This works to the advantage of consumers, sellers, and Priceline, which charges a transaction fee to sellers.

penny (bidding fee) auction

bidder must pay a non-refundable fee to purchase bids

So-called penny auctions are really anything but. To participate in a **penny auction** (also known as a **bidding fee auction**), you typically must pay the penny auction site for bids ahead of time, typically 50 cents to $1 dollar, usually in packs costing $25-$50. Once you have purchased the bids, you can use them to bid on items listed by the penny auction site (unlike traditional auctions, items are owned by the site, not third parties). Items typically start at or near $0 and each bid raises the price by a fixed amount, usually just a penny. Auctions are timed, and when the time runs out, the last and highest bidder wins the item. Although the price of the item itself may not be that high, the successful bidder will typically have spent much more than that. Unlike a traditional auction, it costs money to bid, and that money is gone even if the bidder does not win the auction. The bidder's cumulative cost of bidding must be added to the final price of a successful bid to determine the true cost of the item. The Federal Trade Commission has issued an alert about penny auctions, warning that bidders may find that they spend far more than they intended (Consumer Reports.org, 2013). Examples of penny auction sites include QuiBids, Beezid, and HappyBidDay.

WHEN TO USE AUCTIONS (AND FOR WHAT) IN BUSINESS

There are many different situations in which auctions are an appropriate channel for businesses to consider. For much of this chapter, we have looked at auctions from a consumer point of view. The objective of consumers is to receive the greatest value for the lowest cost. Now, switch your perspective to that of a business. Remember that the objective of businesses using auctions is to maximize their revenue (their share of consumer surplus) by finding the true market value of products and services, a market value that hopefully is higher in the auction channel than in fixed-price channels. **Table 10.6** provides an overview of factors to consider.

The factors are described as follows:

- **Type of product:** Online auctions are most commonly used for rare and unique products for which prices are difficult to discover, and there may have been no

TABLE 10.6	FACTORS TO CONSIDER WHEN CHOOSING AUCTIONS
CONSIDERATIONS	DESCRIPTION
Type of product	Rare, unique, commodity, perishable
Stage of product life cycle	Early, mature, late
Channel-management issues	Conflict with retail distributors; differentiation
Type of auction	Seller vs. buyer bias
Initial pricing	Low vs. high
Bid increment amounts	Low vs. high
Auction length	Short vs. long
Number of items	Single vs. multiple
Price-allocation rule	Uniform vs. discriminatory
Information sharing	Closed vs. open bidding

market for the goods. However, Priceline has succeeded in developing auctions for perishable commodities (such as airline seats) for which retail prices have already been established, and some B2B auctions involve commodities such as steel (often sold at distress prices). New clothing items, new digital cameras, and new computers are generally not sold at auction because their prices are easy to discover, catalog prices are high, sustainable, and profitable, they are not perishable, and there exists an efficient market channel in the form of retail stores (online and offline).

- **Product life cycle:** For the most part, businesses have traditionally used auctions for goods at the end of their product life cycle and for products where auctions yield a higher price than fixed-price liquidation sales. However, products at the beginning of their life cycle are increasingly being sold at auction. Early releases of music, books, videos, games, and digital appliances can be sold to highly motivated early adopters who want to be the first in their neighborhood with new products. Online auctions and sales of event tickets from music concerts to sports events now account for more than 50% of all event ticket sales in the United States.

- **Channel management:** Established retailers such as JCPenney and Walmart, and manufacturers in general, must be careful not to allow their auction activity to interfere with their existing profitable channels. For this reason, items found on established retail-site auctions tend to be late in their product life cycle or have quantity purchase requirements.

- **Type of auction:** Sellers obviously should choose auctions where there are many buyers and only a few, or even one, seller. English ascending-price auctions such as those at eBay are best for sellers because as the number of bidders increases, the price tends to move higher.

- **Initial pricing:** Research suggests that auction items should start out with low initial bid prices in order to encourage more bidders to bid (see "Bid increments" below).

The lower the price, the larger the number of bidders will appear. The larger the number of bidders, the higher the prices move.

- **Bid increments:** It is generally safest to keep bid increments low so as to increase the number of bidders and the frequency of their bids. If bidders can be convinced that, for just a few more dollars, they can win the auction, then they will tend to make the higher bid and forget about the total amount they are bidding.

- **Auction length:** In general, the longer auctions are scheduled, the larger the number of bidders and the higher the prices can go. However, once the new bid arrival rate drops off and approaches zero, bid prices stabilize. Most eBay auctions are scheduled for seven days.

- **Number of items:** When a business has a number of items to sell, buyers usually expect a "volume discount," and this expectation can cause lower bids in return. Therefore, sellers should consider breaking up very large bundles into smaller bundles auctioned at different times.

- **Price allocation rule:** Most buyers believe it is "fair" that everyone pay the same price in a multi-unit auction, and a uniform pricing rule is recommended. eBay Dutch Internet auctions encourage this expectation. The idea that some buyers should pay more based on their differential need for the product is not widely supported. Therefore, sellers who want to price discriminate should do so by holding auctions for the same goods on different auction markets, or at different times, to prevent direct price comparison.

- **Closed vs. open bidding:** Closed bidding has many advantages for the seller, and sellers should use this approach whenever possible because it permits price discrimination without offending buyers. However, open bidding carries the advantage of "herd effects" and "winning effects" (described later in the chapter) in which consumers' competitive instincts to "win" drive prices higher than even secret bidding would achieve.

AUCTION PRICES: ARE THEY THE LOWEST?

It is widely assumed that auction prices are lower than prices in other fixed-price markets. Empirical evidence is mixed on this assumption. There are many reasons why auction prices might be higher than those in fixed-price markets for items of identical quality, and why auction prices in one auction market may be higher than those in other auction markets. Consumers are not driven solely by value maximization but instead are influenced by many situational factors, irrelevant and wrong information, and misperceptions when they make market decisions (Simonson and Tversky, 1992). Auctions are social events—shared social environments, in which bidders adjust to one another (Hanson and Putler, 1996). Briefly, bidders base their bids on what others have previously bid, and this can lead to an upward cascading effect (Arkes and Hutzel, 2000). In a study of hundreds of eBay auctions for Sony PlayStations, CD players, Mexican pottery, and Italian silk ties, Dholakia and Soltysinski (2001) found that bidders exhibited **herd behavior** (the tendency to gravitate toward, and bid for, auction listings with one or more existing bids) by making multiple bids on some auctions (coveted comparables), and making no bids at auctions

herd behavior
the tendency to gravitate toward, and bid for, auction listings with one or more existing bids

for comparable items (overlooked comparables). Herd behavior resulted in consumers paying higher prices than necessary for reasons having no foundation in economic reality (Liu and Sutanto, 2012).

The behavioral reality of participating in auctions can produce many unintended results. Winners can suffer **winner's regret**, the feeling after winning an auction that they paid too much for an item, which indicates that their winning bid does not reflect what they thought the item was worth but rather what the second bidder thought the item was worth. Sellers can experience **seller's lament**, reflecting the fact that they sold an item at a price just above the second place bidder, never knowing how much the ultimate winner might have paid or the true value to the final winner. Auction losers can experience **loser's lament**, the feeling of having been too cheap in bidding and failing to win. In summary, auctions can lead to both winners paying too much and sellers receiving too little. Both of these outcomes can be minimized when sellers and buyers have a very clear understanding of the prices for items in a variety of different online and offline markets.

winner's regret
the winner's feeling after an auction that he or she paid too much for an item

seller's lament
concern that one will never know how much the ultimate winner might have paid, or the true value to the final winner

loser's lament
the feeling of having been too cheap in bidding and failing to win

CONSUMER TRUST IN AUCTIONS

Auction sites have the same difficulties creating a sense of consumer trust as all other e-commerce sites, although in the case of auction sites, the operators of the marketplace do not directly control the quality of goods being offered and cannot directly vouch for the integrity of the buyers or the sellers. This opens the possibility for criminal or unreliable actors to appear as either sellers or buyers. Several studies have found that trust and credibility increase as users gain more experience, if trusted third-party seals are present, and if the site has a wide variety of consumer services for tracking purchases (or fraud), thus giving the user a sense of control (Krishnamurthy, 2001; Stanford-Makovsky, 2002; Nikander and Karvonen, 2002; Bailey et al., 2002; Kollock, 1999). Because of the powerful role that trust plays in online consumer behavior, eBay and most auction sites make considerable efforts to develop automated trust-enhancing mechanisms such as seller and buyer ratings, escrow services, buyer and seller insurance, guaranteed money back features, and authenticity guarantees (see the next section).

WHEN AUCTION MARKETS FAIL: FRAUD AND ABUSE IN AUCTIONS

Online and offline auction markets can be prone to fraud, which produces information asymmetries between sellers and buyers and among buyers, which in turn causes auction markets to fail. Some of the possible abuses and frauds include:

- **Bid rigging:** Agreeing offline to limit bids or using shills to submit false bids that drive prices up.
- **Price matching:** Agreeing informally or formally to set floor prices on auction items below which sellers will not sell in open markets.
- **Shill feedback, defensive:** Using secondary IDs or other auction members to inflate seller ratings.
- **Shill feedback, offensive:** Using secondary IDs or other auction members to deflate ratings for another user (feedback bombs).

- **Feedback extortion:** Threatening negative feedback in return for a benefit.
- **Transaction interference:** E-mailing buyers to warn them away from a seller.
- **Bid manipulation:** Using the retraction option to make high bids, discovering the maximum bid of the current high bidder, and then retracting the bid.
- **Non-payment after winning:** Blocking legitimate buyers by bidding high, then not paying.
- **Shill bidding:** Using secondary user IDs or other auction members to artificially raise the price of an item.
- **Transaction non-performance:** Accepting payment and failing to deliver.
- **Non-selling seller:** Refusing payment or failing to deliver after a successful auction.
- **Bid siphoning:** E-mailing another seller's bidders and offering the same product for less.

Auction sites have sought to reduce these risks through various methods including:

- **Rating systems:** Previous customers rate sellers based on their experience with them and post them on the site for other buyers to see.
- **Watch lists:** These allow buyers to monitor specific auctions as they proceed over a number of days and only pay close attention in the last few minutes of bidding.
- **Proxy bidding:** Buyers can enter a maximum price they are willing to pay, and the auction software will automatically place incremental bids as their original bid is surpassed.

eBay and many other auction sites have investigation units that receive complaints from consumers and investigate reported abuses. Nevertheless, with millions of visitors per week and hundreds of thousands of auctions to monitor, eBay is highly dependent on the good faith of sellers and consumers to follow the rules.

10.3 E-COMMERCE PORTALS

Port: From the Latin porta, an entrance or gateway to a locality.

Portals are among the most frequently visited sites on the Web if only because they often are the homepage page to which many users point their browser on startup. The top portals such as Yahoo, MSN, and AOL have hundreds of millions of unique visitors worldwide each month. Portal sites are gateways to the billions of web pages available on the Internet. Facebook also acts as a home page portal to the Web. Millions of users have set Facebook as their home page, choosing to start their sessions with news from their friends, and many stay on Facebook for several hours a day. We have already discussed Facebook in Section 10.1. Perhaps the most important service provided by portals is to help people find the information they are looking for on the Web and, like newspapers, to expose people to information they were not looking for but which they nonetheless may find entertaining or interesting. The original portals in the early days of e-commerce were search engines. Consumers would pass through search engine portals on their way to rich, detailed, in-depth content on the Web. But portals evolved into much more complex websites that provide news, entertainment, maps, images, social networks, in-depth information, and education on a growing variety of topics all contained at the portal site. Portals today seek to be a sticky destination site, not merely a gateway through which visitors pass. In this respect, portals are very much like television networks: destination sites for content supported by advertising revenues. Portals today want visitors to stay a long time—the longer the better to expose visitors to ads. For the most part they succeed: portals are places where people linger for a long time.

Portals also serve important functions within a business or organization. Most corporations, universities, churches, and other formal organizations have **enterprise portals** that help employees or members navigate to important content, such as human resources information, corporate news, or organizational announcements. For instance, your university has a portal through which you can register for courses, find classroom assignments, and perform a host of other important student activities. Increasingly, these enterprise portals also provide general-purpose news and real-time financial feeds provided by content providers outside the organization. Corporate portals and intranets are the subject of other textbooks focused on the corporate uses of web technology and are beyond the scope of this book (see Laudon and Laudon, 2016). Our focus here is on e-commerce portals.

enterprise portals
help employees navigate to the enterprise's human resource and corporate content

THE GROWTH AND EVOLUTION OF PORTALS

Portals have changed a great deal from their initial function and role. As noted above, most of today's well-known portals, such as Yahoo, MSN, and AOL, began as search engines. The initial function provided by portals was to index web page content and make this content available to users in a convenient form. Early portals expected visitors to stay only a few minutes at the site. As millions of people signed on to the Internet in the early 2000s, the number of visitors to basic search engine sites exploded commensurately. At first, few people understood how a web search site could make money by passing customers on to other destinations. But search sites attracted huge audiences, and therein lay the foundation for their success as vehicles for marketing and advertising. Search sites, recognizing the potential for commerce, expanded their offerings from simple navigation to include commerce (the sale of items directly from the website as well as advertising for other retail sites), content (in the form of news at first, and later in the form of weather, investments, games, health, and other subject matter), communications (email, chat, and texting), and distribution of others' content. These four characteristics have become the basic definition of portal sites, namely, sites that provide four functions: navigation of the Web (search), communications, commerce, and content.

Because the value of portals to advertisers and content owners is largely a function of the size of the audience each portal reaches, and the length of time visitors stay on site, portals compete with one another on reach and unique visitors. *Reach* is defined as the percentage of the web audience that visits the site in a month (or some other time period), and *unique visitors* is defined as the number of uniquely identified individuals who visit in a month. Portals are inevitably subject to network effects: The value of the portal to advertisers and consumers increases geometrically as reach increases, which, in turn, attracts still more customers. These effects have resulted in the differentiation of the portal marketspace into three tiers: a few general-purpose mega

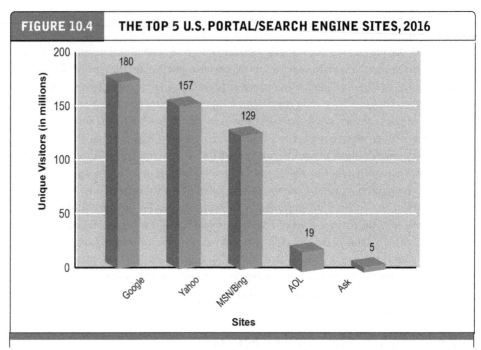

| FIGURE 10.4 | THE TOP 5 U.S. PORTAL/SEARCH ENGINE SITES, 2016 |

SOURCE: Based on data from Compete.com, 2016.

portal sites that garner 60%–80% of the web audience, second-tier general-purpose sites that hover around 20%–30% reach, and third-tier specialized vertical market portals that attract 2%–10% of the audience. As described in Chapter 2, the top five portals/ search engines (Google, Yahoo, MSN/Bing, AOL, and Ask) account for more than 95% of online searches in the United States. A similar pattern of concentration is observed when considering the audience share of portals/search engines (including both desktop and mobile) as illustrated in **Figure 10.4**. However, this picture is changing as large audiences move to social network sites, and millions of users make these sites their opening or home pages and the place where they spend most of their digital time. Social network sites like Facebook are broadening their content with videos, movies, and news, transforming themselves into a hybrid social network and portal.

For more insight into the nature of the competition and change among the top portals, read *Insight on Business: Verizon Doubles Down on Portals.*

TYPES OF PORTALS: GENERAL-PURPOSE AND VERTICAL MARKET

general-purpose portals

attempt to attract a very large general audience and then retain the audience on-site by providing in-depth vertical content

There are two primary types of portals: general-purpose portals and vertical market portals. **General-purpose portals** attempt to attract a very large general audience and then retain the audience on-site by providing in-depth vertical content channels, such as information on news, finance, autos, movies, and weather. General-purpose portals typically offer search engines, free e-mail, personal home pages, chat rooms, community-building software, and bulletin boards. Vertical content channels on general-purpose portal sites offer content such as sports scores, stock tickers, health tips, instant messaging, automobile information, and auctions.

INSIGHT ON BUSINESS

VERIZON DOUBLES DOWN ON PORTALS

In the early years of the Internet, portals were among the most high-profile of business models. AOL and Yahoo were two of the most prominent. In 2000, Time Warner bought AOL for $168 billion and Yahoo was worth about $128 billion. However, as the years passed, Google developed a stranglehold on the search market and social networks such as Facebook have largely usurped the role that portals originally played in online life. Both AOL and Yahoo struggled and undertook various efforts to transform their businesses to make them more relevant in today's online environment.

Over the last few years, Verizon, the U.S. broadband and wireless telecommunications giant, has been facing a similar issue, but for different reasons. Verizon is a direct descendant of the original Bell Telephone Company of the early 20th century. Today, Verizon is the largest wireless cell phone service provider in the United States, with 140 million subscribers (46% of the market), followed by AT&T with 128 million (33%). Other major providers include T-Mobile and Sprint. Verizon also controls around 35% of the landline (wireline) market. In 2015, Verizon generated revenue of $131 billion. Most of this (70%) came from its wireless cell phone network segment. The rest comes from its wireline segment, which owns and operates the copper and fiber optic cables in buildings, underground, and under the sea that are used by major corporations and Internet providers.

Despite Verizon's obvious size and market dominance, it is facing troubled times in the wireless business. Competitors like AT&T, Sprint, and T-Mobile have put a lid on the fees Verizon can charge wireless customers. Revenue in the wireless segment grew only 4% in 2015, while the wireline segment lost 1.5%. Microsoft, Google, Apple, Skype, and Facebook offer alternative communications over the Internet that drain revenue from all of the wireless telephone networks. The growth of Wi-Fi connections in urban areas also competes with Verizon cellular wireless networks. Smartphones typically default to Wi-Fi when available. The market for wireless experienced extraordinary growth following the introduction of the Apple iPhone in 2007, but the market for connecting people with mobile cell voice, text, and video is approaching saturation, and is no longer a growth story. It has become clear that there's more money in owning the media content, the audience, and the brand than owning the pipes. So in a remarkable, unprecedented corporate makeover, Verizon has decided to become an online media and digital advertising company, a business in which it has no prior experience!

To achieve its plan of becoming a major player in online media and advertising, Verizon needs to build an audience. To attract the audience, it needs digital content, preferably video, which seems to have an insatiable online audience. The plan target is 2 billion viewers by 2020. With billions of eyeballs, Verizon hopes to become a media and advertising power house that can challenge Facebook and YouTube (Google) for a sizable chunk of the burgeoning online ad market, which is growing at over 20% annually. Now that's high-tech growth country! Analysts wondered how a phone company could become an Internet media and ad company. The answer: buy them.

To put this plan in to action, in 2014, Verizon bought AOL for $4.4 billion. Analysts at the time wondered why Verizon would buy a fading star portal. The answer would soon become clear: an online audience of 400 million and lots of digital content. In addition, AOL also operated one of the

(continued)

largest digital advertising firms (AOL Platforms). With the AOL purchase, Verizon also picked up dozens of Internet content companies that AOL had previously acquired, such as video streaming firms EdgeCast Networks, OnCue, and UpLynk; blogs Engadget and TechCrunch; news sites like Huffington Post, along with three video platforms (5MinMedia, AdapTV, and Vidible); as well as a mobile advertising company Millennial Media, and a social sharing technology company, Thing Labs. If some of these names are unfamiliar, it's because they are mostly small, relatively unknown, short-form, low-budget video production and distribution companies focused on the teen and young adult audience. Verizon has also invested along with Hearst in ComplexMedia, a music and pop-culture site and along with DreamWorks Animation and Hearst in AwesomenessTV. AwesomenessTV started as a YouTube channel and has begun to create original web series, TV shows, and films aimed at teenagers. AwesomenessTV has 150 million subscribers. In 2015, Verizon launched go90, a free, ad-supported streaming service that offers original series such as *The Runner, Tween Fest,* and comedy shows. Verizon customers' accounts will not be charged minutes for using the service. Critics claim this is in violation of the FCC's new net neutrality regulations, which prohibit discrimination on basis of platform or content. Verizon is also pursuing more mainstream content and has been reported to be meeting with Hollywood production studios seeking original long-form programming that is suited to digital distribution. Hulu, Amazon, Netflix, and Google are the targets.

In 2016, expanding on this strategy, Verizon agreed to purchase Yahoo, another failing portal, for $4.83 billion. Yahoo was unsuccessful in developing its own original content, but is the king of display ads and supporting technology, with over 1 billion users worldwide, including 600 million who access the site via a mobile device. The acquisition is scheduled to close sometime during the first quarter of 2017.

If Verizon is successful in attracting 2 billion viewers by 2020, it can enter the rapidly growing business of Internet advertising, and compete with Facebook, Google, Microsoft, and other content companies in the streaming video market. Verizon's geolocation technology, which is built into its mobile network and keeps track of every mobile user around the clock, can be used to target users based on their activities and location. As the leading wireless provider, Verizon knows more about the location of people and things, and how they got there, than the people or things themselves.

There are plenty of doubters that Verizon can effectively manage all these acquisitions and become a multifaceted portal conglomerate. Verizon's supposed unique advantage is that it has a mobile customer base of 144 million customers and knows their location. So do Google Maps and Apple's iPhones. It is unclear at this point if Verizon can compete against the reigning Internet titans who now dominate social networks, web media, and online advertising. But it will be exciting to find out how this bet turns out.

SOURCES: "Yahoo and the Online Universe According to Verizon," by David Gelles, *New York Times,* July 30, 2016; "Verizon to Acquire Yahoo's Operating Business," PRNewswire, July 25, 2016; "The Problem with Verizon-Yahoo," by Erin Griffith, *Fortune,* July 25, 2016; "Inside Verizon's Gamble on Digital Media," by Ryan Knutson and Deepa Seetharaman, *Wall Street Journal,* July 24, 2016; "Verizon Finalizes $4.8 Billion Yahoo Deal," Ryan Knutson and Deep Seetharaman, *Wall Street Journal,* July 24, 2016; "Verizon's Multi-Billion Dollar Play to Take On Netflix, Amazon, Google, and Facebook," by Ainsley O'Connell, *Fast Company,* May 26, 2016; "Verizon Settles With F.C.C. Over Hidden Tracking via 'Supercookies,'" by Cecillia Kang, *New York Times,* March 7, 2016; "Verizon Communications Inc. Form 10-K filed with the Securities and Exchange Commission for the Fiscal Year Ended December 31, 2015," February 23, 2016; "All the Media Companies That Belong to Verizon Now," by Kate Knibbs, Gizmodo, May 12, 2015.

Vertical market portals (sometimes also referred to as destination sites or vortals) attempt to attract highly focused, loyal audiences with a deep interest in either community or specialized content—from sports to the weather. In addition to their focused content, vertical market portals have recently begun adding many of the features found in general-purpose portals. For instance, in addition to being a social network, you can also think of Facebook as a portal—the home page for millions of users, and a gateway to the Internet. Facebook is an affinity group portal because it is based on friendships among people. Facebook offers e-mail, search, games, and apps.

The concentration of audience share in the portal market reflects (in addition to network effects) the limited time budget of consumers. This limited time budget works to the advantage of general-purpose portals. Consumers have a finite amount of time to spend on the Web, and as a result, most consumers visit fewer than 30 unique domains each month. Facing limited time, consumers concentrate their visits at sites that can satisfy a broad range of interests, from weather and travel information, to stocks, sports, retail shopping, and entertainment content.

General-purpose sites such as Yahoo try to be all things to all people and attract a broad audience with both generalized navigation services and in-depth content and community efforts. For instance, Yahoo has become the Web's largest source of news: more people visit Yahoo News than any other news site including online newspapers. Yet recent changes in consumer behavior on the Web show that consumers are spending less time "surfing the Web" and on general browsing, and more time doing focused searches, research, and participating in social networks. These trends will advantage special-purpose, vertical market sites that can provide focused, in-depth community and content.

As a general matter, the general-purpose portals are very well-known brands, while the vertical content and affinity group portals tend to have less well-known brands. **Figure 10.5** lists examples of general-purpose portals and the two main types of vertical market portals.

vertical market portals
attempt to attract highly focused, loyal audiences with a deep interest in either community or specialized content

| FIGURE 10.5 | TWO GENERAL TYPES OF PORTALS: GENERAL-PURPOSE AND VERTICAL MARKET PORTALS |

GENERAL PURPOSE PORTALS	VERTICAL MARKET PORTALS	
	Affinity Group	Focused Content
Yahoo!	Facebook	ESPN.com
MSN	Sina.com	Bloomberg.com
AOL	Sify.com	NFL.com
Ask.com	Law.com	WebMD.com
	Ceoexpress.com	Gamers.com
		Away.com
		Econline.com
		Sailnet.com

There are two general types of portals: general-purpose and vertical market. Vertical market portals may be based on affinity groups or on focused content.

TABLE 10.7	TYPICAL PORTAL REVENUE SOURCES
PORTAL REVENUE SOURCE	DESCRIPTION
General advertising	Charging for impressions delivered
Tenancy deals	Fixed charge for guaranteed number of impressions, exclusive partnerships, "sole providers"
Commissions on sales	Revenue based on sales at the site by independent providers
Subscription fees	Charging for premium content
Applications and games	Games and apps are sold to users; advertising is placed within apps

PORTAL BUSINESS MODELS

Portals receive income from a number of different sources. The revenue base of portals is changing and dynamic, with some of the largest sources of revenue declining. **Table 10.7** summarizes the major portal revenue sources.

The business strategies of both general-purpose and vertical portals have changed greatly because of the rapid growth in search engine advertising and intelligent ad placement networks such as Google's AdSense, which can place ads on thousands of websites based on content. General portal sites such as AOL and Yahoo did not have well-developed search engines, and hence have not grown as fast as Google, which has a powerful search engine. Microsoft, for instance, has invested billions of dollars in its Bing search engine to catch up with Google. On the other hand, general portals have content, which Google did not originally have, although it added to its content by purchasing YouTube and adding Google sites devoted to news, financial information, images, and maps. Facebook users stay on-site and linger three times as long as visitors to traditional portals like Yahoo. For this reason social network sites, Facebook in particular, are direct competitors of Yahoo, Google, and the other portals. Yahoo has struggled in the last three years to grow revenues and earnings despite the fact that its unique visitor count has held steady with Google's. One part of the problem is the falling price of display ads, which are the mainstay of Yahoo's ad platform. Yahoo shows more display ads on its sites than any other web destination. Another key issue is declining user engagement with materials on the site and the amount of time spent on the site. To address these issues, Yahoo has made a number of acquisitions including Aviate, Tumblr, and Flickr, and launched digital magazines like Yahoo Food and Yahoo Tech that curate content from around the Web. The key to display ad revenue is content and engagement: the more you can show users, the longer they stay on your site, the more ad revenue can be generated. So far, Yahoo and the other general portal sites have not been able to compete with social network sites on these dimensions of engagement and time on site. After several years of pursuing unsuccessful new strategies, Yahoo agreed to sell itself to Verizon in 2016.

The survival strategy for general-purpose portals in the future is therefore to develop deep, rich vertical content in order to reach and engage customers at the site. This involves hiring professional journalists rather than relying on bloggers who write listicle articles, and offering more quality entertainment in the form of movies, TV series, and music. The strategy for much smaller vertical market portals is to put together a collection of vertical portals to form a vertical portal network, a collection of deep, rich content sites. The strategy for search engine sites such as Google is to obtain more content to attract users for a long time and expose them to more ad pages (or screens).

eBay Evolves

When you hear someone mention online auctions, the first site that comes to mind is likely eBay. Founded in 1995 as an offbeat, quirky place to buy and sell almost anything via auctions, eBay now derives the majority of its revenue from traditional e-commerce. As the company continues to model its business after competitors such as Amazon and Alibaba, eBay has banned the sales of quirkier services like tarot card readings and magic spells, and has instituted a rewards program with prominent retail chains like Dick's Sporting Goods and Toys "R" Us.

The transformation began in November 2007, when former CEO Meg Whitman exited and was replaced by John Donahoe. The company had already begun to stall, and the trend continued through 2009. For many buyers, the novelty of online auctions had worn off, and they were returning to easier and simpler methods of buying fixed-price goods from retailers such as Amazon, which, by comparison, had steady growth during the same time period. Search engines and comparison shopping sites were also taking away some of eBay's auction business by making items easier to find on the Web.

Donahoe quickly found that dramatically altering the business model of an Internet company is never easy, particularly when that company is one of the most recognizable sites on the Web. His three-year revival plan moved eBay away from its origins as an

© Iain Masterton/Alamy Stock Photo

online flea market, and at first it began to resemble an outlet mall where retailers sold out-of-season, overstocked, refurbished, or discontinued merchandise. From there it was a straightforward progression to partnering with retail chains to simply serve as another channel for current merchandise.

Small sellers were encouraged to shift away from the auction format and move toward the fixed-price sales model. The fee structure was adjusted, listing fees for fixed-price sales were lowered, improvements were made to the search engine, and rather than displaying ending auctions first, a formula was devised that took into account price and seller reputation so that highly rated merchants appeared first and received more exposure.

Unsurprisingly, the growing pains during this period included increasing complaints from sellers about excessive fees and eBay's favoritism toward big retailers. The hundreds of thousands of people who supported themselves by selling on eBay and many millions more who used eBay to supplement their income often felt slighted. With its stock continuing to drop, analysts' faith that Donahoe could turn things around dwindled. This pessimism failed to account for eBay's history of sensible growth marked by a number of canny purchases.

Its signature purchase was, of course, PayPal, whose payment services enable the exchange of money between individuals over the Internet. This acquisition was the key to eBay's endurance through the lean years, protecting it from weakness in its auction business, and the propeller that pushed it towards the future. PayPal has accounted for over 40% of eBay's revenues at its peak, and was a significant factor in eBay's growth.

eBay recognized the coming mobile revolution even before the first iPhone or the establishment of the App Store, according to Olivier Ropars, senior director of Mobile Commerce. This prescience resulted in eBay achieving its 100 millionth app download and 100 millionth mobile listing relatively early on, in 2012. Dating back to 2010, eBay has been actively acquiring companies specializing in mobile technologies, such as barcode scanning app RedLaser, mobile app developer Critical Path, mobile payment and billing firm Zong, and mobile payment startup Fig Card. In 2013, eBay acquired mobile payment gateway Braintree for $800 million. Braintree's technology allows eBay consumers to more easily make payments on smartphones and tablets, and the acquisition also eliminated a major competitor in that space for PayPal. In 2015, eBay introduced an app for the Apple Watch that allows users to see an overview of their notifications and bid statuses. The company also rolled out more updates for their iOS and Android apps that improve the quality of search results. In 2016, eBay remains on the cutting edge of online retail, redesigning its core mobile platform and adding biometric touch identification support, launching its Marketplace app for Android Wear wearable devices, and releasing a virtual reality feature on StubHub that allows customers to see their prospective seats from any angle. Over 50% of eBay's business now involves a mobile device, and the company continues to make improvements to the mobile experience across all of its different services.

While many other acquisitions through the years have also helped to transform eBay from an online garage sale to a mainstream competitor with Amazon, its adoption of the "social, mobile, local" driving theme has been central to its survival. Positioning itself at the center of the online—offline—mobile triangle by offering a wide variety of

SOURCES: "PayPal Introduces an SDK for PayPal Here, Its Square-like Credit Card Reader," by Roberto Baldwin, Thenextweb.com,

September 4, 2014; "eBay's 900 Million Dollar Question," by Chad Henage, Motley Fool, June 17, 2014; "Alibaba Takes on eBay, Etsy with U.S.-based Shopping Site," by Gail Sullivan, *Washington Post,* June 11, 2014; "Web? Store? Mobile? Shoppers Want It All," by Don Davis, Internetretailer.com, June 11, 2014; "Did Panda Really Beat Up On eBay?" by Thad Rueter, Internetretailer.com, June 9, 2014; "eBay Plays the Field," by Katie Evans, Internetretailer.com, June 2, 2014; "How the Once Impregnable eBay Fell Victim to Hackers (and You Can Too)," by Jeremy Quittner, Inc.com, May 30, 2014; "eBay Reports 13% Sales Growth and Rejects PayPal Spinoff," by Katie Evans, Internetretailer.com, January 22, 2014; "Behind eBay's $800M Buy: Braintree will Replace PayPal's Developer Platform," by Kevin Fitchard, Gigaom.com, September 26, 2013; "Amazon, eBay Lead Way as E-Commerce Sales Still Surge," by Brian Deagon, *Investor's Business Daily*, July 2, 2013; "eBay Hits 100m Mobile App Download Mark," by Dervedia Thomas, Dailydealmedia.com, September 29, 2012; "eBay: We Need to Behave More Like a Retailer," by Sarah Shearman, Tamebay.com, September 25, 2012; "eBay Logo Gets a Refresh; The Time Felt Right After 17 Years," by Mark Tyson, Hexus.com, September 14, 2012; "eBay Bans Magic Spells and Potions," by Katy Waldman, Slate.com, August 17, 2012; "Behind eBay's Comeback," by James B. Stewart, *New York Times*, July 27, 2012; "Bill Me Later, eBay's Credit Version of PayPal, Helps Company's Profits but Exposes It to Risk," by Alistair Barr, MercuryNews.com, July 12, 2012; "PayPal Strength Helps eBay Exceed Forecasts," by Somini Sengupta, *New York Times*, April 18, 2012; "eBay Favors Big-Box Retailers in Holiday Promotions," by Ina Steiner, eCommerce-Bytes.com, December, 16, 2011; "How Jack Abraham Is Reinventing eBay," by Danielle Sacks, *Fast Company*, June 22, 2011; "Connecting the Dots on eBay's Local Shopping Strategy," by Leena Rao, Techcrunch.com, May 15, 2011; "eBay CEO Sees Opportunities in Online and Offline Commerce," by Scott Morrison, *Wall Street Journal,* February 10, 2011.

services that enable merchants to more easily integrate their cross-channel retailing has been the key to eBay's resurgence and to its continued success.

In 2016, the company has also started the process of modernizing its platform with analytical tools. First, the company has started to convert its catalog of items from its traditional unstructured "listing" format, where two identical items can appear totally different to shoppers, to a structured data format. This will allow eBay to more easily gain information about different items and about purchasing trends. eBay is also using machine learning to customize, update, and generally improve its product pages, as well as to fine-tune its search capability beyond simply matching search terms with keywords and tags. To support these efforts, in 2016, the company purchased machine-learning startup SalesPredict, whose technology helps businesses predict consumer buying behavior and sales conversion. Finally, the company's revamped Seller Hub will offer many of these analytical tools and metrics to individual sellers, including inventory, order, and listing management, performance insights, and streamlined business process management.

However, eBay's return to prominence is not without continuing challenges. In 2014, eBay was the victim of a hacking attack that compromised the information of nearly 150 million of its customers. Paypal was unaffected, and the company doesn't believe that any financial information was stolen, but the incident underscored the need for eBay to remain vigilant with its security measures. eBay sales decreased steeply in the wake of the breach, dropping 5.4% in 10 days. Competitors are also ramping up their efforts to battle eBay, with Amazon continuing to focus on third-party sales and Alibaba announcing a U.S.-based site to compete with eBay called 11 Main. What's more, Google rolled out an update to its search algorithm, reducing eBay's search traffic by as much as 33%. eBay hopes that standardizing its product pages will also help improve its rankings in Google searches.

In 2015, eBay elected to spin off PayPal as its own separate company, leaving eBay with its Marketplaces segment, its StubHub ticket sales segment, and a handful of other business units. Although Donahoe and the rest of eBay's leadership had resisted a spinoff for years, the move was prompted by a desire for PayPal to distinguish itself from eBay and become more agile within the rapidly-developing marketplace of online payments. Donahoe also stepped down as CEO of eBay to mark the transition, with the former head of its Global Marketplaces unit, Devin Wenig, taking his place. As part of the split, eBay has agreed to route 80% of its sales through PayPal, but PayPal is free to pursue deals with other merchants, potentially boosting its market share even further.

Many investors believed that PayPal had been the true driver of eBay's bottom line. But while analysts had prepared themselves for disappointing earnings, the company has instead posted several straight quarters of sales growth under Wenig as of 2016. This includes a 5.7% increase over its earnings from the previous year in the second quarter of 2016, with $2.23 billion in revenue, up from $2.11 billion in 2015. The company also reported that it expected continued growth for the upcoming quarters. Despite Amazon's ongoing dominance in online retail, eBay remains one of the most trusted online brands and e-commerce leaders, and it has worked hard to improve its marketplace design and offerings for dedicated users, including eBay Now, its new same-day delivery program. Will eBay be able to respond to these new challenges as well as it has to those in the past without PayPal to bolster it? After some ups and downs, eBay appears to be on a winning trajectory once again.

Case Study Questions

1. Contrast eBay's original business model with its current business model.

2. What are the problems that eBay is currently facing? How is eBay trying to solve these problems?

3. Are the solutions eBay is seeking to implement good solutions? Why or why not? Are there any other solutions that eBay should consider?

4. Who are eBay's top competitors online, and how will eBay's strategy help it compete?

10.5 REVIEW

KEY CONCEPTS

■ **Describe the different types of social networks and online communities and their business models.**

- Social networks involve a group of people, shared social interaction, common ties among members, and a shared area for some period of time. An online social network is one where people who share common ties can interact with one another online.
- The different types of social networks and communities and their business models include:
  - *General communities:* Members can interact with a general audience segmented into numerous different groups. Most general communities began as non-commercial subscription-based endeavors, but many have been purchased by larger community portal sites.
  - *Practice networks:* Members can participate in discussion groups and get help or information relating to an area of shared practice, such as art, education, or medicine. These generally have a nonprofit business model in which they simply attempt to collect enough in subscription fees, sales commissions, and limited advertising to cover the cost of operations.
  - *Interest-based communities:* Members can participate in focused discussion groups on a shared interest. The advertising business model has worked because the targeted audience is attractive to marketers. Tenancy and sponsorship deals provide another similar revenue stream.
  - *Affinity communities:* Members can participate in focused discussions with others who share the same affinity or group identification. The business model is a mixture of subscription revenue from premium content and services, advertising, tenancy/sponsorships, and distribution agreements.
  - *Sponsored communities:* Members can participate in online communities created by government, nonprofit, or for-profit organizations for the purpose of pursuing organizational goals. They use community technologies and techniques to distribute information or extend brand influence. The goal of a branded product site is to increase offline product sales. These sites do not seek to make a profit and are often cost centers.

■ **Describe the major types of auctions, their benefits and costs, how they operate, when to use them, and the potential for auction abuse and fraud.**

- Auctions are markets where prices vary (dynamic pricing) depending on the competition among the participants who are buying or selling products or services. They can be classified broadly as C2C or B2C, although generally the term *C2C auction* refers to the venue in which the sale takes place, for example, a consumer-oriented website such as eBay, which also auctions items from established merchants. A *B2C auction* refers to an established online merchant that offers its own auctions. There are also numerous B2B online auctions for buyers of industrial parts, raw materials, commodities, and services. Within these three broad categories of auctions are several major auction types classified based upon how the bidding mechanisms work in each system:

- *English auctions:* A single item is up for sale from a single seller. Multiple buyers bid against one another within a specific time frame with the highest bidder winning the object as long as the high bid has exceeded the reserve bid set by the seller, below which he or she refuses to sell.
- *Dutch Internet auctions:* Sellers with many identical items for sale list a minimum price or starting bid, and buyers indicate both a bid price and a quantity desired. The lowest winning bid that clears the available quantity is paid by all winning bidders. Those with the highest bid are assured of receiving the quantity they desire but only pay the amount of the lowest successful bid (uniform pricing rule).
- *Name Your Own Price* or *reverse auctions:* Buyers specify the price they are willing to pay for an item, and multiple sellers bid for their business. This is one example of discriminatory pricing in which winners may pay different amounts for the same product or service depending on how much they have bid.
- *Penny (bidding fee) auctions:* Bidder pay a non-refundable fee to purchase bids.

- Benefits of auctions include: liquidity, price discovery, price transparency, market efficiency, lower transaction costs, consumer aggregation, network effects, and market-maker benefits.
- Costs of auctions include: delayed consumption, monitoring costs, equipment costs, trust risks, and fulfillment costs.
- Auction sites have sought to reduce these risks through various methods including rating systems, watch lists, and proxy bidding.
- Auctions can be an appropriate channel for businesses to sell items in a variety of situations. The factors for businesses to consider include the type of product, the product life cycle, channel management, the type of auction, initial pricing, bid increments, auction length, number of items, price allocation, and closed versus open bidding.
- Auctions are particularly prone to fraud, which produces information asymmetries between buyers and sellers. Some of the possible abuses and frauds include bid rigging, price matching, defensive shill feedback, offensive shill feedback, feedback extortion, transaction interference, bid manipulation, non-payment after winning, shill bidding, transaction non-performance, non-selling sellers, and bid siphoning.

■ **Describe the major types of Internet portals and their business models.**

- Portals are gateways to billions of web pages available on the Internet. Originally, their primary purpose was to help users find information on the Web, but they evolved into destination sites that provided a myriad of content from news to entertainment. Today, portals serve three main purposes: navigation of the Web (search), content, and commerce.
- Among the major portal types are:
  - *Enterprise portals:* Corporations, universities, churches, and other organizations create these sites to help employees or members navigate to important content such as corporate news or organizational announcements.
  - *General-purpose portals:* Examples are AOL, Yahoo, and MSN, which try to attract a very large general audience by providing many in-depth vertical content channels. Some also offer ISP services on a subscription basis, search engines, e-mail, chat, bulletin boards, and personal home pages.
  - *Vertical market portals:* Also called destination sites, they attempt to attract a highly focused, loyal audience with an intense interest in either a community they belong to or an interest they hold.

Vertical market portals can be divided into two main classifications, although hybrids that overlap the two classifications also exist.

- *Affinity groups:* Designed to serve aggregates of people who identify themselves by their attitudes, values, beliefs, and behavior.
- *Focused content portals:* These sites contain in-depth information on a particular topic that all members are interested in. They can provide content on such broad topics as sports, news, weather, entertainment, finance, or business, or they can appeal to a much more focused interest group such as boat, horse, or video game enthusiasts.

- Portals receive revenue from a number of different sources. The business model is presently changing and adapting to declines in certain revenue streams, particularly advertising revenues. Revenue sources can include general advertising, tenancy deals, subscription fees, and commissions on sales.
- The survival strategy for general-purpose portals is to develop deep, rich vertical content in order to attract advertisers to various niche groups that they can target with focused ads. The strategy for the small vertical market portals is to build a collection of vertical portals, thereby creating a network of deep, rich content sites for the same reason.

QUESTIONS

1. What is an online social network?
2. How does a social network differ from a portal? How are the two similar?
3. What are some ways to measure the business potential and influence of a social network site?
4. List and describe the five generic types of social networks and online communities.
5. How is Twitter changing in an attempt to show a profit?
6. List and describe three social networks focused on messaging.
7. List and describe four different types of auctions.
8. What is trigger pricing and how is it used?
9. How does a Dutch Internet auction differ from an English auction?
10. What role do algorithms play in social networks?
11. Name and describe five types of possible abuses and frauds that may occur with auctions.
12. What three characteristics define a portal site today?
13. Why have the business strategies of portals changed? How has this impacted Yahoo?
14. List and briefly explain the main revenue sources for the portal business model.
15. Why are mobile social networks growing so fast?
16. What is a sponsored community?
17. What are some of the unintended results of participating in auctions?
18. What are the dangers of a penny (bidding fee) auction?
19. What is herd behavior and how does it impact auctions?
20. Why did Verizon acquire AOL?

PROJECTS

1. Find two examples of an affinity portal and two examples of a focused-content portal. Prepare a presentation explaining why each of your examples should be categorized as an affinity portal or a focused-content portal. For each example, surf the site and describe the services each site provides. Try to determine what revenue model each of your examples is using and, if possible, how many members or registered visitors the site has attracted.

2. Examine the use of auctions by businesses. Go to any auction site of your choosing and look for outlet auctions or auctions directly from merchants. Research at least three products for sale. What stage in the

product life cycle do these products fall into? Are there quantity purchasing requirements? What was the opening bid price? What are the bid increments? What is the auction duration? Analyze why these firms have used the auction channel to sell these goods and prepare a short report on your findings.

3. Visit one for-profit and one nonprofit sponsored social network. Create a presentation to describe and demonstrate the offering at each site. What organizational objectives is each pursuing? How is the for-profit company using community-building technologies as a customer relations management tool?

4. Visit one of the social networks listed in Table 10.1 and compare it to Facebook. In what ways is it similar to Facebook, and in what ways is it different? Which do you prefer, and why?

REFERENCES

Arkes, H. R., and L. Hutzel. "The Role of Probability of Success Estimates in the Sunk Cost Effect." *Journal of Behavioral Decisionmaking* (2000).

Bailey, Brian P., Laura J. Gurak, and Joseph Konstan. "Do You Trust Me? An Examination of Trust in Computer-Mediated Exchange," In *Human Factors and Web Development*, 2nd Edition. Mahwah, NJ: Lawrence Erlbaum (2002).

Barnes, Nora, Ava Lescault, and Glenn Holmes. "The 2015 Fortune 500 and Social Media: Instagram Gains, Blogs Lose." University of Massachusetts (Dartmouth) (2015).

Bloomapp.co "About Us." (accessed October 10, 2016).

Compete.com. "August 2016 Unique Visitors." (accessed October 8, 2016a).

comScore. "Top 50 Multi-Platform Properties (Desktop and Mobile) August 2016." (August 2016a).

comScore. "The 2016 U.S. Mobile App Report." (2016b).

Consumerreports.org. "With Penny Auctions, You Can Spend a Bundle But Still Leave Empty-Handed." (June 30, 2014).

Cormen, Thomas H. and Charles E. Leiserson, Ronald L. Rivest, and Clifford Stein. *Introduction to Algorithms, 3rd Edition* (MIT Press) 3rd Edition. MIT Press, 2009.

Data Center Knowledge. "The Facebook Data Center FAQ." Datacenterknowledge.com (September 16, 2016).

Dholakia, Utpal, and Kerry Soltysinski. "Coveted or Overlooked? The Psychology of Bidding for Comparable Listings in Digital Auctions." *Marketing Letters* (2001).

eBay, Inc. "Form 10-K for the Fiscal Year Ended December 31, 2015." Filed with the Securities and Exchange Commission. (February 1, 2016).

eMarketer, Inc. (Cindy Liu). "Worldwide Social Network Users: eMarketer's Estimates for 2016." (June 2016a).

eMarketer, Inc. "US Facebook Users, by Age, 2015–2020." (August 3, 2016b).

eMarketer, Inc. "Net Digital Ad Revenues Worldwide, by Company, 2015–2018." (September 1, 2016c).

eMarketer, Inc. "Instagram Ad Revenue Worldwide, 2014–2019. (September 1, 2016d).

Facebook. "Newsroom/Company Info." (accessed October 5, 2016).

Hafner, Katie. "The Epic Saga of The Well: The World's Most Influential Online Community (and It's Not AOL)." Wired (May 1997).

Hagel, John III, and Arthur G. Armstrong. *Net Gain: Expanding Markets Through Virtual Communities.* Cambridge, MA: Harvard Business School Press (1997).

Hanson, Ward, and D. S. Putler. "Hits and Misses: Herd Behavior and Online Product Popularity." Marketing Letters (1996).

Hillery, George A. "Definitions of Community: Areas of Agreement." *Rural Sociology* (1955).

Hiltzik, Michael. *Dealers of Lightning: Xerox PARC and the Dawn of the Computer Age.* New York: Harper Collins (1999).

Instagram. "Press News." (accessed October 5, 2016).

Kiesler, Sara. "The Hidden Messages in Computer Networks." *Harvard Business Review* (January–February 1986).

Kiesler, Sara, Jane Siegel, and Timothy W. McGuire. "Social Psychological Aspects of Computer-Mediated Communication." *American Psychologist* (October 1984).

Kollock, Peter. "The Production of Trust in Online Markets." In *Advances in Group Processes* (Vol 16), edited by E. J. Lawler, M. Macy, S. Thyne, and H. A. Walker. Greenwich, CT: JAI Press (1999).

Krishnamurthy, Sandeep. "An Empirical Study of the Causal Antecedents of Customer Confidence in E-tailers." *First Monday* (January 2001).

Laudon, Kenneth C., and Jane P. Laudon. *Management Information Systems: Managing the Digital Firm. 15th edition.* Upper Saddle River, NJ, Prentice Hall (2016).

Liu, Yi, and Juliana Sutanto. "Buyers' Purchasing Time and Herd Behavior on Deal-of-the-Day Group-buying Websites." *Electronic Markets* (June 2012).

Nikander, Pekka, and Kristina Karvonen. "Users and Trust in Cyberspace." In the Proceedings of Cambridge Security Protocols Workshop 2000, April 3–5, 2000, Cambridge University (2002).

Parkes, David C., and Lyle Ungar. "Iterative Combinatorial Auctions: Theory and Practice." *Proceedings of the 17th National Conference on Artificial Intelligence (AAAI-00)* (2000).

Rheingold, Howard. *Hosting Web Communities.* New York: John Wiley and Sons (1998). Also see Rheingold.com for more recent articles by Rheingold.

Rheingold, Howard. *The Virtual Community.* Cambridge, MA: MIT Press (1993).

Rosenbloom, Stephanie. "For the Plugged-In, Too Many Choices." *New York Times* (August 10, 2011).

Simonson, Itamar, and Amos Tversky. "Choice in Context: Tradeoff Contrast and Extremeness Aversion." *Journal of Marketing Research,* Vol. 20, 281–287 (1992).

Stanford Persuasive Technology Lab and Makovsky & Company. "Stanford-Makovsky Web Credibility Study 2002." Stanford Persuasive Technology Lab. (Spring 2002).

United States Patent and Trademark Office. "U.S. Patent 7,827,208 B2." (November 2, 2010).

CHAPTER 11

E-commerce Retailing and Services

LEARNING OBJECTIVES

After reading this chapter, you will be able to:

- Understand the environment in which the online retail sector operates today.
- Explain how to analyze the economic viability of an online firm.
- Identify the challenges faced by the different types of online retailers.
- Describe the major features of the online service sector.
- Discuss the trends taking place in the online financial services industry.
- Describe the major trends in the online travel services industry today.
- Identify current trends in the online career services industry.
- Understand the business models of on-demand service companies.

Souq.com:

The Amazon of the Middle East

© Fenton/Fotolia.com

W hen Souq.com was launched in 2005, e-commerce in the Middle East and North Africa (MENA) region was in its infancy. With no local roadmap to follow, its original parent company Maktoob, a 1998 Internet pioneer that provided the first free Arabic-supported e-mail service, chat, greeting cards, and content channels, opted to follow the successful auction format forged ten years earlier in the West by eBay. A souq, or souk, is a traditional Arab marketplace at which a wide range of products from wood carvings and rugs to spices and food are exchanged through a bargaining process between buyer and seller. In spite of the apropos name, Dubai-based Souq struggled to thrive, especially after Maktoob was purchased by Yahoo in 2009 and Souq was left to fend for itself.

Transactions between Gulf States with different currencies, laws, and regulations complicated trans-country shipping, often necessitating bank accounts in each country and requiring local business partners. Inventory management was also a challenge. And customers were reluctant to use online payment systems, preferring cash on delivery (COD) to entering credit card details online. These problems have plagued MENA retail and service e-commerce, and while more consumers in the region than ever are using online payment systems for e-commerce, a full 50% of purchases are still made using COD.

Though Souq initially pursued a model akin to eBay, it soon began cultivating relationships with small businesses, encouraging them to enter online retailing in the cost-effective atmosphere of an online marketplace. Through trial and error, Souq discovered that the "Buy-It-Now" model was superior to the auction format in nations where auctions were not culturally accepted. Now considered the Amazon of the Middle East, Souq has outperformed its peers in both securing investors and encouraging entrepreneurs to launch their businesses through its site. Meanwhile, its original parent company Maktoob ceased operations in 2014.

In 2011, Souq fully switched to the fixed-price model. Souq also revamped its website in 2012, prioritizing improvements to usability and search. Souq also added fulfillment centers and warehouses, hired delivery and warehouse personnel trained in modernized logistics systems, and updated its data storage systems to bolster security.

The Egypt-based Fawry electronic bill payment service helped overcome consumer reluctance to shop online. Buyers can go to an ATM, post office, or one of 3,000 authorized retailers including grocery stores and pharmacies to pay for online purchases. If the customer does not have a bank account, as is common in the region, cash can be deposited into the Fawry network at the local corner store. Souq now also owns its own payment service, Payfort, which it hopes to expand into offline payments and point-of-sale services akin to Square. The company also partnered with MasterCard in 2016 to provide improved payment options for its customers.

E-commerce in the MENA region is still dominated by men, and Souq has made attracting female customers a priority. To that end, Souq purchased Sukar.com, a high-fashion flash sales site, in 2012 to bolster its burgeoning fashion division. Sukar benefitted from the use of Souq's logistics and delivery systems while Souq gained customer service and fashion expertise and reinforced its position as the leading e-commerce site in the region. While women have lagged behind men as e-commerce consumers in the MENA region, increased Internet access at home and increased mobile device usage has led to a growth in e-commerce purchases by women.

The integration of Sukar with Souq and the launch of Souq Fashion positioned Souq to capitalize on this budding market segment. While in the West around 11% to 15% of fashion sales are derived from e-commerce, in the MENA region only a meager 1% of the $30 billion in fashion purchases are online. Supported by the new website design and advised by stylists for prominent stars including Jennifer Lopez and Rihanna, Souq Fashion provides the traditional counterpart to the daily flash sale specials offered on Sukar. High fashion from over 80 designers, including Arabic luminaries such as Dina JSR, Ronald Abdala, and Dima Ayad, are offered at reasonable price points with the additional benefit of advice from stylists.

All of these improving conditions, investments, acquisitions, and upgrades have generated significant interest in Souq from investors. In 2012, South African media group Naspers and New York hedge fund Tiger Global Management purchased a stake in Souq worth an estimated $40 million, with Naspers providing additional funding in 2014 and Tiger in 2015. In 2016, Souq completed its largest round of funding to date, raising more than $275 million from a combination of Tiger, Naspers, and a slew of other high-powered investors. The 2016 round of funding was the largest ever raised in the Middle East and gave Souq a valuation of over $1 billion, making it the first company from the MENA region to achieve the "unicorn" designation for companies worth a billion or more. Later in 2016, Souq began making plans to sell a 30% stake in the company at a valuation of $1.2 billion, but many reports have indicated that Amazon might not only be interested in that stake, but also in purchasing the entirety of Souq for upwards of $1 billion. This would give Amazon the ability to use Souq's local infrastructure to sell to MENA customers without being forced to ship items from overseas as well as a huge new base of customers to market its Amazon Prime video streaming service.

With the influx of cash, Souq has continued to expand its operations in the United Arab Emirates (UAE), Saudi Arabia, and Egypt. It currently features approximately 2 million products. Souq has continued its support for and expansion of its network of 70,000 entrepreneurial sellers such as KAF, a weaving company; NAS, a design-printed T-shirts

SOURCES: "Saudi Sovereign Wealth Fund Launches Noon, Middle East's Take on Amazon," by Angela Gonzalez-Rodriguez, Fashionunited.in, December 15, 2016; "Souq.com to Offer Same Day Delivery Across GCC by H1," Arabiansupplychain.com, December 14, 2016; "Amazon Purchase of Souq.com Would Be Great News for UAE Residents," by Peter Nowak, Thenational.ae, November 30, 2016; "Bumper 'White Friday' Weekend for Souq.com with Surge in Online Shopping," by Andrew Scott, Thenational.ae, November 27, 2016; "Amazon Is Said to Be Discussing a $1 Billion Purchase of Dubai's Souq.com," by Feliz Solomon, *Fortune*, November 25, 2016; "Souq CEO Not Worried by $1bn Rival Noon.com as Sales Weekend Approaches," by Robert Anderson, Gulfbusiness.com, November 16, 2016; "Dubai's Souq.com Said to Plan Stake Sale at $1.2 Billion Value," by Dinesh Nair, Arif Sharif, and Archana Narayanan, Bloomberg.com, September 7, 2016; "Souq.com and MasterCard Partner to Offer a World-Class Payment Experience for Customers," Mastercard.com, April 11, 2016; "The Middle East's First Unicorn: Souq.com's CEO on Leadership, Timing, and Coping with Rejection," by Elizabeth MacBride, *Forbes*, March 25, 2016; "Souq, Amazon of the Middle East, Raises $275M From Tiger and More at a $1B Valuation," by Ingrid Lunden, TechCrunch, February 29, 2016; "Souq, Online company; the Joud Store, a company that creates home accessories, mugs, coaster-art and trays from tiles; and Skinzo, a laptop covers company. The company also announced same-day delivery for the first time in 2016, initially available only in Dubai, but with plans to expand the service to other major regional sities like Abu Dhabi, Riyadh, and Cairo.

Souq has embraced mobile technology and social media as it attempts to increase its worldwide visibility and bolster its branding and marketing efforts. Souq's Facebook page has over 8.2 million likes, and the company maintains multiple active Twitter accounts focused on different areas of operation, like the UAE and Egypt, with flash deals and other useful information. In 2015, Souq launched its app for the Windows 10 operating system, featuring different catalogs for each of Souq's major markets and special deals exclusive to app users. In 2016, mobile customers represented more than half of all traffic on Souq.com and made 70% of purchases in Saudi Arabia, and closer to 60% in other markets of operation, justifying Souq's emphasis on strengthening its mobile platform.

Souq has worked to improve its visibility in the MENA region. In 2013, Souq unveiled its first regional advertising campaigns across its major market segments, displaying colorful characters interrupted by Souq deliveries. Souq established Egypt's first Internet-based youth commerce training academy and has also entered agreements with universities like the Canadian University of Dubai to promote entrepreneurship and help a new wave of young people in the MENA region develop tech skills. Souq has even launched its own hardware, including the QTAB tablet computer, aimed at Arabic consumers.

Given that online purchasing represents a much smaller fraction of total purchases in the MENA region than it does in the rest of the world, still checking in at about 1–2% compared to the mid- to high teens in England, Souq's potential for growth in 2016 and beyond remains strong—e-commerce is growing approximately 60% every year in the Middle East, indicating that the region is destined to catch up quickly. Souq has even outpaced those figures, growing ten-fold in the last three years and with expectations of growing 30% to 40% in 2017. On "White Friday," Souq's version of America's Black Friday shopping period, Souq reported sales of more than 1.2 million units in 2016, more than double the 600,000 units it sold in 2015, with 50% of those sales coming from Souq's mobile app. However, Souq is not the only company targeting this growing market. Other competitors include Noon, a Saudi-backed e-commerce startup that emphatically announced its arrival with initial funding of $1 billion in late 2016; Rocket Internet-backed MENA e-tailer Namshi, which posted improved results in 2016; and a slew of other hopefuls including Wadi.com and JadoPado. This is a growing market with room for multiple winners, and Souq is well positioned to be a force in e-commerce despite its growing competition.

Retailer in Middle East, Gets a $275 Million Boost," by Sara Hamdan, *New York Times*, February 29, 2016; "Souq.com: Riding High on the E-Commerce Wave," by Dina al-Wakeel, Venturemagazine.me, January 28, 2016; "Souq.com Traffic Surges on Rise in Smartphone Use," by Andrew Scott, Thenational.ae, October 15, 2015; "Souq.com Chief Explains One of Dubai's Biggest Online Success Stories," by Jessica Hill, Thenational.ae, October 7, 2015; "Tiger-backed Souq.com Said Worth $1 Billion in Fundraising," by Dinesh Nair, Matthew Martin, and Arif Sharif, Bloomberg.com, April 14, 2015; "Ronaldo Mouchawar: How I Created Souq.com," by Ed Attwood, Arabianbusiness.com, April 5, 2014; "Souq.com, Dubai-based E-commerce Site, Raises $75 Million," by Rory Jones, *Wall Street Journal*, March 24, 2014; "Souq.com Launches Low-cost QTAB Tablet in UAE," telecompaper.com, September 30, 2013; "After Many Slip-Ups, Mideast E-Commerce Gains Its Footing," by Sara Hamdan, *New York Times*, November 7, 2012; "South Africa's Naspers Swoops on Middle East with Souq.com Buy," by Lance Harris, Zdnet.com, October 31, 2012; "Souq Fashion Launches to Boost High-End Online Retail in the Arab World," by Rania Habib, Wamda.com, October 23, 2012; "Souq in Egypt: Not Relinquishing Its Crown Anytime Soon," by Omar Aysha, Wamda.com, October 18, 2012; "Why Middle East E-Commerce Site Souq.com Acquired Sister Site Sukar.com," by Nina Curley, Wamda.com, April 29, 2012; "How to Launch an E-commerce Business," Wamda.com, April 14, 2011; "Refocus of Souq.com Will End Auction Service," by David George-Cosh, Thenational.ae, January 2, 2011.

T he opening case illustrates some of the difficulties that a pure-play startup retail company such as Souq faces, particularly when starting out in a part of the world, such as the Middle East and North Africa, that has not already embraced e-commerce. Pure-play start-up companies often have razor-thin profit margins, lack a physical store network to bolster sales to the non-Internet audience, and are often based on unproven business assumptions that, in the long term, may not bear out. In contrast, large offline retailers have established brand names, a huge real estate investment, a loyal customer base, and established inventory control and fulfillment systems. In Souq's case, it originally adopted a business model based on the assumption that C2C auctions would find ready acceptance in its marketspace, when in fact they did not. Luckily for Souq, it was able to successfully transition to a B2C model and take advantage of some of the benefits that this model offers. For instance, a pure-play B2C company can simplify the existing industry supply chain and instead develop a Web-based distribution system that may be more efficient than traditional retail outlets.

As with retail goods, the promise of online service providers is that they can deliver superior-quality service and greater convenience to millions of consumers at a lower cost than established bricks-and-mortar service providers and still make a respectable return on invested capital. The service sector is one of the most natural avenues for e-commerce because so much of the value in services is based on collecting, storing, and exchanging information—something for which the Web is ideally suited. And, in fact, online services have been extraordinarily successful in attracting banking, brokerage, travel, and job-hunting customers. The quality and amount of information online to support consumer decisions in finance, travel, and career placement is extraordinary, especially when compared to what was available to consumers before e-commerce. The online service sector—like online retail—has established a significant beachhead and now plays a large role in consumer time on the Internet. In areas such as brokerage, banking, and travel, online services are an extraordinary success story and have transformed their industries. In Sections 11.5–11.7 of this chapter, we take a close look at three of the most successful online services: financial services (including insurance and real estate), travel services, and career services. In Section 11.8, we examine the new on-demand services companies, such as Uber, Airbnb, and a whole host of others, that have rocketed to prominence in the last several years. Using a business model that is both local and mobile, this new type of service company provides a platform for consumers to connect with providers who can provide on-demand services, such as transportation, short-term room rental, grocery shopping, and more.

11.1 THE ONLINE RETAIL SECTOR

Table 11.1 summarizes some of these leading trends in online retailing for 2016–2017. Perhaps the most important theme in online retailing is the effort by retailers—both

TABLE 11.1	**WHAT'S NEW IN ONLINE RETAIL 2016–2017**

- Retail mobile e-commerce is exploding, increasing to expected €70 billion in the EU-5 in 2016.
- Social networks such as Facebook, Twitter, Pinterest, and Instagram, together with online retailers, continue to try to understand how best to facilitate social e-commerce, with the introduction of Buy buttons on Facebook, Instagram, and Pinterest.
- Local e-commerce, headlined by new local on-demand service companies such as Uber, skyrockets to over $40 billion in the United States.
- The number of online buyers continues to increase, to over 1.6 billion worldwide in 2016.
- Online retailers remain generally profitable by focusing on revenue growth, increasing the size of average purchase amounts, and improving efficiency of operations.
- Online retail remains the fastest growing retail channel.
- Shopping and buying online has become a normal, mainstream, everyday experience. Almost all Internet users worldwide are now online buyers or shoppers.
- The selection of goods for purchase online continues to increase to include luxury goods, such as jewelry, gourmet groceries, furniture, and wine, as customer trust and experience increase.
- Informational shopping for big-ticket items such as cars and appliances continues to expand rapidly to include nearly all retail goods (both durables and non-durables).
- Specialty retail sites show rapid growth in online retail as they develop customized retail goods and customer online configuration of goods.
- Online retailers place an increased emphasis on providing an improved "shopping experience," including ease of navigation and use, online inventory updates, interactive tools, customer feedback and ratings, and social shopping opportunities.
- Online retailers increase the use of interactive marketing technologies and techniques such as blogs, user-generated content, and video that exploit the dominance of broadband connections and offer features such as zoom, color switch, product configuration, and virtual simulations of households and businesses.
- Retailers are increasingly becoming omni-channel retailers, integrating the multiple retail channels provided by physical stores, the Web, and the mobile platform.
- New virtual merchants such as Birchbox, Naturebox, and others emerge that are using a new subscription-based revenue model for retail.
- Big data and powerful analytic programs begin to be used for predictive marketing by both large and small retailers.

offline and online—to integrate their operations so they can serve customers in the various ways they want to be served.

By any measure, the size of the global retail market is huge: around €21 trillion in 2016. Retail sales in Asia-Pacific account for about 41% of that total, with North America accounting for about 24%, and Western Europe 17%.

THE RETAIL INDUSTRY

The retail industry is composed of many different types of firms. **Figure 11.1** illustrates the major segments of the U.S. retail industry: durable goods, general merchandise, food and beverage, specialty stores, gasoline and fuel, mail order/telephone order (MOTO), and online retail firms. Each of these segments offers opportunities for online retail,

FIGURE 11.1 **COMPOSITION OF THE U.S. RETAIL INDUSTRY**

General Merchandise

Online Retail

Gasoline and Fuel

Consumer Durables

Specialty Stores

MOTO

Food and Beverage

The retail industry can be grouped into seven major segments.
SOURCE: Based on data from U.S. Census Bureau, 2012.

and yet in each segment, the uses of the Internet may differ. Some eating and drinking establishments use the Web and mobile apps to inform people of their physical locations and menus, while others offer delivery via online orders. Retailers of durable goods typically use the online channel primarily as an informational tool rather than as a direct purchasing tool, although this has begun to change.

The MOTO sector is the most similar to the online retail sales sector. In the absence of physical stores, MOTO retailers distribute millions of physical catalogs (their largest expense) and operate large telephone call centers to accept orders. They have developed extraordinarily efficient order fulfillment centers that generally ship customer orders within 24 hours of receipt. MOTO was the fastest growing retail segment throughout the 1970s and 1980s. It grew as a direct result of improvements in the national toll-free call system, the implementation of digital switching in telephone systems, falling long distance telecommunications prices, and of course, the expansion of the credit card industry and associated technologies, without which neither MOTO nor e-commerce would be possible on a large national scale. MOTO was the last "technological" retailing revolution that preceded e-commerce. Because of their experience in fulfilling small orders rapidly, the transition to e-commerce was not difficult for these firms.

ONLINE RETAILING

Online retail is perhaps the most high-profile e-commerce sector. Over the past decade, this sector has experienced both explosive growth and spectacular failures. Many of the early pure-play online-only firms that pioneered the retail marketspace failed. Entrepreneurs and their investors seriously misjudged the factors needed to succeed in this market. But the survivors of this early period emerged much stronger, and along with traditional offline general and specialty merchants, as well as new startups, the e-tail space is growing very rapidly and is increasing its reach and size.

E-commerce Retail: The Vision

In the early years of e-commerce, literally thousands of entrepreneurial web-based retailers were drawn to the marketplace for retail goods, simply because it was one of the largest market opportunities in the U.S. economy. Many entrepreneurs initially believed it was easy to enter the retail market. Early writers predicted that the retail industry would be revolutionized, literally "blown to bits"—as prophesied by two consultants in a famous Harvard Business School book (Evans and Wurster, 2000). The basis of this revolution would be fourfold. First, because the Internet greatly reduced both search costs and transaction costs, consumers would use the Web to find the lowest-cost products. Several results would follow. Consumers would increasingly drift to the Web for shopping and purchasing, and only low-cost, high-service, quality online retail merchants would survive. Economists assumed that the online consumer was rational and cost-driven—not driven by perceived value or brand, both of which are nonrational factors.

Second, it was assumed that the entry costs to the online retail market were much less than those needed to establish physical storefronts, and that online merchants were inherently more efficient at marketing and order fulfillment than offline stores. The costs of establishing a powerful website were thought to be minuscule compared to the costs of warehouses, fulfillment centers, and physical stores. There would be no difficulty building sophisticated order entry, shopping cart, and fulfillment systems because this technology was well known, and the cost of technology was falling by 50% each year. Even the cost of acquiring consumers was thought to be much lower because of search engines that could almost instantly connect customers to online vendors.

Third, as prices fell, traditional offline physical store merchants would be forced out of business. New entrepreneurial companies—such as Amazon—would replace the traditional stores. It was thought that if online merchants grew very quickly, they would have first-mover advantages and lock out the older traditional firms that were too slow to enter the online market.

Fourth, in some industries—such as electronics, apparel, and digital content—the market would be disintermediated as manufacturers or their distributors entered to build a direct relationship with the consumer, destroying the retail intermediaries or middlemen. In this scenario, traditional retail channels—such as physical stores, sales clerks, and sales forces—would be replaced by a single dominant channel: the Web.

Many predicted, on the other hand, a kind of hypermediation based on the concept of a virtual firm in which online retailers would gain advantage over established offline merchants by building an online brand name that attracted millions of customers, and outsourcing the expensive warehousing and order fulfillment functions—the original concept of Amazon.

As it turned out, few of these assumptions and visions were correct, and the structure of the retail marketplace, with some notable exceptions, has not been blown to bits, disintermediated, or revolutionized in the traditional meaning of the word "revolution." With several notable exceptions, online retail has often not been successful as an independent platform on which to build a successful "pure-play" online-only business. As it turns out, the consumer is not primarily price-driven when shopping on the Internet but instead considers brand name, trust, reliability, delivery time, convenience, ease of use, and above all "the experience," as at least as important as price (Brynjolfsson, Dick, and Smith, 2004).

omni-channel

retailers that sell products through a variety of channels and integrate their physical stores with their website and mobile platform

However, the Internet has created an entirely new venue for **omni-channel** firms (those that sell products through a variety of channels and integrate their physical stores with their websites and mobile platform), and in some cases, the Internet has supported the development of pure-play online-only merchants, both general merchandisers as well as specialty retailers. As predicted, online retail has indeed become the fastest growing and most dynamic retail channel in the sense of channel innovation. The Web has created a new marketplace for millions of consumers to conveniently shop. The Internet and the Web have continued to provide new opportunities for entirely new firms using new business models and new online products—such as Blue Nile, as previously described. The online channel can conflict with a merchant's other channels, such as direct sales forces, physical stores, and mail order, but this multi-channel conflict can be managed and turned into a strength.

The Online Retail Sector Today

Although online retailing is one of the smallest segments of the global retail industry, constituting only about 9% of the total retail market today, it is growing at a faster rate than its offline counterparts, with new functionality and product lines being added every day. In the United States, the apparel and accessories category generates the highest percentage of revenue, around $64 billion in 2015 (see **Figure 11.2**). Consumers have a wide choice of online shopping options in this category, such as omni-channel department store chains like Macy's, Nordstrom, Target, and Walmart and specialty retailers like Gap, Zulily, J.Crew, Urban Outfitters, Abercrombie & Fitch, and Ralph Lauren. This is one category where Amazon does not dominate, in part because clothing shoppers tend to identify more strongly with a specific brand than they do with products that are more of a commodity, such as consumer electronics.

The computers and consumer electronics category generates the second-highest percentage of revenue, around $54 billion in 2015. Online shopping options for this category include Amazon, direct-manufacturers such as Apple, Dell, HP, and Lenovo, omni-channel chains such as Best Buy, and catalog merchants such as CDW and PC Connection.

The automobile and automobile parts and accessories category is in third place, generating around $36 billion in 2015, primarily from auto parts and accessories. Currently, U.S. franchising law prohibits automobile manufacturers from selling cars directly to consumers, so automobile retailing is dominated by dealership networks. Automobile manufacturers use the Internet to deliver branding advertising, while dealers focus on generating leads. Consumers typically focus on product and pricing research, which they then use to negotiate with dealers. Direct online automobile sales are currently not common due to the complexity of the vehicle purchasing process, but they are likely to become more commonplace in the future. For example, startup

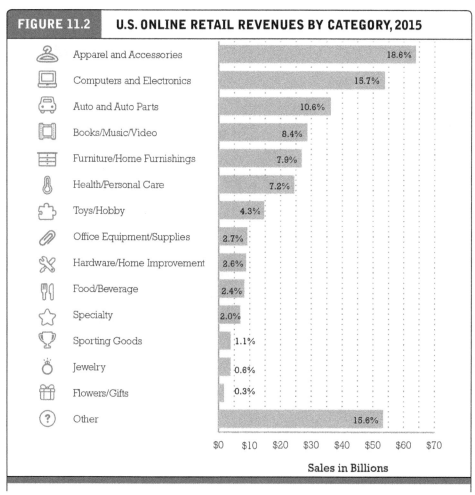

FIGURE 11.2 **U.S. ONLINE RETAIL REVENUES BY CATEGORY, 2015**

Category	Percentage
Apparel and Accessories	18.6%
Computers and Electronics	15.7%
Auto and Auto Parts	10.6%
Books/Music/Video	8.4%
Furniture/Home Furnishings	7.9%
Health/Personal Care	7.2%
Toys/Hobby	4.3%
Office Equipment/Supplies	2.7%
Hardware/Home Improvement	2.6%
Food/Beverage	2.4%
Specialty	2.0%
Sporting Goods	1.1%
Jewelry	0.6%
Flowers/Gifts	0.3%
Other	15.6%

Sales in Billions

Apparel and accessories is the leading online purchase category in terms of revenue generated, accounting for over 18% of all online retail revenues.

SOURCES: Based on data from Internet Retailer, 2016; eMarketer, Inc., 2016a, 2016b; authors' estimates.

Beepi has developed a business model based on eliminating dealers and sells used cars directly to consumers via a mobile app.

Books, music, and video are among the original items sold successfully online. This still popular online category generated about $29 billion in 2015. Leading retailers in this category include Amazon, Apple, Netflix, Google Play, Barnes & Noble, and Hulu.

The furniture and home furnishing category generated about $27 billion in 2015. In the past, the expense of shipping large items such as furniture, mattresses, and rugs was a deterrent to online sales, but that is beginning to change. In addition to Amazon, leading online retailers in this category include other purely online companies such as Wayfair and Overstock, as well as omni-channel retailers such as Williams-Sonoma, Restoration Hardware, Bed Bath & Beyond, and Crate and Barrel.

FIGURE 11.3 THE GROWTH OF ONLINE RETAIL WORLDWIDE

Worldwide online retail revenues will be an estimated €1.8 trillion in 2016 and are expected to increase to €3.8 trillion by 2020.

SOURCES: Based on data from eMarketer, Inc., 2016c

The health and personal care (drugs, health, and beauty supplies) category has also enjoyed steady growth, with about $24.5 billion in revenue in 2015 (eMarketer, Inc., 2016a).

Figure 11.3 illustrates the growth of the online retail revenues worldwide. When we refer to online retail, we will not be including online services revenues such as travel, job-hunting, or the purchase of digital downloads such as software applications and music. Instead, for the purposes of this chapter, online retail refers solely to sales of physical goods over the Internet. The Internet provides a number of unique advantages and challenges to online retailers. **Table 11.2** summarizes these advantages and challenges.

Despite the high failure rate of online retailers in the early years, more consumers than ever are shopping online. For most consumers, the advantages of online shopping overcome the disadvantages. In 2016, it is estimated that 47% of Internet users over the age of 14 worldwide (around 1.6 billion people) will make an online purchase, generating about €1.8 trillion in online retail sales. While the number of new Internet users is not growing as rapidly at it was, this slowdown will not necessarily reduce the growth in online retail e-commerce because the average shopper is spending more on the Internet each year and finding many new categories of items to buy. For instance, in 2003, the average annual amount spent online by U.S. consumers was $675, but by 2016, it had jumped to over $2,255 (eMarketer, Inc., 2016b, 2005). Also, as noted in Chapter 6, millions of additional consumers research products online and are influenced in their purchase decisions at offline stores.

TABLE 11.2	ONLINE RETAIL: ADVANTAGES AND CHALLENGES
ADVANTAGES	**CHALLENGES**
Lower supply chain costs by aggregating demand at a single site and increasing purchasing power	Consumer concerns about the security of transactions
Lower cost of distribution using websites rather than physical stores	Consumer concerns about the privacy of personal information given to websites
Ability to reach and serve a much larger geographically distributed group of customers	Delays in delivery of goods when compared to store shopping
Ability to react quickly to customer tastes and demand	Inconvenience associated with return of damaged or exchange goods
Ability to change prices nearly instantly	Overcoming lack of consumer trust in online brand names
Ability to rapidly change visual presentation of goods	Added expenses for online photography, video, and animated presentations
Avoidance of direct marketing costs of catalogs and physical mail	Online marketing costs for search, e-mail, and displays
Increased opportunities for personalization, customization	Added complexity to product offerings and customer service
Ability to greatly improve information and knowledge delivered to consumer	Greater customer information can translate into price competition and lower profits
Ability to lower consumers' overall market transaction costs	

The primary beneficiaries of this growing consumer support are not only the pure online companies but also the established offline retailers who have the brand-name recognition, supportive infrastructure, and financial resources to enter the online marketplace successfully. **Table 11.3** lists the top U.S. online retail firms ranked by online sales. The list contains pure-play online retailers for whom the Internet is the only sales channel, such as Amazon (in first place) and Newegg; omni-channel firms that have established brand names and for whom e-commerce still plays a relatively small role when compared to their offline physical store channels, such as Walmart, Sears, Macy's, Home Depot, Costco, Best Buy, and Target; and manufacturers of computer and electronic equipment, such as Apple, Dell, and Lenovo. In 2015, Amazon accounted for over 25% of all online retail revenues, the top 10 retailers accounted for almost 55% of all online retail, while the top 500 U.S. retailers accounted for about 85%. The next 500 accounted for an additional 5%, so just 1,000 retailers generated over 90% of all retail e-commerce sales. Many of the fastest growing firms are mid-size merchants, particularly newcomers that focus on a particular niche, such as Blue Apron, which uses a subscription-based sales model for make-at-home meals, and Dollar Shave Club, another company that uses a subscription-based sales model for inexpensive razors (so successful that it was acquired by Unilever for $1 billion in July 2016). Conversely, companies that can't show consumers that they can offer them something of value not available elsewhere are likely to have a difficult time surviving. For pure-play

TABLE 11.3	THE TOP 20 U.S. RETAILERS RANKED BY ONLINE SALES	
RETAILER	ONLINE SALES (2015) (in billions)	TYPE
Amazon	$79.27	Online only
Apple	$18.00	Manufacturer-direct
Walmart	$13.70	Omni-channel bricks and clicks
Staples	$11.03	Omni-channel bricks and clicks
Macy's	$6.21	Omni-channel bricks and clicks
Home Depot	$4.67	Omni-channel bricks and clicks
Sears	$4.65	Omni-channel bricks and clicks
Costco	$4.53	Omni-channel bricks and clicks
Office Depot	$4.39	Omni-channel bricks and clicks
Best Buy	$4.07	Omni-channel bricks and clicks
CDW	$3.95	Catalog merchant
QVC Group	$3.91	Catalog merchant
Dell	$3.68	Manufacturer-direct
Lenovo	$3.38	Manufacturer-direct
Nordstrom	$2.83	Omni-channel bricks and clicks
Kohl's	$2.82	Omni-channel bricks and clicks
Gap	$2.53	Omni-channel bricks and clicks
Newegg	$2.58	Online only
Target	$2.47	Omni-channel bricks and clicks
Williams-Sonoma	$2.38	Omni-channel bricks and clicks

*Does not include revenues derived from the App Store

SOURCES: Based on data from Internet Retailer, 2016; company reports on Form 10-K filed with the Securities and Exchange Commission, 2016; Forbes, 2016; eMarketer, Inc., 2016d; authors' estimates.

firms, the challenge is to turn visitors into customers, and to develop efficient operations that permit them to achieve long-term profitability. Profitability remains a key issue for online-only retailers. Not many of these companies are public and therefore required to report their financial results, but of the few that are, only a handful were profitable in 2015. For traditional firms that are less dependent on e-commerce sales, the challenge is to integrate the offline and online channels so customers can move seamlessly from one environment to another.

Clearly one of the most important e-commerce retail themes of 2016–2017, and into the future, is the ability of offline traditional firms such as Walmart, Target, Macy's, and others to continue to integrate their web and mobile operations with their physical store operations in order to provide an "integrated shopping customer experience" and leverage the value of their physical stores. **Table 11.4** illustrates some of the various ways in which traditional retailers have integrated the Web, the mobile platform, and

TABLE 11.4	RETAIL E-COMMERCE: OMNI-CHANNEL INTEGRATION METHODS
INTEGRATION TYPE	**DESCRIPTION**
Online order, in-store pickup	Probably one of the first types of integration.
Online order, store directory, and inventory	When items are out of stock online, customer is directed to physical store network inventory and store location.
In-store kiosk online order, home delivery	When retail store is out of stock, customer orders in store and receives at home.
In-store retail clerk online order, home delivery	Similar to above, but the retail clerk searches online inventory if local store is out of stock as a normal part of the in-store checkout process.
Order online, in-store returns, and adjustments	Defective or rejected products ordered online can be returned to any store location.
Online catalog	Online catalog supplements offline physical catalog and often the online catalog has substantially more product on display.
Manufacturers use online promotions to drive customers to their distributors' retail stores	Consumer product manufacturers such as Colgate-Palmolive and Procter & Gamble use online channels to design new products and promote existing product retail sales.
Gift card, loyalty program points can be used in any channel	Recipient of gift card, loyalty program points can use them to purchase in-store, online, or via catalog, if offered by merchant.
Mobile order, website and physical store sales	Apps take users directly to specially formatted website for ordering, or to in-store bargains.
Geo-fencing mobile notification, in-store sales	Use of smartphone geo-location technology to target ads for nearby stores and restaurants.

store operations to develop nearly seamless omni-channel shopping. This list is not exclusive, and retailers continue to develop new links between channels.

Rather than demonstrate disintermediation, online retailing provides an example of the powerful role that intermediaries continue to play in retail trade. Established offline retailers have rapidly gained online market share. Increasingly, consumers are attracted to stable, well-known, trusted retail brands and retailers. The online audience is very sensitive to brand names and is not primarily cost-driven. Other factors such as reliability, trust, fulfillment, and customer service are equally important.

The most significant changes in retail e-commerce in 2016 are the continuing growth in social e-commerce, the growing ability of firms to market local services and products through the use of location-based marketing, and not least, the rapidly growing mobile platform composed of smartphones and tablet computers. In retail circles, tablets are being called "the ultimate shopping machine," enabling consumers to browse media-rich online catalogs just like they used to do with physical catalogs, and then buy when they feel the urge.

Social e-commerce refers to marketing and purchasing on social network sites like Facebook, Twitter, Pinterest, Instagram, Snapchat, and others. All of these sites have developed into major marketing and advertising platforms that help direct consumers to external websites to purchase products. And, after trials in 2014, Facebook, Twitter, Pinterest, and Instagram have all introduced their own versions of "buy" buttons that allow consumers to more easily purchase goods on a much wider scale. In 2015, the top 500 retailers in Internet Retailer's Social Media 500 earned about $3.9 billion from social commerce, an over 40% increase over 2014 (Top500guide.com, 2016).

Whereas in the past only large firms could afford to run online marketing and ad campaigns, this has changed with the development of local marketing firms like Groupon, LivingSocial, and dozens of others, which make it possible for consumers to receive discount deals and coupons from local merchants based on their geographic location. Using billions of daily e-mails, these so-called daily deal sites have sold millions of coupons to purchase local goods and services at steep discounts. For the first time, local merchants can advertise their products and services online at a relatively inexpensive cost.

Social and local e-commerce are enabled by the tremendous growth in mobile Internet devices, both smartphones and tablet computers. In 2016, retail m-commerce in the EU-5 generated €70 billion overall. In 2016, over 70% of online buyers in the United Kingdom made a purchase using a mobile device, and it is estimated that this percentage will grow to almost 80% by 2020 (eMarketer, Inc., 2016c, 2016f).

11.2   ANALYZING THE VIABILITY OF ONLINE FIRMS

In this and the following chapters, we analyze the viability of a number of online companies that exemplify specific e-commerce models. We are primarily interested in understanding the near-to-medium term (1–3 years) economic viability of these firms and their business models. **Economic viability** refers to the ability of firms to survive as profitable business firms during the specified period. To answer the question of economic viability, we take two business analysis approaches: strategic analysis and financial analysis.

economic viability
refers to the ability of firms to survive as profitable business firms during a specified period

STRATEGIC ANALYSIS

Strategic approaches to economic viability focus on both the industry in which a firm operates and the firm itself (see Chapter 5, Sections 5.2 and 5.5). The key industry strategic factors are:

- *Barriers to entry*: Can new entrants be barred from entering the industry through high capital costs or intellectual property barriers (such as patents and copyrights)?
- *Power of suppliers*: Can suppliers dictate high prices to the industry or can vendors choose from among many suppliers? Have firms achieved sufficient scale to bargain effectively for lower prices from suppliers?
- *Power of customers*: Can customers choose from many competing suppliers and hence challenge high prices and high margins?
- *Existence of substitute products*: Can the functionality of the product or service be obtained from alternative channels or competing products in different industries? Are substitute products and services likely to emerge in the near future?

- *Industry value chain*: Is the chain of production and distribution in the industry changing in ways that benefit or harm the firm?

- *Nature of intra-industry competition*: Is the basis of competition within the industry based on differentiated products and services, price, scope of offerings, or focus of offerings? How is the nature of competition changing? Will these changes benefit the firm?

The strategic factors that pertain specifically to the firm and its related businesses include:

- *Firm value chain*: Has the firm adopted business processes and methods of operation that allow it to achieve the most efficient operations in its industry? Will changes in technology force the firm to realign its business processes?

- *Core competencies*: Does the firm have unique competencies and skills that cannot be easily duplicated by other firms? Will changes in technology invalidate the firm's competencies or strengthen them?

- *Synergies*: Does the firm have access to the competencies and assets of related firms either owned outright or through strategic partnerships and alliances?

- *Technology*: Has the firm developed proprietary technologies that allow it to scale with demand? Has the firm developed the operational technologies (e.g., customer relationship management, fulfillment, supply chain management, inventory control, and human resource systems) to survive?

- *Social and legal challenges*: Has the firm put in place policies to address consumer trust issues (privacy and security of personal information)? Is the firm the subject of lawsuits challenging its business model, such as intellectual property ownership issues? Will the firm be affected by changes in Internet taxation laws or other foreseeable statutory developments?

FINANCIAL ANALYSIS

Strategic analysis helps us comprehend the competitive situation of the firm. Financial analysis helps us understand how in fact the firm is performing. There are two parts to a financial analysis: the statement of operations and the balance sheet. The statement of operations tells us how much money (or loss) the firm is achieving based on current sales and costs. The balance sheet tells us how many assets the firm has to support its current and future operations.

Here are some of the key factors to look for in a firm's statement of operations:

- *Revenues*: Are revenues growing and at what rate? Many e-commerce companies have experienced impressive, even explosive, revenue growth as an entirely new channel is created.

- *Cost of sales*: What is the cost of sales compared to revenues? Cost of sales typically includes the cost of the products sold and related costs. The lower the cost of sales compared to revenue, the higher the gross profit.

- *Gross margin*: What is the firm's gross margin, and is it increasing or decreasing? **Gross margin** is calculated by dividing gross profit by net sales revenues. Gross margin can tell you if the firm is gaining or losing market power vis-à-vis its key suppliers.

gross margin
gross profit divided by net sales

- *Operating expenses*: What are the firm's operating expenses, and are they increasing or decreasing? Operating expenses typically include the cost of marketing, technology, and administrative overhead. They also include, in accordance with professional accounting standards (see below), stock-based compensation to employees and executives, amortization of goodwill and other intangibles, and impairment of investments. In e-commerce companies, these turn out to be very important expenses. Many e-commerce firms compensated their employees with stock shares (or options), and many e-commerce firms purchased other e-commerce firms as a part of their growth strategy. Many of the companies were purchased at extremely high values using company stock rather than cash; in numerous instances, the purchased companies fell dramatically in market value. All these items are counted as normal operating expenses.

operating margin
calculated by dividing operating income or loss by net sales revenue

- *Operating margin*: What did the firm earn from its current operations? **Operating margin** is calculated by dividing operating income or loss by net sales revenue. Operating margin is an indication of a company's ability to turn sales into pre-tax profit after operating expenses have been deducted. Operating margin tells us if the firm's current operations are covering its operating expenses, not including interest expenses and other non-operating expenses.

net margin
the percentage of its gross sales revenue the firm is able to retain after all expenses are deducted; calculated by dividing net income or loss by net sales revenue

- *Net margin*: **Net margin** tells us the percentage of its gross sales revenue the firm was able to retain after all expenses are deducted. Net margin is calculated by dividing net income or loss by net sales revenue. Net margin sums up in one number how successful a company has been at the business of making a profit on each dollar of sales revenues. Net margin also tells us something about the efficiency of the firm by measuring the percentage of sales revenue it is able to retain after all expenses are deducted from gross revenues, and, within a single industry, it can be used to measure the relative efficiency of competing firms. Net margin takes into account many non-operating expenses such as interest and stock compensation plans.

balance sheet
provides a financial snapshot of a company on a given date and shows its financial assets and liabilities

When examining the financial announcements of e-commerce companies, it is important to realize that online firms often choose not to announce their net income according to generally accepted accounting principles (GAAP). These principles have been promulgated by the Financial Accounting Standards Board (FASB), a board of professional accountants that establishes accounting rules for the profession, and which has played a vital role since the 1934 Securities Act, which sought to improve financial accounting during the Great Depression. Many e-commerce firms in the early years instead reported an entirely new calculation called *pro forma earnings* (also called EBITDA—earnings before income taxes, depreciation, and amortization). Pro forma earnings generally do not deduct stock-based compensation, depreciation, or amortization. The result is that pro forma earnings are always better than GAAP earnings. The firms that report in this manner typically claim these expenses are non-recurring and special and "unusual." In 2002 and 2003, the SEC issued new guidelines (Regulation G) that prohibit firms from reporting pro forma earnings in official reports to the SEC, but still allow firms to announce pro forma earnings in public statements (Weil, 2003). Throughout this book, we consider a firm's income or loss based on GAAP accounting standards only.

assets
refers to stored value

current assets
assets such as cash, securities, accounts receivable, inventory, or other investments that are likely to be able to be converted to cash within one year

A **balance sheet** provides a financial snapshot of a company's assets and liabilities (debts) on a given date. **Assets** refer to stored value. **Current assets** are those assets such as cash, securities, accounts receivable, inventory, or other investments that are likely to be able to be converted to cash within one year. **Liabilities** are outstanding obligations of the firm. **Current liabilities** are debts of the firm that will be due within one year. Liabilities that are not due until the passage of a year or more are characterized as **long-term debt**. For a quick check of a firm's short-term financial health, examine its **working capital** (the firm's current assets minus current liabilities). If working capital is only marginally positive, or negative, the firm will likely have trouble meeting its short-term obligations. Alternatively, if a firm has a large amount of current assets, it can sustain operational losses for a period of time.

liabilities
outstanding obligations of the firm

current liabilities
debts of the firm that will be due within one year

long-term debt
liabilities that are not due until the passage of a year or more

working capital
firm's current assets minus current liabilities

11.3 E-COMMERCE IN ACTION: E-TAILING BUSINESS MODELS

So far, we have been discussing online retail as if it were a single entity. In fact, as we briefly discussed in Chapter 5, there are four main types of online retail business models: virtual merchants, omni-channel merchandisers (sometimes referred to as bricks-and-clicks or clicks-and-bricks), catalog merchants, and manufacturer-direct firms. **Figure 11.4** illustrates the respective shares of 2015 U.S. online retail sales for each of these categories of firms. In addition, there are thousands of small retailers that use the eBay and Amazon sales platforms, as well as affiliate merchants whose

FIGURE 11.4   **SHARE OF U.S. ONLINE RETAIL SALES BY TYPE OF COMPANY**

- Omni-channel Merchants
- Virtual Merchants
- Catalog Merchants
- Manufacturer-Direct

9.3%
16.9%
32.2%
41.6%

Virtual merchants account for over 40% of online retail sales, although this percentage is heavily skewed by the dominance of Amazon, which by itself accounts for almost 25%. However, the percentage accounted for by omni-channel merchants has been steadily increasing over the last few years.
SOURCES: Based on data from eMarketer, Inc., 2016g, 2016h.

primary revenue derives from sending traffic to their "mother" sites. Each of these different types of online retailers faces a different strategic environment, as well as different industry and firm economics.

VIRTUAL MERCHANTS

virtual merchants

single-channel e-commerce firms that generate almost all of their revenue from online sales

Virtual merchants are single-channel e-commerce firms that generate almost all their revenue from online sales. Virtual merchants face extraordinary strategic challenges. They must build a business and brand name from scratch, quickly, in an entirely new channel and confront many virtual merchant competitors (especially in smaller niche areas). Because these firms typically do not have any physical stores, they do not have to bear the costs associated with developing and maintaining physical stores but they face large costs in building and maintaining an e-commerce presence, building an order fulfillment infrastructure, and developing a brand name. Customer acquisition costs are high, and the learning curve is steep. Like all retail firms, their gross margins (the difference between the retail price of goods sold and the cost of goods to the retailer) are low. Therefore, virtual merchants must achieve highly efficient operations in order to preserve a profit, while building a brand name as quickly as possible in order to attract sufficient customers to cover their costs of operations. Most merchants in this category adopt low-cost and convenience strategies, coupled with extremely effective and efficient fulfillment processes to ensure customers receive what they ordered as fast as possible. In the following *E-commerce in Action* section, we take an in-depth look at the strategic and financial situation of Amazon, the leading online virtual merchant. In addition to Amazon, other successful virtual merchants include Newegg, Overstock, Gilt Groupe, Zulily, Wayfair, Rue La La, Blue Nile (profiled in the opening case), Bluefly, Hayneedle, Yoox Net-a-Porter, Shoebuy, and Choxi. Recently, a new group of virtual merchants have emerged that use a subscription revenue model. Examples include Birchbox (personalized beauty samples delivered monthly), Stitch Fix (clothing selected by a personal stylist) (see the *Insight on Technology* case, *Big Data and Predictive Marketing*, on pages 769–770 for more on Stitch Fix), Barkbox (pet supplies), Naturebox (healthy snacks), Bulu Box (supplements and vitamins), and hundreds more. According to Internet Retailer, overall, virtual merchants accounted for over $140 billion (about 42%) of U.S. online retail sales by the Internet Retailer Top 1000 merchants in 2015 (eMarketer, Inc., 2016g, 2016h).

E-COMMERCE IN ACTION

AMAZON

Amazon, the Seattle-based virtual merchant, is one of the most well-known names in the world. As stated in its annual report filed with the U.S. Securities and Exchange Commission, Amazon's objective is to be Earth's most customer-centric company. Exactly what this means, and how it might be possible to achieve it, is a matter of speculation for both customers and investors. Yet in pursuing this goal, Jeff Bezos and his team have built the world's most successful and innovative online retailer.

Few business enterprises have experienced the roller-coaster ride from explosive early growth, to huge losses, and then on to profitability that Amazon has. No Internet business has been both so widely reviled and so hotly praised throughout its development. Its stock reflects these changing fortunes, fluctuating over the past 15 years, from an early high of $106 in 1999, to a low of $6 a share in 2001, then bouncing back and forth between $50–$90 in 2003–2009, and then climbing again to a high of over $810 in 2016. While controversial, Amazon has also been one of the most innovative online retailing stories in the history of e-commerce. From the earliest days of e-commerce, Amazon has continuously adapted its business model based on both its market experience and its insight into the online consumer.

The Vision

The original vision of founder Jeff Bezos and his friends was that the Internet was a revolutionary new form of commerce and that only companies that became really big early on (ignoring profitability) would survive. The path to success, according to founder Bezos, was to offer consumers three things: the lowest prices, the best selection, and convenience (which translates into feature-rich content, user-generated reviews of books and products, fast and reliable fulfillment, and ease of use). Currently, Amazon offers consumers millions of unique new, used, and collectible items in a variety of different categories, both physical and digital. Its physical goods include books, movies, music, and games; electronics and computers; home, garden, and tools; grocery; health and beauty; toys, kids, and baby; clothing, shoes, and jewelry; sports and outdoors; and auto and industrial. Its digital products include unlimited instant videos, digital games and software, MP3s and Cloud Player, Audible audiobooks, and Kindle e-book reader products. And if Amazon does not carry it, it will help you find it at online merchants who "rent space" from Amazon, or even at an external online vendor. In short, Amazon has become the largest, one-stop online merchant, a kind of combined "shopping portal" and "product search portal" that puts it in direct competition with other large online general merchants, eBay, and general portals such as Yahoo, MSN, and even Google. As Amazon succeeded in becoming the world's largest online store, it also expanded its original vision to become one of the largest suppliers of online merchant and search services.

Business Model

Amazon's business is currently organized into two basic segments: North American and International. Within those segments, it serves not only retail customers but also merchants and developers. The retail component of the business sells physical and digital products that Amazon has purchased and then resells to consumers just like a traditional retailer. It also manufactures and sells a variety of versions of its Kindle e-reader and Kindle Fire series of devices, including tablet computers and smart TVs. The Fire smartphone proved unsuccessful, due to a lack of available apps, but the Echo in-home assistant has garnered rave reviews and could be Amazon's next must-have device.

Another major component of Amazon's business is its third-party merchant segment. Amazon Services enables third parties to integrate their products into Amazon's website, and use Amazon's customer technologies. In the early years of its business, Amazon entered into partnerships with large merchants such as Toys"R"Us, Borders, and Target, and created storefronts for these companies within the larger Amazon site. Today, Amazon has increasingly left the enterprise-level business to competitors and instead focused its efforts on small and medium-sized retail merchants.

Thousands of these types of merchants have signed on with Amazon, offering products that in some instances even compete with those that Amazon itself sells. For instance, a single product on the Amazon website may be listed for sale simultaneously by Amazon, by a large branded merchant participant such as Target, and by a business or individual selling a new, used, or collectible version of the product through Amazon Marketplace. For these types of merchants, Amazon is not the seller of record, does not own these products, and the shipping of products is usually handled by the third party (although in some instances, Amazon provides fulfillment services as well). Amazon collects a monthly fixed fee, sales commission (generally estimated to be between 10% and 20% of the sale), per-unit activity fee, or some combination thereof from the third party. In this segment, Amazon acts as an online shopping mall, collecting "rents" from other merchants and providing "site" services such as order entry and payment.

Another major part of Amazon's business is Amazon Web Services (AWS). Through this segment, Amazon offers a variety of web services that provide developers with direct access to Amazon's technology platform and allow them to build their own applications based on that platform. In 2016, AWS is expected to account for $10 billion in revenues, up from nearly $8 billion in 2015 and $4.6 billion in 2014, and delivered more profits than Amazon's retail business. Refer to Chapter 2 for a more detailed examination of AWS.

Despite the profitability of AWS, Amazon still generates the bulk of its overall revenue by selling products. While Amazon started out as an online merchant of books, CDs, and DVDs, since 2002, it has diversified into becoming a general merchandiser of millions of other products. Amazon has turned itself into a major online media and content firm and, following its success with Kindle e-books, has also made a strong move into the music and streaming video business, with Amazon Music and Amazon Instant Video. In 2015, about 20% of its revenue came from media sales while electronics and general merchandise accounted for about 70%. In addition to Amazon.com in the United States, Amazon also operates a number of localized sites in Europe, Asia, and Canada. Although Amazon derived 33% of its gross revenue offshore in 2015, down from 37% in 2014, total international sales still improved—just not as fast as domestic sales.

Financial Analysis

Amazon's revenues have increased from about $600 million in 1998 to an astounding $107 billion in 2015 (see **Table 11.5**). From 2011 to 2015, Amazon's revenues have more than doubled. This is very impressive, explosive revenue growth. However, Amazon's growth strategies have made it difficult for the company to maintain consistent profits in the past. Although it showed a profit of $631 million in 2011, in 2012, Amazon experienced a net loss of $39 million. In 2013, it reversed that loss and reported net income

TABLE 11.5	AMAZON'S CONSOLIDATED STATEMENTS OF OPERATIONS AND SUMMARY BALANCE SHEET DATA 2013–2015		
CONSOLIDATED STATEMENTS OF OPERATIONS (in millions)			
For the fiscal year ended December 31,	2015	2014	2013
Revenue			
Net sales/products.	$79,268	$70,080	$ 60,903
Net sales/services	27,738	18,908	13,549
Cost of sales	$71,651	$62,752	$ 54,181
Gross profit	35,355	26,236	20,271
Gross margin.	33.0%	29.5%	27.2%
Operating expenses			
Marketing	5,254	4,332	3,133
Fulfillment.	13,410	10,766	8,585
Technology and content.	12,540	9,275	6,565
General and administrative	1,747	1,552	1,129
Other operating expense (income), net. . .	171	133	114
Total operating expenses.	33,122	26,058	19,526
Income from operations	2,233	178	745
Operating margin	2.1%	0.2%	1%
Total non-operating income (expense) . .	(665)	(289)	(239)
Income before income taxes	1,568	(111)	506
Provision for income taxes.	(950)	(167)	(161)
Equity-method investment activity, net of tax	(22)	37	(71)
Net income (loss).	596	(241)	274
Net margin	0.05%	–0.3%	0.03%
SUMMARY BALANCE SHEET DATA (in millions)			
At December 31,	2015	2014	2013
Assets			
Cash, cash equivalents, and marketable securities.	19,808	17,416	12,447
Total current assets	36,474	31,327	24,625
Total assets.	65,444	54,505	40,159
Liabilities			
Total current liabilities	33,899	28,089	22,980
Long-term liabilities.	18,161	15,675	7,433
Working capital.	2,575	3,238	1,645
Stockholders' Equity (Deficit)	13,384	10,741	9,746

SOURCE: Amazon.com, Inc., 2016a.

of $274 million but still fell short of analysts' estimates. In 2014, Amazon once again reported a net loss of $241 million, due in large part to operating expenses that rose from $19 billion in 2013 to $26 billion in 2014. But at long last, Amazon registered a string of profitable quarters in 2015, continuing into 2016, with expectations of more to come. Investors who speculated that Amazon would continue to grow and ultimately earn significant profits look to have been proven right. In the second quarter of 2016, Amazon earned $857 million in profit, up from $92 million in the same quarter of 2015.

At the end of December 2015, Amazon had about $19.8 billion in cash and marketable securities. These liquid assets were obtained from sales, sales of stock and notes to the public, venture capital investors, and institutional investors in return for equity (shares) in the company or debt securities. Total assets are about $65 billion. The company emphasizes the strength of its "free cash flow" as a sign of financial strength, suggesting it has more than enough cash available to cover short-term liabilities (such as financing holiday season purchasing). Amazon's current assets should certainly be enough to cover future short-term deficits should they occur.

Strategic Analysis—Business Strategy

Amazon engages in a number of business strategies that seek to maximize growth in sales volume, while cutting prices to the bare bones. Its revenue growth strategies include driving the growth of e-book sales by offering continuing enhancements of its Kindle e-reader and Kindle Fire tablet computer, both in the United States and internationally, as well as new e-book publishing initiatives; expanding further into the device manufacturing business, with Amazon Fire TV and Amazon Echo; expanding its music and streaming video business, with its Amazon Music and Instant Video services; expanding its Amazon Web Services offerings and extending their geographic reach; moving toward a broader trading platform by expanding the third-party seller segment; and moving toward greater product focus by grouping its offerings into major categories called stores. Amazon is still following Walmart's and eBay's examples by attempting to be a mass-market, low-price, high-volume online supermarket where you can get just about anything. To achieve profitability in this environment, Amazon has invested heavily in supply chain management and fulfillment strategies to reduce its costs to the bare minimum while providing excellent customer service and even free shipping.

Specific programs to increase retail revenues are the continuation of free shipping from Amazon Retail (a strategy that has increased order sizes by 25%), Amazon Prime (which for $99 a year provides free two-day shipping and one-day delivery upgrades for $3.99, as well as free access to Prime Music and Prime Video), greater product selection, and shorter order fulfillment times. Amazon Prime membership is steadily increasing, with an estimated 54 million members in the United States in 2016. Usage is also increasing: in 2015, Prime Video streaming hours grew 47% in the United States and 51% internationally, and Prime Music streaming hours tripled in 2015 over the previous year. Amazon offers customers same-day shipping in 14 markets in the United States and now offers its Prime Now one-hour delivery service in nine cities. A ticking clock can be seen next to some Amazon sale items indicating the hours remaining for an order to make it to the customer by the next day.

Amazon has moved strongly into the mobile shopping space as well, with shopping apps for the iPhone, BlackBerry, Android, Windows Phone, and iPad. It also has Deals, Price Check, and Student apps for the iPhone and has opened an Appstore for Android applications. In 2015, it rolled out the initial version of its Amazon Prime Now mobile app, which is quickly expanding across the United States and offers delivery speeds as fast as one hour. Amazon maintains a dominant position in mobile commerce in 2016, with an amazing 93% of smartphone shoppers reporting that they shop on Amazon, with most of those shoppers making the majority of their mobile purchases on Amazon. Amazon has not been as successful in developing its own smartphone, however. In 2015, it withdrew its resources from the continued development of the Amazon Fire phone, which had opened to underwhelming sales in 2014 and never developed an audience.

Amazon has continued to build on the rousing success of its Kindle e-book reader platform, which it has touted as the best-selling product in its history. It has continued to release iterations of the Kindle e-book reader and Fire. According to Amazon, it now sells more Kindle books than all print books combined.

In 2012, Amazon increased its efforts in the entertainment business, adding content to its Instant Video library through an expanded content licensing agreement with NBC Universal and similar arrangements with CBS, Viacom, and nearly every major Hollywood studio. Further agreements were inked with Viacom, PBS, A+E, Scripps Networks, and FX in 2013. In 2014, it added HBO and developed a series of original shows to keep pace with closest competitor Netflix. In 2015, Amazon announced that its content creation arm, Amazon Studios, would begin to develop original movies for theatrical release. These films will move to Amazon Prime within just a month or two of their debut.

On the cost side, Amazon increasingly uses "postal injection" for shipping, in which Amazon trucks deliver pre-posted packages to U.S. Postal System centers. In 2012, Amazon began an aggressive strategy to build warehouses all across the country to improve its delivery speeds. This has continued through 2016, with new fulfillment centers opening in New Jersey, Texas, and North Carolina. Many of Amazon's customers who had previously been exempt must now pay sales tax due to legislation in a number of states. With this competitive advantage evaporating, Amazon is seeking to trump all competitors on delivery speed. The ultimate goal for Bezos and Amazon: same-day delivery in many areas of the country.

To that end, Amazon has taken steps to expand its delivery capability in several ways, including drone delivery and cargo jets. Amazon Prime Air is Amazon's drone delivery project, which would be capable of delivering packages up to 5 pounds in weight—upwards of 80% of all shipments. Until recently, this type of delivery method seemed closer to science fiction than reality, but Amazon appears closer than ever to making it work, despite the engineering and legal hurdles. In 2016, Amazon also agreed to lease 40 Boeing 767 jets to help manage its ever-increasing shipping demands. The company has also purchased a fleet of its own trucks and investigated the development self-driving delivery vehicles. Though it may look like Amazon is trying to take full control of its delivery operations, Amazon isn't likely to end its relationships with FedEx or UPS—the overall volume of its orders has become too high for that. However, these moves could dramatically improve per-order profit margins for the majority of Amazon orders, making life even more difficult for Amazon's traditional bricks-and-mortar competitors.

Strategic Analysis—Competition

Amazon has both offline and online competition. Major competitors include eBay (its primary online competitor) and omni-channel retailers such as Walmart, Sears, and JCPenney. In 2016, Walmart purchased discount Amazon competitor Jet.com for $3.3 billion as it continued to suffer at the hands of Amazon, both falling behind in overall market capitalization and stalling in e-commerce growth as Amazon booms. Amazon also competes in a number of product areas with catalog merchants such as L.L.Bean and Lands' End and with other online bookstores such as Barnesand-noble.com. Insofar as portal sites such as MSN and Yahoo operate online stores, they are also competitors. As Walmart continues to recede as a threat to Amazon, the company's biggest threat may be China-based Alibaba, which handles more business worldwide than eBay and Amazon combined and which went public in 2014. Amazon also competes with web services firms that provide hosting, shopping cart, and fulfillment services. What's more, it has fully engaged iTunes and Netflix in competition by offering video and audio downloads. Amazon Music allows users to store and play music online, offers over 35 million DRM-free MP3 songs from both major music labels and thousands of independent labels, and can be played on virtually any hardware device and managed with any music software. Amazon Instant Video offers over 138,000 movies and TV shows to rent or buy, and Amazon Prime Music, launched in 2014, offers over 1.7 million tracks that users can stream for free.

Strategic Analysis—Technology

Anyone who believes that information technology doesn't make a difference clearly does not know much about Amazon. Amazon arguably has the largest and most sophisticated collection of online retailing technologies available at any single online site. It has implemented numerous website management, search, customer interaction, recommendation, transaction processing, and fulfillment services and systems using a combination of its own proprietary technologies and commercially available, licensed technologies. Amazon's transaction-processing systems handle millions of items, numerous status inquiries, gift-wrapping requests, and multiple shipment methods. Customers can receive orders in single or multiple shipments, based on availability, and track the progress of each order. On the fulfillment side, every warehouse employee carries a shoehorn-sized device that combines a bar code scanner, a display screen, and a two-way data transmitter. It continues to invest heavily in AWS, new versions of the Kindle e-reader, and consumer electronics such as the Kindle Fire devices, as well as projects like drone delivery and the Amazon Echo home assistant, which it hopes will become an indispensable gadget in the home the way that smartphones are outside of it. Powered by its state-of-the-art speech recognition and cloud connectivity, the Echo has a diverse range of features that range from streaming music, doing math, updating to-do lists, getting the weather, playing games, and much more. Echo users can already manage many household appliances with the device, and as more appliances are built with Internet connectivity, this feature will only become more useful. In 2015, Amazon spent over $12.5 billion on technology and new content and is on track to spend even more in 2015.

Strategic Analysis—Social and Legal Challenges

Amazon continually faces lawsuits concerning various aspects of its business. Most common are patent infringement suits, largely settled out of court. Currently, there are several pending patent suits, including some involving the Kindle.

In recent years, Amazon has faced increased challenges from states eager to begin collecting sales taxes from online purchases. Until 2011, only customers in five states were required to pay sales taxes. Between distribution center expansion and state legislation requiring large online sellers to collect sales tax even in the absence of a physical presence, that number has ballooned to 28 states and 84% of all U.S. consumers in 2016. Early on, many states had offered Amazon tax break deals to lure its business, perhaps not expecting that untaxed sales would become billions of dollars in lost tax revenue. As many of those deals expire, Amazon has already begun an aggressive (and costly) expansion of its warehousing infrastructure across the United States to support same-day delivery. The rising costs of shipping expenses, which increased 44% in 2015 to $3.36 billion, represent one of the biggest threats to Amazon's long-term profitability, which explains the company's renewed efforts to explore shipping alternatives.

Future Prospects

In 2016, Amazon finally began to show investors and analysts what they had been waiting years to see—sustainable profitability. The company expects continued strong profitability after its landmark $879 million profit in the second quarter of 2016. The profitability of its AWS unit is also a major positive for Amazon, and that segment showed continued rapid growth. Amazon Prime is also a key component of the company's strong performance. While the company continues to spend heavily on future products and services, Amazon at last appears to have turned the corner to profitability (Amazon, 2016a, 2016b; Manjoo, 2016a, 2016b; Bensinger, 2016a, 2016b; Bensinger and Nassauer, 2016; Berthene, 2016; Roettgers, 2016; Kline, 2016).

OMNI-CHANNEL MERCHANTS: BRICKS-AND-CLICKS

Also called omni-channel merchants, **bricks-and-clicks** companies have a network of physical stores as their primary retail channel, but also have online offerings. Omni-channel firms include Walmart, Macy's, Sears, JCPenney, Staples, OfficeMax, Costco, Target, and other brand-name merchants. While bricks-and-clicks merchants face high costs of physical buildings and large sales staffs, they also have many advantages such as a brand name, a national customer base, warehouses, large scale (giving them leverage with suppliers), and a trained staff. Acquiring customers is less expensive because of their brand names, but these firms face challenges in coordinating prices across

bricks-and-clicks
companies that have a network of physical stores as their primary retail channel, but have also introduced online offerings

channels and handling returns of online purchases at their retail outlets. However, these retail players are used to operating on very thin margins and have invested heavily in purchasing and inventory control systems to control costs, and in coordinating returns from multiple locations. Bricks-and-clicks companies face the challenge of leveraging their strengths and assets to the Web, building a credible website, hiring new skilled staff, and building rapid-response order entry and fulfillment systems. According to Internet Retailer, in 2015, omni-channel bricks-and-clicks retailers accounted for around $109 billion (around 32%) of all the Internet Retailer Top 1000's U.S. online retail sales (eMarketer, Inc., 2016g, 2016h).

Macy's is a prime example of a traditional merchant based on physical stores moving successfully to become an omni-channel retailer. Rowland H. Macy opened the first R.H. Macy & Co. store in New York City in 1858, and moved the flagship store (now the site of the famous Macy's Thanksgiving parade) to Herald Square at 34th Street and Broadway in 1902. Today, Macy's is one of the largest national department store chains, with around 775 Macy's department stores throughout the United States.

Like many traditional retailers, Macy's has had to change its business model to accommodate the Internet. Macy's (then called Federated Department Stores Inc.) jumped into e-commerce in 1995 with the creation of the Macys.com website. In 1999, Federated bought Fingerhut, at that time a leading catalog and direct marketer, in part for its expertise in e-commerce fulfillment and database management. Although the Fingerhut acquisition did not prove to be a financial success, Macy's e-commerce efforts benefitted from the acquisition.

Macy's ranked 6th on Internet Retailer's list of the top 500 online retailers, with about $6.2 billion in online sales in 2015, representing double-digit growth and around 23% of total sales. Growth of its physical store sales pales by comparison, and in 2016, it announced plans to close 100 stores in the coming year as it focuses more and more on its e-commerce operations. In October 2016, it announced plans to launch an e-commerce site in China in 2017. It is already one of the most popular sellers on Alibaba's Tmall Global website, where it began selling in November 2015.

The Macy's website receives around 14 million monthly unique visitors. Website features and functions include an interactive catalog, enlarged product views, and ability to see products in different colors and from alternate views, including via zoom and videos. It also offers product comparisons, product ratings, and product recommendations, as well as a real-time inventory check system. Macy's ranked 6th in the 2016 National Retail Federation Favorite Retail Stores survey of companies with respect to the best e-commerce sites for convenience, safety, and customer service.

Macy's has jumped into social media as well, with a Facebook page that has over 14 million Likes, a Twitter feed with over 940,000 followers, a Pinterest page with 48 different boards, over 925,000 pins, 225,000 followers, and a YouTube channel with over 19 million views. Macy's is also an early adopter of Buyable Pins introduced by Pinterest.

Mobile sales at Macy's are booming, and reached an estimated $1.26 billion in 2015, up 60% from $790 million in 2014 according to Internet Retailer. It has iPhone and Android apps, new versions of which it launched in 2014, and an HMTL5 mobile website powered by Usablenet. In 2016, it plans to enhance its mobile site and apps by adding additional filters so mobile shoppers more easily find what they need. It is also considering ways to provide more information to mobile shoppers such as product reviews and natural language search. It has also tried QR codes, SMS marketing, and augmented reality.

In 2016, Macy's also continues to focus on refining its omni-channel approach, encompassing its physical stores, its website, and the mobile platform. It was among the first retailers to support Apple Pay, Apple's mobile payment system, offering it in addition to Macy's own mobile wallet that allows shoppers to virtually store and access offers and coupons. It offers same-day delivery of products ordered online in 8 major U.S. markets, using Deliv, a crowd-sourced delivery provider. Its Buy Online Pickup In Store program, piloted in 2013, has rolled out to all Macy's stores nationwide. In 2016, it introduced its Macy's On Call mobile app on a pilot basis in 10 stores around the country. The app uses IBM Watson's natural language processing, machine learning and cognitive computing technology, coupled with location-based GPS software to assist shoppers as they move through the store. Macy's has also expanded its use of iBeacons to all of its stores nationwide (see Chapter 7) (Macy's, 2015; Internet Retailer, 2016a; Lindner, 2016; Tong, 2016; Smith, 2016; Gagliordi, 2016).

CATALOG MERCHANTS

Catalog merchants such as Lands' End, L.L.Bean, CDW Corp., PC Connection, and Cabela's are established companies that have a national offline catalog operation, but who have also developed online capabilities. Catalog merchants face very high costs for printing and mailing millions of catalogs each year—many of which have a half-life of 30 seconds after the customer receives them. Catalog merchants typically have developed centralized fulfillment and call centers, extraordinary service, and excellent fulfillment in partnership with package delivery firms such as FedEx and UPS. Catalog firms have suffered in recent years as catalog sales growth rates have fallen. As a result, catalog merchants have had to diversify their channels either by building stores (L.L.Bean), being bought by store-based firms (Sears purchased Lands' End), or by building a strong online presence.

Catalog firms are uniquely advantaged because they already possess very efficient order entry and fulfillment systems. However, they face many of the same challenges as bricks-and-mortar stores—they must leverage their existing assets and competencies to a new technology environment, build a credible online presence, and hire new staff. Nevertheless, in 2015, the Internet Retailer Top 1000 catalog merchants generated combined online sales of over $31 billion in the United States (eMarketer, Inc., 2016g, 2016h).

Arguably one of the most well-known online catalog merchants is LandsEnd.com. Lands' End started out in 1963 in a basement of Chicago's tannery district selling sailboat equipment and clothing, handling 15 orders on a good day. Since then it expanded into a direct catalog merchant, distributing over 200 million catalogs annually and selling a much expanded line of "traditionally" styled sport clothing, soft luggage, and products for the home. Lands' End was one of the first apparel retailers to have an e-commerce-enabled website, launching in 1995 with 100 products and travelogue essays. In 2015, it launched a significantly redesigned website featuring a new online catalog with more brands, improved search and navigation, streamlined checkout, and

catalog merchants
established companies that have a national offline catalog operation that is their largest retail channel, but who have recently developed online capabilities

new payment types such as Visa Pay. In 2016, it plans to launch a new mobile app and make further improvements to its website in time for the holiday season (Lands' End, Inc., 2016; Maple, 2016). Located in Dodgeville, Wisconsin, it has since grown into one of the Web's most successful apparel sites.

Lands' End has always been on the leading edge of online retailing technologies, most of which emphasize personal marketing and customized products. Lands' End was the first e-commerce website to allow customers to create a 3-D model of themselves to "try on" clothing. Lands' End "Get Live Help" enables customers to chat online with customer service representatives; Lands' End Custom allows customers to create custom-crafted clothing built for their personal measurements. While customized clothing built online was thought to be a gimmick in the early years of online retailing, today, 40% of Lands' End clothing sold online is customized. In 2003, Lands' End was purchased by Sears (which itself was purchased by Kmart in 2004) and then was spun off as an independent company again in 2014. In 2016, Lands' End was 19th on Internet Retailer's 2016 Top 500 online retailers and 15th on the National Retail Foundation's Favorite 50 survey (Internet Retailer, 2016; Smith, 2016). Features that garner praise include live video chat, product recommendations that reflect a shopper's preferences, content display based on the shopper's location and referral source, and iPhone and iPad apps that deliver Lands' End catalogs to mobile users. The digital catalogs contain exclusive content, including stories written by Lands' End employees. Shoppers can also visit Lands' End on Facebook, where it has over 1.2 million Likes. Lands' End also has a Twitter presence, where it has about 65,000 followers, and 38 different Pinterest boards with 12,500 followers (Lands' End, Inc., 2016b).

MANUFACTURER-DIRECT

manufacturer-direct
single- or multi-channel manufacturers who sell directly online to consumers without the intervention of retailers

Manufacturer-direct firms are either single- or multi-channel manufacturers that sell directly online to consumers without the intervention of retailers. Manufacturer-direct firms were predicted to play a very large role in e-commerce manufacturers, but this has generally not happened. The primary exceptions are computer hardware, such as Apple, Dell, and Hewlett-Packard, and apparel manufacturers, such as Ralph Lauren, Nike, Under Armour, Carter's, Tory Burch, Deckers, Kate Spade, Jones Retail, and Vera Bradley. Nike is the only consumer brand manufacturer whose direct-to-consumer website was ranked in the NRF's Favorite 50 2016 survey, coming in at 17th, up from 33rd in 2015 (Smith, 2016). Most consumer products manufacturers do not sell directly online, although this has started to change. For instance, Procter & Gamble offers Pgshop, which carries over 50 different Procter & Gamble brands. Overall, manufacturer-direct firms accounted for over $57 billion (about 17%) of Internet Retailer's Top 1000 online retail sales in the United States (eMarketer, Inc., 2016g, 2016h).

channel conflict
occurs when retailers of products must compete on price and currency of inventory directly against the manufacturers

Manufacturer-direct firms sometimes face channel conflict challenges. **Channel conflict** occurs when retailers of products must compete on price and currency of inventory directly against the manufacturer, who does not face the cost of maintaining inventory, physical stores, or sales staffs. Firms with no prior direct marketing experience face the additional challenges of developing a fast-response online order and fulfillment system, acquiring customers, and coordinating their supply chains with market demand. Switching from a **supply-push model** (where products are made prior to orders received based on estimated demand and then stored in warehouses awaiting sale) to a **demand-pull model** (where products are not built until an order is received) has proved extremely difficult for traditional manufacturers. Yet for many products, manufacturer-direct firms have the advantage of an established national brand name, an existing large customer base, and a lower cost structure than even catalog merchants because they are the manufacturer of the goods and thus do not pay profits to anyone else. Therefore, manufacturer-direct firms should have higher margins.

supply-push model
products are made prior to orders received based on estimated demand

demand-pull model
products are not built until an order is received

One of the most frequently cited manufacturer-direct retailers is Dell Inc., the world's largest direct computer systems supplier, providing corporations, government agencies, small-to-medium businesses, and individuals with computer products and services ordered straight from the manufacturer's headquarters in Austin, Texas. Although sales representatives support corporate customers, individuals and smaller businesses buy direct from Dell by phone, fax, and via the Internet, with about $3.7 billion in sales generated online to consumers in 2015 (ranking 2nd only to Apple among consumer brand manufacturers) (Internet Retailer, 2016).

When Michael Dell started the company in 1984 in his college dorm room, his idea was to custom-build computers for customers, to eliminate the middleman, and more effectively meet the technology needs of his customers. Today, the company sells much more than individual computer systems; it also offers enterprise systems, desktop, and laptop computers, as well as installation, financing, repair, and management services. By relying on a build-to-order manufacturing process, the company achieves faster inventory turnover (five days), and reduced component and finished goods inventory levels; this strategy virtually eliminates the chance of product obsolescence.

The direct model simplifies the company's operations, eliminating the need to support a wholesale and retail sales network, as well as cutting out the costly associated markup, and gives Dell complete control over its customer database. In addition, Dell can build and ship custom computers nearly as fast as a mail-order supplier can pull a computer out of inventory and ship it to the customer.

To extend the benefits of its direct sales model, Dell has aggressively moved sales, service, and support online. Each month, the company typically has about 10 million unique visitors at the Dell website, where it maintains an estimated 80 country-specific websites. Dell's Premier service enables companies to investigate product offerings, complete order forms and purchase orders, track orders in real time, and review order histories all online. For its small business customers, it has created an online virtual account executive, as well as a spare-parts ordering system and virtual help desk with direct access to technical support data. Dell has also continued to broaden its offerings beyond pure hardware product sales, adding warranty services, product integration and installation services, Internet access, software, and technology consulting, referring to them as "beyond the box" offerings. These include nearly 30,000 software and peripheral products from leading manufacturers that can be bundled with Dell products. Dell has also embraced social media. It has a corporate blog, called Direct2Dell, and a presence on Facebook (with over 9.6 million Likes), Pinterest (with 7 boards), and

Twitter (with 600,000 followers). It posts Twitter-exclusive sales for those who follow Dell Outlet. It also has a channel on YouTube that it calls the Dell Vlog Channel, with over 55,000 subscribers. In 2011, it released mobile apps for the iPhone and Android that featured in-app purchasing, customer ratings and reviews, product comparison, order tracking, a Shopping Advisor, and easy access to various customer support options. Dell promoted the release of the app via both a standard e-mail campaign and one optimized for mobile viewing, and discovered that the open rate for the mobile e-mail was twice that of the standard version, and the clickthrough rate was more than five times higher. In December 2014, it replaced its mobile website with one that uses responsive design, allowing the site to automatically adapt to consumers' devices, driving a 50% increase in conversion rate and a 70% increase in consumer satisfaction. In 2016, after an 18-month web platform overhaul that left its website with a cluttered home page that took 14 seconds to load, it revamped the site once again, focusing on simple navigation, fast performance, site search, and an easy way to compare multiple products, with a home page that now loads in just over one second, topping Internet Retailer's monthly performance index in August 2016 (Internet Retailer, 2016; Evans, 2016; Berthene, 2016b; Zaraban, 2015).

COMMON THEMES IN ONLINE RETAILING

We have looked at some very different companies in the preceding section, from entrepreneurial virtual merchants to established offline giants. Online retail is the fastest growing channel in retail commerce, has the fastest growing consumer base, and has growing penetration across many categories of goods. On the other hand, profits for many startup ventures have been difficult to achieve, and it took even Amazon eight years to show its first profit.

The reasons for the difficulties experienced by many online retailers in achieving profits are also now clear. The path to success in any form of retail involves having a central location in order to attract a larger number of shoppers, charging high enough prices to cover the costs of goods as well as marketing, and developing highly efficient inventory and fulfillment systems so that the company can offer goods at lower costs than competitors and still make a profit. Many online merchants failed to follow these fundamental ideas, lowering prices below the total costs of goods and operations, failing to develop efficient business processes, failing to attract a large enough audience to their websites, and spending far too much on customer acquisition and marketing. By 2015, the lessons of the past have been learned, and far fewer online merchants are selling below cost, especially if they are startup companies. There's also been a change in consumer culture and attitudes. Whereas in the past consumers looked online for really cheap prices, in 2016, they look to online purchasing for convenience, time savings, and time shifting (buying retail goods at night from the sofa). Consumers have been willing to accept higher prices in return for the convenience of shopping online and avoiding the inconvenience of shopping at stores and malls. This allows online merchants more pricing freedom.

A second common theme in retail e-commerce is that, for the most part, disintermediation has not occurred and the retail middleman has not disappeared. Indeed, virtual merchants, along with powerful offline merchants who moved online, have maintained their powerful grip on the retail customer, with some notable exceptions in electronics and software. Manufacturers—with the exception of electronic goods—have used the Web primarily as an informational resource, driving consumers to the traditional retail channels for transactions. Leaving Amazon aside, the most significant online growth has been that of offline general merchandiser giant intermediaries such as Walmart, Sears, Costco, JCPenney, Macy's, Target, and Nordstrom. Many of the first-mover, online pure-play merchants (online intermediaries) failed to achieve profitability and closed their doors en masse as their venture capital funds were depleted. Traditional retailers have been the fast followers (although many of them cannot be characterized as particularly "fast") and are most likely to succeed online by extending their traditional brands, competencies, and assets. In this sense, e-commerce technological innovation is following the historical pattern of other technology-driven commercial changes, from automobiles to radio and television, where an explosion of startup firms attracts significant investment, but quickly fail, and are consolidated into larger existing firms.

A third theme is that in order to succeed online, established merchants need to create an integrated shopping environment that combines their catalog, store, and online experiences into one. Customers want to shop wherever they want, using any device, and at any time. Established retailers have significant fulfillment, inventory management, supply chain management, and other competencies that apply directly to the online channel. To succeed online, established retailers need to extend their brands, provide incentives to consumers to use the online channel (which given the same prices for goods is more efficient to operate than a physical store), avoid channel conflict, and build advertising campaigns using online search engines such as Google, Yahoo, and Bing, and shopping comparison sites.

A fourth theme is the growth of online specialty merchants selling high-end, fashionable and luxury goods such as diamonds (Blue Nile), jewelry (Tiffany), and high fashion (Emporio Armani and Gilt Groupe) or selling discounted electronics (Best Buy), apparel (Gap), or office products (Office Depot). These firms are demonstrating the vitality and openness of the Internet for innovation and extending the range of products available online. Many virtual merchants have developed large, online customer bases, as well as the online tools required to market to their customer base. These online brands can be strengthened further through alliances and partnerships that add the required competencies in inventory management and fulfillment services. Virtual merchants need to build operational strength and efficiency before they can become profitable.

Another theme in 2016 is the continuing extraordinary growth in social commerce, local marketing and commerce, and mobile commerce. In the space of eight years since the first iPhone appeared, the mobile platform has emerged as a retail marketing and shopping tool, which will greatly expand e-commerce, potentially driving e-commerce to 20% of all commerce in the next five years. Local merchants will be a major benefactor of the growing mobile commerce platform. In an equally short time, people have begun to spend an increasing amount of their Internet time on social networks where they share attitudes and experiences about business firms, products, and services. In a few years, social networks may turn into large purchasing venues. For instance, in October 2016, building on the increasing popularity of Facebook groups created to buy and sell merchandise, Facebook introduced Facebook Marketplace, accessed from a Shop icon at the bottom of the Facebook app. Facebook Marketplace is a blend of social, mobile, and local C2C e-commerce intended to make it easy to find, buy, and sell items offered by people in your local community (Facebook, 2016).

A final theme in 2016 is the increasing use by retailers, large and small, of big data in their marketing efforts. The *Insight on Technology* case, *Big Data and Predictive Marketing*, examines this development.

11.4 THE SERVICE SECTOR: OFFLINE AND ONLINE

The service sector is typically the largest and most rapidly expanding part of the economies in advanced industrial nations such as the United States, and many European and some Asian countries. E-commerce in the service sector offers extraordinary opportunities to deliver information, knowledge, and transaction efficiencies.

The major service industry groups are finance, insurance, real estate, travel, professional services such as legal and accounting, business services, health services, and educational services. Business services include activities such as consulting, advertising and marketing, and information processing. Within these service industry groups, companies can be further categorized into those that involve **transaction brokering** (acting as an intermediary to facilitate a transaction) and those that involve providing a "hands-on" service. For instance, one type of financial service involves stockbrokers who act as the middle person in a transaction between buyers and sellers. Online mortgage companies such as LendingTree refer customers to mortgage companies that actually issue the mortgage. Employment agencies put a seller of labor in contact with a buyer of labor. The service involved in all these examples is brokering a transaction.

transaction brokering
acting as an intermediary to facilitate a transaction

In contrast, some industries perform specific hands-on activities for consumers. In order to provide their service, these professionals need to interact directly and personally with the "client." For these service industries, the opportunities for e-commerce are somewhat different. Currently, doctors and dentists cannot treat patients over the Internet. However, the Internet can assist their services by providing consumers with information, knowledge, and communication.

With some exceptions (for example, providers of physical services, such as cleaning, gardening, and so on), perhaps the most important feature of service industries (and occupations) is that they are knowledge- and information-intense. In order to provide value, service industries process a great deal of information and employ a highly skilled, educated workforce. For instance, to provide legal services, you need lawyers with law degrees. Law firms are required to process enormous amounts of textual information. Likewise with medical services. Financial services are not so knowledge-intensive, but require much larger investments in information processing just to keep track of transactions and investments. In fact, the financial services sector

INSIGHT ON TECHNOLOGY

BIG DATA AND PREDICTIVE MARKETING

Big data refers to the deluge of digital data that is being produced by the billions of people using the Internet, smartphones, and smartphones around the world, as well as an explosion of data from the Internet of Things. Estimates vary, but an IBM report claims big data generates 2.5 exabytes (2.5 billion gigabytes) a day. But big data is about more than volume; it is also about velocity (data comes in real-time torrents, loses value quickly, and requires rapid responses), variety (the data deluge contains both structured numeric data and unstructured data such as text documents, e-mail, video, and audio), variability (the flow of data is event driven and leads to peak loads, followed by relative calm), and complexity (the data comes from different sources and requires cleansing, matching, and reformatting in order to be useful). Storing all this data requires new kinds of database technologies and analyzing all this data involves software called business analytics.

Big data is important for business because it can lead to better decisions and competitive advantages for firms that get it right. Big data is influencing the design and marketing of retail products and in-store sales efforts. Big data and powerful analytics programs make possible predictive marketing, the ability to send personalized messages to customers recommending products before they ask. The hope for retail firms is that big data will make us all into big spenders.

Predictive marketing is not entirely new. Skilled salespeople have always been able to size up a customer and predict how much a customer is willing to spend, informing what they decide to show a customer. Predictive marketing is different because it is not based on traditional sales skills but instead on the collection of data and the use of software programs to maximize the likelihood of

a sale. Predictive marketing can scale to millions of customers and make decisions in milliseconds.

Big data and predictive marketing are not just for huge national retailers, but now can be used by much smaller firms as well. Stitch Fix, a women's clothing retailer using a monthly subscription revenue model, is one example. Stitch Fix blends expert styling advice, personalization software, and unique products to deliver an individualized shopping experience for each of its customers. New customers fill out a Style Profile online, which is then analyzed by the firm's proprietary software to identify products that the customer is likely to purchase. The company's 3,000 personal stylists interpret the output of the system and then handpick five clothing items and accessories each month that are unique to the customer's taste, budget, and life style. The customer is not required to purchase the items until they have been received and accepted; the process to return the items is simple.

Over time, the software keeps track of what the customer purchased, and learns to make better predictions based on what customers actually keep (as opposed to what they say they want, a key difference). The more accurately Stitch Fix can predict what its customers will likely buy, the more sales it will generate, but using analytics to better understand its customers also allows Stitch Fix to reduce its inventory costs, to adjust production to better meet demand, and to know its customers better than its competitors do. The data collected in the Style Profile includes basic demographic information, plus a photo section that depicts seven different styles. Customers can respond to each style suggestion to further differentiate themselves in the Stitch Fix software, which runs on Amazon Simple Storage Service. Customers can also share links to their Pinterest profiles to give Stitch Fix even more information. Based on

(continued)

the customer's demographic information and selections of preferred styles, the software predicts which of several thousand products the customer would like.

Stitch Fix uses its customer data in a closed loop to make continual improvements to its machine learning algorithms, which become more accurate as they are exposed to more customer data. If tweaks to the algorithm are shown to be more predictive, they become permanent, whereas changes that fail to improve the algorithm are discarded. The company has a team of 80 data scientists developing new tools and improving its core item selection algorithms. Eric Colson, the chief algorithms officer, joined the company from Netflix, whose recommendation engine is often cited as the gold standard in personalization. Stitch Fix's algorithms synthesize customer feedback, purchase and return decisions, and profile information to quickly generate possible recommendations. Stitch Fix stylists use these results to make their next selections.

For Stitch Fix, the blend of five years of highly granular data, cutting-edge machine learning, and expert human input has been a winning combination. The company is growing explosively, with industry analysts projecting approximately $375 million in revenue in 2016, a 50% increase from its $250 million earnings in 2015. The company is reportedly profitable and has not raised venture capital in two years. Seventy percent of its customers return within 90 days for another fix, and 39% spend half of their clothing budget or more with the company. Stitch Fix already has five distribution centers, and the company is launching a service for men's clothing as well as several in-house brands of clothing by the end of the year.

At the other end of the spectrum, Walmart, the world's largest retailer, is using big data and predictive marketing both online and in its stores. Over 50% of Walmart's web traffic comes from mobile devices. Walmart's strategy is to turn mobile devices into shopping instruments for both online and offline shopping. Its mobile app generates shopping lists automatically for customers based on what they and other customers purchase each week. When the customer is in the store, a proximity marketing feature prompts the user to switch into store mode, and then customers are sent discounts and loyalty offers. Walmart is also currently building what it bills as "the world's largest private cloud" to track and analyze the millions of transactions that take place each day in its stores. Walmart will use that data to automatically respond to fluctuations in demand, inventory, and competitor activity in real-time.

Experience with big data and predictive marketing in retail is still somewhat limited. There are many pilot projects, but little information on how well these systems really work for retail firms. The ability of big data to reverse the reduction in shoppers at physical retail stores that has occurred in the last few years is not certain. So far, there appears to be more data than there is analysis and strategy in predictive marketing. In opinion surveys, firms identify getting value from the data they have as the most challenging aspect of predictive marketing. A key limitation is the scarcity of data scientists who can bring meaning to the data, and managers who can translate these results into sales tactics and strategies.

SOURCES: "The 'Insight-Driven Business': How to Become a Master of the Data Universe," by Doug Black, Enterprisetech.com, October 3, 2016; "Stitch Fix Launches Stitch Fix Men," PR Newswire, September 19, 2016; "How Artificial Intelligence Is Transforming Retail Personalization," by Craig Alberino, Retailcustomerexperience.com, September 16, 2016; "How Stitch Fix Uses Big Data to Disrupt Your Closet," Bloomberg.com, June 29, 2016; "Is Stitch Fix the Goldilocks of Fashion?," by Lauren Sherman, Businessoffashion.com, June 29, 2016; "Stitch Fix: The $250 Million Startup Playing Fashionista Moneyball," by Ryan Mac, *Forbes*, June 1, 2016; "At Stitch Fix, Data Scientists and A.I. Become Personal Stylists," by Sharon Gaudin, Computerworld.com, May 6, 2016; "Subscription Box Service Stitch Fix Fills a Void in Traditional Retail," eMarketer, Inc, April 6, 2016; "Changing the Retail Sector with Big Data," by Bernard Marr, *Forbes*, November 10, 2015; "Stitch Fix Opening Distribution Center in Arizona," Tucson.com, September 10, 2015; "What Stitch Fix Figured Out About Mass Customization," by Simone Ahuja, Hbr.org, May 26, 2015; "Why Sephora's Digital Boss Joined Stitch Fix, the Personal Stylist Startup That's Growing Like Mad," by Jason Del Ray, Recode.net, March 22, 2015; "How America's E-commerce Giants Compare Across the Desktop, Mobile Web, and Mobile App Arenas," by Ariel Rosenstein, Thenextweb.com, January 14, 2015.

is the largest investor in information technology, with over 80% of invested capital going to information technology equipment and services.

Services differ in the amount of personalization and customization required, although just about all services entail some personalization or customization. Some services, such as legal, medical, and accounting services, require extensive personalization—the adjustment of a service to the precise needs of a single individual or object. Others, such as financial services, benefit from customization by allowing individuals to choose from a restricted menu. The ability of Internet and e-commerce technology to personalize and customize service, or components of service, is a major factor undergirding the extremely rapid growth of e-commerce services. Future expansion of e-services will depend in part on the ability of e-commerce firms to transform their customized services—choosing from a list—into truly personalized services, such as providing unique advice and consultation based on a digital yet intimate understanding of the client (at least as intimate as professional service providers).

11.5 ONLINE FINANCIAL SERVICES

The online financial services sector is a shining example of an e-commerce success story, but one with many twists and turns. While the innovative online firms such as E*Trade have been instrumental in transforming the brokerage industry, the impacts of e-commerce on the large, powerful banking, insurance, and real estate firms have been delayed by consumer resistance and the lack of industry innovation. For instance, online-only banks have not displaced traditional banks. But e-commerce has nevertheless transformed the banking and financial industries, as the major institutions have deployed their own online applications to service an increasingly connected online customer base. Insurance has become more standardized and easier to purchase online. Although security is still a concern, consumers are much more willing to trust online sites with their financial information than in the past. Firms such as Mint (now owned by Intuit), SmartyPig, Credit Karma, Moven, and Simple (now owned by Spanish banking giant BBVA) continue to show growth. Multi-channel, established financial services firms—the slow followers—also continue to show gains in online transactions.

ONLINE FINANCIAL CONSUMER BEHAVIOR

Surveys show that consumers are attracted to financial sites and apps because of their desire to save time and access information rather than save money, although saving money is an important goal among the most sophisticated online financial households. Most online consumers use financial services sites and apps for mundane financial management, such as checking balances of existing accounts, and paying bills, most of which were established offline. Once accustomed to performing mundane financial management activities, consumers move on to more sophisticated capabilities such as using personal financial management tools, making loan payments, and considering offers from online institutions. And in the last few years, increasing investments have been made in startup "fintech" companies that aim to unbundle traditional institutional financial services and instead deliver specifically targeted consumer-oriented solutions, often via mobile devices and apps.

ONLINE BANKING AND BROKERAGE

NetBank and Wingspan Bank pioneered online banking in the United States in 1996 and 1997, respectively. Although late by a year or two, the established brand-name national banks have taken a substantial lead in market share as the percentage of their customers who bank online has grown rapidly. The top banks are all large, national banks that also offer online banking: Bank of America, JPMorgan Chase, Citigroup, and Wells Fargo. Major direct banks (those that operate without a network of branches or branded ATMs) include Ally Bank, EverBank, Discover Bank, Capital One 360, Bank of Internet USA, State Farm Bank, and USAA. These direct banks have seen customer deposits grow faster than regular banks, indicating their growing popularity, particularly with younger customers. Several startups have also moved into the online banking and financial services spaces. For instance, Moven offers debit account services linked with online and mobile financial management tools. Simple, owned by Spanish bank BBVA, provides checking accounts linked to debit cards in addition to financial management tools.

In 2016, according to a December 2016 European Commission survey, almost two-thirds of the adult U.K. population use online banking. Mobile banking has become an important banking channel for all age groups, with 55% of U.K. mobile phone users indicating that they use mobile banking. While online banking has become a primary banking channel for all age groups, Millennials (those in the 18- to 34-year-old group) are adopting mobile banking at a much higher rate than those who are older. Top mobile banking activities include checking balances and bank statements, transferring money from one account to another, paying bills, making bill payments, and depositing checks using smartphone apps that snap a photo of the check. Security issues still deter some. A survey by Javelin Strategy & Research found that about 45% of those surveyed cited security concerns as the reason why they did not use mobile banking services (eMarketer, Inc., 2016i, 2015a; Eurostat, 2016; ING, 2016).

From the bank's perspective, online and mobile banking can provide significant cost savings. According to Javelin Strategy & Research, the average in-person transaction at a bank branch costs $4.25, while an online transaction costs 19 cents, and a mobile transaction, just 10 cents (Javelin Strategy & Research, 2013).

The history of online brokerage has been similar to that of online banking. Early innovators such as E*Trade have been displaced from their leadership positions in terms of numbers of online accounts by discount broker pioneer Charles Schwab and financial industry giant Fidelity (which has more mutual fund customers and more funds under management than any other U.S. firm).

According to one survey, about 25% of U.S. Internet users interact digitally with online brokerage firms (eMarketer, Inc., 2015b). The use of mobile devices and apps for this purpose is increasing, particularly among Millennials. According to a recent E*Trade survey, nearly 80% of Millennials reported using a smartphone/investing

TABLE 11.6	TOP U.S. ONLINE BROKERAGES, 2016
FIRM	NUMBER OF UNIQUE VISITORS (IN MILLIONS)
Fidelity	6.86
Vanguard	4.66
Schwab	3.14
TD Ameritrade	1.77
E*Trade	1.74
Scottrade	1.45
ML (Merrill Lynch)	1.34

SOURCE: Based on data from Compete.com, 2016.

app, with 50% doing so more than once a week (eMarketer, Inc., 2015b, 2015c, 2015d). The most frequent activities conducted on mobile devices include monitoring one's portfolio and the market, getting stock quotes, placing and checking on orders, and doing general financial research. The top trading website among U.S. Internet users in 2016 is Fidelity Investments, with around 6.9 million monthly unique visitors (see **Table 11.6**). The major online brokerage firms are investing significantly in search engine marketing, and are among the biggest spenders in the paid search market. They are also increasingly using social media to engage with customers, although they must be careful to comply with all regulations and rules as they do so. For instance, some brokerage firms use Twitter to deliver commentary, company information, marketing, and customer service. A new wave of online financial advisors, sometimes referred to as robo-advisors, offer inexpensive automated investment management tools and advice. Examples of companies that have attracted venture capital interest include Betterment (valued at over $700 million, and managing almost $4 billion assets for around 150,000 customers as of 2016), Wealthfront, and Personal Capital Corp. Similar services are also offered by major online brokerage firms such as Vanguard and Schwab.

Multi-Channel vs. Pure Online Financial Services Firms

Online consumers prefer to visit financial services sites that have physical outlets or branches. In general, multi-channel financial services firms that have both physical branches or offices and solid online offerings are growing faster than pure-online firms that have no physical presence, and they are assuming market leadership as well. Traditional banking firms have literally thousands of branches where customers can open accounts, deposit money, take out loans, find home mortgages, and rent a safety deposit box. Top online brokerage firms do not have the same physical footprint as the banks do, but each has a strong physical presence or telephone presence to strengthen its online presence. Fidelity has walk-in service center branches, but it relies primarily on the telephone for interacting with investors. Charles Schwab has investment centers around the country as an integral part of its online strategy. Pure-online banks and brokerages cannot provide customers with some services that still require a face-to-face interaction.

Financial Portals and Account Aggregators

financial portals

sites that provide consumers with comparison shopping services, independent financial advice, and financial planning

Financial portals are sites that provide consumers with comparison shopping services, independent financial advice, and financial planning. Independent portals do not themselves offer financial services, but act as steering mechanisms to online providers. They generate revenue from advertising, referral fees, and subscription fees. For example, Yahoo's financial portal, Yahoo Finance, offers consumers the ability to track their stock portfolio, market overviews, real-time stock quotes, news, financial advice, and streaming video interviews with financial leaders. Other independent financial portals include Intuit's Quicken, MSN's MSN Money, and CNNMoney. A host of financial portal sites have sprung up to help consumers with financial management and planning such as Mint (owned by Intuit), SmartyPig, and Credit Karma.

account aggregation

the process of pulling together all of a customer's financial (and even nonfinancial) data at a single personalized website

Account aggregation is the process of pulling together all of a customer's financial (and even nonfinancial) data at a single personalized website, including brokerage, banking, insurance, loans, frequent flyer miles, personalized news, and much more. For example, a consumer can see his or her TD Ameritrade brokerage account, Fidelity 401(k) account, Travelers Insurance annuity account, and American Airlines frequent flyer miles all displayed on a single site. The idea is to provide consumers with a holistic view of their entire portfolio of assets, no matter what financial institution actually holds those assets.

The leading provider of account aggregation technology is Envestnet Yodlee. It uses screen-scraping and other techniques to pull information from 14,000 different data sources. A smart-mapping technology is also used so that if the underlying websites change, the scraping software can adapt and still find the relevant information. Today, Envestnet Yodlee is used by over 1,000 leading financial institutions and companies, including 11 of the 20 largest U.S. banks, and this network reaches more than 100 million end users (Envestnet Yodlee, 2016).

ONLINE MORTGAGE AND LENDING SERVICES

During the early days of e-commerce, hundreds of firms launched pure-play online mortgage sites to capture the U.S. home mortgage market. Early entrants hoped to radically simplify and transform the traditional mortgage value chain process, dramatically speed up the loan closing process, and share the economies with consumers by offering lower rates.

By 2003, over half of these early-entry, pure-online firms had failed. Early pure-play online mortgage institutions had difficulties developing a brand name at an affordable price and failed to simplify the mortgage generation process. They ended up suffering from high start-up and administrative costs, high customer acquisition costs, rising interest rates, and poor execution of their strategies.

Despite this rocky start, the online mortgage market is slowly growing; it is dominated by established online banks and other online financial services firms, traditional mortgage vendors, and a few successful online mortgage firms.

Many mortgage shoppers research mortgages online, but few actually apply online because of the complexity of mortgages. Most mortgages today are written by intermediary mortgage brokers, with banks still playing an important origination role but generally not servicing mortgages they originate.

Although online mortgage originations currently represent a small percentage of all mortgages, their number is expected to continue to grow slowly but surely over the next several years. In November 2015, Intuit's Quicken Loans introduced Rocket Mortgage, which allows borrowers to be fully approved for a mortgage in under ten minutes. The applicant only needs to provide a few details, such as birth date, social security number, and home address, and then Rocket Mortgage uses that data to automatically obtain various types of information without the need for the borrower to manually provide any further documentation. The system then displays various loan options, and once the borrower selects one, all necessary documents (except for final closing documents) can be signed online using a secure portal (Prevost, 2015).

Consumer benefits from online mortgages include reduced application times, market interest rate intelligence, and process simplification that occurs when participants in the mortgage process (title, insurance, and lending companies) share a common information base. Mortgage lenders benefit from the cost reduction involved in online processing of applications, while charging rates marginally lower than traditional bricks-and-mortar institutions.

Nevertheless, the online mortgage industry has not transformed the process of obtaining a mortgage. A significant brake on market expansion is the complexity of the mortgage process, which requires physical signatures and documents, multiple institutions, and complex financing details—such as closing costs and points—that are difficult for shoppers to compare across vendors. Nevertheless, as in other areas, the ability of shoppers to find low mortgage rates online has helped reduce the fees and interest rates charged by traditional mortgage lenders. Online lending services have also become popular. The biggest online lenders include Lending Club, which went public in December 2014, but has faced diminishing returns in 2016, Prosper (a peer-to-peer loan marketplace), and Social Finance Inc. (SoFi), which focuses primarily on student loans.

ONLINE INSURANCE SERVICES

In 1995, the price of a $500,000 20-year term life policy for a healthy 40-year-old male was $995 a year. In 2016, the same policy could be had for around $345—a decline of about 65%—while other prices have risen 15% in the same period. In a study of the term life insurance business, Brown and Goolsbee discovered that Internet usage led to an 8%–15% decline in term life insurance prices industry-wide (both offline and online), and increased consumer surplus by about $115 million per year (and hence reduced industry profits by the same amount) (Brown and Goolsbee, 2000). Price dispersion for term life policies initially increased, but then fell as more and more people began using the Internet to obtain insurance quotes.

Unlike books and CDs, where online price dispersion is higher than offline, and in many cases online prices are higher than offline, term life insurance stands out as one product group supporting the conventional wisdom that the Internet will lower search costs, increase price comparison, and lower prices to consumers. Term life insurance is a commodity product, however, and in other insurance product lines, the Web offers insurance companies new opportunities for product and service differentiation and price discrimination.

The insurance industry forms a major part of the financial services sector. It has four major segments: automobile, life, health, and property and casualty. Insurance products can be very complex. For example, there are many different types of non-automotive property and casualty insurance: liability, fire, homeowners, commercial, workers' compensation, marine, accident, and other lines such as vacation insurance. Writing an insurance policy in any of these areas is very information-intense, often necessitating personal inspection of the properties, and it requires considerable actuarial experience and data. The life insurance industry has also developed life insurance policies that defy easy comparison and can only be explained and sold by an experienced sales agent. Historically, the insurance industry has relied on thousands of local insurance offices and agents to sell complex products uniquely suited to the circumstances of the insured person and the property. Complicating the insurance marketplace is the fact that the insurance industry is not federally regulated, but rather is regulated by 50 different state insurance commissions that are strongly influenced by local insurance agents. Before a website can offer quotations on insurance, it must obtain a license to enter the insurance business in all the states where it provides quotation services or sells insurance.

Like the online mortgage industry, the online insurance industry has been very successful in attracting visitors who are looking to obtain prices and terms of insurance policies. While many national insurance underwriting companies initially did not offer competitive products directly online because it might injure the business operations of their traditional local agents, the websites of almost all of the major firms now provide the ability to obtain an online quote. Even if consumers do not actually purchase insurance policies online, the Internet has proven to have a powerful influence on consumer insurance decisions by dramatically reducing search costs and changing the price discovery process. According to a 2015 survey, over 70% of American consumers looked for life insurance information online, with 30% indicating that the Internet was their most valuable source of information. However, consumers also continue to rely on financial advisors as well for advice, with over half seeking information from both sources (LIMRA, 2015). Another survey found that nearly 2 in 3 consumers who own a mobile device said they already have or plan to use those devices to access services to their life insurance policies (LIMRA, 2014a). Other forms of insurance are more likely to be purchased online. For instance, according to a 2015 comScore study, the online channel continues to be consumers' preferred method for shopping for auto insurance policies, with over 70% of shoppers getting an online quote (comScore, 2015). Insurance companies are also making increased use of social media. For instance, a LIMRA survey found that over 90% of life insurance companies had social media programs, up from 60% in 2010. Facebook and LinkedIn are the most popular platforms, both used by over 90% (LIMRA, 2014b). All of the major insurers, such as GEICO, Allstate, State Farm, Progressive, and Travelers, have a significant online presence. Some of the leading online insurance services companies include InsWeb, Insure.com, Insurance.com, QuickQuote, and NetQuote.

ONLINE REAL ESTATE SERVICES

During the early days of e-commerce, real estate seemed ripe for an Internet revolution that would rationalize this historically local, complex, and local agent-driven industry that monopolized the flow of consumer information. Potentially, the Internet and e-commerce might have disintermediated this huge marketspace, allowing buyers and sellers, renters and owners, to transact directly, lower search costs to near zero, and dramatically reduce prices. However, this did not happen. What did happen is extremely beneficial to buyers and sellers, as well as to real estate agents. At one point, there were an estimated 100,000 real estate sites on the Internet worldwide. Many of these sites have disappeared. However, the remaining online sites have started to make headway toward transforming the industry. In addition, most local real estate brokers in the United States have their own agency websites to deal with clients, in addition to participating with thousands of other agencies in multiple listing services that list homes online. Some of the major online real estate sites are Realtor.com and its parent, Move.com (now owned by global media giant News Corp.), Zillow and Trulia (now owned by the same company), HomeGain, ZipRealty, Craigslist, and Redfin. Zillow and Trulia together account for over 35% of all desktop and mobile visits to real estate sites in 2016, while Realtor.com attracts about 12% of traffic (Hitwise, 2016).

Real estate differs from other types of online financial services because it is impossible to complete a property transaction online. Clearly, the major impact of Internet real estate sites is in influencing offline decisions. The Internet has become a compelling method for real estate professionals, homebuilders, property managers and owners, and ancillary service providers to communicate with and provide information to consumers. According to the National Association of Realtors, the first step in the home buying process for nearly all ages of home buyers was to look online. Websites were the most common information source, used by almost 90%, while mobile sites and apps and mobile search were each also used by over 50%. At the same time, 87% also used the services of a real estate agent (National Association of Realtors, 2016).

The primary service offered by real estate sites is a listing of houses available. In 2016, Realtor.com, the official site of the National Association of Realtors, listed over 3 million homes and had around 40 million unique users across desktop and mobile devices in April 2016 (Feeney, 2016). Listings typically feature detailed property descriptions, multiple photographs, and virtual 360-degree tours. Consumers can link to mortgage lenders, credit reporting agencies, house inspectors, and surveyors. There are also online loan calculators, appraisal reports, sales price histories by neighborhood, school district data, crime reports, and social and historical information on neighborhoods. Some online real estate brokers now charge substantially less than traditional offline brokers who typically charge 6% of the sale price. They can do this because the buyers (and in some cases, the sellers) do much of the work of traditional real estate agents, such as prospecting, choosing neighborhoods, and identifying houses of interest prior to contacting an online agent. For instance, Move (the parent company of Realtor.com) also offers a "Find a Neighborhood" feature that allows users to choose the type of neighborhood they want to live in by weighing factors such as the quality (and tax costs) of schools, age of the population, number of families with children nearby, and available social and recreational services. Move also offers mobile apps for the iPad and iPhone, Android, and Windows phones. For instance, the Area Scout function allows users to see the list prices of all homes in a neighborhood on the street level.

Despite the revolution in available information, there has not been a revolution in the industry value chain. Online listings are provided by local multiple listing services supported by local real estate agents. Sometimes, addresses of the houses are not available, and online users are directed to the local listing agent who is hired by the seller. Traditional hands-on real estate brokers will show the house and handle all transactions with the owner to preserve their fees, typically ranging from 5% to 6% of the transaction.

11.6 ONLINE TRAVEL SERVICES

Online travel is one of the most successful B2C e-commerce segments. The Internet has become the most common channel used by consumers to research travel options, seek the best possible prices, and book reservations for airline tickets, hotel rooms, rental cars, cruises, and tours. Today, more travel is booked online than offline. In the United Kingdom in 2016, about 30 million (over two-thirds of all U.K. Internet users) researched travel and about 27 million booked travel online. Worldwide online travel services revenues reached over €525 billion in 2016 and are expected to continue growing to over €760 billion by 2020 (see **Figure 11.5**) (eMarketer, Inc., 2016j, 2016k).

WHY ARE ONLINE TRAVEL SERVICES SO POPULAR?

Online travel sites offer consumers a one-stop, convenient, leisure and business travel experience where travelers can find content (descriptions of vacations and facilities), community (chat groups and bulletin boards), commerce (purchase of all travel elements), and customer service (usually through call centers). Online sites offer much more information and many more travel options than traditional travel agents. For suppliers—the owners of hotels, rental cars, and airlines—the online sites aggregate millions of consumers into singular, focused customer pools that can be efficiently reached through on-site advertising and promotions. Online sites create a much more efficient marketplace, bringing consumers and suppliers together in a low-transaction cost environment.

Travel services are an ideal service for the Internet, and therefore e-commerce business models work well for this product. Travel is an information-intensive product requiring significant consumer research. It is a digital product in the sense that travel requirements—planning, researching, comparison shopping, reserving, and payment—can be accomplished for the most part online in a digital environment. On the travel reservation side, travel does not require any "inventory": there are no physical assets. And the suppliers of the product—owners of hotels, airlines, rental cars, vacation rooms, and tour guides—are highly fragmented and often have excess capacity. Always

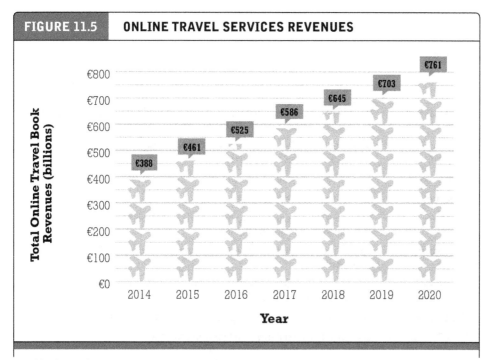

FIGURE 11.5   ONLINE TRAVEL SERVICES REVENUES

Worldwide travel service revenues are expected to reach over €760 billion by 2020.
SOURCE: Based on data from eMarketer, Inc., 2016j.

looking for customers to fill vacant rooms and rent idle cars, suppliers will be anxious to lower prices and willing to advertise on websites that can attract millions of consumers. The online intermediaries—such as Travelocity, Expedia, and others—do not have to deploy thousands of travel agents in physical offices across the country but can instead concentrate on a single interface with a national consumer audience. Travel services do not require the kind of expensive multi-channel "physical presence" strategy required of financial services (although they generally operate centralized call centers to provide personal customer service). Therefore, travel services "scale" better, permitting earnings to grow faster than costs. But these efficiencies also make it hard for reservation sites to make a profit.

THE ONLINE TRAVEL MARKET

There are four major sectors in the travel market: airline tickets, hotel reservations, car rentals, and travel packages. Airline tickets are the source of the greatest amount of revenue in online travel. Airline reservations are largely a commodity. They can be easily described online. The same is true with car rentals; most people can reliably rent a car over the phone or online and expect to obtain what they ordered. Although hotels are somewhat more difficult to describe, hotel branding, supplemented by websites that include descriptions, photographs, and virtual tours, typically provides enough information to most consumers to allow them to feel as if they know what they

TABLE 11.7	MAJOR ONLINE TRAVEL SITES
NAME	**DESCRIPTION**
LEISURE/UNMANAGED BUSINESS TRAVEL	
eDreams OdigO	One of Europe's largest online travel groups, formed by the merger of eDreams, Go Voyages, Opodo, and Travelink.
Expedia	Largest online travel service; leisure focus. Now also owns Orbitz, Travelocity, CheapTickets, Hotels.com, and Hotwire.
Orbitz	Began as supplier-owned reservation system; now owned by Expedia.
Travelocity	Leisure focus. Owned by Expedia.
Priceline	Name Your Price model; leisure focus. Also owns Booking.com and Lowestfare.com, Expedia's primary competitor.
TripAdvisor	Travel review site that also allows you to compare prices and book reservations.
CheapTickets	Discount airline tickets, hotel reservations, and auto rentals. Acquired by Expedia when it purchased Orbitz.
Booking.com	Leading European hotel booking service. Owned by Priceline.
TUI AG	German multinational travel and tourism company.
MANAGED BUSINESS TRAVEL	
GetThere	Corporate online booking solution (COBS). Owned by Sabre Corporation.
BCD Travel	Full-service corporate travel agency.

are purchasing, making them comfortable enough to make hotel reservations online. Travel packages purchased online constituted the smallest percentage of travel sales.

Increasingly, corporations are outsourcing their travel offices entirely to vendors who can provide web-based solutions, high-quality service, and lower costs. Online vendors to corporations provide **corporate online booking solutions (COBS)** that provide integrated airline, hotel, conference center, and auto rental services at a single site.

corporate online booking solutions (COBS)

provide integrated airline, hotel, conference center, and auto rental services at a single site

ONLINE TRAVEL INDUSTRY DYNAMICS

Because much of what travel agency sites offer is a commodity, and thus they face the same costs, competition among online providers is intense. Price competition is difficult because shoppers, as well as online site managers, can comparison shop easily. Therefore, competition among sites tends to focus on scope of offerings, ease of use, payment options, and personalization. Some well-known travel sites are listed in **Table 11.7**.

The online travel services industry has gone through a period of intense consolidation. Expedia now owns Travelocity, Orbitz, CheapTickets, Hotels.com, Hotwire, and meta-search engine Trivago, giving it a 75% market share among U.S. online travel agencies. Its primary competition consists of Priceline, which owns Booking.com, Lowestfare.com, and Kayak. Together, Expedia and Priceline control a whopping 95% of the online travel agency booking market. However, Google is also poised to become a player in the market, with its Google Flights and Google Hotel Finder that also provide booking functionality. The U.S. Department of Justice also cited the TripAdvisor's introduction of an Instant Booking service as a factor in its approval of Expedia's acquisition of Orbitz.

In addition to industry consolidation, the online travel industry has been roiled by meta-search engines that scour the Web for the best prices on travel and lodging, and then collect finder or affiliate fees for sending consumers to the lowest-price sites. Travel aggregator sites include Trivago, Kayak, Fly.com, and Mobissimo. These sites, in the eyes of many industry leaders, commoditize the online travel industry even further, cause excessive price competition, and divert revenues from the leading, branded firms who have made extensive investments in inventory and systems.

Mobile devices and apps used for pre-trip planning, booking, check-in, and context and location-based destination information are also transforming the online travel industry. For instance, in the United States in 2016, about 75 million people are expected to use a mobile device to research travel. Around 59 million are expected to actually book travel using a mobile device in 2016. Smartphones are used slightly more than tablets to both research and book travel (eMarketer, Inc., 2016l, 2016m). Most of the major airlines now have apps for a variety of mobile platforms to enable flight research, booking, and management. Apps from hotels and car rental companies are available from most of the major players such as Hertz and Avis for car rentals, and Best Western, Choice Hotels, Hilton, and Starwood for hotels. Apps may sometimes target specific consumer behavior. For instance, Expedia reports that 25% of its mobile hotel sales are made at properties within 10 miles of the user's current location, indicating that they are searching for and booking rooms on-the-go, as they travel. Mobile devices are also proving to be quite popular for booking at the last minute. Marriott says that 35% of its smartphone bookings are for same-day travel (eMarketer, Inc., 2014).

Social media is also having a big impact on the online travel industry. User-generated content and online reviews are having an increasing influence on travel-buying decisions. The *Insight on Society* case, *Phony Reviews,* examines some of the issues this presents for the industry.

11.7 ONLINE CAREER SERVICES

Next to travel services, one of the Internet's most successful online services has been job services (recruitment sites) that provide a free posting of individual resumes, plus many other related career services; for a fee, they also list job openings posted by companies. Career services sites collect revenue from other sources as well, by providing value-added services to users and collecting fees from related service providers.

The U.S. online job market is dominated by two large players: Monster, with about 17 million unique monthly visitors, and CareerBuilder, with about 14 million. Job listing aggregators, such as Indeed and SimplyHired, both owned by a Japanese-based human resources company, and Glassdoor, which also posts anonymous online reviews of companies by their employees, are also very popular. LinkedIn has also

INSIGHT ON SOCIETY

PHONY REVIEWS

People used to rely on travel agents for professional recommendations about travel destinations, hotels, and restaurants to choose while on vacation. Today, however, sites like TripAdvisor and Yelp have taken over that function. TripAdvisor has been a smashing success, with more than 385 million user-generated reviews, $1.5 billion in revenue, and 108 million members. Yelp has 70 million reviews of restaurants and other services, and a market capitalization of almost $3 billion. The sites have become trusted sources for travelers as they try to decide where to travel, what hotels to book, and where to eat. A good rating can be worth thousands of dollars in bookings. But are all those reviews for real? Can they be trusted?

Although the majority of reviews on TripAdvisor, Yelp, and related sites are trustworthy and 92% of buyers make decisions based on online reviews, fraudulent reviews are commonplace. Hotels pay people to create false identities and post favorable reviews on their properties, a practice known as "astroturfing," and also to slam competing venues. A disgruntled customer with an axe to grind can severely damage the reputation of a small business. Businesses can also tarnish their reputations by mishandling bad reviews, phony or otherwise. An Arizona bakery went viral in 2013 after an unflattering appearance on a reality show drew negative social media attention. The bakery's owners used Facebook, Yelp, and Reddit to make personal attacks against anyone who had posted a negative review and quickly gained unwanted notoriety. In 2014, a British hotel fined two guests after they made a scathing review on TripAdvisor, but after local media scrutiny, the hotel refunded the money and vowed to improve its services.

Travel sites received additional legal backing in 2016, when the House of Representatives passed a bill that bars businesses from forbidding negative reviews in their customer agreements. The Senate passed a similar bill in 2015, so it will likely become law in 2017. Additionally, a federal appeals court ruled in 2016 that Yelp wasn't liable for negative reviews posted on its site about a Washington state locksmith. However, in a separate case, a state court ruled against Yelp in 2014 and demanded the removal of critical posts about a law firm. Even in that case, the Supreme Court is expected to overturn the ruling in 2016.

Although most of these recent rulings empower their users to continue posting honest reviews, even if they are negative, the prevalence of phony reviews still presents a considerable challenge both for businesses and for TripAdvisor and Yelp. Few of these sites verify the identities of their reviewers, which frustrates businesses. In response, restaurants and other retail businesses are trying to popularize the hashtag #noreceiptnoreview, where reviewers post receipts to verify that they were, in fact, customers of the businesses they're reviewing, while retaining a semblance of anonymity. Businesses also bemoan the fact that while a majority of customers use online reviews before making a purchase or travel decision, a very small minority post reviews. One study of adults in the U.K. found that only 11% of travelers reported posting reviews with any frequency. As a result, a few bad eggs in the vocal minority can have a dramatic effect on the well-being of a business, even if most customers are satisfied.

The authenticity of reviews is critically important to the success of Yelp and TripAdvisor, but garnering a high review score is equally important to the businesses listed on the site. Studies have found that if a business can increase its Yelp rating by one star, its revenues will increase anywhere from 5% to 9%, and in March 2014, an industry study found that small businesses using Yelp experienced annual revenue increases of $8,000. This gives businesses ample incentive to post phony reviews praising their own business and slamming their competitors. In 2015, approximately 25% of Yelp reviews are labeled suspicious or not recommended. With this in mind, Yelp continues to develop ways to remove suspect reviews, including those from rings of businesses who work together to fraudulently increase the ratings of each business in the group.

Both Yelp and TripAdvisor use algorithms to automate the identification and removal of phony reviews. Yelp generates notices called Consumer Alerts to inform readers when a review is likely fraudulent, while TripAdvisor employs a team of experts to analyze the integrity of reviews. Nevertheless, these sites have plenty of incentive to downplay the extent of their phony review problems. TripAdvisor has been fined multiple times by regulatory agencies for misrepresenting the authenticity of its reviews, including $610,000 in Italy in 2014 and $484,000 in France in 2011, and the FTC has received well over 2,000 complaints from businesses about Yelp from 2008 to 2014.

In 2015, researchers from Harvard Business School mined and analyzed reviews from these sites to get a better understanding of what makes a review suspicious. Truthful reviewers tend to talk about specific details, while the fraudulent reviewers, not surprisingly, tended to talk more about themselves, reasons for the trip, and traveling companions, lacking actual experience with the venue.

Positive review fraud is driven by sudden dips in reputation, and negative review fraud is driven by changing patterns in competition, like a new restaurant in the area. Most fraudulent reviews are either one or five stars, with very few in between, and fraudulent reviews of chain restaurants are very rare, since these companies are likelier to have sophisticated marketing and branding efforts that go well beyond online review sites.

Will this improved understanding of fraudulent reviews clean up TripAdvisor and Yelp once and for all? Probably not. But review sites and regulators are cracking down on phony reviews with increasing vigor. In 2013, for instance, 19 companies received fines from New York regulators totaling $350,000 for buying and selling fraudulent reviews, and in 2015 Yelp sued a company operating multiple businesses involved in selling fraudulent reviews to restaurants. Amazon is also riddled with phony reviews, and the company has taken legal action against over a thousand individual users for posting fake reviews.

Despite all of the uncertainty surrounding phony and negative reviews, it might be the case that TripAdvisor and Yelp are actually improving service at hotels and restaurants. In Ireland, for example, reviews of hotels improved from 3.6 to 3.8 in 2014, but this was attributable to corresponding improvements in service, not fraud. The best approach is still to take what you read with a grain of salt, discarding both the overwhelmingly positive and the unrelentingly negative reviews.

SOURCES: "Yelp Warns California Lawsuit Could Scrub Critical Reviews," Siliconvalley.com, September 17, 2016; "Yelp, TripAdvisor Gain Legal Cover for Negative Reviews," by Drew Fitzgerald, *Wall Street Journal*, September 13, 2016; "New Bill Would Protect Your Right to Complain in Online Reviews," by Talia Avakian, Travelandleisure.com, September 13, 2016; "Yelp Not Liable for One-Star Review, Appeals Court Rules," by Jacob Gershman, *Wall Street Journal*, September 13, 2016; "Companies Wrestle with New Era of Negative Online Reviews and Spiky Consumers," by Justin O'Brien and Sameer Hosany, Theconversation.com, September 5, 2016; "Online Reviews Are Changing the Nature of Travel," by Elizabeth Matsangou, Businessdestinations.com, July 13, 2016; "Many Rely on Online Travel Reviews, But Only a Vocal Few Post Them," by Helen Leggatt, Bizreport.com, January 19, 2016; "Fake Online Reviews Trip Travelers," by Christopher Elliott, *USA Today*, December 27, 2015; "Are Fake Online Reviews Crushing Consumer Confidence?" by Jen A. Miller, Cio.com, November 30, 2015; "Fake It Till You Make It: Reputation, Competition, and Yelp Review Fraud," by Michael Luca and Georgios Zervas, Harvard Business School, July 2015; "TripAdvisor Reviews Are Now So Powerful They Impact the Tourist Industry of Entire Countries," by Joshua Barrie, Businessinsider.com, March 16, 2015; "Yelp Is Suing a Company for Allegedly Selling Fake Positive Reviews to Restaurants," by Lizzie Plaugic, Theverge.com, February 20, 2015; "Online Reviews: Fakes, Linguistic Analysis & Protecting Children," by Thomas A. Dickerson, Eturbonews.com, February 11, 2015; "Trip Advisor Bad Review 'Fine' to Be Refunded by Blackpool Hotel," Bbcnews.com, November 19, 2014; "Yelp Reviews Brew a Fight Over Free Speech Vs. Fairness," by Angus Loten, *Wall Street Journal*, April 2, 2014; "A Virginia Court Slams Phony Reviews," by Jill Krasny, Inc.com, January 10, 2014; "Leaving Negative Reviews Online Is Not as Safe as It Used to Be," by Alex Goldman, Onthemedia.org, January 9, 2014; "Amy's Baking Co. Meltdown Begs the Question: Is Yelp Bad for Small Business?" by Caitlin Dewey, *Washington Post*, May 17, 2013.

become an increasingly important player in this market (see the opening case in Chapter 10).

Traditionally, companies have relied on five employee recruitment tools: classified and print advertising, career expos (or trade shows), on-campus recruiting, private employment agencies (now called "staffing firms"), and internal referral programs. In comparison to online recruiting, these tools have severe limitations. Print advertising usually includes a per-word charge that limits the amount of detail employers provide about a job opening, as well as a limited time period within which the job is posted. Career expos do not allow for pre-screening of attendees and are limited by the amount of time a recruiter can spend with each candidate. Staffing firms charge high fees and have a limited, usually local, selection of job hunters. On-campus recruiting also restricts the number of candidates a recruiter can speak with during a normal visit and requires that employers visit numerous campuses. And internal referral programs may encourage employees to propose unqualified candidates for openings in order to qualify for rewards or incentives offered.

Online recruiting overcomes these limitations, providing a more efficient and cost-effective means of linking employers and potential employees, while reducing the total time to hire. Online recruiting enables job hunters to more easily build, update, and distribute their resumes while gathering information about prospective employers and conducting job searches.

IT'S JUST INFORMATION: THE IDEAL WEB BUSINESS?

Online recruitment is ideally suited for the Web. The hiring process is an information-intense business process that involves discovering the skills and salary requirements of individuals and matching them with available jobs. In order to accomplish this matchup, there does not initially need to be face-to-face interaction, or a great deal of personalization. Prior to the Internet, this information sharing was accomplished locally by human networks of friends, acquaintances, former employers, and relatives, in addition to employment agencies that developed paper files on job hunters. The Internet can clearly automate this flow of information, reducing search time and costs for all parties.

Table 11.8 lists some of the most popular U.S. recruitment sites.

Why are so many job hunters and employers using Internet job sites? Recruitment sites are popular largely because they save time and money for both job hunters and employers seeking recruits. For employers, the job boards expand the geographical reach of their searches, lower costs, and result in faster hiring decisions.

For job seekers, online sites are popular not only because their resumes can be made widely available to recruiters but also because of a variety of other related job-hunting services. The services delivered by online recruitment sites have greatly expanded since their emergence in 1996. Originally, online recruitment sites just provided a digital version of newspaper classified ads. Today's sites offer many other services, including skills assessment, personality assessment questionnaires, personalized account management for job hunters, organizational culture assessments, job search tools, employer blocking (prevents your employer from seeing your posting),

TABLE 11.8	POPULAR U.S. ONLINE RECRUITMENT SITES
RECRUITMENT SITE	**BRIEF DESCRIPTION**
GENERAL RECRUITMENT SITES	
Monster	One of the first commercial online sites in 1994. Today, a public company offering general job searches in 50 countries.
CareerBuilder	Owned by Tegna (formerly Gannett), Tribune, and McClatchy (all newspaper companies). Provides job search for more than 10,000 websites, including AOL, and 140 newspapers; over 1 million jobs listed.
Indeed	Job site aggregator
SimplyHired	Job site aggregator
Craigslist	Popular classified listing service focused on local recruiting
Glassdoor	Best known for anonymous reviews of companies and management posted by current and former employees, but also has listings for millions of jobs.
EXECUTIVE SEARCH SITES	
Futurestep	Korn/Ferry site, low-end executive recruiting
Spencerstuart	Middle-level executive recruiting
ExecuNet	Executive search firm
NICHE JOB SITES	
SnagAJob	Part-time and hourly jobs
USAJobs	Federal government jobs
HigherEdJobs	Education industry
EngineerJobs	Engineering jobs
Medzilla	Biotechnology, pharmaceutical, medical, and healthcare industry
Showbizjobs	Entertainment industry
Salesjobs	Sales and marketing
Dice	Information technology jobs
MBAGlobalNet	MBA-oriented community site

employee blocking (prevents your employees from seeing your listings if you are their employer), and e-mail notification. Online sites also provide a number of educational services such as resume writing advice, software skills preparation, and interview tips.

For the most part, online recruitment sites work, in the sense of linking job hunters with jobs, but they are just one of many ways people actually find jobs. A survey by The Conference Board found that the majority (70%) of job seekers rely equally on both the Internet and newspapers to look for jobs, with about half relying on word-of-mouth leads, and about a quarter on employment agencies. Given that the cost of posting a resume online is zero, the marginal returns are very high.

The ease with which resumes can be posted online has also raised new issues for both job recruiters and job seekers. If you are an employer, how do you sort through the thousands of resumes you may receive when posting an open job? If you are a job seeker, how do you stand out among the thousands or even millions of others? Perhaps one way is to post a video resume. In a survey by Vault, nearly nine in 10 employers said they would watch a video resume if it were submitted to them, in part because it would help them better assess a candidate's professional presentation and demeanor, and over half said they believed video would become a common addition to future job applications. CareerBuilder became the first major online job site to implement a video resume tool for job candidates, following a previous launch for an online video brand-building tool for employers.

Perhaps one of the most important functions of online recruitment sites is not so much their capacity to actually match employers with job hunters but their ability to establish market prices and terms, as well as trends in the labor market. Online recruitment sites identify salary levels for both employers and job hunters and categorize the skill sets required to achieve those salary levels. In this sense, online recruitment sites are online national marketplaces that establish the terms of trade in labor markets. The existence of online national job sites should lead to a rationalization of wages, greater labor mobility, and higher efficiency in recruitment and operations because employers will be able to quickly find the people they need.

ONLINE RECRUITMENT INDUSTRY TRENDS

Trends for 2016–2017 in the online recruitment services industry include the following:

- **Social recruiting:** According to a recent survey of over 1,600 recruiters and human resource professionals, 87% use social recruiting, with LinkedIn being a primary resource (Jobvite, 2015). LinkedIn, probably the most well-known business-oriented social network, has grown significantly to over 450 million members representing over 170 different industries in over 200 countries as of October 2016. LinkedIn's corporate hiring solutions are used by over 90 of the Fortune 100 companies, and more than 3 million companies have a LinkedIn page. Consumers are using sites such as LinkedIn to establish business contacts and networks. For instance, according to LinkedIn, its members do almost 6 billion professionally-oriented searches on LinkedIn a year. Employers are also using LinkedIn to conduct searches to find potential job candidates that may not be actively job hunting. For instance, LinkedIn offers companies a feature called LinkedIn Talent Solutions that includes tools that help corporate recruiters find "passive talent" (people who are not actively looking for a new job), as well as custom company profiles that are specifically designed for recruitment. According to LinkedIn Talent Solutions, U.S. company reliance on social recruiting to find quality employees has increased by over 50% since 2011, with 44% of those surveyed indicating that social recruiting was the most important source for key positions (LinkedIn Talent Solutions, 2016). Social network sites are also being used by employers to "check up" on the background of job candidates. A study by Harris Interactive of over 2,000 managers and human resource employees found that over 60% are using social networks to screen job candidates, and almost 50% have rejected candidates because of content on a social site. Employers typically search Facebook, Twitter, and LinkedIn. Provocative or inappropriate photos were the biggest negative factor followed by drinking and drug references. However, on the flip side, recruiters also noted that not having any online presence at all also hurts candidates, with more than a third indicating that they would be less likely to interview a job candidate if they cannot find information about that person online (Careerbuilder, 2016).

- **Mobile:** As with other forms of services, career services firms have also moved onto the mobile platform. A recent survey found that mobile devices were the primary devices used by Millennials and Gen X to search for jobs (eMarketer, Inc., 2015e). To reach this audience, CareerBuilder, Monster, LinkedIn, and most of the other major sites all have a mobile website, as well as apps that allow job seekers to create and upload resumes, search jobs by keyword, location, and company, e-mail jobs, browse and apply, and more. LinkedIn's app, for instance, can also recommend jobs based on data you provide on your profile page. In 2016, mobile accounts for about 55% of the unique members visiting LinkedIn.

- **Job search engines/aggregators:** As with travel services, search engines that focus specifically on jobs are posing a new threat to established online career sites. For instance, Indeed, SimplyHired, and Us.jobs "scrape" listings from thousands of online job sites such as Monster, CareerBuilder, specialty recruiting services, and the sites of individual employers to provide a free, searchable index of thousands of job listings in one spot. Because these firms do not charge employers a listing fee, they are currently using a pay-per-click or other advertising revenue model.

- **Data analytics and algorithms:** Companies are increasingly using big data technologies in the hiring process, as well as adaptive algorithms that help them match job seekers to job openings.

- **Hiring by algorithm:** Companies are increasingly using algorithms to sift online job applications, focusing on key words to match job seekers with jobs.

11.8 ON-DEMAND SERVICE COMPANIES

On-demand service companies provide a platform that enables the on-demand delivery of various services, by connecting providers ("sellers") who wish to exploit their "spare" resources, such as cars, rooms with beds, and ability to perform various services via their personal labor, with consumers ("buyers") who would like to utilize those resources and services. Other common phrases sometimes used to describe these online businesses are "sharing economy," "collaborative commerce," "peer to peer consumption," "mesh economy," and "we-commerce." However, unlike traditional sharing where there is no fee charged in the transaction, these firms collect a fee from both sellers and buyers for using their platforms. In the last few years, hundreds of startups have created a plethora of such platforms that allow owners of resources that

TABLE 11.9	EXAMPLES OF ON-DEMAND SERVICE FIRMS
FIRM	SERVICES ENABLED
Airbnb	Lodging
Uber	Transportation
Lyft	Transportation
TaskRabbit	Errand and household tasks
Trusk	Movers
Deliveroo	Restaurant food delivery
ZipJet	Laundry
Postmates	Courier
Zeel	Massages

are underutilized to sell access to those resources to consumers who would prefer not to, or are unable to, buy those resources themselves.

A number of these on-demand service firms have grown exponentially over the last five years. **Table 11.9** describes just a few of the hundreds of firms whose business model is to provide transaction platforms that enable the on-demand delivery of various services.

Collaborative commerce, trading platforms, and peer-to-peer commerce are not new. While eBay involves the sale of items at auction or for fixed prices, on-demand service firms provide sell access to cars, room, spaces, and even skilled people. What is new about these firms is their use of mobile and Internet technology to enable transactions on their platforms. This is especially true of the car and lodging services where transactions are local and mobile. Second, the growth of these firms is supported by the use of online reputation systems based on peer review, to establish a trusted environment where sellers and consumers can feel confident transacting with one another. Online peer review of both the providers and the consumers helps to ensure that both parties have acceptable reputations, and that a high quality of service is provided. These firms have learned from eBay and Netflix the importance of peer reviews and ratings. A third factor is that successful firms lower the cost of services like urban transportation, lodging, office space, and personal errand services. Firms that can do this are highly disruptive of existing firms and business models.

Uber and Airbnb are among the most successful and well-known on-demand service companies. See the opening case in Chapter 1 for a description of Uber and an in-depth discussion of the issues that this business model raises, and the *Insight on Business* case, *Airbnb Takes Off*, for a look at two companies, Airbnb and Wimdu, focused on the short-term lodging market. Deliveroo is another example of the on-demand services model. Similar to Grubhub in the United States, Deliveroo focuses on the on-demand delivery of take-out orders from restaurants. Deliveroo was launched

INSIGHT ON BUSINESS

WIMDU COMPETES WITH AIRBNB

Wouldn't it be nice if every time you went on vacation, you could make a little extra money by renting your apartment to responsible tenants? Or if you had a second property that you could use to make a little extra money without having to make six-month or year-long sublet agreements? And wouldn't it be even better if every time you traveled somewhere, you could find one of these types of apartments for yourself for a deep discount compared to area hotels? This is the inefficiency that short-term C2C real estate rental companies such as Airbnb, Wimdu, and a host of others have attempted to solve with the aid of the new mobile platform. So far, these fledgling "private accommodation service" companies are still finding their footing with regard to profits and losses, but the industry has grown steadily since Airbnb's founding in 2008.

Airbnb is regarded as the biggest player in this emerging field, but it does have some competition. One such competitor is Wimdu. Funded by Rocket Internet and the Samwer brothers (see *Rocket Internet*, the Chapter 1 *Insight on Business* case), Wimdu is very closely modeled after Airbnb, but tailors its business tactics from country to country. Travelers log onto Wimdu, type in their destination and specify their travel dates, and site filters display locations that meet those criteria. Currently, travelers can choose from over 350,000 properties in over 150 countries worldwide. Users can add places to their "favorites" list and submit reviews of hosts and properties. Wimdu has raised almost $100 million in an effort to grow its user base rapidly (currently totaling over 1 million registered users) and reach profitability, but they have struggled to get there. Although Wimdu reported increases in revenue in 2015, the company has

consistently reported losses, including a €48.2 million loss in 2014. The European cities' crackdown on short-term listing sites has further complicated matters for Wimdu. The company first announced plans to merge with rival 9flats in 2016 to better compete against Airbnb in Europe. Only eight weeks later in early 2017, vacation home agency Novasol, the Danish division of Wyndham Hotels, purchased Wimdu, hoping to add Wimdu's 350,000 rental properties to its existing 40,000 listings and to better compete with Airbnb.

Wimdu's takeover was not a surprise. With many clone companies like Wimdu, the end goal is to sell the business to the established leader, which in this case is Airbnb. Although Airbnb founder Brian Chesky admitted coming close to purchasing Wimdu in 2011, the company ultimately decided against it, reportedly due to concerns about Wimdu's business culture and operating style. Airbnb instead opted to enter the German market and compete directly against Wimdu. Airbnb is valued at an astronomical $30 billion, operates in 34,000 cities in 191 countries, raised $1.5 billion in venture funding in 2015, and announced plans to raise $850 million more in 2016. The company has delayed its highly anticipated initial public offering to improve its profitability, but after increasing its revenues 89 percent from 2015 to 2016 to an estimated $1.7 billion, the company may be ready to go public in 2017.

Perhaps the biggest current problem for the private accommodation service industry is governmental interference. Both local and national governments are cracking down on short-term rental services, which enable tenants to elude restrictions that would preclude them from securing permanent housing. In Singapore, law enforcement imposes stiff penalties on any homeowner

(continued)

renting their home via these services. The minimum subletting period is six months. This only applies if money is exchanged. Homeowners can allow friends and relatives to stay over. Berlin is another city that has decided to regulate short-term holiday rentals, hoping to curb the notable increase in the cost of living and scarcity of affordable apartments available for rent in the city dating back to 2007. Munich and Hamburg already have similar laws. In 2017, Copenhagen instituted a cap on the number of days its citizens can rent out their homes on Airbnb, hoping to compromise between full bans of the site and protecting the local hotel industry. Other cities, like Barcelona, have levied fines of $635,000 against Airbnb and its competitors for marketing rentals that did not have permits to host tenants.

In Amsterdam, where individuals are allowed to rent out their property only if they follow certain regulations, the city government has used Airbnb and its competitors to investigate illegal rental properties by combining its own data with listings. An initial government scan found that about 700 of the almost 4,000 listings on Airbnb were illegal hotels. The government also believes that Airbnb and similar businesses fail to comply with local tax legislation. Airbnb contends that it is simply a marketplace, and that its users are the ones responsible for complying with local laws.

New York City and San Francisco are two major U.S. battlegrounds for Airbnb. C2C rental companies argue that their services don't contribute to increases in costs of living, and that outdated laws need to be changed. However, many cities disagree. A 2014 report by the New York City Attorney General indicated that three quarters of Airbnb listings in the city are illegal, and the city continues to push back at Airbnb's attempts to partner with them over reforming housing laws. In 2016, New York passed a bill outlawing apartment listings for stays shorter than 30 days, and San Francisco passed laws requiring anyone listing property on sites like Airbnb to register the property with the city, creating a regulatory burden many renters may be unwilling to take on. Airbnb employs a task force to deal with governments and regulatory agencies. In the same vein, 9flats, Wimdu, and HouseTrip, another Swiss-based rental service, have formed a network to lobby European governments with a unified voice as these services become a more important part of the tourism industry there. Airbnb is not a part of that group, which is perhaps an effort by the European-based companies to compete together against a common enemy. The European network hopes to support tenants and landlords with legal matters and participate in creating regulations and developing solutions to current issues. Still, Airbnb, Wimdu, and their counterparts are united in their desire to see C2C short-term home rental become commonplace, and there are signs that it just might happen.

■■■ **SOURCES:** "Copenhagen Eyes Airbnb Limit," Thelocal.dk, January 11, 2017; "Vacation Home Firm Snaps Up Wimdu, by Christoph Schlautmann, Global.handelsblatt.com, January 10, 2017; "CEO Interview: Why Wyndham Is Going After Urban Rentals," by Patrick Whyte, Skift.com, December 26, 2016; "Airbnb Rivals Wimdu and 9Flats Consolidate," by Natasha Lomas, Techcrunch.com, October 10, 2016; "Wimdu and 9Flats Combine into One Short-Term Rental Company," by Sean O'Neill, tnooz.com, October 10, 2016; "Airbnb Could Be the Biggest IPO of 2017," by Madeleine Johnson, Zacks.com, September 8, 2016; "Airbnb's Revenue Soars 89 Percent," by Tessa Love, Bizjournals.com, September 1, 2016; "Airbnb Raising a Reported $850M at a $30B Valuation," by John Mannes, Techcrunch.com, August 6, 2016; "Airbnb Has a Really Convoluted Process for Being 'Transparent' with New York City," by Alison Griswold, Qz.com, December 15, 2015; "Two-thirds of Berlin's Tourist Flats Now Illegal," Thelocal.de, August 1, 2014; "Rocket Internet's Wimdu Missed Out on Dream Takover by Airbnb—Here's Why," by Georg Rath, Venturevillage.eu, October 14, 2013; "Sharing Verboten: Berlin Puts Kibosh on Airbnb and Co.," by Janko Tietz, Spiegel.de, August 14, 2013; "Will Berlin Follow New York and Rule Airbnb-style Sites Illegal?" by Nina Fowler, Venturevillage.eu, May 30, 2013; "Amsterdam Airbnb Listings Set to Decline Sharply in Illegal Rental Crack Down," by Loek Essers, Cio.com.au, February 19, 2013; "Airbnb Could Be Banned in Amsterdam: Local Authorities Are Now Hunting for Illegal Hotels," by Harrison Weber, Thenextweb.com, February 2, 2013.

in London in 2013, partnering initially with just three Chelsea-based restaurants, but by 2016, had expanded to more 60 cities around the globe in Europe, the Middle East, and Asia, with over 5,000 delivery drivers. The company grew by over 650% in 2016, and in 2016 raised £210 million at a reported valuation of £820 million. However, it faces many of the same issues as other on-demand delivery services. It too is facing challenges over its classification of drivers as self-employed, with law firm Leigh Day announcing in January 2017 that it was advising Deliveroo drivers on potential legal action over their rights, including the right to be paid the national minimum wage and receive holiday pay. (Combes, 2017; Leigh Day, 2017; Cook and Shead, 2016).

OpenTable:
Your Reservation Is Waiting

OpenTable is the leading supplier of reservation, table management, and guest management software for restaurants. In addition, the company operates OpenTable.com, the world's most popular website for making restaurant reservations online. In just over 15 years, OpenTable has gone from a startup to a successful and growing public company that counts around two-thirds of the nation's reservation-taking restaurants as clients.

Today, more than 38,000 restaurants in the United States, Canada, Mexico, the United Kingdom, Germany, and Japan use the OpenTable hardware and software system. This system automates the reservation-taking and table management process, while allowing restaurants to build diner databases for improved guest recognition and targeted e-mail marketing. The OpenTable website, mobile site, and mobile app provide a fast, efficient way for diners to find available tables in real time. The websites and app connect directly to the thousands of computerized reservation systems at OpenTable restaurants, and reservations are immediately recorded in a restaurant's electronic reservation book.

© Justin Sullivan/Getty Images

Restaurants subscribe to the OpenTable Electronic Reservation Book (ERB), the company's proprietary software, which is installed on a touch-screen computer system and supported by asset-protection and security tools. The ERB software provides a real-time map of the restaurant floor and enables the restaurant to retain meal patterns of all parties, serving as a customer relationship management (CRM) system for restaurants. The software is upgraded periodically, and the latest version is designed to provide increased ease of use and a more thorough view of table availability to help turn more tables, enhance guest service, personalize responses to diners, coordinate the seating process, and maximize guest seating. The ERBs at OpenTable's customer restaurants connect via the Internet to form an online network of restaurant reservation books.

OpenTable's revenue comes from two sources. Restaurants pay a one-time fee for on-site installation and training, a monthly subscription fee for software and hardware, and a transaction fee for each restaurant guest seated through online reservations. The online reservation service is free to diners. The business model encourages diners to assist in viral marketing. When an individual makes a reservation, the site "suggests" that they send invites to their dinner companions directly from OpenTable that include a link back to the OpenTable site.

OpenTable is a service-based (software as service, or SaaS) e-commerce company. In other words, customers don't buy software and install it on their computers, but instead go online and get the software functionality through subscriptions. OpenTable is also an online service that does not sell goods, but instead enables diners to make reservations, like social networking sites provide services.

The restaurant industry was slow to leverage the power of the Internet. This was in part because the industry was, and continues to be, highly fragmented and local—made up of more than 30,000 small, independent businesses or local restaurant-owning groups.

The founders of OpenTable knew that dealing with these restaurants as a single market would be difficult. They also realized that the Internet was changing things for diners by providing them with instant access to reviews, menus, and other information about dining options. And there was no method for making reservations online—we all know reserving by phone is time-consuming, inefficient, and prone to errors. In order to make the system work, reach and scale were very important. For diners to use an online reservation system, they would need real-time access to a number of local restaurants, and the ability to instantly book confirmed reservations around the clock. If customers were planning a trip to another city, OpenTable would need participating restaurants in those cities.

When OpenTable was founded, most restaurants did not have computers, let alone systems that would allow online reservations made through a central website. OpenTable's initial strategy was to pay online restaurant reviewers for links to its website and target national chains in order to quickly expand its reach. This got the company into 50 cities, but it was spending $1 million a month and bringing in only $100,000 in revenue. Not exactly a formula for success. OpenTable halted its marketing efforts and narrowed its focus to four cities: Chicago, New York, San Francisco, and Washington, D.C.

The company retooled its hardware and software to create the user-friendly ERB system and deployed a door-to-door sales force to solicit subscriptions from high-end restaurants. The combination of e-commerce, user-friendly technology, and the personal touch worked. The four markets OpenTable targeted initially developed into active, local networks of restaurants and diners that continue to grow. OpenTable has implemented the same strategy across the country, and now includes approximately 38,000 OpenTable restaurant customers. In 18 years, the company has seated approximately 1 billion diners, including 370 million via its mobile solutions, and it is currently averaging 20 million diners per month. In the second quarter of 2016, half of its seating requests in North America originated from a mobile device.

As the company grew, investors began making plans for it to go public. In 2009, the company proceeded with an initial public offering (IPO) despite a terrible economy and worse financial markets. The gamble paid off. On its first day of trading, OpenTable's shares climbed 59% and the share price climbed to over $100 in 2013, more than five times the $20 IPO price.

In 2014, Priceline announced that it would acquire OpenTable for $2.6 billion. OpenTable plans to leverage Priceline's global reach as it continues to expand its business beyond the United States, which has thus far accounted for about 80% of its revenues. Clearly, Priceline believes OpenTable can help it grow even further, this time into restaurant reservations. They might be right: OpenTable is well-positioned for future growth. Its size, track record of growth, and high customer satisfaction rates should continue to work in its favor, and the company hopes to branch out from its main focus of fine dining into other areas like casual dining.

OpenTable has benefited from having e-commerce revenue streams from subscription fees and per-transaction charges, rather than depending on advertising. Furthermore, more than 50% of OpenTable's revenue comes from B2B subscriptions, which are typically part of long-term contracts. Restaurants that have invested in OpenTable's software package are less likely to want to incur the switching costs associated with changing to a different reservation management package.

Another reason for its success is that OpenTable has a large number of satisfied customers. Restaurant owners report that they and their staff members find the software easy to use, and it helps them manage their business better. Specifically, it streamlines operations, helps fill additional seats, and improves quality of service, providing a concrete return on investment. This has led to both high customer satisfaction and high retention rates. By creating an online network of restaurants and diners that transact with each other through real-time reservations, OpenTable has figured out how to successfully address the needs of restaurants and diners.

OpenTable's market also exhibits network effects: the more people use it, the more utility the system delivers. More diners discover the benefits of using the online reservation system, which in turn delivers value to restaurant customers, and helps attract more restaurants to the network.

While OpenTable is the biggest, most successful online player in the restaurant reservations market, it does have competitors. MenuPages offers access to restaurant menus and reviews, but visitors to the site can't make reservations, and the site covers only eight U.S. cities. In 2012, OpenTable partnered with onetime competitor

Urbanspoon, acquiring its reservation management system, Rezbook, and becoming Urbanspoon's reservation provider. Competitors in other countries where OpenTable does not yet operate, such as Restalo in Spain and Italy, and in markets like casual dining, such as NoWait, represent challenges to OpenTable. India-based startup Zomato acquired U.S.-based NexTable in 2015, adding another challenger to the mix, and Reserve and Yelp's SeatMe service also represent potentially formidable competitors for OpenTable. Reserve has undercut OpenTable on price, with a $99 monthly subscription fee for restaurant owners compared to $249 for OpenTable, and has strong venture capital backing, but has less than two percent of the clients that OpenTable has amassed. Yelp may be a more significant immediate threat. OpenTable ended its partnership with Yelp in late 2015; Yelp users had been allowed to book reservations through OpenTable, but OpenTable hopes to improve its reviewing capability and Yelp's launch of SeatMe shows a desire to enter the reservation business.

The company is committed to bolstering its presence on multiple platforms. It has a mobile website, mobile applications that work on all major smartphone platforms, and an iPad app that fully integrates with its ERB software. GPS enables mobile users to locate and make reservations at nearby venues. In 2015, OpenTable launched a version of its app for Apple Watch that reminds diners of their reservations, provides directions, and shows a countdown. It is also testing a premium service that involves paying for an additional fee for last-minute, prime-time reservations at popular restaurants, using a surge pricing algorithm similar to that used by Uber.

OpenTable is attempting to shift its relationship with both diners and restaurants from a "transactional" relationship to an "experiential" relationship, which focuses on the experience of dining. OpenTable launched its first payments feature that allows users to pay for meals completely within the OpenTable app on the iPhone and Android in 2015. In 2016, the company released an improved payment option called Tab, which automatically bills diners without even having to open the app. Though the feature is available in less than 100 restaurants nationwide, the company hopes that Tab's ease of use will make it a popular option for diners in the future. OpenTable is trying to simplify other areas of the dining experience, including picking a venue. In 2016, the company rolled out a feature in its iOS app that allows groups of diners to vote on restaurants in a group text format and then quickly confirm the selected reservation within iMessage. OpenTable also created a Discover option that allows users to pick from restaurants using different criteria: popularity, location, new arrivals, and more. Other improvements to its app included better integration with Apple Maps and Apple Pay. Currently, the app doesn't have a robust personalization engine to generate its recommendations, but OpenTable leadership plans to remedy that in the future.

OpenTable's growth is projected to continue in the United States, Canada, and Mexico despite considerable market penetration. Selective international expansion is planned beyond its current operations in Germany, Japan, and the United Kingdom. OpenTable supports each of these locations with a direct sales force servicing approximately 1,000 restaurants.

The company's international strategy is to replicate the successful U.S. model by focusing initially on building a restaurant customer base. OpenTable believes the

SOURCES: "Fast Facts," Opentable.com, accessed October 1, 2016; "OpenTable for iOS 10: New Ways to Book, Connect, and Pay," by Jonathan Grubb, Blog.opentable.com, September 13, 2016; "OpenTable for iOS 10 Eases the Burden of Group Dinner Reservations," by Whitney Filloon, Eater.com, September 13, 2016; "OpenTable Is Trying to Make Paying for Meals Easier," *Fortune*, July 21, 2016; "OpenTable Launches New Seamless Payment Function Called Tab," by Farley Elliott, La.eater.com, June 23, 2016; "When It Comes to OpenTable, the Restaurant Industry Has Few Reservations," by Nicole Spector, Streetfightmag.com, May 11, 2016; "OpenTable Challenger Reserve Realizes It's Hard to Charge Diners, Shifts Focus to Restaurants," by Alex Konrad, *Forbes*, May 10, 2016; "Restaurant App Challenges Industry Giant OpenTable," by Matthew Flamm, Crainsnewyork.com, May 10, 2016; "OpenTable Launches a Discover Tab in Its iOS App," by April Berthene, Mobilestrategies360.com, April 29, 2016; "OpenTable's New CEO Talks Mobile Payments, Premium Reservations, and More," by Leena Rao, *Fortune*, April 1, 2016; "Yelp and OpenTable End Partnership, As Allies Become Competitors," by Riley McDermid, Bizjournals.com, December 18, 2015; "OpenTable Experiments with Surge Pricing for Restaurant Reservations," by David Kaplan, Skift.com, September 29, 2015; "OpenTable Integrates with Aloha POS Systems, Ramps Up Mobile Payments," by Paolo Lucchesi, Insidescoopsf.com, May 19, 2015; "OpenTable App for Apple Watch Now Available," Opentable.com, April 24, 2015; "Zomato Buys NexTable to Rival OpenTable and Yelp in Reservations," Ingrid Lunden, Techcrunch.com, April 22, 2015; "OpenTable Unveils Rebrand to Deepen Connection with Diners and Restaurants," Opentable.com, March 3, 2015; "OpenTable Seats a Record Two Million Diners in a Single Day," Opentable.com, February 19, 2015; "Priceline Agrees to Buy OpenTable for $2.6 Billion," by Drew FitzGerald, *Wall Street Journal*, June 13, 2014; "OpenTable Is Moving from

'Transactional' to 'Experiential,'" by Ava Seave, Forbes.com, April 22, 2014; "OpenTable's Media Play: Before, During and After Dining," by Ava Seave, Forbes.com, April 21, 2014.

localized versions of its software will compare favorably against competitive software offerings, enabling them to expand across a broad selection of local restaurants.

Case Study Questions

1. Why have OpenTable competitors had a difficult time competing against Open-Table?

2. What characteristics of the restaurant market make it difficult for a reservation system to work?

3. How did OpenTable change its marketing strategy to succeed?

4. Why would restaurants find the SaaS model very attractive?

11.10 REVIEW

KEY CONCEPTS

■ Understand the environment in which the online retail sector operates today.

- The retail industry can be divided into seven major firm types: general merchandise, durable goods, specialty stores, food and beverage, gasoline and fuel, MOTO, and online retail firms. Each type offers opportunities for online retail. The MOTO sector is the most similar to the online retail sales sector.
- During the early days of e-commerce, some predicted that the retail industry would be revolutionized, based on reduced search costs, lower marketing entry costs, the replacement of physical store merchants by online companies, elimination of middlemen (disintermediation), and hypermediation.
- Today, it has become clear that few of the initial assumptions about the future of online retail were correct. Also, the structure of the retail marketplace in the United States has not been revolutionized. The reality is that:
  - Online consumers are not primarily cost-driven—instead, they are as brand-driven and influenced by perceived value as their offline counterparts.
  - Online market entry costs were underestimated, as was the cost of acquiring new customers.
  - Older traditional firms, such as the general merchandising giants and the established catalog-based retailers, are taking over as the top online retail sites.
  - Disintermediation did not occur. On the contrary, online retailing has become an example of the powerful role that intermediaries play in retail trade.

■ Explain how to analyze the economic viability of an online firm.

- The economic viability, or ability of a firm to survive during a specified time period, can be analyzed by examining the key industry strategic factors, the strategic factors that pertain specifically to the firm, and the financial statements for the firm.
- The key industry strategic factors include barriers to entry, the power of suppliers, the power of customers, the existence of substitute products, the industry value chain, and the nature of intra-industry competition.
- The key firm strategic factors include the firm value chain, core competencies, synergies, the firm's current technology, and the social and legal challenges facing the firm.

- The key financial factors include revenues, cost of sales, gross margin, operating expenses, operating margin, net margin, and the firm's balance sheet.

■ Identify the challenges faced by the different types of online retailers.

- *Virtual merchants* are single-channel e-commerce firms that generate all of their revenues from online sales. Their challenges include building a business and a brand name quickly, many competitors in the virtual marketplace, substantial costs to build and maintain an e-commerce presence, considerable marketing expenses, large customer acquisition costs, a steep learning curve, and the need to quickly achieve operating efficiencies in order to preserve a profit. Amazon is the most well-known example of a virtual merchant.
- *Omni-channel merchants* (bricks-and-clicks) have a network of physical stores as their primary retail channel, but also have online operations. Their challenges include high cost of physical buildings, high cost of large sales staffs, the need to coordinate prices across channels, the need to develop methods of handling cross-channel returns from multiple locations, building a credible e-commerce presence, hiring new skilled staff, and building rapid-response order entry and fulfillment systems. Macy's is an example of a bricks-and-clicks company.
- *Catalog merchants* are established companies that have a national offline catalog operation as their largest retail channel, but who also have online capabilities. Their challenges include high costs for printing and mailing, the need to leverage their existing assets and competencies to the new technology environment, the need to develop methods of handling cross-channel returns, building a e-commerce presence, and hiring new skilled staff. Lands' End is an example of a catalog merchant.
- *Manufacturer-direct merchants* are either single- or multi-channel manufacturers who sell to consumers directly online without the intervention of retailers. Their challenges include channel conflict, quickly developing a rapid-response online order and fulfillment system; switching from a supply-push (products are made prior to orders being received based on estimated demand) to a demand-pull model (products are not built until an order is received); and creating sales, service, and support operations online. Dell is an example of a manufacturer-direct merchant.

■ Describe the major features of the online service sector.

- The service sector is the largest and most rapidly expanding part of the economy of advanced industrial nations.
- The major service industry groups are financial services, insurance, real estate, business services, and health services.
- Within these service industry groups, companies can be further categorized into those that involve transaction brokering and those that involve providing a "hands-on" service.
- With some exceptions, the service sector is by and large a knowledge- and information-intense industry. For this reason, many services are uniquely suited to e-commerce and the strengths of the Internet.
- E-commerce offers extraordinary opportunities to improve transaction efficiencies and thus productivity in a sector where productivity has so far not been markedly affected by the explosion in information technology.

■ Discuss the trends taking place in the online financial services industry.

- The online financial services sector is a good example of an e-commerce success story, but the success is somewhat different than what had been predicted in the early days of e-commerce. Today, the multi-channel established financial firms are growing the most rapidly and have the best prospects for long-term viability.
- Multi-channel firms that have both physical branches and solid online offerings have assumed market leadership over pure-online firms.

- Financial portals provide comparison shopping services and steer consumers to online providers for independent financial advice and financial planning.
- Account aggregation is another rapidly growing online financial service, which pulls together all of a customer's financial data on a single personalized website.
- Despite a rocky start, the online mortgage market is slowly growing; it is dominated by established online banks and other online financial services firms, traditional mortgage vendors, and a few successful online mortgage firms.
- Term life insurance stands out as one product group supporting the early visions of lower search costs, increased price transparency, and the resulting consumer savings. However, in other insurance product lines, the Web offers insurance companies new opportunities for product and service differentiation and price discrimination.
- The early vision that the historically local, complex, and agent-driven real estate industry would be transformed into a disintermediated marketplace where buyers and sellers could transact directly has not been realized.
- The major impact of the online real estate industry is in influencing offline purchases and the primary service is a listing of available houses, with secondary links to mortgage lenders, credit reporting agencies, neighborhood information, loan calculators, appraisal reports, sales price histories by neighborhood, school district data, and crime reports.

■ Describe the major trends in the online travel services industry today.

- The Internet has become the most common channel used by consumers to research travel options and book reservations for airline tickets, rental cars, hotel rooms, and tours.
- The major trends in online travel services include consolidation, the rise of meta-search engines, mobile devices, and social media.

■ Identify current trends in the online career services industry.

- Next to travel services, job-hunting services have been one of the Internet's most successful online services because they save money for both job hunters and employers.
- Online recruiting can also serve to establish market prices and terms, thereby identifying both the salary levels for specific jobs and the skill sets required to achieve those salary levels.
- The major trends in the online career services industry are social networking, mobile, job search engines, consolidation, diversification, and localization.

■ Understand the business models of on-demand service companies.

- On-demand service companies provide a platform that enables the on-demand delivery of various services, by connecting providers ("sellers") who wish to exploit their "spare" resources, such as cars, rooms with beds, and ability to perform various services via their personal labor, with consumers ("buyers") who would like to utilize those resources and services. The companies collect a fee both from sellers and buyers for using the platform.
- Uber, a car rental service, and Airbnb, a room rental service, are the most well-known on-demand services companies. They are also among the most disruptive and controversial.

QUESTIONS

1. Why is the slowdown in new Internet users not causing a slowdown in the growth of online retail sales?
2. What is an omni-channel merchant? What advantages do they have? What challenges do they face?
3. What enabled firms in the MOTO retail sector to transition more easily to e-commerce than other sectors?

4. Describe three techniques retail merchants use to integrate their online and offline sales channels, beyond having an online retail store.

5. Why did economists speculate that e-commerce would result in only low-cost, high-service, quality online retail merchants surviving?

6. What is an intermediary? Provide an example of one. What effect has e-commerce had on retail intermediaries?

7. What is Amazon's chief business strategy, and what tactics does it use to achieve these strategies?

8. What unique challenges do manufacturer-direct companies, such as Dell.com, face in retailing online?

9. Identify two key industry strategic factors and describe how they impact the viability of firms operating within an industry.

10. In analyzing the viability of a firm, what questions would you ask to determine how the firm is affected by the technology it uses?

11. Describe three unique challenges that online retailers face compared to offline retailers.

12. Why is the service sector one of the most natural avenues for e-commerce?

13. Why has the mortgage industry been slower to move to online business models than other online financial services industries?

14. Why are online travel services such an ideal service for the Internet?

15. How has the insurance industry been impacted by the Internet?

16. What are two major trends currently affecting the online travel industry?

17. Describe three ways that social networking has affected the online recruitment industry.

18. In addition to matching job applicants with available positions, what larger function do online job sites fill? Explain how such sites can affect salaries and going rates.

19. Describe the business model of on-demand service companies.

20. Why are on-demand service companies viewed as being disruptive and controversial?

PROJECTS

1. Access the EDGAR archives at Sec.gov, where you can review 10-K filings for all U.S. public companies. Search for the 10-K report for the most recent completed fiscal year for two online retail companies of your choice (preferably ones operating in the same industry, such as Staples Inc. and Office Depot Inc., Amazon and Walmart, etc.). Prepare a presentation that compares the financial stability and prospects of the two businesses, focusing specifically on the performance of their respective e-commerce operations.

2. Find an example not mentioned in the text of each of the four types of online retailing business models. Prepare a short report describing each firm and why it is an example of the particular business model.

3. Drawing on material in the chapter and your own research, prepare a short paper describing your views on the major social and legal issues facing online retailers.

4. Choose a services industry not discussed in the chapter (such as legal services, medical services, accounting services, or another of your choosing). Prepare a 3- to 5-page report discussing recent trends affecting online provision of these services.

5. Together with a teammate, investigate the use of mobile apps in the online retail or financial services industries. Prepare a short joint presentation on your findings.

REFERENCES

Amazon.com, Inc. Form 10-K for the fiscal year ended December 31, 2015, filed with the Securities and Exchange Commission (January 28, 2016a).

Amazon.com, Inc. Form 10-Q for the quarterly period ended June 30, 2016, filed with the Securities and Exchange Commission (July 29, 2016b).

Bardhan, Ashok. "The US Economy Grows, But Jobs Don't." Yale Global Online (March 13, 2014).

Benner, Katie. "Airbnb Sues Over New York Law Regulating New York Rentals." *New York Times* (October 22, 2016).

Bensinger, Greg. "Amazon Reveals 'Prime Air' Cargo Jet." *Wall Street Journal* (August 5, 2016a).

Bensinger, Greg. "Amazon Posts Another Blockbuster Quarter." *Wall Street Journal* (July 28, 2016b).

Bensinger, Greg and Sarah Nassauer. "Wal-Mart in Talks to Buy Web Retailer Jet.com." *Wall Street Journal* (August 3, 2016).

Berthene, April. "Amazon.com Is Winning the M-Commerce Game." Mobilestrategies360.com (June 24, 2016a).

Berthene, April. "Dell's E-commerce Site Tops IR's Monthly Performance Index." Internetretailer.com (August 31, 2016b).

Brown, Jeffrey, and Austan Goolsbee. "Does the Internet Make Markets More Competitive? Evidence from the Life Insurance Industry." John F. Kennedy School of Government, Harvard University. Research Working Paper RWP00-007 (2000).

Brynjolfsson, Erik, Astrid Andrea Dick, and Michael D. Smith. "Search and Product Differentiation at an Internet Shopbot," Center for eBusiness@MIT (December, 2004).

Bureau of Economic Analysis, U.S. Department of Commerce. "Table 3: Gross Domestic Product: Level and Change from Preceding Period." www.bea.gov (accessed October 14, 2016).

Careerbuilder. "Number of Employers Using Social Media to Screen Candidates Has Increased 500 Percent Over the Last Decade." (April 28, 2016).

Combes, Jessica. "Disrupted by Deliveroo." Cpifinancial. net (January 26. 2017).

Compete.com. "Site Profiles: Fidelity.com, Scottrade, TDAmeritrade, E-Trade, Vanguard, Charles Schwab, and Merrill Lynch." Accessed October 16, 2016.

comScore. "2015 Online Auto Insurance Shopping Report." (November 18, 2015).

Cook, James and Sam Shead. "Meal Delivery Startup Deliveroo Has Raised $275 Million." Businessinsider. com (August 5, 2016).

Davis, Don. "Mobile Sales Double for Macy's in Fiscal 2015." Internetretailer.com (February 23, 2016).

eMarketer, Inc. "US Retail Ecommerce Sales, by Product Category, 2015–2020." (September 1, 2016a).

eMarketer, Inc. "US Retail Sales Share, by Product Category, 2015–2020." (September 1, 2016b).

eMarketer, Inc. (Cindy Liu). "Worldwide Retail Ecommerce Sales: The eMarketer Forecast for 2016." (August 2016c).

eMarketer, Inc. "Top 10 Apparel Digital Retailers Among Internet Retailer Top 1,000 Retailers Worldwide, Ranked by Retail E-commerce Sales, 2015." (August 26, 2016d).

eMarketer, Inc. "UK Mobile Buyers, by Device, 2015–2020." (October 1, 2016f).

eMarketer, Inc. "Retail Ecommerce Sales for Internet Retailer Top 500 Retailers in North America, by Merchant Type, 2015." (April 13, 2016g).

eMarketer, Inc. "Retail Ecommerce Sales for Internet Retailer Second 500 Retailers in North America, by Merchant Type, 2014 & 2015." (June 1, 2016h).

eMarketer, Inc. "Most Mobile Banking Users Check Balances, Statements." (July 6, 2016i).

eMarketer, Inc. (Cindy Liu). "Worldwide Digital Travel Sales: The Complete eMarketer Forecast for 2016." (July 2016j).

eMarketer, Inc. "UK Adult Digital Travel Researchers and Bookers, 2015–2020." (October 1, 2016k).

eMarketer, Inc. "Millennials Embrace Mobile Banking." (August 18, 2015a).

eMarketer, Inc. "Mobile Tools are Helpful to Investors, but Humans Still Matter." (July 17, 2015b).

eMarketer, Inc. "Types of Financial Institutions/Services Which US Internet Users Interact Digitally, April 2015." (April 27, 2015c).

eMarketer, Inc. "US Millennial Investors Turn to Smartphone Apps for Money Management." (October 7, 2015d).

eMarketer, Inc. (Krista Garcia). "Retailers and Digital Commerce: Trends and Benchmarks for Five Sectors." (June 2015e).

eMarketer, Inc. (Jeremy Kressman). "Travel Purchases on the Go." (June 2014).

eMarketer, Inc. "Recruiters Rely More on Social Media for Talent." (February 26, 2013).

eMarketer, Inc. (Jeffrey Grau). "E-commerce in the US: Retail Trends." (May 2005).

Envestnet Yodlee. "Company." Yodlee.com (accessed October 16, 2016).

Eurostat. "ICT Usage in Households and by Individuals 2016." (December 2016).

Evans, Katie. "How a Dell Executive Learned to Plug Into What Consumers Want." Internetretailer.com (June 8, 2016).

Evans, Philip, and Thomas S. Wurster. *Blown to Bits: How the New Economics of Information Transforms Strategy.* Cambridge, MA: Harvard Business School Press (2000).

Facebook. "Introducing Marketplace: Buy and Sell With Your Local Community." Newsroom.fb.com (October 3, 2016).

Feeney, Caroline. "Zillow Snags More Internet Market Share Than Ever." Inman.com (May 19, 2016).

Gagliordi, Natalie. "Macy's Taps IBM Watson to Improve In-Store Shopping App." Zdnet.com (July 20, 2016).

Hitwise. "Top 10 Multi-Platform Real Estate Websites-September 2016." Marketingcharts.com (October 12, 2016).

ING. "World on the Move for Mobile Banking." (July 2016),

Internet Retailer. "Top 500 Guide 2016 Edition." (2016).

Javelin Strategy & Research. "Javelin Identifies $1.5B in Mobile Banking Cost Savings by Leveraging Omnichannel Approach." (July 8, 2013).

Jobvite. "The Jobvite Recruiter Nation Survey 2016." (2016).

Kline, Daniel B. "How Many Prime Members Does Amazon Have (And Why It Matters)." Fool.com (January 26, 2016).

Lands' End, Inc. Form 10-K for the fiscal year ended January 29, 2016, filed with the Securities and Exchange Commission (April 1, 2016a).

Lands' End, Inc. "About Lands' End." Landsend.com (accessed October 17, 2016b).

Leigh Day. "Leigh Day Announces Potential Legal Action Against Deliveroo." Leighday.co.uk (January 9, 2017).

LIMRA. "Information Seeking in the U.S.: Consumer Internet Use for Retail Insurance in 2015." (2015).

LIMRA. "Disruptive Consumers Want More Mobile Services." (July 9, 2014a).

LIMRA. "Insurers' Use of Social Media Has Jumped More than 50 Percent Since 2010." (July 22, 2014b).

Lindner, Matt. "Macy's Web Sales Grow But An Overall Decline Prompts 100 Store Closures." Internetretailer.com (August 11, 2016).

LinkedIn Talent Solutions. "United States Recruiting Trends 2016." (2016).

Manjoo, Farhad. "Think Amazon's Drone Delivery Idea is a Gimmick? Think Again." *New York Times* (August 10, 2016a).

Manjoo, Farhad. "The Echo from Amazon Brims with Groundbreaking Promise." *New York Times* (March 9, 2016b).

Maple, Tracy. "Lands' End's Sales Declines Stretch Across Online, Catalogs, and Stores." Internetretailer.com (September 3, 2016).

National Association of Realtors. "2016 Home Buyer and Seller Generational Trends." (March 9, 2016).

Prevost, Lisa. "Mortgage Approval Entirely Online." New York Times (December 4, 2015).

Roettgers, Janko. "Amazon Clocks $107 Billion In Revenue In 2015." Variety (January 28, 2016).

Smith, Sandy. "The Favorite 50 2016." Nrf.com (September 1, 2016).

Tong, Frank. "Macy's Plans to Launch an E-commerce Site in China in 2017." Internetretailer.com (October 7, 2016).

Top500guide.com. "Social 500" (accessed October 15, 2016).

U.S. Census Bureau. *Statistical Abstract of the United States 2012* (2012).

U.S. Department of Labor Bureau of Labor Statistics. "Industry Employment and Output Projections to 2024." *Monthly Labor Review* (December 2015).

Weil, Jonathon. "Securities Rules Help to Close the Earning Reports GAAP." *Wall Street Journal* (April 24, 2003).

Zaroban, Stefany. "Dell Banks on a Global E-commerce Platform Overhaul." Internetretailer.com (June 16, 2015).

Zervas, Georgios, Davide Proserpio, and John W. Byers. "The Rise of the Sharing Economy: Estimating the Impact of Airbnb on the Hotel Industry." Working Paper. SSRN (May 7, 2015).

CHAPTER 12

B2B E-commerce

After reading this chapter, you will be able to:

- Discuss the evolution and growth of B2B e-commerce, as well as its potential benefits and challenges.
- Understand how procurement and supply chains relate to B2B e-commerce.
- Identify major trends in supply chain management and collaborative commerce.
- Understand the different characteristics and types of Net marketplaces.
- Understand the objectives of private industrial networks, their role in supporting collaborative commerce, and the barriers to their implementation.

Alibaba:

China's E-commerce King

Alibaba is China's undisputed B2C and B2B e-commerce king. Founded in 1999 by Jack Ma, it began as a B2B exchange, enabling Chinese manufacturers to sell products such as circuit breakers and hydraulic cylinders to international traders and retailers. In the next decade, the Alibaba Group branched out, first into the C2C sector and then into the B2C sector, both of which also proved lucrative.

Today, Alibaba has grown to a size that dwarfs many of the world's established tech giants. In 2014, the company made a splashy initial public offering (IPO) on the New York Stock Exchange, raising $21.8 billion. Since then, Alibaba has continued to post rapid revenue gains, growing approximately 32% in both 2015 and 2016 en route to staggering 2016 revenues of $15.7 billion.

Alibaba operates eBay-like and Amazon-like businesses, and records more trade volume than those two

© Azimuth Interactive, Inc.

companies combined. Alibaba does not hold inventory, manage warehouses, or perform fulfillment, nor does it charge its users. Instead, Alibaba runs platforms that connect sellers and buyers, and earns revenue from commissions and advertising. Alibaba is estimated to control somewhere between 45% to 80% of China's rapidly expanding e-commerce market. The success of the company's IPO propelled Ma's net worth to well over $20 billion, and Ma is worth an estimated $27.7 billion in 2017. Internet penetration in China lags behind that of many Western countries but is rapidly increasing, and by 2020, Chinese e-commerce is projected to become larger than e-commerce in the United States, Great Britain, Japan, Germany, and France combined. This offers Alibaba much room for domestic growth in addition to its international expansion efforts.

Like many early players, Alibaba used an "aggregation of supply" model to connect buyers in North America and Europe to many SME suppliers in China. It created a platform to which sellers would upload their products, businesses would upload their requirements, and supplier–buyer matches would be made. When demand for Chinese goods faltered during the global recession of 2009, Alibaba.com transitioned to recruiting sellers interested in marketing their goods to China, to Japan through its Japanese-language site (Alibaba.co.jp), and to India, where it had opened a branch.

SOURCES: "Alibaba Teams Up with Samsung, Louis Vuitton and Other Brands to Fight Counterfeit Goods," by Jon Russell, Techcrunch.com, January 17, 2017; "Groupon Gains on Alibaba Takeover Rumors," Pymnts.com, January 13, 2017; "Alibaba's Jack Ma Grabs Unusual Spotlight," by Li Yuan, *Wall Street Journal*, January 11, 2017; "Alibaba Looks to Bricks and Mortar with Bid for Mall Operator in China," by Amie Tsang and Paul Mozur, *New York Times*, January 10, 2017; "Alibaba Breaks New Legal Ground in China, Sues Alleged Counterfeit Sellers," by Adam Najberg, Alizila.com, January 4, 2016; "Maersk, Alibaba Team Up to Offer Booking of Ship Places," Reuters.com, January 4, 2017; "Alibaba Will Sell You Anything, Including a Spot on a Container Ship," by Joon Ian Wong, Qz.com, January 4, 2017; "Alibaba Results Boosted by More Users, Mobile Growth," by Alyssa Abkowitz and Anne Steele, *Wall Street Journal*, August 11, 2016; "Alibaba's Jack Ma: The Problem with Counterfeits is They're 'Better Quality' Than Authentic Luxury Goods," by Marc Bain, Qz.com, June 14, 2016; "Alibaba SEC Probe: The Red Flags Fly Higher," by Aaron Back, *Wall Street Journal*, May 25, 2016; "Alibaba Suspended From Anticounterfeiting Group," by Kathy Chu, *Wall Street Journal*, May 13, 2016; "Brands Are Revolting over Alibaba's Membership in an Anti-Counterfeiting Group," by Scott Cendrowski, *Fortune*, May 13, 2016; "Alibaba Is Positioning Itself as Europe's Sales Gateway to China," by Saabira Chaudhuri, *Wall Street Journal*, October 20, 2015; "China's Alibaba Plans to Introduce B2B Platform in Brazil," Macauhub.com, August 4, 2015; "Alibaba Opens B2B Platform in India," Pymnts.com, June 29, 2015; "Alibaba's B2B Plan Could Change the World of Cross-Border Commerce," Pymnts.com, May 7, 2015; "Why Alibaba Says Its

Alibaba has three main B2B divisions. The company's English-language Alibaba.com site handles sales between importers and exporters from over 240 countries. The Chinese language site, 1688.com, focuses on domestic B2B transactions. AliExpress.com serves small businesses, offering wholesale pricing without bulk buying requirements.

Alibaba has invested heavily in global expansion, with new B2B platforms in other growing markets like India, Pakistan, and Brazil. Alibaba is also planning an aggressive expansion into the United States, committing to create 1 million new jobs. There is also speculation that Alibaba may acquire Groupon, the daily deals local e-commerce company, in which it already has a sizeable stake. It is also increasing its involvement in the global logistics business. Its OneTouch platform, which Alibaba acquired in 2010, offers a variety of export services, including customs clearance and financing, and is one of Alibaba's fastest growing units. In December 2016, Alibaba teamed up with Maersk, the world's largest container shipping line, to allow customers to use the OneTouch website to directly reserve space on ships originating from any one of eight Chinese ports and traveling to Europe or Asia, thus bypassing freight forwarders who traditionally act as intermediaries in the process. The company has also bought stakes in a variety of delivery companies, including Cainiao, which handles 70% of mainland China's deliveries, YTO Express, which handles an average of 8 million packages a day, and Singapore's postal service, SingPost. The company is also developing its previously non-existent physical presence for the first time via acquisitions, including a $2.6 billion takeover of Intime Retailer, a Chinese store and mall operator.

Alibaba's site design emphasizes its robust search function, ease of use, and consumer-friendliness. However, the site has dealt with accusations of widespread counterfeiting for years. In 2016, when Alibaba joined an anticounterfeiting group, retailers such as Michael Kors, Gucci, and Tiffany left the group in protest, and Alibaba was eventually suspended from the group after the outcry. Jack Ma has publicly stated that the problem is not that the items are fake, but instead that the quality of fake items is as good as or better than legitimate ones, and buyers of fake items often found that while Alibaba readily refunded customers reporting counterfeit items, sellers were not punished. However, in 2017, Alibaba filed its first lawsuit against counterfeit sellers and announced partnerships with major brands like Samsung and Louis Vuitton to crack down on counterfeiting. Alibaba has also been accused of manipulating its sales figures via fraudulent transactions on its platforms, especially on Singles Day, China's Black Friday equivalent, and was the target of a U.S. Securities and Exchange Commission probe in 2016. These concerns have failed to shake the confidence of most investors, and the company's early 2017 stock price is up 50% from its low in 2015.

As you'll learn in this chapter, the first wave of B2B exchanges fell short when the dot.com bubble of the early 2000s deflated. This latest wave, headlined by Alibaba, has succeeded where its predecessors failed by focusing on cost savings and affordability to meet the needs of small and medium-sized enterprises (SMEs), who aren't able to build their own marketplaces the way large companies can. As the rest of the world hatches new B2B start-ups to serve the SME market, they will have to play catch-up with Alibaba, which has been providing procurement and supply chain efficiencies to such companies for 15 years. Like Alibaba, they must lower transaction costs and identify unique suppliers and products for their buyers by providing a robust store of suppliers and by using matching algorithms, personalization, and big data analytics to help buyers find the supplier with the best product to meet their needs.

Nothing Like Amazon," Pymnts.com, November 5, 2014; "Alibaba, Shrugging Off Slowdown in Chinese Economy, Reports Strong Earnings," by Paul Mozur, *New York Times*, November 4, 2014; "A Soaring Debut for Alibaba," by Michael J. De La Merced, *New York Times*, September 19, 2014.

The Alibaba case illustrates the exciting potential for e-commerce technologies and customer experience to move from the consumer sphere to the business-to-business (B2B) world, where companies buy from hundreds or even thousands of suppliers and in turn sell to hundreds or potentially thousands of distributors and retailers.

This case frames the two sides of B2B e-commerce: the supply (buy) side and the sell side. On the supply side, firms have developed elaborate systems and techniques over many decades in order to manage their supply chains and the procurement process. Large firms can easily have hundreds or even thousands of suppliers of parts and materials. These are referred to as supply chain systems, which are described further in this chapter. These supply chain systems lower production costs, increase collaboration among firms, speed up new product development, and ultimately have revolutionized the way products are designed and manufactured. For instance, in the fashion industry, the combination of high-speed Internet-enabled supply chains coupled with equally high-speed trendy design not only clears shelves (and reduces the likelihood of clearance sales), but increases profits by increasing value to consumers (Zarroli, 2013; Cachon and Swinney, 2011).

The success of Alibaba provides insight into the sell side of B2B e-commerce. All the techniques of marketing, branding, and fulfillment developed in the retail e-commerce marketplace come into play when businesses sell to other businesses. Online websites, display advertising, search engine advertising, e-mail, and social media are just as relevant in B2B e-commerce as they are in B2C e-commerce, and the technologies involved are the same. For example, as consumers have moved to mobile devices to purchase retail goods, so have business procurement and purchasing agents begun to move towards mobile purchasing, inventory management, and marketing.

Alibaba is one kind of B2B Net marketplace, where thousands of suppliers can interact with thousands of business buyers on an Internet-enabled platform. There are many kinds of Net marketplaces described later in the chapter, from simple websites where a single company markets to other businesses, to more complex Net marketplaces where suppliers, producers, and distributors work collaboratively in a digital environment to produce, manufacture, and distribute their products and services.

As you'll learn in Section 12.1, Net marketplaces such as Alibaba have resulted from a decades-long evolution. In the early years of e-commerce, business firms tended to stick with direct purchases from manufacturers who were trusted, long term trading partners rather than participate in public B2B markets. Sellers, in turn, were reluctant to participate for fear of extreme price competition and brand dilution. As a result, B2B e-commerce has evolved much more slowly than B2C e-commerce. Many of the early B2B Net marketplaces that emerged in the late 1990s and 2000s imploded within a few years. We discuss the reasons for these early failures and describe how the new Net marketplaces have learned how to succeed.

Like B2C e-commerce, the B2B marketplace has consolidated, evolved, and moved on to more attainable visions.

In this chapter, we examine some major B2B e-commerce themes: procurement, supply chain management, and collaborative commerce. Each of these business processes has changed greatly with the evolution of B2B e-commerce systems. In Section 12.1, we provide an overview of B2B e-commerce. In Section 12.2, we look more closely at the procurement process, and supply chains. In Section 12.3, we place B2B e-commerce in the context of trends in procurement, supply chain management, and collaborative commerce. The final two sections of this chapter describe the two fundamental types of B2B e-commerce: Net marketplaces and private industrial networks.

Table 12.1 summarizes the leading trends in B2B e-commerce in 2016–2017. Among the most important trends are growing industry concern with supply chain risk and environmental impact, along with a growing public concern with the accountability of supply chains—in particular, violations of developed-world expectations of working conditions in third-world factories that play a key role in the production of goods sold in more developed countries. What many businesses have learned in the last decade is that supply chains can strengthen or weaken a company depending on a number of factors related to supply chain efficiency such as community engagement, labor relations, environmental protection, and sustainability. Many believe that all of these related factors are important to a firm's long-term profitability (Beard and Hornik, 2011). Nearly all of the companies included in the S&P 500 stock index now use B2B e-commerce systems. Half of all revenues of these firms are produced offshore, in part due to the globalization of supply chains. Thousands of smaller firms are also now able to employ B2B e-commerce systems as low-cost cloud computing and software-as-a-service (SaaS) versions have become widely available. Taking advantage of the mobile platform, more and more companies are using smartphones and tablet computers to run their businesses from any location. There are thousands of mobile apps available from enterprise B2B vendors such as SAP, IBM, Oracle, and others that link to supply chain management systems. Social network tools are pushing into the B2B world as well as the consumer world. B2B managers are increasingly using public and private social networks and technologies to enable long-term conversations with their customers and suppliers. Executives at firms large and small are coming to realize that they are competing not just with other firms but with those firms' supply chains as well. **Supply chain competition** refers to the fact that in some industries firms are able to differentiate their product or pricing, and achieve a competitive advantage, due to superior supply chain management. Arguably, firms with superior supply chains can produce better products, more quickly, and at a lower cost than those with simply adequate supply chains (Antai, 2011).

supply chain competition
differentiating a firm's products or prices on the basis of superior supply chain management

12.1 AN OVERVIEW OF B2B E-COMMERCE

The trade between business firms represents a huge marketplace. The total amount of B2B trade in the United States in 2016 is expected to be about $14.5 trillion, with B2B e-commerce contributing about $6.7 trillion of that amount (U.S. Census Bureau,

TABLE 12.1	**MAJOR TRENDS IN B2B E-COMMERCE 2016–2017**

BUSINESS

- B2B e-commerce growth continues to accelerate in 2016 to pre-recession levels as the U.S. economy continues to slowly recover from recession.
- B2B e-distributors adopt the same marketing and sales techniques as successful consumer e-commerce companies such as Amazon.
- Resurgence in Net marketplaces bringing together hundreds of suppliers and thousands of buying firms.
- Risk management: companies heighten their focus on risks in supply chains after being blindsided in recent years by a number of natural and man-made disasters.
- Regional manufacturing: risks of far-flung global networks lead to an increase in regional manufacturing and supply chains, moving production closer to market demand.
- Flexibility: growing emphasis on rapid-response and adaptive supply chains rather than lowest cost supply chains, which typically carry great risks.
- Supply chain visibility: growing calls for more real-time data that would allow managers to see not only across their production, but also into the production and financial condition of their key suppliers.
- Social and mobile commerce and customer intimacy: B2B buyers, like consumers, are tapping into tablets, smartphones, and social networks for purchasing, scheduling, exception handling, and coordinating with their suppliers in order to manage supply chain risk.

TECHNOLOGY

- Big data: global trade and logistics systems are generating huge repositories of B2B data, swamping management understanding and controls.
- Business analytics: growing emphasis on use of business analytics software (business intelligence) to understand very large data sets.
- Cloud: migration of B2B hardware and software to cloud computing and cloud apps, away from individual corporate data centers, as a means of slowing rising technology costs. B2B systems move to cloud computing providers like IBM, Oracle, Amazon, Google, and HP as their core technology.
- Mobile platform: growing use of mobile platform for B2B systems (CRM, SCM, and enterprise), putting B2B commerce into managers' palms.
- Social networks: increasing use of social network platforms for feedback from customers, strengthening customer and supplier relationships, adjusting prices and orders, and enhancing decision making.
- Internet of Things: The number of Internet-connected sensors and other intelligent devices that measure and monitor data continues to grow exponentially and begins to impact how supply chains operate.
- Predictive analytics tools are increasingly being used to identify the most profitable customers.

SOCIETY

- Accountability: growing demands for supply chain accountability and monitoring in developed countries driven by reports of poor working conditions in Asian factories.
- Sustainable supply chains: growing public demand for businesses to mitigate their environmental impact leads from local environmental optimization to consideration of the entire supply chain from design, production, customer service, and post-use disposal.
- Acceptance and growth of B2B platforms: SAP Ariba, one of the largest Net marketplaces, has over 2 million connected businesses, including two-thirds of the Forbes Global 2000 largest companies, that participate in transactions with a value of over $800 billion a year.

2016; authors' estimates). By 2020, B2B e-commerce is expected to grow to about $9 trillion in the United States. Worldwide, B2B e-commerce is estimated to be around €19.8 trillion in 2016 (UNCTAD, 2016).

The process of conducting trade among business firms is complex and requires significant human intervention, and therefore, consumes significant resources. Some firms estimate that each corporate purchase order for support products costs them, on average, at least $100 in administrative overhead. Analysts estimate that the cost of a single manual order entry is about $10.50 when handled by a sales rep on the telephone. A digital order cost is estimated to be 25 to 50 cents. Administrative overhead includes processing paper, approving purchase decisions, spending time using the telephone and fax machines to search for products and arrange for purchases, arranging for shipping, and receiving the goods. Across the economy, this adds up to trillions of dollars annually being spent for procurement processes that could potentially be automated. If even just a portion of inter-firm trade were automated, and parts of the entire procurement and sales process assisted by the Internet, then literally trillions of dollars might be released for more productive uses, consumer prices potentially would fall, productivity would increase, and the economic wealth of the nation would expand. This is the promise of B2B e-commerce. The challenge of B2B e-commerce is changing existing patterns and systems of procurement on the supply chain side, and designing and implementing new marketing and distribution systems on the B2B sell side.

SOME BASIC DEFINITIONS

Before the Internet, business-to-business transactions were referred to simply as *inter-firm trade* or the *procurement process*. We use the term **B2B commerce** to describe all types of inter-firm trade to exchange value across organizational boundaries, involving both the purchase of inputs and the distribution of products and services. B2B commerce includes the following business processes: customer relationship management, demand management, order fulfillment, manufacturing management, procurement, product development, returns, logistics/transportation, and inventory management (Barlow, 2011). This definition of B2B commerce does not include transactions that occur within the boundaries of a single firm—for instance, the transfer of goods and value from one subsidiary to another, or the use of corporate intranets to manage the firm. We use the term **B2B e-commerce** (or **B2B digital commerce**) to describe specifically that portion of B2B commerce that is enabled by the Internet (including mobile apps) (Fauska et al., 2013). The links that connect business firms in the production of goods and services are referred to as the supply chain. **Supply chains** are a complex system of organizations, people, business processes, technology, and information, all of which need to work together to produce products efficiently. Today's supply chains are often global, connecting the smartphones in New York to the shipyards in Los Angeles and Qingdao, and to the Foxconn factories that produce the phones. They are also local and national in scope.

B2B commerce
all types of inter-firm trade

B2B e-commerce (B2B digital commerce)
that portion of B2B commerce that is enabled by the Internet and mobile apps

supply chain
the links that connect business firms with one another to coordinate production

THE EVOLUTION OF B2B E-COMMERCE

B2B e-commerce has evolved over a 35-year period through several technology-driven stages (see **Figure 12.1**). The first step in the development of B2B e-commerce in the

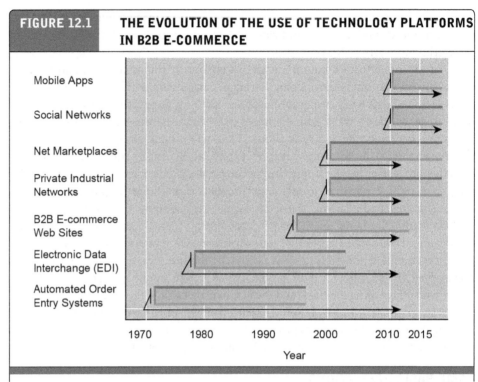

FIGURE 12.1   **THE EVOLUTION OF THE USE OF TECHNOLOGY PLATFORMS IN B2B E-COMMERCE**

B2B e-commerce has gone through many stages of development since the 1970s. Each stage reflects a major change in technology platforms from mainframes to private dedicated networks, and finally to the Internet, mobile apps, and social networks.

automated order entry systems

involve the use of telephone modems to send digital orders

seller-side solutions

seller-biased markets that are owned by, and show only goods from, a single seller

electronic data interchange (EDI)

a communications standard for sharing business documents and settlement information among a small number of firms

mid-1970s was **automated order entry systems** that involved the use of telephone modems to send digital orders to health care products companies such as Baxter Healthcare. Baxter, a diversified supplier of hospital supplies, placed telephone modems in its customers' procurement offices to automate reordering from Baxter's computerized inventory database (and to discourage reordering from competitors). This early technology was replaced by personal computers using private networks in the late 1980s, and by Internet workstations accessing electronic online catalogs in the late 1990s. Automated order entry systems are **seller-side solutions**. They are owned by the suppliers and are seller-biased markets—they show only goods from a single seller. Customers benefited from these systems because they reduced the costs of inventory replenishment and were paid for largely by the suppliers. Automated order entry systems continue to play an important role in B2B commerce.

By the late 1970s, a new form of computer-to-computer communication called **electronic data interchange (EDI)** emerged. We describe EDI in greater detail later in this chapter, but at this point, it is necessary only to know that EDI is a communications standard for sharing business documents such as invoices, purchase orders, shipping bills, product stocking numbers (SKUs), and settlement information among a small number of firms. Virtually all large firms have EDI systems, and most industry groups have industry standards for defining documents in that industry. EDI systems are owned by the buyers, hence they are **buyer-side solutions** and buyer-biased because they aim to reduce the procurement costs of supplies for the buyer. Of course, by automating the transaction, EDI systems also benefit the sellers through customer cost reduction. The topology of EDI systems is often referred to as a **hub-and-spoke system**, with the buyers in the center and the suppliers connected to the central hub via private dedicated networks.

EDI systems generally serve vertical markets. A **vertical market** is one that provides expertise and products for a specific industry, such as automobiles. In contrast, **horizontal markets** serve many different industries.

B2B e-commerce websites emerged in the mid-1990s along with the commercialization of the Internet. **B2B e-commerce websites** are perhaps the simplest and easiest form of B2B e-commerce to understand, because they are just online catalogs of products made available to the public marketplace by a single supplier. In this sense, they mimic the functionality of B2C e-commerce websites. Owned by the supplier, they are seller-side solutions and seller-biased because they show only the products offered by a single supplier.

B2B e-commerce websites are a natural descendant of automated order entry systems, but there are two important differences: (1) the far less expensive and more universal Internet becomes the communication media and displaces private networks, and (2) B2B e-commerce websites tend to serve horizontal markets—they carry products that serve a wide variety of industries. Although B2B e-commerce websites emerged prior to Net marketplaces (described next), they are usually considered a type of Net marketplace. Today, more and more B2B manufacturers, distributors, and suppliers are using B2B e-commerce websites to sell directly to business customers, who most often are procurement/purchasing agents, as discussed in Section 12.2.

Net marketplaces emerged in the late 1990s as a natural extension and scaling-up of B2B e-commerce websites. There are many different kinds of Net marketplaces, which we describe in detail in Section 12.4, but the essential characteristic of a Net marketplace is that it brings hundreds or even thousands of suppliers—each with a digital catalog and potentially thousands of purchasing firms—into a single Internet-based environment to conduct trade. We also use the term Net marketplace to refer to Internet-enabled marketing, distribution, and sales systems.

Private industrial networks also emerged in the last decade as natural extensions of EDI systems and the existing close relationships that developed between large industrial firms and their trusted suppliers. Described in more detail in Section 12.5, **private industrial networks** (sometimes also referred to as a *private trading exchange*, or *PTX*) are Internet-based communication environments that extend far beyond procurement to encompass supply chain efficiency enhancements and truly collaborative commerce where the buyers work with the sellers to develop and design new products.

THE GROWTH OF B2B E-COMMERCE

Figure 12.2 illustrates the growth of B2B e-commerce, as well as that of traditional B2B commerce, during the period 2011–2020. However, let's focus on the growth of B2B e-commerce during the period 2016–2020. During this time, B2B e-commerce is

buyer-side solutions
buyer-biased markets that are owned by buyers and that aim to reduce the procurement costs of supplies for buyers

hub-and-spoke system
suppliers connected to a central hub of buyers via private dedicated networks

vertical market
one that provides expertise and products for a specific industry

horizontal market
market that serves many different industries

B2B e-commerce website
online catalog of products made available to the public marketplace by a single supplier

Net marketplace
brings hundreds to thousands of suppliers and buyers into a sell-side, Internet-based environment to conduct trade

private industrial networks (private trading exchange, PTX)
Internet-based communication environments that extend far beyond procurement to encompass truly collaborative commerce

| FIGURE 12.2 | GROWTH OF B2B E-COMMERCE IN THE UNITED STATES, 2011–2020 |

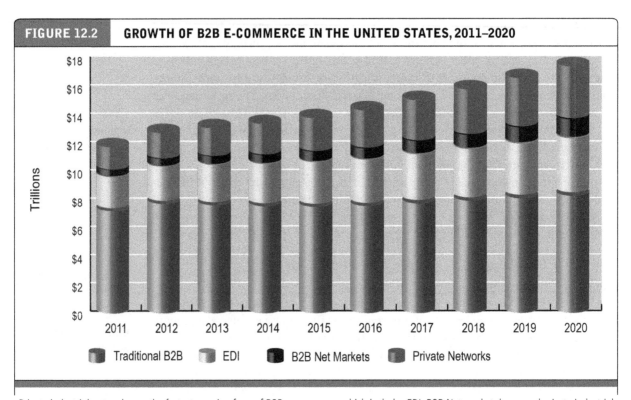

Private industrial networks are the fastest growing form of B2B e-commerce, which includes EDI, B2B Net marketplaces, and private industrial markets.

SOURCES: Based on data from U.S. Census Bureau, 2016; authors' estimates.

projected to grow from about $6.7 trillion in 2016 (about 46% of total B2B commerce in the United States) to $9 trillion (51% of total B2B commerce) in 2020. Several observations are important to note with respect to Figure 12.2. First, it shows that the initial belief that online marketplaces would become the dominant form of B2B e-commerce is not supported even though their growth rate has increased as firms like Amazon and eBay establish Net marketplaces. Second, private industrial networks play a dominant role in B2B e-commerce, both now and in the future. Third, non-EDI B2B e-commerce is the most rapidly growing type of B2B e-commerce. However, EDI remains quite common and continues to be a workhorse of B2B commerce even though its growth is expected to be relatively flat in the five four years.

Not all industries will be similarly affected by B2B e-commerce, nor will all industries similarly benefit from B2B. Several factors influence the speed with which industries migrate to B2B e-commerce and the volume of transactions. Those industries in which there is already significant utilization of EDI (indicating concentration of buyers and suppliers) and large investments in information technology and Internet infrastructure can be expected to move first and fastest to B2B e-commerce utilization. The aerospace and defense, computer, and industrial equipment industries meet these criteria. Where the marketplace is highly concentrated on either the purchasing or selling side, or both, conditions are also ripe for rapid B2B e-commerce growth, as in the energy and chemical industries. In the case of health care, the federal government, health care providers (doctors and hospitals), and major insurance companies are moving toward a national medical record system and the use of the Internet for managing medical payments. Coordinating the various players in the health care system is an extraordinary B2B challenge. Firms like IBM and Microsoft, and B2B service firms like SAP Ariba, are expanding the use of information ecosystems where health providers and insurers can share information.

POTENTIAL BENEFITS AND CHALLENGES OF B2B E-COMMERCE

Regardless of the specific type, B2B commerce as a whole promises many strategic benefits to firms—both buyers and sellers—and impressive gains for the economy. B2B e-commerce can:

- Lower administrative costs
- Lower search costs for buyers
- Reduce inventory costs by increasing competition among suppliers (increasing price transparency) and reducing inventory to the bare minimum
- Lower transaction costs by eliminating paperwork and automating parts of the procurement process
- Increase production flexibility by ensuring delivery of parts just at the right time (known as just-in-time production)
- Improve quality of products by increasing cooperation among buyers and sellers and reducing quality issues
- Decrease product cycle time by sharing designs and production schedules with suppliers
- Increase opportunities for collaborating with suppliers and distributors
- Create greater price transparency—the ability to see the actual buy and sell prices in a market
- Increase the visibility and real-time information sharing among all participants in the supply chain network.

B2B e-commerce offers potential first-mover strategic benefits for individual firms as well. Firms that move their procurement processes online first will experience impressive gains in productivity, cost reduction, and potentially much faster introduction of new, higher-quality products. While these gains may be imitated by other competing firms, it is also clear from the history of B2B e-commerce that firms making sustained investments in information technology and B2B e-commerce can adapt much faster to new technologies as they emerge, creating a string of first-mover advantages.

While there are many potential benefits to B2B e-commerce, there are also considerable risks and challenges. Often real-world supply chains fail to provide visibility into the supply chain because they lack real-time demand, production, and logistics data, and have inadequate financial data on suppliers. The result is unexpected supplier failure and disruption to the supply chain. Builders of B2B supply chains often had little concern for the environmental impacts of supply chains, the sensitivity of supply chains to natural events, fluctuating fuel and labor costs, or the impact of public values involving labor and environmental policies. The result in 2016 is that many Fortune 1000 supply chains are risky, vulnerable, and socially and environmentally unsustainable. Read *Insight on Society: Where's My iPad? Apple's Supply Chain Risks and Vulnerabilities* for a look at the impact the Tohoku earthquake in Fukushima, Japan had on global supply chains, as well as the reputational risk posed by supply chains.

12.2 THE PROCUREMENT PROCESS AND SUPPLY CHAINS

The subject of B2B e-commerce can be complex because there are so many ways the Internet can be used to support the exchange of goods and payments among organizations, efficient supply chains, and collaboration. At the most basic level, B2B e-commerce is about changing the **procurement process** (how business firms purchase goods they need to produce goods they will ultimately sell to consumers) of thousands of firms across the world. In the procurement process, firms purchase goods from a set of suppliers, and they in turn purchase their inputs from a set of suppliers. The supply chain includes not just the firms themselves, but also the relationships among them and the processes that connect them.

procurement process
how firms purchase goods they need to produce goods for consumers

STEPS IN THE PROCUREMENT PROCESS

There are seven separate steps in the procurement process (see **Figure 12.3**). The first three steps involve the decision of who to buy from and what to pay: searching for suppliers of specific products; qualifying both sellers and the products they sell;

| FIGURE 12.3 | THE PROCUREMENT PROCESS |

1	2	3	4	5	6	7
Search	**Qualify**	**Negotiate**	**Purchase Order**	**Invoicing**	**Shipping**	**Remittance Payment**
Catalogs	Research	Price	Order product	Receive PO	Enter into shipper's tracking system	Receive goods
Internet	Credit history	Credit terms	Initiate purchase order (PO)	Enter into financial system	Ship goods	Enter shipping documents into warehouse system
Salespersons	Check with competitors	Escrow	Enter into system	Enter into production system	Deliver goods	Verify and correct invoice
Brochures	Telephone research	Quality	Mail PO	Send invoice	Enter into tracking system	Resend invoice
Telephone		Timing		Match with PO		Cut check
Fax				Internal review		Add corrected invoice to back office systems
				Enter into warehouse system		

The procurement process is a lengthy and complicated series of steps that involves the seller, buyer, and shipping companies in a series of connected transactions.

INSIGHT ON SOCIETY

WHERE'S MY IPAD? GLOBAL SUPPLY CHAIN RISK AND VULNERABILITY

In March 2011, a magnitude 9.0 earthquake occurred offshore of northern Japan. The Tohoku earthquake was the largest in recorded history and immediately created a number of tsunami waves, some of which exceeded 100 feet in height and penetrated up to six miles inland. In their path were six coastal nuclear reactors in the Fukushima Prefecture near the town of Okuma, the largest nuclear power site in the world. Several of the nuclear reactors exploded and began leaking dangerous levels of radiation as fuel rods melted at temperatures exceeding 5,000 degrees.

The Tohoku earthquake exposed significant weaknesses and vulnerabilities in today's modern B2B supply chains. Technology, globalization of trade, and high levels of wage disparity between the developed and undeveloped worlds have led to a massive outsourcing of manufacturing around the world. Today, every component of every manufactured product is carefully examined by company engineers and financial managers with an eye to finding the lowest cost and highest quality manufacturer. Production inevitably tends to concentrate at single firms that are given very high order volumes if they can meet the price. Large orders make lower prices easier to provide because of scale economies. However, when you concentrate production globally with just a few suppliers, you also concentrate risk.

As a result, the world's manufacturing base has become less redundant, flexible, and adaptive than older traditional supply chains. Interdependencies have grown into a tightly coupled machine that is quite fragile. Risk assessment in supply chains has been weak or nonexistent.

Computers, cell phones, tractors, airplanes, and automobiles are just a few of the complex manufactured goods that rely on parts and subassemblies made thousands of miles away from their final assembly plants. Most of these manufacturers know who their first-tier suppliers are but may be less aware about who supplies their suppliers, and so on down the line of the industrial spider's web that constitutes the real world of supply chains. Few firms had considered the impact of an earthquake on their supply chains, or a nuclear meltdown, or even a financial collapse in the global banking system— all typical risks found in the real world.

Take the Apple iPad. In a teardown of an iPad after the earthquake, IHS iSuppli, a market research firm, identified at least five major components sourced from Japanese suppliers, some of whom were located in northern Japan. Not all of these suppliers were directly impacted by the earthquake, but some were, and many had sub-suppliers of various hard-to-replace small components that were directly impacted. For instance, the iPad and iPhone's unusually shaped lithium batteries used a crucial polymer made by Kureha, a Japanese firm in the nuclear contamination zone. Kureha controls 70% of the global production of this polymer. Apple was not the only consumer product manufacturer hit hard: computer chips are built on silicon wafers, and 25% of the world's supply is made by two Japanese manufacturers, both of which had to shut down wafer production. A few years later, in 2015, a tear-down of the iPhone 6 Plus by IHS iSuppli found that Apple had learned its lesson and diversified its supply chain by often having two manufacturers for the same components sourced from different countries, and also having various components manufactured in different parts of the globe. For instance, the retina display screen is manufactured in both Japan and Korea, while the A8 processor is

(continued)

manufactured in both Taiwan and Korea; the NFC chips are made in Holland and Austria, while the audio chip is from United States and the accelerometer chip is from Germany.

Apple was not the only manufacturer that learned a lesson in supply chain risk from the Japanese earthquake: Boeing was without carbon fiber airframe assemblies made in Japan; Ford and GM closed factories for lack of Japanese transmissions; and Caterpillar reduced production at its factories worldwide as it attempted to secure alternative suppliers.

Supply chain risk involves more than disruptions in production, as Apple and many other companies have discovered. Supply chains can produce reputational risks when key suppliers engage in labor and environmental policies and practices that are unacceptable to developed world audiences. For instance, for much of 2012, Apple was under attack in the United States and Europe after an audit by the Fair Labor Association found that workers at several assembly plants operated by Apple contractor Foxconn were exposed to toxic chemicals and forced to work over 60 hours a week under dangerous work conditions.

Also in 2012, a fire in a clothing factory in Dhaka, Bangladesh, killed 117 workers, mostly women and children. Well-known brands from Europe and the United States, among them Walmart and Spanish giant Inditex, were producing clothing in this factory. Walmart claimed a subcontractor was using this factory without Walmart's knowledge. The fire created a worldwide protest,

and has led to government and industry efforts to certify factory safety in Bangladesh and hold firms responsible for working conditions.

It also isn't just natural disasters and fires that can disrupt supply lines. In 2015, supply lines from Asia to the United States were shut down for nearly a month by a longshoreman's dock strike that resulted in a slowdown of automobile production throughout the United States. This in turn backed up production in Asia of car parts. Thailand, the world's third largest fish exporter, was discovered to be using slave labor to harvest fish, and its product was banned by the European Union. Many American companies had their supplies disrupted, and needed to find other suppliers. Finally a new class of supply chain risk is becoming apparent: cybersecurity risks. With hundreds of suppliers, it is very difficult for any single purchasing firm to assess the security of its suppliers' systems. Reducing the number of suppliers is one method. Working only with trusted partners is another. Yet there remains a large opportunity for cybercriminals and rogue governments to disrupt global supply chains.

One might think that in the so-called global and Internet economy, computer-based supply chains could quickly and effortlessly adjust to find new suppliers for just about any component or industrial material in a matter of minutes. Think again. New supply chains will need to be built that optimize not just cost but also survivability in the event of disasters, as well as meet the ethical demands of the major consuming countries in Europe and the United States.

SOURCES: "Supplier Responsibility 2016 Progress Report," by Apple Inc., Apple.com, March 30, 2016; "Resilinc Special Supply Chain Event Case Study: 2016 Taiwan Earthquake, Assessing the Foreseeable Supply Chain Impact," by Resilinc Inc., Info.reslinc.com, February 2016; "A Look Back at 2015: The Top Ten Supply Chain Disruptions," by DHL.com, February 2016; "Financial Firms Grapple With Cyber Risk in the Supply Chain," by Rachael King, *Wall Street Journal*, May 25, 2015; "Supply Chain Slavery Comes Into Focus for Companies," by Ben DiPietro, *Wall Street Journal*, March 30, 2015; "Asian Supply Lines Hit by West Coast Ports," *Reuters*, February 16, 2015; "Teardown Shows Apple's iPhone 6 Cost at Least $200 to Build," by Arik Hesseldahl, Recode.net, September 23, 2014; "Apple Goes on Hiring Binge in Asia to Speed Product Releases," by Eva Dou, *Wall Street Journal*, March 3, 2014; "Teardown: Apple's Latest iPhones Are Not as Green as the Company Claims," by Roger Chang, Wired.com, September 20, 2013; "Gold iPhone 5S Backordered Online in US, Elsewhere," by Josh Lowensohn, Cnetnews.com, September 20, 2013; "Infographic Breaks Down Apple's iPhone Supply Chain," by Bryan Chaffin, MacObserver.com, August 6, 2013; "Bangladesh Factory, Site of Fire That Trapped and Killed 7, Made European Brands," by Julfikar Ali Manik and Jim Yardley, *New York Times*, January 27, 2013; "Disruptions: Too Much Silence on Working Conditions," by Nick Bilton, *New York Times*, April 8, 2012; "Audit Faults Apple Supplier," by Jessica Vascellaro, *Wall Street Journal*, March 30, 2012; "Under the Hood of Apple's Tablet," by Don Clark, *Wall Street Journal*, March 16, 2012; "In China, Human Costs Are Built Into an iPad," by Charles Duhigg and David Barboza, *New York Times*, January 25, 2012; "Japan: The Business After Shocks," by Andrew Dowell, *Wall Street Journal*, March 25, 2011; "Some Worry the Success of Apple Is Tied to Japan," by Miguel Helft, *New York Times*, March 22, 2011; "Crisis Tests Supply Chain's Weak Links," by James Hookway and Aries Poon, *Wall Street Journal*, March 18, 2011; "Caterpillar Warns of Supply Problems From Quake," by Bob Tita, *Wall Street Journal*, March 18, 2011; "Lacking Parts, G.M. Will Close Plant," by Nick Bunkley, *New York Times*, March 17, 2011.

and negotiating prices, credit terms, escrow requirements, quality, and scheduling of delivery. Once a supplier is identified, purchase orders are issued, the buyer is sent an invoice, the goods are shipped, and the buyer sends a payment. Each of these steps in the procurement process is composed of many separate business processes and subactivities. Each of these activities must be recorded in the information systems of the seller, buyer, and shipper. Often, this data entry is not automatic and involves a great deal of manual labor, telephone calls, faxes, and e-mails.

TYPES OF PROCUREMENT

Two distinctions are important for understanding how B2B e-commerce can improve the procurement process. First, firms make purchases of two kinds of goods from suppliers: direct goods and indirect goods. **Direct goods** are goods integrally involved in the production process; for instance, when an automobile manufacturer purchases sheet steel for auto body production. **Indirect goods** are all other goods not directly involved in the production process, such as office supplies and maintenance products. Often these goods are called **MRO goods**—products for maintenance, repair, and operations.

Second, firms use two different methods for purchasing goods: contract purchasing and spot purchasing. **Contract purchasing** involves long-term written agreements to purchase specified products, with agreed-upon terms and quality, for an extended period of time. Generally, firms purchase direct goods using long-term contracts. **Spot purchasing** involves the purchase of goods based on immediate needs in larger marketplaces that involve many suppliers. Generally, firms use spot purchasing for indirect goods, although in some cases, firms also use spot purchasing for direct goods.

According to some estimates, about 65% of inter-firm trade involves contract purchasing of direct goods, and 35% involves spot purchasing of indirect goods (Ariba, 2014; Kaplan and Sawhney, 2000). There are, of course, differences among industries. Purchases of direct goods play a dominant role in the extraction and metal industries, for instance. This finding is significant for understanding B2B e-commerce.

Although the procurement process involves the purchasing of goods, it is extraordinarily information-intense, involving the movement of information among many existing corporate systems. The procurement process today is also very labor-intensive, directly involving millions of employees around the world, not including those engaged in transportation, finance, insurance, or general office administration related to the process. The key players in the procurement process are the purchasing managers. They ultimately decide who to buy from, what to buy, and on what terms. Purchasing managers ("procurement managers" in the business press) are also the key decision makers for the adoption of B2B e-commerce solutions. As purchasing managers have become more familiar and comfortable with B2C e-commerce in their personal lives, they are increasingly coming to expect the same type of purchasing experience in the B2B arena. As a result, B2B manufacturers, suppliers, and distributors are finding that in order to effectively compete, they must pay more attention to the online customer experience, just as their B2C counterparts do. Features that B2B customers now expect include enhanced search functionality, up-to-date product pricing and availability information, product configurators, mobile support, apps along

direct goods
goods directly involved in the production process

indirect goods
all other goods not directly involved in the production process

MRO goods
products for maintenance, repair, and operations

contract purchasing
involves long-term written agreements to purchase specified products, under agreed-upon terms and quality, for an extended period of time

spot purchasing
involves the purchase of goods based on immediate needs in larger marketplaces that involve many suppliers

with websites, online support forums, live customer service reps, and a database that contains their corporate purchasing history, shipping preferences, and payment data, and provides support for repeat orders.

MULTI-TIER SUPPLY CHAINS

Although Figure 12.3 captures some of the complexity of the procurement process, it is important to realize that firms purchase thousands of goods from thousands of suppliers. The suppliers, in turn, must purchase their inputs from their suppliers. Large manufacturers such as Ford Motor Company have over 20,000 suppliers of parts, packaging, and technology. The number of secondary and tertiary suppliers is at least as large. Together, this extended **multi-tier supply chain** (the chain of primary, secondary, and tertiary suppliers) constitutes a crucial aspect of the industrial infrastructure of the economy. **Figure 12.4** depicts a firm's multi-tier supply chain.

The supply chain depicted in Figure 12.4 is a three-tier chain simplified for the sake of illustration. In fact, large Fortune 1000 firms have thousands of suppliers, who in turn have thousands of smaller suppliers. The real-world supply chain is often many layers deep. The complexity of the supply chain suggests a combinatorial explosion. Assuming a manufacturer has four primary suppliers and each one has three primary suppliers, and each of these has three primary suppliers, then the total number of suppliers in the chain (including the buying firm) rises to 53. This figure does not include the shippers, insurers, and financiers involved in the transactions.

Immediately, you can see from Figure 12.4 that the procurement process involves a very large number of suppliers, each of whom must be coordinated with the

multi-tier supply chain

the chain of primary, secondary, and tertiary suppliers

FIGURE 12.4	**THE MULTI-TIER SUPPLY CHAIN**

Tier 3   Tier 2   Tier 1

SELLERS   **BUYER**

The supply chain for every firm is composed of multiple tiers of suppliers.

TABLE 12.2	CONCEPTS AND CHALLENGES IN SUPPLY CHAIN MANAGEMENT
CONCEPT/CHALLENGE	**DESCRIPTION**
Visibility	Ability to monitor suppliers, orders, logistics, and pricing
Demand forecasting	Informing your suppliers of future demand
Production scheduling	Informing your suppliers of the production schedule
Order management	Keeping track of orders to your suppliers
Logistics management	Managing your logistics partners based on your production schedule

production needs of the ultimate purchaser—the buying firm. You can also understand how difficult it is to manage the supply chain, or obtain visibility into the supply chain simply because of its size and scope.

VISIBILITY AND OTHER CONCEPTS IN SUPPLY CHAIN MANAGEMENT

The global, multi-tier nature of supply chains produces a number of challenges for supply chain managers. A central concept of supply chains is **supply chain visibility**, which refers to the ability of a firm to monitor the output and pricing of its first- and second-tier suppliers, track and manage supplier orders, and manage transportation and logistics providers who are moving the products. A supply chain is visible when you know exactly what you have ordered from your suppliers and what their production schedule is, and when you can track the goods through shipping and trucking firms to your in-bound warehouse. With this knowledge, the firm's internal enterprise systems can produce production schedules and develop financial forecasts (Long, 2014; Cecere, 2014; Cecere, 2013). Generally, the more firms invest in digitally enabled supply chains, the greater the visibility managers have into the process (Caridia, et. al., 2010).

supply chain visibility
the extent to which purchasing firms can monitor second- and third-tier suppliers' activities

Other key concepts in supply chain management, and which are also central management challenges, are described in **Table 12.2**.

THE ROLE OF EXISTING LEGACY COMPUTER SYSTEMS AND ENTERPRISE SYSTEMS IN SUPPLY CHAINS

Complicating any efforts to coordinate the many firms in a supply chain is the fact that each firm generally has its own set of legacy computer systems, sometimes home-grown or customized, that cannot easily pass information to other systems. **Legacy computer systems** generally are older enterprise systems used to manage key business processes within a firm in a variety of functional areas from manufacturing, logistics, finance, and human resources. **Enterprise systems** are corporate-wide systems that relate to all aspects of production, including finance, human resources, and procurement. Many large Fortune 500 global firms have implemented global enterprise-wide systems from major vendors such as IBM, SAP, Oracle, and others. Generally enterprise systems have an inward focus on the firm's internal production

legacy computer systems
older mainframe systems used to manage key business processes within a firm in a variety of functional areas

enterprise systems
corporate-wide systems that relate to all aspects of production, including finance, human resources, and procurement

processes, and only tangentially are concerned with suppliers. More contemporary cloud-based dedicated B2B software that can be integrated with existing enterprise systems is growing in importance. Companies such as IBM, Oracle, and SAP have developed SaaS (software as a service) or on-demand cloud-based supply chain management systems that can work seamlessly with their legacy offerings. Cloud-based supply chain management revenues are growing at 25% annually, although many firms prefer to maintain their own supply chain management systems on their private clouds rather than use shared public cloud services (Chao, 2015; Accenture, 2014).

12.3 TRENDS IN SUPPLY CHAIN MANAGEMENT AND COLLABORATIVE COMMERCE

It is impossible to comprehend the actual and potential contribution of B2B e-commerce, or the successes and failures of B2B e-commerce vendors and markets, without understanding ongoing efforts to improve the procurement process through a variety of supply chain management programs that long preceded the development of e-commerce.

supply chain management (SCM)
refers to a wide variety of activities that firms and industries use to coordinate the key players in their procurement process

Supply chain management (SCM) refers to a wide variety of activities that firms and industries use to coordinate the key players in their procurement process. For the most part, today's procurement managers still work with telephones, e-mail, fax machines, face-to-face conversations, and instinct, relying on trusted long-term suppliers for their strategic purchases of goods directly involved in the production process.

There have been a number of major developments in supply chain management over the last two decades that set the ground rules for understanding how B2B e-commerce works (or fails to work). These developments include just-in-time and lean production, supply chain simplification, adaptive supply chains, sustainable supply chains, electronic data interchange (EDI), supply chain management systems, and collaborative commerce.

JUST-IN-TIME AND LEAN PRODUCTION

just-in-time production
a method of inventory cost management that seeks to reduce excess inventory to a bare minimum

lean production
a set of production methods and tools that focuses on the elimination of waste throughout the customer value chain

One of the significant costs in any production process is the cost of in-process inventory: the parts and supplies needed to produce a product or service. **Just-in-time production** is a method of inventory cost management that seeks to reduce excess inventory to a bare minimum. In just-in-time production, the parts needed for, say, an automobile, arrive at the assembly factory a few hours or even minutes before they are attached to a car. Payment for the parts does not occur until the parts are attached to a vehicle on the production line. In the past, producers used to order enough parts for a week or even a month's worth of production, creating huge, costly buffers in the production process. These buffers assured that parts would almost always be available, but at a large cost. **Lean production** is a set of production methods and tools that focuses on the elimination of waste throughout the customer value chain. It is an extension of just-in-time beyond inventory management to the full range of activities that create customer value. Originally, just-in-time and lean methods were implemented with phones, faxes, and paper documents to coordinate the flow of parts in inventory. Supply chain management systems now have largely automated the process of acquiring inventory from suppliers, and made possible significant savings on a global basis. Arguably, contemporary supply chain systems are the foundation of today's global B2B production system.

SUPPLY CHAIN SIMPLIFICATION

Many manufacturing firms have spent the past two decades reducing the size of their supply chains and working more closely with a smaller group of strategic supplier firms to reduce both product costs and administrative costs, while improving quality, a trend known as **supply chain simplification**. Following the lead of Japanese industry, for instance, the automobile industry has systematically reduced the number of its suppliers by over 50%. Instead of open bidding for orders, large manufacturers have chosen to work with strategic partner supply firms under long-term contracts that guarantee the supplier business and also establish quality, cost, and timing goals. These strategic partnership programs are essential for just-in-time production models, and often involve joint product development and design, integration of computer systems, and tight coupling of the production processes of two or more companies. **Tight coupling** is a method for ensuring that suppliers precisely deliver the ordered parts at a specific time and to a particular location, ensuring the production process is not interrupted for lack of parts.

SUPPLY CHAIN BLACK SWANS: ADAPTIVE SUPPLY CHAINS

While firms have greatly simplified their supply chains in the last decade, they have also sought to centralize them by adopting a single, global supply chain system that integrates all the firm's vendor and logistics information into a single enterprise-wide system. Large software firms such as Oracle, IBM, and SAP encourage firms to adopt a "one world, one firm, one database" enterprise-wide view of the world in order to achieve scale economies, simplicity, and to optimize global cost and value.

Beginning in earnest in 2000, managers in developed countries used these new technological capabilities to push manufacturing and production to the lowest cost labor regions of the world, specifically China and South East Asia. This movement of production to Asia was also enabled by the entrance of China into the World Trade Organization in September 2001. Suddenly, it was both technologically and politically possible to concentrate production wherever possible in the lowest cost region of the world. These developments were also supported by low-cost fuel, which made both transoceanic shipping and production inexpensive, and relative political stability in the region. By 2005, many economists believed a new world economic order had emerged based on cheap labor in Asia capable of producing inexpensive products for Western consumers, profits for global firms, and the opening of Asian markets to sophisticated Western goods and financial products.

As it turns out, there were many risks and costs to this strategy of concentrating production in a world of economic, financial, political, and even geological instability. Today, managers need to be more careful in balancing gains in efficiency from a highly centralized supply chain, with the risks inherent to such a strategy (Long, 2014). For

supply chain simplification
involves reducing the size of the supply chain and working more closely with a smaller group of strategic supplier firms to reduce both product costs and administrative costs, while improving quality

tight coupling
a method for ensuring that suppliers precisely deliver the ordered parts, at a specific time and particular location, to ensure the production process is not interrupted for lack of parts

instance, in the global financial crisis of 2007–2009, relying on suppliers in parts of Europe where currencies and interest rates fluctuated greatly exposed many firms to higher costs than anticipated. Suddenly, key suppliers could not obtain financing for their production or shipments. In 2016, the United Kingdom's vote to leave the European Union (commonly referred to as Brexit) is expected to rattle European supply chains. And as you learned in the *Insight on Society* case, the 2011 earthquake and tsunami in Japan had a significant impact on supply chains in a number of industries around the world. In February 2016, another earthquake, this time in southern Taiwan, had a similar impact. Taiwan is the global manufacturing center of integrated circuit wafers, accounting for 70% of the world's production of processor chips used by Apple, IBM, Microsoft, and hundreds of other firms (Resilinc, 2016; DHL, 2016). In recent years, the source of supply chain disruptions has shifted to technology, with major disruptions due to failure of cloud-based services and cyberattacks (Resilinc, 2016; Rossi, 2015; Rowland, 2014; Gusman, 2013; Zurich Insurance, 2012).

adaptive supply chain
allows companies to react to disruptions in the supply chain in a particular region by moving production to a different region

The risks and costs of extended and concentrated supply chains have begun to change corporate strategies (Chopra and Sodhi, 2014). To cope with unpredictable world events, firms are taking steps to create **adaptive supply chains** that allow them to react to disruptions in the supply chain in a particular region by moving production to a different region. Many companies are breaking up single global supply chain systems into regional or product-based supply chains and reducing the level of centralization. Using adaptive supply chains, firms can decide to locate some production of parts in Latin America, for instance, rather than having all their production or suppliers in a single country such as Japan or China. They will be able to move production around the world to temporary safe harbors. This may result in higher short-term costs, but provide substantial, longer-term risk protection in the event any single region is disrupted. Increasingly, supply chains are being built based on the assumption that global disruptions in supply are inevitable, but not predictable. The focus now is on optimal-cost, not low-cost, supply chains, and more distributed manufacturing along with more flexible supply chains that can shift reliably from high-risk to low-risk areas. Regional manufacturing means shorter supply chains that can respond rapidly to changing consumer tastes and demand levels (PriceWaterhouseCoopers and the MIT Forum for Supply Chain Innovation, 2015; Cachon and Swinney, 2011).

ACCOUNTABLE SUPPLY CHAINS: LABOR STANDARDS

accountable supply chain
one where the labor conditions in low-wage, underdeveloped producer countries are visible and morally acceptable to ultimate consumers in more developed industrial societies

Accountable supply chains are those where the labor conditions in low-wage, underdeveloped producer countries are visible and morally acceptable to ultimate consumers in more developed industrial societies. For much of the last century, American and European manufacturers with global supply chains with large offshore production facilities sought to hide the realities of their offshore factories from Western reporters and ordinary citizens. For global firms with long supply chains, visibility did not mean their consumers could understand how their products were made.

Beginning in 2000, and in part because of the growing power of the Internet to empower citizen reporters around the world, the realities of global supply chains have slowly become more transparent to the public. For instance, for much of the past decade, beginning in 1997, Nike, the world's largest manufacturer of sporting goods, has been under intense criticism for exploiting foreign workers, operating sweat shops, employing children, and allowing dangerous conditions in its subcontractor factories. As a result, Nike has introduced significant changes to its global supply chain. Bangladesh is a continuing source of apparel factory fires beginning with the Dhakka fire of 2010, the Rena Plaza factory building collapse of 2013, and the second Dhakka fire in 2015, all of which resulted in deaths and injuries to workers. Around 80% of Bangladesh's exports (and 60% of its total GDP) come from apparel manufacturing for global brands such as Walmart, H&M, JCPenney, Zara, and others (Manik and Yardley, 2013).

With the emergence of truly global supply chains, and political changes at the World Trade Organization, which opened up European and American markets to Asian goods and services, many—if not most—of the electronics, toys, cosmetics, industrial supplies, footwear, apparel, and other goods consumed in the developed world are made by workers in factories in the less developed world, primarily in Asia and Latin America. Unfortunately, but quite understandably, the labor conditions in these factories in most cases do not meet the minimal labor standards of Europe or America even though these factories pay higher wages and offer better working conditions than other local jobs in the host country. In many cases, the cost for a worker of not having a job in what—to Western standards—are horrible working conditions is to sink deeper into poverty and even worse conditions. Many point out that labor conditions were brutal in the United States and Europe in the nineteenth and early twentieth century when these countries were building industrial economies, and therefore, whatever conditions exist in offshore factories in 2016 are no worse than developed countries in their early years of rapid industrialization.

The argument results in a painful ethical dilemma, a terrible trade-off: cheap manufactured goods that increase consumer welfare in developed countries seem to require human misery in less developed countries. Indeed, these jobs would never have been moved to less developed parts of world without exceptionally low, even survival level, wages.

Notwithstanding the argument that having a job is better than being unemployed in low-wage countries, or any country, there are some working conditions that are completely unacceptable to consumers and therefore to firms in developed countries. Among these unacceptable working conditions are slave or forced labor, child employment, routine exposure to toxic substances, more than 48 hours of work per week, harassment and abuse, sexual exploitation, and compensation beneath the minimal standard of living leaving no disposable income. These practices were, and are, in some cases typical, and certainly not atypical, in many low-wage countries.

A number of groups in the last decade have contributed to efforts to make global supply chains transparent to reporters and citizens, and to develop minimal standards of accountability. Among these groups are the National Consumers League, Human Rights First, the Maquila Solidarity Network, the Global Fairness Initiative, the Clean Clothes Campaign, the International Labor Organization (UN), and the Fair Labor Association (FLA). The FLA is a coalition of business firms with offshore production and global supply chains, universities, and private organizations. For member firms, the FLA conducts interviews with workers, makes unannounced visits to factories to track progress, and investigates complaints. They are also one of the major international labor standard-setting organizations (Fair Labor Association, 2012).

In March 2012, the FLA released its investigation of Hon Hai Precision Industry Company (a Taiwan-based company known as Foxconn), which is the assembler of nearly all iPhones and iPads in the world. Foxconn operates what is alleged to be the largest factory in the world in Longhua, Shenzhen, where over 250,000 workers assemble electronics goods. The audit of working conditions at Foxconn was authorized by Apple, a member of the FLA, and was based on 35,000 surveys of workers at the Longhua factory. The report found over 50 legal and code violations (sometimes in violation of Chinese laws) including requiring too many hours of work a week (over 60), failing to pay workers for overtime, and hazardous conditions that injured workers (Fair Labor Association, 2012). Similar violations of labor standards continue to be found in the Middle East and Asia (Fair Labor Association, 2015).

SUSTAINABLE SUPPLY CHAINS: LEAN, MEAN, AND GREEN

Sustainable business is a call for business to take social and ecological interests, and not just corporate profits, into account in all their decision-making throughout the firm (UN Global Compact Office and BSR, 2015). No small request. Since the United Nations World Commission on Environment and Development (WCED) published the first comprehensive report on sustainable business in 1987, firms around the globe have struggled with these concepts and in some cases ignored or resisted them as simply a threat to sustained profitability. The commission's report (*Our Common Future*) argued for a balance of profits, social community development, and minimal impact on the world environment, including, of course, the carbon footprint of business. Today, the consensus among major firms in Europe, Asia, and the United States has become that in the long term, and through careful planning, sustainable business and **sustainable supply chains** are just good business because it means using the most efficient environment-regarding means of production, distribution, and logistics. These efficient methods create value for consumers, investors, and communities (Suering and Muller, 2008).

Notions of sustainable business have had a powerful impact on supply chain thinking. In part, these efforts are good risk management: all advanced countries have substantially strengthened their environmental regulations. It makes good business sense for firms to prepare methods and operations suitable to this new environment.

For instance, all the major textiles brands and retailers have announced plans for a more sustainable supply chain in textiles. One of the world's truly ancient industries, textiles supports millions of workers while consuming extraordinary resources: it takes 1,000 gallons of water to make one pound of finished cotton (your jeans, for instance). While growing cotton has its issues (fertilizer), the subsequent dying, finishing, and cleaning of cotton makes it the number one industrial polluter on Earth. It's not a small matter then that Walmart, Gap, Levi's, Nike, and other large players in the industry are taking steps to reduce the environmental impact of their operations by improving the efficiency of the entire supply and distribution chains.

sustainable supply chain

involves using the most efficient environment-regarding means of production, distribution, and logistics

With the help of IBM, SAP, and Oracle, other firms and entire industries are working to develop sustainable supply chains (IKEA, 2016). McKesson, North America's largest distributor of drugs, uses IBM's Supply Chain Sustainability Management Solution (SCSM) to minimize carbon dioxide emissions throughout its supply chain, while lowering its distribution costs. SCSM (a business analytics package that works with IBM's B2B software) can determine low-cost refrigeration alternatives for certain medicines (such as insulin and vaccines), identify the environmentally least harmful way to bring new products into its distribution network, and determine the best way to transport pharmaceuticals to customers.

ELECTRONIC DATA INTERCHANGE (EDI)

As noted in the previous section, B2B e-commerce did not originate with the Internet, but in fact has its roots in technologies such as EDI that were first developed in the mid-1970s and 1980s. EDI is a broadly defined communications protocol for exchanging documents among computers using technical standards developed by the American National Standards Institute (ANSI X12 standards) and international bodies such as the United Nations (EDIFACT standards).

EDI was developed to reduce the cost, delays, and errors inherent in the manual exchanges of documents such as purchase orders, shipping documents, price lists, payments, and customer data. EDI differs from an unstructured message because its messages are organized with distinct fields for each of the important pieces of information in a commercial transaction such as transaction date, product purchased, amount, sender's name, address, and recipient's name.

Each major industry in the United States and throughout much of the industrial world has EDI industry committees that define the structure and information fields of electronic documents for that industry. Estimates indicate that B2B e-commerce EDI transactions will total about $3.2 trillion in 2016, about 48% of all B2B e-commerce (U.S. Census Bureau, 2016; authors' estimates). In this sense, EDI remains very important in the development of B2B e-commerce (Cecere, 2014).

EDI has evolved significantly since the 1980s (see **Figure 12.5**). Initially, EDI focused on document automation (Stage 1). Procurement agents created purchase orders electronically and sent them to trading partners, who in turn shipped order fulfillment and shipping notices electronically back to the purchaser. Invoices, payments, and other documents followed. These early implementations replaced the postal system for document transmission, and resulted in same-day shipping of orders (rather than a week's delay caused by the postal system), reduced errors, and lower costs. The second stage of EDI development began in the early 1990s, driven largely by the automation of internal industrial processes and movement toward just-in-time production and continuous production. New methods of production called for greater flexibility in scheduling, shipping, and financing of supplies. EDI evolved to become a tool for continuous inventory replenishment. EDI was used to eliminate purchase orders and other documents entirely, replacing them with production schedules and inventory balances. Supplier firms were sent monthly statements of production requirements and precise scheduled delivery times, and the orders would be fulfilled continuously, with inventory and payments being adjusted at the end of each month.

FIGURE 12.5 **THE EVOLUTION OF EDI AS A B2B MEDIUM**

1 **Document Automation**

Purchase Orders / Payments
Shipping Notices / Price Schedules / Invoices
Supplier Computer — Firm Computer

2 **Document Elimination**

Production Schedule / Delivery Schedule
Payment Schedule / Shipping Orders
Supplier Computer — Firm Computer

3 **Continuous Replenishment**

Supplier A Production System
Supplier B Production System
Supplier C Production System
Supplier D Production System
Continuous Replenishment
Payment on Use
Shipping Data
Firm Computer

EDI has evolved from a simple point-to-point digital communications medium to a many-to-one enabling tool for continuous inventory replenishment.

In the third stage of EDI, beginning in the mid-1990s, suppliers were given online access to selected parts of the purchasing firm's production and delivery schedules, and, under long-term contracts, were required to meet those schedules on their own without intervention by firm purchasing agents. Movement toward this continuous real-time access model of EDI was spurred in the 1990s by large manufacturing and process firms (such as oil and chemical companies) that were implementing enterprise systems. These systems required standardization of business processes and resulted in the automation of production, logistics, and many financial processes. These new processes required much closer relationships with suppliers and logistics partners (shipping and ground transporters), who were required to be more precise in delivery scheduling and more flexible in inventory management. This level of supplier precision could never be achieved economically by human purchasing agents. This third stage of EDI enabled the era of continuous replenishment. For instance, Walmart and Toys"R"Us provide their suppliers with access to their store inventories, and the suppliers are expected to keep the stock of items on the shelf within prespecified targets. Similar developments occurred in the grocery industry.

Today, EDI must be viewed as a general enabling technology that provides for the exchange of critical business information between computer applications supporting a wide variety of business processes. EDI is an important industrial network technology, suited to support communications among a small set of strategic partners in direct, long-term trading relationships. The technical platform of EDI has changed from mainframes to personal computers, from corporate data centers to cloud-based software-as-a-service (SaaS) platforms (described below). EDI is not well suited for the development of Net marketplaces, where thousands of suppliers and purchasers meet in a digital arena to negotiate prices. EDI supports direct bilateral communications among a small set of firms and does not permit the multilateral, dynamic relationships of a true marketplace. EDI does not provide for price transparency among a large number of suppliers, does not scale easily to include new participants, and is not a real-time communications environment. EDI does not have a rich communications environment that can simultaneously support e-mail messaging, video conferencing, sharing of graphic documents, network meetings, or user-friendly flexible database creation and management.

MOBILE B2B

Just as with B2C commerce, mobile devices have become increasingly important in all aspects of B2B e-commerce, through all steps of the procurement process and throughout the supply chain. More and more companies have adopted a **Bring Your Own Device (BYOD) policy**, in which employees use their personal smartphone, tablet, or laptop computer on the company's network, which has helped contribute to their growing importance in B2B. Cisco estimates that by 2016, mobile traffic will represent over 25% of all business Internet traffic, up from less than 5% in 2011 (Cisco Systems, Inc., 2015).

Bring Your Own Device (BYOD) policy
employees use their personal smartphone, tablet, or laptop computer on the company's network

On the procurement front, B2B buyers are increasingly using mobile devices for all phases of the purchase process, from discovery to decision-making, to actual purchase. One study found that over 75% of B2B decision-makers surveyed used a mobile device to research products, equipment, services, and suppliers (eMarketer, 2015). B2B buyers want to be able to place orders using mobile devices just as they do in the B2C arena, and increasingly expect B2B e-commerce sites to be readily accessible from such devices, to be able to start an order from a device and finish it on their desktop and vice versa, and to be able to get online customer service on their mobile devices (eMarketer, Inc., 2015).

On the supply chain front, many supply chain network and software providers are enhancing their offerings by providing support for mobile devices and applications. For instance, Elementum provides a variety of mobile apps running on a cloud platform to track various aspects of the supply chain and enable supply chain visibility. For instance, Elementum's Exposure App enables companies to identify and respond to risks in their supply chain, providing real-time alerts on events that may impact the supply, manufacture, or distribution of components of their products. Elementum's Perspective App helps companies monitor the health of their supply chain by providing a dashboard that provides real-time tracking of key performance indicators (KPIs) in the supply chain.

B2B IN THE CLOUD

In the traditional approach to B2B enterprise systems, firms build on their existing on-premise, enterprise production systems that keep track of their manufacturing and distribution processes to include new functionality connecting them to their suppliers' systems. This is a very expensive process that involves connecting suppliers one at a time, establishing the telecommunications channels, and managing the data quality issues, not to mention the cost of building the infrastructure of computers and telecommunications to support coordination of suppliers and B2B transactions. Cloud computing (described in Chapter 2) is increasingly being used to greatly reduce the cost of building and maintaining B2B systems.

FIGURE 12.6   **CLOUD-BASED B2B PLATFORMS**

Participating Firms

Customer Data

Spreadsheet files
XML
EDI
Unstructured data
SAP, Oracle, IBM
   enterprise databases

Data Integration

Business Process Integration

Customer Business Processes

Product information
Inventory
Pricing
Purchase order
Order status
Quotation
Invoice
Shipping notice

Business Partners

Suppliers   Logistics   Distributors   Retail customers   Other firms

Cloud-based B2B platforms integrate a firm's customer data, business processes, and business partners into a cloud-based software system. Businesses are charged for the hardware and software platform on a utilization basis, reducing their costs significantly.

In **cloud-based B2B systems**, much of the expense of B2B systems is shifted from the firm to a B2B network provider, sometimes called a data hub or B2B platform (see **Figure 12.6**). The cloud platform owner provides the computing and telecommunications capability; establishes connections with the firm's partners; provides software on-demand (software-as-a-service or SaaS) to connect the firm's systems to its partners' systems; performs data coordination and cleaning; and manages data quality for all members. Network effects apply here: the cost of these tasks and capabilities is spread over all members, reducing costs for all. B2B network providers also provide communication environments and file storage services that allow partners to work together more closely, and to collaborate on improving the flow of goods and transactions. B2B network providers charge customers on a demand basis, rather than on a percentage of their transactions' value, depending on their utilization of the network. Suppliers of traditional on-premise B2B and supply chain management systems have responded by purchasing cloud-based B2B networks in the last few years. For instance, SAP purchased Ariba, one of the first and largest cloud-based B2B transaction networks, in 2012 for $4.6 billion. SAP Ariba's global network automates more than $700 billion in commercial transactions, collaborations, and business intelligence among a wide range of suppliers, shipping, and logistics firms. SAP, the largest supplier of firm enterprise systems, supplies software that supports internal business processes. Other B2B network providers include E2Open, GT Nexus, and Elementum.

Unlike traditional firm-based B2B systems, cloud-based B2B data networks can be implemented in short periods of time to respond to corporate mergers and rapidly changing markets, as *Insight on Technology: Your Shoes Are in the Cloud* illustrates.

> **cloud-based B2B system**
> shifts much of the expense of B2B systems from the firm to a B2B network provider, sometimes called a data hub or B2B platform

SUPPLY CHAIN MANAGEMENT SYSTEMS

Supply chain simplification, just in time and lean production, focusing on strategic partners in the production process, enterprise systems, and continuous inventory replenishment are the foundation for contemporary supply chain management (SCM) systems. **Supply chain management (SCM) systems** continuously link the activities of buying, making, and moving products from suppliers to purchasing firms, as well as integrating the demand side of the business equation by including the order entry system in the process. With an SCM system and continuous replenishment, inventory is greatly reduced and production begins only when an order is received (see **Figure 12.7**). These systems enable just-in-time and lean-production methods.

Hewlett-Packard (HP) is one of the largest technology companies in the world, with sales of $103 billion in 2015. With operations in over 150 countries, sales in 43 currencies, and 15 languages, HP is truly a global firm with global supply chain issues that became even more complicated as HP expanded by making over 200 acquisitions in the last decade. In 2016, HP has the largest supply chain among information technology manufacturers. To cope with one of the most complex supply chains in the world, HP developed a web-based, order-driven supply chain management system that begins with either a customer placing an order online or the receipt of an order from a dealer. The order is forwarded from the order entry system to HP's production and delivery system. From there, the order is routed to one of several HP contractor supplier firms. The supplier's system then verifies the order with HP and validates

> **supply chain management (SCM) systems**
> continuously link the activities of buying, making, and moving products from suppliers to purchasing firms, as well as integrating the demand side of the business equation by including the order entry system in the process

INSIGHT ON TECHNOLOGY

YOUR SHOES ARE IN THE CLOUD

Have you ever worn Keds, Hush Puppies, Merrells, Sebagos, Sperry Topsiders, or Sauconys? If so, you've had a product made by Wolverine World Wide Inc. on your feet. Although you may not be familiar with its name, Wolverine is one of the world's largest designers, manufacturers, and marketers of footwear for sports, casual wear, and work. The company's business is divided into three segments: its Lifestyle Group includes Sperry Topsider, Stride Rite, Hush Puppies, and Keds. Its Performance Group includes Merrell, Saucony, Chaco, and Patagonia. The Heritage Group comprises brands such as Wolverine, Cat, Bates, Sebago, Harley-Davidson, and HyTest Safety. Wolverine was founded in Grand Rapids, Michigan, in 1883, and originally made the boots that built America's railroads, skyscrapers, and highways. Since then the company has expanded largely by purchasing well-known name brand manufacturers. The company sells its footwear through national retailers, catalog sales, and consumer direct businesses at various e-commerce websites.

In 2015, Wolverine generated almost $2.7 billion in revenue. In 2012, it purchased a total of four brands, including Saucony and Keds, that increased its revenue by $1 billion in a single year. The company has 6,600 employees worldwide. Today, Wolverine sources production of more than 100 million pairs of shoes from 110 factories located in 20 countries. The company's major competitors are Nike (the global giant with $30 billion in revenue) and Deckers (with $1.8 billion in revenue). The global footwear market is estimated to be $248 billion, with a 2.7% annual growth rate.

Like many global consumer goods manufacturers, Wolverine has faced a number of challenges in managing its global supply chain and its retail distribution and sales processes. In the early 2000s, Wolverine's supply chain management capability was based on SAP's BusinessSuite enterprise software. The SAP software centralized and consolidated its operations across all its brands and created an integrated system platform for managing the supply chain, customer relationships, orders, and financial reporting. However, the system could not recognize multiple currencies, languages, or global standards. Signing up new suppliers or retail outlets was an expensive and sometimes lengthy process. Out-of-stock situations were growing as the company could not respond to retailer demands for specific styles. Matching inventory to actual demand was becoming more difficult as fashions changed rapidly. Working with global retailers was difficult at times because the existing system could not work with different languages and currencies. Many of the company's largest global retailers were not comfortable transacting in dollars. In response, Wolverine expanded its SAP enterprise system by adopting the software firm's SAP Retail solutions. This new system had global capabilities that enable different languages and currencies to be used for transactions and communications. The new system also allowed Wolverine managers as well as their retail partners to gain increased, real-time visibility into consumer demand, supply chain, and store operations. As a result, stock outs have declined, and revenues at retail stores have increased 15 to 25% in various segments.

On the supplier side of its operations, Wolverine also faced significant challenges. Its 2012 acquisition of Saucony and Keds brought in an additional $1 billion worth of transactions to process, and might have quickly overwhelmed its domestic supply chain's systems. Its SAP enterprise system was a traditional on-premise, very large system that was designed to enhance Wolverine's supply chain, and not the entire ecosystem of manufacturing, logistics, and financial firms that work with Wolverine to manufacture and distribute shoes. Wolverine in fact had over 200 suppliers in 120 countries that had their own supply chain software, and integrating them into a single platform was unimaginable, costly, and time consuming. There was no easy (or inexpensive) way to scale up its existing supply chain system to include all its partners, and their millions of transactions. It was difficult for its global suppliers to sign up to Wolverine's domestic system, the payment system was outdated, and logistics and finance were not supported in the existing system.

For help Wolverine turned to GT Nexus, a provider of a cloud-based supply chain platform. GT Nexus is a network of supply chain networks that allows firms to tie their own supply chain systems into a global platform and communicate with their partners, who may be manufacturers, shipping companies, finance firms, and retailers. Unlike with traditional enterprise software, Wolverine does not buy the package, or pay monthly rental costs, or host the software on its servers. Instead, GT Nexus provides an on-demand, pay-as-you-go, software-as-a-service (SaaS) model. Some of the services provided include supplier enablement, purchase-to-payment financial tracking, tracking of packing and shipping, financing of transactions, freight contracting, auditing, documentation and customs, and in-transit tracking. GT Nexus bills itself as an on-demand, cloud-based, global supply chain management platform. Currently, GT Nexus supports supply chain management at 25,000 companies, has over 100,000 users, and manages an estimated $100 billion in trades. It also facilitates more than $20 billion in payments between buyers and their suppliers in 90 countries and in eight currencies. In addition to Wolverine, GT Nexus customers include Adidas, Nike, Caterpillar, Columbia Sportswear, DHL, Home Depot, Levi Strauss, Pfizer, and UPS, among many others.

Using GT Nexus, Wolverine can provide its suppliers, retailers, logistics, and financial partners a single login to the global Wolverine supply chain. Wolverine managers and their supply partners can see the entire supply chain from suppliers of raw materials, to manufacturers, transporters, and ultimately retail store orders. With its new supply and distribution systems in place, Wolverine is able to spot under-performing stores and brands. In the past two years, it has closed over 200 outlets, and dropped two brands from its product line.

In August 2015, Infor, one of the world's leading suppliers of enterprise resource planning software, announced that it would acquire GT Nexus for $675 million. Infor's current business focuses on applications within an enterprise, and it currently counts among its customers 18 of the top aerospace companies, all of the top 10 pharmaceutical companies, and 17 of the top 20 industrial distributors. Adding GT Nexus will enable Infor to expand its reach beyond the walls of an organization into its supply chain and allow businesses to better integrate merchandising, marketing, and demand data into supply chain management. Infor currently uses Amazon Web Services to deliver its cloud SaaS ERP software, and plans to add GT Nexus's software to that platform as well.

■■■■ **SOURCES:** "About Us," Wolverineworldwide.com, accessed August 11, 2016; "About GT Nexus," Gtnexus.com, accessed August 1, 2016; Wolverine World Wide, Inc. Form 10k for the fiscal year ended December 31, 2015," March 1, 2016; "Wolverine Worldwide Closing 100 Stores in 2016," by Shandra Martinez, Mlive.com, February 28, 2016; "Global Footwear Manufacturing: Market Research Report," IBISworld.com, January 2016; "Infor Seeks to Strengthen Cloud Footing with $675 Billion GT Nexus Buy," by Katherine Noyes, Cio.com, August 11,2015; "Wolverine Worldwide Warns Investments to Hurt Earnings," by Josh Beckerman, *Wall Street Journal*, January 12, 2015; "Cloud Hub Is a Good Fit for Footwear Company," by Mary Pratt, CIO.com, May 29, 2014; "Wolverine World Wide Achieving Business Clarity to Grow Retail Globally," SAP Transformation Study, SAP.com, May 6, 2014; "Powering the World's Most Responsive and Adaptive Supply Chain Networks," Gtnexus.com/about, May 2014; "Shoe Supply Chain Has Sole Version of Truth," by Jane Bird, *Financial Times*, January 29, 2014.

FIGURE 12.7   **SUPPLY CHAIN MANAGEMENT SYSTEMS**

SCM systems coordinate the activities of suppliers, shippers, and order entry systems to automate order entry through production, payment, and shipping business processes. Increasingly customers, as well as employees working throughout the supply chain, are using smartphones, tablets, and mobile apps to place and coordinate orders.

the ordered configuration to ensure the PC can be manufactured (e.g., will not have missing parts or fail a design specification set by HP). The order is then forwarded to a computer-based production control system that issues a bar-coded production ticket to factory assemblers. Simultaneously, a parts order is forwarded to the supplier's warehouse and inventory management system. A worker assembles the computer, and then the computer is boxed, tagged, and shipped to the customer. The delivery is monitored and tracked by HP's supply chain management system, which links directly to one of several overnight delivery systems. The elapsed time from order entry to shipping is 48 hours. With this system, HP has eliminated the need to hold PCs in inventory, reduced cycle time from one week to 48 hours, and reduced errors. HP has extended this system to become a global B2B order tracking, reporting, and support system for HP B2B customers (Hewlett-Packard, 2015a, 2015b).

It isn't just huge technology companies that use supply chain software. There's nothing quite so perishable as fashionable underwear given the rate of fashion change. Under Armour, which is the world's No. 1 performance athletic brand, uses software from SAP to predict sales, plan inventory, and coordinate suppliers (SAP, 2015; Gilmore, 2014). Prior to using these tools, Under Armour often missed sales because it did not produce enough of popular items, or overproduced items that were not selling.

COLLABORATIVE COMMERCE

Collaborative commerce is a direct extension of supply chain management systems, as well as supply chain simplification. **Collaborative commerce** is defined as the use of digital technologies to permit firms to collaboratively design, develop, build, market, and manage products through their life cycles. This is a much broader mission than EDI or simply managing the flow of information among organizations. Collaborative commerce involves a definitive move from a transaction focus to a relationship focus among the supply chain participants. Rather than having an arm's-length adversarial relationship with suppliers, collaborative commerce fosters sharing of sensitive internal information with suppliers and purchasers. Managing collaborative commerce requires knowing exactly what information to share with whom. Collaborative commerce extends beyond supply chain management activities to include the collaborative development of new products and services by multiple cooperating firms.

A good example of collaborative commerce is the long-term effort of Procter & Gamble (P&G), the world's largest manufacturer of personal and health care products, from Crest toothpaste to Tide soap, to work with suppliers and even customers to develop 50% of its product line over time. In the past, for instance, P&G would design a bottle or product package in-house, and then turn to over 100 suppliers of packaging to find out what it would cost and try to bargain that down. Using Ariba's procurement network, P&G asks its suppliers to come up with innovative ideas for packaging and pricing. Taking it a step further, P&G's website, Pgconnectdevelop.com, solicits new product ideas from suppliers and customers. About 50% of P&G's new products originate with substantial input from its suppliers and customers. P&G is also collaborating with its biggest online customer, Amazon, by co-locating their operations. P&G sets aside warehouse space for P&G products purchased by Amazon customers. Amazon ships the products to its customers directly from the P&G warehouses rather than shipping them first to Amazon warehouses, and then to the consumer. This collaboration results in Amazon reducing its costs of shipping and storing goods, becoming more competitive on price compared to Walmart and Costco, and reducing the time it takes to arrive at consumers' homes. For P&G collaboration means savings on transportation costs incurred trucking products to Amazon warehouses, and Amazon's help in boosting online sales of P&G products. Other well-known companies using collaboration to develop and deliver products include Harley Davidson, Starbucks, and GE's Ecomagination program (Carlozo, 2015; Winston, 2014).

Although collaborative commerce can involve customers as well as suppliers in the development of products, for the most part, it is concerned with the development of a rich communications environment to enable inter-firm sharing of designs, production plans, inventory levels, delivery schedules, and the development of shared products (see **Figure 12.8**).

Collaborative commerce is very different from EDI, which is a technology for structured communications among firms. Collaborative commerce is more like an interactive teleconference among members of the supply chain. EDI and collaborative commerce share one characteristic: they are not open, competitive marketplaces, but instead are, technically, private industrial networks that connect strategic partners in a supply chain.

collaborative commerce
the use of digital technologies to permit organizations to collaboratively design, develop, build, and manage products through their life cycles

| FIGURE 12.8 | ELEMENTS OF A COLLABORATIVE COMMERCE SYSTEM |

A collaborative commerce application includes a cloud repository where employees at several different firms can store engineering drawings and other documents. Workflow software determines who can see this data and what rules will apply for displaying the data on individual workstations.

Collaboration 2.0: Cloud, Web, Social, and Mobile

The technology of collaborative commerce has changed greatly since its inception over thirty years ago with tools like Lotus Notes, which was used almost entirely within firms to establish an environment where employees could share ideas, notes, and ideas, and work on projects together. What's new about collaboration tools today is that the software and data are stored on cloud servers where it is less expensive, and easy to update; social networks like Facebook and Twitter are commonly used by employees in many firms, while other firms deploy their own social network platform; the Web enables very inexpensive collaborative environments; and the mobile platform of smartphones and tablets means that collaboration can take place in many more places and times (Computerworld, 2015; Gohring, 2014). Collaboration technologies have expanded collaboration from a within-the-firm platform to a primary tool of inter-firm B2B collaboration.

Broadband video network systems like Cisco's TelePresence also play a role in enabling frequent, long-distance, collaboration among supply chain partners. TelePresence is one of several high-bandwidth video systems from different vendors that give users the impression they are sharing physical space with other participants who are in fact located remotely, sometimes on the other side of the globe. Cisco TelePresence's Twitter feed enhances the TelePresence experience by adding face-to-face support, scheduling assistance, and demos (Cisco Systems, Inc., 2016b; Cisco Systems, Inc. and Vital Images, 2016). Using Skype video conferencing, even tiny businesses can take advantage of very inexpensive collaborative platforms over the Web, or mobile platforms.

In Section 12.5, we discuss collaborative commerce in greater depth as a technology that enables private industrial networks.

SOCIAL NETWORKS AND B2B: THE EXTENDED SOCIAL ENTERPRISE

It's a short step from collaboration with vendors, suppliers, and customers, to a more personal relationship based on conversations with participants in the supply chain using social networks—both private and public. Here, the conversations and sharing of ideas are more unstructured, situational, and personal. Procurement officers, managers of supply chains, and logistics managers are people too, and they participate in the same social network culture provided by Facebook, Twitter, Tumblr, Instagram, and a host of other public social networks as we all do. Being able to respond to fast moving developments that affect supply chains requires something more than a website, e-mail, or telephone calls. Social networks can provide the intimate connections among customers, suppliers, and logistics partners that are needed to keep the supply chain functioning, and to make decisions based on current conditions (Demery, 2015; Red Prairie, 2012).

Participants in the supply chain network are tapping into their tablet computers, smartphones, and social network sites for purchasing, scheduling, exception handling, and deciding with their B2B customers and suppliers. In many cases, supply chain social networks are private—owned by the largest firm in the supply chain network. In other cases, firms develop Facebook pages to organize conversations among supply chain network members.

Social networks are beginning to be common tools for managers engaged in B2B commerce. Public social network sites like Facebook and Twitter can be excellent for coordinating the flow of information among business partners through the supply chain. Cisco is using its website, Twitter, and Facebook to run new product campaigns for its business customers using social networks exclusively. Dell, like many businesses, uses its YouTube channel to engage suppliers and customers in conversations about existing products, and ideas for new products (Cargill, 2015).

B2B MARKETING

Despite the size of the B2B e-commerce, B2B marketing in 2015 accounted for only a relatively small slice (about $6 billion) of the total amount spent on digital marketing and advertising (about $58 billion) (eMarketer, Inc., 2016a). While some of this disparity results from the slow pace of technological change in supply chain and procurement management, it also reflects the very different nature of much of B2B e-commerce when compared to B2C e-commerce. Long-term sourcing typically involves large purchases with commercial relationships that can last several years or longer. The sellers and buyers may have known about each other for years, even decades; the capabilities and financial situation of the firms are known. Both parties share an understanding of the price and quality of what is being exchanged in the market. In these situations, B2C retail marketing tactics are not appropriate. Instead, interpersonal relationships, networking, brand, and informative content marketing using white papers, videos, podcasts, webinars, blogs, e-books, conferences, and professional associations are the primary and most effective marketing tools (eMarketer, Inc., 2016b). Content marketing refers to using informative media to promote sales rather than advertising the availability and price typical of display and search advertising in B2C markets (see Chapter 6). E-mail and social networks can play a role in content marketing by making potential customers aware of new media content.

However, in spot purchase markets for MRO or other commodity products, B2B marketing uses many of the same marketing tactics and tools found in B2C marketing: display ads, search engine marketing, websites, social network channels, videos, and mobile ads. The use of mobile advertising in B2B marketing has grown as mobile devices play a larger role in workplaces. Almost two-thirds (65%) of B2B marketers use a mobile website or apps that connect customers directly to their marketplaces. Mobile advertising (largely on newsfeeds or display ads on social networks such as LinkedIn), mobile search, and in-app ads are used by roughly 40% of B2B marketers (eMarketer, Inc., 2015). While mobile B2B marketing is growing, it consumes only 5% of B2B marketing budgets, compared to nearly 9% of B2C marketing budgets. One reason is that purchasing agents do not appreciate having their newsfeeds and mobile experience interrupted by their suppliers' mobile messages. Generally, purchasing agents know what they want, and when they want it.

Other trends in B2B marketing include sales enablement systems and the use of predictive analytics. Sales enablement systems keep track of leads developed from websites, e-mail, and mobile apps, and help the salesforce track these prospective customers through the point of purchase (eMarketer, Inc., 2016b). Predictive analytics help B2B marketers estimate the lifetime value of leads based on past marketing data (eMarketer, Inc., 2016c).

12.4 NET MARKETPLACES: THE SELLING SIDE OF B2B

One of the most compelling visions of B2B e-commerce is that of an online marketplace that would bring thousands of fragmented suppliers into contact with hundreds of major purchasers of industrial goods for the purpose of conducting frictionless commerce. The hope was that these suppliers would compete with one another on price, transactions would be automated and low cost, and as a result, the price of industrial supplies would fall. By extracting fees from buyers and sellers on each transaction, third-party intermediary market makers could earn significant revenues. We refer to these online markets as Net marketplaces. Net marketplaces are sell-side digital environments that bring suppliers and buyers together. These Net marketplaces could scale easily as volume increased by simply adding more computers and communications equipment.

In pursuit of this vision, well over 1,500 Net marketplaces sprang up in the early days of e-commerce. Unfortunately, many of them have since disappeared but some still survive, and they are joined by other types of Net marketplaces—some private and some public—based on different assumptions and business models that are quite successful.

TABLE 12.3	CHARACTERISTICS OF NET MARKETPLACES: A B2B VOCABULARY
CHARACTERISTIC	MEANING
Bias	Sell-side vs. buy-side vs. neutral. Whose interests are advantaged: buyers, sellers, or no bias?
Ownership	Industry vs. third party. Who owns the marketplace?
Pricing mechanism	Fixed-price catalogs, auctions, bid/ask, and RFPs/RFQs.
Scope/Focus	Horizontal vs. vertical markets.
Value creation	What benefits do they offer customers or suppliers?
Access to market	In public markets, any firm can enter, but in private markets, entry is by invitation only.

CHARACTERISTICS OF NET MARKETPLACES

There is a confusing variety of Net marketplaces today, and several different ways to classify them. For instance, some classify Net marketplaces on the basis of their pricing mechanisms—fixed prices or more dynamic pricing, such as negotiation, auction or bid/ask—while others classify markets based on characteristics of the markets they serve (vertical versus horizontal, or sell-side versus buy-side), or ownership independent third-party intermediaries (which is most common) or industry-owned consortia. Although the primary benefits and biases of Net marketplaces have to be determined on a case-by-case basis depending on ownership and pricing mechanisms, it is often the case that Net marketplaces are biased against suppliers because they can force suppliers to reveal their prices and terms to other suppliers in the marketplace. **Table 12.3** describes some of the important characteristics of Net marketplaces.

TYPES OF NET MARKETPLACES

Although each of these distinctions helps describe the phenomenon of Net marketplaces, they do not focus on the central business functionality provided, nor are they capable by themselves of describing the variety of Net marketplaces.

In **Figure 12.9**, we present a classification of Net marketplaces that focuses on their business functionality; that is, what these Net marketplaces provide for businesses seeking solutions. We use two dimensions of Net marketplaces to create a four-cell classification table. We differentiate Net marketplaces as providing either indirect goods (goods used to support production) or direct goods (goods used in production), and we distinguish markets as providing either contractual purchasing (where purchases take place over many years according to a contract between the firm and its vendor) or spot purchasing (where purchases are episodic and anonymous—vendors and buyers do not have an ongoing relationship and may not know one another). The intersection of these dimensions produces four main types of Net marketplaces that are relatively straightforward: e-distributors, e-procurement networks, exchanges, and

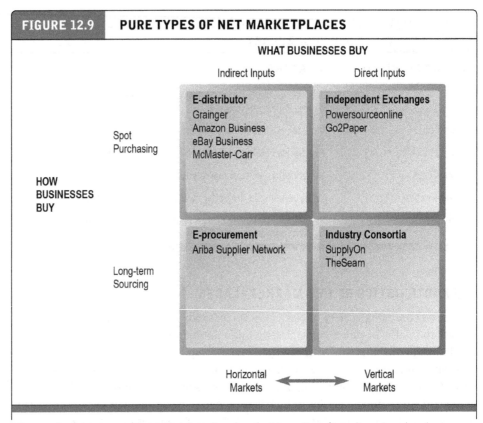

FIGURE 12.9 **PURE TYPES OF NET MARKETPLACES**

There are four main types of Net marketplaces based on the intersection of two dimensions: how businesses buy and what they buy. A third dimension—horizontal versus vertical markets—also distinguishes the different types of Net marketplaces.

industry consortia. Note, however, that in the real world, some Net marketplaces can be found in multiple parts of this figure as business models change and opportunities appear and disappear. Nevertheless, the discussion of "pure types" of Net marketplaces is a useful starting point.

Each of these Net marketplaces seeks to provide value to customers in different ways. We discuss each type of Net marketplace in more detail in the following sections.

E-distributors

E-distributors are the most common and most easily understood type of Net market-place. An **e-distributor** provides an online catalog that represents the products of thousands of direct manufacturers (see **Figure 12.10**). E-distributors are independently owned intermediaries that offer industrial customers a single source from which to order indirect goods (often referred to as MRO) on a spot, as-needed basis. A significant percentage of corporate purchases cannot be satisfied under a company's existing contracts, and must be purchased on a spot basis. E-distributors make money by charging a markup on products they distribute.

e-distributor

provides an online catalog that represents the products of thousands of direct manufacturers

Organizations and firms in all industries require MRO supplies. The MRO function maintains, repairs, and operates commercial buildings and maintains all the machinery of these buildings from heating, ventilating, and air conditioning systems to lighting fixtures.

E-distributors operate in horizontal markets because they serve many different industries with products from many different suppliers. E-distributors usually operate public markets in the sense that any firm can order from the catalog, as opposed to private markets, where membership is restricted to selected firms.

E-distributor prices are usually fixed, but large customers receive discounts and other incentives to purchase, such as credit, reporting on account activity, and limited forms of business purchasing rules (for instance, no purchases greater than $500 for a single item without a purchase order). The primary benefits offered to industrial customers are lower search costs, lower transaction costs, wide selection, rapid delivery, and low prices.

W.W. Grainger is one of the most frequently cited examples of an e-distributor. Grainger is involved in long-term systematic sourcing as well as spot sourcing, but its emphasis is on spot sourcing. Grainger's mission is to become the world's leading source of MRO suppliers. Its revenue model is that of a typical retailer: it owns the products and takes a markup on the products it sells to customers. Grainger's website and mobile apps provide users with a digital version of Grainger's famous seven-pound catalog, plus other parts not available in the catalog (adding up to around 1.4 million parts), as well as a complete ordering and payment system. In 2015, Grainger recorded

FIGURE 12.10   **E-DISTRIBUTORS**

Suppliers   E-distributor Online Catalog   Buyers

E-distributors are firms that bring the products of thousands of suppliers into a single online catalog for sale to thousands of buyer firms. E-distributors are sometimes referred to as one-to-many markets, one seller serving many firms.

$3.3 billion in e-commerce revenues (41% of its total sales), up 14% from 2014 (W.W. Grainger Inc., 2016). McMaster-Carr, a New Jersey-based industrial parts mecca for machinists and manufacturers around the world, is a similar e-distributor. As you learned in the opening case, Amazon also entered the B2B distributor market with AmazonSupply, aiming to leverage its global B2C fulfillment infrastructure into the B2B arena, and in 2015, rebranded it as Amazon Business. Amazon Business primarily engages in spot sales of business products and provides a trading platform for multiple sellers. eBay entered the B2B e-distributors fray by rebranding its eBay Business marketplace in 2016. Other examples of e-distributors include B2Buy and NeweggBusiness.

E-procurement

e-procurement Net marketplace

independently owned intermediary that connects hundreds of online suppliers offering millions of maintenance and repair parts to business firms who pay fees to join the market

An **e-procurement Net marketplace** is an independently owned intermediary that connects hundreds of online suppliers offering millions of maintenance and repair parts to business firms who pay fees to join the market (see **Figure 12.11**). E-procurement Net marketplaces are typically used for long-term contractual purchasing of indirect goods (MRO); they create online horizontal markets, but they also provide for members' spot sourcing of MRO supplies. E-procurement companies make money by charging a percentage of each transaction, licensing consulting services and software, and assessing network use fees (Trkman and McCormack, 2010).

| FIGURE 12.11 | E-PROCUREMENT NET MARKETPLACES |

E-procurement Net marketplaces aggregate hundreds of catalogs in a single marketplace and make them available to firms, often on a custom basis that reflects only the suppliers desired by the participating firms.

E-procurement companies expand on the business model of simpler e-distributors by including the online catalogs of hundreds of suppliers and offering value chain management services to both buyers and sellers. **Value chain management (VCM) services** provided by e-procurement companies include automation of a firm's entire procurement process on the buyer side and automation of the selling business processes on the seller side. For purchasers, e-procurement companies automate purchase orders, requisitions, sourcing, business rules enforcement, invoicing, and payment. For suppliers, e-procurement companies provide catalog creation and content management, order management, fulfillment, invoicing, shipment, and settlement.

E-procurement Net marketplaces are sometimes referred to as many-to-many markets. They are mediated by an independent third party that purports to represent both buyers and sellers, and hence claim to be neutral. On the other hand, because they may include the catalogs of both competing suppliers and competing e-distributors, they likely have a bias in favor of the buyers. Nevertheless, by aggregating huge buyer firms into their networks, they provide distinct marketing benefits for suppliers and reduce customer acquisition costs.

Ariba stands out as one of the poster children of the B2B age, a firm born before its time. Promising to revolutionize inter-firm trade, Ariba started out in 1996 hoping to build a global business network linking buyers and sellers—sort of an eBay for business. With little revenue, the stock shot past $1,000 a share by March 2000. But sellers and buyers did not join the network in large part because they did not understand the opportunity, were too wedded to their traditional procurement processes, and did not trust outsiders to control their purchasing and vendor relationship. In September 2001, Ariba's share price tanked to $2.20. Ariba survived largely by selling software that helped large firms understand their procurement processes and costs. Finally, by 2008, large and small firms had become more sophisticated in their purchasing and supply change management practices, and Ariba's original idea of a global network of suppliers and purchasers of a wide variety of industrial goods came back to life. In 2012, SAP, the largest enterprise software firm, purchased Ariba for $4.3 billion in an effort to strengthen its B2B e-commerce suite. Today, SAP Ariba is a leading provider of collaborative business commerce solutions that includes an e-procurement Net marketplace called the Ariba Supplier Network. Other players in this market segment include Perfect Commerce, BravoSolution, A.T. Kearney Procurement & Analytic Solutions, and IBM Emptoris Sourcing.

Exchanges

An **exchange** is an independently owned online marketplace that connects hundreds to potentially thousands of suppliers and buyers in a dynamic, real-time environment (see **Figure 12.12**). Although there are exceptions, exchanges generally create vertical markets that focus on the spot-purchasing requirements of large firms in a single industry, such as computers and telecommunications, electronics, food, and industrial equipment. Exchanges were the prototype Internet-based marketplace in the early

value chain management (VCM) services
include automation of a firm's entire procurement process on the buyer side and automation of the selling business processes on the seller side

exchange
independently owned online marketplace that connects hundreds to potentially thousands of suppliers and buyers in a dynamic, real-time environment

FIGURE 12.12 **EXCHANGES**

Buyer
Firms

Digital
Marketplace

Suppliers

Market Maker's Proprietary Software Envelope

Independent exchanges bring potentially thousands of suppliers to a vertical (industry-specific) marketplace to sell their goods to potentially thousands of buyer firms. Exchanges are sometimes referred to as many-to-many markets because they have many suppliers serving many buyer firms.

days of e-commerce; as noted previously, over 1,500 were created in this period, but most have failed.

Exchanges make money by charging a commission on the transaction. The pricing model can be through an online negotiation, auction, RFQ, or fixed buy-and-sell prices. The benefits offered to customers of exchanges include reduced search cost for parts and spare capacity. Other benefits include lower prices created by a global marketplace driven by competition among suppliers who would, presumably, sell goods at very low profit margins at one world-market price. The benefits offered suppliers are access to a global purchasing environment and the opportunity to unload production overruns (although at very competitive prices and low profit margins). Even though they are private intermediaries, exchanges are public in the sense of permitting any bona fide buyer or seller to participate.

Exchanges tend to be biased toward the buyer even though they are independently owned and presumably neutral. Suppliers are disadvantaged by the fact that exchanges put them in direct price competition with other similar suppliers around the globe, driving profit margins down. Exchanges have failed in the past primarily because suppliers have refused to join them, and hence, the existing markets have very low liquidity, defeating the very purpose and benefits of an exchange. **Liquidity** is typically measured by the number of buyers and sellers in a market, the volume of transactions, and the size of transactions. You know a market is liquid when you can buy or

liquidity

typically measured by the number of buyers and sellers in a market, the volume of transactions, and the size of transactions

TABLE 12.4	EXAMPLES OF INDEPENDENT EXCHANGES
EXCHANGE	FOCUS
PowerSource Online	Computer parts exchange, new and used computer equipment
Converge	Electronic components
IronPlanet	Used heavy equipment
EquipNet	Used industrial equipment and online auctions
Intercontinental Exchange	International online marketplace for over 600 commodities

sell just about any size order at just about any time you want. On all of these measures, many exchanges failed, resulting in a very small number of participants, few trades, and small trade value per transaction. The most common reason for not using exchanges is the absence of traditional, trusted suppliers.

While most exchanges tend to be vertical marketplaces offering direct supplies, some exchanges offer indirect inputs as well, such as electricity and power, transportation services (usually to the transportation industry), and professional services. **Table 12.4** lists a few examples of some current independent exchanges.

The following capsule descriptions of two exchanges provide insight into their origins and current functions.

Global Wine & Spirits (GWS) is unique among independent exchanges, not only as a startup that has managed to survive, but also as a latecomer to the B2B e-commerce community. GWS opened in 1999, but did not begin to trade products online until May 2001. Based in Montreal, Quebec, GWS is operated by Mediagrif Interactive Technologies Inc., a Canadian company that operates a number of independent exchanges in a variety of industries. GWS offers a spot marketplace for wines, where wine and spirit producers offer wines for sale; a call for tenders market, where members make offers to purchase wines and spirits; a trade database with listings of thousands of industry professionals; and a wine and spirits catalog with over 35,000 products and 6,700 companies (Globalwinespirits.com, 2016).

Inventory Locator Service (ILS) has its roots as an offline intermediary, serving as a listing service for aftermarket parts in the aerospace industry. Upon opening in 1979, ILS initially provided a telephone and fax-based directory of aftermarket parts to airplane owners and mechanics, along with government procurement professionals. As early as 1984, ILS incorporated e-mail capabilities as part of its RFQ services, and by 1998, it had begun to conduct online auctions for hard-to-find parts. In 2016, ILS maintains an Internet-accessible database of over 85 million aerospace and marine industry parts, and has also developed an eRFQ feature that helps users streamline their sourcing processes. The network's 23,000 subscribers in 93 different countries access the site over 75,000 times a day (Inventory Locator Service, 2016).

FIGURE 12.13 | **INDUSTRY CONSORTIA**

Industry consortia bring thousands of suppliers into direct contact with a smaller number of very large buyers. The market makers provide value-added software services for procurement, transaction management, shipping, and payment for both buyers and suppliers. Industry consortia are sometimes referred to as many-to-few markets, where many suppliers (albeit selected by the buyers) serve a few very large buyers, mediated by a variety of value-added services.

Industry Consortia

industry consortium
industry-owned vertical market that enables buyers to purchase direct inputs (both goods and services) from a limited set of invited participants

An **industry consortium** is an industry-owned vertical market that enables buyers in the industry to purchase direct inputs (both goods and services) (see **Figure 12.13**). Industry consortia emphasize long-term contractual purchasing, the development of stable relationships (as opposed to merely an anonymous transaction emphasis), and the creation of industry-wide data standards and synchronization efforts. Industry consortia are more focused on optimizing long-term supply relationships than independent exchanges, which tend to focus more on short-term transactions. The ultimate objective of industry consortia is the unification of supply chains within entire industries, across many tiers, through common data definitions, network standards, and computing platforms.

Industry consortia sprang up in part as a reaction to the development of independently owned exchanges, which were viewed by large industries (such as the automotive and chemical industries) as market interlopers that would not directly serve the interests of large buyers, but would instead line their own pockets and those of their venture capital investors. Rather than "pay-to-play," large firms decided to "pay-to-own" their markets. Another concern of large firms was that Net marketplaces would work only if large suppliers and buyers participated, and only if there was liquidity. Independent exchanges were not attracting enough players to achieve liquidity. In addition, exchanges often failed to provide additional value-added services that would transform the value chain for the entire industry, including linking the new marketplaces to firms' ERP systems.

Industry consortia make money in a number of ways. Industry members usually pay for the creation of the consortia's capabilities and contribute initial operating capital. Then industry consortia charge buyer and seller firms transaction and subscription fees. Industry members—both buyers and sellers—are expected to reap benefits far greater than their contributions through the rationalization of the procurement process, competition among vendors, and closer relationships with vendors.

Industry consortia offer many different pricing mechanisms, ranging from auctions to fixed prices to RFQs, depending on the products and the situation. Prices can also be negotiated, and the environment, while competitive, is nevertheless restricted to a smaller number of buyers—selected, reliable, and long-term suppliers who are often viewed as strategic industry partners. The bias of industry consortia is clearly toward the large buyers who control access to this lucrative market channel and can benefit from competitive pricing offered by alternative suppliers. Benefits to suppliers come from access to large buyer firm procurement systems, long-term stable relationships, and large order sizes.

Industry consortia can force suppliers to use the consortia's networks and proprietary software as a condition of selling to the industry's members. Although exchanges failed for a lack of suppliers and liquidity, the market power of consortia members ensures suppliers will participate, so consortia may be able to avoid the fate of voluntary exchanges. Clearly, industry consortia are at an advantage when compared to independent exchanges because, unlike the venture-capital-backed exchanges, they have deep-pocket financial backing from the very start and guaranteed liquidity based on a steady flow of large firm orders. Yet industry consortia are a relatively new phenomenon, and the long-term profitability of these consortia, especially when several consortia exist for a single industry, has yet to be demonstrated. In fact, the number of firms that can be defined as purely industry consortia has declined since the early 2000s, with many firms broadening their mission to encompass more than one industry, or more commonly, being sold by the original industry founders to private investors. For example, GHX, originally founded in 2000 by companies in the pharmaceutical and medical supply industry, is now owned by a private equity firm. E2open, originally founded by IBM, Seagate, and Hitachi as an industry consortium for companies in the high technology industries, has since become a public company and now provides a cloud-based B2B platform and services for a wide variety of industries.

However, a number of industry consortia do remain. One example is The Seam, which was founded in 2000 by leading global agribusiness companies such as Cargill, Louis Dreyfus, and others. The Seam focused initially on creating a cotton trading exchange, and has since added peanuts, grains, and excess USDA farm commodities.

TABLE 12.5	INDUSTRY CONSORTIA BY INDUSTRY
INDUSTRY	NAME OF INDUSTRY CONSORTIA
Agribusiness	The Seam
Automotive	SupplyOn
Chemical	Elemica
Food	Dairy.com
Hospitality	Avendra

The Seam has handled over $5 billion in transactions since inception and more than 90% of the cotton buyers in the United States are active participants in its Cotton Trading system. **Table 12.5** lists some additional examples.

12.5   PRIVATE INDUSTRIAL NETWORKS

Private industrial networks are the most prevalent form of B2B e-commerce in terms of transaction volume, and are expected to continue to be so into the foreseeable future. Private industrial networks can be considered the foundation of the extended enterprise, allowing firms to extend their boundaries and their business processes to include supply chain and logistics partners.

As noted at the beginning of this chapter, private industrial networks are direct descendants of existing EDI networks and are closely tied to existing ERP systems used by large firms. Like EDI, private industrial networks are owned by the buyers and are buyer-side solutions with buyer biases, but they offer significant benefits for suppliers as well. Inclusion in the direct supply chain for a major industrial purchasing company can allow a supplier to increase both revenue and margins because the environment is not competitive—only a few suppliers are included in the private industrial network. A private industrial network is a web-enabled network for the coordination of trans-organizational business processes (sometimes also called collaborative commerce). A **trans-organizational business process** requires at least two independent firms to perform (Laudon and Laudon, 2016). For the most part, these networks originate in and closely involve the manufacturing and related support industries, and therefore we refer to them as industrial networks, although in the future they could just as easily apply to some services. Private industrial networks can be viewed as extended enterprises in the sense that they often begin as ERP systems in a single firm, and are then expanded to include the firm's major suppliers. **Figure 12.14** illustrates a private industrial network originally built by Procter & Gamble (P&G) in the United States to coordinate supply chains among its suppliers, distributors, truckers, and retailers.

trans-organizational business process
process that requires at least two independent firms to perform

FIGURE 12.14	PROCTER & GAMBLE'S PRIVATE INDUSTRIAL NETWORK

Procter & Gamble's private industrial network attempts to coordinate the trans-organizational business processes of the many firms it deals with in the consumer products industry.

In P&G's private industrial network shown in Figure 12.14, customer sales are captured at the cash register, which then initiates a flow of information back to distributors, P&G, and its suppliers. This tells P&G and its suppliers the exact level of demand for thousands of products. This information is then used to initiate production, supply, and transportation to replenish products at the distributors and retailers. This process is called an efficient customer response system (a demand-pull production model), and it relies on an equally efficient supply chain management system to coordinate the supply side (Gartner, Inc., 2015). In 2015 P&G began the process of transforming its supply chain system into a fully integrated, end-to-end supply base that enables the creation of joint business plans with its suppliers. Coordinating this supply base is a control tower environment, replete with wrap-around room monitors, where real-time supply data is continuously analyzed by teams of analysts (Banker, 2015). P&G's distribution goal is to deliver products within one day of shipping to 80% of its retailers. P&G is the world's largest consumer goods manufacturer, and for many years has been ranked as the leading supply chain manager.

GE, Dell, Cisco, Volkswagen, Microsoft, IBM, Nike, Coca-Cola, Walmart, Nokia, and Hewlett-Packard are among the firms operating successful private industrial networks.

OBJECTIVES OF PRIVATE INDUSTRIAL NETWORKS

The specific objectives of a private industrial network include:

- Developing efficient purchasing and selling business processes industry-wide
- Developing industry-wide resource planning to supplement enterprise-wide resource planning
- Increasing supply chain visibility—knowing the inventory levels of buyers and suppliers

- Achieving closer buyer-supplier relationships, including demand forecasting, communications, and conflict resolution
- Operating on a global scale—globalization
- Reducing risk by preventing imbalances of supply and demand, including developing financial derivatives, insurance, and futures markets

Private industrial networks serve different goals from Net marketplaces. Net marketplaces are primarily transaction-oriented, whereas private industrial networks focus on continuous business process coordination between companies. This can include much more than just supply chain management, such as product design, sourcing, demand forecasting, asset management, sales, and marketing. Private industrial networks do support transactions, but that is not their primary focus.

Private industrial networks usually focus on a single sponsoring company that "owns" the network, sets the rules, establishes governance (a structure of authority, rule enforcement, and control), and invites firms to participate at its sole discretion. Therefore, these networks are private. This sets them apart from industry consortia, which are usually owned by major firms collectively through equity participation. Whereas Net marketplaces have a strong focus on indirect goods and services, private industrial networks focus on strategic, direct goods and services.

For instance, True Value is one of the largest retailer-owned hardware cooperatives with operations in 54 countries, 4,500 stores, and 12 regional distribution centers. The logistics are staggering to consider: they routinely process over 60,000 domestic inbound loads, and over 600 million pounds of freight. True Value imports roughly 3,500 containers through 20 international ports and 10 domestic ports. The existing inbound supply chain system was fragmented, did not permit real-time tracking of packages, and when shipments were short or damaged, could not alert stores. The supply chain was "invisible": suppliers could not see store inventory levels, and stores could not see supplier shipments. Using a web-based solution from Sterling Commerce (an IBM company), True Value created its own private industrial network to which all suppliers, shippers, and stores have exclusive access. The network focuses on three processes: domestic prepaid shipping, domestic collect, and international direct shipping. For each process the network tracks in real time the movement of goods from suppliers to shippers, warehouses, and stores. The system has led to a 57% reduction in lead time needed for orders, a 10% increase in the fill rate of orders, and an 85% reduction in back orders. If goods are delayed, damaged, or unavailable, the system alerts all parties automatically (True Value, 2016; IBM, 2011).

Perhaps no single firm better illustrates the benefits of developing private industrial networks than Walmart, described in *Insight on Business: Walmart Develops a Private Industrial Network*.

PRIVATE INDUSTRIAL NETWORKS AND COLLABORATIVE COMMERCE

Private industrial networks can do much more than just serve a supply chain and efficient customer response system. They can also include other activities of a single large manufacturing firm, such as design of products and engineering diagrams, as well as marketing plans and demand forecasting. Collaboration among businesses can take

INSIGHT ON BUSINESS

WALMART DEVELOPS A PRIVATE INDUSTRIAL NETWORK

Walmart is a leader in the application of information technology to coordinate its supply chain. Walmart's supply chain is the secret sauce behind its claim of offering the lowest everyday prices. Walmart is able to make this promise because it has one of the most efficient B2B supply chains in the world. It also doesn't hurt to be the largest purchaser of consumer goods in the world. With sales of $479 billion in 2015, Walmart has been able to use information technology to achieve a decisive cost advantage over competitors. As you might imagine, the world's largest retailer also has the world's largest supply chain, with more than 100,000 suppliers worldwide. In the United States, Walmart has more than 5,200 retail stores (including Sam's Clubs). The larger stores stock as many as 200,000 different items. Internationally, Walmart has over 6,200 additional stores in 27 countries, giving it a total of over 11,500.

In the late 1980s, Walmart developed the beginnings of collaborative commerce using an EDI-based SCM system that required its large suppliers to use Walmart's proprietary EDI network to respond to orders from Walmart purchasing managers. In 1991, Walmart expanded the capabilities of its EDI-based network by introducing Retail Link. This system connected Walmart's largest suppliers to Walmart's own inventory management system and required large suppliers to track actual sales by stores and to replenish supplies as dictated by demand and following rules imposed by Walmart.

In 1997, Walmart moved Retail Link to an extranet that allowed suppliers to directly link over the Internet into Walmart's inventory management system. In 2000, Walmart hired an outside firm to upgrade Retail Link from being a supply chain management tool toward a more collaborative forecasting, planning, and replenishment (CFPR) system. Using demand aggregation software, Walmart purchasing agents were now able to aggregate demand from all of Walmart's separate stores in the United States into a single RFQ from suppliers. This gave Walmart tremendous clout with even the largest suppliers. The software helped Walmart purchasing agents select a winning bid and negotiate final contracts. In addition, the software enabled suppliers to immediately access information on inventories, purchase orders, invoice status, and sales forecasts, based on 104 weeks of data, with data available by item, by store, and by hour. The system did not require smaller supplier firms to adopt expensive EDI software solutions. Instead, they could use standard browsers and PCs loaded with free software from Walmart. In 2002, Walmart switched to an entirely Internet-based version of EDI, and the result was a radical reduction in communications costs.

Beginning in 2012, and continuing through 2015, Walmart began a transition to a new supply and inventory management platform called Retail Link 2.0 or Global Replenishment System (GRS). It has currently been deployed to about 80 vendors, with the goal to bring all vendors on board by the end of 2015, and close down the existing Retail Link by 2018. Retail Link 2.0 has all the functionality of the first Retail Link and builds on that foundation with real-time, online data and analytics that is available over the Web to vendors and employees.

Retail Link 2.0 uses Microsoft SharePoint, which is a collaborative web-based collection of software services that can store and share documents, keep track of changes, and provide corporate search and enterprise social networking tools

(continued)

to connect employees with one another. SharePoint is integrated with Office 365. In Walmart's Retail Link 2.0, the SharePoint platform is used to create an online web-based facility that enables vendors to respond to orders, track shipments, and sales in a near-real time manner. Vendors and Walmart managers can use business intelligence tools to predict sales rather than simply react to empty shelves or low inventory.

The transition to Retail Link 2.0 requires a massive retraining effort for Walmart's 100,000 suppliers, and tens of thousands of Walmart managers. Problems have developed in the supply chain as the number of new products in stores has mushroomed. Without a history of sales that can be used to predict future sales, some stores have too much inventory, and others not enough.

Despite its success in building a world-class supply chain to support its retail stores, Walmart was not well prepared to deal with online sales or to compete with the online champion, Amazon. From the beginning, Walmart separated out its fledgling e-commerce operation as a separate company with a much lower priority for investment than its physical stores. It was late to invest in an Internet supply chain because the separate companies could never agree on whether it was a good investment. As a result, Walmart's Internet supply chain remains a work in progress, relying on employees at some of the stores to pick online orders and ship from the store, while other orders are handled by a few Internet order warehouses. In 2015, Walmart had $13.7 billion in online sales (up 12%) (compared to Amazon's $107 billion), representing only about 3% of its $479 billion in sales. In 2013, Walmart finally began creating a new inventory and logistics system that will combine the inventory information from its stores and warehouses and then decide the most efficient way to pick and ship online orders. In 2016, Walmart customers can pick up grocery orders placed online at 150 locations. In the works: using drones in its large distribution centers to speed up fulfillment of online orders.

Like other large global firms, Walmart's global supply chain has been criticized for exploiting labor in underdeveloped countries where it buys products and in home markets where it sells them, bribing officials to look the other way, destroying environments, and wasting energy. In response to critics, Walmart has taken a number of steps. Walmart has set a goal of reducing carbon emissions in its supply chain by 20 million metric tons by 2015, and a goal of 100% renewable energy use in the United States. Walmart has made less progress in its labor policies: In 2012, the ABP pension fund blacklisted Walmart for failing to comply with the United Nations' Global Compact principles that include a set of core values relating to human rights, labor standards, the environment, and anti-corruption efforts. In 2014, the National Labor Relations Board issued a complaint against Walmart claiming that it had illegally retaliated against workers who took part in protests about working conditions and a U.S. Department of Justice investigation into allegations that Walmart bribed Mexican officials to expand its stores and supply chain in Mexico remains ongoing. In 2015, to counter critics of its labor policies, Walmart launched a billion dollar program to raise wages, improve health care policies, and improve scheduling for work.

SOURCES: "Corporate & Financial Facts," Walmart.com, accessed August 9, 2016; "Walmart Looks to Drones to Speed Distribution," by Rachel Abrams, *New York Times*, June 2, 2016; "Walmart Loses Ground to Amazon in E-Commerce Battle," by Phil Wahba, *Fortune*, February 18, 2016; "Wal-Mart Curbs Inventory Growth," by Paul Page, *Wall Street Journal*, February 18, 2016; "Wal-Mart Shrinks the Big Box, Vexing Vendors," by Sarah Nassauer, *Wall Street Journal*, October 25, 2015; "Wal-Mart Builds Supply Chain to Meet E-Commerce Demands," by Kim Nash, *Wall Street Journal*, May 7, 2015; "Walmart U.S. CEO: Fresher Food, Fill Empty Shelves and Lower Prices," by Phil Wahba, *Fortune*, April 2, 2015; "Wal-Mart Acknowledges Inventory Woes in U.S. Stores, Seeks 'Fresh' Fix," by Kim Souza, Thecitywire.com, February 12, 2015; "The Supply Side: Welcome to the Supply Chain Revolution," by Kim Souza, Thecitywire.com, February 2, 2015; "The Scoop on Retail Link 2.0," by Sheldon Cwinn, Linkedin.com/pulse, September 15, 2014; "Biggest Lessons Listed for New Wal-Mart Suppliers," by Kim Souza, Thecitywire.com, November 20, 2013; "The Trouble Lurking on Walmart's Empty Shelves," by Bill Saporito, *Time Business*, April 9, 2013; "Walmart's Secret Sauce: How the Largest Survives and Thrives," by Chris Petersen, Retailcustomerexperience.com, March 27, 2013.

FIGURE 12.15 | **PIECES OF THE COLLABORATIVE COMMERCE PUZZLE**

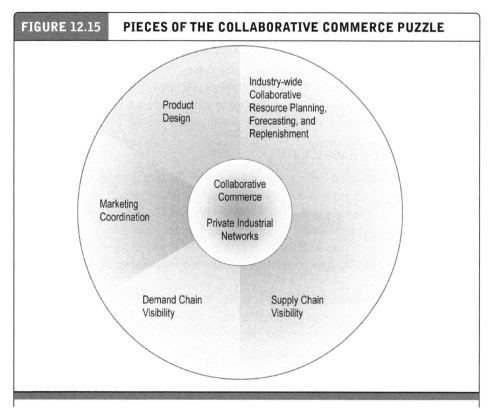

Collaborative commerce involves many cooperative activities among supply and sales firms closely interacting with a single large firm through a private industrial network.

many forms and involve a wide range of activities—from simple supply chain management to coordinating market feedback to designers at supply firms (see **Figure 12.15**).

One form of collaboration—and perhaps the most profound—is industry-wide **collaborative resource planning, forecasting, and replenishment (CPFR)**, which involves working with network members to forecast demand, develop production plans, and coordinate shipping, warehousing, and stocking activities to ensure that retail and wholesale shelf space is replenished with just the right amount of goods. If this goal is achieved, hundreds of millions of dollars of excess inventory and capacity could be wrung out of an industry. This activity alone is likely to produce the largest benefits and justify the cost of developing private industrial networks.

A second area of collaboration is *demand chain visibility*. In the past, it was impossible to know where excess capacity or supplies existed in the supply and distribution chains. For instance, retailers might have significantly overstocked shelves, but suppliers and manufacturers—not knowing this—might be building excess capacity or supplies for even more production. These excess inventories would raise costs for the entire industry and create extraordinary pressures to discount merchandise, reducing profits for everyone.

A third area of collaboration is *marketing coordination and product design*. Manufacturers that use or produce highly engineered parts use private industrial networks

collaborative resource planning, forecasting, and replenishment (CPFR)

involves working with network members to forecast demand, develop production plans, and coordinate shipping, warehousing, and stocking activities to ensure that retail and wholesale shelf space is replenished with just the right amount of goods to coordinate both their internal design and marketing activities, as well as related activities of their supply and distribution chain partners. By involving their suppliers in product design and marketing initiatives, manufacturing firms can ensure that the parts produced actually fulfill the claims of marketers. On the reverse flow, feedback from customers can be used by marketers to speak directly to product designers at the firm and its suppliers. For the first time, closed loop marketing (customer feedback directly impacting design and production) can become a reality.

IMPLEMENTATION BARRIERS

Although private industrial networks represent a large part of the future of B2B, there are many barriers to its complete implementation. Participating firms are required to share sensitive data with their business partners, up and down the supply chain. What in the past was considered proprietary and secret must now be shared. In a digital environment, it can be difficult to control the limits of information sharing. Information a firm freely gives to its largest customer may end up being shared with its closest competitor.

Integrating private industrial networks into existing enterprise systems and EDI networks poses a significant investment of time and money. The leading providers of enterprise systems to Fortune 500 companies (Oracle, IBM, and SAP) do offer B2B modules, and supply chain management capabilities, that can be added to their existing software suites. Nevertheless, implementing these modules is a very expensive proposition in part because the procurement side of many Fortune 500 firms is so fragmented and out-of-date. For smaller firms, cloud computing and software as a service (SaaS) alternatives are appearing on the market, which offer far less-expensive supply chain management capabilities.

Adopting private industrial networks also requires a change in mindset and behavior for employees. Essentially, employees must shift their loyalties from the firm to the wider trans-organizational enterprise and recognize that their fate is intertwined with the fate of their suppliers and distributors. Suppliers in turn are required to change the way they manage and allocate their resources because their own production is tightly coupled with the demands of their private industrial network partners. All participants in the supply and distribution chains, with the exception of the large network owner, lose some of their independence, and must initiate large behavioral change programs in order to participate (Laudon and Laudon, 2016).

CASE STUDY

Elemica:
Cooperation, Collaboration, and Community

It may seem unusual to refer to an entire industry as a community, a word reserved typically for collections of people who more or less know one another. Trade associations are one example of an industrial community. Trade associations form in an effort to pursue the interests of all members in the community although usually they do not include customers in the community. Elemica is a B2B cloud-based, supply chain platform aiming to revolutionize the entire supply chain of the chemical, tire and rubber, energy, and other process industries worldwide. Elemica's purpose is not just to foster cooperation on a one-to-one inter-firm basis, or just to foster collaboration on multi-firm projects, but instead to lift all boats on an industry tide by providing an inter-firm platform for communicating B2B information, and thereby making all firms more efficient. Elemica calls itself a supply chain operating network ecosystem. Elemica is one of the few survivors of the early B2B e-commerce years. Elemica today processes approximately $400 billion in annual transactions across more than 7,500 process industry trading partners. Clients include BASF, BP, Continental, The Dow Chemical Company, DuPont, The Goodyear Tire & Rubber Company, LANXESS, Michelin, Shell, Solvay, Sumitomo Chemical, and Wacker. In terms of the framework we use to understand B2B Net marketplaces, Elemica can be characterized as an industry consortium.

Elemica was founded by 22 leading corporations in the chemical industry (including oil and industrial gases) to provide cloud-based order management and supply chain applications and services. A single platform provides one-stop shopping so that companies can buy and sell products to one another through their own enterprise systems or using a web alternative. It also helps companies automate all of their business processes, creating efficiencies and economies of scale that lead to an improved bottom line. In 2016 Elemica was purchased by Thoma Bravo, a private equity firm. With additional capital resources, Elemica is planning to expand its trading ecosystem to a broader range of industries.

How does Elemica achieve community among a diverse, global collection of firms where firms are often both customers and vendors to one another? It unites community members by linking together their enterprise systems. This is the "social glue" that sets Elemica apart. This "super platform" permits companies to communicate with one another and to conduct transactions, handle logistics, and keep the books. The Elemica commerce platform has effectively standardized industry business transactions for all network members regardless of the type of enterprise system they have, and it's leveled the playing field for trade partners who are less technically sophisticated. This neutral platform facilitates millions of transactions for industry suppliers, customers, and third-party providers. In this sense, Elemica is one of the most sophisticated technology platforms in the B2B space.

One of the largest investments for a company is its enterprise system. Despite these investments, intercompany relationships—the backbone of its supply chain—are often left to outdated and unreliable processes. These shortcomings cost billions in lost productivity, revenue, and profit. Elemica's eCommerce platform changes that. It helps its clients leverage their enterprise system investment by incorporating transactions to external trade partners. Elemica's QuickLink ERP connectivity enables companies to link their internal IT systems through a neutral platform so that information is moved into each company's database while maintaining confidentiality and security. The chemical and oil industries were among the first users of enterprise systems (referred to in the early years as manufacturing resource planning systems). These large-scale systems were developed by single firms in order to rationalize and control the manufacturing process. They achieved this objective by identifying the outputs, inputs, and processes involved in manufacturing and automating key elements including inventory control and planning, process control, warehousing and storage, and shipping/logistics. If a company needed to produce 10 tons of polyethylene plastic, its enterprise system could tell it precisely how many tons of petrochemical inputs were required, when they should be delivered to manufacturing, the machinery and labor force required to manufacture the product, how long it would take, where it would be stored, and sometimes how it would be shipped. The systems can estimate the cost at any stage.

Elemica facilitates transactions of all types including order processing and billing, and logistics management. However, unlike some other companies in the field, Elemica does not buy, sell, or own raw material products. Instead it acts as an intermediary, or network, linking companies together to automate confidential transactions. Like eBay or a credit card company, Elemica's revenue comes from charging transaction fees on a per-transaction basis. Its network of clients opens the door for companies to do business with all other connected buyers and sellers.

Elemica offers a variety of services for suppliers, customers, and logistic partners, enabling them to automate both their business processes and internal purchasing. A modular, cloud-based solution simplifies sales, procurement, and financial processes; integrates supply chain partners to diminish communication barriers; and reduces overhead and errors.

Elemica integrates information flow among global trading partners using a cloud-based business process network called the QuickLink network. This is often referred to as platform as a service (PaaS). Each client needs only a single connection to Elemica, and Elemica manages the connections to that company's external trade partners. That means a company needs only maintain one connection to Elemica (important when it's time for enterprise system maintenance or upgrade) rather than maintain a variable number of connections and infrastructure to all its trade partners. Once a company connects to Elemica, it can have access to thousands of other trading partners, including suppliers, customers, and logistics firms. Clients are charged for the service based on volume of usage. This is much more efficient than older EDI solutions to inter-company transactions. Elemica provides the platform for collaborative commerce through a fully automated integrated network of suppliers, customers, and third-party providers.

Elemica offers cloud-based solutions for four areas: Logistics Management, Customer Management, Supplier Management, and Sourcing Management. Using these solutions, companies can automate ordering, invoicing, shipment tracking, and day-to-day business operations. Companies can sign up for one or more solutions depending on their needs. The software applications are software as a service (SaaS) applications residing on Elemica cloud servers, and therefore do not require participating firms to buy any hardware or software. Firms are charged on the basis of how much of the service they use, on a demand basis.

Here's an example of how Elemica works. Let's say you need to order vinyl acetate from one of your suppliers. You put the order into your internal enterprise system, the order is automatically routed to Elemica's QuickLink network, Elemica routes the order to your supplier's internal enterprise system, and you get a confirmed receipt of the order. Elemica's QuickLink Network ensures the accuracy of the item number and purchase order number and sends an alert if there's an issue. Once an order is confirmed, Elemica's platform can be leveraged to plan and coordinate delivery and automatically send an invoice and submit payment. For small or medium firms that may not have an enterprise system, Elemica has a web portal with online software that allows firms to participate in the community with suppliers and customers. The platform offers a closed-loop process, end to end, from the purchase order, to acknowledgments, load tenders and responses, carrier status updates, and dock scheduling. All of this takes place in a few seconds with little or no human intervention. Elemica has even developed a solution that allows a customer to send a purchase order via e-mail or a print driver (alleviating fax processes) that is then routed to Elemica. The company then routes it to the supplier in its preferred format, integrated with its enterprise system as though it were a true electronic order. This holistic approach to order management allows suppliers to automate the process with both strategic and core customers, without asking its customers to change their processes. It's a win-win situation for suppliers and customers. Elemica's QuickLink Network is sometimes referred to as "Come As You Are" network because it allows firms to use whatever communication tools they currently use, such as EDI, XML, and even e-mail, or formats associated with their enterprise systems.

Unlike the automobile industry or the airline industry, where a few companies dominate, the $5 trillion global chemical industry is made up of many companies of all sizes. In addition, unlike many other industries, chemical companies often buy the output from other chemical companies to use as raw materials for their products. Thus, chemical companies are often customers of one another as well as competitors.

Senior leaders at some of the larger chemical companies were aware of changes in technology that made the adoption of information technology and the tools of e-commerce more appealing. The questions were how to best use these advances to benefit their businesses and how to establish industry standards for electronic transactions to make them accessible and attainable for all. Leaders from companies such as Dow Chemical and DuPont began discussing this subject and determined that a cooperative alliance would be the most efficient way to move forward. They were met with initial skepticism by marketing and sales staff, worried that online procurement would negatively affect relationships. Further, senior corporate leadership wasn't sure that e-commerce would have any use in the chemical industry at all. And companies were cautious about the expense of investing in the infrastructure necessary for e-commerce.

However, there were compelling opportunities that were impossible to dismiss, including lowering costs, creating closer connections with customers and suppliers, and differentiating companies on something other than price. At the same time, new startups like e-Chemicals and PlasticsNet were making traditional chemical companies nervous. What would happen if their efforts to use information technology to streamline an inefficient supply chain helped them capture market share? In other words, if the more traditional companies didn't move forward, they might end up losing the revenue race.

When Dow began looking at startups that were using e-commerce and talking to their customers, they found that customers were concerned about making an investment to establish online connections with multiple firms. Dow and DuPont decided that the best and most economically efficient option was to offer customers the choice of a neutral one-to-one link. This would remove the obstacle of multiple connections. A strong, third-party network addressed the community concern about loss of control. The two companies decided to create and invest in a neutral e-commerce company, partnering with other companies to create the critical mass needed to make it viable.

In 1999, the corporate boards of Dow and DuPont agreed that there were major advantages to online transaction processing and additional online connections among buyers and sellers. Because time and cost considerations made multiple connections unattractive to customers, a hub concept was adopted. It was also decided that a neutral community was the best approach.

All participants shared the common goal of creating a neutral platform to facilitate inter-company transactions and enhance business processes. Dow and DuPont also reviewed the concept with the relevant regulatory agencies and received up-front approval. Ultimately, 22 global chemical companies were involved in the launch of Elemica.

When Elemica opened its doors in 1999, there were around 50 startup B2B e-commerce companies in the chemical industry. Nearly all of these B2B companies were third-party-owned Net marketplaces suitable at best for short-term sourcing of some direct inputs. In 2016, only a handful of these Net marketplaces for the chemical industry remain. Elemica focuses on building longer-term business relationships by creating committed and contractual supply chains. The company acts only as a facilitator of business transactions and does not directly buy and sell chemical products.

Elemica's business model has been successful primarily because it addresses the needs of chemical, tire and rubber, energy, and selected process companies of all sizes. It does this by offering multiple options for connecting to its hub system, multiple products that can be used alone or in combination, and by ensuring that only one connection integrated with a client's enterprise system is needed for all transactions. Customers can use Elemica, and take advantage of the technology it offers, without purchasing an additional internal system.

With Elemica, companies benefit from improved operational efficiency, reduced costs due to elimination of redundant systems and excess inventory, and a much higher percentage of safe and reliable deliveries. The flexibility of Elemica's solutions and network combines simplification, standardization, and efficiency. And clients have increased their profitability and improved cash flow through faster payment.

A number of very large companies use Elemica's platform. In Europe, Shell Oil started using Elemica after recognizing that it had ongoing problems with the coordination of paperwork processing and deliveries. Truck drivers would arrive at delivery sites and wait up to two hours while paperwork was filled out. These delays were costing Shell money. Once Shell began using Elemica, things improved. Today, paperwork is processed 24 hours a day, and truck waiting time has been cut from an average of two hours to an average of 15 minutes. Given this success, Shell continues to expand its relationship with Elemica.

Dow Chemical began to transition to full procurement automation with Elemica in 2007. More than 300 of their MRO suppliers are now linked to Elemica's platform. Errors are down 75%, and Dow has achieved economies of scale that have led to meaningful financial savings. Elemica helped Dow unify multiple, disparate business processes, reduced the cost of getting contracted items from suppliers, and increased efficiency in procurement, operations, IT, and accounts payable.

Air Products & Chemicals, Inc. is a global provider of gases and chemicals with 22,000 employees worldwide, and $10 billion in revenue. A major customer asked them for online ordering, but the initial method proposed would have required considerable additional work for both parties. Because both companies were connected to Elemica, there was a better option—the Elemica Supply Chain Hosted Solution.

Elemica has also developed a sustainability program. In 2015, Elemica received the Food Logistics 2015 Top Green Provider Award for its efforts in promoting sustainable supply chains. Elemica automated all inbound and outbound invoices for a global chemical company, eliminating over one million paper invoices. Elemica also eliminated the costs of archiving and storing paper records, saving additional costs.

Elemica has added social tools to its Supply Chain Operating Network (SCON). The idea is to give clients the ability to discover, create, and build social business networks—just as Facebook provides its users the ability to build online social networks. SCON provides its clients with a cloud-based network for establishing business relationships and SaaS (software as a service) applications to carry on trading once the relationship is established. Instead of creating hundreds of one-to-one EDI connections with partners, and then building their own software applications, firms can now more easily just connect to the network and find all the tools they need to trade with many partners. And in May 2014, Elemica introduced its Process Control Tower, a graphical interface that offers a consolidated view of transactional data across all a customer's business partners. Based on the metaphor of an airport control tower, the idea is to

SOURCES: "Thoma Bravo Completes Acquisition of Elemica," Elemica, July 7, 2016; "Elemica Shares Eight and a Half Supply Chain Priorities for 2016," Elemica, January 7, 2016; "SmartLink Applications," Elemica, accessed July 8, 2015; "Elemica Is a Supply Chain Operating Network," Elemica, accessed July 8, 2015; "Clients Meet Sustainability Goals by Automating Paper-Driven Processes," Elemica, June 25, 2015; "Elemica Shell Global," Royal Dutch Shell, PLC, June 2015; "Building Effective Business Networks in Process Industries Improving Supply Chain Value Networks," by Lora Cecere, Supply Chain Insights, LLC, January 2015; "Elemica Introduces New Supply Chain Process Control Tower," Elemica, May 7, 2014; "Top Ten Supply Chain Initiatives for 2014 That Are Reimagining How Companies Conduct Commerce," Elemica, January 13, 2014; "Elemica: Shifting From a Shared Services Bazaar to Platform 'PaaS' Standard," by Jason Busch, Spendmatters.com, November 18, 2013; "Elemica Announces Launch of New 'Delivery Schedule' Solution," Elemica, September 24, 2013; "The Social Side of Supply Chain Management," by Adrian Gonzalez, *Supply Chain Management Review*, August 2013; "Next Generation Supply Chain Networks Enable More Robust Collaborative Workflows Across Trading Partners to Increase Value," Becky Boyd, *Market Wired*, July 2, 2013; "Elemica Named to Inbound Logistics Top 100 Logistics IT Provider Awards," *Wall Street Journal*, April 24, 2013; "Elemica Introduces Transportation Management Solution," Elemica, February 16, 2012; "Elemica Procurement Case Study: Dow," Elemica, September 2010; "Elemica Order Management Case Study: BP," Elemica, September 2010; "Elemica Case Study: LanXess," Elemica, September 2010; "Elemica and Rubber-Network Merge," SDCExec.com, August 25, 2009; "Case Study: Elemica," Ebusinesswatch.org, August 25, 2009; "Once Elemica Tackled the Hard Part, the Rest Was Easy," SupplyChainBrain.com, August 5, 2009.

give managers a near real-time view of their entire supply and logistics systems. In the past, and still in many firms today, this kind of supply chain information comes in many different forms, from faxes, to e-mails, spreadsheets, and EDI messages. The Control Tower eliminates these difficult-to-interpret messages, and greatly enhances supply chain visibility.

Case Study Questions

1. If you were a small chemical company, what concerns would you have about joining Elemica?

2. Elemica provides a community for participants where they can transact, coordinate, and cooperate to produce products for less. Yet these firms also compete with one another when they sell chemicals to end-user firms in the automobile, airline, and manufacturing industries. How is this possible?

3. How does the purchase of Elemica by Thoma Bravo, a private equity firm, change how Elemica fits into the B2B framework illustrated in Figure 12.9?

12.7   REVIEW

KEY CONCEPTS

■ **Discuss the evolution and growth of B2B e-commerce, as well as its potential benefits and challenges.**

- Before the Internet, business-to-business transactions were referred to simply as *inter-firm trade* or the *procurement process*. Today, we use the term *B2B commerce* to describe all types of inter-firm trade to exchange value across organizational boundaries, involving both the buying of inputs and the marketing, selling, and distribution of products and services, and the term *B2B e-commerce* to describe specifically that portion of B2B commerce that is enabled by the Internet and mobile apps.
- In order to understand the evolution of B2B e-commerce, you must understand several key stages:
  - *Automated order entry systems*, developed in the 1970s, involved the use of telephone modems to send digital orders.
  - *EDI* or *electronic data interchange*, developed in the late 1970s, is a communications standard for sharing various procurement documents including invoices, purchase orders, shipping bills, product stocking numbers (SKUs), and settlement information for an industry.
  - *B2B e-commerce websites* emerged in the 1990s along with the commercialization of the Internet. They are online catalogs containing the products that are made available to the general public by a single vendor.
  - *Net marketplaces* emerged in the late 1990s as a natural extension and scaling-up of the electronic storefront. Net marketplaces involve the marketing, selling, and distribution side of B2B e-commerce. The essential characteristic of all Net marketplaces is that they bring hundreds of suppliers, each with its own online catalog, together with potentially thousands of purchasing firms to form a single Internet-based marketplace.

- *Private industrial networks* also emerged in the late 1990s with the commercialization of the Internet as a natural extension of EDI systems and the existing close relationships that developed between large industrial firms and their suppliers.
- Potential benefits of B2B e-commerce include lower administrative costs; lower search costs for buyers; reduced inventory costs; lower transaction costs; improved quality of products; decreased product cycle time; increased opportunities for collaborating with suppliers and distributors; greater price transparency; and increased visibility and real-time information sharing among all participants in the supply chain network.
- Potential risks and challenges include lack of real-time data, environmental impacts, natural disasters, labor concerns, and the impacts of economic, financial, and political instability.

■ Understand how procurement and supply chains relate to B2B e-commerce.

- The *procurement process* refers to the way business firms purchase the goods they need in order to produce the goods they will ultimately sell to consumers. Firms purchase goods from a set of suppliers who in turn purchase their inputs from a set of suppliers. These firms are linked in a series of connected transactions. The *supply chain* is the series of transactions that links sets of firms that do business with each other. It includes not only the firms themselves but also the relationships between them and the processes that connect them.
- There are two different types of procurements (purchases of direct goods and purchases of indirect goods) and two different methods of purchasing goods (contract purchases and spot purchases).
- The term *multi-tier supply chain* is used to describe the complex series of transactions that exists between a single firm with multiple primary suppliers, the secondary suppliers who do business with those primary suppliers, and the tertiary suppliers who do business with the secondary suppliers.

■ Identify major trends in supply chain management and collaborative commerce.

- *Supply chain management (SCM)* refers to a wide variety of activities that firms and industries use to coordinate the key players in their procurement process.
- *Just-in-time production* is a method of inventory cost management that seeks to eliminate excess inventory to a bare minimum.
- *Lean production* is a set of production methods and tools that focuses on the elimination of waste throughout the customer value chain.
- *Supply chain simplification* involves reducing the size of the supply chain and working more closely with a smaller group of strategic supplier firms to reduce both product costs and administrative costs, while improving quality
- *Adaptive supply chains* allow companies to react to disruptions in the supply chain in a particular region by moving production to a different region.
- *Accountable supply chains* are those where the labor conditions in low-wage, underdeveloped producer countries are visible and morally acceptable to ultimate consumers in more developed industrial societies.
- *Sustainable supply chains* involve using the most efficient environment-regarding means of production, distribution, and logistics.
- EDI remains very important in B2B e-commerce.
- Mobile B2B has become increasingly important in all aspects of B2B e-commerce, through all steps of the procurement process and throughout the supply chain.
- *Cloud-based B2B systems* shift much of the expense of B2B systems from the firm to a B2B network provider, sometimes called a data hub or B2B platform.

- Contemporary *supply chain management (SCM) systems* are based on supply chain simplification, just in time and lean production, focusing on strategic partners in the production process, enterprise systems, and continuous inventory replenishment.
- *Collaborative commerce* involves the use of digital technologies to permit firms to collaboratively design, develop, build, market, and manage products through their life cycles, and is a direct extension of supply chain management systems, as well as supply chain simplification. Collaborative commerce today involves cloud servers, social business tools, and mobile devices.
- Social networks are providing intimate connections among customers, suppliers, and logistics partners.
- Despite the size of the B2B e-commerce, B2B marketing still accounts for onlya relatively small slice of the total amount spent on digital marketing and advertising, in part due to the slow pace of technological change in supply chain and procurement management and in part due to the very different nature of B2B e-commerce compared to B2C e-commerce. For long-term sourcing, Interpersonal relationships, networking, brand, and informative content marketing using white papers, videos, podcasts, webinars, blogs, e-books, conferences, and professional associations are the primary and most effective marketing tools. However, in spot purchasing markets, B2B marketing uses many of the same marketing tactics and tools found in B2C marketing: display ads, search engine marketing, websites, social network channels, videos, and mobile ads.

■ Understand the different characteristics and types of Net marketplaces.

- Net marketplaces are sell-side digital environments where sellers and buyers are brought together.
- Characteristics of Net marketplaces include their bias (seller-side vs. buy-side vs. neutral), ownership (industry vs. third party), pricing mechanism (fixed priced catalogs, auctions, and RFPs/RFQs), scope/focus (horizontal vs. vertical), value creation (customers/suppliers), and access to markets (public vs. private).
- There are four main types of "pure" Net marketplaces:
  - *E-distributors* are independently owned intermediaries that offer industrial customers a single source from which to make spot purchases of indirect or MRO goods. E-distributors operate in a horizontal market that serves many different industries with products from many different suppliers.
  - *E-procurement Net marketplaces* are independently owned intermediaries connecting hundreds of online suppliers offering millions of MRO goods to business firms who pay a fee to join the market. E-procurement Net marketplaces operate in a horizontal market in which long-term contractual purchasing agreements are used to buy indirect goods.
  - *Exchanges* are independently owned online marketplaces that connect hundreds to thousands of suppliers and buyers in a dynamic real-time environment. They are typically vertical markets in which spot purchases can be made for direct inputs (both goods and services). Exchanges make money by charging a commission on each transaction.
  - *Industry consortia* are industry-owned vertical markets where long-term contractual purchases of direct inputs can be made from a limited set of invited participants. Consortia serve to reduce supply chain inefficiencies by unifying the supply chain for an industry through a common network and computing platform.

■ Understand the objectives of private industrial networks, their role in supporting collaborative commerce, and the barriers to their implementation.

- Objectives of private industrial networks include developing efficient purchasing and selling business processes industry-wide; developing industry-wide resource planning to supplement enterprise-wide resource planning; increasing supply chain visibility; achieving closer buyer-supplier relationships; operating on a global scale; and reducing industry risk by preventing imbalances of supply and demand.
- Private industrial networks are transforming the supply chain by focusing on continuous business process coordination between companies. This coordination includes much more than just transaction sup-

port and supply chain management. Product design, demand forecasting, asset management, and sales and marketing plans can all be coordinated among network members. Some of the forms of collaboration used by private industrial networks include the following:

- *CPFR* or *industry-wide collaborative resource planning, forecasting, and replenishment* involves working with network members to forecast demand, develop production plans, and coordinate shipping, warehousing, and stocking activities.
- *Supply chain and distribution chain visibility* refers to the fact that, in the past, it was impossible to know where excess capacity existed in a supply or distribution chain. Eliminating excess inventories by halting the production of overstocked goods can raise the profit margins for all network members because products will no longer need to be discounted in order to move them off the shelves.
- *Marketing and product design collaboration* can be used to involve a firm's suppliers in product design and marketing activities as well as in the related activities of their supply and distribution chain partners. This can ensure that the parts used to build a product live up to the claims of the market- ers. Collaborative commerce applications used in a private industrial network can also make pos- sible closed-loop marketing in which customer feedback will directly impact product design.

QUESTIONS

1. What factors influence the speed with which industries migrate to B2B e-commerce?
2. Describe the stages of evolution of EDI.
3. Describe three weaknesses of EDI in today's B2B e-commerce environment.
4. What types of ownership models and revenue models do Net marketplaces use?
5. Describe the steps in the procurement process. Which steps are least likely to benefit from automation and e-commerce technologies?
6. What is an accountable supply chain? Why are companies now moving to establish such supply chains?
7. Explain the difference between the supply (buy) side and sell side in B2B e-commerce.
8. Why do firms typically use spot purchasing for indirect goods and contractual purchasing for direct goods?
9. Explain the difference between just-in-time and lean production.
10. What are the risks involved in a global supply chain that pushes manufacturing and production to low-cost labor centers? How can these risks be mitigated?
11. Define sustainable business. What is the business value of a sustainable supply chain?
12. Describe three types of B2B collaboration enabled through private industrial networks.
13. What are the benefits for suppliers in a private industrial network?
14. What role do mobile devices play in B2B marketing?
15. What are the barriers to the complete implementation of private industrial networks?
16. What is a cloud-based B2B platform and what advantages does it offer?
17. What is the main reason why many of the independent exchanges developed in the early days of e-commerce failed?
18. How does collaborative commerce differ from EDI? How is it similar?
19. What does BYOD refer to?
20. How have social networks impacted B2B?

PROJECTS

1. Choose an industry and a B2B vertical market maker that interests you. Investigate the site and prepare a report that describes the size of the industry served, the type of Net marketplace provided, the benefits promised by the site for both suppliers and purchasers, and the history of the company. You might

also investigate the bias (buyer versus seller), ownership (suppliers, buyers, independents), pricing mechanism(s), scope and focus, and access (public versus private) of the Net marketplace.

2. Examine the website of one of the e-distributors listed in Figure 12.9, and compare and contrast it to one of the websites listed for e-procurement Net marketplaces. If you were a business manager of a medium-sized firm, how would you decide where to purchase your indirect inputs—from an e-distributor or an e-procurement Net marketplace? Write a short report detailing your analysis.

3. Assume you are a procurement officer for an office furniture manufacturer of steel office equipment. You have a single factory located in the Midwest with 2,000 employees. You sell about 40% of your office furniture to retail-oriented catalog outlets such as Quill in response to specific customer orders, and the remainder of your output is sold to resellers under long-term contracts. You have a choice of purchasing raw steel inputs—mostly cold-rolled sheet steel—from an exchange and/or from an industry consortium. Which alternative would you choose and why? Prepare a presentation for management supporting your position.

4. You are involved in logistics management for your company, a national retailer of office furniture. In the last year the company has experienced a number of disruptions in its supply chain as vendors failed to deliver products on time, and the business has lost customers as a result. Your firm only has a limited IT department, and you would like to propose a cloud-based solution. Go to the website of GT Nexus. Explore the Why GT Nexus tab, and the Solutions By Industry/Retail tab. Read several case studies on the site. Write a report to senior management why you believe that a cloud-based B2B solution is best for your firm.

REFERENCES

Accenture, Inc. "Supply Chain Management in the Cloud." (June 25, 2014).

Antai, Imoh. "A Theory of the Competing Supply Chain: Alternatives for Development." *International Business Research* Vol 4, No. 1 (January 2011).

Ariba Inc., "Ariba-Spot-Buy-Powered-by-Ariba-Discovery." (May 13, 2014).

Banker, Steve. "Procter & Gamble's Futuristic Control Tower Environment." *Forbes* (July 1, 2015).

Barlow, Alexis. "Web Technologies and Supply Chains." Glasgow Calendonian University, Scotland. In *Supply Chain Management: New Perspectives*, edited by S. Renko. (2011).

Beard, Alison and Richard Hornik, "It's Hard to Be Good," *Harvard Business Review Magazine*, November 2011.

Cachon, Gerard, and Robert Swinney, "The Value of Fast Fashion: Quick Response, Enhanced Design, and Strategic Consumer Behavior." *Management Science* Vol. 57 778–795 (April 2011).

Cargill, Bruce. "10 B2B Brands That Are Killing It on Social Media." Clickz.com (October 7, 2015).

Carlozo, Lou. "Crowdfunding: A New Frontier for Investors." *U.S. News and World Report* (May 6, 2015).

Cecere, Lora. "Supply Chain Visibility in Business Networks." Supply Chain Insights, LLC (March 11, 2014).

Cecere, Lora. "EDI Workhorse of the Value Chain." Supply Chain Insights, LLC (November 20, 2013).

Chao, Loretta. "Supply Chain Management in the Cloud." *Wall Street Journal* (May 22, 2015).

Chopra, Sunil and MamMohan Sodhi. "Reducing the Risk of Supply Chain Disruptions." *MIT Sloan Management Review* (Spring 2014).

Cisco Systems, Inc. "Cisco Visual Networking Index: Global Mobile Data Traffic Forecast Update 2014–2019" (2015).

Cisco Systems, Inc. "Cisco Telepresence." Twitter.com/Telepresence, (accessed August 11, 2016b).

Cisco Systems, Inc. and Vital Images. "Video Conferencing Shrinks the Globe." (July 2016).

Computerworld. "Healthcare IT's Seismic Shift: How Collaboration Is Changing Cyber Insurance and More!" Computerworld.com (May 28, 2015).

Demery, Paul. "Salesforce.com Rolls Out a Portal for Selling B2B Mobile Apps." Internetretailer.com (January 5, 2015).

DHL, Inc. "A Look Back at 2015: The Top Ten Supply Chain Disruptions." (February 2016).

eMarketer, Inc. (Bryan Yaeger) "B2B Content Marketing in the US." (January 2016a).

eMarketer, Inc. (Jillian Ryan) "B2B Sales Enablement." (June 2016b).

eMarketer, Inc. (Jillian Ryan) "Predictive Analytics in B2B Marketing." (April 2016c).

eMarketer, Inc. (Tricia Carr, Rebecca Chadwick, and Jillian Ryan). "Six B2B Mobile Marketing Trends for 2016."(December 2015).

Fair Labor Association, "Independent External Monitoring of the Hestle, Olan, and Balsu Hazelnut Supply Chain in Turkey, 2014–2015. (2015).

Fair Labor Association. "Independent Investigation of Apple Supplier, Foxconn Report Highlights." Fairlabor.org (March 30, 2012).

Fauska, Polina, Natalia Kryvinska, and Christine Strauss. "E-commerce and B2B Services Enterprises." 2013 International Conference on Advanced Information Networking and Application Workshops, IEEE (2013).

Gartner, Inc. "Gartner Announces Rankings of Its 2015 Supply Chain Top 25: Amazon Takes the Top Spot in Top 25 Rankings; Apple and P&G Move into New Masters Category." (May 14, 2015).

Gilmore, Dan. "Under Armour's Athletic Supply Chain." *Supply Chain Digest* (April 3, 2014).

Globalwinespirits.com. "About GWS." Globalwinespirits.com (accessed August 9, 2016).

Gohring, Nancy. "Collaboration 2.0: Old Meets New." *Computerworld* (April 10, 2014).

Gusman, Phil. "Most 2012 Supply-Chain Disruptions Were from Tech-Related Events, Not Weather." *Property Casualty Journal* (September 9, 2013).

Hewlett-Packard. "Form 10-K for the fiscal year ended October 31, 2015." (December 16, 2015b). Hewlett-Packard.

Hewlett-Packard Enterprise. "Fact Sheet: Realize Better Outcomes." (2015a).

IBM Corporation, "True Value Company: True Value Optimizes Their Inbound Supply Process with IBM Sterling Supply Chain Visibility." (July 2011).

Inventory Locator Service LLC. "About Us." ILSmart.com (accessed August 9, 2016).

Kaplan, Steven, and Mohanbir Sawhney. "E-Hubs: The New B2B Marketplaces." *Harvard Business Review* (May–June 2000).

Laudon, Kenneth C. and Jane P. Laudon. *Management Information Systems: Managing the Digital Firm.* 14th edition. Upper Saddle River, NJ, Prentice Hall (2016).

Long, Gene, Jr. "Supply Chain Resiliency: From Insight to Foresight: Sustaining Shareholder Value by Hardening the Enterprise Against External Risks." *IHS Quarterly* (March 2014).

Manik and Yardley, 2013. [To come]

PriceWaterhouseCoopers and the MIT Forum for Supply Chain Innovation. "Making the Right Risk Decisions to Strengthen Operations Performance." (2015).

Red Prairie, Inc. "The B2B SoLoMo Imperative." (September 2012).

Resilinc Inc. "Resilinc Special Supply Chain Event Case Study: 2016 Taiwan Earthquake, Assessing the Foreseeable Supply Chain Impact." (February 2016).

Rossi, Ben. "How to Protect the IT Supply Chain From Cyber Attacks." Information Age (March 24, 2015).

Rowland, Daryk. "Combating Cyber Risk in the Supply Chain." Scmagazine.com (November 11, 2014).

SAP, Inc., "Under Armour: Finding a Simple Solution to a Complex Problem with SAP HANA®." SAP Business Cases, 2015.

Suering, Stefan and Martin Muller. "From a Literature Review to a Conceptual Framework for Sustainable Supply Chain Management." *Journal of Cleaner Production* (June 12, 2008).

Trkman, P. and McCormack, K. "Estimating the Benefits of Implementing E-Procurement," Engineering Management, IEEE Transaction, Volume 57, Issue 2 (May 2010).

True Value. Annual Report 2015. (March 2016).

UN Global Compact Office and BSR. "Supply Chain Sustainability: A Practical Guide for Continuous Improvement." (2015).

UNCTAD (United Nations Conference on Trade and Development). "New Initiative to Help Developing Countries Grasp the Opportunity of E-commerce-Worth Around $22.1 Trillion in 2015-or Risk Falling Behind." Unctad.org (July 19, 2016).

U.S. Census Bureau. "eStats." (June 8, 2016).

Winston, Andrew. "GE Is Avoiding Hard Choices About Ecomagination." *Harvard Business Review* (August 1, 2014).

W.W. Grainger, Inc. Form 10-K for the fiscal year ended December 31, 2015, filed with the Securities and Exchange Commission (February 29, 2016).

Zarroli, Jim. "In Trendy World Of Fast Fashion, Styles Aren't Made To Last." Npr.org (March 11, 2013).

Zurich Insurance. "Outsourcing Failures Now in Top 3 as Causes of Supply Chain Disruption." *Insurance Journal* (November 8, 2012).

Index

A bolded page number indicates that the term is defined on that page

Credits

CHAPTER 1
p.45, Uber, © Lenscap/Alamy Stock Photo; p.86, Puma, © René van den Berg/Alamy Stock Photo.

CHAPTER 2
p.95, Augmented Reality, © skdesign/123RF; Figure 2.10, © Visualware, Inc., 2014; Used with permission.

CHAPTER 3
p.175, HTML5, © Azimuth Interactive, Inc.; Figure 3.12, screenshot of WebTrends Analytics 10, © WebTrends, Inc., 2014. Used with permission.

CHAPTER 4
p.239, CyberAttack, © Rafal Olechowski/Fotolia; Figure 4.4, © keith morris/Alamy Stock Photo, Figure 4.13, based on data from eMarketer, Inc., © 2016, used with permission; p.308, Apple Pay, © Anatolii Babii/Alamy Stock Photo.

CHAPTER 5
p.323, Eyewear, © nomadsoul1/123RF; p.367, Pandora.com, © NetPhotos/Alamy Stock Photo.

CHAPTER 6
p.377, Mobile Advertising, © fotografiedk/Fotolia. com; Figure 6.1, adapted from Kotler and Armstrong, *Principles of Marketing*, 13e, 2009. Reprinted by permission of Pearson Education, Inc., Upper Saddle River, NJ; Figures 6.5 and 6.8, based on data from eMarketer, Inc.,© 2016, used with permission; Table 6.4, based on data from eMarketer, Inc., © 2016, used with permission; p.453, RTB/Programmatic, © Azimuth Interactive, Inc.

CHAPTER 7
p.465, Pinterest, © Blaize Pascall/Alamy Stock Photo; Figures 7.8 and 7.9, based on data from eMarketer, Inc., © 2016, used with permission; p.535, Exchange-HunterJumper.com, © 2014 Eohippus, LLC.

CHAPTER 8
p.537, Google and the Right to be Forgotten, © Lee Avison/Alamy Stock Photo; p.611, Pirate Bay, © Tommy (Louth)/Alamy Stock Photo.

CHAPTER 9
p.625, Spotify, © Felix Choo/Alamy Stock Photo; Figure 9.17, based on data from eMarketer, Inc., © 2016, used with permission; p. 683, Netflix © Digitallife/Alamy Stock Photo.

CHAPTER 10
p.693, Social Networks Around the World, © gigra/Fotolia.com; Figure 10.2, based on data from eMarketer, Inc., © 2016, used with permission; p.728, eBay, © Iain Masterton/Alamy Stock Photo.

CHAPTER 11
p.737, Globe with focus on Africa, Middle East, Europe, © Fenton/Fotolia.com; Figures 11.3 and 11.5, based on data from eMarketer, Inc., © 2016, used with permission; p.792, OpenTable, © Justin Sullivan/Getty Images.

CHAPTER 12
p.803, B2B, © Azimuth Interactive, Inc.

Video Cases

Learning Tracks

E-commerce 2017 Companion Web Site